STATISTICAL QUALITY CONTROL & QUALITY MANAGEMENT

TENTH EDITION

R.C. Gupta

KHANNA PUBLISHERS
Operational Office
B-35/9, G.T. Karnal Road, Industrial Area,
(Near Telephone Exchange), Delhi-110033
Phones : 011-27224179, 011-45033819 • *Mob*. 09811541460
email : contactus@khannapublishers.in

Published by :

Romesh Chander Khanna & Vineet Khanna
for **KHANNA PUBLISHERS**
2-B, Nath Market, Nai Sarak
Delhi- 110 006 (India)

Website : www.khannapublishers.in

Hologram & Description

To all readers of our books, to prevent yourself from being defrauded by piraters, please make sure that there is an Hologram on the cover of our books with the below specifications. If you find any book without Hologram and Description, please mail us at **contactus@khannapublishers.in**

Thanking you

ISBN No. 978-81-7409-111-4

First Edition : 1974
Tenth Edition : 2021

***Price :* ₹ 459.00**

PREFACE

This is a text-book-cum working manual on Statistical Quality Control (SQC) and Quality Management. These two subjects are distinct from each other yet closely related as SQC techniques are central to Quality Management.

Hence the book is divided into two parts:

PART-1 : STATISTICAL QUALITY CONTROL

PART-2 : QUALITY MANAGEMENT

PART-1 primarily deals with Shewhart Control Charts (often called the Statistical Process Control (i.e. ***SPC***) and various types of Scientific Acceptance Sampling (*SAS*).

PART-2 : Deals with various types Quality Management Techniques in which SQC (i.e. *SPC* and *SAS*) play a significant role.

These are simple but powerful techniques, widely used in various industries and in many countries throughout the world to improve product and service quality and to reduce costs. The most effective use of these techniques depends upon their being adequately understood by production, inspection, engineering and quality management personnel.

Hence, the object has been to write this book for immediate use by all these groups. It is, therefore, not meant to be of much help to theoretical statistician or the mathematician. The aim has been to give just enough theory to provide the framework of practical working rules so as to enable the user to recognize the limitations of the methods alongside their manifold utility. This book should, therefore, also be equally valuable for seminars and self-study.

A ***distinct*** and ***bonus feature*** of the present edition of this book is that at the completion of text portion in each chapter, a large number of questions—**objective**, **optional one line answer**, **short answer** and **responsive questions** of the fundamental and practical nature have been answered under the head **Solved Questions**. This is meant to help the students, teachers and professionals as the selected question have been picked up from various examinations and interviews on the subject conducted world wide. Each selected question for answer brings out various critical point(s) related to the topic. Just as in previous editions, the changes from the previous edition have been made in part to improve the presentation of text to make it more interesting and practical and in part to keep the various topics up-to-date. Readers who have gone through some other text on the subject will find the present edition of equal utility to them.

However, this edition partly follows the general pattern of nine earlier editions. The author wishes to acknowledge with thanks his gratitude to the number of users both from academic and industrial worlds, for offering valuable comments and suggestions, *most of which have been incorporated* in the present edition. Nevertheless, the final responsibility for the selection and treatment of material must be that of the author and he should receive the blame of any deficiency.

1st January, 2021

R.C. Gupta

Dedication

God : Vishwakarma

Maa : Sarswati

Maa : Laxmi

CONTENTS

PART-1 : STATISTICAL QUALITY CONTROL

PART-2 : QUALITY MANAGEMENT

PART-1

STATISTICAL QUALITY CONTROL

PART-1(A)

INTRODUCTION

CHAPTER

1 Introduction to Quality and Overview

1.1 THE MEANING AND DEFINITION OF QUALITY

When we use the expression "quality product" in common parlance, we usually intend to think in terms of a good or excellent product with a higher price. However this is not so. In fact, some of the cheapest items in every day life can have very high quality. Consider the paper used in a copying machine. For little less than a ₹ a page, we can buy smooth white paper, less than one hundredth of an inch thick and of uniform size. We have come to expect such high quality in copier paper that we don't examine individual pages before loading it into a copier. We wouldn't think of measuring the thickness of each page to make sure that it was thin enough not to jam the copier, but thick enough so that we could print on both sides and not have the two images interfere with each other.

The copy paper example gives us a clue to a working definition of ***quality***. Things that are of high quality are those that work in the way we expect them to. As *Quality Guru* Joseph M. Juran has put it, *quality* implies *fitness for use*. In this sense, *quality means conformance to requirements*. Note that this is not quite the same as conformance to specifications. Copy paper that is cut to size for American copy machines won't fit European machines that demand the slightly narrower A4 metric format.

Note that idea of "things that work in the way we expect them to" points out that quality is defined by customers as well as by producers. As we shall see, meeting the need of customers is central to TQM (Total Quality Management). Working definition of quality vary in different contexts, especially when we contrast goods and services. But in keeping with our notion of conformance to requirements, most working definitions of quality will include the concepts of *consistency*, *reliability* and *lack of errors and defects*.

However, the **most modern definition of quality** is:

Quality is inversely proportional to variability. We may note that this definition implies that if variability in the important characteristics of a product decreases, the quality of the product increases and hence the expression.

1.2 VARIABILITY IS THE ENEMY OF QUALITY

When a craftsman makes something by hand, there is a continuous process of checking measuring, and reworking. If we had watched Michelangelo completing a sculpture, we wouldn't have seen a final "quality control' step before he shipped his artwork to his patron. Indeed, quality control is not an issue when we are producing goods and services that are essentially unique. However, when *mass production* became common during the nineteenth century, it was soon realized that individual pieces could not be identical —a certain amount of variation is inevitable. But this leads to a problem: With too much variation, parts that are supposed to fit together won't fit! In this sense, we can see why variability is the enemy of quality.

1.2.1 Two Types of Variation– Random and Systematic (non random)

The key to managing for quality is to believe that excessive variability is not inevitable. When the output of some process is found to be unreliable, not always conforming to requirements, we must carefully examine the process and see how it can be controlled.

In the 1920s, Walter A. Shawhart, a researcher at Bell Labs created a system for tracking variation and identifying its causes. Shewhart's system of statistical process control (SPC) was developed further and championed by his one time colleague, W. Edwards Deming–A well known another *Quality Guru*.

Let's look at some basic ideas of Shewart's statistical process control (*i.e.* SPC). Consider a production line that makes driveshafts for automobiles. Requirements for well-functioning shafts have been established. We would like to monitor and improve the quality of the shafts we produce. The shafts are made in large quantities on an automatic lathe. If we measured the diameter of each shaft after manufacture, we would expect to see some variability (perhaps a normal distribution) of the measurements around a mean (or average) value. These observed random variations in the measurements could result from variations in the hardness of the steel used for the shafts, power surges affecting the lathe, or even errors in making the measurements on the finished shafts.

But imagine what happens as the cutting tool begins to dull. The average diameter will gradually increase unless the lathe is recalibrated. And if the bearings on the lathe wear over time, the cutting edge might move around. Then some shafts would be too large, and some too small. Although the mean diameter might well be the same, the variability in the measurements would increase. It would be important to note such nonrandom (or *systematic*) variation, to identify its source, and to correct the problem.

From this discussion, we can see that there are *two kinds of variation* that are observed in the output from most processes, in general and from our automatic lathe, in particular:

- **Random variation** (sometimes called *chance* or *common* or *inherent*, variation)
- **Systematic variation** (sometimes called *assignable* or *special cause*, variation)

These two kinds of variation call for different managerial responses. Although one of the goals of quality management is *constant improvement* by the reduction of inherent variation, this cannot ordinarily be accomplished without changing the process. And we should not change the process until we are sure that all assignable variation has been identified and brought under control. So the idea is this:

If the process is *out-of-control* because there is still some special cause variation present, identify and correct the cause of that variation. Then when the process has been bought *in-control*, quality can be improved by redesigning the process to reduce its inherent variability.

1.2.2 Controlling Variability : Inspection vs. Prevention

How should we deal with variability? Think about a stack of two-by-fours in a lumberyard. Most of them will conform to requirements, but some won't because of twisting and warping as they dried, splitting when the saw hit a knot,or sundry other causes. One approach to mass production says it's cheaper to push material through the process and sort out the defects at the end. This leads our lumberyard to have an inspector examine two-by-fours as they come out of the drying kiln. Defective pieces go to the scrap heap.

In the early days of mass production, sorting out defects became the chief method of quality control Armies of white-coated inspectors tested goods at the end of a production line and released only some of them to customers. It was widely believed that the cost of a few rejects didn't amount to much because the marginal cost of each unit was small. But by the late 1970s, people were pointing out that the costs of defects were much higher than supposed. The armies of inspectors had to be paid, and if defective products slipped through, there were warranty costs and loss of customers goodwill.

They argued that it is simply cheaper to do things right the first time. They preached the concept of *zero defects*. If our electrical power was 99 percent reliable, we would spend a lot of time resetting our clocks. A major airline with a 99.9 percent safety record would have several crashes each week! If we demand near-perfect performance from power companies and airlines, perhaps we should expect no less from the producer of all our goods and services.

When poorly made parts are passed down a production line, all subsequent work is wasted when the final product is rejected by quality control inspectors. But it's expensive to keep inspecting component to make sure they conform to requirements. Imagine how much time would be wasted if we had to examine each piece of paper for defect before loading a copier. This leads to the goal of preventing defects at each stage of manufacturing a product or delivering a service. To accomplish this , the people who make things are given the responsibility to check their work before it is passed on rather than just letting sloppy work slide by to be caught at a final inspection. This also has the benefit of giving workers a greater investment of pride in the work they are doing—in this sense, they are more like craftsmen.

1.3 SOME OTHER APPROACHES TO DEFINE QUALITY

As there is no clear or agreed definition of quality various definitions of quality can be categorized into ***five*** approaches as follows

The Transcendent Approach : This approach views quality as synonymous with innate excellence. A 'quality' car is a Rolls Royce. Using this approach, quality is being defined as the absolute the best possible, in terms of the product's or service specification.

The Manufacturing-based Approach : This approach is concerned with making products or providing services that are free of errors and that conform precisely to their design specification. A car which is less expensive than a Rolls Royce, or a Swatch Watch, although not necessarily the 'best' available, is defined as a 'quality' product provided it has been built or delivered precisely to its design specification.

The User-based Approach : This approach is about making sure that the product is fit for its purpose. This definition demonstrates concern not only for its adherence to specification but also with appropriateness of that specification for the customer. A watch that is manufactured precisely for its design specification yet falls to pieces after two days is clearly not fit for its purpose.

The Product-based Approach : This approach views quality as a precise and measurable set of characteristics. A watch, for example, may be designed to run, without the need for servicing for at least five years while keeping time correct to within five seconds.

The Value-based Approach : This approach contends that quality should be perceived in relation to price. A customer may be willing to accept something of a lower specification quality, if the price is low.

1.4 THE FOCUS OF THIS BOOK

The major focus of this book is about the use of *Statistical Techniques* and various *Quality Philosophies* to improve the quality of products which is central to Quality Management. This book has therefore two distinct parts :

PART-1 : STATISTICAL QUALITY CONTROL
PART-2 : QUALITY MANAGEMENT

PART-1 deals with Statistical Quality Control of which *SPC* (*i.e.* Statistical Process Control) and *SAS* (*i.e.* Scientific Acceptance Sampling) form the major pasts PART-1(B) deals with SPC while PART-1(C) deals *SAS*.

PART-2 deals with *Quality Management* (*QM*) in which SPC & SAS form the major quality improvement techniques, and also the different quality philosophies of the world recognized *Quality Gurus* leading to TQM and Six Sigma techniques etc.

1.5 THE CONTROL-CHART VIEWPOINT

One purpose of this book is to explain the control-chart point of view in some detail. PART-1(B) titled "Statistical Process Control," (SPC) is primarily devoted to this exposition. In spite of the apparent simplicity of the control chart, many people involved in trying to manage and improve quality find that its use calls for entirely new point of view. Briefly stated, the main principles are these :

1. Measured quality of manufactured product is always subject to a certain amount of variation as the result of chance.
2. Some "constant system of chance causes" is inherent in any particular scheme of production and inspection.
3. Variation within this stable pattern is inevitable.
4. The reasons for variation outside this stable pattern may be discovered and corrected.

These simple principles provide the foundation of statistical process control (SPC).

The *constant system of chance causes* referred to by Shewhart also has been called a *stable system* or defined *as statistical stability*. W. Edwards Deming referred to these constant or stable systems as *common causes of variation*, constantly operating within a system. Variation outside this stable system called *assignable cause* variation by Shewhart and *special causes* variation by Deming, may be detected using control charts and its cause(s) eliminated through analysis and corrective action. Often these actions result in substantial improvement in the quality of products and services and reductions in spoilage, rework, and error rates. Moreover, by identifying certain quality variations as inevitable chance variations, the control chart tells when to leave a process alone and thus prevents unnecessarily frequent adjustments that tend to increase variability rather than decrease it.

Through its disclosure of the natural capabilities of a production process, the control-chart technique permits better decisions on engineering tolerances and better comparisons between alternative designs and between alternative production or service methods.

1.6 SOME STATISTICAL PROCESS CONTROL i.e. (*SPC*) TOOL

Many of the techniques developed by mathematical statisticians for the analysis of data may be used in the control of product quality. The expression *statistical quality control* may be used to cover all uses of statistical techniques for this purpose. However, it often relates particularly to **five** separate but related techniques that constitute the most common working statistical tools in quality control. These tools are :

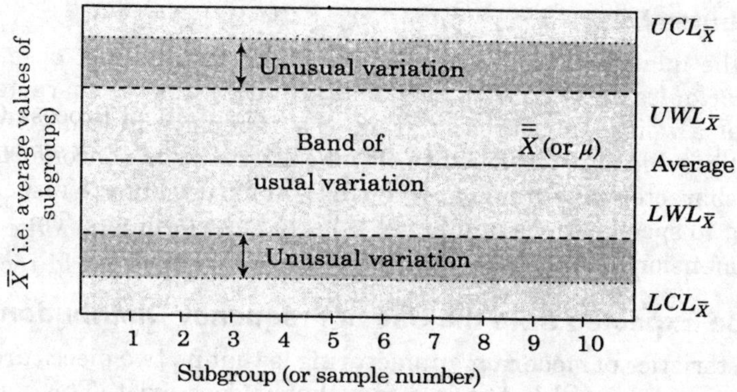

FIGURE 1.1 A sample of control chart for variables ($\overline{X}$ Chart)

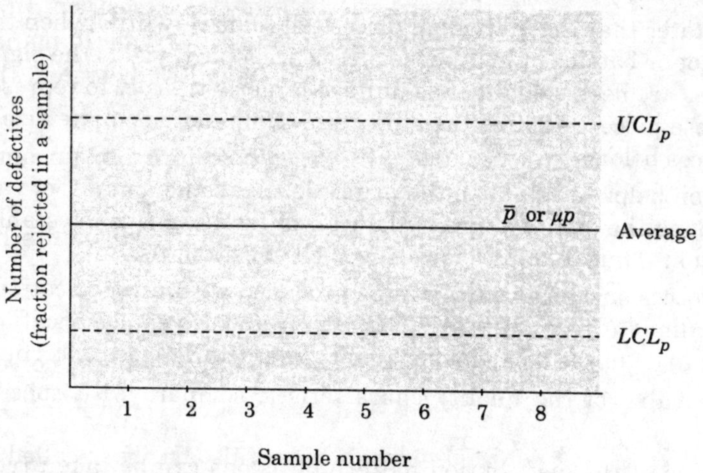

FIGURE 1.2 A sample of control chart for attribute (p chart)

1. The frequency distribution for measurable quality characteristics primarily used for presentation and analysis of data and also for computation of certain statistical measures.
2. The Shewhart control charts for measurable quality characteristics. In technical language of the subject, these are described as charts for variables, or as charts for $\overline{X}$ and R (sample average and range) and charts for $\overline{X}$ and s (sample average and standard deviation)*. Figure 1.1 shows one such chart for averages i.e. $\overline{\overline{X}}$.
3. The Shewhart control chart for fraction rejected, or p chart. Figure 1.2 shows one such p-chart.
4. The Shewhart control chart for number of nonconformities, or c chart.
5. The portion of sampling theory that deals with quality protection given by any specified sampling acceptance procedure.

PART-1(B) of this book deals with (1), (2), (3), and (4) and also introduces some other statistical techniques for comparing processes. PART-1(C) deals with (5) and includes a number of procedures for sampling acceptance, many of which may be used as an aid in sampling for process control purposes. In the use of statistical methods to control product quality, these are the tools for cost reduction and quality improvement that are the most widely applied.

---

* The symbol $\overline{X}$ is read as "X bar" or as "bar X". The bar over any symbol always indicates an average. Thus $\overline{X}$ means an average of the X's. R and s are alternative measures of the dispersion of a set of data. Their calculation and meaning are explained in Chaps. 2 and 3.

1.6.2 Variables and Attributes Data

Data that are collected for the quality control purposes are obtained by direct observation and are classified as either *variables* or *attributes*. Variables are those quality characteristics which are measurable such as a weight measured in gram or a dimension in mm. Attributes are those quality characteristics which are classified as either conforming or nonconforming to specifications. Many quality characteristics which are variables in nature but are inspected as conforming or nonconforming to specifications and hence reported as attributes. This applies for example, to gauging of dimension of machine parts by go and not-go gauges.

1.6.3 Some Benefits to be Expected from the Use of Frequency Distributions

One of the established characteristics of modern manufacturing is that no two pieces are made exactly alike. The variation may be small but it is a fact that it does exist. This variation generally takes a definite frequency pattern, which cannot be known by examining a few pieces. The frequency distribution states that the individual pieces tell relatively little when they are studied by themselves. The lot or batch of which these pieces are a part, yields the significant information. Individual pieces arc best thought of as units of larger lot. Truly to represent the quality characteristics of these pieces requires the study of a sample of adequate size drawn from the lot to which the pieces belong.

The frequency distribution helps to establish the principle that some amount of variation must always be expected among the manufactured product and further helps to establish the general nature of this variation. Thus it helps answering such questions as :

1. Is the variation in a process such that parts can be produced within specification limits i.e. upper specification limit (designated as USL_X or U) and lower specification limit (designated as LSL_X or L) as far as a particular quality characteristic is concerned ?
2. How does the average value of the quality characteristic compare with specification limits?

Depending upon the shape of the distribution pattern decisions can be taken regarding acceptability of lot and regarding adjustment of the process centering and thus reducing the scrap to minimum possible.

1.6.4 Some Benefits to be Expected from the Use of Control Charts for Variables

Trouble is a common state of affairs in manufacturing. Whenever the trouble consists of difficulty in meeting quality specifications that are expressed in terms of variables, the Shewhart control charts for $\bar{X}$ and R are indispensable tools in the hands of the troubleshooter. They provide information on three matters, all of which need to be known as a basis for action. These are :

1. Basic variability of the quality characteristic
2. Consistency of performance
3. Average level of the quality characteristic.

1.6.5 Some Benefits to be Expected from the Use of Control Charts for Fraction Rejected (i.e. *p*-charts)

The ratio of the number of items rejected to the number of items inspected is known as fraction rejected*.

---

* It is commonly expressed as a decimal fraction, such as 0.025. The decimal fraction may be multiplied by 100 to convert it into percent rejected, such as 2.5%.

The Shewhart control charts for fraction rejected (known as *p* chart) generally makes use of data that either are already available for other purposes or can readily be made available. Simple statistical calculations provide control limits that tell whether assignable causes of variation appear to be present or whether the variations from day to day (or lot to lot, supplier to supplier, or whatever the classification basis may be) are explainable on chance grounds. The introduction of *p* chart results in substantial reductions in average fraction rejected. The *p* chart is also of great value in dealing with outside suppliers.

1.6.6 Some Benefits to be Expected from the Use of Control Charts for Nonconformities

This type of control chart known as *c* chart applies to two rather specialized situations. One is the case where a count is made of the number of defects or nonconformities of such type as blemishes in a painted or plated surface of a given area, weak spots in the insulation of rubber-covered wire of a given length, or imperfections in a bolt of cloth. The other is the case of inspection of fairly complex assembled units in which there are a great many opportunities for occurrences of nonconformities of various types, and the total number of nonconformities of all types found is recorded for each unit.

As in other types of control charts, the control limits are set in a way to detect the presence or absence of assignable causes of variation, and they therefore tell when to take action on the process and when not to do so. Experience indicates that erratic variation in inspection standards and inspection practices seems particularly likely to exist in this type of inspection and that the control chart for nonconformities generally proves helpful in standardizing inspection methods.

Figure 1.3 summaries the current industrial practice of using the control charts for variables and attributes depending upon the same size (n).

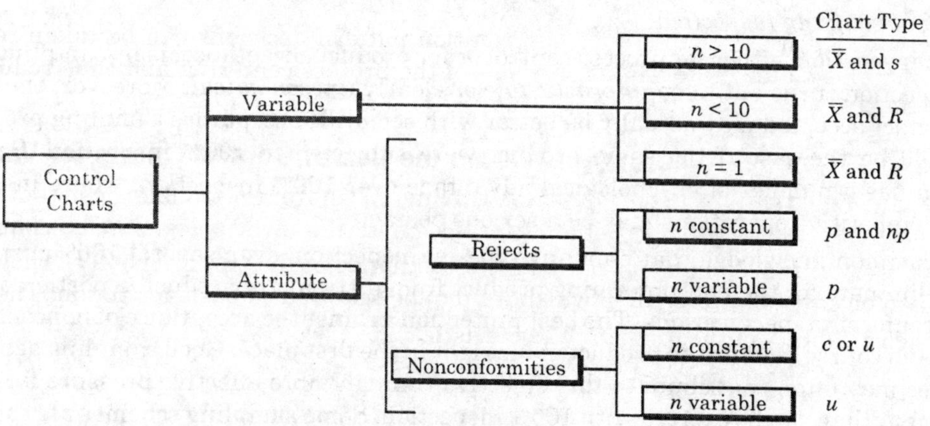

FIGURE 1.3 Various types of control charts

1.7 SCIENTIFIC ACCEPTANCE SAMPLING (*SAS*)

Acceptance inspection is an essential part of manufacturing for quality improvement. Inspection can occur at many points in a manufacturing cycle. Acceptance sampling, defined as the inspection and classification of a sample of units selected at random from a larger batch or lot and the ultimate decision about disposition of the lot.

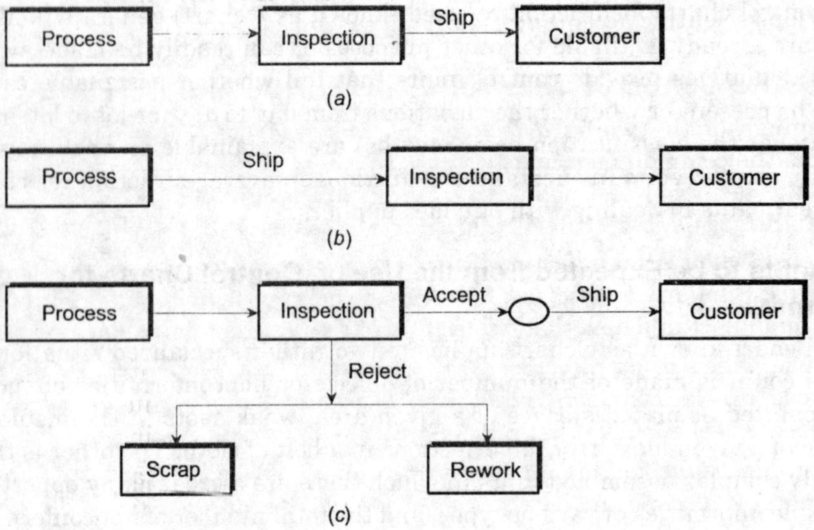

FIGURE 1.4 Variations of acceptance sampling. (*a*) Outgoing inspection; (*b*) Receiving incoming inspection; (*c*) Disposition of lot

Several different variations of acceptance sampling are shown in Fig. 1.3. In Fig. 1.3 (*a*), the inspection operation is performed immediately following production, before the product is shipped to the customer. This is usually called *outgoing inspection*. Figure 1.3 (*b*) illustrates *incoming inspection* ; that is, a situation where lots or batches of product are sampled as they are received from the supplier. Various lot dispositioning decisions are illustrated in Fig 1.3 (*c*). Sampled lots may either be accepted or rejected. Items in a rejected lot are typically either scrapped or recycled, or they may be reworked or replaced with good units. This later case is often called *rectifying inspection*.

Much inspection, either for process control or for product acceptance, is by sampling. Often 100% inspection turns out to be *impracticable or* clearly *uneconomical*. Moreover, the quality of the product accepted may actually be better with scientific acceptance sampling procedures than would be the case if the same product were subjected to 100% inspection. Sampling inspection has a number of psychological advantage over 100% inspection, where inspectors' fatigue on repetitive operations may be a serious obstacle.

It is common knowledge that on many types of inspection, even several 100% inspections will not eliminate all the nonconforming product from a stream of product, a portion of which does not conform to specifications. The best protection against the acceptance of nonconforming product is, of course, having the product made right in the first place. Good sampling acceptance procedures may often contribute to this objective through more effective pressure for quality improvement than can be exerted with 100% inspection. Some sampling schemes also provide a better basis for diagnosis of quality troubles than is common with 100% inspection. It should be recognized that although statistical sampling acceptance procedures are generally superior to traditional sampling methods established without reference to the laws of probability, anyone who uses acceptance sampling must face the fact that whenever a portion of the stream of products submitted for acceptance does not conform to specifications, some nonconforming items are likely to be passed by any sampling acceptance scheme. The statistical approach to acceptance sampling frankly faces this fact. It attempts to evaluate the risk assumed with alternative sampling procedures and to make a decission as to the degree of protection needed in any instance. It is then possible to choose a sampling acceptance scheme that gives a desired degree of protection with due consideration for the various costs involved. PART 1(C) of this book deals with various scientific acceptance sampling schemes.

1.8 MEANINGS AND USAGE OF THE WORDS DEFECTIVE AND DEFECT

The technical meanings of the words *defective* and *defect* as used in the manufacturing industries differ from the common meanings of these words as used in every day speech. This difference between the technical and popular meanings of these words has been a source of misunderstanding in litigation, particularly in product liability suits.

- In technical sense when a manufactured article fails to conform to specification(s) it is known as *defective*. Similarly a *defect* is a failure of the part or article to conform to some one specification. A manufactured item that is defective may contain one defect or several of them.
- In popular sense, when a manufactured article is unsatisfactory with reference to its intended purpose, it is known as *defective*. Similarly a *defect* of a manufactured article is some characteristic of the article that makes it unsatisfactory for its intended purpose.

  Obviously it is impossible for manufacturers to take any action that will change the popular meanings of *defective* and *defect*. The one way the confusion between the technical and popular meanings can be eliminated is to substitute other words or phrases when the technical meanings are intended. An article that does not conform to specifications in some respect can be described as *nonconforming* rather than a *defective*. A failure to conform to a particular specification can be called a *nonconformity* or *nonconformance* rather than a defect. In describing the results of acceptance inspection, it is possible to say percent *rejected* or *nonconforming* rather than *percent defective*.

PART 1(B) of this book deals with various aspects of process control, with particular emphasis on the contributions that can be made by the different types of control charts. In this portion of the book, it has been possible to eliminate the words *defective* and *defect* in nearly all cases.

PART 1(C) of this book describes a number of acceptance sampling systems that use the words *defective* and *defect* in their technical sense. While some of the commercial versions of standards for acceptance sampling have replaced them, the more frequently used military versions have retained them. As long as these words continue to be used in the official documents describing such systems, writers explaining the systems will also need to use the words.

1.9 REASONS FOR USE OF THE ADJECTIVE STATISTICAL

The word *statistics* has generally two quite different meanings. In one sense, it refers to any facts that stated in terms of numbers; in this sense, it is a plural noun. Thus one may say "statistics are kept in the sales department regarding all branch office sales." In the other sense, it refers to a body of methods by which useful conclusions can be drawn from numerical data. In this sense, it is a singular noun. Thus one may say "Satatistics is based in large part on the law of large numbers and the mathematical theory of probability." It is in this second sense that the adjective *statistical* is accurately used in the expression *statistical quality control*.

The control of quality of manufactured product is a function that existed long before statistical methods were applied to the analysis of quality data and that exists today whether or not statistical techniques are used. Properly used, the expression *quality control* applies to a function much broader than the expression *statistical quality control*. The use of *quality* control, or *Q.C.*, in the sense of *statistical quality control* inevitably leads to confusion as to the meaning of the expression.

In the long run this confusion is likely to be more serious than any troubles introduced by the use of an extra word. For this reason, throughout this book the expression *quality* control is always used in the broader sense of the control of quality of product by whatever methods may be used and the adjective *statistical* is always employed where the control of product quality by statistical methods is referred to.

1.10 SOME SITUATIONS NOT REQUIRING STATISTICAL QUALITY CONTROL

Merely installing the statistical quality control techniques may not help in reducing the nonconforming product or improving the quality. The matter must be considered thoroughly in order to decide upon a plan. Such preliminary thinking may indicate that statistical quality control is not applicable to the majority of portions in the plant.

For example, in stamping out non-precision metal blanks on punch presses, it will be sufficient for the operator or foreman to give the product an occasional spot check for burrs and scratch marks. This will be sufficient to detect deficiencies in the blanking die or material and ensure a satisfactory product. Generally speaking, any elaborate statistical quality control is uncalled for on product or operations where all the following conditions exist :

1. Nonconforming work is unlikely.
2. The quality of the product can be checked quickly.
3. The product is a non-precision product.

SOLVED QUESTIONS

Q. 1.1: *Choose the correct statement.*

(*i*) Variablility is the enemy of quality, yet we can avoid it.
(*a*) True (*b*) False

(*ii*) Quality means excellent product
(*a*) True (*b*) False

(*iii*) Which of the following is ***not*** an aspect of quality
(*a*) Luxuriousness (*b*) Fitness for use
(*c*) consistency
(*d*) Conformance to requirement development

(*iv*) Person responsible for conformance to requirement development control chart is
(*a*) Shewhart (*b*) Deming
(*c*) Pareto (*d*) all of (a), (b) & (c)

(*v*) Quality and grade are _________ things
(*a*) Same (*b*) Different

(*vi*) The quality is customer focussed.
(*a*) Yes (*b*) No

(*vii*) Design quality is :
(*a*) Specification meeting customer requirements
(*b*) Output meeting specification
(*c*) Process producing to specification

(*viii*) Conformance quality is :
(*a*) Output meeting specification
(*b*) specification meeting customer requirements
(*c*) process producing to specifications

(ix) Operational quality is :

(a) Output meeting specification

(b) process producing to specification

(c) specification meeting customer requirements

(x) Service quality

(a) cannot be measured (b) is a matter of opinion

(c) is not important

(xi) SQC aims at

(a) zero defect (b) minimum defect

(c) optimum defect

(xii) TQM gives emphasis on

(a) customer-driven focus (b) Employee involvement

(c) continuous improvement (d) All (a), (b) & (c)

(xiii) For which of the following, control chart is used to monitor variable (*i.e.*, X)

(a) Controlling process variability (b) ensuring output within specification

Ans: (i) (a) (ii) (d) (iii) (a) (iv) (a) (v) (b) (vi) (a) (vii) (a) (viii) (a) (ix) (b) (x) (b) (xi) (c) (xii) (c) (xiii) (b).

Q. 1.2 : *State whether the following statements are True (T) or False (F) :*

(i) Statistical process control was originally developed in Japan and brought to the United States after World War II.

(ii) TQM is now being applied in services industries as well as manufacturing industries.

(iii) Controlling variability is an essential aspect of maintaining quality.

(iv) C ontrol charts help us to detect inherent variation.

(v) Quality is always measured using samples.

(vi) Quality is measured through inspection.

Ans: (i) (F) (ii) (T) (iii) (T) (iv) (F) (v) (F) (vi) (F)

Q. 1.3: *List four reasons why quality is important in manufacturing.*

Ans: (1) competitive advantage, (2) survival, (3) influence on cost and (4) influence on image.

Q. 1.4: *List four reasons why quality is important in services.*

Ans: (1) influence on cost, (2) influence on image, (3) Influence on paymasters, (4) social responsibility.

Q. 1.5: *List four reasons why quality is important in not-for-profit organizations.*

Ans: (1) influence on cost, (2) influence on image, (3) influence on paymasters, (4) social responsibility.

Q. 1.6: *Is there any relationship between quality costs and quality levels ?*

Ans: There is no simple relationship.

Q. 1.7: *Is there is any optimum quality level ?*

Ans: No.

Q. 1.8: *Simply define "quality".*

Ans: A simple definition of quality is 'conformance to requirements". However a better definition is "the totality of features and characteristics of a product or service that bear upon its ability to satisfy stated or implied need.

Q. 1.9: *(a) Simply define* ***(do not describe)*** *the term quality in your own words.*

(b) What can be the other definitions of quality? Be ***brief*** *in your answer.*

(c) Why the word "quality" is often found in the ***mission statement*** *of companies?*

Ans: *(a)* The simplest and perhaps the appropriate definition of quality is "consistent conformance to customers" expectation.

(b) Quality can be defined in several other ways as per the following tabulation:

Approach	*Meaning*
1. Transcendent approach	Innate excellence
2. Factors approach	Free From error
3. User based approach	Fit for use
4. Product based	Measurable set of characteristics
5. Value-based	Balance between cost and price.

(c) Quality has been a dominant theme in management thinking for quite sometime. Consideration of quality is a fundamental part of business strategy and now in the age of *force* competition, quality is must for so.

Q. 1.10: *What is SPC ?*

Ans: SPC is the application of statistical methods to the measurement and analysis of variation of any process.

Q. 1.11: *What is a statistical control chart ?*

Ans: A statistical control chart is a graphical comparison of process-performance data to computed statistical control limits drawn as limit lines on the the chart.

Q. 1.12: *What is the function of a control chart ?*

Ans: A control chart is used to separate random causes of variation in product quality frcm non-random 'assignable' causes of poor quality (*e.g.* operator error, faulty set up poor materials etc).

Q. 1.13: *Simply define "quality policy".*

Ans: The overall quality intentions and direction of an operation as regards quality, as formally expressed by top management.

Q. 1.14: *(a) Of the many definitions of 'quality' which one is the most quoted accepter definition of 'quality'? Who gave this definition?*

(b) Mention briefly ***(do not describe)*** *the different elements of this definition.*

Ans: *(a)* There has been remarkable change in the business scenario since two to three decades. One major change has been the switch in the emphasis away from quantity towards quality. Consumer and customers have become more sophisticated and discerning in their requirements.

Hence the definition of quality in industrial context was given by Juran as follows: Quality is defined as fitness for use.

(*b*) This definition of quality by Juran has two distinct elements:

- Quality of design, which can include the customer satisfactions built into the product.
- Quality of conformance, in the other words a lack of detects in the finished goods.

Quality must be considered from the viewpoint of both the consumer and the producer (or service provider).

The consumer– according to Deming the consumer is the most important part of the production line. Quality should be aimed at the needs of the consumer, present and future. This is driven by what the consumer wants and will pay for.

The producer– the product should be designed to meet or exceed the customer's expectations. Once a product has been properly designed the role of operation's manager is to ensure that the product actually produced meet the design specifications.

Q. 1.15: *Which of the following is most true about quality? State the reason (s) for selecting your option and also the reason(s) for rejecting other options.*

(*a*) *It will cost more money to build quality into the product.*

(*b*) *It will cost less money to build quality into the product process.*

(*c*) *Quality is inspection-driven.*

(*d*) *Quality is prevention-driven.*

Ans: The correct option is (*d*)

Reason: Quality is prevention-driven. Quality wants to complete the work correctly the first time in order to prevent poor results, a loss of time and a loss of funds.

The options (*a*) and (*b*) are incorrect. There is no guarantee that a product will cost more or less depending on the amount of expected quality. Incidently, lack of quality will likely to cost more because of the cost of nonconformance. Option (*c*) is incorrect because the quality is planned into a product, not inspected in.

Q. 1.16: *Mention the strategic importance of Quality.*

Ans: Quality is important to any organization due to its impact on cost and competitiveness. However, quality may also play a direct part in the strategy of any organization. World-class competition requires business to produce quality products or services efficiently.

1. Organisations may pursue a strategy of differentiation based on quality, whether by providing a better product at the same price as competitors or with a higher-quality product at a premium price.
2. Quality attributes may be critical success factors in a given market, such as reliability of cars.
3. A vital part of strategy development is to identify the customer and what their quality requirements are.

Q. 1.17: *Write a brief historical note on the development of SQC.*

Ans: The key to managing for quality is to believe that excessive variability is **not** inevitable. When the output of some process is found to be unreliable, not always conforming to requirement we must carefully examine the process and see how it can be controlled.

In the 1920's, Walter A. Shewhart, a researcher at Bell Labs, created a system for tracking variation and identifying its causes. Sherwhart's system of statistical process control (or SPC) was developed further and championed by his one-time colleague, W. Edwards Deming. For many years, Deming was a prophet without honour in the United States, but when Japan was rebuilding its economy after World War II, Japanese Mangers incorporated Deming's ideas into their management philosophy. Many American industries, including automobiles and consumer electronics, encountered severe competitive pressure from the Japanese in the late 1970's and 1980s. As a result , the contributions made to quality control by Deming and others were reconsidered by American Mangers.

Also when Shewhart was at Bell Lab, his colleague Harold F. Dodge was working on the development of sampling schemes for mass produced product. He is best remembered for his many developments in the use of table and procedures for the product accepted on the mathematics of probability which ultimately led to several types of ready-made inspection schemes depending upon customer requirement for quality protection.

Q. 1.18: *Define the term quality and its two key components.*

Ans: Quality : fit for its intended, purpose, at an appropriate cost. Two factors are :

- Quality of design, and
- Quality of conformance.

Q. 1.19: *What is the main difference between SPC and SAS ?*

Ans: Statistical process control (SPC) is the periodic sampling and analysis of units, items or activity, to determine if the system is performing as expected, according to some pre-determined target or within design limits. The primary purpose of SPC is to analyse the process to verify that it is operating correctly. It is *not* to analyse the produced units to see if they conform to specifications. This is the objective to scientific acceptance sampling (SAS).

Q. 1.20: *What are the functions of SPC charts ?*

Ans: Statistical process control charts are useful for measuring the current quality generated by the process and for detecting whether the process has changed to the deteriment of quality. The R-charts are used to monitor process variability, $\overline{X}$ and p-charts identify abnormal variations in the process average. The presence of abnormal variation triggers a reason for assignable causes.

Q. 1.21: *What are the basic statistical methods of controlling the quality ?*

Ans: The two major approaches to controlling quality are scientific acceptance sampling (SAS) of incoming or outgoing products and statistical process control (SPC) of the actual transformation activities. Both methods involve statistical sampling techniques. However, SAS methods reply upon estimating the levels of defective items before or after process has been completed. SPC is more useful during a process to ensure that production is not outside the acceptance limits. The primary means of SPC is via the use of control charts.

Q. 1.22: *Draw a simple diagram to indicate the types of control charts used in practice.*

Ans: There are seven types of control charts used in practice. Variables data generally require two control charts be used in pairs–one to monitor the process average i.e. $\overline{X}$ chart and the other to monitor process variation *i.e. R* chart. Attribute charts, on the other hand, require only one chart. Fig. 1.3 (Page 11) shows all the seven types of charts used in SPC at a glance.

Q. 1.23: *Why a determining whether the cause of a variation is a "common" (also called usual or chance) cause or an "assignable" (also called unusual or special) cause is important?*

Ans: Common variations, which are likely to occur in a random manner and about which comparatively little can be done. Assignable variations, which occur less frequently and can normally be traced to same "external" cause, such as tool wear, faulty materials etc. "Common" variations are normally of a lesser magnitude than "assignable" variations and, since they result from some inherent process variability, they occur randomly and can be described by the normal probability distribution. Quality controllers define limits within which variations are acceptable and beyond which they are either unacceptable, or necessitate some examination. Such limits are called control limits. For example, for a normal probability distribution, 99.73% of all chance or usual variations would be expected to occur within limits placed at 3 ± sigma from the mean value of the variable. Therefore, any variation occurring beyond such limits would, very likely, have resulted from some other unusual or assignable cause and would merit some investigation.

Q. 1.24: *Describe the various usual meanings given to the word "quality".*

Ans: The word "quality" has come to have a set of different meanings in addition to "fitness for use". Much confusion results when the word "quality" is uttered by person who has one of these meanings in mind, only to have the word intepreted in a variety of ways by different listeners.

Experience indicates that the most usual meanings given to the word "quality" include :

Fitness of use This is the historic meaning. In earlier times, fitness for use referred to the degree to which a specific product or services satisfied the requirements of a specific user. In our times there is still a lot of this face to face meeting over fitness for use. Increasingly, however commerce is transacted through a distribution chain, requiring the concept of specification, and creating two parameters of fitness of use :

1. quality or design, or grade
2. quality or conformance.

   With the proliferation of complex, long-life products, two added parameters of fitness for use have arisen :

3. availablity, i.e. the extent to which the user can secure containing use of the product
4. customer service i.e. the extent to which the manfacturer and the distribution chain make good in the event of product failure.

Grade This is the degree to which a class or category of product possesses satisfaction for people generally. The term "quality of design" sometimes used as synonymous with grade. The term "brand" is often used to describe a producer's designation for a particular grade.

Quality of conformance This is the degree to which a specific product conforms to a design or specification.

Quality characteristic This is any distinguishing feature of a grade or a product, i.e., appearance, dimension, performance, length of life, dependability, reliability, durability, maintainability, taste odour etc.

The quality function This is the name for that area of responsibility in industrial units through which we achieve fitness for use.

A department Some industrial units have names containing the word "quality", e.g. quality control department and these names may be abbreviated to the single word "quality". In the literature of statistical quality control the word 'quality' is usually related to some measurement made on the items produced, a good quality item having one which conforms to standards specified for the measurements.

Q. 1.25: *Why are statistical methods of quality control so important ?*

Ans: The most effective way that has so far been developed for getting at the facts about quality characteristics is to use statistical methods. Often the statistical methods are referred to as tools for dealing with quality problems. As a matter of fact these are much more than that. As Dr. Walter A. Shewhart puts it, they provide us with a looking at the universe. They pervade all phases of existence. They lead us to a better understanding of universal truth:

Inherent variability is present in all things

It is this that prevents us from ever achieving an "exact" measurement of any thing. We have nothing "exact" to measure with ! As Dr. W. Edwards Deming puts it, the science of exactness becomes the science of dealing most effectively with inexactness. Statistical methods offer us the most effective means of dealing with inexactness.

Q. 1.26: *Suggest some general ways to diagonse the quality problems.*

Ans: The quality problem can be diagonsed by using appropriate control tools depending upon the meaning or perception of "quality". At a broad level, quality is best modelled as the gap between customers' expectations concerning the product or service and their perceptions concerning the product or service. Modelling quality this way will allow the development of a diagnostic tool which is based around the perception-expectation gap. If such a gap exists it is likely to be caused by one or more of the gaps between factors which influence expectations and perceptions.

There are four main gaps :

1. the gap between a customer's specification and the operation's specification;
2. the gap between the product or service concept and the way the organization has specified it;
3. the gap between the way quality has been specified and the actual delivered quality;
4. the gap between the actual delivered quality and the way the product or service has been described to the customer.

It is the third gap (between the specification of quality and the actual quality delivered) which of particular concern to operations managers.

Q. 1.27: *Distinguish clearly between quality control and inspection.*

Ans: For any organization associated with manufacturing activities, both inspection and quality are essential. However, there is marked difference between the two. In the inspection activity, the emphasis is placed on the quality of past output. For example, if the production schedule calls for manufacture of 1,000 couplings with a length of 10.000 ± 0.250 cm., the inspector will concern himself only with whether the couplings that have been produced to this specification. Those do not, will be rejected and production will continue until the required number, *i.e* 1,000 couplings have been produced.

As opposed to this, the emphasis in the quality control activity is on the quality of future output. There are various ways of controlling this quality. However, one of the most important methods is based on techniques of a statistical nature. For example in the case of above couplings, as the coupling are produced, periodic samples might be taken of the output and the coupling in each sample inspected. If the quality of the items in a particular sample is satisfactory, production will be allowed to continue. But if it is not, corrective action will be immediately taken. In brief, what is learned from the inspection of a sample of the product is used as a basis for deciding whether any changes should be made in production process.

Q. 1.28: *(a) Why most quality control inspections be on a sample basis only?*

(*b*) What are the three main parts at which inspection is usually carried out?

Ans : (*a*) Some important reasons for carrying out quality control inspection on a sample only are:

- Inspection may cause damage or destruction.
- Accuracy may be diminished if inspection is repetitive and for long period of time.
- Inspection may be hazardous procedure.
- Handling the products may result in their deterioration.
- Lengthy inspection periods may be unurse due to perishability or deterioration of goods.

(*b*) Inspection is usually carried out at the following three parts:

- Receiving inspector for raw materials and purchased components.
- Floor or process inspector for *WIP*.
- Final inspection or testing for finished goods.

Q. 1.29: *(a) List out some reasons why quality is important in manufacturing.*

(*b*) List some reasons why quality is important in (i) services (ii) not-for-profit organizations.

(*c*) Statistical process control is concerned with :

(i) controlling process variability

(ii) ensuring output is within specifications

Advice the ***incorrect*** *statement in part (c).*

Ans : (*a*) Some important reasons for importance of quality in manufacturing are :

1. survival
2. competitive advantage
3. influence on cost
4. influence on image

(*b*) Some reasons for important of quality in services and not-for-profit organizations are :

1. influence on cost
2. influence on image
3. influence on pay masters
4. social responsibility

(*c*) (*i*)

Q. 1.30: *(a) How can statistical process control help quality planning and control ?*

(*b*) *Mention briefly the various statistical control charts in SQC work.*

Ans : (*a*) Statistical process control (SPC) involves using control charts to track the performance of one or more quality characteristics in the operation. The power of control charting lies in its ability to set control limits derived from the statistics of the natural variation of processes. These control limits are often set at ± 3 standard deviations of the natural variation of the process samples.

Control charts can be used for either attributes or variables. An attribute is a quality characteristic which has two states (for example, right or wrong). A variable is one which can be measured on a continuously variable scale.

Process control charts allow operations managers to distinguish between the 'normal' variation inherent in any process and the variations which could be caused by the process going out of control.

(*b*) Statistical process control charts are useful for measuring the current quality generated by the process and for detecting whether the process has changed to the detriment of quality. Thus *R* charts are used to monitor process variability, $\bar{X}$ charts and *p* charts identify abnormal variations in the process average, and *c*-charts are used for controlling the number of defects when a product or service process could result in several defects. The presence of abnormal variation triggers a search for assignable causes.

Q. 1.31: *"Quality control is fine, but my product is different. It is not easily subject to control. It is too complicated". Such types of remarks came from a person who sought examples of modern statistical quality control.*

Is he justified ? Why or why not ?

Ans : The remarks seem to be unjustified because the difference is almost always superficial. There is no field of human material experience that does not function in a statistical manner. As long as the materials, men, methods, and machines are used, the problems of quality variation exists. As long as these exists, the methods of statistical quality control are needed.

If a detailed analysis of scrap and rework in terms of money is made and the cost of nonconforming products in terms of customer good-will and reputation is realized, one will certainly come to the conclusion that it is better to spend some portion of this amount to bring about a greater reduction in losses and an improved competitive position.

Q. 1.32: *In what types of production units the statistical techniques of quality control are applicable ?*

Ans : (*a*) Broadly speaking these techniques are applicable only to manufacturing units organized on a quality or mass production basis. Whenever production is repetitive, either in a continuous flow or lot by lot, these quality control techniques will prove to be of ultimate benefit.

As a matter of experience it is found that the method is not economic if an individual lot runs for less than two-hour or three eight-hour shifts through the production process to be "quality controlled". There are exceptions of course. Where small batches repeat constantly, e.g. in aircraft production on short orders, quality control is still applicable. The original application of quality control to a machine shop took place in a precision engineering firms where the average batch size was around 500-1,500 piece parts.

The basic control chart methods are also applicable to product inspection, as distinct from process inspection. It is in this sphere, rather than in that of quality control proper, that the use of these methods leads to the greatest economics in inspection effort and, therewith, to corresponding saving in manpower.

Q. 1.33 : *Comment on the following statement :*

"Control of quality by statistics is the recording of the actual fluctuations in the dimensions of the product of the machines and the statistics so compiled are then available for future guidance. Quality control charts and records can only serve a useful purpose by having as their object the reduction of scrap material and wastage of time, but as the chart is recorded after the event, it is difficult to understand how even this would be achieved".

Ans : (*a*) The statements cited above is an almost perfect example of what quality control is not. The one who has made this statement has clearly failed to grasp the fact that the quality control is essentially news and not history. The outstanding and characteristic feature of the quality control chart is its practical value as a signalling device, indicating to all concerned the onset of impending troubles, and providing objective evidence upon which the appropriate preventive measures may be based. Perhaps the best definition of quality control is that it puts process inspection on a sound basis.

Q. 1.34: *Some of the commonly encountered criticisms of quality control are :*

1. *Quality control reduces engineering limits, i.e. the working tolerances.*
2. *Production is slowed down, by stopping jobs that are according to drawing.*
3. *Statistics must be kept involving time and paper.*
4. *Overheads are increased by spending time and money in measuring parts whose dimensions are within the specified limits.*

Are these objections justified ? Why or why not ?

Ans : (*a*) ***Objection 1*** is by far the most common and arises quite clearly from a misconception as to the relation between control limits and engineering limits. The fact that the former lie inside the latter in no way means that the production process is being controlled within narrower working limits, for these two sets of limits are not directly comparable. The control limits apply only to the *average value* of the several measurement comprising the patrol inspector's "sample". As long as successive samples average fall inside their control limits—the criterion of a stable process level—the corresponding individual measurements will fall inside certain other limits which define the inherent precision of the production process. It is these latter limits, and not the former, which are directly comparable with the tolerance or engineering limits. They are the so-called stability limits for the product and are, in fact, the "limits of accuracy" inherent in production process. The point to bear in mind in interpreting the control charts ($\overline{X}$ and *R*) is, then, that the control limits cannot be referred directly to the engineering limits, for these two sets of limits relate to two different kinds of dimensional values. They can only be compared through "Relative Precision Index" (R.P.I).

Objection 2 attacks the basic operational principle of the control chart as means for taking corrective action before nonconforming items are produced. It is likewise founded on the misconception that control limits are merely "narrower working limits", and that a point on the control chart falling inside the engineering limits thus represents a "job that is according to drawing".

Objections 3 and ***4*** are readily met by pointing out that any system of practical and permanent value requires paper work as well as time and money spent in running it. One does not object on that score to production control or stock control systems—so why object to a quality control system ? Provided such a system pays for itself by reducing scrap and rejected parts, why should it not be introduced into inspection.

Q. 1.35 : *(a) How would you answer an operator who said that 'quality is the inspector's responsibility'?*

(b) How far it can be said that quality is everybody's business ? Do you agree with this concept?

Ans : (*a*) An inspection can only measure work to see whether or not it is right. No amount of inspection will put right that which an operator has incorrectly made.

(*b*) After giving due considerations to the consumer's requirements, the design of the product will go to the production planners, where the following will probably take place.

1. The design will be examined for any obvious inconsistencies.

2. The sequence of operations will be decided, and for each :
   (*i*) a detailed method will be prepared,
   (*ii*) any special jigs or other equipment will be designed, manufactured and checked,
   (*iii*) machines and other process equipment will be specified and made available,
   (*iv*) supplies of raw materials will be arranged,
   (*v*) supervisor will obtain and train suitable operators.

When all is ready, the job will be loaded onto the workshops for the manufacture of each operation in turn. This will inevitably involve a large number of operators, inspectors, supervisors etc. Indeed practically everyone in a company contributes in some way to the quality produced, so that it is often said that 'quality is every body's business'.

Whilst this concept is perfectly true, it does present difficulties. If quality is everybody's business, there is a real risk that it will become nobody's reponsibility. To offset this, the present day practice is to employ someone to coordinate the quality effort. His title may be quality manager or chief inspector etc. and the department he controls may be called the quality assurance department, quality control department or inspection department.

Q. 1.36 : *(a) Why most quality control inspections be on a sample basis only?*

(b) A production engineer once remarked, "It is no good trying to set quality standards for everythings, we expect our operators to use their common sense". How would you have answered him ?

(c) a company produced a component made of soft rubber, in which the drawing called for a hole ***0.100 ± 0.001*** *inch in diameter. This was checked with a plug gauge, but there were endless arguments between the operators and inspection. Discuss why this might be, and what should be done about it.*

Ans : (*a*) In principle, the consumer sets the quality standard. The designer merely interprets the consumer's requirements into manufacturing drawings and specifications.

(*b*) In order to keep a check, some sort of quality standard is almost always better than no standard at all.

(*c*) Soft rubber probably will not hold tolerances as tight as this, especially to check with a plug gauge, so that the result depends on how much pressure the inspection uses. If tolerance as tight as this are really necessary, then a method of measurement must be found which does not deform the rubber.

Q. 1.37: *(a) What is the traditional approach to quality? What problems do you see with this approach? Highlight the important issues in your opinion.*

(*b*) *What does the abandonment of mass inspection to assess quality imply?*

Ans : (*a*) There has been a rise in awareness of quality and the systems that support it, to the extent that it has become of *strategic significance.* Quality is now considered to be of fundamental importance to many organizations. Indeed, many firms pursue a *strategy of differentiation based on high quality*

There was a time when quality was not measured as an output target, and when managers considered it something to be added on to a product rather than something that was integral to it. Quality control applied largely to manufacturing and meant inspection, or identifying when defective items are being produced at an unacceptable level.

There are many problems with this approach.

(*i*) The inspection process itself does not add value; if it could be guaranteed that no defective items were produced, there would be no need for a separate inspection function.

(*ii*) The production of substandard products is a waste of raw materials, machine time, human effort and overhead cost.

(*iii*) The inspection department takes up possibly expensive land and warehousing space.

(*iv*) The production of defects is not compatible with newer production techniques such as just-in-time: there is no time for inspection.

(*v*) Working capital is tied up in inventories that cannot be sold.

In other words the mass inspection approach builds waste into the process, which is not acceptable: the resources it consumes can be put to better use.

(*b*) The abandonment of mass inspection to assess quality implies that quality must be built in from the beginning, not added on at the end.

Q. 1.38: *The boss of XY Umbrellas Ltd. believes that customers want robust umbrellas, so she makes one entirely out of titanium apart from some gold decoration. 'It is a bit heavy I suppose', she says, showing on example, but it's perfectly made, look at the gold pins and look at the perfect, flawless finish. Why don't people want it?*

Ans: (*a*) Quality characteristics can be seen as comprising *functionality, appearance, reliability, durability, recovery* and *contract* etc.

(*b*) (*i*) *Control* is the totality of all means whereby we establish and achieve a standard of performance.

(*ii*) *Quality control* is the totally of all meant whereby we establish and achieve a quality specification/(SQC).

(*iii*) *Statistical quality control/(SQC)* is that part of the means for establishing and achieving a quality specification, which requires uses of the tools of statistics.

Q. 1.39: *(a) Which of the following is responsible for success of Japanese industries*

(b) State the core issue in:

(i) Product design (ii) Process design (iii) Process control

Ans: (*a*) (*i*)

(*b*) **(*i*) Core issues in produce design**

(*i*) Asses consumer needs

(*ii*) Design a product to meet those needs at the least cost

(*iii*) Involve customers, suppliers and manufacturing personnel.

(*iv*) Set-product specifications.

(*ii*) Core issues in produce design

(*i*) Process must be designed to meet final product design specification

(*ii*) Design process while product is being designed to avoid inefficiencies in production or the need to redesign the product.

(*iii*) SET-process limits.

(*iii*) Core issues in process control

(*i*) Ensure that the process actually produces a product that meets specification.

(*ii*) This will happen if the process was designed correctly and if it is kept in control

(*iii*) Keep the process within limits.

Q. 1.40: *(a) What is the ordinary meaning of quality? How this meaning is different in industrial context?*

(b) Quality is to be considered from the important of both customers and producers. How ?

Ans: (*a*) Quality is defined as the totality of features and characteristics of a product which bears on its ability to meet stated or implied needs. Ordinarily quality implies same degree of excellence or superiority.

In an industrial context, it is defined in a much more functional way. Here quality is more concerned with 'fitness for purpose' or 'fitness for use'. Fitness for use includes two elements : Quality of design which can include the consumer satisfactions built into the product. Quality of conformance in other words is a lack of defects/non-conformities in the finished goods.

(*b*) Quality must be considered from the viewpoint of both the consumer and the producer (service provider)

The customer – according to *Deming* the customer is the most important part of the production line. Quality should be aimed at the needs of the customer, present and future. This is driven by what the consumer wants and will pay for.

The producer – the product should be designed to meet or exceed the customer's expectations. Once a product has been properly designed, the role of operations, manager is to ensure that the product actually produced meet the design specification. This is done through product design, process design, process control and conformance to specification.

Q. 1.41: *(a) What is meant by quality policies of a company?*

(b) Can you highlight the various quality policy statements found in companies? Add a brief description to each.

Ans: (*a*) Quality policies define the overall intentions and directions of an organization related to quality as formally expressed by top management.

(*b*) Statement of quality policy may be divided into three types:

(*i*) The mission statement is a brief statement of overall quality policy and commitment set down at the most senior level of management. It will probably refer to customer satisfaction, ISO 9000 and the importance of good quality practice.

(*ii*) The corporate policy statement expands upon the mission statement. The eight quality principles already mentioned provide a good basis for drafting this policy. Additionally it should also conform to five requirements.

1. It should be appropriate to the needs of the organization and its customers.
2. It should involve all members of the organization.
3. It should provide an outline of the organization's goals and objectives.
4. It should be communicated and implemented throughout the organization.
5. It should be understood by everyone involved.

(*iii*) *Process-specific policies* will relate directly to the organization's processes and quality requirements. These should be adequate to manage quality in all key processes.

Q. 1.42: *Mention in simple terms how will you judge the quality of a product or service? What are the implications of you criteria set for judging the quality of a product or service?*

SOLUTION : In simple terms, the quality of a product or service can be judge on the following criteria.

(*i*) How well made a product is, or how well performed if it is a service.

(*ii*) How well it serves its purpose.

(*iii*) How it measures up against its rivals.

The implications of above criteria can be

- That quality is something that requires care on the part of the provider.
- That quality is largely subjective - it is in the eye of the beholder, the customer.

Q. 1.43: *Differentiate between quality and grade.*

Ans: Quality and grade are **not** the same. Quality is the sum of the characteristics of a product that allow it to meet the demands or expectations of the customer. Quality is all about fulfilling requirements.

Grade, is a category or rank given to entities having the same functional use but different technical characteristics. For example, there are different grade of paint, different grades of metal, and even different grades of travel.

Low quality is always a problem, but low grade may not be. Depending on the requirements of the customer, low grade may be completely acceptable, but low quality never is.

Q. 1.44: *What is 'gold plating' with respect to quality and what are its implications?*

Ans: The customer while drawing the specifications for the product he/she wishes to buy also fixes the price to be paid for the product. *Gold plating* is the process of adding extra features that may drive up costs and alter schedules. The vendor should strive to deliver what was expected. Figure 1.5 shows a curve relating cost and level of quality and gold plating.

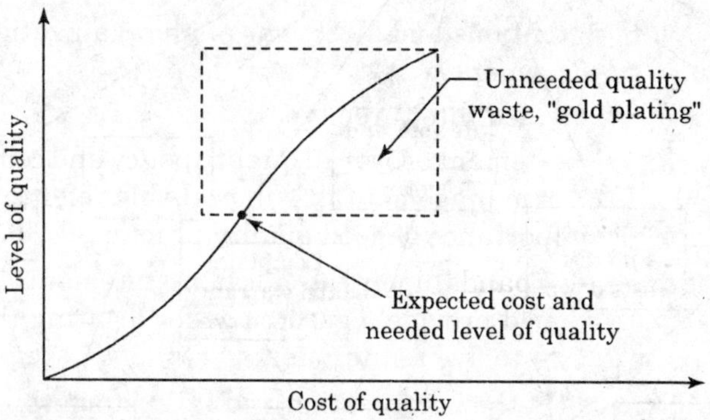

FIGURE 1.5 Gold Plating

Q. 1.46: *(a) What is conveyed by quality characteristics?*

(b) Define briefly the following:

(i) control (ii) quality control (iii) statistically quality control.

Ans: (*a*) Quality characteristic can be seen as comprising *functionality, appearance, reliability, durability, recovery* and *contract* etc.

(*b*) (*i*) *Control* is the totality of all means whereby we establish and achieve a standard of performance.

(*ii*) *Quality control* is the totality of all meant whereby we establish and achieve a quality specification.

(*iii*) *Statistical quality control (SOC)* is that past of the means for establishing specifications, which requires uses and achieving of statistics.

Q. 1.46: *(a) What are the consequences of low quality?*

(b) Mention some potential benefits of quality control?

(c) Mention only ***(do not describe)*** *the key feature of world-class manufacturing?*

Ans: (*a*) Consequences of low quality can be follows:

- Excessive costs are incurred in correcting defects (or non-conformities) and adding or improving features to make the system.
- User confidence is undermined.
- Business efficiency is harmed and harmful effects on customer satisfaction and thence on profitability and even on the continuing existence of the organization or industrial unit.

(*b*) The benefits of quality control come from savings in quality-related costs from improvements in customer relations and hopefully (because of the facial product) increased sales due to increased sales demand. As a bonus feature of this, the production schedules are met with.

(*c*) A strong *customer focus* and *flexibility* to meet customer requirements.

Q. 1.48: *How quality has beneficial effect on profit?*

Ans: There are many benefits of high quality or quality improvement. All these benefits ultimately lead to higher profit thorough different routes as depicted in Fig. 1.6.

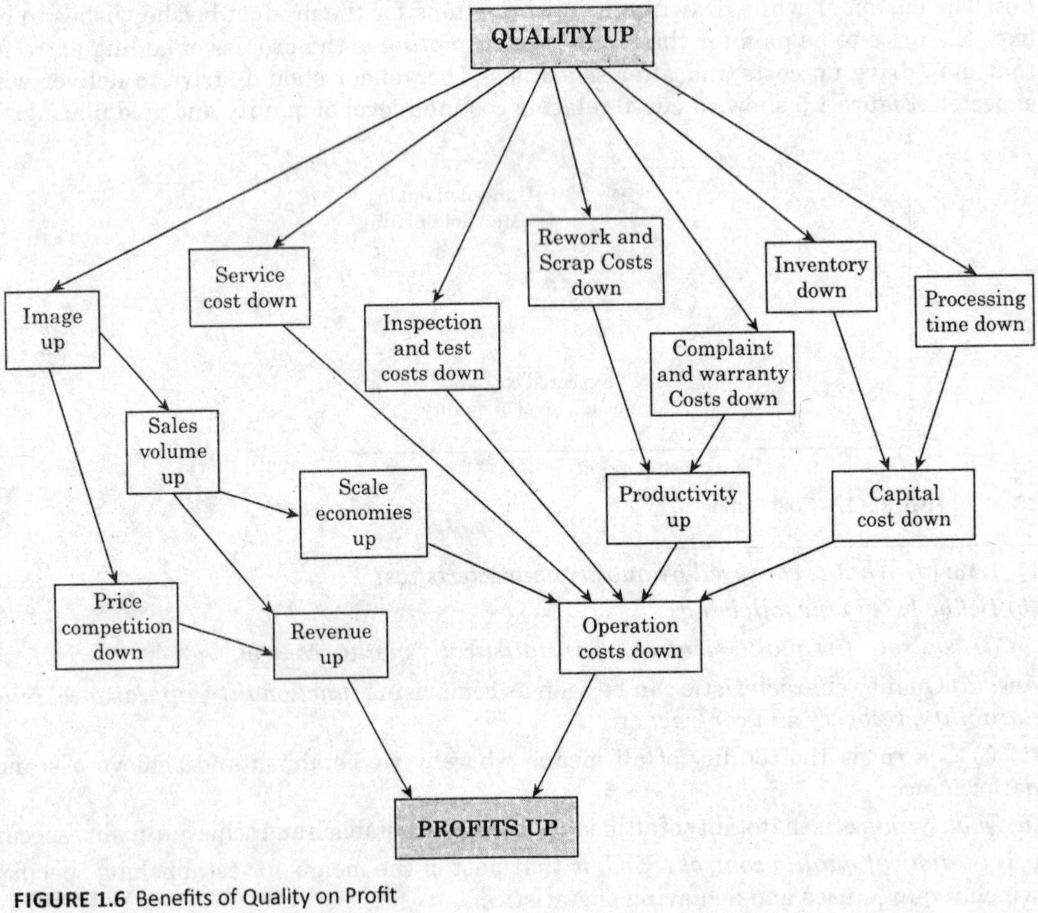

FIGURE 1.6 Benefits of Quality on Profit

PART-1(B)

STATISTICAL PROCESS CONTROL (*SPC*)

CHAPTER

2 Some Statistical Concepts

2.1 NEED FOR UNDERSTANDING STATISTICAL PRINCIPLES

This chapter and the one that follows deal with the principles behind control charts for variables. Experience indicates that the lack of understanding the fundamentals and principles of statistics may lead to costly mistakes and eventually may lead to problems rather than any benefit. However as the quality control personnel are not expected to be familiar with advanced mathematics, the theory developed in this and subsequent chapters, therefore, will emphasize an *intuitive* approach rather than a purely *mathematical* approach. Much of the theory presented uses ordinary arithmetic with occasional assistance of algebra.

The use of statistics in quality control works involves collecting, tabulating, analyzing, interpreting and presenting the quantitative data.

There are ***two*** phases of statistics.

1. *Descriptive* or *deductive statistics,* which endeavours to describe and analyze a subject or group.
2. *Inductive statistics,* which endeavours to determine from a limited amount of data (sample) an important conclusion about a much larger amount of data (universe). Since these conclusions or inferences cannot be stated with absolute certainty, the language of *probability* is often used.

2.2 DESCRIPTION OF PATTERNS OF VARIATION

As already stated in Chap. 1, variation seems inevitable in nature. Manufacturing processes are no exception to this. In fact one of the characteristics of modern manufacturing is that no two pieces are ever made exactly alike. Whether we are attempting to control a dimension of a part which is to form an integral part of an assembly, the resistance of a relay, the acidity of a solution used for dyeing textiles, or any other quality of a manufactured product, it is certain that quality will vary. The variations may be *small*—as in the case of famous Johanson blocks, which have been guaranteed to two millionths of an inch, or they may be *large*—as in the case of hand lathes, annealing furnaces, or painting machines.

Some variations are so great that they are immediately shown by modern measuring equipment. Other variations are so minute that successive readings on measuring equipment will reflect primarily the variation of the measuring equipment themselves rather than that of the part. Among the types of variation, ***three*** following classifications useful for analytical purposes.

1. *Variations within the part itself,* are illustrated by a small shaft which is out of round at one end and within tolerance at the other end.

2. *Variations among parts produced during the same period of time,* as illustrated by the variations in the length of studs produced by a screw machine during 10 minutes period.
3. *Variations among parts produced at different period of time* as illustrated by the variation in length between studs produced at the beginning of the first shift as compared with those produced the at end of the shift.

There are many factors that contribute to any or all of these variations. Among them are tool wear, bearings that loosen, machine vibration, faulty jigs and fixtures, poor raw materials, careless or untrainted operators, and weather changes.

Industry has long recognized the inevitability of these variations. It therefore includes on drawings and specifications, tolerance which designate the permissible deviation from the standard shape, thickness, colour and size etc. The above arguments sufficiently tell us that whatsoever the reasons may be, it is *certain that quality characteristic will vary.*

It follows that it is necessary to have some simple methods of describing patterns of variation. Statisticians and engineers have developed such methods. One useful method involves a *frequency distribution.* Another involves the finding of a measure of the *central tendency* of a distribution (that is an *average* or *mean*) combined with some measure of the *dispersion*, or *spread*, of the distribution.

This chapter explains and illustrates these important methods of describing patterns of variation. It explains that there may be both *stable* and *unstable* patterns of variation ; it points out that the practical conclusions to be drawn from frequency distributions, averages, and measures of dispersion depend on the stability of the pattern of variation. The control chart, which is a test for this stability, is illustrated in Chap. 3 of this book.

2.2.1 Data Gathering

In order to present the patterns of variation for a particular quality characteristic, it is necessary to gather the correct and relevant data concerning only the particular quality characteristic. As the data form the basis for analysis and further action, it is necessary to take good care while collecting the data.

Data may be collected by direct observation or indirectly through written or verbal questions. The latter technique is used extensively by market research personnel and public opinion pollsters. Data that are collected for quality control purposes are obtained by direct observation and are classified as either variables or attributes :

- *Variables* are those quality characteristics which are measurable such as a weight in grams.
- *Attributes* are those quality characteristics which are classified as either conforming or nonforming to specifications.

A variable that is capable of any degree of subdivision is referred to as *continuous*. The weight of a grey iron casting which can be measured as 11 kg, 11.33 kg, or 11.3398 kg, depending on the accuracy of the measuring instrument, is an example of continuous variable. Measurements such as meters, litres, and pascals (pounds per square inch) are examples of continuous data. Variables that exhibit gaps are called *discrete*. The number of defective rivets in a travel trailer can be any whole number, such as 0, 3, 5, 10, 96, ...; however, there cannot be, say, 4.65 defective rivets in a particular trailer. In general, continuous data are *measurable*, while discrete data are *countable*.

Sometimes it is convenient for verbal or non numerical data to assume the nature of a variable. For example, the quality of the surface finish of a piece of furniture can be classified as poor, average, or good. The poor, average, or good classification can be replaced by the numerical values of 1, 2, or 3, respectively.

While many quality characteristics are stated in terms of variables, there are many characteristics which must be stated as attributes. Frequently, those characteristics which are judged by visual observation are classified as attributes. The wire on an electric motor is either attached to the terminal or it is not; the words on this page are correctly spelled or they are incorrectly spelled; the switch is on or it is off; and the answer is right or it is wrong. The examples given in the previous sentence show conformance to a particular specification or nonconformance to that specification.

It is frequently desirable for variables to be classified as attributes. Factory personnel are primarily interested in knowing if the product they are producing conforms to the specifications. For example, the numerical value for the weight of a package of sugar is not as important as the information that the weight is within the prescribed limits. Therefore, the data, which are collected on the weight (*i.e.* variable) of the package of sugar, are reported as acceptable or unacceptable (*i.e.* attribute).

In collecting data the degree of accuracy of the numerical figures is a function of the intended use of the data. For example, in collecting data on the life of light bulbs, it is acceptable to record 995.6 h; however, recording a value of 995.632 h is too accurate and unnecessary. Similarly, if a keyway specification has lower limit of 9.52 mm and an upper limit of 9.85 mm, then data would be collected to the nearest 0.001 mm and rounded to the nearest 0.01 mm.

The rounding of data requires that certain conventions be followed. In rounding the numbers 0.9531, 0.9532, 0.9533, and 0.9534 to the nearest thousandth, the answer is 0.953, since all the numbers are closer to 0.953 than they are to 0.954. And in rounding the numbers 0.9536, 0.9537, 0.9538, and 0.9539, the answer is 0.954, since all the numbers are closer to 0.954 than to 0.953. But in rounding the number 0.9435, we find it to be equidistant from 0.953 and 0.954. Therefore, to minimise cumulative rounding errors, it is the practice to round *up* if the integer preceding the 5 is *odd* and to *truncate* the 5 if the integer preceding it is *even*. The number 0.9535 would be rounded to 0.954 and the number 0.9545 would also be rounded to

0.954. This convention is statistically more desirable since it is unbiased, *i.e.*, it is reasonable to suppose that in a large mass of data as many numbers ending in 5 will be rounded 'down' as many are rounded 'up'.

2.2.2 Counting the Frequencies of Different Observations

Table 2.1 gives the results of measurement of weights of 110 steel shafts. Clearly these data, in this ungrouped or raw data form, are difficult to use and are not effective in describing data's characteristics.

One way to organize such figures to show their pattern of variation is to count the number of times each value occurs. This may be done conveniently on a check sheet (or tally sheet, as more popularly known) such as Fig 2.1. The results of such a count are called a *frequency*

TABLE 2.1: WEIGHT OF STEEL SHAFTS
(Weight in kilograms)

2.559	2.556	2.566	2.546	2.561
2.570	2.546	2.565	2.543	2.538
2.560	2.560	2.545	2.551	2.568
2.546	2.555	2.551	2.554	2.574
2.568	2.572	2.550	2.556	2.551
2.561	2.560	2.564	2.567	2.560
2.551	2.562	2.542	2.549	2.561
2.556	2.550	2.561	2.558	2.556
2.559	2.557	2.532	2.575	2.551
2.550	2.559	2.565	2.552	2.560
2.534	2.547	2.569	2.559	2.549
2.544	2.550	2.552	2.536	2.570
2.564	2.553	2.558	2.538	2.564
2.552	2.543	2.562	2.571	2.553
2.539	2.569	2.552	2.536	2.537
2.532	2.552	2.575 (*max*)	2.545	2.551
2.547	2.537	2.547	2.533	2.538
2.571	2.545	2.545	2.556	2.543
2.551	2.569	2.559	2.534	2.561
2.567	2.572	2.558	2.542	2.574
2.570	2.542	2.552	2.551	2.553
2.546	2.531(*min*)	2.563	2.554	2.544

Weight	*Tally*	*Weight*	*Tally*	*Weight*	*Tally*
31	/	46	////	61	////
32	//	47	///	62	//
33	/	48		63	/
34	//	49z	//	54	///
35		50	////	65	//
36	//	51	~~////~~ ///	66	/
37	//	52	~~////~~ /	67	//
38	///	53	///	68	//
39	/	54	//	69	///
40		55	/	70	///
41		56	~~////~~	71	//
42	///	57	/	72	//
43	///	58	///	73	
44	//	59	////	74	//
45	////	60	////	75	//

FIGURE 2.1 Tally sheet to determine the frequency distribution from data of Table 2.1.

distribution. In order to be more efficient, the weights are coded from 2.500 kg. which is a technique to simplify data. Therefore, a weight with a value of 31 is equivalent to 2.531 (*i.e.* 2.500 + 0.031 kg).

The frequency distribution immediately tells us where most of the data are grouped (the data are centered about a weight of 2.551) and how much variation there is in the data (weight runs from 2.531 to 2.575). The centering and amount of variation in large set of data would not readily apparent from an original data sheet. The frequency distribution spotlights this information.

The frequency distribution usually enjoys a better initial reception in the shop when it is called a *tally*. Its record forms may be termed *tally cards*. A wide variety of forms are used for these tallies. Figure 2.2 shows one of the most widely used format for tally cards.

2.2.3 Definitions Relative to Frequency Distributions

- A *grouped frequency distribution* of a set of observations is an arrangement that shows the frequency of occurrence of the values of the variable in ordered classes.

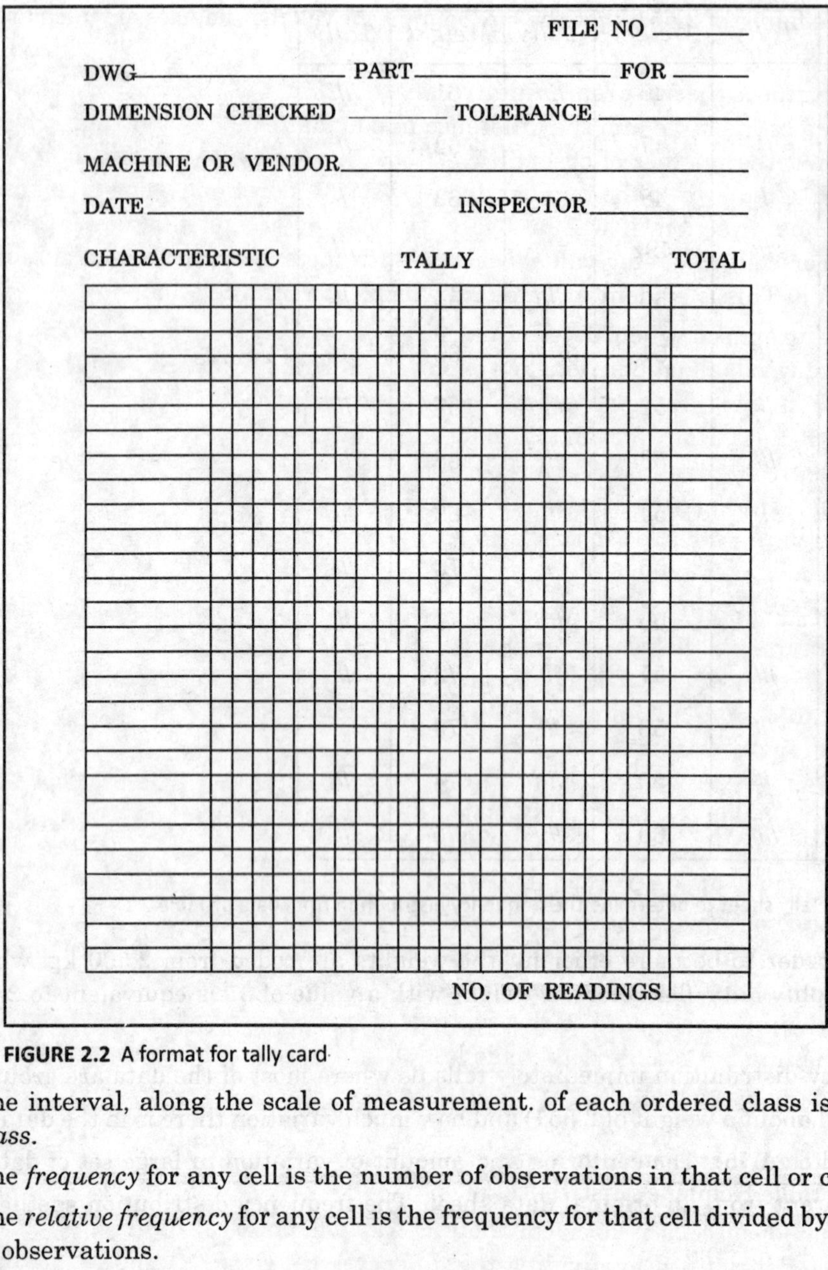

FIGURE 2.2 A format for tally card

- The interval, along the scale of measurement. of each ordered class is termed a *cell* or *class*.
- The *frequency* for any cell is the number of observations in that cell or class.
- The *relative frequency* for any cell is the frequency for that cell divided by the total number of observations.

2.2.4 CELLS, CELL BOUNDARIES AND CELL LIMITS

In Table 2.1, each measured weight was recorded to one thousandth of a kg; as no greater precision measurement was required for the purpose in hand. This is a case of continuous variables. For example, the weight of a given shaft recorded by this measuring process as measured 2.559 does not necessarily measure 2.559 kg. If more precise methods of measurement were used, it might be found to have a weight of 2.5592 kg or any other value which is nearer to 2.559 than it 2.558 or 2.560. The statement in the frequency distribution that 8 shafts had a weight 2.551 really means that weight of each of the 8 shafts was somewhat between 2.5505 and 2.5515 kg. The figure of 2.551 kg is the *midpoint* of the cell, boundaries of which are 2.5505 and 2.5515.

The midpoint value is the most representative value within a cell provided that the number of observations in a cell is large and the difference in boundaries is not too great. Even if this condition is not met, the number of observations above and below the midpoint of a cell will frequently be equal. And even if the number of observations above and below a cell midpoints is unbalanced in one direction, if will probably be offset by an unbalanced in the opposite direction of another cell. Midpoint values should be to the same degree of accuracy as the original observation. This is evident in Table 2.2 which shows the cell midpoints.

Care must be exercised when determining the cell or cell boundaries. For example, a number of pieces of wood, about 6 in. long, were measured with an ordinary ruler and recorded as 5.9, 5.8, 6.1, 6.0 in. etc. If these are stated to be the nearest 0.1 in., then the cell boundaries are 5.75, 5.85, 5.95 in etc. However, an alternate convention is to state completed tenths only,' i.e., fractions of tenths are ignored. Then the cell boundaries are 5.8 to 5.9^-, 5.9 to 6.0^-, 6.0 to 6.1^- etc., where the minus sign indicates 'upto but excluding. Using this convention a rod whose length is 5.898 in. will be included in the cell 5.8 to 5.9^- in., but if the length is 5.900 in., it will be included in the next cell 5.9 to 6.0^-.

Finally, when grouping the discrete data, another term must be introduced, namely cell *limits*. The cell limits are the highest and lowest discrete values included in each cell. For example, if the discrete values 0, 1, 2, etc., upto 99 are grouped into 20 cells of equal width, cell limits would be 0 to 4, 5, to 9, 10 to 14, etc., while the cell boundaries would be – 0.5 to +4.5, 4.5 to 9.5, 9.5 to 14.5 etc., with cell midpoints 2, 7, 12 etc.

In grouping the data into a frequency distribution, the question often arises as to how many cells there should be and where the cell boundaries should be placed. For the given data the choice of the number of cells and hence the width of the cell interval is largely a matter of common sense and judgement. When the number of cells is large, the true picture of the distribution is distorted by cells having an insufficient number of items or sometimes none at all. Or, when the number of cells is small, too many items are concentrated in a few cells and the distribution is also distorted. A useful guide is to divide the data into between 5 to 20 cells depending upon the number of data or observations. A useful and practical guideline is to use 5-9 cells when the number of observations is less than 100, use 8-17 cells when the number of observations is between 100 and 500, and 15-20 cells when the number of observations is greater than 500. To provide flexibility, the number of cells in the guidelines are over-lapping. It is emphasized that these guidelines are *not rigid* and can be adjusted when necessary to present an acceptable frequency distribution.

Once the number of cells is decided, the cell width or interval (difference between cell midpoints) can be determined by dividing the difference between the highest value and the lowest value of the variable by the number of cells. For example in case of Table 2.1 the maximum value is 2.575 and the minimum is 2.531. Their difference, usually known as range, is 0.044. If it is decided to have 15 cells, the cell interval will become $\frac{0.044}{15} \approx 0.003$. In case of 9 cells, this cell interval will become 0.005 and in case of 5 cells, the cell interval will become 0.009.

Table 2.2 illustrates an appropriate way to present a frequency distribution of Table 2.2 showing cell boundaries and cell midpoints for 9 cells. It illustrates also the effect of a coarse grouping, *i.e.*, using less number of cells or higher cell width or interval of 0.009.

TABLE 2.2: EXAMPLES OF GROUPED FREQUENCY DISTRIBUTION SHOWING CELL MID POINTS AND CELL BOUNDARIES
(Data of Table 2.1 on weights of shafts in kg.)

(a) Finer grouping			**(b) Coarse grouping**		
Cell boundaries	*Cell midpoint*	*Observed frequency*	*Cell boundaries*	*Cell midpoint*	*Observed frequency*
2.5255—2.5305	2.528	—	2.5215—2.5305	2.526	—
2.5305—2.5355	2.533	6	2.5305—2.5395	2.535	14
2.5355—2.5405	2.538	8	2.5395—2.5485	2.544	19
2.5405—2.5455	2.543	12	2.5485—2.5575	2.553	32
2.5455—2.5505	2.548	13	2.5557—2.5665	2.562	27
2.5505—2.5555	2.553	20	2.5665—2.5755	2.571	18
2.5555—2.5605	2.558	19	2.5775—2.5845	2.580	—
2.5605—2.5655	2.563	13			
2.5655—2.5705	2.568 11				
2.5705—2.5755	2.573	8			
2.5755—2.5805	2.578	—			
Total		110	Total		110

It may be observed that grouping the data as one in Table 2.2 condenses the original data but some detail is lost. For example, the Table 2.2 indicates that only 6 shafts have weight between 2.5305 and 2.5355 kg. but it does not indicate as how many shafts out of these 6 have weight of 2.535. Such details are further lost when the grouping is still coarser as is again evident from Table 2.2. In order to avoid such problems it is always preferable and recommended to keep the original data.

2.3 GRAPHICAL REPRESENTATION OF A FREQUENCY DISTRIBUTION

The object of tabulating and grouping the data is to make it easier to see the overall pattern of the variation involved. This can often be done by representing the data graphically. Three most common ways of graphical representation of data for the purpose of presentation of frequency distributions are shown in Fig 2.3. Of these, the *frequency histogram* of Fig 2.3(*a*) is easily understood by shop people and executives and is the best in some respects.

Frequency Bar Chart. The simplest form of graphical representation of frequency distribution is simple bar charts using bars erected at the cell midpoints, the heights of the bars are proportional to the frequency in respective cells.

Frequency Histogram. A frequency histogram consists of rectangles with bases that represent cell boundaries and with heights that represent the frequency at the midpoints of the cells.

Figure 2.3(*a*) is the histogram of Table 2.2(*a*) (finer grouping). If desired, the sides of the rectangles may be omitted between the inside of the horizontal steps and the base line. As far as possible, it is desired to keep the cell width equal for all cells. However in certain situations this may not be feasible, particularly when the range of the data in the histogram is to be kept at its exact value only. Histogram affords to accommodate such situations also by allowing the cell width to be altered to k times the original cell width but height for this particular cell to be $\frac{1}{k}$ times of that would have been if the original cell width had been retained. It is obvious that cell heights (also areas of the cells) are either equal or proportional to the frequency in the cell. The histogram represents a visual display of the data in which four properties are exhibited :

- Shape
- Central tendency
- Scatter or spread
- Capability of the process to meet the specification limits.

Essentially, a histogram is a *postmortem* picture in that it portrays a situation that has already occurred. For illustrating variation patterns or for indicating shift or improvement, the histogram is unexcelled. However histogram fails to reveal the times when the process shifts are taking place.

Frequency Polygon. It is of less importance than the histogram, but still an effective way of presenting a picture of a frequency distribution is shown in Fig 2.3 (*b*) for the data in Table 2.2(*a*).

It consists of a series of straight lines joining dots placed over the cell midpoints with a height proportional to cell frequencies. The figure is extended to include an additional cell midpoint at each cell in order to for the figure to be closed. If it is desired to show the frequency of occurrence in terms of both number of items and percentages of items, it is suggested that two vertical scales be placed on the opposite side of the chart as illustrated in Fig. 2.3(*b*). A simple geometrical concept will indicate that the total area in the rectangles of a histogram and that of a frequency polygon are equal. Hence both in fact represent the total frequency.

Whether a frequency polygon or a histogram should be used is largely a matter of preference; however a frequency polygon can generally be used to better advantage if two or more distributions are to be shown on the same diagram. However, a histogram has several other advantages and generally better understood by both the shop people and the executives. A mere look at any histogram will give some idea of the concerned frequency distribution. It is interesting to note that while the frequency polygon implies that all the values in an interval

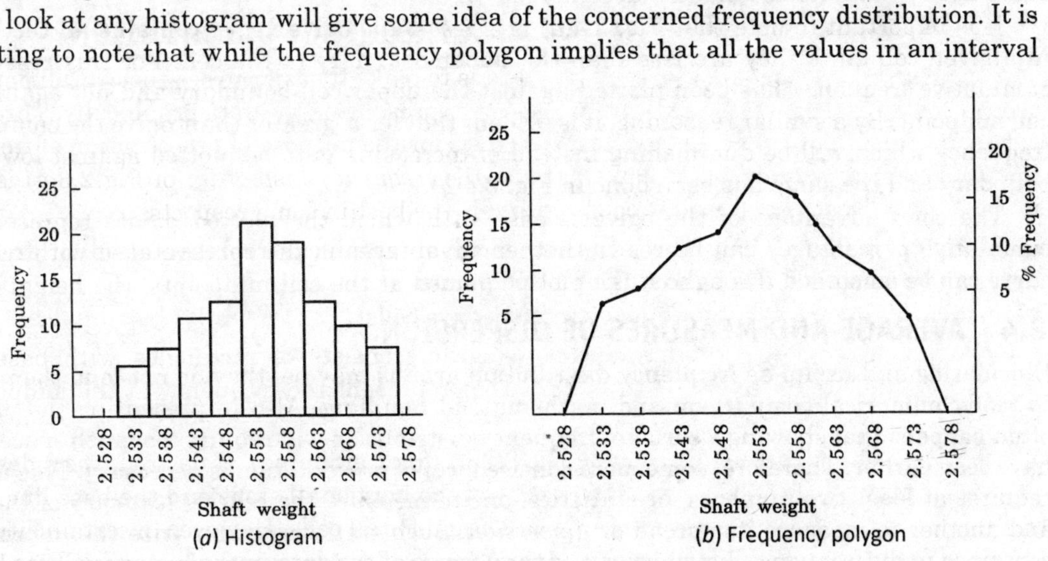

(*a*) Histogram (*b*) Frequency polygon

FIGURE 2.3 Methods of graphical representation of a frequency distribution of data in Table 2.2

TABLE 2.3: EXAMPLE OF CUMULATIVE FREQUENCY DISTRIBUTIONS
(Data of Table 2.1 an weights of steel shafts.)

Weight	*Number of shafts having less than given weight*	*Percentages of shafts having less than given weight*	*Weight*	*Number of shafts having greater than given weight*	*Percentage of shafts having greater than given weight*
2.5755	110	100.00	2.5755	0	0.00
2.5705	102	92.73	2.5705	8	7.27
2.5655	91	82.73	2.5655	19	17.27
2.5605	78	70.91	2.5605	32	29.09
2.5555	59	53.64	2.5555	51	46.36
2.5505	39	35.45	2.5505	71	64.55
2.5455	26	23.64	2.5455	84	76.36
2.5405	14	12.73	2.5405	96	87.27
2.5355	6	5.45	2.5355	104	94.55
2.5305	0	0.00	2.5305	110	100.00

are concentrated at the midpoints, the histogram implies that they are spread uniformly over the cell interval. However, in practice both the implications are usually incorrect.

It is sometimes advantageous to calculate the frequencies of values *less* than or *greater* than the respective cell boundaries. Table 2.3 illustrates this. It shows both the number of shafts and the percentage of shafts having less than and greater than a given weight. Such a *cumulative frequency distribution* may be represented graphically in the manner shown in Figs. 2.4 (*a*) and (*b*). These types of graphs are called *ogive* because of their similarity to ogee curve used by architects and dam designers.

It is important to note that Fig. 2.4(*a*) is a *'less than'* ogive *i.e.*, it contains all the values in a given cell since they are less than the upper boundary of the cell. For this reason the cumulative frequency has been plotted against the upper cell boundary and not against the cell midpoint. By a similar reasoning, it is evident that for a 'greater than' ogive the cumulative frequency which will be diminishing instead of increasing is to be plotted against lower cell boundary and the same has been done in Fig. 2.4(*b*).

The chief advantage of the ogive is ease with which the plotted points represent the cumulative percentages can be read. Another advantages is the relative ease with which a curve can be smoothed throughout the plotted points.

2.4 AVERAGE AND MEASURES OF DISPERSION

Elucidating and useful as frequency distribution graphs may be, they do not lend themselves to ready numerical comparison and mathematical handling. Also in presenting the data, it often happens that showing a series of frequency distribution will require too much space as we have seen earlier. Therefore, some more concise form of presentation is necessary. This always requires at least two numbers, or statistics, one to measure the *central tendency* of the data and another to measure its spread or *dispersion*. Such statistics summarize the information contained in the frequency distribution and therefore may suppress some important information contained in it.

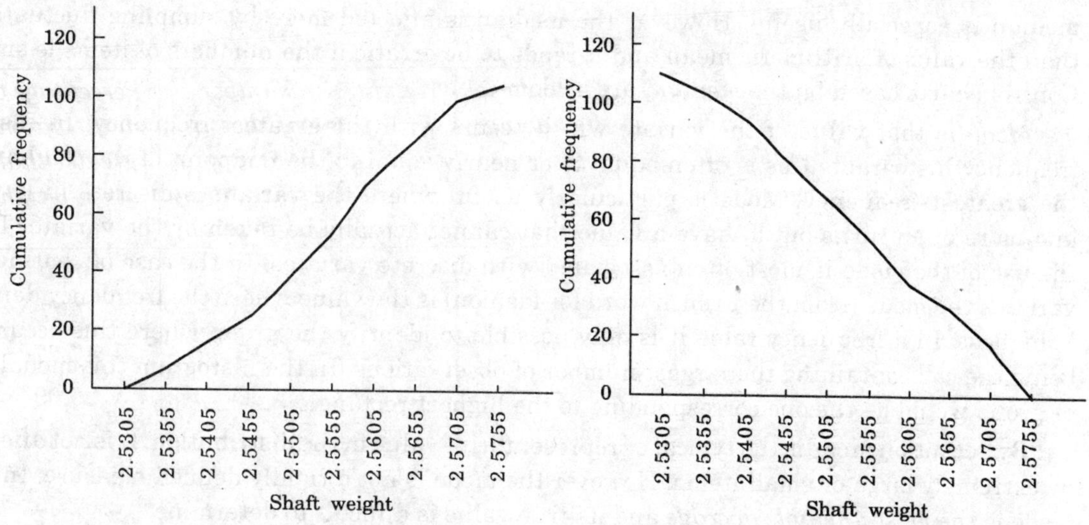

(a) "Less than" ogive

(b) "More than" ogive

FIGURE 2.4 'Less than' and 'More than' ogives for the data in Table 2.3.

The most commonly used measures of central tendency are the *median*, the *mode*, and the *mean* or, more correctly, the arithmetic mean. In popular language, the word *average* usually, implies the technical *arithmetic mean.* Such usage is also common in the literature of quality control. In this book the word *average* means *arithmetic mean* unless otherwise qualified.

The *arithmetic mean* of a set of n numbers is the sum of the numbers divided by n. Expressed algebraically

$$\bar{X}_j = \frac{X_1 + X_2 + X_3 + \dots + X_n}{n} = \frac{1}{n}\sum_{i=1}^{n} X_i \qquad \dots(2.1)$$

where the symbol $\bar{X}_j$ represents the arithmetic mean of any subgroup of consists of n items; X_1, X_2, and so forth, represent specific numbers; and the Greek capital letter Σ (sigma) is the mathematical symbol for the taking of a sum.

The other important measures of central tendency mentioned earlier i.e. median and mode of the data have found relatively less use in quality control work.

Median is that value of the variate which divides the total frequency exactly in half, *i.e.* half the values of the variate are greater, and half of the values are less than the median value.

If there is an odd number $(2n + 1)$ of observations of the variate , and they are arranged in ascending order, then the median is the $(n + 1)$th value.

If the number of observations in even $(2n)$ then the median is by convention taken to be average of the two middle values when arranged in ascending order, that is,

$$\text{Median} = \frac{nth + (n+1)th \text{ observation}}{2} \qquad \dots(2.2)$$

As compared to the mean, the median is not influenced by the magnitude of extreme deviations from it. Hence very often when extreme values are present in a set of observations, the median is a more satisfactory measure of the central tendency than the mean. Also in skewed distributions where the arithmetic mean would be distorted by extreme values the median is especially useful. However the median is affected more by sampling fluctuations than the value of arithmetic mean and it tends to be erratic if the numbers of items is small. Control charts based on the *median*, are seldom used.

Mode is that value of the variate which occurs with the greatest frequency. In case of frequency histograms this is often equal to or nearly equal to the midpoint of the cell having the greatest frequency. Mode is particularly useful where the variate is discrete in nature and more often turns out to have a value that cannot actually be taken by the variate. Thus the use of the mode is most often associated with discrete variates. In the case of continuous variates the mode (from the French word for fashion) is the value where the frequency density is highest. In a frequency table it is only possible to identify the group where this occurs, it being the cell containing the largest number of observations. In the histogram this modal cell or group would be the one corresponding to the highest rectangle.

By definition mode is the typical or representative value in the distribution. It is not affected by extremely large or small items. However the mode is not a rigidly defined measure. In fact mode is the *most unstable average* and its true value is difficult to determine.

A distribution in which the values of mean, median and mode coincide is known as a *symmetrical distribution.* Conversely stated when the values of mean, median and mode are not equal, the distribution is known as *asymmetrical* or *skewed.*

It can be shown that when a distribution is only moderately skewed there is an approximate relationship between the three measures of central tendency which may be expressed as:

$$Mean - Mode = 3\ (Mean - Median) \quad ...(2.3)$$

Two measures of dispersion or scatter that are extremely useful in statistical quality control are the *range R* (sometimes written as *w*, also) and the *sample standard deviation s*. Use of the range as a measure of dispersion, and its importance in control charts for variables is introduced in Chap 3. The range is almost *never used for large subgroups*, that is, for subgroups of more than 10 or 15 items. Expressed algebraically

$$R = X_{max} - X_{min}\ (or\ X_{highest} - X_{lowest}) \quad ...(2.4)$$

where X_{max} is the largest number and X_{min} is the smallest number in the set. The sample standard deviation of a set of numbers from their arithmetic mean is designated in this book by *s*. Expressed algebraically,

$$s = \sqrt{\frac{(X_1 - \bar{X}_1)^2 + (X_2 - \bar{X}_2)^2 + ... + (X_n - \bar{X})^2}{n-1}}$$

$$= \sqrt{\frac{\Sigma(X_i - \bar{X})^2}{n-1}} \quad ...(2.5)$$

While the sample standard deviation is less frequently used as a measure of dispersion of subgroups in control charts for variables, it is often used in measuring the dispersion of a frequency distribution such as might be pictured in a histogram. This is true particularly when the data have not been recorded in subgroups in order of production. The mathematical formula for *s* is applicable whether we are talking about a subgroup drawn for control-chart purposes or any other group of data.

Still another measure of dispersion is the *sample variance*. This measure is the sum of the squares of the deviations from the arithmetic mean divided by $n - 1$. In other words, the variance is square of the standard deviation *i.e.* s^2. The variability in the sample data is measured by sample variance. If there is no variability in the sample ; than each sample observation $X_i = \bar{X}$, and the sample variance $s^2 = 0$. Generally, the larger the sample variance s^2, the greater the variability in the sample data.

The units of the sample variance s^2, are the square of the original units of the data. This is often inconvenient and difficult to interpret, and we prefer to use square root of s^2, i.e. the standard deviation s. The primary advantage of the sample standard deviation is that it is expressed in the original units of measurement. To assist in understanding how the standard deviation describes variability, consider the two samples below :

Sample 1	Sample 2
$X_1 = 1$	$X_1 = 1$
$X_2 = 3$	$X_2 = 5$
$X_3 = 5$	$X_3 = 9$
$\bar{X} = 3$	$\bar{X} = 5$

Obviously *sample* 2 has more scatter than *sample* 1. This is reflected in the computed values of standard deviation, for both samples.

Sample 1 : $$s = \sqrt{\frac{(1-3)^2 + (3-3)^2 + (5-3)^2}{2}} = \sqrt{4} = 2$$

Sample 2 : $$s = \sqrt{\frac{(1-5)^2 + (5-5)^2 + (9-5)^2}{2}} = \sqrt{16} = 4$$

Thus the larger variability is *sample* 2 is reflected by its larger standard deviation. Now consider a third sample, say *sample* 3, for which

$$X_1 = 101$$
$$X_2 = 103$$
$$X_3 = 105$$
$$\bar{X} = 103$$

The standard deviation for *sample* 3 is also equal to 2, which is identical to the standard deviation of *sample* 1. Comparing the two sample, we see both samples have identical scatter about the average, and that is why they have the same standard deviation. This leads to an important conclusion :

- *The standard deviation does not reflect the magnitude of the sample data, it reflects only the scatter about the average.*

A possible source of confusion to persons who read two or more books that deal with principles or applications of statistics may be the different names, symbols, and formulae that writers use in connection with measures of mean square deviation. This somewhat troublesome topic involves the relationship between the dispersion of samples of a finite size and the dispersion of the "universe" from which, in concept, samples are assumed to have been drawn. At this point in our discussion, we have not yet dealt with sampling theory and are merely defining the sample standard deviation of a set of numbers as given in Eq. (2.5).

It may be noted that while discrete and continuous data are summarized numerically by means of *central tendency* and measures of *spread* while *categorical* and *ordinal data* are summarized by *tables, bar graphs,* and *pie -charts* only.

2.4.1 Calculation of a Subgroup Sample Average Standard Deviation and Range

Computation of the statistics for a small number of observations may be illustrated by reference to the five weights (considered to be sample No. 1) in the first column of Table 2.1.

Using Eq. (2.1) to find the sample mean :

$$\bar{X} = \frac{1}{n}\sum_{i=1}^{n} X_i$$

$$= \frac{1}{5}(2.559 + 2.570 + 2.560 + 2.546 + 2.568)$$

$$= 2.5606$$

Using Eq. (2.4) to find the sample range,

$$R = (X_{max} - X_{min}) = 2.570 - 2.546 = 0.024$$

Using Eq. (2.5) to find the sample standard deviation,

$$s = \sqrt{\frac{(2.559 - 2.5606)^2 + (2.570 - 2.5606)^2 + (2.560 - 2.5606)^2 + (2.546 - 2.5606)^2 + (2.568 - 2.5606)^2}{5 - 1}}$$

$$= 0.0095$$

Note the simplicity in the calculation of R in comparison with that of s.

A useful alternate form for Eq. (2.5) is

$$s = \sqrt{\frac{X_1^2 + X_2^2 + \ldots + X_n^2 - n\bar{X}^2}{n - 1}}$$

$$= \sqrt{\frac{\Sigma X_i^2 - n\bar{X}_i^2}{n - 1}} \qquad \ldots(2.6)$$

$$s = \sqrt{\frac{(2.559)^2 + (2.570)^2 + (2.560)^2 + (2.546) + (2.568)^8 - 5(2.5606)^2}{4}}$$

$$= 0.0095$$

This form of the equation may prove more convenient, especially where a desk calculator or computer is available.

2.4.2 Shifting the Origin to Simplify the Arithmetic

One possible trick useful in simplifying the arithmetic and also in reducing the number of significant figures that must be carried throughout the calculations is to shift the measuring scale to new zero point. Such a trick was used in the preparation of Fig 2.1 by shifting the origin to a new zero point of 2.500 kg. Also for the present case, a new origin of 2.560 could have been chosen for the variable in the preceding calculations. The new variable of interest would be the excess weight above 2.560 kg. Thus the calculations of $\bar{X}$ and s would have proceeded as follows:

$$\bar{X} \text{ (above the origin 2.560)} = \frac{-0.001 + 0.010 + 0.0 + 0.014 + 0.08}{5} = 0.0006$$

$$\bar{X} \text{ (above the origin 0)} = 2.560 + 0.0006 = 2.5606$$

Had an assumed origin of 2.500 been used :

$$\bar{X} \text{ (above the origin 2.500)} = \frac{0.059 + 0.70 + 0.060 + 0.046 + 0.068}{5} = 0.0606$$

$$\bar{X} \text{ (above the origin 0)} = 2.500 + 0.0606 = 2.5606$$

Likewise, the addition or subtraction of a constant from all of any set of numbers does not change s. Assuming an origin of 2.560, the calculation of s becomes

$$s = \sqrt{\frac{(-0.001)^2 + (0.010)^2 + (0)^2 + (-0.014)^2 + (0.008)^2 - 5(0.006)^2}{4}}$$

$$= 0.0095$$

The reader will note a considerable saving in the calculation time compared with the previous calculation of s.

2.4.3 Calculation of Sample Average and Standard Deviation of Grouped Frequency Distribution—Long Method

Although Eqs. (2.1) and (2.5) might be applied to the actual measured weights in computing the average and standard deviation of the 110 observed weights of Table 2.1, the computation would be time consuming, and the chances of an error in calculations would be great. To get the average, one would add the 110 individual values

$$\bar{X} = \frac{\Sigma X_i}{n} = \frac{280.995}{110} = 2.554 \text{ kg.}$$

The first step in calculating the standard deviation would be the squaring of each of the 110 numbers. This long calculation is not illustrated here.

The same results could be obtained with less effort by considering the numbers grouped into a frequency distribution. This is illustrated in Table 2.4.

$$\bar{X} = \frac{\Sigma fX}{n} = \frac{280.995}{110} = 2.554 \text{ kg.}$$

$$s = \sqrt{\frac{\Sigma fX^2 - n\bar{X}^2}{n-1}}$$

$$= \sqrt{\frac{7.17.6101 - (110)(2.554)^2}{109}} = 0.0108$$

An inspection of Table 2.4 will show that 280.919 is necessarily the same sum that would be obtained if the 110 numbers were added one by one, and 717.6105 is necessarily the same sum that would be obtained if each of the 110 numbers was separately squared and squares were then added. Consider the numbers in any cell of the frequency distribution. For example,

TABLE 2.4: COMPUTATION OF AVERAGE AND STANDARD DEVIATION OF FREQUENCY DISTRIBUTION-LONG METHOD.
(Data of Tables 2-1 and 2-2 (*a*) on weights of shaft in kg.)

Weight, kg (midpoint of cell) X	*Frequency* f	*Total weight* fX	*Sum of squares or cell* fX^2
2.533	6	15.198	38.4966
2.538	8	20.304	51.5312
2.543	12	30.516	77.6021
2.548	13	33.124	89.4000
2.553	20	51.060	130.3562
2.558	19	48.602	124.329
2.563	13	33.319	85.3966
2.568	11	28.248	72.5409
2.573	8	20.584	52.9626
Totals.......	110	280.995	717.6101

consider the cell corresponding to a weight of 2.538 kg. The 8 observations of 2.538 kg, if added one by one, would contribute 8 × 2.538 = 20.304 to the sum of the numbers. As the square of 2.538 is 6.4414, these 8 observations would contribute 8 × 6.4414 = 51.531 to the sum of the squares.

Although less laborious than calculations from the same data without grouping, calculations of the type of Table 2.4 are still wasteful of time. Table 2.4 has been introduced at this point primarily to provide a transition to the common short-cut calculations for frequency distributions from the direct calculations that use the basic formulae defining average and standard deviation. These short-cut calculations are illustrated in Table 2.5. If the reader fully understands Table 2.4, no difficulty should be experienced in understanding Table 2.5.

2.4.4 Calculation of Average and standard Deviation of Grouped Frequency Distributions-Short Method

Just as the shift of origin simplified the arithmetic in the calculation from ungrouped data, so also may a shift of origin greatly simplify calculations of average and standard deviation of frequency distributions. Another change in direction of simplification is a change of units; one cell is equal to one unit throughout the calculations. At the end of the calculation in cell units from the assumed origin, the results for average and standard deviation are converted into units of the original measurements by multiplying by the value of one cell unit. The average is then converted to its original origin by adding the value of the assumed zero point. This is illustrated in Table 2.5

A further shortcut, which may be used when a rapid calculation is more important than accuracy, may be obtained by grouping the frequencies into larger cells. This could be accomplished by using the grouping of Table 2.2 (*b*) which has 0.005 kg rather than 0.009 kg as the cell interval.

TABLE 2.5: COMPUTATION OF AVERAGE AND STANDARD DEVIATION OF FREQUENCY DISTRIBUTIONS-SHORT METHOD
(Data and Table 2-1 and 2-2(*a*) on weights of shafts in kg.)

Weight, kg, (midpoint of cell)	*Frequency f*	*Deviation in cells from assumed origin d*	*fd*	*fd²*
2.533	6	–4	–24	96
2.538	8	–3	–24	72
2.543	12	–2	–24	48
2.548	13	–1	–13	13
2.553	20	0	0	0
2.558	19	1	19	19
2.563	13	2	26	52
2.568	11	3	33	99
2.573	8	4	32	128
Totals	110		25	527

$$\bar{X} \text{ (in cells from origin of 2.553)} = \frac{\Sigma fd}{n} = \frac{25}{110} = 0.227$$

$\bar{X}$ *(in original units from true origin)*

$$= \text{Assumed origin} + \frac{\Sigma fd}{n} \text{(cell width)}$$

$$= 2.553 + 0.227\,(0.005) = 2.554 \text{ kg.}$$

$$s \text{ (in cell unit)} = \sqrt{\frac{\Sigma fd^2 - \Sigma(fd)^2/n}{n-1}}$$

$$= \sqrt{\frac{527 - 5.628}{109}} = 2.18$$

$$s \text{ (in original units)} = (s \text{ in cell units}) \times \text{(cell width)}$$

$$= 2.18 \times 0.005 = 0.0108 \text{ kg.}$$

In all calculations from grouped data, the assumption is made that the true values of variable are concentrated at the centre of the cell in which they fall. Even in the finer grouping of Table 2.2(*a*), this assumption does not agree with the known facts. For example, for the cell with the midpoint 2.558 it is know these are 6 occurrences in the lower half of the cell and 2 exactly at the mid point and 11 in the upper half. In most cases some error will be introduced whenever a coarser grouping is used to shorten computions. In general, it is desirable that the least count of the measuring instrument be such as to permit grouping the data into at least 20 cells.

2.5 CONCEPT OF UNIVERSE AND A SAMPLE

At this point in the chapter, it is desirable to examine the concept of a universe and a sample. In order to construct a frequency distribution of the weights of steel shafts, a small portion, or a *sample*, is selected to represent all the steel shafts. The *universe* is the whole collection of a measurements and in this case the universe would be all the steel shafts. When averages, standard deviations and other measures are computed from the samples they are referred to as statistics. Since the composition of sample will fluctuate, the computed statistics will be larger or smaller than their true universe value or *parameters*. Parameters are considered to be fixed reference (standard) values or the best estimate of these values which is available at a particular time.

The universe may have a finite number of items, such as a day's production of steel shafts. It may be infinite or almost infinite, such as the number of rivets in a year's production of jet airplanes. The universe may be defined differently depending on the particular situation. Thus, a study of a product could involve the universe of an hour's production, a week's production 5,000 pieces, and so on.

Since it is rarely possible to measure all of the universe, a sample is selected. Sampling is necessary when it may be impossible to measure the entire universe; when the expense to observe all the data is prohibitive ; when the required inspection destroys the product ; or when a test of the entire universe may be too dangerous, as would be the case with a new medical drug. Actually, an analysis of the entire universe may not be as accurate as sampling. It has been shown that 100% manual inspection is not as accurate as sampling. This is probably due to fact that boredom and fatigue cause inspectors to prejudge each inspected item as being acceptable.

2.5.1 Sampling Statistics and Universe Parameters

Many of the useful actions that may be taken in manufacturing are related of future production rather than completed lots of items. The knowledge that must be gained from the sampling procedure is knowledge of the pattern of variation of the production process from which the sample was drawn.

Statisticians use particular words and phrases to define the unknown pattern of variation from which the known sample has been drawn. It is frequency called the *universe*, *parent distribution*, or *population*. Some of the recent texts in mathematical statistics refer to it as the *sample space* or *description space*. The *true, but unknown, numerical values* that describe the universe are called *parameters*.

In order to draw conclusions about an unknown universe, it is necessary to rely on numerical values derived from samples drawn from that universe. Such numerical values which include the sample mean, median, RMS or standard deviation, range, variance, and so forth summarize the information contained in the sample data. Each is referred to as a *statistic* of the sample and may be used to estimate the corresponding *parameter* of the unknown universe.

While statistics literature has adopted no uniform standard for notation, Greek letters have been widely used to identify the parameters of a distribution. Most often the lowercase Greek letter mu (μ) is used to identify the parametric value of the mean and the lowercase sigma (σ) to identify the parametric value of the standard deviation.

In the development of the techniques of statistical quality control in the Bell Telephone Laboratories in the 1920s and 1930s, the prime (′) symbol was adopted to identify a parameter of a universe. Thus the symbols $\bar{X}'$ (read "X Bar prime") and σ′, (read "sigma prime") identified the parametric values of the arithmetic mean and standard deviation, respectively, for a given universe. These symbols, and similar ones for attributes data, have been in use for many years. They and other symbols, terms, and definitions were adopted in the "ASTM Manual on the Presentation of Data" in 1937 and in 1941 in the American War Standards on

Quality Control. The earliest standards in quality control, promulgated by the then American Standards Association (now American National Standards Institute), incorporated them as did the American Society for Quality Control. Thus for over 50 years, as well as the earlier editions of this book they were standard symbols in the literature of quality control.

The 1978 revision of ANSI/ASQC Z1.5 changed to the use of the Greek notation for the mean and standard deviation. However, the other standards have retained the use of the prime notation. Certain other changes introduced by this standard and by the 1976 revision of the ASTM Manual are discussed and implemented in Chap. 3.

The parametric symbols may be applied to a known distribution or, when analyzing data from all items in a production lot. More commonly, parameters are estimated from one or more samples drawn from an unknown universe. Thus $\bar{X}$, the average of a sample of size n, may be used to estimate the parametric mean μ. Often a "caret" or "hat" (^) symbol is used above the Greek letter to differentiate more clearly the estimator from the parametric value. Thus an estimate of the parametric mean obtained from $\bar{X}$ will be designated by $\hat{\mu}$.

2.5.2 Using Samples to Make Estimates about a Universe

Assume that measurements are made on some variable and that it is proposed to base some actions on these measurements. In considering the merits of various proposals for action, it usually is helpful to think of the measurements as one or more samples taken from a universe (or perhaps from several universes). If the variable is some quality characteristic of a manufactured product (such as a dimension, weight, or electrical resistance), the universe may be thought of as the potentially unlimited output of the manufacturing process in question. Or, in some instances, the universe may be viewed as a particular lot of manufactured articles from which one or more samples have been taken.

It is appropriate to consider the following types of questions before making decisions about proposals for action.

1. Does it appear that we have only one universe? Or, more realistically, is it good enough for practical purposes to take action as if we had a single universe ?
2. If the answer to the first question if "Yes," how much do we know about the universe? More specifically, what do we know about its centering and dispersion ? What are our best estimates of its parameters μ and σ, and how satisfactory are these estimates as a basis for action?

2.5.3 Inferences about Pattern of Variation to be Drawn from Sample Average and Standard Deviation

It clearly would be advantageous if substantially all the information contained in a frequency distribution could be packed into *two* figures, such as a *measure* of *central tendency* and a *measure of the spread of dispersion*. Under favourable circumstances it is possible to come close enough to this ideal for many purposes. A practical problem is to judge whether the circumstances are favourable.

Mathematical statisticians have discovered that the best measure of central tendency for this purpose is the *arithmetic mean* (referred to in this book as the average). A useful measure of dispersion for this purpose is the *standard deviation*.

The ideal would be to be able to say, given any average and standard deviation, just what proportion of the measurements fell within any specified limits. For example, if μ were 28.70 mm for some dimension of a manufactured part and σ were 0.05 mm, it would then be possible to tell what proportion of the parts fell between the limits $\mu \pm 2\sigma$, that is, between 28.60 and 28.80 mm. Or it would be possible to tell the proportion that fell between $\mu - 4\sigma$ and $\mu - 2\sigma$, that is, between 28.50 and 28.60 mm, or between any other desired limits. If this could be done, one could completely reconstruct a frequency distribution provided one knew only two figures, its average and its standard deviation.

For this to be possible, the equation of a frequency curve that described the pattern of variation of the particular quality characteristic would need to be fully defined once the average and standard deviation were known. These two numbers are, in fact, sufficient to define the so-called *normal curve*. Many observed frequency distributions of measured qualities of manufactured product,and many other frequency distributions found in nature, do correspond roughly to this normal curve.

2.6 THE FREQUENCY CURVE AND THE NORMAL CURVE

Figure 2.3 (a) showed a graphical representation of a frequency distribution by means of a frequency histogram. The area contained in each column of the histogram is proportional to the frequency within its cell. *If there were enough observed numbers in the frequency distribution, the number of cells might be increased more and more and the width of a cell made smaller and smaller. The series of steps that constitutes the top of the histogram would then approach a smooth curve. The height of the curve at any point would be proportional to the frequency at the point, and the area under it between any two limits would be proportional to the frequency of occurrence within those limits. Such a curve is called a frequency curve or reference distribution.*

One can imagine frequency curves of any different shape. Mathematicians have developed equations that exactly define many common types. The most useful of these curves is the normal curve. This curve is variously called the *normal law*, the *normal curve of error*, the *probability curve*, the *gaussian curve*, the *laplacian curve*, and the *normal distribution curve*. Its bell-shaped symmetrical form is illustrated in Fig. 2.5. Although most of the area under it is included within the limits $\mu \pm 3\sigma$, the curve extends from $-\infty$ (minus infinity) to $+\infty$ (plus infinity). The curve is fully defined by μ and σ. μ

Much of the variation in nature and in industry follows the frequency distribution of the normal curve. Thus, the variations in the weight of elephants, the speed of antelopes, and the height of human beings will follow a normal curve. Also, the variations found in industry, such as the weight of grey iron castings, the life of 60-W light bulbs, and the dimensions of a steel piston ring, will be expected to follow the normal curve. When considering the heights of human beings, we can expect a small percentage of them to be extremely tall and a small percentage to be extremely short, with the majority of human heights clustering about the mean value. The normal curve is such a good description of the variations which occur to most quality characteristics in industry that it is the basis for many quality control techniques.

The most commonly quoted limits in connection with the normal curve are as follows.

Limits	*Percent of total area within specified limits*
$\mu \pm 0.6745\sigma$	50.00
$\mu \pm \sigma$	68.26
$\mu \pm 2\sigma$	95.45
$\mu \pm 3\sigma$	99.73

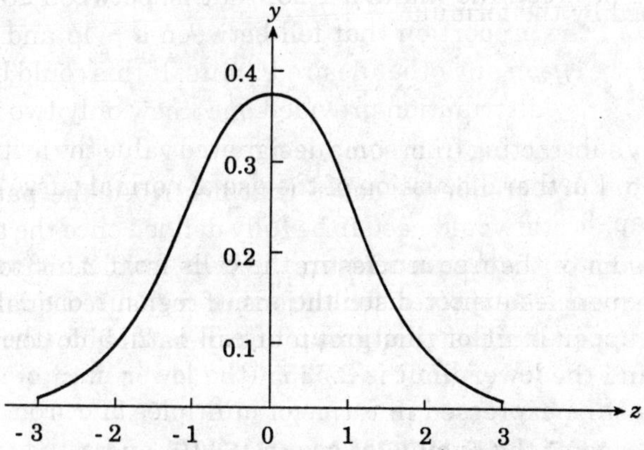

FIGURE 2.5 Normal curve wiht a mean of zero and standard deviation of 1.

This means that in those distributions that roughly approximate the normal curve, about two-thirds of the occurrences fall within one standard deviation on either side of the average, all but about 5% within two standard deviations, and practically all fall within three standard deviations.

Table A, Appendix 1, gives to four decimal places the proportion of the total area under the normal curve that occurs between $-\infty$ and any chosend point expressed in terms of multiples of σ on either side of μ. It can be used to find the area between any two chosen points. For example. the area between $\mu + 1.00\sigma$ and $\mu - 1.75\sigma$ is found as follows :

Table A reading for + 1.00 = 0.8413

Table A reading for – 1.75 = 0.0401

Area enclosed = 0.8012

The mathematical equation for the normal curve is given by the formula

$$y = \frac{1}{\sqrt{2\pi}} e^{-\left(\frac{X-\mu}{\sigma}\right)^2 / 2}$$

where y = height of the curve at any point x along the scale of variable.

σ = standard deviation of the population

μ = mean of the population

π = 3.14159

e = 2.71828

If $z = \dfrac{X-\mu}{\sigma}$, then the formula becomes

$$y = \frac{1}{\sigma\sqrt{2\pi}} e^{-z^2/2} \quad ...(2.7)$$

The variable z is a *normalised* statistic or *standardized normal value*. The constant $\frac{1}{\sqrt{2\pi}}$ has been chosen to ensure that the area under this curve is equal to unity or probability 1.0. This allows the area under the curve between any two values of z to represent the probability that any time chosen at random will fall between two values of z. Figure 2.5 shows the normal curve in its standard form, which is with a mean of zero and a standard deviation of 1. It may be observed that the curve is asymptotic at $z = -3$ and $z = +3$.

Mathematically, Table *A* is described by the formula

$$F(z) = \frac{1}{\sqrt{2\pi}} \int_{-\infty}^{z} e^{-x^2 2} dx \qquad ...(2.8)$$

where *z* is a *normalized* statistic found by subtracting from some designated value the arithmetic mean μ and dividing this difference by σ. Further discussion of the use of normal curve and its limitations on its use is deferred to Chap. 3.

Suppose it is desired to check the sum of the frequencies in the cells from 2.538 to 2.553 inclusive in Table 2.2 (a), with the frequencies expected for the same region from a normal curve having the same μ and σ. The upper limit of this group of cell is 2.5555 (the upper limit of the cell with midpoint 2.553) and the lower limit is 2.5355 (the lower limit of the cell with mid point 2.538). These points must be expressed in terms of multiples of σ from μ. The estimators of μ and σ are $\overline{X}$ (the average of the sample of size $n = 110$) and s the (sample standard deviation).*

From either Table 2.4 or Table 2.5

$$\hat{\mu} = \overline{X} = 2.5540 \text{ and } \hat{\sigma} = s = 0.0108$$

Thus, for the lower limit,

$$z_1 = \frac{2.5355 - 2.5540}{0.0108} = -1.713$$

and for the upper limit,

$$z_2 = \frac{2.5555 - 2.5540}{0.0108} = 0.139$$

Table *A* reading for 0.139 = 0.5553 (by interpolation)
Table *A* reading for − 1.713 = 0.0433 (by interpolation)
Area included = 0.5120

The total frequency in Table 2.2 (a) is 110 : this multiplied by the figure of 0.5120 gives a frequency of 56 cases (that is, occurrences of the variable) to be expected in cells 2.538 to 2.553 if the distribution were normal. This compares favourably with an actual frequency count of 8 + 12 + 13 + 20 = 53 cases observed in these cells.

2.6.1 RELATION TO THE AVERAGE AND STANDARD DEVIATION

As seen by the formulae for the normal curve, there is a definite relationship among the mean, the standard deviation, and the normal curve. In fact, the normal curve is fully defined by the mean, which locates the normal curve, and the standard deviation, which describes the shape of the normal curve. Figure 2.6 shows three normal curves with different mean values; it is noted that the only change is in the location. Figure 2.7 shows three normal curves with the same mean but different standard deviations. This figure illustrates the principal that the larger the standard deviation, the flatter the curve (data are widely dispersed), and the smaller the standard deviation, the more peaked the curve (data are narrowly dispersed). If the standard deviation is zero, all values are identical to the mean and there is no curve.

* Those familiar with statistical inferences know that, when the standard deviation is estimated from the sample, Student's *t* distribution theoretically is more correct than the normal distribution when the samples are drawn from a normally universe. However, as *n* gets large, say, 100 or more, Student's *t* converges to the normal distribution. Hence, it is reasonable to use the normal in this and similar cases.

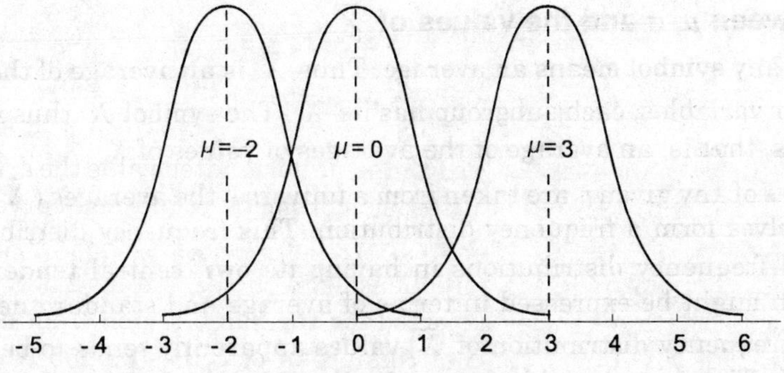

FIGURE 2.6 Normal curve with different averages but identical standard deviations.

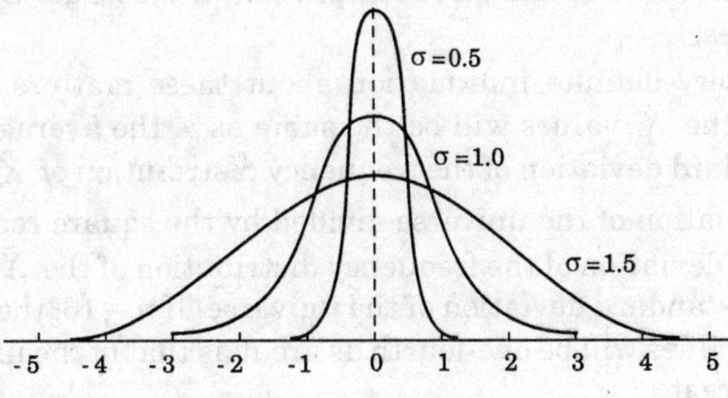

FIGURE 2.7 Normal curve with different standard deviation but identical means.

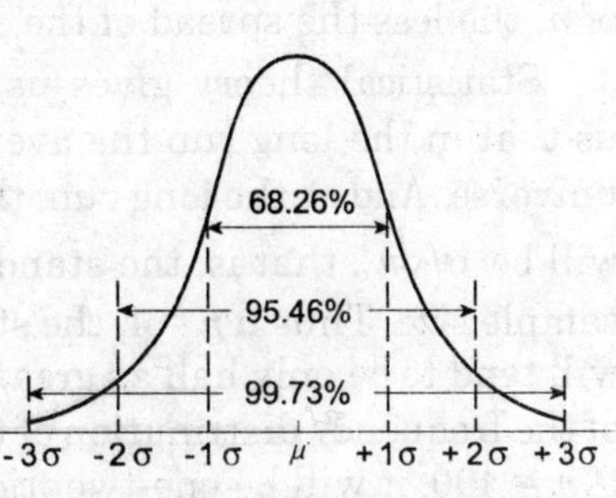

FIGURE 2.8 Percent of items included between certain values of the standard deviation.

A relationship exists between the standard deviation and the area under the normal curve as shown in Fig. 2.8. This figure shows that is a normal distribution 68.26% of the items are included between the limits of $\mu - 1\sigma$ and $\mu + 1\sigma$, 95.46% of the items are included between the limits $\mu + 2\sigma$ and $\mu - 2\sigma$, and 99.73% of the items are included between $\mu + 3\sigma$ and $\mu - 3\sigma$. One hundred percent of the items are included between the limits $+\infty$ and $-\infty$. These percentages hold true regardless of the shape of of the normal curve. The fact that 99.73% of the items are included between $\pm 3\sigma$ is the basis for control charts, which are discussed in Chap. 4.

2.6.2 Testing the Data for Normality

A convenient way to examine variable data is to plot it in a cumulative form on probability paper. This enables the proportion of items outside a given limit to be read directly from the diagram. It also allows the data to be tested for normally if it is normal the cumulative frequency plot will be a straight line.

The probability paper is readily available. The variable is marked along the linear vertical scale, with the horizontal scale shows the percentage of items below that value. The method of using probability paper depends upon the number of values available.

2.6.3 Special Notation for Normal Distribution

The normal distribution is widely used that often special notation is used to describe it. The notations $X \sim N(\mu, \sigma^2)$ or $X \sim N(\mu, \sigma)$ imply that X is normally distributed with mean μ and variance σ^2 or standard deviation σ.

2.6.4 Relationship between μ, σ and the values of $\bar{X}$

In statistics. the bar above any symbol means an average. Thus $\bar{X}$ is an average of the values of X. In the control chart for variables, each subgroup has its $\bar{X}$. The symbol $\bar{\bar{X}}$ thus refers to an average of the $\bar{X}$ values, that is. an average of the averages of values of X.

If many random samples of any given n are taken from a universe, the averages ($\bar{X}$ values) of the samples will themselves form a frequency distribution. This frequency distribution of $\bar{X}$ values is similar to all frequency distributions in having its own central tendency and dispersion or spread, which might be expressed in terms of average and standard deviation. The average $\bar{\bar{X}}$ of such a frequency distribution of $\bar{X}$ values apparently tends to be near μ, the average of the universe. The spread of this frequency distribution of $\bar{X}$ values seems to depend not only on the spread of the universe but also on to sample size n; the larger the value of n, the less the spread of the $\bar{X}$ values.

Statistical theory gives us some very definite information about these matters. It tells us that in the long run the average of the $\bar{X}$ values will be the same as μ, the average of the universe. And in the long run, the standard deviation of the frequency distribution of $\bar{X}$ values will be $\sigma/\sqrt{n}$. that is, the standard deviation of the universe divided by the square root of the sample size. Thus if $n = 4$, the standard deviation of the frequency distribution of the $\bar{X}$ values will tend to be only half as great as the standard deviation of the universe. If n = 16, the spread of the frequency distribution of the $\bar{X}$ values will be one-fourth as great as that of the universe. If $n = 400$, it will be one-twentieth as great.

This standard deviation of the expected frequency distribution of the averages is represented by the symbol $\sigma_{\bar{X}}$. It is referred to in textbooks on statistics as the *standard error of the mean*, or standard error of the average. Regardless of the form of the universe whether normal or otherwise, it is true that expected

$$\sigma_{\bar{X}} = \sigma/\sqrt{n} \qquad \text{...(2.9)}$$

$$\bar{\bar{X}} = \mu \qquad \text{...(2.10)}$$

In the universe is normal, statistical theory tells us that the expected frequency distribution of the $\bar{X}$ values also will be normal. Also the distribution of average of samples tends to be approximately normal even though the samples are drawn from non normal universe.

2.6.5 Relationship between σ and $\bar{s}$

If many sub groups of the same size are taken from a normal universe then in the long run, the sample standard deviations of samples of any size from a normal universe will follow a chance pattern that can be predicted by mathematics. Statistical theory also predicts the ratio between $\bar{s}$, the average of the s deviations of samples of any given size, and σ, the standard deviation of the universe from which the samples are taken. This ratio, represented by the normal c_4*, is given Table C, App. 1.

* Insofar as possible the symbols used in this book are those generally used in statistical quality control work. Unfortunately, the lowercase form of the latter c is commonly used with three different meanings, c_4 is used for the ratio of $\bar{s}$ to σ is used to represent number of nonconformities in the control chart for nonconformities per unit : c, c_1 and c_2 are used to indicate acceptance numbers in the Dodge-Romig single and double sampling tables. The first two uses have the authority of the American National Standards Institute and the American Society for Quality : the third is common in the literature and usage of sampling tables. As the possible confusion arising from departure from standard usage seems more serious than the confusion from the use of the same symbol is different ways, c is used in all three senses in this book. The three uses relate to such different situations that the context should always make clear which meaning of C is intended.

$$\hat{\sigma} = \frac{\bar{s}}{c_4} \qquad \text{...(2.11)}$$

Also larger the number of samples included in the calculation of $\bar{s}$ the greater is the confidence in the estimate of unknown standard deviation of universe from $\bar{s}$.

2.6.6 Relationship between σ and $\bar{R}$

Given n, the samples or subgroup size, statistical theory gives the expected value of the ratio between $\bar{s}$ and σ in random sampling from a normal universe. Similarly, it gives the expected value of the ratio between the average range $\bar{R}$ and σ. This latter ratio, designated as d_2, also is given in Table C, App. 1. Thus

$$\hat{\sigma} = \frac{\bar{R}}{d_2} \qquad \text{...(2.12)}$$

One practical use of this d_2 factor is to provide alternative method of estimating an unknown universe standard deviation σ from a series of samples or subgroups.

Often reasons are advanced in favour of using R because of its ease of computation in comparison with s. However with the technological development of calculators and computers, this is no longer valid. However in control chart work this ease of calculation of R usually is much more important than any slight theoretical advantage that the context should always make clear which meaning of c is intended that might come from the use of s as a measure of dispersion of subgroups. However, in some cases where the measurements themselves from a limited number of tests be as reliable items) and it is necessary that the inferences from a limited number of tests be as reliable as possible the extra cost of calculating for each subgroups may be justified.

2.7 OTHER FREQUENCY CURVES

The normal curve is useful in many ways as an external reference distribution in solving practical problems in industry. Some of these ways will be developed in succeeding chapters. Its general pattern, with a concentration of frequencies about a midpoint and with small numbers of occurrences at the extreme values, repeats itself again and again. Nevertheless, the normal curve is frequently misused; it is not safe to assume that unknown distributions are necessarily normal.

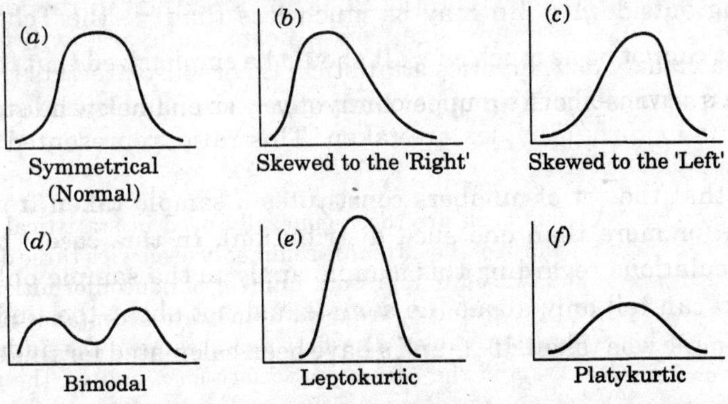

FIGURE 2.9 Different type of frequency distribution curves

There are many other frequency patterns that are like the normal in that frequencies decrease continuously from the center to the extreme values but—unlike the normal are not *symmetrical*. Extreme values occur more frequently in one direction from the center than in the other. Two such distributions are illustrated in Fig. 2.9 (*b*) and (*c*). In the technical language of statistics, these lopsided frequency curves are known as *skewed* curves. Figure 2.9 (*b*) is positively skewed or skewed to the right: that is, extreme variations occur more frequently above the mode than below it. Figure 2.9 (*c*) is negatively skewed or skewed to the left.

Another characteristics of data concerns the number of *modes* or *peaks* of the data. There can be one mode, two modes (bimodal), or multiple modes. Figure 2.9 (*d*) shows a bimodal frequency curve. When the curve is quite peaked i.e. frequency difference between cells is quite large, it is referred to as *leaptokurtic* as the one in Fig. 2.9 (*e*), and when it is flatter, it is referred to as *platykurtic*, the one in Fig. 2.9 (*f*).

As already emphasized the frequency distributions can give sufficient information about a quality control problem, to provide a basis for decision making without further analysis.

2.8 WHAT THE AVERAGE AND STANDARD DEVIATION OF A SET OF NUMBERS REALLY TELL

It has been pointed out that it would be convenient if the combination of sample average and standard deviation could tell us just what proportion of a set of numbers fell within any specified limits. It has also been pointed out that this combination does supply such information in those cases where it is known that the numbers are distributed according to the normal curve.

What do $\bar{X}$ and *s* tell if nothing whatever is known about the pattern of variation? One answer to this question is given by ***Tchebycheff's inequality***. This mathematical theorem states that more than $1 - (1/t^2)$ of any set of finite numbers must fall within closed range $\mu \pm t\sigma$ (where *t* is not less than 1). For example, if $t = 3$, this means that more than $1-\frac{1}{3^2}$ or $\frac{8}{9}$, of any set of numbers must fall within the limits $\mu \pm 3\,\sigma$, where μ and σ have been computed from the numbers themselves. In other words, less than $\frac{1}{9}$ of the numbers can fall outside these limits. In this case, μ is calculated using the formula for $\bar{X}$, Eq. (2.1). The formula for σ is similar to Eq. (2.5) for *s* except that *n* is used in the denominator rather than $n - 1$. The reason for this is that the mean of the set of numbers is known if the entire set is known.

The actual fraction falling outside $\mu \pm 3\,\sigma$ may be much less than $\frac{1}{9}$; the Tchebycheff inequality simply states that it cannot be as much as $\frac{1}{9}$. It should be emphasized that this limit of $\frac{1}{9}$ applies to the *sum* of the fractions above an upper limit of $\mu + 3\sigma$ and below a lower limit of $\mu - 3\sigma$.

Frequently it is the case that the set of numbers constitutes a sample taken from some unknown parent distribution (or more than one such distribution). In this case, the same formulae apply. However, calculations regarding this sample apply to the sample only. That is, the calculations of μ and σ can tell only about the *sample* and not about the underlying distribution from which the sample was taken. If $\bar{X}$ and *s* have been calculated for this sample, $\mu = \bar{X}$ and $\sigma = \sqrt{(n-1)/n}\,s$.

Usually it is desired to have $\bar{X}$ and σ tell more about a distribution than can be determined from Tchebycheff's inequality. An adaptation of the inequality by ***Camp and Meidell*** states that under certain circumstances more than $1 - (1/2.25\, t^2)$ of any distribution will fall within the closed range $\bar{X} \pm t\sigma$. These circumstances are

- the distribution should be unimodel i.e. have one mode only; and
- frequencies must decline continuously on both sides of the mode.
- Many distribution that are not normal do actually come close enough to meeting these conditions for the Camp-Meidell inequality to be applied with confidence.

The percentages indicated by the normal curve and by the two inequalities are compared as follows :

Limits	*If the distribution is roughly normal, approximately the following percentages of cases will be o outside the limits*	*If the Camp-Meidell conditions apply, less than the following percentages of cases will be outside the limits*	*Under any and all circumstances, less than the following percentages of cases will be outside the limits*
$\bar{X} \pm 2\sigma$	4.55	11.1	25.0
$\bar{X} \pm 2.5\sigma$	1.24	7.1	16.0
$\bar{X} \pm 3\sigma$	0.27	4.9	11.1
$\bar{X} \pm 3.5\sigma$	0.05	3.6	8.2
$\bar{X} \pm 4\sigma$	0.006	2.8	6.3
$\bar{X} \pm 4.5\sigma$	0.0007	2.2	4.9
$\bar{X} \pm 5\sigma$	0.00006	1.8	4.0

The rules summarized in the foregoing tabulation are given in many books on statistics. It sometimes happens that the readers of such books misinterpret these rules as pertaining to the relationship between the statistics obtained from samples and the parameters of the universe from which the samples are drawn. It should be emphasized that the rules apply merely to any set of numbers, whether those numbers are viewed as constituting a sample or a universe. For example, Tchebycheff's inequality tells us that it is impossible to construct any set of numbers in which 4.0% or more of the numbers are more than 5σ away from the arithmetic mean.

SOLVED QUESTIONS

Q. 2.1: *Choose the correct statement from each of the following.*

(*i*) A variable is

(*a*) a characteristic that can have numerically different values

(*b*) a characteristic that always has the same numerical value

(*c*) a characteristic that never has the same numerical value

(ii) The frequency is

(*a*) another word for a variable (*b*) a qualitative characteristic

(c) number of times a variable occurs (*d*) the total number of observations

(iii) A histogram is

(*a*) another word for a bar chart

(*b*) a graphical representation of a cumulative frequency table

(*c*) another form of component bar chart

(*d*) a graphical representation of a frequency table

(iv) An ogive is

(*a*) a graphical representation of a cumulative frequency table

(*b*) a graphical representation of a frequency table

(*c*) another type of bar chart

(*d*) another name of a component bar chart

(v) In a set of data the median is

(*a*) the most frequently occuring observation

(*b*) the middle observation

(*c*) the weighted average

(vi) In a set of data the mode is

(*a*) the most frequently occuring observation

(*b*) the middle observation

(*c*) the weighted average

(vii) The measure of location which can be used for further mathematical process is the

(*a*) mean (*b*) median

(*c*) mode

(viii) The measure of location which can be affected by extreme values as the

(*a*) mean (*b*) median

(*c*) mode

(ix) The measure of location which uses every value in the data set is the

(*a*) mode (*b*) median

(*c*) mean

(x) When a frequency distribution is symmetrical than the

(*a*) mean is bigger than the median

(*b*) mode is bigger than the mean

(*c*) mean, median and mode have the same value

(xi) The standard deviation measures the spread around

(*a*) the mean (*b*) the mode

(*c*) the median

Ans: (*i*) (*a*) (*ii*) (*c*) (*iii*) (*d*) (*iv*) (*a*) (*v*) (*b*) (*vi*) (*a*) (*vii*) (*a*) (*viii*) (*a*) (*ix*) (*c*) (*x*) (*c*) (*xi*) (*a*)

Q. 2.2: *Fill in the gaps with suitable word/words.*

1. In a histogram, frequencies are represented by ________.
2. For a discrete data the mode is the values corresponding to the highest ________.
3. Two distributions can be easily compared graphically by means ________.
4. The ________ and the ________ are two methods of data arrangement.
5. Dividing data into similar classes and counting the number of observations in each class will give a ________ distribution.
6. A graph of a cumulative frequency distribution is called a ________.
7. If a curve can be divided into two equal parts that are mirror images, it is ________ if it cannot be divided in this way, it is ________.
8. The symbol $\bar{X}$ denotes the means of a ________ μ denotes the mean of a ________.
9. If two values in a group of data occur more often than any others, the distribution of the data is said to be ________.
10. The measure of the average squared distance between the mean and each item in the population is the ________. The positive square root is the ________.

Ans: **1.** Area of rectangles/ height of rectangles if the cell or class width of each cell is equal, **2.** Frequency, **3.** Frequency polygon, **4.** Order (increasing/decreasing), Frequency distribution, **5.** Frequency, **6.** Ogive, **7.** Symmetrical, skewed, **8.** Sample, population, **9.** Bimodal, **10.** Variance, standard deviation.

Q. 2.3: *State whether the following statements are TRUE (T) or FALSE (F) ?*

1. In comparison to a data array, the frequency distribution has the advantage of representing data in compressed form.
2. A "more-than" ogive is S-shaped and slopes down and to the right.
3. A histogram is a series of rectangles, each proportional in width to the number of items falling within a specific class of data.
4. A single observation is called a data point, whereas a collection of data is known as a tabular.
5. The classes in any relative frequency distribution are both all-inclusive and mutually exclusive.
6. When a sample contains the relevant characteristics of a certain population in the same proportions as they are included in that population, the sample is said to be a representative sample.
7. A population is a collection of all the elements we are studying.
8. If we were to connect the midpoints of the consecutive bars of a frequency histogram with a series of lines, we would be graphing a frequency polygon.
9. Before information is arranged and analyzed, using statistical methods, it is known as preprocessed data.
10. One disadvantage of the data array is that it does not allow us to easily find the highest and lowest values in the data set.
11. Discrete data can be expressed only in whole numbers.
12. As a general rule, statisticians regard a frequency distribution as incomplete if it has fewer than 20 classes.

13. It is always possible to construct a histogram from a frequency polygon.
14. The vertical scale of an ogive for a relative frequency distribution marks the fraction of the total number of observations that falls into each class.
15. A data array is formed by arraying raw data in order of time of observation.
16. A "less-than" ogive is S-shaped and sloped down and to the right.
17. One advantage of a histogram in comparison with a frequency polygon is that it more clearly shows each separate class in the distribution.
18. $\bar{X} = \dfrac{\Sigma X}{n-1}$
19. A frequency distribution organizes data into groups of values describing one or more characteristics of the data.
20. A series of rectangles, each proportional in width to the range of values within a class and proportional in height to the number of items falling in the class, is called a frequency polygon.
21. The class widths of a frequency distribution are of equal size.

Ans: **1.** (T), **2.** (T), **3.** (F), **4.** (F), **5.** (T), **6.** (T), **7.** (T), **8.** (T), **9.** (F), **10.** (F), **11.** (F), **12.** (F), **13.** (T), **14.** (T), **15.** (F), **16.** (F), **17.** (T), **18.** (F), **19.** (T), **20.** (F), **21.** (F).

Q. 2.4: *Match the following terms to the correct definition*

Mean	(*i*) The value which occurs most often in a data set
Median	(*ii*) The answer derived by dividing the sum of a set of values by the number of values
Mode	(*iii*) The middle of a set of values

Ans: Mean – (*ii*), Median – (*iii*), Mode – (*i*)

Q. 2.5 : *Select the correct word to complete the sentences*

(i) The mean/median/mode is the value which appears with the highest frequency.

(ii) The mean/median/mode is calculated by adding all the values and dividing the total by the number of values.

(iii) The mean/median/mode is the middle of a set of values.

Ans: (*i*) mode, (*ii*) mean, (*iii*) median

Q. 2.6 : *Consider the three averaging calculations:*

(a) Mean (b) Median (c) Mode.

Match the following ***disadvantages*** *to the method it relates to.*

(i) Data has to be arranged in order of size which is time consuming.

(ii) It may give undue weight or be influence by extreme runs

(iii) Data has to be arranged to ascertain which figures appears the most often.

Ans: (*i*) – Median; (*ii*) – Mean, (*iii*) – Mode.

Q. 2.7: *Select the correct answer (s) from the following:*

1. All the following expect one are advantages of using the standard deviation to measure spread. Which is incorrect?

(a) It is not distorted by skewed data

(b) It is well known and widely used

(c) It uses all the data

(d) Its formula lends itself to mathematical manipulation **Ans.**

2. What types of frequency curves are shown in charts (X) and (Y) in Fig. 2.10? Allocate one or more the following titles to each chart:

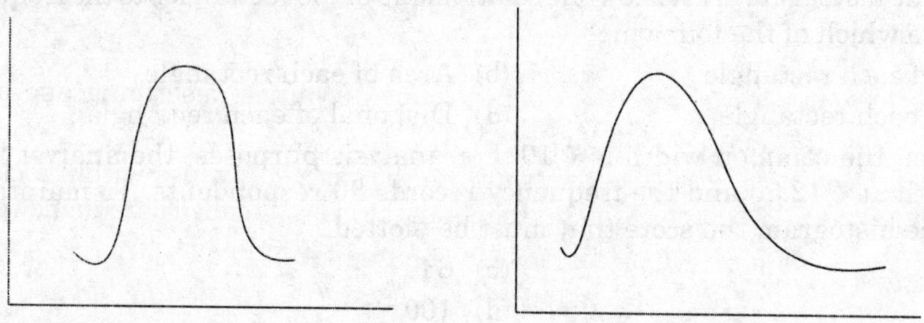

Chart (X) Chart (Y)

FIGURE 2.10

(i) Normal (ii) Symmetrical

(iii) Negatively skewed (iv) Positively skewed

(v) Uniform **Ans.**

3. In a histogram, one class interval is twice the width of the others. For that class, the height to be plotted in relation in the frequency is

(a) × 2 (b) × 0.5

(c) × 1 (d) × 0.25 **Ans.**

4. Match the following statistics to the charts that may be used to directly estimate them

Statistics	*Charts*
(a) The mean	(i) None
(b) The median	(ii) Histogram
(c) The mode	(iii) Ogive

Ans.

5. What information is provided by frequency densities?

(a) The points which must be plotted for an ogive

(b) The heights of the bars in a histogram

(c) The areas of the bars in a histogram

(d) The area under a frequency polygon **Ans.**

6. In a positivity skewed distribution, which of the following is/are generally true?

(a) The mean is larger than the median

(b) The mode is larger than the median

(c) The median is smaller then the mode

(d) the mode is the smallest of the three commonly used averages **Ans.**

Ans: 1. (a); **2.** Chart (X) – (i) & (ii), Chart (Y) – (iv); **3.** (b); **4.** (a) – (i); (b) – (iii), (c) – (ii); **5.** (b); **6.** (a) & (d)

Q. 2.8 : *Select the right option in the following giving a brief reason/justification.*

1. A graphical presentation of classified data in which the number of items in each class is represented by the area of the bar is called:
   (a) an ogive (b) a histogram
   (c) a bar chart (d) a compound bar chart
2. A histogram uses a rectangles to represent a grouped frequency table. To be correctly represented, the histogram must show the relationship of the rectangles to the frequencies by reference to which of the following?
   (a) Height of each rectangle (b) Area of each rectangle
   (c) width of each rectangle (d) Diagonal of each rectangle
3. In a histogram, the common width is ₹ 10. For analysis purposes, the analyst has set one class width at ₹ 12.50 and the frequency records 80 respondents. To maintain the accuracy of the histogram the score that must be plotted:
   (a) 80 (b) 64
   (c) 80 (d) 100
4. In a histogram, one class is 3/4 of the width of the remainity classes. If the score in that class is 21, the correct height to plot on the histogram is:
   (a) 15.75 (b) 21
   (c) 28 (d) 42
5. A frequency distribution of a sample of monthly incomes is as follows:

₹	Frequency
400 and less than 800	7
800 and less than 1,000	16
1,000 and less than 1,200	28
1,200 and less than 1,300	21
1,300 and less than 1,400	8
	80

   If the rectangle representing incomes between ₹ 800 and ₹ 1000 has a height of 8 cm. What is the height of rectangle 1,000 and 1,200?
   (a) 10 (b) 12
   (c) 14 (d) 16
6. Cumulative frequencies are plotted against
   (a) the mid-point (b) the lower class boundary
   (c) the upper class boundary (d) Any of the above
7. An ogive is
   (*a*) another name for a histogram
   (*b*) a chart showy any linear relationship
   (*c*) a chart showy a non-linear relationship
   (*d*) a graph of a cumulative frequency distribution

Ans: 1. (*b*);

Reason: An ogive does not have bars. A bar chart looks similar to a histogram but in bar chart the height of the bar represents the frequency. In a histogram this is only the case if the classes are of equal width. In general the area of the bar is a histogram represents class frequency.

2. (*b*);

Reason: The histogram must show the relationship of the rectangles to the frequencies by reference to the area

3. (*b*);

Reason: The interval is 12.50/10.00 = 1.25 times the standard width so the score to be plotted is 80/1.25 = 64.

4. (*c*);

Reason: The correct high is $21/(3/4) = 28$

5. (c);

Reason: Scale = 1 cm for 2 frequencies, then 28 have a height of 14.

6. (c);

Reason: Cumulative frequencies are plotted against the upper class boundaries.

7. (d);

Reason: In an ogive, the cumulative frequency associated with each interval is graphed on the upper limit of the interval (or class or cell).

Q. 2.9: *An entity is investigating the cost of absenteeism without its production department. Computes records have revealed the following data.*

Day absent last year	*Number of people*
0	94
1-5	203
6-10	105
11-20	68
21-30	15
31-40	10
41 +	5
Total	500

(a) Complete the following cumulative frequency distribution table (**A, B, C**) *using same of the options provided:*

500	505	11 and < 21	12 and < 21	485	475

No. of days absent	*Cumulative number of people*
0	94
1 and < 6	297
6 and < 11	402
A	470
21 and < 31	B
31 and < 41	425
41 and < 51	C

(b) Briefly mention the reason for the selected option.

Ans: (*a*) The completed table is

No. of days absent	Cumulative no. of people
0	94
1 and < 6	297
6 and < 11	402
11 and < 21	470
21 and < 31	485
31 and < 41	425
41 and < 51	500

(*b*) **Reason:** The intervals follow the previous patterns so A is 11 and less than 21. The cumulative frequency *B* is 40 + 15 and *C* is the total frequency 500.

Q. 2.10: *Explain*

(*a*) *Why statistics calculated from raw data are more nearly accurate than statistics calculated using the frequency table ?*

(*b*) *If this is the case why does one use the frequency table as a basis for calculating statistics?*

(*c*) *Why for a given set of data, is the median sometimes smaller than the mean ?*

(*d*) *What are the benefits of presenting data in a table ?*

(*e*) *When are percentages more useful in a table than the original figures ?*

Ans: (*a*) Assumes data evenly spread around mid-point, if this is not true then the statistics calculated from the frequency table will not be as accurate.

(*b*) Calculations can be done more quickly

(*c*) When there are a few very large observations.

(*d*) A properly constructed table can help the reader to understand a set of data better and can assist the reader in making comparisons between two different subjects to the variables.

(*e*) Percentages are useful in a table when the sets of data to be compared are of different sizes.

Q. 2.11: *(a) What are the advantages and disadvantages of the arithmetic mean.*

(b) Which two parameters are most commonly used to summarise a set of numerical data?

(c) What is the relationship between mean, mode and median for a normal distribution ?

Ans: (*a*) **Advantages**—The arithmetic mean (or average) is simple to compute and easy to understand.

Disadvantages—It may not correspond to any particular value in a set and is affected by extreme values.

(*b*) The arithmetic (i.e. the mean) average and standard deviation conveniently summarise a set of data.

(*c*) They all have the same value, *i.e.* they coincide for a Normal distribution.

Q. 2.12: *Identify the measures of the variation in a set of numerical data. Which is the simplest to calculate, and what is its limitation ?*

Ans: (*a*) Two measures of variation are (1) Range and (2) standard deviation. The range (R) is the simplest measure but it is affected by extreme values in the set of data and by definition uses only two values regardless of how many the data set contains.

Q. 2.13: *(a) In a newly constructed hotel, the number of support calls given each day during the last 64 days quarter which is representative, is shown below in the table and the chart Fig. 2.11.*

No. of Calls	*Frequency*
0-9	Nil
10-19	5
20-29	10
30-39	20
40-49	15
50-59	10
60-69	4
70+	Nil
Total	64

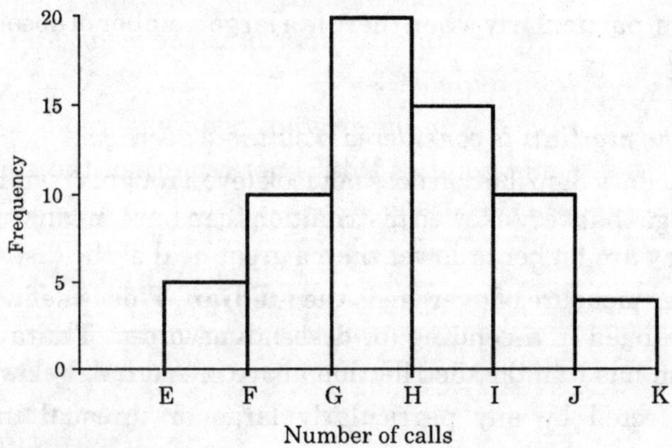

FIGURE 2.11

(a) What type of chart is being used?

(i) Bar chart, (ii) Ogive, (iii) Multiple bar chart, (iv) Histogram, (v) Pareto chart.

(b) What are the values represented by the letter E-K?

Ans: (*a*) (*iv*) Histogram.

(*b*) (E) 9.5, (F) 19.5, (K) 69.5.

Q. 2.14: *(a) How the normally distributed data can be presented with help of curve? How many data points fill within*

(*i*) $\mu \pm 1\sigma$ (*ii*) $\mu \pm 3\sigma$ (*iii*) $\mu \pm 6\sigma$

(b) When can you use a normal distribution?

(c) What distribution is used for variable control charts?

Ans: (*a*) Normally distributed data can be represented by a bell shaped normal curve as in Fig. 2.12

(*i*) % data between $\sigma \pm 1\sigma = 68.25$

(*ii*) % data between $\sigma \pm 3\sigma = 99.73$

(*iii*) % data between $\sigma \pm 6\sigma = 99.99966$

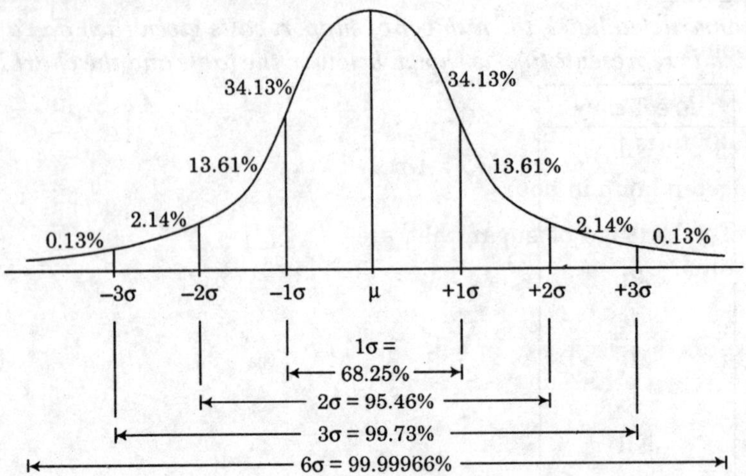

FIGURE 2.12 Normal Curve.

(*b*) In a wide range of applications, particularly when there is a large number of observations.

(*c*) The normal distribution

Q. 2.15: *Define the situation when the* **median** *is considered a suitable average.*

Ans: In skewed distributions the frequency distribution does not look (even roughly) symmetric. It is a criticism of the mean as an average that very skewed distributions can have mean values that appear unrepresentative, in that they are higher or lower than a great deal of the distribution.

To address this problem, another measure of average is the **median**. This is defined as the middle of a set of values, when arranged in ascending (or descending) order. This overcomes the above problem, since the median has half the distribution above it and half below.

Similarly the median is unaffected by any particularly large or unusual individual measurements whereas as the means would be.

Q. 2.16: *Which of the following statements are true about the mode are true? Give the reasons for rejected option(s)*

(a) It is most widely used average

(b) It is a measure of dispersion.

(c) It gives the most common values

(d) A distribution can have several modes.

(e) A distribution can have more than one mode.

Ans: Options (*c*), (*d*) and (*e*) are true.

- Option (*a*) is false because the most widely used average is the mean.
- Option (*b*) is false as mode is an averaging measure. Measure of dispersion are the range, and standard deviation.

Q. 2.17: *(a) Define clearly the following distributions*

(i) Continuous distribution (ii) discrete distribution

(b) Categories each of the following variables as either discrete or continuous with reasons.

		Discrete	Continuous
(*a*)	Age of 5 years	☐	☐
(*b*)	Time of 2-5 hours	☐	☐
(*c*)	Output of 12,000 kg	☐	☐
(*d*)	Output of 5,000 units	☐	☐
(*e*)	the life of tungsten lamp in hours	☐	☐
(*f*)	The weight of 1 kg bags of sugar that are falled by machine.	☐	☐
(*h*)	Dress sizes	☐	☐
(*i*)	the number of days sick leave an employee can take even When a half day sick leave is allowed.	☐	☐
(*j*)	Salaries	☐	☐

Ans: (*a*) (*i*) When the variable data expressed on a continuous scale, it is continuous distribution scale, it is continuous distribution. For examples the diameter of a piston ring can be 100.1, or 100.01 or 100.001 mm i.e., it is continuous depending upon the subdivisions of measuring scale.

(*ii*) When the variable can take an certain values such an integers 0, 1, 2 etc, it is discrete distribution. For example the number of defective pieces in a batch of pieces can be 1, 2, ... etc. i.e., it cannot be 1.2, 1.3, 1.33 etc.

(*b*) Continuous : (*a*), (*b*), (*c*), (*e*), (*f*), (*j*), usually considered to be continuous

Discrete : (*d*), (*g*), (*h*), (*i*),

Reason: Though, the data in (*a*), (*b*), (*c*) and (*e*) give the impression of discrete, a little thought on these data will reveal that they these are continuous as the age in (*a*) can be 5 years, or 5 years 2 days, 5 years 1 hour etc. An output of 5,000 unit in (*d*) is definitely discrete as the output can be complete unit, it cannot be 5000.2 units.

Q. 2.18: *The head of the finance section of a large company spot checks the number of invoices left unprocessed at the end of each day. At the end of the first period of this check (26 working days), he has collected the following data.*

1	5	3	3	2
3	0	4	1	4
3	3	2	1	2
1	1	0	3	6
5	0	3	4	2
3				

(a) Tally the above data.

(b) How often there are more than four (4) invoices left unprocessed at the end of the day?

Ans: (*a*) the data in tally form are shown below:

0	///	3
1	~~////~~	5
2	////	4
3	~~////~~ ///	8
4	///	3
5	//	2
6	/	1
	Total	26

The totals in the above data are called the frequencies and the table is called the frequency distribution.

(*b*)

Number of invoices left unprocessed (less than or equal)	*Frequency*	*Cumulative Frequency*
0	3	3
1	5	8
2	4	12
3	8	20
4	3	23
5	2	25
6	1	26

We can now use this information how often more than 4 invoices remains unprocessed.

26 – 23 = 3 occasions out of 26; that is 11.5%.

Q. 2.19: *(a) For n number of data, the mean is calculated to* $\overline{X}$. *Later on it was discovered that the digits of one practical datum were written wrongly e.g. 65 was taken as 56. What the correct mean of the data?*

(b) The arithmetic mean, the mode and the median of a group of 75 observations were calculated to be 27, 34 and 29 respectively. It was later discovered that one observation was wrongly read as 43 instead of the correct value 53. Examine to what extent the calculated values of the three averages will be affected by the discovery of this error.

Ans: (*a*) The correct mean $= \dfrac{n(\overline{X}) - 56 + 65}{n}$

(*b*) $\Sigma X = 27 \times 75 = 2025$

Correct $\Sigma X = 2025 - 43 + 53 = 2035$

Correct $\overline{X} = \dfrac{2035}{75} = 27.13.$

The values of median and mode will not be affected by this error because these are positional averages and the median value is 29 which is far away from the 43 and 53. Similarly, the values of mode would not be affected by error since mode is 34 which is also for away from the values 43 and 53.

Q. 2.20: *The mean of the following set of numbers is 5 and the mode is 4*

3 7 X 9 4 2 Y

(a) What are the values of X and Y

(b) What is the median

Ans: (*a*) Since the mean is 5 and the total number of observations is 7, then sum of the observations $5 \times 7 = 35$

Therefore $3 + 7 + X + 9 + 4 + 2 + Y = 35$

or $X + Y = 35 - (3 + 7 + 9 + 4 + 2)$

i.e. 10

As mode is the most frequently occurring observation and its value is 4 and it is occuring only once in the given data, and if it is the mode, then it must occur more than once, hence if it is assumed that $X = 4$, then $Y = 6$.

(*b*) Considering X = 4 and Y = 6, let us arrange the data in ascending order in order to find median : 2, 3, 4, 4, 6, 7, 9

The middle value is 4. Hence the median is 4.

Q. 2.21: *A company's assistant management accountant is analysing the number of orders placed by its 10 main customers. He has found the following working which has been compiled by his manager. He can see from the following working that median was calculated to be 29.*

13 42 X 7 51 69 28 33 14 8

(a) What is the value of X ?

(*i*) 25? (*ii*) 29? (*iii*) 30? (*iv*) 32?

Ans: In order of magnitude without *X*, the values are 7, 8, 13, 14, 28, 33, 42, 51, 69

Including *X*, there are ten values so the median of 29 the average of the fifth & sixth. The only possible solution is that *X* lies between 28 and 33 and has a value such that $(28 + X)/2 = 29$. Hence, $X = 30$. Hence option (*iii*) is correct.

Q. 2.22: *In a moderately asymmetrical distribution the mode and the mean are 32.1 and 35.4 respectively. Calculate the median.*

Ans: From the relation between mean, mode and median,

$$(\text{Mean} - \text{Mode}) = 3(\text{Mean} - \text{Median})$$

$$\text{Mode} = 3\ \text{Median} - 2\ \text{Mean}$$

$$32.1 = 3\ \text{Median} - 2(35.4)$$

or $$\text{Median} = \frac{102.9}{3} = 34.3.$$

Q. 2.23: *(a) What is the purpose of a histogram ? Can you draw conclusions of the stability of the process by looking at histogram ?*

(*b*) *Draw a histogram for the following data.*

Time	*Frequency*
15 – under 17	3
17 – under 19	5
19 – under 21	10
21 – under 23	7
23 – under 25	4
25 – under 27	1

Ans: (*a*) The purpose of the histogram is to give us an overall impression of how a particular quality characteristic results are scattered around the mean or average.

It is **not** advisable to draw conclusions from a histogram, without inspecting an *X* chart of the data. Because the *X* chart preserves the ordering of the data, it may reveal instability of the process, which would not be evident from a histogram.

(*b*) Figure 2.13 shows the histogram

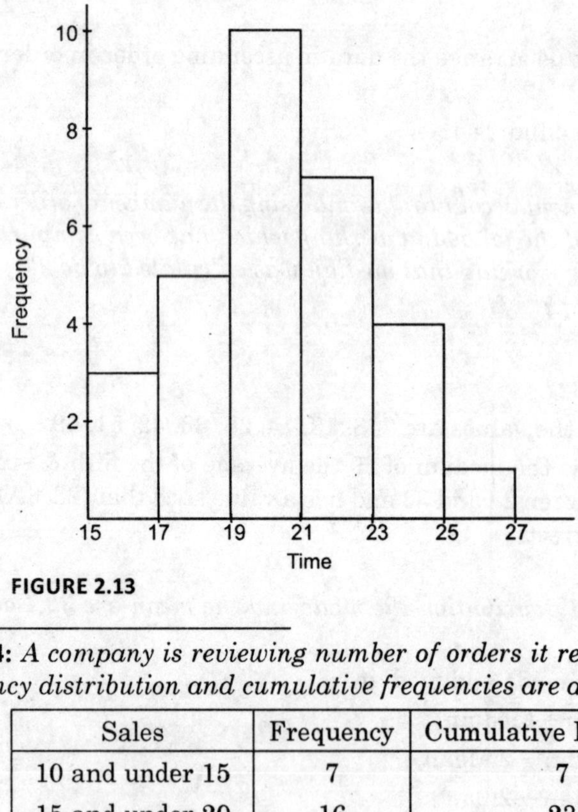

FIGURE 2.13

Q. 2.24: *A company is reviewing number of orders it received daily over a 40 day period. The frequency distribution and cumulative frequencies are as follows:*

Sales	Frequency	Cumulative Frequency
10 and under 15	7	7
15 and under 20	16	23
20 and under 25	13	36
25 and under 30	4	40

Based on this following ogive in Fig. 2.14 has been drawn. Find the values corresponding to letters K to S.

Ans:

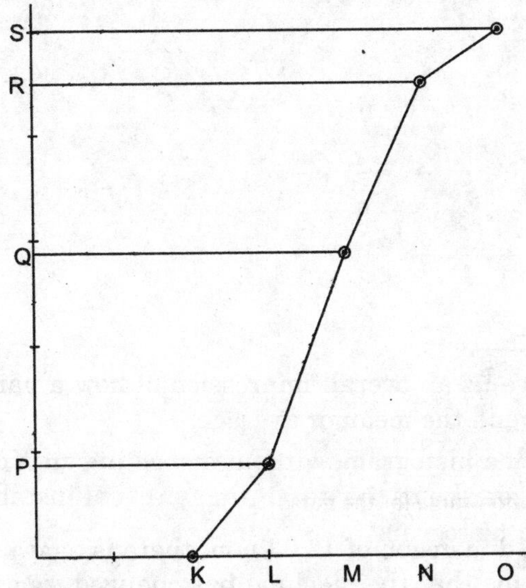

FIGURE 2.14

The values corresponding to letters K to S are as follows:

K = 10, L = 15, M = 20, N = 25, O = 30, P = 7, Q = 23, R = 36, S = 40.

Q. 2.25: *(a) A machine was set to produce a diameter to specification limits of* ***12.00 ± 0.05 mm.*** *It ran for approximately 7 hours, making 1 piece a minute, and then the whole output was checked with the following results.*

Dimension (X)	*No. of pieces (f)*
11.97	1
11.98	7
11.99	49
12.00	103
12.01	102
12.02	43
12.03	20
12.04	38
12.05	39
12.06	15
12.07	2
12.08	1

(a) Plot a histogram and also a frequency distribution curves of the data in the same diagram.

(b) Comment upon the shape of the curves obtained.

Ans: (*a*) Considering the (X) values as midpoint of the cells, histogram and a frequency distribution curve (in dotted) are shown in Fig. 2.15.

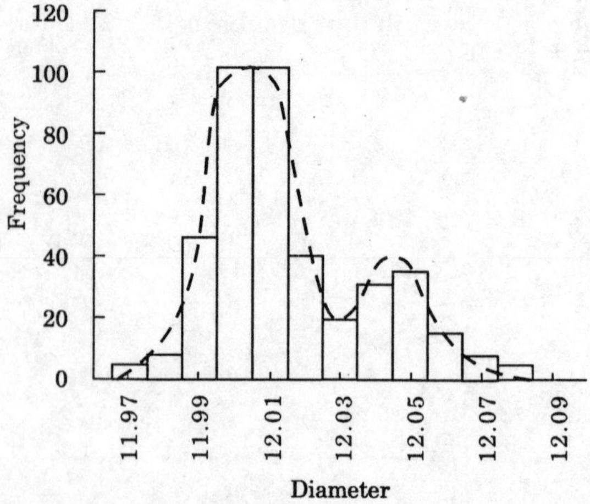

FIGURE 2.15 A histogram and a frequency distribution curve for the data.

(*b*) From Fig. 2.15 it is evident that after a dimension of 12.03 mm, there is again rise in frequency for the dimension of 12.04. This means that the machine has changed its average from 12.00 to around 12.05. This change is for the last 105 pieces accounted for as follows :

One half of frequency at 12.03 i.e. (20) × $\left(\frac{1}{2}\right)$ = 10 pieces

Frequency from 12.04 onwards i.e. 38 + 39 + 15 + 2 + 1 = 95 pieces.

Total pieces = 105 pieces

Since the machine produces 1 piece a minute for 7 hours, total number of pieces produced is 7 × 60 = 420. Since 105 is 25% of 420, it can be concluded that the machine *appears to have changed its average* from 12.00 to 12.05 for 25% of its run time.

Q. 2.26: *One thousand **100** kg drums of a chemical were weighed to the nearest kilogram and the following frequency distribution obtained :*

Weights	*Frequency*
90 kg. and less than 92 kg.	1
92 kg. and less than 94 kg.	5
94 kg. and less than 96 kg.	15
96 kg. and less than 98 kg.	50
98 kg. and less than 100 kg.	150
100 kg. and less than 102 kg.	272
102 kg. and less than 104 kg.	215
104 kg. and less than 106 kg.	165
106 kg. and less than 108 kg.	85
108 kg. and less than 110 kg.	25
110 kg. and less than 112 kg.	12
112 kg. and less than 114 kg.	5

*Construct a relative frequency histogram of the above data and from it estimate the proportion of drums having a weight of at least **106** kg.*

Ans. : (*a*) Relative frequency of any cell = $\dfrac{\text{Frequency of that particular cell}}{\text{Total frequency}}$

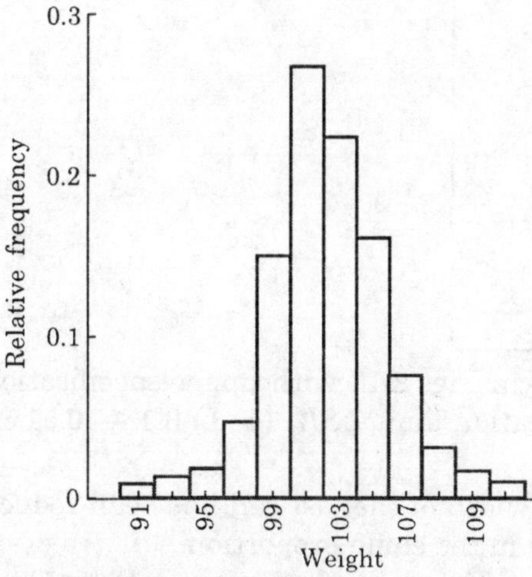

Figure 2.16 Relative frequency histogram for the data

As the total number of drums is 1,000, for the cell 90-92 kg. the relative frequency will be $\frac{1}{1000}$ *i.e.* 0.001 and for the cell 92-94 it will be $\frac{5}{1000}$ i.e. 0.005.

A histogram constructed with these frequencies is called the relative frequency histogram. Figure 2.16 shows the relative frequency histogram with cell mid points 91, 93... 113.

From the relative frequency histogram it is evident that relative frequency of drums having a weight of at least 106 kg. is the sum of frequency of cells whose mid points are 107 kg. to 113 kg., *i.e.*, 0.085 + 0.025 + 0.012 + 0.005 = 0.127. This, when expressed in percent becomes 12.7%.

Q. 2.27: *An assembled product consists of two main components A and B having resistance R_1 and R_2 the resistance of the assembly then being $R_1 + R_2$ Random samples of the components, each consisting of 30 items, were drawn from stock and their resistance (in ohms) measured.*

Component A ;	3.14	3.17	3.21	3.15	3.22	3.13	3.15
Resistance R_1	3.09	3.18	3.19	3.16	3.24	3.11	3.22
	3.17	3.06	3.23	3.14	3.12	3.27	3.19
	3.17	3.14	3.20	3.19	3.13	3.25	3.16
	3.11	3.17					
Component B:	2.09	2.05	2.10	2.02	2.06	2.13	2.11
Resistance R_2	2.07	2.08	1.99	2.07	2.12	2.10	2.03
	2.05	2.08	2.08	2.00	2.07	2.05	2.13
	2.09	2.05	2.07	2.04	2.15	2.09	2.05
	2.13	2.08					

Group the data to form frequency distribution and hence draw histograms for the resistances of the two components A and B. A and B have specified resistance of 3.1 ± 0.15 ohms and 2.05 ± 0.07 ohms respectively. what conclusions do you draw from the frequency distributions of sample resistance ?

Ans: (*a*) The grouping of the data for the component *A* is shown in the following table :

Cell Boundaries	*Cell midpoint*	*Frequency*
3.055-3.085	3.07	1
3.085-3.115	3.10	3
3.115-3.145	3.13	6
3.145-3.175	3.16	8
3.175-3.205	3.19	5
3.205-3.235	3.22	4
3.235-3.265	3.25	2
3.265-3.285	3.275	1

The histogram for the component *A* is shown in Fig. 2.17 with upper specification limit USL_X (*or U*) 3.1 + 0.15 *i.e.* 3.25 and lower specification limit LSL_X (*or L*) 3.1 — 0.51 *i.e.* 2.95 marked on the histogram itself

In Fig. 2.17, it will be seen that since the cell width of the last cell has been reduced, the height of the vertical rectangle has been increased in the same proportion.

Also from Fig. 2.17. it is also obvious that the process is capable of meeting the specified tolerance but the centre of the distribution is not correctly set. Correct centre of distribution can be determined as follows :

From Fig. 2.17, it can be seen that the centre of distribution can only be shifted towards the left. Minimum shifting will be such that all the components outside the upper specification limit *i.e.* *U* should come within the specification limit.

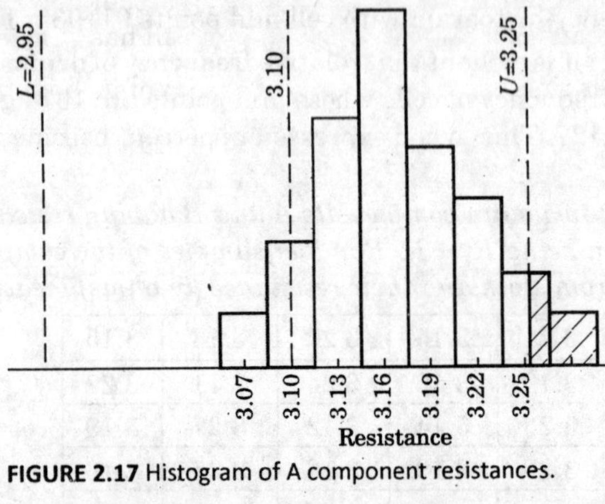

FIGURE 2.17 Histogram of A component resistances.

Cell upper boundary = 3.285

Upper specification limit (U) = 3.10 + 0.15 = 3.25

Minimum shift = 3.285 − 3.250 = 0.035

Cell lower boundary = 3.055

Lower specification limit (L) = 3.10 − 0.15 = 2.95

Maximum allowable shift = 3.055 − 2.950 = 0.105

Since minimum allowable shift is 0.035, the balance shift to be divided into two equal parts remains to be 0.070 ohm.

$$\text{Hence the shift towards left} = 0.035 + \frac{0.070}{2} = 0.070 \text{ ohm.}$$

Similarly for component *B*, by drawing the histogram, it will be seen that the process is not capable of holding the specified tolerances but the percentage of the resistances produced outside the limits can be minimized by reducing the centering of the process by about 0.02 ohm *i.e.* to 2.03 ohms.

Q. 2.28: *In order to make production in a factory more efficient, the manager called in consultants to do an investigation. An analysis, indicated the distribution of ages of the workers, was as follows:*

Ages,	16-19	20-29	30-39	40-49	50-59
Frequency,	15	46	49	32	28

Calculate the mean and median. Draw a histogram of the data and indicate on it both the mean and median.

As a result of this study all those aged 60 and over, together with 6 others who are 59, were made redundant. Find the new mean and median.

Ans: Treating the data as discrete one, the cell limits for the given groupings will be 15.5-19.5; 19.5-29.5; 29.5-39.5; 39.5-49.5; 49.5-59.5; 59.5-64.5. From this grouping it is evident that the first and last cells have different cell width from the rest of the cells. If the same cell width is to maintained throughout the cell limits for the first cell will be 9.5-19.5 and that of the last cell will be 59.5-69.5.

Histogram for the given data is shown in Fig. 2.18. Remembering that the frequencies are represented by the areas of the rectangles, it is evident that since the last cell has the width half of that preceding it and also has frequency exactly one half of that preceding it, its height in the histogram will be same as that of preceding it *i.e.* 28. If the width of this cell is considered same as that of other cells, *i.e.* 10, its height in the histogram will be its actual height *i.e.* 14. This fact has been shown as dotted in the histogram. Similarly the first cell has width of 4 *i.e.* $\frac{1}{2.5}$ times of that of the remaining cells, its height will be 2.5 times of that of its actual height *i.e.* $2.5 \times 15 = 37.5$ in the histogram. If the cell width for this cell is to be retained same as that of other cells i.e. 10, its height in the histogram will be its actual height i.e. 15. This fact has been shown as dotted in the histogram. But doing this will ignore the fact that no workers are of age less than 16 or more than 64.

Cell midpoints of the given data are 17.5, 24.5, 34.5, 44.5, 54.5 and 62.0 respectively.

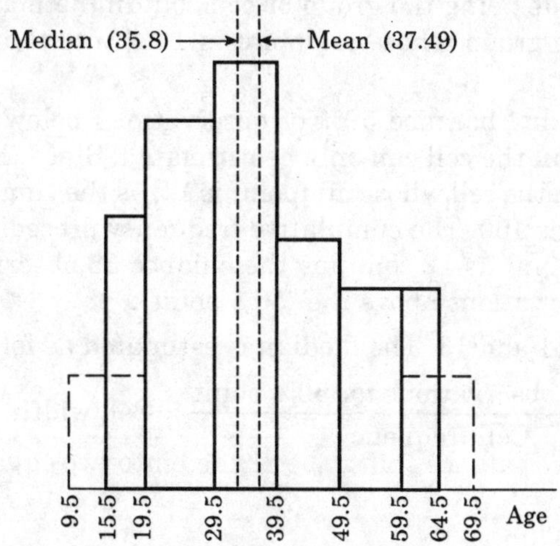

FIGURE 2.18 Histogram for the data.

$$\text{Mean } \overline{X} = \frac{(15 \times 17.5) + \ldots + (14 \times 62.0)}{15 + \ldots + 14} = \frac{6897.5}{184} = 37.49 \text{ years}$$

Since the total frequency is 184, the "50% point" is at 92. Also since the sum of frequencies of the first three cells exceeds 92, the median lies in the third cell whose limits are 29.5 to 39.5. Sum of the frequencies of the first two cells is 61. The balance of 31 for "50% point" lies in the third cell. The median is estimated as follows:

$$\text{Median} = \text{Cell lower limit} + \frac{\text{Balance observations for "50\% point"}}{\text{Cell frequency}} \times \text{Cell width}$$

$$= 29.5 + \frac{31}{49} \times 10 = 35.8 \text{ years}$$

Both the median and the mean are located in the histogram of Fig. 2.16

In ignoring those aged 60 and over, the last cell (59.5-64.5) will be totally eliminated and in ignoring 6 others who are 59, the cell (49.5 - 59.5) will have new limits from 49.5 to 58.5 (and cell midpoint as 54.0) has a frequency reduced by 6 *i.e.*, 28 – 6 = 22.

$$\text{New mean } \overline{X} = \frac{(15 \times 17.5) + \ldots + (22 \times 54.0)}{15 + \ldots + 22} = \frac{5692}{164} = 34.71 \text{ years}$$

Since the total frequency is 164, "50% point" is 82. Hence the new median is $29.5 + \frac{21 \times 10}{49}$ = 33.78 years.

Q. 2.29: *The following frequency table records the diameters of 200 grains of moulding sand in appropriate units.*

Diameter	8	10	12	14	16	18	20
Frequency	25	40	67	35	23	7	3

State the group in which the mode occurs, estimate the median and draw a histogram for the distribution. Choose a suitable assumed mean and hence calculated the mean and standard deviation(s) of the distribution.

The standard deviation calculated from the original measurements (before grouping) was 2.88. Why is there a discrepancy between this and your computed value of s?

Ans: This is a case of continuous data, the mode being the group or cell containing maximum number of observations. In this case it is the group whose midpoint is 12. (Note that given diameters represent the midpoints of the cells.)

The median is described as the "50% point" because 50% of observations below it and 50% above it. The position of the median within the cell can only be estimated. Since the total frequency in this case is 200, the median lies in the cell whose midpoint is 12, as the cumulative frequency of the cells including this cell exceeds 100. The cumulative frequency preceding this cell is 25+40 i.e. 65. Hence the cell with midpoint as 12 contains the balance 35 observations below the "50% point" and 67 – 35 i.e. 32 observations above the "50% point".

Cell boundaries with midpoint of 12, are 11 and 13. The median is estimated as follows.

$$\text{Median} = \text{Cell lower boundary} + \frac{\text{Balance observations for 50\% point}}{\text{Cell frequency}} \times \text{Cell width}$$

$$= 11 + \frac{35}{67} \times 2 \approx 12$$

Figure 2.19 shows the histogram for the distribution.

Following the short method, and assuming the origin at 14, the mean ($\bar{X}$) and standard deviation(s) are computed to be 12.24 and 2.76 respectively.

The difference between this value of s (i.e. 2.76) and that of original measurements i.e. 2.88 is explained by assuming that in grouping all the observation within a particular cell have their values as the midpoint of that cell, whereas it is very unlikely that this was the case with the original data.

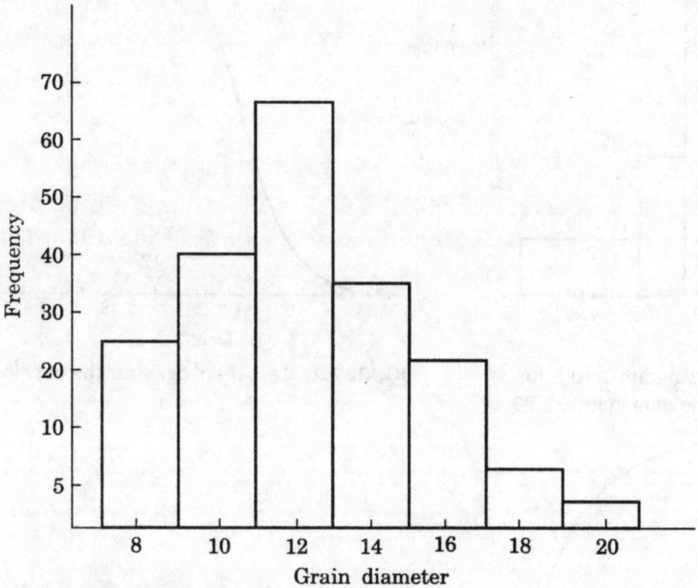

FIGURE 2.19 Histogram for the data.

Q. 2.30: *10,000 rods, normal length 7 in, were measured to the nearest 0.1 and the results were tabulated as follows:*

Cell Boundaries	*Cell midpoint*	*Frequency*
6.75-6.85	6.8	780
6.85-6.95	6.9	1640
6.95-7.05	7.0	5470
7.05-7.15	7.1	1570
7.15-7.35	7.25	540
Total...		10,000

1. *Draw the histogram for the data.*
2. *Draw the following ogive curves :*
   (a) 'less than' the cell upper boundary ;
   (b) 'more than' the cell lower boundary.

Ans: From the given data, it is evident that the last cell interval (i.e. 7.35 − 7.15 = 0.20) is twice the width of the other cells (i.e. 0.10), consequently we reduce the height of this cell by half. This will amount to the assumption that 540 is divided equally into 270 in the interval 7.15 to 7.25 and 270 in the interval 7.25 to 7.35. Since this is only a assumption as the exact situation is not known, we omit the vertical line dividing this column into two, each of width equal to the other two. The histogram is shown in Fig 2.20.

To draw a 'less than' ogive, the data are tabulated below :

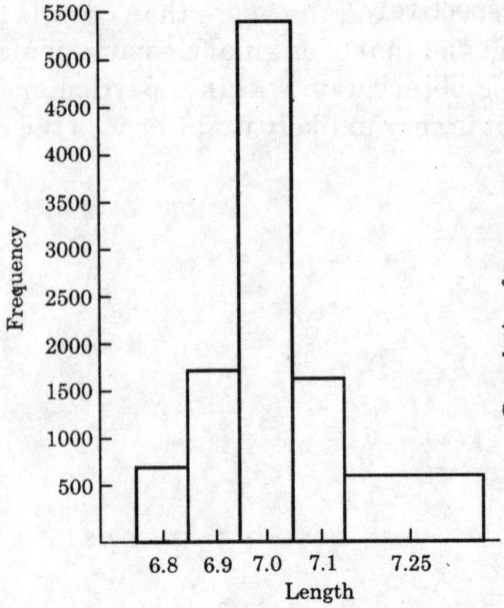

FIGURE 2.20 Histogram of rods for the data in Prob 2.20.

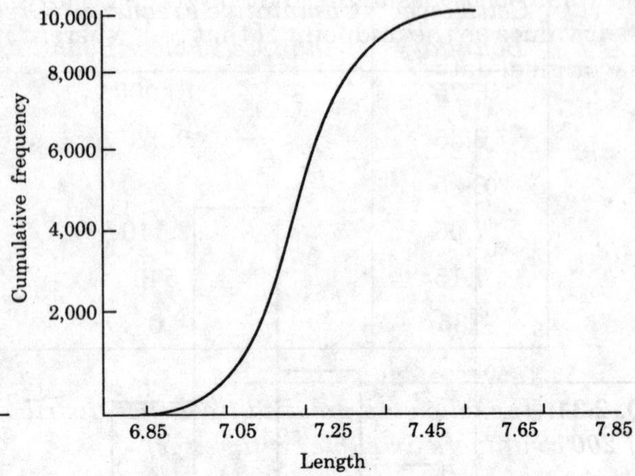

FIGURE 2.21 'Less than' ogive for the data in Prob 2.20.

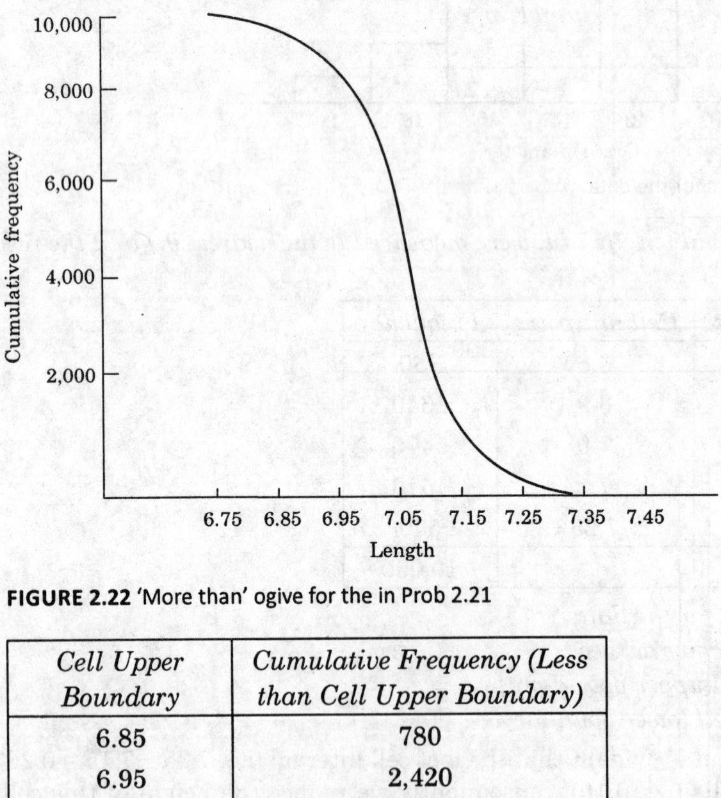

FIGURE 2.22 'More than' ogive for the in Prob 2.21

Cell Upper Boundary	*Cumulative Frequency (Less than Cell Upper Boundary)*
6.85	780
6.95	2,420
7.05	7,890
7.15	9,460
7.35	10,000

Figure 2.21 shows the 'less than' ogive curve.

To draw 'more than' ogive, data are tabulated below and the 'more than' give is shown in Fig. 2.22.

Cell Lower Boundary	*Cumulative Frequency (Greater than Cell Lower Boundary)*
6.75	10,000
6.85	9,220
6.95	7,580
7.05	2,110
7.15	540
735	0

Q. 2.31: *The following grouped frequency distribution describes the measurements of contents of 200 containers (in cubic centimetres).*

(a) Draw of histogram for these data and thus determine the modal volume.

(b) Draw of cumulative frequency curve and estimate from it the median value of volume.

Volume of containers (in c.c)	*Number of containers*
6 and less than 7	2
7 and less than 8	6
8 and less than 9	49
9 and less than 10	121
10 and less than 11	19
11 and less than 12	3
Total	200

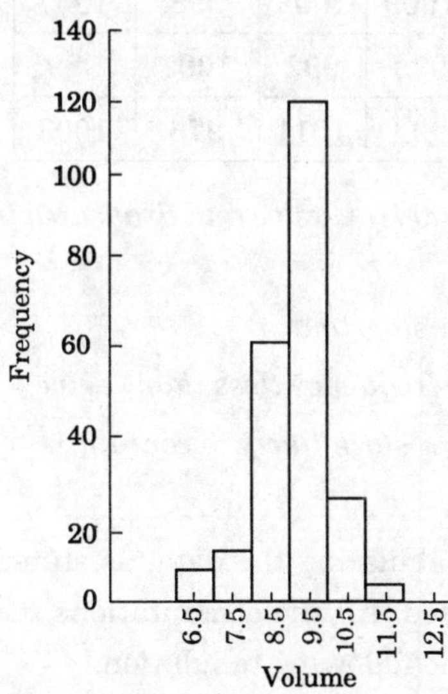

FIGURE 2.23 Histogram

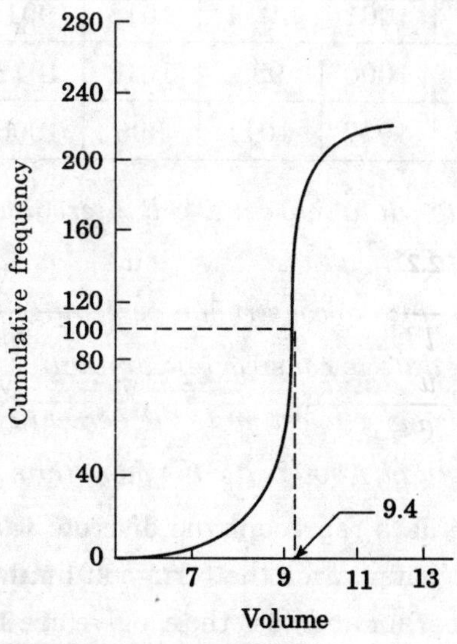

FIGURE 2.24 'Less than' ogive

Ans: (*a*) The histogram for the given data is shown in Fig. 2.23. The modal volume is one having the highest frequency. From Fig. 2.23 it is evident it is the cell whose mid point is 9.5. Hence the modal volume is represented by the cell "9 and less than 10 cc".

(*b*) A cumulative frequency of 'less than' ogive for the data is shown in Fig. 2.24. As previously stated, the cumulative frequencies have been plotted against cell upper boundaries. The medium volume is 50% point that is volume above and below which the frequencies are equal i.e. one half of the total frequency. From Fig. 2.24 it is evident that for a cumulative frequency of 100 (*i.e.* one half of the total of 200,) the volume is 9.4 c.c. approximately. Hence 9.4 c.c, is the median volume.

Q. 2.32: *Bolts are supplied by a certain manufacture in boxes containing a nominal* ***1000****. In fact, the bolts are not counted when packed, the system used is to simple fill the box—consequently the actual number varies from box to box.*

100 *boxes were taken at random, from stock and their contents counted, with the results tabulated below.*

No. of bolts per box (100 boxes)									
992	1007	1001	1010	1001	1008	1013	1010	995	1003
1009	990	1003	1008	999	1002	992	990	998	1013
1014	992	991	1006	998	1001	991	998	1011	985
986	996	1010	1008	1008	1024	995	1023	1001	998
998	1004	1010	1000	1002	997	1013	1005	1006	1015
994	1002	999	1008	1025	998	1005	1008	992	1016
1003	981	1005	982	997	1004	1013	1018	984	1004
1009	1001	1014	1018	991	997	1009	1003	998	1007
1028	1000	988	1012	1012	1001	979	992	1002	989
1010	1017	1011	996	1006	1009	994	1011	976	1003

(*a*) *Group the data into equal cell interval-e.g.,* ***1000-1004*** *inclusive and draw up a frequency table.*

(*b*) *Use the data to construct a percentage frequency histogram.*

(*c*) *Use the data to construct a cumulative percentage frequency (less than) ogive*

(*d*) *Use this ogive to estimate the percentage of boxes in stock likely to contain :*

(*i*) *less than* ***1,000*** *bolts.* (*ii*) *more than* ***1010*** *bolts.*

Ans: Since the data represent the discrete variable, in tabulating the data, as stated earlier, instead of cell boundaries the term cell limits will be used. All the computations required to draw the histogram and 'less than' ogive are shown in the following tabulation.

Cells	*Cell limits*	*Cell midpoint*	*Frequency*	*% Frequency*	*Cumulative % Frequency less than cell upper limit*
975-979	974.5-979.5	977	2	2	2
980-984	979.5-984.5	982	3	3	5
985-989	984.5-989.5	987	4	4	9
990-994	989.5-994.5	992	12	12	21
995-999	994.5-999.5	997	16	16	37
1,000-1,004	999.5-1004.5	1,002	20	20	57
1,005-1,009	1,004.5-1,009.5	1,007	18	18	75
1,010-1,014	1,009.5-1,014.5	1,012	16	16	91
1,015-1,019	1,014.5-1,019.5	1,017	5	5	96
1,020-1,024	1,019.5-1,024.5	1,022	2	2	98
1,025-1,029	1,024.5-1,029.5	1,027	2	2	100

Figure 2.25 shows the percentage frequency histogram for the data.

(Note: The top portion of the rectangles are slightly *curved* to give a *better look* and *less fatigue* to eyes; particularly when the *number of cells is large*.)

Figure 2.26 shows the cumulative percentage 'less than' ogive for the given data.

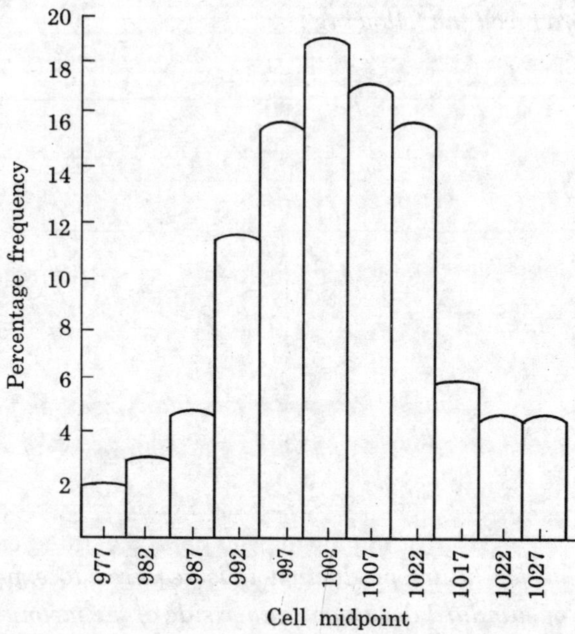

FIGURE 2.25 Percentage Frequency histogram for the data

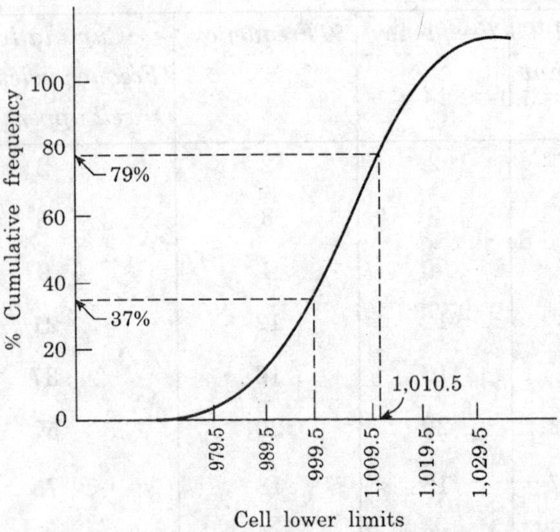

FIGURE 2.26 'More than' ogive for the data

Since all the boxes below the upper cell limit of 999.5 will contain less than 1,000 bolts, from Fig. 2.26 the pércentage cumulative frequency at cell upper limit of 999.5 is 37%. Hence the percentage of boxes containing less than 1,000 bolts is 37%.

"Also from the same curve, the percentage of boxes having less than 1010 (cell limit of 1010.5) bolts is 79%. Hence the percentage of boxes having more than 1010 bolts is 21%.

Q. 2.33: *A machine manufactures metal discs. The particular discs being made are of a nominal diameter of 3 cm. to a tolerance of – 0.06; + 0.07 cm. In other words, diameters between 2.94 and 3.07 are acceptable.*

Measurement of a production run produced the following :

Dia in cm	Discs
2.90-2.92	3
2.92-2.94	29
2.94-2.96	73
2.96-2.98	142
2.98-3.00	176
3.00-3.02	137
3.02-3.04	88
3.04-3.06	64
3.06-3.08	30
3.08-3.10	15
3.10-3.12	1

To assist in scheduling the machine for future production it is required to express the tolerance range in terms of the number of standard deviations either side of the mean. What is the tolerance range in this form ?

Ans: For the given data $\overline{X}$ and are computed values of $\overline{X}$ and s are

Assume $\hat{\sigma} = s = 0.0368$

Acceptable variation below the mean = 3.0 – 2.94 = 0.06 cm and thus expressed in standard deviation is 0.06/0.0368 = 1.63 $\hat{\sigma}$

Acceptable variation above the mean = 3.07 – 3.0 = 0.07 cm and this expressed in standard deviation is 0.07/0.0368 = 1.90 $\hat{\sigma}$

Hence tolerance range in the standard deviation form is

$$- 1.90\ \sigma$$
$$\mu + 1.63\ \sigma$$

Q. 2.34: *Calculate the mean and standard deviation of the melt flow rate data given below (g/10 min).*

If the process specification is 3.0 to 3.8 g/10 min, comment on the capability of the process.

3.2	3.3	3.2	3.3	3.2	3.5	3.0	3.4	3.3	3.7
3.0	3.4	3.5	3.4	3.3	3.2	3.1	3.0	3.4	3.1
3.3	3.5	3.4	3.3	3.2	3.2	3.3	2.7	3.3	2.6
3.2	2.9	3.1	3.2	3.5	2.4	3.5	3.3	3.6	3.5
3.6	3.0	3.1	3.4	3.1	3.6	3.2	3.4	3.3	3.6
3.1	3.4	3.5							

Ans: Using standard formulae and $n = 53$, the computations are $\overline{X} = 3.28, s = 0.242$

Assuming $\hat{\mu} = \overline{X} = 3.28$ and $\hat{\sigma} = s = 0.242$

$$\hat{\mu} + 3\hat{\sigma} = 3.28 + 3(0.242) = 4.006$$
$$\hat{\mu} - 3\hat{\sigma} = 3.28 - 3(0.242) = 2.554$$

Obviously with centering at 3.28, the process is not capable of meeting the specification. Even if the centering is changed to midpoint of specifications i.e. 3.4, then the spread of tolerance, is 3.8 –3.0 *i.e.* 0.8 while the spread of the process 6σ^ i.e..6(0.242) = 1.452. Hence the process is not capable of meeting the specifications.

Q. 2.35: *(a) Mention briefly the relationship among various measures of dispersion indicating which measures of dispersion are generally used in quality control work.*

*(b) Tests made on electrical contacts to determine the number, out of 12, which failed to open (due to welding) before a reversal rate of **1000** cycles per minute had been reached, yielded the following results :*

No. of contacts welded	0	1	2	3	4	5
Frequency	10	13	13	8	4	2

Calculate :

(i) the mean *(ii) the variance*

(iii) the mean deviation from the mean of the number of contacts failing to open.

Determine also :

(iv) the median, and

(v) the mode.

Ans: (*a*) There are four measures of dispersion:

- Range
- Standard deviation
- Mean deviation
- Quartile deviation.

Out the above four, only the first two i.e. Range and Standard deviation are frequently used in quality control work.

The primary advantage of the range is in providing a knowledge of the total spread of the data. It is also valuable when the amount of data is too small or too scattered to justify the calculation of a more precise measure of dispersion. The range is the only measure of dispersion that is not a function of a measure of central tendency. As the number of observations increases, the accuracy of the range decreases, since it becomes easier for an extremely high or low reading to occur. It is suggested that the use of the range be limited to a maximum of 15 observations.

The standard deviation is used when a more precise measure is desired. It is also a very common measure of the dispersion for quality control work and is used when subsequent statistics are to be calculated. When the data have an extreme value for the high or the low, the standard deviation is more desirable than the range.

The mean deviation is not used to any great extent in quality control even though the calculations are simpler and easier to understand. When extreme variations are present in the data, they may unduly influence the standard deviation, and therefore the mean deviation would be more appropriate. For data that are symmetrical or moderately skewed, the mean deviation is approximately 80% of the standard deviation.

The quartile deviation is also not used to any great extent in quality control. It has its greatest use when the median is a measure of the central tendency or when the middle 50% of the data is of the most interest. When the data are symmetrical or moderately skewed, the quartile deviation is approximately 67% of the standard deviation.

(*b*) (*i*) The Mean $\bar{X} = \dfrac{(0 \times 10) + (1 \times 13) + (2 \times 13) + (3 \times 8) + (4 \times 4) + (5 \times 2)}{50} = 1.78$

$$s^2 = \frac{\Sigma fX^2 - n\bar{X}^2}{n-1} = \frac{250 - 50(1.78)^2}{49} \text{ i.e. } 1.89$$

(*iii*) Mean deviation

$$= \frac{10|0-1.78| + 13|1-1.78| + 13|2-1.78| + 8|3-1.78| + 4|4-1.78| + 2|5-1.78|}{50} = 1.12$$

(*iv*) As the number of observations is even *i.e.* 2*n*, the median is the value of $\dfrac{n + (n+1)}{2}$ when the observations are arranged in ascending order.

Hence $\quad$ median $= \dfrac{2+3}{2} =$ i.e. 2.5

(*v*) Mode is the most frequent value of the variate. In this case the distribution is bimodal i.e. it has two modes i.e. 1 and 2.

Q. 2.36: *(a) Name one disadvantage of arithmetic mean. Inspite of this, it is still used as a measure of control tendency in quality central work. Why?*

(b) What is the advantage of using sample averages as a measure of a population characteristic?

(c) Describe in brief and convenient method of drawing a normal curve for a given data.

(d) How will you choose the number of cells or classes while preparing a histogram.

(e) Which two graphical methods are generally used to display data to shop personnel and management ?

Ans: (*a*) One of the disadvantages of the arithmetic mean is that it can sometimes gives a false impression as a result of being influenced by extreme observations. In the industrial quality control work, the observations are taken under controlled conditions and the probability of extreme observations is very small. Moreover when the extreme observations occur, the situation is considered to be out of control and such extreme observations are not considered in decision making. Hence arithmetic mean is used in quality control work.

(*b*) The sample averages will have their own distribution and regardless of the type of universe or population, the average of these sample averages *i.e.* $\bar{}$ of such a frequency distribution tends to be near μ (the parametric value of the population).

(*c*) In order to draw a normal curve, it is often a practice to first draw a histogram of the data by choosing reasonable number of cells and then to join the midpoints of these cells by a smooth curve, which will be in the form of normal curve.

(*d*) Ideally, the histogram will create a picture that shows the variations of data values and simultaneously provide a reasonable level of detail. If too few cells are chosen, little of the shape (except perhaps a few large bars) will be seen. Conversely, if too many cells are chosen, the shape of the data will be lost since some of the cells will be empty, resulting in a comb-like toothed appearance. In order to avoid such situations, it is recommended to divide the data into cells as per the following table :

Number of data	*Number of cells or classes*
Less than 50	5-7
50-100	6-10
100-250	7-12
over 250	10-20

Sometimes Sturgess Rule is used to determine the number of cells. This rule is mathematically represented as

$$K = 1 + 3.3 \log 10\ N$$

where K = number of cells

N = number of observations

The rule when simplified yields the following tabulation :

Number of data	Number of cells or classes
0-9	4
10-24	5
25-49	6
50-89	7
90-189	8
190-399	9
400-799	10
800-1599	11
1600-3200	12

However, often the practical considerations lead to final decision for selecting the number cells.

(*e*) Shop personnel generally prefer histogram of the data. The management people require histogram and to make some quick analysis and estimate, the frequency curves are also required by them.

Q. 2.37: *(a) Advise whether the following statements are TRUE (T) or FALSE (F) :*

1. For a normal distribution, the mean always lies between the mode and the median.

2. A distribution where the mean and median have different values can never be a normal distribution.

3. Area by normal curve is always one.

(b) Answer the following questions (Time allowed : 1 minute).

1. For a normal with $\hat{\mu}$: 55 and $\hat{\sigma} = 10$, how much area will be found under the curve to the right to value 55 ?

(a) 1.0 (b) 0.68 (c) 0.5 (d) cannot be determined from the given information.

2. Which of the following is NOT a valid reason for measuring the dispersion of a distribution?

(a) It provides an indication of the reliability of the statistic used to measure central tendency.

(b) It enables us to compare several samples with similar averages.

(c) It uses more data in describing a distribution.

(d) It draws attention to problems associated with very small or very large variability in distributions.

3. For which of the distributions of Fig. 2.27 is the mean more representative of the data as a whole ?

4. A firm using two different methods to ship orders to its customers found the distributions as in Fig. 2.27 of delivery time for the two methods, based on past records. From available evidence, which shipment method would you recommend?

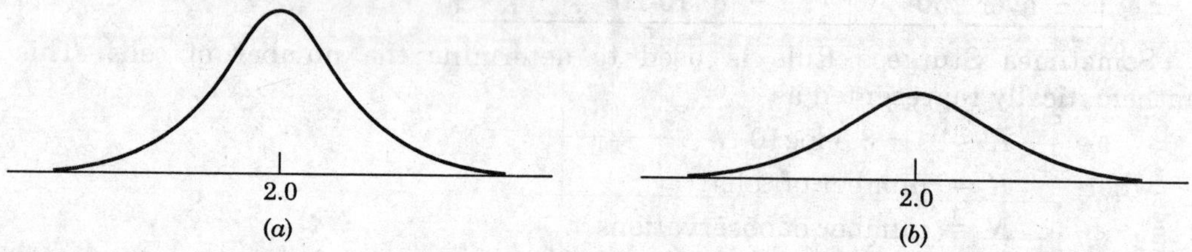

FIGURE 2.27

Ans: (*a*) 1. (F) 2. (T) 3. (T)

(*b*) 1. (*c*) 2. (*a*) 3. (*b*) 4 (*a*)

Q. 2.38: *(a) What is a probability paper? What is the use of this type of paper in quality control ? Mention any additional advantage of this type of paper.*

(b) Figure 2.28 shows frequency curves A, B, C and D. Identify these frequency curves as normal, skewed etc. How these curves will appear on a probability paper?

Ans: The probability paper is a sort of graph paper having a special scale in one direction. The probability paper provides a way of quickly checking the normality of a distribution. For a normal variate, when percentage cumulative frequencies (*i.e.* ogive) are plotted on normal probability paper they give *straight line*. Hence in quality control work, the probability paper is used to check whether a distribution is normal or otherwise. Plot of cumulative frequencies resulting in a straight line indicate that the given distribution is normal.

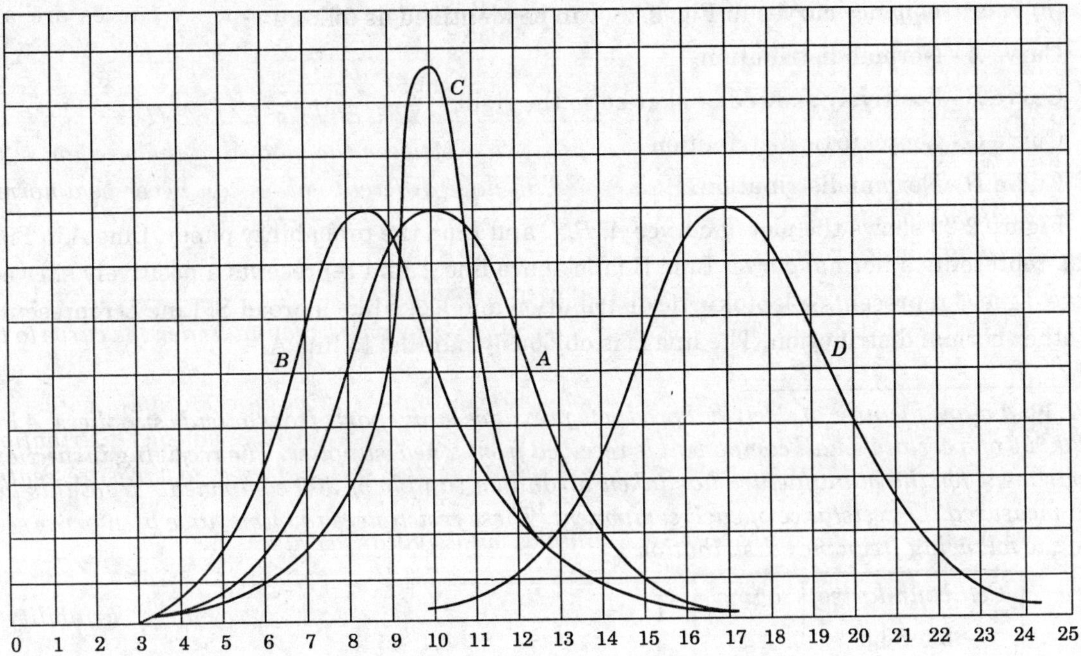

FIGURE 2.28 Frequency curves of Prob. 2.30.(b)

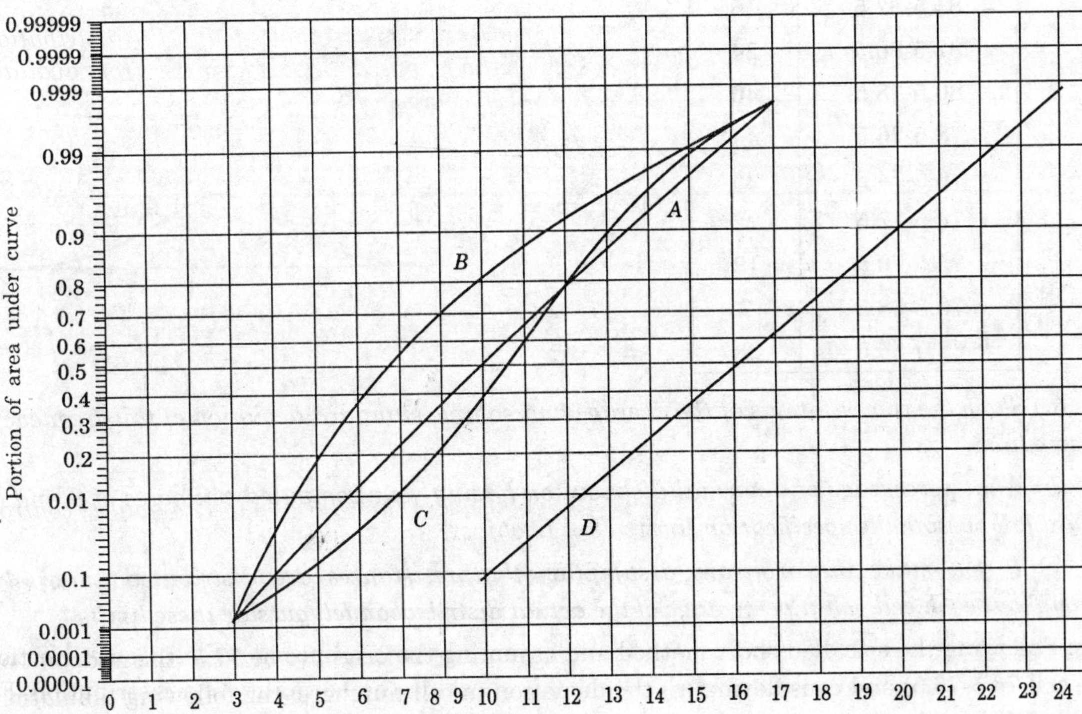

FIGURE 2.29 Plot of Curve A, B, C, and D on probability paper.

An additional advantage of probability paper is that two or more distributions may be drawn on the same diagram without any overlapping of the curves as illustrated by curves *A* and *D* in Fig. 2.29.

(*b*) Four frequency curves in Fig. 2.28, can be identified as follows:

Curve *A* - Normal distribution

Curve *B* - Positively skewed or skewed to the right

Curve *C* - Leptokurtic distribution

Curve *D* - Normal distribution.

Figure 2.29 shows the plot of curves *A, B, C* and *D* on the probability paper. Line *A* in Fig. 2.29, represents a normal curve. Line B falls above line A and represents a positively skewed curve. Line C represents a leptokurtic distribution and looks like a broad *S*. Line *D* represents an other normal distribution. The line D is obviously parallel to line A.

Q. 2.39: *A manufacturer of electrical products purchase many parts from outside suppliers. A lot of 20,000 of a certain small component is received from a new supplier. The receiving inspection department for the manufacture has taken a random sample of 200 components from this lot and measured the resistance of each component. These resistances in ohms have been arranged into the following frequency distribution :*

Cell boundaries	*ohms*
88.5-86.5	2
86.5-84.5	5
84.5-82.5	16
82.5-80.5	24
80.5-78.5	40
78.5-76.5	44
76.5-74.5	25
74.5-72.5	22
72.5-70.5	13
70.5-68.5	7
68.5-66.5	2

(a) Show the computations of the average and sample standard deviation of this frequency distribution.

(b) What percentage of a normal distribution having your computed estimates of μ *and* σ *would fall outside the specification limits* 75 ± 10 *ohms?*

(c) If you make the arbitrary assumption that resistances are distributed uniformly throughout each cell, what percentage of the actual distribution fell outside these limits ?

Ans: Following the so called short method and assuming the origin to be 77.5 (the midpoint of the cell 78.5-76.5) and considering (*d*) the deviation in cell numbers, the following tabulation will help in computation.

Resistance, ohms (midpoint of cell)	*Frequency*	*Deviation in number of cells from assumed origin*		
(X)	*(f)*	*(d)*	*(fd)*	*(fd²)*
87.5	2	5	10	50
85.5	5	4	20	80
83.5	16	3	48	144
81.5	24	2	48	96
79.5	40	1	40	40
77.5	44	0	0	0
75.5	25	− 1	− 25	25
73.5	22	− 2	− 44	88
71.5	13	− 3	− 39	117
69.5	7	− 4	− 28	112
67.5	2	− 5	− 10	50
Total	200		20	802

$\bar{X}$ (in cells numbers from assumed origin of 77.5) $= \dfrac{\Sigma fd}{n} = \dfrac{20}{200} = 0.1$

(*a*) $\bar{X}$ (in original units from true origin) = assumed origin + $\sqrt{\dfrac{\Sigma fd}{n}}$ (cell width)

$$= 77.5 + 0.1(2) + 77.7 \text{ ohms}$$

$$s \text{ (in cell units)} = \sqrt{\frac{\Sigma fd^2 - (\Sigma fd)^2/n}{n-1}} = \sqrt{\frac{802 - 400/200}{199}}$$

$$= \sqrt{4.020} = 2.005$$

s (in original units) = (*s* in cell units) (cell width) = 2.005 (2) = 4.01 ohms

(*b*) $\hat{\mu} = \bar{X} = 17.7;\ \hat{\sigma} = s = 4.01$

$U = 75 + 10 = 85;$

$L = 75 - 10 = 65$

For the *U* of 85, $z_1 = \dfrac{85 - 77.7}{4.01} = +1.820$

For the *L* of 65, $z_2 = \dfrac{65 - 77.7}{4.01} = -3.167$

Table *A* reading for z_1 of + 1.820 = 0.9656

Table *A* reading for z_2 of − 3.167 = 0.00077 (by extrapolation)

Area included = 0.95483

Hence Area outside the specification limits = 1 – 0.95483 *i.e.* 0.04517

Percentage outside the specification limits = 4.52%

(*c*) The frequency distribution in the given table shows that all the components are above the *L* of 65. Also *U* of 85 is within the cell whose boundaries are 86.5 to 84.5. Considering a uniform distribution of frequency within the cell, only one component can be considered to account for resistance of 85 ohms. Hence the number components with resistance more than 85 ohms is (5 – 1) + 2 *i.e.* 6. Therefore the percentage outside the specification limits is = $\frac{6}{200} \times 100$ i.e. 3%.

Q. 2.40: *(a) The variability of a dimension produced by a manufacturing process is normally distributed with a standard deviation of* **0.05** *mm. The mean can be held practically constant. If this dimension is to be as high as possible, provided that hardly any exceed* **60** *mm, at what value should the mean be set?*

(b) If in the same process the components are required to be **60 ± 0.12** *mm, what percentage would be out of limit : (i) If the mean is correctly set at* **60.00** *mm? (ii) If the mean is incorrectly set at* **60.05** *mm.*

Ans. : *(a)* USL_X (or U) = 60.00 mm.

As practically all components fall within $\mu \pm 3\sigma$, therefore

$$\mu + 3\sigma = U \text{ i.e. } 60.00 \text{ mm}$$

Hence $\mu = U - 3\sigma$ *i.e.* 60.00 – 3(0.05) *i.e.* 59.85 mm.

(b) (i) USL_X (or U) = 60.12

LSL_X (or L) = 59.88

For the mean (μ) of 60.00 and σ of 0.05 mm, the area of the normal curve above U is 0.0082 and the area below L is also 0.0082. Hence the proportion outside the $(U - L)$ limits is 0.0082 + 0.0082 *i.e.* 0.0164 or 1.64%.

(ii) For the mean μ of 60.05 mm and σ of 0.05 mm, the area of the normal curve above U is 0.0808 and below L is 0.0034. Hence total proportion outside the $(U - L)$ limits is 0.0808 + 0.00034 *i.e.* 0.08114 *i.e.* 8.11%.

Q. 2.41: *In a study of the variation of a critical dimension of electric contacts, measurements of this dimension were made on a sample of* **1,000** *such contacts. The results are shown here in the form of a frequency table.*

cell midpoint (cm)	10.3	10.4	10.5	10.6	10.7	10.8	10.9	11.0	11.1	11.2
Frequency	5	30	120	180	227	185	150	70	30	3

(i) Describe exactly how this distribution would be represented by a histogram, making it clear where the bases of the rectangles would have their end points.

(ii) Using coding, calculate the mean, variance and standard deviation of this distribution.

(iii) What theoretical frequency for the interval whose midpoints is **10.7** *would be given by a fitted Normal model (i.e. one with the same mean, standard deviation and total frequency as the data)?*

Ans: *(i)* The interval between cell midpoints is 0.1 *i.e.* the cell (or rectangle) width is 0.1. The upper cell boundary of the first cell (or rectangle) is exactly at the middle of first and second cell midpoints i.e. 10.35 and the lower cell boundary of first cell is 10.35 – 0.1 i.e. 10.25.

Hence the cells or rectangles of the histogram should have their end points at 10.25, 10.35, ...11.25.

As the width of cells are equal, the heights (and the areas) are proportional to the frequencies within the cells or rectangles.

(*ii*) By coding the data from 10.0 and taking the deviation d from 10.0 and multiplying with respective frequencies.

$$\Sigma fd = 730.0.$$

Hence $\bar{X} = 10.0 + \dfrac{730.0}{1000}$ *i.e.* 10.73 cm

Also $\Sigma fd^2 = 561.8.$

The standard deviation s is calculated as below.

$$s = \sqrt{\frac{\Sigma fd^2 - (\Sigma fd)^2/n}{n-1}}$$

$$= \sqrt{\frac{561.8 - (730)^2/1000}{999}}$$

$$= 0.17 \text{ cm.}$$

$$\text{Variance} = s^2 = (0.17)2 = 0.0289 \text{ cm}^2$$

(*iii*) Now based upon the assumption that $\hat{\mu} = \bar{X}$ and $\hat{\sigma} = s$, z_1 corresponding to upper cell boundary of 10.75 is $0.11764 \approx 0.1177$ and z_2 corresponding to lower cell boundary of 10.65 is – 0.4705.

From Table *A*, reading for z_1 of + 0.1177 = 0.5468 (by interpolation)

From Table *A*, reading for z_2 of – 0.4705 = 0.3190 (by interpolation)

Area included = 0.2278

As the total frequency is 1,000; this multiplied by 1000 gives a frequency of 227.8 ≈ 228.

Q. 2.42: *In order to estimate the process capability of a machine making resistors, the resistances of 1,000 successive items from it were checked as follows :*

Resistance in ohms	*Frequency*
150.00-150.49	5
150.50-150.99	17
151.00-151.49	44
151.50-151.99	92
152.00-152.49	150
152.50-152.99	192
153.00-153.49	192
153.50-153.99	150
154.00-154.49	92
154.50-154.99	44
155.00-155.49	17
155.50-155.99	5

(a) Plot the data as an ordinary histogram.

(b) State whether the data appear to be normally distributed, giving reasons

(c) Use the curve to estimate the mean and standard deviation.

(d) If a customer demands that resistors should be between 140 and 145 ohms.

(i) To what mean value should the machine be adjusted?

(ii) What is the approximate quality level i.e. what percentage of resistors would be outside the specification limits.

Ans: (*a*) The histogram would have rectangles with cell boundaries 149.995-150.495; .....155.495 to 155.995 and heights proportional to frequency of each cell as cell widths are equal.

(*b*) A mere look at the data indicates that the data are symmetrical distributed. However in order to determine whether the data are normally distributed, it is required to plot the data on probability paper. A plot of cumulative frequency on probability paper will show a straight line indicating that the data are normally distributed.

(*c*) Simple computations yield

$$\bar{X} = 152.995 \text{ and } s = 1$$

(*d*) (*i*) In order to minimize the quantity outside the specification limits, it is best to adjust the machine at $\frac{U+L}{2}$ *i.e.* $\frac{145+140}{2} = 142.5$ ohms.

$$\text{i.e. } \mu = 142.5$$

(*ii*) $\hat{\sigma}$ = s then

$$z_1 \text{ for } U \text{ of } 145 = \frac{145-142.5}{1.0} = 2.5$$

$$z_2 \text{ for } L \text{ of } 140 = \frac{140-142.5}{1.0} = -2.5$$

Area of curve for z_1 of + 2.5 = 0.9938

Area of curve for z_2 of – 2.5 = 0.0062

Hence area of curve above $U = 1 - 0.9938 = 0.0662$.

Similarly area of curve below $L = 0.0062$

Hence area of curve outside $(U - L) = 0.0062+0.0062$ *i.e.* 0.0124

Therefore acceptable quality level is 0.0124 *i.e.* 1.24%.

Q. 2.43: *Samples of polythene bags from two manufacturers A and B are tested by a prospective buyer for bursting pressure with the following results :*

Bursting Pressure	*Number of Bags*	
(lb)	*A*	*B*
5.0 - 9.9	2	9
10.0 - 14.9	9	11
15.0 - 19.9	2	18
20.0 - 24.5	54	32
25.0 - 29.9	11	27
30.0 - 34.5	5	13
Total	110	110

Which set of the bags has highest average bursting pressure ? Which has more uniform pressure? If prices are the same, which manufacturer's bags would be preferred by buyer? Why?

Ans: For determining which set of bags has the highest average bursting pressure, we shall find arithmetic mean and to the uniformity pressure, coefficient of variation will be the deciding factor.

Manufacturer A

For the given data, computed values of average and standard deviation are :

$$\bar{X} = 21$$

$$s = 4.875$$

Assuming $\hat{\mu} = \bar{X} = 21$ and $\hat{\sigma} = s = 4.875$

$$\% \text{ Coefficient of variation} = \hat{\sigma}/\hat{\mu} \times 100 = \frac{4.875}{21} \times 100$$

$$= 23.21$$

Manufacturer B

$$\hat{\mu} = 21.81 \text{ and } \hat{\sigma} = s = 7.07$$

$$\% \text{ Coefficient variation} = \hat{\sigma}/\hat{\mu} \times 100 = \frac{7.0745}{21.81} \times 100$$

$$= 32.40$$

Since the average bursting pressure is higher in case of manufacturer *B*, the bags of this manufacturer have a higher bursting pressure. The bags of manufacturer A have more uniform pressure since the coefficient of variation is less for manufacturer A. If the prices are the same, the bags of manufacturer A should be preferred because of consistency.

Q. 2.44: *In the inspection of a mass-produced item, limit gauges are used to reject everything below a certain size. The dimension being controlled is normally distributed with coefficient of variation 20%, and 15% of items produced are rejected by the gauge. It is considered desirable to reduce this proportion to 5%. The coefficient of variation cannot be altered without installing new machinery but the mean value of the controlled dimension can be increased or decreased by a modification of the existing production process. What percentage change in this mean value will achieve the required reduction in rejects?*

Ans: Let σ be the standard deviation and μ_1 be the mean when the rejection is 15%, and μ_2 be the mean when the rejection is reduced to 5%.

Since coefficient of variation is invariable,

$$\frac{\sigma_1}{\mu_1} = \frac{\sigma_2}{\mu_2} = 0.2, \text{ from which}$$

$$\sigma_1 = 0.2\,\mu_1$$

$$\sigma_2 = 0.2\,\mu_2$$

Let X_1 be the critical dimension, below which the limit gauges start rejection. In first case the rejection is 15%. This means that the area of the normal curve below the X_1 value is 0.15. From Table *A*, z value corresponding to this area is – 1.0365. Since

$$z = \frac{X_1 - \mu_1}{\sigma_1}$$

$$-1.0365 = \frac{X_1 - \mu_1}{\sigma_1}$$

or $$X_1 = \mu_1 - 1.0365\,\sigma_1$$

Eliminating σ_1

$$X_1 = \mu_1 - 1.0365(0.2\,\mu_1) = 0.7927\,\mu_1$$

Similarly when the rejection is 5% by way of altering the mean,

$$X_1 = \mu_2 - 1.645(0.2\,\mu_2) = 0.6710\,\mu_2$$

Equating the above two expressions for the critical dimension gives $\frac{\mu_2}{\mu_1} = \frac{0.7927}{0.6710} = 1.18.$

This means that an 18% increase in the mean value is required.

Q. 2.45: *(a) State some of the characteristics of Normal distribution.*

(b) The mean value of the modulus of the rupture of large number of test specimens of green sitka spruce has been found to be 5,600 psi. Assuming the distribution to be approximately normal and standard deviation to be 8,40, find for what fraction or percentage of the specimen the modulus of rupture will lie between (a) 5,000 and 6,000 ? (b) above 4,000 ? (c) below 3,500 ?

Ans: (*a*) Main characteristics of the normal distribution are :

1. The normal distribution, when depicted graphically, is bell-shaped and symmetrical. Also, it is continuous in the sense that the variable can assume all the values on a continuous scale.
2. It represents a population of infinite size
3. If its mean is shown as zero, the magnitude of the involved range varies from minus to plus infinity.
4. It can be described completely in terms of its mean and standard deviation.
5. It has the same value of mean, median and mode.

(*b*) Table *A*, App. 1 give the area of the normal curve from $-\infty$ upto the specified limit. The area from $-\infty$ to $X = 5{,}000$ can be calculated by first calculating *z*.

$$z = \frac{X - \mu}{\sigma}$$

$$= \frac{5{,}000 - 5{,}600}{840} = -0.714$$

Area of the normal curve = 0.23766.

Similarly when $X = 6{,}000$, $z = 0.476$ and the area of the normal curve from $-\infty$ to *X* of 6,000 is 0.68224.

Therefore, net area of the normal curve between 6,000 and 5,000 = 0.68224 – 0.23766 = 0.44458 or, 44.46% of the specimen will have the modulus of rupture between 5,000 and 6,000 psi.

(*c*) For finding the percentage above *X* of 4,000, the area of curve from $-\infty$ to $X = 4000$, can be calculated. It is found to be 0.0287. Therefore, the fraction above *X* of 4000 is

$$1 - 0.0287 = 0.9713 \text{ i.e. } 97.1\%$$

(*d*) Similarly the fraction below 3,500 is found to be only 0.0062 i.e. 0.62%.

Q. 2.46: *11 coils from a coil winding machine have the following resistances:*

121, 120, 118, 123, 121, 124, 120, 121, 119, 123, 121 *ohms.*

(a) Estimate the average and standard deviation

(b) Assuming that the mean resistance of the coils can be held steady at 121 ohms. What are the tightest tolerances to which the machine could be expected to work ?

(c) If a consumer demanded the coils be within the limits of 119 to 123 ohms, what percentage of production would be acceptable, still assuming that the mean resistance can be correctly set and held there.

Ans: (*a*) Average $(\bar{X}) = \dfrac{121 + 120 + \dots + 123 + 121}{11} = \dfrac{1331}{11}$ *i.e.* = 121 ohms

Standard deviation (s)

$$= \sqrt{\frac{(121-121)^2 + (120-121) + \dots + (123-121)^2 + (121-121)^2}{10}}$$

$= 1.71$

(b) Assuming that $\hat{\mu} = \bar{X} = 121$ and $\hat{\sigma} = s = 1.71$ and the product is normally distributed, the tightest tolerances to which the machine can be expected to work are $\pm 3\sigma$. Hence

Upper tolerance = $\hat{\mu} + 3\hat{\sigma} = 121 + 3(1.71) = 126.13$

Lower tolerance = $\hat{\mu} - 3\hat{\sigma} = 121 - 3(1.71) = 115.87$.

(*c*) Since this is a case of continuous variable, the resistances 120, 121 ohms etc. represent the mid points of cells 119.5 - 120.5, 120.5 - 121.5 ohms etc. In order to find the resistance between 119 and 123 ohms, z values to calculated for upper cell boundaries of 119.5 and 123.5.

z_1 corresponding to $123.5 = \dfrac{123.5 - 121}{1.71} = 1.462$

z_2 corresponding to $119.5 = \dfrac{119.5 - 121}{1.71} = -0.877$

Table A reading for z_1 of 1.462 = 0.9282

Table A reading for z_2 of − 0.877 = 0.1902

Area enclosed = 0.7380

Hence, the % of product between 119 and 123 is 73.8.

Q. 2.47: *The bottle filling machine at Peter's Sauces is being used to fill 15 oz bottles of their Spicy Sauce. The actual bottles will hold 15.6 oz. The machine has been set to discharge an average of 15.2 oz. It is known that the amount discharged follows a normal distribution with a standard distribution of 0.2 oz.*

(i) What proportion of the bottles overflow?

(ii) The overflowing of bottles causes considerable problems and it has therefore been suggested that the average discharge should be adjusted to 15.1 oz. However in order to meet weights and measures regulations no more than 1 in 40 bottles. on average must contain less than 14.6 oz. If the average discharge is adjusted to 15.1 oz are the weights and measure regulations being contravened?

Ans: For the normal curve of distribution,

$$\mu = 15.2 \text{ oz.}, \sigma = 0.20\text{oz}$$

(*i*) As the bottles with fill more than 15.6 oz will overflow, the area of the normal curve between 15.6 oz and + ∞ will give the proportion of overflowing bottles. Area of normal curve from − ∞ to 15.6 is first calculated.

$$z = \frac{15.6 - 15.2}{0.2} = 2.0$$

Area of normal curve between − ∞ up to 15.6 oz i.e. for a z value to 2.0 is 0.9773. Therefore area of normal curve beyond 15.6 oz is 1.0000 − 0.9773 *i.e.* 0.0227 *i.e.* 2.27%

Hence the proportion of bottles which overflow is 2.27%.

(*ii*) The statement that no more than 1 in 40 bottles, on average must contain less than 14.6 oz implies that the area of the normal curve from 14.6 oz to $-\infty$ is not more than $\frac{1}{40}$ i.e. 0.025, which corresponds to a z value of -1.96

Therefore, $$-1.96 = \frac{14.6 - \mu}{0.2}$$

Hence $$\mu = 14.992 \text{ oz}$$

Since the average discharge is adjusted to 15.1 oz in place to 14.992 oz, the proportion of bottles containing less than 14.6 oz. is still lesser than 0.025, which can be seen by drawing the curves or from the following calculations.

For μ of 15.1 and X of 14.6 and $\sigma = 0.2$,

$$z = \frac{14.6 - 15.1}{0.2} \text{ i.e. } -2.5$$

Corresponding to a z of -2.5, the area of the curve is 0.0062 which is substantially less than 0.025 i.e. the proportion of bottles containing less than 14.6 oz. is lesser than 1 in 40.

Hence the weights and measures regulations are not being contravened.

Q. 2.48: *In a cigarette-making process the specifications demand that the individual cigarette weight shall be below the nominal weight of* ***1.2*** *grams on only one occasion in* ***100****. At present the cigarette-making machine produces to any required mean cigarette weight with a standard deviation of* ***.01*** *gram. A new cigarette-making machine is available which makes to a more consistent weight, the standard deviation of weights being* ***.008*** *gram. Both machines can make* ***2,000*** *cigarettes per minutes and will be required to operate for a* ***40*** *hour week* ***50*** *weeks per year. Tobacco costs Rs.* ***1,000*** *per kilogram. Find the annual saving made possible by the new machine and compare it to the new machine purchase price of Rs.* ***12,50,000****.*

Ans: The statement "the individual cigarette weight shall be below the nominal weight of 1.2 grams on only one occasion in 100" means that the probability of individual cigarette weight under 1.2 grams is only $\frac{1}{100}$ *i.e.* 0.01 or the area of normal curve from $-\infty$ to 1.2 gram is 0.01.

Let the present cigarette making machine be designated as M/c-1 and the new machine be M/c-2

For M/c-1, $\sigma_1 = 0.01$ gram. and the average is μ_1

For M/c-2, $\sigma_2 = 0.008$ gram. and the average is μ_2

The normal curve area of 0.01 corresponds to a z value of -2.3267 (by interpolation).

Now for M/c-1, $$-2.3267 = \frac{1.2 - \mu_1}{0.01}$$

or $$\mu_1 = 1.223267 \text{ grams}$$

Similarly M/c-2 $$\mu_2 = 1.218614 \text{ grams.}$$

As μ_2 of M/c-2 is less than μ_1 of M/c-1, there is saving in quantity of tobacco per cigarette. Average saving of in quantity of tabacco per cigarette = $\mu_1 - \mu_2$ *i.e.* 0.004653 grams

Total annual saving is ₹ = $$\left(\frac{0.004653}{1{,}000}\right) \times (1{,}000)(2{,}000 \times 60 \times 40 \times 50) \text{ i.e. } 11{,}16{,}720$$

Cost of M/c-2 is ₹ 12,50,000

In view of above calculations, it is obvious that saving is less than the cost of M/C-2.

Q. 2.49: *A machine is producing components whose lengths are normally distributed about a mean of 6.50 cm. An upper tolerance limit of 6.54 cm has been adopted and, when the machine is correctly set, 1 in 20 components is rejected as exceeding this limit. On a certain day, it is found 1 in 15 components is rejected for exceeding this limit.*

(a) *Assuming that the mean has not changed but that the production has become more variable, estimate the new standard deviation.*

(b) *Assuming that the standard deviation has not changed but the mean has moved, estimate the new mean*

(c) *If 1,000 components are produced in a shift, how many of them may be expected to have lengths in the range 6.48 to 6.53 cm if the machine is set as in (a)?*

Ans: (*a*) When the production becomes more variable, area of the curve above the upper tolerance limit of 6.54 is $\frac{1}{15}$ i.e. 0.0667. Hence the area of the curve up to the tolerance limit is 1.00 − 0.0667 = 0.9333. From Table *A*, corresponding to the area of 0.9333, *z* value is 1.5. If the changed standard deviation is σ, then

$$1.5 = \frac{6.54 - 6.50}{\sigma}$$

or $$\sigma = 0.0266$$

(*b*) When the machine is correctly set, 1 in 20 components are rejected *i.e.* are a of the curve above the upper tolerance limit is 0.05. Hence the area of the curve up to tolerance limit is 0.95. From Table A, corresponding to the area of 0.95, *z* value is 1.645.

If σ is the standard deviation, then $1.645 = \frac{6.54 - 6.50}{\sigma}$

or $$\sigma = 0.0243$$

Since the production becomes more variable because of change in the mean value, let the new mean be μ. Now the area of the curve upto tolerance limit is 0.9333 and the corresponding *z* value is 1.5. Hence

$$1.5 = \frac{6.54 - \mu}{0.0243}$$

or $$\mu = 6.504$$

(*c*) $$\mu = 6.50, \sigma = 0.0266$$

$$z \text{ corresponding to } 6.53 = \frac{6.53 - 6.50}{0.0266} = 1.128$$

$$z \text{ corresponding to } 6.48 = \frac{6.48 - 6.50}{0.0266} = -0.752$$

Table *A* reading for + 1.128 = 0.8704

Table *A* reading for − 0.752 = 0.2260

Area enclosed = 0.6444

From above it is evident that in production of 1,000 components, about 644 will have the length between 6.48 and 6.53 cm.

Q. 2.50: *Find the mean and standard deviation of the following set of 500 measurements. Find also the expected frequencies in each cell for a normal distribution having the same mean and standard deviation. Draw frequency polygons for this and the original distribution.*

Measurement (mm)	29.6	29.7	29.8	29.9	30.0	30.1	30.2	30.3	30.4
Frequency	7	18	54	106	115	96	73	22	9

Ans: Since this is a case of continuous variable, the given measurements i.e. 29.6, 29.7 .... represent the cell mid-point of the cell boundaries 29.55-29.65, 29.65-29.75 etc.

The mean and standard deviation are computed to be

$$\overline{X} = 30.01; s = 0.163$$

In order to find the expected frequencies in each cell for a normal distribution having the mean (μ) = 30.01 and standard deviation (σ) = 0.163, z values are to be computed for the upper cell boundaries. For example, to find the frequency upto 29.6, z is calculated for upper cell boundary of 29.65. z corresponding to 29.65 is – 2.208. Table A reading corresponding to z of – 2.208 is 0.136. This multiplied by total frequency of 500 i.e. 0.136 × 500 = 6.8 gives the expected frequency upto 29.6. Similarly the calculated frequency upto 29.7 is 27.65. Hence the frequency is the cell (29.65 – 29.75) is 27.65 – 6.8 = 20.85. Proceeding in a similar manner, the frequency in each cell is calculated and tabulated below.

Measurement (mm)	≤29.6	29.7	29.8	29.9	30.0	30.1	30.2	30.3	≥30.4
Frequency	6.8	20.85	53.8	96.8	120.5	104.1	62.3	25.9	9.2

Frequency polygons of the above data and the original distribution are shown in Fig. 2.30.

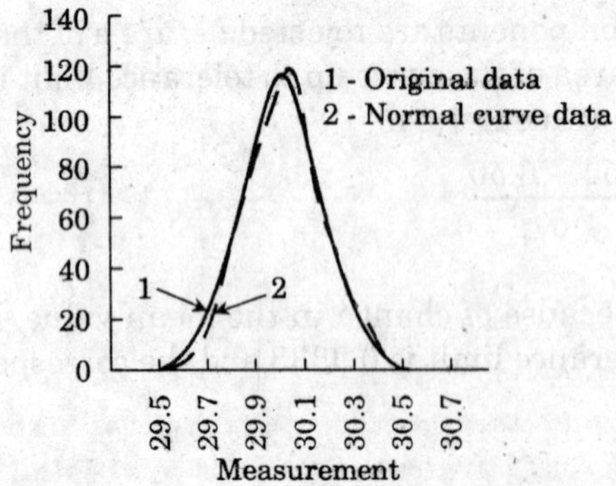

FIGURE 2.30 Frequency polygons for the original data and the normal curve data

Q. 2.51: *A scutcher is a machine used in the textile industry to open and clean new cotton and form it into a continuous fibrous layer called a lap. From a large number of weighings made in the past it is known that the weights of 20 kg. finisher laps produced on a particular type of scutcher can be assumed to be normally distributed with σ of 75 gm. The mean μ of the distribution depends on the adjustment of the scutcher. All laps differing from 20 kg by more than 200 gm. have to be reprocessed. For what value of μ will the percentage of laps requiring reprocessing be a minimum ? Find this minimum percentage.*

Narrowing the tolerance limits for lap weight would, of course, result in more reprocessing. Where could the limits i.e. set if the reprocessing of up to 2% of laps is acceptable ?

Ans: Since the laps differing from 20 kg by more than 200 gm have to be reprocessed and the distribution is normal, setting the μ at 20 kg will minimise the reprocessing.

Evidently laps above 20 kg + 200 g and below 20 kg - 200 g will require reprocessing.

$$z_1 \text{ corresponding to (20 kg - 200 gm)} = \frac{(20\text{kg} - 200\text{gm}) - 20\,\text{kg}}{75\text{gm}} \quad i.e. -2.67$$

$$= -2.67$$

z_1 corresponding to (20 kg + 200 gm) = $\dfrac{(20\text{kg} + 200\text{gm}) - 20\,\text{kg}}{75\text{gm}}$ *i.e.* 2.67

$$= 2.67.$$

From Table *A*, area of the curve for a z of – 2.67 is – 0.0038.

Similarly, area of the curve for a z of 2.67 is – 0.9962.

Area of the curve above the upper limit of (20 kg + 200 gm)

$$= 1.0 - 0.9962 = 0.0038.$$

Minimum reprocessing = Area of the curve below the lower limit + Area of the curve above upper limit

$$= 0.0038 + 0.0038 = 0.0076.$$

Minimum percentage of reprocessing

$$= 100 \times 0.0076 = 0.76.$$

With distribution as normal and μ at 20 kg, let the lower limit be L and the upper limit be U so that the area of the curve below L is 1% and above U is also 1%. From Table *A*, z value corresponding to 1% area of the curve by interpolation = – 2.327. Hence,

$$-2.327 = \frac{L - 20\text{ kg}}{75\text{ gm}}$$

$$L = 20\text{ kg} - 174.5\text{ gm}.$$

Since the distribution is symmetrical about the mean,

$$U = 20\text{ kg} + 174.5\text{ gm}.$$

Hence the laps differing from 20 kg by more than 174.5 gm would require reprocessing.

Q. 2.52: *Preparations from either of two sources, A and B, contain component X in concentrations which are described by normal distributions (280 ; 10) and (270 ; 5) respectively. If it is necessary to attribute source to a batch of items on the basis of the concentration of X in a single item ; what value should be used as the 'watershed' between A and B ? In what way, if any, is the situation changed by basing the decision of the mean of the concentrations of X in a composite sample drawn from 4 preparations ?*

Ans: Decision rule is to be of the kind : If measured concentration of X is less than X_w classify as 'source B', otherwise classify as 'source A' ($270 \le X_w \le 280$). It is reasonable to choose X_w so to minimise the proportion of batches misclassified. The probability of misclassifying a genuine source A batch is given by the area of the lower end tail of the distribution N (280, 10) cut off at X_w and the probability of misclassifying a genuine source B batch is given by the area of the upper tail of the distribution N (270, 5) cut off at X_w.

Thus for $X_w = 275$,

$$z_A = \frac{280 - 275}{10} = 0.5.$$

From Table *A* area of the normal curve is 0.6915.

Hence the required probability is 1 – 0.6915 = 0.3085.

$$z_B = \frac{275 - 270}{5} = 1.00$$

Again from Table *A*, area of the normal curve is 0.8413.

Hence the required probability is 1 – 0.8413 = 0.1587.

Evidently for X_w = 275, 30.85% of genuine source *A* batches and 15.87% of genuine source *B* batches will be misclassified. If equal numbers of batches come from each source the average misclassified rate = $\frac{1}{2}$ (30.85 + 15.87) i.e. 23.36%

Calculations for selected value of X_w give

X_w	*Average misclassification rate*
275	23.36%
276	22.99%
277	23.15%
278	23.78%

This suggests that X_w should be chosen as approximately 276. For sample of size 4 according to the formula, $\sigma_{\bar{X}} = \frac{\sigma}{\sqrt{n}}$ the standard deviations are reduced to 5 and 2.5 respectively. Similar computations show that for X_w = 274 a minimum misclassifications rate of 8.50% is obtained.

Q. 2.53: *Assume that a product cannot accept a component with a particular dimension in excess of 2.57 mm and that samples of size 4 can be taken. The process mean and average range are, generally, 2.5 mm and 0.1 mm respectively. What is the probability of the process producing a value less than or equal to 2.57 if the process mean changes from 2.45 to 2.65 mm in steps of 0.05 mm? What is probability of the mean of the sample being less than or equal to 2.57 for the same variation in the process mean.*

Ans: The data indicate that μ varies from 2.45 to 2.65 but $\bar{R}$ = 0.1 remains constant.

$$\sigma = \frac{\bar{R}}{d_2} \text{ i.e. } \frac{0.1}{2.059} \text{ from Table } C \text{ of App. 2, for } n = 4 \text{ factor } d_2 = 2.059)$$

$$\sigma_{\bar{X}} = \frac{\sigma}{\sqrt{n}} = \frac{0.1}{2.059\sqrt{4}} \text{ i.e. } \frac{0.05}{2.059}$$

For μ of 2.45 and X = 2.57, $z = \dfrac{2.57 - 2.45}{\left(\dfrac{0.1}{2.059}\right)}$ = *i.e.* 2.4708

Similarly for μ of 2.50 and X = 2.57 z = 1.4413

for μ of 2.55 and X = 2.57 z = 0.4118

for μ of 2.60 and X = 2.57 z = − 0.6177

for μ of 2.65 and X = 2.57 z = − 1.6472

Also for μ of 2.45 and $\bar{X}$ = $\dfrac{2.57 - 2.45}{\left(\dfrac{0.05}{2.059}\right)}$ = *i.e.* 4.94

Similarly for μ of 2.50 and $\bar{X}$ = 2.57 z = 2.88

for μ of 2.55 and $\bar{X}$ = 2.57 z = 0.82

for μ of 2.60 and $\bar{X}$ = 2.57 z = − 1.234

for μ of 2.65 and $\bar{X}$ = 2.57 $z = -3.39$

Now from Table *A* of App. 1, following probabilities can be computed.

μ	*Probability of* $X \le 2.57$	*Probability of* $\bar{X} \le 2.57$
2.45	0.9932	1.000 (approx.)
2.50	0.9253	0.9980
2.55	0.6598	0.7939
2.60	0.2669	0.1086
2.65	0.0498	0 (approx.)

Q. 2.54: *How the distribution curve is influenced by variability ?*

Ans: The shape of the distribution curve is influenced by two important features of variability :

1. The frequency with which parts close the mean size occur.
2. The 'spread' either side of the mean-size, called the range.

Q. 2.55: *(a) How the normally distributed data can be presented with the help of a curve?*

(b) How many data fall within

(i) $\mu \pm 1\sigma$ *(ii)* $\mu \pm 3\sigma$ *(iii)* $\mu \pm 6\sigma$

(c) State some characteristics of the Normal distribution.

Ans: *(a)* Normally distributed data can be represented by a bell shaped normal curve in Fig.

(b) (i) % data between $\mu \pm 1\sigma = 68.25$

(ii) % data between $\mu \pm 3\sigma = 99.73$

(iii) % data between $\mu \pm 6\sigma = 99.99966$

(c) Main characteristics of the normal distribution are :

1. The normal distribution, when depicted graphically, is bell-shaped and symmetrical. Also, it is continuous in the sense that the variable can assume all the values on a continuous scale.
2. It represents a population of infinite size
3. If its mean is shown as zero, the magnitude of the involved range varies from minus to plus infinity.
4. It can be described completely in terms of its mean and standard deviation.
5. It has the same value of mean, median and mode.

CHAPTER

3 Control Charts for Variables

3.1 SOURCES OF VARIATION

No two products or services are exactly alike because the processes that produce them contain many sources of variation, even if the process is working as it was intended. For example, the diameter of two crankshafts may vary because of differences in tool wear, material hardness, operator skill, or temperature during the period in which they were produced. Similarly, the time required to process a credit card application varies because of the load on the credit department, the financial background of the applicant, and the skills and attitudes of the employees. Nothing can be done to eliminate variation in process output completely, but management can investigate the causes of variation to minimize it.

3.2 VARIATION - THE AXIOM OF MANUFACTURE

Due to different sources of variations present in the manufacture, one of the axioms or truisms of manufacturing is that no two objects are ever made exactly alike. The variation may be quite large and easily noticeable, such as the height of humans, or the variation may be very small, such as the weight of fibre-tipped pens. When variations are very small, it may appear that items are identical; however, precision instrument will show differences. If two items appear to have the same measurement, it is due to the limits of our measuring instruments. As measuring instruments have become more refined, variation has continued to exist, only the increment of variation has changed. The ability to measure this variation in the product is necessary before it can be controlled. There are following ***three*** distinct categories of variations in the mass manufactured product.

- With-in-piece variation
- Piece-to-piece variation
- Time-to-time variation

Experience and analysis of recorded data indicate that four major contributors to these variation are

- Processes
- Materials
- Operators
- A set of miscellaneous factors

The *first* contributor is *process.* This source includes tool wear, machine variation, work holding device positioning and hydraulic and electric fluctuations. When all these variations are put together there is a certain capability or accuracy within which the process operates. Even supposedly identical machines will have different capabilities and this fact becomes a very important consideration when scheduling the manufacture of critical parts.

FIGURE 3.1 Distinction between chance and assignable causes of variation.

The *second* source of variation is the *material*. Since variation occurs in the finished products, it must also occur in the raw material (which was someone else's finished product).

The *third* and possibly the greatest source of variation is *operator*.

The *fourth* source of variation is *miscellaneous*. The sources includes environmental factors such as heat, light and humidity etc.

As long as these four contributors to variations fluctuate in a normal or expected manner a stable pattern of many ***chance causes*** (also called ***common causes***) of variation develops. Chance causes of variation are inevitable and because they are very small in magnitude they are difficult to identify. These causes of variation which are large in magnitude and therefore readily identified are classified as ***assignable causes*** (also called ***special causes***). The distinction between these two types is depicted in Fig 3.1. *When only chance causes are present in a process, the process is considered to be in control.* However, *when an assignable cause of variation is also present, the variation will be excessive and the process is classified as out of control or beyond the expected normal variation.* The objective of quality control is to restrict the causes only of variation to the chance causes only by detecting and eliminating the causes and sources of assignable causes.

3.2.1 Common Causes

Common causes of variation are the purely random and hence also called random causes. These are due to unidentifiable sources of variation that are unavoidable with the current process. For example, a machine that fills cereal boxes will not put exactly the same amount of cereal in each box. If we weighed a large number of boxes filled by the machine and plotted the results in a scatter diagram, the data would tend to form a pattern that can be described as a distribution. Such a distribution may be characterized by its mean (or average), spread, and shape.

1. The **Mean** (or arithmetic average) is the sum of the observations divided by the total number of observations. This is same as mentioned in Chap 2.

$$\bar{X}_j = \frac{1}{n}\sum_{i=1}^{n} X_i \qquad ...(3.1)$$

where X_i = observation of a quality characteristic (such as weight)

n = total number of observations in a subgroup or sample.

$\bar{X}_j$ = the mean of any subgroup j

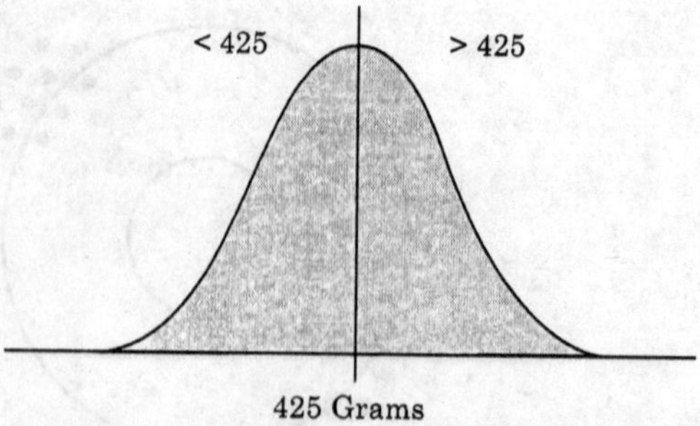

FIGURE 3.2 Process distribution for the box-filling machine when only common causes of Variation are Present.

2. The spread (or *dispersion*)is a measure of the dispersion of observations about the mean. Two measures commonly used in practice are the range and the standard deviation. The ***Range*** is the difference between the largest observation in a sample and the smallest *i.e.*

$$R_j = X_{max} - X_{min} \qquad \text{...(3.2)}$$

and the ***standard deviation*** (σ) may be calculated as

$$\sigma = \sqrt{\frac{\Sigma(X_i - \bar{X})^2}{n-1}} \qquad \text{...(3.3)}$$

Where σ = standard deviation

n = total number of observations

$\bar{X}$ = mean of subgroup

X_i = observation of a quality characteristic

Relatively small values for the range or the standard deviation imply that the observations are clustered near the mean.

3. Two common shapes of process distributions are symmetric and skewed. A symmetric distribution has the same number of observations above and below the mean. A skewed distribution has a preponderance of observations either above or below the mean.

If process variability comes solely from common causes of variation, the distribution is typically symmetric, with most observations near the center. Figure 3.2 shows the distribution for the box-filling machine when only common causes of variation are present. The mean weight is 425 grams, and the distribution is symmetric relative to the mean.

3.2.2 Assignable Causes

The second category of variation, assignable causes of variation, includes any variation causing factors that can be identified and eliminated. Assignable causes of variation include an employee needing training or a machine needing repair. Let's return to the example of the box-filling machine. Figure 3.3 shows how assignable causes can change the distribution of output for the box-filling machine. The Curve (1) is the process distribution when only common causes of variation are present. Curve (2) depict a change in the distribution because of assignable causes. In Fig. 3.3 (*a*), the curve (2) indicates that the machine put more cereal than planned in all the boxes, thereby increasing the average weight of each box. In Fig. 3.3 (*b*), an increase in the variability of the weight of cereal in each box affected the spread of the distribution. Finally, in Fig. 3.3 (*c*), the curve (2) indicates that the machine produced more lighter than heavier boxes. Such a distribution is skewed—that is, no longer symmetric to the average value.

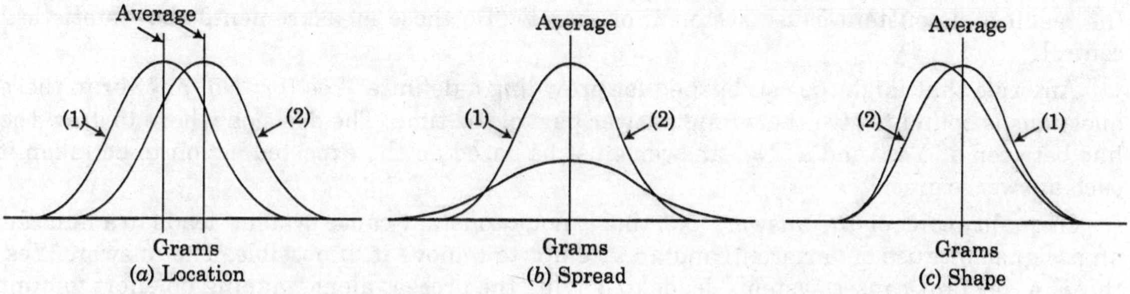

FIGURE 3.3 Effects of assignable causes on the process distribution for the box-filling machine.

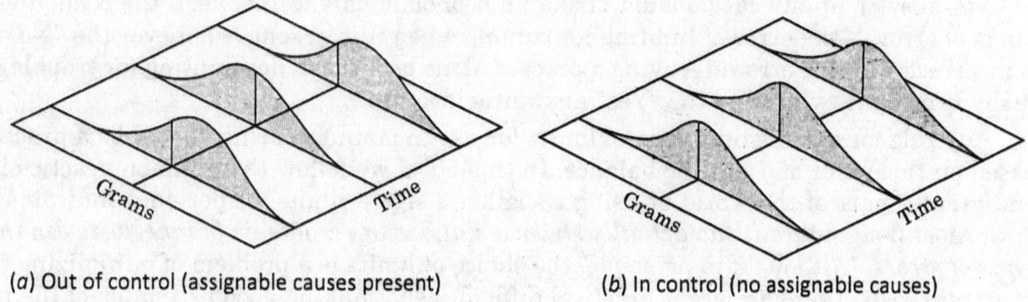

FIGURE 3.4 Effects of assignable causes on process control.

- *A process is said to be in statistical control when the dimensions of its distribution don't change over time.*
- After the process is in statistical control, we can use SPC procedures to detect the onset of assignable causes so that they can be eliminated and variability can be reduced further.

Figure 3.4 shows the differences between a process that is in statistical control and one that isn't. In Fig. 3.4 (*a*), the machine is generating different distributions of cereal box weight over time, indicating assignable causes that need to be eliminated. In Fig. 3.4 (*b*), the distributions of weight are stable over time. Consequently, the process is in statistical control. Later, we discuss how SPC techniques can be used in continuous improvement projects to reduce process variability.

3.3 THE INSPECTION PROCESS

Many companies use quality inspection improperly, merely to weed out the defectives before they reach the customer. This approach is doomed to failure because of the internal and external failure costs discussed in PART-2, Chap 16. In contrast, *world-class* companies combine early inspection with SPC to monitor quality and detect and correct abnormalities. Important decisions in implementing such a programme include how to measure quality characteristics, what size sample to collect, and at which stage in the process to conduct inspections.

3.4 THE USE OF CONTROL CHARTS TO JUDGE WHETHER OR NOT A CONSTANT SYSTEM OF CHANCE CAUSES IS PRESENT

Control charts for $\overline{X}$, R, and s supply a basis for judgement on a major question of practical importance. This question might be phrased in different ways, such as, "Were all these samples drawn from the same population?" or "Is there one universe from which these samples appear to come ?" or "Do these figures indicate a stable pattern of variation?" or "Is this variation the result of a constant-cause system?" or merely "Do these measurements show statistical control?"

Any rule that might be established for providing a definite "Yes" or "No" answer to these questions is bound to give the wrong answer part of the time. The decision where to draw the line between a "Yes" and a "No" answer must be based on the expected action to be taken if each answer is given".

In quality control, the answer, "No, this is not a constant-cause system" leads to a hunt for an assignable cause of variation, and an attempt to remove it, if possible. The answer, "Yes, this is a constant-causes system," leads to leaving the process alone, making no effort to hunt for causes of variation. The rule for establishing the control limits that will determine the "Yes" or "No" answer in any case should strike an economic balance between the costs due to two kinds of errors—the error of hunting for trouble when it is absent (whenever the "No" answer is incorrect) and the error of leaving a process alone because of not hunting for trouble when it really is present (whenever the "Yes" answer is incorrect).

Any rule for establishing control limits for use in manufacturing should be a practical one based on this point of economic balance. In this book, we follow the common practice in India and greater part of the world of using so-called 3-sigma limits. Experience indicates that in most cases 3-*sigma limits do actually strike a satisfactory economic balance between these two types of errors*. (Although, in principle, the choice of limits is a problem of minimizing the sum of certain costs, there are great practical difficulties in making good estimates of the relevant unit costs.)

3.5 THE CONTROL CHART METHOD

In order to indicate when observed variations in quality are greater than could be left to chance, the control chart method of analysis and presentation of data is used. The control chart method for variables is a means of visualizing the variations that occur in the central tendency and dispersion of a set of observations. It is a graphical record of the quality of a particular characteristic.

An example of a control chart is given in Fig 3.5. This particular chart is referred to as an $\bar{X}$ chart and is used to control the variation in the mean or average value of samples or

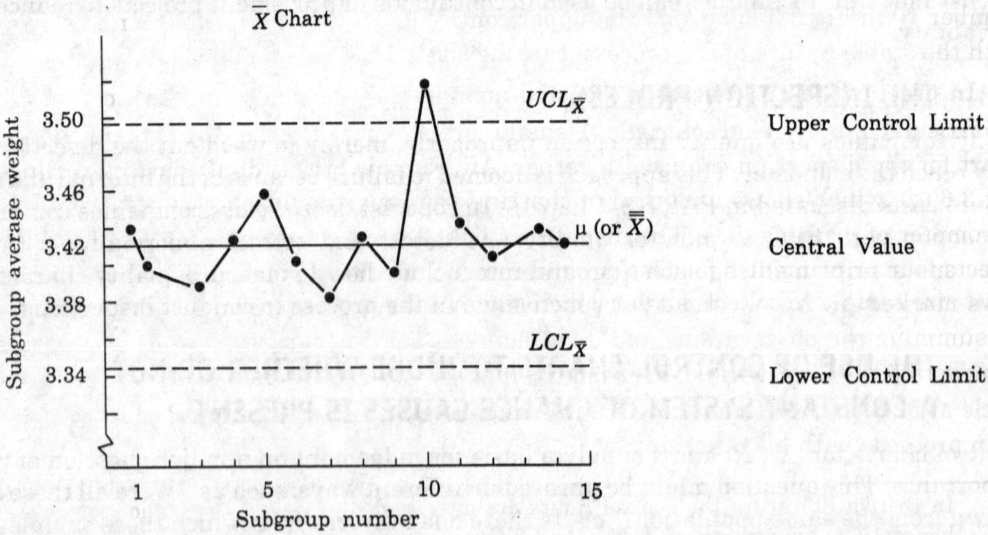

FIGURE 3.5 Example of a control chart.

subgroups. Other charts, such as the *R* chart (range), $\tilde{X}$ chart (median), or *s* (or σ) chart (standard deviation), would have also served for explanation purposes. The horizontal axis is labelled "Subgroup Number," which identifies a particular sample consisting of a fixed number of observations. These subgroups are in order, with the first one inspected being 1 and the last one inspected being 14. The vertical axis of the graph is the variable, which in this particular case is weight measured in kilograms.

Each small solid circle represents the average value within a subgroup. Thus, subgroup number 5 consists of, say, four observations: 3.46, 3.49, 3.45, and 3.44, and their average or mean is 3.46 kg. This value is the one posted on the chart for subgroup number 5. *Averages* are used on control charts rather than *individual* observations because *average values will indicate a change in variation much faster*. Also, with two or more observations in a subgroup, a measure of the dispersion can be obtained for a particular subgroup.

The solid line in the center of the chart is the central value. In this type of chart, it is the universe mean. The central value can also be defined as the mean of the subgroup means (*i.e.* $\bar{\bar{X}}$).

The two dashed outer lines are the upper and lower control limits*: These limits are established to assist in judging the significance of the variation in the quality of the product. Control limits are frequently confused with *specification limits*, which are the permissible limits of a quality characteristic of each *individual* unit of a product. However, *control limits* are used to evaluate the variations in quality from subgroup to subgroup. Therefore, for the $\bar{X}$ chart, the control limits are a function of the subgroup averages. A frequency distribution of the subgroup averages can be determined with its corresponding mean and standard deviation. The control limits are then established at ± 3 standard deviations from the mean. One recalls, from the discussion of the normal curve, in Chap. 2, that the number of items between $+3\sigma$ and -3σ equals 99.73%. Therefore, it is expected that over 997 times out of a 1,000, the subgroup values will fall between the upper and lower limits, and when this occurs, the process is considered to be in control. When a subgroup value falls outside the limits, the process is considered to be out of control and an assignable cause for the variation is present. Subgroup number 10 in Fig 3.5 is beyond the upper control limit; therefore, something has gone wrong with the stable nature of the process, causing the out-of-control point.

In practice, control charts are posted at individual machines or work centers to control a particular quality characteristic. Usually, an $\bar{X}$ chart for the central tendency and an *R* chart for the dispersion are used together. An example of this dual charting is illustrated in Fig 3.6 (*a*), which shows a method of charting and reporting inspection results for the rubber durometer of printing dies. The inspector stops at work center number *XYZ*-77 at 8:30 a.m., selects four printing dies for testing, and records the observations of 55, 52, 51, and 53 in the rows marked X_1, X_2, X_3, and X_4, respectively. A subgroup mean value ($\bar{X}$) of 52.8 is obtained by summing the observations and dividing by 4, and the range value (*R*) of 4 is obtained by subtracting the lowest value, 51, from the highest value, 55. The inspector places a small solid circle at 52.8 on the $\bar{X}$ chart Fig 3.6 (*b*), and a small cross at 4 on the *R* chart, Fig. 3.6 (*c*) and then proceeds with his other duties.

---

* In British literature the control limits are often called as *action limits* (not control limits) and hence $UCL_{\bar{X}}$ is written as $UAL_{\bar{X}}$ and $LCL_{\bar{X}}$ is written as $LAL_{\bar{X}}$ and are placed at 3.09 sigma away from the mean.

$\bar{X}$ AND R CHART (Data format)

Work Center Number *XYZ*-77 (Date ....)

Time	8:30 am	9:30 am	10:40 am	11:50 am	1:30 pm					
Subgroup	1	2	3	4	5	6	7	8	9	10
X1	55	51	48	45	54					
X2	52	52	49	43	50					
X3	51	57	50	45	46					
X4	53	50	49	43	51					
Sum	211	210	196	176	201					
$\bar{X}$	52.8	52.5	49	44	50.2					
R	4	7	2	2	5					

(*a*) Data Recording Format

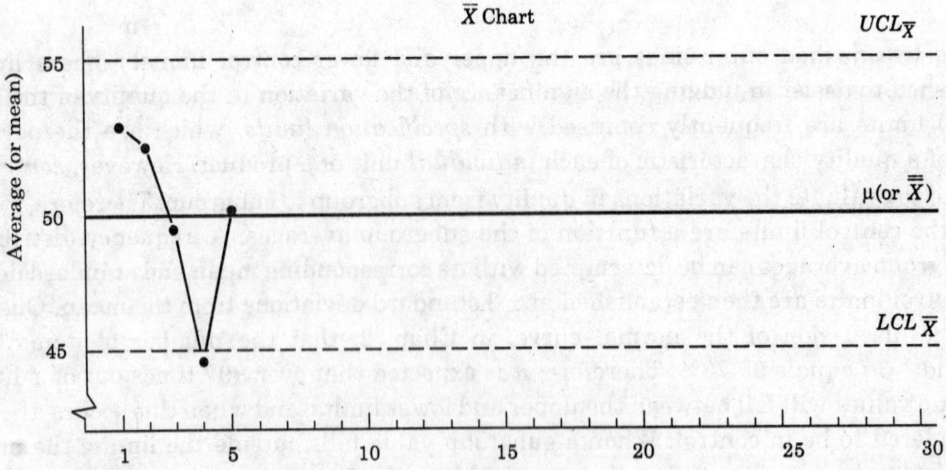

(*b*) $\bar{X}$ Chart

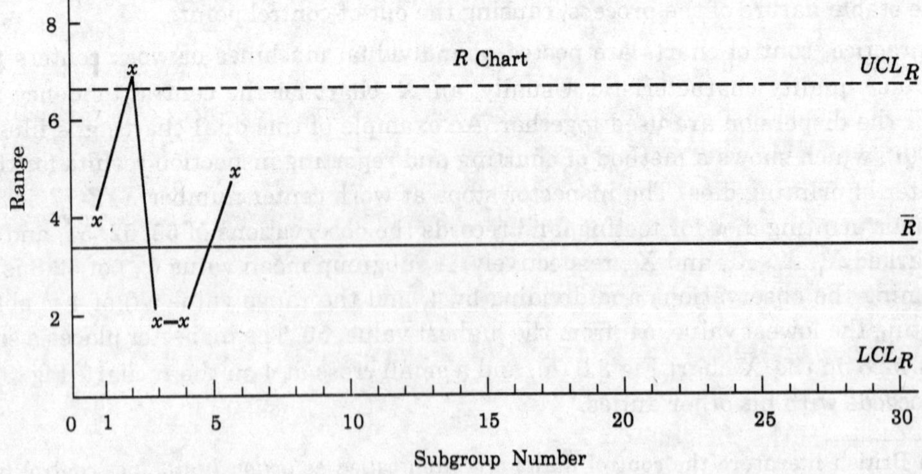

(*c*) R Chart

FIGURE 3.6 Example of a method of reporting inspection results and X & R central charts.

An inspector's routine or the frequency that he inspects a product at a particular machine or work center is determined by the quality of the product. When the process is in control and no difficulties are being encountered, fewer inspections may be required, and, conversely, when the process is out of control, more inspections may be needed. The inspection frequency at a machine or work center is also determined by the number of other work centers that must be inspected or the time that must be spent on non-inspection duties. In this example, the inspection frequency appears to be every 65 or 70 minutes. Inspectors should avoid too fixed a routine, since the operator can, in some cases, influence the reporting of the quality if he knows the exact time the inspector will arrive at the work center.

At 9:30 a.m. the inspector returns and performs the activities for subgroup 2 in the same manner as for subgroup 1. It is noted that the range value of 7 falls right on the upper control limit. Whether to consider this in control or out of control would be a matter of company policy. It is suggested that it be classified as in control, and a cursory examination for an assignable cause be conducted by the operator.

The inspection results for subgroup 2 shows that the third observation has a value of 57, which exceeds the upper control limit. The reader is cautioned to remember the earlier discussion on control limits and specifications. In other words, the 57 value is an individual observation and does not relate to the control limits. Therefore, the fact that *an individual observation is greater than or less than a control limit is meaningless.*

Subgroup 4 has an average value of 44, which is less than the lower control limit of 45. Therefore, subgroup 4 is out of control, and the inspector will report this fact to the departmental supervisor. The operator and supervisor will then look for an assignable cause and, if possible, take corrective action. Whatever corrective action is taken will be noted by the inspector on the X and R chart or on a separate form. The control chart indicates when and where trouble has occurred; the identification and elimination of the difficulty is a production problem.

The control chart is used to keep a continuing record of a particular quality characteristic. When the chart is completed, it is replaced by a fresh chart, and the completed chart is stored in an office file. The information from the chart can be used for process capability studies, to assist in the detection and correction of assignable causes of variation, in the investigation of customer complaints, and as data in periodic quality reports for management.

3.6 CHECKLIST OF NECESSARY STEPS IN USING $\bar{X}$ AND R CHARTS

The $\bar{X}$ and R chart is the most sensitive control chart for tracing and identifying causes. The R pattern is read first and from this it is possible to identify many causes directly. The $\bar{X}$ pattern is read in the light of the R chart, and this makes it possible to identify other causes. Finally, the $\bar{X}$ pattern and R pattern are read jointly, which gives still further information.

It is helpful to visualize the decisions and calculations that must be made and the actions that must be taken as occurring in a sequence somewhat as follows :

I. Decisions preparatory to the control charts

A. Some possible objectives of the charts

B. Choice of the variable

C. Decision on the basis of subgrouping

D. Decision on the size and frequency of subgroups
E. Setting up the forms for recording the data
F. Determining the method of measurement

II. Starting the control charts

A. Making and recording the measurements and recording other relevant data
B. Calculating the average $\bar{X}$ and range R for each subgroup
C. Plotting the $\bar{X}$ and R charts

III. Determining the trial control limits

A. Decision on required number of subgroups before control limits are calculated
B. Calculation of trial control limits
C. Plotting the central lines and limits on the charts

IV. Drawing preliminary conclusions from the charts

A. Indication of control or lack of control
B. Interpretation of processes in control
C. Relationships between processes out of control and specification limits
D. Suggestions about preliminary conclusions and actions based on the control charts

V. Continuing to use the charts

A. Revision of central lines and control limits
B. Use of the control chart as a basis for sorting sublots into homogeneous grand lots
C. Use of the control charts for action on the process
D. Use of the control charts for acceptance inspection
E. Use of the control charts for action on the specifications

3.6.1 Decisions Preparatory to the Control Charts

A. Some Possible Objectives of the Charts

In general where control charts for variables, either $\bar{X}$ and R, or $\bar{X}$ and s (or σ), are undertaken, some or all of the following purposes are present.

1. To provide information for current decisions in regard to recently produced items. Thus, the control chart is used as one source of information to help decide whether an item should be released to the customer or some alternative disposition made, such as starting and repairing.
2. To provide information for current decision in regard to the production process. Thus, the control chart is used to decide when a normal pattern of variation occurs and the process should be left alone, and when an unstable pattern of variation is occurring, which requires action to find and eliminate the disturbing or assignable causes.

3. To provide information for decisions in regard to product specifications, production processes, or inspection procedures. Thus, data from the control charts can be used to establish the product specifications, or to evaluate the production process, or to change the inspection procedures.
4. To provide a method of instructing the operating and supervisory personnel in the techniques of quality control.

Control charts for variables should be established to achieve a particular purpose and their use should be discontinued when the purpose or objective has been achieved.

B. Choice of Variable

The variable chosen for control charts for $\bar{X}$ and R must be a quality characteristic that is measurable and can be expressed in numbers, such as resistance, dimension, weight, strength etc. In any manufacturing plant there are an innumerable number of variables which make up the product and only a few of these present the quality or performance problems. Obviously, these are the legitimate candidates for $\bar{X}$ and R charts. The real basis of choice is always the prospect of reducing or preventing costs. From the standpoint of the possibility of reducing *production* costs a candidate for a control chart is any characteristic that is causing rejections or rework involving substantial costs and time. From the *inspection and acceptance* standpoints destructive testing always suggests an opportunity to use the control charts to reduce costs. In selecting variables for initial application of the control chart technique, it may be important not only to select those with opportunities for cost savings but to select carefully a type of saving that everyone in a supervisory or managerial capacity will readily accept as being a real saving. This usually—although not always—suggests starting where the spoilage and rework are high.

C. Decision on the Basis of Subgrouping

The key idea in the Shewhart method is the division of observations into what Shewhart called *rational subgroups*. The success of the Shewhart technique depends in large measure on the discrimination used in the selection of these subgroups. The principles of subgroup selection are discussed in Chap 7. However, briefly are stated below the two basic methods for selecting the subgroup samples:

1. The first method is to select the subgroup samples from product produced at one instant of time or as close to that instant as possible. Four consecutive parts from machine or four parts from a tray of recently produced part would be an example of this subgrouping technique. The next subgroup samples would be similar but for product produced at a later time — say, one hour later. This method will be called the *instant-time* method.
2. The second method is to select produced product over a period of time so that it is representative of all the product. For example, an inspector makes a visit to a circuit breaker assembling process once every hour. The subgroup sample, of say four, is randomly selected from all the circuit breakers produced in the previous hour. On his next visit, the subgroup is selected from the product produced between visits and so forth. This method will be called the *period-of time* method.

In comparing the two methods, the instant-time method will have a minimum variation with a in subgroup and a maximum variation *among* subgroups. The period-of-time method will have a maximum variation *within* a subgroup and a minimum variation *among* subgroups. Some numerical values may help to illustrate this difference. Thus, for the instant time method, subgroup mean values ($\bar{X}$'s) could be from, say, 26 to 34, with subgroup range values (R's) from 0 to 4; while for the period-of-time method, the subgroup mean values ($\bar{X}$'s) would be from 28 to 32 with the subgroup range values (R's) from 0 to 8.

The instant-time method is the one most commonly used since it provides a particular time reference for determining assignable causes. It also provides a more sensitive measure of changes in the process average. The advantage of the period-of-time method is that it provides better overall results and, therefore, quality reports will present a more nearly accurate picture of the quality. It is also true that because of process limitations the later method may be the only practical method of obtaining the subgroup samples. In some situations, it may be desirable to use both subgrouping methods. When this occurs, two charts with different control limits are required.

Regardless of the scheme used to obtain the subgroup, the lots from which the subgroups are chosen must be homogeneous. By homogeneous is meant that the pieces in the lot are as alike as possible—same machine, same operator, same mould cavity and so on. Similarly, a fixed quantity of material, such as that produced by one tool until it wears out and is replaced or resharpened, should be a homogeneous lot. Homogeneous lots can also be designated by equal time intervals, since this technique is easy to organize and administer. No matter how the lots are designated, the items in any one subgroup should have been produced under essentially the same conditions.

This desirable scheme of subgrouping to make each sample as homogeneous as possible may sometimes need to be modified either because of practical difficulties in taking homogeneous samples or because the control chart is intended to serve several different purposes. For instance, if one of the purposes of control chart is to provide a basis for acceptance, it may be desirable to have each subgroup as nearly representative as possible of the production over a given period of time. For this purpose it would be better to inspect five items selected at random from the production in some given a period of time than to inspect five items produced in succession at the beginning or end of the period. Or, if each item takes a considerable period of time to produce, it may be more convenient for the items inspected for each subgroup is to be spaced approximately uniformly over the production of a given period.

D. Decision on the Size and Frequency of Subgroups

Shewhart suggested *four* as the ideal subgroup size. In the industrial use of control charts, *five* seems to be the most common size. Because the essential idea of the control chart is to select subgroups in a way that gives minimum opportunity for variation *within* a subgroup, it is desirable that subgroups be as small as possible. On the other hand, a size of four is better than three or two on statistical grounds; the distribution of $\bar{X}$ is nearly ***normal*** for *subgroups of four or more (i.e., $n \geq 4$) even though the samples are taken from a* ***nonnormal universe***; this fact is helpful in the interpretation of control-chart limits. A reason sometimes advanced for the use of five is ease of computation of the average, which can be obtained by multiplying the sum by two and moving the decimal point one place to the left, as illustrated below :

$$
\begin{array}{rl}
73 + 69 + 47 + 55 + 61 = 305 & \text{Sum of the five observations} \\
305 & \\
\hline
610 & \text{Adding same figure is equivalent to multiplying by 2} \\
61.0 & \text{Average obtained by shifting decimal point one place to the left.}
\end{array}
$$

However, with the use of inexpensive electronic hand calculators and computers, the reason of 'ease of computation' is no longer valid.

Subgroups of two or three may often be used to good advantage, particularly where the cost of measurements is so high as to veto the use of larger subgroups. Such a situation arises particularly when the inspection of item results in destruction of the item. One such example is thermal fuse, often used in oil refinery and petrochemical plant.

Large subgroup such as 10 or 20 are sometimes advantageous when it is desired to make the control chart sensitive to small variations in the process average. The larger the subgroup size, the narrower the control limits on charts for $\bar{X}$ and the easier it is to detect small variations; this is true only if subgroups are selected in a way that these variations in process average occur between and not within subgroups. Generally speaking, the larger the subgroup size, the more desirable it is to use standard deviation rather than range as a measure of subgroup dispersion. A practical working rule is to use $\bar{X}$ and s or σ charts rather than $\bar{X}$ and R charts whenever the subgroup size is greater than 15 (*i.e.* $n > 15$). In certain problems of process control, the issue of subgroup size may be viewed as an economic problem that is closely related to the issue of the tightness of control limits.

In the introduction of the control-chart technique in any organization, charts for variables are often applied to data already collected for some other purpose. Where the control chart analysis is applied to the part data already tabulated, this may necessitate much larger subgroups than would ordinarily be selected.

No general rules may be laid down for frequency of subgroup. Each case must be decided on its own merits, considering both the cost of taking and analyzing measurements and the benefits to be derived from action based on the control charts. In the initial use of a control chart for analyzing a process, it may be desirable to arrive at conclusions quickly by taking frequent samples. Later on, after the troubles have been diagnosed and corrected and the function of the control chart has become the maintenance of process control on current production, it may be advisable to reduce the frequency of sampling. The frequency of taking a subgroup may be expressed either in terms of time, such as once an hour or as a proportion of the items produced such as 5 out of each 100.

E. Setting up the Forms for Recording the Data

Although the exact details of forms used will vary from one organization to another. However the one already shown in Fig 3.6 (*a*) is most commonly used. This form can further be modified to

Chart No.	Code	CONTROL CHART	Specification	Department
Layout No.	Sample size n =	Operation	Max.	Machine
DRAWING NO.	Frequency	Characteristic	Nom. Min.	Approved By

AP 510-D (7-52)			DATA SHEET FOR $\overline{X}$ AND R CHART								
Product Characteristic									Date Dept.		
1	2	3	4	5	6	7	8	9	10	11	12
TOTAL											
$\overline{X}$											
R											
13	14	15	16	17	18	19	20	21	22	23	24
TOTAL											
$\overline{X}$											
R											

FIGURE 3.7: A format for $\overline{X}$ and R charts

include computations for $\overline{X}$, $\overline{R}$ and s and control limits. It is preferable to leave some blank space to include notes which help in investigating the assignable causes. One such improved form is shown in Fig. 3.7.

F. Determining the Method of Measurement

Decision must be made as to the measuring instruments to be used and the way in which the measurements are to be made and recorded. Usually it is desirable to prepare definite written instructions on this point.

3.6.2 Starting of the Control Charts

A. Making and Recording the Measurements and Recording other Relevant Data

The actual work of the control charts starts with the first measurements. It should always be remembered that the information given by the control chart is influenced by variations in measurement as well as by variations in the quality being measured. Any method of measurement will have its own inherent variability; it is important that this not be increased by mistakes in reading measuring instruments or errors in recording data. It is also important that notes be made about any occurrences which, if the control chart later shows lack of control, might provide help on investigation of assignable causes of variation.

B. Calculating the Average and Range for Each Subgroup

The average for each subgroup $\bar{X}$ is calculated by summing the individual measurements in the subgroup and dividing by the number of measurements. The central line for the $\bar{X}$ chart is found by summing the averages and dividing by the number of subgroups. When n is the subgroup size and m the number of subgroups, the formulae for these calculations are

$$\bar{X}_j = \frac{\sum_{i=1}^{n} X_i}{n} \qquad \text{...(3.4)}$$

$$\bar{\bar{X}}_j = \frac{\sum_{j=1}^{m} \bar{X}_j}{m} \qquad \text{...(3.5)}$$

To find the range for each subgroup, the highest and lowest numbers in the subgroup must first be identified. With large subgroups it is helpful to mark the highest value with the letter *H* and the lowest with the letter *L*. The subgroup range is computed by subtracting the lowest value from the highest. The central line for the *R* chart is found by summing the subgroup range values and dividing by the number of subgroups. Formulae for these calculations are

$$R_j = X_{j.\,\max} - X_{j.\,\min} \qquad \text{...(3.6)}$$

$$\bar{R} = \sum_{j=1}^{m} \frac{R_j}{m} \qquad \text{...(3.7)}$$

C. Plotting the $\bar{X}$ and R charts

$\bar{X}$ and *R* charts have been illustrated in Figs. 3.5 and 3.6 (*b*) and (*c*) and many others are given through out this book.

The vertical scale at the left is used for the statistical measures $\bar{X}$ and *R*. The horizontal scale is used for subgroup numbers. Dates, hours, or lot numbers may also be indicated on the horizontal scale. Each point may be indicated on the chart by a dot, circle, or cross. In this book the general practice is to use a dot for points on $\bar{X}$ charts and a cross for points on *R* charts; there are some exceptions, however. There is no standard practice in industry in this regard. Points on control charts may or may not be connected. In this book they are generally connected by firm or dotted lines except at some places where the connecting lines does not serve any purpose.

Points on both $\bar{X}$ and *R* charts should be kept plotted up to date. This is particularly important where the charts are posted in the shop and are used by machine operators, setters, and foremen.

The objectives of the control chart can sometimes be fully served by the $\overline{X}$ chart alone. In such cases the R chart may be omitted.

3.6.3 Determining the Trial Control Limits

A. Decision on required Number of Subgroups before Control Limits are Calculated.

The determination of the minimum number of subgroups required before control limits are calculated is a compromise between a desire to obtain the guidance given by averages and control limits as soon as possible after the start of collecting data and a desire that the guidance be as reliable as possible. The fewer the subgroups used, the sooner the information thus obtained will provide a basis for action but the less the assurance that this basis for action is sound.

On statistical grounds it is desirable that control limits be based on at least 25 subgroups. Moreover, experience indicates that first few subgroups obtained when a control chart is initiated may not be representative of what is measured later; the mere act of taking and recording measurements is sometimes responsible for a change in the pattern of variation.

For these reasons if 25 subgroups can be obtained in a short time, it is desirable to wait for 25 or more subgroup; this would be true, for example, where a new subgroup was measured every hour.

However, where subgroups are obtained slowly there is a natural desire on the part of those who initiated the control charts to draw some conclusions from them within a reasonable time. This impatience for an answer frequently leads to the policy of making preliminary calculations of control limits from the first 8 or 10 subgroups, with subsequent modification of limits as more subgroups are obtained.

B. Calculation of Trial Control Limits

When the grand average of the subgroups X and the average of the ranges R have been calculated, the factors contained in Table *D*, App. 1, are used to calculate control limits. These formulae are

$$UCL_{\overline{X}} = \overline{\overline{X}} + A_2\overline{R}$$

$$LCL_{\overline{X}} = \overline{\overline{X}} - A_2\overline{R}$$

$$UCL_{\overline{R}} = D_4\overline{R}$$

$$LCL_{\overline{R}} = D_3\overline{R}$$

The trial limits thus obtained are appropriate for analysing the past data that were used in their calculation. They may require modification before extending them to apply to future production.

The preceding formulae for limits for $\overline{X}$ and R assume a constant subgroup size. Chapter 8 explains the necessary calculations where the subgroup size is variable.

C. Plotting the Central Lines on the Charts

The central line on the R chart should be drawn as a solid horizontal line at $\overline{R}$. The upper control limit should be drawn as a dashed horizontal line at the computed value of UCL_R. If the subgroup size is seven or more, the lower control limit should be drawn as a dashed horizontal line at LCL_R. If the subgroup size is six or less, the lower control limit for R does not exist.

The central line on the $\bar{X}$ chart should be drawn as a solid horizontal line at $\bar{X}$. The upper and lower control limits for $\bar{X}$ should be drawn as dashed horizontal lines at the computed values.

3.6.4 Drawing Preliminary Conclusions from the Charts

A. Indication of Control or Lack of Control

Lack of control is indicated by points falling outside the control limits on either the $\bar{X}$ or the R charts. Some users of the control charts identify such out-of-control points by a special symbol. For instance, if each point is represented by a circle, a cross is made in the circles designating out-of-control points; if each point is represented by a dot, or a cross a circle may be drawn around the dot for out-of-control points, practice followed in this book.

When, because points fall outside the control limits, we say that a process is "out of control," this is equivalent to saying, "Assignable causes of variation are present; this is not a constant-cause system." As explained earlier, we can make this statement with considerable confidence that it is correct; a constant cause system will seldom be responsible for points falling outside control limits set.

In contrast to this, when all points fall inside the control limits, we cannot say with the same assurance, "*No* assignable causes of variation are present; this is a constant-cause system." No statistical test can give us this positive assurance. When we say, "This process is in control," the statement really means, "For practical purposes, it pays to act as if no assignable causes of variation were present."

Moreover, even in the best manufacturing processes, occasional errors occur that constitute assignable causes of variation but that may not constitute a basis for action. This fact may lead to various practical working rules on the relationship between satisfactory control and the number of points falling outside limits. One such rule is to consider not more than 1 out of 35, or 2 out of 100, points outside control limits as evidence of control.

Even though all points fall within control limits, lack of control may be indicated by runs of seven or more points in succession on the same side of the central line, or by the presence of other extreme runs such as those listed later in Subsec 3.11.1.

The actions suggested by the evidence of the control chart depend on the relationship between what the process is doing and what it is supposed to do. That is, the apparent universe pattern of variation implied by the control chart needs to be compared with the specifications. This comparison is simplest and most meaningful if the process appears to be in control.

B. Interpretation of Processes in Control

With evidence from the control chart that a process is in control, we are in a position to judge what is necessary to permit the manufacture of product that meets the specifications for the quality characteristic charted. The control-chart data give us estimates of :

1. The centering of the process (μ may be estimated as $\bar{\bar{X}}$)
2. The dispersion of the process (σ may be estimated as $\bar{R}/d_2$)

As discussed in Chap. 2 that estimates of μ and σ are subject to sampling errors. For this reason, any conclusions obtained from a short period (such as 25 points on the control chart) must be regarded as tentative subject to confirmation or change as the control chart is continued and as more evidence becomes available. However, the reasonable thing to do at any stage in the proceedings is to make the best interpretation possible of the data already available. Once it is evident what actions are suggested by this interpretation, a decision can be made whether action should be taken at once or whether it should await more data. In applying the following analysis of processes in control, the limitations of the current estimates if μ and σ always be kept in mind.

In Chap. 2 it is pointed out that practically all (all but 0.27 %) of a normal distribution falls within limits of $\mu \pm 3\sigma$; (and it is for this reason, we call 3 sigma limits as 0.0027 probility limits i.e. 0.00135 out side $\mu + 3\sigma$ and 0.00135 outside $\mu - 3\sigma$) that is, for practical purposes the spread of the distribution may be thought of as approximately 6σ. In the preliminary analysis of control-chart data, there is hardly enough evidence to permit judgment as to whether the distribution is approximately normal. Certainly the evidence is seldom sufficient to tell whether 0.27% or 0.8% or 1.2% or some other small percentage of the distribution will fall outside $\mu \pm 3\sigma$. Evidence of the exact form of the frequency distribution and the percentage of the distribution outside these limits may be obtained only after a long accumulation of data under control. In the meantime a satisfactory rough guide to judgment is provided by the assumption that 6σ is a measure of the spread of the process.

Actions based on the relationship between the specifications and the centering and dispersion of a controlled process depend somewhat on whether there are two specification limits, a maximum or upper specification limit USL_X (U) and a minimum or lower specification limit LSL_X (L), as is always true of dimensions, or only one specification limit, either LSL_X or USL_X, as might be true of a specified minimum tensile strength, or minimum weight of the contents of a container, or maximum percentage of a particular chemical impurity. Some of the various possible situations that may exist with two limits are shown in Figs. 3.8 to 3.10. Some situations that may exist with a single limit are shown in Figs. 3.11 to 3.13.

Possible Relationships of a Process in Control to Upper and Lower Specification Limits

When a controlled process must meet two specification limits on individual values, USL_X and LSL_X all possible situations may be grouped into three general classes, as follows :

1. The spread of the process (6σ) is appreciably less than the difference between the specification limits ($USL_X - LSL_X$).
2. The spread of the process (6σ) is approximately equal to the difference between the specification limits ($USL_X - LSL_X$).
3. The spread of the process (6σ) is appreciably greater than the difference between the specification limits ($USL_X - LSL_X$).

The first situation is illustrated in Fig. 3.8, in which the specification limits are shown by the upper and lower horizontal lines. This is most desirable situation. Frequency curves A, B, C, D, E, and F indicate various positions in which the process might be centered. Since the

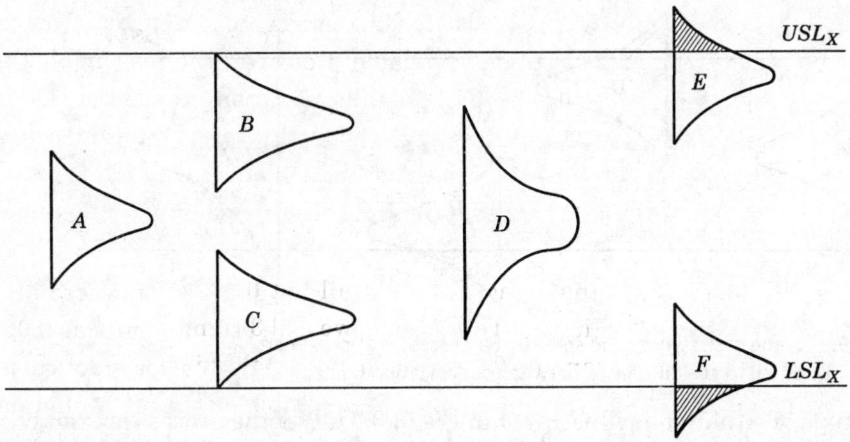

FIGURE 3.8: Some cases where the spread of the spread (i.e. 6σ)of a process in less than the difference between specification limits.

specifications are appreciably greater than the process spread, no difficulty is encountered even when there is a substantial shift in the process average as shown by the distribution at *B*. At *D*, a shift in the dispersion is indicated, and all the individual values are between specifications.

In general, the conditions represented in Fig. 3.8 *A*, *B*, *C*, and *D* represent the ideal manufacturing situation. When the control chart shows that any of these conditions exists, many different possible actions may be considered; the choice among the various actions is a matter of relative economy.

For example, it may be considered economically advisible to permit *X* to go out of control if it does not go too far; that is, the distribution may be allowed to move between positions *B* and *C*. This may avoid the cost of frequent machine set-ups and of delays due to hunting for assignable causes of variation that will not be responsible for unsatisfactory product. In Chap. 8, the use of so called "modified control limits" for this purpose is explained. Again even if the average remain unchanged, greater dispersion may be allowed. Such a situation exists particularly when the tool wear takes place and also the costs of sophisticated inspection may be saved by using less precise methods.

Or, where acceptance has been based on 100% inspection, it may be economical to substitute acceptance based on the control chart for $\overline{X}$ and *R*.

Or, if there is an economical advantage to be gained by tightening the specification limits, such action may be considered.

If none of these things is to be done, it may be economical to discontinue the use of the control chart or at least to increase the time interval between control chart inspections. The larger the ratio of ($USL_X - LSL_X$) to the process spread (6 σ), the more favourable is the situation of getting product without assistance from any control chart.

With the process in position *E* of Fig. 3.8 some product will fall above the upper specification limit, in position *F* some product will fall below the lower specification limit. In either case the obvious action is to try to change the centering of the process bringing it closer to position *A*. Once this has been done consideration may be given to the various actions just enumerated.

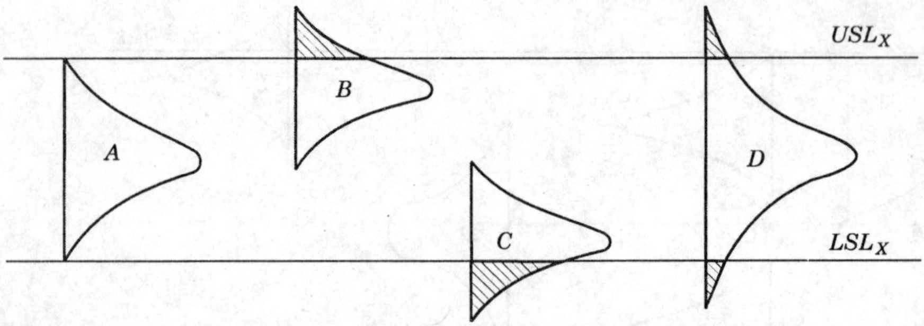

FIGURE 3.9: Some cases where the spread of a process is approximately equal to the difference between specification limits.

The second type of situation is illustrated in Fig. 3.9. Only if the process is exactly centered between the specification limits as in position *A*, will all the product be good. If the distribution shifts away from this exact centering, as in *B* or *C*, some of the product will fall outside the specification limits. Also clearly, no further increase in dispersion should be allowed, otherwise nonconforming product will be produced as shown at *D*.

Here the obvious action is to take all steps possible to maintain the centering of the process and not to allow any increase in the dispersion. This usually calls for continuous use of control charts for $\bar{X}$ and R with subgroups at frequent intervals and immediate attention to the points out of control. If fundamental changes can be made to reduce dispersion, they, will ease the pressure. Consideration should also be given to the question of whether tolerances are tighter than is really necessary.

The third type of situation is illustrated in Fig. 3.10. Here the specification limits are so tight that even with the process in control and perfectly centered as in position *A*, some nonconforming product will be made. This calls for discussion with production engineer for the possibility of increasing the difference between the upper and lower specifications. This solution may require reliability studies with mating parts to determine if the product can function with increased specification differences.

Another solution is to change the process dispersion so that a more peaked distribution occurs as shown at *B*. To obtain such a substantial shift in the dispersion might require new material, a more experienced operator or retraining, a new or overhauled machine, or possibly automatic in process control. But it is still important to maintain the centering of the process; the curves in position *C* and *D* show how a shift in process average will increase the percent nonconforming product.

If 100% inspection is possible, the nonconforming product may be sorted out and eliminated. This is not an attractive proposal, but it may be the most economical or only one. But if such 100% sorting is impossible because acceptance is based on destructive testing, there is no chance to obtain product all of which conforms to specifications.

Still another solution is to shift the process average so that all of the nonconforming product occurs at one tail of the frequency distribution as indicated at *E* of Fig. 3.10. To illustrate this solution, assume that a shaft is being ground to tight specifications. If too much metal is removed, the part is scraped; if too little is removed, the part must be reworked. By shifting

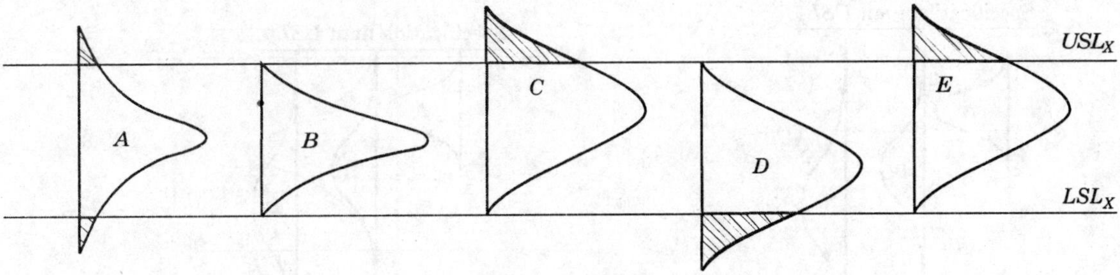

FIGURE 3.10: Some cases where the spread of a process is greater than the difference between specification limits.

the process average the amount of scrap is eliminated and the amount of rework in increased. A similar situation exists for an internal member such as a hole or keyway except that scrap occurs above the upper specification and rework occurs below the lower specification. This type of solution is feasible when the cost of the part is sufficient economically to justify the reworking operation.

From above, it is quite evident that if the specification tolerance $USL_X - LSL_X$ for a component is considerably less than 6σ for the process used to produce the component, the production of some nonconforming pieces is inevitable; the precision of the process is low compared with the precision required, *i.e.* of low relative precision. If the specification tolerance is about equal to 6σ then very few nonconforming pieces would be expected; the process is said to have medium relative precision. Thirdly, if the specification tolerance is considerably greater than 6σ then the process is said to have high relative precision and 'modified' control charts for averages can be used to maintain the quality of production.

Sample average range $\bar{R}$ when divided by the factor d_2 *i.e.* $\bar{R}/d_2$, gives a good estimate of σ. Consequently, for samples of a given number of pieces (n), $\bar{R}$ is proportional to σ and specification tolerance divided by sample average range is a measure is relative precision, and is called the relative precision index (R.P.I.)

$$\text{Relative precision index (R.P.I.)} = \frac{\text{Specification Tolerance}}{\text{Sample Average Range}} = \frac{USL_X - LSL_X}{\bar{R}}$$

$$\text{or } \frac{U - L}{\bar{R}} \qquad \text{...(3.8)}$$

The values of R.P.I., for various sample sizes (n), which indicate low, medium and high relative precision are indicated in Table 3.1.

TABLE 3.1: RELATIVE PRECISION INDEX FOR SUBGROUP SIZE FROM 2 TO 6.

Subgroup size (n)	*Relative Precision Index*		
	Low	*Medium*	*High*
2	< 6.0	6.0 to 7.0	> 7.0
3	< 4.0	4.0 to 5.0	> 5.0
4	< 3.0	3.0 to 4.0	> 4.0
5 or 6	< 2.5	2.5 to 3.5	> 3.5

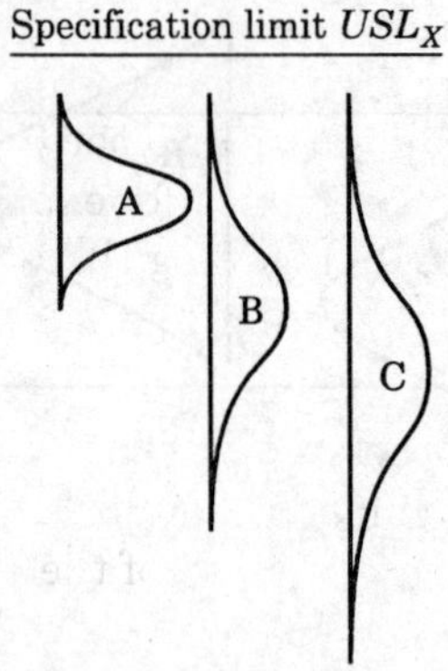

FIGURE 3.11: Some cases where the high value of the process distribution is approximately below the specification maximum.

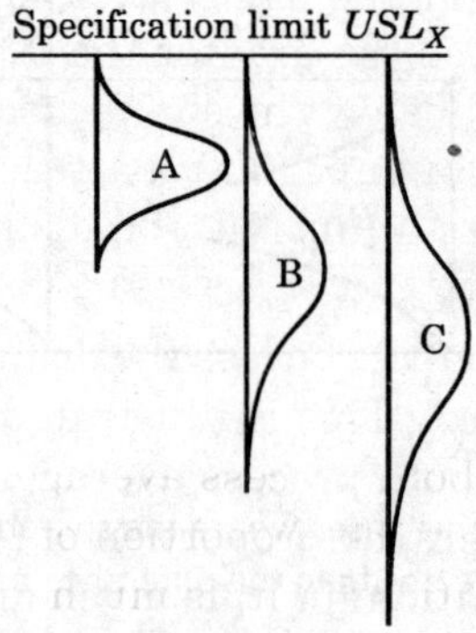

FIGURE 3.12: Some cases where the high value of process distribution is at the specification maximum.

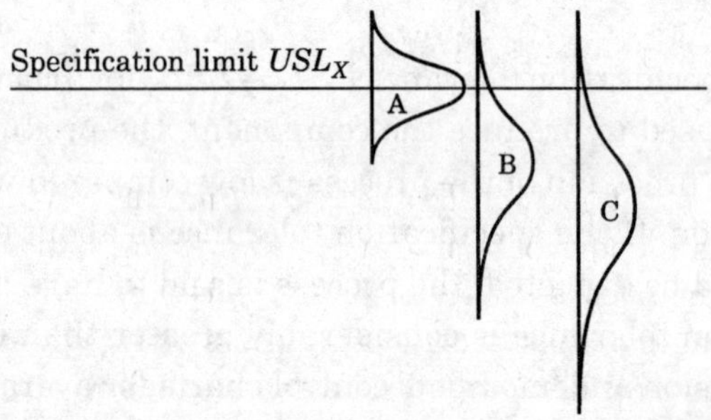

FIGURE 3.13: Some cases where the high value of the process distribution is above the specification maximum.

Possible Relationships of a Process in Control to a Single Specification Limit.

The key to the most useful classification of the situations involving two specification limits was the process dispersion. A similar key to the classification of situations involving a maximum limit is the position of $\mu + 3\sigma$ with respect to USL_X. Again three situations may be considered :

1. The high value of the process distribution ($\mu + 3\ \sigma$) is appreciably below USL_X. This is illustrated in Fig 3.11.
2. The high value of the process distribution ($\mu + 3\ \sigma$) is approximately at USL_X. This is illustrated in Fig. 3.12.
3. The high value of the process distribution ($\mu + 3\sigma$) appreciably above USL_X. This is illustrated in Fig. 3.13.

The first situation is one in which there is a margin of safety, the second is one in which the specification is just barely met as long as the process stays in control, and the third is one in which some nonconforming product is inevitable unless a fundamental change is made in the process. The fundamental change may be either a decrease in process dispersion or a decrease in the process average.

Three curves — A, B, and C, — with different dispersion have been shown in Figs. 3.11 to 3.13 to emphasize the interrelationship of process average, process dispersion, and specification maximum limit. All three distribution —A, B and C, — have the same high value. However, distribution B with a greater dispersion must have a smaller process average than A for the high points to be at the same level; similarly C must have a smaller process average than B. It is evident that the greater the dispersion the lower must be the average for the entire distribution to fall below the specification maximum limit. This relationship between average and dispersion is an important matter related to costs in many instances ; for example, in the filling of containers an increase in dispersion many reduce cost by reducing the average over fill.

On the other hand, the less the dispersion the more important it is that the process average not go out of control. This is illustrated by comparing distributions A and C in Figs. 3.12 and 3.13. In Fig. 3.13 both process averages have shifted an equal amount above their position in Fig. 3.12., However, the proportion of bad product as indicated by the area of the distribution above the specification limit, is much greater in A than in C.

The preceding discussion has related to a single upper specification limit $USL_{\overline{X}}$, with no lower limit. Similar reasoning would apply if there were a lower limit with no upper limit.

C. Relationships Between Processes out of Control and Specification Limits

If the control chart shows lack of control one obvious step is to hunt for the assignable causes of variation and try to correct them. Some guidance is given in Sec 3.8 and 3.9 on the statistical aspects of detection of assignable causes.

It is also pertinent to inquire into the process centering and dispersion that may be expected if control is obtained. If the out-of-control points on the R chart are eliminated, what evidence does the control chart give about process dispersion? In view of this process dispersion and of the specification limits, where ought the process average to be? The same type of analysis of the relationship between process average, process dispersion, and specification limits that was discussed for controlled processes is appropriate for processes not yet brought under control. The practical differences are that it may not be certain whether control can actually be attained and there is less basis for confidence in the estimates of μ and σ at which control might be attained.

D. Suggestions about Preliminary Conclusions and Actions Based on the Control Charts

If the R chart shows control, estimate σ as $\overline{R}/d_2$. If there is an upper specification limit, compare $(\overline{\overline{X}} + 3\sigma)$ with USL_X. If there is a lower specification limit, compare $(\overline{\overline{X}} - 3\sigma)$ with LSL_X If there are two specification limits, also compare 6σ with $(USL_X - LSL_X)$. Determine from these comparisons which type of condition is applicable of the various types illustrated in Figs. 3.8 to 3.13. Consider the possible actions suggested in our discussion of these figures.

If the charts show lack of control, try to judge from the charts and all other pertinent information what may be the assignable causes and whether or not it is likely that they can be eliminated. After removing the subgroups that showed lack of control on the R chart, calculate a revised $\overline{R}$ and new control limits for R. If these limits show additional subgroups out of control, remove those subgroups and repeat the calculation. Estimate σ as $\overline{R}/d_2$, using the final revised $\overline{R}$ after all out-of-control values of R have been eliminated. Consider this as a value of σ that might conceivably be obtained if the process were brought into control.

Consider whether or not the process average can readily be set at any desired level. (In some cases, as in dimensions resulting from machining operations, this may be merely a matter of machine setting; in other cases, as in tensile strengths or percentages of chemical impurities, this may be a difficult matter involving costly changes in the process.) If so, decide on the desired value of $\overline{X}_0$ at which to aim, assuming that control could be maintained with σ as estimated. If not, in the light of the known value of $\overline{\overline{X}}$, decide on an attainable $\overline{X}_0$. Use the values of $\overline{X}_0$ and σ thus obtained as a basis for an analysis of the relationship of the specification limits to the process average and dispersion.

Decisions as to whether to take action now on the basis of the control chart data already at hand, or to defer action until more data are obtained, should give weight to the uncertainties in the estimates of μ and σ and to the costs and possible consequences of the proposed action.

3.6.5 Continuing to use the Charts

A. Revision of Central Lines and Control Limits

The trial control limits served the purpose of determining whether past operations were in control. The continuing use of the control chart, with each out-of-control point used as a possible basis for hunting for an assignable cause of variation and taking action to eliminate that cause, may require revised limits.

If the process has been in control with both average and dispersion satisfactory from the standpoint of the specification limits, the trial control limits should be extended to apply to future production. As more data accumulate, the limits may be reviewed from time to time and revised whenever necessary. It is desirable to establish regular periods for this review, such as once every week, once every month, or once every 25, 50, or 100 subgroups.

If the dispersion has been in control, as evidenced by the R chart, but the average $\overline{X}$ has been out of control, the trial central line and trial limits on the R chart should continue to be used, and control limits on the $\overline{X}$ chart should continue to be a distance of $A_2\overline{R}$ on either side of the central line. The location of the revised central line on the $\overline{X}$ chart calls for a decision whether this should be at an aimed-at level(sometimes called a standard level or target level), designated as $\overline{X}_0$, or whether it should be based on the past data, a revision of $\overline{\overline{X}}$. When making this choice it should be recognized that wherever the central line (that is, the assumed process average for the purposes of the control chart) is placed, a point outside control limits is interpreted as meaning, "This variation is more than would be expected as a matter of chance if the assumed process average is maintained."

If the process average may be changed by a fairly simple adjustment of the manufacturing process, such as a machine adjustment influencing a dimension, it is nearly always desirable to decide on a standard or aimed-at value $\overline{X}_0$. This aimed-at process average should be determined by consideration of the relationship between process average, process dispersion, and specification limits, along the lines already discussed. Where there are upper and lower specification limits and product falling outside one limit may be reworked whereas product falling outside the other limit must be scraped, the aimed-at average should be chosen with due consideration for the difference between costs of spoilage and rework.

Unless the process average can be changed by a definite adjustment, $\overline{\overline{X}}$ is likely to be the result of a complex set of factors, with the influence of each factor not clearly known. In such instances, a control chart based on an aimed-at value of $\overline{X}_0$ that was different from the past $\overline{\overline{X}}$ might show many points out of control; these out-of-control points would simply indicate that the aim had been poor without giving much hope in correcting it. For this reason it is more sensible in such cases to use the past $\overline{\overline{X}}$ as the new central line, or possibly a revised

$\bar{X}$ corrected by the elimination of the past out-of-control points. Then if different changes in the process are undertaken one after another with the purpose of finding a way to bring the process average to a new desired level, the control chart based on the past process average will give evidence whether each change constitutes an assignable cause of variation from past performance. If these assignable causes move the process average closer to the desired average, they should be continued rather than eliminated. Each change that is continued may call for a new central line on the $\bar{X}$ chart based on the changed performance.

Where the R chart shows that the process dispersion is out of control, it is desirable to estimate the value of $\bar{R}$ and σ that might be attained if the dispersion were brought into control. This estimate is necessary even though it cannot be made with great assurance that it is correct. One possible method is to eliminate the values of $\bar{R}$ above the control limits and make a new calculation of $\bar{R}$. If new limits calculated from this $\bar{R}$ throw more points above the control limits, the calculation of a revised $\bar{R}$ may be repeated again. This method is illustrated later in Example. 3.1.

This revised $\bar{R}$ may be used as the new central line on the R chart, as the basis for calculating the new limits on the R chart and for calculating $A_2\bar{R}$ to get the distance of the control limits from the central line on the $\bar{X}$ chart. This has the effect of tightening the limits on both the R and the $\bar{X}$ charts, making them consistent with a σ that may be estimated from the revised $\bar{R}$ as $\bar{R}/d_2$. This σ may also serve as a basis for a preliminary analysis of the relationship among process average, process dispersion, and specification limits, as outlined in our discussion of Figs. 3.8 to 3.13.

Where both R and $\bar{X}$ are out of control and new limits on the $\bar{X}$ chart are to be based on an aimed-at $\bar{X}_0$, the calculation of the revised $\bar{R}$ should be made before making a decision regarding the value of $\bar{X}_0$ to be used.

Revised limits should be reviewed from time to time as additi nal data are accumulated.

B. Use of the Control Chart as a Basis for Sorting Sublots into Homogeneous Grand Lots

If some quality of a manufactured product shows unsatisfactory variability, and if th control chart shows that lack of control is responsible for this variability, the natural action seems to be to make a strong effort to bring about a state of control. However, it may turn out that for some reason it is impracticable to achieve control. Sometimes a satisfactory alternative may exist in the sorting of sublots of product into grand lots that seem to be statistically homogeneous. The variability from one grand lot to another may then become the basis for different correction factors somehow applied in the use of each grand lot. Conceivably, even though control could actually be obtained at a cost, it might be more economical to carry out this sorting.

This sorting is a possible procedure, for example, in the case of artillery ammunition. Experience shows that the variation in ballistic properties from one lot to another may be greater than the variation within any lot. (In other words, the averages show lack of statistical control.) Successive lots, the samples from which, under ballistic tests, all fall within control-chart limits, may be treated as sublots of one grand lot. Different corrections in the powder charge, or in the firing tables used by the artillery operator, could then be made for each grand lot.

In the case of chemical or bacteriological tests that different laboratories make of the same product, experience shows that it is often impracticable to get control. The variation from one laboratory to another will be greater than the variation in successive tests made by any one laboratory. Here also, correction factors might be applied to the results given by any laboratory that did not seem to be part of the grand lot.

Although the control chart provides the best way to sort sublots into homogeneous grand lots, it sometimes happens that people who do not fully understand the principles behind the control chart use it for sorting in ways that are incorrect.

C. Use of the Control Charts for Action on the Process

In continuing the use of the control charts, there may be three different kinds of action on the process, as follows :

1. Action to remove assignable causes of variation that are brought to attention by out-of-control points
2. Action to establish the process average
3. Action to establish the process dispersion

Once a process is brought into control with a satisfactory average and dispersion, an important purpose of the control chart is to help continue this happy state of affairs. The most common routine use of the control chart for variables is for this purpose. This involves simply leaving a process alone as long as it stays in control, and hunting for and removing assignable causes of variation whenever the control charts show lack of control.

Actions to establish a process average at some desired level follow the lines that we have suggested. It should be emphasized that whenever an aimed-at value X0 is used for the central line on the control chart, there should be an actual effort made to aim at that value in the process itself. It does no good to put such a line on the control chart unless this forms a basis for action by those who carry out the operations.

Actions to reduce process dispersion often call for fundamental changes in machine or methods. Action may also be undertaken to match various process dispersions with different jobs to be undertaken. The information given by control charts about the natural tolerances that will be held by various machines or various production methods may make it possible to fit the process dispersion to the job in hand. Operations calling for close tolerances may be assigned to the machines that will hold the close tolerances, and operations on which wide tolerances are satisfactory may be assigned to those machines that will hold only wide tolerances. This use of the control chart in production planning may be its chief contribution in some jobbing shops.

D. Use of the Control Charts for Acceptance Inspection

Our discussion of the interesting and important subjects of the strategy and tactics of acceptance inspection and sampling is deferred until Part Three of this book.

We shall see there that one useful concept in acceptance sampling is that an overall decision with respect to the acceptance or rejection of a manufacturing process often is superior to a series of unrelated decisions regarding acceptance or rejection of separate lots of product.

Control charts may give evidence that a process is in statistical control with satisfactory centering and dispersion and thus provide a rational basis for the acceptance of the process.

In PART-2 (Quality Management) we shall see that another useful concept is that the best way to obtain satisfactory product is to have it made right in the first place—that it usually is difficult or impossible to "inspect quality into a product."

E. Use of the Control Charts for Action on the Specifications

The control charts for variables may influence specifications in two ways.

They may be used to determine the capabilities of a manufacturing process before the specification limits are set. This is often a sensible procedure and is discussed in Chap. 8

They may also be used to give evidence that, because of the inability of a manufacturing process to meet existing specification limits even when it is in control, a review of specification limits is called for.

A general principle applicable here is that the basis of all specification limits should be the prospective use of the part or product for which the limits are specified. Ideally, all specification limits should be exactly right from the standpoint of what is really needed. Actually, many specification limits are made tighter than really necessary, often because no time or effort has been given to finding out what is necessary. Moreover, in most cases there is no one right value of specification limits that can be settled independently of cost factors involved; these cost factors cannot be properly judged without information regarding the capabilities of the manufacturing process such as is given by the control chart. For these reasons, many cases exist in which the appropriate conclusion from the control chart is to change the specifications.

3.7 ILLUSTRATION OF $\overline{X}$, *R*, AND *s* CONTROL CHARTS

The $\overline{X}$, $\overline{R}$, and *s* control charts are often used on a manufacturing operation to find out the possible causes (*i.e.* assignable causes) of troubles for the quality characteristic in question. In controlled conditions of manufacture high percentage of rejects often offer the first opportunity to make use of these control charts for variables. Example 3.1 will now illustrate the control chart technique.

EXAMPLE 3.1 : *Controlling the depth of key way in shafting.*

Facts of the case high percentage of rejections for many of the parts of the machine shop of an automobile industry indicated the need for examination of the reasons for trouble. As most of the rejections were for failure to meet dimensional tolerances, it was decided to try to find the causes of trouble by the use of $\overline{X}$ and *R* charts.

The quality characteristic in question was the depth of the keyway in shafting. It was decided to conduct a study in order to establish suitable tolerance limits.

Because of the many general considerations favouring four as the subgroup size, the size was adopted. It was considered essential that wherever possible all measurements be made at the point of production. As lots of four of these large parts did not accumulate at the machine, it was decided that one part would be measured out of approximately every 20 produced, and that a subgroup would consist of four such measurements.

Data sheet for $\bar{X}$ and R charts

Product : Shafts *Dept. No:* M/c-999, *Order No:* IA/PEC:118

Characteristic : Depth of keyway Special Instructions: measurements to be coded from 6.00 mm.

Unit of measure: mm.

Sub-group Number	Date	Time	Measurements				Average $\|\bar{X}_j\|$	Range Sample R_j	Standard deviations	Comments
			X_1	X_2	X_3	X_4				
1	23/06	8 : 50	35	40	32	33	6.35	0.08	0.031	
2		11 : 30	46	37	36	41	6.40	0.10	0.042	
3		1 : 45	34	34	40	34	6.30	0.06	0.023	*New operator*
4		3 : 45	69	64	68	59	6.65	0.10	0.045	*Temporary operator*
5		4 : 20	38	34	44	40	6.39	0.10	0.042	
6	27/06	8 : 35	42	41	43	34	6.40	0.09	0.042	*New operator*
7		9 : 00	44	41	41	46	6.43	0.05	0.021	
8		9 : 40	33	41	38	36	6.37	0.08	0.032	
9		1 : 30	48	52	49	51	6.50	0.04	0.016	
10		2 : 50	47	43	36	42	6.42	0.11	0.043	
11	28/06	8 : 30	38	41	39	38	6.39	0.03	0.012	
12		1 : 35	37	37	41	37	6.38	0.04	0.017	
13		2 : 25	40	38	47	35	6.40	0.12	0.044	
14		2 : 35	38	39	45	42	6.41	0.07	0.025	
15		3 : 55	50	42	43	45	6.45	0.08	0.031	
16	29/06	8 : 25	33	35	29	39	6.34	0.10	0.041	
17		9 : 25	41	40	29	34	6.36	0.12	0.048	
18		11 : 00	38	44	28	58	6.42	0.30	0.109	*Damaged oil line*
19		2 : 35	33	32	37	38	6.35	0.06	0.025	
20		3 : 15	56	55	45	48	6.51	0.11	0.044	*Bad material*
21	30/06	9 : 35	38	40	45	37	6.40	0.08	0.031	
22		10 : 20	39	42	35	40	6.39	0.07	0.025	
23		11 : 35	42	39	39	36	3.39	0.06	0.021	
24		2 : 00	43	36	35	38	6.38	0.08	0.031	
25		4 : 25	39	38	43	44	6.41	0.06	0.025	
		Total					160.25	2.19	1.006	

$$\Sigma\bar{X}_j = 160.25 \qquad \Sigma R_j = 2.19 \qquad \Sigma s = 1.006$$

The type of form used for recording the data is also illustrated above where only a record of the deviations only from a base value of 6.00 mm is maintained as this is found to be more suitable.

Now, before proceeding further, it is necessary to know the various methods of calculating the control limits. Following explanations will help in determining the methods of computation based on the available data and ease of calculation.

3.7.1 Calculation of 3-sigma limits on Control Charts for $\bar{X}$

Once the data are collected, Table *C*, *D*, and *E* of App 1 can be used for computation of control limits for $\bar{X}$ chart. After calculating the averages and ranges of subgroups, the next step in the calculation of limits is to find $\bar{\bar{X}}$ and *R*. These are

$$\hat{u} = \bar{\bar{X}} = \frac{\Sigma \bar{X}_j}{25} = \frac{160.25}{25} = 6.41 \text{ mm}$$

$$\bar{R} = \frac{\Sigma R_j}{m} = \frac{2.19}{25} = 0.09 \text{ mm}$$

If Table *C* is to be used, the next step is to estimate σ. For this it is necessary to find in Table *C* the d_2 factor for the subgroup size. In this case $n = 4$, and Table *C* gives $d_2 = 2.059$

Estimate of σ i.e., $\hat{\sigma} = \dfrac{\bar{R}}{d_2} = \dfrac{0.09}{2.059} = 0.0437$

Then $3\sigma_{\bar{X}}$ can be calculated from the relationship $\sigma_{\bar{X}} = \hat{\sigma}/\sqrt{n}$

$$3\sigma_{\bar{X}} = \frac{3\hat{\sigma}}{\sqrt{n}} = \frac{3(0.0437)}{2} = 0.07$$

Upper control limit for $\bar{X}$ Chart $\bar{X}(UCL_{\bar{X}}) = \bar{\bar{X}} + 3\sigma_{\bar{X}} = 6.41 + 0.07 = 6.48$

Lower control limit for $\bar{X}$ Chart $\bar{X}(LCL_{\bar{X}}) = \bar{\bar{X}} - 3\sigma_{\bar{X}} = 6.41 - 0.07 = 6.34$

The two steps in the calculation of $3\sigma_{\bar{X}}$ might be consolidated as

$$3\sigma_{\bar{X}} = 3\frac{\bar{R}}{d_2\sqrt{n}} = \frac{3R}{2.059\sqrt{4}} = 0.73\bar{R} = 0.73(0.09) = 0.07$$

To shorten the calculation of control limits from $\bar{R}$, this factor $3/d_2\sqrt{n}$, the multiplier of $\bar{R}$ in the preceding calculation has been computed for each value of *n* from 2 to 20 and tabulated in Table *D* of Appendix 1. This factor is designated A_2. The formulae for 3-sigma control limits on charts for $\bar{X}$ then become

$$UCL_{\bar{X}} = \bar{\bar{X}} + A_2\bar{R}$$

$$LCL_{\bar{X}} = \bar{\bar{X}} - A_2\bar{R}$$

If the control limits are to be calculated from s rather than from $\bar{R}$, the calculations are as follows :

$$\bar{\bar{X}} = 6.41$$

$$\bar{s} = \frac{\Sigma s_i}{25} = \frac{1.006}{25} = 0.041$$

Using the c_4 factor from Table *C* to estimate σ,

Estimate of σ i.e. $\hat{\sigma} = \dfrac{\bar{s}}{c_4} = \dfrac{0.041}{0.9213} = 0.0436$

$$3\sigma_{\bar{X}} = \frac{3\hat{\sigma}}{\sqrt{n}} = \frac{3(0.0436)}{2} = 0.07$$

$$UCL_{\overline{X}} = 6.41 + 0.07 = 6.48$$
$$LCL_{\overline{X}} = 6.41 - 0.07 = 6.34$$

As in the calculation from $\overline{R}$, the two steps in the calculation of $3\sigma_{\overline{X}}$ can be consolidated as

$$3\sigma_{\overline{X}} = \frac{3}{c_4\sqrt{n}}\overline{s} = 1.63(0.041) = 0.07$$

To shorten the calculations for control limits from $\overline{s}$, the factor $3/c_4\sqrt{n}$, the multiplier of s in the above calculation has been computed for each value of n from 2 to 25 , then by 5' s to 100, and tabulated in Table E of App. 1. This factor is designated $A3$. The formulae for 3-sigma control limits using this factor are

$$UCL_{\overline{X}} = \overline{\overline{X}} + A_3\overline{s}$$
$$LCL_{\overline{X}} = \overline{\overline{X}} - A_3\overline{s}$$

For those situations, where it is desired to calculate control limits directly from known or standard value of σ and μ the factor $3/\sqrt{n}$ has been computed and tabulated in Table F, App. 2. This factor is designated as A. The formulae for 3.-sigma control limits using this factor are

$$UCL_{\overline{X}} = \mu + A\,\sigma \text{ or } \overline{X}_0 + A\,\sigma_0$$
$$LCL_{\overline{X}} = \mu - A\,\sigma \text{ or } \overline{X}_0 - A\,\sigma_0$$

The various, equations for central lines and 3-sigma limits on control charts for $\overline{X}$, R, and s are assembled for convenient reference in Table 3.2. The factors (such as A, A_2, and so on) referred to are given in Tables C to F of Appendix 1. The reader will note that the spread of the limits on $\overline{X}$ charts as well as on R or s charts depends on the process dispersion. Limits on all the charts may be calculated directly from a known or assumed σ by estimating σ from either $\overline{R}$ or $\overline{s}$. In most cases in industrial practice, limits are computed from R for ease of computation.

TABLE 3.2: EQUATIONS FOR COMPUTING 3-SIGMA LIMITS ON SHEWHART CONTROL CHARTS FOR VARIABLES

(Table references for required factors pertain to Appendix 1. *CL*= central line)

Method	$\overline{X}$ chart	R chart	s chart
μ and σ known or assumed	$CL = \overline{X} = \mu$ $UCL_{\overline{X}} = \mu + A\sigma$ $LCL_{\overline{X}} = \mu - A\sigma$	$CL = \overline{R} = d_2\sigma$ $UCL_R = D_2\sigma$ $LCL_R = D_1\sigma$	$CL = \overline{s} = c_4\sigma$ $UCL_s = B_6\sigma$ $LCL_s = B_5\sigma$
	Table F	Tables C and F	Tables C and F,
μ and σ estimated from $\overline{\overline{X}}$ and $\overline{R}$	$CL = \overline{\overline{X}}$ $UCL_{\overline{X}} = \overline{\overline{X}} + A_2\overline{R}$ $LCL_{\overline{X}} = \overline{\overline{X}} - A_2\overline{R}$	$CL = \overline{R}$ $UCL_R = D_4\overline{R}$ $LCL_R = D_3\overline{R}$	
	Table D	Table D	
μ and σ estimated from $\overline{\overline{X}}$ and $\overline{s}$	$CL = \overline{X}$ $UCL_{\overline{X}} = \overline{X} + A_3\overline{s}$ $LCL_{\overline{X}} = \overline{X} - A_3\overline{s}$		$CL = \overline{s}$ $UCL_s = B_4\overline{S}$ $LCL_s = B_3\overline{s}$
	Table E		Table E

3.7.2 Control Charts for Range and Sample Standard Deviation

A general formula for the control limits on the $\bar{X}$ chart is $\mu \pm 3\sigma_{\bar{X}}$. Similarly, general formulae for control charts for measures of subgroup dispersion are :

Standard, aimed-at, or target values of $\mu(\bar{X}_0)$ may be substituted for μ or $\bar{\bar{X}}$; likewise, targets (R_0 or s_0) may be substituted for $\bar{R}$ or $\bar{s}$.

1. For the R chart: $\bar{R} \pm 3\sigma_R$
2. For the s chart: $\bar{s} \pm 3\sigma_s$

However, when these three formulae are applied to the calculation of lower control limits such limits will turn out to be less than 0 where n is 6 or less for R chart and where n is 5 or less for the s chart. Because R and s cannot be less than 0, the lower control limit is either not indicated or is marked as 0 in these cases. The marking of lower limit in such cases will keep a little control on the operators for lesser dispersion or better quality.

For the control chart shown in Fig 3.14, the computations for control limits for R chart are as follows :

$$UCL_R = D_4\bar{R} = 2.28(0.09) = 0.20$$

$$LCL_R = D_3\bar{R} = 0(0.09) = 0$$

If it was required to plot the s chart, the control limits on the s chart would be computed as follows:

$$UCL_s = B_4\bar{s} = 2.27(0.041) = 0.093$$

$$LCL_s = B_3\bar{s} = 0(0.041) = 0$$

The trial control limits for $\bar{X}$ and R charts calculated earlier are now used to draw the control charts for overages (means) and ranges. Figure 3.14 shows the control charts.

Most industrial processes are not in control when first analyzed. An analysis of Fig. 3.14 shows that there are out-of-control points on the $\bar{X}$ chart at subgroups 4, 9, and 20 and an out-of-control point on the R chart at subgroup 18. It also appears that there are a large number of points below the central line, which is no doubt due to the influence of the extreme high points. A review of the preliminary data as given in Fig. 3.14 shows that some of the out-of-control subgroups have an assignable cause. Subgroups 4, 18, and 20 had an assignable cause while the out-of-control condition for subgroup 9 does not. It is assumed that subgroup 9's out-of-control state is due to a chance cause and is part of the normal variation. Subgroups 4, 18, and 20 are not part of the normal variation and are discarded from the data and new $\bar{X}$ and R values computed with the remaining data.

There are **two** techniques used to discard the data. If either $\bar{X}$ or the R value of a subgroup is out of control and has an assignable cause, *both* are discarded, or *only the out-of-control* value of a subgroup is discarded. In this case the later technique was followed, thus when an $\bar{X}$ value was discarded, its corresponding R values was *not* discarded and vice-versa. Thus discarding the $\bar{X}$ values of 6.65 and 6.51 for subgroups 4 and 20, and discarding the R value of 0.30 for subgroup 18.

$$\bar{\bar{X}}_{new} = \frac{160.25 - (6.65 + 6.51)}{25 - 2}$$

$$= 6.40 \text{ mm}$$

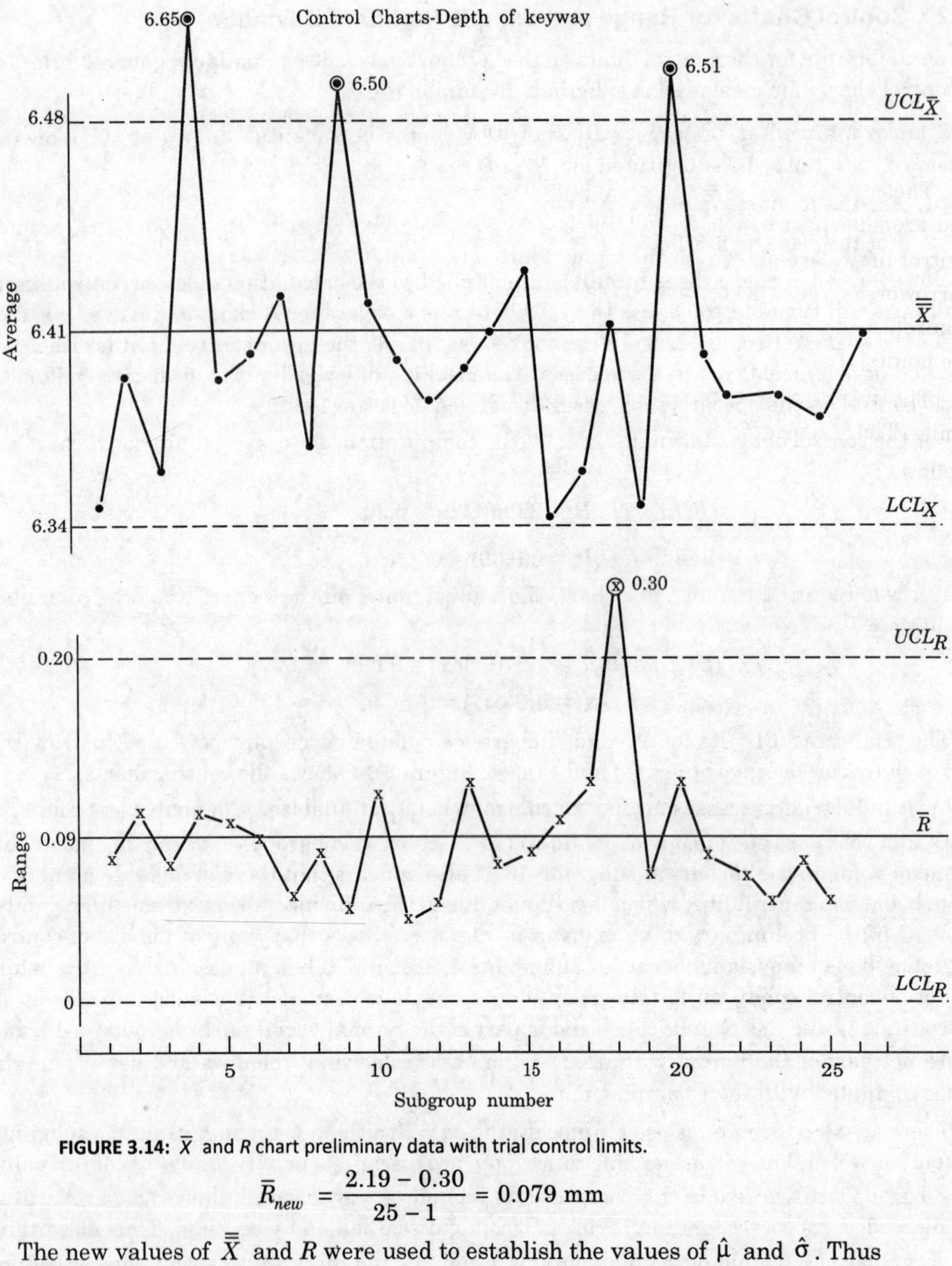

FIGURE 3.14: $\bar{X}$ and R chart preliminary data with trial control limits.

$$\bar{R}_{new} = \frac{2.19 - 0.30}{25 - 1} = 0.079 \text{ mm}$$

The new values of $\bar{\bar{X}}$ and R were used to establish the values of $\hat{\mu}$ and $\hat{\sigma}$. Thus

$$\hat{\mu} = \bar{\bar{X}}_{new} = 6.40 \text{ mm}; \hat{\sigma} = \frac{\bar{R}}{d_2} = \frac{0.079}{2.059} = 0.038 \text{ mm}.$$

The revised control limits based upon $\bar{\bar{X}}_{new}$ and $\bar{\bar{R}}_{new}$ are computed be as follow :

$$UCL_{\bar{X}} = \bar{\bar{X}}_{new} \text{ i.e } + A_2\bar{R}_{new}\ 6.40 + 0.73(0.079) = 6.46 \text{ mm}$$

$$LCL_{\bar{X}} = \bar{\bar{X}}_{new} \text{ i.e } - A_2\bar{R}_{new}\ 6.40 - 0.73(0.079) = 6.34 \text{ mm}$$

$$UCL_R = D_3\ \bar{R}_{new} \text{ i.e. } 2.28(0.079) = 0.18$$

$$LCL_R = D_4\ \bar{R}_{new} \text{ i.e. } 0(0.079) = 0$$

The central lines and control limits are drawn on the $\bar{X}$ and R charts for the next period and are shown in Fig 3.15. For illustrative purposes the trial control limits and the revised control limits are shown on the same chart. The limits for both the $\bar{X}$ and R charts became narrower, as was expected. No change occurred in LCL_R because the subgroup size is less than 7. Figure 3.15 also illustrates a simple charting technique in that lines are not drawn between the points.

The preliminary data for the initial 25 subgroups are not plotted with the revised control limits. These revised control limits are for reporting the results of future subgroups. To make

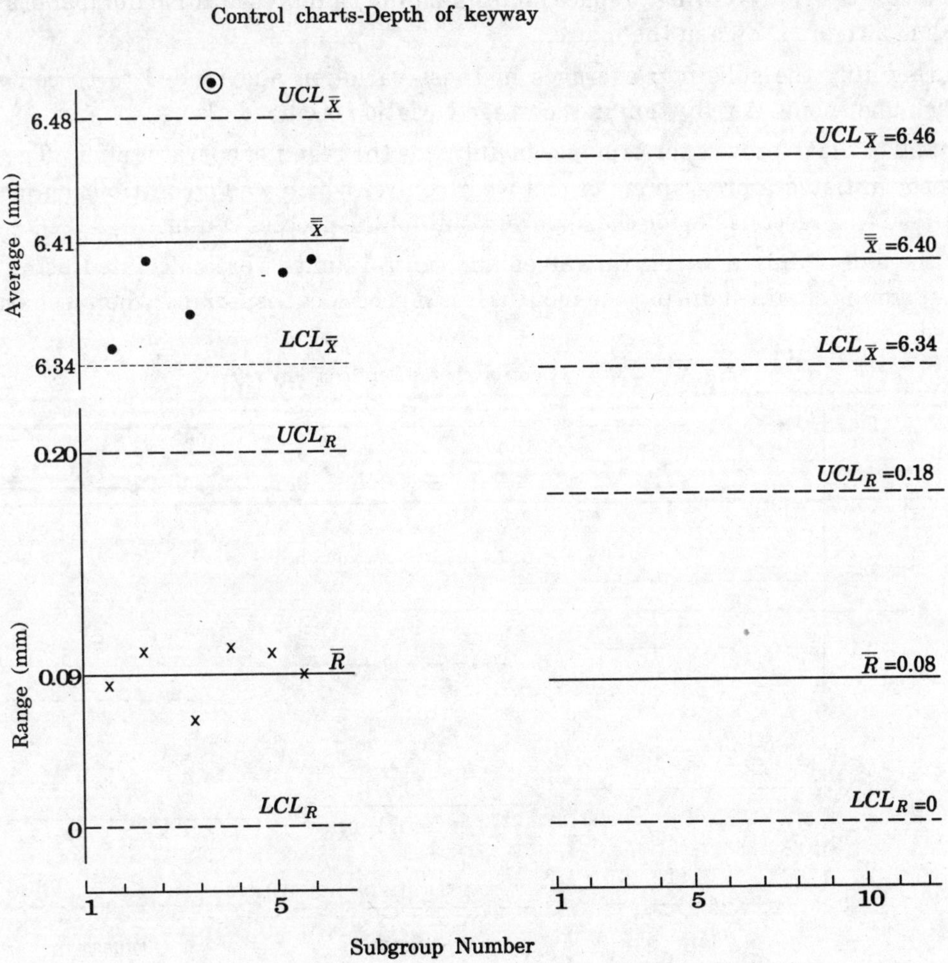

FIGURE 3.15: Trial control limits and revised control limits for *X* and *R* charts.

effective use of the control chart during production, it should be displayed in a conspicuous place where it can be seen by operators and supervisors.

To the diligent reader, it is apparent that when standards are known (μ and σ), the control limits and central values may be calculated immediately, saving considerable work. Therefore, the collecting of 25 subgroups of data, calculation of trial control limits, and estimation of $\bar{X}$ and s are unnecessary.

3.7.3 Continue the use of the Charts

When control charts are first introduced at a work station, an improvement in the process performance usually occurs. This initial improvement is especially noticeable when the process is dependent on the skill of the operator. The posting of quality control chart appears to be a psychological signal to the operator to improve his performance. Most workers want to produce a quality product; therefore, when management shows an interest in the quality, the operator responds.

Figure 3.16 illustrates the initial improvement which occurred after the introduction of the $\bar{X}$ and R charts in July. Owing to space limitations, only a representative number of subgroups for each month are shown in the figure.

During July the subgroup averages had less variation and tended to be centered at a slightly higher point. A reduction in the range variation occurred also.

Not all of the improved performance in July was the result of operator effort. The first-line supervisor initiated a programme of tool wear control which was a contributing factor. This programme was responsible for the apparent shift of the process center.

At the end of July new central values and control limits were calculated using the data from subgroups obtained during the month. It is a good idea, especially when a chart is being initiated,

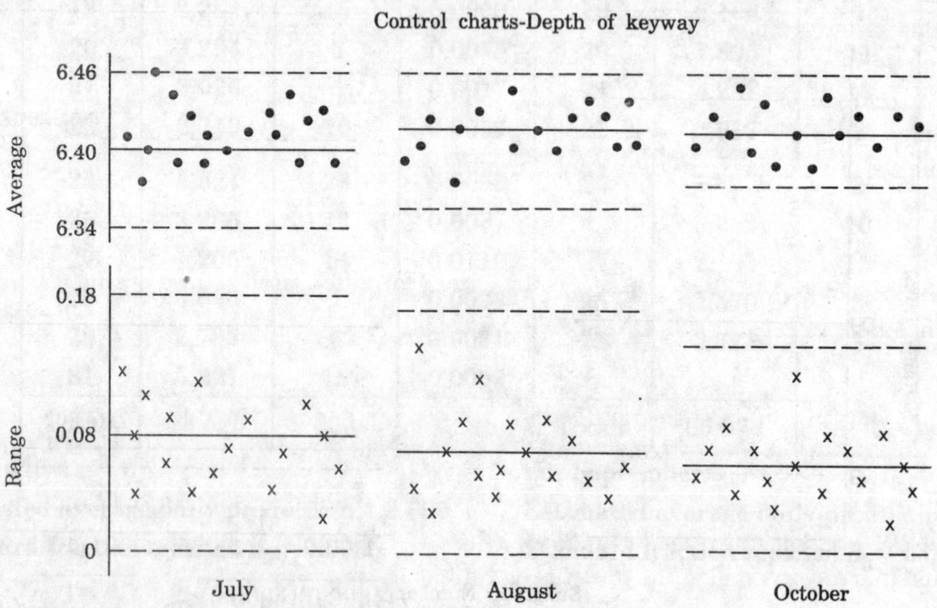

FIGURE 3.16 Continuing use of control charts, showing improved control.

to calculate the process mean ($\bar{X}$) and standard deviation (s) periodically to see if any changes have occurred. This revaluation can be done for every 25 subgroups, and the results compared to the previous values.

New control values and control limits were established for the $\bar{X}$ and R chart for the month of August. During the ensuing months the maintenance department replaced a pair of worn gears; purchasing changed the material supplier; and tooling modified a workholding device. All these improvement were the result of investigations that tracked down the cause for out-of-control conditions.

At the end of September, the periodic evaluation of the past performance showed the need to revise the central values and the control limits. The performance for the month of October and subsequent months showed a normal pattern of variation; therefore, the process was considered to be in control.

As the control chart continues in use, a periodic review is necessary. This review should not only include the standards but the frequency of inspection. If the process performance is satisfactory, the amount of inspection can be reduced and the inspector assigned to other activities. The periodic review should also evaluate the need for both charts. Occasionally, a process will have control problems only with the central tendency or only with the dispersion. In such a case the R chart or the $\bar{X}$ chart may be eliminated. When the objective for initiating the charts has been achieved, its use should be discontinued and efforts directed toward the improvement of some other quality characteristic.

3.7.4 The Sample Standard Deviation Control Chart

While the $\bar{X}$ and R charts are the most common charts for variables, some companies prefer the standard deviation as the measure of the subgroup dispersion. In comparing an R chart with a s chart, an R chart is easier to compute and easier to explain. On the other hand, the subgroup standard deviation for the s chart is calculated using all the data rather than just the high and the low value as done for the R chart. A s chart is therefore more nearly accurate than an R chart. When subgroup sizes are less than 10, both charts will graphically portray the same variation as evident in Fig 3.17. However, as subgroups sizes increase to 10 or more, extreme values have an undue influence on the R chart. Therefore, at larger subgroup sizes the s chart is used.

The steps necessary to obtain the $\bar{X}$ and s trial control and revised control limits are the same as those used for the $\bar{X}$ and R chart except for different formulae. Using the preliminary data in Example 3.1, $\bar{\bar{X}} = 6.41$ and $\bar{s} = 0.041$

$$UCL_{\bar{X}} = 6.48$$

$$LCL_{\bar{X}} = 6.34$$

$$UCL_s = 0.093$$

$$LCL_s = 0$$

Figure 3.17 shows the control charts for $\bar{X}$ and s.

Just like the revision in the control and control limits of $\bar{X}$ and R charts after the elimination of out of control points, $\bar{X}$ and s charts will have the revised control limits after elimination of out of control points.

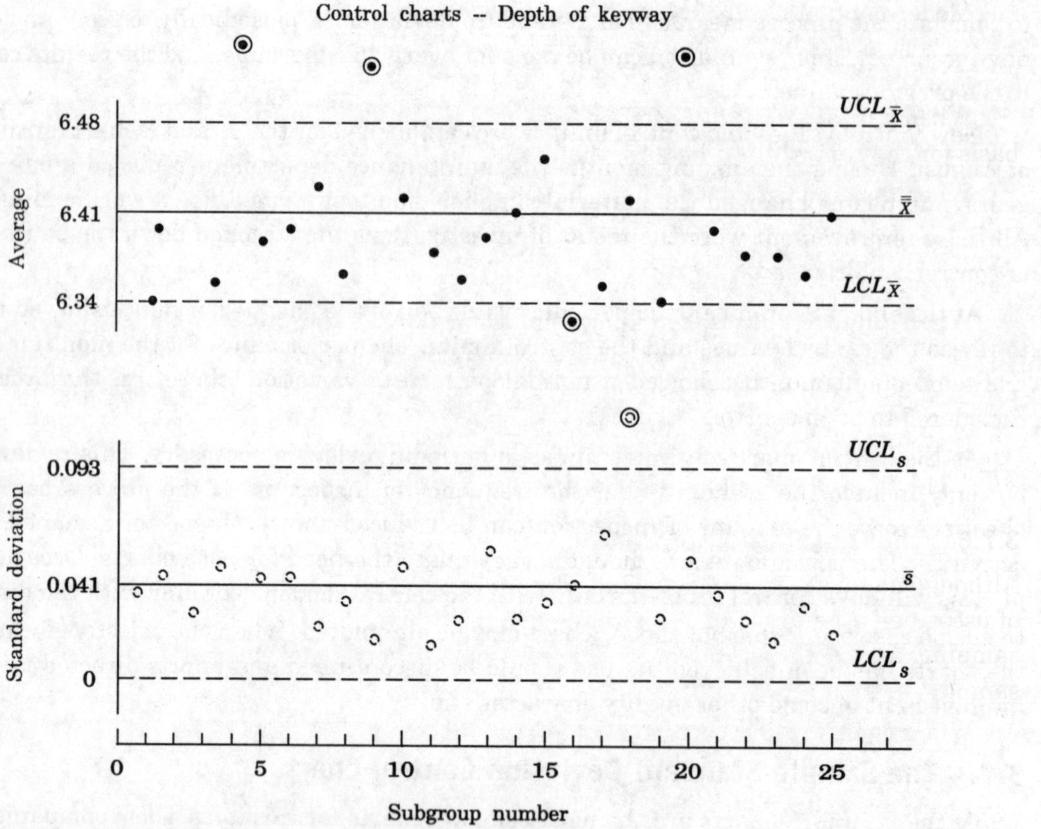

FIGURE 3.17 X and s chart for preliminary data with trial control limits.

3.7.5 The Distribution of the Standard Deviation

Just as each universe has its average and standard deviation, also does each distribution of averages, standard deviations, or ranges have its own average and standard deviation. In case of distribution of $\bar{X}$, the statistical theory gave the expected average μ and the expected standard deviation $\sigma/\sqrt{n}$, both of which are independent of the form of the universe. Moreover, theory told us that if the universe distribution were normal the distribution of $\bar{X}$ values would be normal regardless of sample size, and that even if the universe distribution were not normal, the distribution of $\bar{X}$ values would approach normality as sample size increased.

However, if the universe is normal, statistical theory tells us that expected average and the expected standard deviation of the distribution s. This expected average $\bar{s}$ is $c_4\,\sigma$. A commonly used approximate estimate of σ_s, the expected standard deviation of the distribution of s for samples from a normal universe is $\sigma/\sqrt{2(n-1)}$. It also is known that, as n increases the distribution of s becomes closer and closer to a symmetrical distribution.

Theoretical knowledge of the distribution of s in samples from a normal universe is the basis for 3-sigma limits on the control chart for s. The central line on the control chart is set at $\bar{s}$. The limits are set at $\bar{s} \pm 3\sigma s$.

The approximate value of σ_s for a normal universe is

$$\sigma_s = \frac{\sigma}{\sqrt{2(n-1)}} \qquad ...(3.9)$$

Modern statistical theory gives the exact value as

$$\sigma_s = \sqrt{1 - c_4^2}\,\sigma \qquad ...(3.10)$$

When n is large, the difference between (3.9) and (3.10) is negligible. Equation (3.10) is the basis for the control limit factors where n is 25 or less; Eq. (3.9) is used where n exceeds 25.

When 3-sigma limits on a chart for s are calculated from an observed $\bar{s}$, they are

$$UCL_s = \bar{s} + 3\sigma_s = B_4\bar{s}$$

$$LCL_s = \bar{s} - 3\sigma_s = B_3\bar{s}$$

When limits are based on a known or assumed value of universe standard deviation σ, they

$$UCL_s = c_4\sigma + 3\,\sigma_s = B_6\sigma$$

$$LCL_s = c_4\sigma - 3\,\sigma_s = B_5\sigma$$

In computing σ_s for the B_4 and B_3 factors given in Table E of Appendix 1, σ is assumed to be $\bar{s}/c_4$. The B_6 and B_5 factors are given in Table F.

3.7.6 The Distribution of Ranges

Although no simple formula gives either the expected average range R or the standard deviation of use range σ_R, statistical theory does give the ratio of these figures to universe standard σ in sampling from a normal universe. Therefore also fully defines the expected distribution of R in sampling from a normal universe.

When 3-sigma limits are calculated from an observed R, they are

$$UCL_R = \bar{R} + 3\sigma_R = \bar{R} + 3\frac{d_3}{d_2}\bar{R} = D_4\bar{R}$$

$$LCL_R = \bar{R} - 3\sigma_R = \bar{R} - 3\frac{d_3}{d_2}\bar{R} = D_3\bar{R}$$

When limits are based on a known or assumed value of universe standard deviation σ they are

$$UCL_R = d_2\sigma + 3\sigma_R = d_2\sigma + 3d_3\sigma = D_2\sigma$$

$$LCL_R = D_2\sigma - 3\sigma_R = d_2\sigma - 3d_3\sigma = D_1\sigma$$

In these formulae, the d_2 factor expresses numerically the expected value of $\bar{R}/\sigma$ and the d_3 factor expresses the standard deviation of this relationship. Values of d_2 and d_3 are given in Table C, App. 1. The factors necessary to calculate control limits appear in Tables D and F.

3.8 PROCESS IN CONTROL

When the assignable have been eliminated from the process to the extent that the points plotted on the control chart remain within the control limits, the process is in a state of control. No higher degree of uniformity can be attained with the existing process. Greater uniformity can, however, be attained through a change in the basic process.

When a process is in control, there occurs a normal pattern of variation which is illustrated in Fig 3.18. This natural pattern of variation has (1) about two-thirds of the points near thecenter solid line or central value, (2) a few points closer to the control limits, (3) points located back and forth across the center line, (4) points balanced on both sides of the center line or central value, and (5) no points beyond the control limits. The natural pattern of the points or subgroup values forms its own frequency distribution, which follows a normal curve. As the number of plotted points increases, the frequency distribution will take on the appearance of a smooth polygon. The dashed normal curve at the left end of Fig. 3.18 represents the distribution of the points when a process is in control.

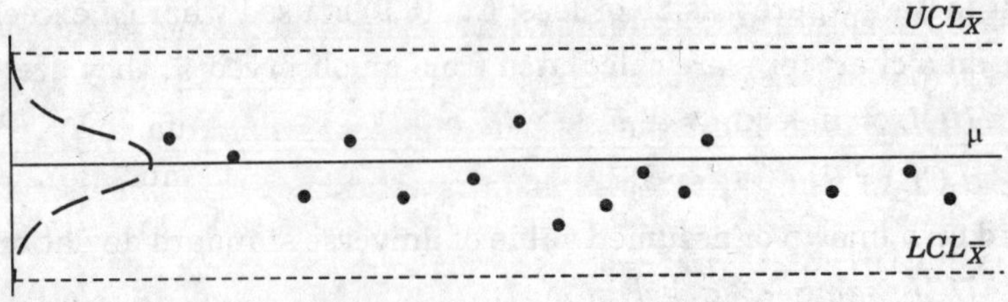

FIGURE 3.18: Natural pattern of variation of a control chart.

Control limits as stated previously, are usually established at 3-sigma from the central value. They are used as a basis to judge whether there is evidence of lack of control. The choice of 3 sigma control limits is an economic one with respect to two types of errors that can occur. One error, called *Type I* by statistician, occurs when looking for an assignable cause of variation when in reality a chance cause is present. When the limits are set at 3-sigma a ***Type I*** (or α) error will occur 0.27% (3 out of 10,000) of the time. In other words when a point is outside the control limits, it is assumed to be due to an assignable cause even though it would be due to a chance cause 0.27% of the time. The other type error, called ***Type II*** (or β, as usually called) error occurs when assuming that a chance cause of variation is present when in reality there is as assignable cause. In other words, when a point is inside the control limits, it is assumed to be due to a chance cause even though it might be an assignable cause. Abundant experience since 1930 in all types of industry indicates that 3 sigma control provide an economic balance between the costs resulting from the two types of errors. Unless there are strong practical reasons for doing otherwise, the ± 3 sigma limits should be used.

When a process is in control, only chance causes of variation are present. Small variations in machine performance, operator performance, and material characteristics are expected and are considered to be part of a stable process.

When a process is in control, certain practical advantages accrue to the manufacturer and purchaser.

- Individual units of the product will be more uniform or, stated another way, there will be less variation among parts.
- Since the product is more uniform, fewer samples are needed to judge the quality. Therefore, the cost of inspection can be reduced to a minimum. This advantage is extremely important when 100% conformance to specifications is not essential.
- The process capability or spread of the process is easily attained from 6σ or by multiplying the square root of the sample size by the difference between the control limits *i.e.* $\sqrt{n}\,(UCL - LCL)$ With a knowledge of the process capability, a number of reliable decisions relative to specification can be made, such as :

(*a*) To decide the product specification.

(*b*) To decide the amount of rework or scrap when there is insufficient tolerance.

(*c*) To decide whether to produce the product to tight specifications and permit interchangeability of components or to produce the product to loose specification and use selective matching of components.

The percentage of product that falls within any pair of values may be predicted with the highest degree of assurance. For example, this advantage can be very important when adjusting filling machines to obtain different percentage of items below, between or above particular values or limits.

When a process is in control, it permits the purchaser to use the manufacturer's data (with consent) and, therefore, to test only a few subgroups as a check on the manufacturer's records.

3.9 PROCESS OUT OF CONTROL

When a point (subgroup value) falls outside its control limits, the process is out of control. This means that an assignable cause of variation is present. Another way of viewing the out-of-control point is to think of the subgroup value as coming from a different universe than the one from which the control limits were obtained. Figure 3.19 shows a frequency distribution of subgroup averages for cereal boxes which was developed from a large number of subgroups and, therefore, represents the universe mean $\mu = 450$ g, and the universe standard deviation for the averages $\sigma_{\bar{X}} = 8$ g. The frequency distribution for subgroup averages is shown by a dashed line, which represents a smooth curve. The out-of-control point has a value of 483 g. This point is so far away from the 3-sigma limits (99.73%) that it can only be considered to have come from another universe. In other words, the process that produced the subgroup average of 483 g is a different process than the stable process from which the 3σ control limits were developed. Therefore, something has gone wrong with the process; some assignable cause of variation is present. This assignable cause must be found and corrected before a normal, stable process can continue.

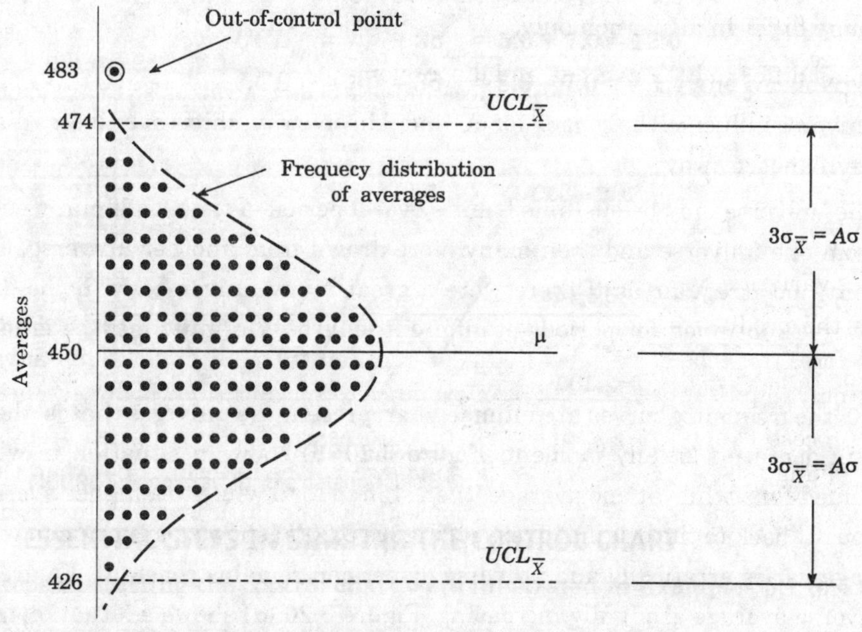

FIGURE 3.19 Frequency distribution of subgroup averages with control limits.

3.10 CONTRIBUTION OF THE CONTROL CHART TO ELIMINATION OF CAUSES OF TROUBLE

As stated earlier, actions based on the control chart for variables are of many kinds. Some of these actions, particularly those related to specifications and tolerances need to start from evidence that a process is in control. Other useful actions start from evidence of the control chart that a process is out of control. Trouble shooting in manufacturing is a particularly important example of this. In this type of control-chart application, the control chart sometimes says, "Leave this process alone", and at other times it says, "Hunt for trouble and try to correct it".

A major virtue of the control chart is that it tells—within reasonably satisfactory limits—when to hunt for the cause of variation. It is always helpful to know when; sometimes this may be sufficient to indicate where to look. Nevertheless, there is often a fair amount of hard work between the decision to hunt for trouble and the actual discovery and correction of the root cause of the trouble. This fact is responsible for often quoted statement that "*statistical quality control is 50% engineering and only 50% statistics*".

3.10.1 A classification of Ways in which Lack of Control may occur

In the preceding sections it has been made amply clear that out of statistical control situation implies change in universe or shift in universe. It is helpful to give separate consideration to three ways in which universes may differ, as follows:

1. They may differ in average only.
2. They may differ in dispersion only.
3. They may differ in both average and dispersion.

Shifts in universe influence the control for $\overline{X}$ and R in one way; shifts in universe dispersion influence them in another way.

Shifts in the universe may be sustained shifts over a period of time, as if many subgroups were drawn from one universe and then many more drawn from another universe. Or shifts may be frequent and irregular as if there were a great many universes with the drawings from each universe continued for periods of different lengths. Or shifts may be gradual and systematic.

In Fig. 3.20, the frequency curves are intended to represent the universe that is, the chance cause system in operation at any moment. Figure 3.20 (*a*) shows a situation in which the universe continued for a while at one average, then shifted for a while to a higher average, and finally was brought back to the original average. Figure 3.20(*b*) shows a situation in which the universe average varies erratically and universe dispersion remains constant. Figure 3.20 (*c*) shows the universe average gradually increasing. Figure 3.20 (*d*) shows a situation in which, although the universe average remained unchanged, the universe dispersion doubled. Figure 3.20 (*e*) shows universe average and dispersion both varying erratically.

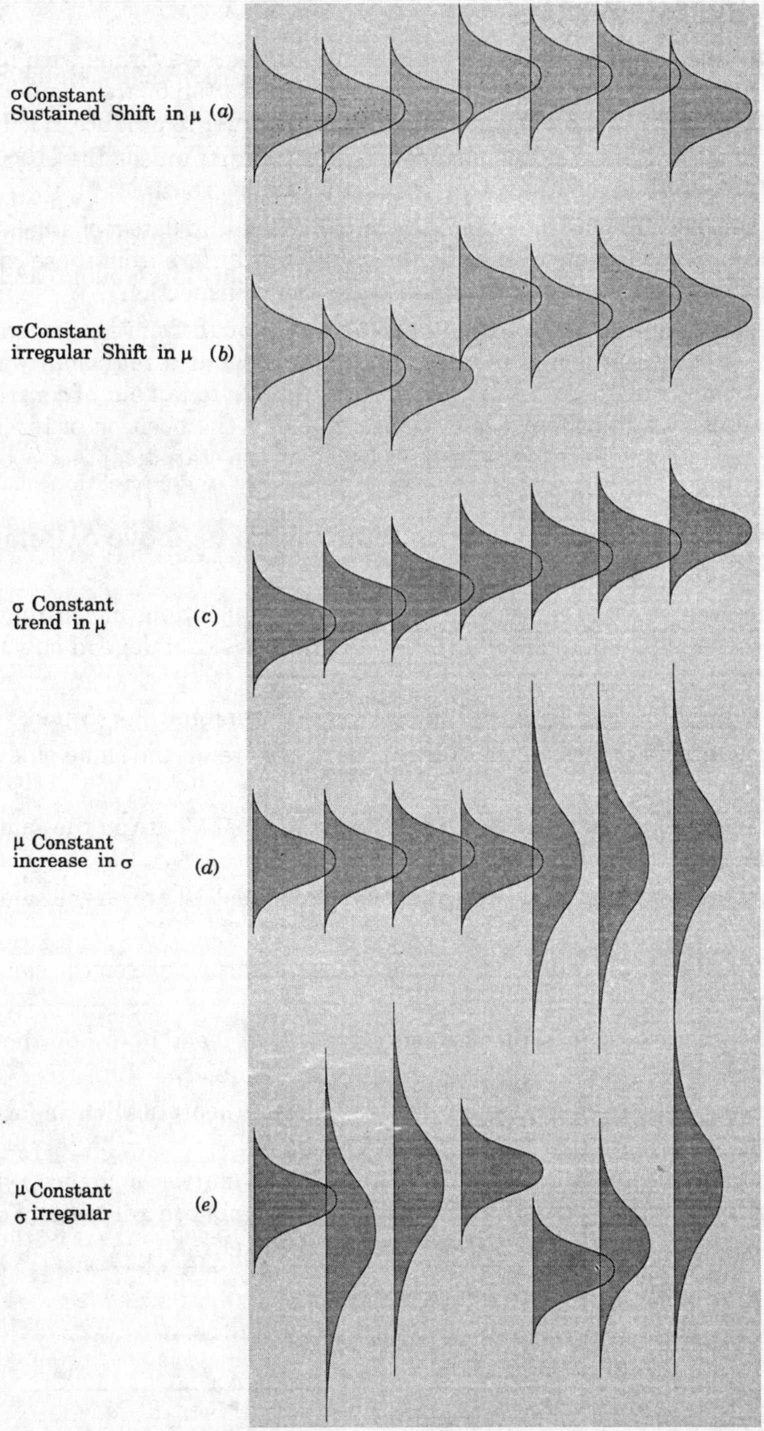

FIGURE 3.20: Chance cause systems (represented here by frequency curves) may change in different ways: (*a*) temporary jumps shift in universe average with constant spread ; (*b*) irregular shifts in universe average with constant spread ; (*c*) steady trend in universe average with constant spread ; (*d*) change in universe spread with no change in average ; (*e*) irregular changes in both average and spread.

3.11 CHANGES IN UNIVERSE AVERAGE

A common type of lack of control in manufacturing is a shift in universe average with little or no change in universe dispersion. In such cases, the control chart is often of great value to the machine setter, helping the setter to center the machine setting in order to produce at a desired process average. This type of lack of control is shown on the $\bar{X}$ chart; unless the changes in universe average take place within a subgroup, the R chart will show control.

In those cases where the main reason for keeping a control chart is to detect changes in the universe average, the appropriate scheme of selection of subgroups differs from those cases in which the control chart has several purposes, including acceptance inspection.

Because, as previously explained, control limits are set far enough from the central line on the chart for there to be very few points outside the limits without a real change in the universe, small shifts in universe average will not cause many points to fall out of control. For this reason, it is often useful to supplement the evidence given by the position of the points relative to the control limits with evidence given by tests based on the statistical theory of runs or sequences.

3.11.1 Some Tests for Lack of Control Based on Runs of Points Above or Below the Central Line on the Control Chart

In order to detect shifts in a universe parameter in the common applications of control charts in manufacturing, the most practical plan is to use a few simple rules that depend only on the extreme runs. The following are suggested :

Consider that grounds exist for suspicion that the universe parameter has shifted :

- Whenever, in 7 successive points on the control chart, all are on the same side of the central line
- Whenever, in 11 successive points on the control chart, at least 10 are on the same side of the central line
- Whenever, in 14 successive points on the control chart, at least 12 are on the same side of the central line
- Whenever, in 17 successive points on the control chart, at least 14 are on the same side of the central line
- Whenever, in 20 successive points one the control chart, at least 16 are on the same side of the central line

The first three situations have been depicted in Fig. 3.21. The theoretical basis for these rules is discussed in Chap. 4.

The sequences mentioned in each of these rules will occur as a matter of chance, with no change in the universe, more frequently than a point outside of 3-sigma control limits. For this

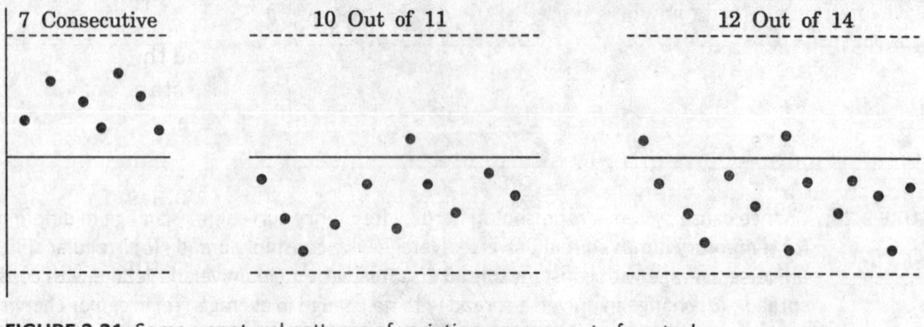

FIGURE 3.21: Some unnatural patterns of variation-process out of control.

reason they provide a less reliable basis for hunting for trouble than the occurrence of a point outside of control limits.

Moreover, if all these different rules are used to judge whether the universe parameter has shifted, the chances of the false indication of a shift are greater than if only one of the rules were used.

Sequences of points on one side of a central line can be useful in relation to possible action on the control chart even where they are not used for hunting for trouble in the process. They are particularly helpful in the special case where the lower control limit is zero. For instance, a reduction in the value of σ calls for a change in the location of the upper and lower control limits on the $\bar{X}$ chart and a change in the center line and limits on the R chart. But in all R charts for which the subgroup size is not more than six, it is impossible for the change in σ to be shown by a point falling below the lower control limit of zero. However, and indication of the decrease in process dispersion can be obtained by applying the theory of runs.

There are many other unnatural patterns, and it is important to remember the conditions of normality. One technique for recognizing unnatural patterns is to divide the control chart into six equal imaginary bands. Three equal bands are between the central value, and the lower control limit and three equal bands are between the central value and the upper control limit. A normal pattern of variation occurs when (1) about 34% of the points fall in each of the bands adjacent to the center value, (2) about $13\frac{1}{2}$% of the points fall in each of the two middle bands, and (3) $2\frac{1}{2}$% of the points fall in each of the three outer bands. Any significant divergence from the normal pattern, such as 2 out of 3 consecutive points in the outer band, would be an unnatural pattern and would be classified as an out-of-control condition.

3.11.2 Nelson Rules for Control Chart Interpretation

Basically control charts can be interpreted by looking at the control limits (which are at ±3 standard deviation (σ)] around the mean; if there are any points outside these limits, then there is an indication that the process outcome is affected by a special cause. However, more complex set of rules for control chart interpretation have been developed such as the Nelson rules shown in Table 3.3 below:

Table 3.3 : The Nelson rules for Control Chart Interpretation

Rule	Chart pattern	Interpretation
1.	One point is more than 3 standard deviations from the mean on either side (within the special cause variation area).	One sample is grossly i.e. too much out of control.
2.	Nine (or more) points in a row are on the same side of the mean.	Some prolonged bias exists.
3.	Six (or more) points in a row are continually increasing (or decreasing)	A trend exists. This is directional and the position of the mean and size of the standard deviation do not affect this rule.
4.	Fourteen (or more) points in a row alternate in direction, increasing then decreasing.	This much oscillation is beyond normal noise. This is directional and the position of the mean and size of the standard deviation do not affect this rule.

...(Cont.)

5.	Two (or three) out of three points in a row are more than 2 standards deviations from the mean in the same direction.	There is a medium tendency for samples to be out of control.
6.	Four out of five points in a row are more than 1 standard deviation form the mean in the same direction.	There is a strong tendency for samples to be slightly out of control.
7.	Fifteen points in a row are all within standard deviation of the mean and the points are in both directions from the mean.	With 1 standard deviation, greater variation would be expected.
8.	Eight points in a row exists with none within 1 standard deviation of the mean and the points are in both directions from the mean.	Jumping from above to below whilst missing the first standard deviation band is rarely random.

3.12.3 Interpretation of Some Typical Patterns on $\overline{X}$ and *R* charts

We have noted previously that a control chart can indicate an out-of-control condition even though no single point plots outside the control limits, if the pattern of the plotted points exhibits nonrandom or systematic behavior. In many cases, the pattern of the plotted points will provide useful diagnostic information on the process, and this information can be used to make process modifications that reduce variability (the goal of statistical process control). We shall now briefly discuss some of the more common patterns that appear on $\overline{X}$ and *R* charts, and indicate some of the process characteristics that may produce these patterns. To effectively interpret $\overline{X}$ and *R* charts, the analyst must be familiar with both the statistical principles underlying the control chart and the process.

In interpreting patterns on the $\overline{X}$ chart, we must first determine whether or not the *R* chart is in control. Some assignable causes show up on both the $\overline{X}$ and *R* charts. If both the $\overline{X}$ and R charts exhibit a nonrandom pattern, the strategy is to eliminate the *R* chart assignable causes first. In many cases, this will automatically eliminate the nonrandom pattern on the $\overline{X}$ chart. Never attempt to interpret the $\overline{X}$ chart when the *R* chart indicates an out-of-control condition.

Cyclic patterns occasionally appear on the control chart. A typical example is shown in Fig. 3.22. Such a pattern on the $\overline{X}$ chart may result from systematic environmental changes such as temperature, operator fatigue, regular rotation of operators and/or machine, or fluctuation on voltage or pressure or some other variable in the production equipment. *R* charts will sometimes reveal cycles because of maintenance schedules, operator fatigue, or tool wear

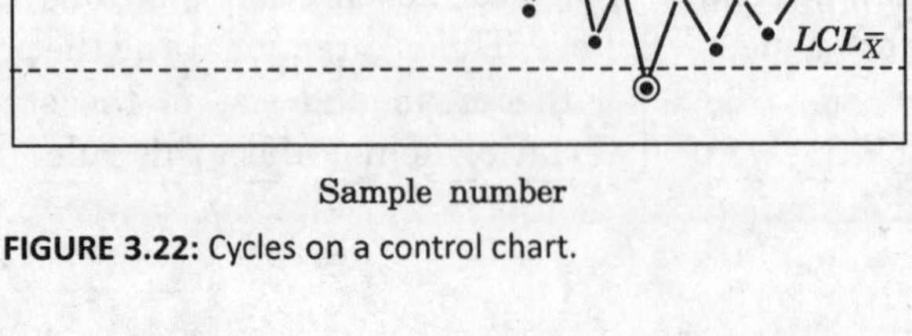

FIGURE 3.22: Cycles on a control chart.

resulting in excessive variability. In one study in which this author was involved, systematic variability in the fill volume of metal container was caused by the on-off cycle of a compressor in the filling machine.

A mixture is indicated when the plotted points tend to fall near or slightly outside the control limits, with relatively few points near the center line as shown in Fig. 3.23. A mixture pattern is generated by two (or more) overlapping distribution generating the process output. The probability distributions that could be associated with the mixture pattern in Fig. 3.23 are shown on the right-hand side of that figure. The severity of the mixture pattern depends on the extent to which the distributions overlap. Sometimes mixtures result from "overcontrol," where the operators make process adjustments too often, responding to random variation in the output rather than systematic causes. A mixture pattern can also occur when output product from several sources (such as parallel machines) are fed into a common stream which is then sampled for process monitoring purposes.

A **shift in process level** is illustrated in Fig. 3.24. These shifts may result from the introduction of new workers, methods, raw materials, or machines, a change in the inspection method or standards, or a change in either the skill, attentiveness or motivation of the operators.

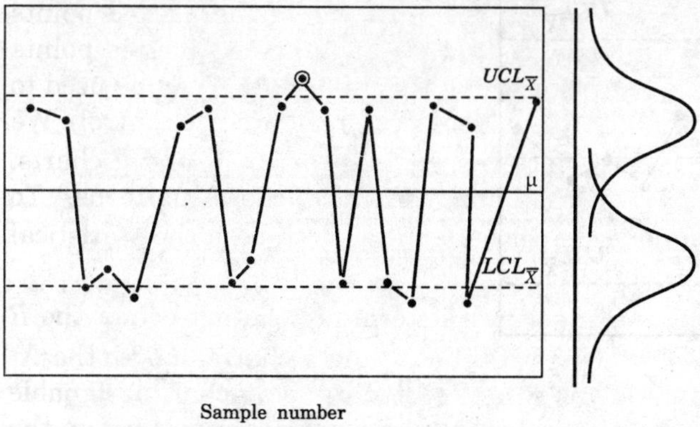

FIGURE 3.23: A mixture pattern.

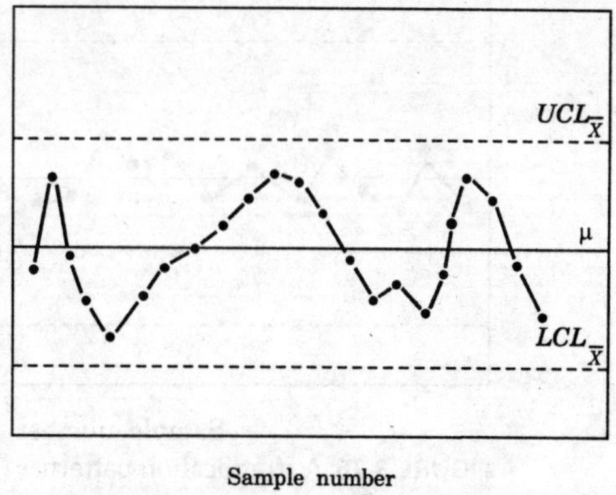

FIGURE 3.24: A shift in process level.

Sometimes an improvement in process performance is noted following introduction of a control chart programme, simply because of motivational factors influencing the workers.

A **trend**, or **continuous movement in one direction**, is shown on the control chart in Fig. 3.25 Trends are usually due to a gradual wearing out or deterioration of a tool or some other critical process component. In chemical processes they often occur because of settling or separation of the components of a mixture. They can also result from human causes, such as operator fatigue or the presence of supervision. Finally, trends can result from seasonal influences, such as temperature. When trends are due to tool wear or other systematic causes of deterioration, this may be directly incorporated into the control chart model. The modified control chart as discussed in Chap. 8, is used when the process exhibits tool wear.

Stratification or a tendency for the points to cluster artificially around the center line, is illustrated in Fig. 3.26 . We note that there is a marked lack of natural variability in the observed pattern. One potential cause of stratification is incorrect calculation of control limits. This pattern may also result when the sampling process collects one or more units from several different underlying distributions within each subgroup. For example, suppose that a sample of size five is obtained by taking one observation from each of five parallel processes. If the largest and smallest units in each sample are relatively far apart because they come from two different distributions, then $\overline{R}$ will be incorrectly inflated, causing the limits on the $\overline{X}$ chart to be too wide. In this case $\bar{R}$ incorrectly measures the variability between the different underlying distributions, in addition to the chance cause variation that it is intended to measure.

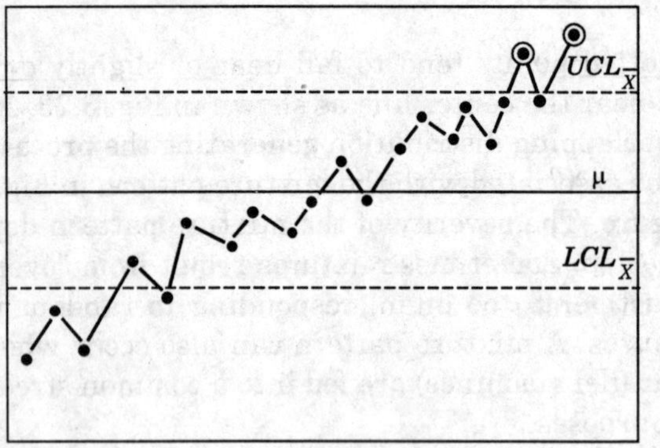

Sample number

FIGURE 3.25: A trend in process level.

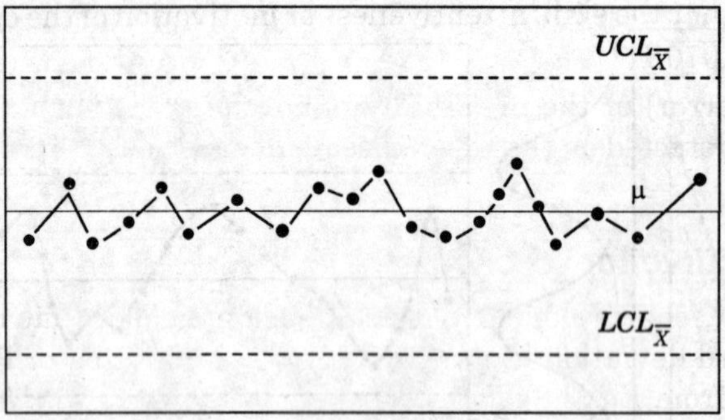

Sample number

FIGURE 3.26: A stratification pattern.

In interpreting patterns on the $\bar{X}$ and R charts, these two charts should be considered jointly. If the underlying distribution is normal, then the random variables $\bar{X}$ and R computed from the same sample are statistically independent. Therefore, $\bar{X}$ and R should behave independently on the control chart. If there is correlation between the $\bar{X}$ and R values, that is, if the points on the two charts "follow" each other, then this indicates that the underlying distribution is skewed. If specification have been determined assuming normally, then those analyses may be in error.

3.13 THE OPERATING CHARACTERISTICS (*OC*) OF *X* AND *R* CHARTS

The ability of the $\bar{X}$ and R charts to detect shifts in process quality *i.e. average* is described by their operating characteristic (*OC*) curves. Consider the *OC* curve for an $\bar{X}$ chart with the process mean at μ and dispersion of σ. If the mean shifts to a new value, say $\mu_1 = \mu_0 + k\sigma$, the probability of *not* detecting the shift on the first subsequent sample or the β error (or *Type II*) is

$$\beta = P\,[LCL_{\bar{X}} \leq \bar{X} \leq UCL_{\bar{X}} \mid \mu = \mu_1 = \mu_0 + k\sigma] \qquad ...(3.11)$$

where P is the probability of $\bar{X}$ falling between $LCL_{\bar{X}}$ and $UCL_{\bar{X}}$.

Since, $\bar{X}$ has a normal distribution with mean μ_0 and standard deviation $\sigma_{\bar{X}}$ *i.e.* $\sigma/\sqrt{n}$ and the upper and lower control limits are $L\sigma_{\bar{X}}$ away from the mean then $UCL_{\bar{X}} = \mu_0 + L\sigma_{\bar{X}}$ *i.e.* $\mu_0 + L\sigma/\sqrt{n}$. Similarly $LCL_{\bar{X}} = \mu_0 - L\sigma/\sqrt{n}$,then the Equation 3.11 can be expressed

$$\beta = z\left[\frac{UCL_{\bar{X}} - (\mu_0 + k\sigma)}{\sigma/\sqrt{n}}\right] - z\left[\frac{LCL_{\bar{X}} - (\mu_0 + k\sigma)}{\sigma/\sqrt{n}}\right]$$

$$= z\left[\frac{\mu_0 + L\sigma/\sqrt{n} - (\mu_0 + k\sigma)}{\sigma/\sqrt{n}}\right] - z\left[\frac{\mu_0 - L\sigma/\sqrt{n} - (\mu_0 + k\sigma)}{\sigma/\sqrt{n}}\right]$$

$$= z\left[L - k/\sqrt{n}\right] - z\left[-L - k/\sqrt{n}\right] \quad \ldots(3.12)$$

To illustrate the application of Eq. (3.12), suppose we are using an $\bar{X}$ chart with usual 3-sigma limits *i.e.* $L = 3$, the sample size $n = 5$ and it is required to determine the probability of detecting a shift to $\mu_1 = \mu_0 + 2\sigma$ on the first sample following the shift. Then, since $L = 3$, $k = 2$ and $n = 5$, we have

$$\beta = z\left[3 - 2\sqrt{5}\right] - z\left[-3 - 2\sqrt{5}\right]$$

$$= z[-1.47] - z[-7.37]$$

Table *A* reading for $-1.47 = 0.0708$

Table *A* reading for $-7.37 = 0$

Area included $= 0.0708$

This is the β-risk, (*i.e. Type II* error) or the probability of not detecting such a shift. The probability that such a shift will be detected on the first subsequent sample is $1 - \beta = 1 - 0.0708$ *i.e.* 0.9292

3.13.1 Construction of the OC curve for $\bar{X}$ chart

To construct the OC curve for the $\bar{X}$ chart, plot the β-risk against the magnitude of the shift to be detected (expressed in standard deviation units) for various sample sizes *n*. These probabilities may be evaluated directly from Eq (3.8). This *OC* curve is shown in Fig. 3.27 for the case of 3-sigma limits ($L = 3$).

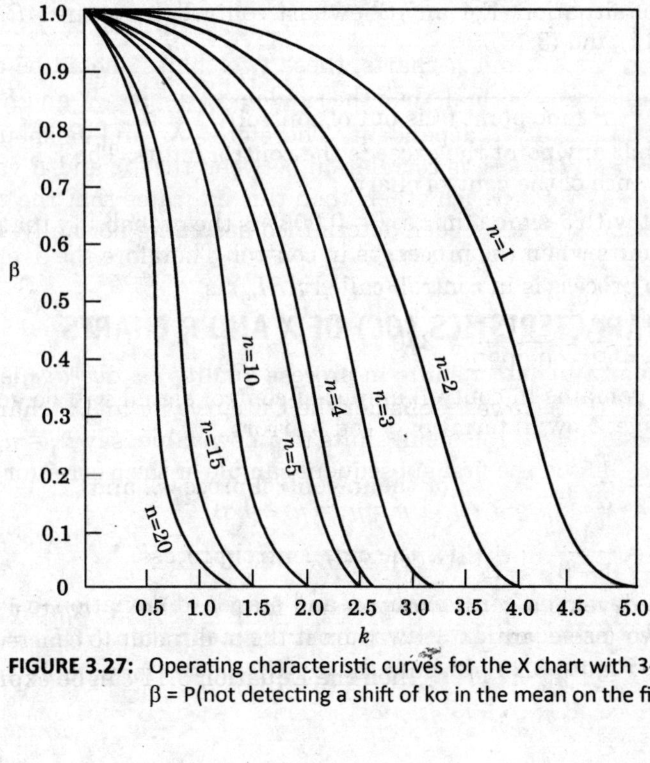

FIGURE 3.27: Operating characteristic curves for the X chart with 3-sigma limits.
β = P(not detecting a shift of kσ in the mean on the first sample following the shift)

Figure 3.27 indicates that for the typical sample sizes of 4, 5, and 6, the $\bar{X}$ chart is not particularly effective in detecting a small shifts—say, those of the order of 1.5 σ or less—on the first sample following the shift. For example, if the shift is 1.0 σ and $n = 5$. then from Fig. 3.27, we have $\beta = 0.75$, approximately. Thus, the probability that the shift will be detected on the first sample is only $1 - \beta = 0.25$. However, the probability that the shift is detected on the second sample is $\beta(1 - \beta)$ *i.e.* 0.75(0.25) *i.e* 0.19, whereas the probability that it is detected on the third sample is $\beta^2(1 - \beta) = (0.75)^2 (0.25) = 0.14$. Thus, the probability that the shift will be detected on the rth subsequent sample is simply $(1 - \beta)$ times the probability of not detecting the shift on each of the initial $(r - 1)$ samples, or

$$\beta^{r-1}(1 - \beta)$$

In general, the expected number of samples taken (or the points plotted on the $\bar{X}$ chart) before the shift is detected is just the ***average run length (ARL)***, or

$$ARL = \sum_{r=1}^{\infty} r\beta^{r-1}(1 - \beta) = \frac{1}{1 - \beta} \quad ...(3.13)$$

Therefore, in our example, using Eq. (3.10), we have

$$ARL = \frac{1}{1 - \beta} = \frac{1}{0.25} = 4$$

In other words, the expected number of samples taken to detect a shift of 1.0σ with $n = 5$ is four.

The above discussion provides a supportive argument for the use of small sample sizes on the $\bar{X}$ chart. Even though small sample sizes often result in a relatively large β-risk, because samples are collected and tested periodically, there is a very good chance that the shift will be detected reasonably quickly, although perhaps not on the first sample following the shift.

3.14 THE AVERAGE RUN LENGTH (ARL) FOR THE $\bar{X}$ CHART

The average run length (*ARL*) is the average number of points that must be plotted before a point indicates an out of control situation. For any Shewhart control chart, the *ARL* can be calculated easily using Eqs. (3.11) and (3.13).

$$ARL = \frac{1}{P \text{ (one point falls out of control)}} \quad ...(3.14)$$

where P is the probability that any point the exceeds the control limits. The Eq. (3.11) can be used to evaluate the performance of the control chart.

To illustrate for the $\bar{X}$ chart with 3-sigma limits, $P = 0.0027$ is the probability that a single point falls outside the control limits when the process is in control. Therefore the average run length of the $\bar{X}$ chart when the process is in control (called ARL_0) is

$$ARL_0 = \frac{1}{P} = \frac{1}{0.0027} = 370$$

That is, even if the process remains in control, an out-of-control signal will be generated every 370 samples, on the average. Now in terms of α and β errors,

$$ARL_0 = \frac{1}{\alpha} \quad \text{(for the in-control process), and} \quad ...(3.15)$$

$$ARL_1 = \frac{1}{1 - \beta} \quad \text{(for the out–control process).} \quad ...(3.16)$$

Since it is relatively easy to develop a general expression for β for the $\bar{X}$ control chart to detect a shift in the average of $k\sigma$ (see equation 3.12), then it is not difficult to construct a set of *ARL* curves for the $\bar{X}$ chart. Figure 3.28 presents these *ARL* curves for sample sizes of n

= 1, 2, 3, 4, 5, 7, 9 and 16 for the $\bar{X}$ chart, where the *ARL* is in terms of the expected number of *samples* taken in order to detect the shift. To illustrate the use of Fig. 3.28, note that if we wish to detect a shift of 1.5 σ using a sample size of n = 3, then the average number of samples required will be ARL_1 = 3. Note also that we could reduce the ARL_1 to approximately 1 if we increased the sample size to n = 16.

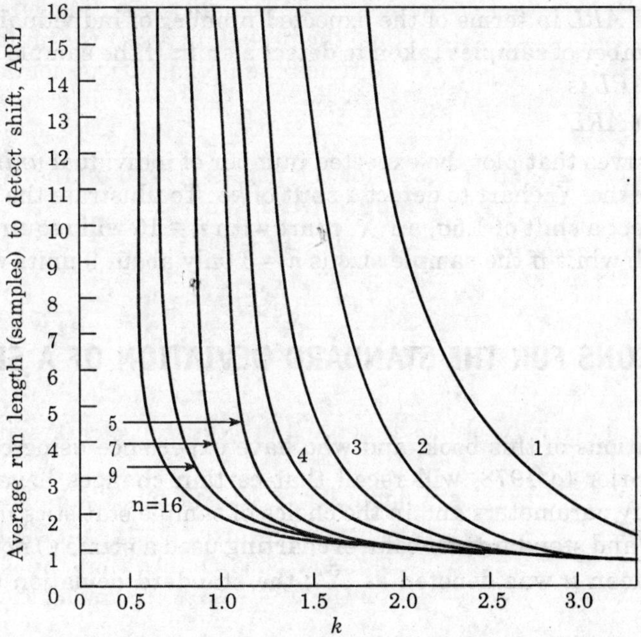

FIGURE 3.28: Average run length (samples) for the $\bar{X}$ chart with 3-sigma limits, where the process mean shifts by kσ.

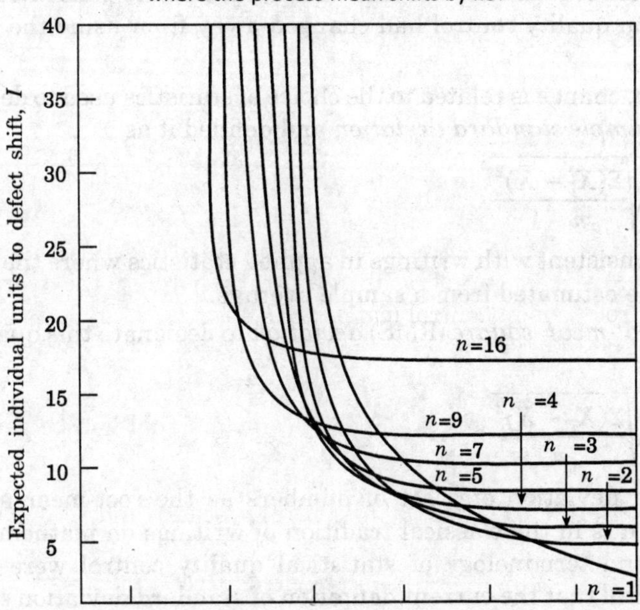

FIGURE 3.29: Average run length (individual units) for the $\bar{X}$ chart with 3-sigma limits, where the process mean shifts by kσ.

Two other performance measures based on ARL are sometimes of interest. The **average time to signal** is the number of time periods that occur until a signal is generated on the control chart. If samples are taken at equally spaced intervals of time h, then the average time to signal (or ATS) is

$$ATS = ARL\ h \qquad \text{...(3.14)}$$

It may be useful to express the ARL in terms of the expected number of individual units sampled [say I] rather than the number of samples taken to detect a shift. If the sample size is n, the relationship between I and ARL is

$$I = n\ ARL \qquad \text{...(3.15)}$$

Figure 3.29 presents a set of curves that plot the expected number of individual *units* say, I that must be sampled in order for the $\bar{X}$ chart to detect a shift of $k\sigma$. To illustrate the use of the curve, note that in order to detect a shift of 1.5σ, an $\bar{X}$ chart with $n = 16$ will require that approximately 16 units be sampled, while if the sample size is $n = 3$ only about 9 units will be required, on the average.

3.15 CONFLICTING EXPRESSIONS FOR THE STANDARD DEVIATION OF A SET OF NUMBERS

Persons familiar with previous editions of this book, and who have experience using control charts for variables dating back prior to 1978, will recall that certain changes have been made in the symbols used to identify parameters and in the choice of sample statistics used to describe dispersion. Early writings and standards for control charting used a prime (′) notation to denote parameters. Thus the mean μ was denoted as $\bar{X}'$; the standard deviation σ was denoted as σ'.

The change was consistent with changes instituted by ASQC and ANSI beginning in 1978. However, the latest revision of the ASTM manual STP 15D (1976) retains the prime notation. By 1990, most books and articles on quality control had changed away from using the prime notation.

The second, and more confusing, change is related to the choice of statistics used to describe dispersion. We have named s the *sample standard deviation* and defined it as

$$s = \sqrt{\frac{\Sigma(X_i - \bar{X})^2}{n-1}}$$

This name and definition are consistent with writings in applied statistics where the mean of an unknown distribution must be estimated from a sample average.

In early editions we used the *root-mean-square* (RMS) *deviation* to designate this quantity, where

$$\sigma_{RMS} = \sqrt{\frac{\Sigma(X_i - \bar{X})^2}{n}}$$

The definition of the standard deviation of a set of numbers as the root-mean-square deviation from the arithmetic mean is in the classical tradition of writings on mathematical statistics. When the techniques and terminology of statistical quality control were being developed in the 1920s, it was natural that the current definition of standard deviation should be used. Moreover, because an estimate of σ is so important in judging process capability, and because σ_{RMS} and s both give biased estimates of σ, neither has any mathematical advantage over the other.

This usage of σ_{RMS} was introduced into the "ASTM Manual on Presentation of Data" (STP 15 A), along with tables of factors to be used in control charting, in 1937 and adopted in 1941 in the American War Standards on Quality Control. The original (1951) version of ASQC Standard A 1, "Definitions and Symbols for Control Charts," followed suit and adopted the definitions and tables of the ASTM Manual. In the first revision of the ASQC Standard, s was defined as the sample standard deviation and was recommended to replace σ_{RMS}. The 1976 revision of the ASTM Manual (STP 15 D) followed the ASQC lead.

An unbiased estimator of obtained from *s* was given as

$$\hat{\sigma} = \frac{\bar{s}}{c_4}$$

Since $$\sigma_{RMS} = \sqrt{\frac{(n-1)}{n}}\,s; \qquad \sigma_{RMS} = \sqrt{\frac{n-1}{n}}\,\bar{s}$$

Thus $$\hat{\sigma} = \frac{\sigma_{RMS}}{c_4\sqrt{(n-1)/n}}$$

The σ_{RMS} symbol was used in the last edition of this book. In earlier editions, and in most quality control literature, σ was the symbol used. The RMS subscript was not used. Thus σ was defined as the root-mean-square statistic and, after correction, was used to estimate the parameter σ′. Tables of factors, like those in App. 1, were used to calculate control limits and estimate dispersion.

SOLVED QUESTIONS

Q. 3.1 : *State whether the following statements are TRUE (T) or FALSE (F).*

(*i*) Outliers (points outside the control limits) can sometimes be a result of inherent variation.

(*ii*) The grand mean $\bar{X}$, captures more information than the individual sample means.

(*iii*) In a control chart *CL* denotes either of the two control limits.

(*iv*) Controlling variability is an essential aspect of maintaining quality.

(*v*) *R*-charts are used to monitor the level of process output.

(*vi*) After the causes of outliers have been identified, those points should be discarded and the control chart should be redone.

(*vii*) The lower limit on *R*-chart is always zero.

(*viii*) A sample of 4 or 5 is sufficient to ensure reasonable to the normality even in non normal population.

(*ix*) The use of 3-sigma control limits on $\bar{X}$ Chart used produce an α risk of 0.0027.

(*x*) With 3-sigma limits on *R*-Chart, α risk of 0.0027.

Ans: (*i*) (T) (*ii*) (T) (*iii*) (F) (*iv*) (T) (*v*) (F) (*vi*) (T) (*vii*) (F) (*viii*) (T) (*ix*) (T) (*x*) (F)

Q. 3.2 : *Fill in the blanks appropriate technically correct word.*

(*i*) Observations falling beyond the ________ are known as outliers.

(ii) ________ are used in statistical process control to monitor the output of a product or service and see whether it is meeting standards.

(iii) The use of 3-sigma limits as an $\bar{X}$-chart will produce an α risk of ________.

(iv) ________ is the enemy of quality.

(v) Nonrandom patterns in control charts indicate the presence of ________ variation.

Ans: (i) Control limits, (ii) Control charts, (iii) 0.0027, (iv) Variability, (v) Systematic (assignable, special cause)

Q. 3.3: *In the following statements advice the technically correct statement*

(i) You look at a process and note that the chart for averages has been in control. If the range suddenly and significantly increases, the mean will

(a) always increase (b) stay the same (c) always decrease
(d) occasionally show out of control of either limit (e) none of the above.

(ii) On an $\bar{X}$ -chart, we always show

(a) specification limits (b) natural tolerance limits
(c) rejection limits (d) control limits

(iii) $\bar{X}$-chart is used alone when

(a) dispersion is in control (b) management does not need other charts
(c) $\bar{X}$ values are out of control (d) when sample size is 4.

(iv) Control limits are

(a) set by the designers of the items being produced
(b) set by the users of items produced
(c) set by the standards institutions
(d) are based on past and current data and accepted formulae.

(v) $\bar{X}$–chart alone are used when

(a) it is difficult to calculate sample standard deviation
(b) sample range is not a representative measure of dispersion
(c) lack of control is seen to be due to causes that affect standard deviation
(d) lack of control is because of factors affecting $\bar{X}$ only.

(vi) Which of the following is ***not*** a control chart for variables.

(a) $\bar{X}$ -Chart (b) σ-chart
(c) R-chart (d) Flow chart

Ans: (i) (d); (ii) (d); (iii) (a); (iv) (d); (v) (d); (vi) (d).

Q. 3.4: *Ray Mandal reproduces antique chairs. His apprentices turn spindles for the chair backs on manual lathes. The beads on the spindles are to have average diameters of $\frac{7}{8}$ inch at their widest points. Ray monitors the apprentices' work with control charts. Which of the following patterns Fig. 3.30 (a) and (b) is he likely to see on the R chart for a new apprentices ? Explain.*

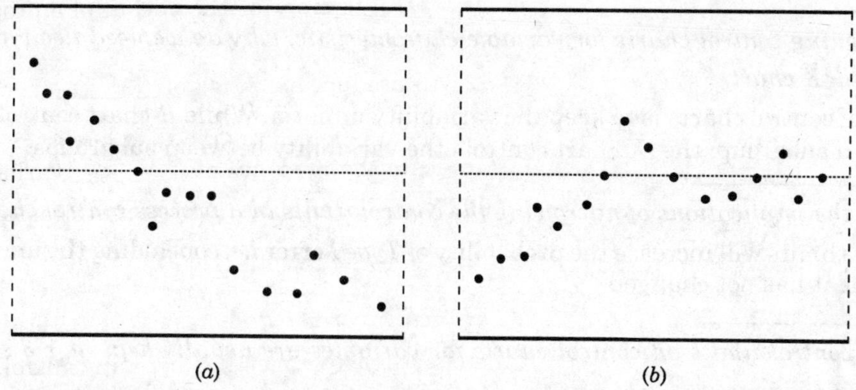

FIGURE 3.30

Ans: We would expect the spindles produced by a new apprentices to show a relatively large variability in diameters initially, with this variability decreasing as the apprentices becomes more experienced. Pattern (*a*) conforms to this expectation.

Q. 3.5: *Why sample size in* $\overline{X}$*-charts and R-charts be more than one?*

Ans: The sample size must be greater than 1 to distinguish between accuracy and precision, and minimum 4, unless the process parameter is known to be normally distributed.

Q. 3.6: *What are the pros and cons of increasing sample size for an X-chart ?*

Ans:
1. As the sample size *i.e., n* increases, the control limits become closer to the process mean (*i.e.,* $\overline{X}$ or μ). This makes the control chart more sensitive to the detection of small variation in the process average.
2. As the sample size increases, the inspection costs per sample may increase. One should question whether the greater sensitivity justifies any increases in cost.
3. The sample size should not exceed 12, if the range is to be used to measure process variability. With larger samples the resulting mean range (i.e. $\overline{R}$) does not give a good estimate of the standard deviation and s charts should be used.

Q. 3.7: *In* $\overline{X}$*-charts how often the samples are taken ?*

Ans: No general rules for the frequency of sample taking exist, but frequency is clearly related to the inherent period of process stability.

Q. 3.8: *What is the main purpose of control charts. What are the additional informations these charts can provide ?*

Ans: The main purpose of the control charts is to indicate changes in quality (i.e. information of the variability) of a manufacturing process and help to identify assignable causes of variation so that same are attended to and process readjusted before large quantities of scrap are generated. Additionally they can be useful for:

Showing the inherent capabilities of a process for producing components of a particular accuracy, *i.e.,* they give a profile of the inherent accuracy of a machine or process.

Recording the degree of accuracy of incoming materials which are subject to 'acceptance sampling'.

Allowing a feed-back of information which can be used for planning and control purposes. This information can be used to help improve product quality and reduce production costs.

Q. 3.9: *When designing control charts for variable characteristic, why do we need two types of charts (R chart and $\bar{X}$ chart) ?*

Ans: The purpose of control charts is to keep the variability uniform. While *R*-chart controls the variability within a subgroup, the $\bar{X}$ chart controls the variability between subgroups.

Q. 3.10: *What are the implications of narrowing the control limits in a process control chart ?*

Ans: Narrowing the limits will increase the probability of *Type I* error *i.e.* concluding the universe has changed, while it has not changed.

Q. 3.11: *Why the control limits on control charts for variables are usually kept at ± 3 sigma away from μ ?*

Ans: Keeping the limits are ± 3 sigma away from the mean μ will strike a rational balance between *Type I* and *Type II* errors.

Q. 3.12: *Why control charts are sometimes associated with quality assurance and acceptance sampling as quality control ?*

Ans: Sampling is not concerned with controlling the quality of parts or products during the manufacturing operations. It is the use of control charts for variables that indicates the presence of assignable causes and steps may be taken to *prevent* that production of nonconforming and substandard items. Hence this can be regarded as quality *assurance function*, as opposed to the *quality control* exercised by acceptance sampling as it is after the product is made.

Q. 3.13: *Why a determining whether the cause of a variation is a "common" (also called usual or chance) cause or an "assignable" (also called unusual or special) cause important?*

Ans: Common variations, which are likely to occur in a random manner and about which comparatively little can be done. Assignable variations, which occur less frequently and can normally be traced to same "external" cause, such as tool wear, faulty materials etc. "Common" variations are normally of a lesser magnitude than "assignable" variations and, since they result from some inherent process variability, they occur randomly and can be described by the normal probability distribution. Quality controllers define *limits* within which variations are acceptable and beyond which they are either unacceptable, or necessitate same examination. Such limits are called *control limits*. For example, for a normal probability distribution, 99.73% of all chance or usual variations would be expected to occur within limits placed at 3 ± sigma from the mean value of the variable. Therefore, any variation occurring beyond such limits would, very likely, have resulted from some other unusual or assignable cause and would merit some investigation.

Q. 3.14: *(a) What is the significance of ARL of an X-chart ?*

(b) Clearly state the meaning of ARL.

Ans: (*a*) *ARL* of an $\bar{X}$-chart indicates the performance or power of the chart in detecting changes.

(*b*) The ARL (abbreviation for Average Run Length) is simply a statement of how many sample points, on average will be plotted on the chart before specific change is detected.

Q. 3.15: *What is meant by a 'significant change' to a process ?*

Ans: The change occurred more frequently than would have been expected on a statistical basis.

Q. 3.16: *Why is statistical process control important ?*

Ans: Because it avoids unnecessary adjustments to the process.

Q. 3.17: *What distribution is used for variable control charts ?*

Ans: The normal distribution.

Q. 3.18: *If the range chart goes out of control, what can this signify ?*

Ans: A fundamental problem, with the process itself, which will not be curable by a 'quick fix'.

Q. 3.19: *Why a plot of sample means ($\overline{X}$) preferable to a plot of individuals (X) ?*

Ans: Because regardless of the shape of the population, the means of samples ($\overline{X}$) tend towards normal distribution.

Q. 3.20: *What is indicated by relative capability ?*

Ans: It enables us to provide an index indicating how well a process should be able to meet the specification tolerance.

Q. 3.21: *A control chart is established with limits of ± 2 standard errors (i.e. ± 2-sigma limits), for use in monitoring samples of size n = 20. Assume the process is in control.*

(a) Would you expect many individual values to lie outside these limits.

(b) How likely would be sample mean fall outside the control limits.

(c) What kind of error would be committed in erroneously concluding that the process is out of control.

Ans: (*a*) Yes, The control limits are set to control the mean values, not individual values.

(*b*) Assuming roughly a normal distribution, about 95.46 percent of the sample means are within $\overline{\overline{X}} \pm 2\sigma_{\overline{X}}$, so that about 4.54 percent of the sample means would lie outside.

(*c*) Type *I* would be committed *i.e.* concluding the process as out of control when really it is not.

Q. 3.22: *What are the functions of SPC charts ?*

Ans: Statistical process control charts are useful for measuring the current quality generated by the process and for detecting whether the process has changed to the deteriment of quality. The *R*-charts are used to monitor process variability, $\overline{X}$ and *p*-charts identify abnormal variations in the process average. The presence of abnormal variation triggers a reason for assignable causes.

Q. 3.23: *What are the design parameters of SPC charts ?*

Ans: Subgroups or sample size and Control limits

Q. 3.24: *Account for the following procedures in control chart analysis, stating clearly any assumption involved :*

(a) A sample of size 5 is ordinarily used in control chart,

(b) The range is used instead of standard deviation, and

(c) The three sigma limits are used for control limits instead of exact probability, whatever be the type of quality characteristics.

Ans: (*a*) Ease of calculation of process mean etc.

(*b*) It is easier to compute range rather than standard deviation. Also with smaller sample size, range is preferred.

(*c*) Using of 3-sigma limits on control charts gives economic balance between Type-*I* and Type-*II* errors.

Q. 3.25: *What is Motorola Corporation's six sigma quality programme ?*

Ans: This programme popularized by Motorola Corporation has a goal of reducing the process variation such that the spread between specification limits is 12 σ and the process mean is centered on exactly mid-way the specifications. This means that the specification limits are six sigma from the mean. Six sigma translates into a $C_{pk} = 2$.

Q. 3.26: *Explain how a process can be in statistical control but still produce bad or unacceptable products.*

Ans: If the process is centered at μ, the natural variation is from $\mu + 3\sigma$ to $\mu - 3\sigma$. Hence total spread is 6σ. If the specification limits U and L are such that $U - L$ is $< 6\ \sigma$, some product is bound to be beyond tolerance limits as the process is not capable of meeting these specifications.

Q. 3.27: *Why frequent adjustment of process is not recommended ?*

Ans: Excessive adjustment of process based on individual tests or measurements causes overall increase in variability.

Q. 3.28: *Describe a control chart for variable briefly.*

Ans: • A control chart is a time-ordered values plot of sample statistic that helps to detect assignable causes of variation in a process. It monitor the performance of a process over time, recognize and control variation in a process.

• A control chart may indicate at out-of-control condition when one or more points fall beyond the control limits, or when the plotted points exhibit some non-random patterns of behaviour. A control chart that has not triggered any out of control condition is considered stable and operating in a state of statistical control. The variation depicted on the chart is due to common-cause variation.

Q. 3.29: *Figure 3.31 shows a control chart for variable. Is the process under control? Why or why not?*

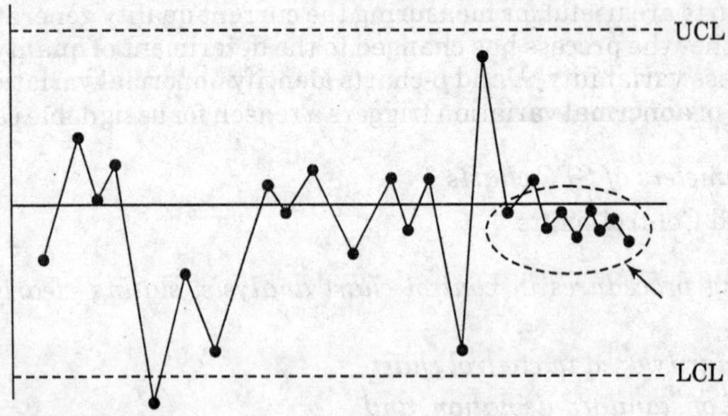

FIGURE 3.31

Ans: The control chart shows that process is out of control. There is very strong evidence for the same as (*i*) one point lies below LCL_X and (*ii*) seven consecutive points all lie on one side of the mean. This is known the 'Rule of seven' and is an assignable cause.

Q. 3.30: *Fig. 3.32 (a) to (d) shows the control charts for variable. What are your comments on there charts?*

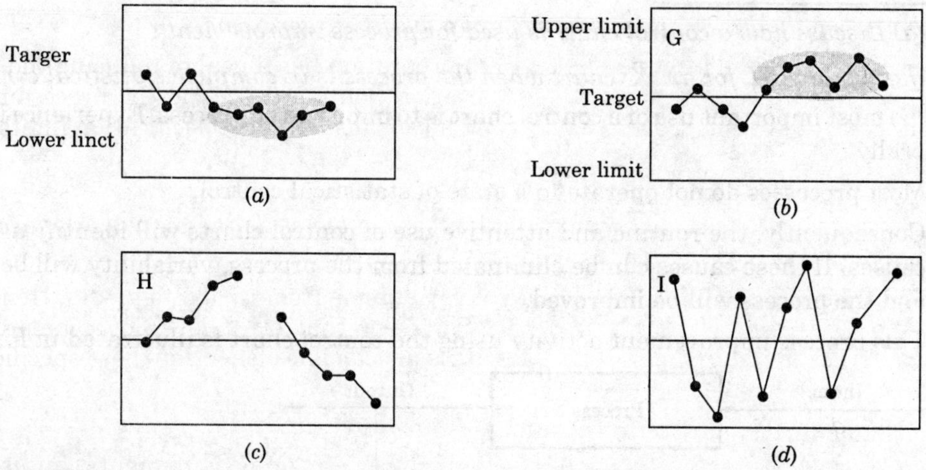

FIGURE 3.32

Ans: All the charts indicate out of control situation for the reasons given below:

Chart (*a* & *b*): *Six to one side of target.* While being well within the control limits, the results are suggesting that the process needs adjustment. Again, the reason for the drift should be established. The number on one side that will trigger investigation will depend on experience with the process.

Chart (*c*): *Trends.* Clear trends, which can be confirmed by collecting more date immediately, show that the output is likely to move out of range shortly. Immediate adjustment may be required. Again, the cause of the pattern should be sought.

Chart (*d*): *Erratic behaviour.* This may be the expected pattern for the process and all is well. Yet , it does suggest that the machine is not good enough to operate within the chosen limits. It would be very difficult to control.

Q. 3.31: *(a) State very briefly, what is meant by:*

(i) a process in statistical control

(ii) a process out of control ?

(b) What is the goal of statistical process control.

(c) State at least five reasons for popularity of control charts.

Ans: (*a*) (*i*) When a process is operating with only chance (or common) causes of variation it is said to be in statistical control.

(*ii*) When a process is operating in the presence of assignable (or special) causes it is said to be out of control.

(*b*) The eventual goal of statistical process control is the elimination of variability in the process. It may not be possible to completely eliminate variability, but the control chart is an effective tool in reducing the variability as much as possible.

(*c*) Control charts are popular for the following reasons :

1. Control charts are proven technique for improving productivity.
2. Control charts are effective in defect (nonconformity) prevention
3. Control charts prevent unnecessary process adjustment
4. Control charts provide diagnostic information
5. Control charts provide information about process capability.

Q. 3.32: *(a) Discuss how a control chart is used for process improvement ?*

(b) What is the ARL for an $\overline{X}$ chart when the process is in complete statistical control ?

Ans: (*a*) The most important use of a control chart is to improve the process. Experience indicates that generally :

1. Most processes do not operate in a state of statistical control.
2. Consequently, the routine and attentive use of control charts will identify assignable causes. If these causes can be eliminated from the process, variability will be reduced and the process will be improved.

   This process improvement activity using the control chart is illustrated in Fig. 3.33.

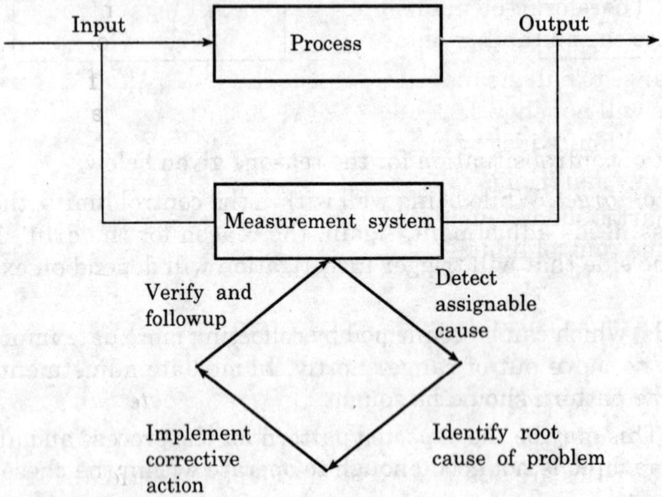

FIGURE 3.33 Process improvement using the control chart

3. The control chart will only detect assignable causes. Management, operator, and engineering action will usually be necessary to eliminate the assignable causes. In identifying and eliminating assignable causes, it is important to find the underlying root cause of the problem and to attack it. A cosmetic solution will not result in any real, long-term process improvement. Developing an effective system for corrective action is an essential SPC implementation.

We may also use the control chart as an *estimating device*. That is, from a control chart that exhibits statistical control, we may estimate certain process parameters, such as the mean, standard deviation, fraction nonconforming or fallout, and so forth. These estimates may then be used to determine the *capability* of the process to produce acceptable products. Such *process-capability studies* have considerable impact on many management decision problems that occur over the product cycle, including make or buy decisions, plant and process improvement that reduce process variability, and contractual agreements with customers or vendors regarding product quality.

(*b*) The *ARL* (average run length) designated as ARL_0 of the $\overline{X}$ chart when the process is in control is

$$ARL_0 = \frac{1}{P} = \frac{1}{0.0027} = 370$$

That is, even if the process remains in control, an out-of-control signal will be generated every 370 samples, on the average.

Q. 3.33: *(a) One process has eight variables of known importance. Another process has fifteen variables of known importance. Is the control chart equally appropriate for these two processes ?*

(b) A technical change in a process has cut the average range on the control chart in half. Does this mean that the chart for averages will now show lack of control if it previously showed control ? Why or why not ?

(c) A machine is producing a product that shows control on the control chart. A new source of raw material fed into the machine is substituted for the regular sources. What are the two possible indications of this change on the control chart ?

Ans: (*a*) In most manufacturing operations the objective is to make many pieces at satisfactory quality level, all the pieces being essentially alike. This is the very thing the quality control chart is designed to measure. Therefore, the number of variables in the manufacturing process is of no concern with respect to the suitability of the quality control chart for this purpose.

(*b*) Cutting the average range to half means reduced variability to one half. In this situation, the control chart for averages will not show lack of control because the probability that a point will fall outside the new control limits just by chance is the same as it was before.

(*c*) When a new source of raw material is substituted for the regular source, the one possible indication of this on the $\bar{X}$ chart is sudden jumps in process level and the other is that subgroup average fall near or outside the control limits.

Q. 3.34: *(a) Name a few (at least five) variable quality characteristics which are suitable for $\bar{X}$ and R charts.*

(b) Discuss briefly the method of measurement of any quality characteristic to be controlled by $\bar{X}$ and R charts.

Ans: (*a*) Many quality characteristics are suitable for $\bar{X}$ and R charts. A few of these are :

1. Length
2. Tensile strength
3. Resistance
4. Filled weight (for containers)
5. Hardness
6. Percentage of impurities in chemical solutions.

(*b*) Quality control charts for variables reflect differences in item measurements on a single quality variable. Obviously, such measurements are made on a continuous scale of measurement. Hence, the measuring instrument used must be capable of direct measurement of such a quality variable on a continuous scale to the required degree of fineness.

Q. 3.35: *Is it essential that the process be 'normal' if it is to be controlled by control charts for variables ?*

Ans: The whole theory of control charts for variables (intended to control such measurable quality characteristics) rests upon the assumption that the production process (universe) has a stable pattern. A nonnormal process may have a stable variation pattern. For a given nonnormal process, this means that the pattern of variation must be identified and the probabilities of given specific variations computed. This requires considerable time and effort. Moreover, for any other nonnormal process, the same procedure for measuring the variation pattern must be re-enacted. This is costly and undesirable. Nevertheless, it can be done so ; process normalcy is not absolutely required. However, if a process is normal, it has a stable variation pattern, with known tabled probabilities for specific amounts of variation. Every normal distribution has the same variation pattern. Hence, the laborious, costly, time-consuming job of measuring the variation pattern is eliminated in advance if the process distribution can be shown to be normal. Thus, having a normal process is vastly preferable to having a nonnormal process Consequently, process normalcy should be investigated before doing anything else in undertaking to indicate the use of variables quality control charts in a factory situations.

Q. 3.36: *Discuss briefly the advantages gained in selecting a subgroup of 4 while working on control chart for variables. Is it always necessary to make a sample of 4 or 5 ?*

Ans: The sample size may be anything from 2 to upwards. If it is possible, it is generally desirable to avoid the sample size of 2 or 3. If perchance it is essential to take a sample of two or three items, serious considerations should be given to grouping two consecutive such samples to form a subgroup of four or six. One disadvantage connected with the subgrouping of two or three items is the frequent computation of group averages and ranges. The other disadvantage is that if the universe is markedly non-normal, the distribution of group average of two's or three's will also be definitely non-normal, whereas for group sizes of four or more the distribution of group average is essentially normal, virtually without regard to the shape of the parent distribution. Thus for group sizes of four or more, the 3-sigma limits for averages are valid even though parent population is definitely nonnormal.

One advantage in using a sample of four instead of some larger number is that points are plotted more frequently and indication of lack of control thereby caught more quickly. But this is partly offset by the fact that smaller groups sizes are less sensitive to small shifts in process levels than are larger groups because the variability of group average varies inversely as the square root of group size.

Another advantage is that a small subgroup size will be more likely to contain only inherent variability than a larger subgroup. Still another is that where the individuals items are approximately normally distributed and it is desired to check them, the control limits for individuals can be very easily computed since they are exactly twice as far from the central line as the control limits for average of four.

It is not always necessary to take a sample of 4 or 5. The selection of the sample size depends upon the following consideration.

- A sample of 4 or 5 is close to optimum if the shifts to be detected are relatively large e.g., if the assignable causes produce a shift of 2σ or more. But to detect a smaller shift, a sample of 15 or 16 is more economical.
- When the shifts in the process average results in high rate of loss, i.e., high relative to the cost of inspection, it is better to take a smaller sample 4 or 5 frequently than a large sample less frequently.
- When the cost of inspection is high, economy results in taking a sample of 12 or more at relatively long intervals with narrow control limits.

Q. 3.37: *What factors should be taken into consideration by a firm when determining (a) the sample size, (b) the manner in which items should be selected for inclusion in the sample, (c) the frequency of sampling, and (d) the operations to be controlled by control charts for variables.*

Ans: (*a*) *The sample size.* It has been observed that the nature of most populations generated by manufacturing processes is such that a minimum sample size of 4 will probably be required to obtain an approximately normal distribution of sample averages. But the firm must make a decision concerning whether the sample size in a given case should be this minimum number or something greater.

It is known that the larger the sample size, the less likely it is that an error will be made when passing judgement on the universe on the basis of the characteristics of the sample. However,as the sample size is increased, the higher will be the cost of sampling, particularly if destructive testing is involved. Consequently the one factor encourages the firm to adhere to large sample size and the other to smaller ones. Hence a judicious balance must be struck between the two. Since the magnitudes of the costs of sampling are often very difficult to estimate the sample size is usually selected on the basis of judgement, a very common practice in industry is to take samples of size 5.

(*b*) Manner of items selection for a sample. The samples should be random, but it is also important that all the items included in the sample be drawn from the same universe. The need for this becomes apparent when the very purpose of drawing a sample is fully understood. When a sample is taken its characteristics are used as a basis of inferring the characteristics of the universe from which it comes. If one sample comes from one universe and a second from another, the probability of detecting a difference between the two universe relatively is high. But if one sample contains items from one universe but the second sample contains items from both universes, the probability of detecting a difference between the two universes is somewhat less. The probability is still smaller if one sample contains items from both universes and a second sample contains items from both universes. Since it is desired that the detection of a change in the population to be maximum, it is necessary that the samples taken should contain items from a single universe.

(*c*) Frequency of sampling. The frequency of sampling, though depends upon the quality control Engineer, yet in general the frequency depends on unit processing times and how well the operation is going. In a typical firm, at the time of control charts have been established, the analyst may take a sample every hour if unit processing times permit this. However, if the process remains in control for two or three days the frequency may be reduced to one every three or four hours. If the process continues in control for a period of a few weeks, the frequency may be reduced still further. On the other hand., if difficulties are encountered in keeping the process in control, more frequent samples are taken. But above all the cost of sampling and difficulties encountered in will decide the frequency of sampling.

(*d*) The operations to be controlled by control charts. The control charts for variables i.e. $\bar{X}$ and R charts, though applicable to any operation that is generating a substantial amount of product that must be reworked or scrapped and if the method of inspection yields a measure for the variable involved. If little or no difficulty is experienced in meeting specifications at a particular work station there will be no good reason for maintaining control charts for this operation.

Therefore these charts should be introduced only where the conditions warrant. Once the causes of troublesome operations are indicated by charts and investigated thoroughly and corrective action taken, it is not unusual to discontinue these charts. Sometimes it is found that care must be taken to keep the universe average in control, whereas the dispersion never is a matter for concern. In those cases, the $\bar{X}$ chart is maintained, but the R chart is discontinued. Hence in brief, no specific rules can be established and adhered to.

Q. 3.38: *(a) When the control are first initiated, it is usual to take 25 subgroups of size 5. Explain the reasons for such a practice.*

(b) Suppose you do not find the process in control after first 25 subgroups, what is your decision regarding the values of control limits ?

Ans: (*a*) The practice of taking 25 subgroups of size five on the first initiation of control charts is mainly from the point of view of reliability of central lines and control limits for further use of these charts.

Since the probability of crossing either of the 3-sigma $UCL_{\bar{X}}$ or $LCL_{\bar{X}}$ of an $\bar{X}$ chart, in random sampling of a normal universe, is 0.00135, the probability of obtaining an $\bar{X}$ falling on either control limit in consecutive samples is given by the binomial or repeated trial theorem, of elementary probability. With $n > 7$, the lower control limit of the $\bar{R}$ chart cannot be crossed in such sampling, the probability of crossing UCL_R, with $n = 5$, is 0.0049. Hence in the same way as for the $\bar{X}$ chart, the probability of obtaining an R beyond UCL_R is obtained for any m consecutive samples. These are respectively probabilities of k (k any integer) points out of m, out of control.

For $m = 25$, $n = 5$ the probability for the controlled process of obtaining no points out of control is 0.8270, with chance governing the random sampling. For none on the $\bar{X}$ chart and one on the R chart, out of control, the probability is 0.0018. For one point out of control on $\bar{X}$ chart and none on the R chart, the probability is 0.0560. For all other possible paired numbers of points out of control on $\bar{X}$ and R charts, with m = 25, n = 5, the probabilities are respectively all less than 0.01.

Hence, when initiating $\bar{X}$ and R charts for the first time, 25 subgroups of 5 items each sampled at random from a normal process and the process in control if, and only if, the maximum number of points out of control on both charts combined is one. Even one point out of control on each chart is too many.

This is important because the 25 subgroups of 5 items each must find the process in control for the resulting, calculated central line and control limit values to be reliable.

(*b*) If the process is not so found in control when samples as in (*a*), then the safe thing to do is to look for existent assignable causes and eliminate them when found, following this by another set of 25 random subgroups as before, to see if the process control an reliable central line and control limit values may then be obtained. Only when such sampling shows the process in control may one depend on the control limits computed in continuing the use of the control charts as judge of process quality.

Q. 3.39: *(a) Does an ostensibly out-of-control process always denote quality trouble ? If so, what does this mean ? If not, what alternative exists, and what action should then follow ?*

(b) Why should the control limits on $\bar{X}$ and R charts be regularly reviewed ?

Ans: (*a*) An ostensibly out-of-control process always does not denote quality trouble. Instead of actual quality trouble, the point out-of-control may simply be the result of the use of nonrandom samples or of worn out-of-adjustments inspection instruments. Or, the inspector may have misunderstood the inspection standards, or have applied them in a lax, inaccurate manner. He may also have been careless or dishonest. Or, he may have made errors in reading or recording measurements or in computing or plotting $\bar{X}$ and R values. Finally, the operator may have altered the set-up of the process or machine, made originally by an expert set-up man, believing it had gone out of adjustment when actually it was not the case. Such possibilities must be considered along with the possibility of real quality trouble whenever a control chart indicates that a process is out of control.

(*b*) As long as process remains in control according to the control charts, the central line values on them remain unchanged in value and may be continued in force along with the original control limits. Nevertheless, control limits and central line values should be regularly reviewed for two reasons :

1. Adding more subgroup data may yield more nearly accurate control limits.
2. Process quality levels and variation pattern may change as time goes on, which would require adjustment of control limits and central line values.

The frequency of review of control limits and central line values depends upon many factors. However, in industry today a review is common after every fifty subgroups, although it may be done only once each month.

Q. 3.40: *With respect to an $\bar{X}$-chart, is it possible to go out of control limits and get back in without doing anything to the process.*

Ans: Quality level shifts that are of small magnitude or of short duration can readily occur without immediately revealing themselves. Shifts may be gradual or sudden, uniformly in one direction or erratic, controlled or uncontrolled. Any combination of these conditions may occur with any degree of intensity. Shifts that are of slight magnitude but long duration may result in only an occasional point falling out of control limits. Thus, if the manufacturer makes no deliberate change in the process during this time, it appears to him that the process has gone out of control and back in without any effort on his part. The truth is that the process has probably not been in control at the previous level or with the same magnitude of inherent variability as previously at any time during the period involved.

The greater the shift that occurs, the greater will be the likelihood of a point falling outside control limits, and more serious the situation will be. Any point that falls outside control limits should be regarded as a danger signal, and every effort made (within economically practicable limits) to determine the reasons for the indication of lack of control. Only very rarely do indication of lack of control occur without an assignable cause.

Q. 3.41: *The control limits have been revised and now a point is outside limits, whereas formerly it would have been within limits. Why is this point not considered a satisfactory condition ?*

Ans: Each plotted point on the control chart tells a most eloquent story in relation to its own control limits. Thus two points widely separated on the chart may have the same numerical value, but different meanings. Suppose the first of these points falls within control limits. We can assume from this fact only that the product is continuing to be made in a controlled manner. Before the second point with which we are concerned occurs, many other points are accumulated which reveal that control has been achieved at a higher level. When the second point occurs it may now fall below the new lower control limit. It signifies that control is probably not being maintained at the new level. Any indication of lack of control must always be regarded as a danger signal regardless of when or where the indication occurs. In addition to our interest in the point's numerical value, we are also interested in its position relative to the control limits which apply to it.

Q. 3.42: *Why is going above the $UCL_{\bar{X}}$ undesirable when working to a specification minimum ? Is this not a great deal better than can be expected ?*

Ans: If the point that goes above the $UCL_{\bar{X}}$ is preceded by a gradual upward trend of the group averages in what appears to be a controlled manner, there is little likelihood of nonconforming material being produced. If, however, a point suddenly jumps out of the $UCL_{\bar{X}}$ without any fore-warning, it probably represent a condition of lack of control. When the manufacturing process is out of control, almost anything can happen, including a sudden drop in quality. Frequently, such high points are followed almost immediately by test failures. While a high level of quality is desirable, it is also very important that control be maintained. Without control we cannot expect to have a uniform product.

Q. 3.43: *If points of averages are permitted to go above their* $UCL_{\bar{X}}$ *to encourage shifts to higher levels, why are not points for ranges permitted to go above their* UCL_R *?*

Ans: The function of the averages is to reveal the level on which the process is operating. The function of the ranges is to reveal the amount of variability inherent in the process. The ranges do this independently of the process quality level and reveal nothing about this quantitative value. The average range $\bar{R}$, however, does enable us to establish the 3 sigma control limits an $\bar{X}$ chart within which virtually all the group averages should fall. These limits are then placed above and below the process averages quality level. Any given group average then indicates both a quality level and whether there is any indication of lack of control. Any given group range reveals both variability and any indication of lack of control. Thus, group averages that go above $UCL_{\bar{X}}$ may possibly be the result of a gradually rising quality level, but a range that goes above UCL_R can indicate only a lack of control.

Q. 3.44: *Is not an uncontrolled product at a higher level more desirable than a controlled product at a lower level ?*

Ans: While the average level of the process is important, the degree of control in effect at that level is also important—in fact virtually important. Without the existence of controlled operations, we can never be certain without what limits future observations will be likely to lie, within what limits untested material already made lies (when the control chart is derived from samples), or whether the existing level of average quality will be maintained.

In general, source *B* of Fig 3.34 would be definitely preferred to source *A*, inspite of the fact that the average quality level shown for *B* is lower than for *A*. Since *A* shows several indications of being out of control, we cannot be sure that the average quality level shown is the true quality level for all material made during the period involved. Nor can we be sure as to the amount of untested material that would also fall outside the control limits, or what portion of it, if tested,

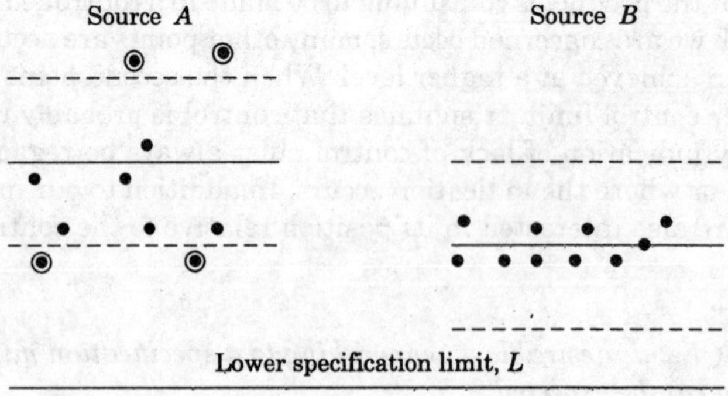

FIGURE 3.34: Contrast of level and control. Source A has a higher level for the items tested but there is no telling what the rest of the lot is like and there is no basis for predicting the future. Source B would normally be preferred.

would fall below the specification minimum, or what the future level or variability will be. On the other hand, in the case of source *B* we have a high degree of assurance that the quality average and variability of the untested material are essentially the same as for the tested material; that extremely little, if any, of the untestd material would fall below the specification minimum ; and that the existing level and amount of variability probably will be maintained in the immediate future.

Q. 3.45: *(a) What good is a control chart on a certain property if it is a different property in which we are interested ?*

(b) If the level of averages is high enough (when working to a minimum only), is it not possible for point to fall at least a little below the lower control limit without danger of failure?

Ans: (*a*) If the two properties are not related such a chart will **not** be helpful. In some cases two different properties are closely related although it is possible to measure only one of them. Wherever the two properties are related, such a chart can be very useful.

(*b*) In this situation there may be no immediate danger of failures on the quality characteristic charted. If there are a number of related quality characteristics of importance, trouble may be encountered with one or more of them. The safe thing is never to ignore indications of lack of control.

Q. 3.46: *Explain why $\overline{X}$ chart and not X chart is generally used in quality control techniques ? Illustrate your answer with suitable examples.*

Ans: Since the primary purpose of a control chart is to reveal the presence of assignable causes of variation so that a prompt action be taken to control or eliminate such causes, it is desirable that the control chart limits be based on only the variability that is inherent in the process. If we group all the data together and compute the standard deviation of the individual measurements, we shall include in that determination all the assignable causes as well as chance causes of variation. As a result, our estimate of variability will be too large if the process is not actually in control. If the process is in control (few processes are when first investigated) it will not make much difference. Since we cannot know the degree of control until after the chart is constructed, we must always avoid lumping all the data and computing the standard deviation of the individual items on this basis.

The data below shows the estimated σ (i.e. ˆ) of a controlled and an uncontrolled process as computed on the bases of the lumped individual items and as grouped into successive five's in the usual control chart procedure. Each series consisted of 125 successive observations.

Process	*Estimated $\hat{\sigma}$*	
	Lumped Individuals	*Grouping of 5 items*
Controlled	1.58	1.56
Uncontrolled	2.88	1.53

It will be noted that when there is lack of control the individual values increase in their scatter to such an extent that they give an abnormally high estimate of population variability. Actually in the above illustration, three different levels of quality were being produced during collection of the 125 uncontrolled process observations. The inherent variability at each of the three levels, however, was the same.

Still another reason for using $\bar{X}$ chart rather than X chart is that former will average fewer measurements before giving an indication of a shift in process average. In other words the efficiency of X chart is less as compared with that for $\bar{X}$ chart in detecting the assignable causes of variation. It may be illustrated in the following way :

Suppose a process which has just been in control suddenly affected by assignable causes making μ to $\mu + 1\,\sigma$. If the sample size of 4 units is used to detect this shift on $\bar{X}$ chart, then computation can be made to find the efficiencies of $\bar{X}$-chart and X-chart in detecting this shift, in terms of minimum number of units inspected before shift is detected. For computing the number inspected, it is necessary compute ARL and then, $I = n\ ARL$.

Since $ARL = 1/(1 - \beta)$, we use Eq. (3.8) to compute β both for X and $\bar{X}$ charts. For X chart $n = 1$ and $k = 1$ and using 3 sigma limits, β is found to be 0.9773 and hence $(1 - \beta) = 0.0227$. Similarly for $\bar{X}$ chart $n = 4$ (sample size) and $k = 1$ and using again 3 sigma control limits, $\beta = 0.8413$ and hence $(1 - \beta) = 0.1587$.

For X chart : $ARL = 1/(1 - \beta)$ *i.e.* $1/0.0227 = 44$ samples

For $\bar{X}$ chart : $ARL = 1/(1 - \beta)$ i.e. $1/0.1587 = 6$ samples.

For X chart : $I = n\ ARL$ *i.e.* $(1)(44) = 44$

For $\bar{X}$ chart : $I = n\ ARL$ *i.e.* $(4)(6) = 24$

The results obtained above clearly indicate that $\bar{X}$ chart is more efficient than X chart.

Q. 3.47: *State the four possibilities in the outcome of control charts.*

Ans: For the Control Charts for variables *i.e.* $\bar{X}$ and R-charts (and also for attribute control charts : p-chart, c-chart) the following summarises the possible outcomes of the sampling results from any of these types of charts.

Samples means lie close to the centre line The sample means lie close to (hug) the centre line, which indicates that the process is well in control. This is the expectation in the Taguchi Methods of quality control. Under this situation, one should tighten up the control limits (bring them closer to the centre line).

Sample means within limits, but wide variation The sample means are within limits, but there is wide fluctuation, which means that, although this indicates that the process is in control, the variation is too much and the process is sloppy. An analysis should be made to find out why this is happening.

Sample means within limits, but there is an alarming trend This means that, although the samples are at present that the process will soon be out of control. The process should be stopped and investigated.

Sample out of control The sample means are beyond upper limit, which shows that, from the beginning, the process is out of control. The system should be shut down and investigated.

Q. 3.48: *(a) Fill in the blanks :*

(i) $\bar{X}$ *chart monitors .... sample variability.*

(ii) R chart measures.... sample variability.

(iii) Control limits are based on .... sample variability only.

Relate (i) and (ii) above to time aspect.

(b) Is it also necessary to use 3-sigma control limits ? State some situations where a slight departure from this existing practice can be tolerated.

Ans: *(a)* *(i)* $\bar{X}$ chart monitors between sample variability *i.e.* variability in the process over time.

(ii) R chart measures *within* sample variability *i.e.* the instantaneous process variability at a given time.

(iii) The control limits are based on *within* sample variability only.

(b) The use of 3-sigma control limits on the $\bar{X}$ and R charts is a widespread practice based on the economic balance between *Type I* and *Type II* errors. However, there are situations when departures from this customary choice of control limits are helpful. For example, if false alarms or *Type I* errors (an out-of-control signal is generated when the process is really in control) are very expensive to investigate, then it may be best to use wider control limits than 3-sigma- perhaps as wide as 3.5-sigma. However, if the process is such that out-of-control signals are quickly and easily investigated with a minimum of lost time and cost, then narrower control limits, perhaps at 2.5-sigma, are appropriate.

Q. 3.49: *(a) What is the purpose of SPC ?*

(b) Why lower limit for R is to be drawn ? That is, why would any one want to signal that the variability might have gotten signifiantly smaller, since consistency in the process is a goal?

Ans: *(a)* Information from samples can be used in SPC to infer something about the proper functioning of the process through which itoms have been ; or are to be, run. SPC is important in quality control because it helps keep the processes running correctly so that defective items are seldom produced. That is SPC helps maintain high-quality operations where quality is built into the product the first time.

(b) A company would probably want to find the assignable causes for the improvement and standardize the improved method. A new value of R should be calculated and new will established for $\bar{X}$ so that probability of Type I error will remain at the established level.

Q. 3.50: *(a) When a process is 'in control' or 'stable', what type of variations are present in the process ?*

(b) Enumerate a few advantages of the situation when the process is in control.

Ans: *(a)* When a process is in control, only chance causes of variation are present. Small variation in machine performance, operator performance, and material characteristics etc. are expected and are considered to part be of a stable process.

(b) When a process is in control, certain practical advantages are inherent to the manufacturer and purchaser.

1. Individual units of the product will be more uniform, or stated another way, there will be less variation among parts and lesser amount of inspection is involved.
2. Since the product is more uniform, relatively fewer samples are needed to judge the quality. Therefore, the cost of inspection can be reduced to a minimum. This advantage is extremely important when 100 percent conformance to specification is not essential.
3. The process capability or speed of the process is easily attained from 6σ or by multiplying the square root of the sample size by the difference between the control limits. With a knowledge of process capability, a number of reliable decisions to specification can be made, such as:
   (i) To decide the product specifications/tolerances etc.
   (ii) To decide the amount of rework or scrap when there is insufficient tolerance.
   (iii) To decide whether to produce the product to tight specifications and permit interchange ability of components or to produce the product to loose specifications and use selective machining of components.

4. The percentage of product that will fall within any pair of values can be predicted with the highest degree of assurance. For example, this advantage can be very important when adjusting filling machines to obtain different percentages of items below, between, or above particular levels.
5. When a process is in control, it permits the purchaser to use the manufacturer's data (with consent) and, therefore, to test only a few subgroups as a check on the manufacturer's records.
6. ISO 9000 requirement is also met with and hence commercial advantages.

Q. 3.51: *(a) A steel bar is being turned to a given diameter on a CNC lathe. Causes of variation of diameter are given below. Classify these causes into :*

(i) inherent process variation causes

(ii) special causes

1. *Fluctuations of temperature.*
2. *Variations in material properties.*
3. *Variations in the coolant supply.*
4. *Variable amounts of eccentric running of bar.*
5. *Vibrations caused by the cutting.*
6. *Errors of tool setting.*
7. *Tool wear.*

(b) Consider the $\overline{X}$ *control charts shown in Fig. 3.35 Does the pattern appear random ?*

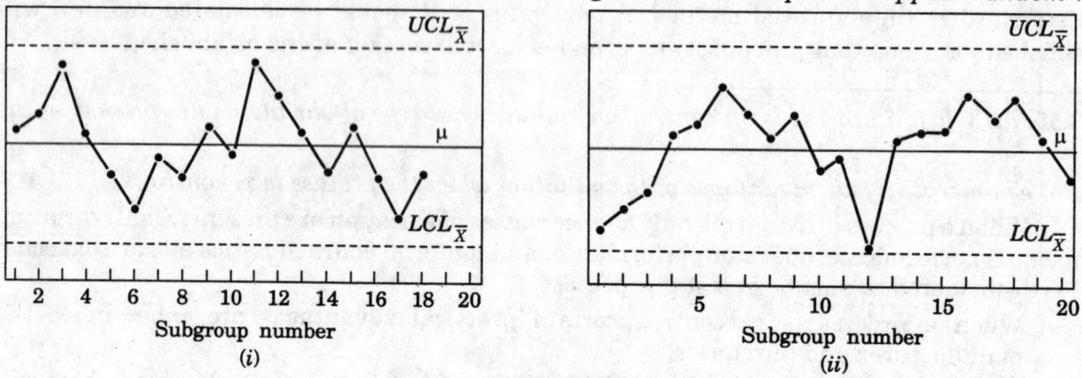

FIGURE 3.35

Ans: (*a*) (*i*) Items (1) to (5) are unlikely to follow any regular pattern and may be regarded as the causes of inherent process variation or chance causes or common causes.

(*ii*) Items (6) and (7) are special causes or assignable causes of variation. An error in tool setting will give rise to a discrepancy between the mean-size achieved and the mean size of the tolerance band. Tool wear will cause a gradual drift of the mean size of consecutive samples across the tolerance band :

(*b*) Figure 3.35 (*i*) exhibits a random pattern

Figure 3.35 (*ii*) exhibits a nonrandom pattern and a cyclic pattern.

Q. 3.52: *(a) What are the natural tolerance limits of a process ?*

(b) Is there any relationship between control limits on the $\overline{X}$ *and R charts, and the specification limits ?*

(c) How are $\overline{X}$ *distributed in a nonnormal distribution.*

Ans: (*a*) It is customary to define the upper and lower natural limits as 3-sigma (σ) above and below the process mean *i.e.* $\mu \pm 3\sigma$.

(*b*) There in no relationship between the control limits on the $\bar{X}$ and R charts and the specification limits on the process. The control limits are driven by the natural variability of the process (measured by process standard deviation σ), that is, by the natural tolerance limits of the process. The specification limits, on the other hand, are determined externally. They may be set by management, the manufacturing engineers, the customers, or by product developers/designers. Of course one should have knowledge of inherent process variability when setting specifications but there is no mathematical or statistical relationship between the control limits and specification limits.

(*c*) Even in a nonnormal distribution the $\bar{X}$ values of subgroups are distributed in a normal manner.

Q. 3.53: *The following 22 subgroups of data represent the average and range of five measurements made each day for one month. Plot the control chart.*

Date	*Average* ($\bar{X}$)	*Range (R)*	*Date*	*Average* ($\bar{X}$)	*Range (R)*
1	1.85	0.28	16	1.68	0.10
2	1.81	0.14	17	1.81	0.29
3	1.75	0.23	18	1.69	0.23
4	1.76	0.35	21	1.78	0.22
7	1.83	0.26	22	1.57	0.05
8	1.76	0.25	23	1.72	0.23
9	1.71	0.21	24	1.74	0.23
10	1.80	0.08	25	1.55	0.32
11	1.73	0.19	28	1.57	0.47
14	1.79	0.39	29	1.61	0.20
15	1.82	0.36	30	1.71	0.23

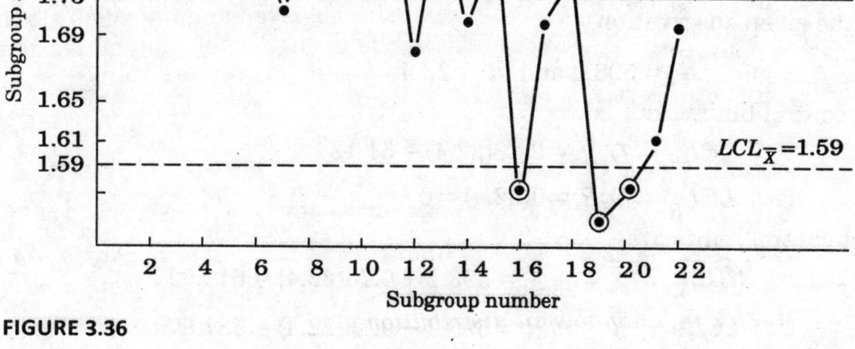

FIGURE 3.36

Do the data show control ? Is there any evidence of shift in process level during the month ? If so, when does it appear that the shift occurred ?

Ans: $\bar{R} = \dfrac{0.28 + 0.14 + ... + 0.20 + 0.23}{22} = 0.241$

$$\bar{\bar{X}} = \frac{1.85 + 1.81 + ... + 1.61 + 1.71}{22} = 1.73$$

$$UCL_{\bar{X}} = \bar{X} + A_2R = 1.73 + 0.58 \times 0.241 = 1.87$$

$$LCL_{\bar{X}} = \bar{X} + A_2R = 1.73 - 0.58 \times 0.241 = 1.59$$

$\bar{X}$ chart of the data is shown in Fig. 3.36.

The data do not show the control because first six points are above the $\bar{X}$ line and averages for subgroups No. 16, 19, and 20 are below, $LCL_{\bar{X}}$, indicating the out of control situation. A close examination of the chart will immediately indicate that after subgroup No. 11, the process level is shifting gradually downwards.

Q. 3.54: *(a) When designing control charts for a variable characteristic, what two types of charts are generally used ? Why we need these two types of charts?*

(b) The ABC Electric Company produces incandescent light bulbs. The following data on the number of lumens for 40-watt light bulbs were collected when the process was in control.

Sample	*Observation*			
	1	*2*	*3*	*4*
1	604	612	588	600
2	597	601	607	603
3	581	570	585	592
4	620	605	595	604
5	590	614	608	604

(i) Calculate control limits for an R-chart and an $\bar{X}$-chart.

(ii) Since these data were collected, some new employees were hired. A new sample obtained the following readings: 570, 603, 623 and 583. The average (i.e. X bar) of this sample is 594.75, which is well with in control limits. Is the process in control ? Why or why not?

Ans: (*a*) Process variability should be in control before process average control charts are constructed. The reason is that the average range i.e. $\bar{R}$ is used in the calculation of control limits for process average control charts. Hence we need two type of charts:

(*b*) (*i*) From the given observation,

$$\bar{\bar{X}} = 598.2 \text{ and } \bar{R} = 22.4$$

The *R*-chart control limits are :

$$UCL_R = D_4\bar{R} = 2.28(22.4) = 51.12$$

$$LCL_R = D_3\bar{R} = 0(22.4) = 0$$

The $\bar{X}$-chart control limits are:

$$UCL_{\bar{X}} = \bar{\bar{X}} + A_2\bar{R} = 598.2 + 0.73(22.4) = 614.53$$

$$LCL_{\bar{X}} = \bar{\bar{X}} - A_2\bar{R} = 598.2 - 0.73(22.4) = 581.87$$

(*ii*) First check to see whether the variability is still in control on the new data. The range of new sample (*i.e.* 623 – 570 = 53), is outside the UCL_R of 51.12. Even though the sample mean 594.75, is within the control limits for the process average, process variability is not in control. A search for assignable causes must be conducted.

Q. 3.55: *(a) Distinguish clearly between SPC and SAS*

(b) State whether the following statements are TRUE (T) or FALSE (F).

(i) Even if all observations are within limits, it does not guarantee that assignable variations are not present, that is, that there is a problem with the process.

(ii) Even if all observations appear outside one of the control limits, this does not guarantee that assignable variations are present.

(iii) If 2σ limits are used, 95.5 per cent of sample means should be within limits and 4.5 percent outside limits when only random variations are present.

Ans: (*a*) Statistical process control (SPC) is the periodic sampling and analysis of units, items or activity, to determine if the system is performing as expected, according to some pre-determined target or within design limits. The primary purpose of SPC is to analyze the process to verify that it is operating correctly. It is not to analyze the produced units to see if they conform to specifications. This is the objective of scientific acceptance sampling (SAS).

(*b*) (*i*) T (*ii*) T (*iii*) T

Q. 3.56: *Fill in columns of the table with codes with one of the following statements:*

Type I, Error (Code 1)
Type II, Error (Code 2)
No Error (Code 3)

		In reality, if we looked at everything the process made, we would know that it	
		Changed	Not changed
The sample suggested that the process had:	changed	1	2
	Not changed	3	4

Ans: Considering the *Type I* error designated as code 1 etc., the four columns will have the following codes :

Column	Code
1	3
2	1
3	2
4	3

Q. 3.57: *(a) What are the two types of decision errors are possible in sampling. Mention these in brief for a layman.*

(b) Which error can lead to legal action from the consumer for a defective product that caused bodily injury?

(c) How will you reduce the type of error in (b)?

Ans: (*a*) Two kinds of decision errors are always possible in sampling.

Suppose that the process is running perfectly but the sample data indicate that something is wrong. We decide to stop the process to make adjustments. This is a *Type I* error. Suppose that the process was not running perfectly and was making defective products. However, the sample data did not indicate that anything was wrong. We did not stop the process and set it right. This is a *Type II* error. Both types of errors are possible in sampling

(*b*) *Type II* error can lead to legal action form the consumer for a defective/non conforming product that caused bodily injury.

(*c*) For a given sample size, reducing the chance of a one type of error will increase the chance of the other. Increasing the sample size or the frequency of sampling reduces the probability of errors but increases the cost of inspection. Many companies determine the size of the errors they are willing to accept according to the overall cost of making the errors plus the cost of inspection. If, for example, a *Type I* error is very expensive in terms of product recalls or legal suits, the company may be willing to make more *Type I* errors, to sample more, or even to go to 100% inspection (if possible) on very critical items to ensure that the company is not accepting defective materials as good and passing them on to the customer. The inspection should take place immediately after the processing.

Q. 3.58: *In order to meet government regulation, the contained weight of a product must at least equal the labeled weight 98% of the time. Control charts for* $\overline{X}$ *and* σ *are maintained on the weight in ounces of the contents using a subgroup size of 10. After 20 subgroups,* $\Sigma\overline{X}$ = *731.4 and* Σs = *10.95. Compute 3-sigma control limits for* $\overline{X}$ *and s and estimate the value of* σ *assuming the process is in statistical control. If the label weight is 36 oz, and assuming the process generates a normal distribution, does it meet governmental requirement ?*

Ans:

$$\overline{\overline{X}} = \frac{\Sigma\overline{X}}{20} = \frac{731.4}{20} = 36.57$$

$$\overline{s} = \frac{\Sigma s}{20} = \frac{10.95}{20} = 0.5475$$

For a sub-group size of 10, Table *E*, App 2, gives the following factors :

$$A_1 = 1.03, B_3 = 0.28\ B_4 = 1.72$$

$$UCL_{\overline{X}} = \overline{X} + A_1\overline{s} = 36.57 + (1.03 \times 0.5475) = 37.134$$

$$LCL_{\overline{X}} = \overline{X} - A_1\overline{s} = 36.57 - (1.03 \times 0.5475 = 36.006)$$

$$UCL_s = B_4\overline{s} = 1.72 \times 0.5475 = 0.9417$$

$$LCL_s = B_3\overline{s} = 0.28 \times 0.5475 = 0.1528$$

For a sub-group size of 10, Table *C* gives c_4 0.9727

$$\hat{\sigma} = \frac{\overline{s}}{0.9727} = \frac{0.5475}{0.9727} = 0.563$$

Labeled weight = 36 oz.

In order to fund out the product below 360 oz.

$$z = \frac{36.00 \quad 36.57}{0.563} = -1.012$$

From Table *A*, when $z = -1.012$, area of the normal curve is 0.1557. It means that about 15.57% of the product will be below the specification limit of 36 oz. while the government requirement is that at least 98% of the products should meet the specification or a maximum of 2% of the products can be tolerated below the specification limit. Hence obviously the regulation is not met with.

Q. 3.59: *A confectionery company is St. Etienne, France, has an automatic filling machine which allows 250 grams of sweets to be put into plastic bags before they are sealed. The company is concerned about the reliability of this machine and decides to carry out a statistical process control study. First, the filling line is shut down and adjusted according to specifications. The line is then put into operation and 20 random samples each of 25 units, are taken during eight hours of operation. For each of the samples taken, the average weight is determined, and the maximum and minimum weight is also recorded. This information is given in Table.*

Average, maximum and minimum weights (g) of confectionery samples

Sample No.	*Average weight*	*Maximum weight*	*Minimum weight*
1	253.00	262.00	232.00
2	248.00	261.00	232.00
3	254.20	269.00	242.00
4	256.00	265.00	248.00
5	253.20	262.40	247.00
6	246.20	261.40	235.00
7	250.00	254.00	230.00
8	247.50	265.00	229.00
9	254.30	275.00	242.00
10	252.00	258.00	241.00
11	246.10	278.00	237.00
12	250.00	265.00	235.00
13	247.00	265.20	241.00
14	248.20	263.20	242.10
15	251.30	270.0	247.20
16	251.30	265.20	248.10
17	253.60	257.20	248.80
18	252.70	259.20	248.20
19	254.30	259.00	247.90
20	255.20	260.10	251.00

Required

(a) Develop the two appropriate control charts to analyse this filling operation.

(b) What are the conclusions from these control charts?

(Note: When subgroup size (n) is 25 or more than 1)

$$A_2 = 0.751/\sqrt{\ }$$
$$D_3 = 0.45 + 0.001n$$
$$D_4 = 1.55 - 0.001n$$

Ans: (*a*) While $\overline{X}$ values are given for each sample, the R value of each can be computed as maximum and minimum weights are given. following computations can be made

$$n = 25,\ \overline{X} = 251.21,\ \overline{R} = 22.54,\ A_2 = 0.153,\ D_3 = 0.46,\ D_4 = 1.54$$

For $\overline{X}$ chart: $UCL_{\overline{X}} = 254.65$ $LCL\overline{X} = 247.76$

For R chart: $UCL_R = 34.71$ $LCL_R = 10.37$

$\overline{X}$ chart and R-charts can be plotted with above data and $\overline{X}$ data given in the table.

(*b*) Both charts illustrate that there is a problem with the filling machine. In the $\overline{X}$ chart the early results are erractic, some falling within the range, and samples 4 and 6 falling outside. As the sampling proceeds, the average weights are erring on the high side and the 20 th sample indicates that the average weight is outside the limit. Although this would not be of concern to the consumer, it is costing more than is necessary to the producer. The machine should be shutdown and checked for operation.

Q. 3.60: *The following data (pertaining two subgroups of size 4), is from two different machines which are supposed to be alike. Plot the necessary charts to show whether their product would support this assumption. If they do not support this assumption, does this prove the machines are not essentially alike ?*

MACHINE 1			MACHINE 2		
Subgroup	*Average* ($\overline{X}$)	*Range (R)*	*Subgroup*	*Average* ($\overline{X}$)	*Range (R)*
1	2.77	0.06	1	2.53	0.12
2	2.70	0.29	2	2.67	0.30
3	2.78	0.19	3	2.66	0.17
4	2.67	0.12	4	2.57	0.25
5	2.75	0.34	5	2.60	0.24
6	2.77	0.23	6	2.60	0.05
7	2.75	0.17	7	2.70	0.30
8	2.73	0.06	8	2.56	0.04
9	2.76	0.23	9	2.70	0.19
10	2.63	0.20	10	2.67	0.08
11	2.73	0.17	11	2.60	0.11
12	2.73	0.28	12	2.63	0.14
13	2.74	0.26	13	2.71	– 0.24
14	2.72	0.13	14	2.63	– 0.31
15	2.73	0.13	15	2.75	0.17

Ans: For Machine No. 1

$$\overline{R} = \frac{0.06 + 0.29 + \ldots + 0.13 + 0.13}{15} = 0.191$$

$$\overline{\overline{X}} = \frac{2.77 + 2.70 + \ldots + 2.72 + 2.73}{15} = 2.73$$

$$\hat{\sigma}_1 = \frac{\bar{R}}{d_2} = \frac{0.191}{2.059} = 0.0927$$

$$UCL_{\bar{X}} = \bar{\bar{X}} + A_2\bar{R} = 2.73 + (0.73 \times 0.191) = 2.87$$

$$LCL_{\bar{\bar{X}}} = \bar{\bar{X}} - A_2\bar{R} = 2.73 - (0.73 \times 0.196) = 2.59$$

For Machine No. 2

$$\bar{R} = \frac{0.12 + 0.30 + ... + 0.31 + 2.17}{15} = 0.181$$

$$\bar{\bar{X}} = \frac{2.53 + 2.67 + ... + 2.63 + 2.75}{15} = 2.64$$

$$\hat{\sigma}_2 = \frac{\bar{R}}{d_2} = \frac{0.181}{2.059} = 0.088$$

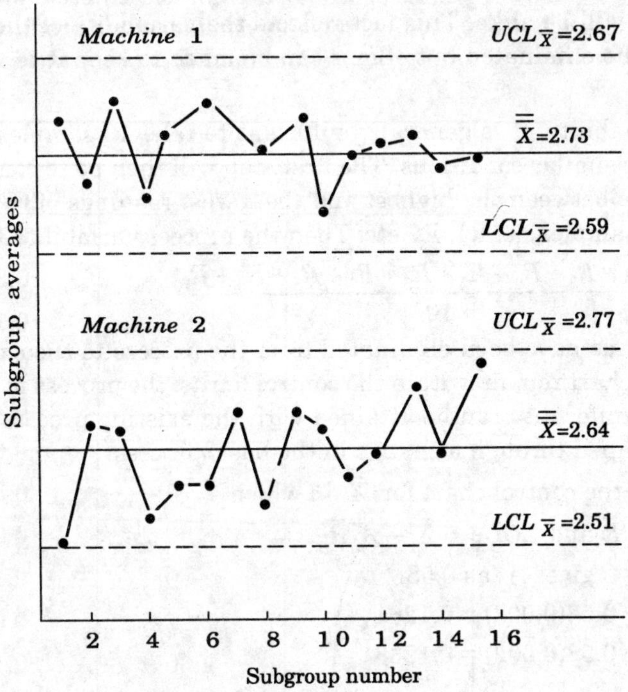

Figure 3.37: *$\bar{X}$ chart for the date for machines 1 and 2*

$$UCL_{\bar{X}} = \bar{\bar{X}} + A_2\bar{R} = 2.64 + (0.73 \times 0.181) = 2.77$$

$$LCL_{\bar{X}} = \bar{\bar{X}} - A_2\bar{R} = 2.64 - (0.73 \times 0.181) = 2.51$$

$\bar{X}$ charts for both the machines are shown in Fig. 3.37

From the $\bar{X}$ charts it is evident that these two machines are not alike. Machine No. 2 shows somewhat rising trend.

Assuming that variation in the dimensions is due to machines only, $\hat{\sigma}$ of the universe produced by these machines are 0.0927 and 0.088 respectively which are different and therefore the machines are not essentially alike.

Q. 3.61: *(a) What do you understand by the term "process variability" ? Explain fully.*

(b) What is meant by "process in control" ?

(c) A large manufacturer of watches makes some of his own parts and buys some other parts from a vendor. The vendor submits lots of parts that meet the specifications of the horologist. The vendor thus wishes to keep a continuous check on his production of watch parts. One gear has been a special problem. A check of 25 samples of 5 pieces gave the following data on a key dimension :

$$\bar{X} = 0.125 \text{ inch.}$$
$$R = 0.002 \text{ inch.}$$

What criterion should be set up to determine when the process is out of control ? How should this criterion compare with specifications ?

Ans: *(a)* Process Variability. The idea of process variability is derived from the consideration that no process can turn out an identical product. Even with the best equipment and the most skilled operation, no two pieces will be alike. This fact reflects the variability of the process. This natural variability cannot be eliminated but efforts can be made to keep it to minimum or within specification limits.

To compute the process variability, it is generally sufficient to take 10 samples of equal number of items produced under similar conditions. The first step will then be to compute the sample range (*R*)—the difference between the highest and the lowest readings of the sample. Similarly compute R for all the samples i.e. R1, R2 etc. Then the process variability will be

$$\bar{R} = \frac{R_1 + R_2 + R_3 + R_4 + R_5 + R_6 + R_7 + R_8 + R_9 + R_{10}}{10}$$

(b) When the assignable causes have been eliminated from the process to the extent that the points plotted on the control chart remain within the control limits, the process is in a state of control. No higher degree of uniformity can be attained with the existing process. Greater uniformity can, however, be attained through a change in the basic process.

(c) The vendor should set up the control chart for $\bar{X}$ in which

$$UCL_{\bar{X}} = \bar{X} + A_2\bar{R} \text{ and } LCL_{\bar{X}} = \bar{X} - A_2\bar{R}$$

For a sample size of 5, Table *C* gives A_2 as 0.58.

$$UCL_{\bar{X}} = 0.125 + 0.58(0.002) = 0.1261$$
$$LCL_{\bar{X}} = 0.125 - 0.58(0.002) = 0.1238$$

$$\hat{\sigma} \text{ for this process} = \bar{R}/d_2 = \frac{0.002}{2.326} = 0.00086.$$

To start with, both the $\bar{X}$ and *R* charts are to be plotted. If the subgroups ranges are in control, 0.00086 represents a true value of $\hat{\sigma}$ of the key dimension and hence all the dimensions are expected to fall between $\bar{\bar{X}} \pm 3\hat{\sigma}$. If the specifications are same as $\bar{\bar{X}} \pm 3\hat{\sigma}$, then control limits of 0.1261 and 0.1238 can be used. If the tolerance are tighter than $\bar{\bar{X}} \pm 3\hat{\sigma}$, then a basic change in process is needed. If the tolerances are more relaxed than $\bar{\bar{X}} \pm 3\hat{\sigma}$, and still many pieces are nonconforming, it indicates that the process is not centered correctly. Depending upon the process adjustments available, adjustments can be made so that the nonconforming product is minimised.

Q. 3.62: *A textile mill's development group determines that it must have a fiber which, among other properties, has a minimum strength of 1,800 grams in which 95% of the fiber used. Manufacturer A offers to supply such a fiber and a contract is arranged.*

(a) Manufacturer A knows that the standard deviation (σ) of its process is 0.015 gram. What minimum aimed-at value of the mean ($\bar{X}_0$) is required to assure compliance with the contract ?

(b) Control chart for $\bar{X}$ are to be maintained based on a subgroup size of 6. Determine the central line and control limits for $\bar{X}$ chart.

Ans: (*a*) Since a minimum tensile strength of 1,800 grams is being possessed by 95% of the fiber, 5% of the fiber will be having a strength of less than 1,800 grams.

From Table *A*, corresponding a area of 0.05, the value of $z = -1.645$. If $\bar{X}_0$ is the aimed at value, then

$$-1.645 = \frac{1800 - \bar{X}_0}{0.015}$$

$$\bar{X}_0 = 1800.0247 \text{ grams}$$

(*b*) For a subgroup size of 6, Table *F* gives the following factor :

$$A_1 = 1.22$$

$$UCL_{\bar{X}} = \bar{X}_0 + A_1\sigma = 1{,}800.4047 + (1.22 \times 0.015) = 1800.2077$$

$$LCL_{\bar{X}} = \bar{X}_0 - A_1\sigma = 1{,}800.4047 - (1.22 \times 0.015) = 1{,}799.8417$$

Q. 3.63: *$\bar{X}$ and R charts based on a subgroup size of 5 have been maintained on process for the long period of time. During the past month, no points have fallen outside the control limits. The resulting month's data yield $\bar{\bar{X}} = 0.7505$ and $\bar{R} = 0.0045$.*

(a) Estimate the current value of (i.e. $\hat{\sigma}$) for this process.

(b) Ten of the last eleven points on the R chart are above the central line. Based on this evidence, does the process appear to be operating in statistical control ?

Ans: (*a*) Since no points have fallen outside the control limits,

$$\bar{R} = 0.0045$$

$$\hat{\sigma} = \frac{\bar{R}}{d_2}$$

$$= \frac{0.0045}{2.326} = 0.00193$$

(*b*) Since ten of the eleven points on *R* chart are above the central line, this is a case extreme runs. It gives strong evidence of lack of control and the process does not appear to be operating in statistical control manner.

Q. 3.64: *A process has a target mean of 40 g with a known σ. Samples of size 4 are drawn and results plotted on Shewhart Mean and Range Charts*

(a) What are the appropriate control limits for these charts ?

(b) Comment on the practical implications of the following results which appear on the Shewhart Mean Chart :

(i) A reading of 42.4 g.

(ii) A reading of 35.8 g.

(iii) Two successive reading of 44.7 g. and 43.8 g.

(iv) Two successive reading of 44.5 g. and 35.7 g.

Ans: $\bar{X}_0 = 40$

$\sigma = 4$

$$\sigma_{\bar{X}} = \frac{4}{\sqrt{4}} = 2$$

(*a*) $UCL_{\bar{X}} = 40 + 3(2) = 46$

$LCL_{\bar{X}} = 40 - 3(2) = 34$

$\bar{R} = d_2\sigma$

From Table *C*, for a sample size of 4, $d_2 = 2.059$

Hence $\bar{R} = 2.059 \times 4 = 8.24$

$UCL_R = D_4\bar{R} = 2.28 \times 8.24 = 18.78$

$LCL_R = D_3\bar{R} = 0 \times 8.24 = 0$

(*b*) (*i*) A reading of 42.4 g is indicates only a chance variation.

(*ii*) A reading of 35.8 is near the $LCL_{\bar{X}}$ indicate a danger signal of shifting the process average downwards.

(*iii*) Two successive readings of 44.7 and 43.8 are above the $\bar{X}_0$ and indicate shift in process average upwards.

(*iv*) Two successive readings of 44.5 and 35.7 are near the $UCL_{\bar{X}}$ and $LCL_{\bar{X}}$ respectively and indicate change in process average or the situation of over control.

Q. 3.65: *The mean weight of a large loaf produced at bakery was found in a series of quality control checks to be 30 ounces, with a standard deviation of 1 ounce. Sample batches of 4 loaves were then taken from the travelling oven at 2-hourly intervals and the following are the averages of the last 6 consecutive sample batches :*

29.6, 29.4, 29.9, 30.2, 30.3, 30.1

(a) Draw the control chart for averages and enter the figures on the chart.

(b) What proportion of loaves would you expect to fall below the legal minimum weight of 28 pounds ?

Ans: $\mu = 30$

$\sigma = 1$

$$\sigma_{\bar{X}} = \frac{1}{\sqrt{4}} = 0.5$$

$UCL_{\bar{X}} = \mu + 3\sigma_{\bar{X}} = 30 + 3(0.5) = 31.5$

$LCL_{\bar{X}} = \mu - 3\sigma_{\bar{X}} = 30 - 3(0.5) = 28.5$

(*a*) On drawings an $\bar{X}$ chart, and plotting the six sample averages it will be seen that first three averages are below the μ and the next three are above the μ, giving an indication of jumps in process level. The reasons may be either change in raw material, or change in balance or measuring machine, or change in basic process, or substitution of new workers.

(*b*) Proportion below the legal limit of 28 ounces, can be found by using Table *A*

$$z = \frac{28 - 30}{1} = -2$$

From Table corresponding to *z* of – 2, are a below the limit of 28 is 0.0228.

Hence 2.28% of loaves would fall below the legal of 28 ounces.

Q. 3.66: *(a) A quality control scheme is in operation for a process producing ball-bearings. It has been established that when the process is under control the average diameter of the bearings is 1 cm with a standard deviation of 0.003 cm. Samples of 9 bearings are taken every hour and the diameters measured. Draw a control chart to be used for recording the average diameter of each sampling, inserting 95% inner control limits and 99% outer control limits.*

(b) The average diameters, in cm, of ten successive sample are 1.0006, 0.9997, 0.9992, 1.0012, 1.0008, 1.0012, 1.0018, 1.0016, 1.0020 and 1.0022. Plot these points in your chart and comment briefly on what conclusions you draw.

(c) If the process goes out of control so that the average diameter changes to 1.001 cm, the standard deviation remaining the same, calculate the probability that the average diameter of a single sample of 9 bearings would be such as to lead to the process being investigated. Calculate the probability of the process being investigated if samples of 25 bearings have been taken throughout.

Ans:

$$\mu = 1.0000$$

$$\sigma = 0.003$$

$$\sigma_{\bar{X}} = \frac{\sigma}{\sqrt{n}} = \frac{0.003}{\sqrt{9}} = 0.001$$

(*a*) 95% limits mean area of the normal curve between μ & UCL is 0.95/2 i.e. 0.475 and between μ and LCL is also 0.475. From Table *A*, these limits are at ± 1.96 sigma from the mean i.e. $\mu \pm 1.96\ \sigma_{\bar{X}}$ *i.e.*, 1.0020 and 0.9980

Similarly, 99% outer limits are $\mu \pm 2.58\ \sigma_{\bar{X}}$ *i.e.*, 1.0026 and 0.9974

(*b*) On plotting the control chart for averages, it will be noticed that all the sample averages except first two are on the same side of the central line indicating that process average has shifted from 1.00 cm to a slightly higher value. Further, both 9th and 10th sample averages are outside the same inner limit ($\mu \pm 1.96\,\sigma_{\bar{X}}$), giving a strong indication that process averages has shifted.

(*c*) When the process mean shifts to 1.001 cm but σ remains the same, the probability that the average diameter of a single sample of 9 bearings would be such as to lead to the process being investigated is equal to the area of the normal curve beyond the upper 99% control limits of $\mu \pm 2.58\ \sigma_{\bar{X}}$

New process average = 1.001 cm = $\mu + 1\sigma_{\bar{X}}$

For $UCL_{\bar{X}}$ $$z = \frac{(\mu + 2.58\sigma_{\bar{X}}) - (\mu + 1\sigma_{\bar{X}})}{\sigma_{\bar{X}}} = 1.58$$

For $LCL_{\bar{X}}$ $$Z = \frac{(\mu + 2.56\sigma_{\bar{X}}) - (\mu + 1\sigma_{\bar{X}})}{\sigma_{\bar{X}}} = -3.58$$

From Table *A*, when z = 1.58, area of the normal curve is 0.9429. Therefore are of the normal curve beyond the upper 99% control limit is equal to 1.0000 – 0.9429 = 0.0571. Also area of normal curve below LCL is = 0.

Hence the required probability is 0.0571

When the sample size is 25,

$$\sigma_{\bar{X}} = \frac{0.003}{\sqrt{25}} = 0.0006$$

New process average $z = 1.001 = \mu$ *i.e.* 1.1667 $\sigma_{\bar{X}}$

$$z = \frac{(\mu + 2.58\sigma_{\bar{X}}) - (\mu + 1.667\sigma_{\bar{X}})}{\sigma_{\bar{X}}} = 0.913.$$

From Table *A*, when $z = 0.913$, area of the normal curve is 0.8194. Therefore area of the normal curve beyond the upper 99% control limit is equal to $1.000 - 0.8194 = 0.1806$. The area below the lower 99% control limit is ≈ 0.

Hence the required probability is 0.1806.

Q. 3.67: *A chemical plant produces acid in a continuous process. Samples of the product are taken at regular intervals and their specific gravity is measured. It may be assumed that these observations are from a normal population with mean 1.18 and variance (σ2) 0.025. After every five observations the average value of the specific gravity is obtained and plotted on a quality control chart.*

Draw a two-sided control chart for this process which has inner control lines containing 95% of the sample means and outer control lines containing 99.5% of the sample means. Twelve such successive means were given below. Plot them on your chart and comment briefly on your findings.

1.29, 1.08, 1.16, 1.18, 1.25, 1.28, 1.22, 1.35, 1.13, 1.38, 1.41.

If the process mean falls to 1.15 what is the probability that a sample mean will fall below the lower inner control line ? For what value of the process mean is the probability that sample a mean will fall below the lower outer control line equal to 0.95 ?

Ans: $\mu = 1.18, \sigma^2 = 0.025$

$$\sigma_{\bar{X}} = \frac{\sigma}{\sqrt{n}} = \frac{\sqrt{0.025}}{\sqrt{5}} = 0.0707$$

95% inner control limits are $\mu \pm 1.96\,\sigma_{\bar{X}}$ *i.e.* 1.32 and 1.04

99.5% outer control limits are $\mu \pm 2.82\,\sigma_{\bar{X}}$ *i.e.* 1.38 and 0.98.

On plotting the sample means on the $\bar{X}$ chart, it will be noticed that the point (1.38) is above the inner control limit and (1.41) is above the upper control limit. Such a situation firmly indicates that the process is now out of control.

when $\mu = 1.15$, and inner $LCL_{\bar{X}} = 1.15$

$$z = \frac{1.04 - 1.15}{0.0707} = -1.556$$

From Table *A* ; when $z = -1.556$, area of the curve is 0.0598. Hence the probability that a sample mean will fall below the lower inner control line is 0.0598.

Let the process mean now shift to a value μ_1 such that the probability of a sample mean falling below the lower outer control limit is 0.95.

From Table *A*, When the area of the curve is 0.95, $z = 1.645$.

$$1.645 = \frac{0.98 - \mu_1}{0.0707}$$

from which $\mu_1 = 0.86$.

Q. 3.68: *The following data refer to a controlled operation on a machine. Samples of four were taken at intervals and the dimension of a specific diameter in millimeters above or below 300 mm is recorded for each item in each of twelve samples :*

Sample	1	2	3	4	5	6	7	8	9	10	11	12
	22	– 2	– 12	– 6	2	– 10	– 16	– 2	– 16	2	– 8	0
	2	6	– 6	– 6	– 2	– 4	– 4	– 2	– 2	– 2	6	6
	12	14	– 8	2	8	8	– 10	0	0	6	2	0
	0	6	– 16	– 10	2	– 2	– 2	4	10	8	12	24

Calculate the grand mean $\bar{\bar{X}}$ and the mean range $\bar{R}$ of the samples and, using the estimate $\hat{\sigma} = K\bar{R}$ for the standard deviation with K = 0.0486, calculate the inner (95%) and (99.8%) control limits for the sample means.

Draw up a quality control chart for means of samples of four and on it plot means of the above 12 samples and of a further 18 samples (13 to 30) as follows :

Sample	13	14	15	16	17	18	19	20	21
	14	– 6	2	10	6	– 2	14	16	4
	– 4	– 12	6	12	0	– 4	– 6	– 6	– 10
	– 20	– 4	– 8	16	14	– 2	12	12	2
	0	2	– 12	0	10	– 2	12	– 10	– 14
Sample	**22**	**23**	**24**	**25**	**26**	**27**	**28**	**29**	**30**
	– 8	– 8	4	2	0	– 8	10	4	24
	– 14	– 2	0	– 2	4	12	0	0	– 2
	– 4	2	– 10	– 8	8	18	– 6	16	12
	8	22	14	14	18	2	16	14	14

Discuss the desirability of an adjustment to the machine after the 19th sample and after the 30th sample.

Calculate tolerance limits to which the machine appears to be capable of working and for tolerances 270 to 330 mm, insert a line on the chart showing the allowable width of control limits.

(Note : Intrepret 'allowable width of control limits' as referring to the outer controls).

Ans: In order to calculate $\bar{\bar{X}}$ and $\bar{R}$, the results of first 12 samples are computed as follows :

$$\Sigma\bar{X} = 4, \Sigma R = 188$$

Continuing 300 as reference value.

$$\bar{\bar{X}} = \frac{4}{12} = \frac{1}{3} = 0.33$$

$$\bar{R} = \frac{188}{13} = 15.67$$

$$\hat{\sigma} = K\bar{R} = 0.486 \times 15.67 = 7.61$$

$$\sigma_{\bar{X}} = \frac{\hat{\sigma}}{\sqrt{n}} = \frac{7.62}{\sqrt{4}} = 3.81$$

95% inner control limits are $\bar{\bar{X}} \pm 1.96\,\sigma_{\bar{X}}$ *i.e.* 7.80 and – 7.13

99.8% outer control limits are $\bar{\bar{X}} \pm 3.09\,\sigma_{\bar{X}}$ *i.e.* 12.10 and – 11.43

$\bar{X}$ and R values from samples 13 to 30 are computed and tabulated below :

Sample No.	**13**	**14**	**15**	**16**	**17**	**18**	**19**	**20**	**21**
$\bar{X}$	– 2.5	– 5.0	– 3.0	9.5	7.5	– 2.5	8	3	–4.5
R	34	14	18	16	14	2	20	26	18
Sample No.	**22**	**23**	**24**	**25**	**26**	**27**	**28**	**29**	**30**
$\bar{X}$	– 4.5	3.5	2	1.5	7.5	6	5	8.5	12
R	22	30	24	22	18	26	22	16	26

The $\bar{X}$ control chart with means for samples 13 to 30 plotted on it is shown in Fig. 3.38 Looking at the control chart and observing the trend, adjustment after 19th sample is not advisable. Further as 29th and 30th sample means are both outside the upper 1.96 $\sigma_{\bar{X}}$ limit, with 30th almost at the outer control limit, adjustment is desirable after 30th sample.

Tolerance limits to which the machine appears to be capable of working are $\mu \pm 3\hat{\sigma}$

Taking 300 as reference value,

$$\mu = 300 + 0.33 = 300.33 \text{ mm}$$

$$3\hat{\sigma} = 3(7.61) = 22.83 \text{ mm}$$

$$\mu + 3\hat{\sigma} = 300.33 + 22.83 = 323.16 \text{ mm}$$

$$\mu - 3\hat{\sigma} = 300.33 - 22.83 = 277.50 \text{ mm.}$$

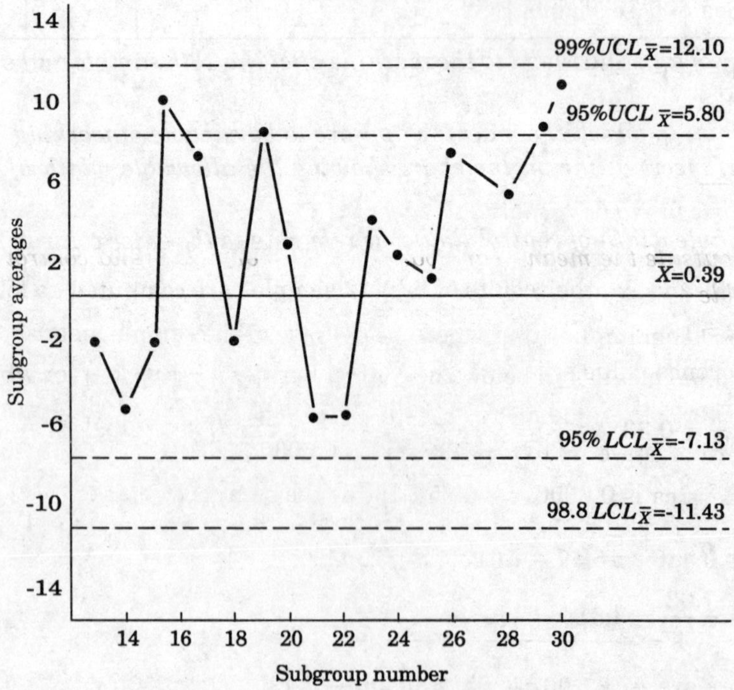

FIGURE 3.38: $\bar{X}$-Chart showing the 95% and 99.8% control limits and averages for subgroups No. 13 to 30 plotted on it.

Q. 3.69: *An average and range chart based on a sample size of five has been run with the following control limits :*

Control limits	$\overline{X}$ *-chart*	*R-chart*
Upper control limit	78.0	8.0
Average value	75.8	3.8
Lower control limit	73.6	0

How large an increase in the overall process average would have to occur in order to have a 30 percent chance that a sample average will exceed the upper control limit ?

Ans:

$$\overline{R} = 3.8$$

$$\hat{\sigma} = \frac{\overline{R}}{d_2}$$

From Table *C*, for a sample size of 5,

$$d_2 = 2.326$$

$$\sigma_{\overline{X}} = \frac{\hat{\sigma}}{\sqrt{n}} = \frac{3.8}{2.326\sqrt{5}} = 0.7306$$

Let the new process average be μ_1, so that area of the normal curve beyond upper control limit of 78.0 now becomes 0.30, resulting in 30 percent chance that a sample average will exceed the upper control limit. Hence, the area of the curve upto $UCL_{\overline{X}}$ is 0.70.

Corresponding to an area of 0.70, Table *A* gives $z = 0.524$.

Therefore,
$$0.524 = \frac{78 - \mu_1}{0.7306}$$

$$\mu_1 = 77.6172.$$

Q. 3.70: *Quality control charts are to be prepared with sensitivity that a mean shift of* **0.6** σ *will cause* $\frac{2}{5}$ *of samples to fall outside the mean chart warning limits of* **1.96** *sigma control limit. What sample size is advisable ?*

Ans: The statement of the problem implies that when the average of the sample means (μ) shift to $\mu - 0.6\,\sigma$, $\frac{2}{5}$ or 40% of sample means fall below the control limit of $\mu - 1.96\,\sigma_{\overline{X}}$. or when the average shifts to $\mu + 0.6\,\sigma$, 40% of sample means be above the control limit of $\mu + 1.96\,\sigma_{\overline{X}}$. In other words, area of the normal curve up to $\mu + 1.96\,\sigma_{\overline{X}}$ is 0.6000.

From Table *A*, when the area is 0.6000, $z = 0.253$. If *n* is the sample size, then

$$\sigma_{\overline{X}} = \frac{\sigma}{\sqrt{n}}$$

$$z = \frac{(\mu + 1.96\sigma_{\overline{X}}) - (\mu + 0.6\sigma)}{\sigma_{\overline{X}}} = 0.253$$

or,
$$\frac{1.96\sigma_{\overline{X}} - 0.6\sigma}{\sigma_{\overline{X}}} = 0.253$$

$$\text{or,}\quad \frac{1.96\frac{\sigma}{\sqrt{n}} - 0.6\sigma}{\frac{\sigma}{\sqrt{n}}} = 0.253$$

$$\text{or,}\quad n = 8.09$$

Since n is a whole number, hence we take $n = 8$.

Q. 3.71: *$\bar{X}$ and R charts have been maintained on a certain quality characteristic. All points have fallen within control limits on both charts. A sudden change in the process occurs that increases μ by 1.5 σ but does not change σ. In answering the following questions, assume that the quality characteristic is normally distributed both before and after the change and that the control limits are based on observations made before the shift in process centering.*

(a) If the subgroups size of 3, approximately what percentage of point would you expect to fall outside control limits on the $\bar{X}$ chart because of change in μ ? What percentage on the R chart ?

(b) Answer the same question assuming a subgroup size of 5.

(c) Answer the same question assuming a subgroups size of 8.

(d) Relate the answers to the above questions to Type II error and the effect of subgroup size on the detection of shifts in μ on the $\bar{X}$ chart.

Ans: Figure. 3.39 shows the $\bar{X}$ chart before and after the changes in μ with the control limits based on μ only.

When the process shifts to $\mu + 1.5\ \sigma$, and control limits remaining the same i.e., $\mu \pm 3\ \sigma_{\bar{X}}$, area of the curve between $UCL_{\bar{X}}$ and $LCL_{\bar{X}}$ can be calculated with the help of Table A.

When $\quad UCL_{\bar{X}} = \mu + 3\sigma_{\bar{X}}$

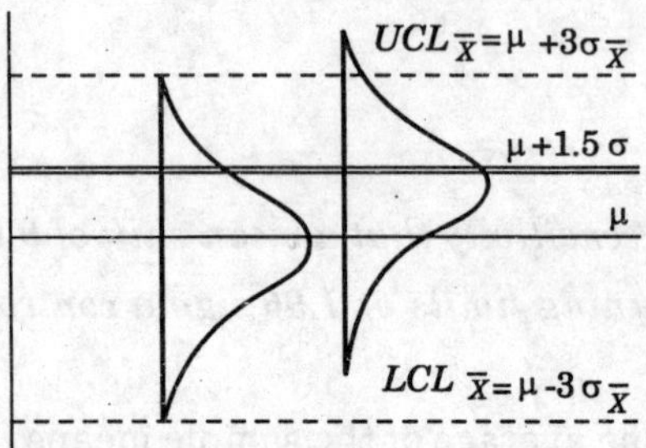

FIGURE 3.39: $\bar{X}$-chart before and after the change of limit in μ.

$$z = \frac{(\mu + 3\sigma_{\bar{X}}) - (\mu + 1.5\sigma)}{\sigma_{\bar{X}}}$$

$$= \frac{3\sigma_{\bar{X}} - 1.5\sigma}{\sigma_{\bar{X}}}$$

$$= \frac{3\sigma_{\bar{X}} - 1.5\sigma_{\bar{X}}\sqrt{n}}{\sigma_{\bar{X}}}$$

$$= 3 - 1.5\sqrt{n}$$

Similarly when $LCL_{\bar{X}} = \mu - 3\sigma_{\bar{X}}$

$$z = -3 - 1.5\sqrt{n}$$

(*a*) When $n = 3$

Value of z corresponding to $UCL_{\bar{X}} = 3 - 1.5\sqrt{3} = 0.402$

Value of z corresponding to $LCL_{\bar{X}} = -3 - 1.5\sqrt{3} = -5.598$

From Table A, the area of curve upto $LCL_{\bar{X}}$ is negligible and area of curve upto $UCL_{\bar{X}}$ is 0.6560. Hence the area of curve beyond the control limits is 1.0000 – 0.6560 = 0.3440 or about 34.4% of the points will fall outside the control limits.

(*b*) When $n = 5$

Following the above procedure and taking the value of n as 5, it can found that 63.8% of the point will fall outside the control limits.

(*c*) When $n = 8$

Percentage of points falling outside the control limits is 89.3%.

It may be noted that in all the above cases, the quality characteristic is normally distributed and σ and hence $\bar{R}$ remains the same. Therefore the number of points falling beyond the control limits or R chart is same as before the shift.

(*d*) If we conclude that universe has not changed, when it really has changed, this conclusion is described as *Type II* error.

In all the above cases the universe has changed. In (*a*) about 34.4% of the points outside the control limit or 65.6% of the points fall within the control limits. When the points fall within the control limit we will be concluding that universe has not changed even when it has really changed. Hence the probability of *Type II* error is 65.6%. Similarly in (*b*) this probability is 36.2% and in (*c*) it is 10.7% only.

From above it can be concluded that an increase in sub-group size reduces the amount or frequency of *Type II* error.

Q. 3.72: *$\bar{X}$ and R charts have been maintained on a process with a subgroup size 4. Past data indicates an μ of 20.0 and a σ of 2.00. The following 3-sigma limits are used :*

$$UCL_{\bar{X}} = 23.0;\ LCL_{\bar{X}} = 17.0$$
$$UCL_R = 9.4;\ LCL_R = 0.$$

A suggestion is made to increase the sample size from 4 to 5 but to maintain the same limits as before on the $\bar{X}$ and R charts "so that we shall not appear to be tightening up on the process".

Discuss the consequences that you would expect if this suggestion were followed. If the suggestion is adopted, would points be more or less likely than before to fall outside the control limits on the $\bar{X}$ chart ? On the R-chart ? Explain your answers.

Ans: When $n = 4,$

$$\mu = 20,\ \sigma = 2.0$$
$$UCL_{\bar{X}} = 23.0,\ LCL_{\bar{X}} = 17.0,$$
$$UCL_R = 9.4,\ LCL_R = 0.$$

For a subgroups size of 4, $D_4 = 2.28$

$$UCL_R = D_4\bar{R} = 9.4$$

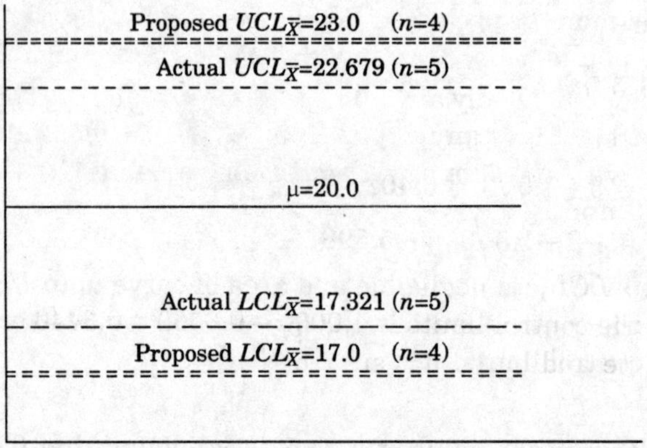

FIGURE 3.40: Position of control limit based on subgroup sizes of 4 and 5 on $\bar{X}$ chart.

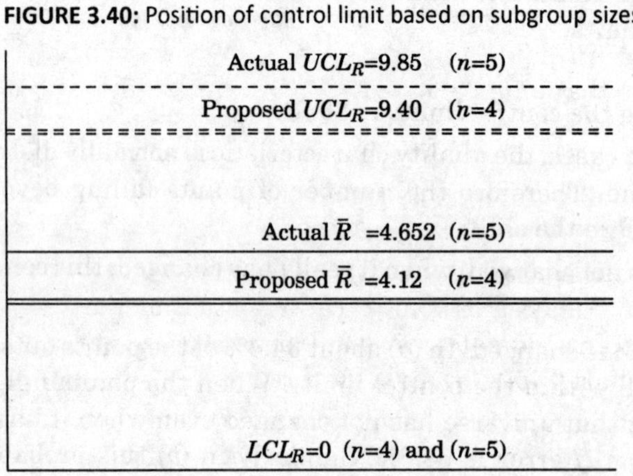

FIGURE 3.41: Position of control limits based on subgroup sizes 4 and 5 on R chart.

$$\bar{R} = \frac{9.4}{D_4} = \frac{9.4}{2.25} = 4.12$$

When $n = 5$ and σ remains unchanged,

$$\begin{aligned}
\bar{R} &= d_2\,\sigma \\
&= 2.326 \times 2 = 4.652 \\
LCL_R &= D_3\bar{R} = 0 \\
UCL_R &= D_4\bar{R} = 2.11 \times 4.625 = 9.85 \\
\sigma_{\bar{X}} &= \frac{\sigma}{\sqrt{n}} = \frac{2}{\sqrt{5}} = 0.893 \\
UCL_{\bar{X}} &= 20 + 3(0.893) \\
&= 22.679 \\
LCL_{\bar{X}} &= 20 - 3(0.893) \\
&= 17.321
\end{aligned}$$

In Fig. 3.40 double dotted lines represent the control limits for subgroup size of 4, (*i.e.* proposed control limits when the subgroup size is 5) single dotted and lines represent the real control limits for subgroup size of 5 on an $\bar{X}$ chart.

When the subgroup size has been increased from 4 to 5 the distribution of subgroup averages will more nearly be normal and again when the control limits are based on the subgroup size of 4 instead of 5, the control bandwidth is more than it should have been. Both the condition lead to the conclusion that more and more points will now be falling between the control limits.

Consequences. If the suggestion is adopted, hardly any point will fall beyond the proposed control limits of 23.0 and 17.0. As a matter of fact any point above 22.679 or below 17.321 indicates an out of control situation but with the proposed control limit in many instances (whenever the point falls between 22.679 and 23.0 ; and 17.321 or 17.0) even out of control situation will be misinterpreted as controlled situation. The chart will now be less sensitive to the detection of shifts in process average or Type II error will be increased.

In Fig. 3.41 double dotted lines show the central and control limits for subgroup size of 4, and broken lines represent the central line and UCLR for subgroup size of 5 on an R chart. LCL_R in both the cases is 0.

When the subgroup size is changed to 5, the central line on R chart should have been at 4.652 but the proposed central line is at 4.12 only. Many points (points falling between 4.562 and 4.12) which are actually below the central line will now be indicated as above the central line, and the resulting conclusion will be that either the dispersion has increased or the chart is going out of control. Since the proposed UCL_R is 9.40 instead of its actual value of 9.85, any point falling between 9.85 and 9.40 will indicate the out of control situation through really it is not. Also since points are expected to fall upto 9.85 but the control limit is set at 9.40 more points will now be falling outside UCL_R of 9.40.

Consequence. In the portion above the central line of the *R*-chart *Type I* will increase because any point falling above 9.40 would indicate the out of control situation but as a matter of fact the process is in control if the points do not cross the limit of 9.85. Similarly in the portion below the central line of the *R*-chart *Type II* error will increase.

Q. 3.73: *You are shown what purports to be a control chart for $\bar{X}$ on a certain quality characteristic of a manufactured product. This control chart contains 50 subgroups. You observe that all the $\bar{X}$ values are close to the central line on the chart and none are near the 3-sigma limits. Infact when you draw 1-sigma limit (only one-third of the distance from the central line to the control limits shown), all the points fall within these narrow limits. (This is called hugging) Would such a chart make you suspicious that something was wrong ? Why ? What possible explanations occur to you that might account for an $\bar{X}$ chart of this type ?*

Ans: There is definitely something wrong. Because in a perfectly controlled process about 68.26% of the occurrences must fall within 1-sigma control limits but according to the observation made for the chart all the points fall within 1-sigma control limits.

One of the possible reasons for this type of situation is that control limits may have been determined on the basis of one universe but the plotted observations are from other universe which has only one-third dispersion of the former universe.

The other possible reason is that after preliminary investigation and control limit determination, there has been considerable improvement in the process so that its dispersion reduces to one-third of its previous value.

Still another possible and most probable reason is that 3-sigma control lines might have been marked on the basis of subgroup size of *n* but while plotting the chart, the subgroup size has been overlooked and it has been kept as 9*n*. The validity of this argument may be proved mathematically as follows :

$$\sigma_{\bar{X}} = \frac{\sigma}{\sqrt{n}}$$

Let $\sigma_{\bar{X}_1}$ denote the standard deviation of when the subgroup size is n and $\sigma_{\bar{X}_2}$ denote the same when the subgroup size is $9n$.

$$3\sigma_{\bar{X}_1} = \frac{3\sigma}{\sqrt{n}}$$

$$3\sigma_{\bar{X}_2} = \frac{3\sigma}{\sqrt{9n}} = \frac{\sigma}{\sqrt{n}}$$

From above, it is obvious that $3\sigma_{\bar{X}_2}$ is equal to one third of $3\sigma_{\bar{X}_1}$. Hence when the subgroup size increase from n to $9n$, the 3-sigma control limits must be kept at only-third distant from the central line to the control limits for the subgroup of size n.

This reasoning seems to be more convincing because a reduction in universe dispersion cannot always be attainable, and, if at all, to a very small extent. This argument presupposes that there is no change in machines, measurements and other variables.

Q. 3.74: *Design an $\bar{X}$ control chart for a process with an in control capability for $\mu = 1.0000$, $\sigma = 0.0020$, with the following specifications :*

Type I or α error to be 0.05

Risk of Type II or β error when $\mu = 1.004$ to be 0.10

Ans: If we conclude that universe has changed when it really is unchanged is known as *Type I* or α error. Obviously the area of the normal curve above the $UCL_{\bar{X}}$ and below the LCL_{X} represent this type of error. Hence the area of the normal curve above $UCL_{\bar{X}} = \frac{\alpha}{2} = \frac{0.05}{2} = 0.025$ or the area of the curve upto $UCL_{\bar{X}} = 0.975$. From Table *A*, the corresponding value of $z = 1.960$.

Again, if we conclude that universe has not changed when it really has changed, is known as *Type II* or β error. Since it is given to be 0.10 when μ shifts to 1.0004, it means that area of the curve outside the control limits be 0.10 or the area of curve upto $UCL_{\bar{X}}$ is $1 - \frac{0.10}{2}$ *i.e.*, 0.95. From Table *A*, the corresponding value of $z = 1.645$.

The above arguments leads to the following equations :

$$1.960 = \frac{UCL_{\bar{X}} - 1.000}{0.0020/\sqrt{n}}$$

$$1.645 = \frac{UCL_{\bar{X}} - 1.004}{0.0020/\sqrt{n}}$$

Solution of these equations and taking n as a whole number, yields

$$UCL_{\bar{X}} = 1.00065 \text{ and } n = 40.$$

Q. 3.75: *In coming steel to be used in process is tested to see that it is of the right chemical composition before it is machine. Dimensions of the machined parts are inspected prior to the heat treating operation. An automatic heat treatment furnace is set at a temperature which hardens the parts. The temperature is so set that the average force required to break the part is 32000 pounds the inherent variability of the heat treating process produces a standard deviation of the breaking force of 3000 pounds Establish the control limits for $\bar{X}$ so that α = 0.10 when samples of size n = 4 are taken.*

Ans:

$$\sigma_{\bar{X}} = \sigma/\sqrt{n} = \frac{3000}{4} = 1500$$

$$z_1 - \frac{\alpha}{2} = z_{0.95} = 1.645$$

$$UCL_{\bar{x}} = \mu + z\sigma_{\bar{x}} = 32000 + 1.645(1500) = 34467.5$$
$$LCL_{\bar{X}} = \mu - z\sigma_{\bar{x}} = 32000 - 1.645(15\ 0\ 0) = 29532.5$$

Q. 3.76: *A process is in control at μ = 25 and σ = 1 and there are 4 observations in each subgroup. Compute 3-sigma control limits for an $\bar{X}$-chart. What is the Type I error for this chart ? If the mean shifts to 27, and undetected, find the magnitude of Type I and Type II errors.*

Ans:
$$\sigma = 1$$
$$3\sigma_{\bar{X}} = \frac{3 \times 1}{\sqrt{4}} = 1.5$$
$$UCL_{\bar{X}} = 25 + 1.5 = 26.5$$
$$LCL_{\bar{X}} = 25 - 1.5 = 23.5$$

The *Type I* error is the area of the normal curve outside the control limits. Clearly in this case it is 0.0027.

When the mean shifts to 27, the area between the control limits of 26.5 and 23.5 is only 0.1587. This area can be computed by using Table *A*.

Now if a point falls between control limits, we will conclude that universe has not changed but in reality it has changed. This is described as Type *II* error and in this case it is 0.1587.

Hence the *Type I* error is 1 – 0.1587 = 0.8413.

Q. 3.77: *A process is normally distributed with mean of 1,000 and a standard deviation of 50. What is the probability of detecting a change of process to 1,080 ?*

(a) Using a control chart for single sample values ?

(b) Using a control chart for means of samples for four in each case, using 3-sigma control lines only on the chart.

Ans: In order to find the required probability, let us derive one general formula.

The original mean μ and its associated $UCL_{\bar{X}}$ is $\mu + 3\sigma_{\bar{X}}$ or $\mu + \frac{3\sigma}{\sqrt{n}}$. If the process is in control the probability of a sample mean lying beyond $UCL_{\bar{X}}$ is 0.00135. Suppose the process mean now moves up *K* standard deviation *i.e.*, the new mean is at $\mu + K\sigma$.

$$z = \frac{\mu + \frac{3\sigma}{\sqrt{n}} - (\mu + K\sigma)}{\sigma_{\bar{X}}}$$
$$= \frac{\mu + \frac{3\sigma}{\sqrt{n}} - (\mu + K\sigma)}{\frac{\sigma}{\sqrt{n}}}$$
$$= 3 - K\sqrt{n}$$

The probability of a subgroup average lying beyond $UCL_{\bar{X}}$, given a change in average to $(\mu + K\sigma)$ is equal to [1.00 — (area of the normal curve corresponding to this value of *z*)].

In this case, when the mean shifts to 1080 the value of

$$K = \frac{80}{50} = 1.6$$

(*a*) For a sample size of 1,

$$z = 3 - 1.6\sqrt{1} = 1.4$$

From Table *A*, area of the curve upto for a *z* value of 1.4 is 0.9192.

Hence the required probability

$$= 1.0000 - 0.9192 \text{ i.e. } 0.0808$$

(*b*) Similarly for a sample size of 4,

$$z = 3 - 1.6\sqrt{4} = -0.2$$

Area of the normal curve for a corresponding value of z of – 0.2, is 0.4207

Hence required probability

$$= 1 - 0.4207 \text{ i.e. } 0.5793$$

Q. 3.78: *In a production programme, the control chart for averages is maintained to detect the out of control situations. Due to tool wear and other causes of similar nature the process average shifts from $\mu + 1.5\sigma$ but σ remains unchanged.*

Find the probability of detecting the shift in the process average when the subgroup size is

(a) 4;

(b) 16.

Ans: As from Q. 3.77., we have

$$z = 3 - K\sqrt{n}$$

$$K = 1.5$$

$$\therefore \quad z = 3 - 1.5\sqrt{n}$$

(*a*) When $n = 4$

$$z = 0$$

the required probability is 0.5.

(*b*) When $n = 16$,

$$z = 3 - 1.5\sqrt{16} = -3$$

Area of normal curve for a corresponding value of z of –3, is 0.00135

Hence required probability

$$1 = - 0.00135$$

$$= 0.99865$$

Q. 3.79: *A manufacturer of dustless chalk is concerned with the density of his product. Previous analysis has shown that his chalk has the required characteristic only if the density is between 4.4 gm/cc and 5.0 gm/cc. If a sample of 100 pieces gives an average of 4.8 gm/cc and a standard deviation of 0.2, is his process aimed at the proper density ? If not, what should the aim be ? Is the process capable of meeting the density requirements.*

Ans:

$$\bar{X} = 4.8, \ \hat{\sigma} = 0.2.$$

$$U = 5.0, L = 4.4$$

$$U - L = 5.0 - 4.4 = 0.6$$

$$6\hat{\sigma} = 6 \times 0.2 = 1.2$$

It is evident that natural tolerances of this process are considerably greater than the specified tolerances. Hence some nonconforming product is inevitable. In order to reduce the nonconforming product to minimum, the process should be centered exactly at the middle U and L *i.e.*. $\bar{X}_0 = 4.7$. Hence it is evident that at present the with $\bar{X}$ of 4.8, the process is not aimed at proper density. Even with centering at 4.7, the process will produce 6.68% below L and 6.68% above U and hence a total of 13.36% nonconforming product is likely to be produced. Obviously the process is not capable of meeting the density requirements.

Q. 3.80: *In the production of an electrical device operated by a thermostatic control, five control switches were tested each hour to determine the "on" temperature at which the thermostat actually operated under a given setting. Results of the test over 4-day production were as follows:*

Date	*Subgroup number*	*"On temperature at which thermostatic switch operates (temperature units not specified)"*					*Subgroup statistics*
		a	*b*	*c*	*d*	*e*	*R*
June 25	1	54	56	56	56	55	2
	2	51	52	54	56	49	7
	3	54	58	50	57	55	7
	4	56	55	56	53	50	6
	5	53	54	57	56	52	5
	6	53	47	58	55	54	11
	7	52	55	54	55	56	4
	8	56	53	53	54	55	3
	9	55	52	53	56	55	4
	10	50	54	53	55	55	5
June 26	11	57	54	53	52	53	5
	12	52	52	54	53	55	3
	13	54	53	55	52	52	3
	14	54	55	54	53	55	2
	15	56	53	57	56	54	4
June 27	16	58	57	56	54	54	4
	17	55	55	55	56	53	3
	18	54	57	54	55	54	3
	19	54	53	56	53	55	3
	20	53	53	57	54	53	4
	21	53	55	57	56	55	4
	22	59	54	53	54	55	6
	23	54	55	58	55	54	4
	24	56	53	51	55	59	8
	25	56	55	55	55	55	1
June 28	26	54	53	54	55	54	2
	27	53	52	55	54	53	3
	28	53	52	53	57	53	5
	29	53	51	55	50	55	5
	30	57	54	56	54	55	3
Totals	30						129

On plotting the $\overline{X}$ and R charts, it was noticed that all points on $\overline{X}$ chart fell within the control limits ; one point on the R chart fell outside the limits. Compute a revised $\overline{R}$ eliminating the out-of-control value of R. From this revised $\overline{R}$, estimate the value of σ that might be expected if the process dispersion could be held under statistical control.

The specification for the "on" temperature of this thermo-statistically controlled switch is 54 ± 4. If the process could be centered at 54, with the σ you have just estimated, and if statistical control could be maintained, what percentage of switches would you expect to fall outside their specification limits ? Assume that the normal distribution is applicable. Among the 150 switches observed, how many actually fell outside the specification limit.

Ans: From the given subgroup ranges, it is evident that subgroup 6 fell outside the UCL_R. Hence eliminating this subgroup.

$$\overline{R}_{revised} = \frac{\Sigma R - 11}{(30-1)}$$

$$= \frac{129-11}{29} = \frac{118}{29}$$

$$= 4.0689 \approx 4.07$$

$$\hat{\sigma} = \frac{\overline{R}}{d_2} = \frac{4.07}{2.326} = 1.75$$

$$U = 54 + 4 = 58$$

$$L = 54 - 4 = 50$$

Also $\mu = 54$

Area of the curve below L of 50 from Table A is found to be 0.0111.

Similarly area of the curve above U is 0.0111

Hence percentage outside the specification limits is 2.22%.

Following tabulation gives the items which are outside the specification limits *i.e.*, either below L of 50 or above U of 58.

Date	*Subgroup number*	*Item number*	*"On" temperature value*
June 25	2	*e*	49
	6	*b*	47
June 27	22	*a*	59
	24	*e*	59
Total		4	

Since out of 150, only 4 items are outside the specification limits. Hence about 2.66% or about 2.7% fell outside the specification limits.

Q. 3.81: *A manufacturer makes metal washers, and a large number of samples of 5 items have been kept. The mean range of washers is 0.0002 cm. The firm receives an order for washers within the tolerance limits of 1 + 0.0003 cm. Should the order be accepted ?*

Ans: Assuming a normal distribution, and in order to have the maximum washers be within the tolerance band, the aimed - at process average to $\overline{X}_0$

Therefore, $$\bar{X}_o = 1 + \frac{0.0003}{2} \text{ i.e. } 1.00015$$

$$\hat{\sigma} = \frac{0.0002}{2.326} = 0.000086$$

With $\bar{X}_0$ of 1.00015 and $\hat{\sigma}$ of 0.000086, the percentage of product above U is 4.05% and also below L is 4.05%. Hence about 8.10% product is nonconforming. The order therefore may not be accepted, due to large scale nonconforming product but commercial viability be considered before arriving at the final decision.

Q. 3.82: *The dimension of a certain manufactured part is specified as **2.050 ± 0.020**. If the dimension falls below L, the part must be scrapped, if above U, rework is required. Control charts for $\bar{X}$ and R are maintained on this dimension. The subgroup size is 4. After 20 subgroups, $\Sigma\bar{X} = 41.340$ and $\Sigma R = 0.320$.*

(a) Compute the values of 3-sigma control limits for $\bar{X}$ and R charts and estimate the value of σ.

(b) If the process is in statistical control and normally distributed, what can you conclude regarding its ability to meet the specifications ? Can your make any suggestion for improvement?

(c) What is R.P.I of the process.

Ans: (*a*) $$\bar{\bar{X}} = \frac{41.340}{20} = 2.067$$

$$\bar{R} = \frac{0.320}{20} = 0.016$$

Using $A_2 = 0.73$ and $D_4 = 2.28$, the control limits on the $\bar{\bar{X}}$ and R charts are computed to be as follows :

$$UCL_{\bar{X}} = 2.079,\ LCL_{\bar{X}} = 2.055$$

$$UCL_R = 0.360,\ LCL_R = 0$$

$$\hat{\sigma} = \bar{R}/d_2 = \frac{0.016}{2.059} = 0.0078$$

(*b*) $$6\hat{\sigma} = 0.0078 \times 6 = 0.0468$$

$$U = 2.050 + 0.020 = 2.070$$

$$L = 2.050 - 0.020 = 2.030$$

As $6\hat{\sigma}$ is more than $(U - L)$ and the centering is not maintained midway of U and L *i.e.* 2.050 and as it is more towards U, some product is liable to be outside the U. With centering at 2.067 and $\hat{\sigma}$ of 0.0078, the area of normal curve above U is 0.3502 *i.e.* 35% product is above U and practically no product below L as centering is more than 3σ away from L.

The situation can be improved by shifting the process centering so that $(\bar{X}_0 - 3\sigma) = L$

i.e. $$\bar{X}_0 = 2.0534$$

with this aimed at value of centering, the area of above the U is found to be 0.0066. Hence rework is 0.66%

From above it is evident that shifting in the process centering will improve the situation to a great extent.

$$R.P.I = \frac{U - L}{\bar{R}} = \frac{0.040}{0.016} = 2.5$$

For a subgroup size of 4, R.P.I of 2.5 indicates that this is a low precision process.

Q. 3.83: *Automatic machinery is used to fill and seal ten-ounce cans of a certain liquid product. The process standard deviation is **0.20** oz. To ensure that every can meets or exceeds this **10.0** oz minimum, the company has set a target value of the process of **11.0** oz.*

*(a) At this process average of **11** oz, what percent of the cans well have less than **10.5** oz of product ? Assume contained weights are normally distributed ?*

(b) If the quality control section samples these cans in subgroups of four, what will 3σ control limits be for the $\bar{X}$ chart ?

*(c) Assuming that ±3σ natural tolerance limits on the process cover virtually all of the filled cans, what is the minimum value to which the process average may be lowered in order to ensure that virtually no cans are filled with less than a minimum of **10** oz ?*

Ans: $\bar{X}_0 = 11.0, \sigma = 0.20$

$$\sigma_{\bar{X}} = \frac{0.20}{\sqrt{4}} = 0.10$$

$$3\alpha_{\bar{X}} = 0.30$$

(*a*) From Table A, the percentage of cans below the lower limit of 10.5 *oz* is computed to be 0.62%

(*b*) $UCL_{\bar{X}} = \bar{X}_0 + 3\sigma_{\bar{X}} = 11.3$

$LCL_{\bar{X}} = \bar{X}_0 - 3\sigma_{\bar{X}} = 10.7$

(*c*) Let μ_1 be the minimum value to which the process average may be lowered in order to ensure that virtually no cans are filled with less than a minimum value of 10z, then

$$\mu_1 - 3\sigma = 10$$

or $\mu_1 - 3(0.20) = 10.$

or $\mu_1 = 10.6$ oz.

Q. 3.84: *The volume of beer dispensed by a beer bottling machine is governed by the machine setting. When processing one pint bottles the company sets a lower limit on volume of **20.20** fluid ounces, i.e. a lower tolerances limit, as a safeguard against giving short measure. At the beginning of a bottling run to process **4,800** one pint bottles the machine was set at **20.4** fluid ounces. Twenty samples each of four bottles were then collected and the sample means and ranges computed :*

Sample No.	**1**	**2**	**3**	**4**	**5**	**6**	**7**	**8**	**9**	**10**
Mean	– 0.09	0.01	– 0.05	– 0.06	0.01	– 0.05	0.05	0.02	– 0.02	0.01
Range	0.21	0.42	0.30	0.05	0.15	0.18	0.22	0.18	0.14	0.27
Sample No.	**11**	**12**	**13**	**14**	**15**	**16**	**17**	**18**	**19**	**20**
Mean	0.03	0.01	0.13	– 0.05	– 0.02	0.02	0.03	– 0.13	0.13	0.03
Range	0.36	0.26	0.14	0.18	0.10	0.21	0.21	0.21	0.24	0.12

*The figures for sample means are each the true mean minus (**20.4** fl. oz).*

*Is the initial setting correct and if not, what should it be on the assumption that at population variance is not altered by changing the setting ? (The machine may be set to the nearest **0.05** fl. oz.)*

Ans: The machine has been set at 20.4 oz. In order to check whether the machine has correctly set, the average ($\bar{\bar{X}}$) is to be checked.

$$\bar{\bar{X}} = \frac{20.4 + (-0.09 + 0.01 + ... + 0.03)}{20}$$
$$= 20.3925$$

Since the computed $\bar{\bar{X}}$ is different from 20.4, the machine setting is slightly incorrect.

Also, $\Sigma R = 0.21 + 0.42 + ... + 0.24 + 0.12 = 4.15$

$$\bar{R} = 4.15/20 = 0.2075$$
$$\hat{\sigma} = \bar{R}/d_2 = 0.2075/2.059 = 0.100$$

Let the machine be set at $\bar{X}_0$ in order to meet the lower specification limit of 20.20 oz. As variance is not altered, therefore $\hat{\sigma}$ also remains unchanged when machine setting is changed.

Therefore $20.20 = \bar{X}_0 - 3\hat{\sigma}$

or $\bar{X}_0 = 20.50$ oz.

Since it is seen that at any setting, the process average results in a lower value than its aimed value by an amount (20.4 – 20.3925) i.e. 0.0075. So it is imperative that the aimed-at process average should be set higher by a minimum amount of 0.0075. Since the minimum step available for average setting is 0.05, which is more than 0.0075, hence the new aimed-at value

$$\bar{X}_0 = 20.50 + 0.05 = 20.55 \text{ oz.}$$

Q. 3.85: *In a statistically controlled container filling process L = 32 C.C. Control charts for $\bar{X}$ and s are maintained. The subgroup size is 10. The value of $\bar{X}$ and s are computed for each subgroup. After 18 subgroups $\Sigma\bar{X}$ = 595.8, and Σs = 8.24.*

(a) Compute control limits for $\bar{X}$ and s charts.

(b) It is desired to hold the over fill to as low a value as possible consistent with meeting this specification. What was the overfill during the period covered by the control chart ? What percentage of containers you would expect to contain less than 32 c.c. Assume normal distribution is applicable. If it were possible for 4% to be below 32 c.c., how much could the average overfill be reduced below its present value ?

Ans:
$$\bar{\bar{X}} = \frac{595.8}{18} = 33.1$$

$$\bar{s} = \frac{8.24}{18} = 0.458$$

From Table C, for $n = 10$, $c_4 = 0.9727$

$$\hat{\sigma} = \frac{\bar{s}}{c_4} = \frac{0.458}{0.9727} = 0.4508$$

(a) For computation of control limits on $\bar{X}$ and s charts, Table E gives following factors for $n = 10$

$A_3 = 0.98$, $B_3 = 0.28$, $B_4 = 1.72$

$$UCL_{\bar{X}} = X_{\bar{X}} + A_{3\bar{s}} = 33.1 + 0.98(0.458) = 33.55$$
$$LCL_{\bar{X}} = X_{\bar{X}} - A_{3\bar{s}} = 33.1 - 0.98(0.458) = 32.65$$
$$USL_s = B_4\bar{s} = 1.72(0.458) = 0.788$$
$$LSL_s = B_3\bar{s} = 0.28(0.458) = 0.128$$

(b) Since the specified limit is 32 c.c., therefore, average overfill = 33.1 – 32.0 = 1.1 c.c.

Percentage of containers containing less than 32 c.c. is the area of the curve upto 32. From Table A, this is calculated to be 0.975%.

If the containers having content below 32 c.c. are 4%, then the area of normal curve upto 32 c.c. should be 0.04 . From Table A, this is possible only when $z = -1.75$.

$$-1.75 = \frac{32.0 - \bar{X}}{0.4708}$$

or $\bar{\bar{X}} = 32.824$

Therefore, overfill reduced by 33.1 – 32.824 i.e. 0.276 c.c.

Q. 3.86: *A machine produces spark plugs to tolerance limits of 25 thousandths of an inch ± 2 thousandth. Plugs outside this range would give erratic running of the engine. It is decided to set up control charts for the machine. Records reveal that the average range for samples of 5 items is 1, and the mean of the means is 25.1. Set up the mean and range charts.*

(a) Find the minimum tolerances to which the machine will operate.

(b) Find the range of shifts that could occur in the process centering before there was danger of exceeding the tolerances.

Ans: $\bar{\bar{X}} = 25.1,\ \bar{R} = 1,\ n = 5$

$$\hat{\sigma} = \bar{R}/d_2 = \frac{1}{2.326} = 0.429$$

Using A_2, D_4 and D_3 for sample size of 5

$$UCL_{\bar{X}} = 26.676,\ LCL_{\bar{X}} = 24.524$$

$$UCL_R = 2.11,\ LCL_R = 0$$

(*a*) Minimum tolerance to which the machine will operate

$$= 25 \pm 3\hat{\sigma} = 25 \pm 3(0.429) = 25 \pm 1.287$$

(*b*) $U - L = 27 - 23 = 4.$

$$6\hat{\sigma} = 6(0.429) = 2.574$$

It is evident that natural tolerances of the process are considerable less than the specified tolerance. Hence shifts in the process centering can be allowed.

If $\bar{X}_{0\ max.}$ is the maximum value of process centering without the danger of exceeding U then

$$U - 3\hat{\sigma} = \bar{X}_{0\ max.}$$

or

$$\bar{X}_{0\ max} = U - 3\hat{\sigma}$$

$$= 25.713$$

If $\bar{X}_{0\ min}$ is the minimum value of the process centering without danger of going below L, then

$$L + 3\hat{\sigma} = \bar{X}_{0\ min}$$

or

$$\bar{X}_{0\ min} = L + 3\hat{\alpha}$$

$$= 24.287$$

From above it is evident that process centering can vary from 25.713 to 24.287 before there is a danger of exceeding the tolerances.

Q. 3.87: *Control charts for* $\bar{X}$ *and R are maintained on the outside diameter of the shaft. The subgroup size is 4. The values of* $\bar{X}$ *and R are computed for each subgroup. After 20 subgroup* $\Sigma X = 41.283$, $\Sigma R = 0.280$. *The dimension specification for the product is* **2.050 ± 0.020**. *If the* *dimension falls above the specification limit, rework is required ; if below the specification limit, the shaft must be rejected. If the process is in statistical quantity control and normally distributed, what can you conclude regarding its ability to meet the specification ? Can you make any suggestion ?*

Ans: $USL_x = 2.050 + 0.020 = 2.070$

$LSL_x = 2.050 - 0.020 = 2.030$

Simple computations result in

$$\bar{\bar{X}} = 2.064\ ,\ \bar{R} = 0.014\ ,\ \hat{\sigma} = 0.007\ ,\ 6\hat{\sigma} = 0.042.$$

As natural tolerance i.e. 0.042 are greater than specified tolerance of 0.040, some product is likely to fall beyond specifications. With the present centering at 2.064, practically no product will fall below L of 2.030 but the amount of product above U of 2.070 is quite high i.e. 19.57% as (computed using Table *A*). Since rework is possible for the product above U and the product below L is to be scrapped considering it is economical to avoid scrap and spend on rework, the aimed at $\bar{X}_0$ should be such that there should be practically no scrap from the process. Hence

$$\bar{X}_0 - 3\hat{\sigma} = L$$

or $$\bar{X}_0 = 2.051$$

With above centering, the percentage of product above U is of the order of 2.07% only.

Q. 3.88: *Control charts for* $\bar{X}$ *and* σ *are maintained on the resistance in ohms of certain electrical parts. For 20 subgroups* $\Sigma X = 1612.9$ *and* $\Sigma s = 71.4$. *If the size of the subgroup is 25, and the resistance is specified as* 80 ± 6 *ohms, find :*

(a) the process capability (6 sigma value)

(b) the percentage expected above U

(c) the percentage expected below L

You can assume that the process is in statistical control and normally distributed.

Describe and justify the action you would like to recommend in order to reduce the rejection to minimum.

Ans: Simple computation yield the following :

$$\bar{\bar{X}} = 80.645\ ;$$

$$\bar{s} = 3.57\ ;$$

$$\hat{\sigma} = \frac{\bar{s}}{c_4} = \frac{3.57}{0.9896} = 3.61$$

$$3\hat{\sigma} = 10.83$$

$$U = 86\ ,\ L = 74$$

(*a*) Process capability = $6\hat{\sigma} = 6 \times 3.61 = 21.66$

(*b*) With the present centering at 80.645 percentage of product above U is found to be 6.95%

(*c*) Also percentage below L is 3.3%.

It is evident that the natural tolerance of this process are considerably greater than the specified tolerances, some nonconforming product will be produced.

To have minimum rejection, the area of the normal curve outside the specified limits should be minimum or the area between the specified limits should be maximum. This is possible only when the centering is done exactly at the middle of the two specified limits. So in this case centering should be done at $\frac{86 + 74}{2}$ i.e., at 80. With centering at 80, the percentage of the product below U is 4.85% and above U is also 4.85%.

It can be observed that even by shifting the process centering, there is hardly any reduction in the percentage rejection.

In order to reduce the rejection to minimum, there should be basic change in the process so that it should have a σ of 2, and if it is not possible to make changes in the process, reworking be resorted to in case the same is feasible.

Q. 3.89: *A control chart has been used to monitor a certain process during a considerable period of time. The process is sampled in subgroups of four at intervals of about two hours, and the $\overline{X}$ control chart has 3σ control limits of 121.0 and 129.0 with the target $\overline{X}_0$ at 125.0*

(a) If the product is sold to a user who has a specification of 127.0 ± 8.0, what per cent of the product will not meet this specification assuming a normally distributed output ?

(b) If the target value of this process can be shifted without effect on the process standard deviation, what target value would minimize the amount of product being produced outside the specification values ?

(c) At this new target value, what percent of the product will not meet the required specifications ?

Ans:
$$\overline{X}_0 = 125.0,\ UCL_{\overline{X}} = 129.0,\ LCL_{\overline{X}} = 121$$
$$3\sigma_{\overline{X}} = 129.0 - 125.0 = 4$$

Since
$$3\sigma_{\overline{X}} = \frac{\hat{\sigma}}{\sqrt{n}},$$
$$3\hat{\sigma} = 3\sqrt{n}(3\sigma_{\overline{X}}) = \sqrt{4} \times 4 = 8$$
$$\hat{\sigma} = 8/3.$$

(*a*)
$$U = 127.0 + 8.0 = 135.0$$
$$L = 127.0 - 8.0 = 119.0$$

With U of 135.0, $\overline{X}_0$ of 125.0 and $\hat{\sigma}$ of $\frac{8}{3}$, as computed from Table A, no item will fall above U

Similarly, with L of 119.0, about 1.22% of items will below L

(*b*) Since the process target value can be changed without affecting the process standard deviation and $3\hat{\sigma}$ for the process is exactly equal to the tolerance limit of 8, setting the process average midway of the U of 135.0 and L of 119.0 i.e. at 127.0, will result in minimum product outside these specification limits.

(*c*) Since U is at $\overline{X} + 3\hat{\sigma}$ and L is at $\overline{X} - \hat{\sigma}$, percentage of product outside the specification limits is only 0.27.

Q. 3.90: *Samples of 4 items each taken from Hardy Motors' manufacturing process at regular intervals. A certain quality characteristic (i.e. diameter, width, etc.) is measured and $\overline{X}$ (mean) and R (range) values are computed for each sample. After 25 samples, $\overline{X}$ = 15,610 and ΣR = 411.4.*

(a) Compute limits (3 sigma) for $\overline{X}$ (mean) and R (range) charts.

(b) Suppose that all the points on the $\overline{X}$ and R charts fell within control limits. Tolerance requirements for this particular quality characteristics are 15,610 ± 15. If the quality characteristic is normally distributed with the distribution centered at $\overline{\overline{X}}$ (i.e. mean of the sample means), what of the product, if any, would you expect to find outside the specified tolerances ?

(c) Any item that falls below the lower tolerance limit of 15,595 must be scrapped, whereas any above the upper tolerance limit of 15,625 may be brought within specifications by rework

operation. It is suggested that the process ought to be centered at a level so that not more than 0.1 percent of the product will be scrapped. If the quality characteristic is normally distributed with the dispersion indicated by the control data, and if it is believed that statistical control can be maintained, what should be the aimed at value $\overline{X}_0$ (i.e the centering of the process) to make this scrap exactly 0.1 percent ? What percentage of the rework should be expected with this centering ?

Ans:

$$\overline{\overline{X}} = 15{,}610$$

$$\Sigma R = 411.4$$

$$\overline{R} = \frac{411.4}{25} = 16.456$$

$$\hat{\sigma} = \frac{16.456}{2.059} = 7.992 \approx 8$$

$$\hat{\sigma}_{\overline{X}} = \frac{8}{\sqrt{4}} = 4$$

$$3\sigma_{\overline{X}} = 12$$

(*a*)

$$UCL_{\overline{X}} = 15610 + 12 = 15622$$

$$LCL_{\overline{X}} = 15610 - 12 = 15998$$

$$UCL_R = D_4\overline{R}$$

$$= 2.28 \times 16.456 = 37.52$$

$$LCL_R = D_3\overline{R}$$

$$= 0 \times 16.456 = 0.$$

(*b*)

$$U = 15610 + 15 = 15625$$

$$L = 15610 - 15 = 15595$$

$$6\hat{\sigma} = 6 \times 8 = 48$$

It is evident that the natural tolerance of this process is considerably greater than the specified tolerance and hence some nonconforming product will be produced. When the process is centered at $\overline{\overline{X}}$ of 15,610, area of the normal curve upto L as determined from Table A is 0.0304. Similarly area of the curve above U is 0.0304. Hence about 6% of nonconforming product will be produced.

(*c*) Let the process be centered at $\overline{X}_0$, so that the scrap is 0.1%. This means that area of the normal curve below L should be 0.001. From Table A the corresponding value of z is – 3.09.

Hence
$$-3.09 = \frac{15{,}595 - \overline{X}_0}{8}$$

$$\overline{X}_0 = 15{,}619.72$$

With the process centering at 15619.72, area of the normal curve above U of 15,625 works out to be 0.2546. Hence about 25.5% of the products will need rework.

Q. 3.91: *The diameter of one end of a gyro drive shaft is required within 1,140 ±10. The control charts $\overline{X}$ and R are initiated. After 30 subgroups of 5 shafts each have been examined, $\Sigma\overline{X}$ = 34,290 and ΣR = 330.*

(a) Estimate the mean and standard deviation of the process assuming that it is in statistical control.

(b) Determine R.P.I. of the process

(c) Determine the 3-sigma limits for $\bar{X}$ and R charts

(d) Determine the natural specification limits of the process

(e) Shafts with diameters less than 1,130 must be scrapped, shafts with diameters greater than 1,150 can be reworked but the rework operation must be done by skilled lathe operators. The resulting cost is as great as the direct cost of manufacture.

1. *Determine the percentage of rework and of scrap product assuming a normal distribution for the process.*
2. *100 percent inspection has been carried on up to this point. What would be your advice regarding the level of inspection, centering etc., for the immediate future ?*
3. *A material Review Committee, made up of representatives from the plant and the customer, has reviewed the situation and has decided that shafts can be used successfully with diameters as large as 1,155. How would this information affect your decision in (2) ?*

Ans: (*a*)

$$\bar{\bar{X}} = \frac{34290}{30} = 1{,}143,$$

$$\bar{R} = \frac{330}{30} = 11$$

$$\hat{\sigma} = \frac{\bar{R}}{d_2} = \frac{11}{2.326} = 4.73$$

(*b*)

$$U = 1140 + 10 = 1150$$

$$L = 1140 - 10 = 1130$$

$$U - L = 1150 - 1130 = 20$$

$$R.P.I. = \frac{U - L}{\bar{R}} = \frac{20}{11} = 1.818$$

(*c*)

$$UCL_{\bar{X}} = 1{,}149.38$$

$$LCL_{\bar{X}} = 1{,}136.62$$

$$UCL_R = 23.21$$

$$LCL_R = 0$$

(*d*) Upper natural specification limit = $\bar{\bar{X}} + 3\hat{\sigma}$ = 1143 + 14.19 = 1157.19

(*e*) Lower natural specification limit = $\bar{\bar{X}} - 3\hat{\sigma}$ = 1143 − 14.19 = 1128.81

1. With process centering at 1143, as determined from Table *A*, scrap = 0.30% and rework = 6.97%
2. Since the specification limits are quite tight in relation to the process dispersion, it is appropriate to continue 100 percent inspection in near future. Also since the resulting cost of rework is same as the direct cost of manufacture, in order to achieve the maximum economy, it is judicious to have the maximum product within the specification limits. This will result when the process centering is done exactly at the middle of *U* and *L* i.e. 1,140.
3. Even when there is a relaxation of accepting the shafts with diameters as large as 1,155, the specification limits are still quite tight in relation to process dispersion, it is appropriate to continue 100 percent inspection in near future. Further it can be determined from Table *A* that maximum economy (minimum area outside the specification) results when the process centering is again shifted to the middle of

U and L *i.e.* $\dfrac{1155 + 1130}{2} = 1142.50$. With this process centering, scrap is only 0.4 percent and the rework is also 0.4 percent.

Q. 3.92: *The head of an automobile engine must be machined so that both the surface that meet the engine block and the surface that meets the valve covers are flat. These surfaces must also be 4.875 inches ±0.001 inch apart. Presuming that the valve cover side of the head is finished correctly, compare the capabilities of two processes for performing the finishing of the engine block side of the head. A broach set to do the job gave an average thickness of 4.877 inches with an average range of 0.0005 inch for 25 samples of 4 each. A milling machine gave an average of 4.875 inches and average range of 0.001 inches for 20 samples of 4 each.*

Ans:

$$U = 4.875 + 0.001 = 4.876$$
$$L = 4.875 - 0.001 = 4.874$$

In case of broach,

$$\mu = 4.877$$
$$\bar{R} = 0.0005$$
$$\hat{\sigma} = \frac{0.0005}{2.059} = 0.00024$$
$$\mu + 3\hat{\sigma} = 4.877 + 3(0.00024) = 4.87784$$
$$\mu - 3\hat{\sigma} = 4.877 - 3(0.00024) = 4.87628$$

In case of milling machine,

$$\mu_1 = 4.875$$
$$\bar{R} = 0.001$$
$$\hat{\sigma}_1 = \frac{0.001}{2.059} = 0.00048$$
$$\mu_1 + 3\hat{\sigma}_1 = 4.875 + 3(0.00048) = 4.87644$$
$$\mu_1 - 3\hat{\sigma}_1 = 4.875 - 3(0.00048) = 4.87356$$

From above results, it is evident that in the case of broach, most of the product will be outside the specification limits while in the case of milling machine most of the product will be within the specification limits. Hence milling operation is preferable.

Q. 3.93: *Construct control charts for $\bar{\bar{X}}$ and R for the following data on the basis of samples of fuses, 5 being taken every hour (each set of 5 has been arranged in ascending order of magnitude). Comment on the state of control, assuming that these are the first data. What will be the future control limits on $\bar{X}$ and R charts.*

42	42	19	36	42	51	60	18	15	69	64	61
65	45	24	54	51	74	60	20	30	109	90	78
75	68	80	69	57	75	72	27	39	113	93	94
78	72	81	77	59	78	95	42	62	118	109	109
87	90	81	84	78	132	138	60	84	153	112	136

Ans: Since there are 60 observations in all and each subgroups consists of 5 observations, therefore we have 12 subgroups of samples. For case of calculations data are arranged as follows:

Sample No.	*Sample observation (X)*					ΣX	$\bar{X}$	R
1	42	65	75	78	87	347	69.4	45
2	42	45	68	72	90	317	63.4	48
3	19	24	80	81	81	285	57.0	62
4	36	54	69	77	84	320	64.0	48
5	42	51	57	59	78	287	57.4	36
6	51	74	75	78	132	410	82.0	81
7	60	60	72	95	138	425	85.0	78
8	18	20	27	42	60	167	33.4	42
9	15	30	39	62	84	230	46.0	69
10	69	109	113	118	153	562	112.4	84
11	64	90	93	109	112	468	93.6	48
12	61	78	94	109	136	478	95.6	75
Totals							859.2	716

$$\bar{\bar{X}} = \frac{\Sigma \bar{X}}{12} = \frac{859.2}{12} = 71.6\,;\ \bar{R} = \frac{\Sigma R}{12} = \frac{716}{12} = 59.67$$

$$UCL_{\bar{X}} = \bar{\bar{X}} + A_2\bar{R} = 71.6 + 0.58 \times 59.67 = 71.6 + 34.6 = 106.2$$

$$LCL_{\bar{X}} = \bar{\bar{X}} - A_2\bar{R} = 71.6 - 0.58 \times 59.67 = 71.6 - 34.6 = 37.0$$

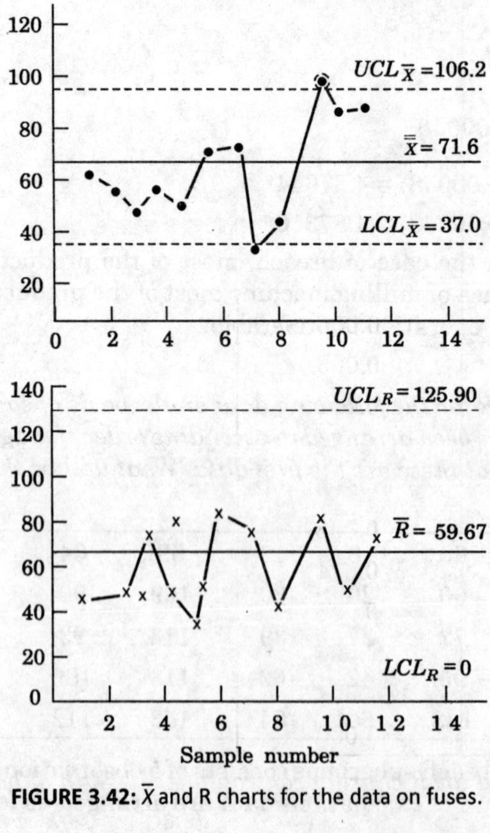

FIGURE 3.42: $\bar{X}$ and R charts for the data on fuses.

$$UCL_R = D_4\bar{R} = 2.11 \times 59.67 = 125.90$$
$$LCL_{\bar{R}} = D_3\bar{R} = 0$$

Figure 3.42. shows the $\bar{X}$ and R charts.

The control charts in Fig. 3.42 indicate that no point on R chart falls beyond the control limits while the points for subgroups 8 and 10 fall below $LCL_{\bar{X}}$ and above $UCL_{\bar{X}}$ respectively. Eliminating these points from $\bar{X}$ chart only.

$$\bar{X}_{revised} = \frac{859.2 - (33.4 + 112.4)}{(12 - 2)} = \frac{713.4}{10} = 71.34$$

Now $UCL_{\bar{X}} = 71.34 + A_2\bar{R} = 71.34 + 34.6 = 105.94$

New $LCL_{\bar{X}} = 71.34 - A_2\bar{R} = 71.34 - 34.6 = 36.74$

As no point on R chart is beyond the control limits, the control limits for future use on R chart will remain unchanged *i.e.* 125.9 and 0.

Also since these are initial data from the process, out-of-control points cannot be assumed as chance causes and it is justified to eliminate then for future control limits.

Q. 3.94: *The following are the mean and ranges of 20 samples of 5 each. The data pertain to the overall lengths of a fragmentation bomb manufactured during the war by the American Stove Company. The measurements are in inches.*

Sample No.	$\bar{X}$	R
1	0.8372	0.010
2	0.8324	0.009
3	0.8318	0.008
4	0.8344	0.004
5	0.8346	0.005
6	0.8332	0.011
7	0.8340	0.009
8	0.8344	0.003
9	0.8308	0.002
10	0.8350	0.006
11	0.8380	0.006
12	0.8322	0.002
13	0.8356	0.013
14	0.8322	0.005
15	0.8304	0.008
16	0.8372	0.011
17	0.8282	0.006
18	0.8346	0.006
19	0.8360	0.004
20	0.8374	0.006

(a) From these data, set up $\bar{X}$ *chart and an R chart of control for the length of bomb bases produced in the future.*

(b) The above samples were taken every 15 minutes in order of production. The production rate was 350 units per hour and the specification limits were 0.820 and 0.840 inches.

On the assumption that the length of the bomb bases were normally distributed what percentage of the bomb base would you estimate to have length outside the specification limits when the process is under control at the levels indicated by the above data? In other words what is the percentage of nonconforming defectives of the above process operating at the levels indicated? Could the percent nonconforming product be reduced to zero by changing the process average?

(c) What would happen to the percent nonconforming product if the process average should shift to 0.8370 ?

(d) What is R.P.I. of the process ?

Ans: *(a)*

$$\bar{X} = \frac{0.8372 + .. + 0.8374}{20} = \frac{16.6796}{20} = 0.83398$$

$$\bar{R} = \frac{0.010 + 0.009 + ... + 0.006}{20} = \frac{0.134}{20} = 0.0067$$

Trial control limit on $\bar{X}$ and R charts :

$$UCL_{\bar{X}} = \bar{X} + A_2\bar{R} = 0.83398 + (0.58 \times 0.0067) = 0.8379$$

$$LCL_{\bar{X}} = \bar{X} - A_2\bar{R} = 0.83398 - (0.58 \times 0.0067) = 0.8301$$

$$UCL_R = D_4\bar{R} = 2.11 \times 0.0067 = 0.01414$$

$$LCL_R = D_3\bar{R} = 0 \times 0.0067 = 0$$

From the given data, it is known that the values of $\bar{X}$ corresponding to subgroups 11 and 17 are above $UCL_{\bar{X}}$. Excluding these points.

$$\bar{\bar{X}}_{revised} = \frac{16.6796 - (0.8380 + 0.9287)}{(20 - 2)} = 0.834077$$

Since no point on R chart falls outside the control limits, there is no revision in $\bar{R}$ and the control limits on R chart remain unchanged.

Control limits for production :

$$UCL_{\bar{X}} = \bar{\bar{X}}_{revised} + A_2\bar{R} = 0.834077 + 0.003886 = 0.8380$$

$$LCL_{\bar{X}} = \bar{\bar{X}}_{revised} - A_2\bar{R} = 0.834077 - 0.00386 = 0.8302$$

$$UCL_R = D_4\,R = 0.1414, \text{ same a s earlier one}$$

$$LCL_{\bar{R}} = D_3\bar{R} = 0$$

(b)

$$U = 0.840$$

$$L = 0.820$$

$$\hat{\sigma} = \frac{\bar{R}}{d_2} = \frac{0.0067}{2.326} = 0.0029$$

$$6\hat{\sigma} = 6 \times 0.0029 = 0.0174$$

$$U - L = 0.840 - 0.828 = 0.020$$

It is evident that the natural tolerance of this process is less than the specified tolerance, the percent nonconforming product can practically be reduced to zero. At the present level ($\bar{\bar{X}} = 0.834077$), as determined from Table *A* percentage of product below *L* is practically zero, but above *U*, it is 2.1 per cent.

If the process average is shifted exactly midway of the specification limits i.e. at 0.8300, percentage of product above *U* and below *L* is practically zero.

(c) When the process average shifts to 0.8370, as determined from Table A, percentage of product below L is practically zero, but above U, it is about 15.87%. Hence the percent nonconforming product is more than earlier.

(d) $$R.P.I = \frac{U - L}{\bar{\bar{R}}} = \frac{0.020}{0.0067} = 2.99$$

Q. 3.95: *The following table gives the coded measurements obtained from 20 subgroups of 5 each.*

Subgroups No.	*Statistics*	$\bar{X}$	*R*
1	– 1, 2, 1, 0, 1	0.6	3
2	2, 0, 1, 0, 1	0.8	1
3	1, 1, 0, 0, 1	0.6	1
4	2, 1, 0, – 1, 0	0.4	3
5	1, – 1, 0, 0, – 1	– 0.2	2
6	1, – 1, 2, 0, – 2	0.0	4
7	– 1, – 1, 0, – 2, 1	– 0.6	3
8	1, 1, 2, – 1, 0	0.6	3
9	2, 1, – 1, 0, 0	0.4	3
10	– 2, 1, – 2, 2, 1	0.0	4
11	0, 1, – 3, 2, 1	0.2	5
12	2, 1, – 1, 0, 0	0.4	3
13	0, 1, – 3, 2, 1	0.2	5
14	0, 0, – 1, 0, 1	0.0	2
15	– 1, 2, 1, 1, 2 1	0	3
16	1, – 1, 2, 0, – 2	0.0	4
17	2, 1, – 1, 0, 0	0.4	3
18	2, 0, 1, 0, 1	0.8	2
19	0, 1, 1, – 1, 1	0.4	2
20	3, – 3, 1, 1, 1	0.6	6

(a) Construct the $\bar{X}$ and R charts and plot the points on the charts.

(b) What will be the control limits on $\bar{X}$ and R charts for immediate future use ?

(c) Estimate the value of σ.

(d) Assuming that the process is just able to meet its specifications, estimate R.P.I.

Ans:

$$\bar{\bar{X}} = \frac{0.6 + 0.8 + ... + 0.6}{20} = 0.33$$

$$\bar{R} = \frac{3 + 1 + ... + 6}{20} = \frac{62}{20} = 3.1$$

$$UCL_{\bar{X}} = \bar{X} + A_2\bar{R} = 0.33 + (0.58 \times 3.1) = 2.13$$

$$LCL_{\bar{X}} = \bar{X} - A_2\bar{R} = 0.33 - (0.58 \times 3.1) = -1.47$$

$$UCL_R = D_4\bar{R} = 2.11 \times 3.1 = 6.54$$

$$LCL_R = D_3\bar{R} = 0 \times 3.1 = 0$$

(*a*) Control charts for $\overline{X}$ and R are shown in Fig 3.43.

(*b*) Since no point on either chart falls beyond control limits, the process is in the state of control and hence there is no change in control limits for immediate future.

(*c*)
$$\hat{\sigma} = \frac{\overline{R}}{d_2} = \frac{3.1}{2.326} = 1.33$$

(*d*) Since the process is just able to meet its specification, its $(U - L) = 6\hat{\sigma}$ *i.e.* 7.98

$$RPI = i.e.\ \frac{7.98}{3.1} = 2.57$$

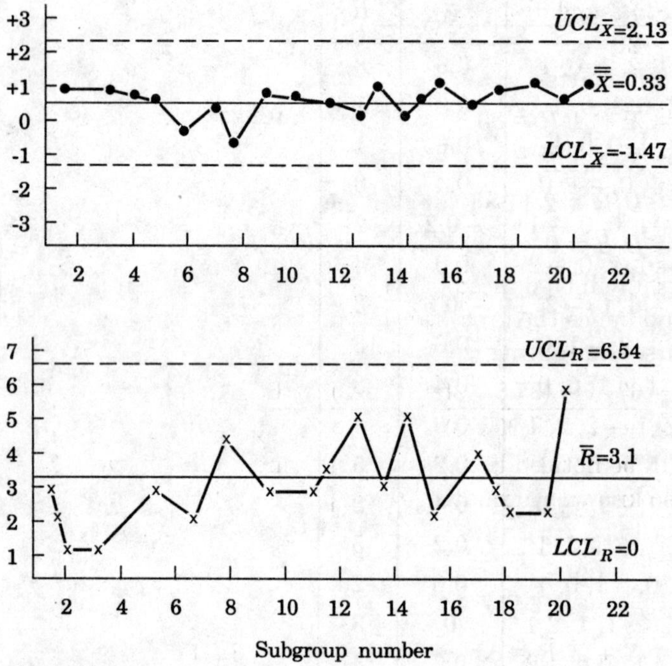

FIGURE 3.43

Q. 3.96: *The following are the* $\overline{X}$ *and R values for 20 subgroups of 5 readings. The specifications for this product characteristic are 4.037 ± 0.0010. The values given are the last two figures of the dimension reading ; i.e., 31.6 should be 0.40316.*

Subgroup	$\overline{X}$	*R*	*Subgroup*	$\overline{X}$	*R*
1	34.0	4	11	35.8	4
2	31.6	4	12	38.4	4
3	30.8	2	13	34.0	14
4	33.0	3	14	35.0	4
5	35.0	5	15	33.8	7
6	32.2	2	16	31.6	5
7	33.0	5	17	33.0	5
8	32.6	13	18	28.2	3
9	33.8	19	19	31.8	9
10	37.8	6	20	35.6	6

(a) Determine the control limits for $\bar{X}$ and R charts for future use, eliminating all the out of control points.

(b) Will the process be able to meet the specification ?

(c) What is R.P.I. of the process ?

(d) Will you recommend shifting of the process centering ?

Ans:

$$\bar{\bar{X}} = \frac{\Sigma\bar{X}}{20} = \frac{34.0 + ... + 35.6}{20} = \frac{671}{20} = 33.6$$

$$\bar{R} = \frac{\Sigma\bar{R}}{20} = \frac{4 + ... + 6}{20} = \frac{124}{20} = 6.20$$

Trial control limits on $\bar{X}$ and R charts

$$UCL_{\bar{X}} = \bar{\bar{X}} + A_2\bar{R} = 33.6 + (0.58 \times 6.20) = 37.20$$

$$LCL_{\bar{X}} = \bar{\bar{X}} - A_2\bar{R} = 33.6 - (0.58 \times 6.20) = 30.00$$

$$UCL_R = D_4\bar{R} = 2.11 \times 6.20 = 13.08$$

$$LCL_R = D_3\bar{R} = 0 \times 6.20 = 0$$

On plotting the control charts it will be noticed that subgroups 10, 12 fall above $UCL_{\bar{X}}$ and subgroup 18 falls below $LCL_{\bar{X}}$ and hence the process is out of control. Since assignable causes are known for out of control points, eliminating these points,

$$\bar{X}_{revised} = \frac{671.0 - (37.8 + 38.4 + 28.2)}{(20 - 3)} = \frac{566.6}{17}$$

On plotting the R chart, it will be noticed that subgroups 9 and 13 fall above UCL_R. Since assignable causes for this are also known eliminating these points,

$$R_{revised} = \frac{124 - (19 + 14)}{(20 - 2)} = \frac{91}{18} = 5.06$$

(*a*) Control limits for future use :

$$UCL_{\bar{X}} = \bar{\bar{X}} + A_2\bar{R} = 33.3 + (0.58 \times 5.06) = 33.3 + 2.93 = 36.23$$

$$LCL_{\bar{X}} = \bar{\bar{X}} + A_2\bar{R} = 33.30 - 2.93 = 30.97$$

$$UCL_R = D_4\bar{R} = 2.11 \times 5.06 = 10.67$$

$$LCL_R = D_3\bar{R} = 0 \times 5.06 = 0$$

(*b*)

$$\hat{\sigma} = \frac{\bar{R}}{d_2} = \frac{5.06}{2.326} = 2.175$$

Upper natural specification limit = $\bar{\bar{X}} + 3\hat{\sigma} = 33.3 + 3(2.175) = 39.825$

Lower natural specification limit = $\bar{\bar{X}} - 3\hat{\sigma} = 33.3 - 3(2.175) = 26.775$

In terms of actual data the natural specifications will be 0.4040 and 0.4027. Since the specification limits are 0.4047 and 0.4027, it is evident that the process will be able to meet the specifications

(*c*) In terms of actual data, $\bar{R} = 0.0005$,

$$R.P.I = \frac{U - L}{\bar{R}} = \frac{0.0020}{0.0005} = 4$$

(*d*) Since the process is able to meet is specifications, it is not advisable to shift the process centering, provided the process remains in control at the above level i.e., 0.4033.

Q. 3.97: *Nominal 100 watt electric light bulbs are being manufactured by an automatic machine. Ten random samples each of 4 bulbs, were tested to determine accurately their electrical power consumption, with the following results :*

Sample No.	*Power (watts-difference from nominal)*				$\bar{X}$	R
1	0.1	0.8	0.2	1.1	0.55	1.0
2	– 0.1	– 0.2	0.2	0.7	0.15	0.9
3	0.5	0.1	0.0	– 0.6	0.00	1.1
4	1.2	– 0.8	– 0.7	0.3	0.00	2.0
5	– 0.7	–0.2	0.1	0.4	– 0.10	1.1
6	– 0.3	0.3	– 0.1	– 0.1	– 0.05	0.6
7	0.7	1.1	– 0.2	0.0	0.40	1.3
8	0.0	0.7	0.2	0.3	0.20	0.9
9	0.5	– 0.1	0.0	0.2	0.15	0.6
10	1.1	– 0.7	1.4	0.6	0.35	1.8

Use these data to set up control charts suitable to detect any change in wattage in the future output of the machine.

If the averages of next three samples are ***101.1, 100.9 101.5*** *respectively, what do you conclude about the process ?*

Ans: For the given situations $\bar{X}$ and R control charts will serve the purpose.

$$\bar{\bar{X}} = \frac{0.55 + ... + 0.35}{10} = \frac{1.65}{10} = 0.165$$

$$\bar{R} = \frac{1.0 + ... + 1.8}{10} = \frac{11.3}{10} = 1.13$$

Trial control limits

$$UCL_{\bar{X}} = \bar{\bar{X}} + A_2\bar{R}$$
$$= 0.165 + (0.73 \times 1.13) = 0.990 \text{ watts}$$
$$LCL_{\bar{X}} = 0.165 - (0.73 \times 1.13) = -0.660 \text{ watts}$$
$$UCL_R = -D_3\bar{R} = 2.28 \times 1.13 = 2.576$$
$$LCL_R = D_3\bar{R} = 0 \times 1.13 = 0$$

Since none of the points fall outside the control limits on either chart, the above control limits will be adopted for future output.

In terms of actual values,

$$UCL_{\bar{X}} = 100 + 0.990 = 100.99 \text{ watts}$$
$$LCL_{\bar{X}} = 100 - 0.660 = 99.34 \text{ watts}$$

Out of the next three samples, first sample (101.1) is above $UCL_{\bar{X}}$, the second sample (100.9) is near the $UCL_{\bar{X}}$ and the third sample (101.5) is again above $UCL_{\bar{X}}$. This indicates that the process is badly out of control.

Q. 3.98: *The estimation procedure (25 samples of size 5 each) is being followed in a case in which the involved variable is breaking strength of an item. Twenty five samples of size 5 are taken, and the average and range of the breaking strength of the units in each sample were ascertained. The sum of the sample average is found to be 255 kg and the sample ranges to be 50 kg.*

Three-sigma trial control limits are calculated for the $\overline{X}$ and R charts, and it is found that two sample averages and three sample ranges exceed these limits. The sample averages are 12.8 kg and 8.2 kg and the sample ranges are 6, 5 and 7 kg.

After the control limits have been revised it is found that no sample range but one sample average exceeds these limits. The value of the average is 9.2 kg. Consequently, a third set of trial control limits is computed. Then values are such that all the remaining points fall within these limits.

(a) What are the values of the trial and final control limits ?

(b) If the specifications call for a minimum breaking strength 9.0 kg and it is assumed that the universe is normally distributed what percentage of nonconforming output can be expected if the indicated universe continuous to be produced ?

(c) What are the natural specification of this process ?

Ans: (*a*) The values of final control limits will be such that no point goes beyond the control limits on either $\overline{\ }$-chart or *R*-chart.

$$\overline{X} = \frac{255}{25} = 10.2 \text{ kg}$$

$$\overline{R} = \frac{50}{25} = 2 \text{ kg}.$$

First set of trial control limits :

$$UCL_{\overline{X}} = \overline{X} + A_2\overline{R} = 10.2 + (0.58 \times 2) = 11.36$$
$$LCL_{\overline{X}} = \overline{X} - A_2\overline{R} = 10.2 - (0.58 \times 2) = 9.04$$
$$UCL_R = D_4\overline{R} = 2.11 \times 2 = 4.22$$
$$LCL_R = D_3\overline{R} = 0 \times 2 = 0$$

Discarding the out of control points on $\overline{X}$ and *R* charts,

$$\overline{X}_{revised} = \frac{255 - (12.8 + 8.2)}{(25 - 2)} = \frac{234}{23} = 10.174$$

$$\overline{R}_{revised} = \frac{50 - (6 + 5 + 7)}{(25 - 3)} = 1.455$$

Second set of trial control limits

$$UCL_{\overline{\overline{X}}} = \overline{\overline{X}} + A_2\overline{R} = 10.174 + (0.58 \times 1.455) = 11.018$$
$$LCL_{\overline{\overline{X}}} = \overline{\overline{X}} - A_2\overline{R} = 10.174 - (0.58 \times 1.455) = 9.330$$
$$UCL_R = D_4\overline{R} = 2.11 \times 1.455 = 3.070$$
$$LCL_R = D_3\overline{R} = 0 \times 1.455 = 0$$

Since no point on *R* chart now falls outside the control limits, these are adopted as final control for *R* chart.

Also on $\overline{X}$ chart one point (9.2 kg.) falls below $LCL_{\overline{X}}$, discarding this point,

$$\overline{\overline{X}}_{revised} = \frac{234 - 9.2}{(23 - 1)} = 10.218$$

$$UCL_{\overline{X}} = \overline{\overline{X}}_{revised} + A_2\overline{R} = 10.218 + (0.58 \times 1.455) = 11.062$$
$$LCL_{\overline{X}} = \overline{\overline{X}}_{revised} - A_2\overline{R} = 10.218 - (0.58 \times 1.455) = 9.374$$

Since no point now falls outside the control limits, these are adopted as final control limits for $\overline{X}$ chart.

(b) $$\hat{\sigma} = \frac{\bar{R}}{d_2} = \frac{1.455}{2.326} = 0.626$$

Lower natural specification limit of the process = $\bar{X} - 3\hat{\sigma}$

$= 10.218 - (3 \times 0.626) = 8.34$

Since L is 9.0 kg, some products are likely to fall below L. This can be calculated from Table A and found to be 2.58%.

(c) Upper natural specification limit = $\bar{X}_{revised} + 3\hat{\sigma}$

$= 10.218 + (3 \times 0.626) = 12.096$

Lower natural specification limit $\bar{X}_{revised} - 3\hat{\sigma}$

$= 10.218 - (3 \times 0.626) = 8.34.$

Q. 3.99: *(a) What is meant by the "natural tolerances of the process" ?*

(b) Control charts for $\bar{X}$ and R are to be established at a workstation at which a hole of a certain diameter is being drilled in a part. The analyst begins by estimating the magnitude $\bar{X}$ and R. He does this by taking 25 samples of size 5, measuring the diameter of the holes contained in each samples, and calculating the sample average and ranges. These averages and ranges are given in the following table :

Sample Number	*Sample average ($\bar{X}$) in.*	*Sample range (R) in.*
1	3.5492	0.005
2	3.5546	0.005
3	3.5488	0.009
4	3.5464	0.008
5	3.5516	0.015
6	3.5496	0.006
7	3.5496	0.007
8	3.5544	0.010
9	3.5506	0.003
10	3.5470	0.005
11	3.5534	0.008
12	3.5526	0.012
13	3.5468	0.020
14	3.5480	0.004
15	3.5488	0.008
16	3.5506	0.007
17	3.5534	0.009
18	3.5496	0.010
19	3.5608	0.011
20	3.5540	0.023
21	3.5506	0.005
22	3.5498	0.011
23	3.5476	0.006
24	3.5546	0.010
25	3.5514	0.006
Total	88.7738	0.222

1. *Compute the following :*

$$\bar{\bar{X}},\quad UCL_{\bar{X}},\quad \hat{\sigma}\quad LCL_{\bar{X}}\quad UCL_{R},\quad LCL_{R}$$

2. *What is the natural tolerance of this process ?*
3. *What are the upper and lower natural specification limits for the process ?*
4. *The specification for the dimension under consideration are 3.5500 ± 0.0076. If the individual items are normally distributed, what percentage defective output can the firm expect if the process remains in control at present level ?*
5. *What is the R.P.I. of this process ?*

Ans: (*a*) *Natural Tolerances.* Sometimes it is found that nothing can be done to bring about a desired change in the average or dispersion of the universe of parts produced by a given manufacturing process. This may be true for economic or technological reasons. In those cases, the attainable $\pm 3\sigma$ values are referred to as natural tolerances of the process.

(*b*) With reference to the given data,

1.
$$\bar{\bar{X}} = \frac{88.7738}{25} = 3.5510$$

$$\bar{R} = \frac{0.222}{25} = 0.00888$$

$$\hat{\sigma} = \frac{\bar{R}}{d_2} = \frac{0.00888}{2.326} = 0.00382$$

$$UCL_{\bar{X}} = \bar{\bar{X}} + A_2\bar{R} = 3.5510 + (0.58 \times 0.00888) = 3.5562$$

$$LCL_{\bar{X}} = \bar{\bar{X}} - A_2\bar{R} = 3.5510 - (0.58 \times 0.00888) = 3.5458$$

$$UCL_R = D_4\bar{R} = 2.11 \times 0.00888 = 0.0188$$

$$LCL_R = D_3\bar{R} = 0 \times 0.00888 = 0$$

2. Natural tolerance, $= \pm\, 3\hat{\sigma} = \pm\, 3 \times 0.00382 = \pm\, 0.01146$

3. Upper natural specification limit = 3.5510 + 0.01146 = 3.5625

   Lower natural specification limit = 3.5510 − 0.01146 = 3.5395

4.
$$U = 3.5500 + 0.0076 = 3.5576$$

$$L = 3.5500 - 0.0076 = 3.5424$$

$$U - L = 3.5576 - 3.5424 = 0.0152$$

$$6\hat{\sigma} = 6 \times 0.0382 = 0.02292$$

Since $6\hat{\sigma}$ is more than the specified tolerance, some nonconforming product is likely to be produced. This can be calculated by using Table *A*.

$$z \text{ conesponding to } L = \frac{3.5424 - 3.5510}{0.00382} = -2.251$$

From Table *A*, area of the curve below *L* is 0.0122

$$z \text{ conesponding of } U = \frac{3.5576 - 3.5510}{0.00382} = 1.728$$

From Table *A*, area of the curve up to *U* is 0.9581. Hence area of the curve above *U* is 0.04190.

Total are outside the specification limits = 0.0122 + 0.0419 i.e., 0.0541.

Hence about 5.41% nonconforming product will be produced if the process in control at the present level.

5. $$R.P.I = \frac{U - L}{\overline{R}} = \frac{0.0152}{0.00888} = 1.71.$$

Q. 3.100: *A component used as a part of a power transmission unit is manufactured using a lathe. Twenty samples, each of five components, are taken at half hourly intervals. For the most critical dimension, the process mean ($\overline{\overline{X}}$) is found to be 3.500 cm, with a normal distribution of the results about the mean, and a mean sample range ($\overline{\overline{R}}$) of 0.0007 cm.*

(a) Use this information to set up suitable control charts for $\overline{X}$ and R using 3-sigma control limits and 2-sigma warning limits for $\overline{X}$ chart and 3-sigma limits for R chart. Specifically indicate on the charts as "Mean chart" and "Range chart" for immediate recognitian by managment

(b) If the specified tolerance is 3.498 cm to 3.502 cm, what is your reaction ? Would you consider any action necessary ?

(c) The following table shows the operator's results over the day. The measurements were taken using a comparitor set to 3.500 cm and are shown in units of 0.001 cm. The means and ranges have been added to the results. What is your interpretation of these results ? Do you have any comments on the process and/or the operator ?

(Record of results recorded from the lathe operation)

Time	1	2	3	4	5	Mean	Range
7.30	0.2	0.5	0.4	0.3	0.2	0.32	0.3
7.35	0.2	0.1	0.3	0.2	0.2	0.20	0.2
8.00	0.2	– 0.2	– 0.3	– 0.1	0.1	– 0.06	0.5
8.30	– 0.2	0.3	0.4	– 0.2	– 0.2	0.02	0.6
9.00	– 0.3	0.1	– 0.4	– 0.6	– 0.1	– 0.26	0.7
9.05	– 0.1	– 0.5	– 0.5	– 0.2	– 0.5	– 0.36	0.4
Machine stopped tool clamp readjusted							
10.30	– 0.2	– 0.2	0.4	–0.6	–0.2	–0.16	1.0
11.00	0.6	0.2	– 0.2	0.0	0.1	0.14	0.8
11.30	0.4	0.1	– 0.2	0.5	0.3	0.22	0.7
12.00	0.3	– 0.1	– 0.3	0.2	0.0	0.02	0.6
Lunch							
12.45	– 0.5	– 0.1	0.6	0.2	0.3	0.10	1.1
13.15	0.3	0.4	– 0.1	– 0.2	0.0	0.08	0.6
Re-set tool by 0.15 cm							
13.20	– 0.6	0.2	– 0.2	0.1	– 0.2	– 0.14	0.8
13.50	0.4	– 0.1	– 0.5	– 0.1	– 0.2	– 0.10	0.9
14.20	0.0	– 0.3	0.2	0.2	0.4	0.10	0.7
14.35							
Batch finished—machine re-set							
16.15	1.3	1.7	2.1	1.4	1.6	1.62	0.8

Ans: (*a*) **The distribution is known to be normal and process is in statistical control with:**

$$\bar{\bar{X}} = 3.5000 \text{ cm}, \ \bar{R} = 0.0007 \text{ cm, and } n = 5$$

From, Table *D* of App. 2, for $n = 5$

$A_2 = 0.58$, and hence 2/3 of $A_2 = 0.39$ (to be used for warning limits)

$$D_4 = 2.11 \ D_3 = 4$$

$$UCL_{\bar{X}} = \bar{\bar{X}} + A_2\bar{R} = 3.50041 \text{ cm}; \ LCL_{\bar{X}} = \bar{\bar{X}} - A_2\bar{R} = 3.49959 \text{ cm.}$$

$$UWL_{\bar{X}} = \bar{\bar{X}} + \frac{2}{3}A_2\bar{R} = 3.50027 \text{ cm}; \ LCL_{\bar{X}} = \bar{\bar{X}} - \frac{2}{3}A_2\bar{R} = 3.49973 \text{ cm.}$$

$$UCL_R = D_4\bar{R} = 0.0015 \text{ cm}$$

$$LCL_R = D_3\bar{R} = 0$$

(*b*) The process is correctly centered. From Table *C*, for $n = 5$, $d_2 = 2.326$.

$$\hat{\sigma} = 0.0007/2.326 = 0.0003 \ ; \ 6\hat{\sigma} = 0.0018$$

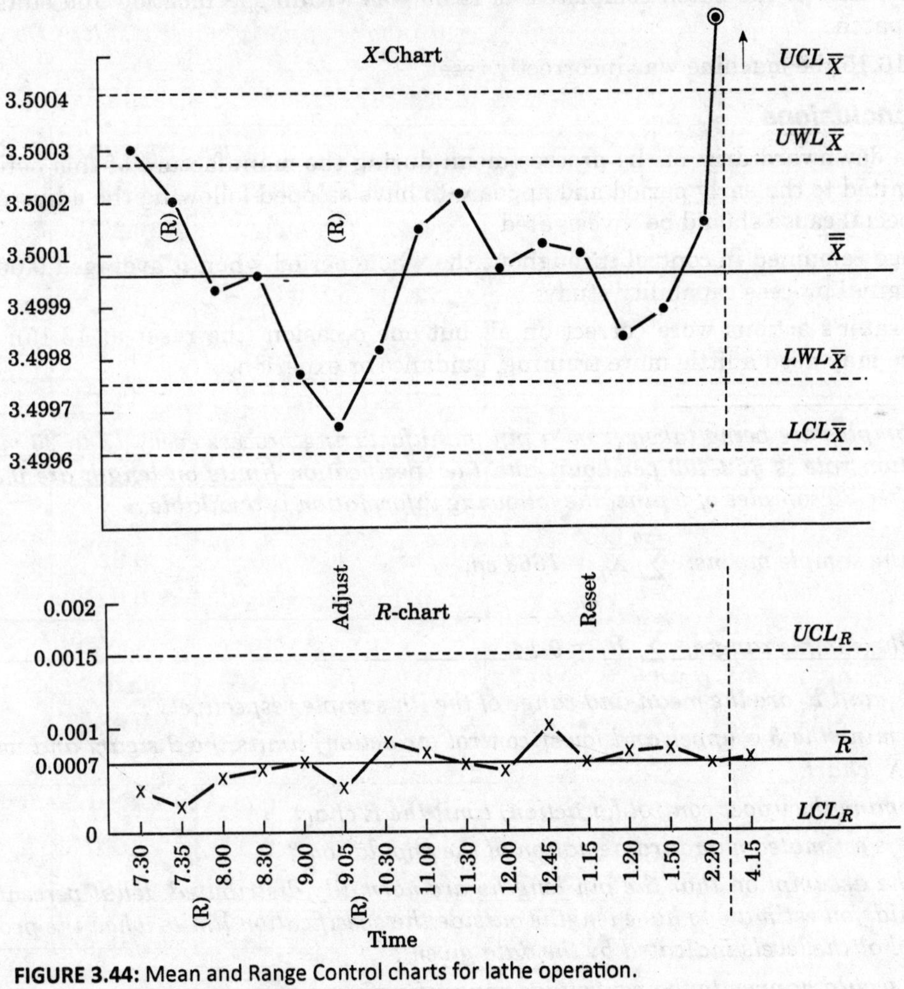

FIGURE 3.44: Mean and Range Control charts for lathe operation.

Also $U - L = 3.502 - 3.498$ *i.e.* 0.004.

Hence the process is capable of meeting the tolerance. If $\bar{X}$ and R charts are used for its control, significant changes should be detected by the first sample taken after the change. No further immediate action is suggested.

(c) The $\bar{X}$ and R values of the given table are plotted in Fig. 3.44.

Observations on the control charts

1. The 7.30 sample required a repeat sample to be taken to check the mean. The repeat sample at 7.35 showed that no adjustment was necessary.
2. The 9.00 sample mean was within the warning limits but was the fifth result in a downwards trend. The operator correctly decided to take a repeat sample. The 9.05 mean result constituted a double warning since it remained in the downward trend and also fell in the warning zone. Adjustment of the mean, was therefore, justified.
3. The mean of the 13.15 sample was the fifth in a series above the mean and should have signalled the need for a repeat sample and not an adjustment. The adjustment, however, did not adversely affect control.
4. The whole of the batch completed at 14.35 was within specification and suitable for despatch.
5. At 16.15 the machine was incorrectly reset.

General conclusions

There was a downward drift of the process mean during the manufacture of this batch. The drift was limited to the early period and appears to have stopped following the adjustment at 9.05. The special cause should be invesigated.

The range remained in control throughout the whole period when it averaged 0.0007 cm, as in the original process capability study.

The operator's actions were correct on all but one occasion (the reset at 13.15); a good operator who may need a little more training, guidance or experience.

Q. 3.101: *Samples are being taken from a pin manufacturing process every 15 to 20 minutes. The production rate is 350-400 per hour, and the specification limits on length are 0.82 and 0.840 cm. After 20 samples of 5 pins, the following information is available :*

Sum of the sample means, $\sum_{j=1}^{j=20} \bar{X}_j = 1668 \text{ cm}$

Sum of the sample ranges, $\sum_{j=1}^{j=20} R_j = 0.14.$

where $\bar{X}_j$ *and* R_i *are the mean and range of the ith sample respectively :*

(a) Determine the 3 σ upper and lower control (or action) limits the 2 sigam and warning limit of the $\bar{X}$ *chart.*

(b) Determine the upper control (or action) limit the R chart.

(c) What is estimated standard deviation of the population ?

(d) On the assumption that the pin lengths are normally distributed, what percentage of the pins would you estimate to have lengths outside the specification limits when the process is under control at the levels indicated by the data given ?

(e) What would happen to the percentage nonconforming pins if the process average should change to 0.837 cm ?

(f) What is the probability that you could observe the change in (e) on your control chart on the first sample following the change ?

(Assume Factor $A_2 = 0.58$, $D_4 = 2.11$ $d_2 = 2.326$)

Ans: (*a*)
$$\bar{\bar{X}} = \frac{16.88}{20} = 0.834 \text{ cm.}$$

$$\bar{R} = \frac{0.14}{20} = 0.007 \text{ cm}$$

Using factor A_2 for control or action limits and $\frac{2}{3} A_2$ for, warning limits for $\bar{X}$ chart and D_4 for R chart,

$$UCL_{\bar{X}} = 0.838;$$
$$LCL_{\bar{X}} = 0.830$$
$$UWL_{\bar{X}} = 0.837;$$
$$LWL_{\bar{X}} = 0.831$$

(*b*) $UCL_R = 0.0148$ cm

(*c*) $\hat{\sigma} = 0.007/2.326$ *i.e.* 0.003

(*d*) for U of 0.84,
$$z_1 = \frac{0.82 - 0.834}{0.003} = 2$$

for L of 0.82,
$$z_2 = \frac{0.82 - 0.834}{0.003} = -4.67$$

Using Table A area above U is 0.0227 and area below L is zero for all practical purposes Hence the percentage outside specifications 2.27%

(*e*)
$$z = \frac{0.84 - 0.834}{0.003} = 1$$

Therefore the percentage outside $UCL_{\bar{X}}$ will increase to 15.87%.

(*f*) $n = 5,$

$$\mu_1 = 0.837,$$

$$\sigma_{\bar{X}} = \frac{0.003}{\sqrt{5}}$$

i.e. $= 0.0018$

Probability of detecting the shift on the first sample after the shift, is the area of normal curve above $UCL_{\bar{X}}$ as the area below the $LCL_{\bar{X}}$ is almost zero. The area of the curve above $UCL_{\bar{X}}$ of 0.838 is 0.2209.

Also any point falling above 2-sigma warning limits signals a shift. In this case $\mu_1 = UWL_{\bar{X}}$ and hence the area of the curve above $UWL_{\bar{X}}$ is 0.5. Therefore probability of detecting the shift from 2-sigma warning limits is 0.5.

[*Note.* The same results could be obtained using Eq. (3.8) with $L = 3$ for 3-sigma control limits, $L = 2$ for 2-sigma warning limits, and $k = 0.837 - 0.834 / 0.003$ *i.e.* 1]

Thus the probability of observing the change to $\mu 1$ of 0.837 cm on the first sample after the change is as follows :

(*i*) 0.50—50% outside warning limits

(*ii*) 0.2209—22.1% outside control limits

Q. 3.102: *(a) Using the bale weight data below, calculate the control limits and warning limits for the $\bar{X}$ and R charts to be used with that data.*

(b) Using these control limits, plot the mean and range values onto the charts.

(c) Comment on the results obtained.

$$(Use\ A_2 = 0.73,\ D_4 = 2.28,\ D_3 = 0)$$

(Bale Weight data record-kg)

Sample number	*Time*	*1*	*2*	*3*	*4*	*Mean* ($\bar{X}$)	*Range (R)*
1	10.18	34.07	33.99	33.99	34.12	34.04	0.13
2	10.03	33.98	34.08	34.10	33.99	34.04	0.12
3	10.06	34.19	34.21	34.00	34.00	34.15	0.21
4	10.09	33.79	34.01	33.77	33.82	33.85	0.24
5	10.12	33.92	33.98	33.70	33.74	33.84	0.28
6	10.15	34.01	33.98	34.20	34.13	34.08	0.22
7	10.18	34.07	34.30	33.80	34.10	34.07	0.50
8	10.21	33.87	33.96	34.04	34.05	33.98	0.18
9	10.24	34.02	33.92	34.05	34.18	34.04	0.26
10	10.27	33.67	33.96	34.04	34.31	34.00	0.64
11	10.30	34.09	33.96	33.93	34.11	34.02	0.18
12	10.33	34.31	34.23	34.18	34.21	34.23	0.13
13	10.36	34.01	34.09	33.91	34.12	34.03	0.21
14	10.39	33.76	33.98	34.06	33.89	33.92	0.30
15	10.42	33.91	33.90	34.10	34.03	33.99	0.20
16	10.45	33.85	34.00	33.90	33.85	33.90	0.15
17	10.48	33.94	33.76	33.82	33.87	33.85	0.18
18	10.51	33.69	34.01	33.71	33.84	33.81	0.32
19	10.54	34.07	34.11	34.06	34.08	34.08	0.05
20	10.57	34.14	34.15	33.99	34.07	34.09	0.16
Totals						680.0	4.66

Ans: *(a)*

$$\bar{\bar{X}} = \frac{680.00}{20}$$

$$= 34.00 \text{ kg.}$$

$$\bar{R} = \frac{4.66}{20}$$

$$= 0.233 \text{ kg.}$$

Using the given factor, the following control and warning limits are computed :

$$UCL_{\bar{X}} = 34.17,$$

$$LCL_{\bar{X}} = 33.83$$

$$UWL_{\bar{X}} = 34.11,$$

$$LWL_{\overline{X}} = 33.89$$
$$UCL_R = 0.531$$
$$LCL_R = 0$$
$$UWL_R = 0.354$$
$$LWL_R = 0$$

(*b*) The data are plotted in Fig 3.45.

(*c*) Following tabulation shows the action that could have been taken had the charts been available during the production period.

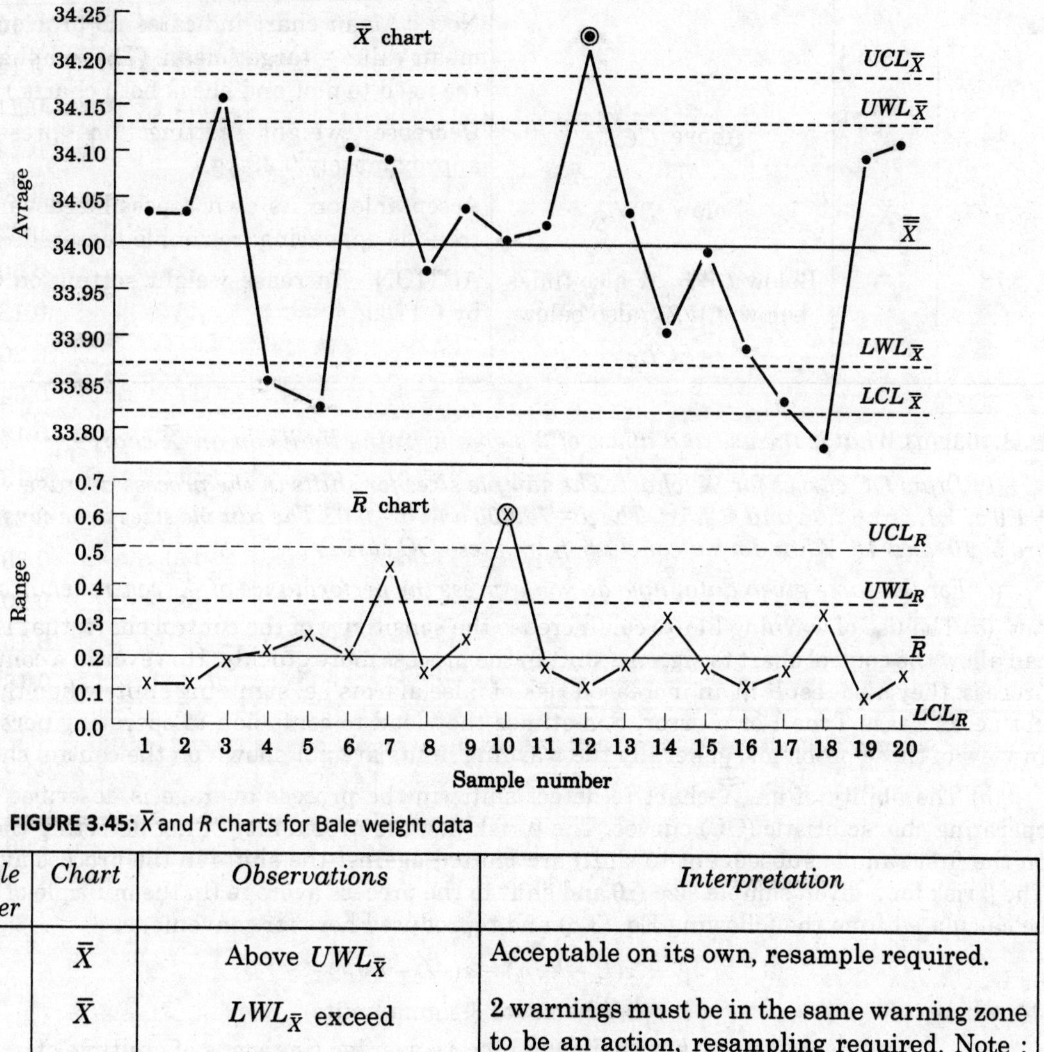

FIGURE 3.45: $\overline{X}$ and R charts for Bale weight data

Sample number	*Chart*	*Observations*	*Interpretation*
3	$\overline{X}$	Above $UWL_{\overline{X}}$	Acceptable on its own, resample required.
4	$\overline{X}$	$LWL_{\overline{X}}$ exceed	2 warnings must be in the same warning zone to be an action, resampling required. Note : Range chart has not picked up any problem.
5	$\overline{X}$	Second times below $LWL_{\overline{X}}$	ACTION - increase weight setting on press by approximately 0.15kg.
7	R	Above UWL_R	Acceptable on its own ; resampling required

...(*Contd.*)

8	R	O.K.	No action required—sample 7 was a statistical event.
10	R	Above UCL_R	Possible actions could involve additional information but some possible actions could be (*a*) check crumb size and flow rate (*b*) cleans bale press (*c*) clean fabric bale cleaner Note : Mean chart indicates no problem the mean value = target mean. (This emphasizes the need to plot and check both charts.)
12	$\bar{X}$	Above $UCL_{\bar{X}}$	Decrease weight setting on press by approximately 0.23 kg.
17	$\bar{X}$	Below $LWL_{\bar{X}}$	Acceptable on its own a possible downward trend is appearing; resample required.
18	–	Below LWL_R & also times below $LWL_{\bar{X}}$ /also below $LCL_{\bar{X}}$	ACTION - Increase weight setting on press by 0.17 kg.

Q. 3.103: *(a) What is the use and abuse of 2-sigma warning limits on an $\bar{X}$ chart ?*

(b) Draw OC curves for $\bar{X}$ chart. The sample sizes for shifts in the process average + 0.5 σ, + 1.0 σ, + 1.5 σ, + 2.0σ and + 2.5 σ. The μ = 74.000 and σ = 0.01 The sample sizes to be considered are 5, 10, and 15. What do you conclude from these OC curves ?

(c) For the same given data, how do you express the performance of $\bar{X}$ control charts ?

Ans: (*a*) The use of warning limits can increase the sensitivity of the control chart; that is, they can allow the control chart to signal a shift in the process more quickly. However in a controlled process, they also result in an increased risk of false alarms i.e. signaling shifts when they are not i.e. increase Type I or α error. Sometimes they lead to confusion to operating personnel. In view of these problems, generally the warning limits are not shown on the control charts.

(*b*) The ability of an $\bar{X}$-chart to detect shifts in the process average is described by its operating characteristic (OC) curves. The β risk (i.e. the probability of not detecting the shift on the first sample subsequent to shift) are plotted against the shifts in the process average. The β risk for a given sample size (n) and shift in the process average (in the multiple of σ) can be calculated from the following Eq. (3.8) and reproduced here for convenience

$$\beta = z(L - k\sqrt{n}) - z(-L - k\sqrt{n})$$

where L = 3, (the usual 3-sigma limits)

k = change in process average (in term s of multiple of σ)

n = sample size

Considering various values k for a given sample size the curves can be plotted.

In this case μ = 74.000 and σ = 0.01. An increase of 0.5σ will increase the mean to 74.005 and so on. Using β risk relation and choosing various k values, the probabilities are computed and the curves are drawn for three sample sizes n = 5, 10 and 15, in Fig 3.46. The probability of detecting a shift on the first sample subsequent to shift is obviously 1 − β. Note that for the same value of k, the β risk is more for smaller sample size and lesser for larger sample size. In other words the probability of detecting a shift i.e. $(1 - \beta)$ increases as the sample size n increases. From the above curves it can be concluded that if the process shift is relatively large, then we should use smaller sample size than that would employed if the shift were relatively smaller.

(*c*) It is convenient to express the performance of the control chart is terms of its ATS (average time to signal). If the samples are taken at fixed intervals of time that are h hours apart, then

$$ATS = ARL\ h$$

Suppose in case of (*b*), the mean shifts to 74.015 and a sample of 5 is used every hour. β is found to be 0.5 and hence $1 - \beta = 1 - 0.5$ *i.e.* 0.5.

$$ARL = \frac{1}{(1-\beta)} = \frac{1}{0.5} = 2 \text{ samples}$$

That is, the control chart will require two samples to detect the process shift, on the average and since the time interval between samples is h = 1 hour, the average time required to detect this shift is

$$ATS = ARL\ h = 2(1) = 2 \text{ hours.}$$

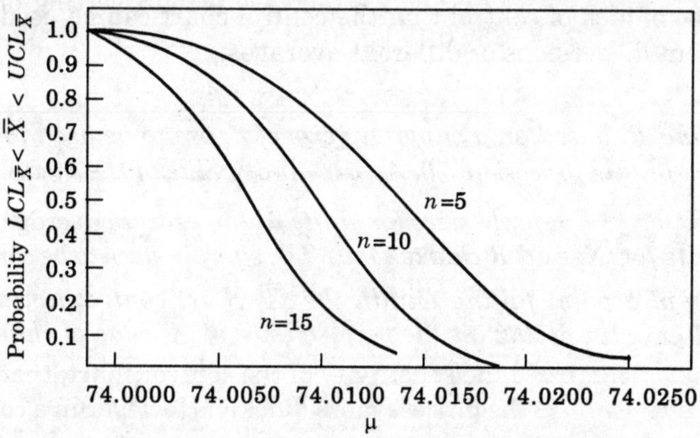

FIGURE 3.46: Operating-characteristic curves for an $\bar{X}$ chart.

Suppose due to excessive generation of scrap etc., the above is not acceptable and lesser time is required to detect this out of control situation. If the consider a larger sample of 10, then $\beta = 0.1$ and $1 - \beta = 0.9$.

$$ARL = \frac{1}{0.9} = 1.11$$

$$ATS = 1.11(1) = 1.11 \text{ hours}$$

Thus the larger sample size would allow the shift to be detected about twice as quickly as the old one.

Q. 3.104: *A component has the specification 720±20. The quality characteristic can be judged by destructive tests only. Control charts were plotted using each set of tests as a sub-group. These exhibit good control and σ was found to be 18. The manufacturer now receives the order for supplying some of these components with some closer tolerance of 720±6 while the rest with tolerance of 720±20. To meet this new situation it was proposed that the process should not be changed but to add two inner limits to the control chart. The limits were to be set at a distance* *from $\bar{\bar{X}}$ equal to the tolerance limits divided by $\sqrt{n}$ i.e., at 723 and 717. Then whenever the average of the sample plotted within the inner limits, the lot was to be classified as meeting the specifications of 720±6 and whenever the average of the sample plotted within control limits but above 723 or below 717, the lot was to be classified as meeting the specifications of 720±20.*

Does the scheme for sorting products into classes seem to be reasonable? Why or why not ?

Ans: The scheme as mentioned in the problem is not reasonable. For when $\bar{X}$ and R-charts for some quality characteristic of a manufactured product exhibit control over a long period, it reflects that the successive subgroups behave like random samples taken from a single universe. The existence of control indicates that universe has remained unchanged throughout the period. If each subgroup is a small sample from a large lot, the evidence is that the large lots are practically alike. The variation from one subgroup to another is simply a chance variation to be expected in random sampling.

The control limits on $\bar{X}$ chart are $720 \pm \frac{18}{\sqrt{4}}$, *i.e.* 729 and 711. With all the points falling between the limits 729 and 711, the fact that the sample from one lot has an $\bar{X}$ of 722 and the sample from the next lot has an $\bar{X}$ of 720 is an indication that the lots are alike, not that they are different. It is only in the case of lack of control that the control chart can be used to sort lots into grand lots having different dispersions or different averages.

Q. 3.105: *Control charts for $\bar{X}$ and R, based on a subgroup size of 4, are to be used to control a process. The standard deviation of this process is 10. An aimed-at value of the mean ($\bar{X}_0$) is to be 250.*

(a) Determine the control limits for $\bar{X}$ and R charts.

(b) Determine the probability of a point falling within the $\bar{X}$ chart control limits of the actual μ is 0.5 σ below the aimed-at value of 250.

(c) If it is 1.0 σ below 250

(d) If it is 2.0 σ below 250

(e) If it is 2.5 σ below 250

(f) Sketch the probabilities as a function in the location of the true mean (horizontal scale) and comment on the usefulness of this diagram in relation to the detection of shifts in the mean.

Ans: *(a)*

$$\bar{X}_0 = 250$$

$$\sigma = 10$$

$$\sigma_{\bar{X}} = \frac{10}{\sqrt{4}} = 5$$

$$3\sigma_{\bar{X}} = 3 \times 5 = 15.$$

$$UCL_{\bar{X}} = 250 + 15 = 265$$

$$LCL_{\bar{X}} = 250 - 15 = 265$$

Also
$$\sigma = \frac{\bar{R}}{d_2}$$

$$\bar{R} = \sigma \times d_2 = 10 \times 2.059 = 20.59$$

$$UCL_R = D_4\bar{R} = 2.28 \times 20.59 = 46.945$$

$$LCL_R = D_3\bar{R} = 0 \times 20.59 = 0$$

(*b*) Actual mean (μ) = 250 – 0.5 σ = 245

With μ of 245, and $\sigma_{\bar{X}}$ of 5, area of the curve between the control limits of 265 and 235 as calculated from Table A is 0.9772. Hence the probability of a point falling between the control limits is 0.9772.

(*c*) Similarly when the mean shifts to 250 – 1.0 σ *i.e.* 240, the area of the curve between the control limits of 265 and 235 is 0.8413 and hence the probability is 0.8413.

(*d*) With mean shifting to 250 – 2.0 σ, the probability is 0.1587.

(*e*) With mean shifting to 250 – 2.5σ, the probability is 0.0227.

(*f*) Figure 3.44 shows the plot of above probabilities (vertical scale) as a function in the location of the true mean (horizontal scale).

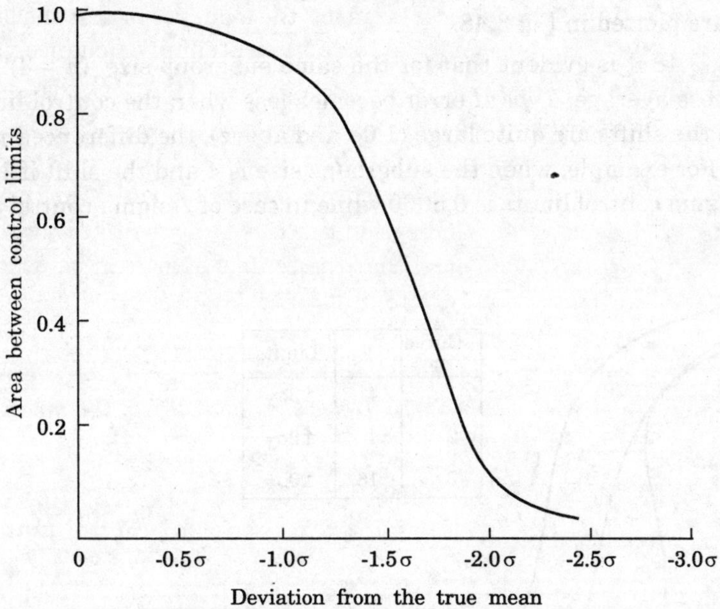

FIGURE 3.47: A lot of area of the normal curve between control limits on $\bar{X}$ chart and the deviation from the mean.

From the curve in Fig 3.47 it is evident that when the shifts in the process average are in the vicinity of 1σ and more, the area between the control limits goes on reducing. In fact when the process average shifts by 2.0 σ, the area between the limits is only about 0.1587. In other words with larger shifts in process average, the Type *II* error becomes quite less and the $\bar{X}$ becomes quite efficient in detecting the shifts.

Q. 3.106: *A plot of Type II error probability as a function of shift magnitude in multiples of σ is a useful tool in illustrating the sensitivity of various control charting schemes. Assuming a normal distribution, find the probability of Type II error for an* $\bar{X}$ *chart for shift magnitude 0+σ , 0.5σ , 1.0σ , 1.5σ , and 2.0σ for the following cases :*

(a) 3-sigma control limits and a subgroup size of 4

(b) 2-sigma control limits and a subgroup size of 4.

(c) 3-sigma control limits and a subgroup size of 16.

(d) Sketch these three curves on a single graph with Type II error probability on the ordinate scale and shift magnitude on the abscissa. Discuss these curves.

Ans: With the help of Table *A*, the results for cases (*a*), (*b*), and (*c*) are tabulated below:

Shift	*Case (a)*	*Probability of Type II Error*	
		Case (b)	*Case (c)*
0σ	0.9973	0.9545	0.9973
0.5σ	0.9773	0.8399	0.8413
1.0σ	0.8413	0.5000	0.1587
1.5σ	0.5000	0.1587	0.00135
2.0σ	0.1587	0.0228	0.0

(*d*) The above results are plotted in Fig 3.48.

From the curves of Fig 3.48 it is evident that for the same subgroup size, ($n = 4$), and for the same shifts in the process average, *Type II* error becomes less when the control limits are relatively narrower. When the shifts are quite large (1.0σ and above), the difference in *Type II* error is quite appreciable. For example, when the subgroups size is 4 and the shift if 1.5σ, the *Type II* error in case of 3-sigma control limits is 0.5000 while in case of 2-sigma control limits it is only 0.1587. Also for the same control limits band i.e. $\pm 3\sigma_{\bar{X}}$, but different subgroup sizes, there is appreciable difference in the *Type II* error even when the shifts are quite small. For example in case of 3-sigma control limits, when the shift is only 0.5σ, *Type II* error in subgroup size of 4 is 0.9773 while it is 0.8413 in case of subgroup size of 16. For larger shifts, the difference in the *Type II* error becomes quite appreciable. This is evident when the shifts are 1.0σ and higher.

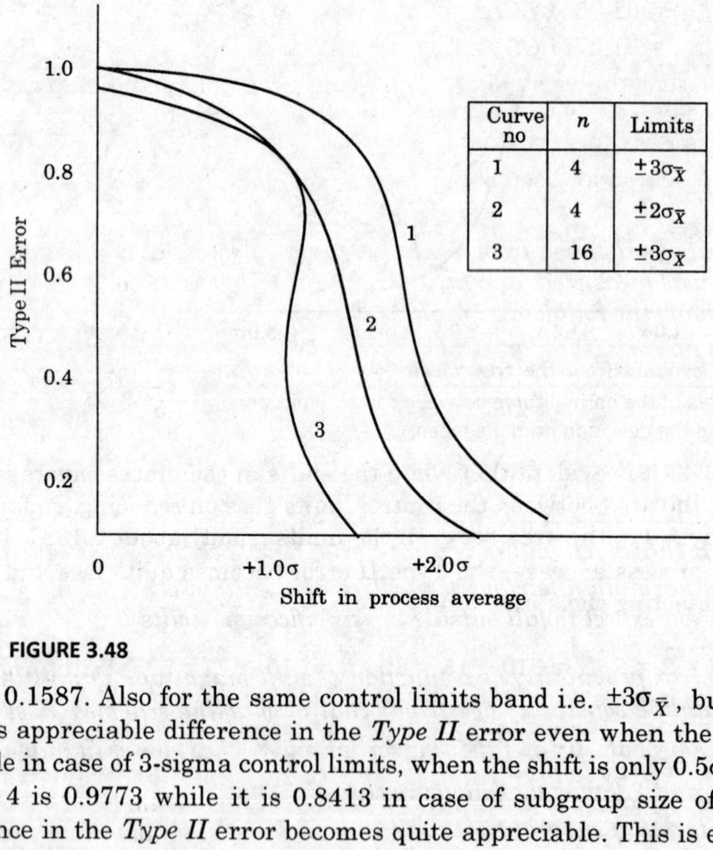

FIGURE 3.48

It can also be concluded that when the shifts are 1.0 σ and higher, control chart with higher subgroup size will be more efficient than a chart with smaller subgroup size or a chart with the small subgroup size but narrower control limits.

Q. 3.107: *The Philips company produces incandesant light bulbs. The following data on the number of lumens for 40-watt light bulb collected when the process was in control.*

Sample	*Observation*			
	1	*2*	*3*	*4*
1	604	612	588	600
2	597	601	607	603
3	581	570	585	592
4	620	605	595	588
5	590	614	608	604

(a) Calculate control limits for an R chart and an $\bar{X}$ chart.

(b) Since these data were collected, some new employees were hired. A new sampler obtained the following readings : 570, 603, 623, and 583. Is the process still in control?

Ans: (*a*) Simple calculations show that

$$\bar{\bar{X}} = 598.2 \quad \text{and} \quad \bar{R} = 22.4$$

and

$$UCL_{\bar{X}} = 614.55; \; LCL_{\bar{X}} = 581.85$$

$$UCL_R = 51.07; \; LCL_R = 0$$

(*b*) First check to see whether the variability (*R*) is still in control for the new data. The *R* for new data is 53 (*i.e.* 623 – 570), which is outside the upper control limit of the *R* chart. Even though the sample average (594.75) of the new data is within control limits of $\bar{X}$ chart, process variability is not in control. A search for assignable causes must be conducted.

Q. 3.108: *Samples of four units were taken from a manufacturing process at regular intervals, The width of a slot on a part was measured, and the average and range were computed for each sample. After 25 samples of four, the following coded results were obtained :*

	Averages	*Ranges*
Upper control limit	*UCL* = 626	*UCL* = 37.5
Average value	$\bar{\bar{X}} = 614$	$\bar{R} = 16.5$
Lower control limit	*LCL* = 602	*LCL* = 0

All points on the $\bar{X}$ and R charts fell within control limits. The specifications requirements are 610 ± 15. If the width is normally distributed and the distribution centered at $\bar{\bar{X}}$, what percentage of product would you expect to fall outside the specification limits ?

Ans: $3\sigma_{\bar{X}} = 12$; $\hat{\sigma} = 4\sqrt{n} = 4 \times 2 = 8$. $U = 610 + 15 = 625$ $L = 610 - 15 = 595$. With $\bar{X}$ of 614, the total area outside *U* and *L* is = 9.4%.

Q. 3.109: *A machine is operated so as to produce ball bearings have a mean diamater of 0.574 inches and which a standard deviation of 0.008 inches. To determine whether the machine is in proper working order a sample of six ball bearings is taken every half-hours and the mean diameter of the six is computed.*

(a) Design a decision rule whereby one can be fairly certain that the ball bearings constantly meet the requirements.

(b) Show how to represent the decision rule graphically.

(c) How could even better control of the process be maintained ?

Ans: (*a*) $\sigma = 0.008$, $n = 6$, $\overline{\overline{X}} = 0.574$

$$3\sigma_{\overline{X}} = \frac{3(0.008)}{\sqrt{6}} = 0.10$$

$$UCL_{\overline{X}} = 0.574 + 0.010 = 0.584$$

$$LCL_{\overline{X}} = 0.574 - 0.010 = 0.564$$

A high degree of confidence will exist if the process can be shown to be in statistical control and capable. A measure of statistical control can be established if the sample lie with $\overline{\overline{X}} \pm 3\sigma_{\overline{X}}$ i.e. 0.584 and 0.564 inches.

To establish, the capability of the process, the specifications i.e. U and L must be known. This information is however not given in the part (*a*).

(*b*) Set up $\overline{X}$ chart with both 3-sigm control and 2-sigma warning limits.

(*c*) With an additional use of R chart, better control of the process can be mainted.

Q. 3.110: *The Canine Gourmet Company produces delicious dog treats for canines with discriminating tastes. Management wants the box-filling lint to be set so that the process average weight per packet is 43.5 grams. To make sure that the process is in control, an inspector at the end of the filling line periodically selects a random box of eight packets and weighs each packet. When the process is in control, the range in the weight of each sample has averaged 10 grams.*

(a) Design an R chart and an $\overline{X}$ *chart for this process.*

(b) The results from the last five samples of eight packets are

Sample	$\overline{X}$	R
1	44	14
2	40	10
3	46	12
4	45	8
5	48	15

Is the process in control ? Explain.

Ans: (*a*) $\overline{X}_0 = 43.5$ $\overline{R} = 10$ and $n = 8$

Simple computations yield :

$$UCL_{\overline{X}} = 47.20; \; LCL_{\overline{X}} = 39.80$$

$$UCL_R = 18.60 \; ; \; LCL_R = 1.40$$

(*b*) A plot on the charts or otherwise clearly indicate that although range is in control but process average ($\overline{X}$) is out of control (sample 5).

CHAPTER

4 Some Fundamentals of the Theory of Probability

4.1 PROBABILITY HAS A MATHEMATICAL MEANING

The statement that you will probably receive *A* in this course is perfectly clear and understandable, whether you agree with it or not. So also is the statement that suman is more likely than Neera to be selected for the post. In general, the words such as *probable, probably, likelihood, likely* and *chance* are used regularly in everyday speech in a qualitative sense, and there is no difficulty in their interpretation as all these refer to the chance that something like this will happen. But consider a statement that the probability is 0.95 that the shaft is made within the specified limits, provided the statistical control is maintained on the machining operation. Or, consider a statement that if a sample of 5 is taken at random from a lot of 50 pieces that contains exactly 3 nonconforming pieces, the probability is 0.724 that the sample will contain no nonconforming pieces. In such statements, *probability* is used in its quantitative or mathematical sense. It is evident that some special explanation of the meaning of *probability* is necessary before these statements can be understood. A critical consideration will show that the two statements not only call of more explanation but they need somewhat different explanations.

Two different traditional definitions of *probability* in its mathematical sense may be given One may be described as the *frequency definition*, the other as the *classical definition.*

4.1.1 Traditional Definitions of Probability

From the standpoint of its useful applications in industry, probability may be thought of as relative frequency in the long run. This may be phrased somewhat more precisely as follows :

Assume that if a large number of trials be made under the same essential conditions, the ratio of the number of trials in which a certain event happens to the total number of trials will approach a limit as the total number of trials is indefinitely increased. This limit is called the probability that the event will happen under these conditions.

Mathematically, this definition may be expressed as follows : Let the letter E represent the occurrence of some event and $n(E)$ represent the total number of times E occurs in n trials. Then the probability of the event E, $P(E)$, equals $n(E)/n$ as n increases without bound.

It may be noted that this limit is always a fraction (or decimal fraction), which may vary from 0 to 1. A *probability of* 0 corresponds to an event that *never happens* under the described conditions; a *probability of* 1 corresponds to an event that *always happens.*

It is because *probability* describes relative frequency in the long run that the concept is so useful in practical affairs. But its use would be severely limited if the only way to estimate any probability were by a long series of experiences. Most mathematical manipulation of probabilities are based on another definition, which may be stated as follows :

If an event may happen in **a** *ways and fail to happen in* **b** *ways, and all of these ways are mutually exclusive and equally likely to occur, the probability of the event happening is* **a/(a+ b)**, *the ratio of the number of ways favourable to the event to the total number of ways.*

This is called the *classical definition.* It represents the approach to the subject developed by the classical writers on the mathematics of probability, many of whom wrote particularly about probabilities associated with games of chance. Experience shows that where properly used, this definition permits the successful forecasting of relatively frequency in the long run without the necessity of a long set of trials prior to each forecast.

The statement in the preceding section about the probability of a given shaft within specified limit could only be justified on the basis of a considerable record of measurements of the dimensions on the shaft; it would be impossible to enumerate a number of equally likely ways in which the dimension could be above or below the specified limit. On the other hand, the statement about the sample of 5 from the lot of 50 is based on a counting of equally likely ways in which the sample of 5 might contain no nonconforming or one or more such articles ; even though not based on the evidence of actual trials, a statement of this sort may be made with strong confidence that the stated *probability is really the relative frequency to be expected in the long run.*

4.1.2 Axiomatic Definition of Probability

It is possible to raise philosophical and practical objections to both the traditional definitions of probability. For example, in the frequency definition how long a series of trials should one have to estimate relative frequency in the long run ? In the classical definition, how can one tell which ways are equally likely ? Such types of objections have led many of the modern writers on probability to view it merely as a branch of abstract mathematics developed from certain axioms or assertions. The establishment of any relationship between actual phenomena in the real world and the laws of probability developed from the axioms is viewed as an entirely separate matter from the mathematical manipulations leading to the probability theorems.

In spite of the different definitions that have been used by mathematicians, the same probability theorems are developed from all the definitions. Generally speaking, persons who use control charts, acceptance sampling procedures, and other statistical techniques in industry will find it satisfactory to think of *probability as meaning relative frequency in the long run.*

4.2 THEOREMS OF PROBABILITY

Modern writers on probability theory prefer a foundation in set theory as a basis for the development of probability theorems. However, in industry, it is usual not to go into deep modern mathematics but understand these theorems in a simplified manner. Keeping this in view a brief and simplified description of various probability theorems applicable to quality control work is given below.

Theorem 1. Probability is expressed as a number between 1 and 0, where a value of 1.00 is a certainty that an event will occur and a value of 0 is a certainty that an event will not occur. Probability of any event *cannot* be *greater* than 1 and also it *cannot* be *less* than 0.

Theorem 2. If $P(A)$ is the probability that event A will occur, then the probability that A will not occur is $1 - P(A)$. For example, if the probability of obtaining a defective socket is 0.04, the probability of obtaining an acceptable socket $P(B)$ is

$$P(B) = 1.00 - P(A) \qquad \text{...(4.1)}$$

$$= 1.00 - 0.04 = 0.96.$$

Theorem 3. This theorem relates to the probability of ***mutually exclusive events***. Mutually exclusive means that the occurrence of one event makes the other event impossible. Thus, if on one toss of a die a 3 occurred (event A), then event B, say a 5, could not possibly occur.

If A and B are two mutually exclusive events, then the probability that either event A or event B will occur is the sum of their respective probabilities.

$$P(A \text{ or } B) = P(A) + P(B) \qquad ...(4.2)$$

For example, if the probability of obtaining 1 defective in a sample of 5 is 0.08 and the probability of obtaining 2 defectives in a sample of 5 is 0.03, the probability of obtaining either 1 or 2 defectives in a sample of 5 is

$$P(1 \text{ or } 2) = P(1) + P(2)$$
$$= 0.08 + 0.03 = 0.11$$

This theorem is frequently referred to as the ***additive law of probability***.

Theorem 4. This theorem relates to the probabilities of independent events. An inde- pendent event is one where its occurrence has no influence on the probability of the other event or events.

If event A and event B are independent events, then the probability of either event A or event B or both is given by

$$P(A \text{ or } B \text{ or both}) = P(A) + P(B) - P(A \text{ and } B) \qquad ...(4.3)$$

For example, the probability of obtaining a jack or a diamond on one draw of a deck of cards is determined as follows :

$$P(A \text{ or } B \text{ or both}) = P(A) + P(B) - P(A \text{ and } B)$$
$$= \frac{4}{52} + \frac{13}{52} - \frac{1}{52} = \frac{16}{52} = 0.308$$

Theorem 5. The sum of the probabilities of the events of a situation is equal to 1.

$$P(A) + P(B) + P(C) + \ldots\ldots + P(N) = 1.00 \qquad ...(4.4)$$

For example, an inspector examines three products in a subgroup to determine if they are defective. From past experience it is known that the probability of finding no (zero) defective in the sample of 3 is 0.89, the probability of 1 defective in the sample of 3 is 0.06, and the probability of finding 2 defectives in the sample of 3 is 0.03. The probability of finding 3 defectives in the sample of 3 is determined as follows.

$$P(0) + P(1) + P(2) + P(3) = 1.00$$
$$0.89 + 0.06 + 0.03 + P(3) = 1.00$$
$$P(3) = 0.02$$

Theorem 6. If a compound event is made up of a number of separate and independent subevents, and the occurrence of the compound event is the result of each of the subevents happening, the probability of occurrence of the compound event is the product of the probabilities that each of the subevents will happen.

Thus if a compound event is made up of two separate independent events A and B, the probability of the compound event happening is the product of the probabilities of A and B happening *i.e.*,

or $$P(AB) = P(A) \times P(B)$$

or $$P(A \text{ and } B) = P(A) \times P(B) \qquad ...(4.5)$$

The above is also known as theorem of ***compound probabilities or multiplication theorem*** or ***multiplication law of probabilities.*** For example, if an order contains two sub-orders (being manufactured in separate independent shops), and the probability that first order is rejected is 0.30 and probability that the second order will also be rejected is 0.10, then the probability that complete order will be rejected is

$$P(AB) = P(A) \times P(B)$$
$$= (0.30) \times (0.10) = 0.03.$$

Still another example of a compound event is usual sampling scheme. Consider a sample 10 contains 3 defective pieces. The probability of drawing two defective pieces drawn in succession with the second drawn after the first has been returned to the sample and sample thoroughly stirred. The events A and B are defined as

A = Occurrence of a defective piece on the first draw

B = Occurrence of a defective piece on the second draw

In the case $P(A) = P(B) = \frac{3}{10}$. The two draws, or events are independent since the occurrence of one does no affect the probability of occurrence of the other. The event of drawing a defective piece on both draws is the compound event AB and has probability

$$P(AB) = P(A) \times P(B) = \left(\frac{3}{10}\right) \times \left(\frac{3}{10}\right) = \frac{9}{100} = 0.09 = 0.09$$

Theorem 7: If a compound event is made up of two (or more) dependent subevents, the probability of occurrence of the compound event is the product of the probability of first multiplied by the probability that if the first has occurred the second will also happen.

Thus if A and B are two dependent events, the probability of both A and B occurring is the product of the probability of A and the probability that A has occurred, then B will occur also.

$$P(A \text{ and } B) = P(A) \times P(B \mid A) \qquad \text{...(4.6)}$$

The symbol $P(B \mid A)$ is defined as the probability of event B provided that event A has occurred. A dependent event is one whose occurrence influences the probability of the other event or events. This theorem is sometimes referred to as the ***conditional theorem*** since the probability of second event depends upon the result of the first event.

For example, if a box contains 50 gears and 3 of them are defective, if a sample of 2 is drawn, the probability that both will be defective is determined as follows :

The probability of the first one being defective (event A) is $P(A) = \frac{3}{50}$

As this has *not been put back* in the box, on the second draw, there are only 49 gears with 2 defective (since one defective gear was removed on the first draw); therefore $P(B \mid A) = \frac{2}{49}$

$$P\,(A \text{ and } B) = P(A) \times (B \mid A)$$
$$= \left(\frac{3}{50}\right) \times \left(\frac{2}{49}\right) = 0.002$$

Returning to earlier sample of 10 with 3 defectives case of Theorem 6, $P(B \mid A) = 2/9$

$$P(A \text{ and } B) = P(A) \times P(B \mid A) = \left(\frac{3}{10}\right) \times \left(\frac{2}{9}\right)$$
$$= 0.667$$

Note that this conditional form could have been used to describe the case explained following Theorem 6. The example could have been stated

$$P(A) = \frac{3}{10}$$

$$P(B \mid A) = \frac{3}{10}$$

$$P(AB) = P(A) \times P(B \mid A) = \left(\frac{3}{10}\right)^2$$

Theorem 6, therefore is a special case of Theorem 7 where the events A and B are independent. The mathematical statement equating the two cases yields the definition of *statistical independence*. Thus

$$P(AB) = P(A) \times P(B \mid A)$$

if and only if $P(B \mid A) = P(B)$; that is, the two events are independent.

Theorems 3, 4, 6 and 7 are stated in terms of two events. They can also be stated in terms of three or more events. The additive and multiplicative theorems are the most important for quality control work.

4.3 COUNTING OF EVENTS

Many probability problems, such as those where the events are uniform, probability distributions, can be solved using counting techniques. There are three counting techniques which are quite often used in the computation of probabilities.

4.3.1 Simple Multiplication

If an event *A* can happen in any of n_1 ways or outcomes, and after it has occurred another event *B* can happen in n_2 ways or outcomes, the number of ways that both events can happen is $n_1 n_2$.

For example, if there are 4 possible inspection routes for an inspector in the morning and 5 possible inspection routes in the afternoon, the total number of different inspection routes possibilities is $n_1 n_2$ *i.e.*, (4)(5) = 20

4.3.2 Permutations

A permutation is an ordered arrangement of a set of objects. The permutations if the word "cup" are cup, cpu, upc, ucp, puc and pcu. In this case there are 3 objects in the set and we arranged them in groups of 3 to obtain six permutations. This is referred to as a permutatun of *n* objects taking *r* at a time where $n = 3$ and $r = 3$. For the solution of many problems in probability it is necessary to know how many different sets of *r* objects can be chosen from *n* objects.

For example, consider a lot of 50 pieces from which a sample is to be drawn. How many different ordered sets of 5 can be drawn? (In other words, how many sets are possible that differ either in the pieces included or in the order in which the pieces were drawn ?) The first draw might be any one of 50; the next, any one of the remaining 49 ; the next, any one of 48; the next, any one of 47; and the final draw any one of 46. The total number of possible ordered sets is obviously the product of these numbers; this is called the number of permutations. The symbol P50 is read as "the number of permutations of 50 things taken 5 at a time." This is

$$P_5^{50} = (50)(49)(48)(47)(46) = 254{,}251{,}200$$

In general, the number of permutations of n things taken r at a time is given by the formula

$$P_r^n = (n)(n-1)(n-2)...(n-r+1) = \frac{n!}{(n-r)!} \quad ...(4.7)$$

(P_r^n is sometimes written as ${}^nP_r$)

Here the expression $n!$, read as "factorial n" or "n factorial," is used for the product of the first n integers. By definition, $0! = 1$. From this an expression may be written for the number of permutations of n things taken all at a time :

$$P_n^n = \frac{n!}{(n-n)!} = \frac{n!}{0!} = n!$$

4.3.3 Combinations

Sets without regard to the order of drawing are called combinations. To find the number of different combinations of 5 that may be drawn from a lot of 50, it may first be noted that any one combination of 5 has $5! = (5)(4)(3)(2)(1) = 120$ possible permutations. As each combination includes 120 possible permutations, the total number of combinations can be computed by dividing the total number of permutations by 120 :

$$C_5^{50} = \frac{50!}{5!45!} = \frac{(50)(49)(48)(47)(46)}{(5)(4)(3)(2)(1)} = \frac{254251200}{120} = 2,118,760$$

In general, the number of combination of n things taken r at a time is given by the formula

$$C_r^n = \binom{n}{r} = \frac{n!}{r!(n-r)!} \quad ...(4.8)$$

(C_r^n is sometimes written as ${}^nC_r$)

Of the three techniques, combinations are the most commonly used.

4.3.4 Application of the Combination Formula to Probability Problems

Consider a lot of 50 articles containing 3 nonconforming articles. A sample of 5 is selected at random from the lot. What are the respective probabilities of 0, 1, 2, and 3 nonconforming articles occurring in the sampling of 5 ?

The total number of different samples of 5 has already been calculated as 2,118,760. If the sample is selected at random, all these may be considered to be equally likely. To compute the respective probabilities we must find how many of these different possible samples contain exactly 0, 1, 2, and 3 nonconforming articles.

Consider a sample containing 0 nonconforming articles. Such a sample must come from the 47 articles that conform to specifications. From these articles the number of different possible samples of 5 is

$$C_5^{47} = \frac{47!}{5!42!} = \frac{(47)(46)(45)(44)(43)}{(5)(4)(3)(2)(1)} = 1,533,939$$

A sample containing exactly 1 nonconforming article must include 4 articles from the 47 acceptable ones and 1 article from the 3 rejectable ones. Thus there are

$$C_4^{47}\, C_1^3 = \frac{47!3!}{4!43!1!2!} = \frac{(47)(46)(45)(44)}{(4)(2)} = 535,095$$

A sample containing exactly 2 nonconforming articles must include 3 articles from the 47 good ones and 2 articles from the 3 bad ones. Of such samples, there are

$$C_2^{47}\, C_2^3 = \frac{47!3!}{4!44!2!1!} = \frac{(47)(46)(45)}{2} = 48.645$$

A sample containing exactly 3 nonconforming articles must include 2 articles from the 47 good ones and all 3 bad articles. There are

$$C_3^{47}\ C_3^3 = \frac{47!}{2!45!} = \frac{(47)(46)}{2} = 48,645$$

The respective probabilities are

$$P_0 = \frac{1,533,939}{2,118,760} = 0.72398$$

$$P_1 = \frac{535,095}{2,118,760} = 0.25255$$

$$P_2 = \frac{48,645}{2,118,760} = 0.02296$$

$$P_3 = \frac{1,081}{2,118,760} = 0.00051$$

$$\text{Total} \qquad = 1.00000$$

(Here P_0 means the probability of exactly 0 nonconforming articles, P_1 means the probability of exactly 1 nonconforming article, etc.)

As the probabilities of all mutually exclusive alternatives have been computed, their sum must be unity. This check should be made for all such calculations.

4.3.5 Handling Factorials

Factorials are very large numbers. For instance 15! = 1,307,674,368,000. Many small pocket calculators will handle up to 69!; others, even programmables, made no provision for the direct calculation of factorials. Most mini-and microcomputers are limited to about 35! before an overflow condition occurs. Needless to say all computers and many programmable pocket calculators require that special programs be written (or software acquired) to calculate factorials.

When probability calculations involving factorials are made infrequently, it is convenient to use logarithms of factorials such as those given in Table *H*, App. 2.

As an illustration, consider the calculations of P0 from the preceding discussion.

$$\frac{C_5^{47} C_0^3}{C_5^{50}} = \frac{47!\,45!}{42!\,50!}$$

Solving this problem by logarithms of factorials from Table H,

log 47!	59.4127	
log 45!	56.0778	115.4905
log 42!	51.1477	
log 50!	64.4831	115.6308
log P_0		9.8597 – 10

and

$P_0 = 0.724$

4.4 THE HYPERGEOMETRIC PROBABILITY DISTRIBUTION

The example used in the preceding discussion involved drawing a sample of size $n = 5$ from a lot of $N = 50$ that contained $D = 3$ nonconforming items. The probabilities associated with drawing r nonconforming items in the sample were calculated where r varied from 0 to 3. Such problems are sufficiently common that the mathematical formula describing them has been named the hypergeometric probability law :

This law of probability may be stated as follows :

$$P(r \mid N, D, n) = \frac{C_r^D C_{n-r}^{N-D}}{C_n^N} = \frac{\binom{D}{r}\binom{N-D}{n-r}}{\binom{N}{r}} \qquad \text{...(4.9)}$$

which says : the probability of r nonconforming items in a sample of size n is equal to the product of the possible combinations of nonconforming items, (C_r^D), times the possible combinations of conforming items, (C_{n-r}^{N-D}), divided by the possible combinations of samples of size n that can be drawn from lots of size N, (C_n^N). N, D, and n are parameters of the probability law; they must be known, or hypothesized, ahead of time.

The vertical line in $P(r \mid N, D, n)$ stands for given that; and the statement itself reads to as "the probability of r occurring given that N, D, and n are specified."

The previous statement of the hypergeometric probability law is usually referred to as the *probability density function* (p.d.f.) or *mass function*. While tables of such functions are published by many sources, *cumulative density functions*, or *cumulative distribution functions* (c.d.f.), are more common and frequently more useful.

As an illustration of the use of the cumulative distribution functions, consider the example $N = 50$, $D = 3$, $n = 5$ used previously. We would like to find the probability that no more than 1 nonconforming item will be found in the sample of 5. To do so, two terms of the hypergeometric probability law will have to be calculated and summed. In general, the mathematical expression is

$$P(r \le c \mid N, D, n) = \sum_{r=0}^{c} \frac{\binom{D}{r}\binom{N-D}{n-r}}{\binom{N}{r}} \qquad \text{...(4.10)}$$

Substituting the values for the example,

$$P(r \le 1 - 50, 3, 5) = \sum_{r=0}^{1} \frac{\binom{3}{r}\binom{50-3}{5-r}}{\binom{50}{r}}$$

$$= \frac{\binom{3}{0}\binom{47}{5}}{\binom{50}{2}} + \frac{\binom{3}{1}\binom{47}{4}}{\binom{50}{5}}$$

$$= 0.724 + 0.253 = 0.977$$

If the value $c = 1$ were used as an acceptance number for a plan that specified testing samples of 5 drawn from lots of 50 items, then lots containing 3 nonconforming items would be accepted with probability equal to 0.977.

Special computer programs are available through ASQC and others for computing hypergeometric probabilities. Many of these programs take advantage of the fact that any calculations may contain no more than $c + 1$ terms and successively multiply and divide individual terms of factorials in an iterative sequential procedure. Since factorials are not calculated directly, hypergeometric probabilities may be calculated for very large values of N.

4.4.1 Change in Probabilities due to Partial Exhaustion of a Lot by a Sample

The problems in the three preceding sections that were solved with the help of the combinatorial formula might also have been solved by computing the probabilities on each draw and applying the theorem of conditional probabilities.

This may be illustrated by again considering the calculation of the probability that a sample of 5 will contain 0 nonconforming items if drawn from a lot of 50 containing 3 such items. The probability that the first article drawn will be acceptable is $\frac{47}{50}$. If the first draw is acceptable, the probability that the second will be acceptable is $\frac{46}{49}$. If the first and second are both acceptable, the probability that the third will be acceptable is $\frac{45}{48}$ etc. This gives the probability that all 5 are acceptable as

$$P_0 = \left(\frac{47}{50}\right)\left(\frac{46}{49}\right)\left(\frac{45}{48}\right)\left(\frac{44}{47}\right)\left(\frac{43}{46}\right) = \left(\frac{45}{50}\right)\left(\frac{44}{49}\right)\left(\frac{43}{48}\right) = 0.72398$$

It is evident that, because each new drawing changes the proportion of acceptable and rejectable articles in the remaining portion of the lot, the probability changes from draw to draw. This partial exhaustion of the lot by the sample is recognized by the above type of calculation, or by calculations that use the combinatorial formula in the way previously illustrated. However, if the lot is large enough compared to the sample, the change in probability from one draw to the next is of negligible importance. Consider a sample of 5 taken from a lot of 5,000 containing 300 nonconforming items. The probability that this sample contains 0 nonconforming items is

$$P_0 = \left(\frac{4,700}{5,000}\right)\left(\frac{4,699}{4,999}\right)\left(\frac{4,698}{4,998}\right)\left(\frac{4,697}{4,997}\right)\left(\frac{4,696}{4,996}\right) = 0.73381$$

For all practical purpose, this is $(4,700/5,000)^5$, or $(0.94)^5$, which equals 0.73390.

The foregoing calculation provides a good transition from the case of the finite universe to the case of the infinite universe. It is evident that in taking a small sample from a finite universe of 5,000 items 6% nonconforming, no appreciable error is introduced if calculations are simplified by assuming that the probability of a nonconforming item is 0.06 on every draw. In other words, calculations are made assuming an infinite universe 6% nonconforming. We shall introduce the subject of the infinite universe by examining the very useful binomial distribution.

4.5 THE BINOMIAL AS A PROBABILITY DISTRIBUTION

Probability problems in which the probability of occurrence of an event may be assumed to be constant may be solved by the use of a formula that depends on the familiar binomial theorem. The reader may recall from algebra that

$$(a+b)^n = a^n + \binom{n}{1} a^{n-1}b + \binom{n}{2} a^{n-2}b^2 + \ldots + b^n$$

$$= \sum_{k=0}^{n} \binom{n}{k} a^{n-k}b^k$$

This binomial expansion is the basis of a probability distribution that is of great importance in statistical quality control.

Let p be symbol for the *probability* that a particular event *will happen*. In applications to statistical quality control, this generally is the probability of a rejectable item, that is, an item not conforming to specifications.

Let q be the symbol for the *probability* that the same event will *not happen*. In applications to statistical quality control, this generally is the probability of an acceptable article, that is, of an item conforming to specifications. Because $p + q = 1$, it follows that $q = 1 - p$.

By substitution and a slight rearrangement of the terms in the binomial expansion, we have

$$(p+q)^n = \sum_{k=0}^{n} \binom{n}{k} p^k q^{n-k}$$

The p.d.f. for the binomial distribution may be stated as

$$p(r \mid n, p) = \binom{n}{r} p^r q^{n-r} \quad \text{...(4.11)}$$

and the c.d.f. as

$$P(r \le c \mid n, p) = \sum_{r=0}^{c} \binom{n}{r} p^r q^{n-r} \quad \text{...(4.12)}$$

In the literature of statistics, the binomial as probability distribution frequently is described as the point binomial or as the Bernoulli distribution.

Table 4.1 illustrates the use of the p.d.f. Eq. (4.11) to calculate the probabilities of exactly r (0 through 5) occurrences in n (equals 5) trials when the probability of occurrence p is 0.06. The reader should note that the probability of 0 occurrences in Table 4.1 using the binomial formula is exactly the value found in Sec. 4.4.1 when it is assumed that there is no depletion of the lot by withdrawing the sample of 5.

4.5.1 Average and Standard Deviation of the Binomial

If a product is 6% rejectable ($p = 0.06$) and many samples of 5 are drawn from this product, it seems obvious that the expected average number of rejectable items per sample will be (5)(0.06) = 0.3. This may be verified in a particular case by a calculation using the binomial distribution of Table 4.1

TABLE 4.1: ILLUSTRATION OF THE BINOMIAL AS PROBABILITY FORMULA
(Probability of exactly *r* occurrences in *n* trials)

r	*General expression*	*Value when p = 0.06 and n = 5*
0	$\binom{n}{0}p^0q^{n-0}$	$(0.94)^5 = 0.7339040224$
1	$\binom{n}{1}p^1q^{n-1}$	$5(0.06)(0.94)^4 = 0.2342246880$
2	$\binom{n}{2}p^2q^{n-2}$	$10(0.06)^2(0.94)^3 = 0.0299010240$
3	$\binom{n}{3}p^3q^{n-3}$	$10(0.06)^3(0.94)^2 = 0.0019085760$
4	$\binom{n}{4}p^4q^{n-4}$	$5(0.06)^4\,(0.94)^1 = 0.0000609120$
5	$\binom{n}{5}p^5q^{n-5}$	$(0.06)^5 = 0.0000007776$
		Total = 1.0000000000

*Number of rejectable items**	*Relative frequency that is probability of occurrence*	*Rejects items × relative frequency*
0	0.7339040224	0.0000000000
1	0.2342246880	0.2342246880
2	0.0299010240	0.0598020480
3	0.0019085760	0.0057257280
4	0.0000609120	0.0002436480
5	0.0000007776	0.0000038880
Totals	1.000000000	0.3000000000

* Average number of rejectable items = 0.3/1 = 0.3.

Where many sets of n trials are made of an event with a constant probability of occurrence p, the expected average number of occurrences in the long run is np; that is, np is the average of the binomial. Translated into terms of a problem in statistical quality control, if many random samples of size n are taken from a product having a fraction rejectable p, the expected number of rejectable items per samples is np. Hence.

$$\mu_p = p \qquad ...(4.13)$$

and

$$\mu_{np} = np \qquad ...(4.14)$$

The expression for standard deviation of the frequency distribution that results from the binomial is derived in standard works on mathematical statistics. It is $\sqrt{npq} = \sqrt{np(1-p)}$.

In the case where n is 5 and p is 0.06, the standard deviation is

$$\sigma_{np} = \sqrt{0.372-(0.3)^2} = \sqrt{0.372-0.09} = \sqrt{0.282} = 0.531037$$

The standard deviation given by the formula may be checked by the following calculation from the distribution :

Fraction rejectable	*Number of rejectable items*	*Rejectable items squared*	*Relative frequency*	*Relative frequency × rejectable items squared*
0.00	0	0	0.7339040224	0.0000000000
0.20	1	1	0.2342246880	0.2342246880
0.40	2	4	0.0299010240	0.1196040960
0.60	3	9	0.0019085760	0.0171771840
0.80	4	16	0.0000609120	0.0009745920
1.00	5	25	0.0000007776	0.0000194400
Totals	..	..	....	0.3720000000

$$\sigma_{np} = \sqrt{0.372 - (0.3)^2} = \sqrt{0.372 - 0.09} = \sqrt{0.282} = 0.531037$$

As stated earlier the standard deviation is :

$$\sigma_{np} = \sqrt{np(1-p)} \qquad ...(4.14)$$

It is important to distinguish between the average number of occurrences of the event in n trials np and the relative proportion of occurrence or probability of occurrence p. In statistical quality control, this is a distinction between average number of rejectable items in the sample and the average fraction rejectable. In any sample, the fraction rejectable is the number of rejectable items divided by the sample size n. The standard deviation of the fraction rejectable items, $\sqrt{npq}$ divided by the samples size n. This is

$$\sigma_p = \frac{\sqrt{npq}}{n} = \sqrt{\frac{pq}{n}} = \sqrt{\frac{p(1-p)}{n}} = \frac{\sqrt{p(1-p)}}{\sqrt{n}} \qquad ...(4.15)$$

This is an important formula in connection with the control chart for fraction rejected. Its mathematical development may be drawn from

4.5.2 The Binomial as a Basis for Approximate Estimates of Probabilities in Sampling from Finite Lots

The binomial describes the situation that exists when the probability of nonconforming items is constant from draw to draw. As already pointed out, this is never quite true in sampling from finite lots. Nevertheless, the binomial often provides a good enough approximation to serve as a practical basis for judgments about various sampling plans.

Our illustration of the use of the combination formula gave the probabilities of 0, 1, 2, and 3 nonconforming items in drawing samples of 5 from lots of 50 that were 6% nonconforming. Table 4.1 gave the probabilities of 0, 1, 2, 3, 4, and 5 nonconforming items in drawing samples of 5 from an infinite lot that was 6% nonconforming. Where these probabilities are expressed only to three decimal places, the differences between them do not seem to be serious.

Nonconforming items	*Probabilities from lot of 50*	*Probabilities from infinite lot*
0	0.724	0.734
1	0.252	0.234
2	0.023	0.030
3	0.001	0.002

In general, the more the lot tends to be exhausted by the sample, the greater the difference between the correct probabilities and the approximate ones computed by the binomial theorem on the assumption of an infinite lot. From the standpoint of practical action based on these probabilities, it may well be true that *it is satisfactory to assume that the probabilities that apply to an infinite lot also apply to samples of 5 from finite of 50 or more.*

4.6 THE POISSON LAW AS A PROBABILITY DISTRIBUTION

Certain types of frequency distributions occur in nature, both in quality control work and elsewhere that are closely fitted by a formula known as the Poisson law, named after Simeon Poisson, who described it in 1837. This is also a discrete probability distribution and is applicable to many situations that involve an observations per unit of time. For example, the number of cars arriving at a highway toll booth in 1-minute intervals ; the number of machine breakdowns in 1 day, and the number of shoppers entering a grocery store in 5-minute intervals. The distribution is also applicable to situations involving the number of observations per unit of amount. For example, the number of weaving defects in 1,000 square meters of cloth, the number of defects per lot of product, and the number of rivet defects in a mobile home.

In each of the preceding situations, there are many equal opportunities for the occurence of an event. Each rivet in a recreational vehicle has an equal opportunity to be defective ; however, there will only be a few defective out of the hundreds of rivets. The Possion is applicable when n is quite large and p is small.

If c is the count of the occurrences of some event of interest, and μ_c is the parametric value of the rate of occurrence, then the Poisson p.d.f. may be stated as

$$p(c \mid \mu_c) = \frac{\mu_c^c}{c!} e^{-\mu_c} \qquad \text{...(4.16)}$$

and the c.d.f. as

$$P(r \leq c \mid \mu_c) = \sum_{r=0}^{c} \frac{\mu_c^r}{r!} e^{-\mu_c} \qquad \text{...(4.17)}$$

4.6.1 The Poisson Distribution as an Approximation to the Binomial

Calculations involving the use of binomials are often burdensome; this is particularly true if many terms are involved and if n is large. Fortunately, a simple approximation may be obtained to any term of the binomial. This approximation is often called *Poisson's exponential binomial limit.* The larger the value of n and the smaller the value of p, the-closer the Poisson approximation. It is admirably suited to the solution of many problems that arise in industrial quality control .

The Poisson formula may be derived from the binomial theorem in the following manner.

In the formula, let $c = np$, then

$$\frac{n!}{r!(n-r)!} p^r (1-p)^{n-r} = \frac{n!}{r!(n-r)!}\left(\frac{c}{n}\right)^r \left(1-\frac{c}{n}\right)^{n-r}$$

$$= \frac{n!}{(n-r)!\,n^r}\left(\frac{c}{r!}\right)^r \left(1-\frac{c}{n}\right)^n \left(1-\frac{c}{n}\right)^{-r}$$

At this stage, the limit of each term is taken, allowing n to go to infinity and holding $c = np$ constant.

$$\lim_{n\to\infty} \frac{n!}{(n-r)!\,n^r} = 1$$

$$\lim_{n\to\infty} \frac{c^r}{r!} = \frac{c^r}{r!}$$

$$\lim_{n\to\infty} \left(1 - \frac{c}{n}\right)^n = e^{-c}$$

where e is 2.71828⁺, the base of natural or napierian logarithms ; and

$$\lim_{n\to\infty} \left(1 - \frac{c}{n}\right)^{-r} = 1$$

Thus, as n increases without bound, the limiting case of the binomial distribution stated

$$B(r \mid n, p) = \binom{n}{r} p^r (1-p)^{n-r}$$

is the Poisson distribution

$$P(r \mid c = np) = \frac{c^r}{r!} e^{-c} = \frac{(np)^r}{r!} e^{-np}$$

It will be remembered that $\mu_{np} = np$ is the average value of the expected number of occurrences. For ordinary use in discussion of the Poisson law throughout this book, $\mu_c = c$ is used for this average instead of μ_{np}

4.6.2 Use of Tables and Computer Programs for Solution of Poisson Problems

Molina's tables give individual terms and summation terms of the Poisson formula to six decimal places for values of μ_c (μ_{np}) up to 100. Table *G* in Appendix 2 of this book gives summation terms to three decimal places, following the formula

$$P(r \le c \mid \mu_c) = \sum_{r=o}^{c} \frac{\mu_c^r}{r!} - \mu_c$$

Individual Poisson terms must be obtained by substracting adjacent summation terms. Thus

$$p(c \mid \mu_c) = P(r \le c \mid \mu_c) - P(r \le c - 1 \mid \mu_c)$$

In Table *G* the values of μ_c go by intervals of 0.02 from 0 to 0.10, by intervals of 0.05 from 0.10 to 1.00, by intervals of 0.1 from 1.0 to 2.0, by intervals of 0.2 from 2.0 to 8.0, by intervals of 0.5 from 8.0 to 15.0, and by intervals of 1 from 15 to 25. The approximate Poisson distribution corresponding to any value of μ_c under 25 that is not given in Table G may be obtained by interpolation between the distributions for the two adjacent values of μc that are given in the table. A value for μ_c equals 5.28, for example, is assumed to be 0.4 [that is, (5.28 – 5.20)/(5.40 – 5.20)] of the way from the 5.20 value to the 5.40 value. Such a linear interpolation in Table *G* will generally give values that are either correct or in error by not more than one unit in the third decimal place. Individual Poisson terms must be obtained by subtracting the adjacent summation terms.

4.6.3 Average and Standard Deviation of the Poisson

The average (expected value) and standard deviation of the Poisson distribution are $\mu_c = \mu_{np}$ and $\sqrt{\mu_c} = \sqrt{\mu_{np}}$, respectively. These parameters may be derived by considering the Poisson either as the limiting case of the binomial or as a distribution in its own right.

The mean and standard deviation of the binomial were found to be $\mu_{np} = np$ and $\sigma_{np} = \sqrt{np(1-p)}$, respectively. In the limiting case where $E(c) = E(np)$, a constant,

$$\text{Mean} = E(np) = np = E(c) = c \qquad \text{...(4.18)}$$

$$\sigma_c = \sqrt{np(1-p)}$$

$$= \sqrt{c\left(1 - \frac{c}{n}\right)}$$

$$= \sqrt{c} \qquad \text{...(4.19)}$$

Considered in its own right, the mean of the Poisson may be derived from

$$E(r) = \sum_{r=0}^{\infty} r \frac{\mu_c^r}{r!} e^{-\mu_c}$$

and the standard deviation from

$$\sigma_c = \sqrt{\text{Var}(r)} = \sqrt{\mu_c}$$

where

$$\text{Var}(r) = E[(r-\mu_c)^2] = \sum_{r=0}^{\infty} r^2 \frac{\mu_c^r}{r!} e^{-\mu_c} - \mu_c^2$$

The Poisson is therefore a distribution for which the standard deviation $\sqrt{\mu_c}$ is always the square root of the average μ_c.

4.7 THE NORMAL DISTRIBUTION

The basic probability distribution underlying the calculation of Shewhart control chart limits for variables data is the *normal* or *gaussian* distribution. The p.d.f. for this distribution is

$$f(x) = \frac{1}{\sqrt{2\pi}} e^{-x^2/2} \qquad \text{...(4.20)}$$

A plot of this function over its full range $-\infty$ to $+\infty$ produces the familiar symmetrical bell-shaped curve. It is a continuous curve over its full range and has a mean value of zero and a standard deviation of one. Fortunately, almost the entire area under this curve lies on the range of z between -3 and $+3$. Table A of App. 2 tabulates the area under this curve from $-\infty$ to the value of z indicated in the left-hand column, that is, from $z = -3.59$ to $z = +3.59$. The c.d.f. for the table values is

$$F(z) = \int_{-\infty}^{z} \frac{1}{\sqrt{2\pi}} e^{-x^2/2} dx \qquad \text{...(4.21)}$$

In mathematical terms, the table is referred to as a tabulation of the cumulative left-hand standard normal curve, usually designated $N(0,1)$, that is, $N(\mu = 0, \sigma = 1)$.

For practical usage, however, it is necessary to convert from mean values and standard deviations other than zero and one, respectively. This procedure, called *normalizing*, involves substituting

$$z = \frac{X - \mu}{\sigma}$$

into the general formula, yielding

$$F(z) = \int_{-\infty}^{(x-\mu)/\sigma} \frac{1}{\sqrt{2\pi}} e^{-x^2/2} dx$$

Thus the values read from the table represent the area under the curve from $-\infty$ to $z = (X-\mu)/\sigma$.

Two important mathematical relationships may be developed from the mean μ and standard deviation σ of the normal distribution. First, the expected value of the average of a sample of size n equals the expected value of an individual measurement μ. This may be demonstrated as follows :

$$\mu_{\bar{X}} = E(\bar{X}) = E\left(\frac{1}{n}\Sigma X_i\right) = \frac{1}{n}E(\Sigma X_i)$$

Since E is a linear operator. Thus

$$\mu_{\bar{X}} = \frac{1}{n}(n\mu X) = \mu_X$$

The second important relationship is that between the variance of distribution of sample average and that of the distribution of individual items σ^2. Remembering that Var is a second-degree operator,

$$\text{Var }(\bar{X}) = \text{Var}\left(\frac{1}{n}\Sigma X_j\right) = \frac{1}{n^2}\text{Var}(\Sigma X_i)$$

$$= \frac{1}{n^2}\Sigma\text{Var }(X_i) = \frac{1}{n^2}(n\sigma^2) = \frac{\sigma^2}{n}$$

Thus the standard deviation of the distribution of sample averages is equal to the standard deviation of the distribution of individual measurements divided by the square root of the sample size. This relationship has already been extensively used in the development of $\bar{X}$ control charts.

4.7.1 The Central Limit Theorem

From the standpoint of process control, the central limit theorem is one of the most powerful tools of mathematical statistics. It has been and will be used extensively throughout this book. Simply stated, the theorem says :

Irrespective of the sample of the distribution of a universe, the distribution of average values, $\bar{X}$, of subgroups of size n, $(\bar{X}_1, \bar{X}_2, \bar{X}_3, ..., \bar{X}_k)$, drawn from that universe will tend a normal distribution as the subgroup size n grows without bound.

Thus we may use the normalized statistic $z = \sqrt{n}(\bar{X} - \mu)/\sigma$ and a normal table such as Table A of Appendix 1 to evaluate probabilities related to the distribution of sample averages.

The reader will recognize that the $\bar{X}$ statistic is used for the control chart for means. As discussed in Chap. 3 for distributions of sample averages from normal or non normal universe, the value of n does not have to be very large before the normal distribution may be applied.

4.7.2 The Normal Curve as an Approximation to the Binomial

One of the several common derivations of the normal curve is as a limit of the binomial distribution as n is increased indefinitely. The greater the value of n, the better the estimate of the binomial that can be made from a normal curve area table such as Table A, Appendix 1. It should be recognized, however, that the normal curve is always a symmetrical distribution. The binomial is symmetrical only in the special case where $\mu_p = p = \frac{1}{2}$. For a given value of n the normal curve gives a better approximation when p is close to $\frac{1}{2}$ than when p is close to 0 or 1.

However, if n is large enough—say in the hundreds or more — the normal curve may be used for a wide range of values of p and will give an *approximation to the binomial that is good enough for practical purpose in many problems in industrial sampling.* Where p is close to 0 or 1, the approximation will be considerably less reliable in the extreme tails of the distribution than near the center of the distribution.

4.8 DECIDING ON THE METHOD TO BE USED FOR CALCULATING PROBABILITIES IN INDUSTRIAL SAMPLING PROBLEMS

In the attributes inspection of industrial product, each item either conforms to specifications or fails to conform. In sampling for acceptance purpose, the decision on acceptance or rejection of the product sampled will commonly depend on the number of nonconforming items in the sample or samples. In judging the merits of any proposed sampling acceptance scheme, it is appropriate to calculate the probabilities of acceptance assuming a number of different percentages of nonconforming items in the product sampled. Some calculations of this type have already been illustrated; many more are given in the chapters on acceptance sampling by attributes in PART 1(C) of this book.

In one type of problem it is specified that a random sample of size n is to be drawn from a lot of size N containing a specified percentage of nonconforming items. It is desired to find the probability that the sample will contain exactly r nonconforming items or, perhaps, r or more or r or less. In this type of problem, the theoretically correct answer requires consideration of lot size N as well as sample size n. Methods of making such calculations were illustrated in Sec. 4.4, probabilities so calculated are described as *hypergeometric probabilities*. As pointed out in subsec 4.4.1, in problems of this type it is often good enough for practical purpose to assume that the sample is drawn from an infinite lot rather than from a finite lot and to use the binomial to give an approximation to the desired hypergeometric probabilities.

In another type of problem the random sample of size n is assumed to be drawn from a stream of product containing a specified percentage of nonconforming items. Here the binomial is applicable in principle rather than as an approximation.

While the use of mini-and microcomputers at the workstation is gaining widespread acceptance, there are still many instances in which lack of access to such equipment may delay important action. The use of approximation methods and readily available tables such as Tables *A* and *G* may be quicker and easier for finding a first-cut solution. The hand calculation of hypergeometric probabilities, for example, is extremely tedious and should be avoided.

No simple general rules can be laid down as to when to use approximate methods. It is always a matter of balancing the savings in time and cost of calculations against the error introduced by the approximation. The following suggestions are merely intended to give some general guidance.

1. In principle, hypergeometric probabilities are required whenever a sample is drawn from a finite lot of stated size N. The decision on whether to compute hypergeometric probabilities or to assume and infinite lot should be influenced by the size of N, by the ratio n/N, and by the number of values of r for which calculations are required. The smaller the ratio of sample size to lot size, the less the error introduced by assuming that the sample is drawn from an infinite lot. The amount of time saved by an approximation is relatively small if calculations are required for only one or two values of r and much greater if many values of r are involved. A possible rule of thumb is to view the binomial as giving an acceptable approximation to hypergeometric prob- abilities whenever n/N does not exceed 0.1.
2. Whenever the binomial applies in principle or is considered to give a satisfactory approximation to hypergeometric probabilities, the decision must be made among (*a*) calculation by the binomial, (*b*) use of the Poisson distribution as an approximation to the binomial, and (*c*) use of the normal curve as an approximation to the binomial. For anyone who has the sets of binomial tables (with sufficient values of n and p) or the computer access that we have mentioned, it is simple to use the binomial. Without these tables, or for values of n and p not given, a decision for or against calculation by the binomial depends in part on the number of terms to be evaluated. If many terms are to

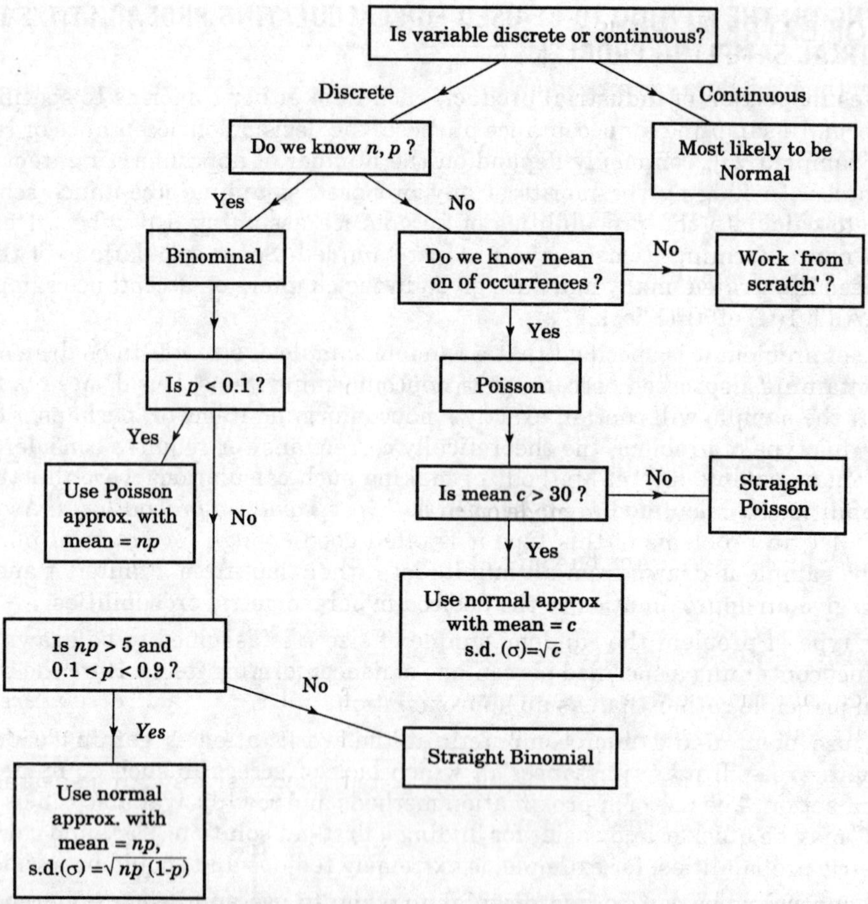

FIGURE 4.1: Summary of the methods to be used for probability calculations.

be evaluated in an "r or more" or "r or less" type of problem, it is usually more practical to use an approximate method.

3. The great timesaver in all such calculations is the Poisson distribution. With a table such as Molina's table or Table G, approximate answers can be obtained very rapidly. This statement applies to calculations of the probability of exactly r occurrences as well as to "r or more" or "r or less" occurrences. In many industrial sampling problems, the approximate values given by the Poisson distribution are good enough. The larger the n and the smaller the p ($p < 0.1$), the closer the approximate answer will be to the true probability.
4. The normal curve as an approximation to the binomial gives a more rapid answer than the Poisson approximation only when the μ_{np} of the problem is greater than the maximum μ_{np} in the available Poisson table or diagram. (This maximum is 25 in Table G and 100 in Molina's tables). The normal curve is somewhat better adapted to rapid calculation of cumulative terms than of individual terms. The larger the n and the nearer the p to 0.5, the closer the approximate answer will be to the true probability. A rough working rule of thumb is to avoid using the normal curve as an approximation to the binomial whenever np is less than 5, or as an approximation to the Poisson when np is less than 10.

The flow diagram in Fig 4.1 summarizes the above and also gives suitable guidance on the method of probability calculations in quality control work.

4.9 THEORY OF EXTREME RUNS

If, in tossing a coin, the probability of a head on 1 toss is $\frac{1}{2}$, the probability of heads on both of 2 successive independent tosses is $\left(\frac{1}{2}\right)^2$. Similarly, the probability of heads on all of 7 successive independent tosses is $\left(\frac{1}{2}\right)^7 = \frac{1}{128} = 1$. As the probability of tails on every toss for 7 tosses is also $\frac{1}{128}$, the probability of a run of either 7 heads or 7 tails in any given set of 7 tosses is $\frac{1}{128} + \frac{1}{128} = \frac{1}{64}$.

The *median* of a set of numbers has been defined (Chap. 2) as the midnumber, the one so located that half the numbers are above it and the other half below it. If numbers were written on a set of chips, the probability is $\frac{1}{2}$ that a single chip drawn at random would fall above the median. Or if measurements are made on a quality characteristic that is statistically controlled, the probability is $\frac{1}{2}$ that any one measurement will be above the universe median. Whenever a frequency distribution is symmetrical, the median and average (arithmetic mean) are the same. In this case, the probability is $\frac{1}{2}$ that any one measurement will fall above the universe average, or that the average of any subgroup will fall above the universe average. Extreme runs of subgroup averages above or below the average are as likely as extreme runs of heads or tails in coin tossing. Thus the probability is $\frac{1}{64}$ that 7 successive subgroup averages will fall on the same side of the universe average.

This type of reasoning is the basis for the rules given in Chap. 3 regarding interpretation of extreme runs on a control chart. For example, if the probability is assumed as $\frac{1}{2}$ that any subgroup average will fall above the universe average, the probability that at least 10 out of 11 subgroups would fall on the same side of the universe average can be computed by adding the first two and last two terms of the binomial, $\left(\frac{1}{2}+\frac{1}{2}\right)^{11}$.

P_{11}, the probability of all 11 above $= \left(\frac{1}{2}\right)^{11} = \frac{1}{2{,}048}$

P_{10}, the probability of exactly 10 above $= 11\left(\frac{1}{2}\right)^{10}\left(\frac{1}{2}\right) = \frac{11}{2{,}048}$

P_1, the probability of exactly 10 below (1 above) $= 11\left(\frac{1}{2}\right)\left(\frac{1}{2}\right)^{10} = \frac{11}{2{,}048}$

P_0, the probability of all 10 below (0 above) $= \left(\frac{1}{2}\right)^{11} = \frac{1}{2{,}048}$

The probability that 10 or more out of 11 will fall on the same side of the universe average $= \frac{24}{2{,}048}$

$\frac{24}{2{,}048} = 0.0117$ or approximately $\frac{1}{85}$

As many distributions of industrial quality characteristic are not symmetrical, it is not strictly correct to state that the probability is always $\frac{}{64}$ that, with no change in the universe, 7 successive subgroup averages will be on the same side of the universe average, or that the probability is always $\frac{1}{85}$ that at least 10 out of 11 will be on the same side. Just as the control-chart limits are best interpreted as rules for action rather than as means of estimating exact probabilities, so also should the extreme runs mentioned in Chap. 3 be interpreted in this way.

As pointed out in Chap. 3, these runs may be expected to occur as a matter of chance with no change in universe average oftener than would a departure from 3-sigma limits. The relative frequencies of the runs and the out-of-control points may be judged by noting that, assuming a normal universe, the probability of a point outside 3-sigma limits is 0.0027 or about $\frac{1}{370}$. If it were desired to set up rules for extreme runs that were as unlikely as departures from 3-sigma limits, such runs could readily be calculated. For example, 9 points in a row on the same side of the average have a probability of $\frac{1}{256}$; 10 points have a probability of $\frac{1}{512}$.

Significant extreme runs are not necessarily with reference to the central line of the control chart. It is suggested in Chap. 8 that two points in succession beyond a 2-sigma limit constitute an extreme run that is a more significant indication of an assignable cause than a single point outside of 3-sigma limits. The statement may be verified by the following calculations. If the probability of one point *above* the *upper* 2-sigma limit is 0.0228, the probability of two in a row is (0.0228)2 = 0.00052. As the probability of two points in a row *below* the *lower* 2-sigma limit is also 0.00052, the probability of two points in succession outside the *same* 2-sigma limit (either above the upper limit or below the lower limit) is 0.00052 + 0.00052 = 0.00104, or about $\frac{1}{960}$.

SOLVED QUESTIONS

Q. 4.1 : *Match the definitions and the examples to the type of probability being described*

Type		*Definition*		*Example*
Exact	(*i*)	These are based on judgement	(*a*)	The probability of wiring new contract
Emperical	(*ii*)	These can be calculated from samples of observation from the past	(*b*)	Selecting a card from a back of cards
Subjective	(*iii*)	These can be applied to the population of outcomes	(*c*)	The likely level of sales in a week.

Ans: Exact – [(*iii*), (*b*)]; Emperical – [(*ii*), (*c*)]; Subjective – [(*i*), (*a*)]

Q. 4.2 : *Select the correct answer:*

(*i*) The lengths of a certain bushing are normally distributed with mean μ. How many standard deviation units, symmetrical about μ, will include 80 percent of the lengths ?

(a) ±1.04 (b) ±0.52 (c) ±1.28 (d) ±0.84.

(*ii*) An inspection plan is set up to randomly sample three feet of a 100 foot cable and accept the cable if no flaws are found in the three-foot length. What is the probability that a cable with an average of one flaw per foot will be rejected by the plan ?

(a) 0.05 (b) 0.95 (c) 0.72

(d) 0.03 (e) 0.10.

(iii) When using the Poisson an approximation to the binomial, the following conditions apply for the best approximation

(a) larger sample size and larger fraction defective

(b) larger sample size and smaller fraction defective

(c) smaller sample size and larger fraction defective

(d) smaller sample size and smaller fraction defective

(iv) Probability of finding a defective item in a large lot varies from

(a) zero to 1 (b) $-\infty$ to $+\infty$ (c) $-\infty$ to 1

(d) + 1 to ∞ (e) -1 to $+1$

(v) A process is producing material which is 40 percent defective. Four pieces are selected at random for inspection, What is the probability of exactly one good piece being found in the sample ?

(a) 0.870 (b) 0.575 (c) 0.346

(d) 0.130 (e) 0.154.

(vi) The probability of observing at least one defective in a random sample of size ten drawn from a population that has been producing, on the average, ten percent defective units is

(a) (0.10)10 (b) (0.90)10 (c) 1 – (0.10)10

(d) 1 – (0.90)10 (e) (0.10) (0.90)9.

(vii) A process is turning out end items that have defects of type A or type B or both in them. If the probability of a type A defect is 0.10 and of a type B defect is 0.20, the probability that an end item will have no defects is

(a) 0.02 (b) 0.28 (c) 0.30

(d) 0.72 (e) 0.68.

(viii) A trip is contemplated with an automobile equipped with four well-used tires on the wheels plus an equally well-used spare. Because of the poor condition of the five tires, the probability that any tire will experience a blowout during the trip is estimated to be 0.50. What is the expected probability of a successful trip (in the sense that no more than one blowout will occur, so that it would not be necessary to purchase a tire enroute)?

(a) 0.0625 (b) 0.5000 (c) 0.0313 (d) 0.3125.

Ans. (*i*) (c); (*ii*) (b); (*iii*) (b); (*iv*) (a); (*v*) (e); (*vi*) (d); (*vii*) (d); (*viii*) (d).

Q. 4.3 : *Give the missing word in each case.*

(*i*) Probability is measured on a scale from 0 to ________.

(*ii*) Probabilities that are obtained by measurement are called ________ probabilities.

(*iii*) Probabilities that are obtained by gusses are called ________ probabilities.

(*iv*) A binomial is an example of a ________ distribution.

(*v*) Poison distribution is used when events occur at ________.

(*vi*) The normal curve is ________ about the mean.

(*vii*) The total area under the normal curve is ________

(*viii*) The normal curve is an example of a ________ distribution.

(*ix*) As the standard deviation gets larger the spread of the curve ________.

(*x*) The standard normal distribution has a mean of ________.

Ans: (*i*) 1 or 100%; (*ii*) Empirical; (*iii*) Subjective; (*iv*) Discrete; (*v*) Random;

(*vi*) Symmetrical; (*vii*) 1 or 100%; (*viii*) Continuous; (*ix*) Increases; (*x*) 0

Q. 4.4: *State whether the following statements are technically TRUE or FALSE*

(*i*) Probability cannot exceed 1 or 100%.

(*ii*) The shape of the binomial distribution with $n = 10$ and $p = 0.01$ will be symmetrical.

(*iii*) The normal distribution is a 'bell' shape.

(*iv*) If the area in the right-hand tail of the normal distribution is 5%, then the area to the left of this tail 95%.

Ans: (*i*) True; (*ii*) False; (*iii*) True; (*iv*) True

Q. 4.5: *Write the meaning of the following briefly:*

(*a*) *Independent events* (*b*) *Mutally exclusive events*

(*c*) *Conditional probability* (*d*) *Expected value*

Ans: (*a*) Two events are independent if the outcome of the first does not affect the outcome of the second.

(*b*) Two events are mutually exclusive if they cannot occur together.

(*c*) The conditional probability is the probability of one event happening, given that another event has already happened.

(*d*) An expected value is the average value, or outcome which would result over a long period of time.

Q. 4.6: *When can the binomial distribution be useful in its own right ?*

Ans: When a situation can be classified into two mutually exclusive categories, e.g., present or absent, and when the number in the sample is not much bigger than $n = 20$.

Q. 4.7: *When can it reasonably be approximated to the normal distribution ?*

Ans: When p is approximately equal to q and n is greater than about 20, ideally greater than 30. If p is not very equal to q then n must be even larger, for a reasonable approximation.

Q. 4.8: *"The hypergeometric distribution provides exact results when sampling is without replacement". True or False ? Give reasons.*

Ans: True–It takes into account the changing probabilities caused by non replacement, and uses both the sample size 'n' and the batch size 'N' in the calculations. It must be used when N is small, e.g. when N is upto 15.

Q. 4.9: *When can you use a Poisson distribution ?*

Ans: Poisson distribution can used when events occur infrequetly and at random. The events. must be indepedent, the probability of an event happening in an interval is propatioal to the length of the interval, and an infinite number of events should be possible in an interval.

Q. 4.10: *When can you use a Poisson distribution as an approximation to a binominal distribution?*

Ans: When the number of events is large and the probability of success is small, so that $np < 5$.

Q. 4.11: *When can you use a normal distribution ?*

Ans: In a wide range of applications, particularly when these is a large number of observations.

Q. 4.12: *What is the most obvious difference between a normal distribution and a binomial or Poisson distribution ?*

Ans: The binomial and Poisson distributions are discrate, while normal is continuous.

Q. 4.12: *A company has three production departments. From a sample of 361 items it has compiled the following data about the production of faulty or acceptable items.*

	Departments			
	P	Q	R	Total
Faulty	6	13	3	22
Acceptance	94	195	50	339
Total	100	208	53	361

Use the data to answer the following question. Give all answers to form decimal places.

A. What is the probability than an item is faulty.

B. What is the probability that an item is from either department P or Q?

C- What is the probability that 2 items are both faulty.

Ans:

$$P_{Faulty} = 22/361 = 0.0609$$

$$P_{(P \text{ or } Q)} = (100 + 208)/361 = 0.8532$$

$$P(\text{two items both family}) = \frac{22}{361} + \frac{21}{360} = 0.0036$$

Q. 4.13: *An entity produces 62% items in dept. A and the rest in dept B. In A, 4% of production is faulty whereas in B the proportion is 5%. Complete the following table giving answer correct to decimal places:*

	Dept A	**Dept B**	**Total**
Faulty			
Acceptable			
Total			

Ans: 4% of production *A* is faulty means (4/100) × 62 i.e. 2.48, So Acceptable 62 – 2.48 = 59.50. Similarly for *B* 5% faulty many (5/100) × 38 = 1.9. Hence, acceptable for *B* = 38 – 1.9 = 36.1. Hence the complete table is as follows:

Faulty	2.48	1.90	4.38
Acceptable	59.52	36.10	95.62
Total	62.00	38.00	100.00

Q. 4.14: *A quality control engineer claims that the probabilities that a large consignment of glass bricks 0, 1, 2, 3, 4, or 5 nonforming bricks are **0.11, 0.23, 0.37, 0.16, 0.09, and 0.05** respectively. Explain why there must be a mistake in the above statement ?*

Ans: If P_0, P_1....... are the probabilities of 0, 1, ... nonconforming bricks and P_6 or more the probability of 6 or more nonconforming bricks, then

$$P_0 + P_1 + P_2 + P_3 + P_4 + P_5 + P_{6\text{ or more}} = 1$$

i.e $0.11 + 0.23 + 0.37 + 0.16 + 0.09 + 0.05 + P_{6\text{ or more}} = 1$

i.e. $1.01 + P_{6\text{ or more}} = 1$

or $P_{6\text{ or more}} = -0.01$

As the $P_{6\text{ or more}}$ has a value between 0 and 1, the above statement therefore is not correct.

Q. 4.15: *Prove that the sum of the probabilities of all possibilities in two independent events amounts to certainty.*

Ans: Let the probability of success and failure in the first event be P_1 and Q_1 and of the second event be P_2 and Q_2. Then

1. The probability of success in first event followed by success in the second event = $P_1 \times P_2$.
2. The probability of success in first event followed by failure in the second event = $P_1 \times Q_2$.
3. The probability of failure in the first event followed by success in the second event = $Q_1 \times P_2$.
4. The probability of failure in first event followed by failure in the second event = $Q_1 \times Q_2$.

Sum of all the above possibilities

$$= P_1P_2 + P_1Q_2 + Q_1P_2 + Q_1Q_2$$
$$= P_1(P_2 + Q_2) + Q_1(P_2 + Q_2)$$
$$= (P_1 + Q_1)(P_2 + Q_2)$$

But $P_1 + Q_1 = 1$ and also $P_2 + Q_2 = 1$

Sum of all possibilities = 1.

Q. 4.16: *The histogram of Fig. 4.2 records the incidence of rejects obtained in checking of 10 items each from 100 lots. Assuming the quality is maintained, calculate the probability that:*

(a) the next sample shall contain more than 2 rejects,

(b) the next two samples shall be perfect,

(c) the next sample contain at least 1 reject while the one following it shall contain no more than 2 rejects ?

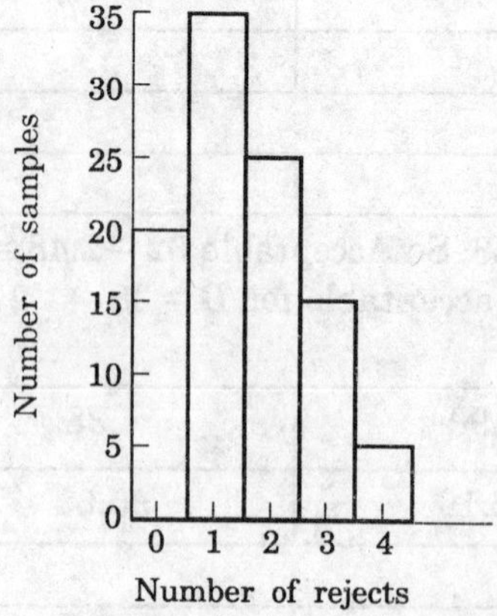

FIGURE 4.2: Histogram of the of rejectables per sample

Ans: Since the probability describes relative frequency in the long run, we can estimate the probabilities of 0, 1, 2, 3, and 4 rejects per sample from the given histogram. Thus

$$P_0 = \frac{20}{100} = \frac{1}{5}$$

$$P_1 = \frac{35}{100} = \frac{7}{20}$$

$$P_2 = \frac{25}{100} = \frac{1}{4}$$

$$P_3 = \frac{15}{100} = \frac{3}{20}$$

$$P_4 = \frac{5}{100} = \frac{1}{20}$$

(*a*) Probability that the next sample contain more than 2 rejects

$$= P_3 + P_4 = \frac{3}{20} + \frac{1}{20} = \frac{1}{5}$$

(*b*) Probability that the next two samples shall be perfect *i.e.* contain no rejects

$$= (P_0)^2 = \left(\frac{1}{5}\right)^2 = \frac{1}{25}$$

(*c*) Probability that the next sample contain at least 1 reject while the one following it shall contain no more than 2 rejects

$$= (1 - P_0)(P_0 + P_1 + P_2) = \left(\frac{4}{5}\right)\left(\frac{16}{20}\right) = \frac{16}{25} = 0.64$$

Q. 4.17: *Micro-electronic circuit components are tested and failure is traced to three sources-resistance fault, R; capacitor fault, C; transistor fault, T. Records of 1,000 components tested were analysed and the failure determined as follows :*

Fault	*none*	*R*	*C*	*T*	*R & C*	*R & T*	*C & T*	*R, C & T*
Number	689	77	121	76	14	9	13	1

(*a*) *Show that these results are approximately in accordance with the probability of failure being:*

R = 0.1; C = 0.15; T = 0.1

(*b*) *After considerable modification the following were obtained in 1,000 tests,*

Fault	*none*	*R*	*C*	*T*	*Others*
Number	753	66	75	84	22

Use the first four results in this table to find the probability of a defective due to R, to C, or to T respectively, and hence divide the remaining 22 components into their probable classifications.

Ans: (*a*) Probability of failure due to $R = \frac{77}{689 + 77} = 0.101 = 0.1$

Probability of failure due to $C = \frac{121}{689 + 121} = 0.149 \approx 0.15$

Probability of failure due to $T = \frac{76}{689 + 76} = 0.101 \approx 0.1$

The above results are approximately with the probability of failure being :

$$R = 0.1 \; ; \; C = 0.15; \; T = 0.1.$$

(*b*) After modification, probability of failure due to $R = \dfrac{66}{753 + 66} = 0.08$

Similarly, probability of failure due to C and T will be 0.09 and 0.1 respectively.

Probability of failure due to R and C $= 0.08 \times 0.09 = 0.0072$

Probability of failure due to R and T $= 0.08 \times 0.1 = 0.008$

Probability of failure due to C and T $= 0.09 \times 0.1 = 0.009$

Probability of failure due to R, C and T $= 0.08 \times 0.09 \times 0.1 = 0.0007$

Number of components failing due to R and C $= 0.0072(753 + 66 + 75) \approx 6$

Number of components failing due to R and T $= 0.008\,(753 + 66 + 84) \approx 7$

Number of components failing due to C and T $= 0.009(753 + 75 + 84) \approx 8$

Number of components failing due to R, C, and $T = 0.0007\,(1{,}000) \approx 1$

Q. 4.18: *(a) In what way does the 'hypergeometric' distribution differ from the 'binomial' distribution as far as the application to sampling is concerned ?*

(b) Determine the probability that a lot of 150 pieces containing 8 nonconforming pieces will yield a sample of 10 pieces of which exactly 3 are nonconforming.

Ans: (*a*) The hypergeometric distribution is used for the same situations as the binomial distribution, with one important exception. In the binomial distribution the percent nonconforming items (and therefore, the percent so acceptable items is assumed to be constant throughout the test.) This is true of the lot from which the sample is taken so large that withdrawal of the sample does not affect the fraction of nonconforming items. Or, if the lot is small, it is assumed that when the sample is taken, each item in the sample is replaced before the next one is drawn. If the fraction of nonconforming items cannot be assumed to be constant, a hypergeometric distribution should be used instead.

(*b*) Using the hypergeometric distribution, the probability that a sample of 10, will yield exactly 3 nonconforming pieces is

$$P_3 = \frac{C_3^8 C_7^{142}}{C_{10}^{150}} = 0.00952$$

Q. 4.19: *A quality control scheme requires that random samples of 5 pieces be taken from the production at regular intervals.*

How often would you expect the sample to contain more than 1 nonconforming piece if the process average is

(a) 10 per cent

(b) 30 per cent;

Ans: (*a*) $p = 0.10$, $q = 0.90$

Let P_0 = probability of obtaining sample containing 0 nonconforming item

P_1 = probability of sample containing 1 nonconforming item

P = probability of obtaining sample containing more than 1 nonconforming item

$$P = 1 - (P_0 + P_1)$$

$$P_0 = C_0^5\,(0.10)^0(0.90)^5 = (0.90)^5 = 0.5905$$

$$P_1 = C_1^5\,(0.10)^1(0.90)^4 = 5(0.01)(0.90)^4 = 0.3280$$
$$P_0 + P_1 = 0.5905 + 0.3280 = 0.9185$$
and $$P = 1 - 0.9185 = 0.0815$$

i.e. we would except about 1 in 12 samples to contain more than 1 nonforming pieces.

(*b*) $$P_0 = (0.7)^5 = 0.1681$$
$$P_1 = 5(0.3)(0.7)^4 = 0.3601$$
$$P_0 + P_1 = 0.1681 + 0.3601 = 0.5282$$
$$P = 1 - 0.5282 = 0.4718$$

i.e. we would expect about 5 out of 10 samples to contain more than 1 nonconforming pieces.

Q. 4.20: *Ten percent of the tools produced in a certain manufacturing process turn out to be defective. Find the probability that in a sample of 10 tools chosen at random, exactly two will be defective by using (a) the binomial distribution, (b) the Poisson approximation to the binomial distribution. Comment upon the results obtained. (Take e = 2.7183).*

Ans: $$p = 0.1$$

(*a*) When a binomial distribution is used, probability of 2 defective items in 10 is given by

$$P_2 = C_2^{10}(0.1)^2\,(0.9)^8$$
$$= 0.1937 \text{ or } 0.194$$

(b) When Poisson distribution is used, probability of 2 defective items given by

$$P_2 = (np)^2\,e^{-np}$$
$$np = 10 \times 0.1 = 1$$
$$\therefore \quad P_2 = \frac{(1)^2 e^{-1}}{2!}$$
$$= \frac{1}{2e} = 0.184$$

The results are in close agreement because when $p \leq 0.1$ and $np \leq 5$, Poisson is good approximation to binomial.

Q. 4.21: *If for the inspection of components from a production line, an automatic device is used for detecting and rejecting substandard items, but it is found that there is a 10% chance of it making a wrong classification. To reduce the number of misclassifications, the system is modified so that each component is tested by the device 5 times and only rejected as substandard if so classified by a least 3 of these tests. What percentage of components will now be misclassified?*

Ans: If the component is O.K., probability that the device passes it is 0.9 and rejects it is 0.1. It will classified as substandard if at least 3 tests reject it.

Probability that O.K. components are misclassified = Sum of the last 3 terms of the binomial expansion $(0.9 + 0.1)^5 = 0.00856$. Similarly, probability that faulty components are misclassified as O.K. Components = sum of the last 3 terms of the binomial expansion $(0.9 + 0.1)^5 = 0.00856$.

Hence (0.00856 + 0.00856) *i.e.* 0.017 or 1.7% of components will be misclassified.

Q. 4.22: *A mass produced article is packed in cartons each containing 40 articles. Seven hundred cartons were examined for nonconforming articles with the results tabulated below*

Nonconforming articles per carton	*Frequency*
0	390
1	179
2	59
3	41
4	18
5	10
6	3
7 and more	0

(a) Obtain the $\overline{p}$ value.

(b) Assuming that the total number of articles is so large that p can be taken to represent the proportion of nonconforming articles in the population, use the binomial distribution to calculate the probability that a random sample of these articles will contain 2 nonconforming articles

Ans:
$$\overline{p} \text{ or } \mu_p = \frac{(0 \times 390) + (1 \times 179) + ... + (6 \times 3)}{700 \times 40} = 0.02$$

The use of binomial is justified as the article being mass produced, and hence the probability of getting a nonconforming article remains constant.

Probability of getting 2 nonconforming articles = $C_2^5\ (0.02)^2\ (0.98)^3 = 0.00376$

Q. 4.23: *If the probability is 0.033 that a single article will be nonconforming, what are the respective probabilities that a sample of 100 will contain 0, 1, 2, 3, 4, 5, 6, 7, 8, 9, 10, and 11 nonconforming articles ? Assuming the Possion is a satisfactory approximation to the binomial in this case, and solve by interpolation in Table G.*

Ans:
$$\mu_p = 0.033$$
$$\mu_{np} = 100 \times 0.033 = 3.3$$

In Table G,

When $\mu_{np} = 3.2, P_2 = 0.041$

When $\mu_{np} = 3.4, P_0 = 0.033$

Interpolating for $\mu_{np} = 3.3, P_0 = 0.041 - \left(\dfrac{0.041 - 0.033}{2}\right) = 0.037$

Similarly for $\mu_{np} = 3.3, P_0 + P_1 = 1.171 - \left(\dfrac{0.171 - 0.0147}{2}\right) = 0.159$

Since $P_0 = 0.037,$

$P_1 = 0.159 - 0.037 = 0.122$

Similarly $P_2 = 0.201; P_3 = 0.2205; P_4 = 0.182; P_5 = 0.1205; P_6 = 0.0655;$

$P_7 = 0.0315; P_8 = 0.013; P_9 = 0.0045; P_{10} = 0.002; P_{11} = 0.0005$

Q. 4.24: *An accepted procedure calls for taking samples of 80 from very large lots. If no defective are found, the lot is accepted. If 2 or more defective are found, the lot is rejected. If exactly I defective is found, a second sample is required. If a lot 0.4% defective is submitted for acceptance, what is the probability that this lot will be accepted on the very first sample of 80 ? What is the probability that the lot will be rejected on the first sample ? What is the probability that a second sample is required ? Use the approximate method that seems most approximate.*

Ans: $\mu_p = 0.004$, $n = 80$; $np = 80 \times 0.004 = 0.32$

From Table G, the probability of acceptance for np of 0.32 under the column headed "$c = 0$", is 0.727 (by interpolation).

For the lot to be rejected on the first sample, the sample should contain 2 or more defectives. Probability of coming 2 or more defectives = 1 — the probability of coming 0 or 1 defectives.

From Table G, the probability of coming 0 or 1 defective is 0.958. Therefore, the probability that the lot is rejected on the very first sample = 1.000 – 0.958 = 0.042.

Probability that a second is taken is equal to the probability of getting exactly 1 defective in the sample = 0.958 – 0.737 = 0.221.

Q. 4.25: *(a) A random sample of 20 pieces, taken from a large lot of mass produced components, is inspected and found to contain 1 defective. Determine if it is more likely that the lot contains 3 percent or 7 percent defectives.*

(b) If a second random sample, this time of 50 pieces, is taken from the same lot and found to contain 2 defectives, use all the information to decide which is the more likely lot proportion defective now.

Ans: (*a*) From Table G the probability of finding exactly 1 defective in a sample of 20 for p of 0.03 is 0.329 and the corresponding value of probability for μ_p of 0.07 is 0.345.

Hence it is more likely that the lot contains 7 percent defectives as the probability of finding 1 defective in 7 percent defective lot is higher, though marginally.

(*b*) Again from Table G, probability of finding exactly 2 defectives in a sample of 50 for p of 0.03 is 0.251. The probability that first sample of 20 contains 1 defective and the second sample of 50 contains 2 defective is $0.332 \times 0.251 = 0.82579$.

In a similar way the probability can be computed for p of 0.07. From the results it will be found that it is more likely that the lot contains 3 per cent defectives.

Q. 4.26: *A large number of samples of 200 each are taken from a process that produces 10% nonconforming items. What is the expected average number of nonconforming items per sample? What is the upper limit of nonconforming items in a sample that, in the long run, you would expect to find exceeded only 5% of the time assuming no shift in the process average?*

Ans: Here $\mu_p = 0.1$

Average number of nonconforming items per sample ($= \mu_{np}$) $= 200 \times 0.1$ i.e. 20. The stipulated condition means that we have to find that number of nonconforming items, such that the probability more than that number in a sample is 5% (*i.e.* 0.05) or the sum of all probabilities upto that number in a sample is 0.95.

Since there is no shift in the process average μ_p is again 0.1, and $\mu_{np} = 20$. Now from Table G, for μ_{np} of 20 and a probability of 0.948, the number of nonconforming items is 27.

Hence 27 is the upper limit of nonconforming items in a sample, that in the long run would expect to find exceeded only 5% provided the process average remains unchanged.

Q. 4.27: *A complex television component has 1,000 joints soldered by a machine which is known to produce on an average one nonconforming joint in forty (i.e. $\mu_p = 0.025$).*

The components are examined and nonconforming joints corrected by hand soldering. If components requiring more than 35 corrections are discarded, what proportion of components will be thrown away.

Ans: $\mu_{np} = 1{,}000 \times 0.025 = 25$

Since n is quite large and p is very small, we can use Poisson for finding P_{35}.

From Table G, for μ_{np} of 25, $P_{35} = 0.978$

Proportion of components to be thrown = 1 – 0.978 = 0.022 or 2.2%.

Q. 4.28: *A certain sampling procedure calls for the selection of a random samples of 50 items from lots of 2,000 item taken from a continuous manufacturing process. If two or less nonconforming items are found in the sample, the lot from which it was taken is assumed to meet specifications. Find the probabilities of acceptance (number of nonconforming items is less than or equal to two) assuming that the process average fraction rejected is ; (a) 1%, (b) 2%, (c) 5%, (d) 10%, and (e) 20%. Plot the probability of acceptance as a function of the process average fraction rejected and comment on the usefulness of the diagram.*

Ans: Since N (2,000) is quite large as compared to sample size n (50), and p values are also small, we would use Poisson distribution. For various values of p the probabilities of 2 or less in a sample, from Table G are tabulated below.

μ_p	μ_{np}	$P_{2 \text{ or less}}$
0.01	0.5	0.986
0.02	1.0	0.920
0.05	2.5	0.544
0.10	5.0	0.125
0.20	10.0	0.003

The results of about tabulation are plotted in Fig 4.3

The curve plotted in Fig 4.3, is known as operating characteristic (OC) curve of the given sampling plan and shows the ability of the given plan to distinguish between good and bad lots. For example, the above curve tells us that the lots which having upto 1% nonconforming items are to be accepted most of the time and lots which are 2% nonconforming will be accepted 9 times out of 10 times by this sampling plan. Similarly lots which have 10 and 20% nonconforming items will most of the time be rejected as the given sampling plan will accept a 10% nonconforming lot only once out of 10 times and a 20% nonconforming lot only 3 times out of 1000 times. Or stated a little differently, the OC curve shows the longrun percentage of

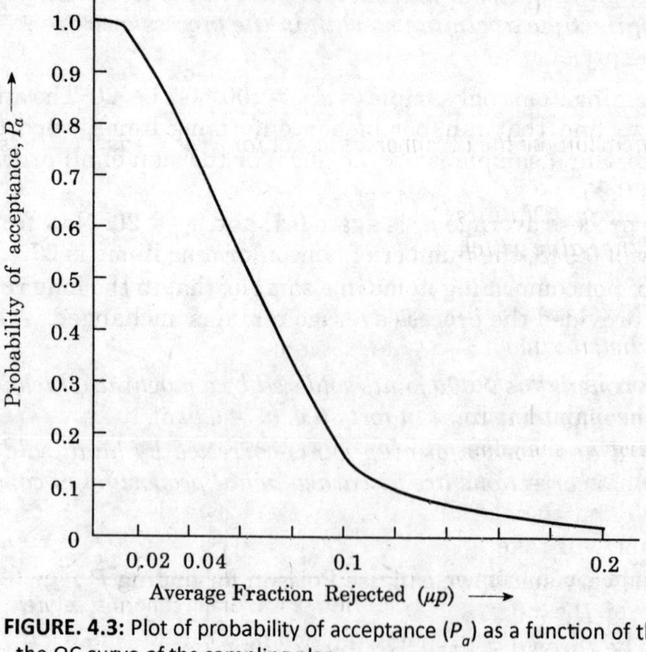

FIGURE. 4.3: Plot of probability of acceptance (P_a) as a function of the process average fraction rejected (μ_p) - the OC curve of the sampling plan.

submitted lots that would be accepted if a great many lots of any stated quality are submitted for inspection. For example this curve tells that when 1000 lots of 5% nonconforming items are submitted for inspection, only 544 will be accepted by this plan.

Q. 4.29: *Define the "arithmetic mean", the "mode" and the "standard deviation" of a probability distribution. Evaluate the mean and standard deviation for each of the following distributions :*

(a) a binomial in which n = 5 and $\mu_p = \frac{1}{5}$

(b) a Poisson distribution with parameter 2 ;

(c) a normal distribution for which the probability of a negative value of the random variable is 0.3085 and the mode is 2.

Ans: ***Arithmetic mean*** of a probability distribution is the ordinary average of all the values of the variate in the sample.

Mode is that value of the variate which occurs with the greatest frequency.

Standard deviation is defined as the square root of the mean of the squares of the deviations of the observations from their mean."

(*a*) For binomial distribution

$$\text{mean} = np = 5 \times \frac{1}{5} = 1$$

$$\text{Standard deviation} = \sqrt{npq} = \sqrt{5 \times \frac{1}{5} \times \left(1 - \frac{1}{5}\right)} = \sqrt{\frac{4}{5}}$$

(*b*) For a Poisson distribution mean (= *c*) = 2; Standard deviation = $\sqrt{c} = \sqrt{2}$

(*c*) In a normal distribution mode is same the mean of the distribution. Hence mean = 2

Any value of variate which is less than 0, has a probability of 0.3085. It implies that when $X = 0$, the area of the normal curve below this value of X should be 0.3085. Corresponding to this value, the value of z from Table A is – 0.5. If σ is the standard deviation of this distribution, then

$$z = \frac{0 - 2}{\sigma} = -0.5$$

Hence $\sigma = 4$

Q. 4.30: *What is meant by the statement 'the observations, X, are approximately normally distributed'? What could be the justification for the common assumption that measurements are normally distributed ?*

If X is normally distributed with mean 100 units and standard deviation 20 units, find the value which in the long run, would be exceeded by 9% of random observations of X. Explain how this value is obtained from tables of standardized normal distribution.

Ans: A universe curve or distribution is developed from a frequency histogram. As the sample size for a histogram gets larger and larger, the class interval or cell width gets smaller and smaller. When the sample size is quite large and the class interval is very small, the histogram will take on the appearance of a smooth polygon or a curve representing the universe. A curve of the normal universe is shown in Fig. 4.4.

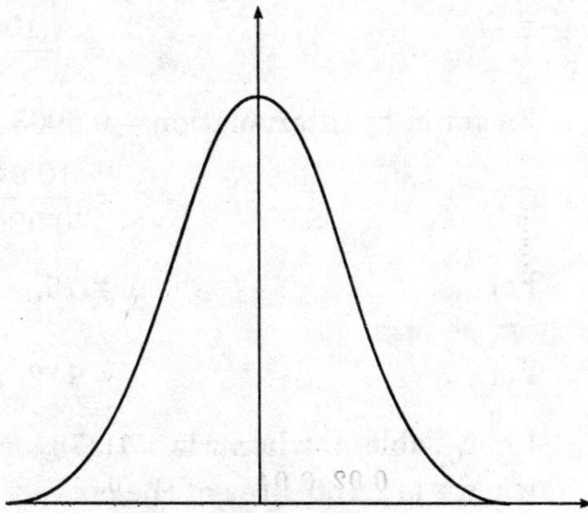

FIGURE 4.4: Graph of normal curve.

Therefore the statement 'the observations, X, are approximately normally distributed' means that even if the observation X come from binomial, hypergeometric or Poisson etc., they can be assumed to come from a normal distribution and their approximate value can be found with the help of normal curve.

Let X_i be the value which in the long run, would be exceeded by 9% of random observation of X. This means that area of the normal curve up to X_i should be 91% or 0.9100. From Table A, the value of z corresponding to this area is 1.304.

Therefore $$1.304 = \frac{X_i - 100}{20}, \text{ from which}$$

$$X_i = 126.08$$

Q. 4.31: *An incoming department receives a shipment of 250 vacuum tubes. The criterion for acceptance is the value of plate current for a given plate voltage, bias, and grid execution. This value is to range between 75 and 112 mA. Twenty seven tubes are drawn randomly from the lot of 250 and tested for plate current, with the following results :*

100	104	98	88	81
78	80	106	77	75
85	92	105	105	80
90	86	101	70	79
103	89	82	73	90
95	77			

What percentage of the total lot is likely to fall within the range of 75 and 112 mA ? Assume that the normal distribution applies?

Ans: Since the normal distribution is assumed, the average and standard deviation of the given 27 diservations will give $\overline{X}$ and s of the universe of which they form the part

$$\hat{\mu} = \frac{\Sigma X}{n} = \frac{100 + 78 + ... + 79 + 90}{27} = 89$$

$$s = \sqrt{\frac{\Sigma(X - \hat{\mu})^2}{n-1}}$$

$$= \sqrt{\frac{(100 - 89)^2 + ... + (90 - 89)^2}{26}} = 10.946$$

Factor c_4 by interpolation = 0.9903

$$\hat{\sigma} = \frac{10.946}{0.9903} = 10.951$$

For $$X = 75, z = \frac{75 - 89}{10.951} = -1.278$$

For $$X = 112, z = \frac{112 - 89}{10.951} = 2.100$$

From Table A, when z is – 1.278, area of the curve = 0.1006

when z is 2.100, area of the curve = 0.9778

Area of the curve lying between these limit = 0.9778 – 0.1006 = 0.8772

Hence 87.72% of the lot is likely to fall between the plate current range of 75 and 112 mA.

Q. 4.32: *(a) A distribution is exactly normal with μ of 50. The frequency of the variable X between 40 and 50 (40 or more but less than 50) is estimated to be 33. Estimate the frequency of the variable between 50 and 60 (50 or more but less than 60).*

(b) In a distribution exactly normal, 6.94% or the items are under 35 and 89.07% are under 63. Find the mean and standard deviation of the distribution.

Ans: *(a)* Since the distribution is symmetrical about the mean ($\mu = 50$) the frequency of the variable between 50 and 60 (50 or more but less than 60) will also be the same as that between 40 and 50. Hence the frequency is 33.

(b) From Table *A*, the values of *z* corresponding to areas of 0.0694 and 0.89 of the normal curve are –1.48 and + 1.23 respectively.

If μ_1 and σ are the mean and standard deviation of the distribution, then

$$\frac{35 - \mu_1}{\sigma} = -1.48$$

$$\frac{63 - \mu_1}{\sigma} = 1.23$$

which give $\mu_1 = 50.3$ and $\sigma = 10.33$

Q. 4.33: *Random samples of 80 items are taken from a continuous process which is known to produce 30% nonconforming items. Determine the probability of finding more than 10 nonconforming items in a sample: (a) Using the normal approximation to the binomial (b) using the Poisson approximation. Which do you think better represents the true value of the binomial and why ?*

Ans: Since it is case of binomial distribution, to use normal distribution, we will have to find the average and standard deviation of binomial distribution.

Average $= np = 80 \times \left(\frac{30}{100}\right) = 24$

Standard deviation $= \sqrt{npq} = \sqrt{80 \times 0.3 \times (1 - 0.3)}$

≈ 4.1

Probability of more than 15 nonconforming articles means the probability of 16 or more nonconforming articles. Since normal curve is a continuous curve, the probability of 16 or more nonconforming articles is to be interpreted to mean the probability of 15.5 or more. To use Table *A*, we will have first to find the value of *z*.

$$z = \frac{15.5 - 24.0}{4.1} = -2.073$$

Area or normal curve for a *z* value of – 2.073 is 0.0191. Therefore, the approximate probability of 16 or more nonconforming articles is 1 – 0.0191 = 0.9809

(b) For using Poisson distribution, Table G gives the probability of 15 nonconforming articles as 0.034. Therefore the probability of more than 15 is 1 – 0.034 = 0.966.

For a given value of *n* (*i.e.* 80), the normal distribution will give better approximate to binomial, as compared to the one, given by Poisson, when *p* is in the vicinity of 0.5. But in this case *p* is 0.3, which is nearer to 0, and when *p* is small the Poisson gives a better approximation of the true probability than the normal distribution.

Q. 4.34: *(a) Discuss briefly the conditions when a binomial distribution may be approximated by a Poisson or a normal distribution.*

(b) Periodic samples of size 100 are taken from the output of a machine which on an average produces 3% defective items. If 5 or more are defective the machine must be inspected. Find the probability that the machine will be inspected even if it is working normally ?

If the ratio of defectives has risen to 4.5% what is the probability that the machine will not be inspected on the assumption that the criterion for inspection is still 5 or more in a sample of 100 ?

(Use both Poisson and Normally approximations.)

Ans: (a) If n is large p is close to zero so that $1 - p$ is close to 1 and np is less than 5, the binomial distribution may be closely approximated by a Poisson distribution whose basic characteristic is that $np \approx np\,q$ (mean variance).

If n is larger and if neither p nor q is close to zero, the normal distribution is a good approximation to the binomial distribution.

(b) The machine will be inspected even if it is working normally when a sample contains 5 or more defectives.

when $p = 0.03$, from Table G, $P_{4 \text{ or less}} = 0.815$

Hence $\quad P_{5 \text{ or more}} = 1 - 0.815 = 0.185$

When using a normal distribution, the probability of 5 or more, is to be interpreted to mean the probability of 4.5 or more.

Since $\quad p = 0.03, q = 0.97$

$$\sqrt{npq} = \sqrt{100 \times 0.3 \times 0.97} = 1.705$$

$$z = \frac{4.5 - 3.0}{1.705} = 0.879$$

From Table A, corresponding to z of 0.897, area of the curve is 0.8104.

Hence the probability of more than 4.5 = 1 – 0.8104 = 0.1896

When $p = 0.045$, the probability that a machine will not be inspected is in fact the probability that the sample contains 4 or less defectives.

From Table G, $P_{4 \text{ or more}} = 0.532$

When using the normal curve, the probability of 4 or less is to be interpreted to mean the probability of 4.5 or less.

$$np = 100 \times 0.045 = 4.5$$

$$\sqrt{npq} = \sqrt{100 \times 0.045 \times 0.955} = 2.07$$

$$z = \frac{4.5 - 4.5}{2.07} = 0$$

From Table A, corresponding to z of 0, area of normal curve is 0.5000. Probability that machine will not be inspected is 0.5000.

Q. 4.35: *A company manufactures and distributes a product which sells at ₹ 20,000. The marginal cost of production is ₹ 11,000 per unit, and unavoidable manufacturing fixed costs are ₹ 70,000 a month. The company employs 128 salesmen and the chances of any salesman getting an order is 1 is 9, but there is no chance of getting more than one order. The firm does not wish to fall below break-even point more than 1 month in 6. How much can be allocated each month for directors' fees, consultancy fees, etc. ?*

Ans: Assume that in the long run sales are normally distributed.

$$\text{Mean number of sales} = \frac{1}{9} \times 128 = 14\frac{2}{9}$$

$$\text{Standard deviation} = \sqrt{128 \times \frac{1}{9} \times \frac{8}{9}}$$

$$= \frac{32}{9} = 3\frac{5}{9}$$

Since the sales are normally distributed and the firm does not wish to fall below break-even point in sales more than 1 month in 6, area of the normal curve upto break-even point is $\frac{1}{6}$ or 0.1667.

From Table *A*, we find this corresponds to a *z* of – 0.97.

$$\text{Therefore} \qquad -0.97 = \frac{X_i - 14\frac{2}{9}}{3\frac{5}{9}}$$

where X_i represents the break-even point for monthly sales and computed to be 10.77 from above.

when 10 sets are sold, Revenue = 20,000 × 10 = 200,000

Total cost = ₹ 70,000 + ₹ 110,000 = ₹ 180,000

Amount available = 200,000 – ₹ 180,000 = 20,000

Similarly when 11 sets are sold, amount available will be ₹ 29,000.

Amount available = ₹ 29,000

Q. 4.36: *A batch of 50 items contains 1 item that does not meet specifications. A random sample of 5 items is drawn from the batch and tested.*

(a) Use the correct probability distribution to calculate the probability that the 1 nonconforming item will be drawn in the sample.

(b) Use the binomial approximation to calculate this probability.

(c) Use the Poisson approximation to calculate this probability.

(d) By what percentage does each of these approximation methods overestimate (+) or underestimate (–) the correct figure ?

Ans: (*a*) The correct probability is $\frac{C_4^{49} C_1^1}{C_5^{50}} = 0.1$

(*b*) The binomial probability is $5(0.02)(0.98)^4 = 0.09224$

(*c*) The Poisson probability from Table *G* is found for *np* of 0.1, to be 0.09.

(*d*) It is obvious that both the probabilities are slightly less than the correct figure.

$$\text{Underestimate in case of } (b) = \left(\frac{0.1 - 0.09224}{0.1}\right) \times 100$$

$$= (-)\ 0.0776\%$$

$$\text{Underestimate in case of } (c) = \frac{(0.1 - 0.09)}{0.1} \times 100$$

$$= (-)\ 0.1\%$$

Q. 4.37: *The diameters of shafts made by a certain manufacturing process are known to be normally distributed with mean 2.500 cm, and standard deviation 0.009 cm. What is the distribution of the sample mean of the nine such diameters selected at random ? Calculate the proportion of such sample means which can be expected to exceed 2.505 cm.*

Ans: From the concept of Central Limit Theorem, the distribution of $\bar{X}$ of samples will be normal with a mean of 2.500 cm, but with a standard deviation of $\sigma/\sqrt{n}$ *i.e.* $0.009/\sqrt{9} = 0.003$ cm. In order to find the proportion of $\bar{X}$ exceeding 2.505, we use Table A. For using Table *A*, we will first have to find the value of *z*.

$$z = \frac{2.505 - 2.500}{0.003} = \frac{0.005}{0.003} = 1.66$$

For value of *z* of 1.66, area of normal curve from Table *A* is 0.9515. Hence the proportion of area for values greater than 2.505 is 1.0000 – 0.9515 = 0.0485.

Q. 4.38: *In Chapter 3, several "decision rules" related to the theory of extreme runs are presented. The statement was: whenever n successive points on a control chart, at least r are on the same side of the central line", where :*

	n	*r*
(*a*)	7	7
(*b*)	11	10
(*c*)	14	12

Assume the probability to be $\frac{1}{2}$ that a subgroup average will fall above the central line. If there has been no shift in the universe average, what probability is associated with the random occurrence of each of these events ?

Ans: Since the probability of a subgroup average, falling above the central line is $\frac{1}{2}$, the probability of the subgroup average falling below central line is also $\frac{1}{2}$.

(*a*) The event of 7 points falling on the same side will happen when all the seven points fall below or above the central line.

The probability of 7 points above the central line $= \left(\frac{1}{2}\right)^7$

The probability of 7 points falling below the central line $= \left(\frac{1}{2}\right)^7$

Hence the probability of the event $= \left(\frac{1}{2}\right)^7 + \left(\frac{1}{2}\right)^7 = 2\left(\frac{1}{2}\right)^7 = \frac{1}{64}$

(*b*) The probability that at least 10 out of 11 points would fall on the same side of the central line can be computed by adding the first two and last two terms of the binomial, $\left(\frac{1}{2} + \frac{1}{2}\right)^{11}$

P_{11}, the probability of all 11 above $= \left(\frac{1}{2}\right)^{11}$

P_{10}, the probability of exactly 10 above $= 11\left(\frac{1}{2}\right)^{10}\left(\frac{1}{2}\right)^{1}$

P_1, the probability of exactly 10 below (1 above) $= 11\left(\frac{1}{2}\right)^{11}\left(\frac{1}{2}\right)^{1}$

P_0, the probability of all 11 below (0 above) $= \left(\frac{1}{2}\right)^{11}$

The probability that 10 or more out to 11 will fall on the same side of the central line

$$= \left(\frac{1}{2}\right)^{11} + \left(\frac{1}{2}\right)^{11} + 11\left(\frac{1}{2}\right)^{11} + 11\left(\frac{1}{2}\right)^{11}$$

$$= \frac{24}{2048} = 0.0117 \approx \frac{1}{85}$$

(*c*) The probability that at least 12 out of 14 points would fall on the same side of the central line can be computed by adding first three and last terms and is found to be $\frac{53}{4096}$ or 0.0129 or $\frac{1}{77}$.

Q. 4.39: *Assuming that the probability is 0.0668 that a point will randomly fall above a 1.5*$\sigma_{\bar{X}}$, *limit on a control chart for* $\bar{\bar{X}}$ *if the universe average has not shifted, develop a decision rule similar to that shown in Q. 4.38 (a) based on the theory of runs that yields a probability of occurrence approximately equivalent to that in Problem 4.38 (a).*

Ans: In Q. 4.38 (*a*), the probability that 7 successive points fall on one side of central line

$$= \frac{1}{128} = 0.0078$$

In this case there are upper and lower 1.5 $\sigma_{\bar{X}}$ limits.

Probability of any point falling above the upper 1.5 $\sigma_{\bar{X}}$ limit = 0.0668.

Probability of any two successive points falling above the upper 1.5 $\sigma_{\bar{X}}$ limits = $(0.0668)^2$ = 0.00446.

Since the probability a point falling below the lower 1.5 $\sigma_{\bar{X}}$ limit is also 0.0668, the probability of two successive points falling below the lower 1.5 $\sigma_{\bar{X}}$ limit will also be 0.00446.

The probability of two points in succession outside the same 1.5 $\sigma_{\bar{X}}$ limit (either above the upper limit or below the lower limit) is 0.00446 + 0.00446 = 00892, which is very near to the stipulated probability of 0.0078.

Hence the 'decision rule' is as follows :

Grounds exist for suspicion that universe parameter has shifted whenever two successive points on an $\bar{X}$ chart are outside the 1.5 $\sigma_{\bar{X}}$ limits (either the upper limit or below the lower limit.)

Q. 4.40: *It has been decided to show both the (2-sigma)* ***warning limits*** *and the (3-sigma)* ***control limits*** *on an* $\bar{X}$ *chart.*

(a) What is the probability that a subgroup average all exceed the upper warning limit but does not exceed the upper control limit when the process is correctly centered.

(b) The quality control supervisor has a policy that he should be notified immediately if two successive subgroup averages exceed one of the warning limits or if one subgroup average exceeds either of the control limits. What is the probability that, when there has been no change in the process, the quality control supervisor will have to be notified based on :

(1) Two successive averages falling between the upper warning and control limit.

(2) A subgroup average exceeding the upper control limit.

(c) If the process average suddenly shifts to $\mu + 1.0\ \sigma_{\bar{X}}$ with no change in σ, what is the probability that two successive points will exceed the upper warning limit but not exceed the upper control limit ?

Ans: (*a*) Since the subgroup averages are normally distributed, the probability of a subgroup average exceeding the upper warning limit ($\mu + 2\ \sigma_{\bar{X}}$) but not exceeding the upper control limit ($\mu + 3\ \sigma_{\bar{X}}$) is the area of the normal curve between these two limits. From Table *A*, this is found to be 0.02135.

(*b*) (1) The probability that two successive subgroup averages falling between the upper warning limit and upper control limit $(0.2135)^2 = 0.00046$.

(2) The probability that a subgroup average exceeding the upper control limit ($\mu + 3\sigma_{\bar{X}}$) from Table *A* is found to be 0.00135.

Probability that the supervisor will be informed = 0.00046 + 0.00135 = .00181

(c) When the process average shifts to ($\mu + 1\sigma_{\bar{X}}$) the probability of a subgroup average still falling between ($\mu + 2\sigma_{\bar{X}}$) and ($\mu + 3\sigma_{\bar{X}}$) can be calculated by finding the area of the normal curve between these two limits but with a process average of $\mu + 1\sigma_{\bar{X}}$ instead of its earlier value of μ

$$z_1 = \frac{(\mu + 2\sigma_{\bar{X}}) - (\mu + 1\sigma_{\bar{X}})}{\sigma_{\bar{X}}} = 1$$

$$z_2 = \frac{(\mu + 3\sigma_{\bar{X}}) - (\mu + 1\sigma_{\bar{X}})}{\sigma_{\bar{X}}} = 2.$$

For $z = 2$ area of the normal curve = 0.9773

For $z = 1$, area of the normal curve = 0.8413

Area between these limits = 0.1360

Probability that will the changed process average, two successive subgroup averages will exceed the upper warning limit but not the upper control limit $1 - (0.1360)^2 = 0.018496$.

Q. 4.41: *Control charts for $\bar{X}$ and R are maintained on dissolved iron content of a certain solution in parts per million (ppm). After 125 hourly samples have been drawn and analysed, the data are organised into 25 subgroups of 5 measurements each maintaining the order of sampling. From these data, $\Sigma \bar{X} = 390$ and $\Sigma R = 84$.*

Assume that the mean of the process shifts to 18 ppm dissolved iron before the next subgroup is drawn. What is the Type II error probability that this shift will go undetected on the next subgroup plotted on the $\bar{X}$ chart ? Assume that no change takes place in the dispersion of the process?

Ans: $\Sigma\overline{X} = 390.8$

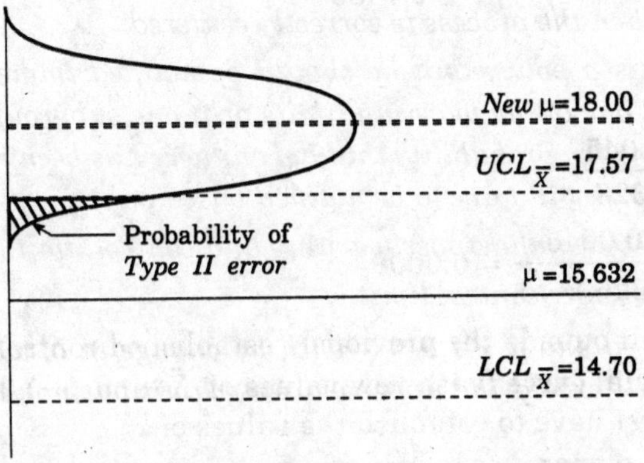

FIGURE 4.8: Probability of Type II error on an $\overline{X}$ chart.

$$\overline{X} = \mu = \frac{390.8}{25} = 15.632$$

$$\Sigma R = 84$$

$$\overline{R} = \frac{84}{25} = 3.36$$

$$\hat{\sigma} = \overline{R}/d_2 = \frac{3.36}{2.326}$$

$$\sigma_{\overline{X}} = \frac{\hat{\sigma}}{\sqrt{n}} = \frac{3.36}{2.326\sqrt{5}} = 0.646$$

Upper control limit = 15.632 + 3(0.646) = 17.57

when the process average shifts to 18.00 and dispersion remaining the same, the distribution of the means will be normal. Now with this new distribution point lying below the limit of 17.57 will give an impression that the process has not changed but as a matter of fact, it has changed. Hence the area of the normal curve below the limit of 17.57 will be the probability of *Type II* error as shown in Fig. 4.8.

To calculate this, we will first find z.

$$z = \frac{17.57 - 18.00}{0.646} = -0.665$$

From Table A, the corresponding area of the normal curve is 0.2530. Hence the probability of *Type II* error is 0.2530.

Q. 4.42: *Based on past month's data, the control limit of for an $\overline{X}$ chart are based on estimate of σ of 0.0015 and an aimed at value of $\overline{X}_0$ of 0.7500. Present month's data based on earlier subgroup size of 5, yield $\overline{X} = 0.7505$ and $\overline{R} = 0.0045$. Find the probability that any given point will outside the previously established $\overline{X}$ chart limits.*

Ans: Established control limits on $\overline{X}$ chart

$$\overline{X}_0 \pm 3\sigma_{\overline{X}}$$

$$\text{Upper control limit} = 0.7500 + \frac{3 \times 0.0015}{\sqrt{5}} = 0.7520$$

Lower control limit $= 0.7500 - \frac{3 \times 0.0015}{\sqrt{5}} = 0.7480$

New $\bar{X} = 7.505$

$\bar{R} = 0.0045$

$$\sigma = \frac{\bar{R}}{d_2} = \frac{0.0045}{2.326}$$

$$\sigma_{\bar{X}} = \frac{\sigma}{\sqrt{n}} = \frac{0.0045}{2.326 \times \sqrt{5}} = 0.0008$$

Probability that any given point will fall outside the previously established control limits of 0.7520 and 0.7480 is the area of the normal curve (with new values of $\bar{X}$ and -), beyond these two limits. To use Table A, we will first have to establish the values of z.

$$z_1 = \frac{0.7480 - 0.7505}{0.0008} = 0.0025 = -3.125$$

$$z_2 = \frac{0.7520 - 0.7505}{0.0008} = \frac{0.0015}{0.0008} = 1.875$$

Area of normal curve corresponding to $z_1 = 0.00088$

Area of normal curve corresponding to $z_2 = 0.9696$

Total area of normal curve beyond the established limits = 0.00088 + (1.0000 – 0.9696)
= 0.03128.

Q. 4.43: *In a bolt factory machines A, B and C are manufacturing 25 percent, 35 percent, and 40 percent of the total production. Of their output 5, 4, 3, 2 pre cents are defective bolts. A bolt is drawn at random for the purpose of thread inspection, from the stream and was found to be defective. What are the probabilities that it was manufactured by machines A, B and C?*

Ans: In order to solve this problem, we apply Bayes' theorem and make the following table :

Hypothesis regarding universe	*Probability that of bolt from m/c*	*Sampling probability of a non defective bolt*	*Conditional probability*	*Probability of bolt from m/c*
Machine A	$\frac{25}{100} = \frac{1}{4}$	$\frac{5}{100} = \frac{1}{20}$	$\frac{1}{4} \times \frac{1}{20} = \frac{1}{80}$	$\frac{\frac{1}{80}}{\frac{69}{2000}} = \frac{25}{69} = 0.363$
Machine B	$\frac{35}{100} = \frac{7}{20}$	$\frac{4}{100} = \frac{1}{25}$	$\frac{7}{20} \times \frac{1}{25} = \frac{7}{500}$	$\frac{\frac{7}{500}}{\frac{69}{2000}} = \frac{28}{69} = 0.405$
Machine C	$\frac{40}{100} = \frac{2}{5}$	$\frac{2}{100} = \frac{1}{50}$	$\frac{2}{5} \times \frac{1}{50} = \frac{2}{250}$	$\frac{\frac{2}{250}}{\frac{69}{2000}} = \frac{16}{69} = 0.232$
Total	1		$\frac{69}{2000}$	

From above table, probabilities that the defective bolt was manufactured by Machines A, B and C are 0.363, 0.405 and 0.232 respectively.

Q. 4.44: *A manufacturing firm produces steel pipes in three different plants with daily production volumes of 500, 1000 and 2,000 units respectively. According to past experience, it is known that fraction rejectable produced by three plants are 0.05, 0.008, and 0.010 respectively. If a pipe is selected at random from a particular day's total production and found to be nonconforming. Determine (a) which plant manufactured this pipe, (b) the probability that it was manufactured in the first plant.*

Ans: Let the three plants be designated by A, B and C. For applying Bayes' theorem, we make the following table :

Hypothesis regarding universe	*Probability of pipe from plant*	*Sampling probability of a nonconforming pipe*	*Conditional probability*	*Probability of nonconforming pipe from plant*
Plant A	$\frac{500}{3500} = \frac{1}{7}$	0.005	$\frac{1}{7} \times 0.005 = 0.00071$	0.00071/0.00870 = 0.0816
Plant B	$\frac{1000}{3500} = \frac{2}{7}$	0.008	$\frac{2}{7} \times 0.008 = 0.00228$	0.00228/0.0087 = 0.2621
Plant C	$\frac{2000}{3500} = \frac{4}{7}$	0.010	$\frac{4}{7} \times 0.010 = 0.00571$	0.00571/0.0087 = 0.6563
Total	1		0.00870	

(*a*) From above tabulation, the greatest probability is 0.6563 for Plant C. Hence it is more probable that the nonconforming pipe came from Plant C.

(*b*) Again, from above tabulation, the probability that it came from Plant A is 0.816.

CHAPTER

5

The Control Charts for Fraction Rejected (*p* charts and *np* charts)

5.1 SOME LIMITATIONS OF CONTROL CHARTS FOR VARIABLES AND OPPORTUNITY FOR INSPECTION BY ATTRIBUTES

In spite of the advantages of the $\bar{X}$ and R charts, both as powerful tools for the diagnosis of quality problems and as a means for routine detection of sources of trouble, it is evident that their use is limited to only a small fraction of the quality characteristic specified for manufactured products. Also inspection by variables, as required for $\bar{X}$ and R charts, is sometimes uneconomical or even impossible. An automatic turning, for instance, may have a dozen dimensions and therefore, may call for a dozen different $\bar{X}$ and R charts. Although any one of these important dimensions could have been measured as a variable and was therefore a possible candidate for $\bar{X}$ and R charts, it is obvious that there could not be one dozen such charts. No dimension should be chosen for $\bar{X}$ and R charts unless there is an opportunity to save costs—costs of spoilage and rework, inspection costs, costs of excess material - or otherwise to affect quality improvement that would in some way more than compensate for the costs of taking the measurements, keeping the charts, and properly analyzing them. An economic and viable solution to the above problem is to check with a "Go" and "Not go" gauge and to keep a record of overall quality by simply noting the percentage of pieces that fail to gauge. Hot forgings for example, have defects such as pits, laps, and cold shuts that are not measurable at all; they can be classified only as 'passable', or 'not passable'. Sometimes product either succeeds or fails a test. Certain types of detonators fall into this category. Frequently at the final inspection of a product there may be so many possible causes for rejection both in dimension and in finish, that a separate record of each cause is out of question. Under such circumstances the best procedure may be to record simply the number of tests performed (by gauging or otherwise) and the number of failures. This is known as inspection by attributes, that is, by classification of the product either good or bad, as either acceptable or not acceptable, as either conforming or nonconforming.

5.2 CONTROL CHARTS FOR ATTRIBUTES

There are several different types of control charts that may be used in either of the cases described in the foregoing paragraphs:

1. The *p* chart, the chart for fraction rejected as nonconforming to specifications.
2. The *np* chart, the control chart for number of nonconforming items.
3. The *c* chart, the control chart for number of nonconformities.
4. The *u* chart, the control chart for number of nonconformities per unit.

The *c* and *u* charts are discussed in Chap. 6.

The cost of collecting data for attributes charts is likely to be less than the cost of collecting the data for $\bar{X}$ and R charts, because the attributes chart generally uses data already collected for other purposes. $\bar{X}$ and R charts on the other hand require special measurements for control chart purposes. The cost of computing and charting may be less since one attributes chart may apply to any number of quality characteristics observed at an inspection station, whereas separate $\bar{X}$ and R charts are necessary for each measured quality characteristic.

In addition to the cost advantages that may be gained, the use of attributes control charts provides management with useful record of quality history. Many managerial decisions need to be based on a knowledge of the quality level currently maintained and on prompt information about changes that occur in the quality level. In government contract work, such information may be required in order to demonstrate capability to meet requirements both prior to award of a contract and later during fulfillment.

5.3 THE CONTROL CHART FOR FRACTION REJECTED

The most versatile and widely used attributes control chart is the *p*-chart. This is the chart for the fraction rejected as nonconforming to specifications (the so-called fraction defective). It may be applied to quality characteristics that can be observed only as attributes. It may also be applied to quality characteristics that are considered as attributes - for example, dimensions checked by 'Go' and 'Not-go' gauges - even through they might have been measured as variables. As long as the result of an inspection is the classification of an individual article as accepted or rejected, a single *p* chart may be applied to one quality characteristic or a dozen or a hundred.

Fraction rejected *p* may be defined as the ratio of the number of nonconforming articles in any inspection or series of inspections to the total number of articles actually inspected. Fraction rejected is nearly always expressed as a decimal fraction.

Percent rejected is 100 *p*, that is, 100 times the fraction rejected. For actual calculation of control limits, it is necessary to use fraction rejected. For charting and for general presentation of results to shop personnel and to management, the fraction is generally converted to percent.

5.4 THE BINOMIAL AS A PROBABILITY LAW THAT DETERMINES THE FLUCTUATIONS OF FRACTION REJECTED

Suppose 10,000 bolts of the same size (except of threading) are placed in a box. Of these 9,500 are with NPT threading and only 500 are with IS-554 type threading. NPT threaded bolts (Ist type) may be considered to represent articles that conform to specifications and IS-554 threading (IInd type) represent nonconforming articles. Let samples of 50 bolts be drawn at random from this box. If the 50 bolts are replaced after each sample has been drawn and all bolts are thoroughly mixed before the next drawing, the theory of probability enables us to calculate the relative frequency in the long run of getting exactly 0, 1, 3, 4, 5, 6, and so on, bolts. As explained in Chap. 4, the binomial gives a very close approximation to these probabilities. If the box held an infinite number of bolts, 5% which were nonconforming, the binomial would apply exactly.

Any one sample of bolts drawn from the box is a sample from a very large quantity of bolts 5% nonconforming. As a matter of chance, variations in the number of nonconforming bolts are inevitable from sample to sample. In a similar way, we may think of a day's or production (or other lot) of any manufactured article or part as a sample from a larger quantity with some unknown fraction that do not conform to specifications. This unknown fraction universe nonconforming depends upon a complex set of causes influencing the production and inspection operations. As a matter of chance, the nonconforming fraction in the sample may vary considerably. As long as the nonconforming fraction in the universe remains unchanged, the relative frequencies of nonconforming fractions in the sample may be expected to follow the binomial law.

5.5 CONTROL LIMITS FOR THE *p* CHART

As a general mathematical model, the Shewhart control chart model with 3-sigma limits may be expressed as

$$UCL_y = E(y) + 3\sigma_y$$
$$\text{Central Line } y = E(y)$$
$$LCL_y = E(y) - 3\sigma_y$$

where y is the random variable to be plotted on the control chart, for example, $\overline{X}$, R, p, c, and so forth, $E(y)$ is the expected value of the statistical variable, and σ_y is the standard deviation of the variable y.

In the case of the control chart for $\overline{X}$, the basic model becomes

$$UCL_{\overline{X}} = \mu_{\overline{X}} + 3\sigma_{\overline{X}}$$
$$\text{Central line } \overline{X} = \overline{\overline{X}}$$
$$LCL_{\overline{X}} = \mu_{\overline{X}} - 3\sigma_{\overline{X}}$$

where the statistical variable $y = \overline{X}$, $E(y) = \mu_{\overline{X}}$ and $\sigma_y = \sigma_{\overline{X}} = \sigma/\sqrt{n}$. The reader will recall that the distribution of the statistic $y = \overline{X}$, even with small subgroup sizes, tends toward a normal distribution because of the power of the central limit theorem. Since the chance (probability) that an exactly normally distributed random variable will fall outside either 3-sigma control limit is 0.0027, such an occurrence purely by chance on an $\overline{X}$ chart would be very rare indeed.

The $\overline{X}$ chart, however, is the only instance in the application of the Shewhart control-chart model for which the distribution of the random variable can be shown to tend toward the normal distribution. In all other cases—for example, the R chart, s chart, p chart, and the like—it is appropriate to say simply that the occurrence of a point falling outside 3-sigma limits at random would be very unlikely*.

The mean, or expected value, of the binomial fraction is p, and its standard deviation is $\sqrt{p(1-p)/n}$ (see Chap. 4) Thus, 3-sigma limits for the p chart are

$$UCL_{\overline{p}} = p + 3\sqrt{\frac{p(1-p)}{n_j}} = p + 3\frac{\sqrt{p(1-p)}}{\sqrt{n_j}} \quad \text{for group } j$$

$$LCL_p = p - 3\sqrt{\frac{p(1-p)}{n_j}} = p - 3\frac{\sqrt{p(1-p)}}{\sqrt{n_j}}$$

* This is not to say that it is impossible to associate probability values with points outside control limits for charts other than the $\overline{X}$ chart. Such calculations are very tedious and time-consuming, especially in p chart applications with varying sample size, and contribute little to the application of the basic decision rule. The general statement may be made, however, that they are of the same order of magnitude as the probabilities of a point falling outside 3-sigma limits in drawing from a normal universe. This is the true power of the Shewhart model.

The value of p in these formulae refers to the parametric, or universe, value of the statistic in question. When combined with the subscript o (that is, p_o), it refers to the standard or aimed-at value chosen for control-chart purposes.

In cases where a standard value is not available, the observed value $\bar{p}$ may be used. The observed value is necessarily used in the calculation of trial control limits. In these cases, the control limits are

$$UCL_p = \bar{p} + 3\sqrt{\frac{\bar{p}(1-\bar{p})}{n_j}} = \bar{p} + 3\frac{\sqrt{\bar{p}(1-\bar{p})}}{\sqrt{n_j}}$$

$$LCL_p = \bar{p} - 3\sqrt{\frac{\bar{p}(1-\bar{p})}{n_j}} = \bar{p} - 3\frac{\sqrt{\bar{p}(1-\bar{p})}}{\sqrt{n_j}}$$

where $\bar{p} = \Sigma r_j/\Sigma n_j$. Each point plot is $p_j = r_j/n_j$, the number of units rejected divided by the number of units inspected in the subgroup.

Industrial practice in the use of the p chart generally bases control limits on either 3 sigma or some other multiple of sigma. Except for very small subgroups, the calculation of probability limits (such as described for $\bar{X}$, R, and s charts in Chap. 8) for a p chart is too burdensome a job. However, if probability limits are desired, they may be obtained by direct use of the binomial distribution.

As in the case of the $\bar{X}$ and R charts, the use of 3-sigma limits rather than narrower or wider limits is a matter of experience as to the economic balance between the cost of hunting for assignable causes when they are absent and the cost of not hunting for them when they are present. Although in most cases 3-sigma limits are best, special cases arise in which the use of narrower limits, such as 2-sigma, is desirable. The need for narrower limits arises out of the use of the p chart as an instrument for executive pressure on quality.

EXAMPLE 5.1: *Illustration of calculation necessary for control charts for fraction rejected for constant subgroup size.*

Facts of the case This example applies to 4-month record of daily 100% inspection of electric hair blower motor. It is intended chiefly as an illustration of how control limits are calculated, and of the setting and revision of standard values for fraction rejected.

When, after a change in design, the production of this part was started early in May, the daily fraction rejected was computed and plotted on a chart. At the end of the month, the average fraction rejected $\bar{p}$ was computed. Trial control limits were computed. A standard value of fraction rejected p_0 was then established to apply for future production. At the end of June, a revised subgroup p_0 was computed to apply to July and again at the end of July, a revised p_0 was computed to apply to August, and the control chart was continued during August with this revised value.

Calculation of trial control limits Table 5.1 shows the number inspected and the number rejected as nonconforming to specifications each day during May. The fraction rejected each day is the number of pieces rejected divided by the number inspected. For example, for May 1,

$$1 = 12/300 = 0.040.$$

At the end of the month, the average fraction rejected p_i is computed. It should be emphasized that the correct way to calculate p_i is to divide the total number rejected in the period by the total number of pieces inspected during the period.

TABLE 5.1: COMPUTATION OF TRIAL CONTROL LIMITS FOR CONTROL CHART FOR FRACTION REJECTED

Data on inspection results of electric hair dryer blower motor

Date	Number inspected n	Number rejected	Fraction rejected p	Date	Number inspected n	Number rejected	Fraction rejected p
May 1	300	12	0.040	May 16	300	3	0.010
2	300	3	0.010	17	300	0	0.0
3	300	9	0.030				
4	300	4	0.013	19	300	5	0.017
5	300	0	0.0	20	300	7	0.023
				22	300	8	0.027
7	300	6	0.020	23	300	16	0.053
8	300	6	0.020	24	300	2	0.007
9	300	1	0.003				
10	300	8	0.027	26	300	5	0.017
11	300	11	0.037	27	300	6	0.020
				28	300	0	0.0
13	300	2	0.007	29	300	3	0.010
14	300	10	0.033	31	300	2	0.007
15	300	9	0.030				
Total	Number inspected = 7,500			Number rejected = 138			

$$\bar{p} = \frac{\text{Total number rejected}}{\text{Total number inspected}} = \frac{138}{7,500} = 0.018$$

$$UCL_p = \bar{p} + 3\sqrt{\frac{\bar{p}(1-\bar{p})}{n}}$$

$$= 0.018 + 3\sqrt{\frac{0.018(1-0.018)}{300}} = 0.041$$

$$LCL_p = \bar{p} - 3\sqrt{\frac{\bar{p}(1-\bar{p})}{n}}$$

$$= 0.018 - 3\sqrt{\frac{0.018(1-0.018)}{300}} = -0.005 \text{ or } 0.0$$

The standard deviation was calculated based on this observed value of $\bar{p}$, 0.018. The lower control limit based on this value of $\bar{p}$ turned out to be negative *i.e.* – 0.005. In practice, a negative fraction rejected would be impossible. Therefore, the lower control limit was kept at zero. The control chart for the month of May is shown in Fig 5.1.

In cases where the lower control limit is positive, it may in some cases be changed to zero for the simple reason *that if the chart is to be reviewed by operating personnel, it would be difficult to explain why a fraction rejected that is below the lower control limit is out of control. In other words, performance of exceptionally good quality would be classified as out of control.* To avoid the need to explain this situation to operation personnel, the lower control limit is changed from a positive value to zero. When the *p-chart is to be used by quality control personnel and by management, a positive lower control limit is left unchanged.* In this manner exceptionally good performance (below the lower control limit) will be treated as out-of-control situation and investigated for an assignable cause. Hopefully, the assignable cause will indicate how the situation can be repeated. Evidently such out-of-controls points (*i.e.* points below the lower control limit) will not be eliminated for computing the revised value of $\overline{p}$ or p_0.

Determination of standard value p_0 If all the points fall within the trial control limits, the standard value p_0 may be assumed to be equal to $\overline{p}$.

In Fig 5.1 one point fell outside the trial control limits. In such cases, the decision as to the value of p0 to be used calls for judgement as to what process average fraction rejected can be maintained in the future, provided the occasional assignable causes of bad quality can be eliminated. An aid to such judgement may be obtained by computing a revised value of $\overline{p}$, eliminating the days on which p fell above the upper control limit.

With May 23, eliminated, the remaining number of rejects is 122 and the remaining number inspected it 7,200. The revised

$$\overline{p} = \frac{122}{7,200} = 0.017$$

Since this value was considered as the best estimate of the standard or universe value, it was decided to keep $p_0 = 0.017$.

Calculation of control limits based on standard fraction rejected, p_0 Based on the value of p_0 as 0.17, the revised control limits for the month of June were

$$UCL_p = p_0 + 3\sqrt{\frac{p_0(1-p_0)}{n}}$$

$$= 0.017 + 3\sqrt{\frac{0.017(1-0.017)}{300}} = 0.039$$

$$LCL_p = 0.017 - 3\sqrt{\frac{0.017(1-0.017)}{300}} = -0.005 \text{ or zero}$$

Control chart for month of June based on these limits indicates that the process is in control.

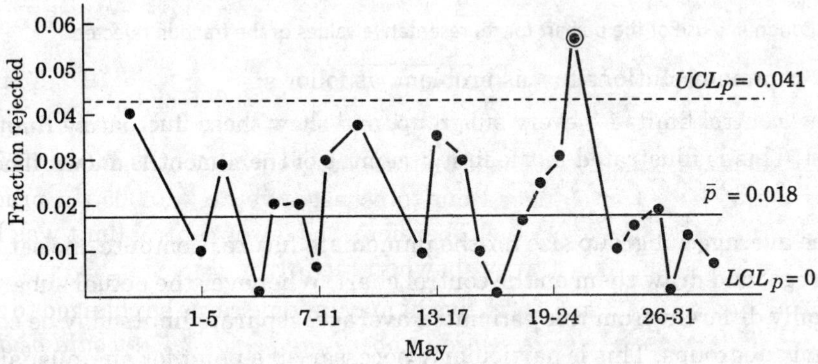

FIGURE 5.1: Control chart for fraction rejected-data from Table 5.1.

Further revision of p_0 During July, the average fraction rejected $\overline{p}$ was calculated to be 0.014. No points fell above the upper control limit. The value, 0.014, was therefore assumed as p_0 to apply to July.

The process quality during July improved even more, and based upon the average fraction rejected $\overline{p}$ was found to be only 0.010. So a p_0 of 0.010 was adopted for the month of August. The control charts for the months of June, July and August are shown in Fig 5.2. For the month of August, the process average $\overline{p}$ was 0.009. This justified a further downward revision of p_0 to for September. The data and the control chart for the September however, are not shown here.

5.6 PROBLEMS INTRODUCED BY VARIABLE SUBGROUP SIZE

The larger the subgroup, the more likely that the fraction nonconforming in the subgroup will be close to the fraction nonconforming of the universe. This obvious general principle is expressed in mathematical terms by the statement that the standard deviation of p, like the standard deviation of $\overline{X}$, varies inversely with $\sqrt{n}$.

For both the $\overline{X}$ chart and the p chart, the appropriate 3-sigma control limits depend on the subgroup size. The practical difference is that because most measurements used for $\overline{X}$ charts are taken for control-chart purposes, it is usually possible to keep subgroup size constant. Many p charts, on the other hand, use data taken for other purposes than the control chart; where subgroups consist of daily or weekly production, the subgroup size is almost certain to vary.

As a practical matter, whenever subgroup size is expected to vary, a decision must be made as to the way in which control limits are to be shown on the p chart.

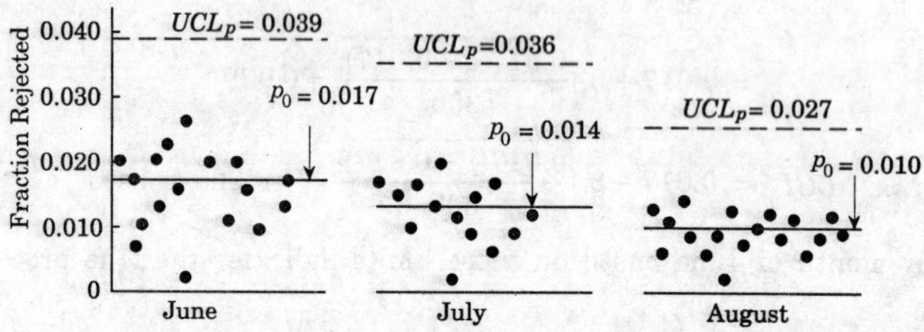

FIGURE 5.2: Continuing use of the *p*-chart for representative values of the fraction rejected.

There are *four* common solutions to this problem, as follows:

1. Compute new control limits for every subgroup, and show these fluctuating limits on the control chart. This is illustrated in the first 3 months of the 4 months shown in Example 5.2.
2. Estimate the average subgroup size for the immediate future. Compute one set of limits for this average, and draw them on the control chart. Whenever the actual subgroup size is substantially different from this estimated average, separate limits may be computed for individual subgroups. This is particularly necessary if a point for an unusually small subgroup falls outside control limits. A practical rule in deciding the situation where to

compute the single set of limits, is that where the maximum and minimum are not more than 25% away from the average, a single set of control limits based on the expected average subgroup size can be used. This scheme is illustrated in the final 2 months of the period shown in Example 5.2. Estimates of future average subgroup size must be revised from time to time; where each day's production is one subgroup, it is customary to revise these estimates monthly.

3. Draw several sets of control limits on the chart corresponding to different subgroup sizes. A good plan is to use three sets of limits, one for expected average subgroup size, one close to the expected minimum, and one close to the expected maximum. In Example 5.2. for instance, limits might be drawn corresponding to subgroup sizes of 1,000, 2,500, and 4,000. This scheme is not satisfactory unless the data are shown on the same sheet with the control chart, with the figures for each subgroup on the same line the plotted point for the subgroup, so that the subgroup size may be seen at a glance. Because with this scheme it is not immediately evident from inspection of the chart which points are out of control, it is desirable to use a special symbol to mark out-of-control points. For instance, if a dot were used for each point on the chart, a circle might be drawn around the dot for each point out of control.

   The main objection raised against separate calculation of correct control limits for each subgroup is the time and effort consumed in calculating and drawing the limits. Actually, even inexpensive pocket or desk calculators provide for automatic extraction of a square root; thus such calculations should take very little time. All process control computer software provides for automatic calculation of limits. Thus hand calculation usually is relegated to the status of a teaching tool in most practical applications.

4. Still another method to meet problem of varying subgroup size is to start the so called 'stabilized' p-chart. Here instead of using the fraction rejected, the expression $(p - \overline{p})/\sigma_p$ is computed and plotted. Clearly, this expression represents the variation in p in terms of standard deviation where the standard deviation itself differs from subgroup due to difference in n. The control limits on this chart will be constant at $\pm$ 3. The stabilized p-chart, though involves laborious calculations, yet simpler in its interpretation. This technique is illustrated in Example 5.3.

EXAMPLE 5.2: *Illustration of calculations necessary for control chart for fraction rejected*

Facts of the case This example applies to a 4-month record of daily 100% inspection of a single critical quality characteristic of a part for an electrical device. It is intended chiefly as an illustration of how control limits are calculated with variable production, and of the setting and revision of standard values for fraction rejected.

When, after a change in design, the production of this part was started early in June, the daily fraction rejected was computed and plotted on a chart. At the end of the month, the average fraction rejected $\overline{p}$ was computed. Trial control limits were computed for each point. A standard value of fraction rejected p_0 was then established to apply to future production. During July new control limits were computed and plotted daily on the basis of the number of parts n inspected during the day. A single set of control limits was established for August, based on the estimated average daily production. At the end of August, a revised p0 was computed to apply to September, and the control chart was continued during September with this revised value.

Calculation of trial control limits. Table 5.2 shows the number inspected and the number rejected as nonconforming to specifications each day during June. The fraction rejected each day is the number of parts rejected (r_j) divided by the number inspected that day (n_j). For example, for June. 6, $p_j = 31/3{,}350 = 0.0093$. The percent rejected is $100p = 0.93\%$.

TABLE 5.2: COMPUTATION OF TRIAL CONTROL LIMITS FOR CONTROL CHART FOR FRACTION REJECTED

(Data on a single quality characteristic of a part of an electrical device)

Date	*Number inspected* n	*Number rejected*	*Fraction rejected* p	$3\sigma_p = 3\frac{\sqrt{\bar{p}(1-\bar{p})}}{\sqrt{n}}$	*UCL* $= \bar{p} + 3\sigma_p$	*LCL* $= \bar{p} - 3\sigma_p$
June 6	3,350	31	0.0093	0.0062	0.0207	0.0083
7	3,354	113	0.0337	0.0062	0.0207	0.0083
8	1,509	28	0.0186	0.0092	0.0237	0.0053
9	2,190	20	0.0091	0.0077	0.0222	0.0068
11	2,678	35	0.0131	0.0069	0.0214	0.0076
12	3,252	68	0.0209	0.0063	0.0208	0.0082
13	4,641	339	0.0730	0.0053	0.0198	0.0092
14	3,782	12	0.0032	0.0058	0.0203	0.0087
15	2,993	3	0.0010	0.0066	0.0211	0.0079
16	3,382	17	0.0050	0.0062	0.0207	0.0083
18	3,694	14	0.0038	0.0059	0.0204	0.0086
19	3,052	8	0.0026	0.0065	0.0210	0.0080
20	3,477	27	0.0078	0.0061	0.0206	0.0084
21	4,051	44	0.0109	0.0056	0.0201	0.0089
22	3,042	70	0.0230	0.0065	0.0210	0.0080
23	1,623	12	0.0074	0.0089	0.0234	0.0056
25	915	9	0.0098	0.0119	0.0264	0.0026
26	1,644	1	0.0006	0.0088	0.0233	0.0057
27	1,572	22	0.0140	0.0090	0.0235	0.0055
28	1,961	3	0.0015	0.0081	0.0226	0.0064
29	2,440	3	0.0012	0.0073	0.0218	0.0072
30	2,086	1	0.00005	0.0079	0.0224	0.0066
Totals ...	60,688	880	....	....	....	....

$$\bar{p} = \frac{\text{total number rejected}}{\text{total number inspected}} = \frac{880}{60,688} = 0.0145$$

$$3\sqrt{\bar{p}(1-\bar{p})} = 3\sqrt{(0.0145)(0.9855)} = 0.3586$$

At the end of the month, the average fraction rejected p is computed. It should be emphasized that the correct way to calculate $\bar{p}$ is to divide the total number rejected in the period by the total number of parts inspected during the period. Whenever the subgroup size (in this case, the daily number inspected) in not constant, it is incorrect to average the values of p_i.

The standard deviation was calculated on the basis of this observed value of $\bar{p}$, 0.0145. Note that the value of $3\sqrt{\bar{p}(1-\bar{p})}$ was calculated only once to apply to all calculations of control limits. Thus, for June 6, the 3-sigma limits are $\pm 0.3586/\sqrt{3,350}$, or $\pm$ 0.0062.

The daily values of pi and the control limits for each day are shown in Fig. 5.3. In this figure, percent rejected (100p) rather than fraction rejected has been plotted. Because percent rejected is more readily understood by both shop and administrative personnel, it is usually desirable for fraction rejected to be converted to percent rejected for all plotting.

Determination of standard value p_0 If all the points fall within the trial control limits, the standard value p_0 may be assumed to be equal to $\bar{p}$.

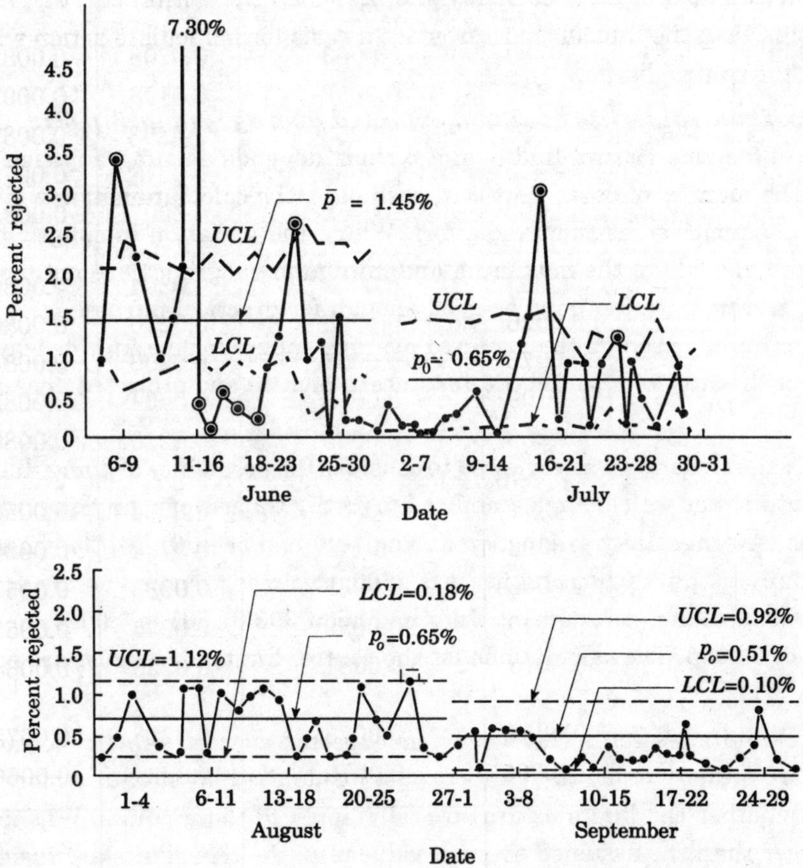

FIGURE 5.3: Control chart for percent rejected — 4 months production of an electrical device.

Here many points fell outside the trial control limits. In such cases, the decision as to the value of p_0 to be used calls for judgment as to what process average fraction rejected can be maintained in the future, provided the occasional assignable causes of bad quality can be eliminated. An aid to such judgment may be obtained by computing a revised value of $\overline{p}$, eliminating the days on which p_i fell above the upper control limit.

With these days — June 7, 12, 13, and 22 — eliminated, the remaining number of rejects is 290 and the remaining number inspected ia 46, 399. The revised $\overline{p}$ = 290/46,399 = 0.0063.

After consideration of this and of the pervious record on similar parts of slightly different design, it was decided to assume p_0 = 0.0065.

Calculation of control limits based on standard fraction rejected p_0 Table 5.3. gives the daily numbers inspected and rejected during July and shows the calculation of control limits based on the standard fraction rejected. This calculation appears to be almost identical with that shown in Table 5.2 . The value of p_0 is used in the calculation of limits in Table 5.3 wherever $\overline{p}$ was used in Table 5.2.

The practical difference is that where $\overline{p}$ is used, no control limits can be computed until $\overline{p}$ is known, that is, not until the end of the period. Where a standard value p_0 is established in advance, the limits can be computed each day and drawn on the control chart as the day's point is plotted. In this way, the control chart provides a basis for immediate action whenever a point goes outside the control limits.

Establishment of control limits based on expected average subgroup size Although the correct position of 3-sigma control limits on a p chart depends on subgroup size (in this case, a subgroup is the number of parts inspected each day), the calculation of new limits for each new subgroup consumes some time and effort. Where the variation in subgroup size is not too great (for example, where the maximum and minimum subgroups are not more than 25% away from the average), it often may be good enough for practical purposes to establish a single set of control limits based on the expected average subgroup size. In this way, limits may be established at the start of a period (for instance, a month) and projected ahead for the entire period.

At the end of July the situation was reviewed to consider the possibility of doing this. It was decided that daily output was well enough stabilized to justify the use of a single set of control limits during August. Average daily production during July had been 61,701/25 = 2,468. The estimated average daily output during August was 2600; this was assumed as the value of n for calculation of control limits. As p during July had been 393/61,701 = 0.0064, no change was made in the p_0 of 0.0065. The calculations for the control limits for August are shown in Table 5.4.

Whenever control limits are set in this way on an expected average value of n, any points on the control that are either outside the limits or just inside the limits require more critical examination to see whether the limits as drawn really apply to these points. Whenever the subgroup size is larger than the assumed average value of n, the true limits are inside those drawn. Whenever the subgroup size is smaller, the true limits are outside.

TABLE 5.3: COMPUTATION OF DAILY CONTROL LIMITS BASED ON STANDARD VALUE OF FRACTION REJECTED p_0

(Data on a single characteristic of a part of an electrical device)

Date	Number inspected n	Number rejected	Fraction rejected p	$3\sigma = 3\frac{\sqrt{p_0(1-p_0)}}{\sqrt{n}}$	$UCLp_0 + 3\sigma$	$LCLp_0 - 3\sigma$
July 2	2,228	4	0.0018	0.0051	0.0116	0.0014
3	2,087	9	0.0043	0.0053	0.0118	0.0012
5	2,088	3	0.0014	0.0053	0.0118	0.0012
6	1,746	2	0.0011	0.0058	0.0123	0.0007
7	2,076	1	0.0005	0.0053	0.0118	0.0012
9	2,164	1	0.0005	0.0052	0.0117	0.0013
10	2,855	5	0.0018	0.0045	0.0110	0.0020
11	2,560	5	0.0020	0.0048	0.0113	0.0017
12	2,545	14	0.0055	0.0048	0.0113	0.0017
13	1,874	1	0.0005	0.0056	0.0121	0.0009
14	2,329	24	0.0103	0.0050	0.0115	0.0015
16	2,744	30	0.0109	0.0046	0.0111	0.0019
17	2,619	77	0.0294	0.0047	0.0112	0.0018
18	2,211	5	0.0023	0.0051	0.0116	0.0014
19	1,746	19	0.0109	0.0058	0.0123	0.0007
20	2,628	28	0.0107	0.0047	0.0112	0.0018
21	2,366	5	0.0021	0.0050	0.0115	0.0015
23	2,954	23	0.0078	0.0044	0.0109	0.0021
24	2,586	32	0.0124	0.0047	0.0112	0.0018
25	2,790	8	0.0029	0.0046	0.011	0.0019
26	2,968	30	0.0101	0.0044	0.0109	0.0021
27	3,100	13	0.0042	0.0043	0.0108	0.0022
28	1,359	4	0.0029	0.0065	0.0130	0.0000
30	3,940	39	0.0099	0.0038	0.0103	0.0027
31	3,138	11	0.0035	0.0043	0.0108	0.0022
Totals	61,701	393	……..	……..	……..	……..

Standard fraction rejected $p_0 = 0.0065$

$$3\sqrt{p_0(1-p_0)} = 3\sqrt{(0.0065)(0.9935)} = 0.241$$

TABLE 5.4. RECORD OF DAILY FRACTION REJECTED WITH CONTROL LIMITS COMPUTED ON STANDARD DAILY PRODUCTION AND ON STANDARD VALUE OF FRACTION REJECTED p_o

(Data on a single quality characteristic of a part of an electrical device)

Date	*Number inspected n*	*Number rejected*	*Fraction rejected p*	*Date*	*Number in-spected n*	*Number rejected*	*Fraction rejected p*
Aug. 1*	3,068	6	0.0020	Sept. 1†	2,539	3	0.0012
2	776	3	0.0039	3	2,425	16	0.0066
3	2,086	16	0.0077	4	1,537	9	0.0059
4	3,652	10	0.0027	5	2,852	17	0.0060
6	2,606	3	0.0012	6	2,953	16	0.0054
7	3,114	21	0.0097	7	2,649	5	0.0019
8	1,768	27	0.0098	8	2,835	4	0.0014
9	3,208	3	0.0012	10	2,752	6	0.0022
10	2,629	21	0.0097	11	892	1	0.0011
11	2,745	22	0.0080	12	3,186	7	0.0022
13	3,114	30	0.0096	13	2,646	5	0.0019
14	1,768	18	0.0102	14	2,714	4	0.0015
15	3,208	29	0.0090	15	2,878	5	0.0017
16	2,629	2	0.0008	17	2,384	6	0.0025
17	3,576	9	0.0025	18	2,639	5	0.0019
18	2,262	15	0.0066	19	3,160	7	0.0022
20	3,294	5	0.0015	20	1,895	11	0.0058
21	3,026	5	0.0017	21	4,287	13	0.0030
22	2,713	10	0.0037	22	2,917	3	0.0010
24	3,824	23	0.0060	25	1,991	2	0.0010
25	3,265	12	0.0037	26	3,280	10	0.0030
27	1,205	14	0.0116	27	2,195	15	0.0068
28	3,035	7	0.0023	28	2,570	3	0.0012
29	2,793	6	0.0021	29	3,323	3	0.0009
31	3,227	18	0.0056				
Totals	73,523	373	....	Totals	65,978	177	

For August:,

Estimated average daily production = 2,600

Standard fraction rejected $p_0 = 0.0065$

$$3\sigma = 3\frac{\sqrt{p_0(1-p_0)}}{\sqrt{n}} = 3\frac{\sqrt{(0.0065)(0.9935)}}{\sqrt{2,600}} = 0.0047$$

$UCL_p = p_0 + 3\sigma = 0.0065 + 0.0047 = 0.0112$

For September:

Estimated average daily production = 2,700

Standard fraction rejected $p_0 = 0.0051$

$3\sigma = 0.0041$

$UCL_p = 0.0051 + 0.0041 = 0.0092$

Such a calculation was made for August 27, when p was 0.0116. This is above the upper control limit of 0.0112 that was computed for the assumed daily production of 2,600. A revised upper control limit for this day based on the actual production of 1,205 is 0.0134. The revised limits for this day are indicated on the control chart (Fig 5.3); they show that the point was actually not out of control.

Further revision of p_0 During August, the average fraction rejected p was 373/73,523 = 0.0051. No points fell above the upper control limit. This value, 0.0051, was therefore assumed as p0 to apply to September. Control limits for September were based on an estimated average subgroup size of 2,700. (Daily production during August had been 73,523/27 = 2,723.) Daily values for September with calculated control limits are shown in Table 5.4, and plotted in Fig. 5.3.

The process quality during September improved even more. Although only two points fell below the lower control limits during the month, confirmation of the existence of a new better level of quality was given by an extreme run for 11 points—from September 7 to 19—below the central line. For the month, the process average $\bar{p}$ was 177/65978 = 0.0027. This justified a further downward revision of p_0 to 0.0027 for October. The data and the control chart for October are not shown here.

EXAMPLE 5.3: *Illustration of calculations are 'stabilized' control chart for fraction rejected.*

This example is intended chiefly as an illustration of the computations for the stabilized control chart; its comparison with an ordinary fraction rejected control chart with variable limits.

Table 5.5 shows the number inspected and the number rejected as nonconforming castings each day during 20 consecutive days. This table also shows the computations for a stabilized p chart, in which case the plot is for $\dfrac{p-\bar{p}}{\sigma_P}$ instead of p.

Based on the data and computation in Table 5.5 Fig. 5:4 shows the stabilized p chart while Fig. 5.5 shows the p chart with variable limits.

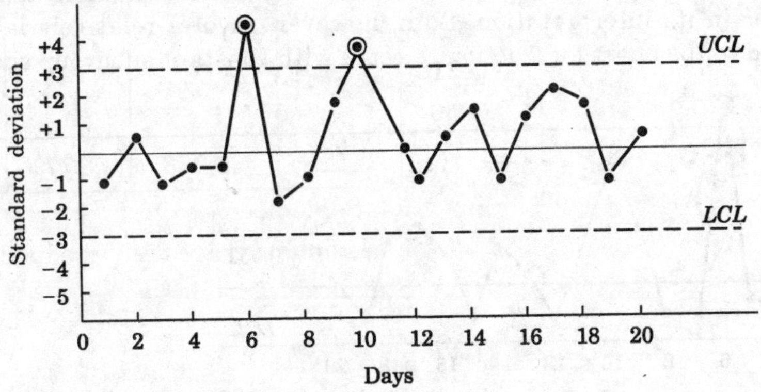

FIGURE 5.4 : Stabilized *p* chart for the data in Table 5.5

TABLE 5.5: DATA OF 20 DAY'S PRODUCTION OF CHARTS

Day	*Number inspected* n	*Number rejected* p	*Fraction rejected*	*Computation for stabilized chart*			*Computation for variable control limits*	
				$p - \bar{p}$ i.e., $p - 0.051$	σ_p	$\frac{p - \bar{p}}{\sigma_P}$	*UCL*	*LCL*
1	42	1	0.024	− 0.027	0.034	− 0.79	0.153	0
2	55	3	0.055	+ 0.004	0.030	+ 0.13	0.141	0
3	60	1	0.017	− 0.034	0.029	− 1.17	0.137	0
4	71	2	0.028	− 0.023	0.026	− 0.88	0.130	0
5	53	2	0.038	− 0.013	0.030	− 0.43	0.142	0
6	49	9	0.183	+ 0.132	0.032	+ 4.13	0.146	0
7	61	0	0.000	− 0.051	0.028	− 1.82	0.136	0
8	93	2	0.022	− 0.029	0.023	− 1.26	0.120	0
9	50	5	0.100	+ 0.049	0.031	+ 1.58	0.145	0
10	65	9	0.138	+ 0.087	0.027	+ 3.22	0.133	0
11	66	5	0.075	+ 0.024	0.027	+ 0.89	0.133	0
12	57	1	0.018	− 0.033	0.029	− 1.14	0.139	0
13	48	3	0.063	+ 0.012	0.032	+ 0.37	0.147	0
14	62	5	0.081	+ 0.030	0.028	+ 1.07	0.135	0
15	59	1	0.017	− 0.034	0.029	− 1.17	0.137	0
16	40	3	0.075	+ 0.024	0.035	+ 0.69	0.156	0
17	46	4	0.087	+ 0.036	0.033	+ 1.09	0.149	0
18	66	5	0.076	+ 0.025	0.027	+ 0.93	0.133	0
19	72	1	0.014	− 0.037	0.026	− 1.42	0.129	0
20	70	4	0.057	+ 0.006	0.026	+ 0.23	0.130	0
	1,285	66		$\bar{p} = \frac{66}{1,285} = 0.051$				

From Fig. 5.4 and 5.5. it is evident that both the charts give the same indication but a stabilized chart is simpler in its interpretation. Both, however, involve relatively laborious computations as compared to the chart for fraction rejected with constant subgroup size.

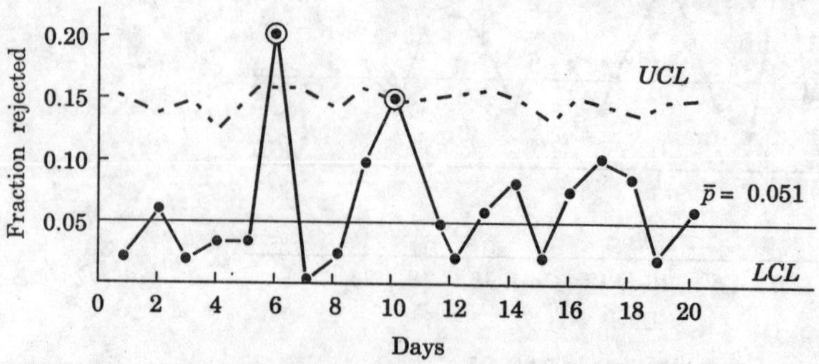

FIGURE 5.5: *p* chart with variable limits for the data in Table 5.5

Comments. The stabilized chart should be read in exactly the same manner as any other conventional control chart. As with other charts, the control lines can be moved to any other desired levels of probability.

Another advantage of this type of chart is that it has a standard format which can be preprinted in quantity, irrespective of the process that has to be monitored. This aspect also helps both operator and management to become familiar with control charting of this nature. A further advantage of this chart is that the trends reflect the quality level. This they may not do when a *p* chart with varying control limits is used because, although the quality may be getting worse, a decrease in sample sizes could make the trend appear to indicate improving quality.

5.7 CHECKLIST OF NECESSARY STEPS IN CONNECTION WITH CONTROL CHART FOR FRACTION REJECTED

It will be helpful in gaining a full understanding of the procedures followed in Examples 5.1 to 5.3 to review the decisions and calculations that must be made and the actions that must be taken in initiating and operating a control chart for attributes data. The major events occur in a sequence somewhat as follows:

1. Decisions preparatory to the control chart

a. Determination of the purpose of the chart
b. Selection of inspection station and quality characteristics to be charted
c. Decisions on the selection of subgroups
d. Choice of type of chart to be used (*p* or *np*)
e. Decision regarding calculation of control limits
f. Setting up the forms for recording and charting the data

2. Starting the control chart

a. Recording the data
b. Calculation of the subgroup control statistics (p_j)
c. Calculation of the average value of the control statistic ($\overline{p}$)
d. Calculation of trial control limits
e. Plotting the points and trial control limits

3. Continuing the control chart

a. Selecting a standard value of the control statistic (p_0)
b. Calculation of control limits
c. Plotting the points and limits
d. Interpretation of lack of control
e. Periodic review and revision of the standard value (p_0)

4. Reports and actions based on the control at a satisfactory level

a. Actions to bring process into control at a satisfactory level
b. Review of specifications in relation to the capabilities of a production process
c. Information to management regarding the quality level

5.8 CHOICE BETWEEN CHART FOR *p* AND CHART FOR *np*

The choice among the control-chart techniques for attributes data is based partially on convenience in interpretation of the chart and partially on the choice of the probability distribution that best fits the circumstances. In Example 5.2, the *p* chart was appropriate because the number of items inspected varied daily and the statistic of interest was the fraction (or percent) rejected. Thus a charting technique based on the binomial distribution was a rational choice.

Whenever subgroup size is variable, the control chart must show the fraction rejected (or proportion rejected) rather than the actual number of rejects. If actual numbers of rejects were plotted, the central line on the chart (as well as the limits) would need to be changed with every change in subgroup size. However, if subgroup size is constant, the chart for actual numbers of rejects may be used. Such a chart is called a chart for *np* or *pn*. (The fraction rejected *p* was obtained by dividing the actual number of rejects by the subgroup size *n*. The actual number of rejects may therefore be represented by *np*, the quantity that, divided by *n*, gives *p*.)

A chart for *np* may be used for data such as those shown in Table 5.6. This table gives the results of inspection of a sheet-metal part for an aircraft turbo supercharger skin. The part was inspected after being shaped by a drop hammer.

As explained in Chap. 4. the standard deviation of the number of occurrences in n trials of an event with a constant *probability* of occurrence *p* (in other words, the standard deviation of the number of rejects) is $\sqrt{np(1-p)}$. The standard deviation of the proportion of occurrences (in other words, the fraction rejected) is $\sqrt{p(1-p)/n}$. Thus the appropriate model for 3-sigma control limits on an *np* chart is

$$UCL_{np} = np + 3\sqrt{np(1-p)}$$

$$LCL_{np} = np - 3\sqrt{np(1-p)}$$

Since no standard value for *p* was established for the data in Table 5.6, the average fraction rejected $\bar{p}$ is used as the best available estimate of *p*.

Figure 5.6 shows a chart for *np* for the data of Table 5.6. If a chart for *p* were drawn for the same data, it would look exactly like the chart for *np* except for the graduations on the vertical scale. Each unit on the vertical scale would represent 1/200 (that is, 1/*n*) as much as it does on the chart for *np*. It is evident that there is no fundamental difference in the appearance of the *np* and the *p* charts or in the information they give.

Where subgroup size is constant, there might be two possible reasons for preferring an *np* chart to a *p* chart. One reason is that the *np* chart saves one calculation for each subgroup, the division of number of rejects r_j by subgroup size n_j to get p_j. The other reason is that some people may understand the *np* chart more readily.

However, it often happens that in a manufacturing plant there are many places where, because of variable subgroup size, only a *p* chart is applicable, and a few places where, because subgroup size is constant, either type of chart may be used. In such cases, the possibility of confusion from having two types of charts might outweigh the slight advantage of the *np* chart, and it would be better to use the *p* charts even for constant subgroup size.

TABLE 5.6: CALCULATIONS FOR *np* CONTROL CHART FOR NUMBER OF REJECTS
(Inspection in drop-hammer department of sheet-metal part)

Production order number	*Lot size n*	*Number of rejects r*
1	200	4
2	200	8
3	200	2
4	200	6
5	200	4
6	200	4
7	200	10
8	200	6
9	200	4
10	200	8
Totals	2,000	56

$$np = \frac{56}{10} = 5.6$$

$$\bar{p} = \frac{56}{2,000} = 0.028$$

$$3\sigma_{np} = 3\sqrt{n\bar{p}(1-p)}$$

$$= 3\sqrt{(200)(0.028)(0.972)} = 7.0$$

$$UCL_{np} = n\bar{p} + 3\sigma_{np} = 5.6 + 7.0 = 12.6$$

$$LCL_{np} = n\bar{p} - 3\sigma_{np} = 5.6 - 7.0 = -1.4 \text{ and considered as zero}$$

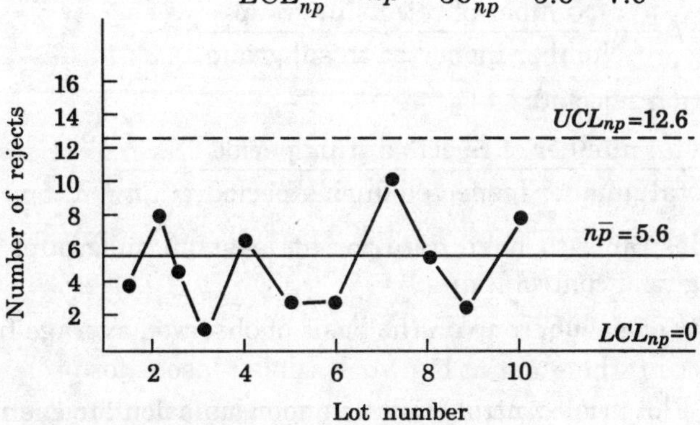

FIGURE 5.6: *np* chart for the data in Table 5.6.

5.9 ESSENTIAL STEPS IN STARTING THE CONTROL CHART

The steps in starting the control chart were illustrated in Examples 5.1 to 5.3. Briefly stated, they are:

A. *Record the data* for each subgroup on number inspected and number of rejects. Any occurrences that might be clues to an explanation of points out of control in a type of format shown in Fig 5.7 or such similar format depending upon the convenience or

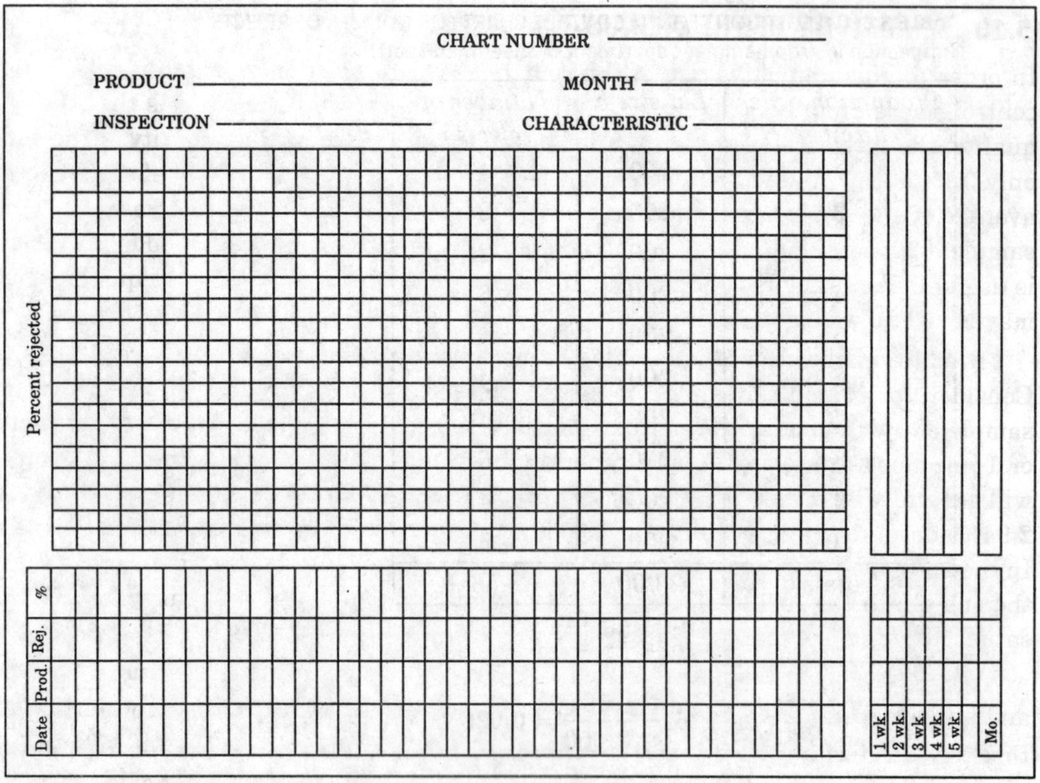

FIGURE 5.7: This format combines p chart data with a control chart.

to changes in the quality level should be noted on the data sheet as supplementary remarks.

B. Compute p for each subgroup: $p = \dfrac{\text{Number of rejects in group}}{\text{Number inspected in subgroup}} = \dfrac{r}{n}$

C. Compute $\overline{p}$, the average fraction rejected:

$$\overline{p} = \frac{\text{total number of rejects during period}}{\text{total number inspected during period}} = \frac{\Sigma r}{\Sigma n}$$

Wherever practicable, it is desirable to have data for at least 25 subgroups before computing $\overline{p}$ and establishing trial control limits.

D. Compute trial control limits for each subgroup on the basis of observed average fraction rejected $\overline{p}$.

E. Plot each point as obtained. Plot trial control limits as soon as calculated, and note whether the process appears to be in control.

It often happens that when the decision is made to use a p chart for any manufacturing operation, data are available for the period immediately past. If so, the steps just outlined should be applied to this past record. This permits putting the p chart to work at once as an effective instrument for process control and avoids a period for which no control limits are currently available.

5.10 SENSITIVITY OF THE *p* CHART

In order to make effective use of the control chart for fraction rejected as a help in process control, there must be same rejects in the sample observed. It is obvious that the better the quality, the larger the sample in order to find some rejects in the majority of the samples. If only 0.1% of the product is rejected, the sample must be at least 1,000 before there will be an average of one reject per sample. In contrast, a sample of 5 will give an average of 1 reject per sample if 20% of the product is rejectable. It is evident that with very good quality, the *p* chart is useful in detecting lack of control only if the sample is large; with poor quality, the *p* chart may be useful with small samples.

In addition, the larger the sample, the more closely it may be expected to reflect the universe. Consider, for example, samples of various sizes drawn from product that is 2% rejectable. A sample of 5 will generally be either 0 or 20% nonconforming (that is, it will contain either 0 or 1 rejects). A sample of 20 will generally be from 0 to 10% nonconforming. A sample of 100 will generally be from 0 to 6% nonconforming. A sample of 2,000 will generally be from 1.06 to 2.94% nonconforming. A sample of 50,000 will generally be from 1.81 of 2.19% nonconforming. In the preceding statements, "generally" applies to 3-sigma limits. For this reason, the smaller the subgroup size, the less sensitive the *p* chart to changes in the quality level and the less satisfactory it is as an indicator of assignable causes of variation.

Where it is desirable to use a control chart for a single measurable quality characteristic and a choice must be made between the *p* chart and the $\bar{X}$ chart, it is important to recognize that the $\bar{X}$ chart will give useful results with a much smaller sample. From a statistical point of view, variables are much superior to attributes; actual measurements on a few parts are as good as gauging on many parts with go and not-go gauges.

5.11 *p* CHARTS ARE NOT SUITABLE FOR ALL DATA ON FRACTION REJECTED

Control limits on the *p* chart are based on the use of the binomial as a probability distribution. As explained in Chap. 4, the binomial assumes a constant probability of occurrence of whatever event is under consideration — in the case of the *p* chart, a constant probability of occurrence of a rejected article or part. If the probability is to be constant from one article to another, each article must be a separate unit independent of the preceding and succeeding articles. With this probability constant, rejections will tend to occur at random rather than in bunches. As long as successive articles continue to be independent of one another and the quality level does not change, practically all the points on the *p* chart will fall within 3-sigma limits.

In some instances, however, it is obvious from the way in which manufacturing or inspection operations are carried on that successive units measured are not independent of one another. In such cases, most of the points on a conventional *p* chart may fall outside control limits. Here the control-chart limits tell—quite correctly—a fact that is already evident without the control chart, namely, that the probability of one article being rejected is influenced by whether or not the immediately preceding articles were rejectable. If this fact is already known and it is evident that nothing can be done about it, the information given by the *p* chart limits is of no practical help. The use of the *p* chart with conventional limits may even do harm, as it may tend to discredit the control chart in the minds of operating personnel and thus handicap the use of the control chart in cases where it would really be helpful.

Four representative cases where conventional p charts were unsuitable because of the foregoing type of difficulty are described in the following paragraphs:

1. In the manufacture of a certain type of rubber belt, a large mould was used that produced 2,500 belts at one time. Conditions of curing varied throughout the mould; if one belt was rejectable, it was likely that many of the adjacent belts also would be rejectable.
2. In the manufacture of a certain type of pile floor covering, daily figures were recorded for total yards produced and for the total yardage of output that was classified as substandard. In this case an imperfection that caused the classification of product as substandard might persist through many successive yards; rejectable yards were not independent of one another. Moreover, there was no natural unit of counting the product (no n for the binomial); for instance, feet or metres might have been used as readily as yards.
3. In the sheet-metal inspection booth of a large aircraft factory, records were kept showing daily numbers of parts inspected and numbers rejected. An average 160,000 parts per day were inspected. Some 1,250 different parts—including practically everything of sheet metal that went into the airplane—were subject to this inspection. Over a period of time the rejections averaged about 3%. Because of the many different parts that passed through this booth, with different cause systems affecting the different parts, it was evident that the probability of a rejectable item could not be constant from part to part. Control limits based on a p of 0.03 and an n of 160,000 would have been 0.0313 and 0.0287. Actual daily fraction rejected varied from about 0.05 to about 0.01.
4. In the 100% inspection of detonators in an ammunition plant, inspection was performed in lots of 10,000. The average fraction rejected was 0.0223. This gave control limits of 0.0268 and 0.0178. Actual lot fractions rejected varied from 0.055 to 0.008 with approximately two-thirds of the points falling outside the control limits. A study of the production process made it evident that quite different cause systems were influencing the different lots.

Even though the conventional p chart cannot be used to advantage in situations like these, it may still be desirable to keep a quality record in the form of a run chart that will be available to production supervision and to management. Generally speaking, this may be done to best advantage simply by plotting percent rejected without control limits.

5.12 COMPARISON OF $\bar{}$ AND R CHARTS WITH p CHART

It is known that the $\bar{X}$ and R charts are the control charts for variables while p-chart is an attribute control chart. The cost for collecting the data for a p-chart is likely to be less than the corresponding cost for $\bar{X}$ and charts. This is due to the fact that p-chart generally uses the data already collected for other purposes, whereas the $\bar{X}$ and R charts generally require special measurement for control chart purposes. The cost of computing and charting the p-chart is less as compared to the corresponding cost for $\bar{X}$ and R charts as one p-chart may be applied to any number of quality characteristics observed on one article at an inspection station, whereas separate $\bar{X}$ and R charts are necessary for each measured quality characteristic. If the inspection is carried out with a view to classifying an article as accepted or rejected, as generally the case is, a single p-chart may be applied to one quality characteristic or a number of them. The p-chart though discloses, the causes of variation, yet it is not as sensitive as the $\bar{X}$ and R charts to the influence of such causes. The p chart is used effectively in the improvement of quality, even through it is much inferior to the $\overline{X}$ and R charts as an instrument for actual diagnosis of causes of trouble.

For a *p*-chart the sample size is generally larger than that for $\overline{X}$ and R charts. So far as the sensitivity in detecting a shift is concerned, a *p*-chart is superior to $\overline{X}$ –chart. When the points on $\overline{X}$ and R chart fall below *LCL*, or many of the points fall below the central line, it is an indication for the out of control situation but in a *p* chart, although the same conclusion would imply but it is definitely a welcoming situation. The variation in sample size influences the $\overline{X}$ and R chart control limits much more than the corresponding influence in a *p* chart. While the *p*-chart has gained easy popularity with the management and shop personnel, the same is not the case with the $\overline{X}$ and R charts.

SOLVED QUESTIONS

Q. 5.1: *State whether the following statements are TRUE (T) or FALSE (F).*

1. p-charts are used to monitor categorical variables with two possible values.

2. The UCL in p chart can never be greater than 1.

3. In a chart, the points falling LCLp indicate the out-of-control situation.

Ans: 1. (T); 2. (T); 3. (T).

Q. 5.2: *Which of the following an attribute control chart in SQC?*

(a) $\overline{X}$ *Chart (b) p chart (c) R chart (d) Flow chart*

State the reasons for not selecting the other options.

Ans: The correct option is (*b*).

Reason: for not selective options (*a*), (*c*) and (*d*) are :

Option (*a*) is incorrect as at is a control chart for variables. Option (*c*) is also a control chart for variables Option (*d*) *i.e.* flow chart slows shows a process moves the rough a system and how the components are related.

Q. 5.3: *Select the correct option*

(*i*) A *p* chart is a type of control chart for

(*a*) plotting bar-stock lengths from receiving inspection samples.

(*b*) plotting fraction-rejected results from shipping inspection samples.

(*c*) plotting defects per unit from in-process inspection samples.

(*d*) answers (*a*), (*b*) and (*c*)

(*e*) answers (*a*) and (*c*) only.

(*ii*) The sensitivity of a *p* chart to changes in quality is

(*a*) equal to that of a range chart

(*b*) equal to that of a chart for averages

(*c*) equal to that of a *c* chart

(*d*) equal to that of a *u* chart

(*e*) none of the above

(*iii*) A *p* chart has exhibited statistical control over a period of time. However, the average fraction defective is to too high to be satisfactory. Improvement can be obtained by

(*a*) a change in the basic design of the product

(*b*) instituting 100 percent inspection

(*c*) a change in the production process through substitution of new tooling or machinery.

(*d*) all of the answers above are correct except (*b*)

(*e*) all of the answers above are correct except (*c*).

(*iv*) *p* or *np* charts are used when

(*a*) records available relate to an attribute in sample size

(*b*) records relate to a variable measurement

(*c*) $\bar{X}$ and *R* charts do not serve the purpose.

(*d*) non-conforming items are known in a sample but sample size is not known.

Ans: (*i*) (*b*); (*ii*) (*e*); (*iii*) (*d*); (*iv*) (*a*).

Q. 5.4: *How do you measure the performance of a p chart chart?*

Ans: *p* charts are not as sensitive as variable control charts for detecting changes in nonconforming processes. *p* chart performance may be measured using the average run length (*ARL*) to detection.

Q. 5.5: *In a factory producing spark plugs, the number rejected found in the inspection of 20 lots of 100 each is given below. Construction appropriate control chart and state whether the process is in control.*

Lot No.	*Number rejected*	*Fraction rejected*	*Lot No.*	*Number rejected*	*Fraction rejected*
1	5	0.050	11	4	0.040
2	10	0.100	12	7	0.070
3	12	0.120	13	8	0.080
4	8	0.080	14	2	0.020
5	6	0.060	15	3	0.030
6	5	0.050	16	4	0.040
7	6	0.060	17	5	0.050
8	3	0.030	18	8	0.080
9	3	0.030	19	6	0.060
10	5	0.050	20	10	0.100
Total No. of rejected = 120					

Ans: Since we are given fraction rejected *p* chart will be suitable for the situation.

$$\bar{p} = \frac{120}{20(100)} = 0.06$$

$$UCL_p = \bar{p} + 3\sqrt{\frac{\bar{p}(1-\bar{p})}{n}} = 0.1311$$

$$LCL_p = \bar{p} - 3\sqrt{\frac{\bar{p}(1-\bar{p})}{n}} = -0.0111$$

Since the fraction rejected *cannot be negative, the* LCL_p *is considered as zero.*

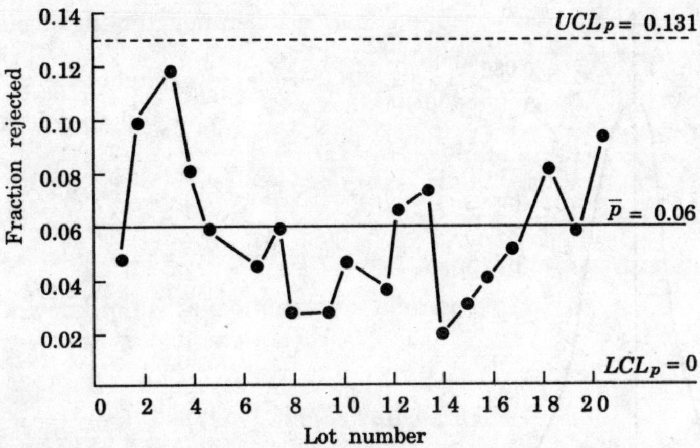

FIGURE 5.8 *p*-chart for the spar-plug data

Figure 5.8 above shows the *p* chart for the given data.

The control chart shows that all the points are within the control limits and variation is random. Hence, the process is in control

Note: Instead of a *p* chart, % *p* chart can also be plotted. Also since the lot size is constant, a *np* chart can also be plotted for the data.

Q. 5.6: *Twenty samples of parts were taken from a production line for gauging each sample containing 100 parts. The following number of nonconforming found in each sample:*

3 4 5 5 5   5 4 7 6 7

6 6 4 3 5   8 5 4 6 5

(a) Calculate the fraction rejected ($\bar{p}$) and draw the distribution.

(b) Calculate the 3 sigma control limits and 2 sigma warning limits. What is your comment on the state of control.

(c) State briefly the main purpose of an attribute control chart.

Ans: (*a*)
$$\bar{p} = \frac{3 + 4 ... + 5}{20 \times 100} = \frac{103}{2000} \text{ i.e. } 0.052$$

In order to draw the distribution it is essential to make a tally chart first. This is shown below:

p	*Tally mark*	*Frequency*
0.03	//	2
0.04	~~////~~	4
0.05	~~////~~ //	7
0.06	////	4
0.07	//	2
0.08	/	1

Figure 5.9 shows the distribution which is approximately normal with $\bar{p}$ = 0.052.

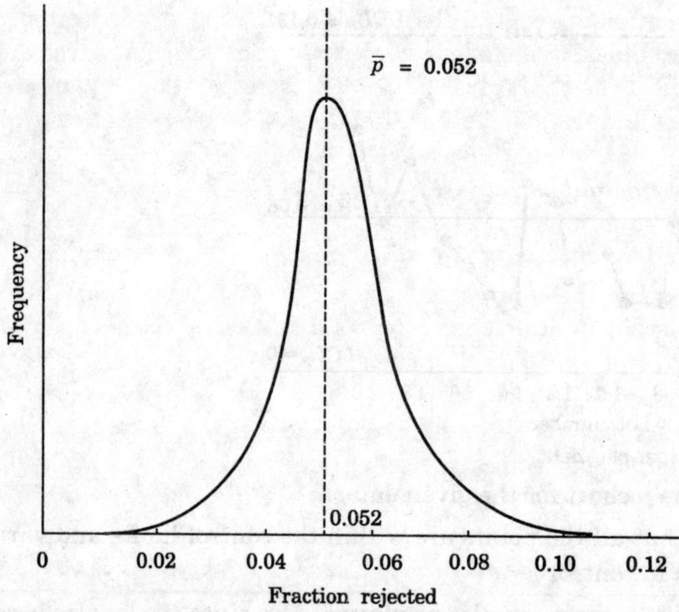

FIGURE 5.9: Distribution of fraction rejected

(*b*)
$$\sigma_p = \sqrt{\frac{\bar{p}(1-\bar{p})}{n}} = \sqrt{\frac{0.052(1-0.052)}{200}} = 0.022$$

$$2\sigma_p = 0.044$$

$$3\sigma_p = 0.066$$

$$UCL_p = 0.052 + 0.066 = 0.118$$

$$LCL_p = 0.052 - 0.066 = -0.014 \ (i.e.\ 0)$$

$$UWL_p = 0.052 + 0.044 = 0.096$$

$$LWL_p = 0.052 - 0.044 = 0.008$$

As all the points are within control limits and mostly the points are within UWL_p, and also the points are randomly distributed, the state of control exists.

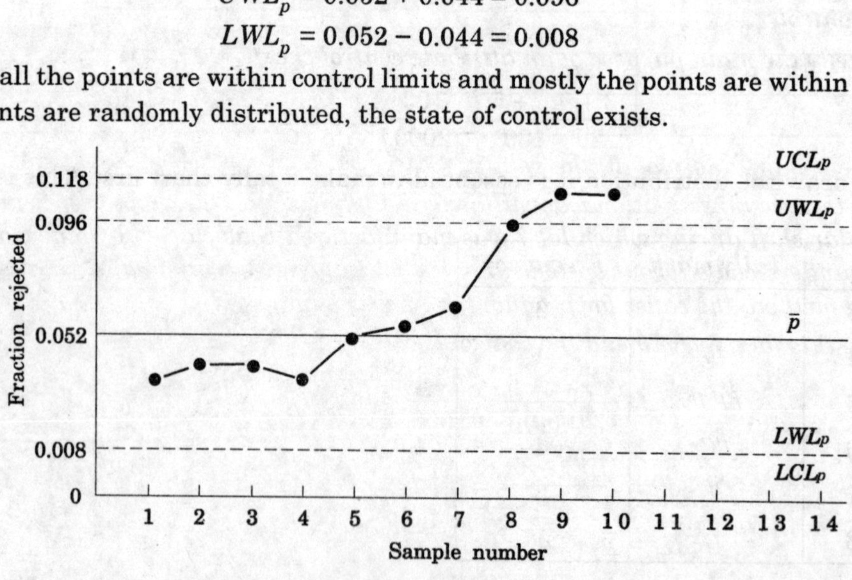

FIGURE 5.10: $\bar{p}$-chart showing the plotted points

(*c*) The main purpose of an attribute control chart such as *p*-chart, is to indicate change in quality so that adjustments can quickly be made to correct the process before large quantities of scrap are produced, *i.e.* in effect the chart gives advance warning of the commencement of a trend towards the production of an increasing number of nonconforming articles.

Q. 5.7: *After computation of control and warning limits, in Q. 5.6 the p control chart in Fig 5.10 shows the plots of fraction rejected for the next 10 samples. All the points are within the control limits. What is your observation on the state of statistical control ?*

Ans: Although all points are within the control limits, the control chart indicates an upward trend and hence the process is not in statistical control. Assignable causes of variation are present.

Q. 5.8: *A manufacturer produces a quantity of 10,000 special valves during a 10-day period. Twice each day he draws a random sample of 50 valves and determines how many nonconforming items are among them. Since this is the first order for this item, the manufacturer wishes to determine if the process is under control and establish control limits for future use.*

Following table lists the number of nonconforming items in each 20 sample lots of 50 valves each.

Lot number	*Number nonconforming*	*p*	*Lot number*	*Number nonconforming*	*p*
1	4	0.08	11	5	0.10
2	3	0.06	12	14	0.28
3	8	0.16	13	9	0.18
4	12	0.24	14	1	0.022
5	7	0.14	15	2	0.04
6	15	0.30	16	9	0.18
7	20	0.40	17	3	0.06
8	13	0.26	18	13	0.26
9	9	0.18	19	6	0.12
10	8	0.16	20	9	0.18

(a) Draw the p chart and plot all the points.

(b) Suppose that an investigation was initiated and the review of the shop records indicated that the particular shift during which lot 7 was manufactured, was started by a new operator and that he misunderstood a torque specification for bolts and after a brief indoctrination of the correct torquing method, the cause for product rejects was eliminated.

Considering this fact, recommend the control limits for future production.

Ans:

$$\bar{p} = \frac{4 + ... + 9}{20(50)} = \frac{180}{1000} = 0.18$$

$$3\sigma_p = \sqrt{\frac{\bar{p}(1-\bar{p})}{n}} = 0.162$$

$$UCL_p = \bar{p} + 3\sigma_p = 0.342$$

$$LCL_p = \bar{p} - 3\sigma_p = 0.018$$

(*a*) *p* chart is shown in Fig. 5.11.

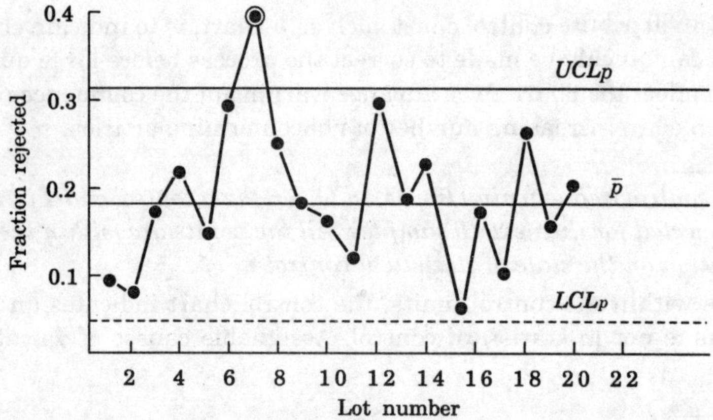

FIGURE 5.11: *p* chart for fraction rejected for valves.

(*b*) Since the reasons for high conforming items in Lot 7 are known and the corrective action taken, eliminating this lot,

$$\bar{p}_{revised} = \frac{(180 - 20)}{(20 - 1)(50)} = \frac{160}{950} = 0.168$$

$$\sigma_p = \sqrt{\frac{0.168(1 - 0.168)}{50}} = 0.053$$

$$UCL_p = 0.168 + 3(0.053) = 0.327$$

$$LCL_p = 0.168 - 3(0.053) = 0.009$$

With these new control limits, all the remaining 19 lots fall between the control limits and are also not clustered above or below the revised *p*. The process is therefore considered under control and hence these control limits will be used for future production.

Q. 5.9: *A police force is concerned that its officers are not responding quickly enough when members of the public telephone to request assistance in non-emergency situations - for example, to report an attempted burglary or a stolen vehicle. Accordingly, senior management has decided that each month a sample of 50 such calls with be monitored, and a chart plotted to show the number within the sample where an officer responded to the call within 30 minutes.*

(*a*) *At present the percentage of calls meeting this criterion is 60 per cent. Where would you place the limits on a control chart if the chart is required to detect departures from the existing position, both improvements and deteriorations?*

(*b*) *Senior management sets a target for the percentage at 80 per cent. Where would the limits be placed if the chart is based on this target?*

(*c*) *Compare the two sets of limits found in (a) and (b), and comment on the results.*

Ans: (*a*) $100\bar{p} = 60$ or $\bar{p} = 0.6$

$$n = 50$$

$$\sigma_p = \sqrt{\frac{0.6 \times 0.4}{50}} = 0.0693$$

$$100\,\sigma_p = 6.93$$

$$UCL_p = 0.6 + 3(0.0693) \approx 0.81$$

$$LCL_p = 0.6 - 3(0.0693) \approx 0.39$$

Hence limits on control chart are = 81% and 39%.

(b) Similarly when $100\,p = 80$, and $n = 50$,

$$UCL_p = 0.9695$$
$$LCL_p = 0.6305$$

Hence limits on control chart are 96.95% and 63.05%.

(c) The limits in both cases are very wide, reflecting the relatively small size of the sample. There is little point in using limits based on a target which is very far from the current level of performance - all that will happen is that many points will fall outside the limits, resulting in much work in 'chasing' these cases and a possible drop in staff morale. It is probably better at this stage to monitor the existing situation while taking steps to achieve gradual improvement, and then change the limits incrementally as improvements occur.

Q. 5.10: *A company makes small inexpensive printed electrical circuits and most of the soldered connections are performed by hand. The company wants to develop a process control chart to see if the operation is in control. Samples of size 100 are withdrawn over a 24-hour period and inspected. These results are shown in the Table given below.*

Table (Printed circuits - results of inspection)

Sample No.	*Number of defective circuits*	*Sample No.*	*Number of defective circuits*
1	7	13	3
2	3	14	4
3	8	15	5
4	2	16	7
5	1	17	3
6	5	18	6
7	2	19	3
8	7	20	4
9	9	21	3
10	2	22	2
11	6	23	8
12	4	24	1

Required

1. *Develop a 3 standard-deviation p-chart, the required control chart.*
2. *Would one conclude that the process in control?*
3. *What comments do you have regarding random sampling for printed circuits?*

Ans: 1. From the data given in the table,

$$\bar{p} = 0.0438$$
$$n = 100$$
$$UCL_p = 0.1051$$
$$LCL_p = 0$$

The p chart can be plotted.

2. Since all the samples fall within the control limits and the distribution is random, the process is considered to be in control

3. One word of caution that should be noted is that, even though the process is in control according to the company's requirements, having even one faulty printed circuit for use in downstream use can have serious consequences to the company (faulty products, poor customer relationship, expensive rework operations.

Q. 5.11: *The data processing of the ANZ Bank has five keypunch operators. Each day their supervisor verifies the accuracy of a random sample of 250 records. A record containing one or more errors is considered defective and must be redone. The results of the last 30 samples are shown in the table. All were checked to make sure that none were out of control.*

Sample	*Number of Defective Records*	*Sample*	*Number of Defective Records*	*Sample*	*Number of Defective Records*
1	7	11	18	21	17
2	5	12	5	22	12
3	19	13	16	23	6
4	10	14	4	24	7
5	11	15	11	25	13
6	8	16	8	26	10
7	12	17	12	27	14
8	9	18	4	28	6
9	6	19	6	29	11
10	13	20	11	30	9
					Total 300

(a) Based on these historical data, set up a p-chart using 3-sigma limits.
(b) Samples for the next four days showed the following.

Sample	*Number of Defective Records*
31	17
32	15
33	22
34	21

What is the supervisor's assessment of the keypunch process likely to be ?

Ans: (*a*)

$$\overline{p} = \frac{300}{(30)(250)} = 0.04$$

$$UCL_p = 0.077 \; ; LCL_p = 0.003$$

(*b*) Samples for the next four days showed the following.

Sample	*Number of Defective Records*	*Proportion (p)*
31	17	17/250 = 0.068
32	15	15/250 = 0.060
33	22	22/250 = 0.088
34	21	21/250 = 0.084

Samples 33 and 34 are out of control. The supervisor should look for the problem and, upon identifying it, take corrective action.

Q. 5.12: *Webster Chemical Company produces mastics and caulking for the construction industry. The product is blended in large mixers and then pumped into tubes and capped. Management is concerned about whether the filling process for tubes of caulking is in statistical control. The process should be centered on 8 ounces per tube. Several samples of right tubes were taken, each tube was weighed, and the weights in the table were obtained.*

(Ounces of Caulking per Tube)

Sample	*Tube Number*							
	1	*2*	*3*	*4*	*5*	*6*	*7*	*8*
1	7.98	8.34	8.02	7.94	8.44	7.68	7.81	8.11
2	8.33	8.22	8.08	8.51	8.41	8.28	8.09	8.16
3	7.89	7.77	7.91	8.04	8.00	7.89	7.93	8.09
4	8.24	8.18	7.83	8.05	7.90	8.16	7.97	8.07
5	7.87	8.13	7.92	7.99	8.10	7.81	8.14	7.88
6	8.13	8.14	8.11	8.13	8.14	8.12	8.13	8.14

(a) Assuming that only 6 samples are sufficient, determine whether the process is in statistical control.

(b) A supervisor notes that the weighing scale was gummed up with caulking. Apparently, a tube was not properly capped. The sticky scale did not correctly read the variation in weights for the sixth sample. Delete that data item and recalculate the control charts. Is the process in statistical control ?

(c) The sticky scale in Part (b) calls management's attention to whether caulking tubes are being properly capped. If a significant proportion of the tubes aren't being sealed, webster is placing its customers in a messy situation. Tubes are packaged in large boxes of 144. Several boxes are inspected, and the following numbers of leaking tubes are found.

Sample	*Tubes*	*Sample*	*Tubes*	*Sample*	*Tubes*
1	3	8	6	15	5
2	5	9	4	16	0
3	3	10	9	17	2
4	4	11	2	18	6
5	2	12	6	19	2
6	4	13	5	20	1
7	2	14	1	Total	72

Calculate p chart three-sigma control limits to assess whether the capping process is in statistical control.

Ans: (*a*) For the given data,

$$\overline{\overline{X}} = 8.067 \text{ and } \overline{R} = 0.38$$

$$UCL_{\overline{X}} = 8.20 \text{ and } LCL_{\overline{X}} = 7.93$$

$$UCL_R = 0.71 \text{ and } LCL_R = 0.05$$

From the data, it can be observed that $\overline{X}$ of sample 2 (i.e. $\overline{X}$ = 8.26) is out of control and $\overline{R}$ of sample 6 (*i.e.* $\overline{R}$ = 0.03) is out of control. Hence the process is not in statistical control.

(*b*) Deleting the data for sample 6, from the computation, revised $\bar{\bar{X}} = 8.054$, $\bar{R} = 0.45$

$$\text{Revised } UCL_{\bar{X}} = 8.22,\ LCL_{\bar{X}} = 7.89$$

$$\text{Revised } UCL_R = 0.837\ LCL_R = 0.063$$

It can again be observed that new while all R values are within control limits, the $\bar{X}$ value of Sample No. 2 (i.e. $\bar{X} = 8.26$) is again out of control and hence the process is not in statistical control.

(*c*)
$$\bar{p} = \frac{72}{144 \times 20} = 0.025$$

$$UCL_p = \bar{p} + 3\sqrt{\frac{\bar{p}(1-\bar{p})}{n}} = 0.025 + 3\sqrt{\frac{0.025(0.975)}{144}} = 0.064$$

$$LCL_p = \bar{p} - 3\sqrt{\frac{\bar{p}(1-\bar{p})}{n}} = 0.025 - 0.0390 \textit{ i.e. } 0.$$

Plot of p values within these limits indicate that process is in statistical control.

Q. 5.13: *The following data refer to the production and number of rejects for 15 consecutive days.*

Day	*Number inspected*	*Number of rejects*
1	400	2
2	400	5
3	400	0
4	400	14
5	400	3
6	400	0
7	400	1
8	400	0
9	400	18
10	400	8
11	400	6
12	400	0
13	400	3
14	400	0
15	400	6
Total	6,000	66

Plot the 100 p or percent rejected control chart. Suppose the reasons for out of control point on 9th day is found and its effect on future production is eliminated what control limits will you adopt for future production?

Ans:
$$\bar{p} = \frac{66}{6{,}000} = 0.011$$

$$100\bar{p} \text{ or } \%\bar{p} = 1.1$$

$$3\sigma_p = 3\sqrt{\frac{\bar{p}(1-\bar{p})}{n}} = 0.0156$$

$$UCL = \bar{p} + 3\sigma_p = 0.0266$$

$$UCL_{100p} = 2.66$$

$$LCL = \bar{p} - 3\sigma_p = 0.011 - 0.0156 = -0.005 \text{ and hence } 0.$$

$$LCL_{100p} = 0$$

It may be noted that percent control limits have been calculated by first calculating UCL_p and LCL_p and then multiplied by 100. However, these can be directly collected by the following formulae which yield the same results.

$$UCL_{100p} = 100\bar{p} + 3\sqrt{\frac{100\bar{p}(100-100\bar{p})}{n}}$$

$$LCL_{100p} = 100\bar{p} - 3\sqrt{\frac{100\bar{p}(100-100\bar{p})}{n}}$$

Converting the fraction rejected into percentage rejected, $\%p$ for 20 days will be 0.50, 1.25, 0.00, 3.50, 0.75, 0.00, 0.25, 0.000, 4.50, 2.00, 1.50, 0.00, 0.75, 0.00 and 1.50 respectively.

Figure 5.12 shows the control chart.

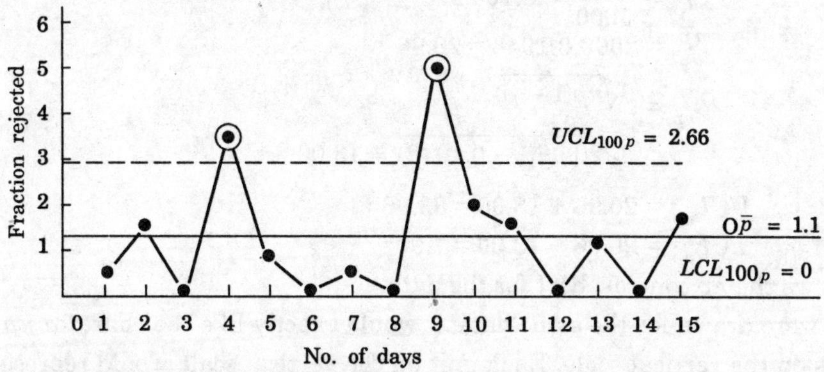

FIGURE 5.12: %p-chart for the data

From the chart or from the data (after determining $\%\bar{p}$ and control limits), it is evident that the points for the 4th and 9th day cross the UCL. Since the causes for out of control only for 9th day are known, only this point can be eliminated for revising $\%\bar{p}$. Hence eliminating this point only

$$\bar{p}_{revised} = \frac{66-18}{6000-400} = 0.0086$$

$$100\bar{p} \text{ or } \%\bar{p}_{revised} = 0.86$$

and the revised control limits will be at 2.25 and 0 respectively.

Q. 5.14: *Data were collected for a large box of bolts containing about 10% nonconforming items. Plot the np chart based on the data given below.*

If a (p) or a (100p) chart is plotted instead of np chart, will it give a different indication?

Subgroup	*Number inspected*	*Number nonconforming*	*Subgroup*	*Number inspected*	*Number non-conforming*
1	200	28	14	200	23
2	200	20	15	200	28
3	200	24	16	200	28
4	200	19	17	200	15
5	200	17	18	200	23
6	200	25	19	200	17
7	200	25	20	200	22
8	200	22	21	200	25
9	200	22	22	200	20
10	200	16	23	200	18
11	200	22	24	200	14
12	200	18	25	200	13
13	200	20			
$N = 5{,}000$ Σ nonconforming bolts = 524					

Ans:

$$\bar{p} = \frac{524}{5000} = 0.1044$$

$$n\bar{p} = 200\times 0.1048 = 20.96$$

$$3\sigma_{np} = 3\sqrt{np(1-p)}$$

$$= 3\sqrt{20.96(1-0.1048)} = 13.00$$

$$UCL_{np} = 20.96 + 13.00 = 33.96$$

$$LCL_{np} = 20.96 - 13.00 = 7.96$$

Figure 5.13 shows the *np* control chart for the data.

If a chart for *p* were drawn for the same data, it would exactly like the chart for *np* except for the graduations on the vertical scale. Each unit on the vertical scale would represent $\frac{1}{200}$ $\left(i.e. \frac{1}{n}\right)$ as much as it does on the chart for *np*. It is evident that there is no fundamental

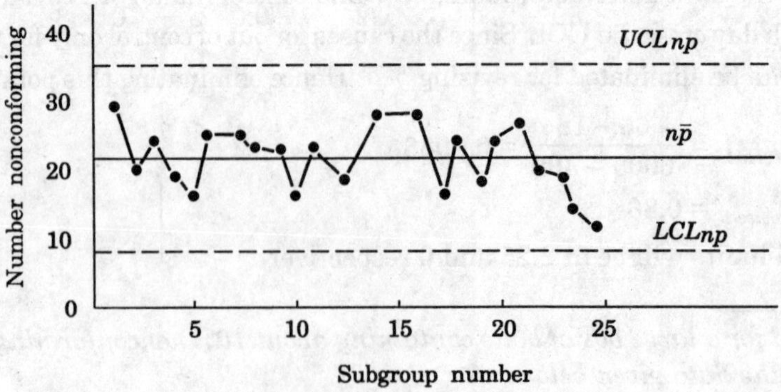

FIGURE 5.13: *np* chart for the data

difference in the appearance of the *np* chart and the *p* charts or in the information they give. Same arguments hold good for 100*p* chart except that each unit on the vertical scale would represent $\frac{100}{200}\left(i.e.\ \frac{100}{n}\right)$ as much as it does on the chart for *np*.

Q. 5.15: *A wheel barrow manufacturer has collected the data on the quality of his product for the end of March and all of April. Subgroup size is one day's inspection results, which is usually the case. The inspection results for 25 subgroups are shown in the first three columns "headed as" subgroups designation, number inspected, and number rejected of the following table. A fourth column for the fraction rejected is calculated by the inspector using the formula p = np/n. The last two columns indicate the computed control limits on the basis that*

$$\bar{p} = \frac{\Sigma np}{\Sigma n} = \frac{1037}{50515} = 0.020$$

and control limits are $\bar{p} \pm 3\sigma_p$.

(a) Draw the p chart plotting the actual control limits for every day.

(b) Suppose that the reasons for out of control situation on March 31 and April 22 are known. What is your recommendation for p?

(c) Suppose that, is decided to base the control limits on the average subgroup size (to be rounded to the nearest one hundred) for future use, what control limits you will recommend for future?

Subgroup	*Number inspected n*	*Number rejected, np*	*Fraction rejected, p*	*UCLp*	*LCLp*
March, 29	2385	47	0.020	0.029	0.011
30	1451	18	0.012	0.031	0.009
31	1935	74	0.038	0.030	0.010
April, 1	2450	42	0.017	0.028	0.012
2	1997	39	0.020	0.029	0.011
5	2168	52	0.024	0.029	0.011
6	1941	47	0.024	0.030	0.010
7	1962	34	0.017	0.030	0.010
8	2244	29	0.013	0.029	0.011
9	1238	39	0.032	0.032	0.008
12	2289	45	0.020	0.029	0.011
13	1464	26	0.018	0.031	0.009
14	2061	49	0.024	0.029	0.011
15	1667	34	0.020	0.030	0.010
16	2350	31	0.013	0.029	0.011
19	2354	38	0.016	0.029	0.011
20	1509	28	0.018	0.031	0.009
21	2190	30	0.014	0.029	0.011
22	2678	113	0.042	0.028	0.012

...(Contd.)

23	2252	58	0.026	0.029	0.011
26	1641	52	0.032	0.030	0.010
27	1782	19	0.011	0.030	0.010
28	1993	30	0.015	0.030	0.010
29	2382	17	0.007	0.029	0.011
30	2132	46	0.022	0.029	0.011
Totals	50,515	1,037			

Ans:

$$\bar{p} = \frac{1037}{50,515} = 0.020$$

(*a*) Figure 5.14 shows the control limits with points plotted for the entire period.

(*b*) From the control chart it is evident that out-of-control situation is present on March 31, April 22, April 26, and April 29. Since the assignable causes are known only for March 31 and April 22 only, these are discarded from the data.

$$\bar{p}_{revised} = \frac{1037 - (75 + 113)}{50.515 - (1935 + 2678)} = 0.018$$

Since this value represents the best estimate of the universe fraction rejected, $\bar{p}$ = 0.018.

(c)

$$n_{average} = \frac{50,515 - (1935 + 2678)}{(25 - 2)} = 1995.73$$

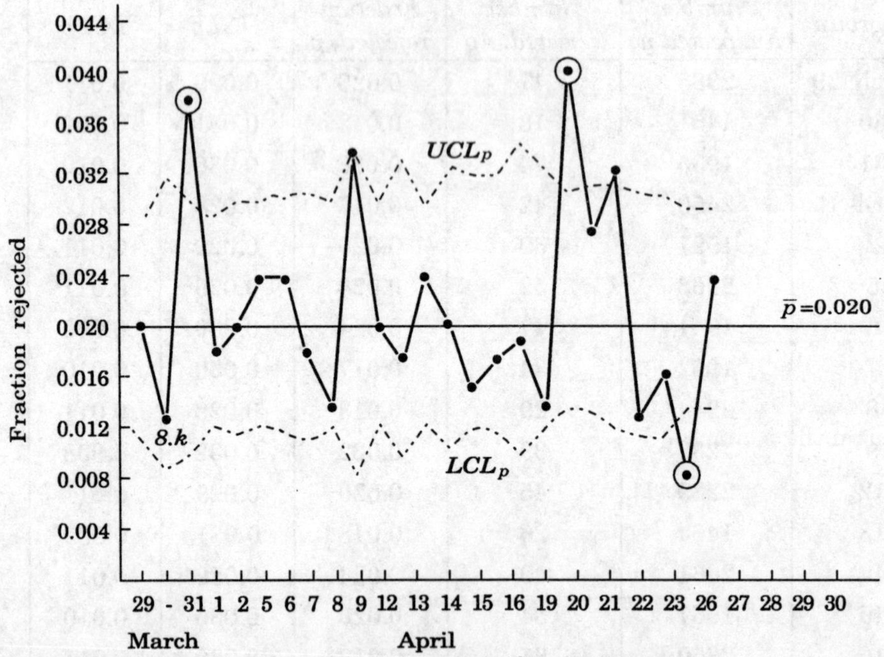

FIGURE 5.14 Control chart for variable subgroup size for wheel barrow.

Rounding this value to nearest one hundred will give n = 2,000

$$3\sigma_p = 3\sqrt{\frac{0.018(1 - 0.018)}{2000}} = 0.009$$

$$UCL_p = \bar{p} + 3\sigma_p = 0.018 + 0.009 = 0.027$$

$$LCL_p = \bar{p} - 3\sigma_p = 0.018 - 0.009 = 0.009.$$

Q. 5.16: *The data given below show the details for the inspection of 10 consecutive batches.*

Batch No.	1	2	3	4	5	6	7	8	9	10
No. of pieces in batch	151	208	174	212	181	162	199	205	220	166
No. of rejected in batch	8	7	4	5	10	5	7	6	8	4

Construct a p-chart showing the 3-sigma upper control and 2-sigma upper warning limits by taking size (n) on one of the axes.

Ans: Total number of pieces = 151 + ... + 166 = 1,878

Total number of rejected pieces = 8 + ... + 4 = 64

$$\bar{p} = \frac{64}{1,878} = 0.034$$

Since the batch size is varying, therefore control limits for every batch will be different. In order to draw the required chart, let us calculate the control and warning limits when batch size varies from 121 to 256. (This is because this range covers all the batch sizes and since σ_p involves $\sqrt{n}$, therefore $\sqrt{121}$, $\sqrt{144}$, etc., are whole numbers and are easy to calculate).

$$\sqrt{p(1-p)} = \sqrt{0.034(1-0.034)} = 0.181$$

Following tabulation gives the values of upper warning and control limits for batch sizes 121 to 256.

Batch size (n)	*Upper warning limit =* $\bar{p} + 2\sqrt{\frac{\bar{p}(1-\bar{p})}{n}}$	*Upper control limit =* $\bar{p} + 3\sqrt{\frac{\bar{p}(1-\bar{p})}{n}}$
121	0.067	0.084
144	0.064	0.079
169	0.062	0.076
196	0.060	0.073
225	0.058	0.070
256	0.057	0.068

Fraction rejected (p) for 10 batches are 0.053, 0.034, 0.023, 0.023, 0.055, 0.031, 0.035, 0.029, 0.036 and 0.024 respectively. Figure 5.15 shows the upper warning and control limits and the points plotted on the p chart.

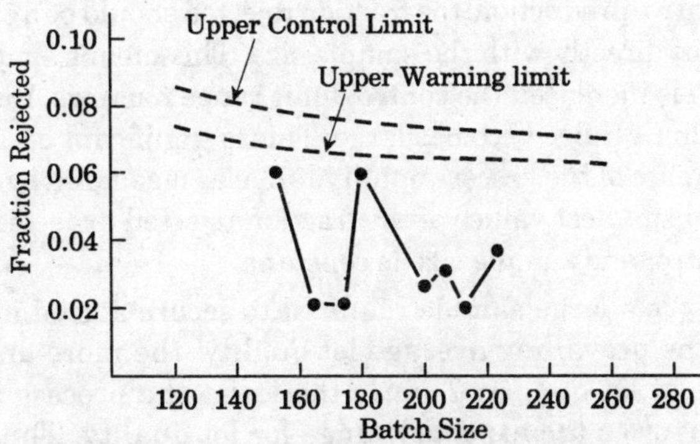

FIGURE 5.15 p chart with variable control limits for the data

Q. 5.17: *Data given below refer to the production programme for 20 days. Set up a suitable control chart and indicate whether assignable causes of variation are present?*

Day	p	σ_p	$p - \bar{p}$	$\frac{p - \bar{p}}{\sigma_p}$
1	0.024	0.034	– 0.027	– 0.79
2	0.055	0.030	+ 0.004	+ 0.13
3	0.017	0.029	– 0.034	– 1.17
4	0.028	0.026	– 0.023	– 0.88
5	0.038	0.030	– 0.013	– 0.43
6	0.183	0.032	+ 0.132	+ 4.13
7	0.000	0.028	– 0.051	– 1.82
8	0.022	0.023	– 0.029	01.26
9	0.100	0.031	+ 0.049	+ 1.58
10	0.138	0.027	+ 0.087	+ 3.32
11	0.005	0.027	+ 0.024	+ 0.87
12	0.018	0.029	– 0.033	– 1.14
13	0.063	0.032	+ 0.012	+ 0.37
14	0.081	0.028	+ 0.030	+ 1.07
15	0.017	0.029	– 0.034	– 1.17
16	0.075	0.035	+ 0.024	+ 0.69
17	0.087	0.033	+ 0.026	+ 1.09
18	0.076	0.027	+ 0.025	+ 0.93
19	0.014	0.026	– 0.037	– 0.42
20	0.057	00.26	+ 0.006	+ 0.23

Ans: The data provided are essentially meant for the use stabilized control chart. Then keeping the central line at 0 and upper and lower control limits at + 3 and – 3 respectively and plotting the points, it will be found that on the 6th and 10th day the point falls above the upper control limit. This indicates that asignable causes of variation are present.

Q. 5.18: *Comment on the statement "A p chart is a somewhat better forecaster of good lot quality than it is a forecaster of bad lot quality".*

Ans: Without the change of process in repetitive production, the fraction rejected should be a constant. If this so, the sensitivity of a *p*-chart varies directly with the sample size. This means simply with *p* unchanging in value, as the sample size is increased the control limit range narrows. But as the sample size becomes smaller, the control limit range becomes large. This is significant because the control limit range constitutes a good estimate of the process quality range as measured by fraction rejected. That is, it defines the largest and smallest values of the fraction rejected expected for the given process as long as it remains in control and sample size is constant.

It can be demonstrated that not only is a large sample required to secure a good indicator of lot quality, but also that the better the prevailing average lot quality, the more any given sample size narrows the possible range of lot quality. That is the lower the process fraction rejected, with sample size fixed, the narrower the expected range for lot quality. Thus, the *p* chart is a somewhat "better forecaster of good lot quality than it is a forecaster of bad quality".

Q. 5.19: *(a) A top executive argues "If the process suddenly makes a lot more nonconforming than usual, we want to know about it, but why should we be concerned if it suddenly makes less than usual and hence there is no need of showing the lower control limit on a p chart".*

Does the above argument seem to be justified ? Why or why not ?

(b) Calculate the control limits for the fraction rejected of a production line where 28 lots of 200 items each gave an average fraction rejected of 0.04. The producer risk is 0.003 and normal inspection may be used.

Ans: *(a)* Opinions regarding showing the LCL_p on the control chart for fraction rejected differ from person to person and industry to industry.

A common practice that has long been adopted in industry and found to be quite successful in situations where skilled and semi skilled persons are engaged in production and inspection, is to avoid showing the LCL_p. But where the purpose of control chart for the purpose of analysis and such a chart is meant for management, it is useful to show the LCL_p on the control chart. The reasons for this are as follows.

1. If the process suddenly makes less nonconforming item than usual, immediate step is to check that the inspection is still going on as planned. The apparent number of nonconforming items will be dropped if,
   (i) a new inspector is put on who, not being fully experienced misses some of the rejectable items he should be finding. If we thereby allow some nonconforming work to go out to the customers the result could be serious and costly.
   (ii) inspection is done for the production also. If due to any reason, the inspection staff is depleted, it may well be that the remaining men temporarily fail to keep up with production. In the case, the number of rejectable items found will be less than usual, not because they have been made less, but because the rest of the rejectable items have not been yet found. They are in the work which have been made but not yet inspected.
2. If the inspection is all right, then may be our process really is temporarily better, in which case there must be some temporary change which caused it. If we can find out what it is, may be we can make that change permanent and so active that there results a permanent reduction in the number or percentage of rejectable. To have any real chance of finding this change in condition however, we need the lower control limits, so that we are informed quickly when it occurs.

(b) $p = 0.04$

Producer's risk = 0.003. This means that the lots of standard quality when submitted by producer should have a probability of rejection of 0.003 only or out of 1000 lots of standard quality not more than 3 lots should be rejected. The 3-sigma limits contain 0.9973 of the area of a normal curve. That is an area about 0.003 lies outside these limits, which is the probability of rejecting the lot of standard quality if 3-sigma limits are used for control. Hence we base the control limits on $3\sigma_p$.

and $$3\sigma_p = 0.042\sigma_p = \sqrt{\frac{0.04(1-0.04)}{200}} = 0.042$$

$$UCL_p = 0.04 + 0.042 = 0.082$$

$$LCL_p = 0.04 - 0.042 = -0.002 \text{ and hence taken zero.}$$

Q. 5.20: *Table below gives the results of daily inspection of a vacuum tubes. The standard value of fraction rejected p_o established at the start of the month was 0.04. The estimated daily average production was 1,600 tubes. Establish a single set of control limits based on these figures and plot a control chart. Compute separate control limits for any points that seem to you to require them. Based on this month's record what would you recommend as the value of p_0 to use for the following month and future.*

Date	Number inspected	Number rejected	Fraction rejected
Nov. 2	531	25	0.0471
3	1,393	62	0.0445
4	1,422	61	0.0428
5	1,500	73	0.0487
6	1,250	46	0.0368
7	2,000	58	0.0290
9	685	28	0.0408
10	2,385	89	0.0373
11	2,150	89	0.0414
12	2,150	58	0.0270
13	2,417	115	0.0476
14	2,549	115	0.0451
16	2,331	75	0.0322
17	2,009	81	0.0403
18	2,198	86	0.0392
19	2,271	67	0.0295
20	1,948	41	0.0210
21	2,150	77	0.0358
23	1,700	49	0.0283
24	2,214	68	0.0307
25	2,394	82	0.0343
26	1,197	56	0.0468
27	850	27	0.0318
28	848	30	0.0353
30	850	33	0.0388
Total	43,392	591	

Ans:

$$p_0 = 0.04$$

$$3\sigma_p = 3\sqrt{\frac{p_0(1-p_0)}{n}} = 3\sqrt{\frac{0.04 \times 0.96}{1,600}} = 0.0147$$

$$UCL_p = p_0 + 3\sigma_p = 0.04 + 0.0147 = 0.0547$$

$$LCL_p = p_0 - 3\sigma_p = 0.04 - 0.0147 = 0.0253$$

Since setting limits on average basis is good enough where the maximum and minimum subgroup are not more than 25% away from the average, the control limits determined above are good enough for any subgroup whose size is 16,00 ± 25% of 1,600 i.e. 1,200 to 2,000.

In the given data, the maximum subgroup size is 2,549. For this size, the control will be 0.05165 and 0.02885.

For all values of n less than 2,549, UCL_p will be higher than 0.05165 and LCL_p will be lower than 0.02835. With these limits, it is seen that point for Nov. 20, falls below LCL_p. But any point falling below LCL_p is not to be discarded. Hence the recommended value of p_0 for the following month will be 0.04. However on plotting the chart it will be noticed that many points falling between p_0 and LCL_p and if this situation is repeated during the next month also, it is a welcoming situation and a lower value of p0 can be considered for subsequent months.

Q. 5.21: *In 25 sample of 50 pieces each, number of rejects was:*

1, 2, 5, 6, 3, 5, 2, 1, 1, 0, 0, 1, 0, 1, 0, 2, 1, 0, 0, 1, 1, 0, 0, 1 and 0.

Is this process in control ? If the consumer is willing to accept lots of this product that are 2.5% or less nonconforming, will the process in present state produces an acceptable lot? From looking at the chart of this process, what do you think happened during the run.

Ans: Total number of pieces inspected = 50(25) = 1250

Total number of rejects = 1 + 2 + ...1 = 34

$$\bar{p} = \frac{34}{1250} = 0.0272$$

$$UCL_p = 0.0272 + 3\sqrt{\frac{(0.0272)(1-0.0272)}{50}}$$

$$= 0.0962$$

On plotting the control chart, it will be found that the process is out of control. As the consumer is not willing to accept lots with more than 2.5% rejects and here the situation is that a lot on an average contains 2.72% rejects, therefore, the process in the present state does not produce an acceptable lot.

On drawing the chart it will be observed that after 6th subgroup only one point (*i.e.* sample have 2 nonconforming items or with $p = 0.04$) crosses the central line. Hence there has been either a substantial improvement in the process or the inspection has been more liberal.

Q. 5.22: *(a) Why an np chart is not recommend when the subgroup size is variable ?*

(b) A p chart is to be used to analyze the September record for 100% inspection of certain radio transmitting tubes. The total number inspected during the month was 2,196, and the total number of rejected was 158. Compute $\bar{p}$. *Compute individual 3-sigma control limits for the following 3 days, and state whether the fraction rejected fell within control limits for each day.*

Date	*Number inspected*	*Number rejected*
Sept. 14	54	8
15	162	24
16	213	3

Ans: *(a)* In case of *np* chart, when the subgroup size is variable, the expected number of rejectable items per subgroup will also change. This means that a different central line as well as different control limits for every subgroup on the chart. This makes the chart very confusing and almost not understandable by shop personnel. Hence when the subgroup size is variable *np* chart is generally not recommended.

(b) $$p = \frac{158}{2,196} = 0.072$$

on Sept. 14, n is 54, $$3\sigma_p = 3\sqrt{\frac{0.072(1-0.072)}{54}} = 0.106$$

on Sept. 15, n is 162, $$3\sigma_p = 3\sqrt{\frac{0.072(1-0.072)}{162}} = 0.061$$

on Sept. 16, n is 213, $$3\sigma_p = 3\sqrt{\frac{0.072(1-0.072)}{213}} = 0.053$$

Following tabulation lists out the fraction rejected, control limits and conclusion whether fraction rejected is within control limits etc.

Date	*Fraction rejected*	*UCL* = $\bar{p} + 3\sigma_p$	*LCL* = $\bar{p} - 3\sigma_p$	*Whether fraction rejected is within control limits*
Sept. 14	8/54 = 0.148	0.178	0	Yes
15	24/162 = 0.148	0.133	0.011	No. (Point above UCL)
16	3/213 = 0.014	0.125	0.019	No. (Point below LCL)

Q. 5.23: *A p chart is maintained for a certain product subject to 100% inspection. Each day's production is responsible for a new point on the chart. New 3-sigma control limits are drawn on the chart at the first of each month based on the standard fraction rejected p set for the coming month. For convenience, the limits shown on the chart are based on the estimated maximum day's output for the coming month. Whenever a point falls outside the limits on the chart, a separate calculation is made to find the limits applicable to the particular day's production.*

(a) For June, p_o *is* ***0.0315*** *and the estimated maximum day's output is* ***1,400*** *units. What control limits should be shown on the chart ?*

(b) During June, 4 points fell outside the control limits drawn on the chart, as follows:

Date	*Number inspected*	*Number of defectives*	*Fraction rejected*
June 7	1100	15	0.0136
14	600	7	0.0117
21	400	22	0.0550
25	900	47	0.0522

Make the necessary calculations to determine on which, if any, of these days the fraction rejected was outside the 3-sigma limits appropriate to the day's output.

Ans:
$$p_0 = 0.0315$$
$$n = 1400$$
$$3\sigma_p = 3\sqrt{\frac{0.0315(1-0.0315)}{1,400}} = 0.0140$$

(a) $$UCL_p = p_0 + 3\sigma_p = 0.031\,5 + 0.0140 = 0.0455$$
$$LCL_p = p_0 - 3\sigma_p = 0.\,0315 - 0.0140 = 0.0175$$

(*b*) Following tabulation lists out the fraction rejected control limits and the conclusion as on which day out of June 7, 14, 21 and 25, the fraction rejected was outside the 3-sigma control limits.

Date	*Number inspected*	*Fraction rejected*	*UCL*	*LCL*	*Whether the fraction rejected is within 3-sigma limits*
June 7	1,100	0.0136	0.0473	0.0157	No
14	600	0.0117	0.0529	0.0101	Yes
21	400	0.0550	0.0577	0.0053	Yes
25	900	0.0522	0.0490	0.0140	No

Q. 5.24: *The Ramington Corporation produces synthetic and natural gut castings for a process meat packer. Natural gut materials are visually inspected upon receipt, graded, and sent to processing. After processing, all finished castings are tested under pressure on a special device to ensure a specified strength before shipping to the meat packer. During the past 25 lots of* **500** *castings each have been subjected to* **100%** *inspection. Total of* **1,000** *castings burst during test.*

(*a*) *Find 3σ limits for a control chart for p.*

(*b*) *Assuming that all points fall within these limits, what is your estimate of the process average fraction nonconforming,* μ_p.

Ans:
$$\bar{p} = \frac{1000}{25(500)} = 0.08.$$

(*a*)
$$3\sigma_p = 3\sqrt{\frac{\bar{p}(1-\bar{p})}{n}} = 3\sqrt{\frac{0.08(1-0.08)}{500}} = 0.036.$$
$$UCL_p = \bar{p} + 3\sigma_p = 0.08 + 0.036 = 0.116$$
$$LCL_p = \bar{p} - 3\sigma_p = 0.08 - 0.036 = 0.044.$$

(b) Since all the points fall within these limits, the process is under control and therefore
$$\hat{\mu}_p = \bar{p} = 0.08.$$

Q. 5.25: *In the manufacture of certain special duty transformers, units are required to meet a number of specifications related to temperature rise, output voltages, voltage and current riple, on-off recovery times, etc. Approximately* **200** *units are produced and subjected to a final inspection daily. At the end of* **20** *working days,* **230** *units have been rejected out of* **4,150** *units produced and inspected.*

(*a*) *Determine 3σ trial control limits for a p-chart based on the estimated average daily production of* **200** *units.*

(*b*) *Only one point on the control chart falls outside limits. On that day,* **30** *nonconforming units were found in* **200** *units inspected. Investigation uncovered the fact that a voltage pot setting was being incorrectly adjusted. What aimed at values of* p_0 *and control limits would you recommend for the following period based on an average daily production of* **200** *units ?*

Ans:
$$\bar{p} = \frac{230}{4,150} = 0.055$$
$$n = 200$$
$$3\sigma_p = 3\sqrt{\frac{\bar{p}(1-\bar{p})}{n}} = 3\sqrt{\frac{0.055(1-0.055)}{200}} = 0.048$$

(a) $UCL_p = \bar{p} + 3\sigma_p = 0.055 + 0.048 = 0.103$

$LCL_p = \bar{p} - 3\sigma_p = 0.055 - 0.048 = 0.007.$

(b) $$p_0 = \frac{230 - 30}{4150 - 200} = \frac{200}{3950} = 0.051$$

$$n = 200$$

$$3\sigma_p = 3\sqrt{\frac{p_0(1-p_0)}{n}} = 3\sqrt{\frac{0.051(1-0.051)}{200}} = 0.047$$

$$UCL_p = 0.051 + 0.047 = 0.098$$

$$LCL_p = 0.051 - 0.047 = 0.004.$$

Q. 5.26: *It is desired to control the output of a certain intergrated circuit production line to maintain a 'yield' of 60 percent, that is a fraction rejected of 40 percent. To this end, daily samples of 100 units are checked to electrical specifications, with the following results:*

Date	*Number of rejected items*	*Date*	*Number of rejected items*	*Date*	*Number of rejected items*
March 12	24	March 26	44	April 9	23
13	38	27	52	10	31
16	62	30	45	13	26
17	34	31	30	14	32
18	26	April 1	34	15	35
19	36	2	33	16	15
20	38	3	22	17	24
23	52	6	34	20	38
24	33	7	43	21	21
25	44	8	28	22	16

Ans: Since the standard value p0 = 0.40, the control limits on a p chart are

$$UCL_p = 0.40 + 3\sqrt{\frac{(0.40)(1-0.40)}{100}} = 0.55$$

$$LCL_p = 0.40 - 3\sqrt{\frac{(0.40)(1-0.40)}{100}} = 0.25$$

The chart for the data is plotted in Fig. 5.16

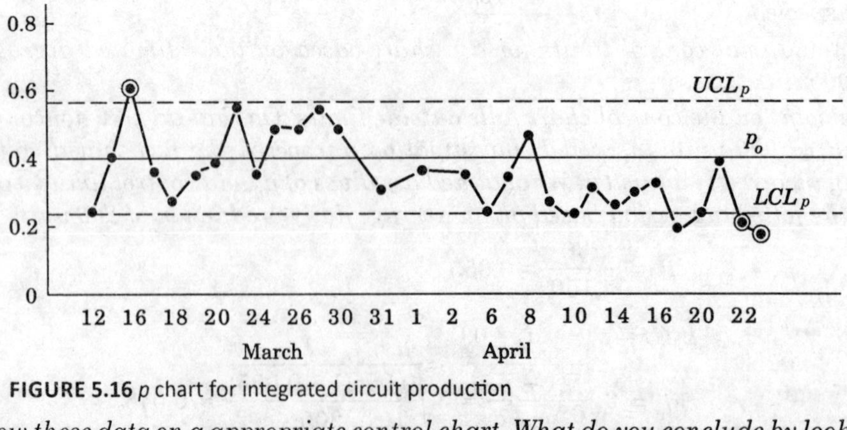

FIGURE 5.16 *p* chart for integrated circuit production

Show these data on a appropriate control chart. What do you conclude by looking at the chart?

The chart shows one point above the UCL_p and seven points below LCL_p. Most of these seven points occured after April 1, and there appears to be general downward trend. In fact, there is an unbroken run of eleven points below the central line after April 7. It appears from this chart that the yield is not stabilized, and that the process is potentially capable of maintaining a yield well above the nominal 60 percent value.

Q. 5.27: *The new item start up procedure of a certain electronics plant calls for **100** percent inspection for at least first four of nonconforming product. A total of **960** units were found to not meet the specifications during the first **20** working days. The number of units produced during this period was **31,985**.*

(a) Determine the trial control limits for a p chart based on the average number of units produced per day.

*(b) After the limits were plotted on the p chart, three points were found to be above the UCLp. On these days, a total of **4,950** items were produced and **232** nonconforming units found.*

(i) What value of an aimed at p_0 would you recommend for the next production period ?

(ii) Give a general formula for calculating control limits during the next production period. Reproduce this formula to the point that only n needs to be found in order to plot the limits.

Ans:

$$\bar{\ } = \frac{960}{31,985} = 0.030$$

$$n = \frac{31,985}{20}$$

$$= 1,599.251 \approx 1,600$$

$$3\sigma_p = 3\sqrt{\frac{\bar{p}(1-\bar{p})}{n}} = 0.0128$$

(a)

$$UCL_p = \bar{p} + 3\sigma_p = 0.030 + 0.0128 = 0.0428$$

$$LCL_p = \bar{p} - 3\sigma_p = 0\ .030 - 0.0128 = 0.0172$$

(b) (i)

$$p_0 = \frac{960 - 232}{31,985 - 4,950}$$

$$= \frac{728}{27,035} = 0.027$$

(ii)

$$3\sigma_p = 3\sqrt{\frac{p_0(1-p_0)}{n}}$$

$$= 3\sqrt{\frac{0.027(1-0.027)}{n}} = \frac{0.486}{\sqrt{n}}$$

$$UCL = p_0 + 3\sigma_p = 0.027 + \frac{0.486}{\sqrt{n}}$$

$$= 0.027\left(1 + \frac{18.01}{\sqrt{n}}\right)$$

$$LCL = p_0 - 3\sigma_p = 0.027 - \frac{0.486}{\sqrt{n}}$$

$$= 0.027\left(1 - \frac{18.01}{\sqrt{n}}\right)$$

General formula for control limits

$$= 0.027\left(1 \pm \frac{18.01}{\sqrt{n}}\right)$$

Q. 5.28: *Assume that process described in Q. 5.27 (a) was found to be in control but that the level of nonconforming product shift from 3 to 4.5%*

(a) Use Table A to estimate the probability that this shift will be detected on the first subgroup drawn after the shift occurs. Base this calculation on the average value of n found in Prob. 5.19 (a).

(b) What is the probability that this shift will be detected within the first three subgroups drawn?

Ans: With change in p_0 from 0.030 to 0.045, σ_p will also change.

$$\text{Now} \qquad \sigma_p = \sqrt{\frac{0.045(1-0.045)}{1,600}}$$

$$= 0.00518$$

The probability of detecting a shift of any subgroup, is the probability of any point falling outside the UCL_p of 0.428. Assuming a normal distribution, the area of normal curve up to UCL_p can now be found.

$$z = \frac{0.0428 - 0.0450}{0.00518}$$

$$= -0.42$$

From Table *A*, the area corresponding to z of – 0.42 is 0.3372.

Hence area outside the UCL_p *i.e.* the probability of detecting a shift is 1.0000 – 0.3372 *i.e.* 0.6672.

(*a*) Probability of detecting a shift on the first subgroup is 0.6672

(*b*) Probability of detecting a shift within the first three subgroups

$$= 0.6672 + 0.6672\ (0.3328) + 6672\ (0.3328)^2$$

$$= 0.9617.$$

Q. 5.29: *Daily inspection records are maintained on production of a special-design electronic device. 100 items have been inspected each day for the past 21 days. A total of 546 items failed during a particularly severe heat stress test. The four highest and lowest values of p are:*

Highest	*Lowest*
0.46	0.18
0.33	0.18
0.31	0.20
0.31	0.21

(a) Compute 3σ trial control limits for a p chart. Is the process operating in control ?

(b) Recommend an aimed-at value p0 and 3σ control limits for continued use of the p chart.

(c) The test results as described above are from a special severe heat stress chamber which is designed in such a way that 25% of the product will fail when, in fact, it is satisfactory for its intended use. If the minimum stress specification is 750 units and the process standard deviation is known to be 12 units, what should be the lower limit of the test ? Assume this stress characteristic to be normally distributed.

Ans:

$$\bar{p} = \frac{546}{21(100)} = 0.26$$

$$3\sigma_p = 2\sqrt{\frac{\bar{p}(1-\bar{p})}{n}} = 0.132$$

(*a*)

$$UCL_p = \bar{p} + 3\sigma_p$$
$$= 0.392$$
$$LCL_p = \bar{p} - 3\sigma_p$$
$$= 0.128$$

(*b*) With the control limits computed in (*a*), only one point ($p = 0.46$) is above UCL_P. Eliminating this point,

$$p_0 = \frac{546 - (0.46 \times 100)}{2{,}100 - 100} = 0.25$$

$$3\sigma_p = 3\sqrt{\frac{p_0(1-p_0)}{n}}$$

$$= 3\sqrt{\frac{0.25(1-0.25)}{100}} = 0.130$$

$$UCL_p = p_0 + 3\sigma_p = 0.380$$
$$LCL_p = p_0 - 3\sigma_p = 0.120$$

(*c*) If the process is normally distributed,

$$L = \bar{X}_0 - 3\sigma$$
$$750 = \bar{X}_0 - 3(12)$$
$$\bar{X}_0 = 786$$

Let L be the test limit such that 25% of the product is below this limit. From Table *A*, for such a situation $z = -0.675$.

Hence $$-0.675 = \frac{L \quad \bar{X}}{}$$

Substituting the values of $\bar{X}_0$ and σ

$$L = 777.9$$

Q. 5.30: *A large number of samples of 200 items each taken from a process that has a percentage nonconforming of 10% .*

(a) What is the expected average number of nonconforming units per sample ?

(b) Find the 3σ control limits for an np chart to control this process.

(c) What is the upper limit in the number of nonconforming items in a sample that, in the long run, you would expect to find exceeded only 5% of the time ? Use a Poisson approximation.

Ans:

$$\bar{p} = 0.10$$
$$n = 200$$

(*a*) Average number of nonconforming units per sample

$$n\bar{p} = 200 \times 0.10$$
$$= 20$$

(*b*)
$$3\sigma_{np} = 3\sqrt{np(1-p)}$$
$$= 3\sqrt{(20)(1-p)} = 12.7$$
$$UCL = n\bar{p} + 3\sigma_{np} = 20 + 12.7 = 32.7$$
$$LCL = n\bar{p} - 3\sigma_{np} = 20 - 12.7 = 7.3$$

(*c*) From Table *G*, for *np* of 20, by interpolation, the number of nonconforming items in a sample that, in the long run we would expect to exceed only 5% (or, in the long run we would expect not to exceed by 95%) is 27.

Q. 5.31: *Batches of 100 components were taken at fixed intervals of time from a production line and tested. The following figures are the number of components found to be nonconforming in each of the batches :*

4 3 2 0 7 5

2 4 1 3 4 6

(a) Calculate the mean proportion rejected.

(b) Draw up a quality control chart for samples of 200 of the components, such that the upper inner limits is equal to the mean plus two standard error and the outer limit is equal to the mean plus three standard errors.

(c) Could your chart be used for batches of 50 components why or why not ?

Ans: (*a*)
$$\bar{p} = \frac{4 + 2 + ... + 4 + 6}{12 \times 100}$$
$$= 0.0342$$

(*b*) When $n = 200$, $np = 200 \times 0.0342 = 6.8$

$$\sigma_{np} = \sqrt{200 \times 0.0342(1 - 0.0342)} = 2.57$$

Inner control limit is $n\bar{p} + 2\sigma_{np} = 6.8 + 2(2.57) = 11.94$

Outer control limit is $= n\bar{p} + 3\sigma_{np} = 6.8 + 3(2.57) = 14.51$

(*c*) The chart cannot be used for batches of 50. The $\bar{p}$ value remains the same even for batches of 50 but σ_p depends upon *n* and will increase as the batch sample size reduces for the same value of $\bar{p}$. Hence the control limits plotted for batch size of 100 cannot be applied to batch size of 50.

Q. 5.32: *A machinist, temporarily in-charge of manufacturing a simple part, is attempting to determine whether the process is in control. Taking a quick look at the control-chart given to him by the quality control department, he sees that the upper control limit has been set 0.062 and the central line at 0.02. Seeking no further information, he takes a sample of 25 parts from the output and determines that the sample contains two nonconforming units. Should he stop the process on the plea that the process is out of control ?*

Ans: Central line at $(\mu_p) = 0.02$

$$UCL_p = 0.062$$

Assuming that UCL_p is 3-sigma away from the central line,

$$0.062 = 0.02 + 3\sqrt{\frac{0.02(1-0.02)}{n}}$$

from which
$$n = 100$$

This is now evident that the upper control limit on the chart given to him is based on the sample size of 100. Since the machinist uses a sample size of 25, the same control limits are not applicable. For the subgroup size of 25,

$$UCL_p = 0.02 + 3\sqrt{\frac{0.02(1-0.02)}{25}} = 0.104$$

Fraction rejected (p) as determined by the machinist in a sample of 25 items $= \frac{2}{25} = 0.08$.

It is evident that a p of 0.08 lies within 3-sigma control limits indicating that the process is in control and therefore the machinist should not stop the process on the plea that the process is out control.

Q. 5.33: *Over the past eight or nine months an assembly line has been producing 400 units of a product per day. Final inspection records show that on an average 20 units a day are nonconforming. A survey of the daily reports show that on an occasional day a few as one or two are nonconforming items.*

(a) Do these records indicate statistical control of quality?

(b) What help might be obtained if any, from these records in improving quality performance at this time?

Ans: 20 nonconforming items in a sample of 400 for substantially long time mean that $\mu_p = 20/400 = 0.05$.

$$3\sigma_p = 2\sqrt{\frac{0.05(1-0.05)}{4,400}} = 0.03$$

$$UCL_p = 0.05 + 0.03 = 0.08$$

$$LCL_p = 0.05 - 0.03 = 0.02$$

A p value of 0.08 indicates 32 nonconforming items in a sample of 400 and a p of 0.02 indicates 8 nonconforming items in a sample of 400.

(a) From the records it is evident that on the average 20 nonforming units and no points fall above UCL_p and only on a occasional day a point fall much below LCL_p. The process therefore is not in statistical control.

(b) As no point falls above UCL_p, but a few points below LCL_p, it indicates a poor estimation of p although it may indicate possible change for the better quality level, and tracking down the assignable causes may enable an improvement to be made in the production process. In either case, points falling below the lower control limit, call for a re-examination of the control chart or the production or the inspection or a combination of these three.

Q. 5.34: *(a) A random sample of 20 articles was drawn from every 100 produced by a certain process. The number of nonconforming articles per sample in the first 20 samples were:*

0, 1, 0, 1, 1, 3, 0, 2, 1, 0, 0, 0, 0, 3, 0, 0, 2, 1, 1, 2,

and in the second 20 samples were:

1, 2, 2, 0, 1, 2, 0, 1, 2, 2, 0, 1, 0, 0, 1, 0, 1, 1, 1, 1

Use the first 20 samples to calculate the mean number of nonconforming articles per sample and by using Poisson distribution obtain a control limit C (whole number) such that the probability of there being C or more nonconforming articles in a sample is less than 1/10. Show all calculations. ($e^{-0.9} = 0.4066$)

(b) Use C to set up a control chart and show that over the whole period during which the samples were drawn the process was under control with a process mean of 4.5% nonconforming.

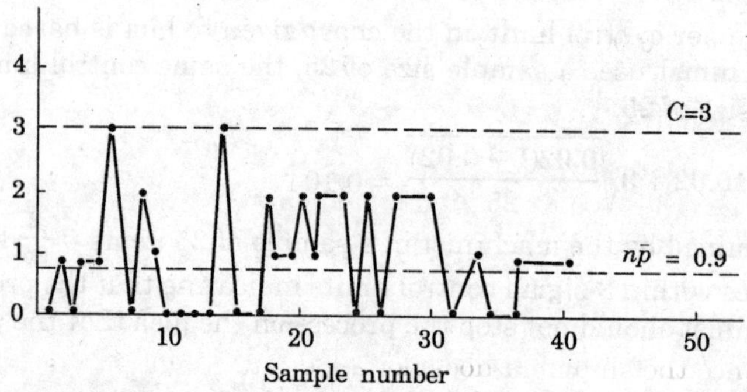

FIGURE 5.17 Control chart for the data.

Ans: (*a*) Number of nonconforming articles in the first 20 samples = 18.

Mean number of nonconforming articles per sample

$$= \frac{18}{20} = 0.9$$

Using the Poisson distribution,

$$e^{-np}, (np)\, e^{-np}, \frac{(np)^2}{2!} e^{-np} \ldots$$

and substitution $np = 0.9$, the probabilities of 0, 1, 2, 3 ...... nonconforming articles per sample are:

0.4066, 0.3659, 0.1647, 0.0494,.....

It is now necessary to decide how many of these probability values must be added together to make a total greater than 9/10. As the sum of the first three probability values is 0.9372, the probabilities of 3 or more nonconforming article per sample is less than 1/10. Thus the required control limit $C = 3$.

(*b*) The control chart for 40 samples is shown in Fig. 5.17.

From the control chart it is evident that no point falls above the control limit of 3 and only 2 out of 40 fall on it and there is no particular trend of the points, the process is under control. In the first 20 samples there are 18 nonconforming articles out of a total of 400. This establishes the process mean as 4.5% and the process is stated to be under control with a process average of 4.5% nonconforming.

Q. 5.35: *The XYZ company purchases small steel balls in cartons that usually contain several thousand balls. Each shipment consists of a number of cartons. As part of the acceptance procedure for these balls, 400 balls are selected at random from each carton and are subjected to visual inspection for certain nonconformities. In a shipment of 10 cartons, the respective percentages of rejectable balls in the sample from each carton are 0.5, 0, 0.75, 2, 0, 0, 0.25, 0, 0.25, and 1.25. Does this shipment of balls appear to exhibit statistical control with respect to the quality characteristic examined in this inspection ?*

Ans: Since the subgroup size in constant,

$$\%\bar{p} = \frac{0.5 + 0 + 0.75 + 2 + 0 + 0 + 0.25 + 0 + 0.25 + 1.25}{10} = 0.5$$

$$\bar{p} = \frac{0.5}{100} = 0.005$$

$$3\sigma_P = 3\sqrt{\frac{0.005(1-0.005)}{400}}$$

$$= 0.0156$$

$$UCL_p = 0.0\ 05 + 0.0106 = 0.0156$$

$$LCL_p = 0.005 - 0.0106 = -0.0056 \text{ and hence taken as zero.}$$

In terms of percentage $UCL = 1.56$

$LCL = 0.$

On plotting the chart, it will be noticed that 4th subgroup falls above UCL_p and 10th subgroup is nearer to UCL_p. Hence the shipment does not appear to exhibit statistical control with respect to the quality characteristic examined in the inspection.

Q. 5.36: *An item is made in lots of 200 each. The lots are given 100% inspection. The record sheet for the first 25 lots inspected showed that a total of 75 items were rejectable*

(a) Determine the trial control limits for an np chart showing number of rejectable in each lot.

(b) Assume that all points fall within the control limits, what is your estimate of the process average fraction nonconforming μ_p ?

(c) If this μ_p remains unchanged, what is probability that the 26th lot will contain exactly 7 rejectable items ? That it will contain 7 or more rejectable items.

Ans:

$$n\bar{p} = \frac{75}{25} = 3$$

$$\bar{p} = \frac{75}{25(200)} = 0.015$$

$$3\sigma_{np} = 3\sqrt{np(1-p)} = 3\sqrt{3(1-0.015)} = 5.157$$

$$UCL_{np} = 3.\ 000 + 5.157 = 8.157$$

$$LCL_{np} = 0.$$

(b) Since all the points fell within the control limits for quite a substantial number of lots, $\mu_{pp} = \bar{p} = 0.015$.

(c) From Table G, the probability of 26th sample for which $np = 3$, containing any number of rejected items up to 7 is 0.088 and probability of any number of rejected items up to 6 is 0.966. Hence the required probability *i.e.*, the sample should contain exactly 7 rejectable items is 0.988 – 0.966 = 0.022 and also the probability that sample contains 7 or more rejectable items is 1.000 – 0.966 *i.e.* 0.034.

Q. 5.37: *A manufacturer of electric heaters uses a p-chart to monitor the number of nonconforming heaters produced that require rework. The manufacturer produces these heaters in lot sizes of 100, and 100% inspection is required. In the past, 5% of the heaters have been nonconforming and have required rework. The quality control group maintains two sets of control limits on the p-chart with ± 2σ limits being used as warning limits and ±3σ limits being used as shutdown limits . The company's policy it that if the fraction rejected of a lots exceed the upper warning limit, then the manufacturing process is shut down and thoroughly inspected.*

(a) Calculate the ± 2σ warning limits and the ± 3σ shutdown limits for this operation.

(b) If the percent rejected suddenly shifts to 7% what is the probability that any one point will exceed the upper shutdown limit ? (Use Table G).

(c) At this 7% rejection level what is the probability that two successive points will fall between the upper warning limit and the upper shutdown limits ?

Ans:

$$p_0 = 0.05$$

$$\sigma_p = \sqrt{\frac{0.05(1 - 0.05)}{100}} = 0.0218$$

$$2\sigma_p = 0.0436$$

$$3\sigma_p = 0.0654$$

(*a*) Upper Warning Limit $= p_0 + 2\sigma_p = 0.05 + 0.0436 = 0.0936$

Lower Warning Limit $= p_0 - 2\sigma_p = 0.05 - 0.0436 = 0.0064$

Upper Shutdown Limit $= p_0 + 3\sigma_p = 0.05 + 0.0654 = 0.1154$

Lower Shutdown Limit $= p_0 - 3\sigma_p = 0.05 - 0.0654 = -0.0154$

therefore zero and hence taken as zero.

(*b*) When the process average shifts to 7%

$$np = 100 \times 0.07 = 7$$

Also a shutdown limit of 0.1154 corresponds to 11.54 nonconforming items. From Table *G*, the probability of 11.54 or more, by interpolation, is 0.039.

Also the probability any point falling above the upper control limit as determined in (*b*) is 0.039.

(*c*) Also as determined in (*b*) probability of a point falling upto upper warning limit of 0.0936 nonconforming items, is 0.856 and probability of any point below the upper shutdown limit *i.e.* 0.1154 nonconforming items is 0.961. From this, the probability of any point between upper warning limit and upper shutdown limit is $0.961 - 0.856 = 0.105$. Hence the probability that two successive points will fall between the upper warning limit and upper shutdown limits is $(0.105)^2 = 0.011$.

Q. 5.38: *A part manufacturer requires that 100% final inspection be performed during the first three months of production on any new or modified part. A total of 750 items were found to be nonconforming to specifications in the first 50 lots of a new item produced in lots of 500 units.*

(a) Compute 3σ trial control limits for an np chart for this purpose.

(b) If the process average remains unchanged, what is the probability that the 51st lot inspected will contain more than 20 nonconforming units ?

(c) If the process average value of np increases by 8, what is the probability that the 51st inspected will exceed the upper control limit found in (a) ? Use Table G.

Ans: (*a*)

$$\bar{p} = \frac{750}{50(500)} = 0.03$$

$$n\bar{p} = 500\ (0.03) = 15$$

$$3\,\sigma_{np} = 3\sqrt{np(1 - p)}$$

$$= 3\sqrt{15(1 - 0.03)} = 11.44$$

$$UCL_{np} = n\bar{p} + 3\,\sigma_{np}$$

$$= 15 + 11.44 = 26.44$$

$$LCL_{np} = n\bar{p} - 3\sigma_{np}$$

$$= 15 - 11.44 = 3.56$$

(*b*) Using Table *G*, with *np* of 15, probability of any sample (in this case 51st sample) containing upto 20 nonconforming items is 0.917. Hence the probability of more than 20 nonconforming items is 1.0 – 0.917 *i.e.* 0.083.

(c) New process average (np) = 15 + 8 = 23

$$UCL_{np} \text{ in } (a) = 26.44$$

Again from Table G, with np of 23, probability upto 26.44 nonconforming (by interpolation) is 0.796. Hence probability that the 51st lot will exceed UCL_{np} of 26.44 is 0.204.

Q. 5.39: *A p chart indicates that the current average is **0.02**. If 50 items are inspected each day. What is the probability of catching a shift in process average to **0.04** on the first day after the shift ? By the end of the third day after the shift ?*

Ans: Current process average of 0.02 means that a sample of 50 items contains one non-conforming item. When the process average shifts to 0.04.

$$np = 50 \times 0.04 = 2$$

From Table G, the probability of having exactly 2 nonconforming items in a samples of 50 is equal to probability of having 0 or 1 or 2 nonconforming item minus the probability of having 0 or 1 nonconforming items. From Table G,

Probability of exactly 0, or 1 or 2 nonconforming items = 0.677

Probability of exactly 0, or 1 nonconforming items = 0.406

∴ Probability of exactly 2 nonconforming items = 0.677 – 0.406 = 0.271

∴ Probability of detecting a shift on the first day = 0.271

Probability of detecting a shift on the third day = (0.406)(0.406)(0.271) = 0.0447.

Q. 5.40: *You are shown a control chart for which* p_o *= **0.05**. You wish a shift to a process average of **0.10** to have approximately a **60** per cent chance of being caught on the first sample after the shift. Determine how large a sample will you use for control chart purpose.*

Ans: The situation given in the problem can be well understood with the help of simple diagram of Fig. 5.18. Assuming that the process is normally distributed about the new process average, the area of the curve below the new process average is 0.50. Also since a 60% chance is the requirement for detecting a shift, area of the curve above the previous UCL_p

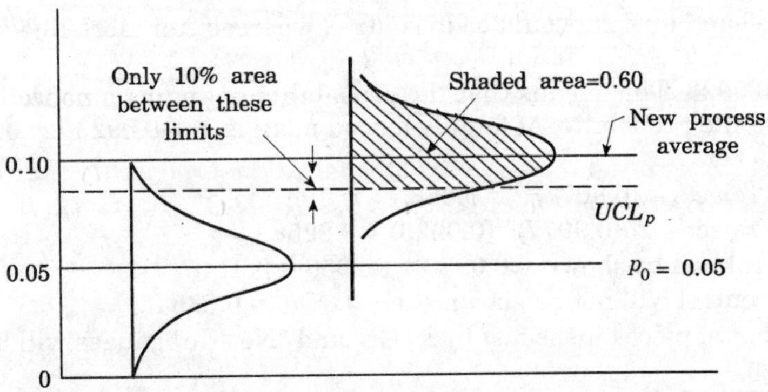

FIGURE 5.18 Diagram illustrates the situation

(*i.e.* $0.05 + 3\sqrt{\frac{0.05(1-0.05)}{n}}$ will be 0.60, or the area of the curve below UCL_p is 0.40. Hence the area of the curve between UCL_p and the new process average is only 0.10. Now it can be determined from Table A that for 10% area to be below the process average, the limit must be 0.2533 σ below the new process average. This is same as UCL_p. Hence, if n is the sample size,

$$0.10 - 0.2533\sqrt{\frac{0.10(1-0.10)}{n}} = 0.05 + 3\sqrt{\frac{0.05(1-0.05)}{n}}$$

This on solution yields $n = 213$.

Q. 5.41: *In the Q. 5.40, if the sample size is limited to 50, determine at what multiple of sigma the control limit be set.*

Ans: Let the control limits be set initially at K-sigma away from the process average of 0.05.

$$\text{Then } 0.05 - K\sqrt{\frac{0.05(1-0.05)}{50}} = 0.10 - 0.2533\sqrt{\frac{(0.10)(1-0.10)}{50}}$$

This on solution gives $K = 1.274$.

Hence the control limits should be set at $\pm\, 1.274\, \sigma_p$.

Q. 5.42: *You are shown a control chart for which $\mu_p = 0.07$. You wish a shift to a process average of 0.12 to have approximately a 0.50 chance of being caught on the first sample after the shift. How large should your daily sample be for control chart purpose ?*

Ans: The calculations of this question is similar to that of Q. 5.41, but numerically simpler as seen from the following equation.

$$0.07 + 3\sqrt{\frac{0.07(1-0.07)}{n}} = 0.12 - 0\sqrt{\frac{0.12(1-0.12)}{n}}$$

or

$$= 0.07 - 3\sqrt{\frac{0.07(1-0.07)}{n}} = 0.12$$

This on solution yields, $n = 234$.

Q. 5.43: *A control chart for rejects is operating at $p_0 = 0.01$. The sample size is 25. Determine the number of pieces inspected by "Go" and "Not–Go" gauges before a shift in p_0 to 0.0932 is detected. Use binomial distribution.*

Ans:

$$p_0 = 0.01,\ n = 25$$

UCL for np-chart

$$= np_0 + 3\sqrt{np_0(1-p_0)}$$

$$= 25(0.01) + 3\sqrt{25(0.01)(1-0.01)} = 1.74$$

Hence 0 or 1 rejects in a sample of 25 would be in control, whereas 2 or more rejects would indicate out of control.

The new value of p_0 is 0.0923. This means that the probability of finding a nonconforming item is 0.0923 and therefore the probability of finding a good piece is 1.0–0.0923 *i.e.* 0.9077.

In a sample of 25.

Probability of finding 0 rejects = $(0.9077)^{25} = 0.088$

Probability of finding 1 reject = $25(0.9077)^{24}(0.0923) = 0.2258$

$\therefore$ Probability that control will be shown = 0.0888 + 0.2258 = 0.3146

$\therefore$ Probability that the control will not be shown = 1 – 0.3146 = 0.6854

Thus the average number of pieces inspected by a "Go" and "Not-Go" gauges will be

$$\frac{25}{0.6854} = 36.$$

Q. 5.44: *During the month of April, samples of 50 items were inspected every day for 27 consecutive days. The number of rejectable items was only 146.*

(a) Determine the fraction rejected.

(b) The upper and lower control limits for a p chart.

(c) Find the probability of p falling within the control limits when p takes the values from 0 to 0.40 sketch the cure with probability on the ordinate and the p values associated with these probabilities on the abscissa .

(For $p \leq 0.10$, use Poison distribution; for $p > 0.10$ use normal distribution).

Ans: (*a*)
$$\bar{p} = \frac{146}{27(50)} = 0.108$$

$$3\sigma_p = 3\sqrt{\frac{\bar{p}(1-\bar{p})}{n}} = 3\sqrt{\frac{0.108(1-0.108)}{50}} = 0.132$$

(*b*)
$$UCL_p = \bar{p} + 3\sigma_p = 0.108 + 0.132 = 0.240$$
$$LCL_p = \bar{p} - 3\sigma_p = 0.108 - 0.132 = -0\ .024 \text{ (considered as 0}$$
$$= -0.024 \text{ (and hence assumed 0).}$$

(c) Following tabulation gives the probability of various p values falling between the upper and lower control limits. In order to have sufficient number of points, the probabilities have been calculated for $p = 0, 0.10, 0.15, 0.20, 0.24, 0.28, 0.30, 0.35$, and 0.40.

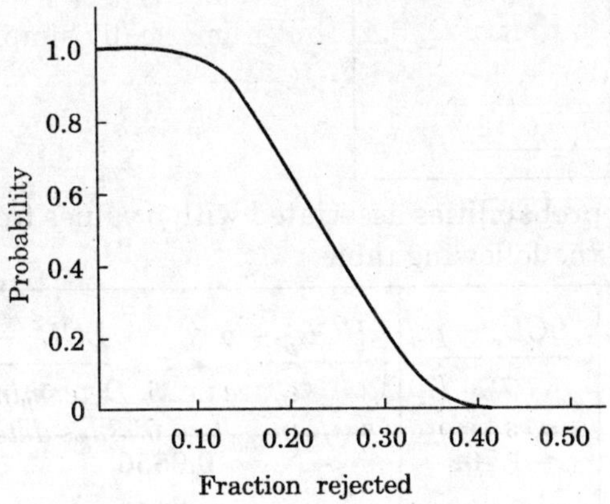

FIGURE 5.19 OC curve for the single unit

p	np	$\sigma_p = \frac{\bar{p}(1-\bar{p})}{n}$	$UCL_p - p$	$\frac{UCL_p - p}{\sigma_p}$	*Probability of p ≤ UCL_p of 0.240*
0	0	—	—	—	1.000 From Table *G*
0.10	5	—	—	—	0.998 From Table *G*
0.15	—	0.0505	0.09	1.782	0.9627 From Table *A*
0.20	—	0.0566	0.04	0.706	0.7598 From Table *A*
0.24	—	—	0	0	0.5000 From Table *A*
0.28	—	0.0635	– 0.04	– 0.630	0.2643 From Table *A*
0.30	—	0.0648	– 0.06	– 0.926	0.1772 From Table *A*
0.35	—	0.0674	– 0.11	– 1.632	0.0514 From Table *A*
0.40	—	0.0693	– 0.16	– 2.309	0.0104 From Table *A*

Figure 5.19 shows the curve between the various *p* values and the associated probabilities. Such a curve is known as the operating characteristic curve (*OC* curve) of the *p* chart.

Q. 5.45: *For a p chart the central line is at $\bar{p} = 0.247$ and control limits are at 0.430 and 0.064 respectively. Subgroup size is 50. Assuming that Poisson is applicable for $p \leq 0.10$ and normal distribution is applicable for $p \geq 0.10$, draw the OC curve for this p chart taking p = 0, 0.01, 0.02, 0.03, 0.04, 0.05, 0.06, 0.08, 0.10, 0.15. 0.25, 0.30, 0.35, 0.40, 0.50, 0.55 and 0.60.*

Ans: The *OC* curve of *p* chart is found by computing the probability of a point falling within the control limits when the actual fraction rejected is at some given value *p*.

Using Poisson distribution for $p \leq 0.10$, the probabilities associated with *p* values upto 0.10 as computed from Table G are given in the following tabulation.

p	np	*Prob.* $(c < 0.43n)$ – *Prob.* $(c \leq 0.064n)$
0	0	0
0.01	0.5	0.002
0.02	1.0	0.016
0.03	1.5	0.057
0.04	2.0	0.125
0.05	2.5	0.216
0.06	3.0	0.319
0.08	4.0	0.528
0.10	5.0	0.700

Using normal distribution for $p > 0.10$, the probabilities associated with *p* values from 0.15 to 0.60 as computed from Table *A* are given in the following table:

p	$\sigma_p = \sqrt{\dfrac{p(1-p)}{n}}$	$\dfrac{UCL_p - p}{\sigma_p}$	$\dfrac{LCL_p - p}{\sigma_p}$	$\left(\dfrac{UCL_p - p}{\sigma_p} < z < \dfrac{LCL_p^2 - p}{\sigma_p}\right)$
0.15	0.0505	5.544	– 1.702	0.9556
0.25	0.0612	2.941	– 3.039	0.9972
0.30	0.0648	2.006	– 3.642	0.9776
0.35	0.0675	1.185	—	0.8820
0.40	0.0693	0.433	—	0.6666
0.43	—	—	—	0.5000
0.50	0.0707	– 0.990	—	0.1611
0.55	0.0704	– 1.704	—	0.0442
0.60	0.0693	– 2.457	—	0.0070

Figure 5.20 shows the OC curve for the *p* chart.

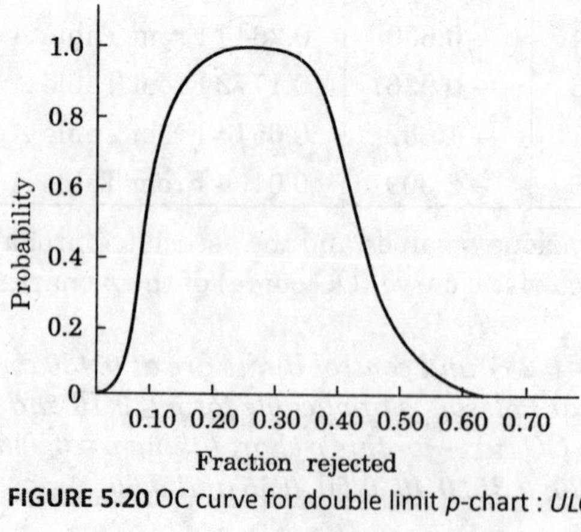

FIGURE 5.20 OC curve for double limit *p*-chart : $ULC_p = 0.430$; $LCL_p = 0.064$; $n = 50$.

Q. 5.46: *Discuss briefly the basis of sample size for a p chart.*

Ans: On some occasions, 100 percent inspection is performed for one or more part characteristics. In this situation the sample size is a function of the plotting frequency. This may be 1 hour, 1 day, or 1 week and is dependent on the problems which may be encountered if a process change is not detected. At other times, the sample size for a p chart is determined by standard sampling plans. This is more apt to occur when material is segregated into lots or batches. It is recommended that samples should be large enough that when no rejects are found in the subgroup, a significant improvement over the standard is indicated. To attain this, it is necessary to have $n > (9 - 9\bar{p}/\bar{p})$.

The graph in Fig 5.21 gives n for $\bar{p}$ values up to 10 percent

It re-emphasised that these sample sizes are intended to reveal a significant improvement when no rejects are found in the sample. In most practical applications, much smaller sample sizes are used with a resulting sacrifice in ability to detect shifts in the process average. Over

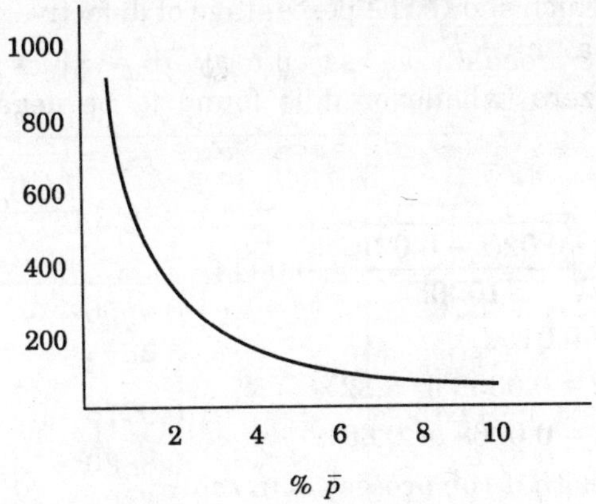

FIGURE 5.21 Relationship between p and n.

some time interval (which may be long), shifts probably will be detected even with small samples based on the theory of runs.

Q. 5.47: *(a) What is a control chart?*

(b) Name any one control chart for attributes? What does this chart show?

(c) What can be the minimum value of LCLp (lower control limit on p-chart)?

(d) A credit company deals with many hundreds of thousands of transactions every week. One of its measures of the quality of service it gives its customers is the dependability with which it mails customers' monthly accounts. The quality standard it sets itself is that accounts should be mailed within two days of the 'nominal post date' which is specified to the customer. Every week the company samples 1,000 customer accounts and records the percentage which were not mailed within the standard time. When the process is working normally only two per cent of accounts are mailed outside the specified period, that is two per cent are 'defective'.

- *Compute the UCL_p and LCL_p.*

(e) Figure 5.22 shows the p-chart of 40 samples with UCLp and LCLp calculated above. Is the process in control?

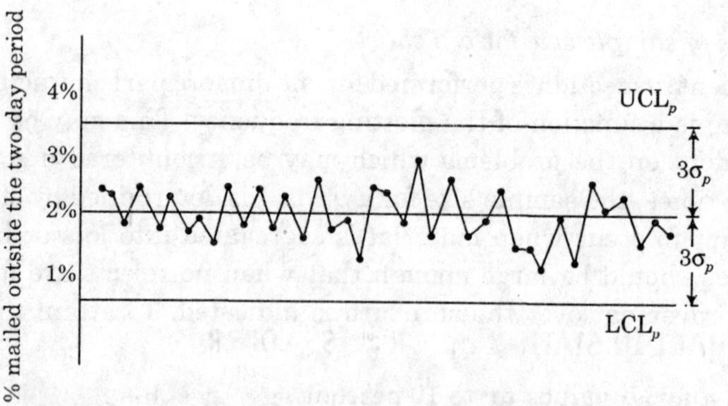

FIGURE 5.25 Control chart for the percentage of customer accounts which were mailed outside their two-day period.

Ans: (*a*) A control chart is the evaluation tool in statistical process control (SPC).

(*b*) Control chart for attributes is *p*-chart, which shows the percentage of defective units in a sample, *c*-charts for the number of defects in a unit.

(*c*) The minimum value of LCL_p can be zero (whenever it is found to be negative in computation).

(*d*)

$$\bar{p} = 0.02$$

$$\sigma_p = \sqrt{\frac{\bar{p}(1-\bar{p})}{n}} = \sqrt{\frac{0.02(1-0.02)}{1000}} = 0.0044$$

$$3\sigma_p = (3)\ (0.0044) = 0.0132$$

$$UCL_p = 0.02 + 0.0132 = 0.0332 \text{ or } 3.32\%$$

$$LCL_p = 0.02 - 0.0132 = 0.0068 \text{ or } 0.68\%$$

(*e*) A mere look at the control chart indicates that the process is in control.

CHAPTER

6

Control Chart for Nonconformities

6.1 THE PLACE OF THE *c* - CHART IN STATISTICAL PROCESS CONTROL

The $\bar{X}$ and R control charts may be applied to any quality characteristic that is measurable. The control chart for p may be applied to the results of any inspection that accepts or rejects individual items of product. Thus both these types of charts are broadly useful in any statistical quality control programme.

The control chart for nonconformities, generally called the c chart, has a much more restricted field of usefulness. In many manufacturing plants there may be no opportunities for its economic use, even though there are dozen of places where $\bar{X}$ and R charts and p charts can be used advantageously.

Nevertheless there are certain manufacturing and inspection situations in which the c chart is definitely needed. To decide whether or not to use a c chart in any individual case, it is first necessary to determine whether its use is appropriate from the viewpoint of statistical theory. If so, then it is necessary to judge whether the c chart is really the best technique to use for the purpose at hand.

Since the c chart is based on Poisson distribution, two conditions must be met. First, *the average number of nonconformities must be much less than the total possible number of nonconformities*. In other words, the opportunity for nonconformities is large, while the chance of nonconformity at any one location is very small. This situation is typified by the rivets on a commercial airplane, where there are a large number of rivets but a small chance of any one rivet being a nonconforming. The second condition specifies that *the area of opportunity for nonconformities should be the same*. For the airplane situation, the type of rivet gun should be the same type used to install all the rivets on the airplane. If different types of rivet guns are used, the opportunity for nonconformities is different at different locations on the airplane.

Other places where a c chart meets these two conditions are: imperfections in a large roll of paper, typographical errors on a printed page, rust spots on steel sheets, seeds or air pockets in glassware, adhesion defects per 1000 square feet of corrugated board, and mould marks on fibreglass cannoes.

6.2 DISTINCTION BETWEEN A NONCONFORMING ARTICLE AND A NONCONFORMITY

As already explained a *nonconforming article* (*a defective* in the restricted technical sense of the word) is an article that in some way fails to conform to one or more given specifications. Each instance of the article's lack of conformity to specifications is a *nonconformity* (a *defect* in the restricted technical sense of the word). Every nonconforming article contains one or more nonconformities. Where it is appropriate to make a total count of the nonconformities in each article, or in each group of an equal number of similar articles, it may be reasonable to use a control chart technique based on the Poisson distribution. This means either a c chart or a u chart.

The np chart, which was explained in Chap. 5, applies to the number of rejected items in subgroups of constant size. In contrast, the c chart applies to the number of nonconformities in subgroups of constant size. Each subgroup for the c chart usually is a single article; the variable c is the number of nonconformities observed in one article. But a c chart subgroup may be two or more articles. It is essential only that the subgroup size be constant in the sense that the different subgroups have *substantially equal opportunity for the occurrence of nonconformities.* When the opportunity for occurrence of nonconformities changes from subgroup to subgroup, the u chart for nonconformities per unit is available.

6.3 APPLICATIONS OF *c* CHART

While the c chart is not as inclusive as the $\overline{X}$ and R or p charts, it is still has a number of applications, some of which have been mentioned. Like the p chart, the c chart can be established for a single quality characteristic or a group of quality characteristics, a single machine or a group of machines, or for the entire product.

The c chart has been used to advantage in different situations.

1. It has been used in short studies to ascertain the variation, in quality of a characteristic or piece
2. It has been used for periodic sampling of production, where a certain number of nonconformities per unit are tolerable.
3. It has been used for 100% inspection where the primary aim is to reduce the cost of rework or scrap.
4. It has been used for scientific sampling procedures based on defects per units.

In all these situations the chart provides information on the current quality level and whether or not a state of control exists.

Because of the limitations of the c chart, many plants and industries do not have occasion to use it in quality control. The c chart has been used in nonmanufacturing situations such as highway accidents and clerical errors.

6.4 CALCULATION OF LIMITS FOR A C CHART

As stated earlier, the c chart is based on the poisson distribution. The standard deviation of the Poisson distribution is $\sqrt{\mu_c}$ (see Chap. 4). Thus 3 - sigma limits on a c chart are as follows:

$$UCL = \mu_c + 3\sqrt{\mu_c}$$

$$LCL = \mu_c - 3\sqrt{\mu_c}$$

When a standard value of average number of nonconformities per unit c_o is not used, μ_c may be estimated as equal to the observed average $\overline{c}$. This is always done in the calculation of trial control limits. In this case the control limits are

$$UCL = \overline{c} \quad \sqrt{\overline{c}}$$

$$LCL = \overline{c} - 3\sqrt{\overline{c}}$$

As the Poisson distribution is not symmetrical, the upper and lower 3-sigma limits do not correspond to l probabilities of a point on the control chart falling outside limits even though there has been no change in the universe. This fact has sometimes been advanced as a reason for the use of probability limits on c charts. The use of 0.995 and 0.005 probability limits has been favoured.

The position of limits corresponding either to these probabilities or to any other desired probabilities may readily be determined from Table G in App. 2. The use of this table is explained in Chap. 4.

The theoretical conditions for the applicability of the Poisson distribution call for the count of the number of occurrences of an event that has an infinite number of opportunities to occur and a very small constant probability of occurrence at each opportunity. (For practical purposes, "infinite" may be interpreted as meaning very large.) As already emphasized, the area of opportunity for occurrence at each count of occurrences must remain constant. However, as we have noted, the count may be of the occurrence of all of several different events, each with its own very large number of opportunities to occur and each with a different small probability of occurrence at every opportunity.

In a large proportion of the applications of the Poisson distribution to statistical quality control (or, for that matter, to all other practical affairs), it is possible to pick minor flaws in the theoretical applicability of the Poisson law to the actual situation. It may be evident that the number of opportunities for the occurrence of a nonconformity (or other event being counted) falls far short of being infinite. Or it may be clear that the unknown probability of occurrence of a nonconformity is not quite constant. Or it may not be possible to keep the area of opportunity exactly constant. As long as these are only minor failures to meet the exact conditions of applicability, the results obtained by assuming that the Poisson distribution is applicable are likely to be good enough for practical purposes.

Slight departures of the actual distribution from the true Poisson law usually will cause the standard deviation to be slightly greater than $\sqrt{\bar{c}}$. Limits based on $3\sqrt{\bar{c}}$ may really be at a little less than 3 sigma. This fact in itself generally does not justify discarding $3\sqrt{\bar{c}}$ or $3\sqrt{c_0}$ as a basis for calculating limits. In some situations to which the c chart is applied, such as records of numbers of nonconformities observed in inspections of complex assemblies, this use of limits a little tighter than 3 sigma may actually be desirable. As pointed out in Chap. 3 the economic basis of any control-chart limits is experience that the procedures used for their computation strike a satisfactory balance between the costs of two kinds of errors, namely, looking for assignable causes when they are really absent and not looking for them when they are really present.

In general, the c chart limits used in this book are based on $3\sqrt{\bar{c}}$ or $3\sqrt{c_0}$.

EXAMPLE 6.1: *Control chart for nonconformities*

Table 6.1 gives the number of nonconformities of a cosmetic nature for plastic canoes by an experienced inspector. These data are collected during the first and second weeks of May by inspecting random production samples. The nonconformities observed in each canoe constitute one subgroup for the control chart. Data shown in Table 6.1 are for 25 canoes, which is the minimum number of subgroups needed for trial control limit calculations. During inspection, the inspector made a note that 76 MY 132 and 76 MY 278 both had production difficulties. The reasoning for such observations is also indicated in Table 6.1.

TABLE 6.1: NUMBER OF COSMETIC NONCONFORMITIES (c) BY CANOE SERIAL NUMBER

Serial Number	*Number of nonconformties*	*Remarks*	*Serial Number*	*Number of nonconformties*	*Remarks*
76MY102	7		76MY198	3	
76MY113	6		76MY208	2	
76MY121	6		76MY222	7	
76MY125	3		76MY235	5	
76MY132	22	Mould sticking	76MY241	7	
76MY143	8		76MY258	2	
76MY150	6		76MY259	8	
76MY152	1		76MY264	0	
76MY164	0		76MY267	4	
76MY166	5		76MY278	14	Fell off skid
76MY172	14		76MY281	4	
76MY184	3		76MY288	3	
76MY185	1				
	Totals...			$\Sigma c = 141$	

The total number of nonconformities for 25 subgroups was 141. The average $\overline{c} = \dfrac{141}{25} =$ 5.64. Trial control limits computed from this average are as follows

$$UCL = \overline{c} + 3\sqrt{\overline{c}} = 5.64 + 3\sqrt{5.64} = 12.76$$

$$LCL = \overline{c} - 3\sqrt{\overline{c}} = 5.64 - 3\sqrt{5.64} = -1.48$$

Since a lower control limit of – 1.48 is impossible it is changed to zero. Figure 6.1 illustrates the control value, $\overline{c}$, the control limits, and the number of nonconformities, *c*, for each canoe of the preliminary data. This chart is only used to determine the revised control limits.

As a few points are falling outside the control limits, this value of $\overline{c}$ cannot be considered as the standard number nonconformities of c_o and discarding only those out of control points for which assignable causes are known (*i.e.* 76 MY 132 and 76 MY 278 only), co is computed as follows :

$$c_o = \frac{141 - (22 + 14)}{25 - 2} = 4.56$$

Based on above value of c_o, the revised control limits for the *c* chart are

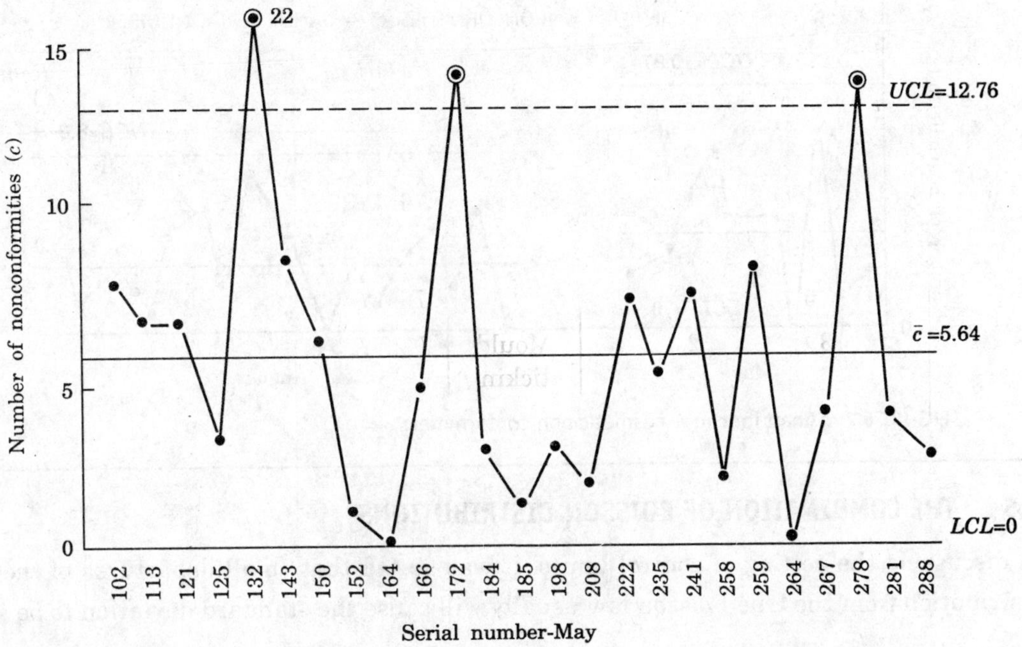

FIGURE 6.1: Control chart for number of defects (c chart), using preliminary data and trial control limits.

$$UCL = c_o + 3\sqrt{c_o}$$

$$= 4.56 + 3\sqrt{4.56} = 10.97$$

$$LCL = c_o - 3\sqrt{c_o} = 4.56 - 3\sqrt{4.56} = -1.85 \text{ or } 0$$

These control limits are used to start the chart beginning with canoes produced during the third week of May as per Table 6.2 and are shown in Fig. 6.2. It is noted that the lower control limit will be negative as long as c_o is less than 9 ; therefore it can be given the value of zero without the necessity of performing the calculations.

If c_o had been known, the data collection and trial control limit phase would have been unnecessary.

Continuing to use the c Chart As with the other types of control charts, an improvement in the quality is expected after the introduction of a chart. At the end of the initial period of use, a better estimate of the universal number of nonconformities can be obtained. Figure 6.2 illustrates the change in c_o and in the control limit for August as the chart is continued in use.

TABLE 6.2: Data for Chart for Canoe Cosmetic nonconformties for the month of May

Type of noncon- formity																											
Scratches	1		2		2		3			1				2					1	2	1		1			1		
Paint Imper-fections						1	2	1				1			3				1				1					3
Inden-tations	1		2						2			1					1		1	2							1	
Scuff Marks	1	1	5		3	4	3	5	2	2		4	1	2		1	2		1	3	1	5	2	1	2	2		3
Total	3	1	5	0	5	5	8	6	4	3	0	6	1	4	3	1	3	0	4	7	2	5	4	1	2	3	1	6
Serial -Number	305	310	321	354	373	409	441	469	485	487			129	150	178	185	209	230	260	283	303	321	347	359	407	471	485	493

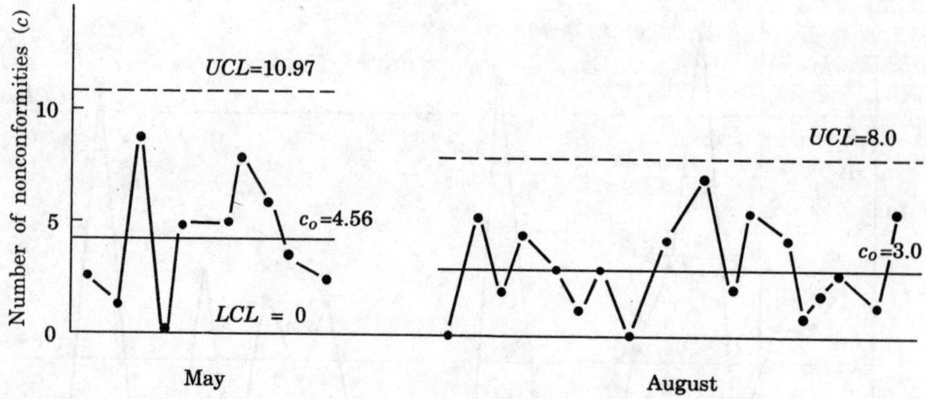

FIGURE 6.2: *c* Chart for canoe cosmetic non-conformities.

6.5 THE COMBINATION OF POISSON DISTRIBUTIONS

In discussing the setting of control limits, it was stated that small departures of the actual distribution from the true Poisson law usually will cause the standard deviation to be slightly greater than $\sqrt{\bar{c}}$. This departure from theoretical justification exists in all applications in which mixtures of inspection units each with different areas of opportunity for nonconformities are included. The effect of this departure is discussed in the following paragraphs.

Assume that the average number of surface imperfections observed in a piece of enameled ware of a certain size is 1.0 and that the frequency of these imperfections follows the Poisson law. If 1,000 such pieces are examined, the expected frequencies of the various numbers of imperfections may be determined from Table *G*, App. 1, to be as follows:

Number of imperfections	*Frequency in 1,000 observations*
0	368
1	368
2	184
3	61
4	15
5	3
Total	1,000

Now assume that the average number of surface imperfections is 3.0 in another piece of enameled ware having three times the area of the first. The expected frequencies of various numbers of imperfections in 1,000 pieces are as follows :

Number of imperfections	*Frequency in 1,000 observations*
0	50
1	149
2	224
3	224
4	168
5	101
6	50
7	22
8	8
9	3
10	1
Total	1,000

Suppose that these two pieces of enameled ware pass the same in inspection station and that the results of the inspection are recorded with no identification of whether the imperfections were observed on the small or the large pieces. If 1,000 pieces of each size pass the station, the expected frequencies in the total of 2,000 will be the sum of the two frequency distributions just given. The average number of surface imperfections per observed piece will of course be 2.0, the average of 1.0 and 3.0.

However, this *combined distribution will not follow the Poisson law*. This may be demonstrated by comparing it with the expected frequency distribution of 2,000 observations on a quality characteristic that does follow the Poisson law and that has on average value *c* of 2.0. Clearly, if the standard deviation of the mixed distribution is calculated from the data in the second column, the result will be numerically greater than the same calculation made from the data of the third column:

Number of imperfections	*Expected frequencies in 2,000 observations*	
	1,000 observations with $\bar{c}$ = 1.0 and 1,000 observations with $\bar{c}$ = 3.0	*2,000 observations with $\bar{c}$ = 2.0*
0	418	270
1	517	542
2	408	542
3	285	360
4	183	180
5	104	72
6	51	24
7	22	8
8	3	2
9	3	0
10	1	0
Totals	2,000	2,000

On the other hand, assume that one small and one large piece of enameled ware are fastened together in an assembly. If many such assemblies are made and inspected for surface imperfections, the average number of imperfections per assembly will, of course, be 1.0 + 3.0 = 4.0. If the pairing of the small and large pieces is done at random, the frequency distribution of the number of imperfections in the assemblies will follow the Poisson law. (This statement can be proved mathematically. However, no simple demonstration of it is given here, similar to the demonstration just given that the sum of two Poisson distributions having different averages is not a Poisson distribution.)

These two illustrations show one kind of combination of Poisson distributions that does not yield a Poisson distribution, and another combination of Poisson distribution that does. In the first case, two products, for which the area of opportunity for a nonconformity was different, passed the same inspection station. This situation is analogous to merging the output of two production lines prior to inspection. The average that may be expected to result from the combination is the weighted average of the two processes. That is,

$$\mu_{comb} = \frac{n_1\mu_{c1} + n_2\mu_{c2}}{n_1 + n_2} \quad ...(6.1)$$

$$= \frac{1{,}000(1.0) + 1{,}000(3.0)}{1{,}000 + 1{,}000} = 2.0$$

The result is a distribution that does not follow the Poisson law and does not have a standard deviation equal to that for the Poisson distribution where $\mu_c = 2.0$, that is, $\sigma_c = \sqrt{2.0}$.

In the second case, where assembly is assumed to take place at random, the resulting combination forms what is called a *linear combination* of random variables each of which follows the same law. This situation may be explained by first considering the drawing of a unit from Part 1, one of the smaller dishes, for example. This dish has d_1 imperfections. We can expect that upon drawing a dish at random from Part 2, the larger dish, and assembling it with the dish selected from Part 1, the combination will have $d_1 + \mu_{c2}$ total imperfections. Expanding this concept to cover all random assemblies of Parts 1 and 2, any assembly at random may be expected to have $\mu_{c1} + \mu_{c2}$ total imperfections. By definition, this type of combination is called a linear combination where

$$\mu_{comb} = \mu_{c1} + \mu_{c2} = 1.0 + 3.0 = 4.0$$

and will be Poisson-distributed with a standard deviation equal to $\sqrt{\mu_{comb}}$ if the parts that make up the assembly are Poisson-distributed.

Because the control chart for *c* uses limits based on the Poisson law, the preceding remarks on various ways of combining Poisson distributions have a bearing on quality control. They indicate that if Poisson limits are to be used, care should be taken to keep approximately constant the area of opportunity for the occurrence of a nonconformity. However, the *c* chart need not be restricted to a single type of nonconformity but may be used for the total of many different kinds of nonconformities observed on any unit. This adds another field of usefulness to those listed already, namely, a count of the total number of nonconformities of all types in complex products such as tractor subassemblies, television sets, computer chips, computer software, and the like.

6.6 ADAPTATIONS OF THE *c* CHART TO VARIATIONS IN THE AREA OF OPPORTUNITY FOR A NONCONFORMITY

The quantity c is the number of nonconformities observed in some specified inspection. Often this inspection is of a single unit of product, such as an airplane, a television set, or a roll of coated paper. In this common case where the subgroup size is unity, c is both the number of nonconformities and the number of nonconformities per unit. As already explained, the units should be alike in size and in the apparent likelihood of the existence of a nonconformity, in order that the area of opportunity for a nonconformity be constant from unit to unit.

However, it is not really necessary that the subgroup be a single unit of product. The unit for control-chart purposes (that is, the subgroup) may be 10 product units, or 100, or any other convenient number. Total nonconformities for each subgroup may be plotted just as if the subgroup were a single unit of product. Control charts for c using a fixed multiple of units are frequently used when the probability of a nonconformity is so small that a single unit of product is likely to have no nonconformities. As long as the number of product units does not change from subgroup to subgroup and each unit is essentially identical with all others, no special problem is created.

Whenever there is an evident change in the area of opportunity for occurrence of a nonconformity from subgroup to subgroup, the conventional c chart showing only total number of nonconformities is not applicable. It is necessary to create some standard measure of the area of opportunity. For example, if a number of units constitute a subgroup of size n, where n varies from subgroup to subgroup, nonconformities per unit (c/n) may be an appropriate control statistic. In such cases, if total nonconformities observed in each subgroup were plotted, the central line on the chart as well as the control limits would have to change from one subgroup to another. This would make the chart confusing and hard to interpret.

The symbol u is used to represent nonconformities per unit c/n where c is the count of nonconformities found and n may be the number of items, the number of square centimeters, or whatever standard unit of measure is used to establish the constant area of opportunity for the occurrence of a nonconformity. The central line on the u chart will be μ_u with standard 3-sigma limits of

$$UCL = \mu_u + \frac{3\sqrt{\mu_u}}{\sqrt{n_i}}$$

$$LCL = \mu_u - \frac{3\sqrt{\mu_u}}{\sqrt{n_i}}$$

Control limit lines on such a chart will vary with subgroup size, just as they do on the $\bar{X}$ chart and p chart. When a standard value of u is to be used, u_o is substituted for μu into the previous equations. When the average value $\bar{u}$ from a series of subgroups is to be used for trial control limits to test for a constant chance cause system and estimate μ_u, $\bar{u}$ is found from

$$\bar{u} = \frac{\Sigma c_i}{\Sigma n_i} = \frac{\text{total nonconformities found}}{\text{total measure units inspected}}$$

and the trial control limits are

$$UCL = \bar{u} + \frac{3\sqrt{\bar{u}}}{\sqrt{n_i}}$$

$$LCL = \bar{u} - \frac{3\sqrt{\bar{u}}}{\sqrt{n_i}}$$

It should be noted that the statistic u does not follow the Poisson distribution. However, the statistic nu does. Thus probabilities may be associated with specific points falling within or outside control limits using Table G in App. 2 and using the values of n for the individual subgroups.

6.7 THE *u* CHART FOR NONCONFORMITIES PER MULTIPLE UNITS

An adaptation of the u chart useful in clerical as well as industrial application is the ku chart for nonconformities per multiple units. An example of this type of chart involves counts of mistakes made per 100 worker-hours. Where nonconformities (or mistake) are very infrequent and the count of units produced is very large, it is necessary to scale the data if useful charts are to be prepared. The control statistic may be defined :

$$ku = \frac{c}{n/k}$$

$$= \frac{\text{no. of nonconformities}}{\text{no. of measure units/scaling factor}}$$

where k is the scaling factor; for example, 100 worker-hours and n is the total worker-hours in the subgroup.

The formulae for control limits are

$$UCL_{ku} = k\,\mu_u + 3\sqrt{\frac{k\,\mu_u}{n/k}}$$

$$LCL_{ku} = k\,\mu_u - 3\sqrt{\frac{k\,\mu_u}{n/k}}$$

A standard value uo or an average value u developed from sampling may be substituted as appropriate for μu in the above formulae.

For a process with a standard value of 4 mistakes per 100 worker-hours, a subgroup of 250 worker-hours would have control limits of

$$UCL_{ku} = 4 + 3\sqrt{\frac{4}{250/100}}$$

$$= 7.79$$

$$LCL_{ku} = 4 - 3\sqrt{\frac{4}{250/100}}$$

$$= 0.21$$

6.8 CLASSIFICATION OF NONCONFORMITIES AND THEIR WEIGHTING

Some defects (that is, nonconformities) are more serious than others. In an overall picture of quality by departments to be presented to management, there may be an advantage in weighting defects according to some scale that measures their seriousness. Such a plan has been in use in many industries, particularly in industries dealing in appliances.

Quality is measured by 'indicators of non-conformance', where defects are classified into four types:

'Critical' (C) — defects dangerous for the user. Will surely cause operating failure of the unit in service which cannot be readily connected on the job, e.g., open induction coil, transmitter without carbon, etc.

'Primary' (P) — defect causing product failure in service. Will surely cause increased maintenance or decreased life

'Secondary' (S) — defects that permit the product to work.

'Tertiary' (T) — aesthetic defects. Will not cause operating failure of the unit in service.

So, for example, the indicators of non-conformance for a washing machine would be as follows:

- the *Safety Index* (SI) is $1000 \times C/N$ where C is the number of critical defects after six working cycles of the product, and N is the number of products tasted;
- the *Quality Index* (QI) is $1000 \times P/N$ where P is the number of serious or major defects after working cycle of the product, and N is the number of products tested;
- the *Confidence Index* (CI) is similar to the preceding index but the defects P are counted after six working cycles;
- the *Reliability Index* (RI) is similar to the preceding index but the defects P are counted after 60 working cycles.
- the *Mean Quality Index* (MQI) taken daily is defined as

  $1000 \times (B + 0.5 \times C + 0.1 \times T)/N$, with P referred to only one working cycle.

Modern procedures often divide the various possible defects of a product (in the sense of nonconformity of specifications) into three or four classes, depending on the seriousness of the different defects. A. V. Feigenbaum describes a fourfold classification as follows.

A *critical* characteristic is one which threatens loss of **life or** property or makes the product nonfunctional if it was outside prescribed limits.

A *major* characteristic is one which makes the product fail to accomplish its intended function if outside prescribed limits.

A *minor* characteristic is one which makes the product fall short of its intended function if outside prescribed limits.

An *incidental* characteristic is one that will have no unsatisfactory effect on customer quality.

Another formal classification of defects is discussed in detail in Sec. 10.11 of Chap. 10.

Once such a classification of all defects is established, demerits may then be assigned to each class of defect. Control charts may be plotted for demerits per unit rather than for defects per unit. Quality rating schemes based on demerits per unit may be an important feature of both supplier rating and quality audit procedures.

6.9 *Q* CHARTS FOR QUALITY SCORES AND *D* CHARTS FOR DEMERIT CLASSIFICATIONS

Two modifications of the *c* chart (or *u* chart) may prove useful where multiple characteristics of varying importance are recorded. Most frequently such charts are used as management tools to indicate where attention should be concentrated and to indicate relative levels of quality over a period of time. They may be applied to incoming materials and products as well as to in-process control.

The first of these charts is the Q chart, or quality score chart. Under this scheme, weighting factors wj are assigned to each defect class j. Defect weights may be based simply on the type of nonconformity or may differ by the extent of the nonconformity as well as by class. For example, one defect class may be a surface scratch. The weighting applied to surface scratches would increase with the length of the scratch as well as its depth or visibility to the customer. Very specific definitions of the weights must be prepared in such cases to achieve uniformity in inspection.

The control statistic for the Q chart is

$$Q_i = \sum_j w_j c_{ij} \text{ for subgroup i}$$

The control limits and central line are

$$UCL_Q = \sum w_j \bar{c}_j + 3\sqrt{\sum w_j^2 \bar{c}_j}$$

$$\bar{Q} = \sum w_j \bar{c}_j$$

$$LCL_Q = \sum w_j \bar{c}_j - 3\sqrt{\sum w_j^2 \bar{c}_j}$$

where $c = \sum_i \bar{c}_{ij}/k$, and $0 < wj < 1$, and i is the sample or subgroup number ($i = 1, 2, \ldots k$). Thus Q is a weighted average of the count of nonconformities. Aimed-at or standard values c_{oj} may be substituted for $\bar{c}_j$ in these calculations.

The demerit control chart, or D chart, formulates identically with the Q chart except in the weighting factors applied. Frequently it is used in conjunction with a formal classification of characteristics such as those described by Dodge and Feigenbaum. Whereas the Q chart applies weightings to nonconformities (perhaps by intensity of the nonconformity), the D chart assigns demerits that usually range between 1 and 100. A possible scheme for these weightings is

Critical—100
Major—40
Minor—20
Incidental—1

The control statistic is

$$D_i = \sum_j d_j c_{ij} \text{ for subgroup}$$

The control limits and central line are

$$UCL_D = \sum d_j \bar{c}_j + 3\sqrt{\sum d_j^2 \bar{c}_j}$$

$$= \sum d_j \bar{c}_j$$

$$LCL_D = \sum d_j \bar{c}_j - 3\sqrt{\sum d_j^2 \bar{c}_j}$$

where $\overline{c}_j = \sum_i C_{ij}/k$ and i is the sample or subgroup number. Aimed-at or standard values c_{oj} may be substituted for $\overline{c}_j$ in these calculations. Using c_{oj} implies an intent to illustrate how a process is performing. Using c_{oj} implies an intent to apply pressure to bring a process to no worse than the stipulated level.

Points out of control on Q and D charts are harder to interpret than on the standard c chart and do not necessarily direct attention to the causes of a problem. It may prove more desirable to use several c charts for process analysis purposes, one for each classification, reserving the Q and D chart for upper-level management reporting.

6.10 USE OF $3\sqrt{c}$ FOR APPROXIMATE CALCULATION OF CONTROL LIMITS IN SITUATIONS INVOLVING THE BINOMIAL DISTRIBUTION

It often happens that a quick calculation of control limits is useful in some situation where no actual control chart has been plotted. If this is needed in any case to which the binomial is applicable as a probability distribution, it is handy to remember that the standard deviation of the Poisson $\sqrt{c}$ is an approximation to $\sqrt{np(1-p)}$. Even though the binomial itself is only an approximation to the correct probability obtainable by the use of combinatorial formulas, $3\sqrt{c}$ often provides a basis for rapid mental arithmetic about control limits that may be good enough for practical purposes.

For example, assume that product submitted under a purchase contract has been 0.4% nonconforming. The question is raised as to what variation in number of nonconforming items may be expected in lots of 1,000. The expected average number of such items in such lots is obviously 4. As $3\sqrt{4} = 6$, the answer is that nonconforming items might generally be expected to fall between 0 and 10 in lots of 1,000. The occurrence of 11 or more nonconforming items in such a lot would be evidence of an assignable cause of variation.

6.11 APPLICABILITY OF *c* CHART TECHNIQUE IN FIELDS OTHER THAN STATISTICAL PROCESS CONTROL

Like all control charts, the c chart gives evidence regarding the quality level, its variability, and the presence or absence of assignable causes of variation. This is useful information as a basis for action in many other fields besides industrial quality control. The universal nature of the Poisson distribution as the law of small numbers makes the c chart technique broadly useful. For example, it may be applied to such diverse phenomena as pollution abatement, industrial accidents, and highway accidents. In all these fields, action should often be based on evidence of assignable causes of variation, and it is important to note changes in the average value of the variable being studied.

6.12 INTERCHANGEABILITY OF *p* AND *c* CHARTS

The subgroup size for a p chart is obviously reasonably large and if the fraction nonconforming is also expected to be small, Poisson provides a good approximation to theoretically more nearly correct binomial earlier. Consequently, provided that the subgroup size is constant, a *c* chart may be plotted instead of a *p* chart by regarding *c* as 'number of nonconforming items per subgroup instead of 'number of nonconformities per unit'. The reverse, plotting of a *p* chart instead of a *c* chart cannot be done since 'number of nonconformities per unit' cannot be expressed as a fraction, the total possible being theoretically infinite.

6.13 OPERATING CHARACTERISTIC FUNCTION

The operating-characteristic (*OC*) curves for both the *c* chart and the *u* chart can be obtained from the Poisson distribution for the *c* chart. The *OC* curve plots the probability of *Type II* error

(β) against the true mean number of nonconformities *c*. The expression for (β) is

$$\beta = P\{X < UCL \mid c\} - P\{X \leq LCL \mid c\}$$

where *X* is a Poisson random variable with parameter *c*.

SOLVED QUESTIONS

Q. 6.1: *Contribute charts for non conformities are used when*

(a) number of items inspected and number of non conformities is known.

(b) Occurrence of an item for unit is known.

(c) data relates to a continuous variate.

(d) there are discontinuities in the value of attributes.

Ans: (*b*)

Q. 6.2: *(a) What is a control chart?*

(b) Name any one control chart for nonconformities. What does this chart show?

(c) What is the basis of a c chart?

Ans: (*a*) A control chart is an evaluation tool in SPC.

(*b*) *c*-chart is one control chart for nonconformities or defects. It shows the number or nonconformities or defects in a unit.

(*c*) Poisson distribution.

Q. 6.3: *(a) You are shown a c chart. You observe that LCL_c is 0 and nearer to mean line as compared to UCL_c from the mean line. What is your explanation to this?*

(b) Is it due to different sigma values for UCL_c and LCL_c?

Ans: (*a*) Since lower control limit on a *c* chart cannot be negative (as the number of defects & cannot be negative). Whenever by calculations, the LCL_c values comes out to be negative, it is considered as zero and hence nearer to the mean lines as compared UCL_c.

(*b*) In a control chart equal $k\sigma$ values is allocated *UCL* and *LCL*. Hence it is not due to different *k* value. The primary reason is explained in (*a*).

Q. 6.4: *Ten airplane wings were inspected for nonconforming welds. The number of nonconforming welds per wing ranged from 26 to 55. The total number of nonconforming welds for the 10 units was 360. Determine the average and the standard deviation of the Poisson distribution as required for a c chart. Also determine UCL and LCL for a c chart.*

Ans: The average number of non conforming welds per wing is

$$\bar{c} = \frac{360}{10} = 36$$

The standard deviation of the Poisson distribution is

$$\sqrt{\bar{c}} = \sqrt{36} = 6$$

The *UCL* and *LCL* for the c chart are the customary ± 3 σ away from $\bar{c}$. Hence,

$$UCL = \bar{c} + 3\sqrt{\bar{c}}$$

$$= 36 + 3\sqrt{36} = 54$$

$$LCL = \bar{c} - 3\sqrt{\bar{c}}$$

$$= 36 - 3\sqrt{36} = 54$$

Q. 6.5: *The following table gives the number of errors of alignment observed at final inspection of a certain model of aeroplane. Prepare a c chart and comment on the picture revealed by the chart.*

Aeroplane number	*alignment errors*	*Aeroplane number*	*Alignment errors*	*Aeroplane number*	*No. of alignment errors*
201	7	210	9	219	13
202	6	211	8	220	7
203	6	212	5	221	8
204	7	213	5	222	15
205	4	214	9	223	6
206	7	215	8	224	6
207	8	216	15	225	10
208	12	217	6		
209	9	218	4		

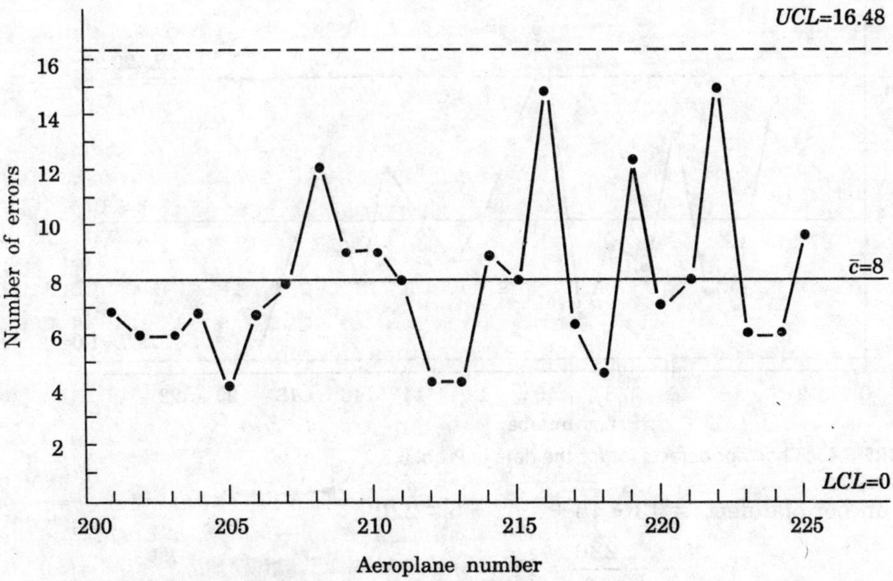

FIGURE 6.3 Control chart for the data in Prob. 6.2.

Ans:

$$\Sigma c = 7 + 6 + \ldots\ldots + 6 + 10 = 200$$

$$\bar{c} = \frac{200}{25} = 8$$

$$UCL = \bar{c} + 3\sqrt{\bar{c}} = 8 + 3\sqrt{8} = 16.24$$

$$LCL = 8 - 3\sqrt{8} = 8 - 3 \times 2.824 < 0 \text{ and hence taken as 0}$$

The control chart for errors is shown in Fig. 6.3.

It is clear from the chart that none of 25 points falls outside the control limits and there is not any particular trend of the points on the chart to create any suspicion, it may be presumed that the process is in a state of statistical control.

Q. 6.6: *The table given below represents a listing of the number of mechanical defects observed on lots of 10 miniature wormgear drives drawn daily from the line. This is a pilot production run lasting 20 days. Construct a c chart and plot the points.*

Suppose the reasons for out of control situation (Lot No. 10) are known, what is your decision regarding the control limits for future use ?

Lot No.	*Number of Defects*	*Lot No.*	*Number of Defects*
1	13	11	17
2	15	12	11
3	19	13	7
4	8	14	11
5	6	15	14
6	17	16	6
7	7	17	16
8	9	18	10
9	3	19	2
10	23	20	6

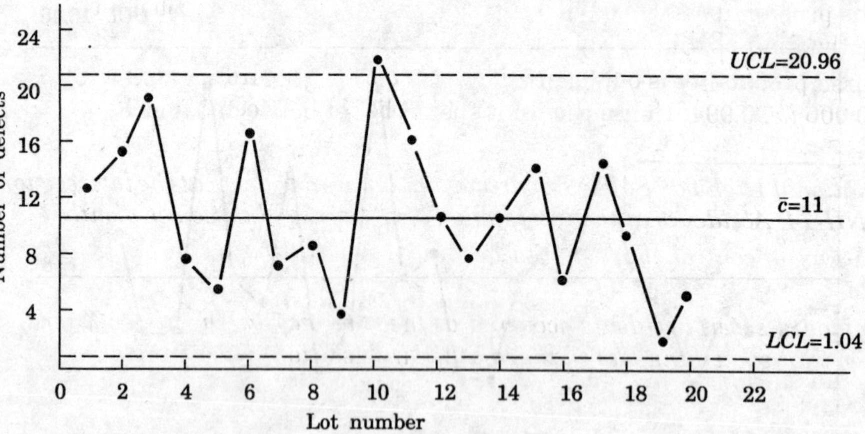

FIGURE 6.4 c Chart for defects lot for the data in Prob. 6.3.

Ans: Total number of defects = 13 + 15 +......2 + 6 = 220

$$\bar{c} = \frac{220}{20} = 11$$

$$UCL = \bar{c} + 3\sqrt{\bar{c}} = 11 + 3\sqrt{11} = 20.96$$

$$LCL = \bar{c} - 3\sqrt{\bar{c}} = 11 - 3\sqrt{11} = 1.04$$

The control chart for the data is shown in Fig. 6.4.

From the chart it is evident that Lot No. 10 is out of control. Since the reasons for out-of-control for this lot are known, eliminating this lot, revised $\bar{c}$ is as follows :

$$\bar{c}_{revised} = \frac{220 - 23}{20 - 1} = \frac{197}{19} = 10.37$$

$$UCL = \bar{c} + 3\sqrt{\bar{c}} = 10.37 + 3\sqrt{10.37}$$

$$= 20.03$$

$$LCL = \bar{c} - 3\sqrt{\bar{c}}$$

$$= 10.37 - 3\sqrt{10.37}$$

$$= 0.71$$

Hence 20.04 and 0.71 are the control limits for future use.

Q. 6.7: *You have been asked to construct a chart to control the number of shut-downs per week on an assembly line in a computer manufacturing plant (the line is shut down when a serious quality problem has been discovered). Over the past two years the average number of shut-downs per week has been 5.2.*

(a) Where would you place the limit on the chart to detect an increase in the number of shut-downs, if the company requires the limit to be exceed only once in a hundred weeks when the process is stable?

(b) If you wished to include a lower limit on the chart to detect significant improvements, and again a level of 1 in 100 is to be used to determine the position of the limit, where would it be placed?

Ans: $\bar{c} = 5.2$

(*a*) Required probability outside the limit is 0.01 or less From Table a, for μ_c of 5.2, we find for *c* of 11, the probability is 1 – 0.986 *i.e.* 0.014 and for *c* of 12 the probability is 1 – 0.993 *i.e.* 0.007. Hence the limit should be set between 11 and 12.

(*b*) Required probability is outside the lower is 0.99. Again from Table *G* for μ_c of 5.2, P_1 or more is 1 – 0.006 *i.e.* 0.994. Hence the limit should be set between 0 and 1.

Q. 6.8: *The National Highway Safety Department monitors accidents at the intersection of Routes NH-12 and NH-14. Accidents at the intersection have averaged three per month.*

(i) Which type of control chart should be used? Construct a control chart with three-sigma control limits.

(ii) Last month seven accidents occurred at the intersection. In this sufficient evidence to justify a claim that something has changed at the intersection?

Ans:

(*i*) The safety department can't determine the number of accidents that did not occur, so it has no way to compute *p* at the intersection. Therefore the administrators must use a *c* chart for which

$$UCL_c = \bar{c} + 3\sqrt{\bar{c}} = 3 + 3\sqrt{3} = 8.20$$

$$LCL_c = \bar{c} - 3\sqrt{\bar{c}} = 3 - 3\sqrt{3} = -2.196$$

There can't be a negative number of accidents, so the lower control limit in this case is adjusted to 'zero'.

(*ii*) The number of accidents last month falls within the upper and lower control limits of the chart. We conclude that no assignable causes are present and that the increase in accidents was due to chance.

Q. 6.9: *Tabulate the expected frequency in 2,000 observations, 1,000 of which come from a Poisson distribution with $\bar{c}$ = 0.5 and 1,000 from a Poisson distribution with $\bar{c}$ = 1.5.*

The $\bar{c}$ of the combined distribution is, of course 1.0. Assume that a c chart is established with UCL at $3\sqrt{\bar{c}}$ above the centre line on the chart. Consult the table prepared by you and indicate how many observations out of 2,000 would fall above this UCL. What objections can you see to the use of a single control chart in this type of situation ?

Ans: From Table G, for $\bar{c}$ = 0.5 and $\bar{c}$ = 1.5, the expected number of nonconformities are tabulated below.

Now, when $\bar{c} = 1.0$

$$UCL = 1 + 3\sqrt{1} = 4.0$$

When $\bar{c}$ = 1.5, frequency of more than 4 defects is

= 15 + 3 + 1 = 19 (from the table).

Hence only 19 observations will fall above the *UCL*.

Nonconformities	*$\bar{c}$ = 0.5 Frequency in 1,000 observations*	*Nonconformities*	*$\bar{c}$ = 1.5 Frequency in 1,000 observations*
0	607	0	223
1	303	1	335
2	76	2	251
3	12	3	125
4	2	4	47
		5	15
		6	3
		7	1
Total	1,000	Total	1,000

Objections: The *c* chart is based on Poisson distribution but in the present case the distribution cannot be classified as Poisson distribution.

In general, a frequency distribution will not follow the Poisson law if some of the frequencies recorded refer to the number of occurrences of one event that follows the Poisson law and the remaining frequencies recorded refer to the number of occurrences of another event that also follow the Poisson law but has a different average. In view of this separate control limits must be used for the two distributions.

Q. 6.10: *Phragyle Products Ltd. supply limitation glass decanters to the hotel trade. Because of the delicate nature of the manufacturing process, each decanter is expected to have some minor blemishes, most of which are completely visible to the naked eye. These very minor blemishes may occur almost every where on the product and are not usually sufficient to lead to the rejection of the item. Nevertheless, the Sales Manager of Phragyle Products is anxious to investigate the* *efforts of recent efforts that the manufacturers claim to have made to improve the manufacturing process and the quality of the products supplied to Phragyle.*

Prior to modifications to the process, each decanter has an average of five almost imperceptible blemishes. The table below shows the number of blemishes on every fifth decanter for a short period after the claimed improvement in manufacture. Comment on the process of adjustments to the supposed manufacturing process.

No. of blemishes per product :

6, 7, 6, 5, 6, 7, 7, 6, 8, 7, 7, 7, 6, 8, 9, 8, 7, 8, 9, 8, 8, 7

Ans:

$$\bar{c} = 5$$

$$UCL = 5 + 3\sqrt{5} = 11.7$$

$$LCL = 5 - 3\sqrt{5} < 0 \text{ and is taken as zero.}$$

Control chart for the number of blemishes per product is shown in Fig. 6.5.

From the control chart, it is evident that even though no point crosses the upper control limit, yet the process is not in control because the distribution of points is not random as no points falls below the central line. Hence the claim made by manufacturer is doubtful.

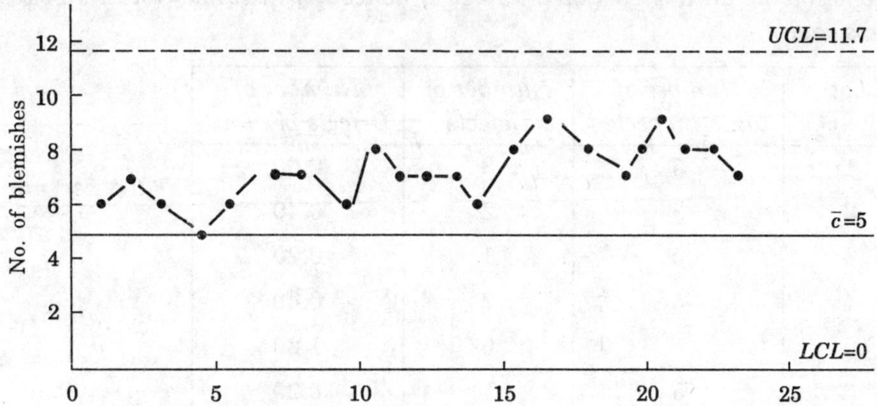

FIGURE 6.5. Control Chart for blemishes of the data

Q. 6.11: *20 samples of cloth, each of equal length and width were examined in order to launch a quality control programme. The number of nonconformities observed per sample are shown below.*

Sample No.	1	2	3	4	5	6	7	8	9	10
No. of Errors	1	4	4	1	6	3	5	10	7	3
Sample No.	11	12	13	14	15	16	17	18	19	20
No. of Errors	2	5	9	8	4	2	7	2	6	4

Draw the control chart. Is the process in control ?

Ans: The appropriate control chart will be the c chart.

$$\Sigma c = 1 + 4 \ldots\ldots + 6 + 4 = 93$$

$$\bar{c} = \frac{93}{20} = 4.65$$

$$UCL = \bar{c} + 3\sqrt{\bar{c}} = 4.65 + 3\sqrt{4.65} = 11.12$$

$$LCL = \bar{c} - 3\sqrt{\bar{c}} = 4.65 - 3\sqrt{4.65} < 0 \text{, therefore } 0$$

The chart is shown in Fig. 6.6.

From the points on the chart, it is evident that process is in state of control.

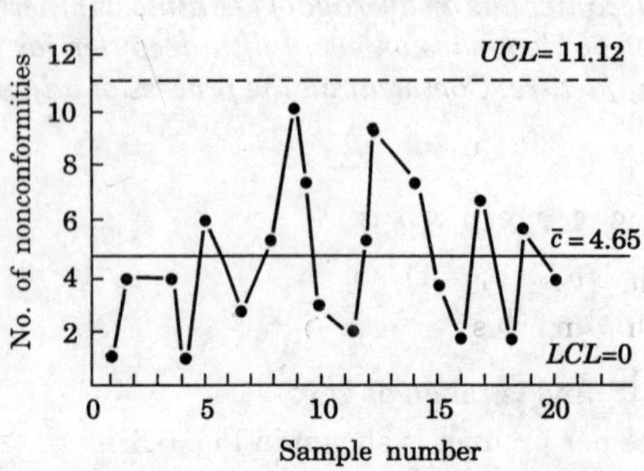

FIGURE 6.6 Control chart for the data in Prob. 6.8

Q. 6.12: *The following data shows the number of nonconformities per lot in 15 successive lots of 5 radio sets each.*

Lot Number	*Number of units Inspected*	*Number of Defects*	*Number of Defects per unit*
1	5	3	0.60
2	5	2	0.40
3	5	1	0.20
4	5	2	0.40
5	5	6	1.20
6	5	1	0.20
7	5	3	0.60
8	5	2	0.40
9	5	0	0.00
10	5	0	0.00
11	5	0	0.00
12	5	0	0.00
13	5	0	0.00
14	5	1	0.20
15	5	2	0.40
	$\Sigma n = 75$	$\Sigma c = 23$	

Plot the control chart based on the above data. Suppose the reasons for out of control point are known and can be eliminated what will you suggest the upper control limit for future production.

Ans: In this case either a *c* chart or a *u* chart can be plotted. For using a *u* chart, the computations are :

$$\bar{u} = \frac{23}{75} = 0.31$$

$$UCL = 0.31 + 3\sqrt{\frac{0.31}{0.5}} = 1.06$$

$$LCL = 0.31 - 3\sqrt{\frac{0.31}{0.5}} < 0, \text{ and hence considered as 0}$$

The control chart is shown in Fig. 6.7.

From the control chart it is evident that lot No. 5 is out of control. Since the assignable causes are known for this out of control, eliminating this for calculation for u_0 future production

$$u_0 = \frac{23-6}{75-5} = \frac{17}{70} = 0.24$$

$$UCL = 0.24 + 3\sqrt{\frac{0.24}{5}} = 0.90$$

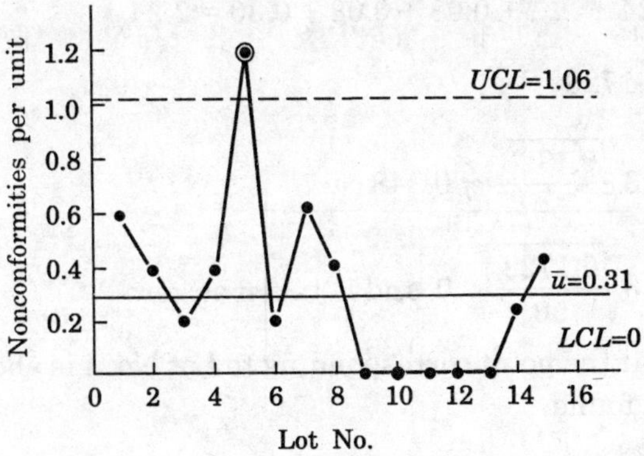

FIGURE 6.7 Control chart for the data

$$LCL = 0.24 - 3\sqrt{\frac{0.24}{5}} < 0. \text{ and hence considered as 0}$$

Q. 6.13: *(a) You are shown 5 control charts for nonconformities for the same product and same quality characteristics. You make the following observations :*

Chart	*Observation*
1	*Two consecutive points fall in the top sixth of the control range*
2	*A trend run of points upward occurs*
3	*An extreme run of points occurs above the central line*
4	*A point outside the upper control limit*
5	*A cyclic run of point*

What common conclusion can you draw regarding these 5 charts ? Give the reason on which your conclusion is based.

(b) Table below refers to the 'average number outlet leaks' per radiator for 13 lots of 50 radiators each.

Lot number	*Number of leaks c*	*Leaks per radiator u*	*Lot number*	*Number of leaks c*	*Leaks per radiator u*
1	10	0.20	8	16	0.32
2	12	0.24	9	4	0.08
3	11	0.22	10	1	0.02
4	20	0.40	11	10	0.20
5	5	0.10	12	4	0.08
6	2	0.04	13	15	0.30
7	2	0.04			

Assume no assignable causes were discovered, establish uo for the future production.

Ans: (*a*) All the 5 charts are *out of control* because there are such unlikely chance in random sampling making it highly probable that assignable causes have entered the process to create quality troubles.

(*b*)

$$\Sigma u = 0.20 + 0.24 + ... + 0.08 + 0.08 + 0.30 = 2.24$$

$$\bar{u} = \frac{2.24}{13} = 0.1723$$

$$UCL = 0.1723 + 3\sqrt{\frac{0.1723}{50}} = 0.348$$

$$LCL = 0.1723 - 3\sqrt{\frac{0.1723}{50}} < 0 \text{ and is taken as zero.}$$

On plotting the chart it will be found that the point corresponding to Lot No. 4 is above the *UCL*. Since no assignable causes have been found,

$$\bar{u} = u_0 = 0.1723$$

Q. 6.14: *A company proposes to modify its paper-making process using pulp from a foreign supplier, rather than its normal domestic suppliers. It wants to be sure that it can use this raw material in its paper-maing operation and obtain the same quality paper as it does not domestic pulp. Prior to running the foreign pulp, it takes paper from its normal suppliers for one week and analyse the blemishes on the paper. On a total of 32 m² of paper tested during one week it found 350 blemishes. The company then ran the paper-making machines with the foreign pulp and in the five bobbins of paper tested it obtained the average blemishes per square metre on the paper as shown in the accompanying table.*

(Average blemishes per square metre on the paper made from the foreign pulp)

Sample No.	*Average blemishes per square metre*
1	*30*
2	*19*
3	*6*
4	*25*
5	*3*

As consultant you are required to:

1. *Establish a c chart for 3s control limits using the domestic paper test. If you computations shown $LCL_c > 0$, is it advisable to deep LCL_c as zero.*
2. *Show the information from the foreign paper on the control chart. What are your comments about the foreign paper ? Do you have any suggestion (s) ?*

Ans: $\bar{c} = \frac{350}{20} = 10.9375 \approx 10.94$

$$\sigma_c = \sqrt{10.9375} = 3.31$$

$$UCL_c = 10.9375 + 3\,(3.31) = 20.86$$

$$LCL_c = 10.9375 - 3\,(3.31) = 1.02$$

With above data, the *c* chart for foreign paper can be plotted now.

2. From the chart it can immediately be observed that the quality of paper seems erratic. Two averages are outside the limits, one is just in the vicinity of the *UCL* an two averages are below the control line. In view of above, the company should analyse the quality of the raw material and perhaps re-evaluate the operating procedures, such as drying time, tension etc., for paper making using the new raw material.

Q. 6.15: *The Zeeland Paper Company produces paper for the newspaper industry. As a final step, the paper passes through a machine that measures various quality characteristics. When the process is in control, its averages 20 defects per roll.*

(a) *Which type of control chart is appropriate in this type of work? Name this chart in SPC parlance.*

(b) *What are the upper and control limits of this chart?*

(c) *What are the 2σ warning (sometimes also called a tight control / warning limits) of this chart?*

(d) *If the latest roll sampled contained 27 defects, is the process in control?*

(e) *If the latest roll contained only 5 defects, is the process in control?*

Ans: (*a*) In this case, "control chart for defects" is the most appropriate. In SPC parlance this is know *c* chart

(*b*) $\bar{c} = 20$

$UCL_c = 20 + 3\sqrt{20} = 33.41$; $LCL_c = 20 - 3\sqrt{20} = 6.39$

(c) 2s Warning limits:

$UWL_c = 20 + 2\sqrt{20} = 33.41$; $LWL_c = 20 - 2\sqrt{20} = 6.39$

(*d*) Because the latest roll had only 27 defects, or les than the upper control limit, the process is in control.

(*e*) Five defects is less than the lower control limit and therefore the process is technically "out of control". However, the control chart indicates that something good has happened. Management should find the assignable causes and exploit it in order to reduce the avaerage number of defects.

Q. 6.16: *A control chart for nonconformities per unit u uses probability limits corresponding to probabilities of 0.975 and 0.025. The central line on the control is at $u_0 = 2.0$. The limits vary with the value of n. Determine the correct position of these upper and lower control limits when n = 5.*

Ans: It is know that u_0 is not Poisson distributed but nu_0 is. Therefore to use Table *G*,

$$c = nu_o = 5 \times 2.0 = 10$$

Entering Table *G* at a c_0 of 10, the following cumulative probabilities are obtained for pertinent value of c_o :

c_o	*Probability*
3	0.010
4	0.029
16	0.973
17	0.986

Interpolating for probability values of 0.025 and 0.975 in the above table, the probability limits are 3.79 and 16.15 respectively.

Hence for *u* chart the probability limits will be $\frac{3.79}{5}$ and $\frac{16.15}{5}$ *i.e.*, 0.76 and 3.23.

Q. 6.17: *A c chart is used to monitor the number of surface imperfections on sheets of photographic film. The chart presently is set up based on a $\bar{c}$ of 2.6.*

(a) Find 3 σ control limits for this process.

(b) Use Table G to determine the probability that a point will fall outside these control limits while the process actually operating at a c of 2.6.

(c) If the process average shifts to 4.8, what is the probability of not detecting the shift on the first sample taken after the shift occurs ?

Ans: (*a*)

$$\bar{c} = 2.6$$

$$UCL = \bar{c} + 3\sqrt{\bar{c}}$$

$$= 2.6 + 3\sqrt{2.6} = 7.44$$

$$LCL = \bar{c} - 3\sqrt{\bar{c}} = 2.6 - 3\sqrt{2.6}$$

$$= -2.2 \text{ and hence taken as zero.}$$

(*b*) Since the *LCL* is zero, the probability for a point to fall outside *UCL* is to be considered only. Entering Table *G* at *c* of 2.6, the probability of a point crossing the *UCL* of 7.44 is 0.005 (by interpolation).

(*c*) When $c = 4.8$, the probability of first sample falling between the control limits is determined by entering Table *G* at *c* of 4.8 and finding the cumulative probability up to 7.44. From Table *G*, by interpolation this is 0.887. Hence the probability that a shift is not detected on the first sample after the shift is 0.887.

Q. 6.18: *Solve the Q. 6.17 using* **0.01** *and* **0.99** *probability limits rather than 3 σ limits. What is the actual probability of a Type I error in this case as opposed to the planned probability* **0.02** *?*

Explain the difference in results obtained in Q 6.13 and this problem.

Ans: As in Q. 6.17, $c = 2.6$.

Entering Table *G* at a $\bar{c}$ of 2.6, the following cumulative probabilities are obtained for pertinent values of *c*.

c	Probability
0	0.074
6	0.983
7	0.995

From above it is evident that *LCL* will be at zero and *UCL* will be at 6.58.

From the definition of Type *I* error, the probability of any point falling beyond control limits is the Type *I* error. Since in this case *LCL* is zero therefore *Type I* error is the probability of any point falling above *UCL*. Since *UCL* is at 0.099 probability limit, the *Type I* error is 0.01 only as opposed to the planned probability of 0.02.

As in Q. 6.17, when the process average shifts to 4.8, from Table *G* by interpolation the probability of first sample falling between the control limits is 0.847. Hence the probability that a shift is not detected on the first sample after the shift is 0.847. The difference in results is evident due to different probability limits in Problem 6.10, and this Problem. In Problem 6.10, 3 sigma limits are approximately 99.73% probability limits, which are more than the probability limits specified in this question.

Q. 6.19: *A c chart is used to monitor surface imperfections on porcelain enameled water heater cabinets. Each cabinet is checked for nonconformities of a certain grade and the count entered on the c chart. Two limits are used on the chart ; a control limit at* $+3\,\sigma$ *and a warning limit at* $+2\,\sigma$. *If a point falls above the control limit, the process is stopped until the problem is corrected. The central line is set at an aimed-at value of* c_0 *of 2.5.*

(a) Find the values of the warning limit and the control limit.

(b) If the process suddenly shifts to mean value of 5, what is the probability that a point will fall above the control limits.

(c) Under the circumstances described in part (b), what is the probability that two points in a row will fall between the warning limit and the control limit ?

(d) What is the combined probability of detection of this shift within the first two units inspected after the shift occurs ?

Ans: $c_0 = 2.5$

(*a*) $+3\,\sigma$ control limit $= c_0 + 3\sqrt{c_0}$

$= 2.5 + 3\sqrt{2.5} = 7.24$

$+2\,\sigma$ warning limit $= c_0 + 2\sqrt{c_0}$

$= 2.5 + 2\sqrt{2.5} = 5.66$

(*b*) When $c = 5$, from Table *G*, the probability of a point above the control limit is 0.883.

(*c*) Probability of a point falling upto warning limit of 5.66, as computed by interpolation from Table G is 0.712.

Hence the probability of any point between warning limit and control limit is 0.883 – 0.712 *i.e.* 0.171.

Probability that two points in a row between control limit and warning limit is $(0.171)^2 =$ 0.029.

(*d*) The probability that a shift is detected within first two samples can be determined by considering the following :

1. First point falls above control limit.

2. First and second points fall between warning and control limits. 3. Second point falls above control limit.

From the calculations made in parts (*b*) and (*c*).
Probability of first point above control limit = 1 – 0.883 = 0.117
Probability of first two points in a row between the warning limit and control limit = 0.029
Probability of second point above control limit = 0.117
Hence probability of shift detection = 0.117 + 0.029 + 0.117 = 0.263.

Q. 6.20: *A textile manufacturer initiates use of a c chart to monitor the number of imperfections found in bolt of cloth. Each bolt is the same length, width, weave, and fibre composition. A total of 191 imperfections were found in the last 25 bolts inspected. The four highest and lowest counts were :*

Count of imperfections	
Highest	*Lowest*
22	4
19	4
14	5
12	5

(a) Calculate 3 σ control limits for this process.

(b) Is the process in control ? If not, what aimed-at value of c0 and control limits would you recommend for the next period ?

Ans:
$$\bar{c} = \frac{\text{ü}}{25} = 7.64$$

(*a*)
$$UCL = \bar{c} + 3\sqrt{\bar{c}} = 7.64 + 3\sqrt{7.64} = 15.93$$
$$LCL = \bar{c} - 3\sqrt{\bar{c}} = 7.64 - 3\sqrt{7.64} = -0.65 \text{ and is taken as zero.}$$

(*b*) Since two points (22 ; 19) are above the control limit and one point (14) just near the control limit, the process is not in control. Discarding the out of control points.

$$c_0 = \frac{191 - (22 + 19)}{(25 - 2)} = \frac{150}{33} = 6.52$$
$$UCL = c_0 + 3\sqrt{c_0} = 6.52 + 3\sqrt{6.52} = 14.18$$
$$LCL = c_0 - 3\sqrt{c_0} = 6.52 - 3\sqrt{6.52} < 0 \text{ and hence considered as 0.}$$

Q. 6.21: *A sheet metal manufacturer records the number of imperfections found on each sheet of metal produced. From these inspections, it has been found that the average number of imperfections per sheet is nine. (a) Compute control limits for a c chart such that the probability of exceeding the UCL is 0.005 and falling below the LCL is 0.21. (b) With these control limits,* *what is the actual probability of assuming that the process is out of control when it really is not? (Use Table G).*

Ans: (*a*) Probability of 0.005 of a point exceeding *UCL* means that *UCL* is at 0.995 probability limit. Using Table *G*, *UCL* = 17. Similarly *LCL* is at 0.021 probability limit. Again using *G*, *LCL* = 3.

(*b*) When the process is in control,

$$UCL = \bar{c} + 3\sqrt{\bar{c}}$$
$$= 9 + 3\sqrt{9} = 18$$
$$LCL = \bar{c} - 3\sqrt{\bar{c}}$$
$$= 9 - 3\sqrt{9} = 0$$

Hence when c is greater than 18 only, the process is out of control but with the control limits in (a) the process will be concluded as out of control, when c < 3 and also when c > 17, even if the process is in control.

Hence the probability of assuming that the process is out of control when it really is not, is estimated as follows :

Probability of $c < 3$	= 0.021
Probability of $17 < c < 18$	= 0.003
Probability of out of control	= 0.024

Q. 6.22: *Both 3 σ control limits and 2 σ warning limits are used on a c chart. The decision rules states that an out-of-control condition will be declared if : (1) one point falls outside of a 3 σ limit, or (2) two points in succession fall between a given set of warning and control limit (e.g., between + 2 σ and + 3 σ. The aimed-at value of* c_0 *is 15.*

(a) Calculate the warning and control limits.

(b) If the process mean suddenly shifts downward to a c of 8.0, what is the probability that the next value of c plotted will fall below the lower control limit ?

(c) In circumstances described in part (b), what is the probability that the next two values of c will fall between the lower warning and control limits ?

(d) What is the combined probability that the shift described in part (b), will be detected within the next two samples ?

Ans: (*a*)

$$c_0 = 15$$
$$UWL = c_0 + 2\sqrt{c_0} = 15 + 2\,(3.87) = 22.74$$
$$LWL = c_0 - 2\sqrt{c_0} = 15 - 2\,(3.87) = 7.26$$
$$UCL = c_0 + 3\sqrt{c_0} = 15 + 3\,(3.87) = 26.61$$
$$LCL = c_0 - 3\sqrt{c_0} = 15 - 3\,(3.87) = 3.39.$$

(*b*) When the process mean shift to 8.0, the probability that the next value of *c* plotted will falls below the lower control of limit of 3.39, from Table *G* is computed to be 0.065.

(*c*) When the process mean shifts to 8, the probability of point falling above the lower warning limit of 7.26, as computed from Table *G* is 0.489. Also from (*b*), the probability of a point falling below lower control limit is 0.065. Hence the probability of a point falling between lower control limit 0.489 – 0.065 *i.e.* 0.42. Probability that the next two points fall between lower warning and control limits is (0.424)2 *i.e.* 0.1798.

(*d*) When the process mean shifts to 8, the probability that a point falls below lower control limit, as determined earlier, 0.065.

Again from Table *G*, probability of a point falling above upper control limit of 22.61 is 0.

Probability of a point falling upto upper warning limit is 1.00. Hence the probability of a point falling between upper warning limit and control limit is 0. These probabilities can now be used to estimate the probability of a shift detection in the next two samples, as follows :

First sample falls above	$UCL = 0.000$
Second sample falls above	$UCL = 0.000$
First sample falls below	$LCL = 0.065$
Second sample falls below	$LCL = 0.065$
First and second samples between UCL and UWL	$= 0.000$
First and second samples between LCL and LWL	$= 0.1798$
Probability of detecting the shift	$= 0.3098$

Q. 6.23: *The number of nonconformities found in one of a group of inspection sample lot is, c = 5. The size of the lot is, n = 20. The basic lot size chosen was 30. Determine the control line and the control limits of the appropriate control chart.*

Ans: Since this is a case of multiple units, the control statistic will be *ku*, where *k* is basic lot size.

$$u_0 = \frac{5}{20}$$

$$ku_0 = \frac{5}{20} \times 30 = 7.5$$

$$UCL = ku_0 + 3\sqrt{\frac{ku_0}{n/k}} = 7.5 + 3\sqrt{\frac{7.5}{20/30}} = 17.56$$

$$LCL = ku_0 - 3\sqrt{\frac{ku_0}{n/k}} = 7.5 - 3\sqrt{\frac{7.5}{20/30}} < 0 \text{ and is taken as zero.}$$

Q. 6.24: *A company starts a new unit for the manufacture of oil cloth. In order to have a quality control programme, the following data from inspection were collected :*

Inspection Lot No.	*Square Yards oil cloth inspected*	*No. of nonconformities*
1	200	5
2	250	7
3	100	3
4	90	2
5	120	4
6	80	1
Total	840	22

Draw an appropriate control chart. Recommend a future value for the control parameter you are using.

Ans: Since the number (quantity) in each sample varies, it is appropriate to draw a u chart. From the given data, it is evident, if the calculations and chart is based on some standard unit of cloth. In this case, it will be good enough to have 100 square yards as a standard unit.

Consequently the basic lot size (k) in this case is 100. Hence the control statistic is $k\,\bar{u}$,

$$\bar{u} = \frac{22}{840}$$

$$k\bar{u} = \frac{22}{840} \times 100 = 2.62$$

The alternative way to calculate $k\,\bar{u}$ will be as follows :

Inspection Lot No.	1	2	3	4	5	6
Lot ku	2.5	2.8	3.0	2.2	3.3	1.3

Now take the weighted average,

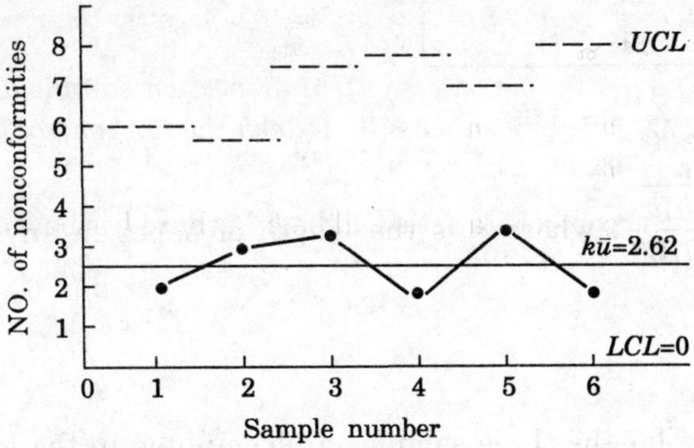

FIGURE 6.8 Control chart for the data

$$k\,\bar{u} = \frac{2.5(2.0) + 2.8(2.5) + 3.0(1) + 2.2(0.9) + 3.3(1.2) + 1.3(0.8)}{2.0 + 2.5 + 1.0 + 1.2 + 0.8}$$

$$= \frac{22}{8.4} = 2.62$$

Control limits for each sample are computed in the following table.

Inspection lot no.	*Quantity n*	$3\sqrt{\dfrac{k\bar{u}}{n/k}}$	$UCL = k\bar{u} + 3\sqrt{\dfrac{k\bar{u}}{n/k}}$	$LCL = k\bar{u} - 3\sqrt{\dfrac{k\bar{u}}{n/k}}$ *Taken as zero is LCL < 0*
1	200	3.43	6.05	0
2	250	3.07	5.69	0
3	100	4.86	7.48	0
4	90	5.12	7.74	0
5	120	4.43	7.05	0
6	80	5.43	8.05	0

The control chart with the points plotted are shown in Fig. 6.8. None of the points is out of control, hence $k\bar{u} = k\bar{u}_0 = 2.62$.

Q. 6.25: *A u chart is to be used to control a corrugated paper product line. End product is produced in rolls of varying length 48 inches wide. Nonconformities include surface imperfections, improper gluing, improper tension setting on the corrugated inner core, etc. The control statistic is nonconformities per 100 ft. with one roll constituting a sample. After 20 rolls have been inspected, the total count of nonconformities is 340 in a total of 9,300 ft. inspected.*

(a) Find the value of $\bar{u}$ in non-conformities per 100 ft.

(b) Set up the formulae for 3 σ control limits and reduce them to the most convenient form for calculating specific limits.

(c) Find the control limits for the following three representative samples and determine if the points are in control.

Length of roll (ft.)	*Count of non-conformities*
250	7
500	34
150	11

Ans: (*a*)

$$k\bar{u} = \frac{100 \times 340}{9,300} = 3.66$$

(*b*) 3 σ control limits $= k\bar{u} \pm 3\sqrt{\dfrac{k\bar{u}}{n/100}}$, where n is the length of paper in any lot. On simplification,

3 σ control limits are $3.66 \pm \dfrac{57.39}{\sqrt{n}}$

(*c*) $k\bar{u}$ value and the control limits for the three samples are computed in the following table.

Sample No.	*Length of roll*	*Sample* $k\bar{u}$	$UCL = 3.66 + \dfrac{57.39}{\sqrt{n}}$	$LCL = 3.66 - \dfrac{57.39}{\sqrt{n}}$ *as zero if LCL < 0*
1	250	2.8	7.29	0.03
2	500	6.8	6.23	1.09
3	150	7.3	8.34	0

It is evident from the above table that sample No. 2 is out of control.

Q. 6.26: *The use of control charts is* **not** *confined to monitoring the quality of a product being manufactured. They have also found application in the laboratory, where they can be used in maintaining the accuracy and precision of analytical methods and measuring instruments. An example of this occurs in the control of radio-assay counting equipment. Suppose that the performance of a low geometry alpha counter is to be checked routinely by recording 10, 1-minute counts on a standard known to have a mean counting rate of 12,960 counts per minute, and then plotting the mean of each 10 counts on a control chart with c0 12,960. In this situation a false* *alarm is less of a nuisance than is usually the case with a manufacturing process so the action limits can allow a 1% risk of it happening. Assuming that recorded counts follow a Poisson distribution, use a suitable approximation to find where the control limits should be placed.*

Ans: $c_0 = 12{,}960$

and $\sqrt{c_0} = \sqrt{12{,}960} = 36\sqrt{10}$

Using the normal approximation, for allowing 1% of risk, the area below the *LCL* should be 0.005 and also the area above the *UCL* should be 0.005. From Table *A*, for the stipulated areas, the control limits should be placed at 2.575 $\sigma_{\bar{X}}$ away from the mean value.

$$\sigma_{\bar{X}} = \frac{36\sqrt{10}}{\sqrt{10}} = 36$$

$$2.575\,\sigma_{\bar{X}} = 2.575 \times 36 = 92.7$$

Upper control limit $= 12{,}960 + 92.7 = 13{,}052.7 \approx 13{,}053$

Lower control limit $= 12{,}960 - 92.7 = 12{,}867.3 \approx 12{,}867$

Q. 6.27: *Table below refers to the computation of mean and variance ($w_i^2 u_i$) per sample for 30 Dial Telephone Assemblies with four classes of defects.*

Class of defect i	*Weight w_i*	*Number of defects $\Sigma_1^{30} c_i$*	*Defects per sample u_i*	*Demerit per sample $w_i u_i$*	*Variance $w_i^2 u_i$*
1	0.64	5	0.1667	0.1083	0.0704
2	0.25	15	0.5000	0.1250	0.0313
3	0.08	75	2.5000	0.2000	0.0160
4	0.02	50	1.6667	0.0333	0.0007
Total	1.00	145	4.8333	0.4666	0.1184

Establish the central line, upper control line and lower control line on cw chart.

Ans: $\sigma = \sqrt{0.1184} = 0.3441.$

Central line should be placed at $w_i c_i$, *i.e.* at 0.4666

$$UCL = 0.4\,666 + 3\,(0.3441) = 1.50.$$

$$LCL = 0.4667 - 3\,(0.3441) = -0.5655 < 0, \text{ and hence } 0.$$

Q. 6.28: *In grading fabric, it is common practice to assign point values to each nonconformity these values varying with the intensity of the nonconformities and being added to give a total point value for each piece graded (The distribution of point values does not follow exactly Poisson distribution, however it is reasonably good approximation). Assume that a mill decides after investigation and establishment of this system that the maximum number of points acceptable for first quality fabric is 80, beyond an 80-point total, the fabric is down-graded to second quality. The question that must be answered is : What must be the average number of points per piece of first quality fabric in order that the mill can be assumed that practically all the fabric will be first quality ? What the mill is actually saying is that the upper control limit for points is 80, so what is the average value of $\bar{c}$?*

Ans:

$$UCL = \bar{c} + 3\sqrt{\bar{c}}$$

$$80 = \bar{c} + 3\sqrt{\bar{c}}$$

or, $$\bar{c} + 3\sqrt{\bar{c}} - 80 = 0$$

To solve for $\bar{c}$, let $\bar{c} = x^2$, so that

$$x^2 + 3x - 80 = 0$$

Solution of above equation leads to

$$x = \frac{-3 \pm \sqrt{329}}{2}$$

$$= \frac{-3 \pm 18.14}{2}$$

Using plus value $$x = \frac{15.14}{2} = 7.57$$

$\therefore$ $$\bar{c} = x^2 = (7.57)^2 = 57.30$$

Thus, the average points representing nonconformities that should warrant approximately all first quality are 57.30.

Q. 6.29: *A chart has the central line at 41.7 and control limits (rounded to the nearest whole number) at 61 and 22 respectively :*

(a) Calculate the probability of a point falling within the control zone if the process average shifts to 15, 18, 20, 22, 27, 30, 42, 50, 55, 61, 70 and 75.

(b) The plot of the probabilities in (a) against process average is known as the OC curve of the chart. Plot this curve with probability on the ordinate scale and shift in process average on the abscissa.

(c) Interpret the curve.

Ans: (*a*) The probabilities of a point falling within the control zone can be computed with the help of Table *G*. But since Table *G* gives probabilities upto *c* of 25, the use of chart for Poisson distribution can be made for c values greater than 25. Following tabulation prepared with the help of Table *G* gives the required probabilities.

Process average	*Probability of* $c \le 61$	*Probability* $c \le 22$	*Probability* $22 < c < 61$	*Process average*	*Probability of* $c \le 61$	*Probability of* $c \le 21$	*Probability* $22 < c < 61$
15	1.000	0.967	0.033	42	0.998	0.001	0.997
18	1.000	0.855	0.145	50	0.944	0.000	0.944
20	1.000	0.721	0.279	55	0.811	0.000	0.811
22	1.000	0.556	0.444	61	0.534	0.000	0.534
27	1.000	0.195	0.805	70	0.155	0.000	0.155
30	1.000	0.081	0.919	75	0.056	0.000	0.056

(*b*) Figure 6.9 shows the *OC* curve for the *c* chart

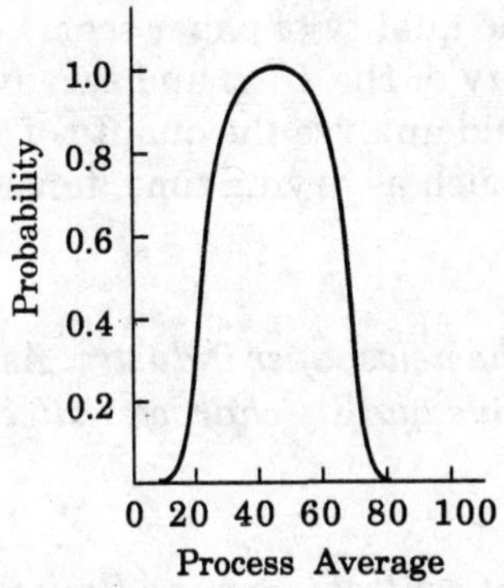

FIGURE 6.9 OC curve for the chart

(*c*) The *OC* of Fig. 6.9 shows that the average number of nonconformities might go as high as 70 or as low as 18 and we would still have more than a 0.10 chance of not catching the shift on a single unit inspected.

Q. 6.30: *A company proposes to modify its paper-making process using pulp from a foreign supplier, rather than its normal domestic suppliers. It wants to be sure that it can use this raw material in its paper-making operation and obtain the same quality paper as it does not domestic pulp. Prior to running the foreign pulp, it takes paper from its normal suppliers for one week and analyses the blemishes on the paper. On a total of 32 m2 of paper tested during one week it found 350 blemishes. The company then ran the paper-making machines with the foreign pulp and in the five bobbins of paper tested it obtained the average blemishes per square metre on the paper as shown in the accompanying table.*

(Average blemishes per square metre on the paper made from the foreign pulp)

Sample No.	*Average blemishes per square metre*
1	30
2	19
3	6
4	25
5	3

As a consultant you are required to ;

1. Establish a c-chart for 3σ control limits using the domestic paper test. If your computations shown $LCL_c > 0$, is it advisable to beep LCL_c as zero.

2. Show the information from the foreign paper on the control chart. What are your comments about the foreign paper ? Do you have any suggestion (s) ?

Ans:

$$\bar{c} = \frac{350}{20} = 10.9375 \approx 10.94$$

$$\sigma_c = \sqrt{10.9375} = 3.31$$

$$UCL_c = 10.9375 + 3\,(3.31) = 20.86$$

$$UCL_c = 10.9375 - 3\,(3.31) = 1.02$$

With above data, the *c*-chart for foreign paper can be plotted now.

2. From the chart it can immediately be observed that the quality of paper seems erratic. Two averages are outside the limits, one is just in the vicinity of the *UCL* and two averages are below the control line. In view of above, the company should analyse the quality of the raw material and perhaps re-evaluate the operating procedures, such as drying time, tension etc., for paper making using the new raw material.

Q. 6.31: *(a) The Zeeland Paper Company produces paper for the newspaper industry. As a final step, the paper passes through a machine that measures various quality characteristics. When the process is in control, its average 20 defects per roll.*

(b) What are the upper and control limits of this chart?

(c) What are the 2σ warning (sometimes also called a tight control/warning limits) of this chart?

(d) If the latest roll sampled contained 27 defects, is the process in control?

(e) If the latest roll contained only 5 defects, is the process in control?

Ans: (*a*) In this case, "control chart for defects" is the most appropriate. In SPC parlance this is known *c*-chart.

(*b*) $\bar{c} = 20$

$$UCL_c = 20 + 3\sqrt{20} = 33.41; LCL_c = 20 - 3\sqrt{20} = 6.39$$

(*c*) 2s Warning limits:

$$UWL_c = 20 + 2\sqrt{20} = 28.94; LWL_c = 20 - 2\sqrt{20} = 11.06$$

(*d*) Because the latest roll had only 27 defects, or less than the upper control limit, the process is in control.

(*e*) Five defects is less than the lower control limit and therefore the process is technically "out of control". However, the control chart indicates that something good has happened. Management should find the assignable causes and exploit it in order to reduce the average number of defects.

CHAPTER 7

Rational Subgrouping, Process Capability and Statistical Tolerances

7.1 THE INFORMATION GIVEN BY THE CONTROL CHART DEPENDS ON THE BASIS USED FOR SELECTION OF SUBGROUPS

One possible view of a control chart is that it provides a statistical test to determine whether the variation from subgroup to subgroup is consistent with the average variation within the subgroups. If it is desired to determine whether or not a group of measurements is statistically homogeneous (that is, whether they appear to come from a constant system of chance causes), subgroups should be chosen in a way that appears likely to give the maximum chance for the measurements in each subgroup to be alike and the maximum chance for the subgroups to differ one from the other.

The basis of subgrouping calls for careful study, with a view to obtaining the maximum amount of useful information from any control chart. As already pointed out in Chap. 3, the most obvious rational basis for subgrouping is the *order of production*.

7.2 TWO SCHEMES INVOLVING ORDER OF PRODUCTION AS A BASIS FOR SUBGROUPING

Where order of production is used as a basis for subgrouping, two fundamentally different approaches are possible :

1. Instant time method
2. Period-of-time method

The first method follows the rule for selection of rational subgroups of permitting a minimum chance for variation within a subgroup and a maximum chance for variation from subgroup to subgroup. It can be expected to give the best estimate of a value of σ that represents the ideal capabilities of a process obtainable if assignable causes of variation, the special causes, from one subgroup to another can be eliminated. Moreover, it provides a more sensitive measurement of shifts in the process average; it makes the control chart a better guide to machine setting or to other actions intended to maintain a given process average. Thus the first method is more ideally suited to analysis of a process and to process control.

However, if subgrouping is by the first method and a change in process average takes place after one subgroup is taken and is corrected before the next subgroup, the change will not be reflected in the control chart. For this reason, the second method is sometimes preferred where one of the purposes of the control chart is to influence decisions on acceptance of product. In such cases a question to be asked before choosing between the two schemes is whether or not two compensating shifts in process average are really likely to occur between subgroups. If so, and if there is no other way to detect bad product that might be produced between subgroups (for instance, failure of a part to fit into an assembly), the second method of subgrouping is desirable in spite of the other advantages of the first method. In machining operations, such compensating shifts between subgroups are more likely to occur in hand-operated machines than on automatic machines.

Where the second method of subgrouping is used, the interpretation of points out of control on the R chart is somewhat different from that in the first method. With the second method a shift in the process average during the period covered by a subgroup may cause out-of-control points on the R chart even though there has been no real change in the process dispersion.

The choice of subgroup size should be influenced, in part, by the desirability of permitting a minimum chance for variation within a subgroup. In most cases, more useful information will be obtained from, say, five subgroups of 5 than from one subgroup of 25. In large subgroups, such as 25, there is likely to be too much opportunity for a process change within a subgroup. Nevertheless, if process changes do not occur within subgroups, large subgroup sizes have the advantage mentioned in Chap. 3 of reducing the risk of so-called *Type II* errors in interpreting control charts. Whenever relatively large subgroup sizes are used for this purpose, it is particularly desirable to use the first method of subgrouping.

In many cases where the first method of subgrouping is really better, it may be necessary to use the second method because of practical reasons associated with the taking of the measurements.

7.3 PRECISION, REPRODUCIBILITY, AND ACCURACY OF METHODS OF MEASUREMENT

The only way in which the value of any quality characteristic—dimensions, hardness, tensile strength, weight, percentage of chemical impurity, and so on—may be determined is by some form of measurement. If measuring devices and those who used them were perfect, it would be possible to make a direct determination of the variability of the true values of the measured quality characteristic. Actually, the measured values reflect errors of measurement as well as variation in the quantity measured.

The *precision* of a method of measurement refers to its variability when used to make repeated measurements under carefully controlled conditions. Otherwise, as in chemical tests or other destructive tests.

The *reproducibility* of a method of measurement refers to the consistency of its pattern of variation. This may be judged to best advantage by control charts for $\bar{X}$ and R or $\bar{X}$ and s. Where repeated measurements show erratic patterns of variation, the method of measurement used is not reproducible. Any statement regarding the precision of a method of measurement implies that the method of measurement is reproducible.

The *accuracy* of a method of measurement refers to its absence of bias — to the conformity of its results to the true value of the quality characteristic being measured. In an accurate method, the average value obtained from a set of measurements should differ from the true value by not more than would be expected as a chance variation in the light of the precision of the particular method.

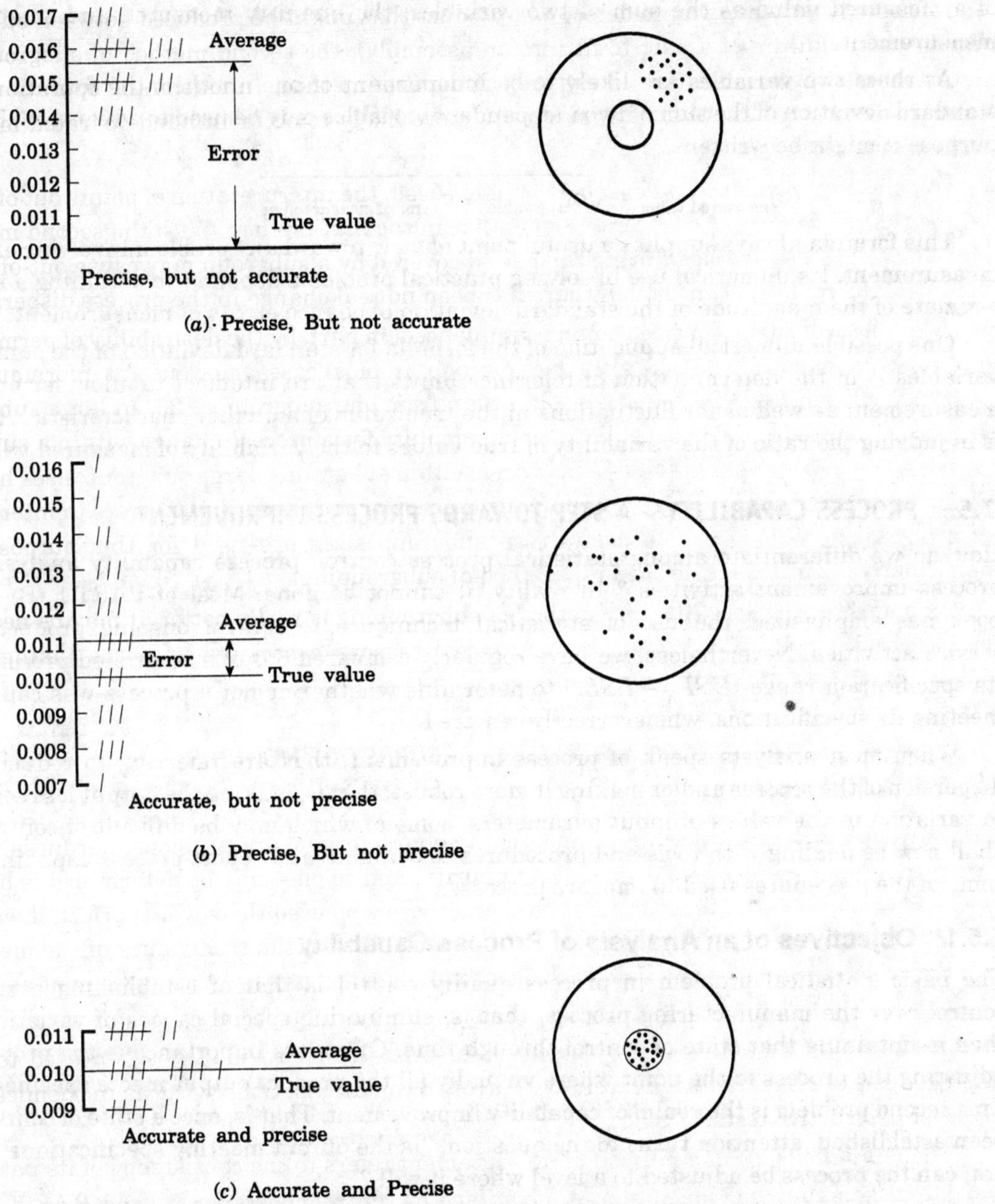

FIGURE 7.1 Distriction between accuracy and precision

Figure 7.1 makes the definition and distinction between these terms abundantly clear.

7.4 RELATIONSHIP BETWEEN THE VARIABILITY OF MEASURED VALUES AND THE PRECISION OF THE METHOD OF MEASUREMENT

The variability observed in measured values of dimensions, hardness, tensile strength, and other quality characteristics of industrial product is due in part to the variability of the product and in part to the variability inherent in the method of measurement. It is helpful to think of a measured value as the sum of two variables, the quantity measured and the error of measurement.

As these two variables are likely to be independent of one another, the formula for the standard deviation of the sum of two independent variables may be used to advantage. For this purpose it might be written

$$(\sigma)_{\text{measured value}} = \sqrt{\sigma^2_{\text{true value}} + \sigma^2_{\text{error of measurement}}} \quad \text{...(7.1)}$$

This formula always supplies a useful point of view toward any problem involving errors of measurement. Its numerical use in solving practical problems depends on obtaining a reliable estimate of the magnitude of the standard deviation of chance errors of measurement.

One possible numerical application of the formula for standard deviation of the sum of two variables is in the determination of tolerance limits that are intended to allow for errors of measurement as well as for fluctuations in the true value of a quality characteristic. Another is in judging the ratio of the variability of true values to the variability of measured values.

7.5 PROCESS CAPABILITY – A STEP TOWARDS PROCESS IMPROVEMENT

How do we differentiate among statistical process control, process capability analysis, and process improvement activities ? In reality, it cannot be done. Most of PART-1 (B) of this book has emphasized the use of statistical techniques to control ongoing production or service activities. Nevertheless, we have regularly compared 6 σ of a controlled process with its specification range ($USL_X - LSL_X$) to determine whether or not a process was capable of meeting its specifications, when correctly centered.

When most analysts speak of process improvement, they are referring to reducing the dispersion of the process and/or making it more robust, that is, making the output less sensitive to variation in the values of input parameters, some of which may be difficult of control. We shall now be dealing with tools and procedures to evaluate and report process capability and some of the procedures used to improve processes.

7.5.1 Objectives of an Analysis of Process Capability

The basic statistical problem in process quality control is that of establishing a state of control over the manufacturing process, that is, eliminating special causes of variation and then maintaining that state of control through time. Of no less importance is the problem of adjusting the process to the point where virtually all the product output meets specifications. This second problem is the realm of capability improvement. That is, once a state of control has been established, attention turns to the question, "Is the output meeting specifications, and if not, can the process be adjusted to a level where it will ?"

Actions that result in a change or adjustment in a process, directed at eliminating common causes, are frequently the result of some form of capability study. The comparison of natural tolerance limits with specification limits and the natural tolerance range with the specification range may lead to any of the following possible courses of action :

1. *No action.* If the natural tolerance limits fall well within the specification limits, usually no action will be required.
2. *Action to adjust centering.* When the natural tolerance range is about the same as the specification range, a relatively simple adjustment to the centering of the process may be all that is necessary to bring virtually all product within specifications.

3. *Action to reduce variability.* This is usually the most complex action.
4. *Actions of change specifications.* This is a design decision but one that should not be ignored by quality control personnel. Simply because specifications are stipulated in writing does not necessarily mean they are inviolate. In some cases, specifications may be set tighter than necessary (*i.e.* ***gold plating***). In others, slight design changes may be less costly, or more feasible, than changes in machinery or tooling. It may be feasible on occasion to totally redesign the product unit within the manufacturer's capability to produce. Needless to say, there are important economic trade-offs between action items 3 and 4 that require close coordination and communication among design, manufacturing, and quality control functions. This was one of the main driving forces behind the development of the Quality Circles concept in Japan, which is now implemented in many reputed companies throughout the world.
5. *Resignation to losses.* When all else fails, management must be content with a high loss rate. Attention at this point focuses on scrap and rework costs, the economical level of control that should be exercised over the production process, and the costs associated with screening all product, realizing that some nonconforming product still is likely to be accepted. It is most important in this case to have good estimates of the form and shape of the distribution of product as an aid to proper process centering.

7.5.2 Steps in the Analysis of Process Capability

The following three basic steps are necessary in performing a capability study.

1. Establish control over the process.
2. Analyze process data.
3. Analyze sources of variation.

7.6 PROCESS CAPABILITY AND PERFORMANCE INDEXES (INDICES)

In many industrial situations, the accuracy is often associated with capability. The factory personnel will often heard saying that machine is capable to produce ± 0.5 mm or its process capability is ± 0.5 mm. This numerical figure of ± 0.5 is in fact ± 3σ capability of the process. Hence the process capability is considered as ± 3σ (or sometimes 6σ).

At many places in this book, the importance of comparing 6σ from a process in statistical control, the so-called natural tolerance of the process, with the specification range ($USL_X - LSL_X$) has been stressed. The smaller 6σ is in relation to ($USL_X - LCL_X$), the more capable the process so long as it is properly centered at the nominal or target dimension. In order to improve the quality more and more, an objective of manufacturing should be to seek methods to continually reduce 6σ even when 6σ is well within ($USL_X - LSL_X$). In the discussion of indexes that follows, we have used the alternative symbol U for USL_X and L for LSL_X in order to simplify the expressions.

The Japanese have formalized this type of comparison into a series of process indexes that are rapidly being adopted universally. The first* of these, designated C_p, is most closely related to *process capability potential* (or capability ratio). It is found from

$$C_p = \frac{U - L}{6\hat{\sigma}} \quad ...(7.2)$$

*(Some writers on SQC consider process capability and capabilities ratio to as same)

At any value greater than 1, a process has the potential for meeting specifications if held in control at an $\overline{X}_0$ of $(U + L)/2$ often firms choose an arbitrary critical value for the process capability ratio such as 1.33 to establish a target for reducing process variability. The value greater than 1.0 will allow for some change in the process distribution before bad output is generated.

The relationship between μ, the estimate of process centering, and the target value $\overline{X}_0$ is designated as k. It is found from

$$k = \frac{|\overline{X}_0 - \hat{\mu}|}{\min(\overline{X}_0 - L, U - \overline{X}_0)} \quad \text{...(7.3)}$$

where the vertical lines (|) around $\overline{X}_0 - \hat{\mu}$ mean the "absolute value," that is, ignore the sign of the value, and min (a, b) means select the minimum value of a or b. The index k always will be greater than or equal to zero and has a target value of zero.

Where specification tolerances are symmetrical about the nominal value, the formula for k reduces to

$$k = \frac{|\overline{X}_0 - \hat{\mu}|}{(U - L)/2} \quad \text{...(7.4)}$$

This is the form in which the index is seen most frequently. However it is *not valid for one-sided specification tolerances* or when there is a single specification limit. Also it should be noted that when one-sided specification tolerances are used, the target value of $\overline{X}_0$ will not equal the nominal dimension unless there is no possible dispersion beyond that dimension.

Three additional indexes, which relate more to process current performance than to potential capability, are as follows :

$$C_{pL} = \frac{\hat{\mu} - L}{3\hat{\sigma}} \quad \text{...(7.5)}$$

$$C_{pU} = \frac{U - \hat{\mu}}{3\hat{\sigma}} \quad \text{...(7.6)}$$

$$C_{pk} = \min (C_{pL}, C_{pU}) \quad \text{...(7.7)}$$

As with the factor k, each of these indexes takes into account the most recent estimate of process centering. C_{pL} and C_{pU} relate the difference between the current estimate of process mean and the respective specification limits, L and U, to half the natural process spread. The minimum target value for each is one. C_{pk} provides the minimum of these two values. If C_{pk} is greater than a critical value of 1.0 (say 1.33) and C_p is greater than its critical value, we can firmly say the process is capable. If C_{pk} is less than 1.0, the process average is close to one of the tolerance limits and generates defective output. The C_{pk} will always be less than or equal to C_p. When C_{pk} equals the C_p, the process is centered between U and L. Companies that have adopted process capability indexes within their own plants frequently specify their usage in supplier purchase contracts, especially C_{pk}.

It should be noted that each index tends to simply that the distribution of product units from a controlled process may be represented by a normal reference distribution; that is, virtually all product will fall between the mean μ and $\pm$ 3 σ. (A check of Table *A*, App. will show that all but 0.27% of the normal curve falls between $\pm$ 3 σ). A histogram of a substantial number of measurements from a controlled process is required to determine whether virtually all product falls within $\pm$ 3σ limits. These symmetrical limits may not fit processes that tend to produce skewed distributions. Also, their usage and target value interpretation must be modified in situations where only a single specification limit, either U or L, is specified.

In testing for steel hardness, for example, there is a metallurgical limit on hardness for various grades of steel alloy. Usually the grade of steel selected for a product is based on this hardness limit (as well as other physical and economic properties). A lower specification limit is indicated with the stated intent to achieve a target as close as possible to the physical limit. In such cases, C_{pL} is the only applicable index and a highly skewed distribution is likely to result.

7.7 TWO STATISTICAL THEOREMS OF GREAT IMPORTANCE IN THE INTERRELATIONSHIP OF TOLERANCES

A dimension on an assembled product may be the sum of the dimensions of several parts. Or an electrical resistance may be the sum of several electrical resistances of parts. Or a weight may be the sum of a number of weights of parts. In this common situation, what should be the relationship of the tolerances of the parts to the tolerances of the sum ? This question may be answered with the aid of a theorem of mathematical statistics that is extremely useful in many problems of quality control. This theorem states that the standard deviation of the sum of any number of independent variables is the square root of the sum of the squares of the standard deviations of the independent variables :

$$\sigma_{\text{sum}} = \sqrt{\sigma_1^2 + \sigma_2^2 + \sigma_3^2 + \ldots + \sigma_n^2} \qquad \ldots(7.8)$$

For example, consider an assembly containing a dimension *AD* that is the sum of the dimensions of parts *AB*, *BC*, and *CD* (see Fig. 7.2). Assume that the dimension of each part is statistically controlled with averages and universe standard deviations as follows :

Part	μ	σ
AB	1.450	0.0010
BC	0.865	0.0008
CD	1.170	0.0007

Assume that upper and lower specification limits are at 4-sigma distance from the average. Specifications are then as follows :

	Specification	*U*	*L*	*Tolerance range (U – L)*
AB	1.450 ± 0.0040	1.4540	1.4460	0.0080
BC	0.865 ± 0.0032	0.8682	0.8618	0.0064
CD	1.170 ± 0.0028	1.1728	1.1672	0.0056
Total		3.4950	3.4750	0.0200

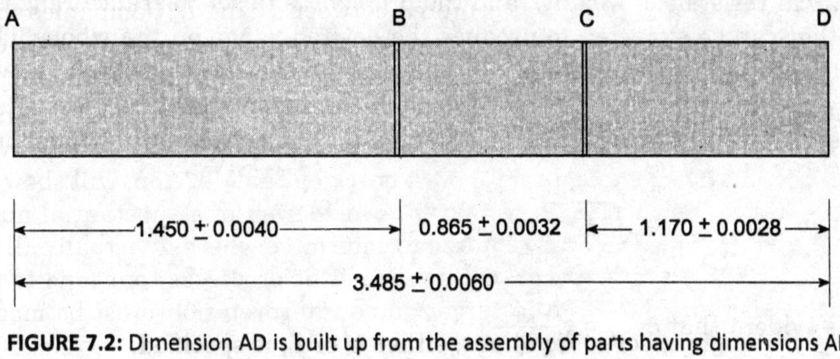

FIGURE 7.2: Dimension AD is built up from the assembly of parts having dimensions AB, BC and CD.

Someone considering merely the specified tolerances and not the distribution pattern of the dimensions might conclude that the appropriate specification for the overall dimension *AD* was 3.485 ± 0.010. This conclusion is incorrect because it fails to recognize the probability aspects of the situation. If the assembly of the parts is at random, large *AB* parts are just as likely to be assembled with small *BC* parts as with large ones. If the probability is small of the occurrence of an extreme maximum value of one part, the probability that three parts all having maximum values will be assembled together is very much smaller. The probabilities of all kinds of combinations of parts are reflected in a simple way by the formula for the standard deviation of the sum of independent variables :

$$\sigma_{AD} = \sqrt{\sigma_{AB}^2 + \sigma_{BC}^2 + \sigma_{CD}^2}$$
$$= \sqrt{(0.0010)^2 + (0.0008)^2 + (0.0007)^2} = 0.0015$$

If the specification limits for the sum AD, like the limits for the parts, are placed at 4-sigma distance from the average (*i.e.*, 4 × 0.0015 *i.e.*, 0.006), the specifications for AD will be 3.485 ± 0.006. This ± 0.006 is in sharp contrast with the ± 0.010 obtained by simple addition of the allowable maximum and minimum values of the parts.

Some individuals in a manufacturing plant may find it difficult to believe that the laws of chance make the appropriate tolerance range for an assembly less than the sum of the tolerance ranges for the component parts. To convince them, it may be helpful to make an experimental verification of the theorem for the standard deviations of the sum of independent variables. Such an experiment at Westinghouse Electric Corporation is reported by *B*. Epstein. Fifty of each of three components of an assembly were drawn at random from storage lots. These were gauged, and averages and standard deviations of the dimension of each component were obtained. The 3-sigma limits on assembled dimensions were then predicted by formula. The components were then selected at random and assembled, and the assemblies were gauged. The 3-sigma limits on the dimensions of the assemblies checked closely with the limits predicted by the use of statistical theory.

Whenever it is reasonable to assume that the tolerance ranges of the parts are proportional to their respective σ values, such tolerance ranges may be combined by taking the square root of the sum of the squares. Thus

$$(U-L)_{AD} = \sqrt{(U-L)_{AB}^2 + (U-L)_{BC}^2 + (U-L)_{CD}^2} \quad ...(7.9)$$
$$= \sqrt{(0.0080)^2 + (0.0064)^2 + (0.0056)^2} = 0.012$$

The actual situation in setting tolerance limits is often the reverse of the one just described. Frequently the desired tolerance range is known for the overall quality characteristic (such as a dimension, electrical resistance, weight), and the problem is to set tolerance ranges on the component parts that can be expected to produce the desired range on the whole. This may be determined without much difficulty by trial-and-error solution of the formula. However, a direct solution is possible if the standard deviations of the various parts are assumed to be equal. In this case the formula for the standard deviation of the sum of *n* independent parts becomes

$$\sigma_{\text{sum}} = \sqrt{n\sigma_{\text{part}}^2} \quad ...(7.10)$$

From this, it is evident that $\sigma_{\text{part}} = \sqrt{\dfrac{\sigma_{\text{sum}}^2}{n}}$

If tolerance ranges are assumed proportional to standard deviations,

$$(U - L)_{part} = \sqrt{\frac{(U - L)^2_{sum}}{n}} \qquad ...(7.11)$$

Another useful theorem of mathematical statistics deals with the standard deviation of the difference between independent variables, which is as follows :

$$\sigma_{1-2} = \sqrt{\sigma_1^2 + \sigma_2^2} \qquad ...(7.12)$$

It will be noted that the standard deviation of the difference is the same as the standard deviation of the sum.

A word of caution is called for on the application of these useful theorems to tolerance problems. The theorems assume independence of the variables being added and subtracted. In some assembly operations this independence does not exist. For example, suppose a dimension on an assembled product is the combined thickness of four metal washers. If these washers all come from the same production process and are assembled in the order of production, the thickness of the four washers in any assembly will not be independent of one another unless the process of producing them is in strict statistical control. Otherwise there will be a tendency for thick washers to be assembled together in some assemblies and thin washers assembled together in others. If this tendency exists, the theorem for the standard deviation of the sum of independent variables is not applicable to the problem of setting tolerances on the overall dimension.

SOLVED QUESTIONS

Q. 7.1: *Discuss the 'order of production' is not always a sufficient basis for subgrouping.*

Ans: The reason why 'order in time' and not the 'order of production' is a good basis of subgrouping is that its use tends to disclose assignable causes of variation that come and go. However, there may be other assignable causes of variation that are not disclosed merely taking subgroups in the order of production.

For example, two or more identical machines may have different process averages, different process dispersions, or other differences in their pattern of variation. If these machines contribute to a stream of product in a way that subgroups taken from that stream contain approximately constant number from each machine, the differences among the machines will not be disclosed by the control charts. The principle here is that assignable causes, if they are to be indicated by the charts, must influence some but not all of the subgroups.

Q. 7.2: *A steel plate that is a part of an assembly, is required to have 4 holes. All these four holes are drilled at the same time and are supposed to have same diameter. A suggestion is made that the variable (X) used for the control charts should be the average of the four hole diameters on a plate and that a subgroup should consist of four such averages. What objections can you see to this suggestion ?*

Ans: When the four holes of a plate are drilled at the same time, the drilling machine must have been incorporated with a system that four drills can work simultaneously. The four drills employed for the purpose may not necessarily have the same characteristics. There may be wide variations. Moreover it is required to control the diameter of each hole rather than the average diameter of the holes of plate. Therefore, the control charts for the successive diameters of the plate must be maintained instead of having the control charts using the average of the diameters of holes.

Q. 7.3: *Explain clearly the meaning of the term "rational subgrouping" in statistical quality control techniques.*

Ans: In order to explain clearly the term "rational subgrouping" let it be assumed that a process gives as initial set of values $X_1, X_2 .... X_n$ and there is no information regarding the stability or lack of stability. If the process changed in its centering during the initial period as for instance in Fig. 7.3. then the computations for $\bar{X}$ and σ for values $X_1, X_2 ... X_n$ are not valid.

In fact we would be pooling observations from two different underlying universes, one with mean μ_1 and the other with μ_2 and our estimates would only be weighted of the statistics averages of both universes. The problem can be overcome by diving the output according to the time at which the process changed. But this is unknown, it may be considered to subdivide the observations into smaller sets each one of which provides estimates of the process characteristic. Then if a change of the type in Fig. 7.3 occurred only one of the subgroups at most would provide invalid estimates.

If the process changes of the type in Fig. 7.4 occurs, the estimates provided by the these subgroups might still be reasonable if the subgroup sizes are small. Then the envelope of the estimates would approximate the actual behaviour of the process.

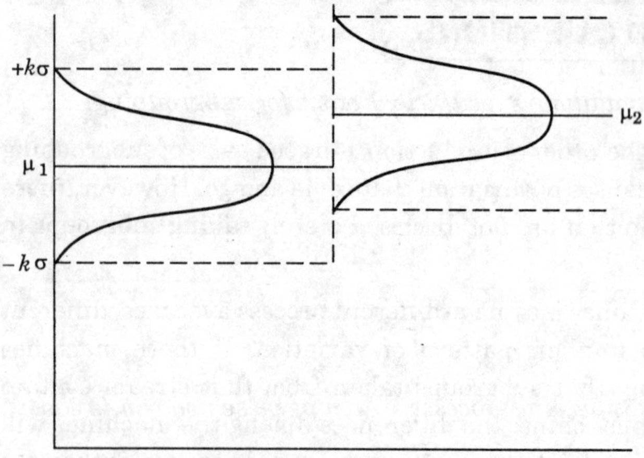

FIGURE 7.3: Effect of change in process centering.

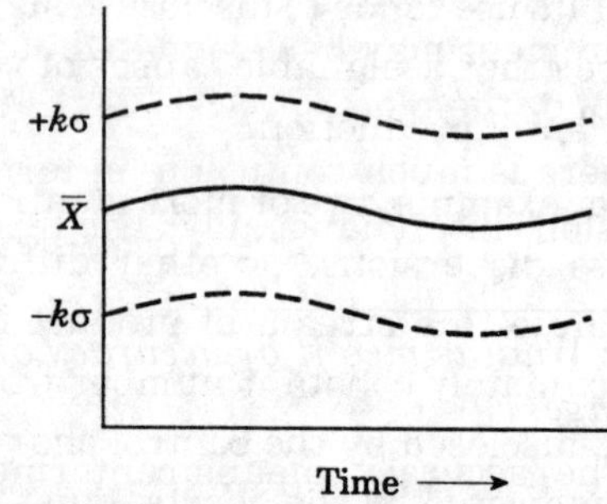

FIGURE 7.4: Continuous slow change in process centering.

If the N observations are divided into (m) subgroups each subgroups consisting of n observations, each preserving the order of observation between subgroups, (m) estimates each of $\bar{X}$ and σ can be computed. Thus it is possible to have two ordered set of statistics as estimate of process behaviour. The value of n is arbitrary and largely depends upon one's expectations as to the likelihood of a process change occurring at all.

If the process is such that if changes occur they are abrupt and of short duration, the sample should be taken over as short a period as possible since it is desirable to ensure that if a change occurs it does so between samples rather than within the sample. If the process is subjected to slow continuous change, then again sample size should be small so that the process variation within the sample be small relative to that between the sample.

Q. 7.4: *The standard deviation of the error of measurement of a certain electric characteristic of a product is determined to be 8 units. The σ of the measured values under a state of control is 42 units. From this information what is your estimation of the true σ of the quality characteristic ?*

It is believed that the standard deviation of the error of measurement could be cut in half by taking the mean of the four measurements on each item of the product rather than by taking only one measurement. If this should be done, what reduction would you expect in the σ of the measured value ?

Ans:

$$\sigma_{measured} = \sqrt{\sigma^2_{true\ value} + \sigma^2_{error}}$$

$$(42)^2 = \sqrt{\sigma^2_{true\ value} + 8^2}$$

or

$$\sigma_{true\ value} = 41.26 \text{ units}$$

$$\sigma_{measured} \text{ in second case} = \sqrt{(41.26)^2 + (4)^2}$$

$$= 41.42$$

Reduction $= 42.0 - 41.0\ 2 = 0.58$ units.

Q. 7.5: *Define the terms "accuracy" and "precision". How will you distinguish between the two?*

Ans: *Accuracy* : The accuracy of an instrument is the extent to which the average of a long series of repeat measurements made by the instrument on a single unit of production differs from the true value of that product. This difference is usually due to a systematic error in the measurement process. In this case, the instrument is said to be "out of calibration".

Precision : The precision of an instrument is the extent to which the instrument respects its results when making repeat measurements on the same unit of product. The scatter of these measurement may be designated as, meaning standard deviation of measurement. The lower value of σ_e the more "precise" is the instrument.

There is much confusion on terminology. Some literature uses the terms "accuracy" and "precision" interchangeably. The term "bias" is sometimes used to indicate a lack of accuracy.

Q. 7.6: *What is meant by accuracy and precision of a process? Which of these two can is easier to change?*

Ans: The 'accuracy' means centering of the process while precision mean the spread to the process.

Accuracy is always easier to change than precision.

Q. 7.7: *(a) Make a diagram for process of $c_p < 1$; $c_p = 1$ and $c_p > 1$.*

(b) What is your conclusion of products with respect to specification limits (U, L) when $c_p < 1$, $c_p = 1$ and $c_p > 1$?

(c) Can the capability ratios be used for bench mark purposes?

Ans: (*a*) Figure. 7.5 shows the situations for $c_p < 1$; $c_p = 1$; $c_p > 1$.

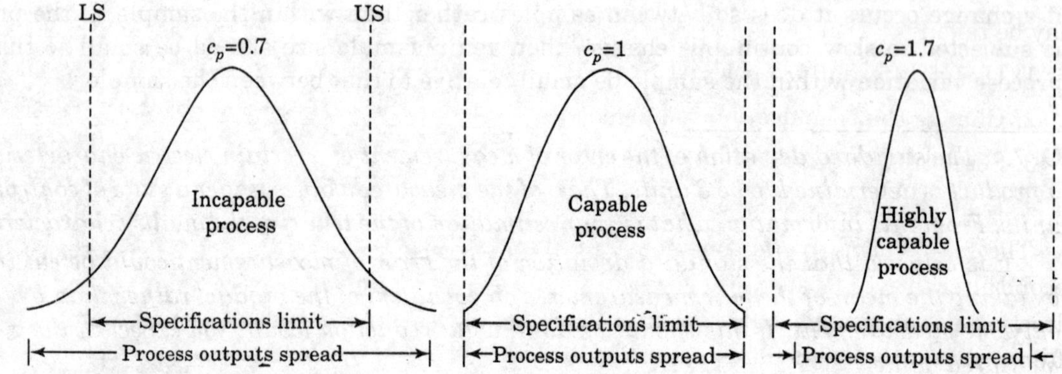

FIGURE 7.5

(*b*) $c_p < 1$**:** The process produces outputs outside the specification limit i.e., $(U-L)$ the lower the c_p value, the more outputs fall out of the specification limits.

$c_p = 1$**:** the process outputs are exactly within the specification limits meaning that sometimes the output is equal (or extremely close) to the specification limits. Although this is considered a capable process, at the slightest drift the outputs will fall outside of the specification limits.

$c_p > 1$ **:** All process outputs fall within the specification and there is a gap between the highest and lowest output and upper and lower specification limits respectively. In this case, even in the case of a drift there is enough space to keep the outputs within the specification limits.

(*c*) Since the capability ratios are unitless, they can be used to compare the capabilities of different processes for benchmark purposes.

Q. 7.8: *(a) Write a brief note on process capability.*

(b) Why range method is generally preferred for process capabilty analysis.

Ans. : (*a*) Process capability may be defined as the "minimum spread of a specific measurement variation which will include 99.73 percent of the measurements from the given process" -in other words, 6 σ. Since a capability study is made to determine natural variation only 6 σ, is used instead of the more familiar directed interval of ± 3 σ.

When making the study it is important to minimize the effects of factors essentially extraneous to the study. Such factors are unnatural material variations, process adjustments, and process deterioration. Hence, homogeneous materials should be used, no process adjustments should be made during the study, and, if within study process deterioration exists, the effects should be calculated and subtracted.

When these conditions have been noted and accounted for, a process capability study may be made by gathering the required data—at least 50 observations and preferably 100 or more if possible—and computing the standard deviation of this data and may be remarked that knowing the capability will not always eliminate the necessity for using a process which will produce defective pieces because of stringent specification requirements. However, the extent of deficiency can be calculated in advance and the steps taken with full knowledge of the consequences. When a process has been shown to be incapable of producing the great majority of units within specification requirements there are four alternative courses of action which may be taken :

1. Use of different process.
2. Change the specification requirements.
3. Screen (100% inspection) for removal of defective units.
4. Leave the process alone.

The first alternative is time consuming and may offset the schedule. In many cases the second alternative is logical, but it is traditionally difficult to get design changes in the relaxation direction. Nevertheless, this second alternative should be considered very thoroughly for it often involves the least total cost. The third should be considered if the cost of inspection is low in comparison to the cost of the other alternatives. The fourth may be resorted to when the units cost is very low, inspection cost relatively high, and the cost (tangible and intangible) of a defective unit in the field is low.

(*b*) For the purpose of calculations of process capability either standard deviation or range method can be used. The range method is preferred for process capability analysis for the following reasons :

1. It is easier to calculate—no square root is involved.
2. Trends occurring in the study or other abnormal conditions can be detected. The range method allows better for trend in process capability determination.
3. When the range method is used, the capability study can serve as a base-period analysis.

Q. 7.9: *(a) When can you use the Process Capability Analysis Tool?*

(b) When do you consider a process as "capable"?

(c) What is process capability analysis and how do you carry out this analysis?

Ans. : (*a*) Once a process is in statistical control and its output are consistent, capability assessment tools can be used to study the process outputs against the required specifications.

(*b*) A 'capable' process is one whose output fall within the specification limits.

(*c*) Process capability analysis is a technique that is used to determine the ability of a process to meet product or service specifications. It is useful tool to evaluate variation within a process and whether improvements can be made to process control. Although a process may be within control limits as determined by control chart data, capability analysis takes things a step further by evaluating the amount of variation in process outcomes (the product or service) compared to the capability of the process.

Capability analyses contain two main parts:

1. The capability histogram which shows the distribution of the outputs of the process, the upper and lower specifications limits and usually the best fit distribution.
2. The capability indices which are numerical values that estimate the capability of the process in respect of the upper and the lower specification limits.

The process capability can be measured using capability ratio or capability $\left(C_p = \dfrac{U - L}{6\sigma}\right)$

C_p is a ratio of the allowed variation of the process (variation within technical specifications) and its real variation. This shows how close the variation of the process is to the desired variation.

C_{pk} is an index of how close the process is delivering within the specification limits taking into accounts its natural variance. C_{pk} calculates the upper variance (above the target) and lower variance (below the target) separately, which is useful when the distribution or specification limits are not symmetrical. The larger the C_{pk}, the fewer the number of occurrences outside the specification limits.

Q. 7.10: *Due to process variability, a continuous performance characteristic X has a normal probability density function with a mean μ and standard deviation σ. However, due to process drift, mean μ can be shifted from target value* $\bar{X}_0$ *by an amount σ i.e.* $\mu = \bar{X}_0 + \sigma$ *Fig. 7.6. Specification limits are* $USL = \bar{X}_0 + 4\sigma$, $LSL = \bar{X}_0 - 4\sigma$. *For* $\sigma = 0, 0.5\sigma, 1.0\sigma, 2.0\sigma, 2.5\sigma, 3.0\sigma$.

(a) *Compute* C_p

(b) *Compute* C_{pk}

(c) *Do you see any advantage* C_{pk} *as compared to* C_p

(d) *Probability of product being rejected.*

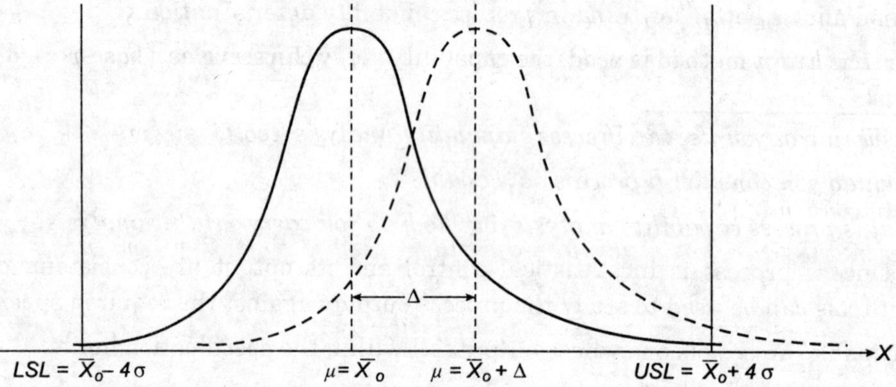

FIGURE 7.6 Shift in mean from target value.

Ans. : when $X = LSL = \bar{X}_0 - 4\sigma$, $\mu = \bar{X}_0 + \Delta$

$$z = \frac{\bar{X}_0 - 4\sigma - (\bar{X}_0 + \Delta)}{\sigma} = -4 - \frac{\Delta}{\sigma}$$

When $X = USL = \bar{X}_0 + 4\sigma$, $\mu = \bar{X}_0 + \Delta$

$$z = \frac{\bar{X}_0 + 4\sigma - (\bar{X}_0 - \Delta)}{\sigma} = 4 - \frac{\Delta}{\sigma}$$

Answers to Parts (*a*), (*b*), (*c*) and (*d*) are given in the following tabulation. We note that as shift Δ increases, the probability of the product being rejected increases rapidly. This change in Δ is not detected by C_p which remains at 1.33. The change is detected by C_{pk} which decreases from 1.33 to 0.33 as the process is increasingly unable to meet the specifications.

Δ	$C_p = \frac{U-L}{6\sigma}$	$C_{pL} = \frac{\mu - L}{3\sigma}$	$C_{pU} = \frac{U-\mu}{3\sigma}$	C_{pk}	*Probability of X below L*	*Probability of X above U*	*Probability of rejection*
0	$\frac{8\sigma}{6\sigma} = 1.33$	$\frac{4\sigma}{3\sigma} = 1.33$	$\frac{4\sigma}{3\sigma} = 1.33$	1.33	0.00003	0.00003	0.00006
0.5 σ	1.33	1.50	1.17	1.17	0	0.00023	0.00023
1.0 σ	1.33	1.67	1.00	1.00	0	0.00014	0.00014
1.5 σ	1.33	1.83	0.83	0.83	0	0.00620	0.00620
2.0 σ	1.33	2.00	0.67	0.67	0	0.02280	0.02280
2.5 σ	1.33	2.17	0.50	0.50	0	0.06680	0.06680
3.0 σ	1.33	2.33	0.33	0.33	0	0.15870	0.15870

Q. 7.11: *Specifications on the dimension of a certain part are* **101.550 ± 0.200**. *Parts produced outside specifications must be scrapped. Two automatic machines produce these parts at a rate of* **100** *units per hour each. Items from both machines are discharged into a single tote box from which the inspector selects a subgroup of 5 parts every half-hour. Adjustments to both machines are made only on the approval of the inspector.*

(a) After **50** *subgroups have been drawn $\Sigma \bar{X}$ = 72.25 and ΣR = 8.80. To simplify the arithmetic* **100** *has been subtracted from each value of X. Determine the control limits for $\bar{X}$ and R charts.*

(b) Assuming no points are outside the control limits on either chart and no significant runs are apparent, based on a normal distribution of the characteristic. What would you estimate the fraction nonconfirming to be ?

(c) Recentering the process would reduce this estimate of fraction nonconforming to what level ?

(d) What is the process capability (± 3 standard deviation) ?

(e) What is capability potential ?

Ans:

$$\bar{\bar{X}} = 100 + \frac{\Sigma\bar{X}}{100} \text{ i.e. } 100 + \frac{72.25}{50}$$

$$= 101.547$$

$$\bar{R} = \frac{8.80}{50} = 0.176$$

(a)

$$UCL_{\bar{X}} = 101.547$$

$$LCL_{\bar{X}} = 101.343$$

$$UCL_R = 0.371$$

$$LCL_R = 0$$

(b)

$$\hat{\sigma} = \frac{\bar{R}}{d_2} = \frac{0.176}{2.326} = 0.0757$$

$$U = 101.550 + 0.200 = 101.750$$
$$L = 101.550 - 0.200 = 101.350$$

Area of the normal curve below L as interpolated from Table A is 0.1047.

Area of the normal curve above U as interpreted from Table A is 0.

Hence fraction nonconforming = 0.1047.

(*c*) Recentering the process exactly the midway *i.e.* at 101.550 well reduce the fraction nonconforming as determined from Table *A*, to 0.0082.

(*d*) Process capability ($\pm$ 3 σ) = $\pm$ 3 (0.0757) = 0.227

(*e*) Capability potential (C_p) = $\dfrac{U-L}{6\hat{\sigma}} = \dfrac{0.4}{6(0.0757)} = 0.88$

As C_p is less than 1, the process is not capable of meeting the specifications.

Q. 7.12: *In order to study the machine capability of a certain machine, the characteristic selected is the diameter of gear blanks which this machine is supposed to produce. The diameter specifications are 1.6950-1.7000 inches. The usual procedure for capability study is followed. The data are coded. The measurement unit is 0.0001 inch, and readings are recorded from a 1.6900 inch zero setting. The* $\bar{X}$ *and R for 20 subgroups of 5 each are recorded as follows:*

Subgroup No.	$\bar{X}$	*R*
1	71	20
2	72	10
3	74	25
4	.67	20
5	79	25
6	78	25
7	70	35
8	80	25
9	72	20
10	83	20
11	81	25
12	74	30
13	72	20
14	71	30
15	70	40
16	75	40
17	74	20
18	64	20
19	66	25
20	68	20

(a) Show the various steps involved in capability study.

(b) Is the machine really capable of meeting the specifications ?
(c) Do you suspect any change in the process by looking at the R chart ?
(d) What is the fraction nonconforming likely to be produced ?
(e) If reworking is allowed, where the process should be centered ?

Ans. : *(a)* Following the usual method of capability study, the following steps would be involved.

1. Compute the maximum allowable tolerance range

$$= 1.7000 - 1.6950 - 0.0050$$

Coded value $= 50.$

Allowable tolerance range

$$= (0.8407)\ (0.75)\ (\text{total tolerance})$$
$$= (0.8407)\ (0.75)\ (50)$$
$$= 31.5$$

Check the ranges for the first five samples

$$R_1 = 20,\ R_2 = 10,\ R_3 = 25,\ \text{R4} = 20,\ \text{R5} = 25$$

Since these values are less than 31.5, proceed to next test.

2. Compute the control limits for the maximum range to test for range stability :

$$UCL_R = D_4\bar{R}$$

$$\bar{R} = \frac{\Sigma R}{5} = \frac{20 + 10 + 25 + 20 + 25}{5} = \frac{100}{5} = 20$$

$$UCL_R = 2.11\ (20) = 42.2$$

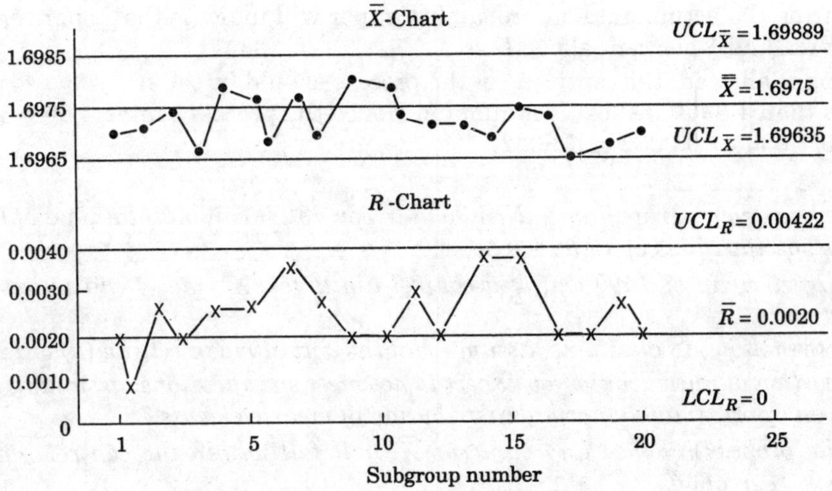

FIGURE 7.7 Average and range chart for gear blank diameter

Project this value of R chart to assess range stability for subsequent subgroups. This is done in Fig. 7.7.

3. Compute the control limits for averages to determine state of control.

$$UCL_{\bar{X}} = 86.56$$
$$LCL_{\bar{X}} = 63.44$$

Project these limits on $\bar{X}$ chart to assess stability for subsequent subgroups. This is done in Fig. 7.7.

4. Test for demonstrated machine capability. The 15 subsequent subgroups as seen from Fig. 7.7 are within the limits projected for averages and ranges. Therefore, the machine capability can be determined by calculating

$$\hat{\sigma} = \frac{\bar{R}}{d_2}$$

$$\bar{R} = \frac{20 + 10 + ... + 20}{20} = \frac{495}{20} = 24.75$$

$$6\hat{\sigma} = \frac{(6)(24.75)}{2.326} = 63.84$$

$$C_p = \frac{U - L}{6\hat{\sigma}} = \frac{50}{63.84} = 0.78$$

(b) Since $C_p < 1$, the machine is not capable.

(c) It is seen from R chart that none of the subsequent ranges were below the estimated $\bar{R}$ and that evidently some change occurred.

(d) Assuming a normal distribution,

z corresponding to $U = \frac{100 - 75}{10.64} = 2.350$

z corresponding to $L = \frac{50 - 75}{10.64} = -2.350$

From Table *A*, the percentage of products below L is 0.94 and above U is also 0.94. Hence fraction nonconforming is 0.0188.

However, plotting the actual data on probability paper will indicate that 2 per cent of the product balls below L and 1 per cent above U.

(e) If reworking is allowed, the centering of the process should be set at $L + 3\sigma$ so that the scrap (blanks less than 1.6950 inches) is minimum. Hence the process center = 50 + 3 (10.64) = 81.92 ≈ 82 *i.e.* at 1.6900 + 0.0082 or 1.6982.

Q. 7.13: *A process has demonstrated that, when held in control, it can maintain a σ of* ***0.15*** *cm. A certain part has specifications of* ***15.00 ± 0.50*** *cm.*

(a) Using a target mean of ***1500*** *cm, find control limits for* $\bar{X}$ *and R charts based on a subgroup size of 4 units.*

In answering the following questions, assume that the actual mean setting (μ) is ***14.90*** *cm.*

(b) What proportion of units would you expect to not meet specifications, assuming that the process generates an approximately normal distribution of measurements ?

(c) What is the probability that any value of $\bar{X}$ *will fall within the control limits (the probability the Type II error) ?*

(d) Test the natural process spread (6 σ) against the specification range. Is this process capable? Also calculate the process capability indexes Cp and C_{pk}.

Ans:

$$U = 15.00 + 0.50 = 15.5\ ;\ L = 15.00 - 0.50 = 14.5$$

$$\bar{X}_0 = 15.00,\ \sigma = 0.15$$

$$UCL_{\bar{X}} = \bar{X}_0 + A\sigma = 15.0 + 1.5(0.15) = 15.225$$

$$LCL_{\bar{X}} = \bar{X}_0 - A\sigma = 15.0 - 1.5(0.15) = 15.225$$

$$UCL_R = D_2\,\sigma = 4.70 \times 0.15 = 0.705$$

$$LCL_R = D_1\,\sigma = 0 \times 0.5 = 0$$

(*b*) When $\mu = 14.90$, the portion above U of 15.50 is almost nil but the portion below L computed to be 0.0038 i.e 0.38%.

(*c*) $$\sigma_{\bar{X}} = \frac{\sigma}{\sqrt{n}} = \frac{0.15}{\sqrt{4}} = 0.075$$

With μ of 14.90, the portion above $UCL_{\bar{X}}$ of 15.225 is almost nil but the portion below $LCL_{\bar{X}}$ of 14.775 is 0.0475. Hence the probability of *Type II* error is $1 - 0.0475$ i.e 0.9525.

(*d*) $U - L = 1.0$ and $6\sigma = 6 \times 0.15$ i.e 0.9.

As $U - L > 6\sigma$, the process is capable.

Also $$C_p = \frac{U - L}{6\sigma} = \frac{1.0}{0.90} = 1.11$$

$$C_{pL} = \frac{\mu - L}{3\sigma} = \frac{14.90 - 14.50}{3 \times 0.15} = 0.89$$

$$C_{pU} = \frac{U - \mu}{3\sigma} = \frac{15.50 - 14.50}{3 \times 0.15} = 1.33$$

$$C_{pk} = \min (C_{pL}, C_{pU}) \text{ i.e } 0.89$$

Q. 7.14: *(a) What do the control limits on control charts indicate?*

(b) Is capability index related to control limits?

(c) Illustrate by diagrams the situations (a) $c_p > 1$; (b) $c_p = 1$; (c) $c_{pk} < 1$; (d) $c_p > 1$.

Ans: (*a*) Control limits on the control charts indicate the expected extent of 'common-cause' variation. If any points lie outside these control limits then the process can be deemed out of control in the sense that variation is likely to be due to assignable causes.

(*b*) Process capability potential is not related to control limits.

(*c*) Figure 7.8 shows the four cases. In (*a*) $c_p > 1$, in (*b*) $c_p = 1$, in (*c*) $c_p < 1$ and (*d*) $c_{pk} < 1$.

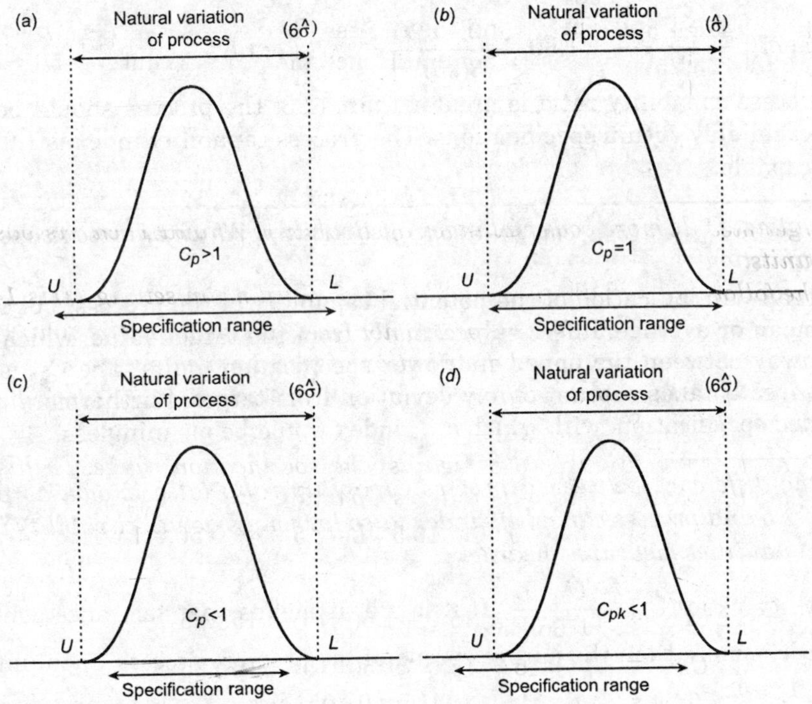

FIGURE 7.8

Q. 7.15: *(a) Explain how a process can be in statistical control but still produce bad products?*

(b) Pioneer Chicken advertises "lite" chicken with 30 percent less calories. (The pieces are 33 percent smaller.) The process average distribution for breasts is 420 calories with a stand deviation of the population of 25 calories. Pioneer randomly takes samples of six chicken breasts to measure calorie content.

(i) Design an $\bar{X}$ -chart, using the process standard deviation.

(ii) The product design calls for the average chicken breast to contain 400 colaries ± 100 calories. Calculate the process capability ratio (target = 1.33) and the process capability index. Interpret the results.

Ans: (*a*) A process can be in statistical control but still not be capable of producing some of the bad products. The process capabilities ratio and the process capability index are quantitative measures used to assess the capability of a process.

(*b*) (*i*)

$$\sigma_{\bar{X}} = \sigma_{\sqrt{n}} = \frac{25}{\sqrt{6}} = 10.2 = 10.2$$

$$UCL_{\bar{X}} = 420 + 3\ (10.2) = 450.6$$

$$LCL_{\bar{X}} = 420 - 3\ (10.2) = 389.4$$

(*ii*) The process capability ratio is

$$C_p = \frac{\text{Upper specification} - \text{Lower specification}}{6\sigma}$$

$$= \frac{500 \text{ calories} - 300 \text{ calories}}{6(25)} = 1.333$$

The process capability index is

$$C_{pk} = \text{Minimum of}\left[\frac{\bar{\bar{X}} - \text{Lower Specification}}{3\sigma}, \frac{\text{Lower Specification} - \bar{X}}{3\sigma}\right]$$

$$= \text{Minimum of}\left[\frac{420 - 300}{3(25)} = 1.60, \frac{500 - 420}{3(25)} = 1.07\right] = 1.07$$

Because the process capability ratio is greater than 1.33, the process should be able to produce the product reliably within specifications. The process capability index is 1.07, so the current process is capable.

Q. 7.16: *Why C_{pk} and not C_p is more powerful index of capability. Which of these two to be used with one sided specification.*

Ans: The C_p index gives an indication of the potential capability of the process, but it can be misleading if the mean or average differs substantially from the target value, which is often assumed to be midway between the upper and lower specification limits. The C_{pk} is a more powerful index because it takes account of any deviation from target. Furthermore it can be used with a one-sided specification, with which a C_p index would be meaningless.

Q. 7.17: *What is the difference between a process capability ratio (also known as potential capability index) of 1.5 and process capability index (also known as actual capability index) of 1.5? What do these quantities measures mean?*

Ans: Process capability ratio (C_p) = $\frac{U - L}{6\sigma}$. If it is 1.5, it means that tolerance zone of the quality characteristic is more than the nature spread of the process. Process Capability index (C_{pk}) = $\min\left(\frac{\mu - L}{3\sigma}, \frac{U - \mu}{3\sigma}\right)$. If the is also 1.5, it mean that the difference between any than the natural spread concerning that limit. When C_p equals C_{pk}, the process is centered between the U and L limits and hence the mean of the process distribution is centered on the nominal value of the design specifications *i.e.* at the mid point of the specification range.

Q. 7.18: *If three sigma quality is equivalent to process capability (C_p) of 1, What is the process capability equivalent to six-sigma quality being followed by Motorola?*

Ans. : If C_p defined as then $\dfrac{U-L}{6\sigma} = 1$. Now if $U - L = \pm\, 6\sigma$, (*i.e.* 12σ) then c_p will be 2.

Q. 7.19: *The Marline Company produces plastic bottles to customer order. The quality inspector randomly selects four bottles from the bottle machine and measures the outside diameter of the bottle neck, a critical quality dimension that determines whether the bottle cap will fit properly. The dimensions (in.) from the last six samples are*

Sample	*Bottle*			
	1	*2*	*3*	*4*
1	0.604	0.612	0.588	0.600
2	0.597	0.601	0.607	0.603
3	0.581	0.570	0.585	0.592
4	0.620	0.605	0.595	0.588
5	0.590	0.614	0.608	0.604
6	0.585	0.583	0.617	0.579

(*a*) *Assuming that using only six samples is sufficient, use the data in the table to determine control limits for an R chart and an $\bar{X}$ chart.*

(*b*) *Suppose that the specifications for the bottle neck diameter are* ***0.600 ± 0.050*** *inch. If the population standard deviation is 0.012 inch, is the process capable of producing the bottle ?*

Ans. : (*a*) Simple computation will yield

$$\bar{\bar{X}} = 0.597 \text{ and } \bar{R} = 0.025$$

Now with $n = 4$,

$$UCL_{\bar{X}} = 0.615 \text{ and } LCL_{\bar{X}} = 0.597$$

$$UCL_R = 0.057 \text{ and } LCL_R = 0$$

(*b*)

$$\hat{\sigma} = \frac{\bar{R}}{d_2} = \frac{0.025}{2.059} = 0.0012$$

$$C_p = \frac{\bar{U} - L}{6\hat{\sigma}} = \frac{0.650 - 0.550}{6(0.012)}$$

$$= 1.39$$

$$C_{pk} = \min.\ (C_{pU}, C_{pL})$$

$$C_{pU} = \frac{0.650 - 0.597}{3(0.012)}$$

$$= 1.47$$

$$C_{pL} = \frac{0.597 - 0.550}{3(0.012)}$$

$$= 1.306$$

Hence $C_{pk} = 1.306$ which is >1. Hence the process is capable of producing the bottles.

Q. 7.20: *The following are measures of the impurity, iron, in a fine chemical which is to be used in phramaceutical products. The data is given in parats per million (ppm).*

Sample	X_1	X_2	X_3	X_4	X_5
1	15	11	8	15	6
2	14	16	11	14	7
3	13	6	9	5	10
4	15	15	9	5	10
5	9	12	9	6	10
6	11	14	11	12	5
7	13	12	9	6	10
8	10	15	12	4	6
9	8	12	14	9	10
10	10	10	9	14	14
11	13	16	12	15	18
12	7	10	9	11	16
13	11	7	16	10	14
14	11	7	10	10	7
15	13	9	12	13	17
16	17	10	11	9	8
17	4	14	5	11	11
18	8	9	6	13	9
19	9	10	7	10	13
20	15	10	12	12	16

Set up the average and range charts and comment on the possibility of using them for future control of the iron content.

Ans. : Simple computations yield

$$\bar{\bar{X}} = 10.8,\ \bar{R} = 7.5 \text{ and } \sigma = \frac{\bar{R}}{d_2} = \frac{7.5}{2.326} \text{ i.e. } 3.2.$$

$$UCL_{\bar{X}} = 10.8 + 0.58\ (7.5) = 15.15$$

$$LCL_{\bar{X}} = 10.8 - 0.58\ (7.5) = 5.65$$

$$UCL_R = (2.11)\ (7.5) = 15.83$$

$$LCL_R = (0)\ (7.5) = 0$$

A plot of $\bar{X}$ values an $\bar{X}$ -chart will indicate that the process is in statistical control.

$$\hat{\sigma} = \frac{\bar{R}}{d_2} = \frac{7.5}{2.326} = 3.22$$

$$C_{pL} = \frac{\bar{\bar{X}} - L}{3\hat{\sigma}}$$

$$C_{pU} = \frac{U - \bar{\bar{X}}}{3\sigma}$$

$$C_{pk} = \text{min.}\ (C_{pL}, C_{pU})$$

Since here we are concerned with maximum amount of impurities which can be tolerated,

$$C_{pk} = C_{pU} = \frac{U - \bar{\bar{X}}}{3\hat{\sigma}}$$

If $\quad C_{pk} = 2$, then $2 = \dfrac{U - 10.8}{3(3.22)}$

i.e. $\quad U = 10.8 + 2 \times 3\ (3.22) = 30.1$ ppm.

Q. 7.21: *Steel pins are purchased in lot sizes of 10,000 and used in the manufacture of textile machinery. The agreed specification for the pin lengths is 30 to 32 mm. Following problems with the lengths of the pins, the supplier was persuaded to carry out a process capability study from which it was concluded that the process was in statistical control with a Cpk of 2.1 (sample size n = 4). The manufacturer further agreed to maintain control of the pin length using mean and range control charts, but was unwilling to supply the details of either the process capability study or the control charts. In addition there were still occasional problems with both short and long pins. A random sample of fifty pins was taken from one delivered batch and the lengths measured. These gave a mean value of 31.2 mm and a standard deviation of 0.4 mm.*

(a) How do you interpret the batch results ?

(b) What percentage, if any, of this batch would lie outside the tolerance band ?

(c) What options are open to both the customer and the supplier ?

Ans. : (*a*) Let us assume that during the capability study the process was centred (this will be the easiest way for the manufacturer to achieve a C_{pk} of 2.1 with $n = 4$). Then:

$$2.1 = C_{pk} = (U - \bar{\bar{X}})/3\sigma = (32 - 31)/3\sigma$$

So $\quad \sigma = (32 - 31)/(2.1 \times 3) = 0.16$ mm

Had the process not been properly centred (i.e. maintained at a value < 31) during the capability study this estimate of the standard deviation would be greater than that observed. If control charts were being used for product classification, and all pins produced prior reaching an $UCL_{\bar{X}}$ were eliminated from the despatches, the probability of finding any pins outside the specification limits would be extremely small-rising to a probability of 0.00135 or 1 in 740 infrequent occasions.

Of course, the standard deviation of the delivered batch (i.e. 0.4 mm) is greater than the standard deviation determined during the process capability study (i.e. 0.16). If we assume that the distribution of the pins in the batch examined was normal, from the properties of the normal distribution we would expect to find only 0.27 per cent of pins outside the plus and minus three standard deviations zone. The batch results indicate that this zone is from :

$31.2 \pm 3\sigma$ *i.e.* $31.2 - (3 \times 0.4)$ to $31.2 + (3 \times 0.4)$

or 30 mm to 32.4

So, at the lower end of the specification (30 mm) there is about 0.00135 change of finding non-conforming pins and at the upper end (32 mm) there is a greater probability. If the distribution was non-normal, one of the tails would be longer than the normal distribution tail and, in either case, there would be even more non-conforming product at that side of the distribution. None of these probabilities of nonduconformance are consistent with the declared C_{pk} and the use of mean and range charts for the control of both the process and the product.

Conclusion

The supplier's claims to have a process in statistical control with a C_{pk} of 2.1, and to be using mean and range charts for process control and product classification are suspect.

(*b*) In order to estimate the proportion of product outside the tolerance zone, we shall be obliged, either to assume that the distribution is normal

The estimates of the mean and the standard deviation based on a random sample of fifty pins taken at random from one batch will be adequate to describe the characteristics of that batch. A similar sampling of several other batches will reveal whether the problem is general or limited to the one batch. If the discussion with the supplier is centred around the characteristics of the only batch studied, the problem may not have been well defined. Either there is a general problem which can be justified by examining several batches selected at random, or the problem relates to isolated batches. These may be different problems arising from different causes and requiring different solutions.

(*c*) While any nonconforming pins should be tabled during the discussion remember that these only provide a convincing demonstration of the effect. The object of the discussion is to persuade the supplier to locate the causes of the effect the eliminate them in order to eliminate the effect.

If similar or identical pins are purchased from other suppliers, repeat the same analysis on several batches of their product, or much better, seek their permission to make use of their process capability and process control chart data. If their capability is good, why should they wish to be shy about it.

The reader will be able to think of other reasons why the preferred option is to prepare for the discussion with the supplier, collect further evidence, and enter the discussions with a coherent and reasonably complete story.

Q. 7.22: *(a) Illustrate clearly various "process capability indices" and the physical significance of them.*

(b) A light-bulb production process yield bulbs with an average life of ***90*** *hours and a standard deviation of 4.8 hours. The nominal value of the tolerance range is* ***100*** *hours. The operation manager wants to determine whether the process is capable of producing the bulbs to specification. What will you advice him ?*

Ans. : (*a*) It is essential to know whether a given process is capable of making a product which meets the specification for that product. Capability indices compare the standard deviation $\hat{\sigma}$ of product characteristic, caused by process variability with the product specification limits *LSL* (or *L*) and *USL* (or *U*).

Potential capability index. Process capability ratio (C_p) also known as is a measure or the theoretical or inherent capability of a process to meet the product specification. It is defined by

$$C_p = \frac{U - L}{6\hat{\sigma}}$$

C_p is used at the process design stage :

If $C_p = 1.0$, process is just potentially capable of meeting the specifications.

If $C_p < 1.0$, process is potentially incapable.

If $C_p > 1.0$ process is potentially capable.

Actual capability index. C_{pk} is a measure of how well the actual process is meeting the product specification, it defined by

$$C_{pk} = \min.\left\{\frac{\hat{\mu} - L}{3\hat{\sigma}}, \frac{U - \hat{\mu}}{3\hat{\sigma}}\right\}$$

i.e. min (C_{pL}, C_{pU})

The values of C_{pk}, have the same meaning as before : if C_{pk} is greater than 1 the process s meeting the specification, if C_{pk} is less than 1 the process is not meeting the specification. However C_{pk} has the advantages over C_p that it can detect a shift in the mean value $\overline{X}$ from the target value X_0. C_p cannot detect this shift and is therefore not suitable for measuring actual process capability. C_{pk} is calculated online from $\hat{\mu}$ and $\hat{\sigma}$.

(*b*) $$C_p = \frac{120 - 80}{6(4.8)} = 1.39 \qquad C_{pL} = \frac{90 - 80}{3(4.8)} = 0.69$$

$$C_{pU} = \frac{120 - 90}{3(4.8)} = 2.08$$

Hence C_{pk} = Minimum of (0.69, 2.08) *i.e.* 0.69.

The potential capability index or capability ratio (C_p) of 1.39 shows that the machine's variability is acceptable relative to the range of the tolerance limit *i.e.* the process is capable of meeting the specification. However, the actual capability index *i.e.* C_{pk} indicates that the distribution of output is too close to the lower specification and that short-lived bulbs will be produced. The manager should look for ways to bring average of the process closer to the nominal value of the design specifications.

Q. 7.23: *(a) Define process capability. What is its purpose? How do you carry out process capability study?*

(b) How do you express process capability?

(c) If the tolerance for the process are 2.50 ± 0.005, and the process is centered. The σ = 0.0027, what is C_p? Is the process capable of ensuring 99.73% of good parts?

(i) If C_p is to be 1, what should be the value of σ? What will it guarantee?

(ii) If the process average shifts to 2.498 and σ is as in (i), what is the process capability? Illustrate the situation with a diagram.

Ans: (*a*) Process capability is a measure of the natural behavior of the process after special causes of variation are eliminated. The basic purpose of process capability is to compare the 'normal variation' of the process against the design tolerances to assess whether the process is able to meet those specifications. Several vehicles exist to conduct a process-capability analysis. Probability plots and histograms, control charts limits, and design of experiments are the most common.

(*b*) Process capability is usually expressed via indexes and ratios that require that the data be distributed normally and that the process be in a state of statistical control. All the known indices relate the normal variation of the process to the engineering specifications.

Following table 4 gives all capability indexes.

TABLE : COMMON PROCESS CAPABILITY INDICES

Index	*Remarks*
$C_p = \dfrac{U - L}{6\sigma}$	Measures the capability of the process if it is centered (*i.e.*, $\bar{\bar{X}} = \mu$). It represents the process potential.
$C_{pU} = \dfrac{U - \mu}{3\sigma}$	Considers unilateral tolerance when only upper specification limit is necessary.
$C_{pL} = \dfrac{\mu - L}{3\sigma}$	Considers unilateral tolerance when only lower specification limit is necessary.
C_{pk} = min	Measures the actual capability when the process is not centered (i.e. $\bar{X} \neq \mu$).

(c) $C_p = \dfrac{U - L}{6\sigma} = \dfrac{2.505 - 2.495}{6(0.0027)} = 0.6173$

This means that the natural variation of the process (6σ) is much larger than the tolerance band given. Then, the process is incapable of ensuring 99.73% of good parts.

(*i*) If C_p is to be 1, the tolerance limits should be set at 2.500 ± 0.0081 and this will guarantee that only 2700 ppm (parts per million) are expected to be defective.

(*ii*) If the process is biased (i.e. the dispersion is the same as before but the average has shifted), which is the case here because process average has shifted from 2.500 to 2.498. In this case the process capability ratio to be used is the C_{pk} = min. (C_{pU}, C_{pL})

$$C_{pU} = \frac{2.505 - 2.498}{3(0.0027)} = 0.8642$$

$$C_{pL} = \frac{2.498 - 2.495}{3(0.0027)} = 0.3704$$

Therefore $C_{pk} = 0.3704$, which means that 2-mil shift in the process average has slashed the capability of the process almost be half! Figure 7.9 illustrated the situation.

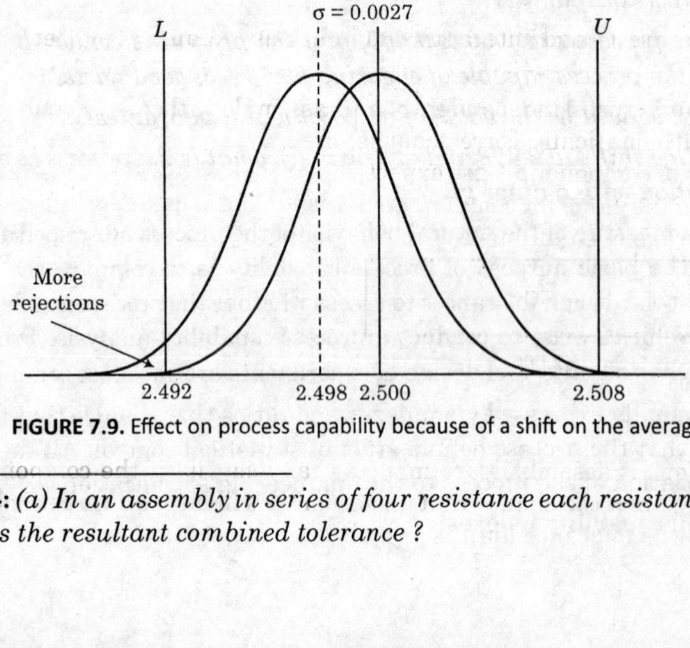

FIGURE 7.9. Effect on process capability because of a shift on the average.

Q. 7.24: *(a) In an assembly in series of four resistance each resistance has a tolerance of ± 3 ohms. What is the resultant combined tolerance ?*

(b) The tolerance for a coated fabic is ± 5 length of an ounce per yard. The finishing plant is able to maintain a tolerance of ± 3 for the weight of coating. What is the tolerance for the uncoated material ?

(c) Tolerances for weight of an airborne component, consisting of 14 parts, are as follows:

1. A tolerance of ± 6 oz. for 3 parts.

2. A tolerance of ± 8 oz. for 5 parts.

3. A tolerance of ± 4 oz. for 6 parts.

What is the assembly tolerance ?

Ans. : *(a)* $(U-L)_{\text{part}} = 3+3 = 6$

$$(U-L)_{\text{sum}} = \sqrt{(6)^2+(6)^2+(6)^2+(6)^2} = 12$$

The resultant combined tolerance

$$= \pm 6 \text{ ohms}$$

(b) $(U-L)_{\text{sum}} = 10$

$$(U-L)_f = 6$$

$$(U-L)_{\text{material}} = \sqrt{(10)^2-(6)^2} = 8$$

Material tolerance = ± 4 tenths oz./yard

(c) $(U-L)_{\text{sum}} = \sqrt{(3\times 12^2)+(5\times 16^2)+(6\times 8^2)} = 45.78$

Assembly tolerance = ± 22.89 oz.

Q. 7.25: *(a) Why the arithmetic addition of tolerances on interacting dimensions is considered to be inaccurate ?*

(b) The standard deviation of an assembly comprising of three components is given by formula:

$$(\sigma)_{assembly} = \sqrt{\sigma_A^2+\sigma_B^2+\sigma_C^2}$$

State the assumption in using this formula.

Ans: Solution. (a) Interacting dimensions are those which mate or merge with other dimensions to create a final result. Considering the simple mechanical assembly shown in Fig. 7.10, the lengths of components *A*, *B*, are *C* and interacting dimensions because they determine the overall assembly length.

If these lengths are manufactured independently and assembled, then approach of adding component tolerances is mathematically correct but is often too conservative. Suppose that about 1 percent of the pieces of component *A* are expected to be below the lower tolerance limit for component *A* and suppose the same for components *B* and *C*. If a component A is selected at random, there is, on the average, 1 chance in 100 that it will be on the low side, and similarly

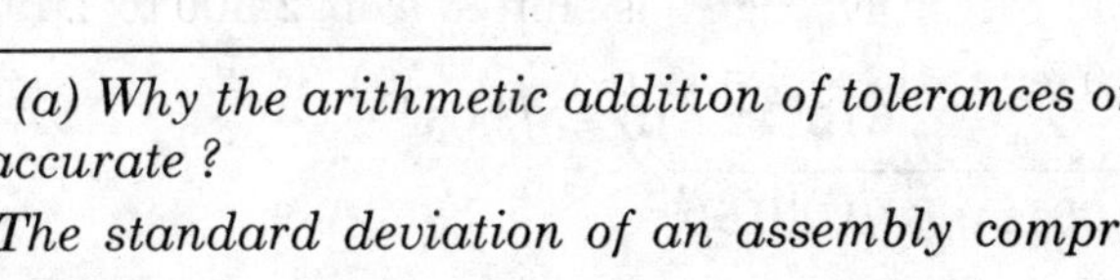

FIGURE 7.10 Mechanical assembly

for components *B* and *C*. Now, if assembles are made at random and if the components are manufactured independently, then the chance that an assembly will have all three components simultaneously below the lower tolerance limit is

$$\frac{1}{100} \times \frac{1}{100} \times \frac{1}{100} = \frac{1}{10,00,000}$$

Thus there is a very small chance that all three components will be too small, resulting in a small assembly. Thus, setting component and assembly tolerances based on the simple addition formula is inaccurate in that it fails to recognize the extremely low probability of an assembly containing all low (or all high) components.

(*b*) In using the formula $\sigma_{assembly} = \sqrt{\sigma_A^2 + \sigma_B^2 + \sigma_C^2}$, the following assumptions are usually made:

1. The component dimensions are independent and the components are assembled randomly.
2. Each component dimension should be normally distributed. Some departure from this assumption is permissible.
3. The actual average for each component is equal to the nominal value stated in the specification.

Q. 7.26: *Two mating parts a and b have dimensions specified as* ***2.610*** *cm and* ***2.615*** *cm respectively. Control chart analysis indicate that the standard deviation of a and b are* ***0.0012*** *and* ***0.0015*** *respectively. If the distributions of a and b are normal and centered about the specified dimensions and if parts are assembled at random. Compute the probability of a greater clearance than* ***0.010*** *inch.*

Ans: The existing clearance

$$= \bar{\bar{X}}_a - \bar{\bar{X}}_b = 2.615 - 2.610 = 0.005$$

$$\sigma_{b-a} = \sqrt{(0.0012)^2 + (0.0015)^2}$$

$$= 0.00192.$$

Both the variations are normally distributed, the difference between the variables is also normally distributed. From this fact the probability of a clearance larger than 0.010 may be calculated.

z corresponding to clearance of 0.010 in. $= \dfrac{0.010 - 0.005}{0.00192} = 2.63$

From Table *A*, the area of the normal curve = 0.9953.

The area of curve beyond the clearance of 0.010 = 1 – 0.9953 = 0.0047.

Hence the probability of clearance greater than 0.010 is 0.0047.

Q. 7.27: *Control chart analysis indicates that the standard deviation of the distributions of the dimensions of two mating parts C and D are* ***0.008*** *in., and* ***0.0020*** *in., respectively. It is desired that the probability of a smaller clearance than* ***0.0020*** *in. should be* ***0.005****. What distance between the average dimensions of C and D should be specified by the designer ? Assume normal distribution and random assembly. With this distance specified, what is the probability that two parts assembled at random will have a greater clearance than* ***0.0120*** *in ?*

Ans:

$$\sigma_{C+D} = \sqrt{(0.0008)^2 + (0.0020)^2}$$

$$= 0.00215.$$

Let, $\bar{X}$ be the average dimension of C + D. If probability of a smaller clearance than 0.0020 is 0.005, it means that the area of the normal curve below the specified limit of 0.0020 is 0.005. From Table *A* the value of z corresponding to the area of 0.005 is – 2.575.

Hence, $$-2.575 = \frac{0.0020 - \bar{X}_{C+D}}{0.00215}$$

$$\bar{X}_{C+D} = 0.0075.$$

z corresponding to a clearance of 0.012, is $\frac{0.012 - 0.0075}{0.00215}$ *i.e.* 2.093. For this value of z, Table A gives the area of the normal curve as 0.9818. Hence the probability that two parts assembled at random have a greater clearance than 0.012 is 1.0 − 0.9818 = 0.0182.

Q. 7.28: *Figure 7.11., shows a shaft (C), two rotating discs (B and D) keyed to the end do the shaft, and a frame (9) which must fit on the shaft between the dises. The specifications are :*

B : 1.000 ± 0.001 inch

C : 5.000 ± 0.004 inch

D : 1.500 ± 0.002 inch.

Assume that all dimensions are normally distributed and the specifications are being met.

(a)What would be a reasonable specification to set on A ?

(b) What are the maximum and minimum possible dimensions for A ?

Ans. : (*a*)

$$(U-L)_{\text{assembly}} = 0.008$$
$$(U-L)_B = 0.002$$
$$(U-L)_D = 0.004$$
$$(U-L)_{\text{assembly}} = \sqrt{(U-L)_B^2 + (U-L)_A^2 + (U-L)_D^2}$$
$$0.008 = \sqrt{(0.002)^2 + (U-L)_A^2 + (0.004)^2}$$
$$(U-L)_A = 0.006$$

Tolerance on $A = +0.003$

$$\bar{X}_A = 5.000 - (1.000 + 1.500) = 2.500$$

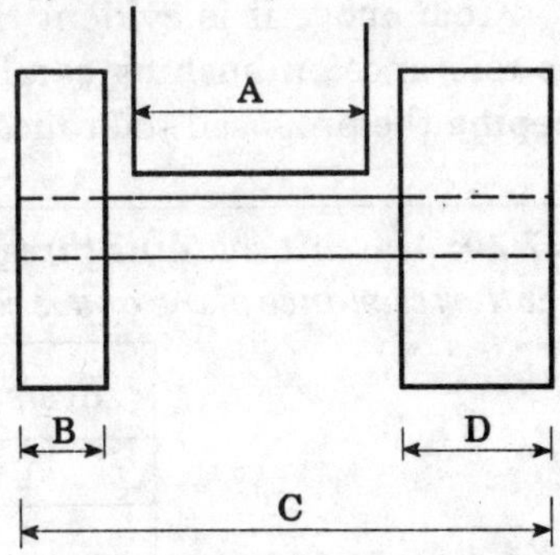

FIGURE 7.11 Assembly for Prob. 7.16

Upper specification on A = 2.500 + 0.003 = 2.503

Lower specification on A = 2.500 − 0.003 = 2.497.

(*b*) Maximum and minimum possible dimensions on A can be calculated conveniently with the help of following tabulation :

	C	B	D	A
Average	5.000	1.000	1.5000	$C - (B + D) = 2.5000$
Tolerance	± 0.004	± 0.001	± 0.002	
Maximum	5.004	1.001	1.502	$C_{MAX} - (B_{MAX} + D_{MIN}) = 0.507$
Minimum	4.996	0.999	1.498	$C_{MIN} - (B_{MAX} + D_{MAX}) = 0.493$

Q. 7.29: *A manufacturer of rotary lawn received numerous complaints concerning the effort required to push its product. Studies soon found that the small clearance between the wheel bushing and shaft was the cause. Designers decided to increase the clearance to allow easy rotation of the wheel (or provide space for a heavy grease coating), yet be "tight enough" to prevent wobbling. Because of a large inventory of wheels and shafts, a decision was made to ream the bushings to a large inside diameter (I.D) and retain the shafts. The following specifications were proposed :*

Shaft diameter = 0.800 ± 0.002 in.

New clearance = 0.008 ± 0.003 in.

Bushing I.D. = 0.808 ± 0.001 in.

A question was asked concerning tolerances for the bushing I.D. Production people said that they could not economically hold such tolerances with their equipment. Design people countered that they had created the product and should know their business. What comment would you make ?

Ans: New clearance tolerance = ± 0.003

$$(U-L)_{new\ clearance} = 0.006$$

$$(U-L)_{shaft} = 0.004$$

$$(U-L)_{new\ clearance} = \sqrt{(U-L)^2_{shaft} + (U-L)^2_{bushing}}$$

$$0.006 = \sqrt{(0.004)^2 + (U-L)^2_{bushing}}$$

$$(U-L)_{bushing} = 0.0045$$

Tolerance on Bushing

$$= \pm\ 0.0022$$

From above it is evident that the bushing tolerance can be increased to ± 0.0022. Hence the tolerance on bushing can be increased to ± 0.0022 if the production people face difficulty keeping the proposed tolerance of ± 0.001.

Q. 7.30: *A circuit contains three resistors in series. Past data show that it is reasonable to assume that the resistance of the above resistors is normally distributed and the data on the resistance are :*

Resistor	*Mean* ($\bar{X}$)	(σ)
1	125	3
2	200	4
3	600	12

What percent of circuits would meet the specification on total resistance of 930± 30 ohms ?

Ans. :

$$\sigma_{circuit} = \sqrt{\sigma_1^2 + \sigma_2^2 + \sigma_3^2} = \sqrt{3^2 + 4^2 + 12^2}$$

$$= 13$$

$$\bar{X}_{circuit} = 125 + 200 + 600 = 925$$

$$U_{circuit} = \bar{X} + 3\sigma_{circuit}$$

$$= 925 + 3\ (13) = 964$$

$$L_{circuit} = \bar{X} - 3\sigma_{circuit} = 925 - 3\ (13) = 886$$

Upper specification limit = 930 + 30 = 960

Lower specification limit = 930 − 30 = 900

From the specification limits, it is evident that some circuits would not be able to meet the lower limit of 900 and some will exceed the upper limit of 960.

For lower limit of 900,

$$z = \frac{900 - 925}{13} = -1.923$$

From Table *A*, percentage of circuits below the lower limit of 900 is 2.72.

For a upper limit of 960,

$$z = \frac{960 - 9.25}{13} = 2.69$$

Again from Table *A*, the percentage of circuits above the upper limit of 960 is 0.36.

Percentage of circuits meeting the specification (930 ± 30)

$$= 100 - (2.72 + 0.36) = 96.92$$

Q. 7.31: *Manufacturer A produces a metal piece the dimension of which is normally distributed with an (μ) of 8.500 inches and an $\bar{R}$ 0.004 inches based on a subgroup size of four. Manufacturer B produces a second metal piece with a dimension that is also normally distributed with (μ) equal to 6.500 inches and an $\bar{R}$ value of 0.005 inches based on a subgroup size of nine. Company C purchases these two parts and assembles them together to obtain a combines dimension of 15.00 inches. What percent of the combined assemblies would you expect to have a dimension in excess of 15.006 inches ?*

Ans. :

$$\mu_A = 8.500 \text{ inch}$$

$$\sigma_A = \frac{\bar{R}_A}{d_2} = \frac{0.004}{2.059} = 0.00194 \text{ inch}$$

$$\mu_B = 6.500 \text{ inches}$$

$$\sigma_B = \frac{\bar{R}_B}{d_2} = \frac{0.005}{2.970} = 0.00168 \text{ inch}$$

$$\mu_{A+B} = 8.500 + 6.500 = 15.00 \text{ inches}$$

$$\sigma_{A+B} = \sqrt{(0.00194)^2 + (0.00168)^2} = 0.00255$$

Upper natural specification of the process

$$= 15.000 + 3\ (0.00255) = 15.00765$$

From above it is evident that some of the product will be above the upper specification limit of 15.006.

z corresponding to 15.006 is $\dfrac{15.006 - 15.000}{0.00255} = 2.353$

Table *A* gives the area of the normal curve as 0.9901. The area of the curve above the specification limit of 15.006 is 1.0–0.990 i.e. 0.0099. Hence 0.99% of the assemblies will have a dimension greater than 15.006 inches.

Q. 7.32: *Two parts, A and B are received in an assembly operation where each part is permanently attached to the other. When the combined width of parts does not meet the required specification of 10.000 ± 0.020 inches, the assembled product must be scrapped. The width of part A is normally distributed with (μ) equal to 3.000 inches and a σ of 0.004 inches. The width of part B is also normally distributed with (μ) equal to 7.00 inches and a σ of 0.006 inches. Assembly is at random. Determine the percentage of the assembled product that will have to be scrapped.*

Ans. :

$$\sigma_{A+B} = \sqrt{(0.004)^2 + (0.006)^2} = 0.0072$$

$$\mu_{A+B} = 3.000 + 7.000 = 10 \text{ inches}$$

Natural specifications of the process = 10 ± 3 (0.0072) = 10 ± 0.0216.

Specification limits = 10 ± 0.020

From above, it is evident that some of the product will be below the lower specification limit of 0.980 inches and because of symmetry the same amount of product will be above the upper specification limit of 10.020.

z Corresponding to 9.980 is $\dfrac{9.980 - 10.000}{0.0072}$ *i.e.* – 2.78

Corresponding to this value of z, Table A gives the percentage of product below the lower specification limit as 0.28.

Similarly the percentage of product above upper specification limit will be 0.28.

Total scrap = 0.56%

Q. 7.33: *It has been suggested that, when extremely high performance of certain missile components is required, a boundary on the stress requirement be set at 6 standard deviations of the stress requirement above two average stress. The average strength requirement of the article would then be set at 5 standard deviations of the strength of the component above this boundary.*

A certain critical electronic component must operate in salt air environment at an average temperature stress of 30 Celsius. The standard deviation of this temperature is believed to be 5°C.

(a) What must be the minimum acceptable average strength, in terms of average failing temperature, of this component ? Assume that the standard deviation of strength in this case is 3°C.

(b) How much of a safety margin does the requirement provide in multiples of the standard deviation of the combined strength–stress characteristic ?

Ans. : (*a*) Minimum acceptable average strength

$$= 30° + 6\,(5°) + 5\,(3°)$$

$$= 75°C$$

(*b*)
$$\sigma_{sum} = \sqrt{5^2 + 3^2} = 5.831$$

$$\text{Safety margin} = 75°C - 30°C = 45°C$$

Safety margin in multiples of the standard deviation of the combined strength-stress characteristic

$$= \frac{45}{5.831} = 7.717$$

Q. 7.34: *Discuss some situations in which statistical dimensioning does not apply.*

Ans: Statistical dimensioning is basically a sound and practical too. However, there are many situations where it does not apply. Some of these situations are :

Skewed Distribution Statistical dimensioning presumes that manufactured parts may have a normal distribution. Some distribution, however, are skewed ; that is, the demensional distributions, is not centered about the nominal dimension size. Instead, parts favour the high limit or low limit. This situation can significantly increase the number of parts gathered around the extreme limits, and thus increase the probability of encountering impossible assemblies. Skewed distributions can result from any of the combinations of improper machine set-up, undetected tool wear or operator's carelessness. Unfortunately most machining and manufacturing process are subject to tool wear, and in practice, operators tend to adjust their tooling and set-ups to accommodate this problem. For example, dies might be made close to high limits on internal dimensions because the tool market knows they will wear with use. Similarly drills and reamers will be ground closer to high limit to obtain longer tool life. Consequently, samplings taken from lots run early in the life of these tools will show a skewed distribution.

When a skewed distribution results from this effect, manufacturing procedures and economics must be examined closely. Perhaps statistical dimensioning should be discarded in favour of the savings from longer tool or die life.

There are also other reasons for skewed distributions. Thermal expansion of a part from heat generated during the machining process can make dimension appear nominal at the time of machining, but later, after the part has cooled, the distributions may be skewed toward the low limits. Other factors could include shrinkage in castings, dimensional changes during heat treatment and contaminants in coolant or materials.

Related Dimensions Dimensions that do not vary randomly of independently or each other cannot be treated by statistical principles. For example, two holes drilled with the same tool fall on the same side of a tolerance. Two surfaces cut with the same fixture are not independent. Nor are several centre distances controlled by the same drilling. Also, two dimensions may be affected by the same human factors.

In all such cases, statistical dimensioning does not represent an accurate picture of dimensional distribution and should be replaced by a more conventional and conservative approach. A good treatment for related dimensions is to add tolerances together and treat them as one "family" dimension. Then this composite dimension can be treated statistically.

Small Production Runs When only a small number of parts are made on a production order, statistical distribution assumptions may not apply. Statistical theory requires a number of samples large enough to provide a sound statistical base.

Machine Capabilities Machine capabilities should be studied thoroughly before setting the tolerances. Engineers should have a knowledge of what tolerances normally can be held by drilling, boring, casting and so forth. Any type of dimensional control breaks down if the machine-capability spread turns out to be greater than tolerances on drawing.

Sophisticated capability studies should be made in a way that eliminates variables and thereby reveals the actual repeatability of a machine. Statistical evaluation must be mixed carefully with a great deal of common sense.

When all else fails and no dimensioning system can be made to work, a remedy may be found in match-machining or selective assembly. Match-reaming or selecting mating parts by trial and error can be costly during assembly, but frequently such procedures are less costly than pursuing a statistical dimensioning application that will not work.

Q. 7.35: *Why the addition of tolerances of different components which are assembled to a final product is* ***inaccurate*** *or* ***conservative*** *for the final product tolerances ?*

A component consisting of a hollow metal core surrounded by a strip of hard rubber is required with specifications as follows :

Component	*Specifications (cm)*	X_{max} *(cm)*	X_{min} *(cm)*	*Range (cm)*
Metal core	2.000 ± 0.081	2.081	1.919	0.162
Rubber strip, First side	0.500 ± 0.027	0.527	0.473	0.054
Rubber strip, second side	0.500 ± 0.027	0.527	0.473	0.054
Assembled platen		**3.135**	**2.865**	**0.270**

Determine the statistically correct six sigma assembly tolerances.

Ans. : Addition of tolerances of components is inaccurate because it disregards completely the probably element in random assembly of components into final assembly product.

Assuming the normal variation and tolerances representing the $\pm 3\sigma$ limits

σ_1 of metal core = 0.027

σ_2 of rubber strip, first side = 0.009

σ_3 of rubber strip, second side = 0.009.

In the present case, by assumption, the rubber, stripping wound around the metal core—a short length—has a constant thickness for any one platen, though variation between one platen and the next is quite possible. The combined diameter of metal core and rubber stripping includes two thicknesses of the latter, for which, accordingly,

$$r_{23} = 1$$

Hence, for rubber strip only,

$$\sigma_{sum} = \sqrt{\sigma_2^2 + \sigma_3^2 + 2r_{23}\,\sigma_2\,\sigma_3}$$
$$= \sqrt{(0.009)^2 + (0.009)^2 + 2 \times 1(0.009)(0.009)}$$
$$= 0.018$$

However, metal core and double thickness of rubber stripping are obviously totally independent random variables. Hence for total assembly,

$$\sigma_{assembly} = \sqrt{\sigma_{sum}^2 + \sigma^2}$$
$$= \sqrt{(0.018)^2 + (0.027)^2}$$
$$= 0.03245$$
$$3\,\sigma_{assembly} = 3 \times 0.03245 = 0.097$$

Thus, the statistically correct six-sigma assembly tolerance range is to be (2.000 + 0.500 + 0.500) ± 0.097 *i.e.* 3.000 ± 0.097.

Q. 7.36: *The design size and tolerances for a hole and a shaft (in ten-thousandths of an inch) are given below :*

	Hole	*Shaft*
Design size	4510	4521
Tolerance	+ 7	+ 0
	− 0	− 4

Determine the expected fit in random assembly for these components.

Ans. : The design size of a part is that size from which the limits to sizes are derived by the application of tolerances. If there is no allowance for fit (clearance or interference), then the design size is the same as the basic size.

Also, $\bar{X}_{hole} = 4513.5$

$\bar{X}_{shaft} = 4519.0$

From above dimensions, it is evident that it is an interference fit with an average value of 5.5 (*i.e.* $\bar{X}_{shaft} - \bar{X}_{hole}$)

$$(U - L)_{fit} = \sqrt{7^2 + 4^2} = \sqrt{65} \approx 8$$

Fit tolerance = ± 4

Expected fit = 5.5 ± 4 i.e. 1.5 to 9.5.

Q. 7.37: *(a) The basic size (in thousandths of an inch) of Bearing, Snap Ring and Groove forming an assembly are 730, 120 and 853 respectively. The respective tolerances on these are* $^{+0}_{-6}$, $^{+2}_{-2}$, $^{+3}_{-0}$. *What are the minimum and maximum clearances ? What are the expected minimum and maximum clearances as a result of random assembly ?*

(b) Sometimes after the start of production, it was found that it would be extremely costly to maintain a tolerance $^{+3}_{-0}$ *(i.e. ± 1.5) on the groove dimension. It was therefore proposed to shift the average groove dimension from 854.5 (i.e. 853 + 1.5) to 853 and open up the tolerance to ± 3.*

On the basis of statistical analysis, do you agree with the proposal ?

(c) What are the bonus advantages of such proposal as in (b) ?

(d) What percentage of the product will be having an interference fit if it is decided to accept the proposal made in (b) ? Show all the details of your calculation.

Ans. : (*a*) Following tabulation gives the results at a glance :

$$(U-L)_{clearance} = \sqrt{6^2+4^2+3^2}$$

Clearance tolerance = ± 3.9

Expected clearance in random assembly 7.5 ± 3.9 *i.e.* 3.6 and 11.4

Hence minimum clearance = 1

Maximum clearance = 14

Minimum expected clearance in random assembly = 3.6

Maximum expected clearance in random assembly = 11.4

	Bearing	*Snap Ring*	*Bearing + Snap Ring*	*Groove width*	
Basic size	730	120		853	
Tolerance ±	0	2		3	
	6	2		0	
Maximum	730	122	852	856	
Minimum	724	118	842	853	
Mating of extremes		852	853	1	
		842	856	14	
Average Dimension	727	120	847	854.5	7.5
Tolerance from average ±	3	2		1.5	

(*b*) New tolerance on Groove = ± 3

New $(U-L)$clearance = $\sqrt{6^2+4^2+6^2} = 9.4$

New clearance tolerance = ± 4.7

New average of Groove = 853

Average of Bearing + Ring = 847

New average clearance = 6

Hence expected clearance = 6 ± 4.7 *i.e.* 1.3 and 10.7

Since this new range of clearance tolerance *i.e.* 1.3 to 10.7 is within the range of 1 to 14, the proposal is acceptable on statistical ground.

(*c*) The dimensions of the *Groove* can be maintained at less cost. Further a practical range of clearances of 1.3 to 10.7 represents a generally superior fit at a wider *Groove* dimension, tolerance.

(*d*) For knowing the percentage of products having interference fit, it is convenient to classify the individual parts into following groups based on the individual tolerance values :

Dimension	*Bearing*	*Snap Ring*	*Groove*
$\bar{X} - 3$	724	—	850
$\bar{X} - 2$	725	118	851
$\bar{X} - 1$	726	119	852
$\bar{X}$	727	120	853
$\bar{X} + 1$	728	121	854
$\bar{X} + 2$	729	122	855
$\bar{X} + 3$	730	—	856

As is evident from above, there are seven Bearing dimensions, seven Groove dimension and five Snap Ring dimensions, the total of possible combination in assembly is 7 × 7 × 5 i.e. 245. Yet, only four of these combinations would yield interference. These are :

Bearing	*Shap Ring*	*Bearing + Ring*	*Groove*
729	122	851	850
730	121	851	850
730	122	852	850
730	122	852	851

$$\text{Percentage of products having interference} = \frac{4 \times 100}{245} = 1.63\%$$

Since the above combinations would occur very rarely in practice, as the number of extreme dimension in each product distribution is only a small fraction of the total product, the maximum percentage of products having an interference fit is only 1.63.

Q. 7.38: *Control chart for* $\bar{X}$ *and R have been maintained to monitor a process for a long time. The process is sampled in subgroups of 4 items at intervals of about two hours. Control limits have been based on an aimed-at mean of 3.750 and an* $\bar{R}$ *of 0.1647.*

(a) Estimate σ from control chart data.

(b) If the standard deviation of error of measurement is known to be **0.0020**, *what is the actual deviation of the process ?*

(c) Assuming the process output to be normally distributed, what actual percentage of product will not meet specifications of 3.810 ± 0.240 ?

(d) In order to minimize scrap loss, it is decided to adjust the process centering to exactly 3 σ above the lower specification limit. Where should the process be centered ?

Ans. :

$$\bar{X}_0 = 3.750$$

$$\bar{R} = 0.1647$$

(*a*)
$$\hat{\sigma} = \frac{\bar{R}}{d_2} = \frac{0.1647}{2.059} = 0.8$$

(*b*)
$$\hat{\sigma} = \sqrt{\sigma_E^2 + \sigma_{actual}^2}$$
$$0.08 = \sqrt{(0.0020)^2 + \sigma_{actual}^2}$$
$$\therefore \quad \sigma_{actual} = 0.066$$

(*c*) Natural specification limits of the process

$$= \bar{X}_0 \pm 3\,\sigma_{actual} = 3.750 \pm 0.198 \text{ i.e. } 3.552 \text{ to } 3.948$$

Specification limits = 3.810 ± 0.240 *i.e.* 3.570 to 4.050. It is evident that some of the product will be below the lower specification limit of 3.570.

$$z \text{ corresponding to } 3.570 \text{ is } \frac{3.570 - 3.750}{0.066} = \text{i.e.} -2.727$$

Corresponding of z to − 2.727 Table *A* gives the percentage of product below the lower specified limit as 0.32%.

(*d*) The centering of process = $L + 3\,\sigma = 3.570 + 3\,(0.08) = 3.810$

Q. 7.39: *In a mechanism a plunger moves inside a cylinder and the difference between the diameters of the plunger and the cylinder must be at least 0.02 cm. Cylinders and plungers are manufactured separately ; the diameters of the cylinders are normally distributed about a mean 4.05 cm with standard deviation 0.004 cm, while the diameters of the plungers are normally distributed about a mean of 4.02 cm with standard deviation 0.006 cm.*

(a) Find the proportion of cylinders that will have inadequate clearance for plungers of diameter 4.02 cm.

(b) Find the proportion of plungers that will have inadequate clearance in cylinders of diameter 4.05 cm.

(c) If plungers and cylinders are assembled at random, find the proportion of pairs in which the clearance is insufficient.

(d) If a set of ten plungers and ten cylinders are taken at random and assembled, find the probability of clearance being sufficient in all cases.

Ans. : (*a*) Plunger diameter = 4.02

Minimum clearance required = 0.02

Hence, minimum cylinder diameter = 4.02 + 0.02 = 4.04

Cylinder mean diameter = 4.05

z corresponding to minimum cylinder diameter

$$= \frac{4.04 - 4.05}{0.004} = -2.5$$

Corresponding to z of −2.5, Table *A* gives area of the normal curve as 0.0062. Hence 0.62% of cylinders will have inadequate clearance.

(*b*) Cylinder diameter = 4.05

Minimum clearance required = 0.02

Hence maximum plunger diameter = 4.05 − 0.02 = 4.03

z corresponding to maximum plunger diameter

$$= \frac{4.03 - 4.02}{0.006} = 1.67$$

From Table *A*, area of the curve corresponding to z of 1.67 is equal to 0.9525.

Area of the curve beyond the limit of 4.03 is equal to 1.0 – 0.9525 *i.e* 0.0475. Hence 4.75% of plungers will have inadequate clearance.

(*c*) In case of random assembly,

$$\sigma_{clearance} = \sqrt{(0.004)^2 + (0.006)^2} \text{ i.e. } 0.0072$$

$$\text{Mean clearance} = 4.05 - 4.02 = 0.03$$

z corresponding to minimum clearance

$$= \frac{0.02 - 0.03}{0.0072} = -1.39$$

From Table *A*, area of the curve corresponding to z of – 1.39 is equal to 0.0823. Hence the proportion of pairs in which the clearance is insufficient is 8.23 percent.

(*d*) Probability of insufficient clearance = 0.0823

Probability of sufficient clearance = 1 – 0.0823 = 0.9177

Probability of ten pairs having sufficient clearance

$$(0.9177)^{10} = 0.4218$$

Q. 7.40: *Reels of insulated wire are made such that the lengths are normally distributed with a mean length of 1000 yards and a standard deviation of 10 yards. Two of these reels are selected at random and would together to make a turn flex package. When one of the reels contributing to this package runs out of wire remaining on the other package is regarded as waste. What average waste may be expected?*

It is decided that a check will be kept on the amount of waste by actually measuring the waster from package sampled at fairy frequent intervals. Set up a control chart and design record forms to do this.

Ans. : $\mu = 1000; \sigma = 10 \text{ and } 3\sigma = 30$

Spread = 6σ *i.e.* from 1030 to 970

When two reels, (X and Y) are selected at random and both together form a flex package, the new standard deviation will be

$$\hat{\sigma}_{X+Y} = \sqrt{10^2 + 10^2} \text{ i.e. } 14.14$$

The new distribution will have a mean of 1000 and $\hat{\sigma}$ of 14.14. The portion outside the lower limit of 970, will be wastage. From Table *A*, this is computed to be 0.017 *i.e.* wastage is about 1.7%.

Control charts for $\bar{X}$ and σ will be used to keep a check on wastage.

CHAPTER

8

Some Special Process Control Procedures

8.1 SOME MISCELLANEOUS TOPICS

This chapter deals with a number of more or less related topics that should form part of SPC. Some of these are variations to conventional $\bar{\bar{X}}$, R and p charts while other topics deal with schemes for plotting and analysis that are based on other statistical procedures or were devised with principal objectives other than control of a process.

8.2 SOME SPECIAL TOPICS ON SHEWHART CONTROL CHARTS FOR VARIABLES

This section deals with a group of variations on the basic Shewhart charts for variables. They include corrections needed when subgroups size is not constant, places where $\bar{\bar{X}}$ charts are not appropriate, the use of warning limits and zone tests, and plotting subgroup totals rather than averages.

8.2.1 Control Charts with Variable Subgroup Size

Wherever possible it is desirable to have a constant subgroup size. If this cannot be done, the limits on both $\bar{\bar{X}}$ and R charts (or $\bar{\bar{X}}$ and s charts) should be variable limits.

Once σ has been estimated, these limits for various sample sizes may be obtained by using the factors and formulae of Table *F*, App. 1. Where the data used to estimate σ include subgroups of various sizes, a satisfactory working rule (although not precisely correct as a matter of statistical theory) is to calculate R/d_2 for each subgroup, using the appropriate d_2 factor from Table *C*, App. 1, for the size of the subgroup in question. The estimate of σ is the average of these values of R/d_2. If sample standard deviation, rather than range, is the measure used for subgroup dispersion, s/c_4 may be computed for each subgroup ; the estimate of σ is the average value of s/c_4.

8.2.2 *R* Charts or *s* Charts Where $\bar{X}$ charts Are Not Appropriate

In some cases subgroups may be comparable in their dispersion even though not comparable in their averages. This is true, for example, of many standard chemical analyses that are made in duplicate, triplicate, or quadruplicate. Each two, three, or four analyses of a given sample may be thought of as a subgroup. If samples having somewhat different chemical content are analyzed, the averages of the subgroups are not comparable. The dispersion of the subgroups, however, reflects the ability of an analyst and an analytical procedure to reproduce results by several similar determinations. The control chart for *R* or s provides a basis for judging whether this dispersion seems to be influenced by a constant-cause system. Calculations for the central lines and control limits for *R* or *s* are no different from such calculations for any other control charts.

8.2.3 Warning Limits on Control Charts

Some writers on statistical quality control have advocated the use of two sets of limits on $\overline{\overline{X}}$ charts. The outer limits, sometimes called *action limits,* are the conventional limits, usually at 3 sigma. The inner limits are recommended as *warning limits* and are usually at 2 sigma.

On the conventional $\overline{\overline{X}}$ chart with only one set of limits, the chart seems to give only two kinds of advice. Either it says, "Look for trouble," or it says, "Leave the process alone." This has the virtue of definiteness. However, any such definite advice is sure to be wrong part of the time. Limits placed at 3 sigma are seldom wrong when they say, "Look for trouble," but are much more often wrong when they say, "Leave the process alone."

The inner limits or warning limits seem to add a third kind of advice. This might be phrased, "Start being suspicious that trouble is brewing."

At first thought, the idea of having warning limits on $\overline{\overline{X}}$ charts may seem attractive. Nevertheless, there is a sound reason for the common practice of having only one set of limits and having these limits at or near 3 sigma. This reason is the greater definiteness of a single set of limits. Two sets of limits tend to be confusing with regard to the exact action to be taken when a point falls between the inner and the outer limits. This is particularly true if many of the people in a facility who are using the $\overline{\overline{X}}$ and R control charts as a basis for action are not fully clear as to the principles underlying these charts. Inner limits will be exceeded at least 5% of the time as a matter of chance. If a single point just outside the inner limits is to be used as a basis for hunting for trouble, there is bound to be unproductive hunting that may tend to destroy confidence in the control charts. Usually so much trouble really exists that it does not pay to hunt for trouble without strong evidence that it is present.

Nevertheless, even though inner limits should not be drawn on most control charts, they can be extremely useful in the sophisticated interpretation of control charts by people who understand control-chart theory. Here the clue to action is given not by a single point outside either of the inner limits but rather by two or more points, both outside the same inner limit. This is really a matter of sizing up extreme runs ; it is somewhat comparable to the interpretation of extreme runs on the same side of the central line that was explained in Chap 3. For example, two points in succession outside the same inner limit on an $\overline{\overline{X}}$ chart give even stronger evidence of a shift in process average than a single point outside the outer limit. Two points out of three beyond one inner limit, three out of seven, or four out of ten, may all be considered as appropriate grounds for action.

8.2.4 Problems of Detecting Small but Sustained Shifts

The use of the theory of runs to identify shifts in the universe was discussed briefly in Chap. 3. Later, in Chap. 4, the method of calculating the approximate probabilities associated with runs of points on one side of the central line of an $\overline{\overline{X}}$ chart was presented. Such tests may be useful because an $\overline{\overline{X}}$ chart with 3-sigma limits and a small subgroup size (*e.g.,* two to five) is not sensitive to small shifts in the process centering.

Consider an example in which a controlled and correctly centered process shifts to a new centering + $\frac{1}{2}$ σ greater than the old centering. σ remains constant through the shift, and the centering holds constant at the new level after the shift. A combination rule is used that says: Look for an assignable cause of a shift in a given direction if either of these conditions occurs :

1. A point falls outside a control limit.
2. Eight points in a row fall between the central line and a single control limit.

Assuming that subgroups of four are drawn from a normally distributed universe, the probability that a single point will falls outside a given control limit is 0.00135, and the probability that a point will fall between the central line and one control limit is 0.49865 when $+\frac{1}{2}$ (σ) the process is correctly centered. After the $+\frac{1}{2}$ (σ) shift, the respective probabilities increase to 0.0228 and 0.8186.

Under the rules as stated, it is conceivable that either rule could signal the shift on the first sample after the shift. That is, a single point could fall outside the upper 3-sigma control limit (with probability 0.0228), or the eighth point in a row could be between the central line and the upper control limit (with probability 0.8186) if the previous seven points before the shift had fallen in the same region (with probability 0.49865^7). Thus the approximate combined probability of detection on the first sample after the shift is

$$0.0228 + (0.49865)^7 (0.8186) = 0.0291$$

The probability of detection on the second sample is the probability of not detecting the shift on the first sample multiplied by the sum of the probabilities of a point outside the upper 3-sigma limit and eight points in a row between the central line and the upper limit, or

$$0.9709 [0.0228 + (0.49865)^6 (0.8186)^2] = 0.0321$$

The probability of detection by the second sample is the sum of the respective individual probabilities, or

$$0.0291 + 0.0321 = 0.0612.$$

The following tabulation shows the respective probabilities of detection on the first eight sample subgroups and the cumulative probabilities to and including the subgroup listed. It should be noted that these probabilities are accurate only if the shift is sustained at the new level until detected.

Subgroup number	*Probability of detection*	
	On that subgroup	*By that subgroup*
1	0.0291	0.0291
2	0.0321	0.0612
3	0.0373	0.0985
4	0.0456	0.1441
5	0.0585	0.2026
6	0.0778	0.2804
7	0.1048	0.3852
8	0.1380	0.5232

8.2.5 Precontrol

The precontrol technique attempts to relate the output of a process to the specifications on individual parts and to use the results of the inspection of individual units to control the process. The process is targetted at $\mu_0 = (USL_X + LSL_X)/2$, *i.e.* half way between specifications, precontrol (PC) lines are set at $(USL_X - \mu_0)/2$ and a $(\mu_0 - LSL_X)/2$. The distance between the

PC lines is called the "green" zone. So long as the dimensions of inspected items fall within this zone, the process is left alone. The two zones between PC lines and their respective specification limits, USL_X as LSL_X, are called "orange" zones. If the dimension of an item falls within an orange zone, the next successive item is inspected. In most of instances it is assumed that $USL_X + LSL_X$ is equal to 6 σ and PC lines are set at $\mu_0 \pm 1.5\sigma$.

However the major objections to this technique are :

1. Even under excellent control conditions, it is difficult to assume that the processes generate a normal distribution.
2. The σ may not be constant
3. It may have the dangerous effect of convincing shop personnel and engineers that there is no need to apply even the simplest statistics in "controlling" process that somehow the same results can be obtained but more simply.
4. The application of this technique may lead to over control in case ($USL_X - LSL_X$) is less than 6 σ.

8.3 Control Chart for Individual Measurements

In many industrial situations only a few measurements are taken on a quality characteristic. This may be due to the fact that it is too expensive, too time consuming, or there are a few items to inspect. In such cases an *X* chart will provide some information from limited data, whereas an $\bar{\bar{X}}$ chart would provide no information or information only after considerable delay to obtain sufficient data. Other situation favourable for such a chart is when charts for averages are misunderstood by shop personnel, it is a good idea to not to plot averages at all but rather to plot individual measurements. The central value is the same as one for an *X* chart, and the formulae for the control limits are

$$UCL_X = \mu + 3\,\sigma$$
$$LCL_X = \mu - 3\,\sigma$$

The chart for the dispersion is an *R* chart using a moving range method. To obtain the first range point, the value of X_1 is subtracted from X_2, to obtain the second point, X_2 is subtracted from X_3, and so forth. Each individual value is used for two different point, therefore, the 'moving' range. The range points are placed between subgroup number since they are obtained from both values.

The *X* chart has the advantage of being easier for production personnel to understand and of providing a direct comparison with specifications. It does have the disadvantages of (1) requiring too many subgroups to indicate an out-of-condition, (2) not summarizing the data as well as *X*, and (3) distorting the control limits when the distribution is not normal, (4) having less sensitivity to indicate substantial shifts in process average.

Although greater sensitivity to such shifts may be gained by the use of narrower limits, such sensitivity is gained only by increasing the chance of false indications of lack of control (so-called *Type 1* errors). Unless an *X*-chart is accompanied by a range chart, it is difficult to discover whether there have been changes in process dispersion. In general, charts for individual measurements are inferior to conventional control charts because they fail to give as clear a picture of changes in a process or as quick evidence of assignable causes of variation.

8.4 PROBABILITY LIMITS ON CONTROL CHARTS FOR VARIABLES

8.4.1 Two Questions for Decision Regarding Control Limits on Charts for $\bar{X}$, R, and s

Two questions that often have been debated among statisticians, as well as among persons engaged in quality control work in industry, are as follows :

1. Shall control-chart limits be described as multiples of the standard deviation of the statistic charted or in terms of the estimated probabilities associated with the limits?
2. How far apart should the limits be spaced, all things considered ?

The first question is primarily one of semantics. We have already suggested that, in principle, the second question is primarily an economic one.

8.4.2 Probability Limits on $\bar{X}$ Charts

If we assume that $\bar{\bar{X}}$ values follow the normal distribution when all samples have been taken from the same universe, we can use Table *A* to find the multiple of $\sigma_{\bar{X}}$ associated with any stipulated probabilities. The reader will recall that in Chap. 2 it was pointed out that $\bar{\bar{X}}$ values are normally distributed when the universe is normal; they are approximately normal even from nonnormal universes when the sample size is four or more.

For instance, if it is desired that the probability be 0.001 that without a change in the universe a point will fall above the upper control limit. We look in Table *A* for the multiplier of σ corresponding to 0.001. This is 3.09. Because the factors A_2, A_3. and A in Tables *D, E,* and *F* are based on 3-sigma limits, it is merely necessary to multiply them by 3.09/3 = 1.03 to obtain corresponding factors based on 0.001 that a point will fall below the lower limit. This means a probability of 0.002 of a point outside limits, or 0.998 within limits. The British particularly have used limits based on 3.09 $\sigma_{\bar{X}}$.

Or if it is desired that the probability be 0.025 that a point fall above the upper limit (corresponding to 0.05 that it fall outside limits), Table *A* gives 1.96 as the appropriate multiple of $\sigma_{\bar{X}}$. The multiplier to be applied to the A_2, A_3, and A factors is then 1.96/3 = 0.653. Factors based on 1.96 $\sigma_{\bar{X}}$ have been used by the British as inner control limits or *warning limits.*

8.4.3 Probability Limits on Charts for *R* and *s*

The distribution of $\bar{\bar{X}}$ values, which is normal or approximately so, is symmetrical. Therefore probability limits on an $\bar{\bar{X}}$ chart are like 3-sigma limits in being equidistant from the central

TABLE 8.1 FACTORS FOR PROBABILITY LIMITS TO BE USED IN CONTROL CHARTS FOR SAMPLE STANDARD DEVIATION

(To obtain limits, multiply the estimated value of (σ) by the *B* factor with subscript corresponding to the desired probability)

Size of subgroup n	*Lower limits*			*Upper limits*		
	$B_{0.001}$	$B_{0.005}$	$B_{0.025}$	$B_{0.975}$	$B_{0.995}$	$B_{0.999}$
2	0.00	0.00	0.03	2.25	2.81	3.30
3	0.04	0.07	0.16	1.92	2.30	2.63
4	0.09	0.15	0.27	1.77	2.07	2.33
5	0.15	0.22	0.35	1.67	1.92	2.15
6	0.21	0.28	0.41	1.60	1.83	2.03
7	0.25	0.33	0.45	1.56	1.76	1.93
8	0.29	0.37	0.49	1.52	1.70	1.86
9	0.33	0.41	0.52	1.48	1.65	1.80
10	0.36	0.44	0.55	1.45	1.62	1.76

TABLE 8.2: FACTORS FOR PROBABILITY LIMITS TO BE USED IN CONTROL CHARTS FOR RANGE
(To obtain limits, multiply the estimated value of (σ) by the D factor with the subscript corresponding to the desired probability)

Size of subgroup n	*Lower limits*			*Upper limits*		
	$D_{0.001}$	$D_{0.005}$	$D_{0.025}$	$D_{0.975}$	$D_{0.995}$	$D_{0.999}$
2	0.00	0.01	0.04	3.17	3.97	4.65
3	0.06	0.13	0.30	3.68	4.42	5.06
4	0.20	0.34	0.59	3.98	4.69	5.31
5	0.37	0.55	0.85	4.20	4.89	5.48
6	0.53	0.75	1.07	4.36	5.03	5.62
7	0.69	0.92	1.25	4.49	5.15	5.73
8	0.83	1.08	1.41	4.60	5.25	5.82
9	0.97	1.21	1.55	4.70	5.34	5.90
10	1.08	1.33	1.67	4.78	5.42	5.97

line on the chart. In contrast, because the distributions of R and s are not symmetrical even when the universe is normal, it is necessary to have separate factors for the upper and lower control limits if the probabilities of extreme variations are to be made equal. Table 8.1 gives such factors for probability limits for s charts; Table 8.2 gives them for R charts. Three sets of symmetrical probabilities (giving unsymmetrical limits) are 0.001 and 0.999, corresponding to a 0.002 probability that with no change in the universe a point will fall outside of the limits; 0.005 and 0.995, corresponding to a 0.01 probability of a point falling outside ; and 0.025 and 0.975, corresponding to an 0.05 probability of a point falling outside.

Table 8.1 gives multipliers for σ the assumed or estimated value of σ to obtain limits on a chart for s. σ may be estimated as $\bar{s}/c_4$.

Table 8.2 gives multipliers for the assumed or estimated value of σ to obtain limits on a chart for R. σ may be estimated as $\bar{R}/d_2$.

It should be emphasized that the probabilities given for these limits are strictly accurate only when sampling from a normal universe. They are also based on the assumption that a σ estimated from the data is the true universe standard deviation. For practical control-chart work in industry, where the exact form of the universe is hardly ever known and control limits are often based on the evidence of short series of observations, it must be recognized that these probabilities are approximate rather than exact and may often be substantially in error.

8.4.4 Differing Viewpoints on How to Describe the Limits on Control Charts for Variables

Two points of view are found regarding the best way to describe limits on control charts for $\bar{\bar{X}}$, R, and s.

One viewpoint is that the appropriate decision to make in setting limits is the numerical value of a probability. This should be the probability that, with no change in the universe, a point will fall within the control limits (or, alternatively, beyond the limits). The advocates of this point of view have usually adopted 0.998 as the desired probability of falling within limits of $\bar{\bar{X}}$ charts. This has led to limits of $\bar{\bar{X}}$ (or $\bar{\bar{X}}_0$) ± 3.09 $\sigma_{\bar{\bar{X}}}$.

An alternative point of view is that, even if the probability associated with any limits could be known accurately, the exact numerical value of the probability is only of incidental interest. The important matter is that there be a definite basis for the establishment of limits and that this basis form a suitable guide to the actions that are to be based on the control charts.

In comparing these viewpoints, the reader should recognize that it really is not the exact value of the probability that constitutes a basis for action. For instance, it would be practically impossible to have any sense of the difference between the effect of probabilities of 0.0010 and 0.00135 that a point would fall above the upper control limit by chance. The real basis for acceptance of control limits, whether called 3-sigma limits or something else, is experience that the operational procedure involved in their computation gives limits that provide a satisfactory basis for action. As far as the practical use of $\bar{\bar{X}}$ charts in manufacturing is concerned, it makes very little difference whether limits are at 3 sigma or at 3.09 sigma, and it makes even less difference whether they are called 3-sigma limits or probability limits. Both types of limits are used in the same manner and give very nearly the same results.

8.4.5 Some Special Aspects of Probability Limits on Control Charts for *R* and *s*

Although probability limits on $\bar{\bar{X}}$ charts are like 3-sigma limits in being equidistant from the central line, probability limits on charts for R are not equally spaced with reference of the central line. This statement also applies to the distribution of s values from small subgroups. Both distributions are decidedly skewed.

A point emphasized by some advocates of probability limits is that for the common subgroup sizes of five or less, the lower 3-sigma limit is zero on these charts. In contrast, for the probabilities given in Tables 8.1 and 8.2, a subgroup size of three or more will give a lower control limit greater than zero.

8.5 $\bar{X}$ CHART WITH A LINEAR TREND

8.5.1 $\bar{X}$ Charts for Trended Universe Average with Constant Standard Deviation

The type of trend with which we are here concerned is a gradual shift in quality level which results from an assignable cause that is impossible or impractical to control. Probably the best known such cause is tool wear and its effect upon dimensions. Other causes include such as gradual erosion of furnace linings (*e.g.*, bessember converter and open hearth for making steel), wear of machine parts (usually insignificant in a properly designed and properly lubricated machine), and changes in ambient air temperature or humidity.

It is obvious that conventional control chart limits will be unsatisfactory when dealing with trends, since values will eventually go out of control due only to the trend. It is also apparent that specification limits must be wide enough to allow a marked shift in process level if nonconforming items are to be avoided.

In some machining operations, tool wear occurs at a uniform rate over the period of use of the tool. This tool wear may be one of the factors influencing the average value of some dimension of the product manufactured and may be responsible for a trend in this average. Where subgroups are selected in a way that spaces them uniformly with respect to this wear,

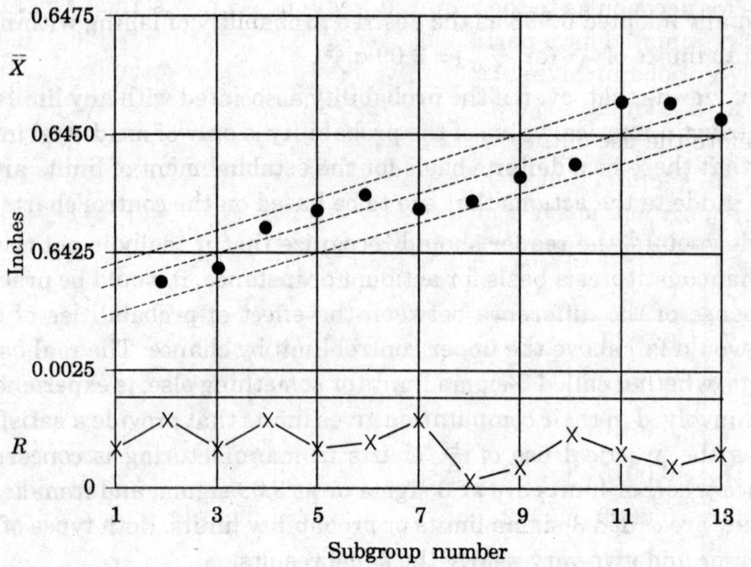

FIGURE 8.1. Illustration of trend line on X chart - Example 8.1.

control charts for $\bar{\bar{X}}$ may look something like Fig. 8.1. The R chart, however, is likely to remain in control yielding a constant estimate of σ.

The central line and control limits for the $\bar{\bar{X}}$ chart, in such a case, should be sloping rather than horizontal. The slope of the central line, or universe average, and $\bar{R}$, estimated from R, are determined from the measurements themselves. Once known, it becomes possible to determine the initial setting and length of run that together will give the maximum period between machine settings consistent with the specified tolerances. The methods of making the required calculations are illustrated in Example 8.1.

EXAMPLE 8.1 : *Determining the initial machine setting when a trend is expected in the value of a dimension.*

Facts the case On certain operations in one machine shop, it was a common experience for a definite steady trend in the average value of dimensions of machined parts to be caused by rapid tool wear. On many specified dimensions the spread of the specification limits, $USL_X - LSL_X$, was substantially greater than the natural tolerance range of the process, 6 σ. This provided an ample margin of safety against the production of nonconforming product as long as the machine setting held the average value of the dimension somewhere close to a point midway between the specification limits. However, the tendency of the average value of a dimension to shift rapidly as a result of tool wear called for frequent new setups to restore the average value to its desired position. Each new setup involved appreciable costs, both for setup expense and for idle machine time.

The introduction of the control-chart point of view provided a basis for reducing the frequency of setups. The average value of the frequency distribution of the variable X (in this case, a dimension) shifted at an approximately uniform rate, but the shape of the frequency distribution and its dispersion (measured by σ) did not change. From control-chart data properly taken, it was possible to estimate σ. It was also possible to estimate the rate of change of the average X and to express this rate of change in terms of an equation.

The estimate of σ made it possible to determine the aimed-at average value for an initial setup to permit the maximum run between setups. The estimate of the rate of change of the dimension provided a basis for decision as to the required frequency of new setups. Once σ and the rate of change of X were estimated for a particular operation, it proved possible to use this information on new jobs. Even jobs involving relatively short runs were benefited, as many such jobs were completed with a single setup in contrast to the two or three setups usually required for similar jobs before the use of the control chart.

Fitting a trend line to an $\bar{X}$ chart Consider the following values of $\bar{X}$ and R for a dimension specified as 0.644 ± 0.004 in. Subgroups of five components were measured every half-hour.

Subgroup number	$\bar{X}$	R	h
1	0.6417	0.0011	−6
2	0.6418	0.0016	−5
3	0.6424	0.0010	−4
4	0.6431	0.0015	−3
5	0.6433	0.0009	−2
6	0.6437	0.0010	−1
7	0.6433	0.0014	0
8	0.6436	0.0004	1
9	0.6441	0.0006	2
10	0.6444	0.0011	3
11	0.6456	0.0009	4
12	0.6457	0.0007	5
13	0.454	0.009	6
Totals	8.3681	0.0131	

$$\bar{\bar{X}} = \frac{8.3681}{13} = 0.6437$$

$$\bar{R} = \frac{0.0131}{13} = 0.0010$$

Certain precautions should be taken in the collection of data to be used for the calculation of a trend line and control limits. The production between successive subgroups should be approximately constant. The components included in a subgroup should be produced in succession so that the trend will have little effect on the range of a subgroup.

On the conventional $\bar{X}$ chart, the central line is horizontal. With an upward trend of $\bar{X}$ values, the central line must be a sloping line. The position of this central line may be described by an equation of the form $\bar{X} = a + bh$, with the symbol h used to represent the subgroup number (preferably with a revised subgroup numbering using the middle subgroup as the origin), a is the value of $\bar{X}$ when $h = 0$, and b is the slope of the line. The method of least squares provides a satisfactory way of finding the values of a and b corresponding to any given set of measurements.

Under certain special circumstances, computing a least-squares trend line is a very simple operation. These circumstances are that the observed values of the variable plotted on the vertical axis of the chart (in this case, values of $\bar{X}$) are uniformly spaced along the horizontal axis of the chart (in this case, on the scale of subgroup numbers h); that there are an odd number of subgroups; and that the origin on the horizontal axis is taken as the midpoint of that axis (that is, the 0 value of h is assumed at the middle subgroup). Under these circumstances $a = \bar{\bar{X}}$, and $b = \Sigma h \bar{X} / \Sigma h^2$. The method of calculation is illustrated in Table 8.3.

TABLE 8.3 CALCULATION OF EQUATION OF LEAST-SQUARES TREND LINE FOR X.

($\bar{X}$ expressed in units of 0.0001 in excess of 0.6400)

Subgroup number	*Revised subgroup number h*	*Subgroup average* $\bar{X}$	$h\bar{X}$	h^2
1	– 6	17	– 102	36
2	– 5	18	– 90	25
3	– 4	24	– 96	16
4	– 3	31	– 93	9
5	– 2	33	– 66	4
6	– 1	37	– 37	1
7	0	33	0	0
8	1	36	36	1
9	2	41	82	4
10	3	44	132	9
11	4	56	224	16
12	5	57	285	25
13	6	54	324	36
Totals	0	481	599	182

$$a = \bar{\bar{X}} = \frac{481}{13} = 37.0$$

$$b = \frac{\Sigma h\bar{X}}{\Sigma h^2} = \frac{599}{182} = 3.29$$

$$\bar{\bar{X}} = a + bh = 37.0 + 3.29\,h$$

For simplicity in calculations, the $\bar{X}$ values in Table 8.3 are expressed in units of 0.0001 in excess of 0.6400. The equation $\bar{X}$ = 37.0 + 3.29 h is, of course, expressed in these units. In terms of the actual dimension in inches, the equation becomes $\bar{X}$ = 0.6437 + 0.000329 h.

To plot this line on the control chart (Fig. 8.3), it is necessary to locate two points on the line and connect them. For example,

$$\bar{X}\begin{cases} 0.06437 + (0.000329)(-6) = 0.6417 \text{ for } h = -6 \\ 0.6437 + (0.000329)(6) = 0.6457 \quad \text{for } h = +6 \end{cases}$$

Interpreting the control chart as a basis for action: The control limits are sloping lines parallel to the central trend line. The upper control limit is $A_2\ \bar{R}$ above the trend line, and the lower control limit is A_2 R below it. In this case, $A_2\ \bar{R}$ = 0.58 (0.0010) = 0.0006. Figure 8.3 shows sloping limits plotted at this distance from the central line.

To decide on the value of the average dimension to be aimed at in the initial machine setting, it is first necessary to estimate σ. This is $\bar{R}/d_2$ = 0.0010/2.326 = 0.00043. The tolerance spread $USL_X - LSL_X$ may then be compared with σ. In this case.

$USL_X - LSL_X$ = 0.6480 – 0.6400 = 0.0080

This is equal to 18.6 σ.

A decision must then be made as to how many multiples of σ the initial setting should be from the lower specification limit. In some instances, this might be 3 σ; in others, it might be a greater multiple of σ such as 4 σ. This decision is a function of the economics involved. Where the tolerance spread is great enough to allow a considerable run between settings, as in this case, the additional margin of safety involved in the use of 4 σ is likely to be justified. The same multiple of σ should be used to determine the time of a new setup. Using 4 σ in this case, we obtain the following directions: On initial setup, aim at

$$\bar{X} = LSL_X + 4\,\sigma = 0.6400 + 0.0017 = 0.6417$$

Make a new setup when trend line $= USL_X - 4\,\sigma = 0.6480 - 0.0017 = 0.6463$.

The slope of the trend line, $b = 0.000329$, is the expected change in average dimension from one subgroup to the next. The interval between setups may be estimated as (0.6463 – 0.6417)/0.000329 = 14 subgroup intervals. With subgroups spaced half an hour apart, this indicates that a new setup is required every 7 h.

Comment in Example 8.1

When a point falls outside control limits on an $\bar{\bar{X}}$ chart with a sloping central line, there are two possible interpretations. One is the conventional interpretation that an assignable cause of variation is responsible for the point falling outside the limits. The other is that the limits are based on a trend line that is wrong. For example, a control chart might be started for a new job using a slope of a trend line determined from a previous similar job; it might turn out that the jobs were really sufficiently different for the slopes to differ. As another example, tool wear is a factor that does not necessarily operate at a uniform rate; on jobs where the rate of change of the average value of a dimension is variable, no straight line fitted to $\bar{\bar{X}}$ values will provide a satisfactory central line for a control chart

8.6 NARROW LIMIT GAUGING

8.6.1 Conditions Favouring the Use of Limit Gauging

Most industrial plants producing large quantities of small piece parts have been accustomed for some time to inspection by the attribute method (Go, Not-Go gauging is a very common form). It may be impracticable in many cases to convert to a system of variable inspection. There may be large investment in existing gauging equipment and necessary standards for checking it, the training of existing personnel to use variables measurements and apply variables quality control charts may be hampered by lack of necessary skills and the cost of hiring new personnel may be prohibitive, or the components may be so small that it is difficult to handle them on a variable measurement basis.

8.6.2 Inadequacy of Patrol Inspection

While patrol inspection generally provides for the taking of any sample size at any time interval (even though some sort of rough schedule may be followed), its greatest weakness lies in the fact that routine samples are seldom large enough to catch any but the most drastic quality level shifts and the system may degenerate to the point where the time intervals are much too large and the standards are much too lax. For example, one inspector took a handful (indefinite quantity) whenever it suited him and passed the sample if it was not over 50 percent defective. The material then continued to flow into production until another sample was taken.

8.6.3 Limit Gauging only a Substitute Method

It should be borne in mind that the limit gauging method is not suggested for wholesale replacement of quality control by measurements where such a system is functioning satisfactorily or where it is feasible to install such a system. Measurements provide the most generally satisfactory means of appraising quality levels and process control.

8.6.4 Permissible Variation in Process Level

Many repetitive operations tend to retain essentially the same variability over long periods of time even though the process level may shift due to tool wear, frequent adjustment of machining process and a similar set of other variables. The limits within which the process level may be permitted to vary for the purpose of limits gauging are illustrated in Fig. 8.2. The distance of four standard deviations from the specification limit to the mean instead to three (minimum generally allowed for a control process in connection with control charts for variables), is to provide an added margin of safety since the aim here is to deal with attribute inspection instead of variable inspection.

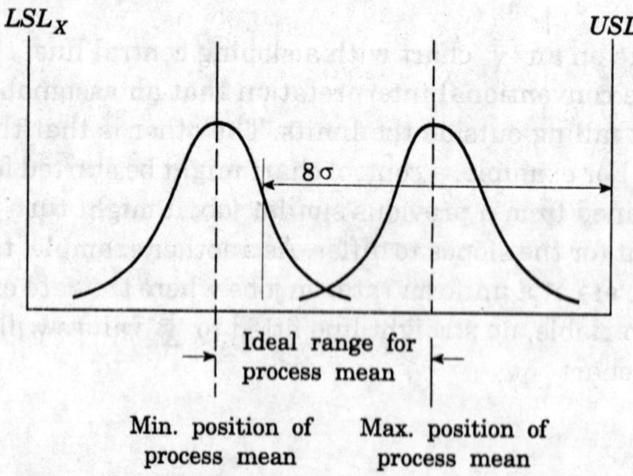

FIGURE 8.2: Ideal range for process mean with limit gauging.

8.6.7 Setting Gauge Limits

The weakness in conventional attribute inspection is that when a process is producing a satisfactory product, it is the general tendency to expect only a few nonconforming items and a vary marked shift in quality before one becomes aware of the situation. For this reason a special limit gauge with closer tolerances than those of the specification, is used. The slope of the normal curve is steepest at ± 1 σ from the mean. Thus with gauge limits at this point, a given shift in quality level will have the maximum effect upon the number of items falling beyond the gauge limits.

Gauge limits for a process just able to meet the specification are illustrated in Fig. 8.3 (*a*). Figure 8.3 (*b*) illustrates the gauge limits for a process able to keep well within the specification limits.

The most sensitive position for the gauge limits varies somewhat with the sample size, but for small samples it is very close to the mean plus and minus one standard deviation. The setting of these limits does not mean that tolerance zone is reduced, but rather a certain portion of items will be expected to fall outside the limit gauge limits when the process is operating under control. This will greatly increase the sensitivity of the attribute inspection to shifts in quality level.

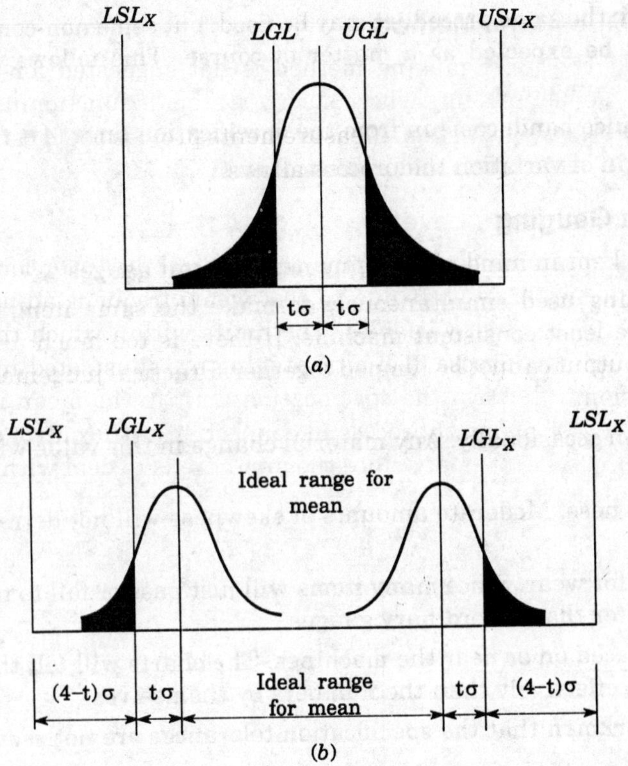

FIGURE 8.3 (*a*) Gauge limits for a process just able to meet the specification.
(*b*) Gauge limits for a process able to keep well specification limits.

Further, a larger sample may be taken than could be handled under variable measurements thus increasing the power of the inspection.

The first step in determining the actual limits is to obtain an estimate of σ of the process. At last 50 to 100 items are measured on variable scale. The process is kept under conditions as constant as possible during the collection of data. A control chart may be started to assure the presence of control. If the standard deviation is $\frac{1}{6}$ to $\frac{1}{8}$ of the specified tolerance, the process is just satisfactory. The gauge limits are then set at the middle of the tolerance range plus and minus t σ.

The values t for sample size (25 to 5) generally used in industry are given in Table 8.4.

TABLE 8.4: VALUES OF T TO BE USED FOR GAUGE LIMITS

Sample size	*Factor t*	*Maximum allowable outside gauge limits*	
		Action limit	*Warning limit*
25	1.08	8	5
20	1.06	7	4
15	1.00	6	4
10	1.14	4	2
5	0.90	3	2

If σ is over – of tolerance band, the same procedure may be used, but some non-conforming (out of specification limits) must be expected as a matter of course. This follows in every inspection method.

If σ is less than $\frac{1}{8}$ of the tolerance band, come in from the specification limit $(4 - t)\ \sigma$. This will take advantage of extra margin of variation the process allows.

8.6.5 Cautions in Using Limit Gauging

Several practical points should be kept in mind when using narrow limit gauges :

1. If several machines are being used simultaneously to make the same item, use the standard deviation from the least consistent machine. If there is too much difference among the machines, their output cannot be lumped together. Practical judgement must be used in making this decision.
2. Check the standard deviation occasionally. Any material change in this value will affect the validity of the limits.
3. Guard against marked skewness. Moderate amounts of skewness will not detract from the value of the procedure.
4. Check the gauge frequently for wear. Since many items will just pass or fail to pass the gauge, the wear will be greater than on ordinary gauges.
5. Plot the results on charts placed on or near the machines. The charts will tell the story of quality trends much more effectively than the numbers by themselves.
6. Be sure to explain to the workmen that the specification tolerances are not reduced by this method.

8.7 REJECTION LIMITS AND MODIFIED LIMITS

8.7.1 Rejection Limits for Averages on $\bar{X}$ charts

One possible method of showing the relationship between $\bar{X}$ values and the specification limits that apply to individual items is through the use of *rejection limits* for the averages. If the assumption is made that σ is known and will not change and that practically all the product will fall within limits of $\mu \pm 3\ \sigma$ (or, for that matter, $\mu \pm$ any other desired multiple of σ), it is easy to calculate the highest and lowest values of μ that will permit practically all product to fall within specification limits. The reject limits for averages are certain control-chart limits that would be appropriate if μ should be at each of these computed values. The derivation of these reject limits is explained here.

Figure 8.4 illustrates the development of such limits. Assume the universe in its highest acceptable position with universe average exactly 3 σ below the upper specification limit (μ_h). On an $\bar{\bar{X}}$ chart with subgroup size n, the upper control limit $UCL_{\bar{X}}$ will be $3\ \sigma/\sqrt{n}$ above the universe average. This will evidently be the highest possible satisfactory value of the upper control limit and is designated as the upper reject limit for averages, abbreviated as $URL_{\bar{X}}$.

The distance of $URL_{\bar{X}}$ below the upper specification limit for individual values is obviously $3\sigma - \left(3/\sqrt{n}\right)$. This may be expressed as $\left[3 - \left(3/\sqrt{n}\right)\right]\sigma$. This factor $\left[3 - \left(3/\sqrt{n}\right)\right]$ is designated as V. Table 8.5 gives values of V corresponding to values of n from 2 to 25. By a similar process of reasoning that assumes the universe in its lowest acceptable position, it may be shown that the lower reject limit for averages, $LRL_{\bar{X}}$, is $V\sigma$ above the lower specification limit.

If an $\bar{X}$ chart shows a state of statistical control and both control limits fall within the two reject limits, this means that practically all the product will fall within specification limits. If the $UCL_{\bar{X}}$ falls above the $URL_{\bar{X}}$, or if the $LCL_{\bar{X}}$ falls below the $URL_{\bar{X}}$, the conclusion is that even though control is maintained, some product will fall outside one of the specifications. In this way, limits telling the conformance of individual values with specifications may be placed on the chart for averages.

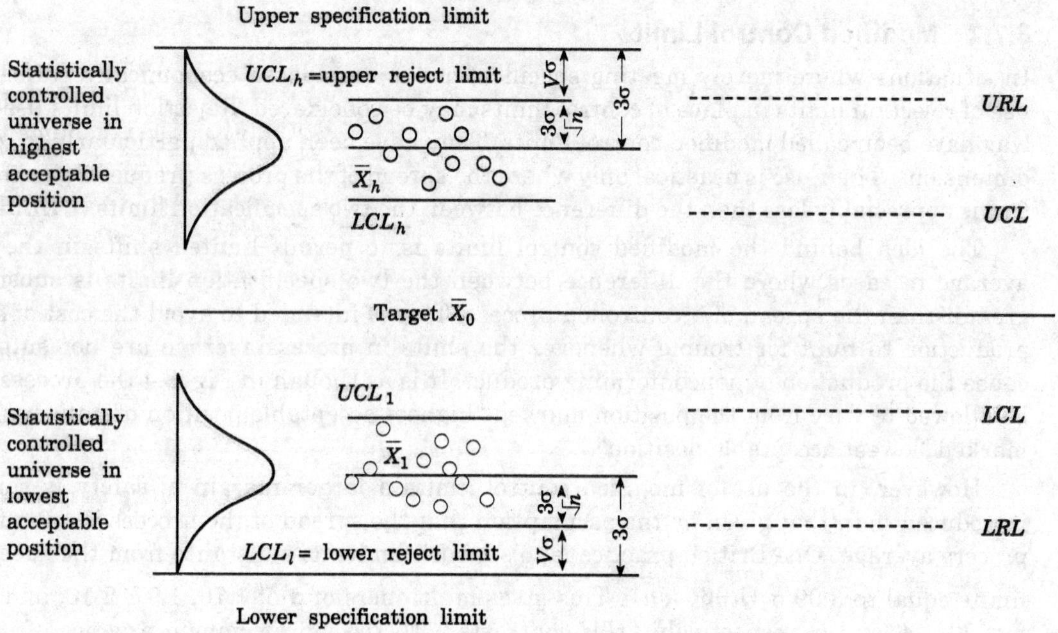

FIGURE 8.4: Relationship among specification limits, control limits, and reject limits.

TABLE 8.5: Values of V, Factor for Reject Limits, for Different Values of N Subgroup Size.

n	V	n	V	n	V
2	0.88	10	2.05	18	2.29
3	1.27	11	2.09	19	2.31
4	1.50	12	2.13	20	2.33
5	1.66	13	2.17	21	2.35
6	1.78	14	2.20	22	2.36
7	1.87	15	2.23	23	2.37
8	1.94	16	2.25	24	2.39
9	2.00	17	2.27	25	2.40

$$URL_{\bar{X}} = USL_{\bar{X}} - V\sigma \qquad \text{... (8.1)}$$

$$URL_{\bar{X}} = LSL_{\bar{X}} + V\sigma \qquad \text{... (8.2)}$$

$$V = 3 - \frac{3}{\sqrt{n}}$$

The right-hand side of Fig. 8.4 shows the positioning of the reject limits in relation to control limits targeted at the midpoint between USL_X and LSL_X. This positioning would be consistent with the drive toward never-ending quality improvement where symmetrical tolerances are specified. Target values could be developed for one-sided specifications and in cases where a linear trend is unavoidable. Whenever reject limits are employed, it must be possible to maintain the R (or s) chart in statistical control. When process dispersion behaves erratically, reject limits are not appropriate.

8.7.2 Modified Control Limits

In situations where merely meeting specifications is considered economically sufficient, the use of rejection limits in place of control limits may be considered. Rejection limits used in this way have been called modified control limits. They have been applied particularly to control of dimensions. Their use is practical only where the spread of the process (frequently estimated as 6 σ) is appreciably less than the difference between the two specification limits ($USL_X - LSL_X$).

The idea behind the modified control limits is to permit limited shifts in the process average in cases where the difference between the two specification limits is substantially greater than the spread of a controlled process. This is intended to avoid the cost of stopping production to hunt for trouble whenever the shifts in process average are not sufficient to cause the production of nonconforming product. It is as though in Fig. 8.4 the process were to be allowed to vary from the position marked "highest acceptable position of universe" to that marked "lowest acceptable position".

However, in the use of modified control limits a larger margin of safety is sometimes introduced than that given by the assumption that the spread of the process is ± 3 σ from the process average. One British practice is to set such limits at a distance from the specification limits equal to 3.09 σ $(1.96\sigma/\sqrt{n})$. This gives multipliers of σ of 1.70, 1.97, 2.10, and 2.21 for n = 2, 3, 4, and 5, respectively ; this contrasts with the more common practice of using the respective V factors of 0.88, 1.27, 1.50, and 1.66 given in Table 8.8 for the same subgroup sizes.

Modified control limits seem to have proved particularly useful as applied to intermittent short production runs in machining operations where process dispersion (6 σ) has been determined from previous runs. The more $USL_X - LSL_X$ exceeds 6 σ, the greater the permissible latitude in machine setting. The use of modified control limits may simplify the problem of maintaining machine settings that are good enough for practical purposes or where a trend exists.

Nevertheless, where the only limits shown on $\bar{\bar{X}}$ charts are modified control limits, users of these charts should recognize that the charts fail to disclose the presence or absence of statistical control in the manufacturing process. Moreover, the protection given by the rejection limits depends on a good estimate of σ after this estimate has been made, the process dispersion must remain in statistical control.

8.8 CUMULATIVE SUM CONTROL CHART FOR AVERAGES

The primary Shewhart control-chart rule, look for trouble if a point falls outside the control limits, is a statistically independent decision rule. That is, the decision is based on a point plot of information taken from one and only one sample or subgroup. When a secondary rule is introduced into the decision process, such as look for trouble if seven points in a row are on the same side of the central line, the decision process becomes, in part, statistically dependent. This statistical dependence results from the fact that one of the decision rules utilizes the results of the six immediately preceding samples as well as the last. The decision process becomes more sensitive to small but sustained shifts in the statistical measure being controlled.

The cumulative sum control chart, frequently called the CuSum chart and sometimes abbreviated *CSCC*, was designed to identify slight but sustained shifts in a universe. The technique incorporates information taken from the latest samples into that taken from a sequence of prior samples.

This chart has an entirely different appearance from any Shewhart control chart. In place of the centerline and symmetrical control limits, a mask is constructed that incorporates a location pointer and two decision lines that angle away from it. Figure 8.5 illustrates the mask and chart for a *CSCC* for sample averages. The horizontal scale represents the counter i on subgroups; the vertical scale represents the cumulative sum of subgroup average deviations from an aimed-at or standard value $\bar{X}_0$. The two-sided control limits for $\bar{X}$ are the edges *AA″* and *BB″*, which are the lower and upper control limits, respectively.

The mask is placed over the control-chart plot in such a way that the point P on the mask lies on the last point plotted and the line *OP* is parallel to the horizontal axis. As long as none of the previous points lie above *AA′* or below *BB′*, the process is assumed to be in control. The basis for the *CSCC* control limits is described in the following paragraph.

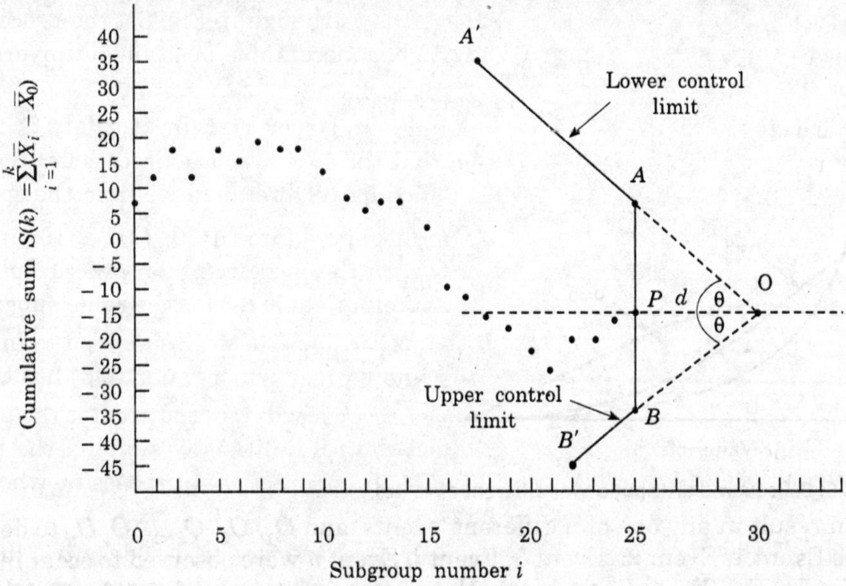

FIGURE 8.5: Cumulative sum control chart for sample averages (X) data from 25 subgroups.

Suppose that, after a sustained period of operation in control at the level $\mu_0 = \bar{X}_0$ the mean suddenly shifts to a new level of $\mu_1 = \bar{X}_1$, which is above X_o. Each new point that successively is added into the cumulative sum of the $(\bar{X}_i - \bar{X}_0)$ will cause the sum to increase and will result in a general upward trend on the chart. If this trend is great enough, sooner or later a point will fall below *BB′*, the upper control limit, signaling an upward shift in the process average. Similarly, if the average shifts downward, the cumulative sum will exhibit a downward trend, which will be signaled be one or more points falling above *AA′*.

Two elements are needed to construct the mask. They are σ, the angle between the horizontal and each control limit line, and the distance *OP* from the vertex of these angles to the locator point *P*.

8.9 SIGNIFICANCE TEST FOR UNKNOWN POPULATION

In an industry turning out large number of components, sometimes it is desirable to know whether a sample differs from the other significantly even if the distribution is known or unknown. A very useful significance test is chi-squared (χ^2) test when the distribution of population is unknown or not normal.

8.9.1 Chi-squared (χ^2) Test

There are many situations in which it is not possible to make rigid assumptions about the shape of the population from which samples are being drawn. For example imagine a large quantity of bolts in a box. It is thought that 50 percent are of length 100 mm, 20 per cent of 50 mm, 20 per cent of 30 mm, and 10 percent of 20 mm. A random sample of 50 bolts is taken and found to contain 28 of length 100 mm (we would have expected 25), 11 of 50 mm (10 expected). 8 of 30 mm. (10 expected) and 3 of 20 mm. (4 expected). Our problem is to decide if the difference between the contents of the sample and what we would have 'expected' is great enough to give reason to doubt our initial assumption. To make this decision we employ the chi-squared distribution. Chi is a Greek letter (pronounced ki, as in kite) and written χ. The values of χ^2 which have only a 5 per cent probability of being exceeded due to differences arising from sampling alone, *i.e.,* if the assumption made initially is correct, are given in Table *B* of App. 1.

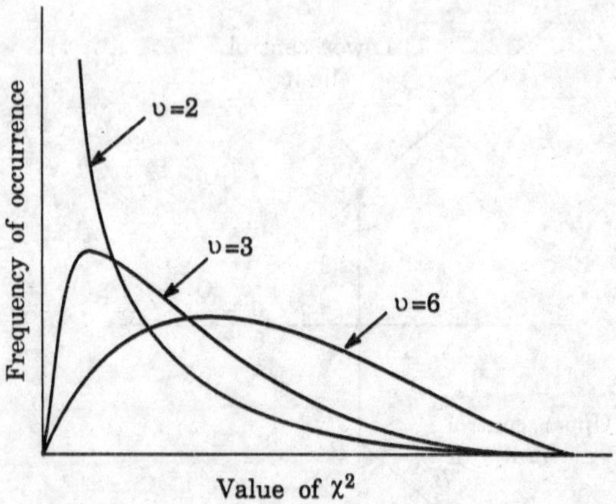

FIGURE 8.6: Chi-squared distribution for different df values.

If a trial can result in any one of n different 'events' and O_1, O_2, O_3......O_i O_n to denote the number of times Event 1, Event 2, Event 3, Event *i*, Event *n* were observed to occur in a series of trials, and E_1, E_2, E_3, *Ei*.........E_n to denote the number of items we would 'expect' them to occur, assuming a given hypothesis to be true, then

$$\chi^2 = \frac{(O_1 - E_1)^2}{E_1} + \frac{(O_2 - E_2)^2}{E_2} - \frac{(O_3 - E_3)^2}{E_3} + \ldots \frac{(O_i - E_i)^2}{E_i} + \ldots \frac{(O_n - E_n)^2}{E_n} \quad \ldots(8.3)$$

and has $n-1$ degrees of freedom. *i.e.* $v = n - 1$)

The reliability of this form of χ^2 increases as the number of trials increases (i.e. as Oi and E_i ; $i = 1, 2, 3 \ldots n$ increases) and should never used when a value of E_i is less than 5. If it is necessary to test a set of observations from which one or more of the 'expected' frequencies fall below 5, the offending frequency are to be combined with another group (or groups) to bring the expected frequency above 5. If this has to be done, the number of degrees of freedom for χ^2 is reduced by one each time a small group is merged into another.

The distribution of χ^2 depends on the degrees of freedom. There is a different χ^2 distribution for each number of degrees of freedom. The distribution is very much skewed to the right for small degrees of freedom, and as the degrees of freedom increase the curve becomes more and more symmetric and becomes approximately normal for larger degrees of freedom as illustrated in Fig. 8.6. The mean of the χ^2 distribution is equal to the number of degrees of freedom (i.e ν) and its standard deviation is the square root of twice the degrees of freedom, *i.e.,* $\sqrt{2\nu}$. We can define the confidence intervals (99%, 95% etc.,) for χ^2 by using Table B for chi-squared. For example, assume that we are interested in 90% confidence interval, then we determine the values of χ^2 namely χ^2 and χ^2 for which 5 percent of the area under the curve lies in each tail. For ν of 4 the graphical interpretation is shown in Fig. 8.7.

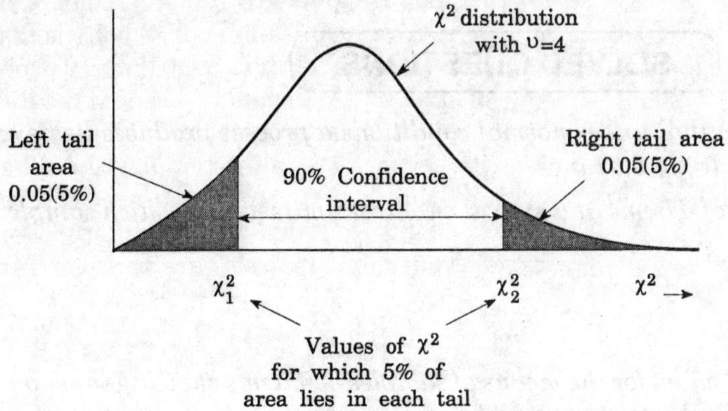

FIGURE 8.7: *Illustration* of chi-squared distribution with df (ICD) of 4 and a 90 per cent confidence interval.

χ^2 -test is one of the simplest and the most general test known. It is applicable to a very large number of problems in practice which can be summed up as follows :

Test of Independence: In order to test whether or not the attributes are associated we take the null hypothesis that there is no association in the attributes under study, or in other words, the two attributes are independent. If the calculated value of χ^2 is less than the table value at a certain level of significance (generally 5 percent), we say that the results of the experiment provide no evidence for doubting the hypothesis or, in other words, the hypothesis that the attributes are not associated holds good.

Goodness of Fit: The χ^2 -test can be used in a similar manner to test the 'goodness of fit' of an observed set of data to a given theoretical distribution. The 'goodness of fit' is tested by comparing the observed frequencies each value of the variate with the frequencies given by the theoretical distribution. The parameters of the theoretical distribution (*e.g.,* mean and standard deviation) are chosen to be the same as those of the observations. χ^2 loses one degree of freedom for each constraint placed on the theoretical frequencies (e.g. $\nu = n - 3$) if the theoretical frequencies are so ordered that they have the same mean, standard deviation and sum of the observed frequencies.

Reliability of Sample Estimate of Population Standard Deviation: It can be shown that

$$\chi^2 = \frac{\nu s^2}{\sigma^2} \qquad \text{...(8.4)}$$

where s is the standard deviation of a sample of n items drawn from a population whose (unknown) standard deviation is σ, is distributed like χ^2 with $(n - 1)$ degrees of freedom.

Consequently we can use this to estimate the greatest value σ is likely to have when the only information available is σ, based on a sample.

Addition Property of χ^2**:** It is possible to combine the independently derived values of χ^2 relating to samples of similar data by the simple process of addition. It enables a better (because more comprehensive) test than could be made using the data of any one sample by itself. The sum of the χ^2 values thus combined will itself have a χ^2 distribution with degrees of freedom equal to the sum of the degrees freedom of the separate χ^2 values. However, while adding the χ^2 values, it must be remembered that the combining of results in a single inclusive test is appropriate when the samples are independent.

SOLVED QUESTIONS

Q. 8.1 : *Experience has shown that under normal conditions a process produces items of mean diameter (σ) 3.00 inches with (σ) of 0.01 inch.*

Find the $\sigma_{\bar{X}}$ *for samples of 4 items and state the control limits within which sample means will lie for:*

(*a*) *95% of samples, and*

(*b*) *virtually all samples.*

Draw up a quality control chart for the means of samples of 4 items showing inner and outer limits. Plot the mean given in the following table on your chart and comment on the picture revealed.

Means of samples of size and taken at 10 min. interval					
Time	3.00	3.10	3.20	3.30	3.40
Mean diameter	3.003	3.004	2.995	3.001	2.992
Time	3.50	4.00	4.10	4.20	4.30
Mean diameter	2.996	3.001	3.003	3.006	3.011
Time	4.40	4.50	5.00	5.10	5.20
Mean diameter	3.005	2.995	2.997	2.993	2.990
Time	5.30	5.40	5.50	6.00	6.10
Mean diameter	2.991	2.992	2.990	2.986	2.984

Ans.

$$\sigma = 0.01$$

$$\sigma_{\bar{X}} = \frac{\sigma}{\sqrt{n}} = \frac{0.01}{\sqrt{4}} = 0.005$$

(*a*) From Table *A*, it is evident that 95% of samples will lie between ±1.96 sigma control limits.

$$1.96 \quad - = 1.96 \times 0.005 \approx 0.010$$

Upper control limit = $\mu + 1.96\ \sigma_{\bar{X}}$ 3.000 – 0.010 = 3.010
Lower control limit = $\mu - 1.96\ \sigma_{\bar{X}}$ 3.000 – 0.010 = 2.990

(*b*) Virtually all samples will lie between ±3 sigma limits

$$3\sigma_{\bar{X}} = 3 \times 0.005 = 0.015$$
$$= \mu + 3 = \sigma_{\bar{X}} = 3.000 + 0.015 = 3.015$$
$$= \mu - 3 = \sigma_{\bar{X}} = 3.000 - 0.015 = 2.985$$

On drawing the $\bar{X}$ chart with above limits it will be evident that only sample taken at 4.30 crosses inner limit while the last two samples cross the lower inner limit. Further the distribution of points is not random. From sample at 3.40 there appears to be some upward adjustment made in the process. Similarly from sample at 4.40 onwards there appears to some downward adjustment. On the whole it can be predicted that the process is not in control.

Q. 8.2 : *A certain company manufactures electronic components for use in television sets. One particular component is made to a critical length of 0.450 in. Based on past production experiences, the standard deviation of this dimension is 0.010 in. Because of the critical nature of the dimension the quality control group maintains warning limits on the $\bar{X}$ control chart as well as the normal 3 σ limits. The $\bar{X}$ chart is based on subgroups of four samples, and warning limits are maintained at two standard deviations from the mean.*

Compute the warning limits and the control limits for the $\bar{X}$ chart and answer to following questions.

(*a*) *What is the probability that a subgroup average will exceed the upper warning limit but not exceed the upper control limit when the process is correctly centered ?*

(*b*) *The quality control supervisor has a policy that he should be notified immediately if two successive subgroup averages exceed one of the warning limits or if one sùbgroup average exceeds either of the control limits. What is the probability that, when there has been no change in the process, the quality control supervisor will have to be notified based on :*

1. *Two successive subgroup averages falling between the upper warning limit and upper control limit.*
2. *A subgroup average exceeding the upper control limit.*

(*c*) *If the process average suddenly shifts to 0.460 with no change in the standard deviation, what is the probability that two successive points will exceed the upper warning limit but not exceed the upper control limit ?*

Ans.

$$\mu = 0.450\ ;\ \sigma = 0.010$$
$$\sigma_{\bar{X}} = \frac{\sigma}{\sqrt{n}} = \frac{0.010}{\sqrt{4}} = 0.005$$

Upper warning limit = $\mu + 2\ \sigma_{\bar{X}}$ = 0.450 + 2(0.005) = 0.460
Lower warning limit = $\mu - 2\ \sigma_{\bar{X}}$ = 0.450 – 2(0.005) = 0.440
Upper control limit = $\mu + 3\ \sigma_{\bar{X}}$ = 0.465
Lower control limit = $\mu - 3\ \sigma_{\bar{X}}$ = 0.435

(*a*) Probability that a subgroup average exceeds the upper warning limit but not exceed the upper control limit is the area of the normal curve between these two limits. From Table *A* this area is 0.02135. Hence the probability is 0.02135.

(*b*) From (*a*) the computed probability of a subgroup average falling between $UWL_{\bar{X}}$ and $UCL_{\bar{X}}$ is 0.02135.

1. Probability that two successive subgroup averages falling between $UWL_{\bar{X}}$ and $UCL_{\bar{X}}$ is $(0.02135)^2$ i.e. 0.00046.
2. Probability that a subgroup average exceeds the $UCL_{\bar{X}}$ is the area of the normal curve above $UCL_{\bar{X}}$. From Table *A*, the area of the curve above $UCL_{\bar{X}}$ is 0.00135. Hence the probability that a subgroup average falling above $UCL_{\bar{X}}$ is 0.00135.

(c) $UCL_{\bar{X}} = 0.465$ and $UWL_{\bar{X}} = 0.460$. When the process average shifts to 0.460,

z corresponding to $UCL_{\bar{X}}$ of $0.465 = 1$

z corresponding to $UWL_{\bar{X}} = 0$

From Table *A*, area of the curve between $UCL_{\bar{X}}$ and $UWL_{\bar{X}}$ is 0.3413. Hence the probability of a subgroup average falling between $UCL_{\bar{X}}$ and $UWL_{\bar{X}}$ after the shift is 0.3413.

Probability that two successive points will exceed the upper warning limit but not exceed the upper control limit

$$= (0.3413)^2 = 0.11649.$$

Q. 8.3: *In the manufacture of the balance wheel for a speed control device, finished wheels are tested for dynamic balance on a test stand at 6,000 r/min. If a vibration force in excess of 85 g cm/s² results, the balance must be remachined.*

Because of the critical nature of this test, control charts for $\bar{X}$ and R are maintained using a subgroup size of four. Warning limits at ± 2 σ are used as well as standard 3 σ control limits. The process has been operating in control at an estimated μ of 74 g cm/s² and a σ of 3.4.

(*a*) *Calculate control limits for both the $\bar{X}$ and R charts and warning limits for the $\bar{X}$ chart.*

(*b*) *With the process centered as indicated, what is the probability that two successive points will fall between the UCL and the UWL on the $\bar{X}$ chart.*

Ans.

(*a*)

$$\mu = 74, \sigma = 3.4$$

$$\sigma_{\bar{X}} = \frac{3.4}{\sqrt{4}} = 1.7$$

$$UCL_{\bar{X}} = \mu + 3\,\sigma_{\bar{X}} = 74 + 3\,(1.7) = 79.1$$

$$UCL_{\bar{X}} = \bar{\bar{X}} - 3\,\sigma_{\bar{X}} = 74 - 3\,(1.7) = 68.9$$

$$UCL_R = D_1\,\sigma = 4.70 \times 3.4 = 15.98$$

$$UCL_R = D_1\,\sigma = 0 \times 3.4 = 0$$

$$UWL_R = \mu + 2\,\sigma_{\bar{X}} = 74 + 2\,(1.7) = 77.4$$

$$UWL_R = \mu - 2\,\sigma_{\bar{X}} = 74 - 2\,(1.7) = 70.6$$

(*b*) Area of the normal curve between and *UWL*, and *UCL* is 0.02135. Hence the probability that two successive points will fall between the *UCL* and *UWL* on $\bar{X}$ chart is $(0.02135)^2$ *i.e.* 0.00046.

Q. 8.4: *In the situation described in Q. 8.3, the mean of the process suddenly shifts to 78 g cm/s².*

(*a*) *At this new mean level, what proportion of the balance wheels will exceed the 85 g cm/s² limit assuming a normal distribution of this characteristic ?*

(b) *What is the probability that this shift in μ will be detected on the first subgroup after the shift occurs ?*

(c) *What is the probability that the shift will be detected on the first two subgroups based only upon two successive points falling between the UCL and the UWL ?*

(d) *What is the combined probability of detecting this shift within the first two subgroups plotted?*

Ans : In the changed situation $\mu = 78$ g cm/s^2 but $\overline{X}$ remains to be the same *i.e.* 3.4.

(*a*) *z* corresponding to 85

$$= \frac{85 - 78}{3.4} = 2.059$$

Area of the normal curve for *z* of 2.059 is 0.98025. Proportion of the balance wheels exceeding the 85 g cm/s^2

$$= 1.0 - 0.98025 = 0.01975.$$

(*b*) $UCL_{\overline{X}}$ as determined in Q. 8.3 is = 79.1

$$z \text{ corresponding} \quad UCL_{\overline{X}} = \frac{79.1 - 78.0}{1.7} = 0.6471$$

Area of the curve for *z* of 0.6471 is 0.7412.

Area of the curve above $UCL_{\overline{X}}$ = 1.0 – 0.7412 = 0.2588

Thus 0.2588 represents the probability of a point falling above $UCL_{\overline{X}}$ after the shift has taken place. Also the probability of a point between central line and $UCL_{\overline{X}}$ is 0.7319. Before the shift, the probability of a point between central line and $UCL_{\overline{X}}$ is 0.49865. Hence probability of detecting the shift on the first subgroup is

$$0.2588 + (0.49865)\,(0.7319) = 0.6307$$

(*c*) Before the shift in the process mean, the probability of a point between $UCL_{\overline{X}}$ and $UCL_{\overline{X}}$ is 0.02315. After the shift, this probability increases to 0.3791. Based upon two successive points, the probability of detecting the shift on first subgroup, after the shift is :

$$(0.3791)\,(0.02135) = 0.0081.$$

The probability of detecting the shift on the second sample after the shift is the probability that after the shift and first and second points fall between $UCL_{\overline{X}}$ and $UWL_{\overline{X}}$. The probability of such an event is :

$$(0.3791)^2 = 0.1437$$

The probability that the shift is detected within first two subgroups is :

$$0.0081 + 0.1437 = 0.1518.$$

(*d*) Combined probability of detecting the shift within first two subgroups plotted is :

$$0.6307 + 0.1518 = 0.7825$$

Q. 8.5 : *For a certain process, the natural tolerance range exceeds the specification range. Slight changes in centering will therefore result in substantial product being produced outside specifications. Some one has suggested the use of 1 σ warning limits in addition to 3 σ control limits on an $\overline{X}$ chart. A shift in process is assumed to have occurred if : (1) a point falls outside one of the 3 σ control limits ; or (2) three points in a row fall outside one of the warning limits.*

(*a*) *What is the probability that the application of rule (2) will lead to hunting for trouble when none exists (Type I error) ?*

(*b*) *Assuming an upward shift is μ of 0.5 σ and a subgroup size of 4, what is the probability that the application of rule 1 will lead to not detecting the shift on the first three subgroups drawn after the shift occurs (Type II error) ?*

Ans: (*a*) Probability of a point between $UWL_{\bar{X}}$ and $UCL_{\bar{X}}$ = 0.15735. Probability that the application of rule (2) will lead to hunting for trouble when none exists

$$= (0.15735)^2 = 0.003896$$

(*b*) After an upward shift of 0.5 σ (*i.e.* 1 $\sigma_{\bar{X}}$) the probability of a point between the warning limit and control limit increases to 0.4773. Probability that 3 points fall in a row is $(0.4773)^3$ *i.e.* 0.109. Hence probability of not detecting the shift

$$= 1.0 - 0.109 = 0.891$$

Q. 8.6: *The tensile strength of a steel bar a nominal value of 450 M N/m2. Specifications are prepared at intervals from the steel bar being produced. The following table shows the tensile strength of ten such specimens.*

442.5 457.5 442.5 450.0 457.5 450.0 457.5 457.5 450.0 457.5

(*a*) *Calculate the average and standard deviation of the process of these values.*

(*b*) *Plot the values on an ordinary chart and insert the 1 in 40 and I in 1,000 limits.*

(*c*) *Plot the values on a cumulative sum control chart.*

(*d*) *Comment on the information shown by each chart.*

Ans: (a) Average

$$\bar{X} = \frac{442.5 + ... + 457.5}{10}$$

$$= \frac{4522.5}{10} = 452.25$$

$$\text{Standard deviation } (s) = \sqrt{\frac{(442.5 - 452.25)^2 + ...(457.5 - 452.25)}{9}} = 6.175$$

(*b*) From Table *A*, 1 in 40 limits are ± 1.96 sigma limits and 1 in 1,000 limits are ± 3.09 sigma limits

$$1.96\ s = 1.96 \times 6.17 = 12.10$$
$$3.09\ s = 3.09 \times 6.1 = 19.08$$

For an ordinary *X* chart, the limits are 452.25 ± 19.10 and warning limits are 452.25 ± 12.10.

(*c*) On plotting the *X* chart it will be noticed that the point are randomly distributed and are within the warning limits and hence this chart will show statistical control.

(*d*) On plotting the cusum chart, a change will be indicated at 7th sample mean.

Q. 8.7: *A small electronic device is designed to emit a timing signal of 200 milliseconds duration. In the production of this device, subgroups of five units are taken at periodic intervals and tested.*

$\overline{X}$ and R are calculated for each subgroup and used to plot the control charts. After inspection of 125 of these devices,

$$\Sigma \overline{X} = 4{,}9908 \; ; \; \Sigma R = 277$$

Find the 95% probability limits for $\overline{X}$ and R control charts.

Ans :

$$\overline{X} = \frac{4990.8}{25} = 199.63$$

$$\overline{R} = \frac{277}{25} = 11.08$$

95% probability limits indicate that area of normal curve between control limits is 0.95. Assuming a symmetrical distribution, area of the normal curve below $LCL_{\overline{X}}$ is 0.025 and also above $UCL_{\overline{X}}$ it is 0.025. From Table A, the multiplier of σ is 1.96. Since the factor A_2 in Table D is based on 3-sigma limit, it is merely necessary to multiply it by 1.96/3 = 0.653.

$$UCL_{\overline{X}} = 199.63 + (0.653)\,(0.58)\,(11.08) = 203.83$$

$$LCL_{\overline{X}} = 199.63 - (0.653)\,(0.58)\,(11.08) = 195.43$$

From Table 8.4, $D_{0.975} = 4.20$ and $D_{0.025} = 0.85$'

$$UCL_R = D_{0.975} \times \sigma = 4.20 \times 4.76 = 19.99$$

$$LCL_R = D_{0.025} \times \sigma = 0.85 \times 4.76 = 4.04$$

Q. 8.8: *Control charts for $\overline{X}$ and s are maintained on the weight in ounces of the contents of a cereal container. The subgroup size is 10. After 18 subgroups, $\Sigma \overline{X} = 595.8$ and $\Sigma s = 7.96$.*

(a) *Compute 3 σ control limits for the $\overline{X}$ chart and estimate the value of σ.*

(b) *A decision is made to use 95% probability limits on the $\overline{X}$ chart rather than 3 σ limits. What would be locations of these limits ?*

(c) *If the mean shifts to 33.4, what is the probability of detecting this shift on the first subgroup after the shift occurs if the 3 sigma limits are used ?*

(d) *What is the probability of detecting the shift described in (c) if 95% probability limits are used ?*

Ans:

$$\Sigma \overline{X} = 595.8;$$

$$\overline{\overline{X}} = \frac{595.8}{18} = 33.1$$

$$\overline{s} = \frac{8.24}{18} = 0.458$$

(a)

$$UCL_{\overline{X}} = \overline{\overline{X}} + A_3\,\overline{s} = 33.1 + 1.03\,(0.458) = 33.57$$

$$LCL_{\overline{X}} = \overline{\overline{X}} + A_3\,\overline{s} = 33.1 - 1.03\,(0.458) = 32.63$$

$$\sigma = \frac{\overline{s}}{c_4} = \frac{0.458}{0.9727} = 0.47$$

(b) For 95% probability limits

$$UCL_{\overline{X}} = \overline{\overline{X}} + (1.96/3)\,A_3\,\overline{s} = 33.41$$

$$LCL_{\overline{X}} = \overline{\overline{X}} - (1.96/3)\,A_3\,\overline{s} = 32.79$$

(c) When the mean shifts to 33.4, the probability of a point falling above $UCL_{\bar{X}}$ can be calculated by first computing

Since $UCL_{\bar{X}} = \bar{X} + 3\,\sigma\bar{X} = 33.57$, and $\bar{X} = 33.1$, hence $\sigma\bar{X} = 0.157$.

The probability of a point falling above $UCL_{\bar{X}}$ after the change is computed to be 0.1394. Probability of a point below the central line is computed to be 0.0281. Hence the probability of a point between the $UCL_{\bar{X}}$ and central line is 1.0 – (0.1394 +0.0281) *i.e.* 0.8325.

Also before the shift, the probability of a point above $UCL_{\bar{X}}$ is 0.00135 and that between central line and $UCL_{\bar{X}}$ is 0.49865.

A shift is indicated either by way of the first subgroup falls above $UCL_{\bar{X}}$ or this becomes the eighth point in a row of previous seven points in a row falling between central line and $UCL_{\bar{X}}$. Thus the combined probability of detection on the first sample after the shift is :

$$0.1394 + (0.49865)^7\,(0.8325) = 0.14578$$

(d) When using 95% probability limits, before shift the probability of a point falling above $UCL_{\bar{X}}$ is 0.025 and that between the central line and $UCL_{\bar{X}}$ is 0.4750. After the shift the respective probabilities are 0.4746 and 0.4973. The probabilities of detecting a shift on the first subgroup is :

$$0.4746 + (0.4750)^7\,(0.4973) = 0.4773.$$

Q. 8.9: *A certain manufacturing process has exhibited a linear increasing trend. Sample averages and ranges for the past 15 subgroups, taken every 15 minutes in subgroups of 5 items, are given in the following table.*

Subgroup	*Average*	*Range*	*Subgroup*	*Average*	*Range*
1	198.8	7	9	209.2	7
2	197.6	2	10	207.8	16
3	204.6	10	11	210.0	9
4	203.8	12	12	214.4	8
5	205.6	17	13	211.8	16
6	204.8	9	14	211.8	6
7	205.4	10	15	213.8	8
8	210.6	9			

Find the linear trend line to these data and plot a trended $\bar{X}$ control chart with 3-sigma limits.

Ans: The following table shows the calculations for least squares line for $\bar{X}$.

Subgroup number	*Revised subgroup number h*	*Subgroup average $\bar{X}$*	$h\bar{X}$	h^2	R
1	–7	198.8	–1391.6	49	7
2	–6	197.6	–1185.6	36	2
3	–5	204.6	–1023.0	25	10
4	–4	203.8	–815.2	16	12
5	–3	205.6	–616.8	9	17
6	–2	204.8	–409.6	4	9

7	–1	205.4	–205.4	1	10
8	0	210.6	0	0	9
9	1	209.2	209.2	1	7
10	2	207.8	415.6	4	16
11	3	210.0	630.0	9	9
12	4	214.4	857.4	16	8
13	5	211.8	1059.0	25	16
14	6	211.8	1270.8	36	6
15	7	213.8	1496.6	49	8
Totals	0	3110.0	291.4	280	146

$$a = \overline{X} = \frac{3110}{15} = 207.33$$

$$b = \frac{\Sigma h\overline{X}}{\sigma h^2}$$

$$= \frac{291.4}{280} \quad 1.0407$$

$$\overline{X} = a + bh = 207.33 + 1.0407\,h$$

$$\overline{R} = \frac{146}{15} = 9.73$$

$$A_2\overline{R} = (0.58)\ (9.73)$$

The upper control limit is $A_2\ \overline{R}$ above the trend line, and the lower central limit is $A_2\ \overline{R}$ below it. The control line on the chart is calculated as follows :

For subgroup 1, $h = -7$,

$$\overline{X} = 207.33 + 1.0407\ (-\ 7) = 200.05$$

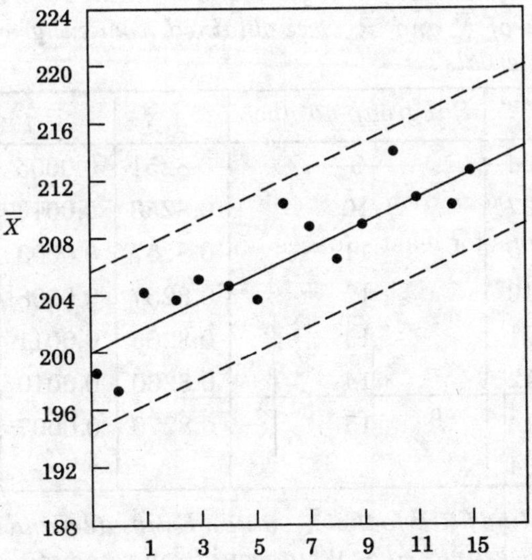

FIGURE 8.8: Trended *X* control chart for the Prob. 8.9.

For subgroup 15, $h = 7$,

$$\bar{} = 207.33 + 1.0407\ (7) = 214.62$$

The line joining the above points is the central line on the chart. Control limits are at 5.64 units away from this line. Figure 8.8 shows the trended X chart with points plotted on it.

Q. 8.10: *Specifications on the process in Q. 8.99 are 200 ± 20. The process may be stopped at any time and readjusted. If upon readjustment the mean is to be set exactly 3 σ above the lower specification and the process is to be stopped for readjustment when the mean reaches a level exactly 3 σ below the upper specification :*

(*a*) Calculate the aimed-at starting and stopping values of $\bar{\bar{X}}_0$.

(*b*) *Estimate the duration of a run between adjustments.*

Ans:

$$U = 200 + 20 = 220$$

$$L = 200 - 20 = 180$$

From Problem 8.16, $\bar{R} = 9.73$

$$\sigma = \frac{\bar{R}}{d^2} = \frac{9.73}{2.326} = 4.183$$

(*a*) Aimed at starting ($\bar{\bar{X}}_0$) = 180 + 3 σ

$$= 180 + 3\ (4.183) = 192.549$$

Aimed-at stopping ($\bar{\bar{X}}_0$) = 220 – 3 σ

$$= 220 - 3\ (4.183) = 207.451$$

(*b*) Interval between setups = 2.07.451 – 192.549/1.0407 = 14.3 subgroup intervals.

With subgroups spaced 15 minutes apart, this means that a new set up is required every 3.5 hours.

Q. 8.11: *A certain dimension was specified as 0.8250 ± 0.0050 in. Experience indicated that tool wear caused a fairly steady trend in the average dimension of parts made on the required type of machining operation. The following values of $\bar{X}$ and $\bar{R}$ were obtained from subgroups of 4 parts taken from the machine at half hour intervals :*

Subgroup number	$\bar{X}$	$\bar{R}$	*Subgroup number*	$\bar{X}$	$\bar{R}$
1	0.8220	0.0004	9	0.8251	0.0005
2	0.8228	0.0007	10	0.8253	0.0013
3	0.8233	0.0005	11	0.8257	0.0003
4	0.8232	0.0010	12	0.8257	0.0008
5	0.8235	0.0011	13	0.8265	0.0011
6	0.8241	0.0012	14	0.8260	0.0010
7	0.8244	0.0014	15	0.8270	0.0007
8	0.8248	0.0004			

Determine the equation of a least squares line fitted to the $\bar{X}$ values. Estimate σ and express the tolerance spread (U–L) as a multiple of the estimated σ. What would you recommend as the aimed-at value of $\bar{X}_0$ in the initial setting if this is to be at 3 σ above the lower specification limit? If a new set up is to be made when the value of the control line on an $\bar{X}$ chart is 4 σ below *the upper specification limit, what would you estimate as the length of production run before a new set up is required ?*

Ans: The following table shows the calculations for least squares line. For simplicity, $\bar{X}$, values in the table are expressed in units of 0.0001 in excess of 0.8200.

Subgroup number	*Revised subgroup number h*	*Subgroup average* $\bar{X}$	$h\bar{X}$	h^2
1	– 7	20	–140	49
2	– 6	28	–168	36
3	– 5	33	–165	25
4	– 4	32	–128	16
5	– 3	35	–105	9
6	– 2	41	–82	4
7	– 1	44	–44	1
8	0	48	0	0
9	+ 1	51	51	1
10	+ 2	53	106	4
11	+ 3	57	171	9
12	+ 4	57	228	16
13	+ 5	65	325	25
14	+ 6	60	360	36
15	+ 7	70	490	49
Totals....	0	694	919	280

$$a = \bar{X} = \frac{694}{15} = 46.3$$

$$b = \frac{\Sigma h\bar{X}}{\Sigma h^2} = \frac{919}{280} = 3.28$$

$$\bar{X} = a + bh = 46.3 + 3.28\,h$$

$$\bar{R} = \frac{\Sigma R}{15} = \frac{0.0124}{15} = 0.0008266$$

$$\sigma = \frac{\bar{R}}{d^2} = \frac{0.0008266}{2.059} = 0.0004$$

$$U - L = 0.8300 - 0.8200 = 0.01$$

$$\frac{U - L}{\sigma} = \frac{0.01}{0.004} = 25$$

or $$U - L = 25\,\sigma.$$

The initial set up $(\bar{X}_0) = L + 4\sigma = 0.8200 + 4\ (0.0004) = 0.8216$

New set up is required at $U - 4\sigma$ *i.e.* $0.8300 - 4\ (0.0004) = 0.8284$

The slope of the trend line, $b = 3.28$ *i.e.* (0.000328 in.) is the expected change in average dimension from one subgroup to the next. The interval between set ups is terms of subgroups is estimated to be $\frac{0.8284 - 0.8216}{0.000328} = 20.73$, with subgroups spaced half an hour apart, the new set up is required at every 10 hours.

Q. 8.12: *In the testing of a certain ballistic characteristics of ammunition, it is desired that all values of this quality characteristic fall between 2,720 and 2,900 units. The quality characteristic has been tested on variable basis with a sample of 4 taken from each lot. $\bar{X}$ and R charts have been plotted from past samples. The chart has shown excellent statistical control with an $R = 51$ units. The $\bar{X}$ chart has shown a decided lack of control. Thus lack of control of $\bar{X}$ is to be expected because past experience with other ammunition has indicated that it is very difficult to control the centering of the production process with respect to this particular characteristic.*

It has been determined that it will be considerably more economical to test 16 items on an attribute basis than 4 on a variable basis. In this connection it is decided to maintain np chart. For this purpose it is desired to conduct the "Go" and "Not-Go" testing using special severe limits. These severe limits are to be established so that the appropriate up is 0.15 for the "above limits" chart (corresponding to the "Not-go" chart) and is also 0.15 for the "below limits" chart corresponding to the "Go" chart.

(a) *With specification limits of 2,720 and 2,900 as stated, what should be the values of these severe test limits ?*

(b) *With 16 items tested in each sample, where should the action limits (3-sigma limits) be placed on the np chart ?*

Ans: *Figure 8.9 depicts te given situation.*

$$U = 2{,}900\ ;\ L = 2{,}700$$

$$U - L = 2{,}900 - 2{,}720 = 180$$

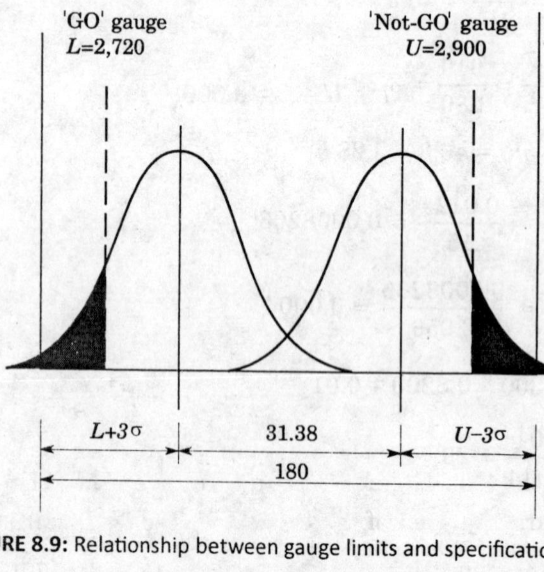

FIGURE 8.9: Relationship between gauge limits and specification limits for the in Q. 8.12 given

$$\bar{R} = 51; \sigma = \bar{R}/d_2 = \frac{51}{2059} = 24.7$$

On the assumption that the distribution is normal, Fig. 8.9 shows that the process centering can vary from L + 3 σ to $U - 3\sigma$ *i.e.* 2794.31 to 2825.69.

(*a*) For the 'Go' gauge chart, $\mu p = 0.15$. This means that the area of the curve below Lower Gauge Limit is 0.15. From Table *A*, the value of z corresponding to the area of 0.15 is – 1.037. If $\bar{X}$ is the value of lower limit, or 'Go' gauge limit, then

$$-1.037 = \frac{X - 2794.31}{24.77}$$

from which $X = 2768.6$

Similarly the value of 'Not-Go' gauge limit is found to be 2851.4.

(b) When 16 items are tested,

$$n\,\mu_p = 16 \times 0.15 = 2.40$$

3-sigma action limits on *np* chart

$$= 2.40 \pm 3\sqrt{2.40(1 - 0.15)}$$

$$= 2.40 \pm 4.28$$

Upper 3-sigma action limit = 2.40 + 4.28 = 6.68

Lower 3-sigma action limit = 0

Q. 8.13: *The internal diameter of a ring has been specified as* **2.00 ± 0.003** *units. The standard deviation of the universe as estimated with* **200** *observations seems to be* **0.0009** *units. The centering of the process has been maintained throughout. It was decided by the quality control department to reduce the cost of inspection by inspecting a small fraction of the lot. For this purpose the suggestion was made to have a "Go" gauge with dimension as* **1.99892** *units and a "Go" "Not-Go" gauge with dimension as* **2.00108**.

Establish μ_p values for "Go" and "Not-Go" charts. Also establish the dimensions of "Go" and "Not Go" gauge when μ_p = **0.1210** *for "Go" chart and μ_p =* **0.1230** *for "Not Go" chart.*

Ans: Since the centering has been maintained and the process is in control, the distribution is assumed to be normal

$$U = 2.003\ ;,\ L = 1.997\ ;,\ U - L = 0.006$$

$$\sigma = 0.0009\ ;\ 6\,\sigma = 0.0054$$

Upper Gauge Limit (*UGL*) = 2.00108

Lower Gauge Limit (*LGL*) = 1.99892

Since $U - L$ is almost equal to 6σ, the shift in the process centering is not allowed.

μ_p value for the "Go" chart is the normal curve below *LGL* of 1.99892.

z corresponding to *LGL*

$$= \frac{1.99892 - 2.00000}{0.0009} = -1.2$$

From Table *A*, the area of the curve corresponding to *z* of –1.2 = 0.1151. Hence the μ_p value for "Go" Chart is 0.1151. Similarly for the "Not-Go" chart the *p* value is found to be 0.1151.

Now when μ_p = 0.1210 for 'Go' chart, the area of the curve up μ_p to *LGL* is 0.1210. From Table *A*, the corresponding value of *Z* is – 1.17. If *X* is the value of "Go" gauge limit, then

$$-1.17 = \frac{X - 2.000}{0.0009}$$

From which, $X = 1.99895$ in.

Similarly when μ_p is 0.1230 for "Not-Go" chart, the area of the curve upto UGL is equal to 1.0000–0.1230 i.e., 8770. From Table A, the corresponding value of z is 1.16. If X is the value of "Not-Go" gauge limit, then

$$1.16 = \frac{X - 2.000}{0.0009}$$

From which, $X = 2.0010$ in.

Q. 8.14: *It is decided to prepare a set of special patrol inspection "Go" and "Not-Go" gauges for process control of a critical machining operation of a plug. Specifications call for a dimension of 9.650 ± 0.150 cm. Previous application of X and R charts indicates an estimate of σ of 0.045 cm and an approximate normal distribution of product when the process is in control. The patrol inspection gauges are to be set at + 1 σ for the "Go" gauge and – 1 σ for the "Not-Go" gauge :*

(a) *Calculate the gauge limits.*

(b) *What proportion of the units should fail each of these tests individually when the process is correctly centered ?*

(c) *Calculate the control limits for the np chart for each gauge based on a subgroup size of 12.*

Ans:

$$U = 9.650 + 0.150 = 9.800 \text{ cm}$$

$$L = 9.650 - 0.150 = 9.500 \text{ cm}$$

$$\sigma = 0.045 \text{ cm.}$$

(a) "Go"gauge limit = 9.650 + 0.045 = 9.695

"Not-Go" gauge limit = 9.650 – 0.045 = 9.605

(b) Since the gauge limits are equidistant from the process centering, the proportion of product below "Go" gauge limit will be exactly equal to proportion of product above the "Not-Go" gauge limit. z corresponding to "Go" gauge limit

$$= \frac{9.605 - 9.650}{0.045} = -1$$

From Table A the area of the curve corresponding to Z of – 1 is 0.1587.

Hence the proportion of the units should fail each of these test individually when the process is correctly centered is equal to 0.1587.

(c)

$$n = 12$$

$$n\mu p = 12 \times 0.1587 = 1.9044$$

Control limits are at $n\mu_p \pm 3\sqrt{n\mu_p(1-\mu p)} = 1.9044 \pm 3.7970$

$$UCL = 5.70$$

$$LCL = 0$$

Q. 8.15: *On a broaching operation a dimension of 0.425 + 0.005 m is being produced. An investigation has shown that the process standard deviation σ is 0.0008 in, and that a progressive increase of 0.001 in. per 50 pieces made is caused by the broaches wearing. Determine modified Pre-control limits (U – 1.5 σ and L – 1.5 σ) suitable for this task and estimate the number of pieces likely to be made between re-sets.*

Ans:

$$U = 0.425 - 0.005 = 0.430$$

$$L = 0.425 - 0.005 = 0.420$$

$$\sigma = 0.0008$$

$$1.5\,\sigma = 0.0012$$

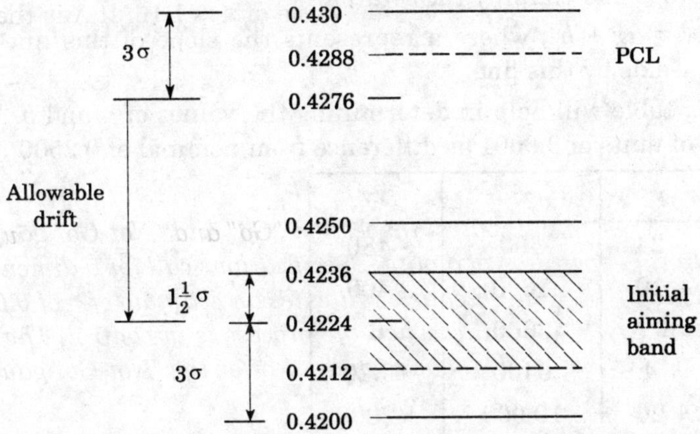

FIGURE 8.10 Modified Pre-control chart showing all the calculations for the data in Prob. 8.23.

Upper $PCL = U - 1.5\sigma = 0.430 - 0.0012 = 0.4288$

Lower $PCL = L + 1.5\sigma = 0.420 + 0.0012 = 0.4212$

Initial aiming size $= L + 3\,\sigma$

$= 0.420 + 3\ (0.0008) = 0.4224$

Upper limit of aiming band $= L + 3\sigma + 1.5\sigma$ *i.e.* $L + 4.5\sigma = 0.4236$

Allowable drift is from $L + 3\,\sigma$ to $U - 3\,\sigma$ *i.e.* 0.4224 to 0.4276.

Available drift $= 0.4276 - 0.4224 = 0.0052$

For a drift of 0.001 the number of pieces made = 50 Hence for a drift of 0.0052 the number of pieces made

$$= \frac{50}{0.001} \times 0.0052 = 260$$

Figure 8.10 shows all the calculations from the average dimension of 0.425 in.

Q. 8.16: *A grinding operation was subjected to an investigation to establish as to what limits it consistently produce and also the progressive rate of change of dimension caused by grinding wheel wear. Fifty pieces were produced, without adjustment and their diameters, in the same sequence as made, were measured to 0.0001 in. and are recorded below. Calculate the approximate number of pieces made per 0.001 in. change in diameter and the process standard deviation.*

Sequence number of piece	20	40	60	80	100
Diameter (in.)	0.2476	0.2490	0.2500	0.2504	0.2520
Sequence number of piece	120	140	160	180	200
Diameter (in.)	0.2524	0.2530	0.2542	0.2542	0.2548

The specification for this operation calls for a dimension of 0.2500 ± 0.0020 in. ; construct a suitable modified Pre-control Chart for this operation, and estimate the number of pieces expected to be produced between successive adjustments (due to wheel wear).

Ans: Since the number of readings in this case is even, it is not possible to adopt the strategy of assigning the number to readings and simplify the solution.

Let the line of best fit be $y = ax + b$; where a represents the slope of this line and b represents the intercept on the y-axis by this line.

Preparation of the following table will help in determining the values of a and b. In this Table y represents the number of units of 0.0001 as difference from nominal of 0.2500.

n	x	y	x^2	xy
1	20	– 24	400	–480
2	40	– 10	1600	–400
3	60	0	3600	0
4	80	+ 4	6400	+ 320
5	100	+ 20	10,000	+ 2000
6	120	+ 24	14,400	+ 2880
7	140	+ 30	19,600	+ 4200
8	160	+ 42	25,600	+ 6720
9	180	+ 42	32,400	+ 7560
10	200	+ 48	44,000	+ 9600
Totals	1,100	+ 176	154,000	32,400

Solution of the simultaneous equations :

$$\Sigma y = a\,\Sigma x + nb$$

$$\Sigma xy = a\Sigma x^2 + b\Sigma x$$

will give the value of 'a' and 'b'

$$n = 10$$

$$\Sigma x = 1100$$

$$\Sigma y = 176$$

$$\Sigma x^2 = 154{,}000$$

$$\Sigma xy = 32{,}400$$

Putting these values in above equations

$$176 = 1{,}100\,a + 10\,b$$

$$32{,}400 = 154{,}000\,a + 1{,}100\,b$$

Solution of these equations yields

$$a = 0.3921 \text{ and } b = -25.5310$$

Hence the line of best fit is given by

$$y = 0.3921x - 25.5310$$

Since $a = 0.3921$, it shows a drift of 0.3921×0.0001 in per. piece.

Therefore, number of pieces made per 0.001 in.

$$= \frac{0.001}{0.3921 \times 0.0001} = 25$$

The process capability can be obtained by calculating the standard deviation (σ) by using the formula

$$\sigma = \sqrt{\left[\frac{1}{n-1}\Sigma(y - \bar{y})^2\right]}$$

where y will be different for each value of $\bar{y}$ and is obtained by calculating the value of y on the Line of best fit at the particular value of x.

That is $\bar{y} = 0.3921x - 25.5310$

By taking $x = 20, 40...200$ and using the above formula σ is found to be 0.0004 in.

Process capability $= \pm 3\,\sigma = \pm 3\,(0.0004) = \pm\, 0.0012$ in.

$$U = 0.2500 + 0.0020 = 0.2520 \text{ in.}$$

$$L = 0.2500 - 0.0020 = 0.2480 \text{ in.}$$

From the readings of the diameters and also since a is positive, it is clear that the diameter of the workpiece increases with tool wear.

The initial aimed-at value $= L + 3\,\sigma$

$$= 0.2480 + 3\,(0.0004) = 0.2492$$

Allowable band for tool wear = $U - 3\,\sigma$ to $L + 3\,\sigma$ *i.e.* 2508 to 0.2492 *i.e.* 0.0016.

$$\text{Number of pieces between re-sets} = \frac{0.0016}{0.3921 \times 0.0001} = 40$$

PCLs are at $L + 1\frac{1}{2}\sigma$ and $U - 1\frac{1}{2}\sigma$ *i.e.* 2486 and 0.2514 in. respectively.

Q. 8.17: *The specifications for a certain quality characteristic are 220 ± 20. It is decided to initiate $\bar{X}$ and R control charts with X charts based on rejection limits. Past evidence indicates that, although the centering of the process shifts from time to time, the dispersion tends to remain constant with a σ of about 9 units. With a subgroup size of 4,*

$$URL_{\bar{X}} = 240 - 1.5(9) = 226.5$$

$$URL_{\bar{X}} = 200 + 1.5(9) = 213.5$$

$$UCL_X = 4.70(9) = 42.3 \text{ and } LCL_R = 0$$

The control chart is initiated. In the first 50 subgroups no points on the R chart are outside the control limits. On the $\bar{X}$ chart, 4 points are above upper rejection limit and 3 points are below the lower rejection limit. The analyst who proposes the charts concludes that the process is "badly out of control ".

Discuss the foregoing case with reference to control chart principles. Is this the type of case in which you would recommend the use of reject limits ? Why or why not ?

Ans: $U = 240,\ L = 200\ ;$

$$U - L = 240 - 200 = 40$$

$$\sigma = 9,\ 6\,\sigma = 54$$

The use of reject limits for controlling the dimension is practical only where $6\,\sigma$ is appreciably less than $U - L$. Hence this is not the fit case for using reject limits.

Further the process is stated to be out of control since the average shifts from time to time, the use of reject limits is not advisable.

Q. 8.18 : *A certain dimension is specified in inches as 3.5100 ± 0.0050. Control charts for X and R indicate that the X shows lack of statistical control but the R chart always shows control. From the R chart the estimate of (σ) chart is 0.0010. If the aimed-at process average* $\bar{X}_0$ *is to be 3.5100, what should be the upper control limit for the X with a subgroup size of 4 ? What should be the upper rejection limit on the X chart assuming the use of 3-sigma rejection limit ?*

Ans:

$$UCL_{\bar{X}} = \bar{X}_0 + 3\sigma_{\bar{X}} = \bar{X}_0 + \frac{3\sigma}{\sqrt{n}}$$

$$= 3.5100 + \frac{3 \times 0.0010}{\sqrt{4}} = 3.5115$$

$$URL_{\bar{X}} = U - V\sigma = (3.5100 + 0.0050) - 1.50 \times 0.0010 = 3.5135$$

Q. 8.19 : *A product is manufactured to meet an upper specification limit of 150.0 and a lower specification limit of 100.0. The process standard deviation is 5.00, and the product is sampled in subgroups of size four. Both* $\bar{X}$ *and R charts are maintained to monitor the product quality. Assume the distribution of the process follows the normal curve.*

(*a*) *To ensure that no more than 0.135% of the product fails to meet each specification limit, what must the control limits of the highest and lowest acceptable* $\bar{X}$ *charts be ?*

(*b*) *Determine reject limits for a modified* $\bar{X}$ *chart. How do these limits compare with those found in (a) ?*

(*c*) *Calculate the central line and the control limits for an R chart for monitoring the dispersion of this process.*

(*d*) *If the R chart were to suddenly indicate lack of control i.e. an upward shift of σ, what effect would this have on the solutions to (a) and (b) ?*

Ans: (*a*) Since 0.135% of the product fails to meet each specification, 3-sigma limits apply. In case of highest acceptable $\bar{X}$ chart,

$$\mu h = U - 3\sigma = 150 - 3(5) = 135$$

$$\sigma_{\bar{X}} = \frac{}{\sqrt{}} = \frac{}{\sqrt{}} = 2.5$$

$$UCL_{\bar{X}} = 135 + 3(2.5)$$

$$= 142.5$$

$$LCL_{\bar{X}} = 136 - 3(2.5) = 127.5$$

In case of lowest acceptable $\bar{\bar{X}}$ chart

$$= L + 3\sigma = 100 + 3(5) = 115$$

$$UCL_{\bar{X}} = 115 + 7.5 = 122.5$$

$$LCL_{\bar{X}} = 115 - 7.5 = 107.5$$

(*b*) Upper rejection limit = $U - V\sigma = 150 - 1.5\,(5) = 142.5$

Lower rejection limit = $L + V\sigma = 100 + 1.5\,(5) = 107.5$

From above it is evident that height $UCL_{\bar{X}}$ is equal to upper rejection limit and lowest $LCL_{\bar{X}}$ is equal to lower rejection limit.

(c) $\overline{R} = d^2 \sigma = 2.059 \times 5 = 10.30$

$$UCL_{\overline{X}} = D_4 \overline{R} = 2.28(10.30) = 23.50$$

$$LCL_{\overline{X}} = D_3 \overline{R} = 0(10.30) = 0$$

(d) If σ increases, in the highest $\overline{X}$ chart, the $UCL_{\overline{X}}$ decreases and $LCL_{\overline{X}}$ increases and $URL_{\overline{X}}$ decreases. In case lowest X chart, the $UCL_{\overline{X}}$ increases and $LCL_{\overline{X}}$ decreases and $URL_{\overline{X}}$ increases.

Q. 8.20 : *The thickness of fiber clutch pads for a certain device must be controlled within specifications of 0.360 ± 0.015 cm. These pads are formed in a semiautomatic machine with an estimated σ of 0.002 cm. It is suggested that reject limits be used for an X chart rather than standard 3 σ control limits about the nominal dimension of 0.360 cm. The subgroup size is 4.*

(a) *Calculate the reject limits.*

(b) *What would be the central line and control limits to control portion of the process using subgroup ranges ?*

(c) *It is suggested that, since the factor V, used to find the reject limits in (a), relies heavily on the assumption of a normal distribution of this product characteristic, the factor 3 be replaced by 4 in the multiplier of σ in the formula. Thus 3 σ $\overline{X}$ reject limits would be based on maintaining the process 4 σ away from specifications. What would be the reject limits in this case ?*

Ans:

$$U = 0.360 + 0.015 = 0.375$$

$$L = 0.360 + 0.015 = 0.345$$

(a) For a subgroup size of 4, $V = 1.50$

$$URL_{\overline{X}} = U - V\sigma = 0.375 - 1.5\ (0.002) = 0.372$$

$$LRL_{\overline{X}} = L - V\sigma = 0.375 - 1.5\ (0.002) = 0.348$$

(b) $\overline{R} = d_2\, \sigma = 2.059 \times 0.002 = 0.004$

$$UCL_R = D_4\ \overline{R} = 2.28\ (0.004) = 0.009$$

$$UCL_R = D_3\ \overline{R} = 0\ (0.004) = 0$$

(c) Formula for $V = 3 - \frac{3}{\sqrt{n}} = 3\left(1 \frac{1}{\sqrt{n}}\right)$

Revised V $= 4\left(1 \frac{1}{\sqrt{n}}\right)$

$$= 4\left(1 \frac{1}{\sqrt{4}}\right)$$

$$= 2$$

$$URL_{\overline{X}} = U - V\sigma$$

$$= 0.375 - 2\ (0.002) = 0.371$$

$$LRL_{\overline{X}} = L + V\sigma$$

$$= 0.345 + 2\ (0.002) = 0.349$$

Q. 8.21 : *A shop decides to use reject limits on a modified control chart for $\bar{X}$ for both product acceptance and for process control. A random sample of 6 items is drawn from a storage cradle and inspected. If the value of $\bar{X}$ falls outside the rejection limits, the tote box is screened for nonconforming units. Previous analysis indicates that this dimension is approximately normally distributed when held in control with an estimated σ of 3.62 mm. The specification range (U – L) is 50.00 mm.*

(a) *Is this process a reasonable candidate for using reject limits ?*

(b) *Calculate the reject limits when U = 1040 mm and L = 990 mm ?*

(c) *If the process is operating at an actual mean value of 1035 mm, what fraction rejected is being produced ?*

(d) *What is the probability of detection on any given subgroup when σ is 1035 mm ?*

Ans: (a) Since $(U - L)$ is 50 mm and this being appreciably more than $6 \times (6 \times 3.62 = 21.72 \text{ mm})$, and the distribution is approximately normal, this process is a reasonable candidate for using reject limits.

(b) For n = 6, the factor $V = 1.78$

$$URL_{\bar{X}} = U - V\sigma = 1040 - 1.78\ (3.62) = 1033$$

$$LRL- = L + V\sigma = 990 + 1.78\ (3.62) = 996.44$$

(c) $\mu = 1{,}035$ mm

z corresponding to $U = \dfrac{1040 - 1035}{3.62} = 1.381$

Area of the curve corresponding to z of 1.381 is 0.9164.

Hence 1– 0.9164 *i.e.* 0.0836 fraction rejected is being produced above U.

z corresponding to $L = \dfrac{990 - 1035}{3.62} = -12.43$

From above it is evident that practically no product lies below L.

Hence fraction rejected = 0.0836.

(d)
$$\sigma_{\bar{X}} = \frac{\sigma}{\sqrt{n}} = \frac{3.62}{\sqrt{6}} = 1.4779$$

z corresponding to $URL_{\bar{X}} = \dfrac{1033.56 - 1035.00}{1.4779} = -0.9744$

From Table A, the area of normal curve corresponding to a z of - 0.9744 is 0.1649. Probability of detection = 1 – 0.1649 + 0.8351.

Q. 8.22 : *(a) A process is required to make pallets whose weights are 2.0 ± 0.5 grams. It is set up and adjusted so that the weights it produces are randomly correct and consistent. A sample of 5 pallets is then taken once per hour, and each is weighed with the following results.*

S. No.	*Weights*					$\bar{X}$	*R*
1	2.1	2.2	2.2	2.0	2.1	2.12	0.2
2	2.0	2.2	2.1	1.9	2.1	2.06	0.3
3	1.9	2.1	2.0	2.0	1.9	1.98	0.2
4	2.2	2.0	2.3	2.1	2.2	2.16	0.3

5	1.9	2.1	1.9	2.0	1.9	1.96	0.2
6	2.1	1.8	2.0	2.1	2.0	2.00	0.3
7	2.0	2.0	2.1	2.1	2.0	2.04	0.1
8	2.1	2.0	1.9	1.9	2.1	2.00	0.2
9	2.0	2.3	2.1	2.1	2.2	2.14	0.3
10	2.1	2.2	2.2	2.1	2.2	2.16	0.1
Totals						20.62	2.2

Determine the reject limits for this process. Also calculate the control limits for R chart.

(b) Sometimes later a consumer asks for pallets with their weights varying as little as possible. Using the above data, calculate the most suitable control limit for working to the best of which the process is capable.

Ans:

$$U = 2.5 \; ; L = 1.5$$

$$\bar{R} = \frac{2.2}{10} = 0.22$$

$$\sigma = \frac{\bar{R}}{d^2} = \frac{2.2}{2.326} = 0.0946$$

For a sample of 5, $V = 1.66$

$$V\sigma = 1.66 \times 0.0946 = 0.16$$

$$URL_{\bar{X}} = U - V\sigma = 2.5 - 0.16 = 2.34$$

$$LRL_{\bar{X}} = L + V\sigma = 61.5 + 0.16 = 1.66$$

$$UCL_R = D_4 \bar{R} = 2.11\,(0.22) = 0.46$$

$$LCL_R = D_3 \bar{R} = 0\,(0.22) = 0$$

(*b*)

$$\bar{X} = \frac{20.62}{10} = 2.062$$

$$3\sigma = 3\,(0.0946) = 0.28$$

Since in a controlled process the minimum variation will be 3 σ from th average of 2.062 grams and not even a single individual reading out of 50 falls beyond the $\bar{X} \pm 3\sigma$, the process can be assumed to have the following specifications :

$$U = \bar{X} + 3\sigma = 2.062 + 0.28 = 2.34$$

$$L = \bar{X} - 3\sigma = 2.062 - 0.28 = 1.78$$

The best working limits which the process is capable of are upper and rejection limits in relation to U of 2.34 and L of 1.76.

$$URL_{\bar{X}} = U - V\sigma = 2.34 - 0.16 = 2.28$$

$$LRL_{\bar{X}} = L + V\sigma = 1.78 + 0.16 = 1.94$$

Q. 8.23 : *A box contains a large quantity of bolts. It is thought 50 percent are of length 100 mm, 20 per cent of 50 mm, 20 per cent of 30 mm and 10 per cent of 20 mm. A random sample of 50 bolts is taken and found to contain 28, 11, 8, and 3 of respective lengths. Have we reasons to doubt our claim ?*

Ans: Using chi-squared test we have :

Bolt length (mm)	100	50	30	20	
Observed frequency (O)	28	11	8	3	Total = 50
Expected frequency (E)	25	10	10	5	Total = 50
$(O-E)$	3	1	– 2	– 2	Total = 0
$(O-E)^2$	9	1	4	4	
$\dfrac{(O-E)^2}{E}$	0.36	0.1	0.4	0.8	Total = 1.66

Thus $\chi^2 = 1.66$ and has 4 1 – 3 degrees of freedom. From Table *B*, for ν of 3, any value of χ^2 in excess of 7.81 is significant at 5 percent level, hence our value of 1.66 is not significant i.e., there is a better than 5 percent chance of obtaining such a sample as ours from a population containing 50 percent of 100 mm, 20 percent of 50 mm, 20 percent of 30 mm and 10 percent of 20 mm, so we have no reason to doubt our claim.

Q. 8.24 : *The strength of 100 test specimens of yarn was distributed according to the details in the following table. The mean and standard deviation were calculated as 44.80 and 5.84 kg respectively and a normal distribution fitted to the data. It is required to examine whether the observed and the expected frequencies are in agreement, thereby testing the goodness of fit of the normal distribution to the observed data :*

Strength, (kg)	*Observed frequening*
25.5 – 30.5	2
30.5 – 35.5	1
35.5 – 40.5	13
40.5 – 45.5	44
45.5 – 59,31	
50.5 – 55.5	4
55.5 – 60.5	2
60.5 – 65.5	3
65.5 and above	–
Total	100

Ans. : For testing the goodness of fit to normal distribution, we will first determine the mid value of the cell, (*i.e.* strength) and with the help of Table A of App. 2 and given of mean and standard deviation 44.80, and 5.84 respectively determine the expected frequency for normal distribution. Thus for 1st row, mid value

$$= 25.5 + \frac{30.5 - 25.5}{2}$$

$$= 28.0$$

For Table *A*,

$$z = \frac{28.0 - 44.80}{5.84}$$

$$= -\frac{16.80}{5.84}$$

$$= -2.88$$

Frequency corresponding to above value of z is 0.0020 Since the total number of observations is 100,

Expected proportional frequency = 0.0020 × 100 = 0.20

Similarly calculating for other classes, and completing the table, we have

Strength	Observed frequency (O)		Expected frequency (E)	
25.5 - 30.5	2		0.20	
30.5 - 35.5	1	16	1.97	12.30
35.5 - 40.5	13		10.13	
40.5 - 45.5	44		25.53	
45.5 - 50.5	31		33.05	
50.5 - 55.5	4		21.04	
55.5 - 60.5	2		6.89	
60.5 - 65.5	3	5	1.10	8.08
65.5 and above	—		0.09	
Total	100		100	

As the expected frequencies in the first two classes and the last two classes are less than 5, they are pooled with the adjoining classes so that the expected frequency in each cell exceeds 5.

Since the normal distribution puts two restraints, the degrees of freedom are reduced by three *i.e.*

$$\nu = 5 - 3 = 2$$

$$\chi^2 = \Sigma(O - E)^2/E$$

$$\chi^2 = \frac{(16.00 - 21.04)^2}{12.30} + \frac{(44.00 - 25.53)^2}{25.53} + \frac{(31.00 - 33.05)^2}{33.05} + \frac{(4.00 - 21.04)^2}{21.04} + \frac{(5.00 - 8.08)^2}{8.08}$$

$$= 1.113 + 13.362 + 0.127 + 13.800 + 1.174$$

$$= 29.576$$

From Table *B* we see that the value of χ^2, with 2 degrees of freedom, which is significant at 1 per cent level is 9.21. Consequently the fit is not considered to be good and the observed data on yarn strength do not follow the normal distribution.

Q. 8.25 : *(a) State the conditions for the validity of χ^2 test.*

(*b*) It is required to make a quick to decision as to the acceptability of a large lot of spacers. To be of any use, the thickness of spacers must not vary by more than ± 0.08 mm. A random sample of 10 spacers from the lot had the following thickness (difference from the nominal in mm).

+0.02	0.00	+0.01	+0.01	0.00
–0.02	+0.01	+0.03	0.00	–0.01

Should the lot be accepted the basis of abo ·e results ?

Ans : (*a*) Condition for the validity of χ^2-test are

1. The sample observations should be independent.
2. Constraints on the cell-frequencies, if any, should be linear.
3. The total frequency should be reasonably large, say greater than 50.
4. No theoretical cell frequency should be less than 5. The χ^2-distribution is essen- tially a continuous distribution but it cannot maintain its character of continuity if a cell frequency is less than 5. If any theoretical cell frequency is less than 5, then for the application of this test, it is pooled with the proceeding or succeeding frequency so that the pooled frequency is more than 5 and finally, adjusted for the degrees of freedom (*i.e.* df) lost in pooling.

(*b*) For the given data, we make the following table :

Difference from nominal mm × 0.01 X	*f*	*fX*	*fX2*
– 2	1	– 2	4
– 1	2	– 2	2
0	3	0	0
1	2	2	2
2	1	2	4
3	1	3	9
Total	10	3	21

$$= \frac{fX}{\Sigma f} = \frac{3}{10} = 0.3$$

Sample average $= 0.3 \times 10^{-2}$ mm

$$s^2 = \frac{\Sigma fX^2}{\Sigma f - 1} - (\overline{X})^2$$

$$= \frac{21}{9}(0.3)^2 = 2.01$$

Sample variance $= 2.01 \times 10^{-2}$ mm

Now $\frac{(n-1)s^2}{\sigma}$ is distributed like χ^2 with $(n - 1)$ degrees of freedom i.e

$$\nu = n - 1 = 9$$

For 95% significant level Table *B* gives χ^2 3.33

That is $\frac{9s^2}{\sigma}$ has a 95 per cent chance of exceeding 3.33 so we can be 95 per cent sure that σ^2 will not exceed $\frac{9s^2}{3.33}$. We can be 95 per cent sure that the population variance (σ^2) will be less than

$$\frac{9 \times 2.01}{3.33} = 5.44$$

95 per cent confidence limits for population tolerance $= \pm 3\,\sigma$

$$= \pm 3\sqrt{5.44} = \pm 7 \times 10 - 2\text{mm}$$

So although we have only inspected 10 spacers we can be 95 per cent sure that the tolerance over the whole lot will not exceed ± 0.07 mm, since this is less than the stipulated ± 0.08 mm, should be accept lot.

PART-1(C)

SCIENTIFIC ACCEPTANCE SAMPLING (*SAS*)

CHAPTER

9

Some Fundamental Concepts in Scientific Acceptance Sampling

9.1 THE IMPORTANCE OF SAMPLING

Adaption of Total quality Management (TQM) techniques implies a goal that the inputs to each stage of an operation should be defect-free because the operations at the preceding stage are under control. But manufacturers often have to accept raw materials and components from suppliers. To be sure that the results of their own operations are of high quality, they must often test inputs to make sure that they conform, to requirements. In most production situations, complete inspection of an entire batch of input is impractical because of time and cost considerations. Instead, a sample of the batch is inspected, and the decision to accept or reject the entire batch is based on the quality of the sample. Hence acceptance sampling is the middle of the road approach between no inspection and 100 percent inspection.

Sampling is invariably used in quality assurance. Even if all items produced or services performed are inspected for conformance to specifications, we are still sampling from the universe of all like items or services that have been or will be produced. In statistical process control (SPC), the objective is to ensure that a single universe exists, that is, to maintain a constant μ and σ at acceptable levels. It is often the case that not all items are inspected and their conformance verified. The SPC techniques in **PART 1(B)** of this book clearly exhibit that samples were drawn from the process flow ; often these samples constituted much less than 100% of the output. The rules and guidelines for forming rational subgroups in Chap 7, were presented and discussed without consideration of the proportion of output being inspected.

9.1.1 Need for Lot-By-Lot Acceptance Sampling

Lot-by-Lot (or batch-by-batch) acceptance sampling by attributes is the most common type of sampling applied to incoming materials of partly finished product at various intermediate stages of the manufacturing process and to final product. With this type of sampling, a predetermined number of units (sample) from each lot is inspected by attributes. If the amount of defective is less than the prescribed minimum, the lot is accepted ; if not, the lot is rejected as being below the set standard. Each lot in the shipment or order is sampled and either rejected or accepted.

The conditions which immediately favour the use of acceptance sampling are :

1. when the cost of inspection is high and the loss arising from the passing of a defective unit is not so high.
2. where the inspection is of destructive nature and it is definitely not possible to carry out 100% inspection.
3. where it is desired to exert more effective pressure on the vendor for improving the quality by rejecting the entire lot on the basis of sampling. Inspection, in the sense of sorting good product from bad, cannot be relied on to ensure that all accepted product is good. Inspection fatigue on repetitive inspection operations will often limit the

effectiveness of 100% inspection. Obviously no sampling procedure can eliminate all defectives. It follows that the best way to be sure that accepted product is good is to have the product made right in the first place.

When a producer does not make product right in the first place and, in effect, relies on the consumer to do screening inspection, it often happens that striking quality improvement can be caused by the outright rejection of entire lots of product on the basis of the number of defectives found in samples. The rejection of entire lots brings much stronger pressure for quality improvement than the rejection of individual articles.

4. when it is desirable to dispose the lot in shorter (calendar) time so that scheduling and delivery are improved even by employing lesser number of inspectors etc.

It is obvious that sampling involves risks but apart from the necessity of acceptance sampling as in the case of destructive testing, advantages of sampling are significant. It may also be remembered that the *purpose of acceptance sampling is to guide the course of action, not to estimate lot quality*. Further *acceptance sampling is not an attempt to 'control' the quality but to 'assure' the quality*. It is the purpose of control charts to control the quality.

9.2 EARLY FORMS OF ACCEPTANCE SAMPLING

Many of the mentioned advantages of sampling over 100% inspection have been long recognized. As a result, sampling was carried on in industry long before its features were publicised by the current attention to the statistical sampling table discussed in Chaps. 10 through 13. Many of these sampling procedures have been relatively crude and makeshift and have not resulted in the advantages over 100% inspection. **'Spot-checking'** is the phrase usually applied to these hit-or-miss procedures.

In some plants, spot-checking has meant a well-regulated and well defined procedure for examining a certain percentage of the pieces in all incoming lots. In other plants, it has meant the occasional examination of a few pieces from those incoming shipment boxes which were easiest to reach or to pry open. In some other plants, spot-checking has resolved, in the final analysis, into a rough examination to determine if the amount of material in the lot corresponds to the amount billed by the vendor.

When, owing to these latter practices, bad material causes quality troubles on the production lines, the amount of inspection may be temporarily increased. This increase in inspection merely constitutes a post mortem step and does not aid in preventing the production of defective work.

The number of parts or the amount of material to be inspected and the size of the lot to be sampled are generally determined in arbitrary fashion under spot-check procedures. Occasionally, too many parts are checked—which is costly. Sometimes too few parts are examined—which may permit defective materials to get into the production line.

In general, little attention is paid to the risk of sampling variation associated with the particular spot-check procedure in use. Nor is there any real understanding as to the quality 'target' that is being aimed at.

Another feature of the usual spot-check is its lack of an agreed upon acceptance or rejection procedure. If a number of defective pieces are found there is often no definitely specified system as to dispose of the lot.

One week, the spot-check of a lot of incoming material show five defective pieces, and the lot may be rejected. A few weeks later, another spot-check on similar material may show six defective pieces, and the lot may be passed on to the manufacturing floor. Such inconsistencies in procedure have as their inevitable results friction between vendor and customer, spotty quality of parts and materials released to the manufacturing floor, and strained feelings between the incoming-material inspectors and the manufacturing supervisors.

9.3 PURPOSE OF THIS CHAPTER

The real problem in most acceptance sampling is to design a satisfactory acceptance sampling system or, more commonly, to select such a system from a number of possible systems already developed by someone else. To judge the suitability of any proposed acceptance sampling system in a particular case, it is desirable to have an understanding of the strategy and tactics built into the various available types of systems.

This chapter is intended to lay the ground work for more detailed discussions in Chaps. 10 through 13 of a number of widely used modern acceptance sampling systems. As a prerequisite for an understanding of such systems, the reader needs to know certain terminology, concepts, and probability calculations involved in acceptance sampling. This chapter uses lot-by-lot acceptance sampling by attributes to develop the terminology and concepts and to illustrate some types of probability calculations. Discussion of acceptance sampling from a continuous stream of product is deferred until Chap. 12. Discussion of acceptance sampling by variables is deferred until Chap. 13.

9.3.1 Use of the Words *Defective* and *Defect* in PART-1(C) of this Book

It was pointed out in Chap. 1 that when these words are used in their technical sense dealing with lack of conformity to specifications, they do not necessarily mean *defective* and *defect* in the popular sense. It is common for specifications to contain a margin of safety; therefore, some product that does not meet specifications can be satisfactory for its intended use. The difference between the technical and popular meanings has been a source of confusion and misunderstanding in law suits involving product liability.

In the interest of clarity in writing and speaking about topics related to quality of manufactured product it would be desirable if everyone concerned with quality matters would abandon the use of defective and defect in the restricted technical sense. In PART-1(B), the author has been able to substitute appropriate words or phrases. For example reference has been made to nonconforming product, *percent rejected*, and numbers of *nonconformities*.

Unfortunately, it does not seem reasonable to continue such substitutions throughout PART-1(C). The acceptance sampling systems that we examine in the following chapters all make considerable use of the words *defective* and *defect*. Therefore the words should be used in explaining the systems. Nevertheless, the reader should understand that in the coming pages these words are used in their restricted technical senses. A defective item is one that does not conform to specifications in some respect; a defect is a nonconformity to some specification.

9.3.2 Need for Designing of Sampling Plans (or Schemes)

The measurements in a sample provide following two types of information :

1. Information about the product in the sample. This permits decisions about the product in the sample itself.

2. Information about the variables present in the manufacturing process. This leads to conclusions about the process at the time the sample was taken.

The knowledge of the process, in turn, gives information about the uninspected product. Acceptance sampling is valid because the uninspected product came from the same process which produced the sample of inspected product. Of course, there are risks.

Suppose that we wish to accept all lots which are not more than 2.5% defective, and we wish to reject all lots which are over 2.5% defective. Along comes a lot of 1,000 pieces, of which 4% are actually defective. An inspector takes a sample of 20 pieces and finds none defective, and so he accepts the lot (the sample shows 0% defective). Clearly the sampling plan has led to a wrong decision, since the lot is actually 4% defective. Actually the sample of 20 pieces could, by the luck of probability have contained 1, 2 etc., even 20 defectives. This sampling variation is critical in the design of sampling plans. Through bad luck in sampling, there can be two errors in decision making.

1. A good lot may be rejected.
2. A bad lot may be accepted.

Modern design of sampling plans quantifies these risks and adjusts the sampling criteria to balance risks in the light of the economic factors involved.

9.4 ECONOMICS OF SAMPLING VERSUS 100 PER CENT INSPECTION

An economic evaluation of sampling versus 100% inspection requires a comparison of total costs under each of the two procedures. Suppose it is assumed that no inspection errors occur and the cost to replace a defective found in inspection is borne by the producer or is small compared to the damage done by a defective in use. Then if

N number of items in lot

n number of items in the sample from this lot

p fraction defective of the submitted lot for inspection

A damage cost incurred if a defective slips through inspection

I inspection cost per item

total cost with 100% inspection = NI and total cost with sampling = $nI + (N - n)\,pA$. If these two costs are equated, a break-even point fraction defective i.e. p_{BEP} can be determined as follows:

$$NI = nI + (N - n)\,p\,A$$

$$p_{BEP} = \frac{(N-n)I}{(N-n)A} = \frac{1}{A} \qquad \text{... (9.1)}$$

If the fraction defective in the lot is less than pb, the total cost will be lowest with sampling. If p is greater than p_{BEP}, then using 100% inspection will result in a lowest total cost.

For example, consider the inspection of pieces of mica film used in condensers. Pinholes or conducting inclusions in the mica cause a short circuit in the finished condenser. It costs ₹ 1 to inspect one piece. If a bad piece of mica is allowed to go into a condenser, a damage costs ₹ 100 is incurred, because the total cost of manufacturing the condenser is lost when it is revived by defective piece of mica.

$$p_{BEP} = \frac{1}{100} = 0.01 = 1.0\%$$

If it is expected that the percent defective will be greater than 1.0%, then 100% inspection should be used. Otherwise, sampling should be instituted.

The variability in quality from lot to lot is important. If past history shows that the quality level is much better than the break-even point and is stable from lot to lot, little if any inspection may be needed. If the level is much worse than the break-even point, and consistently so, it will usually be cheaper to use 100% inspection rather than sample. If the quality is at neither these extremes, then sampling will pay for itself.

9.5 SOME SYMBOLS AND TERMS USED IN RELATION TO ACCEPTANCE SAMPLING PLANS

The probability principles presented in Chap. 4, and the explanation of control charts for fraction rejected and for numbers of nonconformities given in Chap. 5 and 6 provide a background for a discussion of the evaluation of acceptance plans involving sampling by attributes. In discussing such plans, the following symbols are used :

N	number of pieces in a given lot or batch.
n	number of pieces in a sample.
D	number of defective pieces (that is, pieces not conforming to specifications) in a given lot of size N.
r	number of defective pieces (that is, pieces not conforming to specifications) in a given sample of size n.
c	acceptance number, the maximum allowable number of defective pieces in a sample of size n (also denoted by Ac in come cases).
p	fraction defective. In a given submitted lot, this is D/N ; in a given sample, it is r/n.
μ_p	true process average fraction defective of a product submitted for inspection.
$\overline{p}$	average fraction defective in observed samples.
P_a	$L(p)$ = probability of acceptance.
β	consumer's risk, the probability of accepting product of some stated undesirable quality. It is the value of P_a at that stated quality.
α	producer's risk, the probability of rejecting product of some stated desirable quality. $\alpha = 1 - P_a$ at that stated quality.
$p_{0.95}$, $p_{0.50}$, $p_{0.10}$, etc.	fraction defective having a probability of acceptance of 0.95, 0.50, 0.10, and so on, under any given acceptance criteria.

9.6 LOT-BY-LOT ACCEPTANCE USING SINGLE SAMPLING Plan (SSP) BY ATTRIBUTES

In acceptance inspection a defective article is defined as one that fails to cönform to specifications in one or more quality characteristics. A common procedure in acceptance sampling is to consider each submitted lot of product separately and to base the decision on acceptance or rejection of the lot on the evidence of one or more samples chosen at random from the lot. When the decision is always made on the evidence of only one sample, the acceptance plan is described as a single *sampling* plan (SSP) or single sampling scheme (SSS).

Any systematic plan for single sampling requires that three numbers be specified. One is the number of articles N in the lot from which the sample is to be drawn. The second is the number of articles n in the random sample drawn from the lot. The third is the acceptance number c.

This acceptance number is the maximum allowable number of defective articles in the sample. More than c defectives will cause the rejection of the lot. In sampling plans developed without benefit of statistical analysis, c often is specified as zero under the illusion that if the sample is perfect, the lot will be perfect.

In the discussion that follows, sampling acceptance plans of this type are described by only these three numbers *i.e.* N, n, c. For example if a sampling plan is specified as

$$\begin{bmatrix} N = 50 \\ n = 5 \\ c = 1 \end{bmatrix}$$

it is to be interpreted as "Take a random sample of 5 from a lot of 50". If the sample contains more than 1 defectives, reject the lot ; otherwise accept the lot.

9.6.1 The Operating Characteristic (OC) Curve of an Acceptance Sampling Plan Shows the Ability of the Plan to Distinguish between Good and Bad Lots

In judging various acceptance sampling plans it is desirable to compare their performance over a range of possible quality levels of submitted product. An excellent picture of this performance is given by the *operating characteristic curve*, or power curves. Such curves are commonly referred to as OC curves of the sampling plans of schemes. Figure 9.1 shows the OC curve for the sampling plan : $[N = 10{,}000$ (*i.e.* $\approx \infty$), $n = 150,\ c = 4]$

It can immediately be known from this OC curve that a 3% defective lot (considered as good lot) has only 70% (or 0.7) chance of being accepted under this plan. However, a lot 4% defective (though technically considered as 'bad') has the probability of acceptance of only 0.4. Thus for any given fraction defective p in a submitted lot, the OC curve shows the probability P_a that such a lot will be accepted by the given sampling plan.

It should be noted that the OC *curve does not predict the quality of the lots* submitted for inspection. For example, it is wrong to conclude from OC curve of Fig. 9.1 that there is a 40% chance that the lot quality is 4.0% defective. The curve merely tells the chance of accepting lots which are at any given fraction defective before inspection or stated a little differently, the OC curve shows the long run percentage of submitted lots that would be accepted if a great many lots of any stated quality were submitted for inspection.

As explained in this chapter, in most cases OC curves may also be thought of as showing the probability of accepting lots from a stream of product having a fraction defective, p.

Any OC curve (except that for an ideal sampling plan) can be divided into three zones.

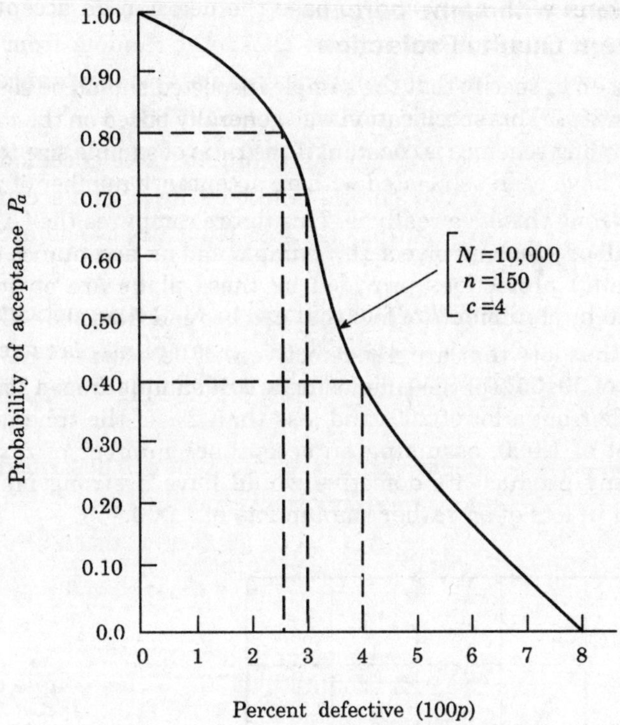

FIGURE 9.1: OC curve of a sampling plan.

Zones of Acceptance and Rejection. Within the zone of acceptance, nearly all lots will be accepted and within the zone of rejection, they will nearly all be rejected. Therefore, the OC curve should be so chosen that its zone of acceptance accepts what is considered to be satisfactory lot and its zone of rejection rejects what is considered to be an unsatisfactory lot.

Zone of Indecision. Within this zone there is no surety whether any particular lot will be accepted or rejected. It may be remembered that unless 100% inspection is done, zone of indecision cannot be eliminated. However its width can be reduced by taking a larger sample, but this will increase the inspection costs and so may or may not be justified. Fortunately, the zone of indecision is not nearly of such a practical disadvantage as it may be supposed on the first thought. A lot in this zone is worse than what is considered as an acceptable lot, and better than what is considered as unacceptable. Its quality is thus borderline, and in most practical cases it will not matter much whether a lot is finally accepted or rejected from this zone.

9.6.2. Constructing the Operating Characteristic Curve

An OC curve can be developed by determining the probability of acceptance for several values of incoming quality, p. The probability of acceptance is the probability that the number of defectives in the sample is equal to or less than the acceptance number for the sampling plan. There are ***three*** distributions—*hypergeometric, binomial* and *Poisson*, which can be used to find the probability of a acceptance. When its assumptions can be met, the Poisson distribution is preferable because of the ease of calculations. The *Poisson distribution yields a good approximation for acceptance sampling when the sampling size is at least 16, the lot size is at least ten times the sample size, and p is less than 0.1.*

9.6.3 Sampling Acceptance Plans with same percent Samples give very different Quality Protection

A common practice in industry has been to specify that the sample inspected should be some fixed percentage of the lot, such as 5, 10, or 20%. This specification was generally based on the mistaken idea that the protection given by sampling schemes is constant if the ratio of sample size to lot size is constant. Such specifications often have been associated with an acceptance number of zero.

Figure 9.2 illustrates just how wrong this idea really is. This figure compares the OC curves of four sampling acceptance plans, all of which involve a 10% sample and an acceptance number of zero. The differences in the quality protections provided by these plans are obvious and impressive. They may be emphasized by statements of fact that can be read from the OC curves.

For example, the curves show that lots that are 4% defective will be accepted 81% of the time using a 10% sample from a lot of 50; 65% of the time using a 10% sample from a lot of 100; 42% of the time using a 10% sample from a lot of 200; and less than 2% of the time (actually 1.35%) by a 10% sample from a lot of 1,000, assuming an acceptance number of zero in all cases. Obviously, a producer making product 4% defective would have a strong motive for trying to have its product inspected in lots of 50 rather than in lots of 1,000.

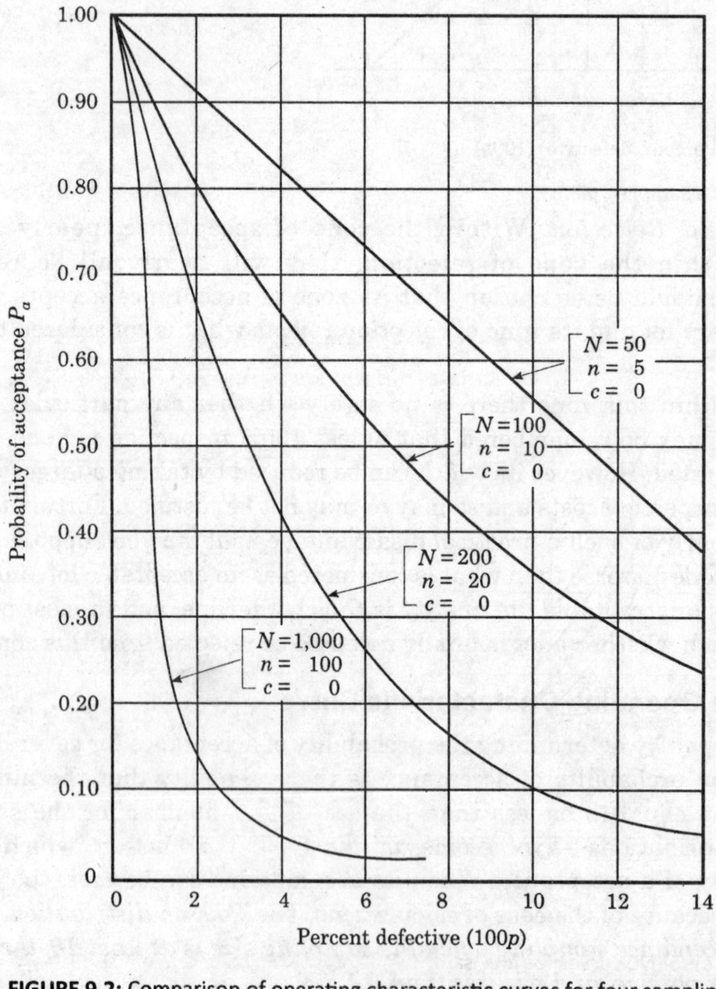

FIGURE 9.2: Comparison of operating characteristic curves for four sampling plans involving 10% samples.

Or, considered in a slightly different way, the curves show the quality of lot that will be passed 50% of the time by each plan. $\begin{bmatrix} N = 50 \\ n = 5 \\ c = 0 \end{bmatrix}$ will pass a 12% defective lot half the time; $\begin{bmatrix} N = 100 \\ n = 10 \\ c = 0 \end{bmatrix}$ a 6% defective lot; $\begin{bmatrix} N = 200 \\ n = 20 \\ c = 0 \end{bmatrix}$ a 3% defective lot; and $\begin{bmatrix} N = 1{,}000 \\ n = 100 \\ c = 0 \end{bmatrix}$ a 0.65% defective lot.

These curves are based on computations such as illustrated earlier in Chap. 4.

9.6.4 Fixed Sample Size Tends toward Constant Quality Protection

From the standpoint of quality protection, the absolute size of a random sample is much more important than its relative size compared to the size of the lot. This fact is illustrated by Fig. 9.3. This figure shows the OC curves of four different sampling plans all having the same sample size 20 but having lot sizes of 50, 100, 200, and 1,000. respectively.

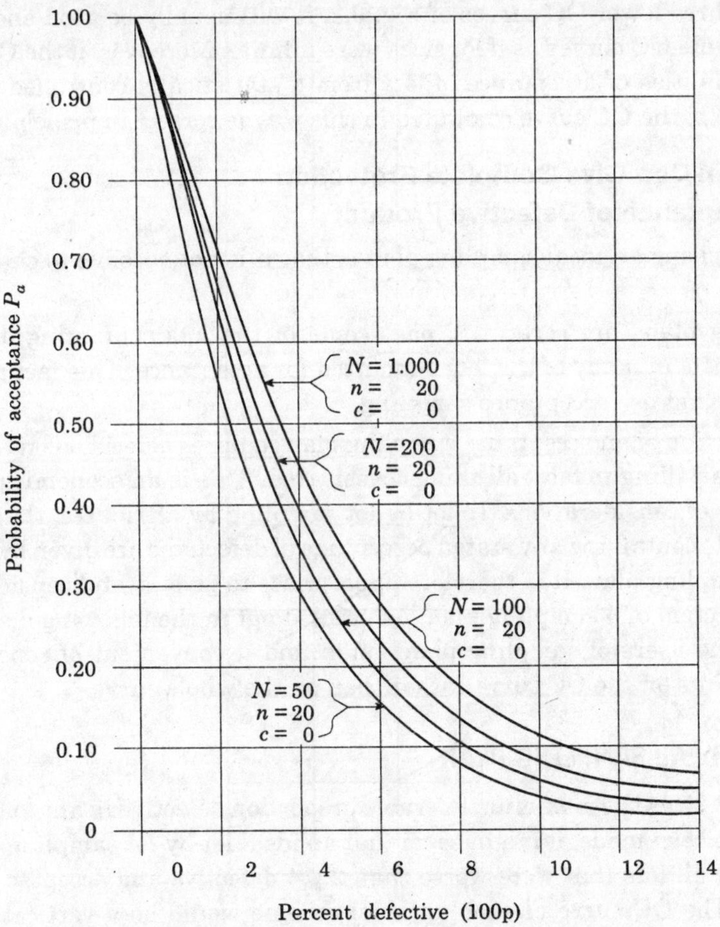

FIGURE 9.3: Comparison of OC curves for four sampling plans involving samples of 20, each with an acceptance number of zero.

The three upper curves, in which the sample size varies from 20 to 2% of the lot, show close agreement. This agreement is in sharp contrast to the great difference among the curves in Fig. 9.2. These two figures together emphasize the point that it is the *absolute size of the sample rather than its relative size that determines the quality protection given by an acceptance sampling plan.* The story told by these two figures is particularly striking because it contradicts many preconceived notions on the subject of sampling.

The upper most curve corresponding to a lot size of 1,000 is practically identical with the OC curve that would be obtained for an infinite lot size. For example, the probability of acceptance of a 5% defective lot when $N = 1000$ is 0.355. When $N = \infty$, the corresponding probability is 0.358. For a 10% defective lot, the respective probabilities of acceptance are 0.119 and 0.122. (These figures are obtained using hypergeometric probabilities for the lot of 1,000 and using the binomial for the infinite lot.) *For a given lot fraction defective and a zero acceptance number the probability of acceptance computed for a finite lot is always less than that computed for an infinite lot because of the recognition of the partial exhaustion of the lot by the sample.* This was very clearly illustrated in Chap. 4.

It is evident that unless a sample is a large proportion of the lot, such as the 10, 20, and 40% samples in the three lower OC curves of Fig. 9.3, it will usually be good enough for practical purposes to compute OC curves as if lot sizes were infinite. Moreover, if the OC curve is viewed as giving probabilities of acceptance of lots from a statistically controlled product having a fraction defective p, the OC curve computed in this way is correct in principle.

9.6.5 No Sampling Plan Can Give Complete Protection against the Acceptance of Defective Product

A practical difficulty in devising an ideal sampling plan is that it is not possible to change the laws of chance.

All lot-by-lot sampling plans are certain to pass some of the lots containing defective product if such product exists in many of the lots submitted for acceptance. This fact needs to be faced by all who specify and use acceptance sampling.

It follows that the selection of an acceptance sampling plan requires a decision on the risks that the user of the plan is willing to face, all things considered. This is an economic decision that depends on a number of considerations. In lot-by-lot sampling by attributes, the risks of acceptance of submitted lots containing any stated percentage of defectives are given by the OC curve of the particular sampling plan. It is therefore appropriate to give careful consideration to the OC curve in the selection of a sampling plan. As pointed out in the following discussion of acceptance sampling, the users of sampling plans often find it convenient of concentrate attention on one or two points on the OC curve rather than on the whole curve.

9.7 OC CURVE OF AN IDEAL SAMPLING PLAN

Suppose it is decided that 2.2% is the maximum tolerable proportion defective in any submitted lots. Once this decision has been made, it might seem that an ideal lot-by-lot sampling scheme would be one that rejected all lots that were worse than 2.2% defective and accepted all lots 2.2% defective or better. The OC curve of such an ideal scheme would be a vertical at p of 0.22 or ($100\ p = 2.2\%$) as shown in Fig 9.4. Of course no such scheme can exist short of 100% inspection executed with 100% perfection.

It is, however, possible to select a sampling plan in which a 2.2% defective lot has some desired probability of acceptance. If it should be decided that the consumer can take 1 chance in 10 that if a 2.2% defective lot is submitted the lot will be accepted, the OC curve of the selected plan should pass through the point $P_a = 0.10$, $p = 0.022$ (or $100\,p = 2.2\%$).

Figure 9.4 shows that the OC curve of the plan $\begin{bmatrix} N = 1,000 \\ n = 100 \\ c = 0 \end{bmatrix}$ passes through this point.

If the product is to be submitted for acceptance in lots of 1,000 articles, this plan is a possible one to give the consumer the desired quality protection against accepting 2.2% defective lots.

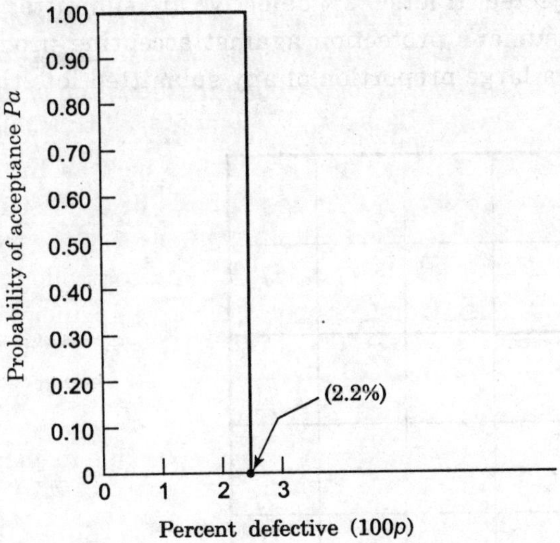

FIGURE 9.4: OC curve of an ideal sampling plan.

9.7.1 Conflicting interests of Consumer and Producer in the Selection of Sampling Plans

There are always two parties to an acceptance procedure, the party submitting the product for acceptance and the party for whom the decision is made regarding acceptance or rejection. In all discussions of acceptance procedures in this book, these parties are concisely referred to as the producer and the consumer. It should be recognized that for many inspection operations the producer and consumer may be part of the same organization; for instance, the producer might be the machine shop and the consumer the assembly department. In a manufacturer's final inspection of its own product, the sales department may be thought of as the consumer. In acceptance inspection of some purchased product, the producer—in the sense used here—may actually be a dealer who had no connection with the original production.

At first impression, it might seem that the producer and consumer should have completely opposite viewpoints toward the selection of sampling plans. The consumer requires protection against the acceptance of too much defective product. The producer, on the other hand, needs to be protected against the rejection of too much product that conforms to specifications.

As an example, assume that a consumer selects the plan $\left| \begin{array}{l} N = 1{,}000 \\ n = 100 \\ c = 0 \end{array} \right.$ in order to be fairly well protected against accepting lots more than 2.2% defective. As already pointed out, if a lot exactly 2.2% defective should be submitted, there is only 1 chance in 10 of its acceptance. The consumer will have even greater protection if lots of poorer quality are submitted.

This plan, however, gives unsatisfactory protection to the producer who submits product considerably better than 2.2% defective. For instance, the OC curve of Fig. 9.5 shows that if the producer submits lots 1% defective, 65% of them will be rejected. (The curve says 35% will be accepted; this is subtracted from 100% to get the percentage rejected.) If lots 0.5% defective are submitted 41% will be rejected. If lots 0.2% defective are submitted 19% will be rejected. It is evident that the consumer's protection against accepting product 2.2% defective is obtained only by rejecting a large proportion of any submitted lots that are of much better quality.

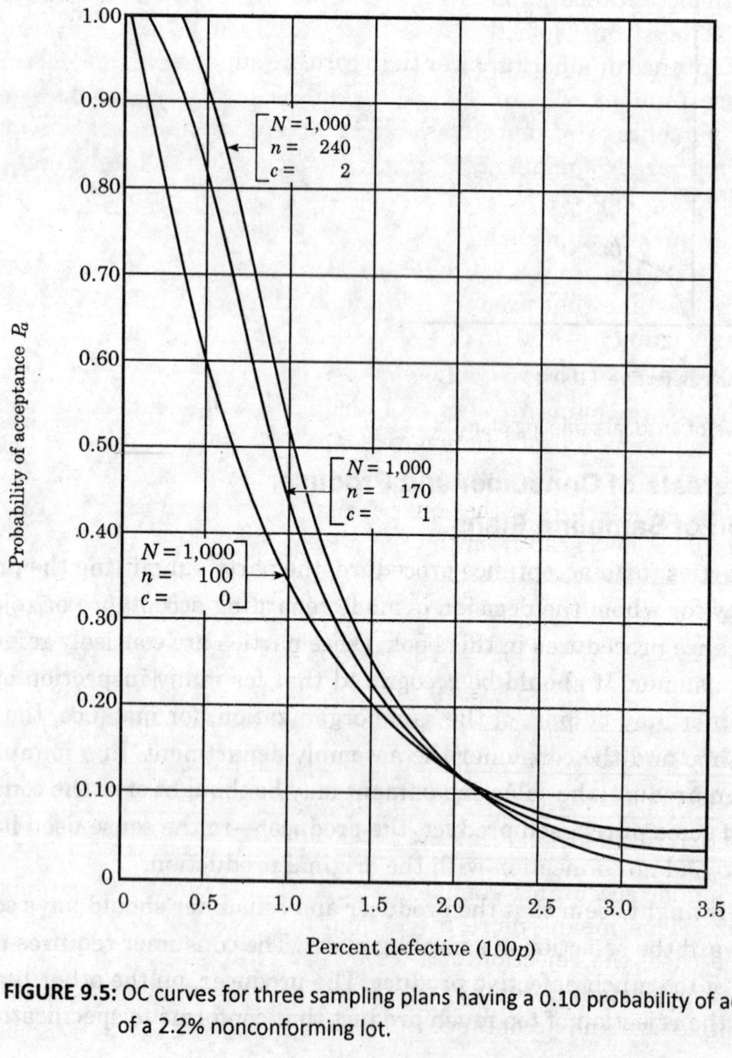

FIGURE 9.5: OC curves for three sampling plans having a 0.10 probability of acceptance of a 2.2% nonconforming lot.

A more critical consideration will show that, where there is a continuing relationship between producer and consumer, such substantial rejections of acceptable product in the effort to exclude product not conforming to specifications are not necessarily in the consumer's interest. The consumer is interested in quality, but also in cost and time. In the long run the costs incident to the rejection of acceptable product tend to be passed on by the producer to the consumer. The consumer may also be interested in having the product now. Any acceptable product rejected by the consumer is not available for immediate use and hence delays.

It seems clear that, even from the consumer's viewpoint, it is not sufficient to ask that a sampling plan protect the consumer against the acceptance of lots having a higher percentage of defectives than some maximum tolerable figure.

9.7.2 The Acceptance Number Need Not Be Zero

Figures 9.2 and 9.3 emphasized the fact that a perfect sample does not ensure a perfect lot. Once this fact is recognized, the objections sometimes raised to permitting lot acceptance with some defectives in a sample may be shown to have no logical foundation.

The users of modern acceptance sampling procedures recognize certain psychological advantages of allowing at least one defective in a sample. Moreover, the operating characteristics of plans with acceptance numbers greater than zero are superior to those of comparable plans with an acceptance number of zero. For a desired protection against accepting lots containing some stated percentage of defectives, larger acceptance numbers involve larger sample sizes. Plans having larger sample sizes have greater ability to discriminate between satisfactory and unsatisfactory lots.

For example, consider our consumer who wants protection against accepting lots of 2.2% defective or worse and insists that any 2.2% defective lots submitted shall have only a 0.10 probability of acceptance. Assume that product is submitted in lots of 1000. This consumer's requirement will be met by using $n = 100$ and $c = 0$, or by using $n = 170$ and $c = 1$, or by using $n = 240$ and $c = 2$, or by various other possible plans.

The OC curves for these three plans are shown in Fig. 9.5. It will be noted that although all three plans give the consumer equal protection against the acceptance of a 2.2% defective lot, the plans with acceptance numbers of 1 and 2 give the producer much better protection against the rejection of lots that are satisfactory in the sense of being greatly superior to 2.2% defective lots. A few figures tabulated below, read from the three curves serve to emphasize this point.

Sampling plan →	$\begin{bmatrix} N = 1{,}000 \\ n = 100 \\ c = 0 \end{bmatrix}$	$\begin{bmatrix} N = 1{,}000 \\ n = 170 \\ c = 1 \end{bmatrix}$	$\begin{bmatrix} N = 1{,}000 \\ n = 240 \\ c = 2 \end{bmatrix}$
Lots 1% defective rejected	65%	51%	44%
Lots 0.5% defective rejected	41%	20%	9%
Lots 0.2% defective rejected	19%	3%	0%

The plans with the higher acceptance numbers and better OC curves have higher sample sizes for a given lot size. This means more inspection and hence more inspection cost. If, however, as is often the case, the rejection of a lot by sampling inspection means that the rejected lot is to be 100% inspected, the total amount of resulting inspection may actually be less with the higher sample size and acceptance number.

9.7.3 Generally Speaking, the Larger the Sample Size, the Steeper the Slope of the OC Curve

It is of interest to compare several plans having different sample sizes and having and the same ratio of acceptance number to sample size (i.e. c/n). Consider the plans $\begin{bmatrix} n = 75 \\ c = 1 \end{bmatrix}$, $\begin{bmatrix} n = 150 \\ c = 2 \end{bmatrix}$ and $\begin{bmatrix} n = 750 \\ c = 10 \end{bmatrix}$. Assume a lot size N of 10,000. This lot size is large enough so that even the largest of these samples is a relatively small fraction of the lot. The OC curves of these three plans are shown in Fig. 9.6.

Although these three plans each permit 1.33% (that is, $\frac{1}{75}$) of the sample to be defective, it is evident that they have quite different OC curves. The larger the sample size, the greater the ability of a sampling plan to discriminate between lots of different qualities. For example, a 3% defective lot, if submitted, has more than 1 chance in 3 of acceptance if $n = 75$ and $c = 1$ but is practically certain to be rejected if $n = 750$ and $c = 10$. The larger sample, which protects the consumer against the acceptance of relatively bad lots, also gives the producer better protection against the rejection of relatively good ones. Thus a 0.7% defective lot has 1 chance in 10 of rejection if $n = 75$ and only 2 chances in 100 of rejection if $n = 750$.

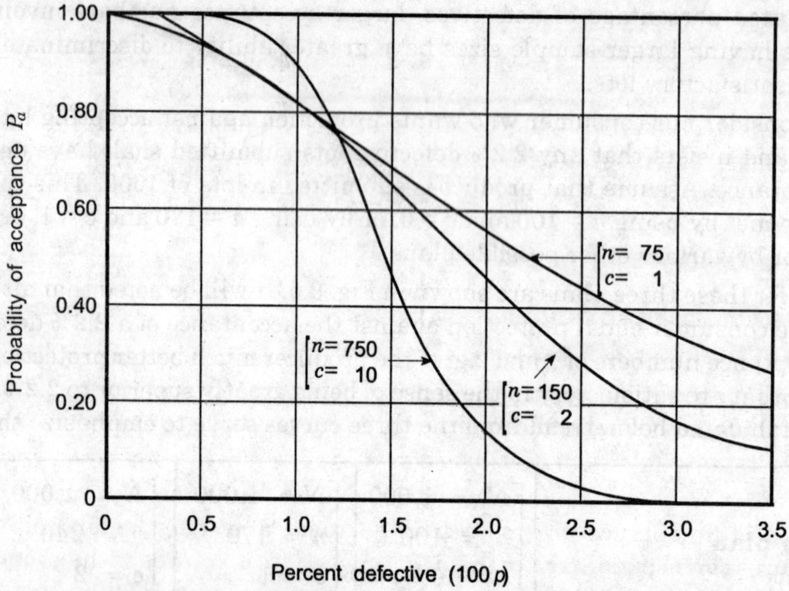

FIGURE 9.6 : Comparison of OC curves with different sample sizes, all permitting the same fraction of the sample to be nonconforming.

9.7.4 Type *A* and Type *B* OC Curves

H.F. Dodge and H.G. Romig make the helpful distinction between two types of OC curves. Type *A* curves give the probabilities of acceptance for various fractions defective as a function of the lot quality of finite lots. In principle, such curves should be computed by hypergeometric probabilities; the binomial or Poisson distributions often give satisfactory approximations. In principle, also, such curves are discontinuous. For example, a lot of 200 items may be 0.5 or 1.0% defective but not 0.8%. In practice, it is common to draw Type *A* curves as continuous.

Type *B* curves give the probabilities of acceptance of a lot as a function of product quality. Such curves are calculated as if the lot size were infinite. For Type *B* curves the binomial is exact and the Poisson distribution often gives a satisfactory approximation. Such curves are correctly viewed as continuous.

In the discussion of Fig. 9.3—which gave Type *A* OC curves for several plans that had an n of 20, a c of 0, and various lot sizes—it was pointed out that there was no practical difference between the OC curve for $N = 1{,}000$ and $N = \infty$. In general, where the sample size n is not more than one-tenth the lot size N, Type *A* and Type *B* curves may be considered as identical for most practical purposes.

In judging the appropriateness of using Type *B* curves where n is more than one tenth N, certain assumptions underlying such uses should be recognized. Assume that a statistically controlled process exists that has some fraction defective μ_p. The lots of size N that come from this process are, in a statistical sense, random samples from the process. Each random sample of size n selected from some lot of N items may therefore be viewed as a random sample from the process that has the fraction defective μ_p. It follows that the Type *B* curve gives the expected results of a given sampling plan over the entire range of possible values of process fraction defective.

In examining a Producer's Risk, it usually is appropriate to adopt the viewpoint of the Type *B* OC curve. That is, it is reasonable for a producer to want to know the percentage of lots that will be rejected by a proposed sampling plan for any given level of process quality.

In constrast, the viewpoint of the Type *A* curve may be desirable in evaluating a Consumer's Risk with respect to individual lots. That is, a consumer reasonably may want to know the risk taken of accepting a relatively bad lot if it is submitted. The Type *A* curve always falls below that of Type *B* in the region of interest to the consumer; thus it follows that the use of Type *B* curves tends to give a conservative figure for Consumer's Risk that is somewhat too high. The easiest way now to calculate and plot the OC curves is through the use of computer programs. Computer softwares are available to compute and plot these curves.

9.7.5 Use of Table *G* for Approximate Calculation of Type *B* OC Curves of Sampling Plans

Although the binomial distribution is correct in principle for computing Type *B* OC curves, it is usually satisfactory and convenient to compute approximate probabilities of acceptance by use of a Poisson distribution table such as Table *G*, App. 1.

Table 9.1 illustrates the use of Table *G* in computing the three OC curves shown in Fig. 9.6. The probabilities of acceptance are read directly from Table *G* (or interpolated where necessary) as the figures corresponding to c (that is, "c or less") occurrences of the event with an average μ_{np}. Table 9.1 gives all probabilities to three decimal places to permit readers to check their use of Table *G*. Nevertheless, it should be recognized that because of the approximate method used, three decimal places are not really justified.

9.8 THE INDEXING OF ACCEPTANCE PLANS BY A SINGLE POINT ON THE OC CURVE

Chapters 10 through 13 include descriptions of a number of different tables of acceptance sampling plans. Certain tables classify acceptance plans in accordance with a single point on the OC curve. Three points on the OC curve have been given particular importance in the design of systems of sampling plans, namely:

TABLE 9.1 : Calculation of Approximate Type B Oc Curves For Three Sampling Plans.

Fraction defective in lot μ_p	*Expected average number of defectives μ_{np} in sample*			*Probability of acceptance P_a*		
	n = 75	*n = 150*	*n = 750*	$n = 75$, $c = 1$	$n = 150$, $c = 2$	$n = 750$, $c = 10$
0.002	0.15	0.30	1.5	0.990	0.996	1.000
0.004	0.30	0.60	3.0	0.963	0.977	1.000
0.006	0.45	0.90	4.5	0.925	0.937	0.993
0.008	0.60	1.20	6.0	0.878	0.879	0.957
0.010	0.75	1.50	7.5	0.827	0.809	0.862
0.012	0.90	1.80	9.0	0.772	0.731	0.706
0.014	1.05	2.10	10.5	0.718	0.650	0.521
0.016	1.20	2.40	12.0	0.663	0.570	0.347
0.018	1.35	2.70	13.5	0.610	0.494	0.211
0.020	1.50	3.00	15.0	0.558	0.423	0.118
0.025	1.875	3.75	18.75	0.441	0.278	0.021
0.030	2.25	4.50	22.5	0.343	0.174	0.003
0.035	2.625	5.25	26.25	0.262	0.106	0.000
0.040	3.00	6.00	....	0.199	0.062	
0.050	3.75	7.50	....	0.112	0.020	
0.060	4.50	9.00	....	0.061	0.006	
0.070	5.25	10.50	....	0.033	0.002	
0.080	6.00	12.00	....	0.017	0.001,	
0.090	6.75	13.50	....	0.009	0.000	
0.100	7.50	....	....	0.004		

1. The lot (or process) quality for which $P_a = 0.95$. In this book, this quality is referred to as $p_{0.95}$. (sometimes referred to as AQL *i.e.* Acceptable Quality Level).
2. The lot (or process) quality for which $P_a = 0.50$. In this book, this is referred to as $p_{0.50}$. (sometimes referred to as point of control or indifference quality or spit risk quality).
3. The lot (or process) quality for which $P_a = 0.10$. To be consistent with the preceding symbols, this is referred to as $p_{0.10}$. In the literature of acceptance sampling, this quality is most frequently referred to as the lot tolerance fraction defective: $100p_{0.10}$ is described as the *Lot Tolerance Percent Defective* (LTPD).

The same acceptance plan may therefore be referred to by several different product quality values, depending on the point of indexing. There are legitimate reasons for this variability in indexing sampling plans. Further comments on this topic is made in next three chapters.

9.9 AVERAGE OUTGOING QUALITY AND THE AOQL

The decision to accept a lot, based on the outcome of one or more samples drawn from the lot, leads to rather obvious results. The decision to reject, however, leads to another series of actions and decisions, usually well stipulated in contractual agreements or standard operating procedures, but nevertheless more complex than the actions required by a decision to accept.

Frequently the result of a decision to reject a lot is 100% inspection of that particular lot. Such action is referred to as *screening inspection*, or *detailing*. This is sometimes described as an acceptance/rectification scheme. Responsibility for screening inspection may rest with either the producer or the consumer.

The accepted lots will contain approximately the percent defective submitted, although they will be slightly improved by the elimination of any defectives found in the samples whenever c is 1 or more. The rejected lots, after screening, presumably will contain no defectives. Thus, at any given level of incoming quality p greater than 0, there is some lower level of *Average Outgoing Quality* (AOQ). The P_a begins at 1.0, when p equals 0.0, and as described by the OC curve, descends continuously to 0.0, when p equals 1.0. Thus the value of the AOQ must begin at 0.0, rise continuously to some maximum value, and then descend continuously to 0.0. That maximum value is referred to as the *Average Outgoing Quality Limit* (AOQL).

A common type of approximate calculation to determine the AOQL is illustrated in Table 9.2. This table refers to the plan $\begin{bmatrix} n = 75 \\ c = 1 \end{bmatrix}$ when N is large compared to n. The probabilities of acceptance were computed in Table 9.1. The right-hand column gives average outgoing quality (AOQ) for each assumed percent defective in submitted lots. The maximum value of the AOQ is 1.12% occurring when submitted lots are 2.2% defective. This maximum value is the AOQL. Figure 9.7 illustrates the variation of AOQ with incoming quality.

TABLE 9.2 Average Outgoing Quality from $\begin{bmatrix} n = 75 \\ c = 1 \end{bmatrix}$ when used as an Acceptance/Rectification Plan

Percent defective in submitted lots, 100p	*Probability of acceptance, Pa*	*Average percent defective in accepted product, AOQ*
0.2	0.990	0.198
0.4	0.963	0.385
0.6	0.925	0.555
0.8	0.878	0.702
1.0	0.827	0.827
1.2	0.772	0.926
1.4	0.718	1.005
1.6	0.663	1.061
1.8	0.610	1.098
2.0	0.558	1.116
2.1	0.533	1.119
2.2	0.509	1.120
2.3	0.486	1.118
2.4	0.463	1.111
2.5	0.441	1.102
3.0	0.343	1.029
3.5	0.262	0.917
4.0	0.199	0.796
4.5	0.150	0.675
5.0	0.112	0.560

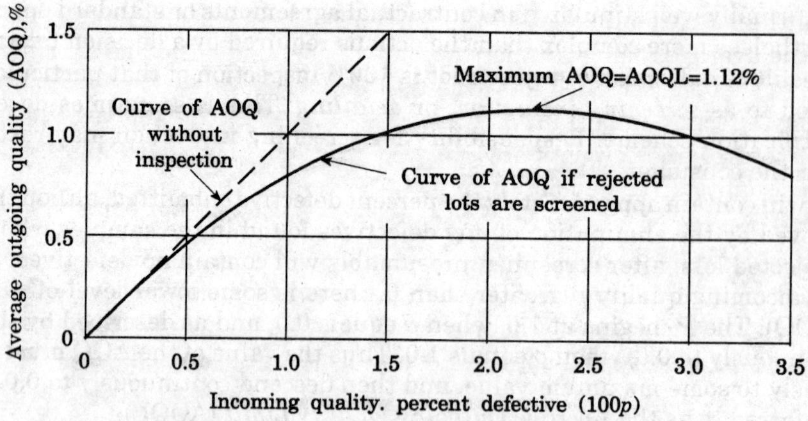

FIGURE 9.7: Average outgoing quality for acceptance/rectification plan $n = 75$ and $c = 1$.

The assumptions underlying Table 9.2 may be explained by examining one particular calculation. Consider that incoming lots come from a process that is 0.6% defective. The probability (Type *B*) that such lots will be accepted on the basis of the sample is 0.925 or 37. In the long run, therefore, only 3 lots out of 40 will be screened. For 40 such lots, 37 will be passed containing, on the average, 0.6% of defectives and 3 will contain no defectives after screening. The approximate AOQ expressed in percent defective will therefore be

$$(P_a)\,(100p) = (0.925)\,(0.6\%) = 0.555\%$$

Several simplifying assumptions in the foregoing calculation are as follows:

1. The lot size N is constant. Thus the 3 screened lots may be assumed to be the same size as the 37 unscreened ones.
2. The screening inspection finds all the defectives in the screened lots, and these defectives are removed.
3. The defective articles removed from the screened lots are replaced with good articles. Thus each screened lot contributes N good articles to the final stream of product.

It should be emphasized that any calculation of average outgoing quality gives the expected quality *in the long run*. As its name implies, the AOQ is an *average*. Over a short period, the outgoing quality may be better or worse than the long-run average. Subject to the limitations of the three simplifying assumptions just stated, any acceptance/rectification plan guarantees that, regardless of the incoming quality submitted, the outgoing quality in the long run will not be worse than the plan's AOQL. *This guarantee, however, does not apply to short periods.*

9.9.1 Some Comments on the Significance of the AOQL

Sampling schemes based on stated AOQL values have gained widespread use in industry. They are used particularly in a manufacturer's inspection of its own product, both in process inspection and in final inspection. They have also been used advantageously in the inspection of lots of purchased product. If the purchaser's sampling inspection takes place in the supplier's plant, the supplier may do the screening of rejected lots and submit a certification of the screening work done.

At various points in our discussion of lot-by-lot acceptance sampling, we shall have occasion to note that the continued use of a sampling scheme tends to be confined to circumstances where most of the time the quality is good enough for nearly all lots to be accepted on the basis of a sample. AOQL plans are no exception to this rule.

Where nearly all the lots are accepted on the basis of the sample, the AOQ will be only slightly better than the average quality in these accepted lots. If submitted lots are badly out of statistical control, so that the screened lots are generally much worse than the unscreened lots, the screening may affect an important improvement in quality. If the submitted product is in good statistical control and few lots are screened, the outgoing quality will not differ greatly from incoming quality. In any event, the AOQ will nearly always be considerably better than the AOQL.

Even though the simplifying assumptions used in the calculation of AOQLs may depart somewhat from actual facts, it follows that this departure is not a matter of great practical importance. Only rarely will the users of schemes based on the AOQL have need to cash in on the guarantee that outgoing quality will not be worse than the computed AOQL.

9.10 DOUBLE SAMPLING PLAN (DSP) OR DOUBLE SAMPLING SCHEME (DSS)

Single sampling calls for decision on acceptance or rejection of a lot on the basis of the evidence of one sample from that lot.

Doubt sampling involves the possibility of putting off the decision on the lot until a second sample has been taken. A lot may be accepted at once if the first sample is good enough or rejected at once if the first sample is bad enough. If the first sample is neither good enough nor bad enough, the decision is based on the evidence of the first and second samples combined. In general, double sampling schemes will involve less total inspection than single sampling for any given quality protection. They also have certain psychological advantages based on the idea of giving a second chance to doubtful lots.

The additional symbols used in connection with double sampling are :

n_1 number of pieces in the first sample.

c_1 acceptance number for first sample, the maximum number of defectives that will permit the acceptance of the lot on the basis of the first sample.

n_2 number of pieces in the second sample.

$n_1 + n_2$ number of pieces in the two samples combined.

c_2 acceptance number for the two samples combined, the maximum number of defectives that will permit the acceptance of the lot on the basis of the two samples.

An example of the use of these symbols to describe a double sampling plan is

$$\begin{bmatrix} N & 1000 \\ n_1 & 36 \\ c_1 & 0 \\ n_2 & 59 \\ c_2 & 3 \end{bmatrix}$$

This may be interpreted as follows :

1. Inspect a first sample of 36 from a lot of 1,000.
2. Accept the lot on the basis of the first sample if the sample contains 0 defectives.
3. Reject the lot on the basis of the first sample if the sample contains more than 3 defectives.
4. Inspect a second sample of 59 if the first sample contains 1, 2, or 3 defectives.

5. Accept the lot on the basis of the combined sample of 95 (*i.e.* 36 + 59) if the combined sample contains 3 or less defectives.
6. Reject the lot on the basis of the combined sample if the combined sample contains more than 3 defectives.

9.10.1. Analysis of a Double Sampling Plan

Figure 9.8 shows three Type *A* OC curves involved in the analysis of this double sampling plan.

There are four possibilities of acceptanceor rejection of a lot submitted for double sampling namely.

1. Acceptance after the first sample
2. Rejection after the first sample
3. Acceptance after the second sample
4. Rejection after the second sample

The lowest of the three OC curves in Fig. 9.8 shows the probability of (1) acceptance after the first sample. This is simple the curve for $\begin{bmatrix} N = 1,000 \\ n = 36 \\ c = 3 \end{bmatrix}$

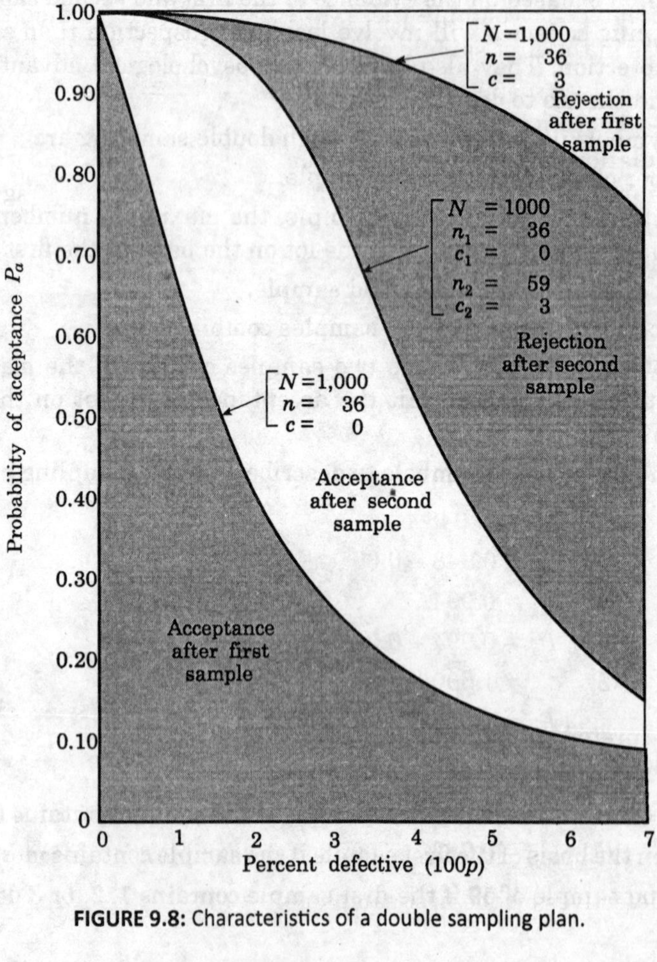

FIGURE 9.8: Characteristics of a double sampling plan.

The highest of the three *OC* curves shows the probability that the lot will not be rejected after the first sample. It is the curve for $\begin{bmatrix} N = 1{,}000 \\ n = 36 \\ c = 3 \end{bmatrix}$. Both these limiting curves may be calculated in the manner illustrated in Chap. 4 for the calculation of curves for all single sampling plans. For any given value of percent defective, the ordinate distance between these two curves corresponds to the probability that for a lot of that percent defective a second sample will be required.

The middle curve of Fig. 9.8 is the actual OC curve of the double sampling plan. To compute points for this curve it is necessary to find the probability that if a second sample is taken, the lot will be accepted.

The lot may be accepted in the following ways:

0 defectives in first sample
1 defective in first sample followed by 0, 1, or 2 defectives in second sample
2 defectives in first sample followed by 0 or 1 defective is second sample
3 defectives in first sample followed by 0 defective in second sample.

The probability of accepting the lot is the sum of the probabilities of these different ways in which it may be accepted. To compute these, it is first necessary to find the probabilities of 0, 1, 2, and 3 defectives in the first sample of 36.

If not set up and solved using a computer program, the hypergeometric distribution calculations required to obtain Type *A* OC curve probabilities are very time consuming. The method for hand calculation, which involves the use of factorials and Table *H*, was illustrated in Chap. 4. If it is assumed that the binomial is applicable to this sampling problem (in other words, that samples are drawn from an infinite lot or that a Type *B* curve is desired) and that the Poisson distribution is a satisfactory approximation to the binomial. Table *G* may be used. The necessary calculations are illustrated for a single point on the *OC* curve corresponding to $\mu_p = 0.010$.

In using Table *G* to compute the respective probabilities of results of the first sample, $\mu_{np} = 36\ (0.010) = 0.36$. Interpolating in Table G between the values for μ_{np} of 0.35 and 0.40, we find

$$P_0 = 0.698$$
$$P_{1 \text{ or less}} = 0.948$$
$$P_1 = 0.948 - 0.698 = 0.250$$
$$P_{2 \text{ or less}} = 0.994$$
$$P_2 = 0.994 - 0.948 = 0.046$$
$$P_{3 \text{ or les}} = 1.000$$
$$P_3 = 1.000 - 0.994 = 0.006$$

If there is one defective on the first sample, calculations regarding the second sample should be based on $\mu_{np} = (59)\left(\frac{9}{964}\right) = 0.55$. Table *G* gives directly

$$P_{2 \text{ or less}} = 0.982$$

If there are two defectives on the first sample, $\mu_{np} = (59)\left(\frac{8}{964}\right) = 0.49$. Table *G* gives

$$P_{1 \text{ or less}} = 0.913$$

and if there are three defectives on the first sample,

$$P_0 = 0.652$$

The probability of acceptance may now be computed. For comparison, the second set of figures shows the results of Type *A* OC curve calculations. Using the theorem of conditional probabilities :

		Type B	Type A
0	defectives in first	= 0.698	0.692
1	defective in first, with 0, 1, or 2 in second = (0.250) (0.982)	= 0.246	0.257
2	defective in first, with 0 or 1 in second = (0.046) (0.913)	= 0.042	0.039
3	defectives in first, with 0 in second = (0.006) (0.652)	= 0.004	0.003
	Probability of acceptance of a lot 1.0% defective	= 0.990	0.991

In this case, the difference was negligible between the result of theoretically correct calculations (Type A) and the result obtained by the approximate method using the Poisson distribution and Table *G*. Although the check between exact and approximate calculations will not usually be as good as this, the OC curve obtained by the use of the Poisson distribution will ordinarily be close enough for practical purposes.

9.11 CHOOSING A SAMPLING PLAN TO MINIMIZE AVERAGE TOTAL INSPECTION

The question of minimum total inspection depends on the number of rejected lots that must be screened (that is, 100% inspected). This, in turn, depends on the quality level of the product submitted. In analyzing and evaluating various sampling plans it is convenient to state the problem in terms of the *ATI, average total inspection*, and the *AFI, average fraction inspected.* For single sampling plans the ATI and AFI may be found from

$$\text{ATI} = nP_a + N(1 - P_a)$$
$$= n + (N - n)(1 - Pa) \quad \text{... (9.2)}$$

and

$$\text{AFI} = \frac{ATI}{N} \quad \text{... (9.3)}$$

Use of these formulae to choose among sampling plans may be illustrated by using the three plans of Fig. 9.5 under different assumptions as to the quality level of incoming lots. Assume that a large number of lots that are 0.5% defective are submitted for acceptance by each plan. The required values are

N	1000	1000	1000
n	100	170	240
c	0	1	2
P_a	0.59	0.80	0.91
$n\,P_a$	59.0	136.0	218.4
$N(1 - P_a)$	410.0	200.0	90.0
ATI	469.0	336.0	308.4
AFI	0.469	0.336	0.308

With the quality level submitted for inspection 0.5% defective, it is evident that the plan $\begin{bmatrix} N = 1,000 \\ n = 240 \\ c = 2 \end{bmatrix}$ requires the least total inspection. However, if the quality level submitted should be 0.2% defective rather than 0.5% defective, the minimum total inspection will be required using $\begin{bmatrix} N = 1,000 \\ n = 170 \\ c = 1 \end{bmatrix}$. This is shown in the following calculation:

N	1000	1000	1000
n	100	170	240
c	0	1	2
P_a	0.81	0.97	1.00
$n\,P_a$	81.0	164.9	240.0
$N(1-P_a)$	190.0	30.0	0.0
ATI	271.0	194.9	240.0
AFI	0.271	0.195	0.240

It should be noted that the amount of sampling inspection always increases with increasing n. The minimization of AFI results from a trade-off between increased sampling inspection and decreased risk of detailing. In those cases where the purchaser charges detailing costs back to the supplier, there may be strong pressure to minimize the sample size rather than the AFI. In the long run such action will prove to be uneconomical.

For a double sampling plan, the formula for average total inspection is

$$\text{ATI} = n_1\,P_a\,(n_1) + (n_1 + n_2)\,P_a\,(n_2) + N\,(1 - P_a)$$

$$= n_1\,P_a + n_2\,P_a\,(n_2) + N\,(1 - P_a) \qquad \text{... (9.4)}$$

where $P_a\,(n_1)$ = probability of acceptance on the first sample

$P_a\,(n_2)$ = probability of acceptance on the second sample

$$P_a = P_a\,(n_1) + P_a\,(n_2)$$

Referring to the double sampling plan of Fig. 9.8 (N = 1,000, n_1 = 36, c_1 = 0, n_2 = 59, c_2 = 3), if incoming lots are 1.0% defective, the AFI is computed from ATI as follows :

$$\text{ATI} = 36\,(0.698) + 95\,(0.292) + 1000\,(1 - 0.990) = 62.87$$

$$\text{AFI} = \frac{62.87}{1,000} = 0.063$$

By varying the value of p for lots entering inspection from 0 to 1, the value of Pa will range from 1 to 0 in accordance with the *OC* curve for the individual plan. Thus the AFI will range from a minimum of n/N (or n_1/N) to a maximum of 1. Analysis of AFI values of alternative sampling plans at specific values of p permits the user to choose that plan with minimum AFI. Such calculations were used as the basis for specifying the plans contained in the Dodge-Romig tables covered in Chap 10.

The mathematical relationship between the AFI and the AOQ is

$$\text{AOQ} = p(1 - \text{AFI}) \qquad \text{... (9.5)}$$

The approximate formula for AOQ given previously is correct for an acceptance number of 0. However, when c is greater than 0, some defective units will be found in samples from accepted lots. Naturally these defectives are removed and usually replaced with good items prior of returning the sample to the lot. This reduces the AOQ by some small amount not accounted for in the formula in Fig (9.2). A popular way to account for this modest reduction for single sampling plans is to introduce the correction factor $(1 - n/N)$. Thus

$$\text{AOQ (in percent)} \doteq \left(\frac{1-n}{N}\right) P_a (100p) \qquad \text{... (9.7)}$$

Whereas the formula without the correction factor tends to overstate the AOQ by a small amount (except when $c = 0$), that with the correction factor tends to understate it by a small amount.

The AOQ value found from the AFI is correct in all cases for all rectifying inspection plans. When complex sampling plans are to be analyzed, this formula is used rather than direct solution for AOQ. For the previous double sampling plan, the simplest approach is to solve for the AOQ as follows:

$$\text{AOQ} = 0.01\ (1 - 0.063) = 0.00937$$

9.12 MULTIPLE AND SEQUENTIAL SAMPLING plans (msp & sesp)

Just as double sampling plans may defer the decision on acceptance or rejection until a second sample has been taken, other plans may permit any number of samples before a decision is reached. The phrase *multiple sampling* is generally used when three or more samples of a stated size are permitted and when the decision on acceptance or rejection must be reached after a stated number of samples. The phrase *sequential sampling* is generally used when a decision is possible after each item has been inspected and when there is no specified limit on the total number of units to be inspected. However, some writers use the two phrases interchangeably. Hence in order to avoid confusion, plans involving the possibility of decision after each item are referred to in this book as item-by-item sequential plans. The design of an item-by-item plan is illustrated in Chap. 11.

Usually multiple or item-by-item sequential plans can be designed to give OC curves closely similar to the OC curve of any given single or double sampling plan. The following single, double, and multiple plans illustrate a set of matched plans having nearly identical OC curves.

Type of plan	*Sample number*	*Individual sample size*	*Combined sample size*	*Acceptance number*	*Rejection number*
Single	1	75	75	2	3
Double	1	50	50	1	4
	2	100	150	3	4
Multiple	1	20	20	*	2
	2	20	40	0	3
	3	20	60	1	3
	4	20	80	2	4
	5	20	100	2	4
	6	20	120	2	4
	7	20	140	3	4

*Acceptance not permitted on first multiple sample.

The foregoing method of describing acceptance sampling plans differs slightly from the one used earlier in this chapter of single and double sampling. It is generally not convenient to use n and c numbers to describe a multiple plan.

Figure 9.9 shows the OC curves for these three attributes plans together with the OC curve for a matched plan using variables criteria. The calculation of the OC curve for the multiple plan follows the same pattern already explained for double sampling. The following calculations apply to a single point on the curve, namely, the probability of acceptance of a 2% defective lot. To simplify the calculation, it is assumed that the lot size is large enough so that the unsampled portion of the lot will still be substantially 2% defective regardless of the results of past samples. Under this assumption, it is not necessary to recalculate μ_{np} based on the number of defectives found in the first sample as was done in Sec. 9.10.1. Each multiple sample consists of 20 articles. To use Table *G*, it should be noted that μ_{np} = (20) (0.02) = 0.4. Table *G* then gives the following useful figures applicable to any sample:

$$P_0 = 0.670$$

$$P_1 = 0.938 - 0.670 = 0.268$$

$$P_2 = 0.992 - 0.938 = 0.054$$

$$P_{3 \text{ or more}} = 1.000 - 0.992 = 0.008$$

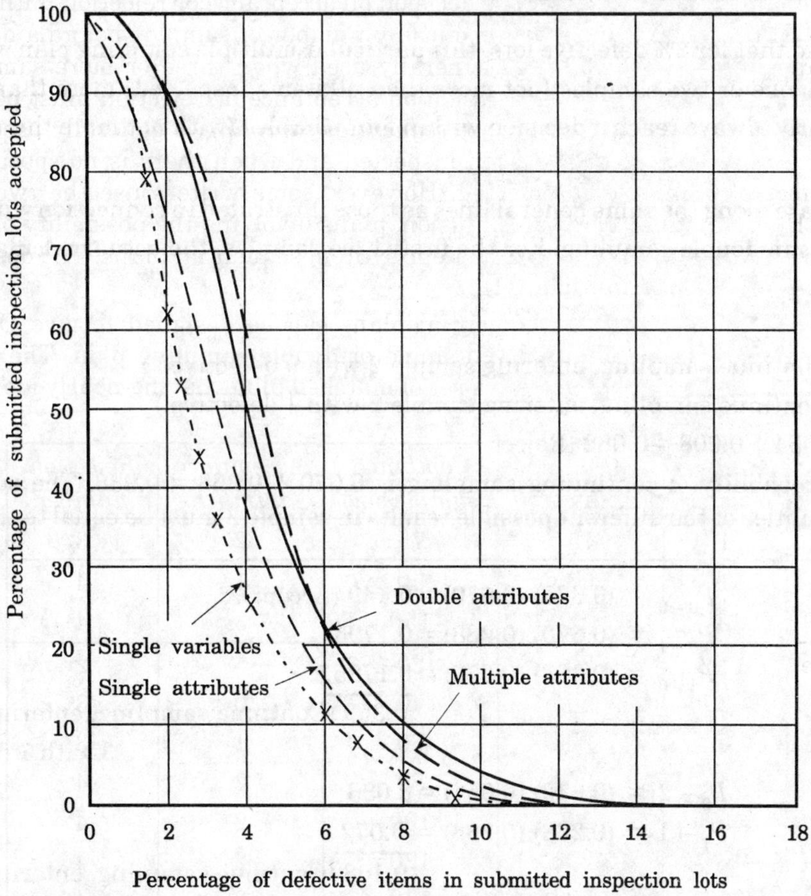

FIGURE 9.9 : OC curve for the single sampling attriutes plan n = 75, c = 2, and curves for three matching sampling plans.

These may be combined by the theorem of conditional probabilities to obtain the following probabilities of acceptance or rejection on each sample:

Sample number	*Probability of*	
	Acceptance	*Rejection*
1	0.000	0.062
2	0.449	0.022
3	0.241	0.058
4	0.113	0.010
5	0.000	0.015
6	0.000	0.010
7	0.013	0.007
	0.816	0.184

It will be noted that for 2% defective lots, this particular multiple sampling plan will arrive at a decision with one or two samples (not more than 40 items inspected) more than half the time and will nearly always reach a decision within four samples (with not more than 80 items inspected).

Calculations are along the same general lines as those illustrated in connection with finding Type *B* OC curves in double sampling. For the first three samples, the actual calculations are as follows:

Sample 1

$P_0 = 0.670$ (Continue sampling, entering sample 2 with 0 defectives.)

$P_1 = 0.268$ (Continue sampling, entering sample 2 with 1 defective.)

$P_{2\ or\ more} = 0.054 + 0.008 = 0.062$ (Reject.)

Note: The probability of continuing sampling is 0.670 + 0.268 = 0.938. The sum of the computed probabilities of the different possible results in sample 2 must be equal to this figure.

Sample 2

P_{0-0} = (0.670) (0.670) = 0.449 (Accept).

P_{0-1} = (0.670) (0.268) = 0.1795

P_{1-0} = (0.268) (0.670) = 0.1795

0.359 (Continue sampling, entering sample 3 with 1 defective.)

$P_0 - 2$ = (0.670) (0.054) = 0.036

$P_1 - 1$ = (0.268) (0.268) = 0.072

0.108 (Continue sampling, entering sample 3 with 2 defectives.)

$$P_{0=3 \text{ or more}} = (0.670)\,(0.008) = 0.005$$
$$P_{1=2 \text{ or more}} = (0.268)\,(0.062) = \underline{0.017}$$
$$0.022 \text{ (Reject.)}$$

Check: 0.449 + 0.359 + 0.108 + 0.022 + 0.938

Note : The probability of continuing sampling is 0.359 + 0.108 = 0.467. The sum of the computed probabilities of the different possible results in sample 3 must be equal to this figure.

Sample 3

$$P_{1-0} = (0.359)\,(0.670) = 0.241 \text{ (Accept.)}$$
$$P_{1-1} = (0.359)\,(0.268) = 0.096$$
$$P_{2-0} = (0.108)\,(0.670) = \underline{0.072}$$

0.168 (Continue sampling, entering sample 4 with 2 defectives.)

$$P_{1-2 \text{ or more}} = (0.359)\,(0.062) = 0.022$$
$$P_{2-1 \text{ or more}} = (0.108)\,(0.330) = \underline{0.036}$$
$$0.058 \text{ (Reject.)}$$

Check: 0.241 + 0.168 + 0.058 = 0.467

It should be clear to the reader that the only reasonable approach to the calculation of probabilities of acceptance and OC curves for multiple sampling plans is through the use of computer programs designed for the purpose.

The topic of the difference in average amount of sampling inspection under single, double, and multiple sampling is discussed in Chap. 10, which also considers other relative advantages and disadvantages of these competing types of sampling.

An explanation of the calculation of the OC curve of the matching variables plan shown in Fig. 9.9 is deferred until Chap. 13.

9.12.1 Rejection Number for First Sample in Double Sampling

The reader will observe that in the double sampling plans discussed in this chapter, the rejection number is the same for the first sample as for the combined samples. This is in contrast to the multiple sampling plan just explained, which had rejection numbers of 2, 3 or 4, depending on the sample number. We shall see that in nearly all multiple sampling plans, two or more rejection numbers are used.

Administrative simplicity is gained by the policy of having only one rejection number for any given double sampling plan. Before 1963, this policy was adopted for the various tables of double sampling plans that were in popular use.

At some sacrifice of administrative simplicity, the average amount of sampling inspection in double sampling can often be reduced for a given quality protection by making the rejection number for the first sample less than the rejection number for the combined samples. Two such rejection numbers are used in most of the double sampling plans in ABC-STD-105, an interna- tional standard for acceptance sampling by attributes adopted in 1963. This ABC standard is discussed in Chap. 10.

9.13 RANDOMNESS IN ACCEPTANCE SAMPLING

The probability calculations used to compute OC curves assume that samples are drawn at random. That is, each item in the lot is assumed to have an equal chance to be selected in the sample. If the items in a lot have been thoroughly mixed, a sample chosen anywhere in the lot meets the requirement of randomness. However, a common condition is that there is no reason to believe that the items have had a thorough mixing. Moreover, it may be impracticable to carry out a thorough mixing because of physical difficulties or excessive costs incident to mixing or for other reasons. Sometimes the best that can be done is drawing a sample is to avoid any obvious type of bias. For instance, if items are packed in layers, it clearly is not sensible to draw the entire sample from the top layers.

If it is practicable to assign a different number to each item in a lot and to draw an item from any place in the lot, a formal scheme for drawing a random sample may be adopted. Such a scheme may use a table of random numbers or some mechanical device for generating random numbers as needed. Computer-generated random numbers may be used so long as a different "seed" number is used each time. Otherwise the same set of pseudo-random numbers will be generated each time the program is run.

9.13.1 Use of Random Numbers to Select a Sample

Random digits can be generated in any way that gives each digit from 0 to 9 an equal chance to be selected. Extensive tables of random digits can be generated rapidly by modern electronic computers. Table *X* in App. 1 contains 2500 random digits reproduced from an extensive table prepared by the RAND Corporation.

Let us illustrate the use of a table of random digits by a numerical example based on Table *X*. Assume that it is desired to select a sample of 15 from a lot of 750 items. Each item in the lot is identified by a number from 1 to 750. Therefore it is necessary to select 15 random three-digit numbers from 001 to 750.

First it is necessary to determine a starting point in the table. Table X contains 50 rows and 50 columns of digits listed in pairs. Assume that a pencil point is placed at random in the table, and the first two-digit number to the right from 1 to 50 determines the row to be selected. The procedure is repeated to determine the starting column. Assume that the 8th row and the 39th column are chosen. Assume that the decision was made in advance that the starting digit chosen will be the first digit of a three-digit number read to the right and that succeeding numbers will be read down the table. The following numbers are obtained. (Numbers that are not between 001 and 750 must be discarded; these are shown in parentheses. A number that has already occurred must also be discarded; there are no such numbers in this example.)

471, 098, 443, 335, 015, 106, (932), 682, (864), 531, 379, (909), 225, 233, 404, (812), 392, (820), (934), 183, (929), 592

The selection of the sample is simplified if the 15 numbers between 001 and 750 are rearranged in order of increasing size as follows:

015, 098, 106, 183, 225, 233, 335, 379, 392, 404, 443, 471, 531, 592, 682

If samplers wish to generate their own random numbers, a convenient method is to use a set of Japanese random dice. Each die is a regular icosahedron. Each digit from 0 to 9 is engraved on two faces so that the 10 digits occur with equal probability. The dice come in sets of three colours. When the dice are used to generate three-digit random numbers, one colour may be assigned to each digit.

In cases where it is deemed imperative to use a formal scheme to ensure a random sample, there may be a psychological advantage in having the person who selects the sample use random dice or some other mechanical device. The use of a device that obviously involves the laws of chance may add interest to the job of selecting the sample. Because of this interest, there may be less tendency for the sampler to disregard a stipulated formal set of rules for randomiza- tion.

9.13.2 Stratified Sampling

The large lots, the difficulties of random selection may be so great that it is advisable to adopt stratified (proportional) sampling . Stratification of the lot with samples drawn from each stratum can be effective substitute for random sampling. The technique is to divide the lot strata or layer as shown in Fig. 9.10. Each stratum is further sub-divided into cubes, as illustrated by stratum 1 within each cube samples are drawn from the entire volume. The dividing of the lot into strata and cubes within each stratum is an imaginary process done by the inspector. By this technique pieces are selected from all locations in the lot.

Such a stratified sample is, of course, different from a random sample. In taking many such stratified samples from a given lot, the average number of defectives will be the same as if samples were drawn at random, but the variation in number of defectives from sample to sample will be less. The result is that the OC curve for any given acceptance criteria will be steeper under stratified sampling than under random sampling. Lots substantially better than those at $p_{0.50}$ will have a somewhat greater chance of acceptance than indicated by the OC curve for random sampling: lots substantially worse than those at $p_{0.50}$ will have a somewhat smaller chance of acceptance. OC curves under stratified sampling cannot be calculated without making an assumption as to the variation of quality from sublot to sublot. Investigations indicate that for practical situations likely to arise in industrial sampling, the use of stratified samples will seldom make much change from the OC curve computed for random sampling.

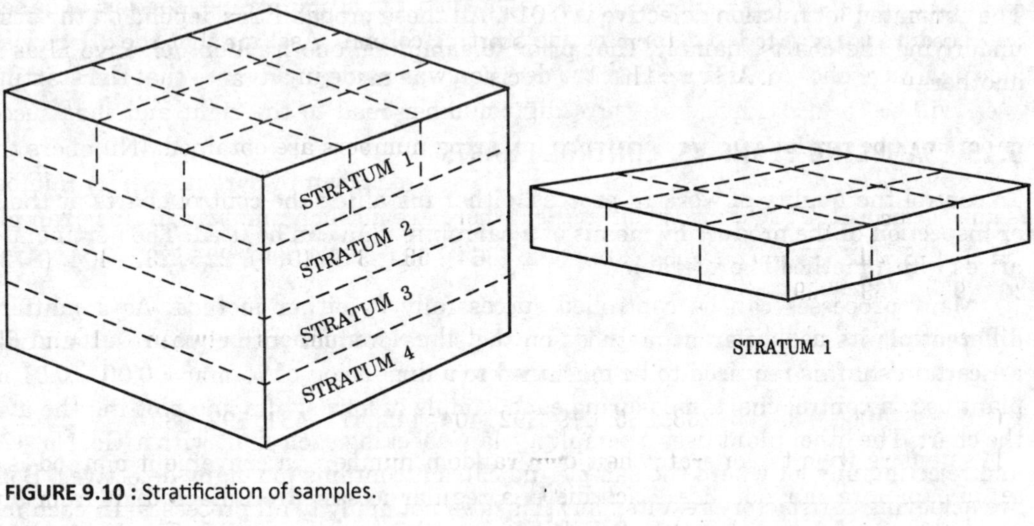

FIGURE 9.10 : Stratification of samples.

9.14 ESTIMATING THE LOT QUALITY FROM THE SAMPLE QUALITY

In lot by lot acceptance sampling, the immediate practical question is what to do with lot. A decision must be made to accept a lot or reject it or perhaps to screen it. Definite criteria are established to settle such decisions. Usually, the estimation of lot quality from sample quality is viewed merely as an academic question. In some instances, however, particularly in dealing with isolated lots and in borderline cases, it may be desired to have an idea of a sampled lot.

If it is desired to estimate from a given sample by attributes the probability that the true lot quality is within given limits, such an estimate requires the use of Bayes' theorem. A solution of this problem was made by General Simon, who has presented this solution in compact form in his *Io* charts. These charts are based on the assumption that prior to sampling, all fraction defective were equally likely. The five charts apply to probabilities of 0.995, 0.9, 0.5, 0.1, and 0.005. For instance, with any given sample size (up to 500) from an infinite or very large lot and with any given number of observed defectives in the sample, the probability is 0.995 that the true fraction defective in the lot is less than a value that may be read from the 0.995 chart.

An illustration of the numerical information given by these charts may help the reader to decide whether they will be useful in dealing with his particular problems. Assume a sample of 240 from a very large lot contains exactly 2 defectives. The charts give the probability as 0.995 that the true fraction defective is below 0.038 and as 0.005 that it is less than 0.0014. In other words, it is a fairly safe estimate (with a 0.99 probability) that the true fraction defective of the lot is between 0.038 and 0.0014. The charts give the probability as 0.9 that the true fraction defective is less than 0.022 and as 0.1 that it is less than 0.0046. In other words, these are four chances out of five that the true fraction defective is between 0.022 and 0.0046. The 0.5 chart gives the estimated lot fraction defective as 0.011. This contrast with the sample fraction defective of $\frac{2}{240} = 0.0083$.

A contrast is afforded by the probabilities for a sample half as big with half as many defectives. Assume a sample of 120 has exactly 1 defectives. The probability is 0.99 that the true fraction defective is between 0.06 and 0.0009, and 0.8 that it is between 0.032 and 0.0043. The estimated lot fraction defective is 0.014. All these probabilities depend on the assumption underlying the charts, namely, that prior to sampling, one fraction defective is as likely as another.

9.15 SAMPLING PLANS VS. CONTROL CHARTS

To control the quality of work in process, either installing the control charts at the machine or inspection of the product by means of a sampling plan can be used. The pertinent question arises which method is preferable ?

Many processes can be controlled successfully by either method. As a matter of fact, different plants use different methods on the same product with equal results. For example : A certain shaft is required to be machined to a dimension of 75 mm + 0.00 – 0.01 mm. One plant uses a control chart, measuring each sample of four shafts and plotting the average on the chart. The other plant uses a sampling plan, checking each shaft with a 'Go, Not-Go' gauge, and rejecting any lot where the sample indicates it contains too many defectives. Both plants are achieving satisfactory results ; but this does not apply to all processes. In each individual case a decision has to be made on the basis of the following facts :

1. The information obtained from control charts is superior to the one obtained from sampling plans, because control charts often sound a warning when a process is going out of control even before defective product occurs. A sampling plans can only tell that the process is out of control after the defectives have already been produced.
2. The sample size is much smaller under the control chart system, but sometimes each sample has to be tested very carefully in order to obtain a precise measurement or pointer reading. Sampling plans, although they require larger sample sizes, involve merely a simple test or visual examination to determine whether each item is satisfactory or defective.
3. The amount of figure work to be done is, of course, greater when control charts is used, since we have to compute sample averages, standard deviation and process variability etc.

The advantages versus disadvantages of control charts and sampling plans are as follows:

Method	Advantages	Disadvantages
Control Charts	Superior Information Small Samples	Work Simple Tests More Pains taking Tests
Sampling Plans	Less Figure Sample Tests	More Figure Work Less Information Bigger

It should be realized that in practice there are many examples where one of the advantages or disadvantages outweighs all the rest. For example, when inspecting chrome plated item, it would be highly impractical to attempt to measure the brightness of finish along a numerical scale. Therefore, it is preferable to classify each article 'satisfactory' or 'defective' and use a sampling plan. On the other hand, when determining yield point and alongation of steel castings, testing is so difficult, costly and time consuming that it is of primary importance to have small sizes. Here the control chart method must be used.

SOLVED QUESTIONS

Q. 9.1: *Select the correct option form the follows:*

(*i*) Probability of finding a defective item in a large lot varies from

(*a*) zero to 1 (*b*) $-\infty$ to $+\infty$ (*c*) $-\infty$ to 1

(*d*) $+1$ to ∞ (*e*) -1 to $+1$

(*ii*) An attribute sampling plan is specified by

(*a*) *n*, *c* (*b*) α, β (*c*) AQL and LTPD

(*d*) AQL and AOQL (*e*) none of these

(*iii*) In a double sampling scheme (DSS) the decision to accept a batch (or lot) is taken

(*a*) always on minimum two samples (*b*) one sample also

(*c*) second sample size always being twice the fast sample

(*d*) acceptance number of second sample is twice of that of the first sample.

(*iv*) On an OC curve we can also locate

(*a*) indifference quality (*b*) AOQL

(*c*) quality requiring maximum inspection (*d*) quality requiring minimum inspection

(v) The steeper the OC curve

(a) the less protection for both producer and consumer

(b) the more protection for both producer and consumer

(c) the lower the AQL

(d) the smaller the sample size.

(vi) For an operation requiring shipments from your vendor of small lots of fixed size, the sampling plan used for receiving inspection should have its OC curve developed using

(a) the Poisson distribution (b) the hypergeometric distribution

(c) the binomial distribution (d) the log normal distribution

(e) the Gaussian (normal) distribution.

(vii) Two quantities which uniquely determine a single-sampling attributes plan are

(a) AOQL and LTPD (b) sample size and acceptance number

(c) AQL and producer's risk (d) LTPD and consumer's risk

(e) AQL and LTPD.

(viii) The probability of accepting material produced at an acceptable quality level is defined as

(a) α (b) β (c) AQL

(d) $1-\alpha$ (e) $1-\beta$.

(ix) The AQL for a given sampling plan is 1.0 percent. This means that

(a) the producer takes a small risk of rejecting product which is 1.0 percent defective or better

(b) all accepted lots are 1.0 percent defective or better

(c) the average quality limit of the plan is 1.0 percent

(d) the average quality level of the plan is 1.0 percent

(e) all lots are 1.0 percent defective or better.

(x) Prior to the use of any sampling plan, one must consider

(a) the consumer's and producer's risks must be specified

(b) the method of selecting samples must be specified

(c) the characteristics to be inspected must be specified

(d) the conditions must be specified (material accumulated in lots or inspected by continuous sampling)

(e) all of the above.

Ans: (i) (a), (ii) (a), (iii) (b), (iv) (a), (v) (b), (vi) (b), (vii) (b), (viii) (d), (ix) (a), (x) (e).

Q. 9.2: *(a) State whether the following statements are TRUE* (T) *or FALSE* (F) *:*

1. For a given lot size, a single sampling scheme is completely specified by the sample size and acceptance number.
2. Consumer's Risk in acceptance sampling is like a Type II error in hypothesis testing.
3. If you use acceptance sampling, your supplier won't be motivated to improve the quality of their output.
4. Increasing the sample size enables you to reduce both consumer's and producer's risks.

5. Double sampling requires larger sample sizes than single sampling in order to achieve the same levels of risk.
6. The AOQ curve tells you how the output quality of an acceptance sampling scheme varies as a function of the input quality of the batches being tasted.

(*b*) *Choose the correct statement :*

1. An OC curve can be used to determine :
   (*a*) Consumer's Risk (*b*) Producer's Risk (*c*) Both Risks (*d*) Neither Risk
2. AOQ stands for :
   (*a*) Approximate outgoing quality (*b*) Average operating quality
   (*c*) Approximate optimal quality (*d*) Average outgoing quality
3. The correct distribution to use to complete Consumer's Risk exactly is the :
   (*a*) Normal (*b*) Hypergeometric (*c*) Poisson (*d*) Binomial

Ans: (*a*) 1. (T) 2. (T) 3. (F) 4. (T) 5. (F) 6 (T)
(*b*) 1. (*c*) 2. (*d*) 3. (*b*)

Q. 9.3: *"The hypergeometric distribution provides exact results when sampling is without replacement". True or False ? Give reasons.*

Ans: True.

Reason: It takes into account the changing probabilities caused by non replacement, and uses both the sample size '*n*' and the batch size '*N*' in the calculations. It must be used when *N* is small, *e.g.* when *N* is upto 15.

Q. 9.4: *Mention one situation where there is no alternative to acceptance sampling ?*

Ans: When destructive testing is involved, acceptance sampling is a must.

Q. 9.5:. *Can SAS provide the estimate of lot quality ?*

Ans: No. It determines with specified risks, an acceptance or rejection of each lot.

Q. 9.6: *How do you achieve a sampling plan which is nearer to ideal sampling plan ?*

Ans: With higher sample size *n* and higher acceptance number *c*, the sampling plan is nearer to ideal sampling plan.

Q. 9.7: *Can the given OC curve predict the quality of a given lots ?*

Ans: The OC curve does not predict the quality of lots submitted for inspection.

Q. 9.8: *Can the given OC curve predict the final quality achieved after all inspections are completed.*

Ans: No.

Q. 9.9: *Simply define a sampling plan.*

Ans: A sampling plan is a decision rule that specifies how large a sample *n* should be taken and the allowable number of defective *c* in the sample.

Q. 9.10: *How do you define Scientific Acceptance Sampling (SAS) ?*

ANS: Scientific acceptance sampling is the process of evaluating a portion of the product in a lot for the very purpose of accepting or rejecting a lot.

Q. 9.11: *Give one simple example each of sampling plan (a) attributes (b) variables.*
Ans: (*a*) *Attribute plan* : Select a random sample of size $n = 40$ and count the number of defectives. It this number is less than or equal to c, accept the batch, otherwise reject it.

(*b*) *Variable plan* : Select a random sample of size n = 40, and measure the (quality characteristic i.e. for example mean tensile strength $\overline{X}$). If $X \geq 12000$ psi, accept the lot, otherwise reject it.

Q. 9.12: *What is an operating characteristic curve of an attribute sampling plan ?*
Ans: An operating characteristic curve is a graphical description of a sampling plan (*n*, *c* combination) which shows the probability that the plan will accept lots of various (possible) quality levels.

Q. 9.13: *(a) What is the general range of producer's risk ?*

(b) If during sampling acceptance, a good lot is rejected, what kind of error it is. If bad lot is accepted, what kind of error it is ?

Ans: (a) It is generally 1 to 5% *i.e.* 0.01 to 0.05.

(*b*) If good lot is rejected it is Type *I* error and if bed lot is accepted it is Type *II* error.

Q. 9.14: *If Producer's risk is α, what is the probability of acceptance of AQL ?*
Ans: 1 – α.

Q. 9.15: *What is AQL ?*
Ans: It is acceptable quality level of a good lot. It is the percent defective that can be considered satisfactory as a process average, and represents a level of quality which the producer wants accepted with a higher probability of acceptance.

Q. 9.16: *Draw a typical OC curve and indicate the two points which are usually specified in choosing a sampling plan.*
Ans: Figure 9.11 shows a typical OC curve and two points usually specified in choosing a sampling plan. These two points are :

1. AQL and Producer's risk (α). The point on the OC curve is therefore [AQL ; 1 – α *i.e.* the (probability of acceptance of a lot of AQL quality)]
2. LTPD and Consumer's Risk (β). (*i.e* the probability of acceptance of a lot of LTPD quality).

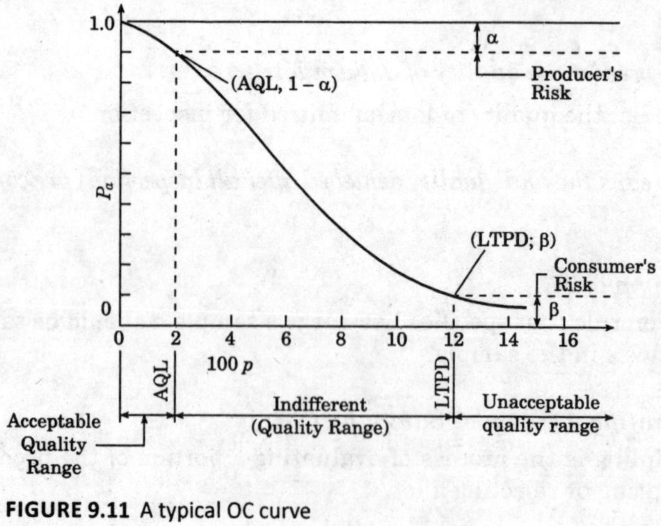

FIGURE 9.11 A typical OC curve

Q. 9.17: *What is Rule-of-thumb sampling plan and what are its basis ? Give you committee.*

Ans: Rule-of-thumb sampling plan is generally the "ten percent sampling rule". For any lot size, a sample equal to ten percent of the lot is selected. If there are no defectives found in the sample, the lot is accepted. If any defectives are found in the sample, the lot is rejected. It is usually presumed that, with the sample always a constant percentage (ten percent) of the lot, the sampling risks will be constant.

Comment: The ten percent rule, however does not provide equal risks.

Q. 9.18: *(a) Show graphically a perfect sampling scheme designed to reject batches containing more than 5 percent defectives.*

(b) Using the same axis as in (a), show how a real sampling scheme deviates from perfection (i) for a reasonably effective scheme, and (ii) for an ineffective scheme.

(c) Why don't firms always use the most effective sampling schemes available ?

Ans: (*a*) A perfect or ideal scheme for rejecting the batches containing more than 5 percent defectives i.e. accepting all batches containing upto 5% defectives is shown at (1) in Fig. 9.12.

(*b*) (*i*) curve at (2) in Fig. 9.12 shows the OC curves of the reasonably effective scheme *i.e.* a sampling scheme having a *very high probability* of acceptance of good batches and low *probability of acceptance* (i.e. *higher probability of rejection of bad batches*).

(*ii*) Curves at (3) and (4) in Fig. 9.12 show the OC curve of ineffective schemes *i.e.* the probability of acceptance of bad lots also remain high. In other words the given schemes do not distinguish between very good lots and very bad lots.

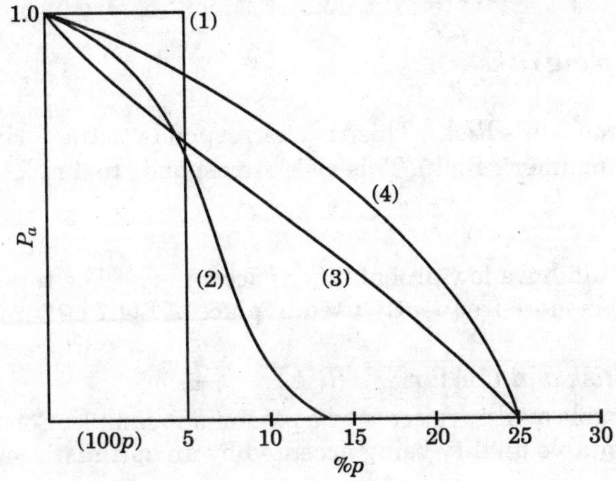

FIGURE 9.12

(c) Most effective schemes i.e. ideal schemes involve nearly 100 percent inspection and even then may **not** serve the intended purpose. Also where destructive testing is involved, the ideal schemes cannot be used.

Q. 9.19: *(a) Draw an OC of the scheme where probability of acceptance of a batch if it contains more than 0.4% defective is zero, and probability of accepting the batch if it contains less than 0.4% defective is 1.*

(b) If a sampling scheme is selected with n = 50 and c = 1, does it meet the requirement exactly ?

Ans: (*a*) Figure 9.13 shows the OC of the scheme in (*a*).

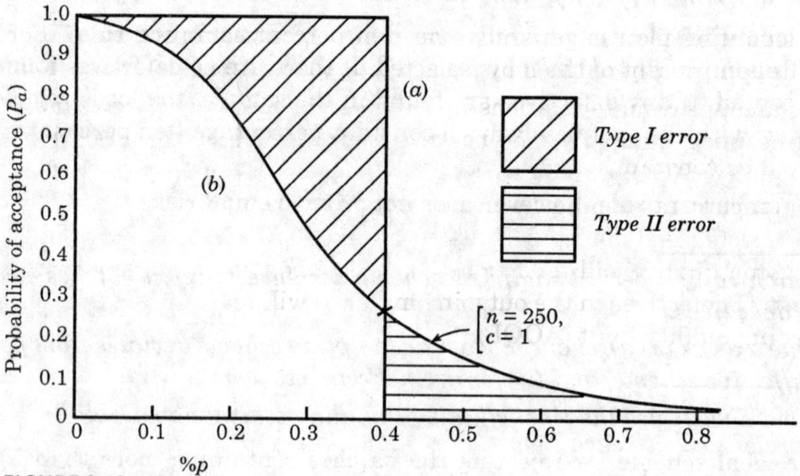

FIGURE 9.13

(*b*) No. The OC curve of the scheme is also shown in Fig. 9.13 (*b*). The scheme will have *Type I* and *Type II* errors. As the procedure, relies on a sample, there will always be a probability of rejecting a good batch because the number of defectives in the sample is 2 or more despite the bach is in fact being acceptable (*Type I* risk shown by the top shaded area). There is also a probability that inspite of accepting a batch (because the number of defectives it contains is zero or one) in its sample the actual number of defectives in the whole batch might be greater than 0.4%.(*Type II* risk shown in the lower shaded area).

Q. 9.20: *What are the two types of sampling risks ?*

Ans: Sampling risks are to two kinds :

1. Good lots can be rejected (the Producer's Risk). This risk corresponds to the α risk.
2. Bad lots can be accepted (the Consumer's Risk). This risk corresponds to β risk.

Q. 9.21: *What is LQL ?*

Ans: It is limiting quality level and should have low probability of acceptance. The term LTPD (*i.e.* lot tolerance percentage defective) is more frequently used in place of LQL.

Q. 9.22: *What is meant by Producer's Risk and Consumer's Risk?*

Ans: Producer's risk (α) is batch of acceptable quality rejected by a pessimistic sample. Consumer's risk (β) is the risk of a batch of unacceptable quality being accepted by an optimistic sample.

Q. 9.23: *The OC curve shows the probability of rejecting batches of differing incoming percentage defective. True or False:*

Ans: False.

Reason : An *OC* curve shows the probability of acceptance (P_a) and $P_r = 1 - P_a$. is a computed data.

Q. 9.24: *State whether the following statements are True or False?*

(*a*) *It costs more to sample to do no inspection at all.*

(*b*) *OC curve shows the optimum quality of batches.*

(*c*) *OC curve can predict the quality of batches.*

Ans: (*a*) False; (*b*) False; (*c*) False.

Q. 9.25: *What do (i) AOQ and (ii) AOQL refer ?*

Ans: (*i*) AQL : The level of defectives at which there must be a very low chance of acceptance. These levels must be continually reduced by proactive measures forming part of TQM.

(*ii*) There exists an approximate relationship between the fraction defective in the material before inspection (incoming quality *p*) and the fraction defective remaining after inspection (average outgoing quality AOQ) : AOQ = $P_a p$. When incoming quality is perfect, outgoing quality will also be perfect (assuming no inspection errors) because the sampling plan will cause all lots to be rejected and detected. Thus, at either extreme–incoming quality excellent or terrible–the outgoing quality will tend to be good. Between these extremes is the point at which the percentage of defectives in the outgoing material will reach its maximum. This point is the average outgoing quality limit (AOQL).

Q. 9.26: *Give four reasons why companies may use samples instead of checking every item. When might a company prefer to check each item.*

Ans: (*i*) Some reasons for sampling are :

1. Sampling is often faster.
2. In destructive testing sampling is essential.
3. It economies inspection
4. Data from 100% inspection may give a false sense of accuracy.

Companies prefer to check each item of the rejected lot which have been on the rejected on the basis of sampling; or when the allowable number of defectives is only a few hundred per million, it may require 100% inspection for most reasonable lot sizes. Automatic testing of items while they are in the process is often the best way to check quality control in this type of situation.

Q. 9.27: *What are non-scientific sampling plans ?*

Ans: Nonscientific sampling plans are generally not based on defined risks assumed by the producer and the consumer and use no scientific tools. One of such scheme is to inspect 10% of the lot and if no defective is found the lot is accepted, otherwise it is rejected.

On the surface this would appear to be a reasonable and effective sampling scheme but its shortcoming becomes quite apparent when the OC curves of such a scheme is examined. For example if $n = 110$, 35, and 15 and $c = 0$ and if the lots are normally 2 percent defective, the chances of acceptance, (as computed from Table *G*) of such a lot by these three schemes is as follows.

n	C	P_a
110	0	0.111
35	0	0.497
15	0	0.741

Since the sample size is function of lot size, the probability of acceptance depends upon the lot size. That is, a production lot of size $N = 1{,}100$ which contains 2 per cent defectives has a 11.1% chance of acceptance using the 10 percent inspection sample scheme, while an equally defective lot of size $N = 150$ would have a 74% chance of acceptance. Using this plan, a producer of product which runs 2 per cent defective would obviously prefer to submit lots of size $N = 150$ for acceptance inspection.

In the case of scientific sampling, no such disparity in risks is present, as the very selection to sampling plans is based on a primary choice of risk levels.

Q. 9.28: *(a) What is scientific acceptance sampling?*

(b) How can scientific acceptance sampling help quality planning and control?

Ans: (*a*) Acceptance sampling is concerned with the decision to accept or reject a batch (or lot) of goods. The design of the acceptance sampling process includes decisions about sampling versus complete inspection, attribute versus variable measures, AQL, α, LTPD, β, sample size, and the acceptable number of defective items in the sample.

Management can select the best plan (choosing sample size n and acceptance number c) by using an operating characteristic (OC) curve.

(*b*) Acceptance sampling helps managers to understand the risks they are taking when they make decisions about a whole batch of products on the basis of a sample taken from that batch. The risks of any particular sampling plan are shown on its operating characteristic (OC) curve.

Some of the assumptions within acceptance sampling (most notably that a certain level of defectives *is 'acceptable'*) are not looked on favourably by proponents of total quality management.

Q. 9.29: *A certain part is made in lots that usually contain a considerable number of defectives. Only about one-fourth of the parts that are classed as defectives are really unsatisfactory for the purpose intended. Any unsatisfactory parts passed on to assembly will be detected there at an estimated average cost of ₹ 95 each. Or 90% of them could be eliminated by 100% inspection at a unit cost of 40 paise for each item inspected. Assume that the type of inspection has an influence on production cost. Assume also that all parts technically defective but actually satisfactory will finally be used in the assembly so that total production will be same either with 100% inspection or with no inspection ; neglect costs of material review procedures to bring this about. At what per cent defective will 100% inspection just break even with no inspection.*

Ans: Let the lots consist of N units each and the fraction defective at which 100% inspection breaks even with no inspection be pb.

$$\text{Defective units} = Np_{BEP}$$

$$\text{Really unsatisfactory units} = \frac{1}{4} Np_{BEP}$$

$$\text{Total cost with no inspection} = ₹\ 95 \times \frac{1}{4} Np_{BEP}$$

Since in 100% inspection, 90% of the defective units are eliminated, therefore, defective units passed to assembly = 0.10 Np_{BEP}.

Since really unsatisfactory units are 0.25 times the defective units, therefore, out of 0.10 Np_{BEP} units, really defective units are 0.025 N_p.

Total cost with 100% inspection = Rs. 0.40 (N) + 95 (0.025 Np_{BEP})

For break even

$$95 \times \frac{1}{4} Np_{BEP} = 0.40\ (N) + 95\ (0.0025\ Np_{BEP})$$

or $$p_{BEP} = 0.0187$$

or $$\%p_{BEP} = 1.87$$

Q. 9.30: *The marketing manager of Roller Bearings International (RBI) estimates that "defective bearings that get into the hands of industrial users cost RBI an average of ₹ 1000 each" in replacement costs and lost business. The production manager counters that "the bearings are only about 2 percent defective now, and the best a sampling plan could do would be to reduce that to*

1 percent defective—but not much better (unless we go to 100 percent inspection)." Should RBI adopt a sampling plan if it costs (a) ₹ 5 per bearing ? (b) ₹ 12.50 per bearing ? (c) How much per bearing can RBI afford to spend on inspection costs before it begins to lose money on inspections ?

Ans: For purposes of illustration, assume that all comparisons are based upon a lot of 100 bearings.

(*a*) Without inspection : Defect cost = 100(.02) (1000) = ₹ 2000

With inspection : Inspection cost = 100(5) = ₹ 500

Defect cost = 100(.01) 1000 = ₹ 1000

₹ 1500

Advantage from inspection : 500 (or ₹ 5 per bearing)

(*b*) Without inspection : Defect cost = ₹ 2000

With inspection : Inspection cost = 100(12.50) = ₹ 1250

Defect cost = ₹ 1000

₹ 2250

Disadvantage from inspection : ₹ 250 (*i.e.* ₹ 2.50 per bearing)

(c) Let X = the inspection cost per bearing. Then the minimum cost is where

Defect cost without inspect = inspect cost + defect cost with inspect

$$100\ (.02)\ (1000) = X(100) + (100)(.01)(1000/\text{bearing})$$

$$X = \frac{2000 - 1000}{100} = ₹\ 10 \text{ per bearing}$$

Q. 9.31: *A single sampling plan uses a sample size of 15, and an acceptance number of 1. Compute the probability of acceptance of a lot of 50 articles 2% defective. Use hypergeometric probabilities.*

Ans: When a lot of 50 articles contains 2% defective articles, it means that only 1 out of 50 is defective. Also the acceptance number is 1. Therefore, whenever a sample of 15 or for that matter any size is drawn at the most it will contain only 1 defective. So the lot will always be accepted. Otherwise also the probability of acceptance can be found by using hypergeometric probabilities.

$$P_0 = \frac{C_{15}^{49} C_0^1}{C_{15}^{50}} = 0.70$$

$$P_1 = \frac{C_{14}^{48} C_0^1}{C_{15}^{50}} = 0.30$$

Therefore, probability of acceptance

$$= 0.70 + 0.30 = 1.00.$$

Q. 9.32: *A manufacturer of pipe fittings produces continuously with an average of 1 defective for every 1,000 fittings. If a sample of 500 pieces is inspected, what is the probability that this sample will be equal to or less than 0.2 per cent defective ? Use Table G, if required.*

Ans: $$p = \frac{1}{1{,}000}$$

The expression "that this sample will be equal to or less than 0.2 per cent defective" means that the sample of 500 should consist of either 0 or $\left(500 \times \frac{0.2}{100} = 1\right)$ defective

Hence we should find the probability that the sample consists of 0 or 1 defective.

Now $$np = 500 \times \frac{1}{1,000} = 0.5$$

From Table G, the required probability is 0.910.

Q. 9.33: *A manufacturer sells his product in large lots to a customer who uses a sampling plan at incoming inspection. The plan calls for a sample of 200 units and an acceptance number of 2. Rejected lots are returned to the manufacturer. If a lot is rejected and returned, the manufacturer has decided to gamble and send it right back to the customer without screening it (and without telling the customer it was a rejected lot). He hopes that another random sample will lead to an acceptance of the lot. What is the probability that a 2 percent defective lot will be accepted on either one or two submissions to the customer ?*

Ans:
$$n = 200, p = 0.02$$
$$np = 200 \times 0.02 = 4$$

Table G gives the probability that the lot is accepted at first submission = 0.238

Probability of rejection = 1 – 0.238 = 0.762

Probability that this lot is accepted again is 0.238.

Hence total probability $= 0.238 + (0.762 \times 0.238) = 0.238\,(1 + 0.762) = 0.419$

Q. 9.34: *A clothing manufacturer regularly takes delivery of batches of zip-fasteners from a supplier in another EU country. In the past there have been problems with some of these zips jamming in use, resulting in complaints from customers and the need to replace the zip, or sometimes an entire garment. A policy of sampling inspection has therefore been introduced: from each batch of 5,000 zips received, 10 will be taken, and subjected to a standard test in which they are mechanically fastened and unfastened 200 times. Any zips which jam during this test are classed as failures, and if one or more zips in the sample fail the test, the whole batch is rejected.*

(a) What is the probability of rejecting a batch in which (i) 5 per cent, (ii) 10 per cent and (iii) 20 per cent of zips are defective?

(b) Sketch the operating characteristic for the scheme and comment on what it reveals.

(c) If the supplier sends 100 batches per year, all with 5 per cent defective, and this scheme is in operation, what is the average number of batches that will be rejected per year? On average, how many satisfactory zips will therefore be sent back?

Ans: (*a*) (*i*) $$\mu_{np} = 10 \times .05 = 0.5$$

Probability of 0 defective = 0.607

Hence probability of rejection $(P_r) = 1 - 0.607$ *i.e.* 0.393

(*ii*) Similarly for $p = 0.01$, $P_r = 1 - 0.368$ *i.e.* 0.632

(*iii*) Similarly for $p = 0.02$, $P_r = 1 - 0.135$ *i.e.* 0.865

(*b*) The OC curve can be drawn assumes different values of p. From the curve it can be concluded that this scheme as it stands results in the rejection of high proportion of batches with reasonable quality (5 percent defective) while allowing through over 13 percent of batches with quality as poor as 20 percent defective.

(c) The probability of rejecting a batch with 5 percent defective is 0.393 as found in (a) (i), so 39.3 percent of 100 batches will be rejected - that is, approximately 39 batches.

Q. 9.35: *A double sampling plan is as follows :*

(a) *Select a sample of 2 from a lot of 20. If both articles inspected are good, accept the lot. If both are defective, reject the lot. If 1 is good and 1 defective, take a second sample of one article.*

(b) *If the article in the second sample is good, accept the lot. If it is defective, reject the lot.*

If a lot 25% defective is submitted what is the probability of acceptance ? Compute this by the method that is theoretically correct rather than by an approximate method.

Ans: When the lot is 25% defective, it means that out of 20 articles, 5 are defective. A lot will be accepted when :

(a) both the articles in the first sample are good or there is no defective,

(b) the first sample contains one good and one defective and the second sample of 1 article is not defective

$$P_a = \frac{C_2^{15} C_0^5}{C_0^{20}} = \frac{21}{38}$$

Probability that a second sample is taken (*i.e.* first sample contains 1 defective)

$$= \frac{C_1^{15} C_1^5}{C_2^{20}} = \frac{15}{38}$$

After drawing a sample that contains 1 good and 1 defective articles, only 18 articles are left in all, out of which 14 are good and 4 are defective.

Probability that a second sample contains no defective is

$$\frac{C_1^{14} C_0^4}{C_1^{18}} = \frac{7}{9}$$

Therefore $$P_a = \frac{15}{38} \times \frac{7}{9} = \frac{35}{114}$$

Hence total probability of acceptance $\dfrac{21}{38} = \dfrac{35}{114}$ = 0.8596 *i.e.* 0.860.

Q. 9.36: *Figure 9.14 sets out an acceptance procedure laid out by a particular specification for concrete to be used in highway structures.*

If the concrete passes (S) the first test, it is accepted outright. If it fails (F) it is subjected to a second test and failure at this stage means outright rejection. Success at the second test, on the other hand gives the concrete a chance of still being accepted by going on a third test. Concrete which passes the third test is accepted, but failure means rejection. Concrete of certain quality has probabilities of P_1, P_2, P_3 of passing tests-1, 2, 3 respectively. By following the appropriate paths in Fig. 9.14. Find the probability of (a) acceptance P_a, (b) rejection P_r

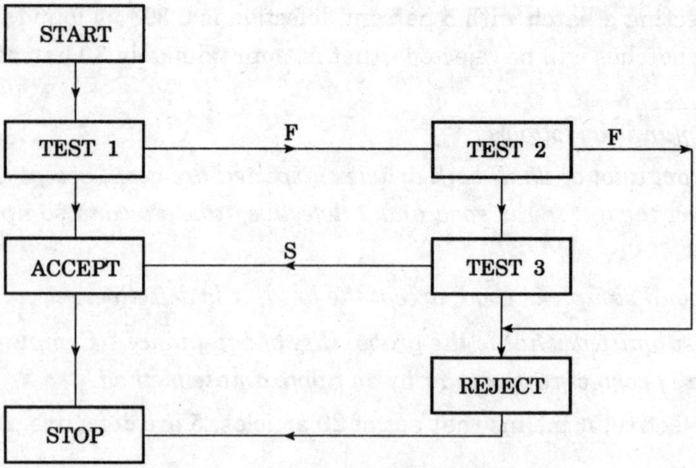

Acceptance procedure for concrete

FIGURE 9.11 : Acceptance procedure for concrete.

Ans: (*a*) The concrete has two paths of being accepted :

(*i*) Pass on Test 1 : the probability is (P_1)

(*ii*) Fail on first test but successively pass through Tests 2 and 3, the probability is $[(1 - P_1)\, P_2\, P_3]$

Hence probability of acceptance = $(P_a) = P_1 + (1 - P_1)\, P_2\, P_3$

(*b*) Similarly total probability of rejection (P_r)

$$= (1 - P_1)(1 - P_2) + (1 - P_1)(P_2)(1 - P_3) = (1 - P_1)(1 - P_2 P_3)$$
$$= (1 - P_1)(1 - P_2 P_3)$$

Q. 9.37: *A random sample of 10 is to be selected from a lot of 600 articles. Each article in the lot has been assigned a number. Table X of App. 1 is to be used to select 10 three-digit numbers between 001 and 600 ; these numbers will determine the articles to be chosen as the sample. A random choice from Table X results in a first number of 376 taken from the 13th, 14th and 15th digit on line 4. The rule established is to read down the table directly below these digits. Select the required 10 three-digit numbers (of course eliminating all numbers above 600) and arrange them in order of increasing magnitude.*

Ans: Consulting Table X of App. 1, the 13th, 14th and 15th digit on line 4 are 3, 7 and 6. So the first number is 376. As per the rule, reading exactly below these digits and forming the number as above, and discarding any number which is repeated or above 600, the next nine numbers are :

157, 072, 571, 051, 325, 529, 288, 507, 517.

Arranging the above ten numbers in order of increasing magnitude, the required numbers are :

051,	072,	157,	288,	325,
376,	507,	517,	529,	571.

Q. 9.38: *A Road Research Laboratory Report (LR 276) suggests an acceptance procedure for rolled asphalt based on comparison with a "Standard Job" which defines, in statistical terms, a reasonable standard of quality as far as both client and producer are concerned. When a sample* *is taken from a batch of material and its composition determined, the results are assessed in relation to those which would be obtained from a "Standard Job". For the latter, limits can be found outside which only 10% of results would occur ; in the acceptance sampling procedure a result outside these 10% limits classifies the sample as defective.*

(a) Suppose that 4 samples are taken and the acceptance criterion is that not more than 1 should be defective. What is the probability of a batch of the same quality as the "Standard Job" being accepted ?

(b) Suppose that, in the case of rolled asphalt wearing course, samples from the "Standard Job" would give, when analysed for % stone content, results which are $N(30, 2^2)$. What are the limits (symmetrically placed with respect to the mean) outside which only 10% of results would occur ?

(c) For a batch of material for which sample analyses of % stone content are $N(32, 2)$, what is the probability of getting a result outside the 10% limits found in (b) and hence classified as defective ? Deduce the probability of such a batch being accepted under the ($n = 4$, $c = 1$) scheme mentioned in (a).

Ans: (*a*) For the given sampling scheme,

$$P_0 = (q)^4 = (0.9)^4$$
$$P_1 = C_1^4\,(0.9)^3\,(0.1) = 4 \times 0.93 \times 0.1$$
$$P_a = P_0 + P_1 = 0.948$$

(*b*) $N(30, 2^2)$ means a normal distribution with an $\mu = 30$ and $\sigma = 2$.

Table *A* indicates a defective of 10% (area of the normal curve 5% below the lower limit and 5% above the upper limit) and can be achieved when the limits are placed at $\mu \pm 1.645\,\sigma$. Therefore the limits are $30 \pm 1.645 \times 2$ i.e., 26.71 and 33.29.

(*c*) Again the calculations from Table *A* will show that for $N(32, 2^2)$, the area outside the limit of 26.71 is 0.0041 and that outside the limit of 33.29 is 0.2611. Hence total area outside these limits is 0.2652. Hence the *p* in this case is 0.2652.

Now with the sampling scheme of $n = 4$, $c = 1$,

$$\hat{\mu}_{nb} = 4 \times 0.2652 = 1.0608$$

Interpolation in Table *G* indicates $P_a = 0.712$.

Q. 9.39: *Specifications require that a certain quality characteristic of a manufactured product have a minimum value of 200 units. The quality characteristic can be tested only by a destructive test. The product is made in batches of several thousand. The past practice regarding accepting inspection has been to test 4 articles from each batch. If all 4 articles met the quality specification of 200, the batch was accepted. If 2 or more failed, the batch was rejected.*

If 1 failed, a second sample of 4 was taken ; with no failure on the second sample, the batch was accepted, otherwise it was rejected.

(a) What is the probability that a batch containing 5% of defectives will be accepted by this procedure ?

(b) Control charts for $\bar{X}$ and R have been plotted from the first samples. These charts indicate that the range stays in statistical control even though the average shifts from batch to batch. The standard deviation of a batch appears to be 10 units. The suggestion is made that the acceptance decision be based on the average value computed from a single sample 4, with the batch accepted if the average is 210 or more. Assuming that the standard deviation continues to

be at 10 units and assuming a normal distribution of the quality characteristic within a batch, what is the probability of accepting of a 5% defective lot ?

Ans: (*a*) Probability for given conditions can easily be computed with the help of Table *G*. In this case it is 0.954.

(*b*) $\sigma = 10$. Since the batch is 5% defective, therefore, 5% of the products do not meet the specification of 200. Also the averages are normally distributed. From this information value of μ can be calculated.

z corresponding to the 5% are of the normal curve is – 1.645.

$$\therefore \quad -1.645 = \frac{200 - \mu}{10}$$

$$\text{or} \quad \mu = 216.45$$

Now the batch is accepted or rejected on the basis of the sample average. If the average is 210 or more the batch is accepted otherwise it is rejected. Also the standard deviation of the sample average is

$$\frac{\sigma}{\sqrt{n}} = \frac{10}{\sqrt{4}} = 5$$

Area of the normal curve below the average of 210 is the area of rejection.

$$z = \frac{210 - 216.45}{5} = 1.29$$

Corresponding this value of *z*, the area of normal curve below 210 is 0.0985.

$\therefore$ Area of normal curve above 210 is 1 – 0.0985 = 0.9015, or, the probability of acceptance is 0.9015.

Q. 9.40: *Where destructive testing is involved, a common acceptance procedure is to test one article from a lot, passing the lot if the article is satisfactory and taking a second sample of one if the article fails the test. If the second article also fails the lot is rejected, if the second article proves satisfactory, the lot is accepted.*

Plot the O.C. curve for this plan, assuming the submitted lot is large enough so that the selection of a defective article on the first does not make any appreciable change in the probability of getting a defective article on the second sample. What do you think of the quality protection given by this common plan ?

Ans: $n = 1, c = 0$

O.C. curve can be plotted when the probabilities of acceptance corresponding to different *p* values are known.

Let the lot 2% defective

$$\mu_{nb} = 1 \times 0.02 = 0.02$$

From Table *G*,

Probability of acceptance of the lot on the very first sample = 0.980.

Probability that a second sample is drawn = 1 – 0.980 = 0.02.

Probability that a second sample is good = 0.980.

$\therefore$ Total probability of acceptance = 0.980 + (0.02) (0.980) = 0.99960

Similarly when the lot is 10% defective.

Total probability of acceptance = 0.98645.

From the foregoing calculations, it may well be concluded that although the fraction defective has assumed an alarming proportion (10%), still the probability of acceptance is very high, and when the percentage of the defectives increases from 2 to 10, there is a minor decrease in the probability of acceptance. So this sampling plan is not good from the quality protection point of view of consumers.

Q. 9.41: *A proposed triple sampling plan for testing the steel girders is as follows : Take a sample of 2. If both good, accept ; if both bad, reject. If 1 good and 1 bad, take a second sample of 2. If both good, accept ; if both bad, reject. If 1 good and 1 bad, take a third sample of 2. If both in third sample are good, accept ; otherwise reject.*

Assuming the lots to be relatively large and 5% defective, find the probability of acceptance of such lots.

Ans: From Table G,

Probability that the first sample contains 2 good girders = 0.905.

Probability that the second sample is taken (*i.e.* the first sample contains 1 good and 1 bad girder) = 0.995 − 0.905 = 0.09.

Probability that the second sample contains 2 good girders = 0.905

Probability that the third sample is taken (*i.e.* the first as well the second both samples contains 1 good and 1 bad girder) = 0.09 × 0.09 = 0.0081.

Probability that the third sample contains 2 good girders = 0.905

∴ Total probability of acceptance = 0.905 + (0.09) (0.905) + (0.0081) (0.905) = 0.994.

Q. 9.42: *A proposed sampling plan is as follows : Take a sample of 3. If none is defective, accept; if 2 are defective, reject. If 2 good and 1 bad, take a second sample so that the total number of pieces inspected in both the samples is 18% of the lot size. If the second sample is free of defectives, accept the lot ; otherwise reject it.*

Find the probability of acceptance of a lot which is exactly 2% defective and contains the minimum number of pieces so as to exactly stipulate the condition of '2% defective'.

Ans: When the lot is exactly 2% defective and contains minimum number of pieces, it means that it must at least contain 50 pieces.

Hence $N = 50$

$$n_1 = 3$$

$$n_1 + n_2 = 18\% \text{ of } 50 = 9$$

∴ $$n_2 = 6$$

Using the correct combinatorial formulae, it will be found that the probability of acceptance of the lot is 1.

Otherwise also, one can see that the probability of acceptance will always be 1 because a 2% defective lot of 50 pieces will contain only 1 defective and according to the acceptance criteria the lot will never be rejected. When the second sample is taken, it will always be accepted because the only one defective which exists in the lot, will already be taken out in the first sample.

Q. 9.43: *A batch of products are believed to be 10 percent defective. A sample of 10 taken at random is found to be perfect. Does this evidence throw any suspicion on the premise that the batch is in fact 10 percent defective ?*

Ans: A sample found to be perfect means that sample did not contain any defective *i.e.* $c = 0$.

In this case $\mu_{np} = 10\ (0.1)$ *i.e.* 1

From Table *G*, for μ_{np} of 1, the chances of having 0 defective in the sample are 0.368 0.37 or stated a little differently, nearly 37% of samples may be found to contain no defectives. Hence the evidence does not throw any suspicion on the premise that the batch is 10 percent defective

---

Q. 9.44: *Sketch the OC curve for the following scheme : A single item is taken at random from the lot and inspected. If it is defective, the lot is rejected ; otherwise the lot is accepted.*

Ans: As $p + q = 1$, for the given conditions,

$$P_a = P_o = (q)^1 = (1-p)^1 = 1-p$$

$$\therefore \quad P_a = (1-p)$$

The above is the equation of st. line. Thus OC curve is straight line as in Fig. 9.15. Any two points on this line can be determined by putting the values of $P_a = 0$ and 1 in the above equation and determining the corresponding values of *p* which are 1 and 0 respectively.

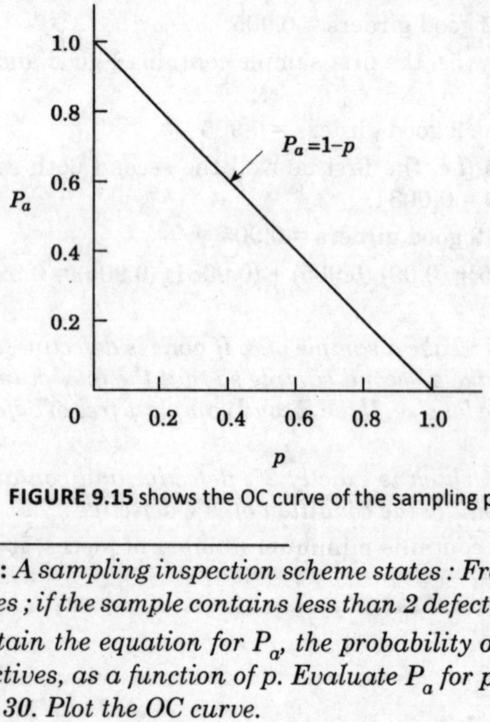

FIGURE 9.15 shows the OC curve of the sampling plan.

Q. 9.45: *A sampling inspection scheme states : From each (large) batch take a random sample of 20 pieces ; if the sample contains less than 2 defectives accept the batch, otherwise reject the batch.*

Obtain the equation for P_a, the probability of accepting a batch containing a proportion p of defectives, as a function of p. Evaluate P_a for p = 0.01, 0.02, 0.03, 0.04, 0.04, 0.07, 0.10, 0.15, 0.20, 0.30. Plot the OC curve.

Ans: Let P_a = Probability of accepting a batch containing a proportion *p* of defectives.

Then $\quad P_a = P_0 + P_1$

Now, for a sample of 20 pieces.

$$P_0 = q^{20}$$

where $q = 1 - p$

$$P_1 = C_1^{20}\, p\, q^{19} = 20\, p\, q^{19}$$

$$P_a = q^{20} + 20\, p\, q^{19}$$

$$= q^{19}\,(q + 20\,p)$$

But $\quad q = 1 - p$

therefore $\quad P_a = (1-p)^{19}\,[(1-p) + 20\,p]$

$$= (1-p)^{19}\,(1 + 19\,p)$$

Substituting any value of p in the above relation, corresponding value of P_a can be calculated substituting $p = 0.01, 0.02$ etc., P_a values are calculated to be as follows.

p	0.01	0.02	0.03	0.05	0.07	0.10	0.15	0.20	0.30
P_a	0.9834	0.9392	0.8803	0.7357	0.5872	0.3918	0.1756	0.0691	0.0075

The OC curve can be drawn based upon computed the data given above.

Q. 9.46: *A double sampling scheme states : 'Take a first sample of 20 ; if 0 or 1 defectives are found, accept the batch ; if 4 or more defectives are found, reject the batch ; if 2 or 3 defectives are found take a further sample of 20 and if, in the combined sample of 40, less than 5 defectives are found, accept the batch ; otherwise reject the batch'.*

Write down the equation of the operating characteristic and plot the curve for values of p of 0.02, 0.03, 0.05, 0.07, 0.10, 0.15, 0.20, 0.25

Read off (a) of Producer's Risk for a p of 0.05

(b) the value of p for Consumer's Risk of 10%.

Ans: From the given conditions, the value of P_a can be calculated as

$$P_a = P_0 + P_1 + P_2\,(P_0 + P_1 + P_2) + P_3\,(P_0 + P_1)$$

where

$$P_0 = (1 - p)^{20}$$

$$P_1 = 20\,p\,(1 - p)^{19}$$

$$P_2 = 109\,p^2\,(1 - p)^{18}$$

$$P_3 = 1140\,p^3\,(1 - p)^{17}$$

Following tabulation gives the values of P_a, P_0 P_1, P_2, P_3 for different values of p. These values can be used for plotting the OC curve

p	P_a	P_0	P_1	P_2	P_3
0.02	0.9977	0.6770	0.2722	0.0528	0.0065
0.03	0.9931	0.5439	0.3364	0.0988	0.0183
0.05	0.9539	0.3584	0.3773	0.1887	0.0596
0.07	0.8662	0.2344	0.3528	0.2523	0.1139
0.10	0.6574	0.1216	0.2702	0.2852	0.1901
0.15	0.3113	0.0388	0.1368	0.2296	0.2432
0.20	0.1115	0.0115	0.0576	0.1368	0.2061
0.25	0.0334	0.0032	0.0210	0.0665	0.1336

From the OC curve, or above tabulation it can be seen that when

$p = 0.05$, $\quad P_a = 0.9539$

(*a*) The Producer's Risk (α) = 1 – Pa

= 0.0461

(*b*) For consumer's Risk (β) of 0.10, value of $p = 0.207$.

Q. 9.47: *(a) Construct the power curve (i.e. OC curve) for the risk of rejecting a batch containing not more than the specified proportion of defectives p, is 0.1 when the sample size n is 50. At the same time we accept the samples when the number of defectives per sample does not exceed 2.*

(b) For approximately the same risk of wrong rejection, establish the decision rule when the sample size n is 150 and construct the power curve for the sampling plan.

Ans: (*a*) Assuming the different values of *p*, the OC curve of the sampling plan $n = 50; c = 2$, can be drawn.

At a specified value of *p*, the risk of wrong rejection is 0.1. It means that at this specified *p* the probability of acceptance is 0.9 when the above sampling plan is operating.

From Table *G*, under the column "headed $c = 2$", when P_a is 0.900, the corresponding value of μ_{np} is 1.1.

Since

$$n = 50$$

$$p = \frac{1.1}{50}$$

$$= 0.022$$

(*b*) Now, at this value of *p i.e.* at a *p* value of 0.022 and n of 150, we have to find the value of *c* such that the probability of acceptance is approximately 0.900 so that the risk of wrong rejection approximately remains same *i.e.* 0.100.

Using Table *G* again,

$$\mu_{np} = 150 \times 0.022 = 3.3$$

Interpolation from Table *G* indicates that at *c* value of 5, the probability of acceptance is 0.883 *i.e.* approx 0.900. Therefore risk of wrong rejection is 0.117.

Hence the sampling plan is

$$n = 150; c = 5$$

Assuming different values of *p* the *OC* curve can be drawn.

Q. 9.48: *A manufacturer knows that a supplier of components produces one defective item in 100. He instructs his quality control department to open each batch delivered and randomly select 100 items. If more than one defective is found, the batch is returned to the supplier. The manager of the quality control department criticises this instruction. Why ?*

Ans:

$$\mu_p = \frac{1}{100}$$

$$\mu_{np} = 100 \times \frac{1}{100} = 1$$

Using Table *G* $\quad P_a = 0.736$

This means that irrespective of the size of the batch, about 26.4 per cent of the batches will be returned. Such a large rejection will not only spoil the relations between the supplier and the manufacturer but also create problems for the manufacturer to meet his schedule.

As it appears that the batch is much larger than the sample size of 100 and it is likely to contain more than 1 defective. In fact larger the batch size, the greater number of defectives it is supposed to contain.

In these circumstances, it would have been much better if the acceptance number would have been specified as 2 in which case the probability of acceptance is 0.920 or on the average only 8 percent of the lots would be returned to the supplier.

The other alternative open is to have some double sampling plan.

Q. 9.49: *An electrical manufacturer receives components from three different suppliers. At present, the user accepts lots based on his own sampling plan. The policy is to draw a random sample equal to 10% of the lot size with a lot being rejected if one or more defective components are found. Suppliers A, B, and C submit components in lots of 100, 250, and 1,000 respectively.*

(a) Use Table G to determine for each supplier the lot fractions defective for which 95%, 50%, and 10% of the lots will be accepted.

(b) Do you consider the user's sampling plan fair ? Why or why not ?

Ans: (*a*) Let us first consider the supplier *A*

$$N = 100$$

$$n = 10\% \text{ of } 100 = 10,\ c = 0$$

$$P_a = 0.95 \text{ or } 95\%$$

Interpolation from Table *G* indicates that when $c = 0$ and $P_a = 0.95$, np 0.05

Hence $$p = \frac{0.05}{10} = 0.005$$

Proceeding in the same way, the following tabulation gives all the results at a glance.

Supplier	*n*	μ_p *when* $P_a = 0.95$	μ_p *when* $P_a = 0.50$	μ_p *when* $P_a = 0.10$
A	10	0.005	0.0065	0.23
B	25	0.002	0.0026	0.092
C	100	0.0005	0.00065	0.023

From above it can be concluded that user's sampling plan is not fair which will be clear from the following explanation :

If we draw the OC curves for three sampling plans and analyse them, we will notice that for any fixed percentage of defectives (for example 4%), P_a for producer *A* is 42%, P_a for producer *B* is 37%, P_a for producer *C* is 1.35%, obviously producer *C* is most adversely affected inspite of the fact that he is making the product of the same quality (*i.e.* 4%).

Or, considering in a slightly different way, the curves will show that for a fixed P_a (for example 50%) the producer *C* has to submit approximately 10 times better lots as compared to producer *A*.

Thus it is concluded that user is using the sampling scheme which gives different Producer's Risk for different lot sizes and it is for this reason that this scheme does not appear to be fair.

Q. 9.50: *The single sampling plan* $n = 35$ *and* $c = 1$ *has* $\alpha = 0.16$ *and* $\beta = 0.14$, *both too large for a company.*

(a) What would happen to α *and* β *if c were increased but n remained at 35 ? If c decreased?*

(b) What would happen if n increased with c constant ? If n decreased ?

(c) Why do we need to increase both n and c to lower both α *and* β *?*

Ans: (*a*) Increasing *c* relaxes the criterion for accepting a lot. Both β and $1 - \alpha$ are acceptance probabilities, so β goes up and α goes down. Decreasing *c* has the opposite effect.

(*b*) Larger *n* means more chances to find enough defectives to reject the lot; so β goes down and α rises. Lower *n* has the opposite effect.

(*c*) Larger *n* gives us more information about the lot.

The cut off level has to be chosen relative to *n*; we are concerned with fraction defective which is measured by *c*/*n*.

Q. 9.51: *Determine the OC curve of the following scheme. 'A sample of 10 items is to be drawn at random from each lot and the lot rejected if any defectives are found'.*

Comment on its desirability.

Ans: OC curve can be determined by assuming various values of p and finding P_a by using either binomial distribution or Poisson distribution.

It may be noted that the lot is acceptable when no defective is found.

Using Table G, following table can be prepared to sketch the OC curve.

μ_p	0	0.1	0.2	0.3	0.4	0.5	0.6	0.7	0.8	0.9	1.0
μ_{np}	0	1	2	3	4	5	6	7	8	9	10
P_a	1.00	0.368	0.135	0.050	0.018	0.007	0.002	0.001	0	0	0

The OC curve is shown in Fig. 9.16. This shape of the OC curve gives a notably poor Producer's Risk.

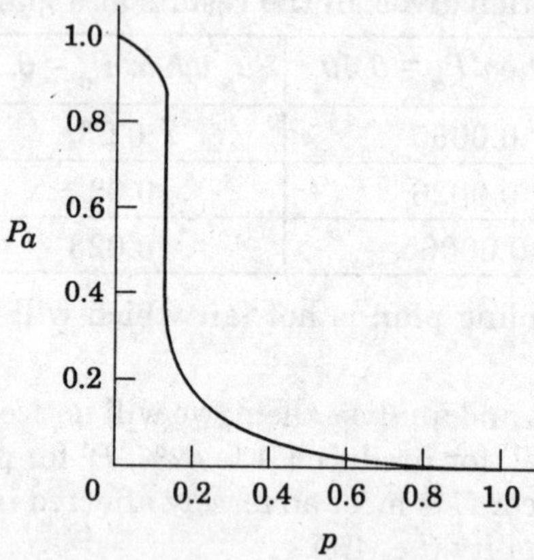

FIGURE 9.16 OC curve of the sampling plan $n = 10$; $c = 0$

Q. 9.52: *(a) State at least one situation where acceptance sampling is not recommended.*

(b) State some situations where acceptance by sampling is a better choice or the only choice.

(c) What is an ideal sampling scheme and why the firms generally do not opt for ideal sampling schemes ?

(d) What should be the quality of any sampling plan ?

(e) What are the two parameters of a sampling plan ?

Ans: (*a*) In precision engineering it is not uncommon for every item in it to be inspected and acceptance sampling is not recommended.

(*b*) There are many situations where for various reasons 100 percent inspection is not feasible and hence acceptance sampling is a better choice. One reason might be that the cost of inspection would be too high. Another might be the inspection involves a destructive test, as in determining the blowing time of a fuse where the fuse, is destroyed by the test. In this case acceptance sampling is the only choice, otherwise nothing will be left.

(*c*) Where a sampling scheme is such that it accepts all the satisfactory lots and rejects all the unsatisfactory lots. The OC curve of such a scheme is a vertical line erected vertically at the maximum acceptable value of p.

Such an ideal scheme is rendered impracticable by the amount of inspection it would require. In order to achieve this ideal complete lot of size N is to be inspected. Hence the firms generally do not opt for ideal sampling schemes which involve 100% inspection.

(*d*) The most we can look for in an acceptance sampling plan is that the probability of acceptance should be high for lots of good quality and low for lots of poor quality. This would mean the OC curve being as near to the ideal as possible within the limitations of the amount of inspection that can be carried out.

(*e*) Any sampling plan is defined by its the two parameters, the sample size (n) and the maximum allowable number of defectives often called the acceptance number (c).

Q. 9.53: *A single sampling inspection scheme for large lot of mass produced flanges states:*

From each lot take and inspect a random sample of 50. If 3 or more defective, inspect the whole lot and remove all defectives, if less than 3 are found accept the lot without further inspection.

Obtain the equation for P_a, the probability that a lot containing a fraction p of defectives will be accepted, in terms of p.

Evaluate P_a for p = 0.01, 0.02, 0.03, 0.05, 0.07, 0.10, 0.15, 0.20, 0.30.

Plot the operating characteristic and average outgoing quality curve.

Estimate : (a) the Producer's Risk at p of $2\frac{1}{2}$ %

(b) the Consumer's Risk for LTPD of 6.0 per cent.

Ans: Let P_a = probability of accepting a lot containing a fraction p of defectives.

P_0, P_1, P_2 = Probability of drawing a random samples containing exactly 0, 1 or 2 defectives respectively.

By addition law of probability $(P_a) = P_0 + P_1 + P_2$

Now, for a sample of 50 pieces,

$$P_0 = q^{50} \text{ where } q = 1 - p$$

$$P_1 = C_1^{50}\, pq^{40} = 50pq^{49}$$

$$P_2 = C_2^{50}\, p^2 q^{48} = \frac{50 \times 49}{1} = p^2 q^{48} = 1225\, p^2 q^{48}$$

$\therefore$ $$P_a = q^{50} + 50pq^{49} + 1225p^2q^{48} = q^{48}\,(q^2 + 50pq + 1225p^2)$$

Since $$q = 1 - p$$

Therefore, $$P_a = (1 - p)^{48}\,[(1 - p)^2 + 50p\,(1 - p) + 1225p^2]$$
$$= (1 - p)^{48}\,(1176p^2 + 48p + 1)$$

therefore, P_a is the probability of obtaining 2 or less successes (*i.e.* find a defective) in 50 trial (inspecting 50 components). Substituting the successive values of p, we tabulate the values of probability as follows :

p = 0.01	0.02	0.03	0.05	0.07	0.10	0.15	0.20	0.25
p_a = 0.9862	0.9216	0.8108	0.5405	0.3108	0.1117	0.0142	0.0013	0.0001

The operation characteristic from these above values is shown in Fig. 9.17. Since the calculations by Binomial (as obtained by the above formula for P_a) are quite tedious and time consuming, the use of Table G (Poisson Distribution) is recommended and the values of P_a corresponding to the various values of p are given below.

p = 0.01	0.02	0.03	0.05	0.07	0.10	0.15	0.20	0.25
P_a = 0.986	0.920	0.809	0.544	0.321	0.125	0.0205	0.003	0.000

(Note the these values or P_a are *not* significantly different from those above.)

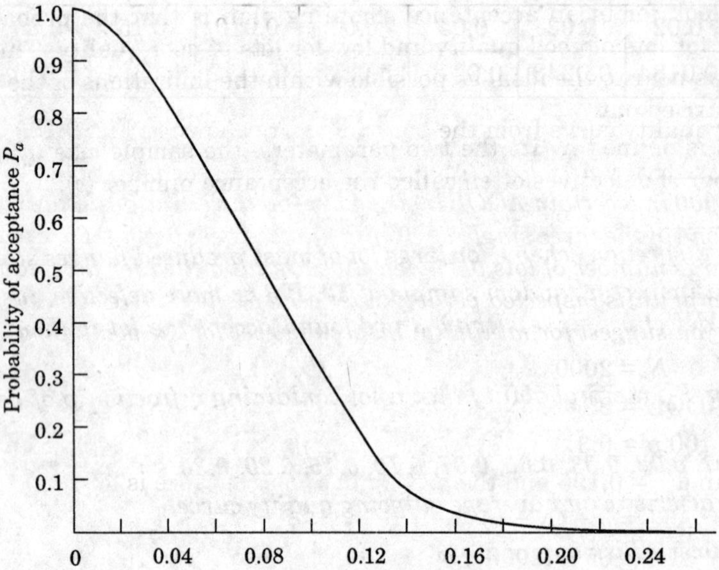

FIGURE 9.17 OC curve of the given sampling plan.

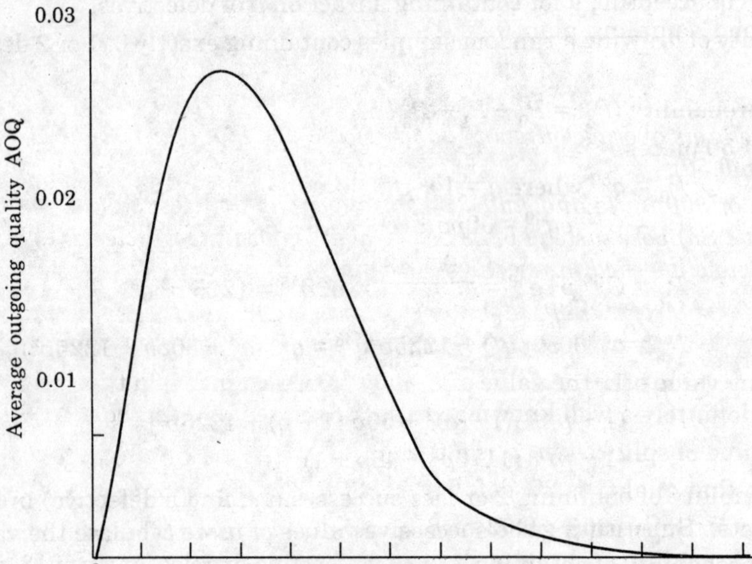

FIGURE 9.18 AOQ curve of the given sampling plan.

From the OC curve,

when $p = 0.025 \quad P_a = 0.88$

$p = 0.060 \; P_a = 0.42$

i.e., Producer's Risk = 100 – 88 = 12%

and Consumer's Risk = 42 percent for LTPD of 6%.

Since it is known that AOQ = $P_{a\,p}$.

Tabulating AOQ for all values of *p* we have

$p = 0.01$	0.02	0.03	0.05	0.07	0.010	0.15	0.20	0.25
$AOQ = 0.0099$	0.0184	0.0243	0.0273	0.0218	0.0112	0.0021	0.0003	0

The average outgoing quality curve from the above data are shown in Fig. 9.18.

Q. 9.54: *The lot size N is 2000 in a certain AOQL inspection procedure. The desired AOQL of 2% can be obtained with any one of the three single sampling plans. These are n = 65, c = 2; n = 41, c = 1 ; n = 18, c = 0. If a large number of lots 0.3% defective are submitted for acceptance, what will be the average number of units inspected per lot under each of these three sampling plans ? Which of three plans will you suggest for minimum inspection cost for the mentioned quality ?*

Ans:

$$N = 2000$$
$$\text{AOQL} = 2\%$$
$$100\,p = 0.3$$

For first sampling plan $\mu_{np} = 0.195$ and the probability of acceptance is 0.999.

$$\text{ATI} = n + (N - n)\,(1 - P_a)$$
$$= 65 + (2000 - 65)\,(1 - 0.999) = 67$$

Similarly the average number of articles inspected per lot for second and third sampling plans are 55 and 121 respectively.

Obviously the second sampling plan (n = 41, c = 1) should be suggested for minimum inspection cost.

Q. 9.55: *Your supplies claims average outgoing quality to be 2%. Plot the OC curve. What is the value of split risk (i.e. p 0.50).*

You take a sample of 900 units and find 33 nonconforming articles. Would you reject his claim ? Why or why not ? Suppose instead of 33 only 5 non-conforming articles are found in the sample of 900. Are you now justified in rejecting his claim?

Ans:

$$\%\text{AOQ} = (100p)\,(P_a)$$
$$2 = (100p)\,(P_a) \qquad \text{...(1)}$$

From Eq. (1), for any value of p, the value of P_a may be determined and thus a curve can be plotted. The curves is definitely a well known geometrical curve, *i.e.* hyperbola.

From above, the value of split risk $p_{0.50}$ is 0.04.

On the assumption that quality is 2% defective,

$$\mu_{np} = 900 \times 0.02 = 18.$$

From Table *G* the probability of obtaining 33 nonconforming articles for *np* of 18, is 1. This means that there is every possibility of obtaining 33 nonconforming articles in a sample of 900 when the quality is 2% nonconforming. Hence the supplier's claim should not be rejected.

Again from Table *G* the probability of obtaining 5 nonconforming articles in a sample of 900 when the quality is 2% nonconforming is 0. Here it is justified to reject his claim.

Q. 9.56: *(a) The values listed below are points on the OC curve of the sampling plan 25 (1/2), (that is, take a sample of 25, accept of 1 or less defectives are found, reject if 2 or more are found). Plot the AOQ curve for the plan. What is the AOQL ?*

(b) If you were asked if the plan guaranteed that the outgoing quality of a lot would never be worse than 3.5% defectives what would you reply ?

Ans: (*a*) Assuming that AOQ = $p\ (P_a)$

Where p = fraction defective

P_a = Probability of acceptance

For the given data

p	0	0.02	0.04	0.06	0.08	0.10	0.15	0.20
P_a	1	0.91	0.74	0.55	0.40	0.27	0.09	0.30
$AOQ = p\ (P_a)$	0	0.0182	0.296	0.0330	0.0320	0.0270	0.0135	0.0060

Figure 9.19 shows the AOQ curve.

From the graph AOQL can be estimated as approximately 0.0335 or 3.35%.

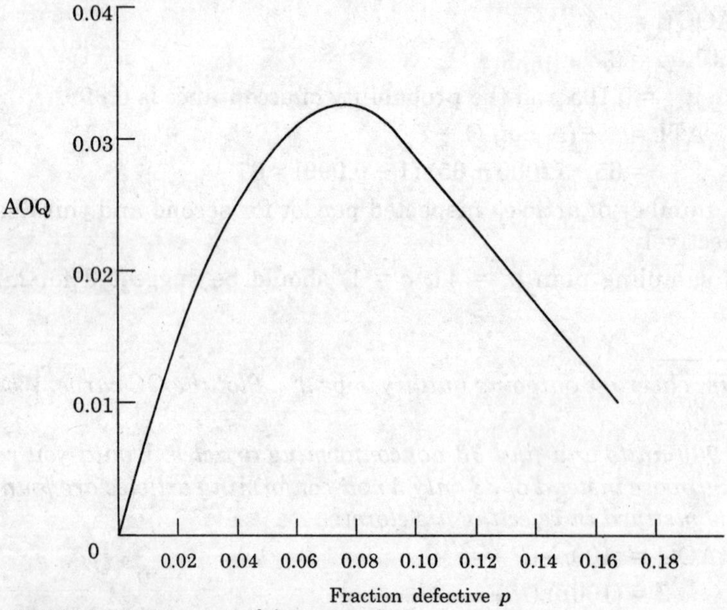

FIGURE 9.19 AOQ curve of the given scheme

Percentage defective (%p)	0	2	4	6	8	10	15	20
Probability of acceptance (P_a)	1 0.91	0.74	0.55	0.40	0.27	0.09	0.03	

(Make an additional assumption that all rejected lots are sorted and detailed).

(*b*) A sampling scheme cannot guarantee individual lot properties, only average lot properties. A 'bad' lot could give a freakishly 'good' sample and be passed undetailed.

Q. 9.57: *If the lots with fraction defective μp are submitted to a given 'single sampling plan'; derive expressions for AOQ assuming the following conditions :*

(a) All the defectives found in accepted samples are discarded and all the rejected lots are fully screened.

(b) If it is desired to maintain the some lot size after and final inspection.

Prove that the ratio of average items inspected in (a) and (b) is (1 − p).

Ans: Let N be the lot size.

n be the sample size.

P_a be the probability of acceptance; and

K be the total number of lots submitted for inspection.

(*a*) Number of defectives in accepted samples

$$= (KP_a)\,[p\,(N-n)]$$

Average lot size of the lot after discarding the defectives

$$= N - pn - p\,(1 - P_a)\,(N - n)$$

$$AOQ = \frac{(P_a K)[p(N-n)]}{K[N - pn - p(1-P_a)(N-n)]}$$

$$= \frac{P_a p(N-n)}{N - pn - p(1-P_a)(N-n)}$$

(*b*) Since the lot size is to remain the same, therefore,

$$AOQ = \frac{P_a p(N-n)}{N}$$

Let ATI_1 be the average number of items inspected per lot in (a), then

$$ATI_1 = n + (1 - P_a)\,(N - n) = N - P_a\,(N - n).$$

Let ATI_2 be the average number of items inspected per lot in (*b*),

then $\quad ATI_2 = n + (1 - P_a)\,(N - n) + p\,[n + (1 - P_a)\,(N - n)] + p^2\,[n + (1 - P_a\,(N - n) + ...$

$$= [n + (1 - P_a)\,(N - n)]\,(1 + p + p^2 + ...),$$

$$= [N - P_a\,(N - n)] \times 1 - p$$

There $\quad \dfrac{ATI_2}{ATI_1} = 1 - p.$

Q. 9.58: *An automobile supplier produces headlight dimmer switches. In order to maintain adequate customer relations, she must maintain an average outgoing quality of 2% or less in lots of 1000 switches. She currently uses an acceptance sampling plan with sample size n = 100 and acceptance number c = 2.*

The AOQ curve for the plan is shown in the Fig. 9.20.

(a) What is the worst average outgoing quality performance her sampling plan will allow ?

(b) The past 20 batches were 100% inspected to determine how the fraction defective varies. The following table describes the result :

Incoming fraction defective	*0.01*	*0.03*	*0.05*	*0.07*
Number of times observed	*3*	*8*	*8*	*1*

Make an estimate of the long-run average outgoing fraction defective.

(c) Compare your answers to parts (a) and (b), and discuss.

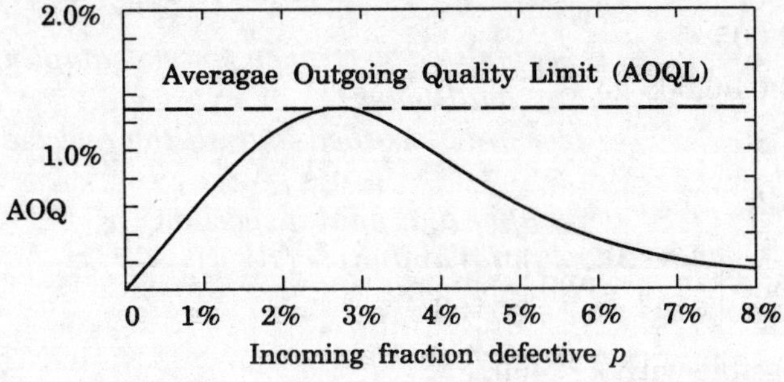

FIGURE 9.20

Ans: (*a*) From Fig 9.20, it is obvious AOQL = 1.23% or 0.0123

(*b*) From Fig 9.17 it is also obvious, that

when $p = 0.01$ (1%), AOQ is 0.8% or 0.008

when $p = 0.03$ (3%), AOQ is 1.2% or 0.012

when $p = 0.05$ (5%), AOQ is 0.6% or 0.006

when $p = 0.07$ (7%), AOQ is 0.2% or 0.002

Long-run average of outgoing fraction defective :

(0.008) (3/20) + (0.012) (8/20) + (0.006) (8/20) + (0.002) (1/20) = 0.0085.

(*c*) AOQL is an upper limit on the long run fraction defective in the outgoing batches. Therefore (*a*) should be higher than (*b*), It is of course there.

Q. 9.59: *Based on the data of Prob 9.58, which of the following statements can be said true or false?*

(*a*) *The outgoing quality of each and every batch is better than 1.23% defective.*

(*b*) *The most likely incoming fraction defective is about 2.3%.*

(*c*) *Incoming batches with 2% defective yield worse outgoing quality than batches with 5% defective on the average.*

(*d*) *An incoming batch with 5% defectives is less likely to be rejected than one with 2% defective.*

(*e*) *Incoming fraction defective is very likely to be above 7%.*

Ans: (*a*) Statement is False

(*c*) Statement is True

(*b*), (*d*) and (*e*) statements cannot be judged from the AOQ curve of Fig. 9.20.

Q. 9.60: *A single-sampling acceptance plan is required for a purchased product. The probability of acceptance must be 0.95 or more if the percent defective is 0.5 percent or less. Find three different combinations of sample size and acceptance number to meet this condition. The sample size must not be greater than 400 items. The Poisson distribution may be used as an approximation.*

Ans:

$$p_a = 0.95 \text{ or more}$$

As Poisson is applicable, using Table G, different combinations of n and c can be used to satisfy the above requirements.

Let us assume $c = 0$

Under the coloumn $c = 0$, when $p_a = 0.961$ (slightly greater than 0.95), $\mu_{np} = 0.04$

As

$$p = 0.005,$$

$$n = 0.04/0.005 \text{ i.e. } 8$$

Hence one combination is $\begin{bmatrix} n = 80 \\ c = 0 \end{bmatrix}$

Similarly, other two combinations $\begin{bmatrix} n = 70 \\ c = 1 \end{bmatrix}$ and $\begin{bmatrix} n = 160 \\ c = 2 \end{bmatrix}$

Other combinations are also possible with $n < 400$.

Q. 9.61: *Suppose that a supplier ships components in lots of size 5,000. A single-sampling plan with n = 50 and c = 2 is being used for receiving inspection.*

(a) *Draw the OC curve for this plan.*

(b) *Find the level of lot quality that will be rejected 90% of the time.*

(c) *Management has objected to the use of the above sampling procedure and wants to use a plan with an acceptance number c = 0, arguing that this is more consistent with their zero-defects program. What do you think of this?*

(d) *Design a single-sampling plan with c = 0 that will give a 0.90 probability of rejection of lots having the quality level found in part (b). Note that the two plans are now matched at the LTPD point. Draw the OC curve for this plan and compare it to the one for n = 50, c = 2 in part (a).*

(e) *Suppose that incoming lots are 0.5% noncon-forming. What is the probability of rejecting these lots under both plans? Calculate the ATI at this point for both plans. Which plan do you prefer? Why?*

Ans: (a) The OC curve can be drawn taking various values of p. For example when $p = 0.01$, $P_a = 0.910$ and $p = 0.1$, the $p_a = 0.125$.

(b) Since the level of lot quality that will be rejected 90% of the time, it means that probability of acceptance of the lot is only 10% or 0.1 *i.e.* $P_a = 0.1$. From Table *G* Under column c = 2, interpolation between μ_{np} of 5.2 and 5.4 will np of 5.32 . Hence $p = 0.106$

(c) This is not a right policy as during manufacture some defectives are likely to occur and keeping $c = 0$, would tantamount to 100% inspection.

(d) Since the probability of rejection is 0.9, therefore, probability of acceptance *i.e.* $P_a = 0.1$. Again using table *G* column c = 0, the $\mu_p \approx 2.3$.. For p of 0.106, $n = 10$ Hence $n = 20$ a_{bd} c = 0. This OC curve will be much steeper than the curve in (*a*)

(e) For $p = 0.5\%$ *i.e.* 0.005

Case (*i*) $n = 50$, $c = 2$ table c_1 gives P_a of 0.998. Hence Probability of rejection is 0.002.

Case (*ii*) $n = 20$, c = 0, table *G* give P_a of 0.905 *i.e.* probability of rejection is 0.095.

ATI in case (*i*) = 50 + (5000 – 50) (1 – 0.998) = 60

ATI in case (*ii*) = 20 + (5000 – 20) (1–0.905) = 493

Hence case (*i*) will be preferred.

Q. 9.62: *(a) Explain the stepwise operation of the following double sampling scheme. 100, $100_{1/4}$*

(b) *Determine the probability of*

(*i*) *acceptance of the lot on the first sample*

(*ii*) *rejection of the lot on the first sample*

(*iii*) *taking a second sample*

of a 2% defective lot under scheme (a).

(c) *How a double sampling scheme is beneficial?*

(d) *The quality protection by scheme in (a) can also be achieved by single sampling scheme as $200_{3/4}$. The how do you compare these two schemes with respect to quantum of inspection?*

Ans: (*a*) The operation of the scheme 100, $100_{1/4}$ is as follows.

Take a first sample of 100,

1. (*i*) If the number of defectives is 0 or 1 accept the lot

   (*ii*) If the number of defectives is 2 or 3, take a second sample

   (*iii*) If the number of defectives is 4 or more, reject the lot.

2. Take a second sample of 100,

   (*i*) If the total number of defectives in two samples is 3 or less accept the lot.

   (*ii*) If the total number of defectives is 4 or more, reject the lot.

(*b*) Using Table *G* and μ_{np} or 2.0 the following probabilities are following :

(*i*) 0.406

(*ii*) 0.143

(*iii*) 1 – (0.406 + 0.143) *i.e.* 0.451

(*c*) The idea behind the double sampling is to reduce the amount of inspection work that has to be done. Good quality work will be accepted immediately and low quanlity work rejected immediately on the first sample. Borderline work will be assessed by the use of the second sample.

(*d*) Though single sampling scheme $200_{3/4}$ *i.e.* (n = 200 and c = 3), will give almost the same quality protection, as double scheme 100, $100_{1/4}$, the amount of inspection in single sampling is more than equivalent double sampling scheme. Where two sampling schemes have identifical or near identical OC curve, they can be compared by their average sample size (more commonly known as average sample number, *i.e.* ASN). The ASN refers to average number of items inspected in sampling. This is different from ATI, which applies only to cases where rejected lots are submitted to 100% inspection.

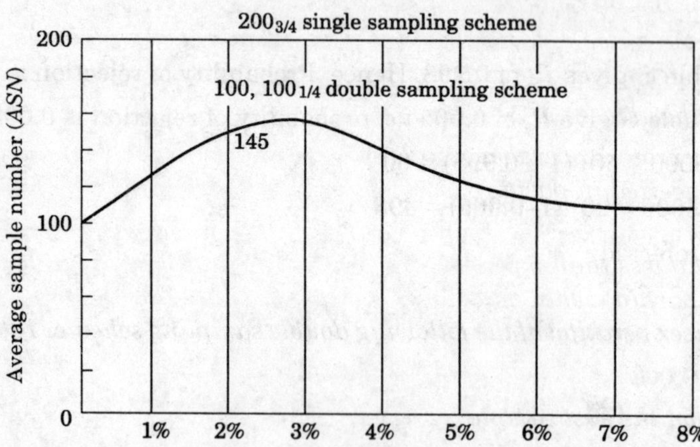

FIGURE 9.20: Graph of average sample number (ASN) vs. % defective.

(**Note.** The concept of ASN is further explained in Chap. 10) In case of single sampling, ASN = n (*i.e.* constant)

In case of double sampling ASN = $n_1 + n_2 \times$ (Probability of taking a second sample) Hence in this case,

ASN (single sampling) = 200

ASN (double sampling) = 100 + 100 (0.51) = 145

Figure 9.18 Shows the comparison of ASN vs. %p for single and double schemes. This figures shows that ASN for double sampling is always less than ASN for equivalent single sampling.

Q. 9.63: *You are responsible for purchasing bearings for the maintenance department of a large airline. The bearings are under contract from a local supplier, and you must devise an appropriate acceptance sampling plan for them. Management has stated in the contract that the acceptable quality level is 1 percent defective. In addition, the lot tolerance proportion defective is 4 percent, the producer's risk is 5 percent, and the consumer's risk is 10 percent.*

(a) Specify an appropriate acceptance sampling plan that meets all these criteria.

(b) Draw the OC curve for your plan. What is the resultant producer's risk ?

(c) Determine the AOQL for your plan. Assume a lot size of 3000.

Ans: (*a*) $p_1 = 0.01$ and $\alpha = 0.005$, *i.e.* $P = 1 - \alpha = 0.95$

$$p_2 = 0.04 \text{ and } P_a = 0.10$$

Using Table *G* and trial and miss method, one suitable sampling plan is : [$n = 280$ and $c = 6$.]

(*b*) The OC curve can be constructed by assuming various value of p ranging from 0 to 0.06. The P_a for p of 0.01 is found to be 0.976. Hence $\alpha = 1 - 0.976$ *i.e.* 0.024.

(c) The %AOQ is $\left(1 - \frac{n}{N}\right) P_a$ (100p). By taking values of p from 0.01 to 0.02, the AOQL is found to be 1.22%.

Q. 9.64: *Your company supplies sterile syrings to a distributor of hospital supplies. The contract states that quality should be no worse than 0.2 percent defective, or 20 parts in 10,000. During negotiations, you learned that the distributor will use an acceptance sampling plan with n = 400 to test quality.*

(a) If the Producer's risk is to be no greater than 5 percent, what is the lowest acceptance number, c, that should be used ?

(b) The syringe production process averages 2.5 defective parts in 10,000. With n = 400 and the acceptance level suggested in part (a), what is the % probability that a shipment will be returned to you ?

(c) Suppose that you want a less than 5 percent chance that your shipment will be returned to you. For the data in part (b), what acceptance number, c, should you have suggested in (a) ? What is the producer's risk for that plan ?

Ans: (*a*) $n = 400$ $p = 0.2\%$ *i.e.* 0.002

$$\mu_{np} = 400 \times .002 = 0.8$$

If Producer's risk is no greater than 5% *i.e.* 0.05, the P_a should be ≥ 0.95.

From Table *G*, for μ_{np} of 0.8, that the for $P_a \geq 0.95$, that $c = 2$, which is the minimum value of c, which gives P_a of 0.953 i.e. it meets the requirement of $P_a \geq 0.95$.

Producer's risk = 1–0.953 = 0.047

(*b*)
$$p = 25/10{,}000 = 0.0025$$
$$\mu_{np} = 400 \times 0.0025 = 1.0.$$

From Table *G*, $P_a = 0.920$

Hence probability of rejection = 0.08 *i.e.* 8%.

(*c*) $P_a \geq 0.95$

with $\mu_{np} = 1.0$, and $P_a \geq 0.95$, from Table *G*, the acceptance number *c* = 3.

In part (*a*) $\mu_{np} = 0.8$. When *c* = 3, $P_a = 0.991$

Hence Producer's Risk = 1 – 0.991 ≡ 0.009

Q. 9.65: *An inspection station has been installed between two production processes. The feeder process, when operating correctly, has an acceptable quality level of 3 percent. The consuming process, which is expensive, has a specified lot tolerance proportion defective of 8 percent. The feeding process produces in batch sizes; if a batch is rejected by the inspector, the entire batch must be checked and the defective items reworked. Consequently, management wants no more than a 5 percent Producer's risk and, because of the expensive process that follows, no more than a 10 percent chance of accepting a lot with 8 percent defectives or worse.*

(*a*) *Determine the appropriate sample size, n, and the acceptable number of defective items in the sample, c.*

(*b*) *Calculate values and draw the OC curve for this inspection station.*

(*c*) *What is the probability that a lot with 5 percent defectives will be rejected ?*

Ans: (*a*) For AQL = 3%, LTPD = 8%, α = 5%, and β = 10%, use Table *G* and trial and error to arrive at a sampling plan. One suitable sampling plan is : [*n* = 180 and *c* = 9.]

$$np = 180\ (0.03) = 5.4$$

$$\alpha = 0.049\ (i.e.\ 4.9\%)$$

$$np = 180\ (0.08) = 14.4$$

$$\beta = 0.092\ (i.e.\ 9.2\%)$$

Other sampling plans that would also work are *n* = 200, *c* = 10 ; *n* = 220, *c* = 11 ; and *n* = 240, *c* = 12.

(*b*) The following table prepared with the help of Table *G* contains the data for the OC curve shown in Fig. 9.21.

Proportion Defective (p)	*np*	*Probability of c or Less Defective* (P_a)	*Comments*
0.01	1.8	1.000	
0.02	3.6	0.996	
0.03 (AQL)	5.4	0.951	α = 1 – 0.951 = 0.049
0.04	7.2	0.810	
0.05	9.0	0.587	
0.06	10.8	0.363	
0.07	12.6	0.194	
0.08 (LTPD)	14.4	0.092	β = 0.092
0.09	16.2	0.039	
0.10	18.0	0.015	

(*c*) According to the table, the probability of accepting a lot with 5 percent defectives is 0.587. Therefore the probability that a lot with 5 percent defects will be rejected is 0.413, 1.00—0.587 or 0.413.

Q. 9.66: *(a) In which circumstances a double-sampling or sequential sampling is preferred to single sampling plan?*

(b) What is an OC curve?

(c) Why the quality level in rectified inspection is generally high?

Ans:

(*a*) Attribute sampling can be done with single-sampling, double-sampling, or sequential-sampling plans. When the lot proportion defective is either very low or very high, the last two have an advantage over single-sampling plans because the average number of items (ANI) needed to make a decision is smaller.

(*b*) When less than 100 percent of the lot is inspected, the sample may not be an accurate representation of the lot.

There are risks of accepting poor quality materials or rejecting good quality materials. The OC curves provide a graphic display of the performance of a sampling plan. They show how the probability of accepting a lot decreases with an increasing proportion defective in the lot.

(*c*) In rectified inspection, the defectives found in the samples of the accepted lots are replaced with good ones and it is for this reason that the material leaving the inspection area (outgoing) will have a very high quality level. The average outgoing quality will depend on the original quality of the lot and the sampling plan used to identify and correct defects. Sampling plan parameters may be adjusted to provide an acceptable average outgoing quality limit

CHAPTER

10 Dodge-Romig : LTPD & AOQL & ABC or MIL-STD 105E : AQL Sampling Plans and Tables

10.1 SELECTING AN ACCEPTANCE INSPECTION PROCEDURE

The great bulk of acceptance inspection is carried out on an attribute basis, with articles classified into those conforming to specifications and those failing to conform. Attributes inspection is well adopted to the establishment of standard sampling procedures. Further any sampling scheme or procedure should essentially consider the *economy in inspection* and at the same time *quality improvement*. Sampling plans have been devised and published based upon the balance between these two essential requisites. For example, the Dodge-Romig sampling plans are based upon the screening the rejected lots and thus leading to quality improvement and also total minimum inspection. Similarly *ABC* system recognizes the fact that if quality is within limits, the amount of inspection can be reduced and if the quality is bad then the amount of inspection should be more than normal. Consumer can choose any one of the plans suitable to his/her requirements or can design his own sampling plan based upon the concepts presented in Chap. 11. However, most of the industrial acceptance schemes are taken from these published plans. This chapter therefore, presents the most widely used systems—Dodge-Romig system and *ABC* system.

10.2 DODGE-ROMIG (D-R) SAMPLING PLANS

The Dodge-Romig (abbreviated as **D-R**) sampling system employs the $p_{0.10}$ point as the index to two sets of tables in the system. The point 100 $p_{0.10}$ is termed as the Lot Tolerance Percent Defective (LTPD), that percent defective which has a probability of acceptance of 0.10. Thus the two sets of tables are indexed on Consumer's Risk —(□), where (□) equal 0.10.

Another set of two tables is indexed on *Average Outgoing Quality Limit* (AOQL). The concept of AOQL was developed in Chap. 9.

All of the sampling plans in the D-R tables aim at minimizing the ATI considering both sampling inspection and screening of the rejected lots. Thus the D-R volume contains four sets of tables, as follows :

I. Single Sampling Lot Tolerance Tables

II. Double Sampling Lot Tolerance Tables

III. Single Sampling AOQL Tables

IV. Double Sampling AOQL Tables

Sets I and II apply to the following lot tolerance percent defectives (LTPD), (assuming Consumer's Risk = 0.10):

0.5%	3.0%	7.0%
1.0%	4.0%	10.0%
2.0%	5.0%	

Sets III and IV apply to the following values of AOQL:

0.1%	1.5%	4.0%
0.25%	2.0%	5.0%
0.5%	2.5%	7.0%
0.75%	3.0%	10.0%
1.0%		

10.2.1 Single Sampling Lot Tolerance Tables

Table 10.1 is representative of Dodge-Romig Set I.

All the sampling plans in this table have the same lot tolerance percent defective (LTPD), namely, 5.0%. However, the plans have different values of AOQL. The tables give the AOQL figure for each plan.

The table contains six columns, each for a different value of process average percent defective. The purpose of these different columns is to indicate the plan that involves the minimum total inspection, considering both the inspection of samples and the 100% inspection of rejected lots.

For example, consider the inspection plans indicated in the table for the lot size range from 801 to 1000. Six different plans, namely,

$$\begin{bmatrix} n = 45 \\ c = 0 \end{bmatrix} \begin{bmatrix} n = 75 \\ c = 1 \end{bmatrix} \begin{bmatrix} n = 105 \\ c = 2 \end{bmatrix} \begin{bmatrix} n = 155 \\ c = 4 \end{bmatrix} \begin{bmatrix} n = 180 \\ c = 5 \end{bmatrix} \text{ and } \begin{bmatrix} n = 225 \\ c = 7 \end{bmatrix} \text{ all have an LTPD of 0.05.}$$

But, as previously explained, if rejected lots are to be detailed, the total amount of inspection of samples and rejected lots under these plans will depend on the quality level of the product submitted for inspection. Table 10.1 simply says that this total inspection will be a minimum for $\begin{bmatrix} n = 45 \\ c = 0 \end{bmatrix}$ if the process average is 0–0.05% defective, that it will be minimum for $\begin{bmatrix} n = 75 \\ c = 1 \end{bmatrix}$ if the process average is 0.06–0.50%, and so forth.

TABLE 10.1: EXAMPLE OF DODGE-ROMIG SINGLE SAMPLING LOT TOLERANCE TABLES
(Lot tolerance percent defective = 5.0%. Consumer's Risk = 0.10)

Lot size	Process average, %																	
	0-0.05			0.06-0.50			0.51-1.00			1.01-1.50			1.51-2.00			2.01-2.50		
	n	*c*	*AOQL* %	*n*	*c*	*AOQL* %	*n*	*c*	*AOQL* %	*n*	*c*	*AOQL* %	*n*	*c*	*AOQL* %	*n*	*c*	*AOQL* %
1-30	All	0	0	All	0	0	All	0	0	All	0	0	All	0	0	All	0	0
31-50	30	0	0.49	30	0	0.49	30	0	0.49	30	0	0.49	30	0	0.49	30	0	0.49
51-100	37	0	0.63	37	0	0.63	37	0	0.63	37	0	0.63	37	0	0.63	37	0	0.63
101-200	40	0	0.74	40	0	0.74	40	0	0.74	40	0	0.74	40	0	0.74	40	0	0.74
201-300	43	0	0.74	43	0	0.74	70	1	0.92	70	1	0.92	95	2	0.99	95	2	0.99
301-400	44	0	0.74	44	0	0.74	70	1	0.99	100	2	1.0	120	3	1.1	145	4	1.1
401-500	45	0	0.75	75	1	0.95	100	2	1.1	100	2	1.1	125	3	1.2	150	4	1.2
501-600	45	0	0.76	75	1	0.98	100	2	1.1	125	3	1.2	150	4	1.3	175	5	1.3
601-800	45	0	0.77	75	1	1.0	100	2	1.2	130	3	1.2	175	5	1.4	200	6	1.4
801-1000	45	0	0.78	75	1	1.0	105	2	1.2	155	4	1.4	180	5	1.4	225	7	1.5
1001-2000	45	0	0.80	75	1	1.0	130	3	1.4	180	5	1.6	230	7	1.7	280	9	1.8
2001-3000	75	1	1.1	105	2	1.3	135	3	1.4	210	6	1.7	280	9	1.9	370	13	2.1
3001-4000	75	1	1.1	105	2	1.3	160	4	1.5	210	6	1.7	305	10	2.0	420	15	2.2
4001-5000	75	1	1.1	105	2	1.3	160	4	1.5	235	7	1.8	330	11	2.0	440	16	2.2
5001-7000	75	1	1.1	105	2	1.3	185	5	1.7	260	8	1.9	350	12	2.2	490	18	2.4
7001-10.000	75	1	1.1	105	2	1.3	185	5	1.7	260	8	1.9	380	13	2.2	535	20	2.5
10,001-20,000	75	1	1.1	135	3	1.4	210	6	1.8	285	9	2.0	425	15	2.3	610	23	2.6
20,001-50,000	75	1	1.1	135	3	1.4	235	7	1.9	305	10	2.1	470	17	2.4	700	27	2.7
50,001-100,000	75	1	1.1	160	4	1.6	235	7	1.9	355	12	2.2	515	19	2.5	770	30	2.8

If there is no basis for estimating the process average, the sampling plan should be selected from the right-hand column of the table. This gives the desired quality protection and gives satisfactory lots a better chance of acceptance. Moreover, it collects data more rapidly to permit reliable estimates of the process average.

In the use of these lot tolerance tables, it should be understood that the tables contemplate the screening of rejected lots. However, the tables give the consumer the stated quality protection regardless of any provision for screening. Even though rejected lots are merely returned by the consumer to the producer with no formal provision for screening by anyone, it is reasonable to suppose that the producer will screen these lots. Under such circumstances, the consumer's use of the process average to determine the acceptance criteria may be thought or as aimed at minimizing the total inspection done by industry as a whole, considering both the consumer's sampling inspection and the screening presumably done by the producer.

10.2.2 Double Sampling Lot Tolerance Tables

Table 10.2 is representative of Dodge-Romig Set II.

Some differences between single and double sampling plans are evident from a comparison of Tables 10.1 and 10.2. These differences may be brought out to best advantage by comparing any single sampling plan with a double sampling plan for the same lot size and process average that gives the same lot quality protection. For example, consider the plans from Tables 10.1 and 10.2 for a lot size of 801-1,000 and a process average of 0.51-1.00% defective :

Single sampling	*Double sampling*	
$n = 105$	$n_1 = 55$	$n_2 = 115$
$c = 2$	$c_1 = 0$	$n_1 + n_2 = 170$
		$c_2 = 4$

The first sample in double sampling is smaller than the one sample in single sampling; in this case it is 55 instead of 105. On the other hand, the combined sample in double sampling is larger —170 compared to 105. The relative number of articles inspected in the samples in the two plans evidently depends on the quality of submitted product. If the product sampled is good enough that very few second samples have to be taken, the inspection will be substantially less with the double sampling plan. If many second samples need to be taken, the single sampling will require less sampling inspection. Dodge and Romig give a diagram that compares the inspection, under single and double sampling for various lot sizes and ratios of process average tolot tolerance fraction defectives. They state that over the portion of the tables most useful in practice, the saving in inspection due to double sampling is usually over 10% and may be as much as 50%.

One characteristic of all the Dodge-Romig double sampling plans is that c_2 is always 1 or more. This means that no lot is ever rejected as a result of only 1 defective.

10.2.3 Single Sampling AOQL Tables

Table 10.3 is representative of Dodge-Romig Set III.

In contrast to Table 10.1 in which all the single sampling plans had the same LTPD, all the plans in Table 10.3 have the same AOQL, namely , 2%. The table gives the lot tolerance percent defective for each plan. It is of interest to note that the larger the sample size and acceptance number for a given AOQL, the lower the LTPD.

Like all the Dodge-Romig tables, columns are given for various process averages; the plan in each column is the one that gives the minimum total inspection for the process average at the head of the column. Thus all the plans on any line of the table are alike in quality protection (as measured by the AOQL) and differ only in total amount of inspection required. As remarked in the discussion of Table 10.1, if there is no basis for estimating the process average, the sampling plan should be chosen from the right-hand column of the table.

10.2.4 Double Sampling AOQL Tables

Table 10.4 is representative of Dodge-Romig Set IV.

Dodge and Romig point out that the lot tolerance concept was first developed and applied in the Bell Telephone System in 1923. The concept of the AOQL was developed and applied in 1927. Thus tables involving both concepts, and involving single and double sampling, have been available within the Bell System for application to all types of inspection for many years. It is significant that Dodge and Romig state that the double sampling AOQL tables, of which Table 10.4 is an example, have proved the most useful of all the tables.

TABLE 10.2: EXAMPLE OF DODGE-ROMIG DOUBLE SAMPLING LOT TOLERANCE TABLES

Lot tolerance percent defective = 5.0% Consumer's Risk = 0.10.

Process average, %

Lot size	0–0.05						0.06–0.50						0.51–1.00					
	Trial 1		Trial 2			AOQL	Trial 1		Trial 2			AOQL	Trial 1		Trial 2			AOQL
	n_1	c_1	n_2	n_1+n_2	c_2	%	n_1	c_1	n_2	n_1+n_2	c_2	%	n_1	c_1	n_2	n_1+n_2	c_2	%
1–30	All	0	—	—	—	0	All	0	—	—	—	0	All	0	—	—	—	0.
31–50	30	0	—	—	—	0.49	30	0	—	—	—	0.49	30	0	—	—	—	0.49
51–75	38	0	—	—	—	0.59	38	0	—	—	—	0.59	38	0	—	—	—	0.59
76–100	44	0	21	65	1	0.64	44	0	21	65	1	0.64	44	0	21	65	1	0.64
101–200	49	0	26	75	1	0.84	49	0	26	75	1	0.84	49	0	26	75	1	0.84
201–300	50	0	30	80	1	0.91	50	0	30	80	1	0.91	50	0	55	105	2	1.0
301–400	55	0	30	85	1	0.92	55	0	55	110	2	1.1	55	0	55	110	2	1.1
401–500	55	0	30	85	1	0.93	55	0	55	110	2	1.1	55	0	80	135	3	1.2
501–600	55	0	30	85	1	0.94	55	0	60	115	2	1.1	55	0	85	140	3	1.2
601–800	55	0	35	90	1	0.95	55	0	65	120	2	1.1	55	0	85	140	3	1.3
801–1000	55	0	35	90	1	0.96	55	0	65	120	2	1.1	55	0	115	170	4	1.4
1001–2000	55	0	35	90	1	0.98	55	0	95	150	3	1.3	55	0	120	175	4	1.4
2001–3000	55	0	65	120	2	1.2	55	0	95	150	3	1.3	55	0	150	205	5	1.5
3001–4000	55	0	65	120	2	1.2	55	0	95	150	3	1.3	90	1	140	230	6	1.6
4001–5000	55	0	65	120	2	1.2	55	0	95	150	3	1.4	90	1	165	255	7	1.8
5001–7000	55	0	65	120	2	1.2	55	0	95	150	3	1.4	90	1	165	255	7	1.8
7001–10,000	55	0	65	120	2	1.2	55	0	120	175	4	1.5	90	1	190	280	8	1.9
10,001–20,000	55	0	65	120	2	1.2	55	0	120	175	4	1.5	90	1	190	280	8	1.9
20,001–50,000	55	0	65	120	2	1.2	55	0	150	205	5	1.7	90	1	215	305	9	2.0
50,001–100,000	55	0	65	120	2	1.2	55	0	150	205	5	1.7	90	1	240	330	10	2.1

Lot size	1.01–1.50						1.51–2.00						2.01–2.50					
	Trial 1		Trial 2			AOQL	Trial 1		Trial 2			AOQL	Trial 1		Trial 2			AOQL
	n_1	c_1	n_2	n_1+n_2	c_2	%	n_1	c_1	n_2	n_1+n_2	c_2	%	n_1	c_1	n_2	n_1+n_2	c_2	%
1–30	All	0	—	—	—	0	All	0	—	—	—	0	All	0	—	—	—	0
31–50	30	0	—	—	—	0.49	30	0	—	—	—	0.49	30	0	—	—	—	0.49
51–75	38	0	—	—	—	0.59	38	0	—	—	—	0.59	38	0	—	—	—	0.59
76–100	44	0	21	65	1	0.64	44	0	21	65	1	0.64	44	0	21	65	1	0.64
101–200	49	0	51	100	2	0.91	49	0	51	100	2	0.91	49	0	51	100	2	0.91
201–300	50	0	55	105	2	1.0	50	0	80	130	3	1.1	50	0	100	150	4	1.1
301–400	55	0	80	135	3	1.1	55	0	100	155	4	1.2	85	1	105	190	6	1.3
401–500	55	0	105	160	4	1.3	85	1	120	205	6	1.4	85	1	140	225	7	1.4
501–600	55	0	110	165	4	1.3	85	1	145	230	7	1.4	85	1	165	250	8	1.5
601–800	90	1	125	215	6	1.5	90	1	170	260	8	1.5	120	2	185	305	10	1.6
801–1000	90	1	150	240	7	1.5	90	1	200	290	9	1.6	120	2	210	330	11	1.7
1001–2000	90	1	185	275	8	1.7	120	2	225	345	11	1.9	175	4	260	435	15	2.0
2001–3000	120	2	180	300	9	1.9	150	3	270	420	14	2.1	205	5	375	580	21	2.3
3001–4000	120	2	210	330	10	2.0	150	3	295	445	15	2.3	230	6	420	650	24	2.4
4001–5000	120	2	255	375	12	2.1	150	3	345	495	17	2.3	255	7	445	700	26	2.5
5001–7000	120	2	260	380	12	2.1	150	3	370	520	18	2.3	255	7	495	750	28	2.6
7001–10,000	120	2	285	405	13	2.1	175	4	370	545	19	2.4	280	8	540	820	31	2.7
10,001–20,000	120	2	310	430	14	2.2	175	4	420	595	21	2.4	280	8	660	940	36	2.8
20,001–50,000	120	2	335	455	15	2.2	205	5	485	690	25	2.5	305	9	745	1050	41	2.9
50,001–100,000	120	2	360	480	16	2.3	205	5	555	760	28	2.6	330	10	810	1140	45	3.0

†Reprinted by permission from H. F. Dodge and H. G. Romig, *Sampling Inspection Tables —Single and Double Sampling,* 2d ed., John Wiley & Sons, Inc., New York, 1959.

TABLE 10.3: EXAMPLE OF DODGE-ROMIG SINGLE SAMPLING AOQL TABLES

(Note: Average outgoing quality limit = 2.0%)

Lot size	Process average, %																	
	0-0.04			0.05-0.40			0.41-0.80			0.81-1.20			1.21-1.60			1.61-2.00		
	n	c	$100p_{0.10}$	n	c	$100p_{0.10}$	n	c	$100p_{0.10}$	n	c	$100p_{0.10}$	n	c	$100p_{0.10}$	n	c	$100p_{0.10}$
1-15	All	0	....	All	0	....	All	0	....	All	0	....	All	0	....	All	0	....
16-50	14	0	13.6	14	0	13.6	14	0	13.6	14	0	13.6	14	0	13.6	14	0	13.6
51-100	16	0	12.4	16	0	12.4	16	0	12.4	16	0	12.4	16	0	12.4	16	0	12.4
101-200	17	0	12.2	17	0	12.2	17	0	12.2	17	0	12.2	35	1	10.5	35	1	10.5
201-300	17	0	12.3	17	0	12.3	37	1	10.2	37	1	10.2	37	1	10.2	37	1	10.2
301-400	18	0	11.8	18	0	11.8	38	1	10.0	38	1	10.0	38	1	10.0	60	2	8.5
401-500	18	0	11.9	18	0	11.9	39	1	9.8	39	1	9.8	60	2	8.6	60	2	8.6
501-600	18	0	11.9	18	0	11.9	39	1	9.8	39	1	9.8	60	2	8.6	60	2	8.6
601-800	18	0	11.9	40	1	9.6	40	1	9.6	65	2	8.0	65	2	8.0	85	3	7.5
801-1000	18	0	12.0	40	1	9.6	40	1	9.6	65	2	8.1	65	2	8.1	90	3	7.4
1001-2000	18	0	12.0	41	1	9.4	65	2	8.2	65	2	8.2	95	3	7.0	120	4	6.5
2001-3000	18	0	12.0	41	1	9.4	65	2	8.2	95	3	7.0	120	4	6.5	180	6	5.8
3001-4000	18	0	12.0	42	1	9.3	65	2	8.2	95	3	7.0	155	5	6.0	210	7	6.5
4001-5000	18	0	12.0	42	1	9.3	70	2	7.5	125	4	6.4	155	5	6.0	245	8	5.3
5001-7000	18	0	12.0	42	1	9.3	95	3	7.0	125	4	6.4	185	6	5.6	280	9	5.1
7001-10000	42	1	9.3	70	2	7.5	95	3	7.0	155	5	6.0	220	7	5.4	350	11	4.8
10001-20000	42	1	9.3	70	2	7.6	95	3	7.0	190	6	5.6	290	9	4.9	460	14	4.4
20001-50000	42	1	9.3	70	2	7.6	125	4	6.4	220	7	5.4	395	12	4.5	720	4	3.0
50000-100000	42	1	93															

10.2.5 Relationship between the Process Average Used in Selecting a D-R Sampling Plan and the OC Curve of the Plan Selected

Tables 10.1 to 10.4 all have six columns, each corresponding to a stated process average. In general, the greater the process average used in entering any Dodge-Romig table, the larger the sample size for any stated lot size. The plans having larger sample sizes have steeper *OC* curves with resulting better discrimination between lots superior to the quality standard and lots worse than the quality standard. This point is illustrated by Figs. 10.1 and 10.2.

Figure 10.1 shows the *OC* curves for the six double sampling plans given in Table 10.2 (LTPD = 5%) for the lot size 4,001-5,000. All these curves naturally show that the probability of acceptance of a 5% defective lot is 0.10. At all other points, however, the *OC* curves differ considerably. The differences are particularly striking at about half the 5% LTPD. Thus a 2.5% defective lot is almost certain to be accepted under the plan corresponding to the process average 2.01-2.50% (curve 6) but has only about a 0.50 probability of acceptance under the plans corresponding to the process averages 0-0.05% and 0.06-0.50% (curves 1 and 2). In general, where submitted lots are as good as the process average used in entering the tables, they are almost certain to be accepted.

Figure 10.2 shows the *OC* curves for the six double sampling plans given in Table 10.4 (AOQL = 2%). A comparison with Fig. 10.1 may be helpful in emphasizing certain similarities and certain differences between using the LTPD and the AOQL as the quality standard. Just as in the LTPD tables, any lots at the assumed process average or better are almost certain of

TABLE 10.4: EXAMPLE OF DODGE-ROMIG DOUBLE SAMPLING AOQL TABLES

Process average, %

Lot size	0–0.04 Trial 1 n_1	c_1	Trial 2 n_2	n_1+n_2	c_2	$100p_{0.10}$	0.05–0.40 Trial 1 n_1	c_1	Trial 2 n_2	n_1+n_2	c_2	$100p_{0.10}$
1–15	All	0	—	—	—	—	All	0	—	—	—	—
16–50	14	0	—	—	—	13.6	14	0	—	—	—	13.6
51–100	21	0	12	33	1	11.7	21	0	12	33	1	11.7
101–200	24	0	13	37	1	11.0	24	0	13	37	1	11.0
201–300	26	0	15	41	1	10.4	26	0	15	41	1	10.4
301–400	26	0	16	42	1	10.3	26	0	16	42	1	10.3
401–500	27	0	16	43	1	10.3	30	0	35	65	2	9.0
501–600	27	0	16	43	1	10.3	31	0	34	65	2	8.9
601–800	27	0	17	44	1	10.2	31	0	39	70	2	8.8
801–1000	27	0	17	44	1	10.2	32	0	38	70	2	8.7
1001–2000	33	0	37	70	2	8.5	33	0	37	70	2	8.5
2001–3000	34	0	41	75	2	8.2	34	0	41	75	2	8.2
3001–4000	34	0	41	75	2	8.2	38	0	62	100	3	7.3
4001–5000	34	0	41	75	2	8.2	38	0	62	100	3	7.3
5001–7000	35	0	40	75	2	8.1	38	0	62	100	3	7.3
7001–10,000	35	0	40	75	2	8.1	38	0	62	100	3	7.3
10,001–20,000	35	0	40	75	2	8.1	39	0	66	105	3	7.2
20,001–50,000	35	0	40	75	2	8.1	43	0	92	135	4	6.6
50,001–100,000	35	0	45	80	2	8.0	43	0	92	135	4	6.6

Lot size	0.41–0.80 Trial 1 n_1	c_1	Trial 2 n_2	n_1+n_2	c_2	$100p_{0.10}$	0.81–1.20 Trial 1 n_1	c_1	Trial 2 n_2	n_1+n_2	c_2	$100p_{0.10}$
1–15	All	0	—	—	—	—	All	0	—	—	—	—
16–50	14	0	—	—	—	13.6	14	0	—	—	—	13.6
51–100	21	0	12	33	1	11.7	21	0	12	33	1	11.7
101–200	24	0	13	37	1	11.0	27	0	28	55	2	9.6
201–300	29	0	31	60	2	9.1	29	0	31	60	2	9.1
301–400	30	0	35	65	2	9.0	33	0	52	85	3	8.2
401–500	30	0	35	65	2	9.0	34	0	56	90	3	7.9
501–600	35	0	55	90	3	7.9	35	0	55	90	3	7.9
601–800	35	0	60	95	3	7.7	38	0	82	120	4	7.3
801–1000	36	0	59	95	3	7.6	38	0	87	125	4	7.2
1001–2000	37	0	63	100	3	7.5	43	0	112	155	5	6.5
2001–3000	41	0	84	125	4	7.0	75	1	115	190	6	6.1
3001–4000	41	0	89	130	4	6.9	80	1	140	220	7	5.8
4001–5000	42	0	88	130	4	6.9	80	1	175	255	8	5.5
5001–7000	44	0	116	160	5	6.4	85	1	205	290	9	5.3
7001–10,000	45	0	115	160	5	6.3	85	1	210	295	9	5.2
10,001–20,000	45	0	115	160	5	6.3	90	1	260	350	11	5.1
20,001–50,000	47	0	148	195	6	6.0	130	2	300	430	13	4.7
50,001–100,000	85	1	185	270	8	5.2	135	2	345	480	14	4.5

Lot size	1.21–1.60 Trial 1 n_1	c_1	Trial 2 n_2	n_1+n_2	c_2	$100p_{0.10}$	1.61–2.00 Trial 1 n_1	c_1	Trial 2 n_2	n_1+n_2	c_2	$100p_{0.10}$
1–15	All	0	—	—	—	—	All	0	—	—	—	—
16–50	14	0	—	—	—	13.6	14	0	—	—	—	13.6
51–100	21	0	12	33	1	11.7	23	0	23	46	2	10.9
101–200	27	0	28	55	2	9.6	27	0	28	55	2	9.6
201–300	32	0	48	80	3	8.4	32	0	48	80	3	8.4
301–400	33	0	52	85	3	8.2	36	0	69	105	4	7.6
401–500	36	0	74	110	4	7.5	60	1	90	150	6	7.0
501–600	37	0	78	115	4	7.4	65	1	95	160	6	6.8
601–800	38	0	82	120	4	7.3	70	1	120	190	7	6.4
801–1000	70	1	100	170	6	6.5	70	1	145	215	8	6.2
1001–2000	80	1	160	240	8	5.8	110	2	205	315	11	5.5
2001–3000	115	2	195	310	10	5.3	160	3	310	470	15	4.7
3001–4000	120	2	255	375	12	5.0	235	5	415	650	20	4.3
4001–5000	125	2	285	410	13	4.9	275	6	475	750	23	4.2
5001–7000	125	2	320	445	14	4.8	280	6	575	855	26	4.1
7001–10,000	165	3	335	500	15	4.5	320	7	645	965	29	4.0
10,001–20,000	170	3	425	595	18	4.4	395	9	835	1230	37	3.9
20,001–50,000	205	4	515	720	22	4.3	480	11	1090	1570	46	3.7
50,001–100,000	250	5	615	865	26	4.1	580	13	1460	2040	58	3.5

†Reprinted by permission from H. F. Dodge and H. G. Romig, *Sampling Inspection Tables—Single and Double Sampling*, 2d ed., John Wiley & Sons, Inc., New York, 1959.

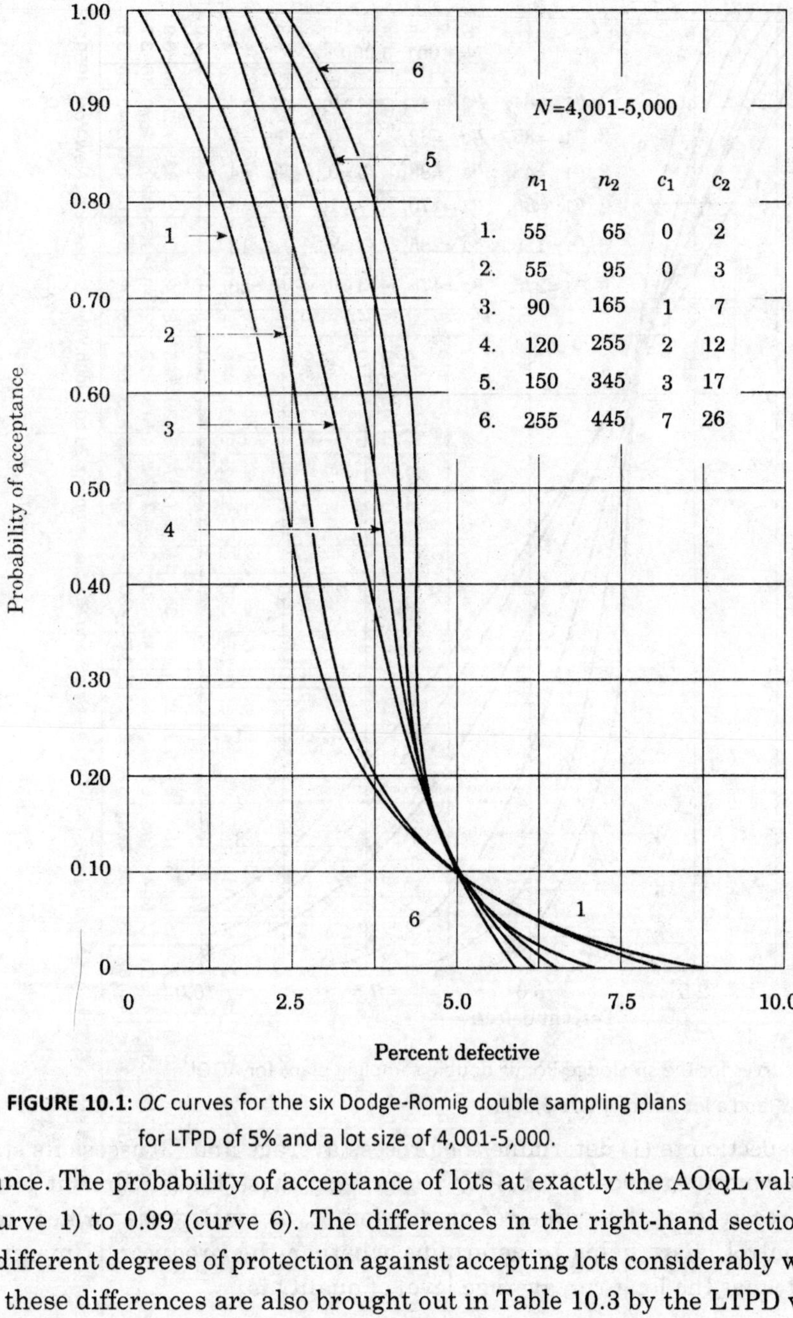

FIGURE 10.1: *OC* curves for the six Dodge-Romig double sampling plans for LTPD of 5% and a lot size of 4,001-5,000.

acceptance. The probability of acceptance of lots at exactly the AOQL value varies from about 0.84 (curve 1) to 0.99 (curve 6). The differences in the right-hand sections of the *OC* curves reflect different degrees of protection against accepting lots considerably worse than the stated AOQL; these differences are also brought out in Table 10.3 by the LTPD values given for each sampling plan.

10.2.6 Determining the Process Average in Dodge-Romig Inspection

The objective of minimizing total inspection depends on selecting the correct plan, which, in turn, depends on making a good estimate of the process average as a basis for the selection. It follows that in all Dodge-Romig inspection, it is advantageous to make systematic use of the

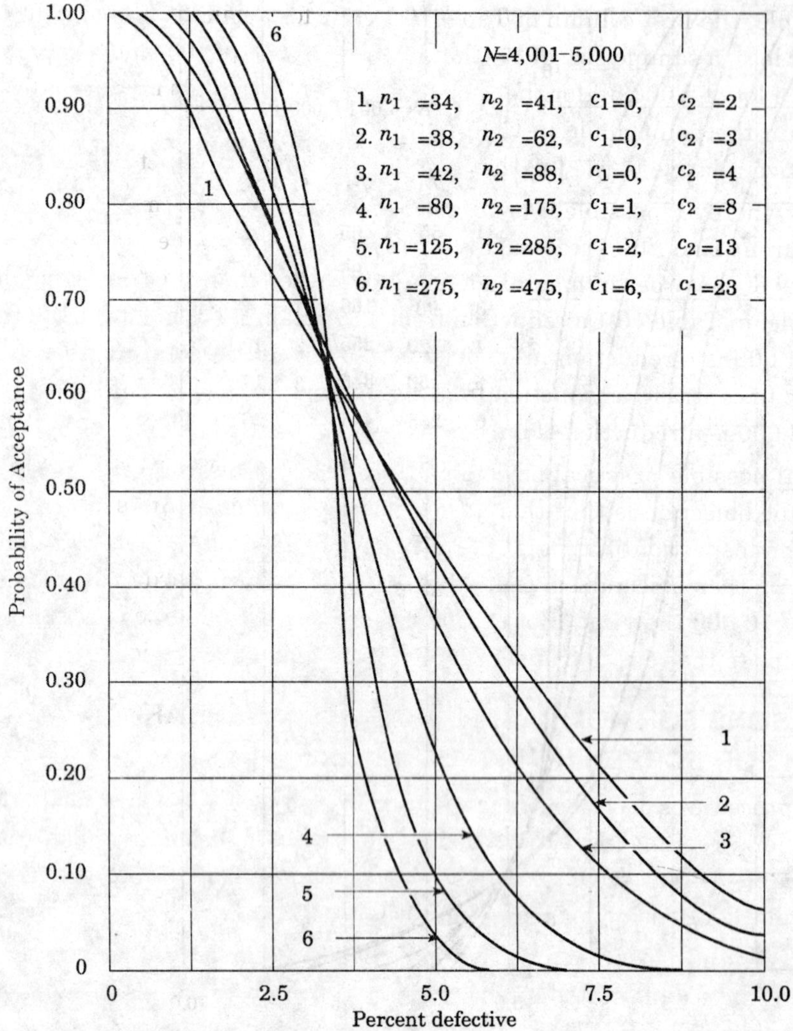

FIGURE 10.2: *OC* curves for the six Dodge-Romig double sampling plans for AOQL of 2% and a lot size of 4,001-5,000.

results of sampling inspection to (1) determine the process average and (2) assess its stability through time. Control charts are useful tools for performing these tasks. Often it is safe to assume that lots are received in their order of production or, at least, were formed in order of production. The control chart helps to determine whether the producer is maintaining statistical control and what the long-run average level of quality is.

10.2.7 Relationship between Lot Size and Sample Size in Dodge-Romig Tables

The D-R tables apply to lot sizes from 1 to 100,000 and may be used for any lots that happen to be subjected to acceptance inspection. It is not necessary that inspection lot sizes be equal to production or shipping lot sizes. Where practicable, it may be advantageous to establish lot sizes for acceptance inspection purposes rather than take lots as they come. The tables help in making a decision on lot size by showing clearly the disadvantage of small lots as compared with large ones from the viewpoint of the amount of sampling necessary for a given quality protection. For example, the first column of Table 10.1 calls for a sample size of "All" (that is, 100%) of a lot of 30 or less, a sample size of 37 (that is, 37%) of a lot of 100, and a sample size of 45 (that is, 2.25%) of a lot of 2,000 all for the same quality protection (as measured by LTPD). This emphasizes again the point made in Chap. 9 that it is the absolute size of the sample, much more than its size relative to the lot, that governs the quality protection.

It is evident that wherever possible it is desirable to avoid the very small lot sizes. At the same time it is apparent that the great saving in inspection for a given quality protection consists in taking lots of the order of magnitude of 1,000 rather than the conventional lots of 50 or 100. For example, in Table 10.1 a reduction from a 37% sample from lots of 100 to a 4.5% sample from lots of 1,000 is a reduction in inspection of 32.5% of the total number of articles submitted in the lots. In contrast, a reduction from a 4.5% sample from lots of 1,000 to a 2.25% sample from lots of 2,000 is a reduction of only 2.25%.

There are several possible practical objections to very large lot sizes such as those from 10,000 to 100,000. One objection is that there are often practical difficulties in bringing such large lots together for inspection purposes; the cost of doing this may more than offset the inspection savings. Another objection is that it is frequently much harder to get a random sample out of a lot of 10,000 than out a lot of 1,000. Moreover the adverse effect on producer consumer relationships to the rejection of very large lots is sometimes serious.

10.3 SOME REASONS FOR NOT BASING A QUALITY STANDARD ON A PROVISION FOR SCREENING INSPECTION

The D-R acceptance procedures described earlier in Sec 10.2 all gave consideration to the effect of a formal provision for screening inspection whenever the results of sampling inspection were sufficiently unfavourable. In the AOQL plans, the stated quality standard (*i.e.* the AOQL) was dependent, in part, on the provision for screening inspection.

Where the producers and consumer are different organizations, there are good reasons why the consumer is unwilling for his stated quality standard to be based on the assumption that such screening inspection will occur. He may consider it impracticable or inadvisable to carry out this screening in all cases, and he may be unwilling to rely on any such screening carried out by the producer. There have been many instances where a lot rejected by the consumer, has been passed on again by producer to the consumer without screening.

Screening inspection by the consumer (either of all the product or rejected lots) may be impracticable because it is unduly costly or because he does not have sufficient inspection facilities or the required personnel or he is not willing to upset his schedules or for many other reasons. Even though practicable, he may deem it inadvisable. If the consumer carries out screening inspection of all products, he may, as a consequence, find himself doing inspection that really should have been done by the producer. Moreover, the pressure for quality improvement exerted by outright rejection of one or more entire lots is much stronger than the pressure exerted by the rejection of individual articles classified as defective by a consumer's 100% inspection because the production man *takes it as a matter of course* if just individual articles are returned to him for repair. But if a whole lot is returned to him and he is required to undertake the entire corrective action, the steady outward flow of product is interrupted.

10.4 DEFINITION OF ACCEPTABLE QUALITY LEVEL (AQL)

The idea of AQL (Acceptable Quality Level) or an allowable percent defective is arrived at from the following considerations. Under the speed of mass production, it is often impossible to continually turn out 100% satisfactory product. It is sure that a certain percentage of defectives will always occur on certain processes, however, if the percentage does not exceed a certain limit, it is often more economical to allow the defectives to go through rather than to screen each lot. This limits known as the *Acceptable Quality Level.*

This definition of AOQL has undergone some changes time to time in different standards which list out various sampling plans based on AQL concept.

The most widely accepted definition of AQL is as follows :

"The AQL is the maximum percent defective (or the maximum number of defects per hundred units) that, for the *purpose of sampling inspection,* can be considered satisfactory as a process average."

The above definition has been adopted by ABC standard, and its commercial counterpart ANSI/ASQC Z1.4 and the latest 1989 version of military standard i.e. MIL-STD-105 E.

It may be noted that in the above definition of AQL, the key words are "for the purposes of sampling inspection". The inclusion of these words emphasize that the choice of an *AQL* is a necessary evil that exists in any sampling inspection : there really is no such thing as an acceptable level of production of defective material. Therefore all above mentioned standards contain a "limitation" statement acknowledging that the choice of an AQL does not imply that right to supply defective material.

10.5 AQL SAMPLING STANDARDS

The first attempt in developing the sampling acceptance standard on AQL resulted in military standard designated as MIL-STD-105. During the years 1960 to 1962, *ABC* standard was prepared by the military agencies of the United States of America, Great Britain and Canada for use in these countries. This is international in character and widely used. Following is the brief summary of various AQL standards and their equivalent.

International standard : ABC-STD-105 (popularly known as ABC standard).

- Its International standards organization designation is ISO 2859.
- For commercial purposes American National Standards Institute designated this as ANSI/ASQC A1.4.
  (Some changes have been incorporated in its latest edition of 1981)
- For defence purposes, the U.S. Department of Defense in the year 1989 with a few substantive changes in *ABC* standard designated it as MIL-STD-105 E. However the tables developed for the *ABC* standard and carried into Z1.4 remain the same. The substantive changes are described at appropriate points in the text. In order to stress the importance of this standard and its international character, it is referred to throughout this chapter as the *ABC* standard (from the name of the working group that prepared it).

10.6 SOME VALID DECISIONS IN THE ESTABLISHMENT OF THE AQL AS A QUALITY STANDARD

Some of the decisions based on the AQL concept as quality standard are as follows :

1. In order to establish acceptable criteria for any particular quality characteristic of a product, it is first necessary to prescribe a maximum percent defective that, *for the acceptance sampling purposes only*, is considered acceptable as a process average. This acceptable quality level usually is abbreviated AQL.
2. In the absence of unsatisfactory quality history or other reasons for misgivings about the quality of submitted product, the acceptance criteria should be selected with the objective of protecting the producer against the rejection of submitted lots from a process that is at the AQL value or better.
3. Such acceptance criteria generally give the consumer unsatisfactory protection against accepting lots that are moderately worse (sometimes considerably worse) than the AQL. For this reason, more severe acceptance criteria designed to protect the consumer must be used whenever the quality history is unsatisfactory or when there are other good reasons for being suspicious about quality. This concept of *tightened inspection* as an alternative to *normal inspection* is at the heart of all acceptance sampling systems based on the AQL. It is an essential part of any acceptance/rejection procedures where the acceptance criteria are chosen to protect the producer under "normal" conditions.
4. The acceptance criteria for serious defects should be more severe than for trivial defects. In other words, relatively low AQL values should be used for those types of defects that would have serious consequences and relatively high AQL values for those defects that are of little importance. The provision for a *classification of defects* is an essential feature of systems based on the AQL.
5. Economics for the consumer can be realized by *permitting reduced inspection* when the quality history is good enough. This permits the concentration of attention of inspectors on those products where attention seems to be needed most.
6. In establishing the relationship between lot size and sample size, weightage should be given to the greater difficulty of obtaining random samples from large lots and the more serious consequences of a wrong decision on acceptance or rejection of a large lot. For this reason, the relationship between lot size and sample size is based more on empirical grounds than on considerations arising from the mathematical theory of probability.

10.7 SOME ASPECTS OF THE MASTER TABLES REPRODUCED FROM THE ABC STANDARD

Tables L to T in App. 2 give sample sizes and acceptance and rejection numbers. To enter any one of these tables, it is necessary to know the AQL and sample size code letter. To determine which table should be used, it is necessary to know whether single, double, or multiple sampling is to be used and to know whether normal, tightened, or reduced inspection is to be used.

The AQL values in the standard may be interpreted either as percent defective or as defects per hundred units depending on whether acceptance criteria are to be based on the number of *defectives* observed in a sample or on the number of *defects*. However, AQL values above 10.0 are interpreted as applying to defects per hundred units. Most of our discussion of the standard will assume the more common acceptance criteria based on numbers of defectives with AQL specified as a percent defective.

All the AQL values are multiples of the numbers 1, 1.5, 2.5, 4.0, and 6.5. These numbers are roughly in geometrical progression ($10^{0.2}$) and correspond to systems of "preferred numbers" in common use for other industrial purposes.

10.8 DETERMINING THE SAMPLE SIZE CODE LETTER

Table *K*, reproduced from the ABC standard, gives the relationship between lot or batch size and the code letter that determines the sample size. The "general inspection levels" on the right-hand side of the table are the ones to use in most cases. The standard states: "Unless otherwise specified, Inspection Level II will be used. However, Inspection Level I may be specified when less discrimination in needed, or Level III may be specified for greater dis- crimination."

The four special levels, S-1 to S-4 at the left-hand side of the table, are included for the special cases where relatively small sample sizes the necessary and large sampling risks can or must be tolerated.

10.8.1 Selecting a Sampling Plan for Normal Inspection

Assume that an *AQL* of 1.5% has been specified for a certain class of defects. Assume normal inspection with a lot size of 1,000 and inspection level II. Table *K* indicates that the sample size code letter is *J*.

Table *L* gives acceptance criteria with normal inspection, single sampling. It tells us that for code letter *J* and a 1.5% AQL, sample size is 80 and the acceptance number is 3. The rejection number is stated as 4. In all these single sampling plans, the rejection number is one more than the acceptance number.

Table *O* gives acceptance criteria with normal inspection, double sampling. Table R gives criteria with normal inspection, multiple sampling. For code letter *J* and an *AQL* of 1.5%, these are:

Sample number	*Sample size*	*Cumulative sample size*	*Acceptance number*	*Rejection number*
Double :				
First	50	50	1	4
Second	50	100	4	5
Multiple :				
First	20	20	■	3
Second	20	40	0	3
Third	20	60	1	4
Fourth	20	80	2	5
Fifth	20	100	3	6
Sixth	20	120	4	6
Seventh	20	140	6	7

■ Acceptance not permitted at this sample size.

The standard gives OC curves for all single sampling plans for normal and tightened inspection. It is stated that "curves for double and multiple sampling are matched as closely as practicable." The various issues involved in choosing among single, double, and multiple sampling are discussed later in this chapter. For our discussion of a number of aspects of the standard, we shall concentrate our attention on single sampling.

10.8.2 Probabilities of Acceptance of Lots Having AQL Percent Defective

In all AQL systems, the acceptance criteria under normal inspection have been chosen to protect the producer against rejection-of lots meeting the quality standard. However, in most AQL systems the Producer's Risk that such lots will be rejected is not the same for all sampling plans.

Figure 10.3 shows a portion of the OC curves for four single sampling plans from the ABC standard all having an AQL of 1%. It is evident that the smaller the sample size, the greater the risk the producer takes that a lot will be rejected when it is exactly 1% defective.

Of course, the Consumer's Risk of accepting a lot much worse than the AQL is also much greater with a small sample size. For example, Fig. 10.3 shows that a 5% defective lot has more than a 0.5 probability of acceptance with $n = 13$ and $c = 0$. In contrast, such a lot is practically certain to be rejected with $n = 500$ and $c = 10$. We have already noted that, when the acceptance number is zero, the OC curve has no point of inflection; it is concave upward through its entire length. If a plan with $c = 0$ were selected to reduce the Producer's Risk of rejection of a 1% defective lot to, say, 0.05, the consumer would have even less protection against accepting bad product than is present with $n = 13$ and $c = 0$. (A P_a of 0.95 for 1% defective product with $c = 0$ would require $n = 5$. With this n, even a 12% defective lot would have a better than even chance of being accepted.)

In designing an AQL system, it is reasonable to give some weightage to the entire OC curve of each of the sampling plans in the system rather than merely to a point near one end of the

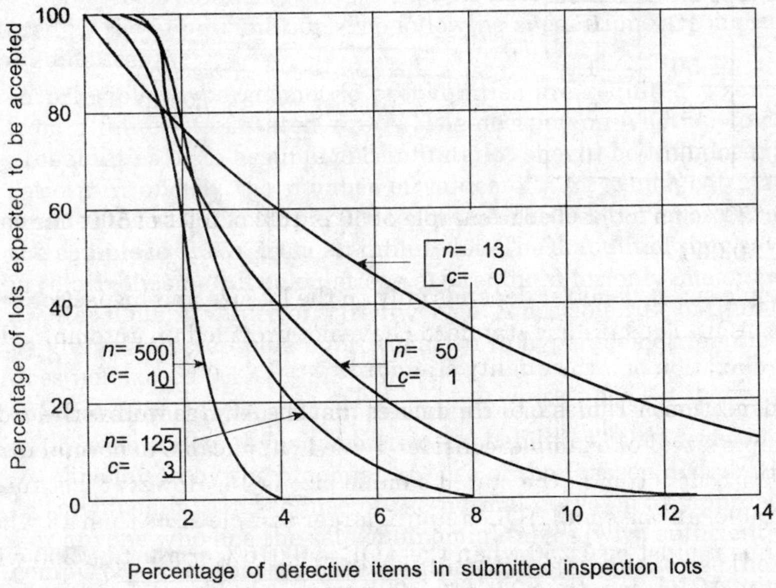

FIGURE 10.3: OC curves for four single sampling plans from the ABC standard, all with an AQL of 1.0%.

OC curve, namely, the P_a at the AQL value. In the ABC system, the probability of acceptance at the AQL value in normal inspection varies from about 0.88 for plans with the smaller sample sizes where $c = 0$ to about 0.99 for the large sample sizes and acceptance numbers.

H.F. Dodge preposed and AQL system, discussed briefly in Chap. 11, that eliminatesthe use of $c = 0$ in single sampling under normal inspection(although $c = 0$ is used in tightended inspection). This elimination makes practicable a standardized aimed-at P_a of 0.95 at the AQL value under normal inspection.

10.8.3 The Relationship between Lot Size and Sample Size in the Military *AQL* Systems

The discussion in Sec. 10.8 illustrated the use of Table *K*, App. 1 to determine the sample size code letter from the lot size and inspection level in the ABC standard. The code letter then determines the sample size as shown in Tables *L* to *T*.

All the military AQL systems have used a somewhat empirical relationship between lot size and sample size. It is true, of course, that unless a sample is a substantial fraction of its lot, the OC curve of the sampling plan is practically independent of lot size, depending almost entirely on sample size and acceptance number. Nevertheless, computed OC curves always assume random sampling. The use of larger samples for larger lots recognizes that it is relatively difficult to get a small random sample from a very large lot. Moreover, large samples with their steeper OC curves give better discrimination between good and bad lots; the larger the lot size, the more important this discrimination is likely to be.

It should be emphasized that, although the absolute sample size increases with lot size in the military AQL systems, the relative sample size decreases. Consider the following lot sizes under inspection level II applicable to the four plans shown in Fig. 10.3 from the ABC standard:

N	n	c
51–100	13	0
281–500	50	1
1201–3200	125	3
35001–150000	500	10

The sample of 13 is 20% of a lot of 65; the sample of 50 is 10% of a lot of 500; the sample of 500 is only 1% of lot of 50,000.

In Table *K*, the sample size code letter depends only on the lot size and inspection level and is not influenced by the AQL. The military standards have not provided an automatic decrease in sample size with a relaxation of a the quality standard.

Nevertheless, an inspection of Tables *L* to *T* indicates that the AQL as well as the code letter may determine the sample size. For example, consider Table L, applicable to normal inspection and single sampling. For code letter *E*, the stated sample size is 13. However, because of the vertical arrows in the table, all the small AQL*s* require larger sample sizes than 13 when code letter *E* is specified. Thus n must be 1,250 when the AQL is 0.010%; n must be 200 when the AQL is 0.065%. When the AQL is less than 0.010% (100 parts per million defective), inspection under the standard is not recommended.

10.8.4 Criteria for Shifting to Tightened Inspection and Requalification for Normal Inspection

In acceptance/rejection systems that make use of normal and tightened inspection, it is customary for normal inspection to be used for the first lots submitted. In effect, the producer is given the benefit of the doubt; if its product meets the stated quality standard for process average, there is relatively little chance that its lots will be rejected.

Because normal inspection will accept nearly all lots submitted that are at the AQL value or better, it will also accept a high percentage of any submitted lots that are moderately worse than the AQL. (The exact protection against such lots is, of course, given by the OC curve, the steepness of which is greatly influenced by sample size.) The consumer's protection against continuing to accept such lots if they are submitted depends on having rules requiring a shift to more severe acceptance criteria whenever there is good evidence that the process quality is worse than the AQL.

The ABC standard states: "*When normal inspection is in effect, tightened inspection shall be instituted when 2 out of 5 consecutive lots or batches have been rejected on original inspection (i.e. ignoring resubmitted lots or batches for this procedure).*"

The statement regarding requalification for normal inspection is as follows: "*When tightened inspection is in effect, normal inspection shall be instituted when 5 consecutive lots or batches have been considered acceptable on original inspection.*" After tightened inspection has been in effect for 10 consecutive lots, sampling inspection under the standard is terminated until action is taken to improve the process.

MIL-STD-105E (1989) calls for discontinuance of sampling inspection after only 5 consecutive lots had been inspected on tightened inspection. Thus, if a return to normal inspection did not occur, inspection under the standard was to be discontinued until corrective action on the process has been taken. Then tightened inspection was to be reinstituted as if the shift to tightened inspection has just occurred.

10.8.5 Acceptance Criteria under Tightened Inspection

In all the military *AQL* systems using sample size code letters, the code letter in tightened inspection is determined just as in normal inspection. The acceptance criteria under tightened inspection in the *ABC* standard are shown in Tables *M, P,* and *S*. The relationship between criteria under normal and tightened inspection may be illustrated with reference to the normal plans for a 1% *AQL* that were shown in Fig. 10.3.

Code letter	Normal		Tightened	
	n	*c*	*n*	*c*
E	13	0	20	0
H	50	1	80	1
K	125	3	125	2
N	500	10	500	8

In the first three cases the criteria under tightened inspection for a 1% AQL are the same as the criteria under normal inspection for the stated code letter for the next lower AQL, namely, 0.65%. In most cases in the ABC standard, the tightened criteria are identical with the normal criteria for the next lower AQL class, although there are a number of exceptions.

Later in this chapter there is an illustration of the difference between the OC curves in normal and tightened inspection. The various AQL systems have differed considerably in this respect.

10.8.6 Criteria for Qualification and Loss of Qualification for Reduced Inspection

Generally speaking, eligibility for reduced inspection should be based on recent quality history indicating average quality considerably better than the AQL. Moreover, it should seem likely that the product to be inspected under reduced inspection will be produced under the same conditions that gave rise to the recent good quality history.

The ABC standard states the following conditions for a shift from normal to reduced inspection:

(a) *The preceding 10 lots or batches (or more, as indicated by the note to Table VIII (or Table W in this book) of App. 1 have been on normal inspection and none has been rejected on original inspection; and*

(b) *The total number of defectives (or defects) in the samples from the preceding 10 lots or batches (or such other number as was used for condition a above) is equal to or less than the applicable number given in Table W. If double or multiple sampling is in use, all samples inspected should be included, not "first" samples only; and*

(c) *Production is at a steady rate; and*

(d) *Reduced inspection is considered desirable by the responsible authority.*

Normal inspection must be reinstated whenever "a lot or batch is rejected" or "production becomes irregular or delayed, or other conditions warrant that normal inspection shall be instituted." A further condition requiring that normal inspection be reinstated is discussed in the next section.

10.8.7 Acceptance Criteria under Reduced Inspection

In all the military *AQL* systems using sample size code letters, the code letter in reduced inspection has been determined just as in normal inspection. The acceptance criteria under reduced inspection in the *ABC* standard are shown in Tables *N*, *Q*, and *T* in App. 2. The relationship between the criteria under normal and reduced inspection may be illustrated with reference to the single sampling normal plans for a 1% *AQL* that were shown in Fig. 10.3.

Code letter	Normal			Reduced		
	n	Accept	Reject	n	Accept	Reject
E	13	0	1	5	0	1
H	50	1	2	20	0	2
K	125	3	4	50	1	4
N	500	10	11	200	5	8

The reader will observe that the acceptance criteria shown for code letters *H*, *K*, and *n* under reduced inspection all have an area of indecision in which the lot is neither accepted nor rejected. The standard states that, whenever the number of defectives falls in this indecision region (for example, if there should be exactly 1 defective in the sample of 20 with code letter

H), the lot in question shall be accepted but reduced inspection shall be discontinued and normal inspection reinstated.

10.8.8 General Comments on Reduced Inspection in Acceptance/Rejection Plans

A provision for reduced inspection is not a necessary part of an acceptance/rejection plan. Nevertheless, such a provision is based on a principle that is economically sound. This principle is to concentrate inspection attention on those products and quality characteristics where the quality history is doubtful and to give less attention where the quality history is very good.

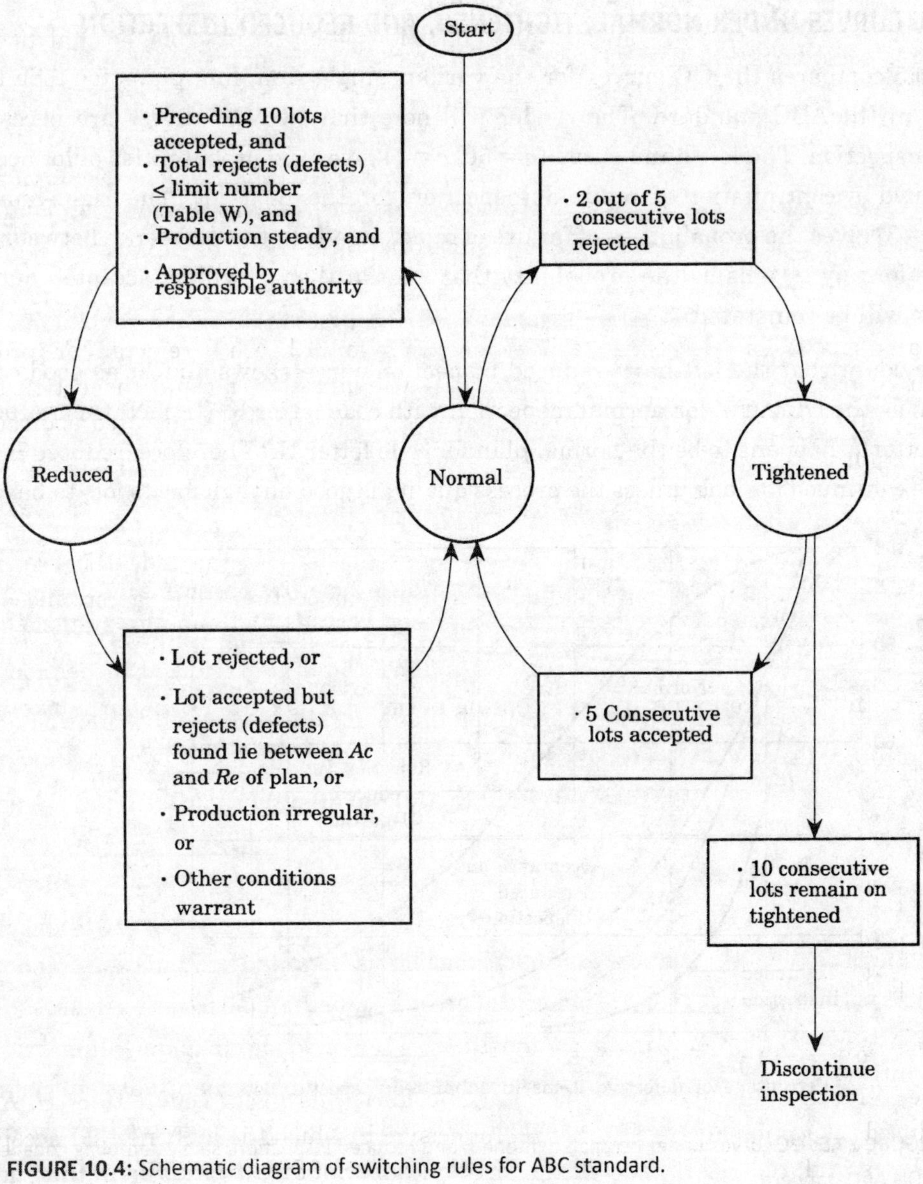

FIGURE 10.4: Schematic diagram of switching rules for ABC standard.

The consumer's savings in inspection costs under reduced inspection are apparent. The producer's advantages are not quite so obvious. However, because the acceptance criteria in reduced inspection are not so stringent, the producer receives added protection against lot rejection. The producer may also have a real sense of accomplishment in having qualified for reduced inspection. Hence, from the consumer's viewpoint, the provisions for reduced inspection in any acceptance programme may provide a useful nonfinancial incentive to the producer to improve quality. Figure 10.4 shows an abbreviated flow diagram of the operation of the switching rules in the *ABC* standard.

10.9 OC CURVES UNDER NORMAL, TIGHTENED, AND REDUCED INSPECTION

Figure 10.5 compares the OC curves for the various single sampling plans for code letter K, 1% AQL, in the ABC standard. The reader will note that two OC curves are necessary for reduced inspection. The left-hand curve ($n = 50$, $c = 1$) gives the probabilities of lot acceptance accompanied by continuation of reduced inspection for the next lot. The right-hand curve ($n = 50$, $c = 3$) gives the probabilities of failure of reject; in effect, the difference between the two Pa values for any μ_p tells us the probability that a lot at that μ_p will be accepted but normal inspection will be reinstated.

It is evident that the left-hand reduced inspection curve shows almost as good consumer protection as the *OC* curve for normal inspection with code letter K. (In fact, this reduced plan for code letter *K* happens to be the normal plan for code letter H.) Therefore, reduced inspection will not be continued for long unless the process quality is good enough for its lots to have passed

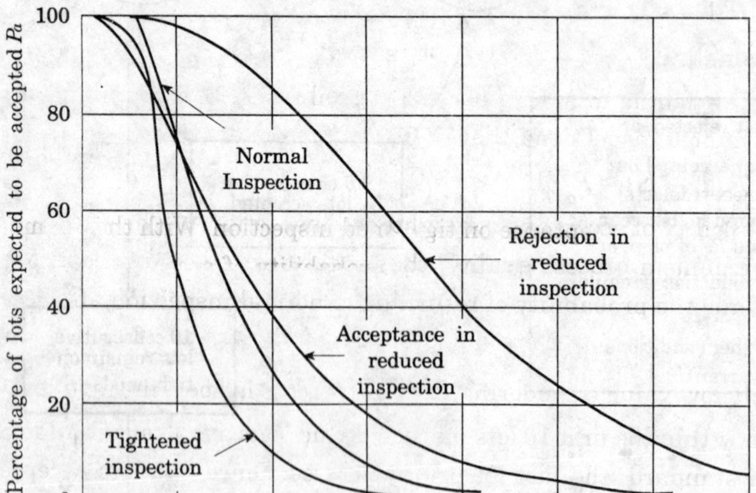

FIGURE 10.5: OC curves under normal, tightened, and reduced inspection; single sampling code letter K, 1% AQL, ABC standard.

normal inspection if normal inspection had been in effect. On the other hand, the right-hand curve shows that any particular lot under reduced inspection has a much greater chance of not being rejected than the same lot would have had under normal inspection.

An examination of the OC curve under tightened inspection makes it clear that lots appreciably worse than the AQL still have a fair chance of acceptance. For example, the indifference quality p0.50 for this 1% AQL tightened plan is about 2.2% defective. It may be desirable to supplement the tightened inspection criteria by less formal pressures based on a current estimate of the process average.

10.9.1 Calculating Probabilities of Switching, N-T-N

Let us assume single sampling under code letter *L* and an AQL of 1.0%. The sample size under normal and tightened inspection is 200. The acceptance numbers are 5 under normal inspection and 3 under tightened.

The probability of switching from normal to tightened inspection after any 5 successive lots are inspected is the probability that 2 (or more) or 5 consecutive lots will be rejected on normal inspection. This may be formulated, using the binomial, as 1 minus the probabilities that 0 or 1 lots will be rejected as follows :

$$P\,(\mathrm{N} \rightarrow \mathrm{T}) = 1 - P^{5}_{a,\,N} - 5\,P_{r,\,N}\,P^{4}_{a,\,N} \qquad \text{...(10.1)}$$

where $P_{a,\,N}$ = probability of acceptance on normal inspection

$P_{r,\,n}$ = probability of rejection on normal inspection

If μ_p = AQL = 0.01 , then $P_{a,\,N}$ = 0.983. Hence, with lots drawn from a process operating at the *AQL*,

$$P\,(\mathrm{N} \rightarrow \mathrm{T}) = 1 - (0.983)^5 - 5\,(0.017.)\,(0.983)^4 = 0.0028$$

This risk is very small.

The probability of switching from tightened to normal inspection after the first 5 lots have been inspected on tightened inspection (that is, 5 consecutive lots accepted) is simply

$$P\,(\mathrm{T} \rightarrow \mathrm{N}) = P^{5}_{a,\,T} \qquad \text{...(10.2)}$$

where $P_{a,\,T}$ = probability of acceptance on tightened inspection. With the example problem given and no improvement in process quality, the probability of acceptance under tightened inspection is 0.857. Thus the probability of returning to normal inspection after 5 lots is

$$P\,(\mathrm{T} \rightarrow \mathrm{N}) = (0.857)^5 = 0.4623$$

This is a relatively low value considering that the process is operating at the AQL.

In order to switch within the first 10 lots inspected, and thus avoid termination of sampling inspection under the standard, the last lot prior to the sequence of 5 lots accepted must be rejected. Prior to that rejected lot in the sequence, it is irrelevant whether the lots are accepted or rejected. This yields a probability of about 0.79 that the switch will be made when μ_p = AQL before inspection is terminated.

A tabulation of switching probabilities at various quality levels for these code letter L, 1.0% AQL, normal and tightened plans gives some insight into the operation of the rules:

Incoming μ_p	½ AQL 0.005	AQL 0.01	2AQL 0.02
$n\mu_p$	1.0	2.0	4.0
$P_{a,N}$	0.999	0.983	0.785
$P_{a,T}$	0.981	0.857	0.433
P (N → T)	≈ 0	0.0028	0.2937
P (T → N)	0.9085	0.4623	0.0152
P (termination)	0.005	0.207	0.942

These figures demonstrate that, when the quality level is at the AQL or better, a switch from normal to tightened inspection is quite unlikely. Even at a quality level twice that of the *AQL* the likelihood of switching within the first 5 lots inspected is not great. However, once the switch is made, the chances are not great that a return to normal inspection will be made unless product quality improves to a level better than the AQL.

Similar calculations for switching to and from reduced inspection are more complicated because of the limit number criterion and thus are not illustrated here.

10.9.2 Normal, Tightened, and Reduced Inspection as a Sampling System

When two or more sampling plans are linked together by a set of rules for switching from one plan to another, as with the ABC standard, the linked group may be considered a "sampling system." Figure 10.4 is typical of system flow diagrams in that it shows the various possible *states* in the inspection system — normal, tightened, and reduced inspection—and the *transition* (switching) rules.

Figure 10.6 shows the system OC curve for the single sampling code letter K, 1.0% AQL, plans illustrated in Fig. 10.5. To reduce the amount of confusion, only the normal-and tightened- plan OC curves have been drawn in. In general, the system curve is much steeper than that for any individual plan. At quality levels better than the AQL, the system probability of acceptance is better than that indicated for normal inspection. This illustrates the effect of reduced inspection if it is permitted. If reduced inspection is not permitted, the system curve traces that for normal inspection at good quality levels.

As quality deteriorates, the system curve moves downward toward that for tightened inspection and becomes asymptotic to it beyond the indifference quality level p0.50. System OC curves are not included in the ABC standard or in its U.S. military equivalent MIL-STD-105E. A note of caution in using system curves should be introduced at this point. Of necessity, such curves assume that lots are formed from a controlled process at a level μ_p and that this level remains constant indefinitely. In calculating the probabilities of shifts to and from tightened inspection in the previous section, the assumption of a constant μp over some specified number of lots was used. Thus some compromise with reality was made. This compromise was minimal, however, in comparison to that made in developing system OC curves.

As was illustrated, once a shift to tightened inspection is made, the P_a is reduced considerably. Five consecutive lots must be accepted in order to return to normal inspection, and this shift must take place within ten consecutive lots inspected on tightened inspection. (This termination rule is not reflected in the system OC curves.) This places heavy pressure on the

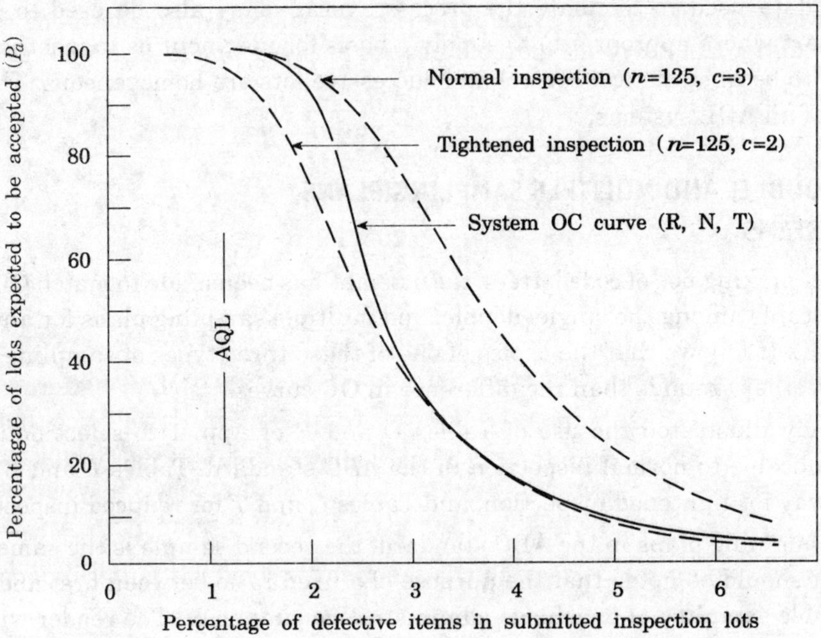

FIGURE 10.6: Comparison of normal and tightened OC curves with system (R, N, T) OC curve, single sampling code letter K, 1% AQL, ABC standard.

producer to improve quality. As a consequence, the assumption of a constant μp is quite unrealistic. Nevertheless, these system curves, when overlaid on curves for the individual plans, may still offer some further insight into the behaviour of systems of sampling plans.

10.9.3 Calculation of Estimated Process Average

Most AQL systems have required a formal estimate of the most recent process average (often from the samples from the past 10 lots) to guide the decisions about shifts back and forth among tightened, normal, and reduced inspection. The ABC standard has simplified the administrative rules regarding such shifts and does not make it imperative that an estimated process average be calculated.

Nevertheless, it is a good idea to require calculation of an estimated process average at regular intervals. It is desirable for both producer and consumer to know whether quality is, on the average, better or worse than the AQL and to know whether quality seems to be improving or deteriorating.

The calculated process average from any series of samples is merely the total number of defective units found divided by the total number of sample units inspected. If single sampling is used, it is customary to inspect the entire sample in all cases even though sometimes enough defectives may be found to cause rejection of a lot before all the sample units have been examined. Otherwise, samples from rejected lots will not be given sufficient weight in computing the process average. For the same reason, it is customary to inspect the entire first sample in double and multiple sampling.

In double and multiple sampling, it has been customary to use only the results from first samples in estimating process average. Otherwise, lots requiring more than one sample tend to be given undue weight in the calculation.

The lot-by-lot data used to calculate the process average may also be used to plot a p chart (or an np chart where appropriate) to supply a basis for judgment as to whether or not the process seems to be in statistical control and successive lots are homogeneous. This is an important aspect of all AQL systems.

10.10 SINGLE, DOUBLE, AND MULTIPLE SAMPLING PLANS IN AQL SYSTEMS

In the *AQL* systems making use of code letters, the attempt has been made to match OC curves as closely as practicable among the single, double, and multiple sampling plans for any stated code letter and AQL. It follows that the choice of one of these three types of sampling usually should be made on other grounds than the difference in OC curves.

We have already illustrated the use of Tables O and *R* of App. 1 to select double and multiple plans applicable to normal inspection in the *ABC* standard. Tables *P* and *S* may be used in a similar way for tightened inspection, and Tables *Q* and *T* for reduced inspection.

In the double sampling plans in the ABC standard, the second sample is the same size as the first sample. It should be noted that the purpose of a fixed ratio between first and second sample size in double sampling is to achieve administrative simplicity. The reader will recall that in the Dodge-Romig tables, designed to minimize total inspection, there was no fixed ratio of sizes of the two samples in double sampling.

Another aspect of the double sampling plans in the ABC standard is that the rejection number for the first sample is usually less than the rejection number for both samples combined. In this respect, the ABC standard reduces the amount of inspection under double sampling at some sacrifice of administrative simplicity.

The multiple sampling plans in the ABC standard all provide for seven samples. In all the military AQL standards, all the individual samples in any multiple sampling plan have been the same size.

For any given code letter in the ABC standard, a sample in double sampling is approximately five-eighths the corresponding single sample size; each sample in multiple sampling is one-fourth the corresponding single sample size. There are a few slight exceptions to the foregoing ratios that are caused by the need to have integral values of sample sizes.

10.10.1 Curtailment of Sampling Inspection in Double and Multiple Sampling

For reasons already mentioned in our discussion of the calculation of the process average, it is customary to inspect the entire first sample in double and multiple sampling.

When the rejection number is reached in the second sample in double sampling, it is customary to discontinue inspection. For example, assume the following plan applicable to normal inspection, 1.5% AQL, code letter *L*, in the ABC standard:

Sample size	Cumulative sample size	Acceptance number	Rejection number
125	125	3	7
125	250	8	9

On the first sample, 6 defectives are found. This requires a second sample. Suppose that 3 more defectives are found by the time 15 items from the second sample have been inspected. Since the rejection number of 9 has been reached, no further inspection is needed. In this instance, curtailment saves inspecting 110 items that would have been examined if the full second sample of 125 had been inspected.

In a similar way it is common to curtail multiple inspection whenever a rejection number is reached on any sample after the first. The advantage of curtailment in double and multiple sampling occurs particularly when product is bad enough to cause a fair percentage of lot rejections.

10.10.2 Comparing the Amount of Sampling Inspection in Single, Double, and Multiple Sampling in the *ABC* Standard

Figure 10.7. taken from the ABC standard, shows the approximate values of *Average Sample Number* (ASN) for double and multiple sampling relative to the sample size in single sampling.

Each of the 15 sets of curves applies to a set of plans characterized by a particular value of c in single sampling. The horizontal scale in each diagram is the product of single sample size and fraction defective. The ABC standard contains the following statement about these curves: "The curves assume no curtailment of inspection and are approximate to the extent that they are based upon the Poisson distribution, and that the sample sizes for double and multiple sampling are assumed to be 0.631 n and 0.25 n respectively, where n is the equivalent single sample size."

A reader who inspects the 15 diagrams in Fig. 10.7 might gain the impression that the average amount of inspection in multiple sampling in the ABC standard is much less than in double sampling. As applied to the portion of the standard that ordinarily will have the greatest use, this is an incorrect impression for the following reasons :

1. The plans from the standard that are likely to be used the most are those corresponding to the relatively low c numbers in single sampling, particularly numbers from 0 to 5. Upon examining Table L, the reader will observe that the higher values of c apply to the relatively high AQL values or to the relatively large sample sizes (or both).
2. It is the left-hand portion of the ASN curve — particularly to the left of the AQL value for normal inspection (shown by vertical arrows in Fig. 10.7) — that is of the most interest from a practical point of view. No AQL acceptance sampling plan is likely to be continued for long if the quality of submitted product is consistently much worse than the AQL.

Consider the portions of the ASN curves to the left of the AQL arrows where c is 1, 2. 3, and 5 in single sampling. (Figure 10.7 does not contain a diagram for $c = 0$ because the standard does not have matching double and multiple plans for this value of c.) Where c is 1, double sampling involves less inspection than multiple sampling because all the multiple sampling plans corresponding to this c value will not accept until the third sample. Where c is 2, 3, or 5, the ASN values in multiple sampling are generally from 80 to 85% of those in double sampling; for these plans, acceptance is possible on the second multiple sample.

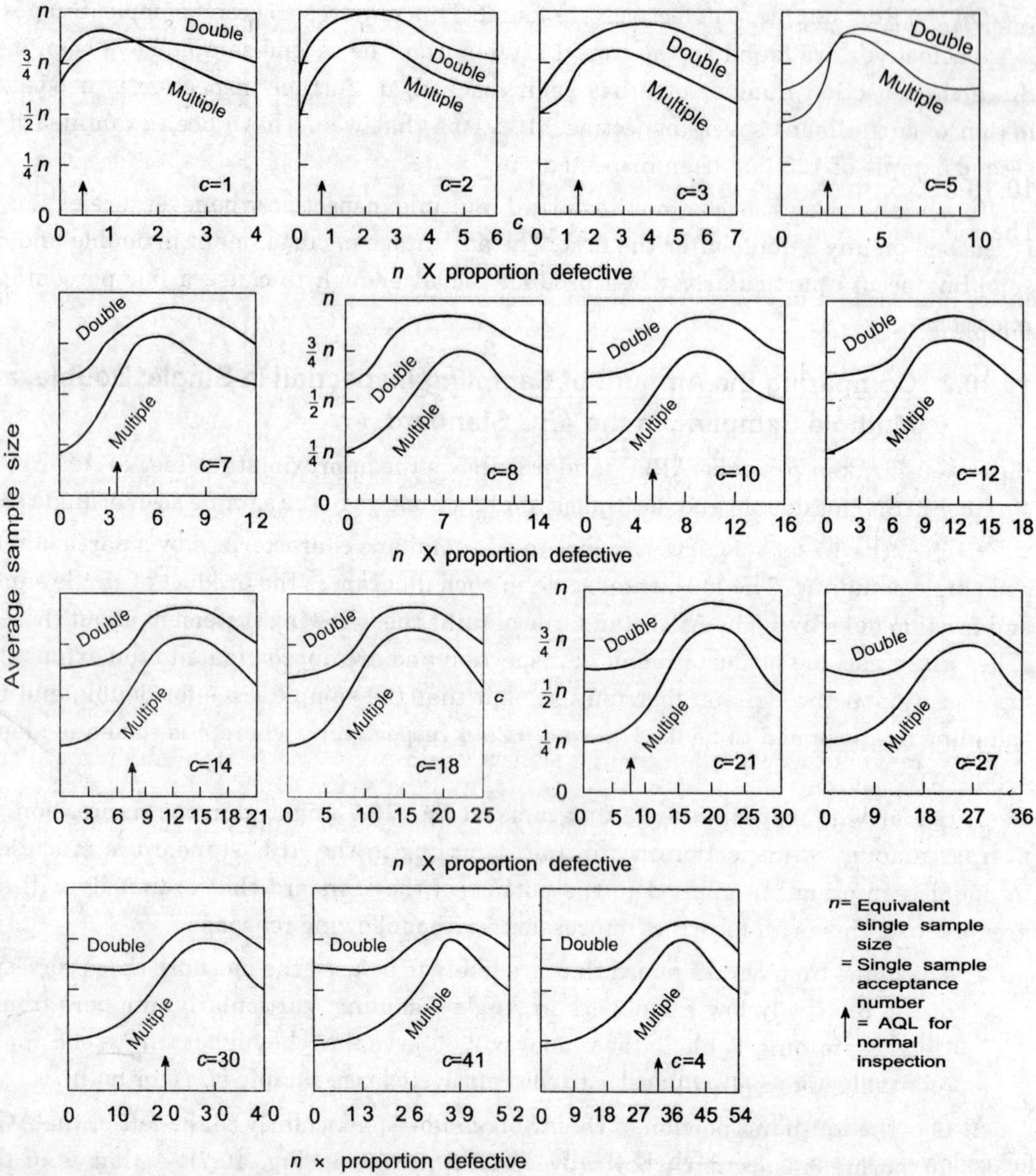

FIGURE 10.7: Table IX of MIL-STD-105E (and ABC standard) showing ratio of average sample size in double and multiple sampling to single sample size (normal and tightened inspection) assuming no curtailment.

It is chiefly where c in single sampling is 7 or more that the multiple sampling plans involve large savings in amount of inspection as compared with the double sampling plans. As previously stated, this advantage occurs chiefly where AQL values are relatively high or sample sizes are relatively large. For example, with an n of 32 in single sampling (code letter G), the AQL is 10% for a c of 7 in normal inspection. For an AQL of 1% and a c of 7 in normal inspection, n is 315 (code letter M).

The reader should note that the average sample number (ASN) is related to but not the same as the average total inspection (ATI) discussed in Chap. 9. As generally used, ASN refers to comparisons between average numbers of items inspected in sampling where other characteristics of the plans, such as their OC curves, are nearly identical. ATI applies only to cases where rejected lots are subjected to 100% inspection. This usage is adhered to consistently in this book. However such is not always the case in general literature of acceptance sampling.

10.10.3 Computing Average Sample Numbers in Double and Multiple Sampling

The following numerical examples are intended to illustrate how to calculate a point on an ASN curve. They also aim to show why each of the 15 graphs in Fig. 10.7 is applicable to the entire family of plans in the ABC standard that corresponds to a particular value of c in single sampling.

Consider the following plans for normal inspection from the *ABC* standard:

Code letter J, 0.065% AQL			Code letter P, 0.065% AQL		
Cumulative sample size	Acceptance number	Rejection number	Cumulative sample size	Acceptance number	Rejection number
Single:			Single:		
80	1	2	800	1	2
Double:			Double:		
50	0	2	500	0	2
100	1	2	1000	1	2
Multiple:			Multiple:		
20	*	2	200	*	2
40	*	2	400	*	2
60	0	2	600	0	2
80	0	3	800	0	3
100	1	3	1000	1	3
120	1	3	1200	1	3
140	2	3	1400	2	3

*Acceptance not permitted at this sample size.

Assume that product 1% defective is being submitted to the double sampling plan shown for code letter *J* and an AQL of 0.65%. To compute the average sample number it is first necessary to find the respective probabilities that a decision will be reached on each sample. (It was explained in Chap. 9 that such probabilities are computed in finding each point on an OC curve in double and multiple sampling.)

Assume that calculations will be based on the Poisson approximation. Then μnp for each sample of 50 is 50 (0.01) = 0.5. Table *G* gives P_0 as 0.607, P_1 as 0.303, and P_2 as 0.090. The probability of a decision on the first sample is the P_a of 0.607 plus the P_r of 0.090 = 0.697. In double sampling, the probability of a decision on the second sample is identical with the probability that a second sample will be taken, in this case 0.303. If there is no curtailment of inspection, 0.697 of the lots will require a sample of 50 and 0.303 will require a sample of 100. It follows that

$$\text{ASN} = 0.697\ (50) + 0.303\ (100) = 65.2$$

For double sampling plans in general,

$$\text{ASN} = [P_a(n_1) + P_r(n_1)]\, n_1 + [P_a(n_2) + P_r(n_2)]\,(n_1 + n_1)$$
$$= n_1 + [P_a(n_2) + P_r(n_2)]\;\; n_2 = n_1 + n_2\, P(n_2) \qquad \text{...(10.3)}$$

where $P_a(n_1)$ = probability of acceptance in n_1, and so on

$P(n_2)$ = probability of drawing n_2.

Calculations regarding the ASN in multiple sampling follow the same lines, although they require considerably more arithmetic. In the multiple sampling scheme for code letter *J* and AQL of 0.65%, each sample is 20. With a μp of 0.01, the μnp for each sample is 0.2. Table *G* gives $P_0 = 0.819$, $P_1 = 0.163$, $P_2 = 0.017$, $P_3 = 0.001$. These figures may be used to compute probabilities of acceptance and rejection on each sample. These probabilities are as follows :

Sample	P_a	P_r	$P_a + P_r$
1st	0.000	0.018	0.018
2nd	0.000	0.045	0.045
3rd	0.549	0.060	0.609
4th	0.000	0.006	0.006
5th	0.220	0.015	0.235
6th	0.000	0.016	0.016
7th	0.058	0.013	0.071
Totals	0.827	0.173	1.000

If it is assumed that there is no curtailment of inspection, the probabilities of a decision (that is, $P_a + P_r$) on each sample may be used to compute the ASN value as follows :

$$\text{ASN} = 20\,(0.018) + 40\,(0.045) + 60\,(0.609) + 80\,(0.006)$$
$$+\, 100(0.235) + 120(0.016) + 140(0.071) = 74.5$$

Now, let us compare the single, double, and multiple sampling plans shown for code letter P and an AQL of 0.065% with the corresponding plans shown for code letter J and an AQL of 0.65%. It is evident that the acceptance and rejection numbers are identical and that all sample sizes in the plans for code letter P are 10 times those for code letter J. If we assume a μ_p of 0.001, one-tenth of the μ_p value used in our calculations for the plan from code letter J, the μ_p values for the sample sizes of 500 and 200 with code letter P will be the same as those with samples of 50 and 20 with J. It follows that, if the Poisson approximation is used, the values of P_a and P_r for each sample will be identical with those calculated for a μ_p of 0.01 with code letter J. The ASN values will be 652 with double sampling and 745 with multiple sampling, exactly 10 times the values calculated for code letter J.

In Fig. 10.7 one ASN curve for double sampling and another for multiple sampling applied to the plans we have analyzed for code letters J and P and to all other plans corresponding to a *c* of 1 in single sampling. The use of one ASN curve to represent many different plans is possible in part, because of the generalized scales used in plotting the curves in Fig. 10.7 and, in part, because of certain unique aspects of the ABC standard.

One relevant aspect of the ABC standard is that there is only one set of acceptance and rejection numbers in double and multiple sampling corresponding to each value of *c* in single sampling. Another aspect is that the ratio of double and multiple sample size to single size is approximately constant for all corresponding plans.

Moreover, the product of single sample size and AQL value in normal inspection is approximately constant for all plans having the same value of c in single sampling. For this reason, it is possible to show arrows indicating AQL values in normal inspection on the graphs in Fig. 10.7. (The graphs without AQL arrows apply to plans used only in tightened inspection.)

10.10.4 Effect of Curtailment on Amount of Sampling Inspection

The curves in Fig. 10.7 assume no curtailment of inspection when the rejection number is reached in the second sample in double sampling or in the second or subsequent samples in multiple sampling. (This assumption simplified the calculation of average sample numbers and made possible the plotting of one set of curves for each value of c.) However, such curtailment is a desirable practice and is commonly used. Economies due to curtailment occur particularly where quality is sufficiently worse than the AQL for a fair percentage of lots to be rejected.

The larger the sample sizes, the greater the possible savings due to curtailment. For this reason, in a comparison the corresponding double and multiple sampling plans, curtailment will cause greater economies in double sampling than in multiple sampling. It follows that, where curtailment is to be used, Fig. 10.7 exaggerates the differences in average amount of inspection between double and multiple sampling, particularly in the right-hand portion of the curves.

10.10.5 Choosing among Single, Double, and Multiple Sampling

It sometimes happens that double and multiple sampling are impracticable. There may be physical reasons why only one sample can be drawn from a lot, or it may not be feasible to provide for the variable inspection load associated with double and multiple sampling. Under such circumstances, it is necessary to use single sampling. More often, however, there is opportunity for choice. In deciding among these three types of sampling, consideration should be given to a number of factors in addition to the expected differences in average amount of inspection. Some of these factors are :

1. The psychological advantages of double advantages
2. The expected differences in costs of administration
3. The difficulties of training inspectors to use multiple sampling correctly
4. The need for quick and reliable estimates of process average for various purposes including decision among normal, tightened and reduced inspection
5. The availability of inspection personnel and facilities.

10.11 CLASSIFICATION OF DEFECTS

In AQL systems for acceptance sampling by attributes, it is common for one AQL to apply to a group of possible defects rather than to have a separate AQL value for each possible way in which product may fail to conform to specifications. Unless trivial defects are to be given the same weightage as serious ones, it is essential to have a classification of defects or classification of characteristics. (These two phrases seem to be used interchangeably.) Such classifications were mentioned in Chap. 6.

The ABC standard calls for defects to be classified as critical, major, and minor. The definitions of these are as follows :

Critical Defect: A critical defect is a defect that judgment and experience indicate is likely to result in hazardous or unsafe conditions for individuals using, maintaining, or depending upon the product; or a defect that judgment and experience indicate is likely to prevent performance of the tactical function of a major end item such as a ship, aircraft, tank, missile or space vehicle.

Major Defect: A major defect is a defect, other than critical, that is likely to result in failure, or to reduce materially the usability of the unit of product for its intended purpose.

Minor Defect: A minor defect is a defect that is not likely to reduce materially the usability of the unit of product for its intended purpose, or is a departure from established standards having little bearing on the effective use or operation of the unit.

Product usually is subject to 100% inspection for critical defects. But there are many types of product with no defects classed as critical; all are either major or minor. It is fairly common to divide minor defects into two groups depending on their relative importance. The more important minors may be designated Minor A; the less important ones, Minor B. (In the original Army Ordnance and Army Service Forces tables, the more descriptive adjective "incidental" was used for the relatively unimportant defects of the type later classified as "Minor B.")

10.11.1 An Illustration of the Use of Classification of Defects in Acceptance Sampling

Assume that the classification of defects for certain bolts includes 5 defects classified as Major, 11 classified Minor *A*, and 8 classified as Minor *B*. Bolts are to be inspected in lots of 10,000 under the *ABC* standard. Double sampling and inspection level II are to be used. The *AQL* is 1.0% for Majors, 4.0% for Minor *A*, and 6.5% for Minor *B*.

The sample size code letter *L* is determined by the lot size and inspection level. In this case, the acceptance criteria are:

Cumulative sample size	*Major*		*Minor A*		*Minor B*	
	Accept	*Reject*	*Accept*	*Reject*	*Accept*	*Reject*
125	2	5	7	11	11	16
250	6	7	18	19	26	27

A first sample of 125 will be drawn from the lot. This sample is inspected separately for each class of defects. The numbers of defective articles found in each class are as follows :

Major 2

Minor *A* 10

Minor *B* 7

Therefore the lot is passed for Major and Minor *B* defects on the basis of the first sample. A second sample of 125 must be drawn and inspected only for Minor *A* defects. If not more than 8 additional bolts containing such defects are found, the lot is passed. If 9 or more are found, the lot is rejected for Minor *A* defects.

In general, it is economical and convenient to inspect the same sample for all classes of defects. However, the acceptance criteria are applied separately for each class. A lot is rejected if it fails to meet the acceptance criteria for one or more classes. All characteristics checked within a class count toward acceptance or rejection within that class.

10.12 PROBLEMS ARISING FROM RESUBMISSION OF REJECTED LOTS

Whenever rejected lots are returned to the producer, the resubmission of these lots for another sampling inspection creates certain problems.

Obviously, it is not in the consumer's interest for lots to be submitted unchanged. This point can be illustrated by a simple probability calculation.

Assume that the probability of acceptance of a lot of given quality is 0.80. This will be the probability of its acceptance not only on the first submission but also on any subsequent submission. The probability of acceptance with a maximum of two resubmissions is as follows:

Probability of acceptance on first submission	0.80
Probability of rejection on first submission followed by acceptance on second submission = (0.20) (0.80)	0.16
Probability of rejection on first and second submission followed by acceptance on third submission = (0.20) (0.20) (0.80)	0.03
Probability of acceptance with not more than three submissions	0.99

Of course, the normal action by a reputable producer is to screen a rejected lot before resubmitting it. The ABC standard contains the following reasonable stipulation: "Lots or batches found unacceptable shall be resubmitted for reinspection only after all units are reexamined or retested and all defective units are removed or defects corrected."

Resubmitted lots that have received 100% inspection by the producer after rejection presumably are considerably better on their second submission than they were on their first submission. Therefore, the results from sampling inspection of resubmitted lots should not be viewed as representative of the process average. Criteria for determining whether normal, tightened, or reduced inspection is to be used should be based solely on the results of original inspection, and the results from any resubmitted lots should be ignored.

10.13 ACCEPTANCE BASED ON NUMBERS OF DEFECTS

A defective article is an article containing one or more defects. In our discussion up to this point, acceptance decisions have been based on the numbers of defectives contained in a sample. Decisions on lot acceptance or rejection have not been influenced by the number of defects observed in each defective article. The sampled article with eight defects has had the same influence on lot acceptance as the sampled article with only one defect; each has counted as a single defective.

Under certain conditions, it may be more reasonable to base acceptance decisions on defects rather than on defectives. For instance, some defects might be tolerable in a bolt of cloth, but it might be desired to limit the average defects per bolt in a shipment of bolts of cloth. In general, the field of application of acceptance based on defects is similar to the field for the c chart discussed in Chap. 6. With acceptance based on defects, AQL values, OC curves, and so forth, are interpreted in terms of defects per hundred units rather than as percent defective.

The entire ABC standard may be used for inspection based on defects as well as for inspection based on defectives. In general, the only changes necessary are to substitute the word *defects* wherever *defectives* is used and to interpret AQLs as defects per hundred units. Of course, the highest AQL values in the standard may be interpreted only as defects per hundred units. For example, it would be meaningless to have an AQL of 150% defective but entirely reasonable to have an AQL of 150 defects per hundred units in sampling inspection of, say, bolts of cloth (that is, 1.5 defects per bolt). Normal, tightened, and reduced inspection can be used in inspection based on defects just as in inspection based on defectives.

The binomial distribution is correct in principle for Type B OC curves based on defectives; in the ABC standard, the binomial is used for OC curves for AQLs of 10.0 or less. The Poisson distribution is correct in principle for OC curves based on defects; in the ABC standard, the Poisson is used for AQLs of 15.0 or more.

10.14 SELECTING AN ACCEPTANCE PLAN FOR AN ISOLATED LOT

The teeth in any AQL system are in the provision for tightened inspection whenever the recent quality record is bad enough. An AQL is enforced through the overall system, not through the lot-by-lot acceptance criteria used in normal inspection. As has been explained, such criteria are chosen to protect the producer by making sure that nearly all lots will be accepted as long as the process average is at the AQL value or better. Therefore, if individual lots considerably worse than the AQL are submitted, such lots have a good chance to be accepted.

Where lots are isolated or infrequent, an overall acceptance sampling system cannot be used to develop pressure for the submission of good quality. The consumer dealing with an isolated lot needs to take a good look at the OC curve of the proposed sampling plan to judge whether it gives adequate protection. If it is required to be protected against product worse than, say, 1% defective, one should not select a sampling plan indexed under an AQL of 1% in any of the various AQL tables. Such a plan will not give the required protection.

At several points we have noted that one of the serious objections to regular 100% inspection by the consumer is that such inspection does not exert enough pressure on a producer to improve the process. Of course, this objection applies only when there is a continuing relationship between producer and consumer; it is not valid when there is only one lot. In general, the consumer should be willing to screen an isolated lot whenever high quality is deemed essential and when such screening is practicable (as in the case of nondestructive test). A possible compromise between the interests of producer and consumer might be to use an acceptance plan for isolated lots based on a stated quality standard at $p_{0.50}$, the indifference quality, with the consumer screening any accepted lot.

The ABC standard stipulates that, when a lot or batch is of an isolated nature, sampling plans should be chosen based on the identification of a Consumer's Risk point associated with the designated AQL. Tables for Consumer's Risks of 5 and 10%, called the *Limiting Quality* (LQ) tables, are contained in the standard. Table 10.5 reproduces the LQ table for a 10% Consumer's Risk. The term LQ, in this instance, is synonymous with the LTPD.

The user enters the table by the designated AQL and searches the column until an acceptable value of LQ ($100p_{0.10}$) is found. The sample size code letter is then read from the left-hand side. In using this table, the choice of a sampling plan is based, in effect, on the choice of two points on the OC curve, a Producer's Risk point (AQL) and a Consumer's Risk point ($100\ p_{0.10}$).

TABLE 10.5: ABC-STD-105 LIMITING QUALITY TABLES FOR WHICH P_a = 10% NORMAL INSPECTION, SINGLE SAMPLING

Code letter	Sample size	In percent defective (100p0.10)															
		Acceptable quality level															
		0.010	0.015	0.025	0.040	0.065	0.10	0.15	0.25	0.40	0.65	1.0	1.5	2.5	4.0	6.5	10
A	2															68	
B	3														54		
C	5													37			58
D	8												25			41	54
E	13											16			27	36	44
F	20										11			18	25	30	42
G	32									6.9			12	16	20	27	34
H	50								4.5			7.6	10	13	18	22	29
J	80							2.8			4.8	6.5	8.2	11	14	19	24
K	125						1.8			3.1	4.3	5.4	7.4	9.4	12	16	23
L	200					1.2			2.0	2.7	3.3	4.6	5.9	7.7	10	14	
M	315				0.73			1.2	1.7	2.1	2.9	3.7	4.9	6.4	9.0		
N	500			0.46			0.78	1.1	1.3	1.9	2.4	3.1	4.0	5.6			
P	800		0.29			0.49	0.67	0.84	1.2	1.5	1.9	2.5	3.5				
Q	1,250	0.18			0.31	0.43	0.53	0.74	0.94	1.2	1.6	2.3					
R	2,000			0.20	0.27	0.33	0.46	0.59	0.77	1.0	1.4						

Code letter	Sample size	In defects per hundred units																									
		Acceptable quality level																									
		0.010	0.015	0.025	0.040	0.065	0.10	0.15	0.25	0.40	0.65	1.0	1.5	2.5	4.0	6.5	10	15	25	40	65	100	150	250	400	650	1000
A	2															120			200	270	330	460	590	700	1000	1400	1900
B	3														77			130	180	220	310	390	510	670	940	1300	1800
C	5													46			78	110	130	190	240	310	400	560	770	1100	
D	8												29			49	67	84	120	150	190	250	350	480	670		
E	13											18			30	41	51	71	91	120	160	220	300	410			
F	20										12			20	27	33	46	59	77	100	140						
G	32									7.2			12	17	21	29	37	48	63	88							
H	50								4.6			7.8	11	13	19	24	31	40	56								
J	80							2.9			4.9	6.7	8.4	12	15	19	25	35									
K	125						1.8			3.1	4.3	5.4	7.4	9.4	12	16	23										
L	200					1.2			2.0	2.7	3.3	4.6	5.9	7.7	10	14											
M	315				0.73			1.2	1.7	2.1	2.9	3.7	4.9	6.4	9.0												
N	500			0.46			0.78	1.1	1.3	1.9	2.4	3.1	4.0	5.6													
P	800		0.29			0.49	0.67	0.84	1.2	1.5	1.9	2.5	3.5														
Q	1,250	0.18			0.31	0.43	0.53	0.74	0.94	1.2	1.6	2.3															
R	2,000			0.20	0.27	0.33	0.46	0.59	0.77	1.0	1.4																

Reproduced from "Military Standard 105E. Sampling Procedures and Tables for Inspection Attributes," pp/28-29, Superintendant of Documents, Government Printing Office, Washington, D.C., 1989.

10.15 IMPORTANCE OF AOQL VALUES IN SAMPLING PLANS BASED ON THE AQL

Tables *U* and *V* in App. 1 are reproduced from the ABC standard. They give AOQL factors for normal and tightened inspection, respectively, for the single sampling plans in the standard. With the exception of those where $c = 0$, the AOQL values in tightened inspection are fairly close to the stipulated AQL values. The AOQL value is significant in an AQL plan because it is reasonable to expect that a reputable producer will screen lots that have been rejected under the sampling plan.

Some persons object to the policy of placing reliance on the quality protection promised by a computed AOQL value on the grounds that one cannot be certain that errors will not be made by the inspector who screen the rejected lots. To be consistent, such persons also should object to all OC curves for sampling inspection plans because such curves assume that the inspectors discovers the defective items in a sample. They also should object to all use of 100% inspection. In general, there is no reason to be more concerned with the possibility of inspectors' errors in screening rejected lots than with the possibility of such errors made in other inspection activities. In fact, it usually is reasonable to expect that more care will be exercised in screening rejected lots than when 100% inspection is used in the first place.

SOLVED QUESTIONS

Q. 10.1: *Select the correct option:*

(*i*) Selection of a sampling plan from the Dodge-Romig AOQL sampling tables

(*a*) requires an estimate of the AOQ

(*b*) requires an estimate of the process average

(*c*) requires sorting of rejected lots

(*d*) requires larger samples than MIL-STD-105E for equivalent quality assurance

(*e*) requires that we assume a consumer's risk of 0.05.

(*ii*) Dodge-Romig sampling schemes aim at

(*a*) minimizing the total inspection (*b*) minimizing the acceptance number

(*c*) minimizing AQL (*d*) minimizing AOQL

(*iii*) Dodge-Romig sampling schemes provide for

(*a*) single, and multiple sampling plans

(*b*) only single sampling plans

(*c*) both single and double sampling plans

(*d*) generally single and double sampling plans but for certain quality level multiple and sequential sampling plans also.

(*iv*) Dodge-Romig sampling schemes provide for

(*a*) minimum total inspection (*b*) minimum AOQL

(*c*) minimum LTPD (*d*) minimum AOQL.

(*v*) Dodge-Romig sampling plans provide sampling schemes indexed on

(*a*) AQL and LTPD (*b*) AOQL and LTPD

(*c*) AOQ and LTPD (*d*) LQ and LTPD

(*vi*) In Dodge-Romig sampling schemes, each LTPD plan gives lists the corresponding

(*a*) AOQL (*b*) indifference quality

(*c*) α and β risks (*d*) AQL

(*vii*) In D-R sampling schemes, each AOQL plan gives corresponding

(*a*) LTPD (*b*) AOQ

(*c*) LQ (*d*) Indifference quality.

Ans: (*i*) (*b*); (*ii*) (*a*); (*iii*) (*b*); (*iv*) (*a*); (*v*) (*b*); (*vi*) (*a*); (*vii*) (*a*)

Q. 10.2: *State whether the following statements are True/False.*

(*i*) One characteristics of D-R double sampling plan (DSP) is that no lot is even rejected as a result of only 1 defective.

(*ii*) In D-R DSP, the first sample is always less than comparable SSP.

(*iii*) LQL is an alternative term for LTPD.

(*iv*) D-R schemes are very much applicable where destructive testing is involved.

Ans: (*i*) True; (*ii*) True; (*iii*) True; (*iv*) False.

Q. 10.3: *What is LQL?*

Ans: It is limiting quality level and should have low probability of acceptance. The term LTPD (*i.e.* lot tolerance percentage defective) is more frequently used in place of LQL.

Q. 10.4: *Why Dodge-Romig AOQL sampling plans are sometimes not acceptable to consumers ?*

Ans: AOQL sampling plans are appropriate only when all rejected lots are 100 percent screened by the producer. As there is no assurance from the producer for this procedure, AOQL schemes are open to question and sometimes not acceptable to consumers.

Q. 10.5: *Describe briefly how Dodge-Romig sampling schemes achieve their aim.*

Ans: All D-R sampling schemes are constructed to minimize the average total inspection (ATI) per lot for product of a given process average.

Suppose a consumer gives the acceptance criteria as follows :

$$\text{LTPD} = 5\% \; i.e. \; (100\,p = 5) \text{ or } p = 0.05$$

Probability of acceptance $P_a = 0.1$

A great many sampling plans meet these criteria; i.e. there are many combinations of sample size and acceptance number that would have an OC curve through this point (0.05, 0.1).

It is obvious that the total number of articles inspected is made up two components :

1. the sample which is inspected for each lot and
2. the remaining part which must be inspected in these lots which fail to pass the sampling inspection.

For small acceptance number (i.e. small *c* value), the total number inspected is high because many lots need to be detailed. For higher acceptance numbers, the total is again high, this time because of the large size of samples. The minimum sum occurs at a point between these extremes. All D-R sampling schemes minimize the ATI.

Q. 10.6: *Can Dodge-Romig acceptance sampling schemes be applied to cases where destructive testing is involved ?.*

Ans: The D-R sampling schemes include detailing of the rejected lots. Where destructive testing is involved, this may not be practical or possible. In these cases D-R schemes may still be used, but the consumer no longer is guaranteed that the average outgoing quality will be better than the AOQL value. In practice, however, the high rate of rejected lots with quality much worse (two times AOQL value) and high rate of acceptance of lots with quality better than the AOQL value will tend to compel the producer in his own interest to maintain a process quality which at worst will be little, if any, poorer than the AOQL.

Q. 10.7: *What is the concept of AOQL ?*

Ans: There exists an approximate relationship between the fraction defective in the material before inspection (incoming quality p) and the fraction defective remaining after inspection (average outgoing quality AOQ) : AOQ = *Pap*. When incoming quality is perfect, outgoing quality will also be perfect (assuming no inspection errors) because the sampling plan will cause all lots to be rejected and detected. Thus, at either extreme–incoming quality excellent or terrible–the outgoing quality will tend to be good. Between these extremes is the point at which the percentage of defectives in the outgoing material will reach its maximum. This point is the average outgoing quality limit (AOQL).

Q. 10.8: *Describe briefly the approach taken by Dodge-Romig in the preparation of sampling schemes.*

Ans: Dodge and Romig pioneered work on sampling inspection in the 1920s and 1930s. Their work on single sampling inspection schemes is concerned with rectifying inspection. In this type of inspection, when a lot is rejected, it is not discarded, sold off cheaply or returned to the producer, but instead is subjected to 100% inspection (or detailed) and all defectives are rectified or replaced. Thus if a lot is rejected all N items are inspected, whereas if a lot is accepted only n items are inspected. Dodge and Romig schemes use the semi-economic approach of minimizing the total amount of inspection, considering both sampling inspection and screening inspection of the rejected lots, considering that the cost of inspection is proportional to the number of items inspected. Thus D-R schemes aim at minimizing

$$\text{ATI} = n\,P_a + N\,(1 - P_a)$$

or

$$N - P_a\,(N - n)$$

with respect to the two parameters n and c of the single sampling plan. In order to determine n and c uniquely a second condition is required, and Dodge Romig considered two possible alternatives leading to (*a*) Lot Tolerance Percent Defective (LTPD) and (*b*) Average Outgoing Quality Limit (AOQL) schemes.

Q. 10.9: (*a*) *When do you recommend LTPD sampling schemes ?*

(*b*) *Why Dodge-Romig AOQL tables do not give any plans for process average which exceed AOQL?*

(c) If a single sampling plan is desired with an AOQL of 1.8% at an incoming quality of 2.5%, what is the common point on the OC curves for a family of sampling plans that meet the AOQL and 100% μp stipulation ?

Ans: *(a)* When it is desired to protect the customer from accepting submitted lots where quality is poorer than he is willing to tolerate, an LTPD sampling scheme is used.

(b) Sampling is uneconomical if the average quality submitted is not considerably better than the AOQL specified. Hence D-R AOQL tables (Tables 10.3 and 10.4) do not give any plans for process average which exceeds AOQL.

(c) Several sampling plans can meet the given conditions. One of the plans D-R Table 10.1 for the stated AOQL of 1.8% is $n = 280$, $c = 9$. Probability of acceptance of 2.5% *i.e.* ($\mu_p = 0.025$) defective lot as computed from Table *G* is 0.830. Hence the OC curves of all such sampling plans will have a common point ($\mu_p = 0.025$; $P_a = 0.830$).

Q. 10.10: *(a) State the basic differences between the D-R LTPD and AOQL sampling schemes.*

(b) A firm is manufacturing a range of electric motors of up to 5 h.p. Batch sizes are typically 500, and one particular customer absorbs approximately 60 per cent of the production capacity. This customer would like to formalize quality control procedures, and he wishes these to be statistically valid. The customer desires to keep the percentage of unacceptable motors in his goods - inward stores at no more than 2 percent on average. The production process is capable of manufacturing 1% defective or less, and current conformance checking procedures involve 100% inspection at various stages of manufacture. Design a single sampling plan and determine the LTPD.

Ans: *(a)* LTPD tables are based on the probability that a particular lot, which has a percent defective equal to or less than LTPD, will be accepted. LTPD schemes give assurance that individual lots of poor material will rarely be accepted.

AOQL sampling schemes limit the amount of poor outgoing quality on an average basis, but give no assurance an individual lots.

(b) $\mu_p = 0.01$ and AOQL = 2%, N = 500.

Table 10.3 gives the sampling plan : $n = 39$, $c = 1$.

The LTPD as read from Table 10.3 for this sampling plan for *N* of 500 and process average of 0.01, is 9.8% i.e. 0.098.

Q. 10.11: *(a) TRUE or FALSE ?*

"Dodge-Romig sampling schemes have provision for multiple sampling."

(b) Why D-R sampling tables are popular for within-plant inspection ?

(c) List out some features of D-R LTPD sampling tables.

Ans: *(a)* FALSE. D-R sampling schemes do not have any provision of multiple sampling.

(b) The principal advantage of the D-R tables is a minimum amount of inspection for a given inspection procedure. This advantage makes the tables desirable within plant inspection.

(c) Some of the notable features of D-R LTPD tables are :

1. For the same process average, as the lot size increases, the sample size decreases *i.e.* it does not increase in the same proportion and hence inspection costs are more economical with larger lots.

2. The tables extend until the process average is one-half of the LTPD. Provision of additional averages is unnecessary since 100% inspection becomes more economical than sampling inspection when the process average exceeds one-half of the LTPD.
3. As the process average increases, a corresponding increase occurs in the amount inspected. Therefore, an improvement in the process average results in a fewer inspections and a lower sampling inspection cost.

Q. 10.12: (*a*) *Discuss some features of the D-R AOQL sampling tables.*

(*b*) *How do you take care of type of defects in the D-R sampling schemes ?*

(*c*) *Do the D-R sampling schemes have the provision of tightened and reduced inspection ?*

Ans: (*a*) Some notable features of the D-R AOQL sampling tables are

1. As the lot size increases, the relative sample size decreases.
2. Sampling plans are not given for process averages which exceed the AOQL, since sampling becomes uneconomical when the process average incoming quality is poorer than the specified AOQL.
3. The lower the process average, the smaller the sample size, resulting in lower sampling inspection cost.

(*b*) The D-R tables do not make a provision for the type of defect, although different LTPD or AOQL values can be used—lower ones for critical defects and higher ones for minor defects. Defects/100 rather than percent defective can be used for the process average; however this is limited to values of 10 or less.

(*c*) The D-R tables do not have any provision for tightened or reduced inspection, although different LTPD or AOQL values can also be used.

Q. 10.13: (*a*) *For the same protection provided by an AOQL scheme and by an LTPD scheme, how will you choose between these two schemes ?*

(*b*) *What single sampling plan should be used for lot size of 325 and an LTPD of 5% with a Consumer's Risk of 0.10, if the process average is estimated as 0.56% ? Use the Dodge-Romig Single Sampling Tables.*

What is the maximum outgoing quality limit ?

(*c*) *What double sampling plan should be used for the condition described in (b) ? What is the maximum outgoing quality limit ?*

Ans: (*a*) The AOQL schemes should be used if interest is in the general level of quality after inspection (although it should be noted that is usually considered better than the AOQL).

However if, it is required that each low quality lot is rejected with a prescribed high probability of at least (1 – β), then the LTPD scheme should be used.

(*b*) For lot size of 325, and process average (0.51 - 1.00) D-R Single Sampling Lot Tolerance Tables (Table 10.1) for LTPD of 5% and consumer's Risk of 0.10, give the following sampling plan : $n = 70$, $c = 1$

Maximum outgoing quality limit (AOQL) given by the Table 10.1 is 0.99%.

(*c*) For the same conditions, Table 10.2 gives the following:

$$n_1 = 55, c_1 = 0$$
$$n_2 = 55, c_2 = 2$$
AOQL is 1.1%.

Q. 10.14: *Assuming that the number of defective items follows the Poisson law, how would you determined the most economical single sampling plan, given N (lot size). Average Outgoing Quality Limit (AOQL) and process quality ($\bar{p}$) ?*

(b) Using the Dodge-Romig tables, determine the double sampling plan for AOQL = 2.0% when the process average is 0.80% and the lot size is 25000. What is p_t ?

(c) What would be the sampling plan if the lot contains a new product and the process average is unknown ? What is LTPD in this case.

Ans: (*a*) Using Dodge-Romig Double sampling AOQL plans, gives the most economic plan as the inspection is reduced to minimum.

(*b*) Using Table 10.4, (Dodge-Romig 2% AOQL double sampling tables, for lot size of 2500 and AOQL of 0.80% the double sampling plan is as follows :

$$n_1 = 41, c_1 = 0, n_2 = 84$$
$$n_1 + n_2 = 125 \text{ and } c_2 = 4$$

Dodge-Romig termed LTPD as 100 p_t. From the table 100 p_t = 7. Hence p_t = 0.07.

(*c*) When the process average is unknown and there is no basis of estimating the same, the samples plan should be chosen from the right-hand column of the table. Hence the sampling plan is :

$$n_1 = 160, c_1 = 3, n_2 = 310$$
$$n_1 + n_2 = 470, c_2 = 15$$

From the table LTPD is 4.7.

Q. 10.15: *What double sampling plan should be used for a lot size of 1,500 and an LTPD of 5% with a Consumer's Risk of 0.10, if the process average is estimated as 0.8% ? Use Dodge-Romig Double Sampling Tables.*

If the quality improves to a point where the process average is 0.6%, what will be the changes in the inspection plan designed when process average is 0.8% ?

Ans: From the Table 10.2, the sampling plan to be used is as follows :

$$n_1 = 55, c_1 = 0 ;$$
$$n_2 = 120, c_2 = 4.$$

According to the Table 10.2 from which the above plan has been taken, if the process average varies from 0.51 to 1.00%, there will not be any change in the sampling plan.

Q. 10.16: *What single sampling plan should be used for a lot size of 900 and an AOQL of 2.0% if the process average is estimated as 0.9% defective ?*

(*i*) *What will be the changes in the sampling plan if the lots start coming in sizes of (a) 1000, (b) 1,100, and the other conditions remain the same ?*

(*ii*) *What will be the changes in (a) and (b) if the process average is known to be exactly 1% defective ?*

Ans: For a lot size of 900, Dodge-Romig Single Sampling AOQL Table 10.3 for an AOQL of 2.0%, for the process average of 0.9% give the sampling plan as

$$n = 65, c = 2$$

(*i*) (*a*) When the lot size changes from 900 to 1,000 the above plan is still applicable, provided other conditions remain the same.

(*b*) When the lot size changes from 900 to 1,100, other conditions remaining the same, the required sampling plan is still valid.

(*ii*) When the process average is known to be exactly 1.0%, and an AOQL is 2.0%, the required sampling plan is still same irrespective of the lot size of 900, 1,000 and 1,100.

Q. 10.17: *What double sampling plan should be used for a lot size of 900 and on AOQL of 2.0%, if the process average is estimated as 0.9% defective. What will be LTPD for this sampling scheme ?*

Ans: From D-R 2% AOQL double sampling Table 10 - 4, the required sampling scheme is

$$n_1 = 38, c_1 = 0;$$

$$n_2 = 87, c_2 = 4.$$

LTPD is 7.2%.

Q. 10.18: *Design a single sampling plan for an AOQL of 2% for the estimated process average of 1% and lot size of 1,000. What percentage of the product will be subjected to sampling inspection in a lot ? Out of 2,000 submitted lots, which are 1% defective, how many would you expect to be subjected to screening to inspection ?*

Ans: From the required Table 10.3 the sampling plan to be used as follows :

$$n = 65, c = 2$$

Since 65 pieces out of 1,000 are inspected, therefore percentage of the product subjected to sampling inspection in a lot is 6.5.

Also when $\mu_p = 0.01$

and $n = 65$

therefore $\mu_{np} = 0.65$

For μ_{np} or 0.65 and $c = 2$, the probability of acceptance from Table *G* is 0.972. Or out of 1,000 lots, 28 will be rejected.

Hence or out of 2,000 lots which are 1% defective 56 lots are expected to be screened.

Q. 10.19: (*a*) *Determine from Table 10.3 the single sampling plans for an AOQL of 2%, an estimated process average of 1% and lot sizes of 200, 1,000 and 5,000 respectively. What percentage of the product will be subjected to sampling inspection with each lot size ?*

(*b*) *Out of 100 submitted lots 1% nonconforming, how many would you expect to be subject to screening inspection for each lot size ?*

(*c*) *Using the answers of (a) and (b), what will be the total percentage of inspection for each of the three lots sizes, considering both sampling inspection and screening inspection of rejected lots ?*

Ans: Consulting Table 10.3 and using Table *G*, the required information for the three lots is as follows.

N	200	1000	5000
n	17	65	125
c	0	2	4
μ_{np}	0.17	0.65	1.25
P_a	0.844	0.972	0.990

Following above tabulation will now give the answers to (a), (b), and (c).

Lot size	*% of product for sampling inspection*	*Out of 100 lots*		*Total percentage of inspection*
		Accepted	*Rejected for screening*	
200	$\frac{17}{200} \times 100 = 8.5$	84	16	$\frac{[(17 \times 84) + (200 \times 16)]100}{(200 \times 100)}$ $= 23.14 \approx 23\%$
1,000	$\frac{65}{1,000} \times 100 = 6.5$	97	3	$\frac{[(65 \times 97) + (1,000 \times 3)]100}{(1000 \times 100)}$ $= 9.3 \approx 9.0\%$
5,000	$\frac{125}{5,000} \times 100 = 2.5$	99	1	$\frac{[(125 \times 99) + (5,000 \times 1)]\,100}{5,000 \times 100}$ $= 3.475 \approx 3.5\%$

Q. 10.20: *A consumer receives lots of 2,000 items and uses a single sampling plan to accept or reject the lots. The plan calls for 200 items to be inspected and for the lot to be accepted if two or less defectives are found. All rejected lots are screened by the consumer and the resultant cost is billed to the producer. Compute the Average Outgoing Quality (AOQ) if 0.8% nonconforming lots are submitted for inspection ?*

Ans: Sample size $n = 200$; $p = 0.008$

$$\mu_{np} = 200 \times 0.008 = 1.6$$

From Table *G*, the probability of acceptance $(P_a) = 0.783$

$$\% \text{ AOQ} = \left(\frac{N-n}{N}\right) p \times P_a \times 100$$

$$= \left(\frac{2,000 - 200}{2,000}\right) \times 0.08 \times 0.783 \times 100$$

$$= 0.564$$

Q. 10.21: *In a double sampling plan, $N = 5,000$, $n_1 = 100$, $c_1 = 0$, $n_2 = 100$ and $c_2 = 1$.*

(a) *Use Table G to compute the probability of acceptance of a 1% nonconforming lot.*

(b) *Assume that a lot rejected by the proposed sampling plan will be 100% inspected. What will be the AOQ if submitted lots are 1% nonconforming ?*

(c) Consider both the inspection of samples and inspection of rejected lots, what will be the average number of articles inspected per lot if the submitted product is 1% defective ?

(d) What is % AOQ ?

Ans: $N = 5000$

Since $n_1 = 100$

∴ $n_2 = 100$

$$\mu_p = 0.01$$
$$\mu_{n_1 p} = 100 \times 0.01 = 1.0$$
$$\mu_{n_2 p} = 100 \times 0.01 = 1.0$$

(*a*) A lot will be accepted when

(*i*) the first sample contains 0 defective.

(*ii*) the first sample contains 1 defective and second sample contains no defective.

From Table *G* probability of such a event is 0.368 + 0.135 = 0.503.

(*b*) % AOQ = (0.503) (1) = 0.503.

(*c*) Suppose *K* lots are submitted. Then out of *K* lots only 0.368 *K* lots will be accepted on the very first sample and, therefore, total number of articles inspected in such lots = 0.368 K (100) *i.e.* 36.8 *K*. Out of the remaining lots, 0.135 *K* lots are accepted on the evidence of second sample while the remaining lots are fully screened.

Number of articles inspected in lots for which second samples are drawn = 0.135 *K* (200) = 27 K.

Number of articles inspected in lots which are fully screened = 0.497 *K* (5,000) = 2,485 *K*

Total number of articles inspected in *K* lots = 36.8 *K* + 27 *K* + 2,485 *K* = 2,549 K

∴ Average number of articles inspected per lot $= 2{,}549 \dfrac{K}{K} = 2{,}549$

otherwise from the formula of ATI,

$$\text{ATI} = n \,.\, P_a(n_1) + (n_1 + n_2)\, P_a(n_2) + N(1 - P_a)$$
$$= 100 \times 0.368 + 2\ 00 \times 0.135 + 5{,}000\ (1 - 0.503)$$
$$= 36.8 + 27 + 2{,}485$$
$$\approx 2{,}549$$

(*d*) To calculate AOQ, first calculate AFI

$$\text{AFI} = \text{ATI/N} = 2{,}549/5{,}000 = 0.5098$$
$$\text{AOQ} = p\,(1 - AFI) = 0\,.\,0\,1\,(1 - 0.5098) = 0.0049$$

%AOQ ≈ 0.5

Q. 10.22: *Using the D-R tables, determine the double sampling plan for AOQL = 2.0% when the process average is 0.80% and the batch size is 2,500. What is LTPD ?*

What would be the sampling plan if the batch contains a new product and the process average is unknown ?

Ans: From Table 10.4 the required sampling plan is as follows :

$$n_1 = 41,\ c_1 = 0$$
$$n_1 + n_2 = 125,\ c_2 = 4$$

LTPD *i.e.* $100p_{0.10} = 7.0$

In case of new product and process average is not known it is suggested to take sampling plan from right hand side of the table. In this case the plan will be :

$$n_1 = 160, c_1 = 3$$
$$n_1 + n_2 = 470, c_2 = 15$$

Q. 10.23: *(a) Electrical bulbs are sold in lots of 2,000. Obtain the single sampling plan that a consumer must operate of he wishes to use the LTPD scheme with an LTPD of 5.0% and β = 0.1, assuming the process average is 0.01.*

(b) For the conditions stipulated in (a) other single sampling plans with different values of n and c are also available. Explain why the consumer will prefer to use the sampling plan as stipulated in Dodge-Romig single sampling tables ?

Ans: *(a)* Table 10.1 gives the required single sampling plan as $n = 130$, $c = 3$.

(b) Dodge-Romig sampling plan will give the same protection with minimum total inspection even considering the screening of rejected lots by the consumer.

Q. 10.24: *(a) If the percent defective from a machining operation is 1.95%. What single sampling plan should be used for a lot size of 26,000 items and an AOQL of 2% ?*

(b) With this single sampling plan, what percentage of product will be subjected to sampling inspection ?

(c) Find the double sampling plan for the lots described in (a) ?

(d) If only one sample is necessary to accept a given lot, what percent of the lot will require sampling using this double sampling plan ?

(e) If both first and second samples are necessary to accept a given lot, what percent of the product will require sampling using this double sampling plan ?

Ans: *(a)* From Dodge-Romig Table for 2% AOQL and single sampling, the required scheme is :

$$n = 720, c = 21$$

(b) % of product subjected to sampling inspection $= \dfrac{720 \times 100}{26,000} = 2.77\%$

(c) Double sampling scheme for lots described in *(a)*

$$n_1 = 480, c_1 = 11$$
$$n_2 = 1,090, c_2 = 46$$

(d) Since the first sample consists in inspecting 480 articles, therefore % inspection

$$= \frac{480 \times 100}{26,000} = 1.86$$

(e) Number of articles in two samples = 480 + 1,090 = 1,570

Therefore % inspection $= \dfrac{1,570 \times 100}{26,000} = 6.04$

Q. 10.25: *A consumer of electrical components receives them in lots of 5,000. Based on past sampling experience he has estimated the process average per cent defective at 1.1% level. The consumer inspects this product under a Dodge-Romig 5% LTPD plan returns all rejected lots to the producer.*

(a) Find the single sampling plan that the consumer should use.

(b) What is the probability of acceptance of a lot 1.1% defective ?

(c) If the producer also inspects each lot before shipment using a Dodge-Romig 2% AOQL plan, what single sampling plan should be used based on a process average percent defective of 1.6%?

(d) What is the probability that a lot 5.0% defective will pass first the producer's plan and then the consumer's plan ?

Ans: (*a*) From D-R 5% LTPD tables, the sampling plan :

$$n = 235, c = 7$$

(*b*) $\mu_{np} = 235 \times 0.011 = 2.585$

From Table *G*, $P_a = 0.995$

(*c*) From D-R 2% AOQL tables, the sampling plan :

$$n = 155, c = 5$$

(*d*) Producer's sampling plan: $n = 155$, $c = 5$

Consumer's sampling plan: $n = 235$, $c = 7$

$$\mu_p = 0.05$$

For Producer's plan $\mu_{np} = 155 \times 0.05 = 7.75$.

From Table *G*, the probability that the lot passes the producer's inspection is 0.216. Again for consumer's sampling plan $\mu_{np} = 235 \times 0.05 = 11.75$. From Table *G*, the probability that the lot passes the consumer's inspection is 0.102.

Probability that the lot passes both the inspections = 0.216 × 0.102 = 0.022.

Q .10.26: *The lot size is 2,000 units in a certain D–R AOQL inspection procedure. The desired AOQL of 2.0% can be obtained with any one of the three single sampling plans. These plans are : (i) n = 65, c = 2 ; (ii) n = 41 ; c = 1 ; and (iii) n = 18, c = 0. Answer the following questions under the assumption that incoming lots contain 0.8% nonconforming items.*

(a) Use Table G to compute the approximate probabilities of acceptance for each plan.

(b) Compute ATI for each plan.

(c) Compute AOQ for each plan.

(d) Taking all three of these measures of effectiveness into account, which plan would you recommend in this case ? Explain.

Ans: Using Table *G*, following tabulation can be prepared for the three sampling plans:

Parameters	*Sampling Plans*		
	(i)	*(ii)*	*(iii)*
N	2000	2000	2000
n	65	41	18
c	2	1	0
P_a	0.984	0.956	0.864
ATI	96	127	287
AFI	0.048	0.0635	0.1435
% *AOQ*	0.77	0.75	0.69

Since all the three plans satisfy the condition of AOQL of 2.0%, the criterion for selection of suitable plan will be to consider the parameters : (*a*) maximum P_a : (*b*) minimum ATI. Since sampling plan (*i*) *i.e.* $n = 65$, $c = 2$, gives maximum P_a (*i.e.* 0.984) and minimum ATI (*i.e.* 96), it is therefore the recommended sampling plan.

Q. 10.27: *A vendor inspects his own product under a Dodge-Romig 2% AOQL plan, screening all rejected lots before shipment. The lot size is 1000 and the assumed process average is 0.75%. Single sampling plan is used.*

The purchaser inspects the same lot under a Dodge-Romig 5% LTPD plan, returning all rejected lots to the vendor. The plan used is taken from the process average column '0.51-1.00'. Single sampling is used.

(a) What is the probability that a 2% defective lot will pass both vendor's and the purchaser's sampling inspection ?

(b) What is the probability that a 5% defective lot will pass both vendor's sampling inspection and be rejected by the purchaser's ?

(c) What is the AOQ in (b) ?

Ans: The vendor inspects the product under a Dodge-Romig 2% AOQL single sampling plan with process average taken as 0.75%. The Table 10.3 gives the sampling plan,

$$n = 40, c = 1$$
$$\mu_p = 0.02, \mu_{np} = 40 \times 0.02 = 0.8$$

For the specified details the sampling plan adopted by purchaser is

$$n = 105, c = 2$$
$$\mu_p = 0 .02 \; ; \mu_{np} \; 105 \times 0.02 = 2.10.$$
$$\mu_{np} = 40 \times 0.2 = 0.8$$

For μ_{np} of 0.8 and $c = 1$, the required probability from Table *G* is 0.809.

Probability that a lot passes the purchaser's inspection can be calculated with μ_{np} of 2.10 and $c = 2$, the required probability is 0.650.

(*a*) Probability that a lot passes both vender's and the purchaser's sampling inspection, therefore is $0.809 \times 0.650 = 0.526$.

(*b*) The product is 5% defective. Therefore $\mu_p = 0.05$.

The sampling plans will remain unchanged.

Probability that a lot passes vendor's inspection will now be 0.406. Probability that a lot passes purchaser's inspection will now be 0.1055 and thus the probability that the lot is rejected by the purchaser is (1 – 0.1055). Probability that a 5% defective lot passes vendor's inspection but rejected by the purchaser's is 0.406 (1 – 0.1055) = 0.363.

(*c*) %AOQ = [(0.406 (0 .1055)] (5) = 0.214.

Q. 10.28: *The following sampling plans are taken from a set of published tables.*

Sampling scheme	*Sampling size*	*Accept/reject Number*	*Probability of acceptance of a 1% defective lot*
1	13	0/1	0.85
2	50	1/2	0.90
3	80	2/3	0.95
4	125	3/4	0.96

(a) Calculate which of these schemes would be the most economic for lots of size (i) 300, (ii) 1,000.

(b) Obtain the lot tolerance percent defective associated with 10% Consumer's Risk for the plan 125 (3/4).

(Assume that 'most economic' is equivalent to least total inspection' and that the solution is to be valid for lots containing 1.0% defective).

Ans: (*a*) The OC curves characteristic of a sampling schemes do not give much weightage to lot size. If the scheme involves total inspection of rejected lots then the larger the lot the more 'wasted' inspection of wrongly rejected lots. For any percentage defectives, ATI required by sampling scheme in which a sample of size n leads to acceptance of a lot of size *N* with probability P_a is calculated as :

$$ATI = n + (1 - P_a)(N - n).$$

Considering the above relation the ATI values for both lots size and all the four schems are tabulated below.

	Sampling Scheme			
	1	2	3	4
ATI (*N* = 300)	56	75	91	132
ATI (*N* = 1,000)	162	145	126	160

(*b*) The LTPD can be obtained from the OC curve or from the cumulative tables of the Poisson distribution (Table G).

LTPD for a consumer's risk of 10% for the plan 125 (3/4) can be calculated as :

In Table *G*, go down in the column of $c = 3$ till the probability of acceptance is 0.10. In this case we find that when $P_a = 0.105$ $np = 6.8$ and when $P_a = 0.093$, $np = 6.8$. So by interpolation for $P_a = 0.10$, we set $\mu_{\hat{np}} = 6.7$

Since

$$n = 125$$

$$\mu_p = 6.7/125$$

$$\approx 0.054$$

If the Poisson distribution tables are not available, and because n is large, the normal distribution approximation may be used. Suppose required LTPD is μ_p. Take $\mu = \mu_p$ and $\mu_{np} = \sqrt{np(1-p)}$ to define teh normal distribution.

It implies that 10% of area corresponds to 3 or less defectives. Because defectives are discrete variables continuity correction (as explained in Chap. 4) leads one to seek the 10% corresponding to less than 3 + 0.5 *i.e.* 3.5 defectives. From Table *A*,

$$z = -1.28$$

Hence

$$-1.28 = \frac{3.5 - 125p}{\sqrt{125p(1-p)}}$$

or, $15830\,p^2 - 1080\,p + 12.25 = 0$ giving two values of p as 0.054 and − 0.014.

Hence, 0.054 is the required LTPD for Consumer's Risk of 10%.

Q. 10.29: (*a*) *TRUE or FALSE ?*

"If AOQL = 3%, no batch will have more than 3% defective items in it, after rectifying inspection." Explain your answer.

(b) Compare the AOQL approach of sampling plans as given by D-R with that of OC approach.

*(c) Select a economic single sampling plan for process average of **0.04** % and lot size of **200** when LTPD = 5.0% and Consumer's Risk = 0.10. Compute % AOQL and compare it with AOQL value of **0.74**% in Table 10.1.*

Ans: (*a*) FALSE. It is possible that a bad batch will yield a good sample (by chance). However, in the long run, averaging over many batches, there will be 3% or fewer defective items after the acceptance sampling process with rectification, regardless of how large the incoming fraction defective p is or how it varies with the time.

(*b*) The goal of each approach to acceptance sampling is to obtain a reliable judgment of whether batch quality is acceptable, based on the inspection of parts of the batch. The OC approach protects the consumer against receiving bad batches, with a certain specified probability of error. The AOQL approach guarantees an average quality level to the consumer but with no specified probability of error.

Protection for the producer is also different. The AOQL plans offered by Dodge and Romig are designed to minimize the number of items inspected whereas the OC approach achieves an acceptably small probability of rejecting good batches.

(*c*) Table 10.1 gives the most economic sampling plan for the given conditions :

$$\left[\begin{array}{l} n = 40 \\ c = 0 \end{array}\right.$$

AOQL is maximum value of AOQ over a given range of p values. It can be determined by drawing a graph of variation of AOQ values with p values. The mathematical formula is quite complex. However a simple way exists to determine the AOQL values when n and N are known.

The AOQL = y $(1/n - 1/N)$. The author has made certain studies and AOQL factor y has been found out for different values of c. The following tabulation gives the factor y to be used in the formula of AOQL.

Acceptance number, c	*AOQL factor (y)*
0	0.3679
1	0.8400
2	1.3711
3	1.9424
4	2.5435
5	3.1682
6	3.8120
7	4.4720
8	5.1457
9	5.8314
10	6.5277

In this particular case when $c = 0$, $y = 0.3679$ and hence

$$\%AOQL = 0.3679\left(\frac{1}{n} - \frac{1}{N}\right) \times 100$$

$$= 0.3679\left(\frac{1}{40} - \frac{1}{200}\right) \times 100 = 0.7358 \approx 0.74$$

This agrees with the table value of % AOQL of 0.74.

Q. 10.30: *(a) TRUE or FALSE ? " Dodge-Romig sampling schemes have provision for multiple sampling."*

(b) Why D-R sampling tables are popular for within-plant inspection ?

(c) List out some features of D-R LTPD sampling tables.

Ans: (*a*) FALSE. D-R sampling schemes do not have any provision of multiple sampling.

(*b*) The principal advantage of the D-R tables is a minimum amount of inspection for a given inspection procedure. This advantage makes the tables desirable withinplant inspection.

(*c*) Some of the notable features of D-R LTPD tables are :

1. For the same process average, as the lot size increases, the sample size decreases *i.e.* it does not increase in the same proportion and hence inspection costs are more economical with larger lots.
2. The tables extend until the process average is one-half of the LTPD. Provision of additional averages is unnecessary since 100% inspection becomes more economical than sampling inspection when the process average exceeds one-half of the LTPD.
3. As the process average increases, a corresponding increase occurs in the amount inspected. Therefore, an improvement in the process average results in a fewer inspections and a lower sampling inspection cost.

Q. 10.31: (*a*) *Discuss some features of the D-R AOQL sampling tables.*

(*b*) *How do you take care of type of defects in the D-R sampling schemes ?*

(*c*) *Do the D-R sampling schemes have the provision of tightened and reduced inspection ?*

Ans: (*a*) Some notable features of the D-R AOQL sampling tables are

1. As the lot size increases, the relative sample size decreases.
2. Sampling plans are not given for process averages which exceed the AOQL, since sampling becomes uneconomical when the process average incoming quality is poorer than the specified AOQL.
3. The lower the process average, the smaller the sample size, resulting in lower sampling inspection cost.

(*b*) The D-R tables do not make a provision for the type of defect, although different LTPD or AOQL values can be used—lower ones for critical defects and higher ones for minor defects. Defects/100 rather than percent defective can be used for the process average; however this is limited to values of 10 or less.

(*c*) The D-R tables do not have any provision for tightened or reduced inspection, although different LTPD or AOQL values can also be used.

Q. 10.32: *The ABC company sells a certain article to the XYZ company. The purchase agreement stipulates that the product will be submitted in lots 1,000, the XYZ will inspect under Dodge-Romig 2% AOQL single sampling plan, and that ABC will be charged for XYZ's cost in the 100% inspection of any lots rejected on the basis of sampling plan. The agreement does not mention the process average to be used in the selection of the sampling plan.*

At the start of this contract XYZ's receiving inspection department used the plan $n = 90$, $c = 3$, taken from the right-hand column of Table 10.3. Because the initial quality was good and all lots were accepted, XYZ shifted to the left-hand column of the table, using $n = 18$ and $c = 0$ in order or reduce inspection costs. Shortly after this change, a lot was rejected by the sampling plan. The lot was screened by XYZ, and ABC was billed for the cost of screening.

This lot of 1,000 actually contained 9 defectives. As a lot of 0.9% defective is substantially better than 2% AOQL, the management of ABC wonders whether it should protest this charge. The management also wonders whether it should request to return to the 'normal' inspection at the right-hand side of the table instead of the 'reduced' inspection of the left-hand side.

Discuss these questions, pointing out the different interests of vendor and purchaser under this type of agreement.

Ans: Not doubt, that the 0.9% defective lot is better than 2% AOQL but to maintain the of AOQL value, it is essential that a lot of whatever quality it may be, if rejected by the sampling plan, must be detailed. Therefore, ABC should not protest the charge.

Before taking the decision, ABC company should consider the following aspects :

1. Larger the sample size and allowable defectives the better is the discrimination between good and bad products. With larger sample size and allowable defectives the probability of acceptance of good lots is higher than the corresponding probability of acceptance obtained with a smaller sample size and smaller number of allowable defectives. If the ABC company is pretty sure of the very small process average of its product, then it may request the XYZ company to return to 'to normal' inspection.
2. If the ABC company knows that the process average may vary a little it should determine which of the two plans gives minimum rejection and should act accordingly.
3. In case the product of the ABC has wide variations in the process average, then the ABC should not make any request at all because it will be in the interest of the ABC if the XYZ uses a small sample size.

In fact when the process average is not mentioned, the purchaser starts taking the sampling plan from the right-hand side column. These plans involve large sample size and large value of allowable defectives as compared with the plans taken from the left hand side column of the same table.

If the vendor's process average is same as is assumed by the purchaser, then most of the lots will be passed by the sampling plan. If the process average is better, still more lots will be accepted. The vendor gains by this way but when the quality worsens, there is much rejection and the fear of charging for screening makes the vendor to improve the quality of the product but certainly on the purchaser's side it will involve more inspection.

The purchaser is interested on reducing the cost of inspection. If the purchaser assumes the process average to be very small and adopts a sampling plan from the left-hand side column, then the probability of acceptance of a lot even with minor process average is less as compared with the situation when the sample size is large. This plan will involve less inspection and will bring pressure on the vendor to improve the quality still further. But when wide variations in process average are encountered, it is in the interest of the vendor if the purchaser uses a small sample size.

Q. 10.33: *Select the correct option:*

(*i*) In MIL-STD-105E, the AQL is always determined at what p on the OC curve ?

(*a*) 0.05 (*b*) 0.10 (*c*) 0.90

(*d*) 0.95 (*e*) none of the above.

(*ii*) ABC standard, MIL-STD-105 D and E have

(*a*) identical tables (*b*) different tables altogether

(*c*) partly similar and partly different (*d*) no tables at all.

(*iii*) ABC standard and MIL-STD-105 E provide for

(*a*) single, double and multiple sampling plans

(*b*) single, double, sequential sampling plans

(*c*) only single and double sampling plans

(*d*) minimum total inspection plans.

(*iv*) ABC standard provides for sampling scheme under

(*a*) Normal, reduced and tightened inspection

(*b*) normal inspection

(*c*) reduced inspection

(*d*) reduced and tightened inspection.

(*v*) In ABC standard it is possible under certain conditions to switch over

(*a*) Normal to reduced inspection (*b*) reduced to tightened

(*c*) tightened to reduce inspection (*d*) no inspection at all.

Ans: (*i*) (*e*); (*ii*) (*a*); (*iii*) (*a*); (*iv*) (*a*); (*v*) (*a*)

Q. 10.34: *In ABC standard or MIL-STD-105 E, when nothing is specified which level of inspection is generally used for selection of sample size code letter ?*

Ans: Level II.

Q. 10.35: *What is the approximate ratio of inspection in three general inspection levels of MIL-STD-105 E ?*

Ans: The three general inspection levels involve inspection in amounts roughly in the ratio 0.4 : 1.0 : 1.6.

Q. 10.36: *Why different inspection levels are provided in ABC standard ?*

Ans: The inspection level concept permits the users to balance the cost of inspection against the amount of protection required.

Q. 10.37:. *When do you use S1, S2, S3 and S4 level inspection ?*

Ans: These four special levels are used when the sample size is to be kept small, for example in destructive testing.

Q. 10.38: *Do the tables of ABC standard, MIL-STD-105 D and MIL-STD-105 E are in complete agreement ?*

Ans: Yes.

Q. 10.39: *In ABC system, what is the range of probability of acceptance in case of normal inspection at AQL ?*

Ans: An ABC system, the Pa at AQL value in normal inspection varies from about 0.88 for plans with the smaller sample size where c = 0 to about 0.99 for the large sample sizes and acceptance number.

Q. 10.40: *What is the rejection number of a sample in ABC standard?*

Ans: It is $C + 1$ i.e. always 1 more than acceptance number.

Q. 10.41: *(a) Define AQL as per ABC-STD-105.*

(b) List several of the areas of application of ABC-STD-105 sampling plans.

Ans: *(a)* The AQL is the maximum percent defective (or the maximum number of defects per hundred units) that, for the purpose of sampling inspection, can be considered satisfactory as a process average. The phrase "can be considered satisfactory" is interpreted as a Producer's Risk, α, equal to 0.05, actually, α varies from 0.01 to 0.10 in the standard.

(b) Sampling plans under ABC-STD-105 are applicable but not limited to inspection of the following:

1. End items
2. Components and raw materials
3. Operations
4. Materials in process
5. Supplies in storage
6. Maintenance operations
7. Data or records
8. Administrative procedure.

Q. 10.42: *(a) What are the indexing parameters of ABC-STD-105 ?*

(b) The agreement between a supplier and consumer is to accept the lots at 3% AQL under ABC-STD-105. Does the producer has a right to supply 2% defective articles knowingly?

(c) The AQL tables in ABC-STD-105 mention sampling plans for preferred AQL. Are these tables also applicable for any other AQL value not mentioned in the tables ?

(d) AQL plans are said to be producer oriented. Why ? Is consumer's protection maintained at any specified value ?

Ans: *(a)* The sampling plans in ABC standard are indexed at AQL together with the sample size code letter.

(b) No. The designation of an AQL does not imply that the supplier has the right to supply knowingly any defective units of product.

(c) No.

(d) AQL plans are basically producer-oriented ; they keep the latter's risk of having lots rejected, even though they meet the specification sampling criteria, to 5% (or to 1 lot in 20). The consumer protection offorded by AQL plans in ABC standard varies considerably from plan to plan. Unlike the producer's protection, it is not maintained at any specific value.

Q. 10.43: *Write a brief summary of various inspection levels in ABC-STD-105.*

Ans: The inspection level determines the relationship between the production lot size and the inspection sample size. A code letter designates the latter. The ABC standard contains three general inspection levels : I, II and II. Unless otherwise directed, inspection level II is used. Inspection level I provides less discrimination (60% less than level II) because it uses smaller sample size, while level III increases the discrimination 1.6 times that of level I inspection because of larger sample size for the same lot. The level I provides for about ½ the amount of inspection while level III provides for about twice the amount of inspection.

When dealing with relatively small sample sizes, the standard provides four special inspection levels : S_1, S_2, S_3 and S_4. Thus there are a total seven levels of inspection which permit the balancing of the cost of inspection against the amount of inspection desired. General levels I, II and III are generally used for a nondestructive types of inspection. Special levels S_1 to S_4 are used when inspection involves destruction of the sample or when the cost of inspection is very high.

Q. 10.44: *Production lots of 1,000 units each are inspected under the following plan :*

AQL = 1.0%, limiting quality plan, Consumer's Risk is 10%, normal inspection, single sampling.

(a) What is the size of the sample ?

(b) What is the limiting quality in percent defectives which corresponds to the Consumer's Risk of 10% ?

(c) What are the accept and reject numbers for this plan ?

(d) What is the probability of lot acceptance if the submitted lots contain 1%, 3% and 4 ½% defectives, respectively ?

(e) Discuss the results.

Ans: For a lot size of 1,000, Table *K* gives the code letter as *J*. From Table *L*, for code letter *J* the sample size is 80 and from Table 10.5 the limiting quality for code letter *J* and AQL of 1.0%, the limiting quality is 6.5%.

Again Table L, for code letter *J* and AQL of 1.0%, the acceptance and reject numbers are 2 and 3 respectively. From Table *G*, the probability of acceptance are computed as under :

n	p	np	P_a
80	0.01	0.8	0.953
80	0.03	2.4	0.570
80	0.045	3.6	0.303

Hence, submitted lots that have about quality level of 1% defective have about 95% chance of being accepted (AQL = 1.0%). This means that, 95 times out of 100, samples of size 80, taken from production lots which are 1.0% defective, which contain not more than 2 defectives will be accepted. Submitted lots which have limiting quality level of 6.5% defective have a 10% chance of being accepted (LTPD = 10%). The consumer is thus assured that if a lot of 1,000 units, for example, contains 65 defective units, this sampling plan will pass such a lot only 10 of 100 times.

The producer is assured that if he submits lots which are 1% defective (10 defective units in a lot of 1,000) he has, on the average, a 95% chance of having such lots accepted.

Q. 10.45: *How many defective units must be found in the required sample to cause rejection of the production lot of size 150 units inspected under ABC-STD-105 with AQL of 0.25%, single sampling, tightened inspection ?*

Ans: Choosing general inspection level II, Table *K* gives the sample-size code letter as F.

Entering Table *M* with code letter F (sample size 20 units), we find there is no accept/reject criterion at the intersection of the horizontal code letter F line and the AQL = 0.25% column. There is, however, an arrow pointing downward. The applicable accept/reject criterion is found at the tip of the arrow ; it is : acceptance number = 0, rejection number = 1.0. As will be noted, this changes the corresponding required sample size from 20 to 80 (new sample size code letter J).

Hence, since the reject criterion is 1.0, the lot of 150 units will be rejected if one or more defective units are found in a sample of 80 units.

Q. 10.46: *A sampling acceptance plan under ABC standard is required to be designed with inspection level II an AQL of 4% and the lot size of 2,500. Suggest the values of sample size and acceptance number under :*

(a) Normal inspection,

(b) Tightened inspection and

(c) Reduced inspection.

If 10,000 lots 4% defective are submitted for inspection under tightened inspection, how many lots are liable to be rejected by the sampling plan in the long run ? After inspecting 5,000 lots under tightened inspection, it was suggested that the remaining lots should be examined using normal inspection. How many lots will now be accepted ?

(Use Table G, if required.)

Ans: Table *K* for lot size of 2,500 and inspection level II give the code letter *K*.

(*a*) For normal inspection Table *L* for code letter K gives :

$$n = 125 \text{ and } c = 10$$

(*b*) For tightened inspection Table *M* for code letter *K* gives :

$$n = 125 \text{ and } c = 8$$

(*c*) For reduced inspection, Table *N* for code letter *K* gives :

$$n = 50 \text{ and } c = 5$$

Since the lots are 4% defective, therefore $\mu_p = 0.04$.

1. When the tightened inspection is used, $\mu_{np} = 125 \times 0.04 = 5.0$.

From Table *G* the probability of acceptance for μ_{np} of 5.0 and *c* of 8, is 0.932.

Lots rejected = 10,000 (1 – 0.932) = 680

2. When the normal inspection is used, $\mu_{np} = 125 \times 0.04 = 5.0$

From Table *G* the probability of acceptance for μ_{np} of 5.0 and *c* of 10, is 0.986.

When 5,000 lots are given tightened inspection, the lots liable to be accepted

$$= 5{,}000\ (0.932) = 4{,}660.$$

When the next 5,000 lots are given normal inspection, the lots liable to be accepted

$$= 5{,}000 \times (0.986) = 4{,}930.$$

The lots accepted $= 4{,}660 + 4{,}930 = 9{,}590.$

Q. 10.47: *The acceptance sampling under the ABC standard, single sampling is to be used with inspection level II, an AQL of 4%, and a lot size of 2,500.*

A series of lots 8% defective are submitted for acceptance. What is the approximate value of the probability that a shift of tightened inspection will be required after the first two such lots ? Assume that no rejections have occurred in the preceding 14 lots.

Ans: For the stated conditions, using Tables *K* and *L*, the acceptance criteria is

$$n = 125 \text{ ; } c = 10$$

When the submitted lots are 8%, $\mu_p = 0.08$,

and $\mu_{np} = 125 \times 0.08 = 10$

Using Table *G*, probability of 10 or less defectives in a sample of 125 is 0.583.

Therefore probability of 11 or more defectives or the probability of rejecting a lot = 1 – 0.583 = 0.417.

Similarly the probability that the second lot is also rejected is 0.417.

As per the criteria for shifting to tightened inspection, the required probability = 0.417 × 0.417 = 0.17.

Q. 10.48: *In acceptance sampling under the ABC standard, single sampling is to be used with inspection level II, an AQL of 4%, and a lot size of 2,500. Assume that tightened inspection is being used. After the rejection of one lot, the product quality improves to the point where lots are now only 4% defective. What is the approximate probability that normal inspection will be reinstated after the next 5 such lots ?*

Ans: For the stated conditions, Table *M* for code letter *K* gives

$$n = 125, c = 8 \text{ and}$$

When the lots are 4% defective, $\mu_p = 0.04$ and $\mu_{np} = 125 \times 0.04 = 5$

Using Table *G*, probability of 8 or less defectives is 0.932.

The statement regarding requalification for normal inspection is as follows :

"When tightened inspection is in effect, normal inspection shall be instituted when 5 consecutive lots or batches have been considered acceptable on original inspection."

Probability that 5 consecutive lots when tightened inspection is in effect, are considered acceptable = $(0.932)^5 = 0.703$.

Q. 10.49: *For a lot size of 2,600 and inspection level II and an AQL of 4%, the ABC standard gives the plan for tightened inspection as*

Sample size = *125*

Acceptance number = *8*

Rejection number = *9*

After the rejection of one lot, the production quality improves to a point where the lots are now 4% defective. Assuming the tightened inspection was being used before the rejected lot, what is approximate probability that normal inspection will be reinstituted after the next

(*a*) *4 lots,*

(*b*) *5 lots.*

Ans: According to ABC standard, "When the tightened inspection is in effect, normal inspection shall be instituted when 5 consecutive lots or batches have been considered acceptable on original inspection."

(*a*) After the rejection of one lot, at least 5 consecutive lots are required to take some decision regarding reinstitution of normal inspection. Therefore after the inspection of 4 lots the probability of returning to normal inspection is zero.

(*b*) Probability that a 4% defective lot when the sample size is 125 and acceptance number is 8, from Table *G* is 0.932. Probability that 5 consecutive lots are acceptable is $(0.932)^5 = 0.703$.

Hence, the probability that a normal inspection is instituted is 0.703.

Q. 10.50: *If a lot 8% defective is submitted under the reduced inspection plan [n = 50, c = 5, and rejection number 8], find the approximate probabilities that*

(*a*) *the lot will be accepted and reduced inspection continued,*

(*b*) *the lot will be accepted but normal inspection will be reinstituted, and*

(*c*) *the lot is rejected.*

Ans: From Table *G* according to given plan, the probability of acceptance of 8% defective lot is 0.785.

(*a*) Probability that a lot is accepted and reduced inspection continued is 0.785.

(*b*) When the lot falls in the indecision zone ($c = 6$ or 7), the lot will be accepted but normal inspection will be reinstated. Probability of such an event is (P_8 or less − P_5 or less)

$$= 0.949 - 0.785 \text{ i.e. } 0.164$$

(*c*) Probability of rejection of the lot is P_8 or more

$$= 1 - 0.949 \text{ i.e. } 0.051$$

Q. 10.51: *A manufacturer receives an invitation to bid on a government contract for special brass insert for air craft use. The contract is for 114,000 inserts and specifies a 1.0% AQL sampling plan. Production and delivery is in weekly batches of 1,200 inserts. Based on ABCSTD-105 requirements, the weekly inspection sample size is n = 80.*

Disregarding quantity discounts, what should the manufacturer's unit price by if past experience, on similar orders showed average production to be 1% defective and if it costs him ₹ 20.00 to produce an insert and ₹ 3.50 to inspect it (overhead costs are included). To cover his profits the manufacturer adds 10% to his total cost figure.

Ans: First, the manufacturer has to determine how many inserts he will have to produce to assure a yield of 114,000 units acceptable by the inspection plan. Since his own product quality matches the required AQL, he is justified to expect 95% of his lots to be accepted and 5% to be rejected. Hence, 114,000/0.95 i.e. 120,000

Therefore, he has to produce 120,000 inserts. The quantity of inserts requiring inspection is 80 per production lot of 1,200. There will be 120,000/1,200 = 100 production lots ; hence, a total of 80 × 100 = 8,000 inserts will be inspected.

The total cost of production plus markup is therefore :

Cost to produce 120,000 inserts	
at ₹ 20.00/Unit	= ₹ 2,400,000
Cost of inspecting 8,000 inserts	
at ₹ 3.5/Unit	= ₹ 28,000
Total	= ₹ 2,428,000
10% profit = ₹ 242,800	
Total	= ₹ 2,670,800
The per-unit insert price	
(not considering quantity discount)	= 2,670,800/114,000
	= ₹ 2,3.43.

Q. 10.52: (*a*) *Find the ABC standard normal inspection plan for inspection level II, an AQL of 1.5%, and a lot size of 1,000 units.*

(*b*) *Assuming no curtailment of inspection, compute the ASN values for process average of 2.9, 4.5 and 8.0%.*

(*c*) *Sketch a curve of ASN as a function of process average over the range 2.0 to 8.0.*

Ans: (*a*) From Table *K* the sample size code letter is J. Table *L* gives the following single sampling plan $n = 80$, $c = 3$, rejection number = 4.

(*b*) Since there is no curtailment of inspection, the ASN for single sampling is same and equal to sample size irrespective of process average. Therefore ASN for 2.9, 4.5, and 8.0% nonconforming lot is 80.

(c) Since ASN is independent of process average, the curve of ASN as a function of process average is just a straight line parallel to the axis of process average at a distance of ASN from process average axis.

Q. 10.53: *In acceptance sampling under the ABC standard double sampling is to be used with inspection level II, an AQL of 1% and a lot size of 750. What are the acceptance criteria under (a) normal (b) tightened and (c) reduced inspection ?*

Ans: For a lot size of 750, inspection level II, Table K gives the code letter J for sampling plan.

(a) From Table O the normal inspection double sampling plan :

$$n_1 = 50,\ c_1 = 0, \text{ rejection number} = 3$$
$$n_2 = 50,\ c_2 = 3, \text{ rejection number} = 4.$$

(b) From Table *P* the tightened inspection double sampling plan :

$$n_1 = 50,\ c_1 = 0, \text{ rejection number} = 2.$$
$$n_2 = 50,\ c_2 = 1, \text{ rejection number} = 2$$

(c) From Table *Q* the reduced inspection sampling plan :

$$n_1 = 20,\ c_1 = 0, \text{ rejection number} = 3$$
$$n_2 = 20,\ c_2 = 0, \text{ rejection number} = 4.$$

Q. 10.54: *In acceptance sampling under the ABC standard, double sampling for inspection level II, an AQL of 1% and lot size of 750, find,*

(a) the probability of accepting lots from 1.5% defective product under

(i) normal inspection,

(ii) tightened inspection.

(b) the probability that a 2% defective lot under reduced inspection will be

(i) accepted and reduced inspection continued,

(ii) accepted but normal inspection will be reinstated, and

(iii) rejected.

Ans: (a) For lot size of 750 and inspection level II with an AQL of 1% the normal double sampling plan :

$$n_1 = 50,\ c_1 = 0, \text{ rejection number} = 3$$
$$n_2 = 50,\ c_2 = 3, \text{ rejection number} = 4.$$
$$\mu_p = 0.015; = \mu_{np} = 0.75.$$

From Table *G* :

$$P_0 = 0.4720$$
$$P_{1 \text{ or less}} = 0.8270$$
$$P_1 = 0.8270 - 0.4720 = 0.3550$$
$$P_{2 \text{ or less}} = 0.9590$$
$$P_2 = 0.9590 - 0.8270 = 0.1320$$

For the second sample $\mu_{np} = 0.75$. From Table *G* :

$$P_0 = 0.4720$$
$$P_1 = 0.3550$$
$$P_2 = 0.1320$$

These probabilities may be used to estimate the probability of acceptance as follows :

0 defective in first = 0.4720

1 defective in first with 0 defective in second = (0.3550)(0.4720) = 0.1680

1 defective in first with 1 defective in second = (0.3550) (0.3550) = 0.1260

1 defective in first with 2 defectives in second = (0.3550) (0.1320) = 0.0468

2 defectives in first with 0 defective in second = (0.1320) (0.4720) = 0.0623

2 defectives in first with 1 defective in second = (0.1320) (0.3550) = 0.0468

(*i*) Probability of acceptance of a lot 1.5% defective = 0.9219

(*ii*) Similarly the probability under tightened inspection will be found to be 0.640.

(*b*) Sampling plan under reduced inspection :

$$n_1 = 20,\ c_1 = 0,\ \text{rejection number} = 3$$
$$n_2 = 20,\ c_2 = 0,\ \text{rejection number} = 4.$$
$$\mu_p = 0.02$$

For the first sample $\mu_{n_1 p} = 0.4$. From Table G :

$$P_0 = 0.670$$

To continue the reduced inspection, the lot should be accepted on the very first sample because the acceptance number of the second sample is also zero.

(*i*) Probability that a lot is accepted and reduced inspection continued is 0.670.

$$P_{1\text{ or less}} = 0.9380$$
$$P_1 = 0.9380 - 0.6700 = 0.2680$$
$$P_{2\text{ or less}} = 0.9920$$
$$P_2 = 0.9920 - 0.9380 = 0.0540$$

For second sample $\mu_{n_2 p} = 0.4$. From Table G :

$$P_0 = 0.6700$$
$$P_{1\text{ or less}} = 0.9380$$
$$P_{2\text{ or less}} = 0.9920$$

The probability that a lot is accepted but normal inspection is reinstated may be calculated as follows :

1 defective in first with 0 or 1 or 2 defectives in second = (0.2680) (0.9920) = 0.2659

2 defectives in first with 0 or 1 defective in second = (0.0540) (0.9380) = 0.0507

(ii) Probability that a lot is accepted but normal inspection reinstated = 0.3166

(iii) Probability that a lot is rejected = 1 − (0.6700 + 0.3166) = 0.0134.

Q. 10.55: *Assume that the double sampling plan of Problem* **10.36** *for normal inspection is being used where process averages are respectively* **0.5, 3,** *and* **6%** *nonconforming. Assuming no curtailment, compute the ASN value for each process average. Use the Poisson approximation to the binomial in your calculation. Express the respective ASN values as a percentage of the single sample size corresponding to this double sampling plan in the ABC standard.*

Ans: From Problem, 10.36 the double sampling plan under normal inspection is

$$n_1 = 50,\ c = 0,\ \text{rejection number} = 3\ ;$$
$$n_2 = 50,\ c = 3,\ \text{rejection number} = 4.$$

Since $p = 0.005$

Then μ_{np} for each sample of 50 is 0.250.

Table G gives $P_0 = 0.779$, $P_1 = 0.195$, $P_2 = 0.0024$, and $P_{3 \text{ or more}} = 0.0002$. The probability of a decision on the first sample is the P_a of 0.779 plus the P_r of 0.002 *i.e.* 0.781. In double sampling, the probability of a decision on the second sample is identical with the probability that a second sample will be taken, in this case it is P_1 of 0.195 plus P_2 of 0.024 *i.e.* 0.219. Assuming that there is no curtailment of inspection, 0.781 lots will require a sample of 50 and 0.219 lots will require a sample of 100. It follows that

$$\text{ASN} = 0.781\ (50) + 0.219\ (100) = 60.95 \approx 61$$

For AQL of 1% and single sampling Table L gives sample size as 80.

$$\text{ASN as percentage of single sampling size} = 61 \times \frac{100}{80} = 76\%$$

Similar calculation will show that for p of 3% and 6%, ASN are 79.3 and 68.6 and respective percentage are 99% and 86%.

Q. 10.56: *Inspection based on defects per hundred units is being conducted under the ABC standard. Single sampling is used with special inspection level S-3, and AQL of 25 defects per hundred units, and a lot size of 200. What are the acceptance criteria under normal, tightened and reduced inspection ?*

Ans: From Table K, for a lot size of 200 and inspection level S-3, code letter is D.

For an AQL of 25 defects per hundred units or 25%, Tables L, M, and N give the acceptance criteria as under :

Table L, Normal inspection : $n = 8$, $c = 5$, Rejection Number = 6

Table M, Tightened inspection : $n = 8$, $c = 3$, Rejection Number = 4

Table N, Reduced inspection : $n = 3$, $c = 2$, Rejection Number = 5

Q. 10.57: *Normal inspection under ABC standard is being conducted using single sampling, code letter L, and an AQL of 0.65%. The preceding 5 lots have all been accepted. The process average shifts to 3% defective. What is the probability that a shift to tightened inspection will be required within the next 3 lots.*

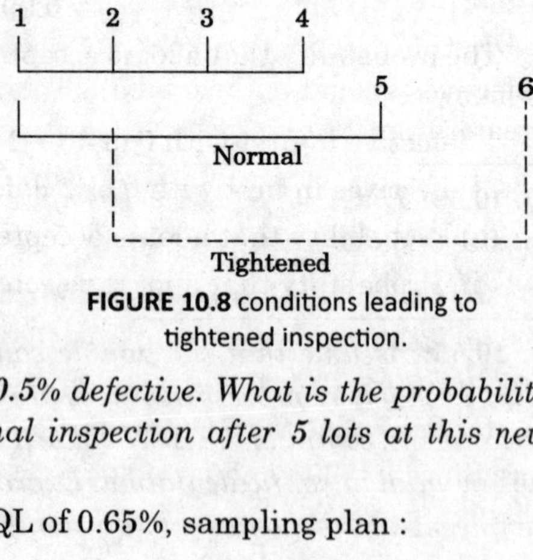

FIGURE 10.8 conditions leading to tightened inspection.

Assuming that the tightened inspection in now is force and the most recent lot has been rejected on original inspection. The process average now shifts by 0.5% defective. What is the probability that the process will qualify for reinstatement of normal inspection after 5 lots at this new average ?

Ans: For normal inspection with code letter L and an AQL of 0.65%, sampling plan :

$n = 200$, $c = 3$ and rejection number = 4.

$\mu_{\hat{p}} = 0.03$

From Table G the probability of acceptance of a lot is 0.151.

According to ABC standard, tightened inspection will be reinstated when 2 out of 5 consecutive lots are rejected on original inspection.

The conditions leading to the shifting to tightened inspection are depicted in Fig. 10.8. These are :

(*i*) When with reference to Fig. 10.8, lots 4, 5, 6 are accepted and lots 7 and 8 are rejected.

(*ii*) When with reference to Fig. 10.8, lots 4, 5, 7 are accepted and lots 6 and 8 rejected.

Since lots 4 and 5 are known as the accepted ones,

$$\therefore \quad P_{(i)} = (0.151)\,(1 - 0.1\,51)\,(1 - 0.151) = 0.109$$

$$P_{(ii)} = (1 - 0.151)\,(\,0.151)\,(1 - 0.151) = 0.109$$

Probability that a shift to tightened inspection will be required

$$= 0.109 + 0.109 = 0.218$$

Tightened inspection plan,

$n = 200$, $c = 2$, Rejection number = 3

$\mu_p = 0.005.$

From Table G the probability of acceptance of a lot is 0.920.

Normal inspection will be reinstated when 5 consecutive lots are accepted on original inspection. The probability of such an event = $(0.920)^5 = 0.6590$.

Q. 10.58: *The single sampling plan n = 200, c = 5 is being used under the ABC standard, code letter L, 1% AQL. The number of defectives observed in samples from the first 10 lots under original inspection are 3, 0, 2, 0, 1, 1, 4, 1, 2 and 3 respectively. Production is at a steady rate. Does this process now qualify for reduced inspection ?*

Ans: To qualify for reduced inspection, the following conditions should be satisfied :

1. The preceding 10 lots must be accepted.
2. The number of defectives in proceeding 10 lots must be less or equal to that shown by Table W.
3. Production is at a steady rate.

In this problem conditions (1) and (3) are satisfied. Table W indicates that total number of defectives should not exceed 14. Total number of defectives in this problem is 15. Since 15 is greater than 14, therefore, this process does not qualify for reduced inspection.

Q. 10.59: *The ABC-STD-105 specifies n = 200 and c = 5 under code letter L, a 1.0% AQL, and a lot size of 5,000 units.*

(*a*) *Use Table G to find the approximate probability of acceptance of lots with a μp of 0.04.*

(*b*) *Rectifying inspection is to be employed with this plan. Compute the ATI for the lots described in part (a).*

(*c*) *Determine the AOQ for the lots described in part (a).*

Ans: Since $n = 200$ and $\mu_p = 0.04$;

$$\mu_{np} = 8$$

(*a*) Table G gives the probability of acceptance as 0.191

(*b*) $$\text{AT I} = n\,P_a + N\,(1 - P_a)$$

$$= 200 \times 0.19\,1 + 5{,}000\,(1 - 0.191) = 4083.2$$

(c) $$\text{AOQ} = p\,(1 - AFI)$$

$$= \left(1 - \frac{ATI}{N}\right)$$

$$= 0.04\,(1 - 0.81664) = 0.0073$$

From the approximate AOQ formula also,

$$\text{AOQ} = p\,P_a = 0.04\,(0.191) = 0.0076.$$

Q. 10.60: *(a) Find the ABC standard single sampling plan for inspection level II, a 1.5% AQL, and a lot size of 400 items for normal inspection.*

(b) An np chart is to be used to plot the results in inspection of incoming lots. Assuming that the AQL value is to be used as the aimed at mean value of μpo, find 3 σ control limits for the chart.

(c) What fraction of nonconforming units does the UCL represent ?

(d) Use Table G to calculate the approximate probability that a point will fall outside the UCL when incoming lots are at the AQL.

Ans: (a) For 1.5% AQL, lot size of 400 and inspection level II, the sample size code letter from Table *K* is H. Table *L* gives the sampling plan as under :

$$n = 50,\ c = 2 \text{ and rejection number} = 3.$$

(b) $$\mu_p = 0.015$$

$$\mu_{np} = 50 \times 0.015 = 0.75$$

$$\text{UCL}_{np} = np + 3\sqrt{np(1-p)}$$

$$= 3.328$$

$$\text{LCL}_{np} = np - 3\sqrt{np(1-p)}$$

(c) $$\text{UCL}_{np} = 3.3285$$

$$n = 50$$

$$p = \frac{3.3285}{50} = 0.0665 \text{ or } 6.65\%.$$

(d) For $\mu_{np} = 0.75$ and a c of more than 3.3285, Table *G* gives the probability of a point falling outside the UCL_{np} as 0.005.

Q. 10.61: *Lots of 1,200 are submitted for inspection under the normal sampling ABC standard. The agreed AQL is 4%. What is the exact average outgoing quality limit ? Suggest a possible way to improve the outgoing quality limit.*

Ans: For the lot size of 1200 and normal inspection (inspection level II) and code letter *J* (From Table *K*), the Table *U* for an AQL of 4%, gives the approximate average outgoing quality limit (AOQL) as 5.6%.

$$\text{Exact AOQL} = \text{approximate AOQL}\left(1 - \frac{\text{sample size}}{\text{lot size}}\right)$$

$$= 5.6\left(1 - \frac{80}{1{,}200}\right)$$

$$= 5.23\%$$

The outgoing quality can be improved by giving a tightened inspection. For the lot size of 1,200 and tightened inspection (inspection level II) the Table V for an AQL of 4%, gives the approximate average out going quality limit (AOQL) as 4%,

$$\text{Exact AOQL} = 4\left(1 - \frac{80}{1,200}\right)$$

$$= 3.74\%$$

Use of inspection level III in tightened inspection will still improve the outgoing quality limit.

Q. 10.62: *(a) Does ABC standard allow the switching over from tightened inspection directly to reduced inspection ?*

(b) Parts for a contract are bought in lots of 2,000 pieces. What AQL must be specified so that lots are rejected when 4 or more defective parts are found in the sample drawn ? Attribute sampling, general inspection level II, and single sampling, and normal inspection apply.

(c) In (b) above, suppose that seven consecutive lots of 2,000 pieces each were subjected to inspection. Lots 1 and 2 through 3 were accepted, lots 4 and 5 were rejected, and lots 6 and 7 were accepted. What were the acceptance and rejection numbers for each of these seven lots ?

Ans: (*a*) No. If the conditions are favourable, the inspection is to return to normal and if the conditions are again favourable then only reduced inspection can be instituted.

(*b*) For lot size of 2,000 and level II, Table *K* gives code letter as *K*. Than from Table *L*, in the row of K, the rejection number 4 occurs under AQL of 1.0%. Hence AQL to be specified is 1.0%.

(*c*) As the normal inspection is in force and out of first 5 consecutive lots 2 lots (lot No. 4 and lot No. 5) are rejected, the tightened inspection is to be instituted for lot 6 and lot 7. Hence the acceptance and rejection numbers for lot 6 and 7 are to be taken from Table M.

The following tabulation summarizes the acceptance and rejection number of lots 1 to 7.

Lot No.	*Acceptance number*	*Rejection number*
1, 2, 3, 4, 5	3	4
6, 7	2	3

Q. 10.63: *Refer to ABC-STD-105 with the following conditions :*

Lot size = 10,000

Inspection level II

Acceptable quality level = 4 percent

(a) State a single sampling plan for normal inspection.

(b) Suppose a lot is sampled and accepted, someone makes the statement : "This means the lot has 4 percent or less defective ". Comment on this statement. (Assume the sample was randomly selected and no inspection errors were made).

(c) Calculate the probability of accepting a 4 percent defective lot under normal inspection.

Ans: (*a*) From Tables *K* and *L*, the following single sampling plan is determined : Sample size 200, Acceptance number 14 and Rejection number 15.

(*b*) The statement is incorrect, because the ABC standard provides about 95% probability of acceptance of lots which have lot quality as AQL.

When a consumer designates some specific value of AQL for a certain defect or group of defects, he indicates to the supplier that his (the consumer's) acceptance sampling plan will accept the great majority of lots that the supplier submits, provided the process average level of percent defective (or defects per hundred units) in these lots be no greater than the designated value of AQL. Thus the AQL is a designated value of percent defective (or defects per hundred units) that the consumer indicates will be accepted most of the time by the acceptance sampling procedure to be used. The sampling plans provided by ABC standard are so arranged that the probability of acceptance at the designated AQL value depends upon the sample size, being generally higher for large samples than for smaller ones for a given AQL. The AQL alone does not describe the protection to the consumer for individual lots but more directly relates to what might be expected from a series of lot.

(*c*) The probability of acceptance under of 4% defective lot (*i.e.* $\mu_p = 0.04$) under the given sampling plan ($n = 200$, $c = 14$) as determined from Table *G* is 0.983.

Q. 10.64: *Refer to ABC or MIL-STD-105E with the following conditions :*

- *Lot size = 10,000*
- *Inspection level II*
- *Acceptable quality level = four percent*

(*a*) *Find a single-sampling plan for normal inspection.*

(*b*) *Suppose that a lot is sampled and accepted. Someone makes the statement. "This means the lot has four percent or less defective." Comment on this statement. (Assume that the sample was randomly selected and no inspection errors were made.)*

(*c*) *Calculate the probability of accepting a four percent defective lot under normal inspection.*

(*d*) *What sample size would be required by MIL-STD-414 (Assume that the inspection level is IV, normal inspection, variability measured by the standard, deviation single specification limit form 1).*

Ans: For lot size 10,000 and inspection level II, Table *K* gives the sample size code letter as L.

From Table *L*, for code letter L, the single sampling plan for AQL of 4% is :

$$n = 200$$

$$Ac = 14 \quad Re = 15$$

(*b*) The choice of an AQL is a necessary evil that exists in any sampling inspection, there really is no such thing as an acceptable level of production of defective material. Choice of an AQL does not imply the right to supply defective material. Hence the statement does not hold good.

(*c*) $n = 200$, $p = 0.04$, $\mu_{np} = 8$

From Table *G*, $P_a = 0.983$

(*d*) $n = 75$

Q. 10.65: *Using MIL-STD 105 E or ABC STD, determine the single sampling plans for the following information :*

	Inspection level	*Inspection*	*AQL*	*Lot size*
(*a*)	II	Tightened	1.5%	1,400
(*b*)	I	Normal	65	115
(*c*)	III	Reduced	0.40%	160,000
(*d*)	III	Normal	2.5%	27

Explain the meaning of the sampling plan determined in (c) if (i) 6 defectives are found in the sample, (ii) if 8 defectives are found, and (iii) if 4 defectives are found.

Ans: ABC STD and MIL-STD 105 E are same in sampling schemes and tables.

(*a*) For lot size of 1400 and inspection level II, the sample size code letter as per Table K is K. From Table M for the AQL of 1.5, the sampling plan as :

Sample size (n) = 125

Acceptance number (A_c) = 3, Rejection number (R_e) = 4

(*b*) Sample size (n) = 8

Acceptance number (A_c) = 10 (*i.e.* defects per 100 units)

Rejection number (R_e) = 11 (*i.e.* defects per 100 units)

(*c*) Sample size (n) = 500

Acceptance number (A_c) = 5, Rejection number (R_e) = 8

(*d*) Sample size (n) = 13

Acceptance number (A_c) = 1, Rejection number (R_e) = 2

In case of (*c*)

(*i*) If 6 defects are found, accept the lot but reinstate the normal inspection.

(*ii*) If 8 defectives are found, reject the lot.

(*iii*) If 4 defective are found, accept the lot and continue the reduced inspection.

Q. 10.66: *A double sampling plan is to be employed to check 1,000 parts for a safety characteristic. Due to the number of the device, the AQL has been set at 0.1 percent, general inspection level III. What plan would be used ?*

Ans: For lot size of 1,000 and general inspection level III, the sample size code letter is K.

From Table *O* for an AQL of 0.1%, the sampling plan is

$$n_1 = 315 \; Ac = 0 \; Re = 2$$

$$n_2 = 315 \; Ac = 1 \; Re = 2$$

Q. 10.67: *For a continuing audit inspection, a multiple sampling plan with an AQL = 2.5 percent is required. Material is submitted in 1,400 piece lots. Specify the appropriate plan. The following results were obtained on the first audit :*

First sample	*1 defective found*
Second sample	*1 defective found*
Third sample	*3 defectives found*
Fourth sample	*5 defectives found*
Fifth sample	*0 defective found*
Sixth sample	*1 defective found*
Seventh sample	*2 defective found*

Evaluate the auditor's procedure and determine the correct final decision. Does he need additional instruction ?

Ans: When inspection level is not specified, it is taken as level II only.

For lot size of 1400, sample size code letter for level II inspection is *K*.

From Table *R*, the multiple sampling normal inspection for 2.5% AQL is as follows :

Sample	*Size*	*Cumulative sample size*	A_c	R_e
First	32	32	0	4
Second	32	64	1	6
Third	32	96	3	8
Fourth	32	128	5	10
Fifth	32	160	7	11
Sixth	32	192	10	12
Seventh	32	224	13	14

As 1 defective is found in First sample, and rejection number is not reached, the second sample is to be taken. As the second sample also contains one defective, and hence total defectives upto 2 samples is 2 against Ac of 1 and Re of 6 has not been reached, take a third sample. As third sample contains 3 defectives and hence total defectives upto third sample is 5 against Ac of 3 and Re of 8, take Fourth sample. As the Fourth sample contains 5 defectives, the total defectives upto Fourth sample is 10 which is more than Ac of 5 but equal to Re of 10, reject the lot on after Fourth sample and stop inspection as soon 10th defective is found.

Auditor should not have inspected after 10th defective was located and there was definitely no need for inspection Fifth, Sixth and Seventh samples.

Further, it was necessary to clearly stipulate normal and level II inspection inorder to avoid any ambiguity.

Q. 10.68: *For a double sampling plan, code letter L, normal inspection, and AQL = 2.5% the number inspected and the number defectives for the last 10 lots are*

	n	*np*		*n*	*np*
I	125	0	VI	125	1
II	125	2	VII	125	1
III	125	0	VIII	125	2
IV	250	6	IX	125	3
V	125	1	X	125	1

(*a*) *If the production is at a steady rate and reduced inspection is authorized, can a change from normal to reduced inspection be initiated ?*

(*b*) *If lot IX has 9 defectives rather than 3 defectives, is a change from normal to reduced inspection warranted ?*

Ans: (*a*) No. of sample units = (125 × 9) + (250 × 1) = 1375

Total number of defective = 2 + 6 + 1 + 1 + 1 + 2 + 3 + 1 = 17

From Table *W*, for AQL of 2.5% the maximum number of defectives can be 24.

As all the conditions are met with, a reduced inspection can be initiated.

(*b*) In case lot IX has 9 defectives and number of pieces inspected remains to be 125 then this lot will be rejected on the first sample itself. Hence the condition : "the preceding 10 lots or batches (or more, as indicated by Table W) have been on normal inspection and more has been rejected on original inspection," is violated and in view of this a reduced inspection is not warranted.

CHAPTER

11 Designing of Sampling Plans and Special Sampling Plans

11.1 PURPOSE OF THIS CHAPTER

Where modern acceptance sampling is to be adopted, the first decision usually should be on the acceptance sampling system to be chosen. Chapter 10 described two types of widely used systems and schemes.

Even where all that is needed is a particular sampling plan that involves certain stated risks, the publications describing existing systems are useful. Such publications generally give the OC curves for each of the many sampling plans included ; usually a plan can be found that comes fairly close to giving a desired OC curve.

But, whenever desired, we can design our own sampling plans that have a stipulated value of the risk of accepting product containing some stated percentage of defectives. The first part of this chapter discusses the design of single sampling plans having a stated value of the 'indifference quality' *i.e.* $p_{0.50}$ and also the design of single sampling plans having stated amount Producer's and Consumer's Risks. Further it discusses item-by-item sequential sampling plans for which again both Producer's Risk and Consumer's Risk are stipulated.

The second part of this chapter gives brief description of three systems of lot-by-lot acceptance sampling by attributes. The first of these is the Philips Standard Sampling System, which uses $p_{0.50}$ as the basis for referencing all its sampling plans. The second is a simplified AQL type system proposed by Harold Dodge. The third, also developed by Dodge, is devised for the special case where sample sizes must be so small that the only practicable acceptance number is zero.

11.2 DESIGNING LOT-BY-LOT ACCEPTANCE SAMPLING PLANS FOR CERTAIN RISKS

This section briefly describes the design basis of attribute acceptance plans where either Consumer's Risk or Producer's Risk or both are stipulated. Essentially the design of such acceptance plans depends upon at least one and maximum two points on the OC curve known to the designer of plans. Nevertheless it is once again emphasized that none of these plans can be ideal and hence involves certain amount of risks.

11.2.1 Designing Single Sampling Attributes Plans having a Stated Value of $p_{0.50}$

The quality $p_{0.50}$, for any lot-by-lot acceptance sampling plan, is the lot or process quality that has a probability of acceptance of 0.50. In the Philips Standard Sampling System, $p_{0.50}$ is called the *point of control*. Some other quality control literatures mention this as an *indifference quality*. It is easy to devise home-made single sampling acceptance criteria for any desired

$p_{0.50}$, using the formula, first given by G.A. Campbell.

$$n = \frac{c + 0.67}{p_{0.50}} \quad ...(11.1)$$

Suppose that lots 2.5% defective or better considered to be acceptable but that it is desired to reject lots that are any worse. With this quality standard, we wish to find a set of single sampling plans for which a lot 2.5% defective will have a P_a of 0.50. Assume values of the acceptance number c from 0 upto any desired number, and solve the foregoing formula for sample size n, using p0.50 as 0.025. The resulting family of acceptance plans is as follows :

c	n	c	n	c	n
0	27	4	187	8	347
1	67	5	227	9	387
2	107	6	267	10	427
3	147	7	307	11	467

Although the OC curves of these 12 single sampling plans all pass fairly close through the one point $p = 0.025$ or 2.5%, and $P_a = 0.50$ the plans having the larger sample size give better discrimination between lots that are somewhat better than 2.5% defective and lots that are somewhat worse. This fact is illustrated in Fig. 11.1. A choice among the various plans requires balancing the extra inspection cots of larger samples against the advantage of better assurance that a lot meeting the quality standard will be accepted and one failing to meet it will be rejected.

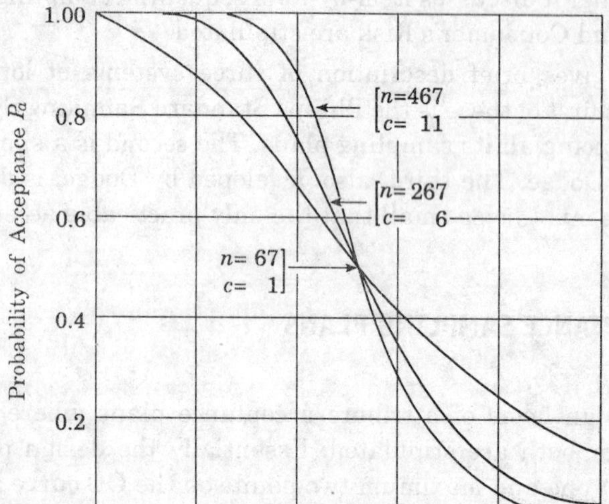

FIGURE 11.1: *OC* curves for three single sampling plans having a p0.50 of 2.5%.

11.2.2 Sampling Plans for Stipulated Producer's Risk

When the Producer's Risk α and its corresponding acceptable quality level (AQL) are specified, a sampling plan or, more precisely, a family of sampling plans, can be determined. For a Producer's Risk, α, of say 0.05 and an AQL of 1.2%, the OC curves for a family of sampling plans as shown in Fig. 11.2, are obtained. Each of the plans passes through the point defined by

TABLE 11.1: GENERALIZED TABLE OF SINGLE SAMPLING PLANS THAT HAVE CERTAIN SPECIFIED PRODUCER'S AND CONSUMER'S RISK

c	$np_{0.99}$	$np_{0.95}$	$np_{0.90}$	$np_{0.50}$	$np_{0.10}$	$np_{0.05}$	$np_{0.01}$	$\frac{p_{0.10}}{p_{0.95}}$
0	0.010	0.051	0.105	0.693	2.303	2.996	4.605	44.890
1	0.149	0.355	0.532	1.678	3.890	4.744	6.638	10.946
2	0.436	0.818	1.102	2.674	5.321	6.296	8.406	6.509
3	0.823	1.366	1.745	3.672	6.681	7.754	10.045	4.890
4	1.279	1.970	2.433	4.671	7.994	9.154	11.605	4.057
5	1.785	2.613	3.152	5.670	9.275	10.513	13.108	3.549
6	2.330	3.286	3.895	6.670	10.532	11.842	14.571	3.206
7	2.906	3.981	4.656	7.699	11.771	13.148	16.000	2.957
8	3.507	4.695	5.432	8.669	12.995	14.434	17.403	2.768
9	4.130	5.426	6.221	9.668	14.206	15.705	18.783	2.618
10	4.771	6.169	7.021	10.668	15.407	16.962	20.145	2.497
11	5.428	6.924	7.829	11.668	16.598	18.208	21.490	2.397
12	6.099	7.690	8.646	12.668	17.782	19.442	22.821	2.312
13	6.782	8.464	9.470	13.668	18.958	20.668	24.139	2.240
14	7.477	9.246	10.300	14.668	20.128	21.886	24.446	2.177
15	8.181	10.035	11.135	15.668	21.292	23.098	26.743	2.122
16	8.895	10.831	11.976	16.668	22.452	24.302	28.031	2.073
17	9.616	11.633	12.822	17.668	23.606	25.500	29.310	2.209
18	10.346	12.442	13.672	18.668	24.756	26.692	30.581	1.990
19	11.082	13.254	14.525	19.668	25.902	27.879	31.845	1.954
20	11.825	14.072	15.383	20.668	27.045	29.062	33.103	1.952
21	12.574	14.894	16.244	21.668	28.184	30.241	34.355	1.892
22	13.329	15.719	17.108	22.668	29.320	31.416	35.601	1.865
23	14.088	16.548	17.975	23.668	30.453	32.586	36.841	1.840
24	14.853	17.382	18.844	24.668	31.584	33.752	38.077	1.817
25	15.623	18.218	19.717	25.667	32.711	34.916	39.308	1.795
30	19.532	22.444	24.113	30.667	38.315	40.690	45.401	1.707
35	23.525	26.731	28.556	35.667	43.872	46.404	51.409	1.641
40	27.587	31	066	33.038	40.667	54.878	57.695	63.231
45	31.704	35.441	37.550	45.667	54.878	57.695	63.231	1.548
50	35.867	39.849	42.089	50.667	60.339	63.287	69.066	1.515

$p_{0.95} = 00.12$ and $P_a = 0.95$ $(1 - \alpha = 0.95)$. Therefore, each of the plans will ensure that product 1.2% defective (good product) will be rejected 5% of the time or, conversely, accepted 95% of the time.

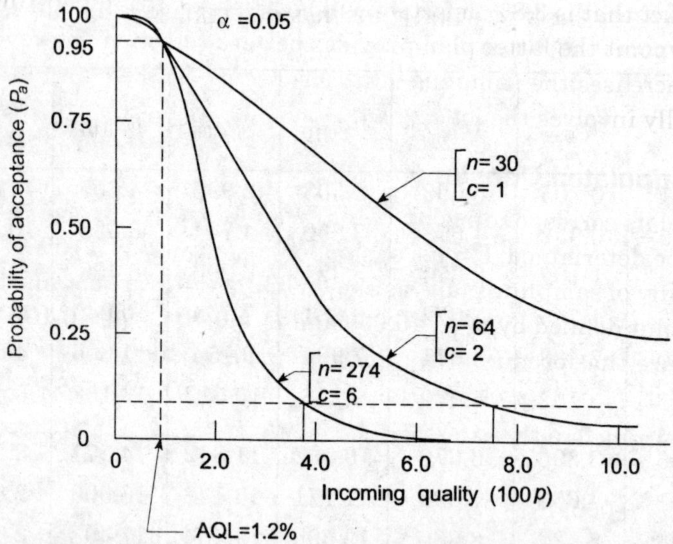

FIGURE 11.2: Single sampling plans for stipulated Producer's Risk and AQL.

The sampling plans are obtained by assuming a value for c and finding its corresponding μ_{np} value from Table G. Then knowing np and p, the sample size n is obtained. In order to find the μ_{np} values Table G, interpolation is required. To eliminate the interpolation operation, np values for $\alpha = 0.05$ and $\beta = 0.10$ are reproduced in Table 11.1. In this table, c is cumulative, which means that a c value of 2 represents 2 or less.

Calculations to obtain the three sampling plans of Fig. 11.2 are as follows :

$$P_a = 0.95$$

$$p_{0.95} = 0.012$$

For $c = 1$, $np_{0.95} = 0.355$ (from Table 11.1)

and
$$n = \frac{np_{0.95}}{p_{0.95}}$$

$$= \frac{0.355}{0.012} = 29.6 \text{ or } 30$$

For $c = 2$, $np_{0.95} = 0.818$ (from Table 11.1)

and
$$n = \frac{np_{0.95}}{p_{0.95}} = \frac{0.818}{0.012} = 64.2 \text{ or } 64$$

For $c = 6$, $np_{0.95} = 3.286$ (from Table 11.1)

and
$$n = \frac{np_{0.95}}{p_{0.95}} = \frac{3.286}{0.012} = 273.8 \text{ or } 274.$$

The sampling plans $c = 1$, $c = 2$, and $c = 6$ have been arbitrarily selected to illustrate the technique.

While all the plans provide the same protection for the prouducer, the Consumer's Risk, at say $\beta = 0.10$, is quite different. From Fig. 11.2 for the plan $c = 1$, $n = 30$, product that is 13% defective will be accepted 10% ($\beta\% = 0.10$) of the time (not shown on the figure) ; for the plan $c = 2$, $n = 64$, the product that is 7.8% defective will be accepted 10% ($\beta = 0.10$) of the time ; and for the plan $c = 6$, $n = 274$, product that is 3.8% defective will be accepted 10% ($\beta = 0.10$) of the time. From the consumer's viewpoint the latter plan provides better protection ; however, the sample size is greater, which increases the sampling cost. The section of the plan to use is a matter of judgment which usually involves the lot size.

11.2.3 Sampling Plans for Stipulated Consumer's Risk

When the Consumer's Risk β and its corresponding lot tolerance percent defective are specified, a family of sampling plans can be determined. For a Consumer's Risk, β, of say 0.10 and LTPD of 6.0%, the *OC* curves for a family of sampling plans as shown in Fig. 11.3, are obtained. Each of the plans pass through the point defined by $p_{0.10} = 0.060$ and $P_a = 0.10$ i.e. ($\beta = 0.10$). Therefore, each of the plans will ensure that product 6.0% defective (bad product) will be accepted 10% of the time.

The sampling plans are determined in the same manner as used for a stipulated Producer's Risk. Calculations are as follows :

$$p_{0.10} = 0.060,\ P_a = 0.10$$

For $c = 1$,

$$np_{0.10} = 3.890 \text{ (from Table 11.1)}$$

$$n = \frac{np_{0.10}}{p_{0.10}} = \frac{3.890}{0.060} = 64.8 \text{ or } 65$$

For $c = 3$,

$$n = p_{0.10} = 6.681 \text{ (from Table 11.1)}$$

and

$$n = \frac{np_{0.10}}{p_{0.10}} = \frac{0.681}{0.060} = 111.4 \text{ or } 111$$

Similarly when $c = 7$, $n = 196$.

The sampling plans for $c = 1$, $c = 3$ and $c = 7$ have been arbitrarily selected to illustrate the technique.

While all the plans provide the same protection for the consumer, the Producer's Risk at say $\alpha = 0.05$, is quite different. From Fig. 11.3 for the plan $c = 1$, $n = 65$, product that is 0.5% defective will be rejected 5% ($\alpha = 0.05$) of the time; for the plan $c = 3$, $n = 111$, product that is 1.2% defective will be rejected 5% ($\alpha = 0.05$) of the time ; and for the plan $c = 7$, $n = 196$, product that is 2.0% defective will be rejected 5% ($\alpha = 0.05$) of the time.

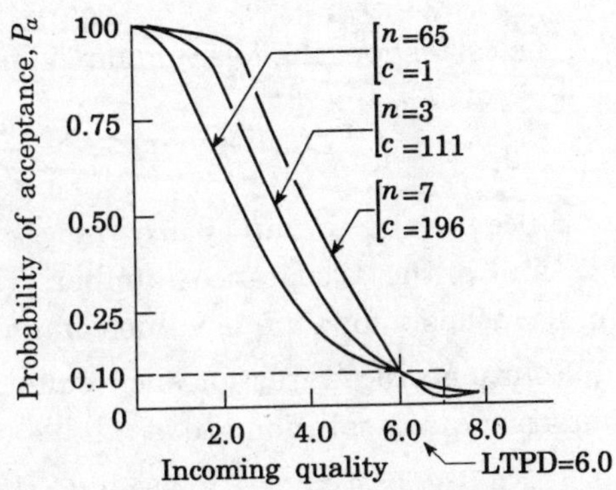

FIGURE 11.3: Single sampling plans for stipulated Consumer's Risk and LTPD.

From the producer's viewpoint the latter plan provides better protection ; however, the sample size is greater, which increases the sampling costs. The selection of the plan is a matter of judgement, which usually involving the lot size.

11.2.4 Designing Single Sampling Plans for Stipulated Producer's and Consumer's Risks

The topic of the choice of a sampling plans based on the assessment of both Consumer and Producer Risks was introduced in Chap. 10. The reader will remember that the definition of AQL, the basis of the ABC standard, related to a high quality (low value of μ_p) considered acceptable as a process average. Once such a value of the AQL is fixed, a definite point on the upper end of the OC curve may be established. The coordinates of this point are $(p_1, 1-\alpha)$, where p_1 is the value of the AQL and α is the Producer's Risk. In the ABC standard system, α ranges from 0.01 to 0.12 with the highest values occurring for those plans where c equals 0.

In the discussion of the LQ tables (Sec. 10.14, Chap. 10), it was pointed out that, in instances where isolated lots of product are to be inspected using a sampling plan, equal attention should be directed to the Consumer's Risk. The LQ tables gave values of μ_p with probabilities of acceptance, that is, Consumer's Risk (β), of 5 and 10%. The tables were organized in such a manner that the user searched and AQL column until an acceptable Consumer's Risk point (p_2, β) was found. Thus the consumer's interest may be most closely associated with the lower end of the OC curve. While this duality in the relationship between the interests of the producer and consumer may be strongest in those cases where judgment must be passed on isolated lots of product, a strong argument could be made that the appropriate balancing of consumer and producer interests in the operating characteristics of a sampling plan is basic to the selection of a good plan.

Mathematically, the selection of two points on an operating characteristic curve uniquely defines a single sampling plan for those points. In practice, this means that the appropriate balancing of consumer and producer interests, as exemplified by the choice of a Producer's Risk point $(p_1, 1-\alpha)$ and a Consumer's Risk, point (p_2, β), leads to a unique single sampling plan. For simplicity, this fact is demonstrated using the Poisson distribution.

Since the producer wishes product with the stipulated quality p_1 accepted with probability $1-\alpha$, the Poisson formula for probability of acceptance describing the stipulated preference is

$$P_a\,(\text{producer}) = \sum_{r=0}^{c} \frac{(np_1)^r}{r!} e^{-np_1} = 1-\alpha \qquad \ldots(11.2)$$

The corresponding formula describing the Consumer's Risk preference is

$$P_a\,(\text{consumer}) = \sum_{r=0}^{c} \frac{(np_2)^r}{r!} e^{-np_2} = \beta \qquad \ldots(11.3)$$

Since $p_1, p_2, 1-\alpha$, and β are known, the two unknowns in these equations are n, the sample size, and c, the acceptance number. These two equations in two unknowns may be solved simultaneously for unique values of n and c, which are essentially to be whole numbers.

Solution procedures for such equations are beyond the scope of this text but two simple courses of quick solution are available.

1. Figure 11.4 shows four plans that are close to meeting the stipulations for $\alpha = 0.05$, $AQL = 0.9$ and $\beta = 0.10$ LTPD = 7.8. The *OC* curves of two plans meet the consumer's stipulation that product which is 7.8% defective (LTPD) will be accepted 10% ($\beta = 0.10$) of the time and comes close to the producer's stipulation. These two plans are shown by the dashed lines in Fig. 11.4 and are $c = 1$, $n = 50$ and $c = 2$, $n = 68$. The other two plans exactly meet the producer's stipulation that product which is 0.9% defective (*AQL*) will be accepted 95% ($\alpha = 0.05$) of the time. These two plans are shown by the solid lines and are $n = 39$, $c = 1$ and $n = 91$, $c = 2$.

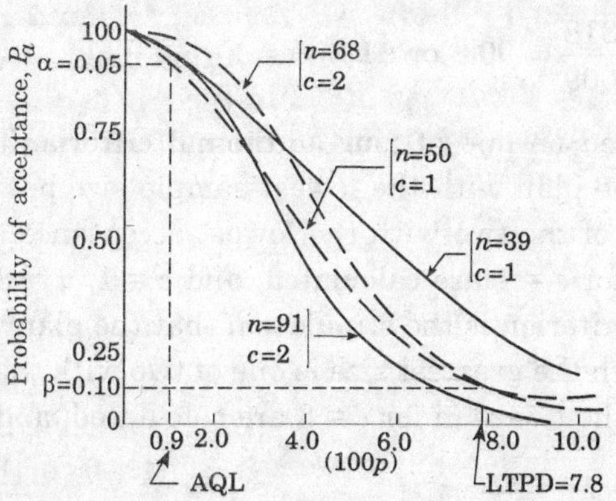

FIGURE 11.4: Sampling plans for stipulated producer's and consumer's risk.

In order to determine the plans the first step is to find the ratio $p_{0.10}/p_{0.95}$ which is

$$\frac{p_{0.10}}{p_{0.95}} = \frac{0.078}{0.009} = 8.667$$

From the ratio column of Table 11.1, the ratio of 8.667 falls between the row for $c = 1$ and the row for $c = 2$. Thus plans that exactly meet the consumer's stipulation of LTPD = 7.8% for $\beta = 0.10$ are

For $c = 1,$

$$p_{0.10} = 0.078$$

$$np_{0.10} = 3.890 \text{ (from Table 11.1)}$$

$$n = \frac{np_{0.10}}{p_{0.10}} = \frac{3.890}{0.078} = 49.9 \text{ or } 50$$

For $c = 2$

$$p_{0.10} = 0.078$$

$$np_{0.10} = 5.322 \text{ (from Table 11.1)}$$

$$n = \frac{np_{0.10}}{p_{0.10}} = \frac{5.322}{0.078} = 68.2 \text{ or } 68$$

Plans that exactly meet the producer's stipulation of AQL = 0.9% for $\alpha = 0.05$ are.

For $c = 1$

$$p_{0.095} = 0.009$$

$$np_{0.95} = 0.355 \qquad \text{(from Table 11.1)}$$

$$n = \frac{np_{0.95}}{p_{0.95}} = \frac{0.355}{0.009} = 39.4 \text{ or } 39$$

From $c = 2,$

$$p_{0.95} = 0.009$$

$$np_{0.95} = 0.818 \qquad \text{(from Table 11.1)}$$

$$n = \frac{np_{0.95}}{p_{0.95}} = \frac{0.818}{0.009} = 90.8 \text{ or } 91$$

Which of the four plans to select is based on one of four additional criteria. The first additional criterion is the stipulation that the plan with the lowest sample size be selected. The plan with the lowest sample size is one of the two with the lowest acceptance number. Thus, in the above case, only the two plans for $c = 1$ are calculated, and $c = 1$, $n = 39$ is the sampling plan selected. A second additional criterion is the stipulation that the plan with the greatest sample size be selected. The plan with the greatest size is one of two with the largest acceptance number. Thus, for this case only the two plan for $c = 2$ are calculated, and $n = 91$, $c = 2$ is the sampling plans selected.

A third additional criterion is the stipulation that the plan exactly meet the consumer's stipulation and come as close as possible to the producer's stipulation. The two plans that exactly meet the consumer's stipulation are $n = 50$, $c = 1$; and $n = 68$, $c = 2$. Calculations to determine which plan is closest to the producer's stipulation of $AQL = 0.9\%$, $\alpha = 0.05$ are :

For $n = 50$, $c = 1$

$$p_{0.95} = \frac{np_{0.95}}{n} = \frac{0.355}{50} = 0.007$$

For $n = 68$, $c = 2$

$$p_{0.95} = \frac{np_{0.95}}{n} = \frac{0.818}{68} = 0.012$$

Since $p_{0.95} = 0.007$ is closest to the stipulated value of 0.009, the plan of $n = 50$, $c = 1$ is selected.

The fourth additional criterion for the selection of one of the four sampling plans is the stipulation that the plan exactly meet the producer's stipulation and comes as close as possible to consumer's stipulation. The two plans that are applicable are $n = 39$, $c = 1$; and $n = 91$, $c = 1$. Calculations to determine which is the closest to the consumer's stipulation of $LTPD = 7.8\%$, $\beta = 0.10$ are :

For $n = 39$, $c = 1$

$$p_{0.10} = \frac{np_{0.10}}{n} = \frac{3.890}{39} = 0.100$$

For $n = 91$, $c = 2$,

$$p_{0.10} = \frac{np_{0.10}}{n} = \frac{5.322}{39} = 0.058$$

Since $p_{0.10} = 0.058$ is closest to the stipulated value of 0.078, the sampling plan $n = 91$, $c = 2$ is selected for the given conditions.

2. Use the following approximate procedure (the mathematical justification of this procedure is beyond the scope of the book.)

Consult the χ^2-distribution table and search for two values χ_1^2 and χ_2^2 such that

$$\chi_1^2 = 2\,np_2 \text{ with } (1 - \alpha) \text{ as significance level} \quad ...(11.4)$$

$$\chi_2^2 = 2\,np_2 \text{ with } \beta \text{ as significance level} \quad ...(11.5)$$

The number of degrees of freedom for χ_1^2 and χ_2^2 is $2(c+1)$. In practice this means examining rows of the χ^2-table until a row is found for which the entries in the $(1-\alpha)$ and β columns are in the ratio p_1/p_2. The number of degrees of freedom corresponding to that row then gives c and either value of χ^2 allows n to be calculated. Note that only rows with even degrees of freedom can be considered. To understand of this approximate procedure let us consider the same risk stipulations as assumed earlier

Thus $p_1 = 0.009,\ 1-\alpha = 0.95$

$p_2 = 0.078,\ \beta = 0.10$

and $p_1/p_2 = 0.009/0.078 = 0.1153$

Following tabulation (extracted from Table *B* of App. 2) shows the relevant portion of $\chi 2$-distribution

Degrees of Freedom	*Significance Level*		*Ratio of*
	0.95	*0.05*	$\chi^2_{0.95}/\chi^2_{0.05}$
2	0.10	5.99	0.0172
4	0.71	9.49	0.0748
6	1.64	12.59	0.1303
8	2.73	15.51	0.2168
10	3.94	18.31	0.2152
12	5.23	21.03	0.2487
14	6.57	23.68	0.2774

The ratio of 0.1303 is the closest to the p_1/p_2 ratio of 0.1153.

Hence, the degrees of freedom = $2(c+1) = 6$ from which $c = 2$. The equations involving n are then

$$2 \times n \times 0.009 = 1.64, \quad n = 91$$

$$2 \times n \times 0.078 = 12.59, \quad n = 81$$

Thus plans with $(n = 91,\ c = 2)$ or $(n = 81,\ c = 2)$ meet approximately the risk requirements specified.

The reader should recognize that because n and c must be whole numbers it is not always possible to find sampling plans which exactly satisfy specified risks. However a choice can always be made depending upon the circumstances stated previously.

11.3 DESIGN OF A SEQUENTIAL SAMPLING PLAN (SeSP) HAVING AN OC CURVE PASSING THROUGH TWO DESIGNATED POINTS

Sequential sampling is similar to multiple sampling except that the sequential sampling can theoretically continue indefinitely. In practice the plan is truncated after the number inspected is equal to three times the number inspected by a corresponding single sampling plan. Sequential sampling, which is used for costly or destructive tests, usually has a subgroup size of 1, thereby making it an item-by-item plan.

Item-by-item sequential sampling is based on the concept of the sequential probability ratio test (SPRT) which was first developed by Wald. The mathematical form that the probability ratio takes is :

$$\frac{p_1(1-p_1)^{n-r}}{p_2(1-p_2)^{n-r}} \quad ...(11.6)$$

If the actual fraction defective of the lot μ_p, is at the level p_1, the lot should be accepted. Thus the P_a associated with the numerator of the equation is $1 - \alpha$ and that associated with the denominator is β. When the value of the probability ratio exceeds the ratio of $B = (1 - \alpha)/\beta$, the lot is accepted. Conversely, if μ_p is at the level p_2, the probabilities of rejection are α and $1 - \beta$, respectively, for the numerator and denominator of the probability ratio. Thus if ther value of the ratio falls below $A = \alpha/(1 - \beta)$, the lot is rejected. B and A are associated with the acceptance and rejection lines, respectively. The solution, in terms of r and n, is found with the use of logarithms.

Figure 11.5 illustrates the sampling plan technique. The "stepped" line shows the number defective for the total number inspected and is updated with the inspection results of each item. If the cumulative results equal or are greater than the upper line, the lot is rejected. If the cumulative results equal or are less than the lower line, the lot is accepted. If neither decision is possible, another item is inspected. Thus, if the 30th sample is found to be defective, the cumulative number of defectives will be five. Since five defectives exceed the rejection line for 30 inspection, the lot is rejected, as shown by the dotted line in Fig. 11.5.

The sequential sampling plan is defined by the Producer's Risk, α and its process quality, p1 and by the Consumer's Risk, β and its process quality, p_2. Using these requirements, the equation (slope intercept form) can be determined for the acceptance line and rejecting line as follows:

Acceptance line : $Ac = sn - h_1$ ...(11.7)

Rejection line : $Re = sn + h_1$ ...(11.8)

To compute s, the slope of these lines, and h_1 and h_2,–the intercepts, certain auxiliary symbols g_1, g_2, a and b are used. The necessary computations are as follows :

$$g_1 = \log \frac{p_2}{p_1} \quad ...(11.9)$$

$$g_2 = \log \frac{1 - p_1}{1 - p_2} \quad ...(11.10)$$

$$a = \log \frac{1 - \beta}{\alpha} \quad ...(11.11)$$

$$b = \log \frac{1 - \alpha}{\beta} \quad ...(11.12)$$

$$h_1 = \frac{b}{g_1 + g_2} \quad ...(11.13)$$

$$h_2 = \frac{a}{g_1 + g_2} \quad ...(11.14)$$

$$s = \frac{g_2}{g_1 + g_2} \quad ...(11.15)$$

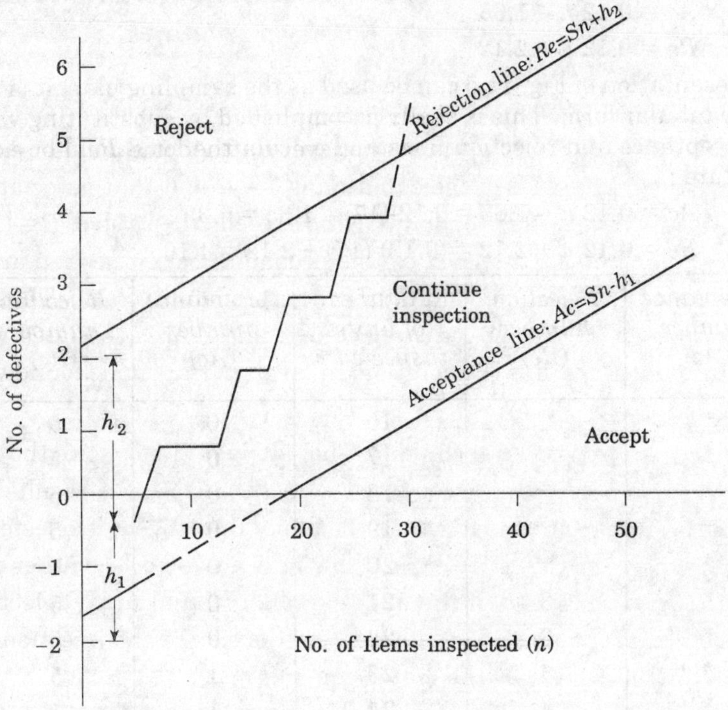

FIGURE 11.5: Graphical presentation of an item-by-item sequential plan.

Thus, the equations for the sequential plan, which are defined by $\alpha = 0.05$, $p_1 = 0.06$; $\beta = 0.10$, and $p_2 = 0.20$, are obtained by the following calculations :

$$h_1 = \frac{b}{g_1 + g_2} = \log\left(\frac{1-\alpha}{\beta}\right) \bigg/ \left[\log\left(\frac{p_2}{p_1}\right) + \log\left(\frac{1-p_1}{1-p_2}\right)\right] \quad \text{...(11.16)}$$

$$= \log\left(\frac{1-0.05}{0.10}\right) \bigg/ \left[\log\left(\frac{0.20}{0.06}\right) + \log\left(\frac{0.94}{0.90}\right)\right]$$

$$= 1.65$$

$$h_2 = \frac{a}{g_1 + g_2} = \log\left(\frac{1-\beta}{\alpha}\right) \bigg/ \left[\log\left(\frac{p_2}{p_1}\right) + \log\left(\frac{1-p_1}{1-p_2}\right)\right] \quad \text{...(11.17)}$$

$$= \log\left(\frac{1-0.10}{0.05}\right) \bigg/ \left[\log\left(\frac{0.20}{0.06}\right) + \log\left(\frac{0.94}{0.80}\right)\right]$$

$$= 2.12$$

$$s = \frac{g_2}{g_1 + g_2} = \log\left(\frac{1-p_1}{1-p_2}\right) \bigg/ \left[\log\left(\frac{p_2}{p_1}\right) + \log\left(\frac{1-p_1}{1-p_2}\right)\right] \quad \text{...(11.18)}$$

$$= \log\left(\frac{1-0.06}{1-0.20}\right) \bigg/ \left[\log\left(\frac{0.20}{0.06}\right) + \log\left(\frac{0.94}{0.80}\right)\right]$$

$$= 0.12$$

Substituting the values of h_1, h_2 and s into the formulae for *Ac* and *Re* we obtain the following equations :

$$Ac = 0.12\,n - 1.65$$
$$Re = 0.12\,n + 2.12$$

While the graphical presentation of Fig. 11.5 can be used as the sampling plan, it is usually more convenient to use the tabular form. This is easily accomplished by substituting values of n into equations for the acceptance and rejection lines and calculate Ac and Re. For example, the calculations for $n = 17$ are :

$$Ac = 0.12\,n - 1.65 = 0.12\,(17) - 1.65 = 0.39$$
$$Re = 0.12\,n + 2.12 = (0.12)\,(17) + 2.12 = 4.16$$

Number of units inspected n	*Acceptance number (Ac)*	*Rejection number (Re)*	*Number of units inspected n*	*Acceptance number (Ac)*	*Rejection number (Re)*
1	*	**	16	0	5
2	*	**	17	0	5
3	*	**	18	0	5
4	*	**	19	0	5
5	*	**	20	0	5
6	*	3	21	0	5
7	*	3	22	0	5
8	*	4	23	1	5
9	*	4	24	1	5
10	*	4	25	1	6
11	*	4	26	1	6
12	*	4	27	1	6
13	*	4	28	1	6
14	0	4	29	1	6
15	0	4	30	1	6

* → Acceptance not possible.

** → Rejection not possible.

Since number of defectives Ac and Re are whole number, the rejection number the next whole number above Re and the acceptance number is the next whole number below Ac. Thus, for $n = 17$, $Ac = 0$, and $Re = 5$. The following tabulation above illustrates the sampling plan for the first 30 samples. The plan would normally be truncated at $n = 150$, since this value is 3 times the value of n for an equivalent single sampling plan, which is a widely accepted norm.

It is sometimes preferable to take the sample in group rather than singly. This is accomplished by using multiples of the desired sample size. Therefore, if the sample size is 5, the acceptance and rejection numbers are determined for n values of 5, 10, 15...

It may be borne in mind that the purpose of adopting the item-by-item sequential sampling is to reduce the average amount of inspection below the amount that would be obtained with a multiple sampling giving about the same quality protection. However, it is always advisable to fix some upper limit to the size of n ; otherwise, an occasional borderline lot might conceivably require the indefinite continuation of sampling.

Five points on the OC curve of an item-by item sequential plan can be found without difficulty. Two of these are the point used in designing the plan. Two more points are established by the knowledge that when $\mu_p = 0$, $P_a = 1.00$ and when $\mu_p = 1$, $P_a = 0$. A fifth point is fixed by the relationship that when $\mu_p = s$, $P_a = h_2/(h_1 + h_2)$.

As previously mentioned, the objective in using item-by-item sequential sampling is usually to minimize the amount of sampling inspection necessary to reach a decision. The *ASN* function is, therefore, an important characteristic of the plan. Sufficiently good OC curves and *ASN* functions often can be sketched from the five points as follows :

Value of μ_p	*OC curve* (P_a)	*ASN*
0.0	1.0	$\dfrac{h_1}{s}$
p_1	$1 - \alpha$	$\dfrac{(1-\alpha)h_1 - \alpha h_2}{s - p_1}$
s	$\dfrac{h_2}{h_1 + h_2}$	$\dfrac{h_1 h_2}{s(1-s)}$
p_2	β	$\dfrac{(1-\beta)h_2 - \beta h_2}{p_2 - s}$
1.0	0	$\dfrac{h_2}{1-s}$

For the sequential plan just computed, the values would be as follows :

μ_p	*OC curve* (P_a)	*ASN*
0.06	0.95	24.35
0.12	0.56	33.13
0.20	0.10	21.79
1.00	0.00	2.41

11.3.1 The Simple Random Walk

An alternative approach to sequential sampling involves the concept of the random walk. Suppose that as each item is inspected a series of points are plotted on a horizontal axis according to the following rules :

1. The zero point is at the centre of the axis.
2. If the item inspected is defective a 'step' of 1 unit to the left is taken (i.e. - 1 unit).
3. If the item inspected, is not defective a 'step' one unit to the right is taken (*i.e.* + 1 unit).
4. When the point + a units is reached sampling stops and the lot is accepted.
5. When the point – b units is reached sampling stops and the lot is rejected.

The fraction defective, p, gives the probability of a step being taken to the left and $(1 - p)$ gives the probability of a step being taken to the right. Providing $p \neq 0.50$ the probability of reaching $+ a$ is given by

$$P_{+a} = \frac{1 - \left(\dfrac{p}{1-p}\right)^{b}}{1 - \left(\dfrac{p}{1-p}\right)^{a+b}} \qquad \text{...(11.19)}$$

Similarly, the probability of reaching $-b$ is given by

$$P_{-b} = \frac{1-\left(\frac{1-p}{p}\right)^{+a}}{1-\left(\frac{1-p}{p}\right)^{a+b}} \qquad \text{...(11.20)}$$

These probabilities are the probabilities of accepting and rejecting a lot respectively. For any value of p the choice of a and b determines the operating characteristic of the scheme.

11.4 THE PHILIPS STANDARD SAMPLING SYSTEM

The Philips standard sampling system was developed by H.C. Hamaker for the Philips Company in Holland. The system uses $p_{0.50}$, as the point of control or indifference quality, as the basis for referencing all the sampling plans.

The system is comprised of one table, which is shown by Table 11.2. This table is indexed by the lot size and the specified product quality of point of control. There are eleven lot size groupings with single sampling being required for lots which are 1,000 or less. Double sampling is required whenever the lot is greater than 1,000. The table provides plans for eight different quality levels : 0.25, 0.5, 1.0, 2.0, 3.0, 5.0, 7.0 and 10.0.

Figure 11.6 shows the OC curves of all the plans in the Philips standard sampling system. Some of the notable features of this standard are :

1. All plans are classified by a particular point on the OC curve, the product quality for which the probability of acceptance is 0.50.
2. Producer and consumer, in effect, share equally in the risk of a "wrong" decision by any sampling plan included in the system. Thus, if a 5% plan is used, product exactly 5% defective is as likely to be accepted as it is to be rejected.
3. As nearly as practicable, all the sampling plans in the system have the same ratio of the slope of the OC curve of $p_{0.50}$ to the value of the quality standard p0.50. In other words, the relativė discrimination between good and bad product is approximately constant at the indifference quality or point of control.
4. A consequence of item 3 is that the Producer's Risk of rejection of product at some stated amount moderately better than the quality standard is roughly comparable to the Consumer's Risk of acceptance of product at the same amount worse than the standard. For instance, consider the 2% plan (n = 85, c = 1) applicable to a lot of 1,000. The Producer's Risk of rejection of a 1% defective lot is approximately 0.21 ; the Consumer's Risk of acceptance of a 3% defective lot is approximately 0.28.
5. Another consequence of item 3 is that the sample size is relatively large for plans designed for maximum consumer protection and decreases as the quality standard is relaxed. For instance, the sample size for a lot of 750 is 225 when the point of control is 0.5% defective and decreases to 55 when the point of control is 5% defective. The poorer the quality that can be tolerated, the smaller the sample size that is needed.
6. Single sampling is stipulated whenever the lot is 1,000 or less. Double sampling is stipulated whenever the lot is greater than 1,000, with n_2 always equal to $2n_1$. Thus for a lot size of 3,500 and the point of control as 3%, the sampling plan is

$$n_1 = 70$$
$$c_1 = 1$$
$$n_2 = 2\,(n_1) = 2\,(70) = 140$$
$$c_2 = 5$$

TABLE 11.2: PHILIPS STANDARD SAMPLING SYSTEM
'A' MEANS INSPECT ENTIRE LOT : FOR SECOND SAMPLE, $n_2 = 2\,n_1$.

Point of control	Lot size	0.25%		0.5%		1%		2%		3%		5%		7%		10%	
		n	c	n	c	n	c	n	c	n	c	n	c	n	c	n	c
Single Sampling	25-50																
	51-100	A	-	A	-	A	-	30	0	20	0	13	0	10	0	7	0
		A	-	A	-	60	0	30	0	20	0	13	0	10	0	7	0
	101-200	A	-	100	-	60	0	35	0	55	1	35	1	25	1	17	1
	201-500	175	0	100	0	135	1	75	1	55	1	35	1	40	2	25	2
	501-1,000	225	0	225	1	150	1	85	1	85	2	55	2	55	3	35	3

Point of control	Lot size	0.25%			0.5%			1%			2%			3%			5%			7%			10%		
		n_1	c_1	c_2	n_1	c_1	c_2	n_1	c_1	c_2	n_1	c_1	c_2	n_1	c_1	c_2	n_1	c_1	c_2	n_1	c_1	c_2	n_1	c_1	c_2
Double Sampling	1001-2,000	330	0	1	150	0	1	110	0	2	55		2	45	0	3	25	0	3	30	1	5	22	1	5
	2,000-5,000	425	0	2	200	0	2	135	0	3	70	1	3	70	1	5	45	1	5	55	2	10	40	2	10
	5,001-10,000	525	0	3	260	0	3	220	1	5	110		5	125	2	10	75	2	10	75	3	15	55	3	15
	10,000-20,000	875	1	5	440	1	5	380	2	10	190	2	10	180	3	15	110	3	15	100	4	20	70	4	20
	20,001-50,000	1,500	2	10	750	2	10	540	3	15	270	3	15	240	4	20	140	4	20	120	5	25	85	5	25
	50,001 and over	2,200	3	15	1,100	3	15	700	4	20	350	4	20	290	5	25	175	5	25	145	6	30	105	6	30

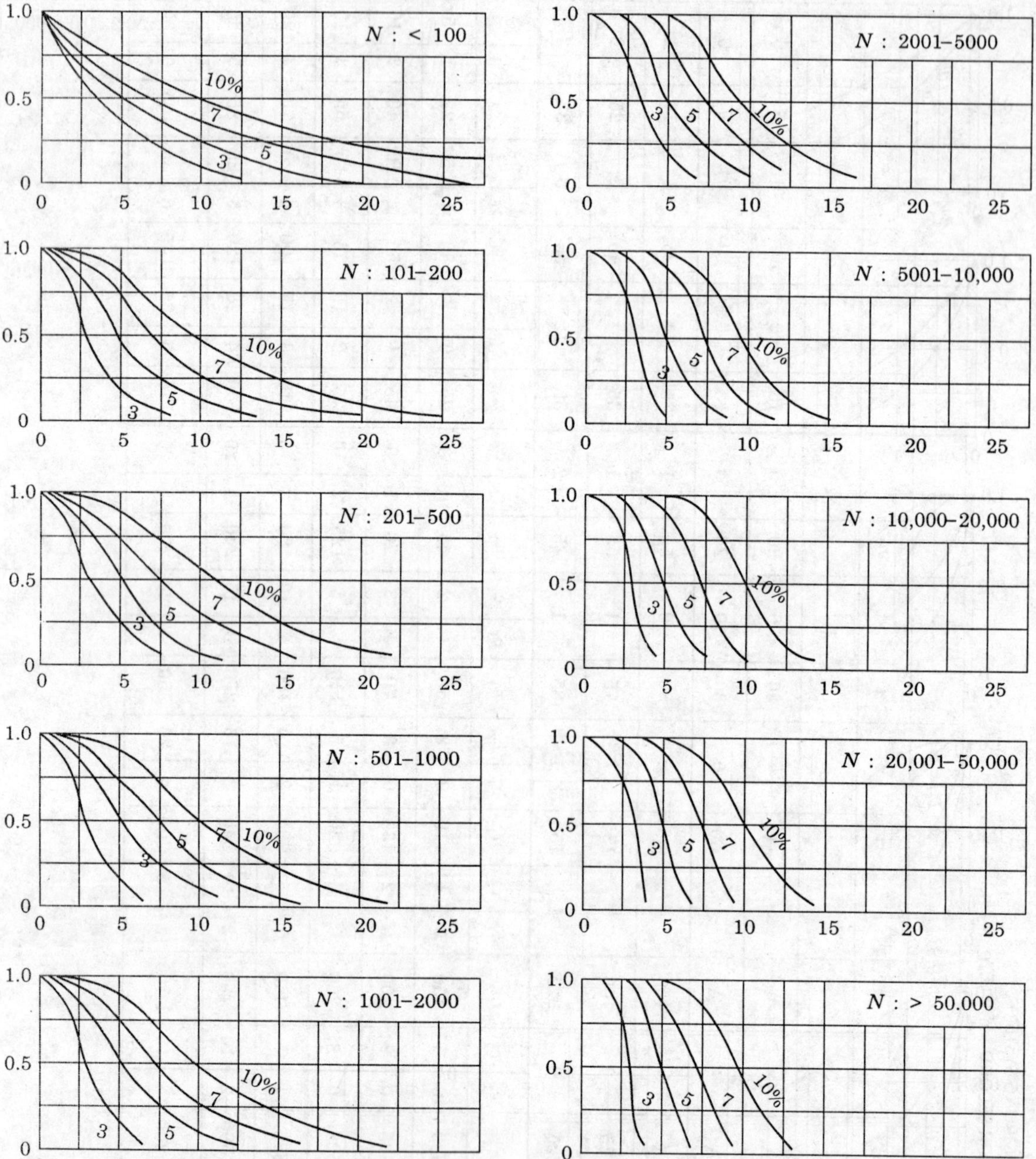
N : < 100
N : 2001–5000
N : 101–200
N : 5001–10,000
N : 201–500
N : 10,000–20,000
N : 501–1000
N : 20,001–50,000
N : 1001–2000
N : > 50.000
3
5
7
10%

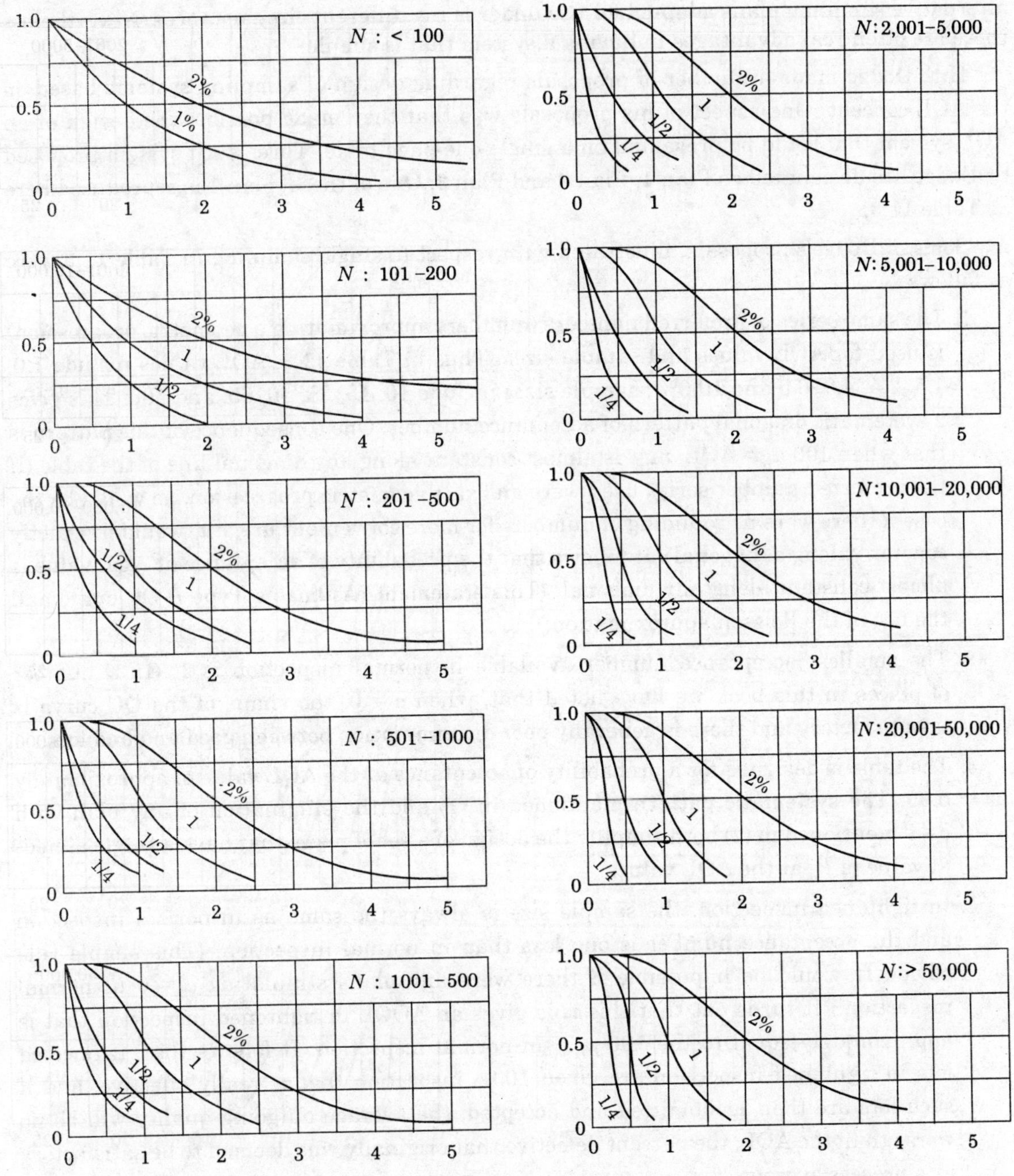

FIGURE 11.6: OC curves for acceptance sampling plans in Philips Standard Sampling System.

11.5 A SIMPLE AQL SYSTEM PROPOSED BY DODGE

The Philips standard sampling system reproduced in Table 11.2 is quite simple. The earlier AQL tables were also quite simple. The *ABC*-STD-105 and MIL-STD-105 E sampling standards illustrated in Chap. 10 involved fairly complex set of tables. Also the D-R tables illustrated in Chap. 10 are quite extensive. The complex tables make it possible to provide many different alternative sampling plans adapted for use under many different circumstances. Nevertheless there are often real advantages in having a system that is simple.

H.F. Dodge made a number of proposals regarding design of sampling systems based on the AQL concept. One aspect of his proposals was that they made possible the design of an AQL system that could be presented on a single one-page table. Three such system proposed by Dodge are designated as Plan 1, Plan 2 and Plan 3. One of these, plan 1 is reproduced here as Table 11.3.

Some of Dodge's proposals, illustrated with respect to single sampling in Table 11.3 were as follows :

1. The same series of preferred numbers (numbers approximating a geometric progression) is used for AQL values and sample sizes. Thus in Table 11.3, AQL values include 1.0, 1.5, 2.5, 4.0, 6.5 and 10.0% ; sample sizes include 10, 15, 25, 40, 65, and 100. This gives a systematic diagonal pattern of acceptance number. One consequence of this pattern is that when 100 μ_p = AQL, $n\mu_p$, is almost constant along any diagonal line of the table (If the preferred number series used were an exact geometric progression, as would be the case if there were no rounding of numbers for more convenient use, $n\mu_p$ would be exactly constant along a diagonal). It follows that the probability of acceptance at AQL value is almost constant along any diagonal. (This statement assumes a Type *B* OC curve and the use of the Poisson approximation.)
2. The smallest acceptance number available in normal inspection is 1. (In a number of places in this book we have noted that, when $c = 0$, the shape of the OC curve is unsatisfactory and there is generally poor discrimination between good and bad lots.
3. The table is designed for a probability of acceptance at the AQL value of approximately 0.95. The systematic pattern mentioned in (1) and the elimination of any plan with $c = 0$ mentioned in (2) both simplify the design of a set of plans that have a single aimed-at value of P_a at the AQL value.
4. In tightened inspection, the sample size is always the same as in normal inspection and the acceptance number is one less than in normal inspection. (This simple rule obviously would be impossible if there were any plans stipulating $c = 0$ in normal inspection.) It turns out that this rule gives an AOQL in tightened inspection that is approximately equal to the 100 $p_{0.95}$ in normal inspection. It follows that, if rejected lots in tightened inspection are given 100% inspection that is really effective, and if such lots are then resubmitted and accepted, the average outgoing quality will be no worse than the AQL, the percent defective that originally was deemed to be satisfactory as a process average.
5. No code letters are used. The lot sizes that correspond to each sampling plan under ordinary circumstances are given in the table. These values given in the table are designated as applying to inspection level II. Where necessary, smaller sample sizes for a given lot size can be used by shifting to the next smaller sample size in the table (inspection level I) ;, larger sample sizes can be used by shifting to the next larger sample size (inspection level III).

TABLE 11.3: COMPOSITE SINGLE SAMPLING TABLE FOR PLAN OF DODGE'S PROPOSED AQL SYSTEM FOR ACCEPTANCE SAMPLING BY ATTRIBUTES

*Lot size, inspection level II***	*Sample size n*	*Acceptance number in normal inspection CN**										
		0.10	*0.15*	*0.25*	*0.40*	*0.65*	*1.0*	*1.5*	*2.5*	*4.0*	*6.5*	*10.0*
3-15	3											↓
16-22	4											1
23-40	6										1	
41-70	10									1		2
71-120	15								1		2	3
121-210	25							1		2	3	5
211-400	40						1		2	3	5	7
401-700	65					1		2	3	5	7	10
701-1300	100				1		2	3	5	7	10	15
1301-3200	150			1		2	3	5	7	10	15	22
3201-15000	250		1		2	3	5	7	10	15	22	
15001-80000	400	1		2	3	5	7	10	15	22		
Over 80000	650		2	3	5	7	10	15	22	↑		

* For tightened inspection, acceptance number $C_T = C_N - 1$

** For inspection level I, use plan with next smaller sample size. For inspection level III, use plan with next larger sample size.

A number of other features of AQL systems, not illustrated in Table 11.3, were also proposed by Dodge. One important proposal was that a shift from normal to tightened inspection be required if 2 of the last 5 (or less) lots under normal inspection were rejected. The reader will recall that this was the rule adopted for the *ABC* standard. Normal inspection was to be reinstated when 5 successive lots were accepted under tightened inspection. Dodge commented regarding these proposed rules as follows :

"The criteria given for shifting from normal to tightened inspection and from tightened back to normal inspection are very simple and easy to apply. Simple criteria have been made possible by holding to a reasonably constant probability pattern for normal inspection and a reasonably constant AOQL pattern for tightened. The rule for shifting to tightened inspection "if 2 of the last 5 lots were rejected" seems appropriate as a *general* rule only so long as all plans under normal inspection have about the same probability of acceptance for AQL quality.

To be effective and to be used, the rules for shifting from normal to tightened inspection must be reasonable, and must appear to be reasonable to inspection personnel. It is the author's observations that the penalty of shifting from normal to tightened inspection has been sufficiently drastic in certain area of existing sampling tables and procedures based on the AQL concept, that there has been a strong tendency to avoid using tightened inspection at all. This constitutes a basic misuse of the procedures ; it undermines and relegates to a position of secondary importance, the consumer's protection against product running at a substandard level of quality. The magnitude of the change in going from normal to tightened inspection in the proposed system is relatively small, and intentionally so, yet it is adequate for the intended purpose here.

The two two factors, ease of application, and less drastic shifts, should be conducive to a more willing acceptance and a better following of the rules and hence a better realization of a major objective - maintenance of quality equal to or better than the AQL.

As indicated..., the maintenance of a control chart showing graphically the results of lot-by-lot inspections, while not required, is highly recommended. Such charts have been found invaluable as an aid to an understanding of the operations of the inspection system, especially when quality difficulties are encountered and shifts in inspection plans are necessary."

11.6 DODGE'S CHAIN SAMPLING INSPECTION PLAN

A special type of lot-by-lot acceptance sampling plan for attributes was developed by H.F. Dodge. The plan was designated, "Chain Sampling Plan Ch SP-1". It is applicable to quality charac- teristics which involve destructive or costly tests.

When tests are destructive or very costly, sampling plans with a small size are used as a matter of practical necessity. Plans with sample sizes of 5, 10, 15, etc. usually have acceptance numbers of 0.

Single sampling plan for $c = 0$ have two undesirable features. One undesirable feature occurs simply because one defective in the sample causes the lot to be rejected. The other undesirable feature is the poor shape of the OC curve, which gives poor discrimination between good and bad lots. Figure 11.7 shows the general shape of single sampling plans for $c = 0$ and $c = 1$ or more. The comparison shows the desirability of plans with acceptance numbers equal to 1 or more.

Chain sampling plans make use of the cumulative result of several preceding samples. The procedure is as follows :

1. For each lot, select a sample of size n and test each for conformance to specifications.
2. If the sample has 0 defective, accept the lot ; and if the sample has 1 defective, it may be accepted provided that there is no defective in the previous i samples of size n.

Thus, for a chain sampling given by $n = 8$, $i = 3$, the lot would be accepted (*a*) by no defectives in the sample of 8, of (*b*) 1 defective in the sample 8 and no defectives in the previous 3 samples of 8.

The value of i, the number of previous samples, is determined by analysis of the operating characteristic curves for a given sample size. Fig. 11.8 shows the *OC* curve for the single sample plan $n = 5$, $c = 0$, and the *OC* curves for Ch SP-1 plans for $i = 1$, 2, 3 and 5. The *OC* curves for the Ch SP-1 plans are obtained from the general formula

$$P_a = P_0 + P_1\,[P_0]^i \qquad \text{...(11.21)}$$

An example will illustrate the technique. For the Ch SP-1 plan $n = 5$, $c = 0$, $i = 2$, the calculations for $p = 0.15$ are

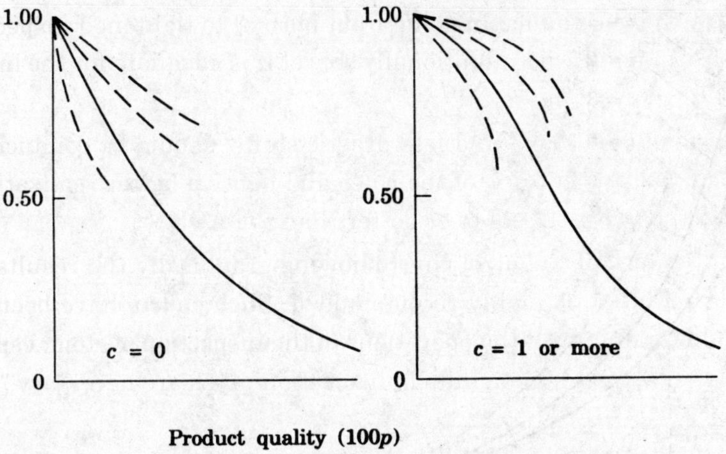

FIGURE 11.7: General Shape of OC curves for single sampling plans.

$$P_0 = \frac{n!}{d!(n-d)!} p^d q^{n-d} \qquad \text{...(11.22)}$$

$$= \frac{5!}{0!(5-0)!}(0.15)^0 (0.85)^{5-0}$$

$$= 0.444$$

$$P_1 = \frac{n!}{d!(n-d)!} p^d q^{n-d}$$

$$= \frac{5!}{1!(5-1)!}(0.15)^1 (0.85)^{5-1}$$

$$= 0.392$$

$$P_a = P_0 + P_1 (P_0)^2$$

$$= 0.444 + (0.392)\,(0.444)2$$

$$= 0.521$$

The point $P_a = 0.521$ is shown in Fig. 11.8.

The curve for $i = 1$ is shown dotted, since it is not a perferred choice. In practice i values of from 3 to 5 will be the most used, since their *OC* curves approximate the single sampling plan *OC* curve. Where the percent defective is small, the Ch SP - 1 plans increase the probability that a sample with one defective will be accepted. This provides for the occasional defective that is expected every now and then.

For appropriate use of the chain sampling technique, the following conditions should be met with :

1. The lot should be one of a continuing series of product which is sampled in substantially the order of its production.

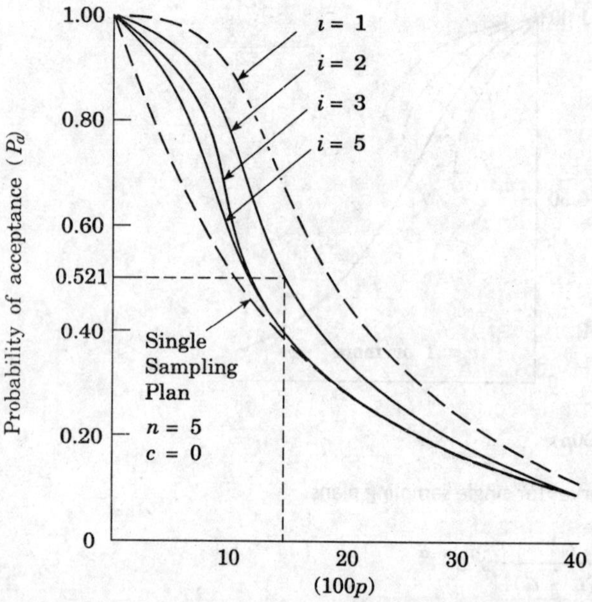

FIGURE 11.8: OC curves for Ch SP-1 plans with values 1, 2, 3, 5 and for single sampling plan $n = 5$, $c = 0$.

2. The consumer can normally expect the lots to be essentially of the same quality.
3. The consumer has confidence in the producer, that he would not occasionally send a bad lot which would have the optimum chance of acceptance.
4. The quality characteristic is one that involves destructive or costly tests, thereby dictating a small sample size.

SOLVED QUESTIONS

Q. 11.1: *Select the correct option:*

(*i*) On an OC curve we can also locate

(*a*) indifference quality (*b*) AOQL

(*c*) quality requiring maximum inspection (*d*) quality requiring minimum inspection

(*ii*) The steeper the OC curve

(*a*) the less protection for both producer and consumer

(*b*) the more protection for both producer and consumer

(*c*) the lower the AQL

(*d*) the smaller the sample size.

(*iii*) For an operation requiring shipments from your vendor of small lots of fixed size, the sampling plan used for receiving inspection should have its OC curve developed using

(*a*) the Poisson distribution (*b*) the hypergeometric distribution

(*c*) the binomial distribution (*d*) the log normal distribution

(*e*) the Gaussian (normal) distribution.

(*iv*) Two quantities which uniquely determine a single-sampling attributes plan are

(*a*) AOQL and LTPD
(*b*) sample size and acceptance number
(*c*) AQL and producer's risk
(*d*) LTPD and consumer's risk
(*e*) AQL and LTPD.

(*v*) The AQL for a given sampling plan is 1.0 percent. This means that

(*a*) the producer takes a small risk of rejecting product which is 1.0 percent defective or better
(*b*) all accepted lots are 1.0 percent defective or better
(*c*) the average quality limit of the plan is 1.0 precent
(*d*) the average quality level of the plan is 1.0 percent
(*e*) all lots are 1.0 percent defective or better.

(*vi*) Prior to the use of any sampling plan, one must consider

(*a*) the consumer's and producer's risks must be specified
(*b*) the method of selecting samples must be specified
(*c*) the characteristics to be inspected must be specified
(*d*) the conditions must be specified (material accumulated in lots or inspected by continuous sampling)
(*e*) all of the above.

Ans: (*i*) (*a*); (*ii*) (*b*); (*iii*) (*b*); (*iv*) (*b*); (*v*) (*a*); (*vi*) (*e*)

Q. 11.2: *Fill in the blanks:*

(*i*) $p_{0.50}$ is also known as ________ quality.
(*ii*) The general range of producer's risk is ________.
(*iii*) In philips standard simplify , all plans are have a probability of acceptance is ________.
(*iv*) Ch SP-1 is applicable where ________ testing is inversed.
(*v*) As the OC curve becomes sleeper, the producer and consumer enjoy ________ protection.

Ans: (*i*) Indifferent; (*ii*) 1 to 5% i.e., 0.01 to 0.05; (*iii*) 50%; (*iv*) destructive; (*v*) more.

Q. 11.3: *Mention briefs the difference between "Prevention and Inspection."*

Ans: Prevention is simply keeping defects from occurring, while inspection is about catching the errors that have occurred before they impact others outside the project.

Q.11.4: *State the difference between attribute sampling and variable samples.*

Ans: Attribute sampling is binary; either a work result conforms to quality or it does not. Variable sampling, on the other hand, measures how well something conforms to quality. Consider, for example, a production facility making prescription drugs. Using attribute sampling, they would define tolerances, a batch of product would be tested, and it would either pass or fail that inspection. Using variable sampling, however, the batch of product would be rated on a continuous scale (perhaps on parts per million) that showed how well the batch conformed to ideal quality.

Q. 11.5: *Mention briefly the SeSP.*

Ans: The sequential sampling plan (SeSP) is similar to multiple sampling plan (MSP). It is an item-by-item inspection plan and is used when destructive inspection is involved and costly.

Q. 11.6: *The indifferent sampling plan is: SeSP orDSP or MSP?*

What do we compute in this plan?

Ans: SeSP

We compute sample size in the indifferent quality plan.

Q. 11.7: (*a*) *Mention briefly the theortical basis of the formula*

$$n = \frac{c + 0.67}{p_{0.50}}$$

(*b*) *For a $p_{0.50}$ of 0.015, what should be the single sample sizes corresponding to acceptance numbers of 0, 1, 3, 5 and 7 respectively.*

(*c*) *Draw the OC curves of these plans. Which is the common point on all these curves ?*

Ans: (*a*) Indifference quality (popularly known as indifference quality level *i.e.* IQL) or point of control, is that value of *p* for which a lot has equal chances of acceptance and rejection. Wetherill and Chiu in 1974 suggested that $p_{0.50}$ should be chosen on economic grounds, being that value of p for which the cost of accepting a lot is equal to the cost of rejecting it.

Using the χ^2-distribution, it can be shown that $2\, n\, p_{0.50}$ is the median of a χ^2-distribution with $(2\, c + 2)$ degrees of freedom. The mean and the mode of such a distribution are $(2\, c + 2)$ and $2\, c$ respectively. So on using the following approximate relationship, which holds for distribution of moderate asymmetry,

$$3 \text{ Median} = 2 \text{ Mean} + \text{Mode}, \qquad \text{...(11.23)}$$

We have the median of such a distribution approximately as $2\, c + \frac{4}{3}$. This is an excellent approximation to the median of the χ^2-distribution, which leads to the relationship.

$$2\, n\, p_{0.50} = 2\, c + \frac{4}{3}$$

$$\therefore \quad n = \frac{c + \frac{2}{3}}{p_{0.50}}$$

$$= \frac{c + 0.67}{p_{0.50}}$$

(*b*) Using $p_{0.50} = 0.015$ and taking *c* values as 0, 1, 3, 5 and 7 the samples sizes are computed to be :

$c = 0$ $n = 46$

$c = 1$ $n = 111$

$c = 3$ $n = 245$

$c = 4$ $n = 378$

$c = 7$ $n = 511$

(*c*) By assuming various values of *p* as 0.001, 0.005, 0.010, 0.015, 0.020, 0.025, 0.030 and determining the corresponding values of Pa from Table G, the OC curves can be constructed. Obviously all these curves will have ($p = 0.015$ and $P_a = 0.50$) as a common point.

Q. 11.8: *Obtain a single sampling plan for inspection of lots of 10,000 items which has a 95% chance of accepting lots with 1.0% defective and an IQL of 0.04.*

Ans: It is obvious that we have to satisfy two conditions :

(*a*) $p = 0.04$ $P_a = 0.50$

(*b*) $p = 0.01$ $P_a = 0.95$

Various plans satisfying condition (1) can be found by using the formula

$$n = \frac{c + 0.67}{p_{0.50}}$$

Choosing $c = 0$, 1, 2, 3 and 4 various values of n computed to be :

$c = 0$ $n = 17$

$c = 1$ $n = 42$

$c = 2$ $n = 67$

$c = 3$ $n = 92$

$c = 4$ $n = 117$

Now with the help of Table *G*, we compute the probability of acceptance of *p* of 0.10 for the all the above plans and select that plan which exactly meets or closely meets the condition of $p_{0.01}$ and $P_a = 0.95$.

No.	*Sampling Plan*	(μ_p)	(μ_{np})	P_a *from Table G*
1	$n = 17$ $c = 0$	0.01	0.17	0.844 (by interpolation)
2	$n = 42$ $c = 1$	0.01	0.42	0.933 (by interpolation)
3	$n = 67$ $c = 2$	0.01	0.67	0.970 (by interpolation)
4	$n = 92$ $c = 3$	0.01	0.92	0.986 (by interpolation)

Since a minimum probability of acceptance required of 0.95, hence the sampling plan $n = 67$, $c = 2$ is most appropriate.

Q. 11.9: *A producer and consumer agree that a single sampling plan will be used to accept and reject lots. The single sampling plan specified will pass through the indifference quality point at 2% defective. (a) Use Table G to define operating characteristic curves for the sampling plans with acceptance of 0, 1, 2, and 3. (b) Disregarding inspection costs, which plan do you feel will provide the consumer with the best protection against poor quality ? (c) If 200 lots of 2.0% defective quality are shipped to the consumer, how many items do you anticipate will be inspected if all the rejected lots of 1,000 items are screened, based on the plan with an acceptance number of 2 ?*

Ans: (*a*) Since the sampling plan is to be based on indifference quality, the plan can be determined by using the formula :

$$n = \frac{c + 0.67}{p_{0.50}}$$

In the above formula indifference quality ($p_{0.50}$) is 2% (*i.e.* 0.02) various sampling plans are:

$c = 0$ $n = 34$

$c = 1$ $n = 84$

$c = 2$ $n = 134$

$c = 3$ $n = 84$

OC curves can now be determined by assuming different values of *p* for various plans and finding the probability of acceptance from table *G*.

(*b*) If inspection costs are disregarded, then naturally the plan having the larger sample size will give better discrimination between lots that are somewhat better than 2.0% defective and lots that are some what worse. Hence the recommended plan to the vendor is :

$$(n = 184 \quad c = 3).$$

(*c*) When the acceptance number is 2, the plan used by consumer is :

$$n = 134, \quad c = 2$$

$$\mu_p = 0.02$$

$$\mu_{np} = 134 \times 0.02 = 2.68$$

Using Table *G*, the probability of acceptance is 0.498 (by inerpolation).

Although the probability of acceptance for this plan theoretically should be 0.50, but the minor difference arises because of (i) computations, (ii) interpolations (iii) making n as whole number against the theoretically correct value of n resulting from the following formula

$$n = \frac{c + 0.67}{p_{0.50}}$$

is found to be 133.5 instead of assumed value of 134.

If 200 lots are submitted, then about 99 or 100 lots are likely to be accepted. Let us assume that 100 lots are accepted. Rejected lots will be 100.

When the rejected lots are fully screened, the anticipated number of items inspected :

(134) × 100 + (1,000) × 100 = 113,4 00

Q. 11.10: *A single sampling acceptance criteria for any desired p0.50 is given by approximate relation*

$$n = \frac{c + 0.67}{p_{0.50}}$$

n = *sample size*

c = *acceptance number*

$p_{0.50}$ = *fraction defective for which the probability acceptance is 0.50.*

Agreed value of $p_{0.050}$ = *0.025. The vendor has 3,000 lots, of which 1,000 are 2% ; 1,000 of 2.5% quality ; and the rest of 3% quality. It has also been agreed that the cost of inspection done by consumer will be borne by the vendor.*

The consumer suggests for acceptance number as 1 while the vendor insists upon c = 0. Why?

Ans:

$$n = \frac{c + 0.67}{p_{0.50}}$$

In the above relation $p_{0.50} = 0.025$

when $c = 0, \quad n = 27$

when $c = 1, \quad n = 67$

From Table *G*, when

$p = 0.02$; $n = 27$; $c = 0$, $P_a = 0.583$

$p = 0.025$; $n = 27$; $c = 0$, $P_a = 0.500$

$p = 0.03$; $n = 27$; $c = 0$, $P_a = 0.444$

$p = 0.02$; $n = 67$; $c = 1$, $P_a = 0.613$

$p = 0.025$; $n = 67$; $c = 1$, $P_a = 0.500$

$p = 0.03$; $n = 67$; $c = 1$, $P_a = 0.404$

when $c = 0$, total accepted lots = 583 + 500 + 444 = 1,527

when $c = 1$, total accepted lot = 613 + 500 + 404 = 1,517.

It can be observed that when $c = 0$, 10 more lots will be accepted by the consumer as compared to the situation when $c = 1$.

Again when the cost of inspection has to be borne by the vendor, the vendor will insist upon lower value of n, which is obtainable when $c = 0$.

Thus choosing $c = 0$, gives two distinct advantages to the vendor.

Q. 11.11: *A consumer has the choice of using an ABC standard single sampling plan or a Philips Standard single sampling plan. The ABC standard would be used with an inspection level II, an AQL of 1.0% and a lot size of 500. The Philips plan would be used with a point of control (indifference quality) of 3%.*

(a) Find the acceptance criteria under both plans with same acceptance number

(b) If the customer's primary concern is the assurance that lots 5% nonconforming are rejected, which plan would give him the best protection ? Explain.

Ans: (*a*) For ABC standard with a lot size of 500 and inspection level II, the code letter is H. Now from Table *L* of App. 2, for code letter H and 1%. AQL, the sample size $n = 50$ and acceptance no. *i.e.* $c = 1$.

The Philips plan for $p_{0.50} = 0.03$ is computed by using the formula :

$$n = \frac{c + 0.67}{p_{0.50}}$$

with $c = 1$, $n = 55$.

(*b*) Under both the above plans the probability of acceptance are interpolated from Table *G* as follows :

ABC STD $\quad P_a = 0.287$ Hence $P_r = 1 - P_a = 0.713$

Philips STD $\quad P_a = 0.240$ Hence $P_r = 1 - P_a = 0.760$

The above computations indicate that Philips plan give the best protection to the consumer.

Q. 11.12: *It is desired that the Producer's Risk of rejecting 0.5% defective shall be 0.05. Use Table 11.1 to find the respective sample sizes for single sampling plans that meet this requirement and have acceptance numbers 1, 2 and 3. For each of these plans, find the percentage defective corresponding to a Consumer's Risk of 0.10.*

Ans: From Table 11.1

When $c = 1$, $np_{0.95} = 0.355$ and $np_{0.10} = 3.890$

Therefore
$$n = \frac{np_{0.95}}{p_{0.95}} = \frac{0.355}{0.005} = 71$$

$$= \frac{np_{0.10}}{n} = \frac{3.890}{71}$$

$$= 0.0547$$

$$100\, p_{0.10} = 5.5\%$$

Again when $c = 2$,
$$n = \frac{np_{0.95}}{p_{0.95}} = \frac{0.818}{0.005}$$
$$= 164$$
$$p_{0.10} = \frac{np_{0.10}}{n} = \frac{5.322}{164}$$
$$= 0.0318$$
$$100\ p_{0.10} = 3.2\%$$

Similarly when $c = 3$
$$n = 273\ ;\ 100\ p_{0.10} = 2.4\%.$$

Q. 11.13: *It is desired that the Consumer's Risk of accepting product 1.2% nonconforming shall be 0.01. Use Table 11.1 to find the respective sample sizes for single sampling plans that meet this requirement and have acceptance numbers of 1, 2, and 3. For each of these plans find the percentage nonconforming corresponding to a Producer's Risk of 0.01.*

Ans: From Table 11.1,

When $c = 1$, $np_{0.01} = 6.638$

Therefore
$$n = \frac{np_{0.01}}{p_{0.01}} = \frac{6.638}{0.012} = 553$$
$$p_{0.99} = \frac{np_{0.99}}{n} = \frac{0.149}{553} = 0.000269$$
$$100\ p_{0.99} = 0.027\%$$

Again when $c = 2$
$$n = 700$$
$$100\ p_{0.99} = 0.062$$

Similarly when $c = 3$
$$n = 837$$
$$100\ p_{0.99} = 0.098$$

Q. 11.14: *It is desired to have a single sampling plan for which the Producer's Risk of rejection of a 1% defective lot is 0.05 and the Consumer's Risk of accepting a 3% defective lot is 0.10. Using Table 11.1, find the plan that exactly meets the stipulation on Producer's Risk and comes as close as possible on Consumer's Risk. For this plan, what percentage defective has a Consumer's Risk 0.10 ?*

Ans:
$$p_{0.95} = 0.01$$
$$p_{0.10} = 0.03$$
$$\frac{p_{0.10}}{p_{0.95}} = \frac{0.03}{0.01} = 3$$

The ratio $p_{0.10}/p_{0.95}$ is 3. The last column of Table 11.1 shows that a ratio of 3.206 is obtained when $c = 6$ and a ratio of 2.957 is obtained when $c = 7$. Since neither of these values is exactly 3, it is not possible to have single sampling plan that has an OC curve passing exactly through the two stipulated points. But we have to choose a plan that exactly meets the stipulation on

Producer's Risk and comes as closely as possible on Consumer's Risk. Using Table 11.1 again, we compute the following plans :

c	$p_{0.95}$	n	$100\, p_{0.10}$
6	0.01	329	3.59%
7	0.01	398	2.96%

The above two plans exactly meet the Producer's Risk. But the plan : $n = 398$, $c = 7$ exactly meet the stipulation an Producer's Risk and comes as closely as possible to the Consumer's Risk.

Also $100\, p_{0.10} = 2.96\%$.

Q. 11.15: *It is desired that a single sampling plan for attributes data satisfy a Producer's Risk of rejection of **1.5%** nonconforming lots of **0.05** and a Consumer's Risk of acceptance **6.0%** nonconforming lots of **0.10**.*

*(a) Use Table **11.1** to find the plan that fits the Consumer's Risk and is as close as possible to the Producer's Risk.*

*(b) What is the percentage nonconforming that has a probability of rejection of **0.05** ?*

Ans:

$$p_{0.95} = 0.015$$

$$p_{0.10} = 0.060$$

$$\frac{p_{0.10}}{p_{0.95}} = \frac{0.060}{0.015} = 4$$

The ratio $\frac{p_{0.10}}{p_{0.95}}$ is 4. The last column of the Table 11.1 shows that a ratio of 4.057 is obtained when $c = 4$ and a ratio of 3.549 is obtained when $c = 5$. Since neither of these values is exactly 4, it is not possible to have single sampling plan that has an *OC* curve passing exactly through the two stipulated points. But we have to choose a plan that exactly meets the stipulation on Consumer's Risk and comes as closely as possible on Producer's Risk. Using Table 11.1 again, we compute the following sampling plans.

c	$p_{0.10}$	n	$100\, p_{0.95}$
4	0.06	133	1.48%
5	0.06	155	1.69%

The above two plans exactly meet the consumer Risk stipulation. But the plan $n = 133$, $c = 4$ exactly meets the Consumer's Risk and comes as closely as possible to the Producer's Risk.

Also $100\, p_{0.95} = 1.48\%$.

Q. 11.16: *A single sampling plan is to be developed based on a Producer's Risk of **0.05** of rejection lots which contains **0.435%** nonconforming items. The consumer's Risk of accepting lots containing **3.30%** nonconforming items should be as close as possible to **0.05**. Use Table **11.1** to determine the plan.*

Ans:

$$p_{0.95} = 0.00435$$

$$p_{0.50} = 0.0330$$

The last column in Table 11.1 gives the ratio of $p_{0.10}/p_{0.95}$ which is in fact the ratio of $n\, p_{0.10}/n\, p_{0.95}$

$$\frac{p_{0.05}}{p_{0.95}} = \frac{0.0330}{0.000435} = 7.586$$

Also the following computations from Table 11.1, indicate that when $c = 2$, the ratio of 7.696 comes closer to the required ratio of 7.586.

c	$np_{0.05}$	$np_{0.95}$	$np_{0.05}/np_{0.95}$
0	2.996	0.051	58.745
1	4.744	0.355	13.363
2	6.296	0.818	7.696
3	7.754	1.366	5.676
4	9.154	1.970	4.647

Since we have to meet the Producer's Risk stipulation exactly, for the calculation of n,

$$np_{0.95} = 0.818$$

$$p_{0.95} = 0.00435$$

$$n = 0.818/0.00435 = 188$$

The required sampling plan is : $n = 188$, $c = 2$.

Q. 11.17: *It is proposed to have a set of single sampling plans in which the percentage defective corresponding to a Consumer's Risk of 0.10 as nearly as practicable, 2.5 times the percentage defective corresponding to a Producer's Risk to 0.05. Use the table given below to find the plan for which 100 p0.10 is 1 % and 100 p0.95 is 0.4% and for which 100 $p_{0.10}$ is 10% and 100 $p_{0.95}$ 4%. Does it seem to you that it is good idea to stipulate that p0.10 shall always be 2.5 times p0.95 ? Why or why not ?*

c	$np_{0.95}$	$np_{0.10}$	$np_{0.10}/np_{0.95}$
6	3.286	10.532	3.206
7	3.981	11.771	2.957
8	4.695	12.995	2.768
9	5.426	14.206	2.618
10	6.169	15.407	2.497

Ans:

$$p_{0.10} = \frac{1}{100} = 0.01$$

$$p_{0.95} = \frac{0.4}{100} = 0.004$$

$$\frac{p_{0.10}}{p_{0.95}} = \frac{0.01}{0.004} = 2.5$$

Consulting the given table, $\frac{p_{0.10}}{p_{0.95}} = 2.497$ for $c = 10$.

Let the acceptance number be 10.

Corresponding to c of 10, $np_{0.10} = 15.407$

As $p_{0.10} = 0.01$, $n = 1540.7$ *i.e.* 1541

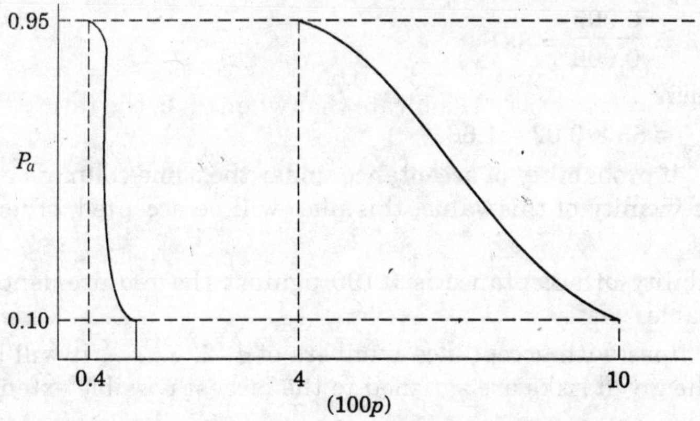

FIGURE 11.9 The OC curves of two sampling plans having $np_{0.10}/np_{0.95} = 2.5$.

The acceptance number based on $np_{0.95}$ and $p = 0.004$ will have $n = 1541$. The other sampling plan will have n of 154. Figure 11.9 shows the approximate plot (i.e. OC curves) for the two sampling plans obtained above.

From Fig. 11.9, it can be concluded that it is not a good idea to stipulate $p_{0.10}$ always 2.5 times $p_{0.95}$. The first sampling plan finds favour with the consumer while the second one with the producer. When the probability of acceptance is 0.95 the difference in the percentage of accepted defectives is 4 – 0.4 = 3.6 % while the difference in the percentage defectives amounts to 9 when the probability of acceptance is 0.10.

However, much depends upon $p_{0.95}$. If it is small, then there is no harm in having $p_{0.10}$ as 2.5 times $p_{0.95}$. If $p_{0.95}$ is higher, the disadvantages of having p0.10 as 2.5 times p0.95 are obvious.

Q. 11.18: *Design a single sampling plan for which the Consumer's Risk of acceptance of 2% defective product is 0.10 and the Producer's Risk of rejection of 0.6% defective is 0.05.*

Determine the value of p0.50 for this sampling plan.

Ans: The solution of this problem can be worked out several ways. Four of them are

1. By use of Table 11.1.
2. By use of χ^2 distribution.
3. By assuming that defectives are normally distributed with a mean μ_{np} and standard deviation $\sqrt{npq}$ and forming suitable equation and solving them for *n* and *c* by using Table *A*. Such a method was used in finding the values of *n* and *c* for one of the problems is Chap. 9.

It may be mentioned that the use of Table 11.1 is limited to those risks only which are mentioned in this table. For other values of risk, this table cannot be used.

χ^2-distribution and normal distribution assumptions mentioned at (2) and (3) involve extensive calculations and give only approximate solution.

4. This hit and trial method makes use of Table *G* and does not involve much calculations and can be used for any risks. Its working is explained below:

Producer's Risk, (α) = 0.05 at p_1 of 0.006, *i.e.* at p_1 of 0.006, $P_a = 0.95$

Consumer's Risk, (β) = 0.10 at p_2 of 0.02 *i.e.* at p_2 of 0.02, $P_a = 0.10$

Let the acceptance number $c = 0$

From the column 'headed $c = 0$' in Table *G*, when $P_a = 0.95$, the $\mu_{np} = 0.05$ (by interpolation).

Since $\qquad p_1 = 0.006$

$$\therefore \qquad n = \frac{0.005}{0.006} = 83$$

If n is to be taken as 83, then

$$\mu_{np2} = 83 \times 0.02 = 1.66.$$

Now with this value of μ_{np2} if probability of acceptance under the same column i.e. column 'headed $c = 0$' is 0.10 or in the vicinity of this value, this plan will be accepted, otherwise we have to go for other values of c.

From Table G, the probability of acceptance is 0.190 against the requirement of 0.10. Therefore this plan is not suitable.

Proceeding on the similar lines with acceptance numbers of 1, 2, 3........, it will be found that with $n = 525$ and $c = 6$, the given risks are satisfied to the largest possible extent. Hence the required sampling plan :

$$n = 525,\ c = 6$$

$p_{0.50}$ for this plan is 0.0127

Q. 11.19: *Find a single defects-unit sampling inspection plan that will come close to u of 6 defects per 1,000 units, a u2 of 2 defects per 100 units, $\alpha = 0.05$ and $\beta = 0.10$.*

Ans: The problem can be worked out in the same manner as the previous one and has the same answer except that c represents and maximum total number of allowable defect.

Q. 11.20: *The designer has been asked to specify a single sampling plan for inspection of large lots (of about 4,000 items) which has a 95% chance of accepting lots with 0.5% defective and a 10% chance of accepting lots with 4.0% defective. The designer has specified the plan :*

"Take a random sample of 134 items. Accept the lot if the sample contains 2 or less defectives. Otherwise reject the lot." When you calculate the probabilities of acceptance for 0.5% and 10% defective lots, figures do not match the figures stipulated above.

Are you in agreement with the designer for the proposed sampling plan ? Why ?

Ans: It is a matter of common knowledge that it is rare that the *OC* curve of any sampling plan will exactly pass through the points $(p_1, 1 - \alpha)$ and (p_2, β). Hence any sampling plan can be accepted if it satisfies the following inequalties :

1. Probability of acceptance of 0.5% defective lot $\geq 1 - \alpha$ *i.e* ≥ 0.95
2. Probability of acceptance of 10% defective lot $\leq \beta$ *i.e* ≤ 0.10

The proposed sampling plan gives the respective probabilities as

1. 0.9694 (which is > 0.95)
2. 0.0974 (which is < 0.10)

Hence the designer's sampling plan is acceptable.

Q. 11.21: *(a) Large lots of items are subjected to inspection by attributes using a single sampling plan with $n = 100$ and $c = 3$. Obtain expressions for the OC curve in terms of (i) binomial and (ii) Poisson probabilities in terms of process average p.*

(b) Also calculate the probability of accepting lots with 1 percent and 10 percent defectives using (i) and (i) and compare their values.

(c) For the process considered above it is required to use a single sampling plan which accepts lots with 1 percent defectives with probability ≥ 0.9 and rejects lots with 5 percent defectives with probability ≥ 0.9. Show that the plan considered above is not suitable and design a suitable plan.

Ans: (*a*) (*i*) Using p.d.f for binomial distribution

$$P_a = \sum_{r=0}^{3} \binom{100}{r} p^r (1-p)^{100-r}$$

(*ii*) Using p.d.f. for Poisson distribution

$$P_a = \sum_{r=0}^{3} \frac{(100p)^{r}}{r!} e^{-100p}$$

(*b*) Now for $p = 0.01$

(*i*) $P_a = 0.9816$ (ii) $P_a = 0.981$

For $p_{0.10}$

(*i*) $P_a = 0.0078$ (ii) $P_a = 0.010$

(*c*) Let us check whether the sampling plan ($n = 100, c = 3$), meets the following requirements.

1. When $p = 0.01$, $P_a \geq 0.9$ and
2. When $p = 0.05$, $P_r \geq 0.9$.

When $p = 0.01$, the given sampling plan gives $P_a = 0.981$ (which is > 0.9) and hence conditions(1) is met with :

When $p = 0.05$, P_a computed form Table *G* is 0.265 and hence $P_r = 1 - 0.265$ *i.e.* 0.735 (which is < 0.5) and conditions(2) is not met with.

Hence the proposed sampling plan is not suitable. We can design the sampling plan following the suggested method in Prob. 11.12 or using Table 11.1.

Using Table 11.1, we get two options

1. For $p_{0.90} = 0.01$ $n = 110$ $c = 2$
2. For $p_{0.10} = 0.05$ $n = 107$ $c = 2$

Out of above two options, option No. (2) *i.e.* $n = 107$, $c = 2$ satisfies both the conditions to the closest possible extent. Hence the required sampling plan is $n = 107$, $c = 2$.

Q. 11.22: *When batches of 1,000 components contain 5% defective, the Consumer's Risk is approximately 5%. The process average percentage defectives is approximately 2% and the AOQL must be less than 0.5%. Suggest a suitable single sampling scheme. What is the Producer's Risk of your scheme ?*

Ans: The sampling scheme should satisfy the following two conditions :

1. For lots of 1,000 pieces, when μ_p is approximately 2%, $AOQL \leq 0.5\%$ *i.e.* 0.005.
2. When *p* is 5% *i.e.* 0.05, β should approximately be 5% *i.e.* 0.05.

If we consider condition (1), the selection of sampling scheme requires published tables for AOQL schemes. However a simple route to avoid all problems is to use a suitable factor *y* for various values of *c* and *N*. These are given in solution of Q. 10.29 (*c*). However the relevant portion is reproduced here for convenience.

$$\text{AOQL} = y\left[\frac{1}{n} - \frac{1}{N}\right]$$

c	*y*
0	0.3679
1	0.8400
2	1.3711

1. Considering $c = 0$, $N = 1{,}000$, and AOQL = 0.005 and $y = 0.3679$, $n = 69$
2. Considering $c = 1$, $n = 144$

with sampling plan No. 1 *i.e.* $n = 69$, $c = 0$, and $p = 0.05$, β found to be 0.031

with sampling plan No. 2 *i.e.* $n = 144$ $c = 1$, and $p = 0.05$, β, is found to be 0.00575 *i.e.* 0.5% which is very much less than 5%.

Hence we select the sampling plan No. 1 (*i.e.* $n = 69$, $c = 0$) which approximately meets the given conditions. With the plan ($n = 69$, $c = 0$) probability of 2% acceptance of defective lot computed to be 0.252. Hence $1 - \alpha = 0.252$, from which $\alpha = 0.748$. Hence Producer's Risk is 0.748.

Q. 11.23: *Design a sequential sampling plan (SeSP) for the following specifications :*

$$\alpha = 0.05$$
$$\beta = 0.10$$
$$p_1 = 0.01$$
$$p_2 = 0.04$$

Also compute :

(*a*) *Average outgoing quality when* $p = p_1$

(*b*) *Minimum number of items inspected for accepting the lot.*

(*c*) *Minimum number of defectives for rejection of the lot.*

(*d*) *Average number of items inspected when the quality of the lot is* p_1.

Ans: For sequential sampling

Acceptance line $(Ac) = sn - h_1$

Rejection line $(Re) = sn + h_2$

where
$$g_1 = \log \frac{p_2}{p_1} = 0.6021$$

$$g_2 = \log \frac{1 - p_1}{1 - p_2} = 0.0133$$

$$a = \log \frac{1 - \beta}{\alpha} = 1.2553$$

$$b = \log \frac{1 - \alpha}{\beta} = 0.9777$$

$$h_1 = \frac{b}{g_1 + g_2} = 1.588$$

$$h_2 = \frac{a}{g_1 + g_2} = 2.0398$$

$$s = \frac{g_2}{g_1 + g_2} = 0.0216$$

Substituting the values in the above relations

$$Ac = 0.0216n - 1.588$$
$$Re = 0.0216n + 2.039$$

(*a*) When $p = p_1$, AOQ $= (1 - \alpha)\, p_1 = (1 - 0.05)\,(0.01) = 0.0095$

(*b*) Minimum number of items n inspected for acceptance $= \frac{h_1}{s} = 74$

(*c*) Minimum number of defectives for rejecting the lot $= h_2 = 2$

(*d*) Average number of items inspected when the lot quality is p_1,

$$= \frac{(1-\alpha)h_1 - \alpha h_2}{s - p_1}$$

$$= \frac{(1-0.05)(1.588)-(0.05)(2)}{(0.0216-0.01)} = 35$$

Q. 11.24: *Find the equations of the decision lines for a sequential sampling plan to meet the requirements :*

$p_1 = 0.10$, $\alpha = 0.05$; $p_2 = 0.30$, $\beta = 0.20$

The table given below shows the acceptance numbers Ac for n up to 24. Check these entries and explain why there is no entry for n = 1-6. Complete the table by finding the corresponding values of the rejection number Re (i.e. the minimum number of defectives which leads to rejection).

n	1-2	3-5	6	7-10	11	12-15	16	17-21	22	23-24
Ac	—	—	—	*0*	*0*	*1*	*1*	*2*	*2*	*3*
Re										

Ans: The equations of acceptance and rejection lines

$$Ac = sn - h_1$$

$$Re = sn + h_2$$

and these are computed to be

$$Ac = 0.186n - 1.154$$

$$Re = 0.186n + 2.054$$

For practical use, these lines are converted into an item-by-item table of acceptance and rejection numbers by substituting values of n = 1, 2, 3...... Computed values of *Ac* and *Re* are generally not whole numbers. In the following tabulation of acceptance and rejection numbers up to n = 24, the rejection numbers is the next whole number above *Re*, and the acceptance number is the next whole number below Ac.

n	*Acceptance number*	*Rejection number*	*n*	*Acceptance number*	*Rejection number*	*n*	*Acceptance number*	*Rejection number*
1	*	+	9	0	4	17	2	6
2	*	+	10	0	4	18	2	6
3	*	3	11	0	5	19	2	6
4	*	3	12	1	5	20	2	6
5	*	3	13	1	5	21	2	6
6	*	4	14	1	5	22	2	7
7	0	4	15	1	5	23	3	7
8	0	4	16	1	6	24	3	7

* Acceptance requires sample of at least 7 items.

\+ Rejection requires a sample of at least 3 items.

From the above it is clear that n must be at least 7 before the condition of the acceptance line is satisfied and it is for this reason that there is no entry for $n = 1 - 6$.

Figure 11.10, shows the graphical representation of the given plan.

From Fig. 11.10, it can be seen that minimum number of items inspected for acceptance $\frac{h_1}{s}$

In this case

$$\frac{h_1}{s} = \frac{1.154}{0.186} = 6.2$$

Hence the next whole number 7 becomes the minimum number of items inspected and it is for this reason there is no entry for n = 1 – 6. With the computed values of acceptance and rejection numbers above, the table given in the problem is completed as given below.

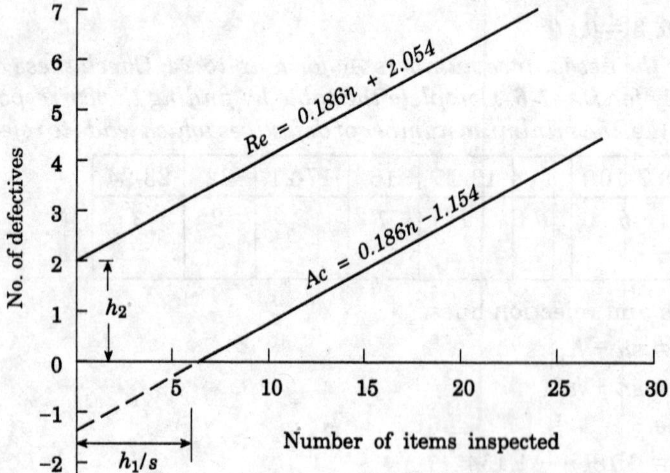

FIGURE 11.10 Graphical representation of Sequential plan for $p_1 = 0.10$, $\alpha = 0.05$, $p_2 = 0.30$, $\beta = 0.20$

n	1-2	3-5	6	7-10	11	12-15	16	17-21	22	23-24
Ac	–	–	–	0	0	1	1	2	2	3
Re	–	3	4	4	5	5	6	6	7	7

Q. 11.25: *(a) Determine the equations of the rejection and acceptance lines for an item-by-item sequential plan in which $p_{0.90} = 0.50$ and $p_{0.20} = 0.15$.*

(b) Find the minimum number of items inspected before the lot is accepted.

(c) Fine the minimum numbers of defectives to reject the lot.

(d) Plot an approximate OC curve for the sequential plan. Prepare an item-by-item table of acceptance and rejection numbers for the values of n from 1 to 50. In this table, make the rejection number the next whole number above Re and the acceptance number the next whole number below Ac.

Ans: (a) For the given data *i.e.*,

$p_1 = 0.05$, $\alpha = 0.10$; $p_2 = 0.15$, $\beta = 0.20$

The equations of acceptance and rejection lines are : $Ac = sn - h_1$; $Re = sn + h_2$

The equations of acceptance and rejection lines are computed to be

$$Ac = 0.092n - 1.243$$

$$Re = 0.092n + 1.719$$

(*b*) Minimum number of items inspected before the lot acceptance

$$= \frac{h_1}{s} = \frac{1.243}{0.092} = 13.5 \text{ i.e. } 14$$

(*c*) Minimum number of defectives to reject the lot = h_2 = 1.791 *i.e.* 2

(*d*) Following tabulation shows the computed values of *Ac* and *Re* up to *n* of 50.

n	*Ac*	*Re*	*n*	*Ac*	*Re*	*n*	*Ac*	*Re*
1	*	+	18	0	3	35	2	4
2	*	+	19	0	3	36	2	5
3	*	+	20	0	3	37	2	5
4	*	2	21	0	3	38	2	5
5	*	2	22	0	3	39	2	5
6	*	2	23	0	3	40	2	5
7	*	2	24	0	3	41	2	5
8	*	2	25	1	4	42	2	5
9	*	2	26	1	4	43	2	5
10	*	2	27	1	4	44	2	5
11	*	2	28	1	4	45	2	5
12	*	2	29	1	4	46	3	5
13	0	2	30	1	4	47	3	6
14	0	3	31	1	4	48	3	6
15	0	3	32	1	4	49	3	6
16	0	3	33	1	4	50	3	6
17	0	3	34	1	4			

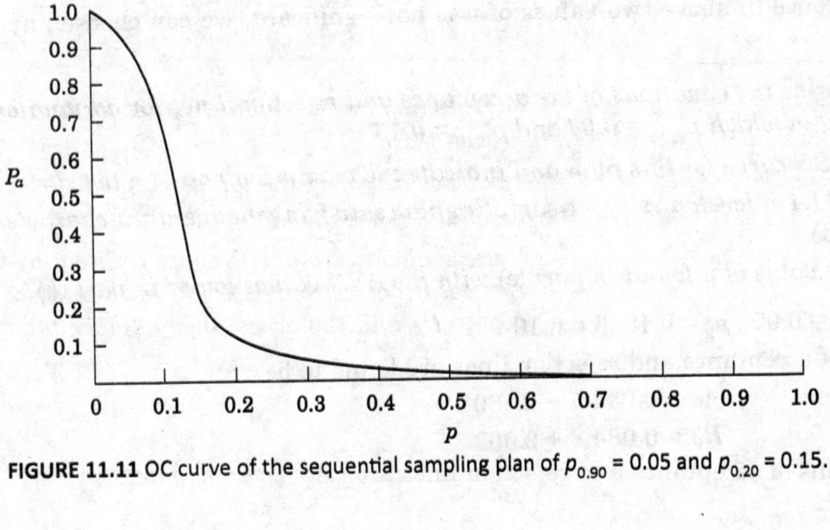

FIGURE 11.11 OC curve of the sequential sampling plan of $p_{0.90}$ = 0.05 and $p_{0.20}$ = 0.15.

Sufficiently good OC curve can be obtained from the following five points Figure 11.11 shows the OC curve

p	P_a
0.0	1.0
$p_1 = 0.5$	$(1 - \alpha) = 0.90$
$s = 0.092$	$\left(\dfrac{h_2}{h_2 + h_2}\right) = 0.58$
$p_2 = 0.15$	0.20
1.0	0

Q. 11.26: *(a) Determine the acceptance and rejection lines for an item-by-item sequential sampling plan in which $p_{0.95} = 0.015$ and $p_{0.10} = 0.059$*

(b) Use Table 11.1 to compute to single sampling plan corresponding to the item-by-item sequential plan found in (a).

Ans: *(a)* $p_1 = 0.15$, $\alpha = 0.05$; $p_2 = 0.059$, $\beta = 0.10$

The equations of acceptance and rejection lines are found to be

$$Ac = 0.0319n - 1.591$$

$$Re = 0.0319n + 2.043$$

(b) The ratio $$\frac{p_{0.10}}{p_{0.95}} = \frac{0.059}{0.015} = 3.933$$

Since this ratio of 3.933 is very close to 4.057 corresponding to the c value of 4 of table 11.1, we take $c = 4$ for the plan. Again from this table $np_{0.95} = 1.970$, and therefore,

$$n = \frac{1.970}{0.015}$$

$$= 131$$

And if we stick to Consumer's Risk then $np_{0.10} = 7.994$, and therefore

$$n = \frac{7.994}{0.059} = 135$$

Since the difference in above two values of n is not significant, we can choose any of the above two plans.

Q. 11.27: *(a) Determine the equations of the acceptance and rejection lines for an item-by-item sequential sampling in which $p_{0.95} = 0.04$ and $p_{0.10} = 0.15$.*

(b) Sketch an ASN curve for this plan and indicate the maximum point on the curve.

(c) Using Table 11.1 to develop a single a sampling plan satisfying the operating characteristics prescribed in part (a).

(d) Compare the value of n found in part (c) with the ASN values found in part (b).

Ans: *(a)* $p_1 = 0.04$, $\alpha = 0.05$; $p_2 = 0.15$, $\beta = 0.10$

The equations of acceptance and rejection lines are found to be

$$Ac = 0.084\,n - 1.560$$

$$Re = 0.084\,n + 2.003$$

(*b*) Following tabulation gives 5 points on ASN curve.

p	*ASN*
0.00	$\frac{h_1}{s} = 18.55$
$p_1 = 0.04$	$\frac{(1-\alpha)h_1 - \alpha h_2}{s - p_1} = 31.41$
$s = 0.084$	$\frac{h_1 - h_2}{s(1-s)} = 40.57$
$p_2 = 0.15$	$\frac{(1-\beta)h_2 - \beta h_1}{p_2 - s} = 24.98$
1.00	$\frac{h_2}{1-s} = 2.19$

Figure 11.12 show the ASN curve. From the plot, the maximum ASN = 42 and it occurs at $p = 0.09$.

(*c*) The ratio $p_{0.10}/p_{0.95} = 0.15/0.04 = 3.75$. The final column of Table 11.1 tells us that a ratio of 4.057 is obtained when c is 4 and 3.549 is obtained when $c = 5$. Because neither of this values is exactly 3.75, it is not possible to have a single sampling plan that has an OC curve passing exactly through the two stipulated points. A choice can be made of one of the following four plans that can be computed from Table 11.1 ; the OC curve of each plan passes through one of the specified points and provides a near miss to the other point.

c	n	$100\, p_{0.95}$	$100\, p_{0.10}$
4	49	4	16.3
5	65	4	14.3
4	53	3.7	15
5	62	4.2	15

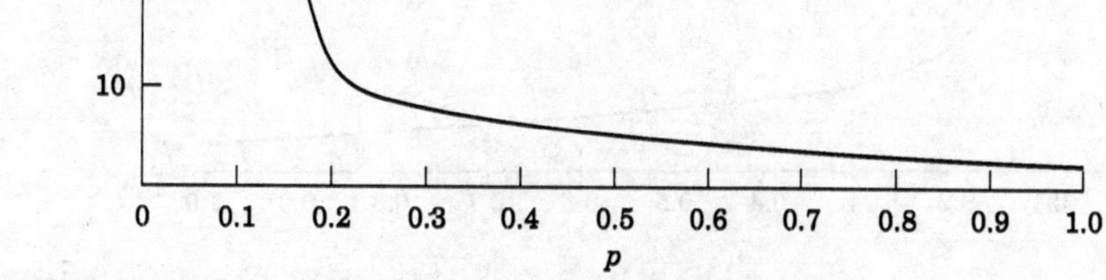

FIGURE 11.12 ASN curve of the plan of $p_{0.95} = 0.04$ and $p_{0.10} = 0.15$.

Sacrificing a little of Consumer's interest, the appropriate plan is $n = 62$ and $c = 5$.

(*d*) Comparing the value of ASN in sequential sampling and n of single sampling plan, we find that it is more in single sampling and hence more inspection cost.

Q. 11.28: (*a*) *Determine the equations of the acceptance and rejection lines for an item-by-item sequential sampling plan in which* $p_{0.95} = 0.015$ *and* $p_{0.10} = 0.10$.

(*b*) *Sketch an ASN curve for this plan and indicate the maximum point on this curve.*

(*c*) *On the assumption that* $p_{0.95}$ *is a reasonable AQL value, find the ABC standard single sampling plan for Code Letter H under normal inspection.*

(*d*) *Compare the value of n found in part (c) with the ASN values found in part (b).*

Ans: (*a*) $p_1 = 0.015$, $\alpha = 0.05$; $p_2 = 0.10$, $\beta = 0.10$.

The equations of the acceptance and rejection lines are found to be

$$Ac = 0.045\,n - 1.133$$

$$Re = 0.045\,n + 1.455$$

(*b*) Following tabulation gives 5 points on ASN curve

p	ASN
0.00	$h_1/s = 25.07$
$p_1 = 0.015$	$\dfrac{(1-\alpha)h_1 - \alpha h_2}{s - p_1} = 33.24$
$s = 0.045$	$\dfrac{h_1 h_2}{s(1-s)} = 38.20$
$p_2 = 0.10$	$\dfrac{(1-\beta)h_2 - \beta h_1}{p_2 - s} = 18.24$
1.00	$\dfrac{h_2}{1-s} = 1.52$

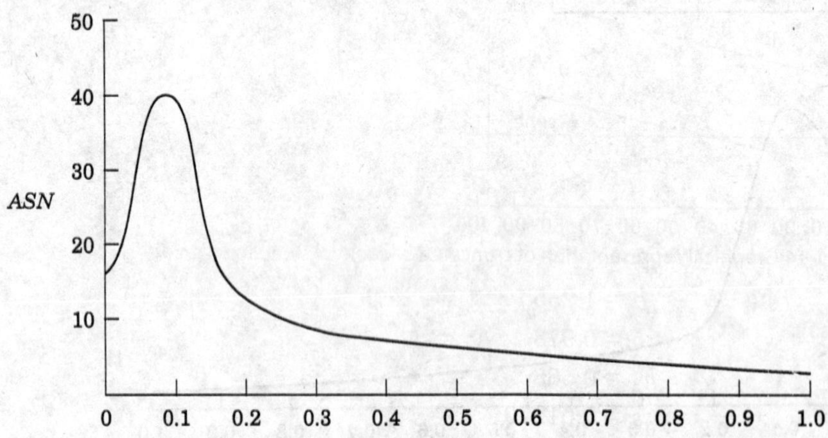

FIGURE 11.13 ASN curve of the plan of $p_1 = 0.015$, $\alpha = 0.015$, $p_2 = 0.10$, $\beta = 0.10$.

Figure 11.13 shows the ASN curve. From the plot, the maximum ASN = 40 and it occurs at $p = 0.06$.

(c) For an AQL of 0.015 (*i.e.* 1.5%) and Code Letter H, Table *L* gives sampling plan as $n = 80$, $c = 2$.

(d) Comparing the value of ASN in sequential sampling and *n* of single sampling plan, we find that it is more in single sampling and hence more inspection cost.

Q. 11.29: (a) *Explain the statement " sequential sampling plans make most efficient use of the information in the sample".*

(b) *Design a truncated sequential sampling plan that will reject only 5 percent of the times ots containing 0.1 per cent defective items, but will reject 90 percent of the time lots containing 5 percent defective items.*

Ans: (a) The total amount of inspection can often be reduced by designing a plan that takes a sequence of small samples rather than taking one large sample. The savings accrue whenever an early decision is possible as a result of exceptionally good (or bad) results.

Wald proposed a plan that has two stopping rules, after each item is inspected :

1. stop and reject the lot if cumulative number of defectives falls above a certain limit; or
2. stop and accept the batch of defectives fall below a second limit.

If neither limit is violated, another sample item is drawn and the process is continued. It has been estimated that sequential sampling may reduce the average number inspected by approximately 50%, by stopping earlier than a single sampling plan. Thus sequential plans make efficient use of the information in the sample.

(b)

$$p_1 = 0.001$$

$$p_2 = 0.05$$

We compute

$$g_1 = 1.69897$$

$$g_2 = 0.2185$$

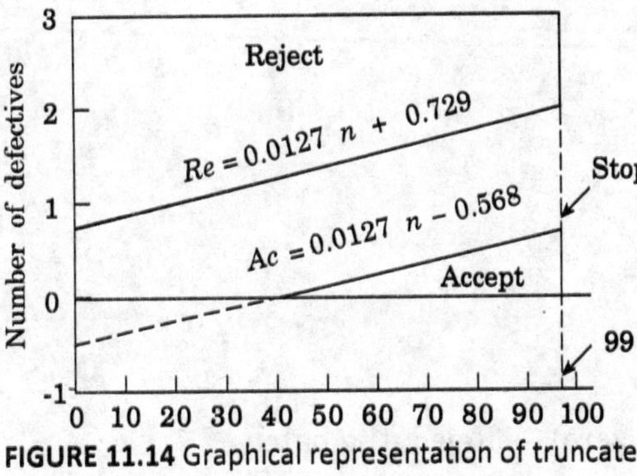

FIGURE 11.14 Graphical representation of truncated sequential sampling plan.

$$a = 1.255$$

$$b = 0.978$$

$$h_1 = 0.568$$

$$s = 0.01270$$

$$n = \frac{3ab}{g_1 g_2} \text{ i.e } 99$$

To truncate the plan, we agree to stop sampling after 99 items have inspected, accepting if the continuing path is closer to the acceptance (lower) line and rejecting if the path is closer to the rejection (upper) line.

Figure 11.14 shows the sampling chart used for a hypothetical sample of 99.

Q. 11.30: *Burnard's Handicap Method is an alternative method of Sequential Sampling and employs two parameters known as the 'Handicap' and the 'Penalty'. After the inspection of each piece the 'Score' is computed.*

Scores (S) = Handicap (H) + Number of 'good' pieces (G) – [Penalty (P) × Number of 'bad' pieces (b)]

i.e., $S = H + G - PB.$

If score reaches a target value equal to twice the handicap, the batch will be accepted. If the score falls to zero or below, the batch will be rejected. In a typical plan of this type,

Handicap H = 175

Penalty = 95

Target value (2H) = 350.

A 'safety valve' is included in the form of a maximum sample size (in this instance 675). If this number of pieces is reached (i.e., G + B = 675) without the target value, or zero, being reached, then the batch would be rejected.

Compute the 'score' for each of the following sequences and state if the batch is accepted or rejected :

(*a*) G, B, 16G, B, 67G, B.

(*b*) 107G, 2B, 180G, B, 241G.

Ans: (*a*) Considering batch (*a*), and computing the 'score' at each stage.

1 good, Score= 175 + 1 = 176

Continue testing

1 bad, Score = 176 – (95 × 1) = 81

Continue testing

16 good, Score = 81 + 16 = 97

Continue testing

1 bad, Score = 97 – (95 × 1) = 2

Continue testing

67 good, Score = 2 + 67 = 69

Continue testing

1 bad, Score = 69–95 = – 26 (below zero) — Reject the batch,

No. of pieces inspected = 1 + 1 + 16 + 1 + 67 + 1 = 87.

(*b*) Now considering the batch (*b*), and computing the 'Score' at each stage.

107 good, Score = 175 + 107 = 282

Continue testing

2 bad, Score = 282 – (95 × 2) = 92

Continue testing

180 good, Score = 92 + 180 = 272

Continue testing

1 bad, Score = 272-(95 × 1) = 177

Continue testing

173 good, Score = 177 + 173 = 350 [Target Value]

Accept the batch at this stage

No. of pieces inspected = 107 + 2 + 180 + 1 + 173 = 463.

Q. 11.31: *The boundary lines for a sequential sampling scheme are*

$$G = 9 + 4B \text{ (Accept)}$$
$$G = -16 + 4B \text{ (Reject)}$$

'Translate' the above scheme into the 'Handicap' form, determine the values of the Handicap, Penalty and Target.

Ans: If the target value is T, then the batch is accepted when score $S \geq T$.

$T = H + G - PB$ (Accept)

Similarly the batch is rejected when $S \leq 0$.

$0 = H + G - PB$ (Reject)

From the above two equations,

$G = (T - H) + PB$ (Accept)

$G = (-H) + PB$ (Reject)

Comparing these equations with the given equations,

$$P = 4$$
$$T - H = 9$$
$$-H = -16$$

Therefore $T = 25$ and $H = 16$.

The statement of the sampling scheme is as under.

If the score reaches a target value of 25, the batch will be accepted. If the score falls to zero or below, the batch will be rejected.

Q. 11.32: *The boundary lines for a sequential sampling scheme are :*

$$G = 9 + 4B \quad \text{(Accept)}$$
$$G = -16 + 4B \quad \text{(Reject)}$$

The following sequences were obtained from a lot ; use the above sequential scheme to decide, whether the lot is acceptable or not.

GGG B G BB GGG B GG BG

B GGG GG B GG BB GG BBB

G B.

Ans: Figure 11.15 shows the 'Accept' and 'Reject' boundary lines and the points plotted. The procedure in such a case is to take a single piece at random. If it is a 'good', plot one unit vertically, if it is a 'bad' plot in continuation one unit horizontally. So long as the position reached lies in the centre band, sampling continues the decision to accept or reject the lot only being made when the plotted point moves into either 'accept' or 'reject' decision region.

In this case, it is seen that the point for 26 piece crosses the 'Reject' boundary and falls in reject zone. Hence the lot will be rejected after inspecting the 26th piece.

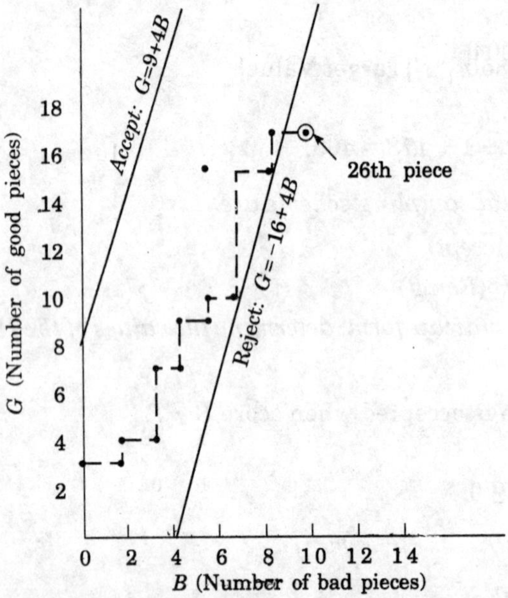

FIGURE 11.15 Graphical representation of the sequential sampling scheme in Prob. 11.27.

Q. 11.33: *In the 'simple random walk' method, a lot of items has p = 0.20. If the sequential scheme is applied with a = 5 and b = 3 what is the probability of this lot being accepted?*

Ans: Acceptance means reaching *a*, *i.e.* + 5

$$P_a = \frac{1-\left(\dfrac{0.20}{0.80}\right)^3}{1-\left(\dfrac{0.20}{0.80}\right)^8}$$

$$= 0.984.$$

Q. 11.34: *Select from Table 11.2 the sampling plan for a point of control of 1% and a lot size of 1,000. Under what AQL value is this plan listed in Table 11.3 ?*

Ans: Table 11.2 shows that for a sample size of 1,000 and point of control of 1%, single sampling plan is to be used. The plan is

$$n = 150,\ c = 1.$$

Table 11.3 shows that this sampling plan is listed under AQL of 0.25%.

Q. 11.35: (*a*) *Select from Table 11.2 the sampling plan for a lot size 400 and a point of control of 2%.*

(*b*) *Use Table G to calculate the percents of nonconforming product for which the probability of acceptance is 0.95 and 0.10.*

Ans: (*a*) From Table 11.2, for a lot size of 400 and point of control of 2%, the sampling plan is $n = 75$, $c = 1$.

(b) In Table G, under the column "headed $c = 1$", when $P_a = 0.951$, $\mu_{np} = 0.35$.

Since $n = 75$

$$p = \frac{0.35}{75} = 0.00466$$

or $100p = 0.466\%$

Similarly in Table G, under the column "headed $c = 1$", when $P_a = 0.10$, $\mu_{np} = 3.9$ (by interpolation).

Since $n = 75$

$$\therefore \quad p = \frac{3.9}{75} = 0.052$$

or $100p = 5.2\%$.

Q. 11.36: *(a) Find the appropriate Philips Standard Sampling System plan for a point of control of 2% and a lot size of 1,500 items.*

(b) Use Table G to compute the approximate probability of acceptance of lots containing 4% nonconforming product.

(c) Campute the ASN for these lots.

(d) Compute the AFI on the assumption that rectifying inspection is to be used.

Ans: (a) For a point of control of 2% and lot size of 1,500, the double sampling plan prescribed in Table 11.2 is as under :

$$n_1 = 55,\ c_1 = 0\ ;$$
$$n_2 = 2\ n_1 = 2 \times 55 = 110,\ c_2 = 2.$$

(b) In using Table G to compute the respective probabilities of results of the first sample,

$$np = 55\ (0.04) = 2.2$$
$$P_0 = 0.111$$
$$P_{1 \text{ or less}} = 0.355$$
$$P_1 = 0.355 - 0.111 = 0.244$$
$$P_{2 \text{ or less}} = 0.623$$
$$P_2 = 0.623 - 0.355 = 0.268$$

Also $P_r = (1 - 0.623) = 0.377$ (P_r 1st sample)

If there is one defective in the first sample, calculations regarding the second sample are based on $\mu_{np} = (110)\ (0.04) = 4.4$

$$P_0 = 0.012$$
$$P_{1 \text{ or less}} = 0.066$$

These probabilities can now be used to estimate the probability of acceptance, as follows :

$P(n_1)$ *i.e.* 0 defective in first	$= 0.111$
$P(n_2)$ i.e. 1 defective in first with 0, or 1 in the second $= (0.244 \times 0.066) - 0.111$	$= 0.016$
2 defectives in first with 0 in the second $= (0.268)\ (0.012) = 0.111$	$= 0.003$
Probability of acceptance of a lot 4.0% defective	$= 0.130$

(c) Probability of decision on the first sample is the P_a of 0.111 plus the P_r of $0.377 = 0.488$. If there is no curtailment of inspection, 0.488 of the lots will require a sample of 55, and the balance 0.512 will require a sample of 110. It follows that

$$ASN = 0.488\ (5\ 5) + 0.512\ (110) = 83.16$$

(*d*) $AFI = ATI/N$

For double sampling

$$ATI = n_1\ P_a\ (n_1) + (n_1 + n_2)\ P_a\ (n_2) + N\ (1 - P_a)$$

$$ATI = 55\ (0.111) + 165\ (0.019) + 1500\ (0.870) = 1314.24$$

$$AFI = 1314.24/1500 = 0.876.$$

Q. 11.37: (*a*) *Using the Philips Standard Sampling System, determine the acceptance if the lot size is 800 and the point of control is 3.0%.*

(*b*) *What is the probability of a rejection of a lot 40% defective for the plan found in (a).*

(*c*) *Find a double sampling plan from the Philips Standard Sampling System for a lot size of 1,200 and a point of control of 5.0%.*

(*d*) *What is the probability of 4.0% defective lot using the plan found in (c) ?*

(*e*) *Compare the ASN values under the two plans if incoming lots are 4.0% defective.*

Ans: (*a*) From Table 11.2, for a lot size of 800 and point of control of 3.0%, the required sampling plan is

$$n = 55, c = 2$$

(*b*) $\mu_{np} = 55\ (0.04) = 2.2$

Table *G* gives $P_a = 0.623$

Therefore $P_r = 1 - 0.623 = 0.377.$

(*c*) Again from Table 11.2, for a lot size of 1,200 and point of Control of 5.0%, the required double sampling plan is

$$n_1 = 25,\ c_1 = 0\ ;$$

$$n_2 = 50,\ c_2 = 3.$$

(*d*) In using Table *G* to compute the respective probabilities of results of the first sample, $\mu_{np} = 25\ (0.04) = 1$. From Table *G*, we find

$$P_0 = 0.368$$

$$P_{1 \text{ or less}} = 0.736$$

$$P_1 = 0.736 - 0.368 = 0.368$$

$$P_{2 \text{ or less}} = 0.920$$

$$P_2 = 0.920 - 0.736 = 0.184$$

$$P_{3 \text{ or less}} = 0.981$$

$$P_3 = 0.981 - 0.920 = 0.061$$

$$P_{4 \text{ or more}} = 1 - 0.981 = 0.01\ 9\ (P_r \text{ of 1st sample})$$

For the second sample $\mu_{np} = 50\ (0.04) = 2\ .0,$

$$P_{2 \text{ or less}} = 0.677$$

$$P_{1 \text{ or less}} = 0.406$$

$$P_0 = 0.135$$

The above probabilities may be used to estimate the probability of acceptance as under, as follows :

0 defective in the first = 0.368

1 defective in the first with 0, 1, or 2 in the second = (0.368) (0.677) = 0.249

2 defectives in the first with 0, or 1 in the second = (0.184) (0.406) = 0.075

3 defectives in the first with 0 in the second = (0.061) (0.135) = 0.008

Probability of acceptance = 0.700

Therefore Probability of rejection = 1.0 – 0.7 = 0.3.

(*e*) For the sampling plan at (*a*), which is a single sampling plan, the decision is reached on the very first sample. It follows that

$$\text{ASN} = n = 55$$

For the sampling plan at (*c*), which is a double sampling plan, the probability of decision on the first sample is the P_a of 0.368 plus the P_r of 0.019 = 0.387. Hence the probability of taking a second sample = 0.613.

It follows that

$$\text{ASN} = 25\ (0.3\ 87) + 50\ (0.613) = 40.33$$

From the two ASN values, it is clear that in this case, ASN for double sampling is less than the ASN for single sampling.

Q. 11.38: *In Dodge's proposed system shown in Table 11.3, what are acceptance criteria in normal and tightened inspection level I, 1.5% AQL, and a size of 1,000. What are the respective probabilities of acceptance under normal and tightened inspection when the process average is at the AQL value ? What is the AOQL under tightened inspection ?*

Ans: From Table 11.3, for inspection level II the lot size of 1,000, the sample size is 100. For inspection level I, we shell be using the plan with next smaller sample size. It follows that the required sampling plan is

$$n = 65,\ c = 2$$

Again for tightened inspection the sample size remains the same but

$$C_r = C_N - 1 \text{ i.e. } 2 - 1 = 1$$

It follows that the required sampling plan is

$$n = 65,\ c = 1.$$

Probabilities of acceptance under these two plans can be calculated by using Table G.

$$n_p = 65 \times (0.015) = 0.975$$

P_a for normal inspection = 0.925

P_a for tightened inspection = 0.745.

By assuming various values of *p* and computing the corresponding P_a values, *AOQL* can be computed for tightened inspection.

Q. 11.39: *A vendor inspects his own product before shipment using the Philips Standard Sampling System, screening all rejected lots before shipment. The lot size is 2,500, and the point of control is 2%. The purchaser inspects the same lots under the Dodge system shown in Table 11.3. He uses inspection level II, normal inspection and as AQL of 1.0%.*

Use Table G to obtain approximate asnwers to the following questions.

(a) What is the probability that a 2.5% nonconforming lot will pass both the vendor's and purchaser's sampling inspection ?

(b) What is the probability that a 2.5% nonconforming lot will bass both the vendor's sampling inspection and be rejected by the purchaser's ?

Ans: From Table 11.2, the vendor's sampling plan is as follows :

$$n_1 = 70, c_1 = 0 ;$$
$$n_2 = 140, c_2 = 3.$$

From Table 11.3, the purchaser's sampling plan is as follows :

$$n = 150, c = 3$$

For a 2.5% nonconforming lot, probability of acceptance given by vendor's double sampling plan is found to be 0.316 and that by purchaser's plan is found to be 0.483.

(*a*) Probability that a 2.5% nonconforming lot will be passed by both the vendor's and purchaser's sampling plan

$$= (0.316)(0.483) = 0.153$$

(*b*) Probability that a 2.5% nonconforming lot will be passed by vendor's but rejected by purchaser's sampling plan

$$= (0.316)(1 - 0.483) = 0.163$$

Q. 11.40: *A vendor inspects his own product before shipment using the Philips Standard Sampling System, screening all rejected lots before shipment. The lot size is 500, and the point of control is 2%. The purchaser inspects the same lots, using single sampling under the ABC standard with inspection level II, normal inspection, and an AQL of 1.5%.*

Use Table G to obtain approximate answers to the following questions :

(a) What is the probability that a 1.5% defective lot will pass both vendor's and purchaser's sampling inspection ?

(b) What is the probability that a 1.5% defective lot will pass vendor's sampling inspection and be rejected by the purchaser's ?

Ans: For specified details the Philips Standard Sampling plans is follows :

$$n = 75, c = 1$$

Purchaser's sampling plan :

$$n = 50, c = 2, \text{rejection number} = 3.$$
$$p = 0.015$$

when $n = 75, \mu_{np} = 1.125$

when $n = 50, \mu_{np} = 0.750$

From Table *G* :

(*i*) The probability that a lot passes vendor's inspection = 0.690

(*ii*) The probability that a lot passes's purchaser's inspection = 0.959

(*a*) The probability that a lot passes both vendor's and purchaser's sampling inspection

$$= (0.690)(0.959) = 0.662.$$

(*b*) The probability that a lot passes vendor's sampling inspection and rejected by purchaser's sampling plan

$$= (0.690)(1 - 0.959) = 0.028$$

Q. 11.41: *'Cork & Flowerpot Pvt. Ltd.' inspects its own product before shipment using the Philips Standard Sampling System, screening all rejected lots before shipment. The lot size is 1,000 and* $p_{0.50} = 3\%$.

The purchaser 'XYZ-55' inspects the same lots under the Dodge sampling plan n = 100, c = 5. Use Table G to obtain approximate answers to the following questions :

(a) What is the probability that a 2.5% defective lot is accepted by 'XYZ-55 and 'Cork & Flowerpot Pvt. Limited ?'

(b) What is the probability that a 2.5% defective lot is shipped back to Cork & Flowerpot Pvt. Ltd.?

(c) If the lots shipped back are screened and defective items be replaced by good ones' find the average outgoing quality for 'XYZ-55.'

Ans: Philips Standard Sampling Plan for $p_{0.50}$ of 3%, and a lot size of 1,000, is :

$$n = 85, c = 2.$$

Dodge plan : $n = 100, c = 5,$

$$p = 0.025.$$

(a) For a p of 0.025, P_a for philips plan is 0.642 and for Dodge plan P_a is 0.9575.

Probability that a 2.5% defective lot is accepted by 'XYZ-55' and 'Cork & Flowerpot Pvt. Ltd.' = (0.642) (0.9575) = 0.627.

(b) Probability that a 2.5% defective lot is shipped back

$$= 1 - 0.9578 = 0.425$$

(c) AOQ for 'XYZ−55' = (0.627)(2.5) = 1.6%.

Q. 11.42: *A manufacturer inspects all of his product before shipment using Dodge's single sampling system shown in Table 11.3. Inspection level II for normal inspection is used. Lots are shipped in quantities of 1,500 under an AQL requirement of 2.5%. On receiving lots, the customer also inspects the material using a plan from the Dodge system. However, the customer uses inspection level III and tightened inspection with the same AQL.*

(a) Find the acceptance criteria for both plans.

(b) Compute the probability that a lot with 3.5% nonconforming will be accepted by both plans consecutively.

Ans: (a) From Table 11.3, the manufacturer's sampling plan is $n = 150$, $c = 7$. Again from the same table, the customer's sampling plan is $n = 250$ and a c of (10 − 1) = 9.

(b) P_a given by manufacturer's plan = 0.839

P_a given by customer's plan = 0.625

Probability that a lot with 3.5% nonconforming will be accepted by both the plans

$$= (0.839)\ (0.625)\ i.e.\ 0.524.$$

Q. 11.43: *A purchase of steel rods uses of chain sampling acceptance plan ChSP-1, since only a limited amount of inspection is possible. The plan in use requires that five rods from each lot be inspected. If no defective rods are found the lot is accepted. If one defective is found, the lot is accepted if the two previous lot samples inspected contained no defectives. Otherwise, the lot is rejected. If the lots received are 5% defective, determine the probability of accepting any given lot.*

Ans:

$$p = 0.05, q = 0.95$$

$$n = 5$$

$$i = 2$$

$$c = 0$$

$$P_0 = \frac{5!}{0!\,(5-0)!}(0.05)^0(0.95)^{5-0}$$
$$= 0.7738$$
$$P_1 = \frac{5!}{1!\,(5-1)!}(0.05)^1(0.95)^{5-1} = 0.2036$$
$$P_a = P_0 + P_1[P_0]i = 0.7738 + 0.2036[0.7738]^2$$
$$= 0.8957.$$

Q. 11.44: *A producer and consumer have agreed to use a Dodge Ch SP-I chain sampling plan in the acceptance procedure for a new electrical component. From each lot of material received, the consumer will sample n items. If no defective are found, the lot will be accepted. If one defective is found, the lot will be accepted only if the previous two lots inspected contained no defectives. Otherwise, the lot will be rejected.*

(a) What value of n will ensure the producer that no more than 10% of the lots will be rejected when incoming lots are 5% defective ?

(b) What value of n will ensure the consumer that no more than 25% of the lots at 25% defective will be accepted ?

(c) Recommend a value of n to come the closest to meeting the producer's and consumer's requirements.

Ans: The probability of acceptance in Ch SP-1 can be written as

$$P_a = (q)^n + n(q)^{n-1}(p)(q)^{in}$$

$(q)^n\,[1 + n\,(p)\,(q)^{in-1})]$

(*a*) In this problem $i = 2$,

$$p = 0.05,\ q = 0.95$$
$$P_a = 0.90 \text{ or more}$$

Also $\qquad P_a = (0.95)^n\,[1 + n(0.05)(0.95)^{2n-1}]$

Since the solution of the about equation is complex, we will try only hit and trial method by assuming certain values of n and comparing the value of P_a thus obtained with the required one.

Since in ChSP-1, the sampling number is small, let us first assume $n = 4$

$$P_a = (0.95)^4[1 + 4(0.05)(0.5)(0.95)^7] = 0.928$$

Let $\qquad n = 5$

$$P_a = (0.95)^5\,[1 + 5(0.05)(0.95)^9] = 0.896$$

Let $\qquad n = 6$

$$P_a = (0.95)^6[1 + 6\,(0.05)(0.95)^{11}] = 0.861$$

The above results indicate that from producer's point of view $n = 4$ will most suitable and the second best choice is $n = 5$ when the probability of acceptance is 0.896.

(*b*) When $p = 0.25$, $P_a = 0.25$ or less

Let $\qquad n = 4$

$$P_a = (0.75)^4\,[+ 4[(0.25)(0.75)^7] = 0.358$$

When $n = 5$ $\qquad P_a = (0.75)^5[1 + 5(0.25)(0.75)^9] = 0.259$

When $n = 6$ $\qquad P_a = (0.75)^6[1 + 6(0.25)(0.75)^{11}] = 0.189$

The above results indicate that from the consumer's point of view $n = 6$ is the best choice and $n = 5$ is the next best choice.

(c) From the results derived at (a) and (b) it is obvious that $n = 5$ will meet closely the consumer's as well as producer's requirements.

Q. 11.45: *(a) Describe briefly how will you select a random sample.*

(b) Compare the single sampling, double sampling, and sequential sampling plans.

Ans: (a) If the theory of probability is to be properly used for calculating the risk of wrong decision resulting from sample analysis, it is very essential that the random sample must be drawn from the universe.

One of the methods used in industries to draw a random sample, is to use tables of random sampling numbers. These tables are collections of the digits 0 to 9 that have been put together in way that our intuition strongly suggests will yield a random arrangement. Table *X* App. 1 is one such table.

Still another one is to employ electronic computer to takes a random sample.

The general rules to be borne in mind in drawing a random sample are :

1. The method of selection should be such that gives every member of the lot an equal chance of being drawn.
2. Any method that associates the selection of an item with the classification of the item being selected, should be avoided.

(b) Depending upon the conditions of inspection, any one of the mentioned sampling plan may be adopted for acceptance sampling. But sometimes the double and sequential sampling is impracticable. There may be physical reasons which warrant only one sample to be drawn from the lot. In comparison among these three types of sampling, the following factors must be considered.

1. *The psychological advantage of double sampling.* There are definite psychological advantages of double sampling. One is that borderline lots are given a 'second chance' to be accepted. The other is that no lot is rejected because of a single defective article.

These above mentioned advantages are also associated with the sequential or multiple sampling plan.

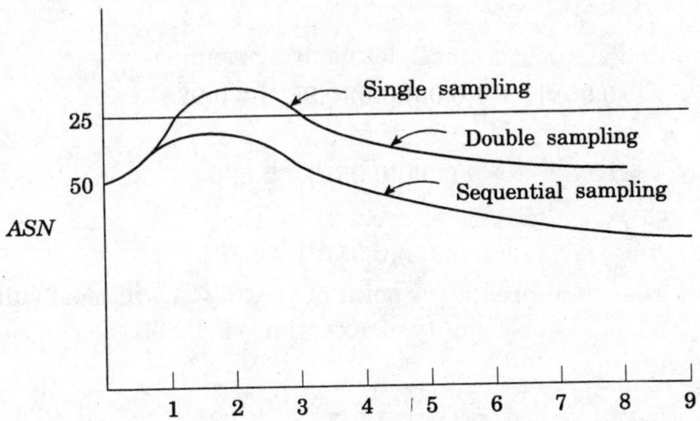

FIGURE 11.16 Comparison of Average amount of sampling (ASN) required single, double and sequential sampling plans having essentially the same OC curve.

2. *The expected differences in cost.* The cost tends to be highest for multiple and sequential plans and lowest for single sampling plan. The more complicated the acceptance plan, the greater the attention needed for inspection and arriving at correct decisions.

In a single sampling plan, the amount of sampling required is constant regardless the quality of submitted lots. In a double and sequential sampling the amount of sampling required varies according to the quality of the submitted lots. Figure 11.16 shows the amount of sampling required in single, double and sequential sampling plans having essentially the same operating curves :

The single sampling plan $n = 75$, $c = 1$. The double sampling plan $n = 50$, $n_2 = 100$, $c_1 = 0$, $c_2 = 2$. The sequential sampling plan $p_1 = 0.005$ $\alpha = 0.05$, $p_2 = 0.05$, $\beta = 0.10$.

Sequential sampling plan shows a marked advantage over single sampling regardless of the quality of lots. It shows very little advantage over double sampling until the percent defective in lot exceeds above 3%. Above 3% defective it shows marked advantage over double sampling.

The curves of Fig. 11.17 strictly apply only to the plan shown. Other plan will produce different curves but in general the same basic relationship will hold.

3. *Difficulty in training the personnel.* The idea of single sampling as compared with other types of sampling is easy to infuse in the minds of the inspectors and other people.

CHAPTER

12

Acceptance Sampling from Continuous Production

12.1 SAMPLING PLANS FOR CONTINUOUS PRODUCTION—CSP-1

Acceptance sampling plans which have been discussed in Chapters 9, 10 and 11 were lot-by-lot plans. Many manufacturing operations do not create lot as a normal part of the production process, since they are produced by a continuous process on a conveyor or other straight line system. In such cases, acceptance sampling plans for continuous production are required.

Plans for continuous production consist of alternating sequences of sampling inspection and screening (100%) inspection. These plans usually begin with 100% inspection, and if a stated number of units (clearance number, i) are free of defects, sampling inspection is instituted. Sampling continues until a specific number of defective units are found, at which time 100% inspection is reinstated.

Sampling plans for continuous production are applicable to attribute, non-destructive inspection of moving product. The inspection must be of such a nature that it is relatively easy and rapid so that no "bottlenecks" occur because of the inspection activity. In addition the process must be capable of manufacturing homogeneous product.

The concept of sampling for continuous production was first devised by H.F. Dodge in 1943, with a sampling plan that has been commonly referred to as CSP-1. This plan and two additional plans CSP-2 and CSP-3, are categorized as single-level plans. In 1955 the theory of multilevel continuous plans was presented by G. Licherman and H. Soloman. Multilevel plans provide for reduced levels of sampling inspection when the quality continues to be superior. Much of this early work was incorporated into MIL-STD-1235 (ORD), which was superseded by MIL-STD-1235 (MU) on June 28, 1974.

12.1.1 Dodge's AOQL Plan for Continuous Production-CSP-1

The procedure for CSP-1 is as follows :

(*a*) At the outset, inspect 100% of the units consecutively as produced and continue such inspection until i units in succession are found clear of defects.

(*b*) When i units in succession are found clear of defects, discontinue 100% inspection, and inspect only a fraction f of the units, selecting individual sample units one at a time from the flow of product, in such a manner as to assure an unbiased sample.

(*c*) If a sample unit is found defective, revert immediately to a 100% inspection of succeeding units and continue until again i units in succession are found clear of defects, as in paragraph (*a*).

(*d*) Correct or replace, with good units, all defective units found.

Figure 12.1 gives the necessary information for the selection of such a plan for any desired AOQL. As an example, suppose the desired AOQL is 2%, and it is desired to establish a plan that calls for inspection of 1 out of every 20 pieces from the conveyor belt. Then *f*, the fraction inspected, is $\frac{1}{20}$, or 0.05, or 5%. In Fig. 12.1, find the value of *i* corresponding to an *f* of 5% on the curve for an AOQL of 2%. This $i = 76$. The acceptance plan is then as follows :

1. Inspect all the units consecutively as produced until 76 units in succession are free from defects.
2. As soon as 76 successive units are free from defects, inspect a sample consisting of only 1 unit out of every 20. Accept all the product as long as the sample is free from defects.
3. Whenever one of these sample units is found defective, resume 100% inspection until 76 units is succession have again been found free from defects. Then resume sampling inspection.

12.1.2 The Dodge-Torrey Modifications of Continuous Sampling Plan 1

H.F. Dodge and M.N. Torrey developed two modifications of CSP-1 referred to as CSP-2 and CSP-3, respectively. They describe CSP-2 as follows:

Plan CSP-2 differs from Plan CSP-1 in that, once sampling inspection is started, 100% inspection is not invoked when each defect is found but is invoked only if a second defect occurs in the next k or less sample units. In other words, if two defects observed during sampling are separated by k or less good inspected units, 100% inspection is invoked. Otherwise sampling is continued.

Although the factor *k* might conceivably be assigned any value, the only CSP-2 plans prepared for use have been those in which $k = i$. Table 12.1 gives values of i in CSP-1 and CSP-2 using 5 and 10% samples and various AOQL values. These values for CSP-2 were obtained from a graph similar to Fig. 12.1 given in the Dodge-Torrey article.

Consider the application of CSP-2 when *f* is 5% and the AOQL is 2%. Table 12.1 gives $i = 96$. The acceptance plan is then as follows :

1. Inspect all the units consecutively as produced until 96 units in succession are free from defects.
2. As soon as 96 successive units are free from defects, inspect a sample consisting of only 1 out of every 20. Accept all the product as long as the sample is free from defects.
3. If one defective is found in this sampling, continue sampling inspection for the time being. However, if a second sample defective is found within the next 96 samples, resume 100% inspection immediately. Continue 100% inspection until 96 units in succession have been found free from defects. Then resume sampling under the foregoing rules.

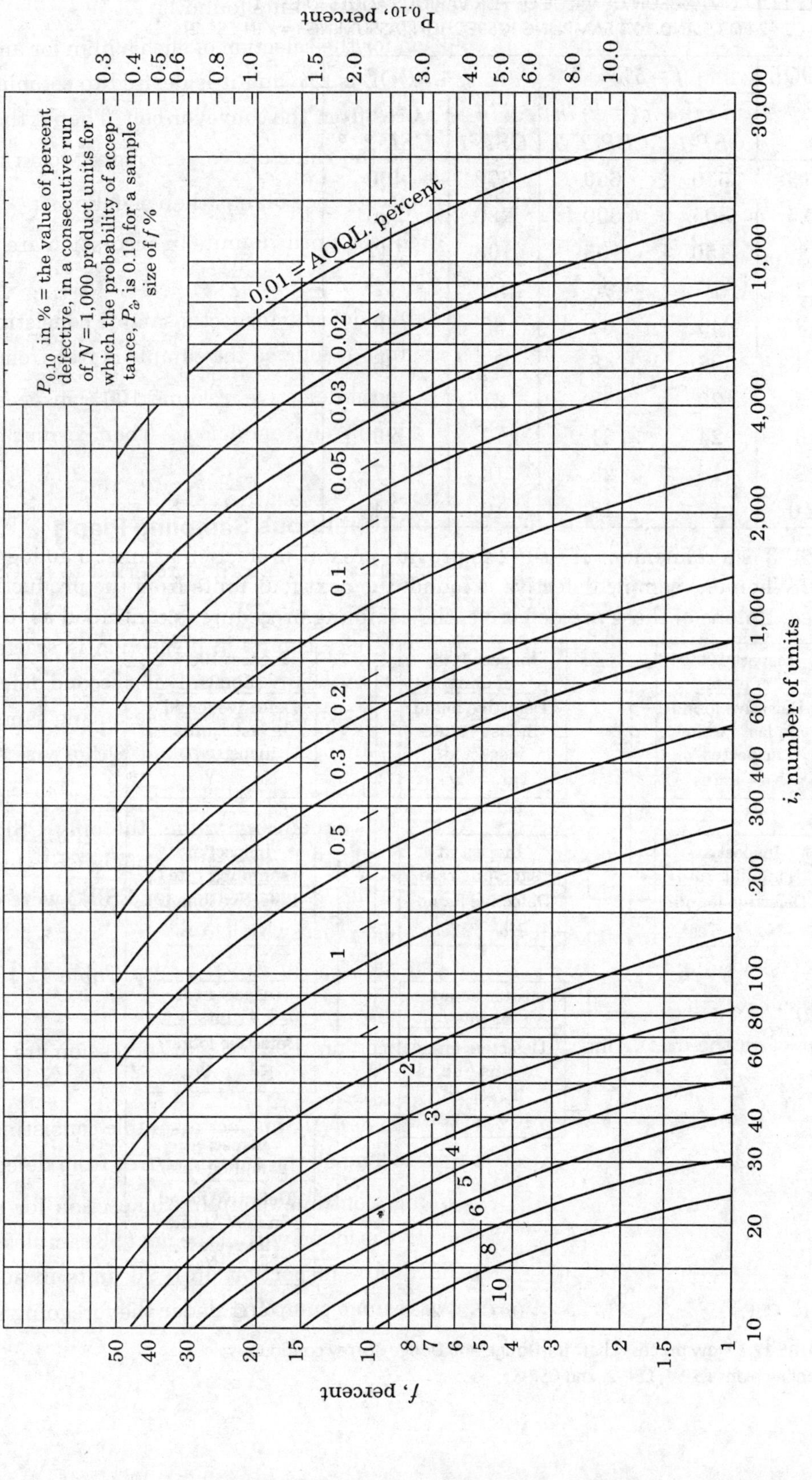

FIGURE 12.1 Curves for determining values of f and i for a given value of AOQL in Dodge's plan for continuous production CSP-1.

TABLE 12.1 COMPARISON OF VALUE OF FOR VARIOUS AOQLS IN CSP-1 AND CSP-2 FOR 5 AND 10% SAMPLING INSPECTION (ASSUMING i = k IN CSP-2).

AOQL %	*f = 5%*		*f = 10%*	
	i in CSP-1	*i (= k) in CSP-2, 3*	*i in CSP-1*	*i (= k) in CSP-2, 3*
0.3	510	650	370	490
0.5	305	390	220	290
1	150	195	108	147
2	76	96	55	72
3	49	64	36	48
4	37	48	27	36
5	29	38	21	29
6	24	31	17	23
8	18	23	13	17
10	14	18	10	14

Plan CSP-3 is a refinement of CSP-2 to provide greater protection against a sudden run of bad quality. When one sample defective is found, the next four units from the production line are inspected. If none of these are defective, the sampling procedure is continued as in CSP-2.

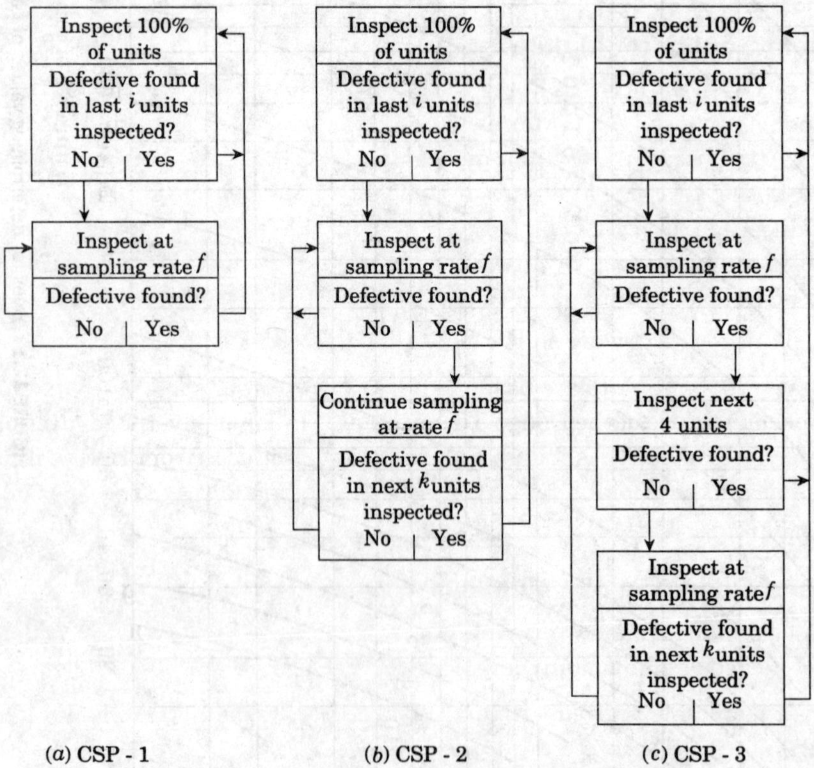

FIGURE 12.2 Flow process chart for Dodge and Dodge-Torrey continuous sampling plans CSP-1, CSP-2, and CSP-3.

If one of the four units is defective, 100% inspection is resumed at once and continued under the rules of CSP-2. In CSP-3, the value of i used for a given f and AOQL is the same as in CSP-2. Figure 12.2 shows as abbreviated flow process chart of the operation of the CSP-1, CSP-2, and CSP-3 plans.

12.2 MULTILEVEL CONTINUOUS SAMPLING PLANS (CSP-M)

Sometimes it is desired to start any sampling inspection with a relatively large fraction sampled, such as $\frac{2}{3}$, $\frac{1}{2}$, or $\frac{1}{3}$. In such cases, economies can be obtained by permitting a subsequent change to a smaller sampling fraction whenever the quality observed on the initial sampling inspection turns out to be good enough. To secure these economies and to obtain certain other advantages, multilevel continuous sampling schemes have been developed that stipulate two or more different sampling fractions and give rules for shifting back and forth among the stipulated fractions.

One particular type of multilevel plans was developed by Lieberman and Solomon. Just as in the CSP plans described the Lieberman and Soloman plans start with 100% inspection that continues until i acceptable units have been found in succession. Then sampling inspection is initiated with a fraction f inspected. If i acceptable units in succession are found under this sampling inspection, subsequent inspection is at the fraction f^2. Another i acceptable units in a row qualify for inspection at f^3, and so on. When a unit is rejected, inspection is shifted back to the next lower level. Any number of levels may be provided from two to an infinite number.

12.2.1 A Convenient Source for Multilevel Plans

In 1956, under a contract with the U.S. Air Force, Stanford University's Department of Industrial Engineering developed a proposed AMC Manual 74 entitled "Multi-level Continuous Sampling Acceptance Plans for Attributes." With minor additions and deletions of certain plans, this set of plans was adopted by the Air Force and later published by the U.S. Department of Defense as "Inspection and Quality Control Handbook (Interim) H 106, Multi-level Continuous Sampling Procedures and Tables for Inspection by Attributes." Table 12.2 combines the plans given in these two pamphlets. (H 106 added plans for AOQL values of 0.35, 0.15, and 0.10% and deleted those for 20 and 4%; plans for $f = \frac{2}{3}$ were shown in the proposed AMC Manual but not in H 106.)

The plans in these two pamphlets are based on the Lieberman-Solomon type of procedure combined with the special feature of the Dodge-Torrey plan CSP-3, namely, the inspection of the next four units whenever a defective is found. Figure 12.3, reproduced from H 106, illustrates the general features of all these plans by giving specific instructions for the operation of a three-level plan using an f of $\frac{1}{2}$.

12.2.2 Selection and Operation of a Multilevel Continuous Sampling Plan

Three decisions must be made in choosing a plan from Table 12.2. The AOQL and f must be selected, and it must be decided how many levels will be permitted.

Assume that a 3-level plan is desired with an AOQL of 2.0% and an f of $\frac{1}{2}$. Table 12.2 gives $i = 40$ for such a plan.

We may use Fig. 12.3 to see how this plan will operate. There will first be 100% inspection until 40 consecutive acceptable units are found. Then sampling inspection will start with half the units inspected. If all goes well and the next 40 sample units are accepted, sampling will then be applied to $\frac{1}{4}$ of the units. If another 40 consecutive sample units are accepted, sampling inspection will be applied to $\frac{1}{8}$ of the units. Inspection of $\frac{1}{8}$ will continue indefinitely until a unit is rejected.

TABLE 12.2 VALUES OF *i* FOR MULTILEVEL CONTINUOUS SAMPLING PLANS.

AOQL, % defective	For $f = \frac{1}{2}$					For $f = \frac{1}{3}$					For $f = \frac{2}{3}$		
	$k = 1$	$k = 2$	$k = 3$	$k = 4$	$k = 5$	$k = 1$	$k = 2$	$k = 3$	$k = 4$	$k = 5$	$k = 1$	$k = 2$	$k = 3$
20.0	*	*	*	*	*	*	*	4	5	6	*	*	*
15.0	*	*	*	4	5	*	4	6	7	8	*	*	*
10.0	*	4	6	8	9	*	7	10	12	13	*	*	*
7.5	*	6	9	11	13	6	11	14	16	18	*	*	*
5.0	5	11	15	18	20	10	18	22	25	27	*	5	8
4.0	7	14	19	22	25	14	23	29	32	34	*	7	11
3.0	11	20	26	31	34	19	32	39	43	46	5	11	16
2.0	18	31	40	47	51	31	48	59	66	71	9	18	25
1.5	25	43	55	63	69	42	66	80	89	95	13	25	34
1.0	39	65	83	95	104	64	100	120	134	142	21	39	52
0.75	54	88	112	128	140	87	134	161	179	191	30	53	71
0.50	82	132	168	193	210	133	202	243	269	287	46	80	107
0.35	119	197	241	275	302	190	290	349	386	408			
0.25	167	269	337	386	422	269	406	488	540	576	96	164	217
0.15	218	446	636	636	706	450	680	815	903	960	706	450	680
0.10	421	675	847	969	1,059	677	1,022	1,224	1,354	1,443			

* Sampling plans not available for values of *i* less than 4.

Figure 12.3 also shows the operating rules whenever a defective unit is found under sampling inspection. One hundred percent inspection is applied to the next 4 units, with the state described as 1 *R*, 2 *R*, or 3 *R* depending on the sampling inspection continues at the previous rate, $\frac{1}{2}$, $\frac{1}{4}$, or $\frac{1}{8}$ as the case may be. If a unit is rejected in the 4 units, there is a shift to 100% inspection if sampling has been at rate $\frac{1}{2}$ or to 4-unit inspection with state 1*R* or 2*R*, respectively, if sampling has been at the rate $\frac{1}{4}$ or $\frac{1}{8}$.

12.3 THE MIL-STD-1235 SYSTEM FOR SAMPLING FROM CONTINUOUS PRODUCTION

In 1959, just less than a year after publication of Handbook H 106 for multilevel continuous sampling, Handbook H 107 was published consisting of three single-level continuous sampling plans. The set included Dodge's CSP-1 and CSP-2 and a plan developed for the U.S. Navy

FLOW PROCESS CHART FOR MULTILEVEL CONTINUOUS SAMPLING PLANS

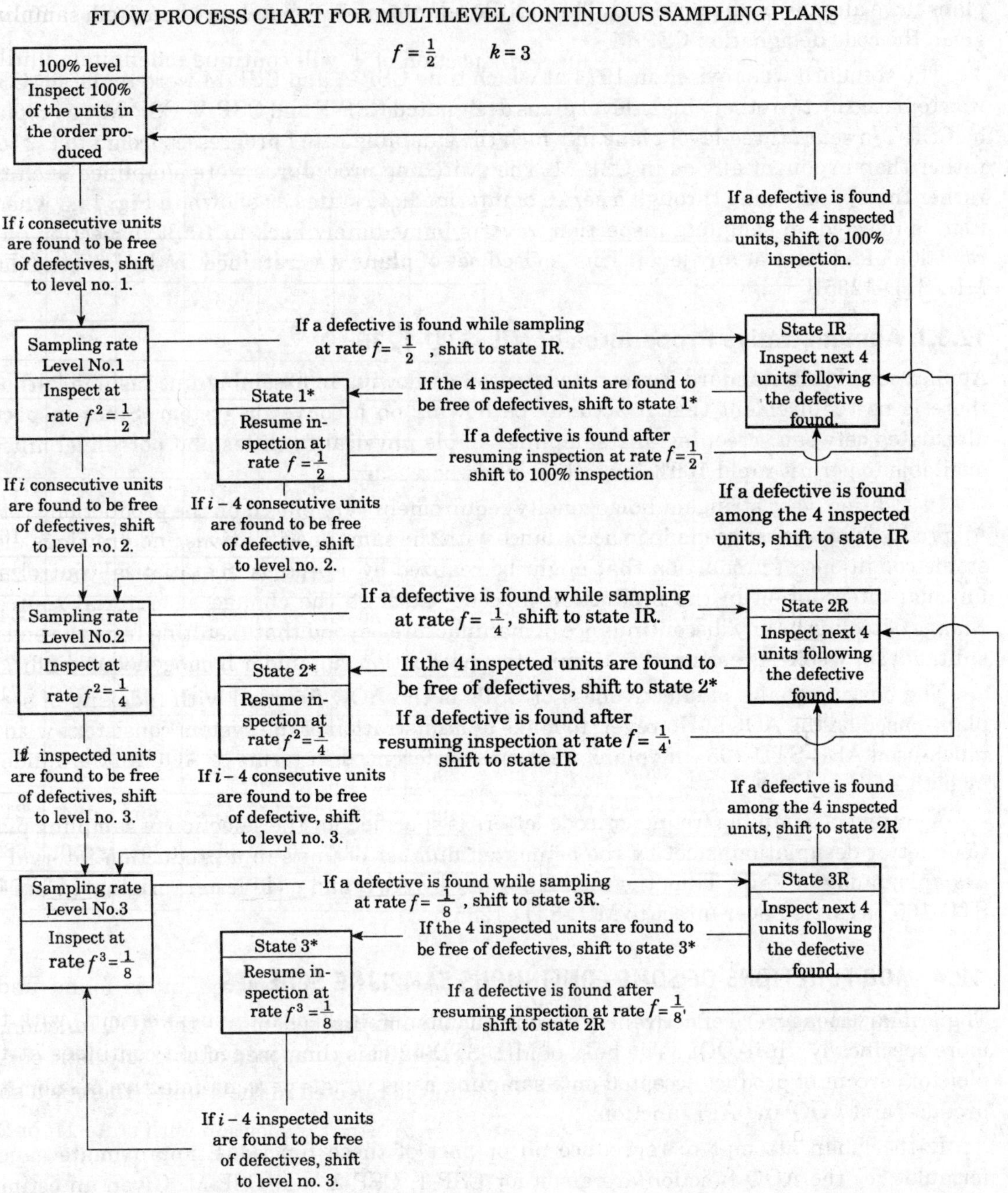

FIGURE 12.3 Example of rules for operating the multilevel continuous sampling plans of Table 12.2, assuming a three-level plan with $f = \frac{1}{2}$

designated CSP-A. Most of the operating procedures of CSP-1 and CSP-2 were identical with those previously discussed with the single exception of a provision for terminating acceptance altogether when 100% (screening) inspection continues for too great a period of time. In 1962 the Handbooks H 106 and H 107 were combined into a single document designated MIL-STD- 1235

(ORD); however H 106 and H 107 continued in use. The main procedural features of these plans have already been presented. The multilevel continuous sampling plans from H 106 were given the code designation CSP-M.

The standard was revised in 1974 at which time CSP-A and CSP-M were replaced. CSP-A was replaced by two other single-level plans designated CSP-F and CSP-V. CSP-M was replaced by CSP-T, a set of three-level plans in which the sampling rate f progresses from f to f /2 to f /4 rather than exponentially as in CSP-M. The switching procedures were simplified such that, rather than progressing through a series of intermediate states as shown in Fig. 12.3 when an item is rejected on sampling inspection, reverts immediately back to 100% inspection on the rejection of an item at any level. This revised set of plans was retained in the latest revision, MIL-STD-1235B.

12.3.1 Administrative Procedures of MIL-STD-1235

Application of this standard is restricted to product flowing in assembly-line fashion, although there is no requirement that it actually be flowing on a conveyor system. Since inspection alternates between screening and sampling, ample physical facilities and personnel must be available to permit rapid 100% inspection when necessary.

In addition, very stringent homogeneity requirements are placed on the production system. All product units must be made in accordance with the same specifications and drawings under stable conditions of production that might be realized by a process in statistical control. Any unusual interruption in the production process—such as the change of material source or change of tooling or any discontinuance of manufacture beyond that resulting from the end of a shift, day, or week—is assumed to terminate a production run under homogeneous conditions.

The basic measure of effectiveness of CSPs is the AOQ function with indexing of sets of plans based on the AOQL. However, to make administration of the system consistent with the much-used ABC-STD-105, the plans were cross-referenced in terms of AQL and are indexed by both AQL and AOQL.

A system of sampling frequency code letters is specified for the selection of sampling plans. Code letter designation is set by the estimated number of units in a production interval, for example, a day or shift. Thus the matrix format by AQL and code letter, originated in MIL-STD-105, is carried over intact to MIL-STD-1235.

12.4 AOQ FUNCTIONS OF SOME CONTINUOUS SAMPLING SCHEMES

The primary measure of effectiveness of continuous sampling schemes is the AOQ function, or, more specifically, the AOQL. The bulk of MIL-STD-1235 is composed of characteristic curves, plots of percent of product accepted on a sampling basis versus percent defective of submitted product, and AOQ and AFI functions.

Rather than attempt to reproduce all or part of these functions, approximate general formulae for the AOQ function are given for CSP-1, CSP-2, and CSP-M. Given an estimate of the process average μ_p, the following formulae may be used to determine the approximate AOQ of product :

CSP-1: $$AOQ = \frac{p(1-f)q^{i-1}}{f+(1-f)q^{i-1}}$$

where p = fraction nonconforming

$q = (1 - p)$

CSP-2: $$\text{AOQ} = \frac{p(1-f)(2q^i - q^{2i})}{fq + (1-f)(2q^i - q^{2i})}$$

CSP-M: $$\text{AOQ} = p\,\frac{\displaystyle\sum_{j=1}^{k}\left(\frac{1}{f_j}-1\right)\left(\frac{q^i}{1-q}\right)^j}{\displaystyle\sum_{j=0}^{k}\left(\frac{1}{f_j}\right)\left(\frac{q^i}{1-q^i}\right)^j}$$

where j = indexes over the number of inspection levels in the plan

k = maximum number of inspection levels in the plan

12.5 SKIP-LOT SAMPLING

Skip-lot sampling, developed by Harold Dodge, is a variation on continuous sampling wherein the inspection unit is a lot or batch rather than an individual item. It may be particularly useful as a quality audit procedure of supplier's material where JIT inventory management is used and receiving lots are small or where inspection is slow and costly. As is the case with chain sampling, discussed in Chap. 11, skip-lot sampling is heavily dependent on the assumption of homogeneity among lots and a good quality history. Thus it is unlikely to give satisfactory results if applied to lots coming from erratic and uncontrolled processes.

Under the plan designated SkSP-1, consecutive lots are 100% inspected until i have been found free of nonconforming items. At this point, inspection shifts to a proportion f of the lots received. As usual, the order of production of the lots must be maintained and lots inspected in that order. The values of i and f are selected from some continuous sampling system such as CSP-1, CSP-2, or CSP-M.

Under SkSP-2, rather than performing 100% inspection on each lot inspected, a *reference sampling plan* is chosen (perhaps from ABC-STD-105 or one of the Dodge-Romig systems), and each lot designated for inspection is subjected to the reference sampling plan. Under either SkSP plan the AOQL is taken to be the AOQL of the continuous sampling plan adopted. The value of the AOQL applies to the long-run average quality of lots.

12.6 FURTHER COMMENT ON CONTINUOUS SAMPLING PLANS

Various other types of continuous sampling AOQL plans may be developed. Some plans start with sampling inspection rather than with 100% inspection. These plans, in effect, give a process credit for such good quality as has been shown in past samples and base the decision regarding the shift from sampling inspection to 100% inspection on cumulative evidence from past samples.

As in all acceptance/rectification schemes, a necessary condition for the successful use of continuous sampling schemes is that the submitted quality should be good enough for most product to be passed without screening. The sampling is intended to give protection against runs of bad quality. If the protection against short runs of bad quality (so-called spotty quality) is to be satisfactory, the sample percentage f should not be too low. The relative weakness of small values of f in this respect is brought out by the scale on the right-hand side of Fig. 12.1 showing values of $p_{0.10}$.

Mention should be made of the practical difference between lot-by-lot acceptance/rectification schemes and most continuous sampling schemes. In lot-by-lot schemes, an infavourable sample from a lot results in the screening inspection of that particular lot. In continuous sampling, a bad sample calls for the screening of subsequent production. In effect, the sample is considered as representative of the production process, and 100% inspection is applied to later articles from the same process. In some instances, where the physical conditions of production permit, a modification of continuous sampling procedures is made to require screening inspection applied to a specified number of units immediately preceding a defective sample.

12.7 UNIQUE FEATURES OF CSP PLANS AS GUIDES FOR SPC SAMPLING

Much of the data collection performed for statistical process control is done on a sampling basis. With the single exception of inspection of critical characteristics, it simply does not make economic sense to conduct 100% inspection of all dimensions and characteristics of production and service processes. This condition is reflected in many of the examples discussed in Parts One and Two of this book.

The procedures discussed in this chapter afford person concerned with statistical process control a quantitative basis on which to determine sampling frequencies and procedures. That important measure of quality protection is the AOQL. Aspects of continuous sampling may be combined with sample sizes chosen from any of the attribute or variables sampling systems discussed in this book, as was discussed in the section dealing with skip-lot sampling, to provide a scientifically justifiable procedure for process control charting.

SOLVED QUESTIONS

Q. 12.1: *In Dodge's CSP-1 it is desired to apply sampling inspection to 1 piece out of every 15 and to maintain an AOQL of 2%. What should be the value of i ? What will be the effect of increasing f on i when AOQL remains the same ?*

Ans: Figure 12.1 can be used for finding i, the clearance number. For using Fig 12.1, % f and AOQL are required.

$$\% f = \frac{1}{15} \times 100 = 6.66$$

AOQL = 2%.

These parameters give the clearance number of 68. Figure 12.1 clearly indicates that with the increase of f the clearance number i decreases for the same AOQL.

Q. 12.2: *In CSP-2 (popularly known as Dodge-Torrey CSP-2), it is desired to apply sampling inspection 1 piece out of every 10 and to maintain an AOQL of 4%. What should be the value of i ?*

Ans: This problem can be solved if we have curves similar to Fig. 12.1 for CSP-2. But the data given in the problem can be analyzed with help of Table 12.1, which shows that for $f = \frac{1}{10}$ and AOQL of 4%,

$$i = 36$$

Q. 12.3: *In the the Dodge-Torrey CSP-3, it is desired to apply sampling inspection to 1 piece out of every 10 and to maintain an AOQL of 5%. Give detailed rules for the operation of the continuous sampling plan.*

Ans: In CSP-3, the value of i used for a given f and AOQL is the same as in CSP-2. Therefore, using Table 12.1, for $f = \frac{1}{10}$ and an AOQL of 5%, the value of $i = 29$.

Operation of the sampling plan. The operation of this sampling plan is similar to Fig. 12.2 (*c*) except that once after starting sampling inspection, when one sample defective is found, the next 4 units from the production line are inspected. If none of these are defective, the sampling procedure is continued as in CSP-2. If one of four units is defective, 100% inspection is resumed at once and continued under the rules of CSP-2. In CSP-3, the value of i used for a given f and AOQL is the same as in CSP-2.

Q. 12.4: *Select from Table 12.2 a four-level continuous sampling plan for an AOQL of 1.0% and an f of $\frac{1}{3}$. If a defective is found shortly after the third level is reached, describe how the plan would operate ?*

Ans: From Table 12.2, for an *AOQL* of 1.0% and $f = \frac{1}{2}$ and $k = 4$, the value of $i = 95$. Figure 12.4 clearly indicates the operation of the plan. At the third stage, we must be inspecting at the rate of $f = \left(\frac{1}{2}\right)^3$, *i.e.* 1 out of every 8 units. If a defective is found while inspecting this level, inspect immediately the next 4 units following the defective found. If the next 4 units are found to be O.K. shift to state 3, *i.e.*, resume the inspection at the rate of $f^3 = \frac{1}{8}$. If now $(i - 4)$, *i.e.* $(95 - 4)$ = 91 units are found to be free of defectives, shift to level 3, *i.e.*, inspect at the rate of $f^3 = \frac{1}{8}$.

If a defective is found in the 4 inspected units or while inspecting at state 3, return to state 2 *R*. Repeat the same as stated above except that at the state 2 and state 2 *R*, the inspection will be at the rate of $f^2 = \frac{1}{4}$ and so on.

Q. 12.5: *It is desired to apply continuous sampling inspection to 1 piece out of every 10 and to maintain a AOQL of 2%.*

(*a*) *Find the value of i for applying Dodge's CSP-1.*

(*b*) *Find the values of i and k for applying Dodge's CSP-2.*

(*c*) *Prepare flow charts of the operation of these plans.*

(*d*) *For the plans found for (a) and (b) compute AOQ when the process is generating 3% nonconforming product.*

Ans: (*a*) CSP-1 from Table 12.1, for f of $\frac{1}{10}$ and *AOQL* of 2% $i = 55$.

(*b*) For CSP-2 from Table 12.1 for f of $\frac{1}{10}$ and *AOQL* of 2% $i = 72$.

(*c*) The flow charts are as per Fig. 12.2 (*a*) and (*b*) respectively where i is 55 and 72 respectively.

(*d*) $p = 0.03$, $q = 1 - 0.03$ *i.e.* 0.97

For CSP-1:
$$\text{AOQ\%} = \frac{0.03\left(1 - \frac{1}{10}\right)(0.97)^{55-1}}{\left(\frac{1}{10}\right) + \left(1 - \frac{1}{10}\right)(0.97)^{55-1}} \times 100$$

$$= 1.90$$

Similarly for CSP-2: AOQ% = 1.99.

CHAPTER

13

Acceptance Sampling by Variables

13.1 SOME ADVANTAGES AND LIMITATIONS OF ACCEPTANCE SAMPLING BY VARIABLES

Thus far we have discussed acceptance sampling by attributes. The latter is based on the classification of an inspected item as either acceptable or defective. Present day industrial practice of acceptance sampling is by attributes and will doubtless continue to be so. Nevertheless, the growth of knowledge of statistical quality control techniques has led to a considerable increase in the industrial use of acceptance sampling by variables. It seems likely that this tendency will continue.

One obvious limitation on the use of variables criteria in acceptance sampling is the fact that many quality characteristics are observable only as attributes. Examples of characteristics that can be observed as attributes are :

1. The presence or absence of a required marking on a fabricated item.
2. The diameter of a metal rod using "Go and Not Go" gauge.

Clearly in such cases, sampling by variables is out of question. Nevertheless, it often turns out to be possible to devise methods of measurement in cases where at first glance it seems that inspection must be by attributes.

For quality characteristics such as temperature rise of an electrical component or the leakage current through insulation, which are obviously measurable, it is usually true that the cost of inspection per item is less by attributes than by variables. Often this is due to greater economy of inspection methods using the Go and Not Go principle. Moreover, clerical costs are usually less with attributes inspection ; it is less expensive to record merely the conformance or nonconformance to specifications than to record an actual measured value and to make computations using that value.

Perhaps the most serious *limitation* on the use of sampling by variables is the fact that acceptance criteria must be applied separately to each quality characteristic. This tends to increase the cost of acceptance inspection. For example, if 10 quality characteristics of a product are to examined at a given inspection station, a single set of attributes sampling criteria can be applied to the acceptance decision. In contrast, if each characteristic is subjected to variables inspection, 10 different sets of variables criteria must be used.

An *additional limitation* on certain types of variables criteria exists in that the computed protection against various percentages of defectives depends on an assumption regarding the form of the underlying frequency distribution of the quality characteristic. This limitation is discussed near the end of this chapter.

In spite of the foregoing limitations, acceptance sampling by variables is often preferable to acceptance sampling by attributes, particularly for those quality characteristics that are the source of troubles. Possibly only 2 of the 10 characteristics mentioned in the preceding paragraph may turn out to be troublesome. If so, it may be that variables criteria can be applied profitably to these even though attributes criteria are used for the remaining 8.

The great advantage of the use of acceptance sampling by variables is that more information is obtained about the quality characteristic is question. This may lead to a number of desirable results, as follows :

1. For a given sample size, better quality protection may usually be obtained with variables criteria than with attributes. Or, stated a little differently, for a given quality protection against various possible percentages of defectives (as reflected in the OC curve) smaller samples may be used with variables than with attributes.
2. The extent of conformance or nonconformance to the desired value of a quality characteristic is given weight where variables criteria are used. This may be important wherever there is a margin of safety in the design specifications or a twilight zone of values of the quality characteristic between clearly satisfactory and clearly unsatisfactory.
3. Variables information usually gives a better basis for guidance toward quality improvement.
4. Variables information may provide a better basis for giving weight to quality history in acceptance decisions.
5. Errors of measurement are more likely to be disclosed with variables informations.

13.2 SOME DIFFERENT TYPES OF ACCEPTANCE CRITERIA INVOLVING VARIABLES

There are many different ways in which the actual measured values of quality characteristics in a sample can be used to influence decisions on acceptance of submitted product. The following general classification of types of variables criteria is intended to provide a convenient basis for discussion of the subject :

1. Criteria in which the decision depends in some way on the frequency distribution of the sample. The Shainin Lot Plot is the example of this type of plan.
2. Criteria using a control chart for variables to divide a series of consecutive inspection lots into "grand lots" with acceptance criteria applied to each grand lot.
3. Criteria in which the decision on acceptance or rejection of a lot is based on the sample average alone. Plans using such criteria may be referred to as *known-sigma* plans or plans with *variability known.*
4. Criteria in which the decision is based on the sample average in combination with a measure of sample dispersion. Such plans may be referred to as *unknown-sigma* or as having *variability unknown.*

Sometimes there are legal or other reasons why variables criteria should not be used for lot rejection even though such criteria are appropriate for lot acceptance. This condition may lead to some combination of variables and attributes criteria. This topic is examined following the discussion of known-sigma and unknown-sigma plans.

13.3 USING PLOTTED FREQUENCY DISTRIBUTION IN ACCEPTANCE SAMPLING

In the technical language of inspection, an article is defective if it fails to conform to specifications. A slight departure beyond specification limits makes the article defective ; so, also, does a large departure beyond the limits. This definition of a defective gives no weight to the extent of the nonconformity to specifications.

Nevertheless, the extent of nonconformity may be a matter of great practical importance. Consider any measurable quality characteristic on which the designer has specified upper and lower limits. There frequently is a twilight zone of values just outside one or both specification limits within which it is satisfactory to accept a moderate percentage of "defective" articles.

In many manufacturing plants, it is common for some purchased lots to be rejected initially under the regular acceptance procedures and then finally to be accepted under some sort of material-review procedure. Sometimes there is a highly formalized procedure involving a material-review board ; in other cases material review may be quite an informal matter, involving a decision by some one individual. In any event, the extent of nonconformity to specifications is usually given consideration in material-review decisions. Extra costs may be avoided and interruptions of production may be prevented by using material-review procedures to accept a product that is good enough for the purpose at hand, even though it is technically nonconforming to specifications.

Where sample frequency distributions for certain quality characteristics are plotted as part of the regular acceptance procedures, one objective usually is the provision of a more rational basis for material review. The frequency distribution is a great aid to judgment on the question of the extent of nonconformity to specifications.

Moreover, the frequency distribution has the advantage that it may disclose certain common types of departure from normality, such as skewed distributions, bimodal distributions, distributions with cut-off points, and distributions containing strays at some distance from the main distribution. The larger the sample, the better the chance to recognize such non-normal distributions when they occur, and the less the danger that a sample really taken from a normal distribution will give a false indication of non-normality.

13.3.1 The Shainin Lot Plot Method

The Shainin lot plot plan is a variable sampling plan used in many industries. It was developed by Dorian Shainin while he was Chief Inspector at Hamilton Standard Division of United Aircraft Corporation. The plan uses a plotted frequency distribution to evaluate a sample for decisions concerning acceptance or rejection of a lot. The most significant feature of the plan is the fact that it is applicable to both normal and non-normal frequency distributions. It is a practical plan for in-house inspection as well as receiving inspection. The method for obtaining the lot plots is as follows :

1. In the lot plot method, the sample size always is 50. Table 13.1 shows the inspection results for such a sample.
2. Five pieces are selected from the original 50 and inspected. The mean, $\bar{X}$, and range R, are obtained from the values of the 5 pieces, which are shown in column 1 of Table 13.1. Calculations are as follows :

$$\bar{X} = \frac{\Sigma X}{n} = \frac{96.75 + 97.78 + 98.42 + 97.41 + 97.08}{5} = 97.49$$

$$R = X_{max} - X_{min} = 98.42 - 96.75 = 1.67.$$

TABLE 13.1 RANDOM SAMPLE OF 50 IN SUBGROUPS OF 5
(Data for the width of a brass plate, in millimeters)

1	2	3	4	5	6	7	8	9	10
96.75	97.04	98.03	97.80	97.54	98.55	98.30	98.28	97.95	97.48
97.78	98.34	99.09	97.24	96.70	97.11	97.70	97.95	97.79	96.55
98.42	97.28	98.32	97.68	98.12	96.81	97.62	97.85	97.80	96.98
97.41	96.52	97.59	98.01	96.69	97.60	98.86	98.10	97.17	97.35
97.08	97.86	97.79	97.48	96.98	96.24	98.04	98.80	98.35	98.48

3. The mean of the subgroup of 5 is established as the assumed mean $\bar{X}_0$, for construction of the frequency distribution and is taken as 97.50. A simple procedure is used to determine the cell interval and the number of cells using the first subgroup of 5. The range of the lot is assumed to be twice the first range and is $2R = 2(1.67) = 3.34$. Knowing the lot range, the cell interval and the number of cells are obtained as discussed in chapter 2. The plan states that the number of cells should be between 7 and 16. Assuming the cell interval to be 0.25, the number of cells in this becomes 13. Since the required number of cells is to be between 7 and 16, the cell interval of 0.25 is satisfactory.
4. The cell midpoint values of the frequency distribution of Fig. 13.1 are established using the assumed mean $\bar{X}_0 = 97.50$ and the cell interval, $i = 0.25$. The figures are shown in the first column. Column 2 of Fig. 13.1 gives the deviation in cell units of the cell mid points from the assumed mean. If the cell mid-point is greater than $\bar{X}_0$, the deviation in cell units is positive ; if less than $\bar{X}_0$, the deviation in cell units is negative.
5. The first subgroup of 5 is recorded on the frequency distribution with the number 1. Additional subgroups of 5 each are inspected and recorded with the appropriate number.
6. For each subgroup of 5, the sum, mean, and range in cell units are recorded in the columns to the right of the frequency distribution. The totals of the subgroup means and ranges are divided by 10, the number of subgroups, to obtain $\bar{\bar{X}} = 0.70$ in cell units from $\bar{X}_0$ and $\bar{R} = 6.5$. The lot mean is shown in Fig. 13.1.
7. Using these values, the upper lot limit and lower lot limit in cell units are calculated as follows :

$$\text{ULL} = \bar{\bar{X}} + 3\frac{\bar{R}}{d_2} \qquad \text{LLL} = \bar{\bar{X}} - 3\frac{\bar{R}}{d_2} \qquad ...(13.1)$$

$$= 0.70 + \frac{(3)(6.5)}{2.325} \qquad = 0.70 - \frac{(3)(6.5)}{2.325}$$

$$= 9.08 \text{ cell units} \qquad = -7.68 \text{ cell units}$$

Midpoint	Cell deviation	Distribution
	+ 10	---------------------- ULL
	+ 9	
	+ 8	
	+ 7	
99.00	+ 6	3
98.75	+ 5	7 8
98.50	+ 4	1 6 10
98.25	+ 3	2 3 6 7 8 9
98.00	+ 2	3 4 5 7 8 8 9
97.75	+ 1	1 2 3 4 4 7 8 9 9 ---- $\overline{\overline{X}}$
97.50	0	1 3 4 5 6 7 10
97.25	− 1	2 4 9 10
97.00	− 2	1 2 5 6 10
96.75	− 3	1 5 5 6
96.50	− 4	2 10
96.25	− 5	
96.00	− 6	
	− 7	
	− 8	---------------------- LLL
	− 9	
	− 10	

	Values in cell units		
No	Sum	$\overline{X}$	R
1	0	0	8
2	− 3	-0.6	8
3	12	2.4	7
4	3	0.6	4
5	− 6	-1.2	6
6	2	0.4	8
7	11	2.2	6
8	13	2.6	4
9	6	1.2	5
10	− 3	-0.6	9
Totals		70	65
Average		0.70	6.5

FIGURE 13.1 Example of lot pot for width of brass plate

In Fig. 13.1 it is clear that the spread of the process somewhat less than the spread of the lot limits and that the process is centered midway between the lot limits.

Once the lot plot and the lot limits are obtained, the decision concerning acceptance or rejection is made. This decision is based on a comparison of the lot plot with 11 different types of lot plot which are shown in Fig. 13.2.

The first four types are applicable to lot plots which are approximately normally distributed. In the Type 1 situation, the lot plot is well within specification limits, and the lot is accepted without the need to calculate the lot limits. If the lot limits are within the specification, as illustrated by Type 2, the lot is accepted. When the lot limits are outside the specification as shown by Types 3 and 4, the percentage of product beyond specifications is obtained and review board determines the final disposition of th stock. In some cases an attribute plan is employed to determine the lot acceptability when one or two values are beyond the lot limits.

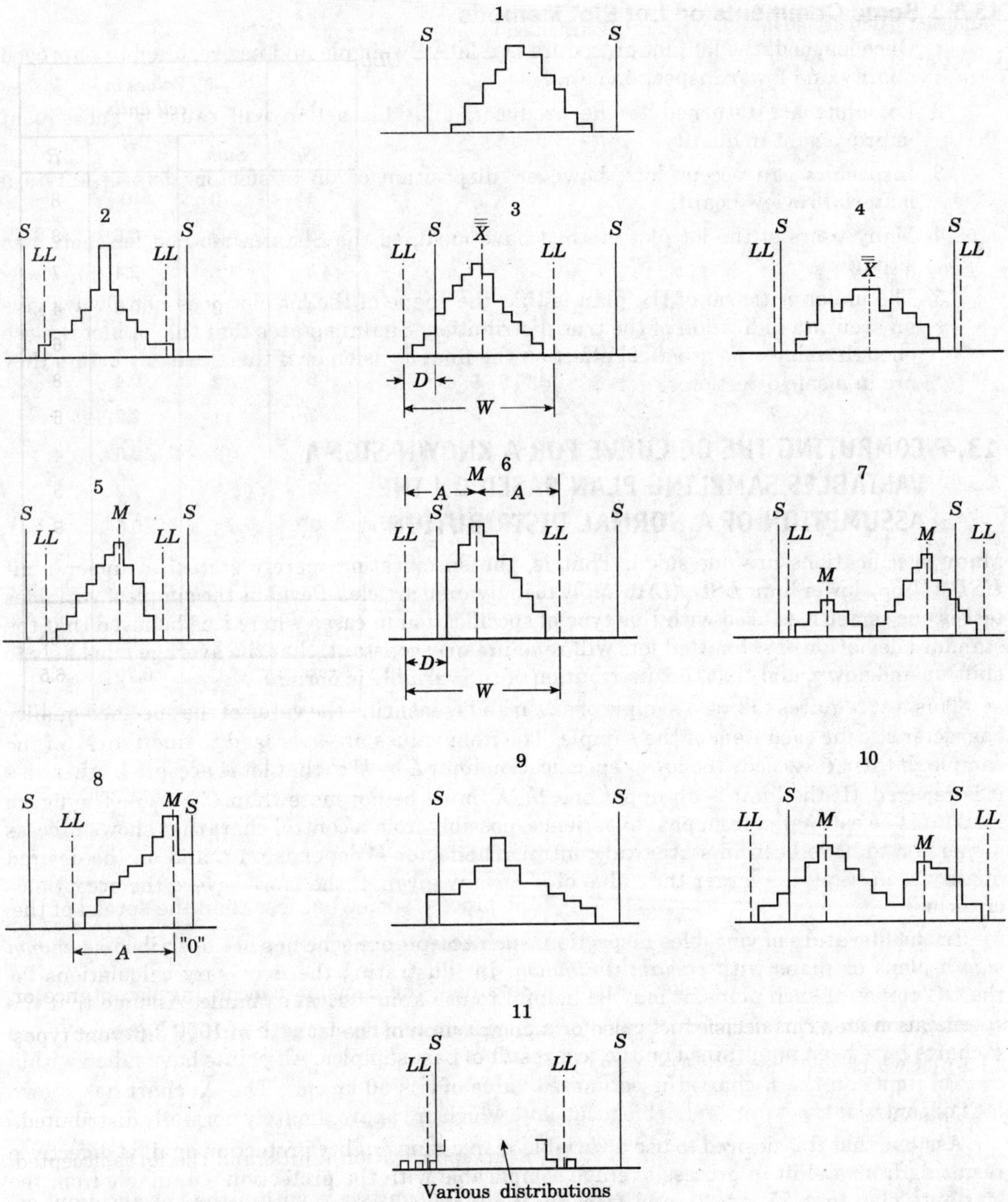

FIGURE 13.2 Eleven different types of lot plots

The other types of lot plots are used for non-normal distributions. For example Type 5 is skewed ; Types 6 and 9 indicate that the lot was screened or sorted ; Types 7 and 10 illustrate the bimodal condition ; and Type 11 is for stray values. Special techniques are specified for analyzing the non-normal lot plots.

13.3.2 Some Comments on Lot Plot Methods

1. Once learned, the lot plot procedure is relatively simple and has resulted in improved quality and lower inspection costs.
2. Lot plots are returned to the producer, and this action will cause a subsequent improvement in quality.
3. Inspectors can accept lots, however, disposition of unsatisfactory lots is left to a material-review board.
4. Many users of the lot plot method have modified the Shainin method for their own situation.
5. The major criticism of the plan is that the shape of the lot plot does not always give an accurate indication of the true distribution. Shainin states that the lot plot is close enough to have no practical effect on the final decision or if there are any errors they are in a safe direction.

13.4 COMPUTING THE OC CURVE FOR A KNOWN-SIGMA VARIABLES SAMPLING PLAN BASED ON THE ASSUMPTION OF A NORMAL DISTRIBUTION

Many specifications are one-sided. That is, the specification merely states an upper limit $USL_X(U)$ or a lower limit $LSL_X(L)$ to apply to individual articles. Perhaps the simplest variables test is one sometimes used with this type of specification in cases where it is believed that the standard deviation of submitted lots will remain fairly constant, that the average μ is likely to shift up and down, and that the distribution of the variable is normal.

This test requires taking a sample of size n and measuring the value of the specified quality characteristic for each item of the sample. The item values are averaged to find the $\bar{X}$ of the sample. If this $\bar{X}$ exceeds the lower specification limit L by $k'\sigma$, that lot is accepted; otherwise it is rejected. (If the limit is an upper one U, $\bar{X}$ must be not more than $U - k'\sigma$). The figure for σ must be estimated from past experience, possibly from a control chart that shows process dispersion to have been in statistical control. The factor k' depends on n and on the desired quality protection; the larger the value of k' for any given n, the more severe the acceptance criteria.

In the literature of variables inspection, such acceptance schemes are described as *known sigma* plans or plans with *variability known*. In illustrating the necessary calculations for the OC curves of such plans, it may be helpful to use a numerical example. Assume that the specification for a certain product calls for a minimum tensile strength of 1000 kg/cm^2. $\bar{X}$ and R charts have been maintained on the test result of past samples. All points have fallen within control limits on the R chart; the estimated value of σ is 50 kg/cm^2. The $\bar{X}$ chart has shown lack of control.

Assume that it is desired to use a variable plan giving quality protection against defectives resulting from a shift in process average comparable with the protection obtainable from the attribute plan (n = 75, c = 2), and from the equivalent double and multiple plans shown in Chap. 9. In their volume on variables acceptance inspection, Bowker and Goode give values of n and k' for known-sigma variables plans that have OC curves corresponding fairly well to many different attributes plans. To match the attributes plan of (n = 75 c = 2), n is given as 16 and k' 1.846. In our particular example this means that the average tensile strength of a sample of 16 test specimens should be at least

$$1{,}000 + 1.846\ (50) = 1{,}092.3 \text{ kg/cm}^2$$

It is not possible to compute an OC curve for such an acceptance plan without making some assumption about the frequency distribution of the quality characteristic in question. The OC curve for this plan that was shown in Fig. 9.9 is based on the assumption of a normal distribution. Figure 13.3 illustrates the calculation of the probability of acceptance of 2.5% defective product. It shows the frequency distribution of individual values and the frequency distribution of averages of samples of 16 when 2.5% of the product falls below the lower specification limit. In this calculation, two questions must be answered. (In the following explanation, μ refers to product average and $\overline{\ }$ to the average of a sample of size n.)

1. *What is μ for the particular percent nonconforming ?* Consult Table A, App. 1 to find the value of $z = (\overline{X}_i - \mu)/\sigma$ corresponding to an area of 0.0250. This table shows that 2.5% of a normal distribution falls below the value $\mu - 1.96\ \sigma$. If 2.5% of the product falls below and lower specification limit L, then μ must be $L + 1.96\ \sigma$. Hence as L is 1,000 kg/cm² and σ is 50 kg/cm²,

$$\mu = 1098.0 \text{ km/cm}^2$$

2. With μ at this figure, what proportion of the $\overline{X}$ distribution will fall above the minimum allowable value of $\overline{X}$? The difference between μ and the minimum $\overline{X}$ must be computed. This is 1098.0 – 1092.3 = 5.7 kg/cm². The standard deviation of $\overline{X}$ must be computed. In this case

$$\sigma_{\overline{X}} = \frac{\sigma}{\sqrt{n}} = \frac{50}{\sqrt{16}} = 12.5 \text{ kg/cm}^2$$

The value 5.7 kg/cm² is 0.456 $\sigma_{\overline{X}}$. Interpolation in Table A shows that 0.6758 of a normal distribution in above the value $\mu - 0.456\ \sigma$. It follows that the probability of acceptance is 0.6758 or approximately 0.68.

Although the preceding calculation used numerical values of L and σ for purposes of illustration, the computed probability of acceptance is, of course, independent of these values and depends only on n and k'.

If K is the minimum allowable $\overline{X}$ value, then, in general, for a lower specification

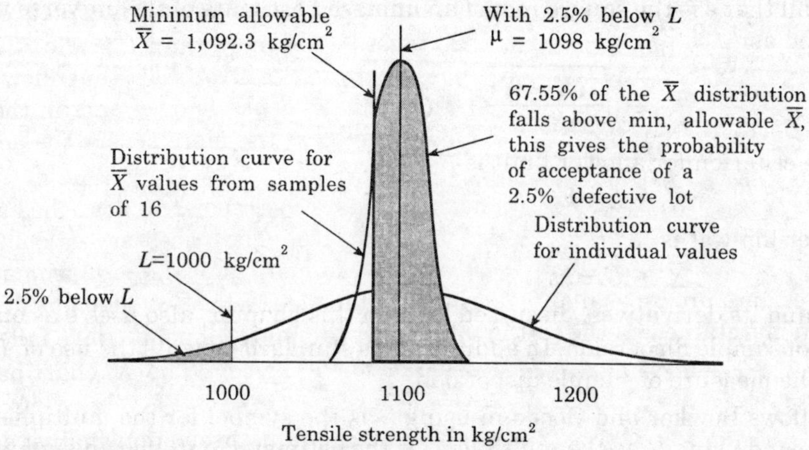

FIGURE 13.3 Diagram illustrating the calculation of the probability of accepting 2.5% defective product under the known-sigma plan n = 16, k' = 1.846.

$$K = L + k'\sigma \quad \text{...(13.2)}$$

For any descried fraction nonconforming μ_p, the mean of the distribution must be

$$\mu = L + Z_p\,\sigma \quad \text{...(13.3)}$$

One advantage of variables sampling is the use of smaller sizes to obtain the same quality protection against a particular type of trouble. In the preceding example, the variables sample was 16 whereas the attributes single sample was 75.

13.4.1 Some Aspects of Unknown-Sigma Variables Sampling Plans Based on the Assumption of a Normal Distribution

The known-sigma plan illustrated in Fig. 13.3 specified a minimum allowable $\bar{X}$ of 1,092.3 kg/cm^2 for a sample of 16. This minimum $\bar{X}$ was computed by adding 1.846σ to the L of 1,000 kg/cm^2 using an estimate that σ was 50 kg/cm^2. If it had been estimated that σ was only, say 10 kg/cm^2, the same OC curve would have been obtained by specifying a minimum $\bar{X}$ of only, 1,018.5 kg/cm^2 for a sample of 16. The smaller the estimate of σ, the closer $\bar{X}$ could be to L. The general relationship among the centering of a process (or lot), its dispersion, a single specification limit, and the fraction nonconforming were first discussed in Chap. 3.

Assume that it is desired to design a variables acceptance plan for a stipulated sample size n and a specified L of 1,000 kg/cm^2. Assume that nothing is known about the σ of the product sampled. Obviously it is necessary to use some measure of sample dispersion to estimate σ. Conceivably this measure might be the s or R of the sample, or if the samples is to be divided into two or more subsamples, $\bar{R}$ may be used. Because σ is unknown, it is not possible to specify any single minimum value of the sample $\bar{X}$ such as 1092.3 or 1018.5 kg/cm^2. In effect, the specification has to be that $\bar{X}$ must exceed L by a stated multiple of some chosen measure of the sample dispersion.

Bowker and Goode's *Sampling Inspection* by *Variables*, already mentioned, is the pioneer treatise on variables sampling plans in which computed OC curve are based on the assumption of a normal distribution. This volume contains a large number of known-sigma and unknown sigma plans having OC curves matched to those of the attributes plans given in the Columbia Statistical Research Group's volume *Sampling Inspection*, mentioned in Chaps. 9 and 10. Bowker and Goode give OC curves for all their unknown-sigma plans based on one-sided specifications.

The unknown-sigma plans in Bowker and Goode use s as the measure of sample dispersion. The reader will recall that s is the square root of an unbiased estimate of the universe variance and that it is defined as

$$s = \sqrt{\frac{\Sigma(X - \bar{X})}{n-1}}$$

The acceptance criterion for a lower limit is

$$\bar{X} \geq L + ks \quad \text{...(13.4)}$$

and for an upper limit, it is

$$\bar{X} \leq U - ks \quad \text{...(13.5)}$$

MIL-STD-414 and its derivatives, discussed later in this chapter, also uses s as one of the possible measures of sample dispersion. In addition, this standard permits the use of $\bar{R}$ (or, in some cases, R) as the measure of sample dispersion.

Our chapter follows Bowker and Goode in using k as the symbol for the multiplier of s in known-sigma plans and using k' as the multiplier for the estimated σ in known-sigma plans.

Where σ may have only one value (such as the 50 kg/cm^2 in Fig. 13.3), there is only one value of μ that will correspond to any particular percent nonconforming in the case of a one-sided specification (such as the 2.5% defective in Fig. 13.3). In contrast, if σ may have any value, there are an infinite number of values of $\bar{X}$ that will correspond to, say, 2.5% nonconforming; each σ will have a different μ for 2.5% nonconforming. It follows that the mathematics of computing OC curves for unknown-sigma plans is more complicated than for known-sigma plans. To compute an OC curve for an unknown-sigma plan, it is necessary to use certain probability distributions not discussed in this book. A simple explanation of the computation of such curves along the lines of Fig. 13.3 is not possible for unknown-sigma plans. Nevertheless, anyone who understands the explanation of Fig. 13.3 can doubtless also see the general reasoning that must underlie the calculation of an OC curve for an unknown-sigma plan.

13.4.2 Known-Sigma and Unknown-sigma Plans for Two-Sided Specifications

Where both an upper limit U and a lower limit L are specified for the quality characteristic and the distribution is normal, the ability of a process to make product meeting specifications depends on the relationship between $U - L$ and the spread of the process, often assumed as 6σ. It also depends on the centering of the process. This point was brought out in Chap. 3.

Where $U - L$ is substantially greater than the spread of the process —say 8.0σ or more and the distribution in a lot is normal, both specification limits will not be exceeded in a single lot. It follows that where a known-sigma plan is used with such relatively loose tolerances, the OC curve of the plan can be computed as if the specification were one-sided in the way illustrated in our discussion of Fig. 13.3. The only difference in the acceptance criterion from the case of the one-sided specification is that there are now two limits on the permissible value of the sample average; $\bar{X}$ may not exceed $U - k'\sigma$ and may not fall below $L + k'\sigma$.

The matter is more complicated in the cases where the tolerances are tight in relation to the process capability. Here some rejects are sure to be produced. For instance, with a normal distribution there will be 0.27% nonconforming even than $U - L = 6\sigma$. The minimum percentage of rejects will occur when the process is centered midway between U and L. With this centering and such tight tolerances, some rejects will be produced above the upper specification limit and others below the lower limit. It follows that in calculating the OC curve for a known-sigma variables acceptance plan for a two-sided specification with tight tolerances, it is necessary to compute percentages of defectives in both tails of the frequency distribution. Except for this need of considering both tails of the distribution, such calculations follow the lines explained in discussion of Fig. 13.3.

Bowker and Goode give values of n and a coefficient designated as k'^* for known-sigma variables plans for two-sided specifications assuming a normal distribution. These plans are to be used where the tolerances are tight in reference to process capability. With these plans, $\bar{X}$ may not exceed $U - k'^*\sigma$ or fall below $L + k'^*\sigma$. Like the other types of variables plans in the Bowker-Goode volume, a plan is provided to match the OC curve of each of the attributes plans in "Sampling Inspection".

Whenever unknown-sigma plans are used for two-sided specifications, the uncertainty regarding σ *always* makes it necessary to consider the possibility of defectives in both tails of the distribution. Procedures in connection with such plans are discussed briefly in our explanation of MIL-STD-414.

13.4.3 Use of the Estimated Lot Percentage Nonconforming in Acceptance-Sampling by Variables.

If one *knew* the μ and σ of a lot and also *knew* that the frequency distribution in the lot was normal, the exact percentage of the lot outside any specification limit could be computed. Similarly, if the $\bar{X}$ of the lot is estimated from the μ of the sample, and if it is assumed that the σ of the lot is known, or if σ is estimated from some measure of sample dispersion, and if the lot is assumed to be normal, it is possible to make an estimate of lot percentage nonconforming. Of course, any such estimate is subject to sampling errors.

We have discussed acceptance criteria in known-sigma and unknown-sigma variables plans that are expressed in terms of the relationship between the sample average and the specification limits. If a normal distribution in the lot is assumed, any such criteria may be converted into criteria expressed in terms of the maximum permissible estimated percentage nonconforming in a lot.

13.5 SOME GENERAL ASPECTS OF MILITARY STANDARD 414

MIL-STD-414 is a lot-by-lot acceptance sampling plan by variables. This standard is indexed by numerical values of the AQL which range from 0.04 to 15.00%. This standard is similar to the series of successive military standards that have been used for many years for attributes sampling. Some points of similarity are that the procedures and tables are based on the concept of the AQL, that they assume lot-by-lot acceptance inspection ; that they provide for normal, tightened, or reduced inspection depending upon the circumstances, that the sample size is greatly influenced by lot size ; that several inspection levels are made available, and that all plans are identified by sample size code letter.

This variable standard is also like the attribute standards in stipulating sampling plans under normal inspection that have been designed to protect the producer by making the probability of rejection of a lot having AQL percent nonconforming relatively small. Just as in the military standards for attributes, the protection to the consumer depends largely on the use of tightened inspection whenever the process average appears to be unsatisfactory or there are other reasons to be suspicious of the process.

The plans in this standard are like those in the Bowker-Goode volume in that OC curves given for all the plans assume a normal distribution of any variable to which the acceptance procedures are to be applied. Tables included in the standard supply a source for estimates of the fraction defective in each inspected lot ; these estimates also assume a normal distribution of the variable.

The standard makes provision for nine different procedures which can be used to evaluate a lot for acceptance or rejection. Figure 13.4 shows the composition of the standard.

This standard can be applied either with a single specification limit, L or U, or with two specification limits. If the variability (σ) of the process is known and stable, the "variability known" plans are the most economical. Unknown sigma plans have been designated as having "variability unknown". In variability unknown plans it is possible to use either the "standard deviation method" or the "range method" in estimating the lot variability. The range method requires a larger sample size, however, the calculations are easier.

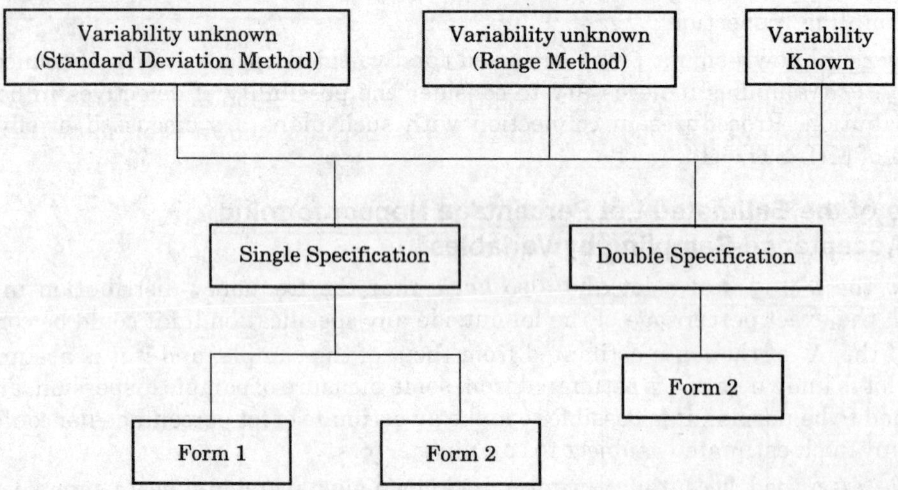

FIGURE 13.4 Composition of MIL-STD-414

Two alternative procedures, Forms 1 and 2, are available and will lead to the same acceptance-rejection decision. In Form 2 the decision on acceptance or rejection requires the use of an auxiliary table that provides an estimate of the lot percentage nonconforming based on a "quality index" computed from certain statistics of the sample. Form 1 is somewhat easier, it is only applicable to single specification situations ; it does not give sufficient information for the normal, tightened, and reduced switching rules. Therefore, Form 2 is the preferred procedure. This standard is divided into four sections. Section A contains a general description, sample-size code letters, and OC curves for the sampling plans. Procedure and examples for the unknown variability-standard deviation method is given in Section B ; procedures and examples for unknown variability-range method are given in Section C; and procedures and examples for known variability are given in Section D. Because this standard is a relatively long one, it is not practicable to reproduce all its tables in this book. The tables that have been reproduced here deal chiefly with the code H, and hence all our discussions and problems relate to this code letter only. Any one who understands the use of the tables and procedures for one code letter should have no difficulty with their use for any other code letter.

13.5.1 Determining the Sample Size Code Letter

To use MIL-STD-414 it is necessary to stipulate an AQL applicable to the quality characteristic being sampled. The standard contains an AQL conversion table (A-1), not reproduced here, that must be used whenever the stipulated AQL falls between two of the AQL values used in the standard.

The standard also contains a table (A-2) similar to Table K of App. 1. This table gives the sample size code letter for any lot size. In contrast to the most recent military standards for attributes, which have had three general inspection levels, the variables standard provides for five such levels. Lot sizes calling for the use of code letter H are as follows :

Inspection level	*Lot size*
I	8001 — 22000
II	1301 — 3200
III	501 — 800
IV	181 — 300
V	66 — 110

It is evident from the foregoing tabulation that the decision on inspection level has an important influence on sample size. This point is perhaps shown even more strikingly in the following tabulation which shows the sample size under "variability unknown-standard deviation method" for lot sizes 501-800 and an AQL of 4.0%.

Inspection level	*Sample size code letter*	*Sample size in normal and tightened inspection*
I	D	5
II	F	10
III	H	20
IV	J	30
V	L	40

The standard states that "unless otherwise specified, inspection level IV will be used". Inspection level V gives a steeper OC curve and therefore reduced consumer's risk can be tolerated, lower inspection levels can be used.

13.5.2 Tables Reproduced from MIL-STD-414

This chapter includes five tables dealing with code letter H.

Table 13.2 gives acceptance criteria in normal, tightened, and reduced inspection for all AQL values for plans based on variability unknown, standard deviation method. This table contains factors taken from Tables B-1 to B-4 of the standard. Table 13.5 contains corresponding criteria for plans based on variability unknown, range method : its factors come from Tables C-1 to C-4 of the standard. Table 13.6 has corresponding factors for plans based on known variability ; these are taken from Tables D-1 to D-4 of the standard.

TABLE 13.2 CONSTANTS REQUIRED TO DETERMINE ACCEPTANCE IN NORMAL, TIGHTENED, AND REDUCED INSPECTION WHEN VARIABILITY IS UNKNOWN— STANDARD DEVIATION METHOD—

Code Letter H of MIL-STD-414

AQL normal and reduced inspection	*AQL tightened inspection*	*Constants in normal and tightened inspection*				*Constant in reduced inspection*			
		Single specification limit, Form 1		*Single limit, Form 2, and double limit*		*Single specification limit Form 1*		*Single limit Form 2, and double limit*	
		n	*k*	*n*	*M*	*n*	*k*	*n*	*M*
0.04	0.065	20	2.69	20	0.135	15	2.53	15	0.186
0.065	0.10	20	2.58	20	0.228	15	2.42	15	0.312
0.10	0.15	20	2.47	20	0.365	10	2.24	10	0.349
0.15	0.25	20	2.36	20	0.544	7	2.00	7	0.422
0.25	0.40	20	2.24	20	0.846	7	1.88	7	1.06
0.40	0.65	20	2.11	20	1.29	7	1.75	7	2.14
0.65	1.00	20	1.96	20	2.05	7	1.62	7	3.55
1.00	1.50	20	1.82	20	2.95	7	1.50	7	5.35
1.50	2.50	20	1.69	20	4.09	7	1.33	7	8.40
2.50	4.00	20	1.51	20	6.17	7	1.15	7	12.20
4.00	6.50	20	1.33	20	8.92	7	0.955	7	17.35
6.50	10.00	20	1.12	20	12.99	7	0.755	7	23.29
10.00	15.00	20	0.917	20	18.03	7	0.536	7	30.50
15.00	—	20	0.695	20	24.53				

Table 13.4 provides a source of estimates of lot percentage defective as a function of the "quality index". This incorporates information from Tables B-5, C-5, and D-5 of the standard.

Table 13.7 contains certain criteria for deciding whether to use tightened or reduced inspection rather than normal inspection for the case of variability unknown, standard deviation method. It includes factors taken from Tables B-6 and B-7 of the standard.

13.6 NUMERICAL DATA TO ILLUSTRATE NORMAL INSPECTION UNDER MIL-STD-414

Assume a one-sided specification for which L = 1,000 kg/cm^2, the AQL is 2.50%, and normal inspection is to be used with code letter H. Tables 13.2, 13.5, and 13.6 indicate respective sample sizes of 20, 25, and 9.

The largest sample size, 25, is the one required for unknown variability, range method. To use the range method this sample must be divided into subsamples of 5, with ranges computed for each subsample. Assume that the respective tensile strengths in kg/cm^2 and the computed ranges are as follows :

Subsample number	*Tensile strength, kg/cm^2*					*Range*
1.	1,101.5	1,090.0	1,049.0	1,037.5	1,074.0	64.0
2.	1,028.5	1,055.5	1,013.5	948.5	1,105.5	157.0
3.	1,137.0	1,061.0	1,065.0	1,096.0	1,052.5	84.5
4.	1,089.0	1,090.0	1,079.0	1,049.5	1,087.0	40.5
5.	1,058.5	1,019.5	1,065.5	1,038.0	1,072.0	52.5
					Sum of ranges	398.5

Assume that the first 20 of the foregoing figures are the tensile strengths obtained for the required sample under the standard deviation method with variability unknown. Assume that the first 9 of the figures are the ones obtained for the required sample with variability known.

13.6.1 Calculation with Variability Unknown - Standard Deviation Method — Form 1

From Table 13.2, it may be determined that an AQL of 2.50% with code letter H calls for an n of 20 and a k of 1.51. In effect, these criteria say that the $\bar{X}$ of a sample of 20 must exceed the L of 1,000 kg/cm^2 by at least 1.51 s, where s is computed from the sample.

The calculation form suggested in MIL-STD-414 is illustrated in the upper part of Table 13.3. The reader will note that the recommended computational procedure for s makes use of the identity

$$\sum(X - \bar{X})^2 = \sum X^2 - n\bar{X}^2$$

The correction factor in line 4 is, of course, equal to $n\ \bar{X}^2$. Obviously the method of calculation shown in Table 13.3 is designed for use on a calculating machine, where there is no loss of significant figures in multiplication or division.

The form refers to s as the "estimate of lot standard deviation".

$$L + ks = 1{,}000 + 1.51\ (40.24) = 1{,}060.76 \text{ kg/cm}^2$$

Since the sample $\bar{X}$ of 1,065.48 kg/cm^2 is not less than this figure, the lot is acceptable.

However, this minimum acceptable value for $\bar{X}$ of 1,060.76 kg/cm^2 is not actually used in the computational procedure illustrated in Table 13.3. Instead of comparing $\bar{X}$ with $L + ks$, the same result is obtained by comparing $(\bar{X} - L)/s$ with k. In Table 13.3, $(\bar{X} - L)/s$ equals 1.627 is not less than the stipulated k of 1.51, the lot is accepted.

TABLE 13.3 ILLUSTRATION OF CALCULATION FORMS USING MIL-STD-414 VARIABILITY UNKNOWN-STANDARD DEVIATION METHOD

Line	*Information needed*	*Value obtained*	*Explanation*
	Single specification limit—Form 1		
1.	Sample Size : n	20	
2.	Sum of measurements : ΣX	21,309.5	
3.	Sum of Squared Measurements : ΣX^2	22,735,511.25	
4.	Correction Factor (CF) : $(\Sigma X)^2/n$	22,704,739.51	$(21,309.5)^2/20$
5.	Corrected Sum of Square (SS) : $\Sigma X^2 - CF$	30,771.74	22,735,511.25 −22,704,739.51
6.	Variance (V) : SS $/(n-1)$	1,619.57	30,771.74/19
7.	Estimate of Lot Standard Deviation $s : \sqrt{V}$	40.24	$\sqrt{1,619.57}$
8.	Sample Mean $\bar{X}$: $\Sigma X/n$	1,065.48	21,309.5/20
9.	Specification Limit (Lower) : L	1,000	
10.	The Quantity : $(\bar{X} - L)/s$	1.627	(1,065.48–1,000)/40.24
11.	Acceptability Constant : k	1.51	See Table 13.2
12.	Acceptability Criterion : Compare : $(\bar{X} - L)/s$ with k	1.627 > 1.51,	
	The lot meets the acceptability criteria, since $(\bar{X} - L)/s > k$		

	Single specification limit—Form 2		
1-9	Same as in Form 1		
10.	Quality Index : $QL = (\bar{X} - L)/s$	1.627	(1,065.48 – 1,000)/40.24
11.	Estimate of lot per cent defective : P_L	4.69%	See Table 13.4
12.	Maximum allowable per cent defective : M	6.17%	See Table 13.2
13.	Acceptability Criterion : Compare P_L with M	4.69 < 6.17%	
	The lot meets the acceptability criterion, since PL is M		

13.6.2 Calculation with Variability Unknown—Standard Deviation Method—Form 2

As indicated in Table 13.3, the first 9 lines are identical in Forms 1 and 2. In effect, the 10th line is also the same except that, in Form 2, $(\bar{X} - L)/s$ is designated as QL, the "quality index".

In Form 2, the quality index is used with an auxiliary table (B-5) to estimate the lot percentage defective. Table 13.4 reproduces part of this auxiliary table. The QL of 1.627 gives us the estimate that the lot is 4.69% defective. Since Table 13.2 states the M, the "maximum allowable percent defective", is 6.17%, the lot is accepted.

As previously stated, the k values used in the Form 1 procedure are consistent with the *M* values used in the Form 2 scheme ; therefore, the decision on acceptance or rejection is not influenced by the choice between Form 1 and Form 2.

TABLE 13.4 ESTIMATES OF LOT PERCENTAGE NONCONFORMING FOR VARIOUS VALUES OF QUALITY INDEX AS DEFINED IN MIL-STD-414

Q_U or Q_L	*Variability unknown-standard deviation method*				*Variability unknown-range method*				*Variability known*
	$n = 7$	$n = 10$	$n = 15$	$n = 20$	$n = 7$	$n = 10$	$n = 15$	$n = 25$	*Any n*
0.00	50.00	50.00	50.00	50.00	50.00	50.00	50.00	50.00	50.000
0.10	46.26	46.16	46.10	46.08	46.29	46.20	46.13	46.08	46.017
0.20	42.54	42.35	42.24	42.19	42.60	42.42	42.29	42.19	42.070
0.30	38.87	38.60	38.44	38.37	38.95	38.70	38.51	38.38	38.209
0.35	37.06	36.75	36.57	36.49	37.15	36.87	36.65	36.50	36.317
0.40	35.26	34.93	34.73	34.65	35.36	35.05	34.82	34.66	34.458
0.45	33.49	33.13	32.92	32.84	33.60	33.27	33.02	32.85	32.636
0.50	31.74	31.37	31.15	31.06	31.85	31.51	31.25	31.07	30.854
0.55	30.01	29.64	29.41	29.32	30.13	29.78	29.52	29.33	29.116
0.60	28.32	27.94	27.72	27.63	28.44	28.08	27.82	27.64	27.425
0.65	26.66	26.28	26.07	25.98	26.78	26.42	26.17	25.99	25.785
0.70	25.03	24.67	24.46	24.38	25.14	24.80	24.56	24.39	24.196
0.75	23.14	23.10	22.90	22.83	23.55	23.22	22.99	22.84	22.663
0.80	21.88	21.57	21.40	21.33	21.98	21.69	21.48	21.34	21.186
0.85	20.37	20.10	19.94	19.89	20.46	20.0	20.01	19.89	19.766
0.90	18.90	18.67	18.54	18.50	18.98	18.75	18.60	18.50	18.406
0.95	17.48	17.29	17.20	17.17	17.54	17.36	17.24	17.17	17.106
1.00	16.10	15.97	15.91	15.89	16.14	16.02	15.94	15.89	15.866
1.05	14.77	14.71	14.68	14.67	14.79	14.73	14.69	14.67	14.686
1.10	13.49	13.50	13.51	13.52	13.50	13.49	13.50	13.52	13.567
1.15	12.27	12.34	12.39	12.42	12.25	12.31	12.37	12.42	12.507
1.20	11.10	11.24	11.34	11.38	11.05	11.19	11.29	11.38	11.507
1.25	9.98	10.21	10.34	10.40	9.91	10.12	10.27	10.39	10.565
1.30	8.93	9.22	9.40	9.48	8.83	9.11	9.32	9.47	9.680
1.35	7.92	8.30	8.52	8.61	7.80	8.16	8.41	8.60	8.851
1.40	6.98	7.44	7.69	7.80	6.83	7.27	7.57	7.79	8.076
1.45	6.10	6.63	6.92	7.04	5.93	6.44	6.78	7.03	7.353
1.50	5.28	5.87	6.20	6.34	5.08	5.66	6.05	6.33	6.681
1.55	4.52	5.18	5.54	5.69	4.30	4.94	5.37	5.68	6.057
1.60	3.83	4.54	4.92	5.09	3.58	4.28	4.74	5.08	5.480
1.65	3.19	3.95	4.36	4.53	2.93	3.68	4.17	4.52	4.947
1.70	2.62	3.41	3.84	4.02	2.35	3.13	3.64	4.00	4.457
1.75	2.11	2.93	3.37	3.56	1.83	2.63	3.16	3.54	4.006
1.80	1.65	2.49	2.94	3.13	1.38	2.19	2.73	3.11	3.593
1.85	1.26	2.09	2.56	2.75	0.99	1.79	2.34	2.73	3.216

(Contd...)

Table 13.4 (Continued)

Q_U or Q_L	*Variability unknown-standard deviation method*				*Variability unknown-range method*				*Variability known*
	$n = 7$	$n = 10$	$n = 15$	$n = 20$	$n = 7$	$n = 10$	$n = 15$	$n = 25$	*Any n*
1.90	0.93	1.75	2.21	2.40	0.67	1.46	1.99	2.38	2.872
1.95	0.65	1.44	1.90	2.09	0.42	1.15	1.68	2.07	2.559
2.00	0.43	1.17	1.62	1.81	0.23	0.89	1.41	1.79	2.275
2.05	0.26	0.94	1.37	1.56	0.10	0.67	1.17	1.54	2.018
2.10	0.14	0.74	1.16	1.34	0.02	0.49	0.96	1.32	1.786
2.15	0.06	0.58	0.97	1.14	0.000	0.35	0.78	1.13	1.578
2.20	0.015	0.437	0.803	0.968	0.000	0.236	0.625	0.954	1.390
2.25	0.001	0.324	0.660	0.816	0.000	0.150	0.495	0.802	1.222
2.30	0.000	0.233	0.538	0.685	0.000	0.089	0.386	0.672	1.072
2.35	0.000	0.163	0.435	0.571	0.000	0.047	0.296	0.558	0.939
2.40	0.000	0.109	0.348	0.473	0.000	0.021	0.223	0.461	0.820
2.45	0.000	0.069	0.275	0.389	0.000	0.007	0.165	0.378	0.714
2.50	0.000	0.041	0.214	0.317	0.000	0.001	0.118	0.307	0.621
2.55	0.000	0.023	0.165	0.257	0.000	0.000	0.083	0.247	0.539
2.60	0.000	0.011	0.125	0.207	0.00	0.000	0.056	0.198	0.466
2.65	0.000	0.005	0.094	0.165	0.000	0.000	0.037	0.157	0.402
2.70	0.000	0.001	0.069	0.130	0.000	0.000	0.023	0.123	0.347
2.75	0.000	0.000	0.049	0.102	0.000	0.000	0.014	0.096	0.298
2.80	0.000	0.000	0.05	0.079	0.000	0.000	0.007	0.074	0.256
2.85	0.000	0.000	0.024	0.060	0.000	0.000	0.004	0.055	0.219
2.90	0.000	0.000	0.016	0.046	0.000	0.000	0.002	0.042	0.187
2.95	0.000	0.000	0.010	0.034	0.000	0.000	0.001	0.031	0.159
3.00	0.000	0.000	0.006	0.025	0.000	0.000	0.000	0.022	0.135
3.10	0.000	0.000	0.002	0.013	0.000	0.000	0.000	0.011	0.097
3.20	0.000	0.000	0.001	0.006	0.00	0.000	0.000	0.005	0.067
3.30	0.000	0.000	0.000	0.003	0.000	0.000	0.000	0.003	0.048
3.40	0.000	0.000	0.000	0.001	0.000	0.000	0.000	0.001	0.034
3.50	0.000	0.000	0.000	0.000	0.000	0.000	0.000	0.000	0.023
3.60	0.000	0.000	0.000	0.000	0.000	0.000	0.000	0.000	0.016
3.70	0.000	0.000	0.000	0.000	0.000	0.000	0.000	0.000	0.011
3.80	0.000	0.000	0.000	0.000	0.000	0.000	0.000	0.000	0.007
3.90	0.000	0.000	0.000	0.000	0.000	0.000	0.000	0.000	0.005
4.00	0.000	0.000	0.000	0.000	0.000	0.000	0.000	0.000	0.003

Whether or not the Form 2 procedure is used to determine the acceptance decision, it is essential to use the quality index to estimate the percentage defective in each lot. These estimates are needed to compute an estimated process average and to determine whether normal, tightened, or reduced inspection should be used. This is true with the range method and with known variability as with the standard deviation method.

13.6.3 Calculations with Variability Unknown—Range Method

Assume normal inspection as before with an AQL of 2.5% and code letter H. Table 13.5 gives the sample size as 25. Using the Form 1 procedure, k is 0.647. For the Form 2 procedure, d_2^* is 2.358 and M is 5.98%. The following discussion illustrates the two types of computational forms given in the standard (such as Table 13.5 for the standard deviation method). The sum of the 25 tensile strengths is 26,563.0. The sum of the 5 ranges in 398.5. In both procedures, $\bar{X}$ and R must be computed.

$$\bar{X} = \frac{\Sigma X}{25} = \frac{26,563.0}{25} = 1,062.52 \text{ kg/cm}^2 \; ; \; \bar{R} = \frac{\Sigma R}{25} = \frac{390.5}{5} = 79.7 \text{ kg/cm}^2$$

Using the Form 1 procedure, $(\bar{X} - L)/\bar{R}$ is computed ; if this computed value is equal to or greater than R, the lot is accepted, otherwise it is rejected. In this case,

$$(\bar{X} - L)/\bar{R} = (1,062.52 - 1,000 .0)/79.7 = 0.784.$$

Since this figure exceeds the stipulated k of 0.647, the lot is accepted. In effect, the $\bar{X}$ of the sample is required to be at least

$$L + k\bar{R} = 1,000.0 + 0.647\ (79.7) = 1,051.57$$

Under the form 2 procedure, it is necessary to compute the quality index Q_L, now defined as $[(\bar{X} - L)d_2^*]/\bar{R}$. In this case,

$$Q_L = \frac{(1,062.52 - 1,000.0)(2.358)}{79.7} = 1.85$$

For this Q_L, Table 13.4 gives an estimated lot percentage defective of 2.73%. Because 2.73 is not greater than the stipulated M of 5.98%, this lot is accepted.

TABLE 13.5 CONSTANTS REQUIRED TO DETERMINE ACCEPTANCE CRITERIA IN NORMAL, TIGHTENED, AND REDUCED INSPECTION WHEN VARIABILITY IS UNKNOWN - RANGE METHOD CODE LETTER H OF MIL-STD-414

AQL, normal and reduced inspection	*AQL, tightened inspection*	*Constants in normal and tightened inspection*					*Constants in reduced inspection*				
		Single specification limit Form 1		*Single limit Form 2 and double limit*			*Single specification limit, Form 1*		*Single limit, Form 2, and double limit*		
		n	k	d_2^*	n	M	n	k	d_2^*	n	M
0.04	0.065	25	1.14	2.358	25	0.125	15	1.04	2.379	15	0.136
0.065	0.10	25	1.10	1.358	25	0.214	15	0.999	2.379	15	0.253
0.10	0.15	25	1.05	2.358	25	0.336	10	0.916	2.405	10	0.23
0.15	0.25	25	1.01	2.358	25	0.506	7	0.702	2.830	7	0.28
0.25	0.40	25	0.951	2.358	25	0.827	7	0.659	2.830	7	0.89
0.40	0.65	25	0.896	2.358	25	1.27	7	0.613	2.830	7	1.99
0.65	1.00	25	0.815	2.358	25	1.95	7	0.561	2.830	7	3.46
1.00	1.50	25	0.779	2.358	25	3.82	7	0.525	2.830	7	5.32
1.50	2.50	25	0.723	2.358	25	3.96	7	0.465	2.830	7	3.47
2.50	4.00	25	0.647	2.358	25	5.98	7	0.405	2.830	7	12.35
4.00	6.50	25	0.501	2.058	25	8.65	7	0.386	2.830	7	17.54
6.50	10.00	25	0.484	2.358	25	12.59	7	0.266	2.830	7	23.50
10.00	15.00	25	0.398	2.358	25	17.48	7	0.189	2.830	7	30.66
15.00	...	25	0.305	2.358	25	23.79					

TABLE 13.6 CONSTANTS REQUIRED TO DETERMINE ACCEPTANCE CRITERIA IN NORMAL, TIGHTENED, AND REDUCED INSPECTION WHEN VARIABILITY IS KNOWN—CODE LETTER H OF MIL-STD-414

AQL normal and reduced inspection	*AQL tightened inspection*	*Constants in normal and tightened inspection*					*Constants in reduced inspection*				
		Single specification limit Form 1		*Single limit, Form 2, and double limit*			*Single specification limit, From 1*		*Single limit, Form 2, and double limit*		
		n	*k'*	*n*	*M*	*v*	*n*	*k'*	*n*	*M*	*v*
0.04	0.065	4	2.65	4	0.111	1.115	3	2.49	3	0.114	1.225
0.065	0.10	4	2.55	4	0.161	1.115	4	2.39	4	0.290	1.155
0.10	0.15	5	2.46	5	0.296	1.118	3	2.19	3	0.369	1.225
0.15	0.25	5	2.34	5	0.445	1.118	2	1.94	2	0.310	1.414
0.25	0.40	6	2.23	6	0.721	1.095	2	1.81	2	0.510	1.414
0.40	0.65	6	2.08	6	1.14	1.095	3	1.69	3	1.94	1.225
0.65	1.00	7	1.95	7	1.75	1.080	3	1.56	3	2.76	1.225
1.00	1.50	7	1.80	7	2.62	1.080	3	1.44	3	3.85	1.225
1.50	2.50	8	1.68	8	3.68	1.069	4	1.28	4	6.99	1.155
2.50	4.00	9	1.49	9	5.68	1.061	4	1.11	4	9.97	1.155
4.00	6.50	10	1.31	10	8.43	1.054	5	0.919	5	15.21	1.118
6.50	10.00	12	1.11	12	12.35	1.045	5	0.728	5	20.80	1.118
10.00	15.00	14	0.906	14	17.36	1.038	6	0.515	6	28.64	1.095
15.00	...	16	0.685	16	23.96	1.033					

13.6.4 Calculation with known Variability

Now assume normal inspection with an AQL of 2.5% code letter H, and an estimated σ of 50 kg/cm^2. (In fact, our sample of values for tensile strengths was taken from a table of normal random deviates, assuming that μ = 1,050 kg/cm2 and σ = 50 kg/cm2). Table 13.6 gives the sample size as 9. Using the form 1 procedure, k' = 1.49. For the Form 2 procedure, M is 5.68% and v is 1.061. The following discussion illustrates the two types of computation procedure but does not reproduce the forms given in the standard.

The sum of the nine measurements is 9,398.0 (These are the values shown on page 711 as of subsample 1 and the first 4 values in subsample 2). Both Form 1 and Form 2 procedures cell for computing the sample average.

$$\bar{X} = \frac{\Sigma X}{9} = \frac{9,098.0}{9} = 1044.2 \text{ kg/cm}^2$$

Under the Form 1 procedure, ($\bar{X}$ – L/σ) is computed. For our sample, this is (1,044.2 – 1,000.0)/50 = 0.884. If this computed value is equal to or greater than the stipulated k', the lot is accepted ; otherwise it is rejected. Since k' is stipulated as 1.49 and 0.884 is less than 1.49 this lot is rejected. In effect, this procedure stipulates a minimum value for the $\bar{X}$ of the sample of $L + k'\sigma$. In our example, the minimum $\bar{X}$ for acceptance is 1,074.5 kg/cm^2.

Under the Form 2 procedure applicable to a single specification limit, a quality index is computed. This index *QL* is now defined as

$$(\bar{X} - L)\, v/\sigma \quad \text{...(13.4)}$$

where v (tabulated in the standard in our Table 13.6 for various value of n) is $\sqrt{n(n-1)}$. For the observed sample of 9,

$$Q_L = \frac{(1{,}044.2 - 1{,}000)(1.061)}{50} = 0.94$$

The quality index is used to enter a table (our Table 13.4) to determine the estimated percentage defective in the lot. In this case, Table 13.4 indicates 17.4% defective for a Q_L of 0.94. If the estimated lot percentage defective is equal to or less than the stipulated maximum *M*, the lot is accepted ; otherwise it is rejected. Since M is 5.68% in this instance, the lot is rejected.

13.7 TIGHTENED INSPECTION IN MIL-STD-414

The standard specifies that the estimated process average at any time "is the arithmetic mean of the estimated lot present defectives computed from the sampling inspection results of the preceding 10 lots or as may be otherwise designated." The process average is needed to determine when shifts shall be made between normal and tightened inspection and between normal and reduced inspection. Tightened inspection is required when the estimated process average is greater than the AQL with more than a certain number *T* of the lots used to compute the process average that have estimates of percentage defective exceeding the AQL.

The standard gives values of *T* assuming that the process average has been computed using the preceding 5, 10 and 15 lots, respectively. The stipulated *T* depends on the sample size code letter and the AQL. Table 13.7 gives values of *T* for code letter H, assuming variability unknown and the standard deviation method. (Most *T* values are the same for the range method and for known standard deviation, although there are a few slight differences.)

The use of Table 13.7 may be illustrated with reference to an AQL of 4.0%, assuming that normal inspection has been in force and that the preceding 10 lots have given the following estimates of process average :

5.51% 3.52% **5.96%** **4.72%** 3.57%

4.06% 3.79% **5.09%** 3.08% **4.37%**

The estimated process average is the arithmetic mean of these 10 figures, namely, 4.34%. Thus one condition for the shift to tightened inspection is met ; the estimated process average is greater than the AQL of 4.00%. However, the second condition is not met ; only 6 of the lots (those in bold) has an estimated percentage nonconforming of more than 4.00, whereas the standard (Table 13.7) stipulates that tightened inspection is not required unless more than 8 out of 10 lots have values of estimated percentage nonconforming above the AQL. Therefore, normal inspection would be continued for the time being.

The acceptance criteria under tightened inspection are shown in Tables 13.2, 13.5, and 13.6 for code letter H. In all instances, these are the criteria under normal inspection for the next smaller AQL class. Once tightened inspection has been initiated, normal inspection is not reinstated until the estimated process averages of the lots under tightened inspection is equal to or less than the AQL.

TABLE 13.7 CRITERIA RELATING TO ESTABLISHMENT AND DISCONTINUANCE OF TIGHTENED AND REDUCED INSPECTION WHEN VARIABILITY IS UNKNOWN STANDARD DEVIATION METHOD - CODE LETTER H OR MIL-STD-414

AQL	*Values of T for tightened inspection*			*Limits of estimated lot per cent non-conforming for reduced inspection*		
	Number of lots			*Number of lots*		
	5	*10*	*15*	*5*	*10*	*15*
0.04	3	5	6	0.000	0.004	0.013
0.065	3	5	7	0.000	0.010	0.029
0.10	3	5	7	0.002	0.023	0.058
0.15	3	6	8	0.005	0.048	0.105
0.25	4	6	8	0.017	0.111	0.215
0.40	4	6	9	0.048	0.225	0.396
0.65	4	7	9	0.123	0.445	0.65
1.00	4	7	9	0.266	0.785	1.00
1.50	4	7	10	0.521	1.31	1.50
2.50	4	7	10	1.14	2.40	2.50
4.00	4	8	11	2.24	4.00	4.00
6.50	4	8	11	4.20	6.50	6.50
10.00	4	8	11	7.40	10.00	10.00
15.00	4	8	11			

13.8 REDUCED INSPECTION IN MIL-STD-414

To initiate reduced inspection, all the preceding 10 lots (or other designated number) must have been accepted and the estimated percentage defective for each of these preceding lots must have been less than a stated lower limit. Moreover, production must be "at a steady rate". For 10 lots with code letter H, unknown variability, the standard deviation method, and an AQL of 4.0%. Table 13.7 shows this lower limit to be 4.0%.

The acceptance criteria for code letter H under reduced inspection are given in Tables 13.2, 13.5 and 13.6. For an AQL of 4.0% with unknown variability and the standard deviation method, *n* is 7 and *k* is 0.955%, for the Form 2 procedure, *M* is 17.35%. Just as in the military standards for acceptance sampling by attributes, if a bad lot is submitted, it has a better chance of acceptance under reduced inspection than under normal inspection.

Reduced inspection must be discontinued and normal inspection reinstated whenever a lot is rejected, whenever the estimated process average exceeds the AQL, whenever "production becomes irregular or delayed" or "other conditions" exist that "may warrant that normal inspection should be reinstated".

13.9 AN UPPER SPECIFICATION LIMIT IN MIL-STD-414

The foregoing numerical examples all have assumed a one-sided specification with a lower limit *L*. The only difference when there is a single upper limit U is that it is necessary to measure down from U rather than up from L ; $U - \bar{X}$ replaces $\bar{X} - L$ in the analysis. This point may be illustrated by noting the definition of the quality indexes Q_L and Q_U for the various procedures.

For unknown variability, standard deviation method, these are

$$Q_L = \frac{\bar{X} - L}{s} \qquad Q_U = \frac{U - \bar{X}}{s}$$

For unknown variability, range method, they are

$$Q_L = \frac{(\bar{X} - L)d_2}{\bar{R}} \qquad Q_U = \frac{(U - \bar{X})d_2}{\bar{R}}$$

For known variability, they are

$$Q_L = \frac{(\bar{X} - L)v}{\sigma} \qquad Q_U = \frac{(U - \bar{X})v}{\sigma}$$

The foregoing definitions of Q_L and Q_U also apply to the case of two-sided specifications.

13.10 TWO-SIDED SPECIFICATIONS IN MIL-STD-414

Only the Form 2 procedure is applicable with a double specification limit. Two types of condition are recognized. In one type, an AQL is assigned to both limits combined. In the other type, different AQLs are assigned to each specification limit.

In both types, sample size code letters are obtained just as for one-sided specifications. Moreover, in both types the same tables used for Form 2 with a single limit are used to find n, M, and — where applicable — d_2 or v. Q_L and Q_U are computed just as for single limits, and the percentage of rejects outside each limit is estimated from a table such as our Table 13.4. These percentages are designated p_L and p_U. The estimated lot percentage nonconforming p is defined as $p_L + p_U$.

Where one AQL has been assigned to both limits combined, if "p is equal to or less than the stipulated maximum allowable percent defective M, the lot meets the acceptability criterion; if p greater than M or if either Q_U of Q_L or both are negative, than the lot does not meet the acceptability criterion."

Where different AQL values have been assigned to L and U, the rules are somewhat more complicated. For example, assume code letter H, normal inspection, with unknown variability and the standard deviation method. Assume an AQL of 2.5% for the lower specification limit and 1.0% for the upper limit.

Table 13.2 tells us that n is 20 for both AQLs and that M is 6.17% for the lower limit and 2.95% for the upper. These values are designated as M_L and M_U, respectively.

Now assume that the sample of 20 has been inspected and that Q_L and Q_U have been computed following the procedure illustrated in Table 13.3. Assume that Q_L if 1.60 and Q_U is 2.10. We may enter Table 13.4 to find $p_L = 5.09\%$ and $p_U = 1.34\%$.

For the lot to be accepted :

1. p_U must be equal to or less than M_U. Since 1.34% is less than 2.95%, this condition is met.
2. p_L must be equal to or less than M_L. Since 5.09% is less than 6.17%, this condition also is met.
3. p must be equal to or less than the larger of M_L and M_U. Here

   $p = 1.34\% + 5.09\% = 6.43\%$

Since 6.43% is greater than 6.17%, this condition is not met and the lot is rejected.

The general rules regarding tightened and reduced inspection are the same for two-sided and one-sided specifications.

MIL-STD-414 contains two auxiliary tables (B-8 and C-8) not reproduced here. These tables provide an aid in judging whether the dispersion of a quality characteristic is too great to meet a stated quality standard even under the most favourable conditions of centering between U and L.

13.11 THE RELATIONSHIP AMONG SAMPLES SIZES UNDER THE STANDARD DEVIATION METHOD. THE RANGE METHOD, AND PROCEDURES ASSUMING KNOWN VARIABILITY

There is no code letter A in MIL-STD-414. For code letters B to G with variability unknown, the standard deviation method and the range method have identical sample sizes under normal inspection, namely 3, 4, 5, 7, 10, and 15, respectively. For code letter H and beyond, sample sizes in normal inspection are from about 12 to 20% smaller in the standard deviation method than in the range method.

For code letters of H and beyond, the choice of the standard deviation method over the range method will cause some saving in inspection cost; choice of the range method presumably will cause some saving in the cost of calculations to apply the acceptance criteria. The relative importance of these cost differences will depend chiefly on the costs per item associated with inspection. Where tests are destructive or otherwise costly, it will usually be more economical to use the standard deviation method.

For any given AQL and code letter, the OC curves for the standard method and the range method are matched as closely as practicable. For this reason the question of quality protection to the consumer should be viewed primarily as a matter of choosing the desired AQL and inspection level rather than as a matter of choice between the standard deviation method and the range method.

In the range method, all sample sizes of 10 or more are multiples of 5 and the sample must be divided into subsamples of 5 each to compute $\bar{R}$. For example sizes of 3, 4, 5, and 7, the R of the entire sample is used as the measure of sample dispersion and no calculation of $\bar{R}$ is required.

The standard deviation method and the range method in MIL-STD-414 are alike in the feature that the sample size under normal inspection depends only on the code letter and is not influenced by the AQL. For example, Tables S and T for code letter H show sample sizes of 20 and 25, respectively, for all AQL values under normal inspection. In contrast, the sample size for a given code letter with known variability changes greatly with the AQL. For this reason, no simple statement applicable to all AQL values can be made about the relationship between sample sizes with known and unknown variability.

For example, Table 13.6 for code letter H shows sample sizes under normal inspection varying from p for an AQL of 0.04% to 16 and an AQL of 15%. This is a variation of from 20 to 80% of the required sample size with the standard deviation method, variability unknown. The paradox that sample size increases with the relaxation of the quality standard arises because the known-sigma plans in the standard were designed to match the OC curves obtained for the unknown-sigma plans.

For the popular AQL value of 1.00% and between the code letters, D and Q, the sample size under normal inspection for known-sigma plans varies from 40 to 32.5% of that required for unknown-sigma plans using the standard deviation method.

13.12 SOME COMMENTS ON TABLE 13.4

This table has been condensed in various ways from Table B-5, C-5, and D = 5 of the standard. Thus the quality index varies by steps of 0.05 in Table 13.4 whereas it varies by steps of 0.01 in the standard. The only values of n given in Table 13.4 for the case of variability unknown are those required for normal, tightened, and reduced inspection with code letter H; the standard, of course, gives all values of n required by a code letter.

The user of Table 13.4 needs to remember that the quality index is defined differently for each of the three parts of the standard. He should also be aware that, given the respective definitions of quality index, Table 13.4 and Tables B-5, C-5, and D-5 of the standard are resources of unbiased minimum variance estimates of lot percentage defective based on the assumption of normality. These tables may therefore be used for other purposes than the application of the acceptance criteria of MIL-STD-414.

For all three Parts of the standard, Table 13.4 starts with an estimate that the lot is 50% nonconforming when the quality index is zero. Of course, a zero quality index occurs when the sample average is the same as the specification limit in question, either L or U. Whenever the sample $\bar{X}$ falls below L or above U, the quality index is negative, implying that more than 50% of the lot is defective. All lots that have negative quality indexes should be rejected without further calculation.

The final column of Table 13.4 applicable to all values of n with variability known, is, in effect, merely a normal curve area table such as our Table *A*.

13.13 THE CHOICE BETWEEN-UNKNOWN-SIGMA AND KNOWN-SIGMA PLANS

In starting to use MIL-STD-414, the Bowker-Goode tables, or other comparable variables procedures for acceptance inspection of a new product, there may be no basis for estimating σ. Where this is true, it is necessary to start with unknown-sigma procedures.

Nevertheless, if many lots are expected from the same production source, it always is a good idea to start gathering data to provide a basis for judgement on the question of whether or not there is statistical control of the dispersion of the quality characteristic being measured. Usually this calls for an control chart for s or R. If such a chart indicated that the lots are coming from a process that is in statistical control with respect to its dispersion, it makes sense to switch from the unknown-sigma procedure to a known-sigma one. In the initial stages of a switch to known-sigma, it will be conservative to estimate σ a little on the high side. Often the estimated σ may be reduced as more evidence is accumulated.

Usually an incidental advantage of the switch to known-sigma will be a reduction in sample size. In the common case where sample sizes is small, a more important advantage is that a much better estimate of σ is obtained from a series of samples that exhibit statistical control of dispersion than can be had from a single small sample. Even where there is not full statistical control, a conservatively chosen σ may be better than unknown-sigma if it is imperative to use a very small sample size. The reader may get a feeling for the unreliability of any estimate of σ from a small sample by examining the variation of any measure of dispersion, such as R, σ, s, or s^2,—in successive samples from a statistically controlled process.

Of course, whenever a known-sigma plan is used, a control chart should be maintained on some measure of dispersion R, σ, s. Such a chart will serve to check the assumption that σ is in statistical control and, as time goes on, may provide a basis for a better estimate of the "known" value of σ that should be used.

13.14 COMPARISON OF SAMPLING COST —SAMPLING BY ATTRIBUTES AND SAMPLING BY VARIABLES

Much has been written on acceptance sampling by variables. Actually, the available literature is disproportionate to the fruitful applications of lot-by-lot variables sampling for acceptance.

In consideration of whether to apply attributes or variables sampling to an inspection characteristic, a surface indication favouring the latter may, upon a cursory cost analysis, result in the selection of former. This may be illustrated with the help of the sampling cost analysis of the plans of Table 13.8. All these plans give equivalent protection.

TABLE 13.8 ATTRIBUTES AND VARIABLES SAMPLING PLANS OF EQUIVALENT PROTECTION

Type of Plan	*Sample size (n)*	*Acceptance criterion*
Attributes	100	$c = 4$
Unknown-sigma for Two Sided Specifications	50	$\bar{X} + 1.689\,\sigma \leq U$ $\bar{X} - 1.689\,\sigma\,Q \geq L$
Known-sigma for Two-sided Specification	20	$\bar{X} + 1.622\,\sigma \leq U$ $\bar{X} - 1.622\,\sigma \geq L$

Sampling cost is composed of the following :

Overhead These are independent of the sample size. They include the cost of administration, and of the recording the computation costs. For a sigma-known plan the cost of maintaining up-to-date information concerning the value of sigma must be included. This could be done by use of a control chart for ranges.

Sampling These are same per unit regardless of the plan.

Inspection These will ordinarily be much more expensive per unit for variable, since measuring costs more than making an attributes decision.

Computation This involves only the negligible cost of counting for an attribute plan, computing a mean for a sigma-known variables plan and mean and standard deviation for a sigma-unknown variables plan.

$$\text{Total cost} = A + (B + C + D)n. \qquad \text{...(13.5)}$$

Following table gives the cost factors *A*, *B*, *C* and *D* for the three plans listed above.

Sampling Plan	*Cost per lot* (₹)	*Cost per Unit* (₹)			
	A	B	C	D	B + C + D
Attributes	50.00	0.04	0.40	0.00	0.44
Unknown-sigma	60.00	0.04	0.80	0.20	1.04
Known-sigma	80.00	0.04	0.80	0.02	0.86

Sampling costs per lot for the three plans, are computed as follows :

Attributes : 50 + (0.44)(100) = ₹ 94.00
Unknown-sigma : 60 + (1.04)(50) = ₹ 112.00
Known-sigma : 80 + (0.86)(20) = ₹ 97.20.

From above analysis, it is evident that the attributes sampling plan is the most economical.

The foregoing is not intended to demean the contribution of variables sampling for acceptance in the job of quality assurance. Rather, it is to place it in proper perspective. If from a total cost standpoint, it is the most economical, it should be used. If it is not the most economical, the attributes plan should be used.

Generally, speaking, where *destructive testing is involved, variables sampling will be the most inexpensive*. In most other situations attributes sampling will be the most economical.

SOLVED QUESTIONS

Q. 13.1: *Using the Shainin lot plot, compute the lot limits and draw the lot plot. The hardness inspection results of 50 sample units using Rockwell C are as follow :*

Subgroup	1	50	49	53	49	46
Subgroup	2	52	50	47	50	51
Subgroup	3	49	49	53	51	48
Subgroup	4	49	52	50	52	51
Subgroup	5	51	53	51	52	53
Subgroup	6	54	50	54	53	52
Subgroup	7	53	51	52	47	50
Subgroup	8	46	55	54	52	52
Subgroup	9	49	53	51	51	50
Subgroup	10	51	48	55	51	52

What type of lot plot does the distribution above represent? Specifications are from 41 to 60. Is the lot accepted and rejected?

Ans: Following the procedure of lot plot, the mean () of first five piece i.e. of subgroup 1 is 49.4 and range is 7. For the purpose of construction of frequency distribution the is taken as 49 and range of the lot is to be taken as 14. Assuming the cell interval to be 1, the number cell is 14. The lot plot is shown in Fig 13.5.

Mid point	Cell division									
58	+ 9									
57	+ 8									
56	+ 7									
55	+ 6	8	10							
54	+ 5	6	6	8						
53	+ 4	1	3	5	5	6	7	9		
52	+ 3	2	4	4	5	6	7	8	8	10
51	+ 2	2	3	4	5	5	7	8	9	10
50	+ 1	1	2	2	4	6	7	9	10	
49	0	1	1	3	3	4	9			
48	– 1	3	10							
47	– 2	2	7							
46	– 3	1	8							
45	– 4									
44	– 5									
43	– 6									
42	– 7									
41	– 8									
40	– 9									

FIGURE 13.5 Lot plot for the data of Q. 13.1

From the lot plot of Fig. 13.5, it is obvious that the lot is approximately normally distributed and falls well within the specification limits of 60 and 41 and there is no need for calculating lot limits and the lot is accepted.

Q. 13.2: *(a) For any code letter in MIL-STD-414, what are the AQL values to be used for determining the acceptance constants for the following AQL values of 0.062%, 0.45%, 1.30%m 12.0%.*

(b) Do the procedures for reduced and tightened inspection of MIL-STD-414 also apply to mixed variable attributes inspection?

Ans: Following the procedure of lot plot, the mean ($\bar{X}$) of first five piece *i.e.* of subgroup 1 is 49.4 and range is 7. For the purpose of construction of frequency distribution the $\bar{X}_0$ is taken as 49 and range of the lot is to be taken as 14. Assuming the cell interval to be 1, the number cells is 14. The lot plot is shown in Fig. 13.5.

From the lot plot of Fig. 13.5, it is obvious that the lot is approximately normally distributed and falls well within the specification limits of 60 and 41 and there is no need for calculating lot limits and the lot is accepted.

TABLE 13.9. AQL CONVERSION TABLE
(Reproduced from MIL-STD-414)

For specified AQL values falling within these ranges	*Use this AQL value*	*For specified AQL values falling within these ranges*	*Use this AQL value*	*For specified values within these ranges*	*Use the AQL values*
— to 0.049	0.04	0.280 to 0.439	0.40	2.80 to 4.39	4.0
0.050 to 0.069	0.065	0.440 to 0.699	0.65	4.40 to 6.99	6.5
0.070 to 0.109	0.10	0.700 to 1.09	1.0	7.00 to 10.9	10.0
0.110 to 0.164	0.15	1.10 to 1.64	1.5	11.00 to 16.4	15.0
0.165 to 0.279	0.25	1.65 to 2.79	2.5		

From Table 13.9, it is evident that for AQL values of 0.062%, 0.45%, 1.30%, 12.0% the AQL values to be used are 0.065%, 0.65%, 1.5% and 15.0% respectively.

(*b*) As per MIL-STD-414, the procedures for estimating the process average and criteria for tightened and reduced inspection based on the inspection results of preceding lots are not applicable for mixed variable attributes inspection.

Q. 13.3: *A known-sigma variables acceptable plan for a one-sided specification uses n = 9 and k' = 1.466. Assuming a normal distribution and a correct estimate of σ, what is the probability of acceptance of a 3.75% nonconforming lot ?*

Ans: If μ is the average for 3.75% nonconforming lot L is the lower speicification limit then from Table *A* an area of 0.0375 corresponds to z of – 1.78. Hence

$$\frac{L-\mu}{\sigma} = -1.78$$

$$\mu = L + 1.78\,\sigma$$

Also
$$\sigma_{\bar{X}} = \frac{\sigma}{\sqrt{n}} = \frac{\sigma}{\sqrt{9}} = \frac{\sigma}{3}$$

Minimum allowable value of $\bar{X} = L + 1.466\sigma$.

With an μ at $L + 1.78\,\sigma$ and minimum value of $\bar{X}$ at $L + 1.466\sigma$, the area of the curve below this minimum value as determined from Table *A* (by using $\sigma_{\bar{X}}$ since we are dealing with the distribution of averages) is 0.1731.

Probability of acceptance = 1 – 0.1731 = 0.8269.

Q. 13.4: *Assume normal inspection MIL-STD-414, variability known code letter H, 2.50% AQL, single specification limit. Compute the probability of acceptance of a normally distributed lot containing 5% of defective product if the σ of the lot is estimated correctly.*

Ans: For MIL-STD-414, under code letter H and known sigma plan for an AQL of 2.50%, $n = 9$ and $k' = 1.49$. Let the lower limit be *L*. Since 5% of the product is defective, area of the normal curve below *L* is 0.05. From Table *A* the corresponding *z*. If μ be the process centre, then

$$\frac{L-\mu}{\sigma} = -1.645$$

$$\mu = L + 1.645\sigma$$

Minimum allowable $\bar{X} = L + k'\sigma = L + 1.49\sigma$

$$z \text{ corresponding to } \bar{X} \text{ of } L + 1.49\sigma = \frac{(L+1.49\sigma)-(L+1.64.5\sigma)}{\frac{\sigma}{\sqrt{9}}} = -0.465$$

Area of the normal curve below the minimum allowable limit of $L + 1.49\sigma$ from Table *A* is 0.3210.

Probability of acceptance = 1 – 0.3210 = 0.6790.

Q. 13.5: *A MIL-STD-414 variables accepting sampling plan uses code letter H and an AQL of 1.5%. Variability is unknown and there is a single upper specification of 6.850.*

(a) What are the required critical numbers using the range method for tightened inspection under both the Form 1 and Form 2 procedures ?

(b) What are the critical numbers using the standard deviation method for normal inspection under both the Form 1 and Form 2 procedures ?

(c) Assuming s = 0.125 for a sample (and is the best estimate of σ), compute the location of the process mean for incoming lots with μ_p of 0.04.

(d) Sketch the distribution of product with respect to U, the distribution of $\bar{X}$ with respect to the acceptance criterion, and compute the probability of acceptance for the lots described in (c). Assume the normal inspection applies.

Ans: (*a*) Form 1 $n = 25, k = 0.779$

Form 2 $n = 25, M = 3.82$

(*b*) Form 1 $n = 20, k = 1.69$

Form 2 $n = 20, M = 4.09$

(*c*) Since $\mu_p = 0.04$, the area of the normal curve above *U* of 6.850 is 0.04 and below *U* is 0.96. From Table *A* corresponding value of *z* is 1.75. Hence, if μ is the process mean, then,

$$\frac{6.850-\mu}{0.125} = 1.75 \quad i.e. \quad \mu = 6.63125$$

(*d*) For an *AQL* of 1.5% and normal inspection and known variability, the critical numbers are

$$n = 8\ k' = 1.68$$

Maximum sample average $= U - k'\sigma$

$$= 6.8\,50 - 1.68\,(0.125) = 6.640$$

$$z = \frac{6.640 - 6.63125}{\frac{0.125}{\sqrt{8}}} = 0.1979$$

Area of the normal curve corresponding to z of 0.1979 is 0.5785. Hence probability of acceptance = 0.5785.

The distribution of X with respect U is shown in Fig. 13.6.

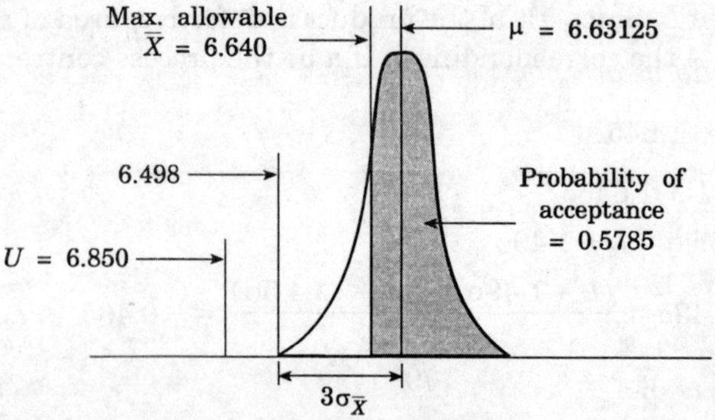

FIGURE 13.6 Diagram illustrating the distribution of X with respect to U in Problem 13.5.

Q. 13.6: *(a) A manufacturer produced a lot of 35 thermostats. The maximum temperature at which the thermostat must actuate is 100°C. A sample of 5 thermostats has shown the actuation temperatures as 95, 99, 100, 97, and 98°C. Determine the acceptability of lot using an AQL of 1.30%, using MIL-STD-414.*

(b) In case you decide to reject the lot, why is it so when all the thermostats in the sample have shown the actuation temperature either less than or equal to the maximum specified temperature ?

Ans: The MIL-STD-414 indicates that for the lot size of 35 and inspection level IV, the sample size code letter is D and for an AQL of 1.30%, the AQL value to be used is 1.50%.

For an AQL of 1.50%, and sample size code letter *D*, and the variability unknown, the sample size is 5 and $k = 1.40$. Using from 1,

$$\bar{X} = \frac{95 + \ldots + 98}{5} = \frac{489}{5} = 97.8 \text{ say } 98$$

$$s = \sqrt{\frac{\Sigma(X - \bar{X})}{n-1}} = \sqrt{\frac{(-3)^2 + (1)^2 + (2)^2 + (-1)^2 + (0)^2}{4}} = 1.936$$

The quantity $(U - \bar{X})/s = (100 - 98)/1.936 = 1.033$. Since the computed value is less than the stipulated value of k and 1.40, the lot is rejected.

(*b*) The lot is rejected even though none of the 5 units exceed the specified 100°C limit because of the inherent variability of the production lot.

Q. 13.7: *Using the same specifications as in Problem 13.6, except that instead of maximum actuation temperature of 100°C, a minimum temperature of 95°C applies. The AQL and the readings of the sample units are likewise unchanged.*

Ans: From Problem 13.6, $n = 5$, $k = 1.40$, $s = 1.936$, and $\bar{X} = 98$.

Quantity $(\bar{X} - L)/s = (98 - 95)/1.936 = 1.549$.

Since the computed value of 1.549 is more than the stipulated value of k of 1.40, the lot is accepted.

Q. 13.8: *The single lower specification limit, L, for tensile strength for a certain wire is 62.0 lb. MIL-STD-414 is used with normal inspection, code letter H, and an AQL of 1.0%. Variability is unknown and the range method and Form 2 procedure are to be used.*

(a) What critical numbers are required for the plan ?

(b) A sample from a lot yields $\Sigma X = 1{,}681$ and $\Sigma R = 32$. Make the necessary calculations to determine whether or not the lot should be accepted.

Ans: (*a*) For code letter H and an AQL of 1.0% variability unknown and range method with Form 2 procedure, the critical numbers from Table 13.5 are

$$d_2^* = 2.358,\ n = 25,\ M = 3.82\%.$$

(b) $\Sigma X = 1681$, $\quad \bar{X} = \dfrac{1.681}{25} = 67.24$

$\Sigma R = 32$, $\quad \bar{R} = \dfrac{32}{5} = 6.4$

$$Q_L = [(\bar{X} - L)d_2^*]/\bar{R} = \frac{(67.24 - 62.0)(2.358)}{6.4} = 1.93$$

For this Q_L, Table 13.4 (by interpolation) gives an estimated lot percentage defective of 2.20. Because 2.20 does not exceed the stipulated M of 3.82%, (Table 13.5) the lot is accepted.

Q. 13.9: *The single lower specification limit on a certain item is 14.5 units. MIL-STD-414 is used with normal inspection, code letter H, and an AQL of 1.5%. Variability is unknown and the range method and Form 2 procedure are to be used.*

(a) What factors from the standard are required to estimate the lot percentage non-conforming and to decide whether or not to accept a lot ?

(b) The required sample of 25 is measured with the following results :

Subgroup	1	45	26	37	33	12
Subgroup	2	29	43	25	22	37
Subgroup	3	33	29	32	30	13
Subgroup	4	40	18	30	11	21
Subgroup	5	18	36	34	26	35

Make the necessary calculations to determine whether or not the lot should be accepted.

(c) What is the probability of acceptance of lots having the proportion of non-conforming product found in (b) ? Use R/d_2^* to estimate σ and the value of k listed for the Form 1 procedure of find P_a.

Ans: (*a*) The factors required from the standard are :

$$= 2.358,\ M = 3.96$$

(*b*) $\quad \Sigma X = 45 + 26 + \ldots.. + 35 = 715$

$$\bar{X} = \frac{715}{25} = 28.6$$

$$\Sigma R = R_1 + R_2 + R_3 + R_4 + R_5$$
$$= 33 + 21 + 20 + 29 + 18 = 121$$
$$\bar{R} = \frac{121}{5} = 24.2$$
$$Q_L = (\bar{X} - L)d_2^*/\bar{R} = \frac{(28.6 - 14.5)(2.358)}{24.2} = 1.3738$$

For this Q_L, Table 13.4 gives an estimated lot percentage nonconforming of 8.68% or 0.0868. Because 8.68% exceeds the stipulated M of 3.96 (Table 13.5), this lot cannot be accepted. (i.e. it is rejected)

(*c*) $$\sigma = \frac{\bar{R}}{d_2^*} = \frac{24.2}{2.358} = 10.26$$

$k = 0.723$ (From Table 13.5)

If 8.68% of the product falls below the lower limit of 14.5, the area of the normal curve upto 14.5 is 0.0868. Corresponding value of z is – 1.36. If μ is the process average, then

$$-1.36 = \frac{14.5 - \mu}{10.26}$$
$$\mu = 28.45$$

Minimum allowable $\bar{X} = L + k\,\sigma$
$$= 14.5 + 0.723\,(10.26)$$
$$= 21.92.$$

z corresponding to 21.92 is $\dfrac{21.92 - 28.45}{\dfrac{10.26}{\sqrt{5}}}$ *i.e.* – 1.5

Area of the normal curve corresponding to z of – 1.5 is only 0.0668.

$$P_a = 0.0668.$$

Q. 13.10: *An ABC standard single sampling plan calls for n = 50 and c = 2 for code letter H, an AQL of 1.5%, and normal inspection.*

(a) What Form 1 MIL-STD-414 variable sampling plan corresponds to this ABC standard attributes plan ? Assume σ is known and that there is a single specification limit for this characteristic.

(b) Fine the probability of acceptance of a lot containing 10% nonconforming items under the plan found in (a).

Ans: (*a*) MIL-STD-414 variable sampling plan corresponding to the attribute plan will have $n = 8$ and $k' = 1.68$. If there is a single specification limit, L, then take a sample of 8 items and compute the average of the quality characteristic of the sample. Compute the quantity $(\bar{X} - L)/\sigma$. If this computed value is equal to or greater than the stipulated k' of 1.68, the lot is accepted ; otherwise it is rejected.

(*b*) If 10% non-conforming product falls below L, the process center is at $L + 1.28\,\sigma$. Minimum value of sample average = $L + 1.68\,\sigma$. Z corresponding to this value

$$= \frac{(L - 1.68\sigma) - (L + 1.28\sigma)}{\dfrac{\sigma}{\sqrt{8}}}$$

$$= 1.13$$

Area of the curve = 0.8708

Probability = 1 – 0.8708 = 0.1292.

Q. 13.11: *The minimum temperature of operation for a certain device is specified as 180°C. A known-sigma variable acceptance plan with a sample size of 9 is to be used. The desired value of 100 $p_{0.10}$ is 4.0% and k' 2.178. If the assumed value of σ is 6°C, will a lot be accepted when the sample items have operating temperatures of 197, 188, 184, 205, 201, 190, 195, 193 and 199° C ?*

Ans:

$$\Sigma X = 197 + 188 + \ldots + 199 = 1{,}752$$

$$\bar{X} = 1{,}752/9 = 195°$$

$$(\bar{X} - L)/\sigma = (19\ 5 - 180)/6 = 2.5$$

Since this computed value is greater than the stipulated value of 2.178, the lot is accepted.

Q. 13.12: *In the absence of adequate information on σ, the unknown-sigma plan (n = 16 , k = 2.018) is to be used for acceptance of the product mentioned in Q. 13.11, will a lot be accepted when the sample items have operating temperatures of 202, 195, 191, 198, 178, 185, 194, 191, 192, 188, 203, 197, 197, 190, 189, and 182°C.*

Ans: $n = 16$, $k = 2.018$

$$\Sigma = 2\ 02 + 195 + \ldots + 182 = 3{,}072$$

$$\bar{X} = \Sigma\frac{X}{n} = \frac{3{,}072}{16} = 192$$

$$s = \sqrt{\frac{\Sigma(X - \bar{X})^2}{n - 1}}$$

$$= \sqrt{\frac{(202 - 192)^2 + \ldots(182 - 192)^2}{16 - 1}} = 6.772$$

$$(\bar{X} - L)/s = (192 - 180)/6.772 = 1.772$$

Since $(\bar{X} - L)/s$ *i.e.* 1.772 is less than acceptability factor k of 2.018, the lot cannot be accepted.

Q. 13.13: *A known-sigma variables acceptance sampling plan has n = 5, and k' = 1.522. When measured against a single upper specification of 950, incoming lots contains 5% non-conforming items. Distribution of product is approximately normal with a σ of 100.*

(a) At approximately what level is this process centered ?

(b) What is the probability of acceptance for these incoming lot ?

Ans: (*a*) Let μ be the center of the process. Since 5% of the project falls above the U of 950, the area of the normal curve upto U is 0.95. Corresponding z value from Table A is 1.645.

Hence, $$\frac{(950 - \mu)}{100} = 1.645$$

$$\mu = 950 - 164.5 = 785.5$$

(*b*) Maximum average of the sample

$$= U - k'\sigma$$

$$= 950 - 1.522\ (100)$$

$$= 797.8$$

Corresponding to the limit of 797.8,

$$z = \frac{797.8 - 785.5}{\frac{100}{\sqrt{5}}}$$

$$= 0.275.$$

Area of the curve upto 797.8 from Table A is 0.6084

Probability of acceptance = 0.6084.

Q. 13.14: *The plan described in Q. 13.13 has a Producer's Risk of 0.05 of rejecting lots with a μp of 0.012 and a Consumer's Risk of 0.10 of accepting lots with a μp of 0.172.*

(a) What plan is recommended in MIL-STD-414 for code letter H, an AQL of 1.0%, and normal inspection using the Form 1 procedure when σ is known ?

(b) What is the probability of acceptance of lots containing 5% nonconforming items under this plan ?

(c) What percentage of non conforming has a 10% probability of acceptance (Consumer's Risk point) under this plan ? Comment on the reasons for the difference between this value and that stated for the plan described lin Q. 13.13.

Ans: (*a*) Take a sample of 7 items. Compute the average of the quality characteristic of the sample. Compute the value of $(U - \bar{X})/\sigma$. If the computed value of this quantity is less than the stipulated k' of 1.80, the lot is rejected otherwise it is accepted.

(*b*) If 5% of the product falls above the upper specification limit of U, the process center must be at $U - 1.645\ \sigma$. Maximum value of the sample average quality characteristic is $U - 1.80\sigma$.

$$Z = \frac{(U - 1.80\sigma) - (U - 1.645\sigma)}{\frac{\sigma}{\sqrt{7}}} = -0.41$$

Area of the curve from Table *A* is 0.3409.

(*c*) Maximum value of the sample average quality characteristic $= U - 1.80\sigma$. If the probability of acceptance is 10%, the area of the normal curve is 0.10. Corresponding z value from Table *A* is – 12.8. If process is centered at $U - t\ \sigma$, then

$$= \frac{(U - 1.80\sigma) - (U - t\,\sigma)}{\frac{\sigma}{\sqrt{7}}} = -1.28$$

or $\quad (t - 1.8\ 0)\sqrt{7} = -1.28$

or $\quad t = 1.316$

Process center $= U - 1.316\sigma$

Area of the normal curve above U will be the μ_p for a probability of acceptance of 10%. z corresponding to $U = \dfrac{U - (U - 1.316\sigma)}{\sigma} = 1.316$

From Table *A*, area of the curve upto $U = 0.9059$

Hence, $\mu_p = 1 - 0.9059 = 0.0941$

The difference between the values of μp is because of the fact that attributes plan is based on binomial distribution and the normal distribution is only a approximate to the binomial distribution and the OC curves of variable sampling plans match the OC curves of attribute sampling plan approximately.

Q. 13.15: *A lot of 200 transformers has a critical specification for excitation current. The latter must fall between 12 and 16 milliamperes. An AQL = 2% and inspection level IV applies. A sample of 20 transformer has shown $\bar{X}$ = 14.6 and s = 1.14. Determine the acceptability of the lot.*

Ans: From MIL-STD-414, the sample code letter is H and the AQL to be used is 2.5%.

$$Q_L = \frac{\bar{X} - L}{s} = \frac{14.6 - 12}{1.14} = 2.28$$

$$Q_U = \frac{U - \bar{X}}{s} = \frac{16 - 14.6}{1.14} = 1.23$$

From Table 13.4, for Q_L of 2.28, the computed value of p_L is 0.73% and for Q of 1.23, the computed value of p_U = 11.0%, Estimate lot percentage defective $p = p_L + p_U$ *i.e.* 0.738 + 11.0 = 11.738%. Stipulated value of M = 6.17%. Since *p* is more than *M*, the lot does not meet the acceptability criterion.

Q. 13.16: *Under normal inspection, MIL-STD-414, variability unknown, standard deviation method, code letter H, 0.40 AQL, single specification limit, the most recent 10 lots have been accepted with the following estimated percentages reject : 0.97, 0.47, 0.01, 0.21, 0.82, 0.57, 0.00, 0.52, 0.08, 1.05. Is a shift from normal to tightened inspection required at this time ? What are the Form 1 and Form 2 acceptance criteria (constants) under tightened inspection.*

Ans: The estimated process average

$$= \frac{0.97 + 0.47 + \ldots 1.05}{10}$$

$$= 0.47\%$$

Since 0.47% > AQL of 0.40%, so one condition of shifting to tightened inspection is met.

From Table 13.7, the number of the lots required to have percentage defective more than the AQL is 5. Actual number of lots having percentage reject more than the AQL of 0.40% is 6. Thus the second condition is also met with. Hence a shift from normal to tightened inspection is required at this stage.

Form 1 criteria : The constants for tightened inspection for AQL of 0.40% are n = 20, k = 2.24.

Form 2 criteria : The constants for tightened inspection for AQL of 0.40% are n = 20, M = 0.846.

Q. 13.17: *Under normal inspection, MIL-STD-414, variability unknown, standard deviation method, code letter H, 1.50% AQL, single specification limit, the most recent 10 lots have been accepted with the following estimated percentages rejects : 0.00, 0.05, 0.83, 0.77, 0.04, 1.44, 0.09, 0.13, 0.22, 1.05. Is a shift to reduced inspection permissible ? What are the Form 1 and Form 2 acceptance criteria under reduced inspection ?*

Ans: In order to initiate reduced inspection the lower limit for each of the most recent 10 lots from Table 13.7, is 1.31. Since one of the lots is having percentage rejects is 1.44 which is greater than 1.31, the condition for reduced inspection is not met.

Form 1 criteria : The constants reduced inspection for AQL of 1.50% are $n = 7$, $k = 1.33$.

Form 2 criteria : The constants for reduced inspection for AQL of 1.50% are $n = 7$, $M = 8.40$.

Q. 13.18: *A mixed variable attributes sampling plan stipulates the following procedures.*

(1) Draw a sample of 20 items from the lot and calculate the average of the sample : if $(\bar{X} - L)/\sigma \geq 2.0$, accept the lot, otherwise (2) draw a second sample of 100 items : if the number of nonconforming items in this samples does not exceed 2, accept the lot, otherwise reject the lot. Assume the lot size is 3,000, σ is 100, the lower specification limit (L) is 1000, and that incoming lots contain 3% nonconforming items.

(a) Assuming that this process is approximately normally distributed, what is the centering of the process from which these lots are formed ?

(b) Find the probability of acceptance on the first sample.

(c) Find the total probability of acceptance under this plan.

(d) Control charts for $\bar{X}$ and σ are to be maintained on the data from first samples. Find the values of the central lines and control limits assuming 3% non-conforming items.

Ans: (*a*) Since the lots contain 3% nonconforming items which are below the lower specification limit L, the area of the normal curve below L is 0.03. From Table A, corresponding value z is – 1.88. Also if μ is the process center, then

$$-1.88 = \frac{1{,}000 - \mu}{100}$$

$$\mu = 1{,}188.$$

(*b*) Minimum acceptance sample average is governed by the condition $\dfrac{\bar{X} - L}{\sigma} = 2$

Hence
$$\bar{X} = L + 2\sigma$$
$$= 1{,}000 + 2(100)$$
$$= 1{,}200$$

Since sample size is 20,

$$\sigma_{\bar{X}} = \frac{100}{\sqrt{20}}$$

z corresponding to minimum value of $\bar{X}$ of 1,200

$$= \frac{1{,}200 - 1{,}188}{\frac{100}{\sqrt{20}}}$$

$$= 0.537$$

Area of the normal curve up to $\bar{X}$ of 1,200 from Table A is 0.7044.

Hence the probability of acceptance on the first sample

$$= 1 - 0.7044$$
$$= 0.2956.$$

(*c*) Probability that a second sample is taken = 0.7044

$$\mu_{np} = 100 \times 0.03 = 3$$

From Table G, the probability that a sample contains either 0, or 1, or 2 non-conforming items = 0.423.

Total probability of acceptance = 0.2956 + 0.7044 (0.423) = 0.5936

(*d*) $\overline{X}$ -Chart : Central line = μ = 1,188

$$UCL_{\overline{X}} = \mu + A\sigma = 1{,}188 + 0.67\ 100 = 1{,}255$$

$$LCL- = \mu - A\sigma = 1{,}188 - 0.67\ (100) = 1{,}121$$

σ-Chart : Central line = $c_2\sigma = 0.9619 \times 100 = 96$

$$UCL_{\sigma\ RMS} = B_2\sigma = 1.43 \times 100 = 143$$

$$LCL_{\sigma\ RMS} = B_1\sigma = 0.49 \times 100 = 49$$

Q. 13.19: *A company uses a combined variable attribute sampling plan to inspect large batches of incoming lots. Items are inspected against of single upper specification limit of 3.00 units on a certain characteristic. On receiving a new lot, a random sample of 9 items is selected. If the average of the measurements of this characteristic is 2.90 or less, the lot is accepted. Otherwise, a new random sample of 25 items is selected. If no item in this sample exceeds 3.00 when tested, the lot is accepted otherwise the lot is rejected. In answering the following questions, assume a normal distribution underlies this characteristic and that σ is 0.20 units.*

(a) What is the probability of acceptance on the first sample for a lot containing 10% non-conforming items ?

(b) What is the probability of taking a second sample ?

(c) What is the total probability of acceptance of this lot ?

Ans: (*a*) Area of the normal curve above the upper specification limit of 3 is 0.10. Hence the area of the curve upto specification limit is 0.9. Corresponding value of z = 1.282. If μ is the process center, then

$$1.282 = \frac{3 - \mu}{0.20}$$

$$\mu = 2.7436$$

z corresponding to $$2.90 = \frac{2.90 - 2.7436}{\dfrac{0.20}{\sqrt{9}}}$$

Area of the normal curve corresponding to z of 2.346 is 0.9905. Hence the probability of acceptance on the first sample is 0.9905.

(*b*) Probability of taking of the second sample = 1 – 0.9905 = 0.0095.

(*c*) $$\mu_{np} = 25 \times 0.1 = 2.5$$

Probability of 0 defective from Table G is 0.083.

Total probability of lot acceptance = 0.9905 + 0.0095 (0.083) = 0.9913.

Q. 13.20: *The $\overline{X}$ control chart reject limits constitute a special case of known-sigma variables acceptable criteria. The rejection limit factor (V) for n of 16 is 2.25. Assume that these values of V and n are being used for an $\overline{X}$ chart that show only reject limits. Assume that the process is centered so that 2% of the product is outside one specification limit and no product is outside the other specification limit. What is the probability that the first $\overline{X}$ value from a process so* *centered will fall within the reject limits ? Assume a normal distribution and a correct estimate of σ.*

Ans: If L is the lower specification limit and the process is so centered that 2% of the product falls below this limit, Table A gives the process center (μ) = $L + 2.054\sigma$. Since no product falls above the upper specification limit, it can be assumed that this limit is more than 3σ away from the process center.

The lower reject limit $= L + V_\sigma$

$= L + 2.25\sigma$

Also $$\sigma_{\bar{X}} = \frac{\sigma}{\sqrt{n}} = \frac{\sigma}{\sqrt{16}} = \frac{\sigma}{4}$$

Area below the lower reject limit can be found by first finding z.

$$z = \frac{L + 2.25\sigma - (L + 2.054\sigma)}{\sigma_{\bar{X}}} = \frac{0.196\sigma}{\sigma_{\bar{X}}} = \frac{0.196\sigma}{\frac{\sigma}{4}} = 0.784$$

Area of the curve below lower reject limit = 0.781

Area of the curve above upper rejection limit will not be of any significance.

The area of the curve between reject limits = 1 – 0.781 = 0.219

Hence the probability that the first $\bar{X}$ value from this process will fall between two reject limits is 0.219.

CHAPTER

14

Reliability and Life Testing

14.1 BACKGROUND AND IMPORTANCE OF PRODUCT RELIABILITY

In recent decades the complexity of equipment used for military, space, and commercial applications has increased manifold. The more complex a piece of equipment, the less reliable it is and the more likely it is that one or more of its parts may fail.

Military electronic gear which fails, when needed, may adversely affect the outcome of an engagement and cost lives. Downtime on commercial computers or process control devices could cause extensive financial losses, while failures in medical electronics or safety equipment could endanger life. Hence there has been great emphasis on enhancing the reliability of the equipment in recent times. It is with this view that it is one of the purposes of this chapter to understand the fundamentals of the reliability.

14.2 MEANING AND DEFINITION OF RELIABILITY

Simply stated, *reliability* is quality for performing the intended purpose) over the long run. Quality is the condition of the product during manufacturing or immediately afterward, whereas reliability is the ability of the product to perform its intended function over a period of time. A product that "works" for a long period of time is a reliable one. Since all units of a product will fail at different times, reliability is a probability.

A more precise definition is : *Reliability is the probability that a product will perform its intended function satisfactorily for a prescribed life under certain stated environmental conditions.* From the definition, there are four factors associated with reliability : (1) numerical value, (2) intended function, (3) life, and (4) environmental conditions.

The numerical value is the probability that failure of the product will **not** occur during a particular time. Thus, a value of 0.93 would represent the probability that 93 of 100 products would function after a prescribed period of time and 7 products would fail before the prescribed period of time. Particular probability distributions can be used to describe the failure rate of units of product.

The second factor concerns the intended function of the product. Products are designed for particular applications and are expected to be able to perform those applications. For example, an electric hoist is expected to lift a certain design load; it is not expected to lift a load that exceeds the design specification.

The third factor in the definition of reliability is the intended life of the product; in other words, how long the product is expected to last. Thus, the life of automobile tyres is specified by different values, such as 40 months or 50,000 km., depending on the construction of the tyre. Product life is specified as a function of usage, time, or both.

The last factor in the definition involves the environmental conditions. A product that is designed to function indoors, such as an upholstered chair, cannot be expected to function reliably outdoors in the sun, wind, and precipitation. The area of environmental conditions also includes the storage and transportation aspects of the product. These aspects may be more severe than the environmental conditions while the product is in use.

14.2.1 Achieving Reliability

Emphasis Increased emphasis is being given to product reliability. One of the reasons for this emphasis is due to the Consumer Protection Act. Another reason is the fact that products are more complicated. At one time the washing machine was a simple device that agitated the clothes in a hot, soapy solution. Today, a washing machine has different agitating speeds, different rinse speeds, different cycle times, different water temperatures, different water levels, and provisions to dispense a number of washing ingredients at precise times in the cycle. An additional reason for the increased emphasis on reliability is due to automation ; people are, in many cases, not able to manually operate the product if an automated component fails.

System Reliability As products become more complex (have more components), the chance of failure increases. The method of arranging the components affects the reliability of the entire system. Components can be arranged in series, parallel or a combination. Figure 14.1 illustrates the various arrangements.

When components are arranged in series, the reliability of the system is the product of the individual components. Thus, for the series arrangement of Figure 14.1(*a*), the series reliability, R_s, is calculated as follows :

$$\begin{aligned} R_s &= (R_A)(R_B)(R_C) \\ &= (0.95)(0.75)(0.99) \\ &= 0.71 \end{aligned}$$

As components are added to the series, the system reliability decreases.

When components are arranged in series, the failure of any component causes failure of the system. This is not the case when the components are arranged in parallel. When a component fails, the product continues to function using another component until all parallel components have failed. Thus, for the parallel arrangement in Fig. 14.1 (*b*), the parallel reliability, R_p, is calculated as follows :

$$\begin{aligned} R_p &= 1 - (1 - R_I)(1 - R_J) \\ &= 1 - (1 - 0.75)(1 - 0.84) \\ &= 0.96 \end{aligned}$$

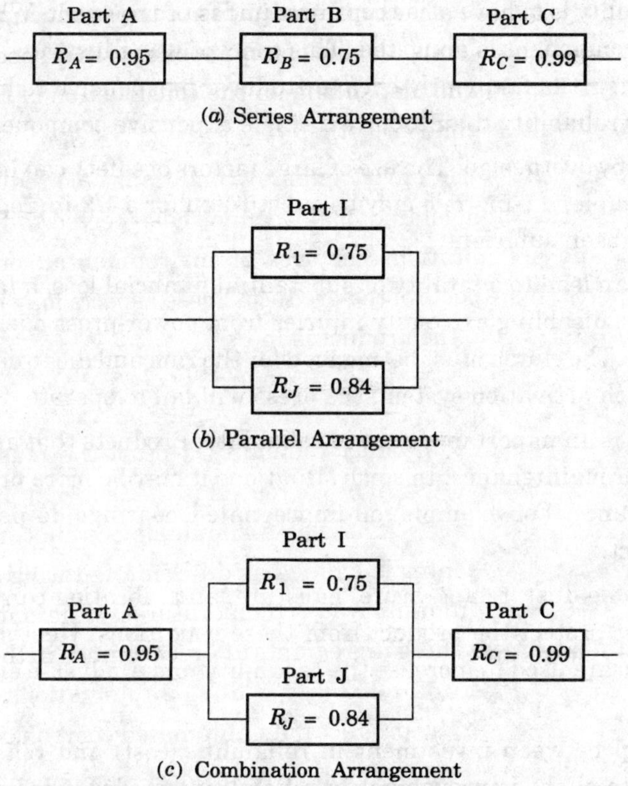

FIGURE 14.1: Methods of arranging components : (*a*) Series arrangement ; (*b*) Parallel arrangement ; (*c*) Combination arrangement.

As the number of components in parallel increases, the reliability increases. The reliability for a parallel arrangement of components is greater than the reliability of the individual components.

Most complexed products are a combination of series and parallel arrangements of components. This is illustrated in Fig. 14.1(*c*), wherein part B is replaced by the parallel components, part *I* and part *J*. The reliability of the combination, R_c, is calculated as follows :

$$R_c = (R_A)(R_{I,J})(R_C)$$
$$= (0.95)(0.96)(0.99)$$
$$= 0.90$$

Product reliability depends on its *design, manufacture, transportation*, and *maintenance*.

Design The most important aspect of reliability is the design. It should be as simple as possible. As previously pointed out, the greater the number of components, the greater the chance of product failure. If a system has 50 components in series, and each component has a reliability of 0.95, the system reliability is

$$R_s = R^n = 0.96^{50} = 0.08$$

The fewer the components, the better the reliability.

Another way of achieving reliability is to have a backup or redundant component. When the primary component fails, another component is activated. This concept was illustrated by the parallel arrangement of components. It is frequently cheaper to have inexpensive redundant components to achieve a particular reliability than to have a single expensive component.

Reliability can also be achieved by overdesign. The use of large factors of safety can increase the reliability of a product. For example, a 1-in. rope may be substituted for a 1/2-in. rope even though the 1/2-in. rope would have been sufficient.

When the failure of a product can lead to a fatality or substantial financial loss, a fail-safe type of device should be used. Thus, disabling extremity injuries from power-press operations are minimized by the use of a clutch. The clutch must be engaged for the ram and die to descend. If there is a malfunction of the clutch-activation system, the press will fail to operate.

The maintenance of the system is an important factor in reliability. Products that are easy to maintain will likely receive better maintenance. In some situations it may be more practical to eliminate the need for maintenance. For example, oil-impregnated bearings do not need lubrication for the life of the product.

Environmental conditions such as dust, temperature, moisture, and vibration can be the cause of failure. The designer must protect the product from these conditions. Heat shields, rubber vibration mounts, and filters are used to increase the reliability under adverse environmental conditions.

There is a definite relationship between investment in reliability (cost) and reliability. After a certain point, there is only a slight improvement in reliability for a large increase in product cost. For example, assume that a ₹ 500 component has a reliability of 0.75. If the cost is increased to ₹ 1,000, the reliability becomes 0.90 ; if the cost is increased to ₹ 2,000, the reliability becomes 0.96. As can be seen by this hypothetical example, there is a diminishing reliability return for the investment rupee.

Manufacturing. The manufacturing process is the second most important aspect of reliability. Basic quality control techniques that have been described in earlier chapters will minimize the risk of product failure. Emphasis should be placed on those components which are least reliable.

Manufacturing personnel can take action to ensure that the equipment used is right for the job and investigate new equipment as it becomes available. In addition, they can experiment with process conditions to determine which conditions produce the most reliable product.

Transportation. The third aspect of reliability is the transportation of the product to the customer. No matter how well conceived the design or how carefully manufactured, the actual performance of the product by the customer is the final evaluation. The reliability of the product at the point of use can be greatly affected by the type of handling the product receives in transit. Good packaging techniques and shipment evaluation are essential.

Maintenance. While designers try to eliminate the need for customer maintenance, there are many situations where it is not practical or possible. In such cases, the customer should be given ample warning. For example, a warning light or buzzer when a component needs a lubricant. Maintenance should be simple and easy to perform.

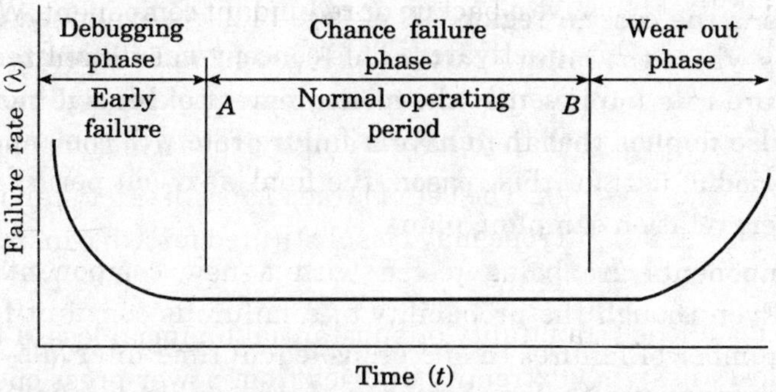

FIGURE 14.2 Typical life history of a complexed product for an infinite number of items.

14.3 LIFE HISTORY CURVE

Figure 14.2 shows a typical life-history curve of a complexed product for an infinite number of items. The curve, sometimes referred to as the "bathtub". curve, is a comparison of failure rate with time. It has three distinct phases : *debugging phase*, *chance failure phase*, and the *wear-out phase*.

The **debugging phase**, which is also called the **burn-in** or **infant-mortality** phase, is characterized by marginal and short-life parts that cause a rapid decrease in the failure rate. This phase is depicted by many visits to the repair shop. While the shape of the curve varies somewhat due to the type of product, the Weibull distribution with shaping parameters less than 1, $\beta < 1$, is used to describe the occurrence of failures. Since the debugging phase is not necessarily as operational phase, it is rarely studied.

The **chance failure phase** (or **normal operating period**) is shown in the figure as a horizontal straight line, thereby making the *failure rate constant*. Failures occur in a random manner due to the constant failure rate. The assumption of constant failure rate is valid for most products ; however, some products may have a failure rate that decreases or increases with time.

The exponential distribution and the Weibull distribution with shape parameter equal to 1 are used to describe this phase of the life history. When the curve increases or decreases, a Weibull shape parameter greater or less than 1 can be used: Reliability studies and sampling plans are, for the most part, concerned with the chance failure phase.

The third phase is the **wear-out phase**, which is depicted by a sharp rise in the failure (i.e. not conforming to specification) rate. Usually the normal distribution is the one that best describes the wear-out phase. However, the Weibull distribution with shape parameters greater or less than 3.5 can be used depending on the type of wear-out distribution.

The curve shown in Fig. 14.2 is the type of failure pattern exhibited by most products; however, there will be some products that deviate from this curve. It is important to know the type of failure pattern so that known probability distribution can be used for analysis and prediction of product reliability.

14.4 THE RELATIONSHIP BETWEEN A CONSTANT FAILURE RATE AND MEAN LIFE OR MEAN TIME BETWEEN FAILURES

Assume that the probability of a failure of a component or complex device is constant per unit of time. That is, the failure rate is independent of the numbers of hours the component or device has been operated. This is the case in region *AB* of Fig. 14.2. As explained earlier in the chapter, that in those cases where the failure pattern of Fig. 14.2 is believed to apply, the assumption of a constant failure rate implies that the measurement of life will not start before time *A*. This assumption also implies that the uniform failure rate will continue for a longer time than the intended period of use; for this reason, the final wear-out period can be disregarded in the design and interpretation sampling plans.

Consider that, say, 100 components are being tested with a new component being substituted whenever one fails. Even though the probability of a failure is constant for any stated time interval, the actual number of failures in successive equal time intervals will be subject to chance fluctuations. When we use the mathematics of probability to compute OC curves for acceptance sampling plans used in life testing we are recognizing the inevitability of these chance fluctuations.

Two related quantities that we shall use in computing OC curves are as follows :

- λ failure rate, i.e., the probability of a failure in a stated unit of time. Conceivably, any unit of time could be adopted. However, for consistency throughout this chapter; we shall arbitrarily select 1 hour as the time unit in all instances.
- (θ) the arithmetic mean or average of the lives (of components), usually referred to in the literature of reliability as the *mean life*, or *mean time to failure* (MTTF). As applied to complex devices, (θ) is interpreted as the *mean time between failures* (sometimes designated as mtbf or MTBF). (θ) should be expressed in the same time units that are used for λ.

For our special case of the constant failure rate : $(\theta) = 1/\lambda$. (It is pointed out later in this chapter that this reciprocal relationship between (θ) and λ depends on the use of a time unit that is a relatively small fraction of the mean life.)

Although our discussion in this chapter is based on failure rates and mean lives expressed in units of time, it should be mentioned that other units than time may be used in certain instances. For example, the number of operating cycles of certain switching devices is a more appropriate unit for measuring life than the number of operating hours.

14.5 OC CURVE COMPUTATION AND CONSTRUCTION

The operating characteristic (OC) curve is constructed in a manner similar to that given in Chap. 9. However, the fraction defective p is replaced by the mean life (θ). The shape of the OC curve as shown in Fig. 14.3 is different than those of Chap. 9. If lots are submitted with a mean life of 5,000 h, the probability of acceptance is 0.697 using the sampling plan described by the OC curve of Fig. 14.3.

An example problem for a constant failure rate will be used to illustrate the construction. A lot-by-lot acceptance sampling plan with replacement is as follows. Select a sample of 16 units from a lot and test each item for 600 h. If 2 or less items fail, accept the lot; if 3 or more items fail, reject the lot. In symbols, the plan is $n = 16$, $T = 600\ h$, $c = 2$, and $r = 3$. When an item fails, it is replaced by another one from the lot. The first step in the construction of the curve is to assume values for the mean life (θ). These values are converted to the failure rate, λ, as shown in the second column of Table 14.1. The expected average number of failures is obtained by multiplying a constant $[nT = H = (16)(600) = 9{,}600\ h]$ with the failure rate as shown in the third column of the table. This value $H\lambda$ performs the same function as the value of np which was

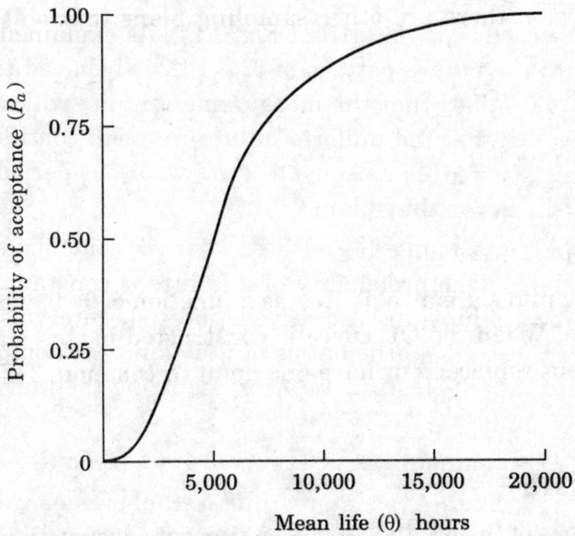

FIGURE 14.3: *OC* curve for the sample plan $n = 16$, $T = 600$ h, $c = 2$, and $r = 3$.

previously used for the construction of an OC curve. Values for the probability of acceptance of the lot are found in Table *G* for $c = 2$. Typical calculations are as follows. Assume that (θ) = 2,000:

$$\lambda = \frac{1}{(\theta)} = \frac{1}{2{,}000} = 0.0005$$

$$nT\lambda = (16)(600)(0.0005) = 4.80$$

From Table *G* for $nT\lambda = 4.80$ and $c = 2$,

$$P_a = 0.143$$

Additional calculations for other assumed values of θ are shown in Table 14.1.

TABLE 14.1: CALCULATIONS FOR THE OC CURVE FOR THE SAMPLING PLAN

($n = 16$, $T = 600$ h, (i.e. $H = 9{,}600$) $c = 2$, and $r = 3$)

Mean Life θ	*Failure Rate,* $\lambda = 1/\theta$	*Expected Average Number of Failures,* $H\lambda$	P_a
20,000	0.00005	0.48	0.985
10,000	0.0001	0.96	0.927
5,000	0.0002	1.92	0.698
2,000	0.0005	4.80	0.143
1,000	0.0010	9.60	0.004
4,000	0.00025	2.40	0.570
6,000	0.00017	1.60	0.783

Since this OC curve assumes a constant failure rate, the exponential distribution is applicable. The Poisson distribution is used to construct the OC curve since it approximates the exponential.

Because of the constant failure rate, there are other sampling plans that will have the same OC curve. Some of these are :

$n = 4$, $T = 2{,}400$ h, $c = 2$

$n = 8$, $T = 1{,}200$ h, $c = 2$

$n = 16$, $T = 600$ h, $c = 2$

$n = 24$, $T = 450$ h, $c = 2$

$n = 32$, $T = 300$ h, $c = 2$

OC curves for reliability sampling plans are also plotted as a function of θ/θ0, which is the actual mean life/acceptable mean life. When the OC curve is constructed in this manner, all OC curves for life tests with or without replacement have one point in common. This point is the producer's risk α and $\theta/\theta_0 = 1.0$.

14.6 TYPES OF RELIABILITY TESTS

Since reliability testing requires the use of the product and sometimes its destruction, the type of test and the amount of testing is usually an economic decision. Testing is normally done on the end product ; however, components and parts can be tested if they are presenting problems. Since testing is usually done in the laboratory, every effort should be made to simulate the real environment under controlled conditions.

Life tests are of three types, as described below.

Failure-Terminated: These life-test sample plans are terminated when a preassigned number of failures occur to the sample. Acceptance criteria for the lot are based on the accumulated item test times when the test is terminated.

Time-Terminated: This type of life-test sampling plan is terminated when the sample obtains a predetermined test time. Acceptance criteria for the lot are based on the number of failures in the sample during the test time.

Sequential: A third type of life-testing plan is a sequential life-test sampling plan whereby neither the number of failures nor the time required to reach a decision are fixed in advance. Instead, decisions depend on the accumulated results of the life test. The sequential life-test plans have the advantage that the expected test time and the expected number of failures required to reach a decision as to lot acceptability are less than the failure-terminated or the time-terminated type.

Testing may be conducted with replacement of a failed unit or without replacement. *With replacement* occurs when a failure is replaced with another unit. Test time continues to be accumulated with the new sample unit. This situation is possible when there is a constant failure rate and the replaced unit has as equal chance of failure. The *without-replacement* situation occurs when the failure is not replaced.

Tests are based on one or more of the following characteristics :

1. *Mean life* — the average life of the product.
2. *Failure rate* — the percentage of failures per unit time or number of cycles.
3. *Hazard rate* — the instantaneous failures rate at a specified time. This varies with age except in the special case of a constant failure rate wherein the failure rate and

hazard rate are the same. The Weibull distribution is applicable and the hazard rate increases with age if the shape parameter β is greater than 1 and decreases with age if the shape parameter is less than 1.

4. *Reliable life* — the life beyond which some specified portion of the items in the lot will survive. The Weibull distribution and the normal distribution as they pertain to the wear-out phase are applicable.

14.7 HANDBOOK H 108

Quality Control and Reliability Handbook *H* 108 gives sampling procedures and tables for life and reliability testing. Sampling plans in the handbook are based on the exponential distribution. The handbook provides for the three different types of tests: failure-terminated, time-terminated, and sequential. For each of these types of tests, provision is made for the two situations: with replacement of failed units during the test, or without replacement. Essentially, the plans are based on the mean-life criterion, although failure rate is used in one part of the handbook.

14.8 ESTIMATING MEAN LIFE AT VARIOUS STAGES IN A LIFE TEST

Assume the existence in a lot or process of an unknown constant failure rate per item hour λ. We wish to estimate this probability of failure in an item hour. On the basis of all the information from life tests from the lot or process available at any moment, our best estimate is

$$\text{Estimated } \lambda = \frac{\text{number of failures observed}}{\text{number of item hours of test}}$$

This equation simply applies the frequency definition of probability and assumes that all trials of the event in question (that is, failure) are made "under the same essential conditions." If the probability of a failure does not depend on the age of the item tested, each item hour of test should be viewed as providing the same amount of information as any other item hour. For example, 1,000 item hours obtained from testing 1,000 items each for 1 h give just as good a basis for estimating λ as if only 10 items were tested (with replacement) for 100 h each.

The greater the number of item hours, the more confidence it is reasonable to have in the resulting estimate of λ. However, in this connection, it may be pointed out that a small number of trials may occasionally, by chance, give an estimate closer to the true probability than will be obtained from a larger number of trials.

Because mean life is the reciprocal of failure rate, as estimate of θ in hours may be made at any time during a life test as follows :

$$\text{Estimated } \theta = \frac{\text{number of item hours of test up to the time of estimate}}{\text{number of failures up to the time of estimate}}$$

Table 14.2 shows a series of estimates of mean life such as might have been made at various times during a life test. It should be noted that, in such a test made without replacement, the number of item hours of test at any time can be computed by adding the lives in hours ti of the items that have failed (r in all) up to the moment of estimate to the number of item hours of life observed t for the items that have not yet failed $(n - r)$. For example, the estimate after 4 h could be computed as follows :

TABLE 14.2: SOME ESTIMATES OF MEAN LIFE

Hours of test at moment of estimate	*Failures up to moment of estimate*	*Item hours of test up to moment of estimate*	*Estimate of mean life h*
4	11	461	41.9
5	17	570	33.5
6	17	673	39.7
8	19	878	46.2
10	23	1,078	46.9
15	31	1,556	50.2
20	41	1,970	48.0
30	55	2,696	49.0
171	120	5,912	49.3

$$\text{Estimated} \quad \theta_r = \frac{\sum_{i=1}^{r} t_i + (n-r)}{r}$$

$$= \frac{1+1+1+1+2+2+2+3+4+4+4+4(120-11)}{11}$$

$$= \frac{25+436}{11} = \frac{461}{11} = 41.9 \text{ h.}$$

In examining the successive estimates of mean life shown in Table 14.2, the reader should keep in mind that the data were generated using a failure rate of 0.02 per hour. This failure rate corresponds to a "true" mean life of 50 h.

14.9 ACCEPTANCE SAMPLING PLANS INVOLVING THE COMBINATION OF SAMPLES FROM A SERIES OF LOTS

Consider the case of, say, an electronic component to be used in a service where it is desired to have a failure rate of not more than 0.00001 per hour. (Sometimes it is desired to avoid the use of very small decimal fractions; if so, a rate of 0.00001 per hour might be stated as 1% per 1,000 h.) Such a specification tells us that the mean life must be at least 100,000 h.

The need to combine the evidence of the samples from a series of successive lots is particularly great when one is dealing with a requirement for such an extremely low failure rate. Otherwise, if the decision on each lot is to be made solely on the evidence of the sample from the lot itself, the required item hours of test from each lot may be extremely high and the test may be extremely costly.

The following plan illustrates one possible method of combining the results of samples from successive lots. The plan is one of a set that has been suggested for use in acceptance sampling for certain long-lived electronic components. The sample size and acceptance numbers in this particular plan are related to a desired mean life of at least 1,00,000 h.

1. The plan starts with a qualification sample requiring 418,000 item hours of test (say, 836 items for 500 h). Not more than 3 failures are allowed in this sample. The sample

size and acceptance number are chosen to give a Consumer's Risk of 0.40 of accepting product having a mean life of 100,000 h. (In some of the literature of reliability, such a Consumer's Risk is referred to as a "confidence level" of 0.60.)

2. After qualification has been obtained, a sample of 44 items from each lot is tested for 250 h, a total of 11,000 item hours. Not more than 1 failure is allowable to pass the lot.
3. The item hours and failures of the samples from each set of 10 successive lots are to be cumulated. The total item hours from the 10 lots will be 10 (11,000) = 110,000. If a total of more than 2 failures is found at any time during the 110,000 item hours, reduced inspection is discontinued and a new qualification sample is required. If lots are held and accepted or rejected in sets of 10, these criteria give a Producer's Risk of 0.10 of rejecting product that has a mean life of 100,000 h.
4. Item hours and failures from successive samples are cumulated until 418,000 item hours, the number used in the qualification test, have been observed. If a total of more than 3 failures is found, reduced inspection is discontinued and a new qualification sample is required.

The reader will note that three different OC curves are relevant in judging how a scheme of this type affects the producer and consumer. Nevertheless, because the criteria of paragraph (1) are also applied cumulatively in (4), the OC curve of the qualification sample is the one of greatest interest to the producer. Unless the producer can make product that has a mean life considerably longer than 100000 h, there is a substantial risk that the producer cannot qualify in the first place. (The producer has 6 chances out of 10 that its product will not qualify if its λ is exactly 0.00001.) The producer also takes the same risk that, if its product qualifies, it will be disqualified before one cycle of procedure (paragraph 4) has run its course.

Although the OC curve of the acceptance plan in paragraph (1) measures the consumer's protection relative to qualification, the consumer needs to look at the OC curve of the plan in (2) to evaluate the worst condition faced in the short run (that is, protection against accepting an individual lot after a producer achieves qualification). All things considered, it is evident that the consumer takes substantial risks of accepting product that has a failure rate much worse than the desired 0.00001.

The foregoing type of acceptance procedure has been included in this chapter to emphasize the difficulties that inevitably arise in devising acceptance sampling schemes when tolerable failure rates are extremely low. In meeting these difficulties, it is desirable that all parties concerned recognize the need for quite large sample sizes and for a substantial sharing of risks between producer and consumer.

14.10 THE "EXPONENTIAL" RELIABILITY FUNCTION THAT RESULTS FROM THE ASSUMPTION OF A CONSTANT FAILURE RATE

If successive trials of an event that have a constant probability 0.02 that a failure would occur on any single trial, the probability that any one trial will not result in a failure is $1 - 0.02 = 0.98$. If trials are to be continued until a failure occurs, we can apply the theorem of conditional probabilities to determine the probability of survival (that is, of no failure) after any stipulated number of trials. For example, the probability of survival after 10 trials is

TABLE 14.3: AN ILLUSTRATION OF THE VALIDITY OF THE NEGATIVE EXPONENTIAL FORMULA TO ESTIMATE RELIABILITY (THAT IS PROBABILITY OF SURVIVAL UNDER THE ASSUMPTION OF A CONSTANT FAILURE RATE

Age H, (hours)	*Ratio of age to mean life,* $H/\theta = H\lambda$	*Probability of survival*		
		By theorem of conditional probabilities $(1-\lambda)^H$	*By negative exponential* $e^{-H\lambda}$	*Actual fraction surviving among the 120 days*
2	0.04	0.960	0.961	0.94
4	0.08	0.922	0.923	0.91
6	0.12	0.886	0.887	0.86
8	0.16	0.851	0.852	0.84
10	0.20	0.817	0.819	0.81
15	0.30	0.739	0.741	0.74
20	0.40	0.668	0.670	0.66
30	0.60	0.546	0.549	0.54
40	0.80	0.446	0.449	0.42
50	1.00	0.364	0.368	0.37
60	1.2	0.298	0.301	0.30
70	1.4	0.243	0.247	0.26
80	1.6	0.199	0.202	0.23
90	1.8	0.162	0.165	0.22
100	2.0	0.133	0.135	0.18
120	2.4	0.089	0.091	0.10
140	2.8	0.059	0.061	0.05
160	3.2	0.039	0.041	0.02
180	3.6	0.026	0.027	0.00
200	4.0	0.018	0.018	0.00

$(0.98)^{10} = 0.817$. In general, if λ represents a constant probability of failure per hour, the probability of an item surviving for H hours is $(1 - (\lambda)^H$.

Early in this chapter, several formal definitions of reliability were quoted. Although the phrasing differed slightly, all the definitions viewed reliability as being the probability of no failure throughout some specified period of time. In this sense, the third column of Table 14.3 gives reliability values corresponding to a λ of 0.02 and to the various possible "specified periods of time" from 2 to 200 h that are given in the first column of the table. In examining Table 14.3, it is of interest to note the fairly close agreement between the computed probabilities of survival $(0.98)^H$ given in the third column and the observed fractions surviving given in the fifth column based on the experiment.

Nevertheless, although our experiment employed a constant failure rate of 0.02 per trial, it failed in one minor respect to simulate the results that would occur in an actual life test where the failure rate was constant. A constraint in our test was that we could obtain only integral values of lives; no fractional values were possible. That is, we could find a life of 5 h (5 trials with each trial interpreted as an hour) or 6 h but not, say, 5.37 h. Of course, in an actual life test, failure may occur at any moment, not merely at the end of an hour. This point bears on the relative merits of the methods of computing probability of survival illustrated in the third and fourth columns of Table 14.3.

The fourth column of Table 14.3 gives values of $e^{-H\lambda}$ for our λ of 0.02. The reader will recall from the discussion of the binomial and Poisson distributions in Chap. 4 that e^{-np} is a limit of $(1-p)^n$ as n increased and p decrease with product np held constant, or, stated a little differently, e–np gives a satisfactory approximation to $(1 - p)^n$ provided p is small enough and n is large enough. Of course, the symbols that we employ are purely arbitrary; it is equally appropriate to view $e - H\lambda$ as an approximation to $(1 - \lambda)^H$. By comparing the values in the third and fourth columns of Table 14.3, we can see that this approximation is fairly close with a λ of 0.02. For smaller values of λ, the approximation would be even better.

The theorem of conditional probabilities used in the manner illustrated in Table 14.3 is correct in principle for an artificial experiment in which lives can be only integers. However, the concept of a constant failure rate applied to actual lives presumably means a constant instantaneous failure rate; for such a rate, the negative exponential formula for probability of survival is correct in principle.

Although the expression $e^{-H\lambda}$ is more precisely described as negative exponential, the literature of life testing and reliability usually refers to it simply as "exponential". With one exception (the discussion of a graph reproduced from a source that uses "negative exponential"). the word exponential is the one used throughout the remainder of this chapter.

SOLVED QUESTIONS

Q. 14.1: *Select the right/appropriate option for the following*

(i) From the definition of reliability, it follows that in any reliability programme there must be

(a) a quantification of reliability in terms of probability

(b) a clear statement defining successful performance

(c) a definition of the environment in which the equipment must operate

(d) a statement of the required operating times between failures

(e) all of the above.

(ii) When reliability people say they are breaking the monopoly of the designer, they mean

(a) they are relieving the designer of responsibility for the design

(b) they intend to review the design in conjunction with other experts

(c) they insist on having final approval of the design

(d) they intend to put the reliability engineer one level higher than the design engineer in the organization.

(iii) It is Reliability's job to see that all the tasks outlined in the reliability programme are

(a) carried out by reliability engineers

(b) carried out by the department having the primary responsibility

(c) defined, making sure that quality control does its job

(d) done, including those jobs that the primary responsible departments are incapable of doing.

(*iv*) The process of dividing up or budgeting the final reliability goal among the subsystems is known as

(*a*) reliability estimation (*b*) reliability prediction

(*c*) reliability apportionment (*d*) all of the above.

(*v*) Reliability prediction is

(*a*) a one-shot estimation process

(*b*) a continuous process starting with paper predictions

(*c*) a process to be viewed as an end in itself in fulfillment of a contract

(*d*) none of the above.

(*vi*) Reliability prediction and measurement is primarily useful in

(*a*) evaluating feasibility (*b*) establishing reliability goals

(*c*) evaluating overall reliability (*d*) defining problem areas

(*e*) all of the above.

(*vii*) Preventive maintenance is defined as

(*a*) actions performed as a result of failure

(*b*) repair of an item to a specified condition

(*c*) actions performed on a scheduled or routine basis to retain an item in a specified condition

(*d*) maintenance performed for detection and prevention of incipient failure.

(*viii*) Reliability testing of parts is performed to yield which of the following types of information ?

(*a*) application suitability (*b*) environmental capability

(*c*) measurement of life characteristics (*d*) all of the above.

(*ix*) If a system reliability of 0.9998 is required, what reliability of two components in series is required ?

(*a*) $R_a = 0.99$ (*b*) $R_a = 0.999$

(*c*) $R_a = 0.98$ (*d*) $R_a = 0.9999$

(*e*) $R_a = 0.998$.

(*x*) The reliability of a device comprised of various parts functionally in series is

(*a*) the sum of the probabilities of the unreliabilities

(*b*) the product of the unreliabilities

(*c*) the sum of the reliabilities

(*d*) the product of the reliabilities

(*e*) the sum of the combinations and permutations.

(*xi*) The flat portion of the bathtub curve is a region of chance failures therefore, the reliability equation, $R = e^{-H\lambda}$

(*a*) does not apply to this region (*b* only applies to this region

(*c*) applies to the wear-out region as well as the flat region

(*d*) applies to the entire bathtub curve.

(*xii*) If a component has a known constant failures rate of 0.0037 failure per hour, the reliability of two of the these components in a series arrangement would be

(a) less than 99 percent
(b) dependent on the wear-out rate of a mating subsystem
(c) insufficient information to solve the problem
(d) 99.63 percent.

(xiii) Assuming an exponential failure distribution, the probability of surviving an operating time equal to twice the MTBF is
(a) practically zero (b) about 14 percent
(c) about 36 percent (d) none of the above.

(xiv) Unless repair or maintenance action is taken, the probability of failure of a device which has progressed to the point of wear-out will
(a) decrease (b) increase (c) not change.

Ans: (i) (a); (ii) (b); (iii) (b); (iv) (c); (v) (b); (vi) (e); (vii) (c); (viii) (d); (ix) (b); (x) (d); (xi) (b); (xii) (e); (xiii) (b); (xiv) (b).

Q. 14.2: *What is a suitable definition of 'reliability' ?*

Ans: Ability to perform to stated specification under stated conditions for the required time.

Q. 14.3: *Give a simple definition of 'reliability'.*

Ans: The probability that a piece of equipment continues to operate during a specified time period.

Q. 14.4: *Identify the three key categories of failure.*

Ans: Sudden, intermittent and catastrophic.

Q. 14.5: *What is meant by terms 'hazard' and 'hazard rate' ?*

Ans: Hazard is the ratio of failure in a period to survivors at the start of that period. Hazard rate is the hazard per unit time.

Q. 14.6: *What is the difference between failure and failure rate ?*

Ans: Failure rate is the number of failures per unit time.

Q. 14.7: *How are MTBF and failure rate related ?*

Ans: MTBF is the reciprocal of failure rate.

Q. 14.8: *In a negative exponential distribution, what is the standard deviation equal to ?*

Ans: The standard deviation is equal to the mean. The distribution has a constant rate of decrease.

Q. 14.9: *If wear is suspected as a failure cause, what might be a suitable distribution ?*

Ans: Normal

Q. 14.10: *What is meant by 'series' and 'parallel' connections ?*

Ans: Elements in series are connected end to end each other. Elements in parallel have a common input and a common output.

Q. 14.11: *What is meant by active parallel redundancy ?*

Ans: The system will still function when some of its elements fail.

Q. 14.12: *If a number of components are put in parallel is the reliability of the system increased or decreased ?*

Ans: Increased

Q. 14.13: *Do you think that the likely maintenance cost for a machine will decrease over time ?*

Ans: No.

Q. 14.14: *If wear is suspected as a failure cause, what might be a suitable distribution ?*

Ans: The normal distribution.

Q. 14.15: *It is not possible to get higher reliability from a system than those of its elements. True or False ?*

Ans: False : Connection in parallel achieves higher reliability.

Q. 14.16: *Define the following : (i) Hazard rate (ii) Reliable life.*

Ans: (*i*) **Hazard rate:** It is the instantaneous failure rate at a specified time. This varies with age except in the special case of a constant failure rate wherein the failure rate and hazard rate are the same. The Weibull distribution is applicable and the hazard rate increases with age if the shape parameter β is greater than 1 and decreases with age if the shape parameter is less than 1.

(*ii*) **Reliable life:** The life beyond which some specified portion of the items in the lot will survive. The weibull distribution and the normal distribution as they pertaion to the wear-out phase are applicable.

Q. 14.17: *Distinguish between reliability and quality control.*

Ans: All the definitions of reliability that we have given involve the element of time. To say, for example, that the probability of survival of a given piece of equipment is 95% for 100 hours of operation indicates that, on the average, 95 of 1000 such pieces would operate without failure for 1,000 hours.

The incorporation of a *time constraint in the reliability definition is not unusual*. No product lasts forever ; after its useful life period is over, it begins to show signs of wearing out, and a rapidly rising failure rate. The manufacturer therefore restricts his prediction of the reliability of the product to a time span and does not reach into the wear-out region of the life of the equipment.

Product quality, on the other hand, is not mathematically linked to a time period, nor is it stated in terms of a probability of performance. It may best be defined as the degree of conformance of the product to the applicable specifications, standards, and workmanship criteria.

It should also be understood that the high quality of an item in not necessarily synonymous with high reliability. For instance, a component used in an assembly, or system, may have been exposed to all the necessary quality control and have met all of its specification requirements and yet run into unforeseen difficulties when working as part of the overall equipment. This difficulty may stem, for example, from a lack of recognition of adverse electrical or mechanical interactions between components.

Q. 14.18: *Given component reliabilities as indicated, calculate the probability of survival of the assembly.*

Component	Reliability
A	0.999
B	0.98
C	0.99
D	0.87
E	0.92
F	0.84

Ans: Assuming the components are arranged in series to form the required assembly, the series reliability, R_s is calculated as follows :

$$R_s = (R_A)(R_B)(R_C)(R_D)(R_L)(R_F)$$

$$= (0.999)\ (0.98)\ (0.99)\ (0.87)\ (0.92)\ (0.84) = 0.6516$$

Q. 14.19: *The resistance tolerance of a 100 ohm resistor, as purchased, is± 10%. This type of resistor may drift up to ± 15% in resistance value after 2 years of operation. What are the worst case considerations for the application of this resistor ?*

Ans: The lowest resistance value, as purchased could be

$$= 100 - 0.1\ (100)$$

$$= 90 \text{ ohms}$$

The lowest resistance value after 2 years could be

$$= 90 - 0.15\ (90)$$

$$= 76.5 \text{ ohms.}$$

The highest resistance value as purchased could be

$$= 100 + 0.1\ (100)$$

$$= 110 \text{ ohms.}$$

The highest resistance value after 2 years could be

$$= 110 + 0.15\ (110)$$

$$= 126.5 \text{ ohms.}$$

Therefore, unless the circuit is designed to be sufficiently tolerant to a variation of this 100 ohm resistor, ranging from a possible 76.5 to 126.5 ohm, there could be a circuit malfunction.

Q. 14.20: (*a*) *A filter and an amplifier comprise a system that is to operate with a probability of success of 90% for 1000 h. The amplifier has a probability of survival of 95% for 1000 h. What probability of survival is required for the filter ?*

(*b*) *What is the reliability of the system shown in Fig 14.4? Assume that* $P_A = P_B = P_C = P_D = P_E = P_F = 0.9$.

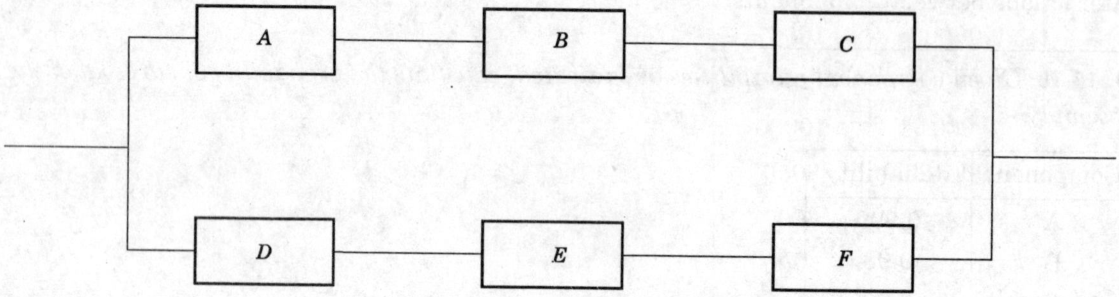

FIGURE 14.4: System of Prob. 12.20.

Ans:

$$R_{\text{system}} = P_{\text{filter}} \times P_{\text{Amplifier}}$$
$$0.90 = P_{\text{filter}} \times 0.95$$
$$P_{\text{filter}} = 0.90/0.95 = 0.947$$

(*b*)

$$R_{\text{System}} = 1 - (1 - 0.9^3)^2$$
$$= 1 - (1 - 0.729)^2 = 1 - 0.271^2 = 0.92656$$

Q. 14.21: *An assembly, through simplification, can be reduced from six components to three components. The reliability of the six components is 0.98. Presuming no change in component reliabilities, what would be the change in the assembly reliability with this reduction of components.*

Ans: From the statement of the problem, it is obvious that the assembly must contain at least three components in series. Assuming that each of these components was having one redundant component

$$R_c = [1 - (1 - 0.98)^2]^3$$
$$= [0.9996]^3 \quad \textit{i.e.,} \quad 0.9988$$

After the reduction of components the reliability of the system is

$$R_s = (0.98)^3 = 0.9412$$

$$\% \text{ change in reliability} = \left(\frac{0.9988 - 0.9412}{0.9988}\right) \times 100 = 5.77\%$$

Q. 14.22: *In one of the plans from H 108, 10 items were to be tested for 500 h with replacement and with an acceptance number of 1. Using values of* λ *that seem to you to be appropriate, make a calculation similar to Table 14.1 to find enough points to define the OC curve of this plan. Plot your OC curve showing probability of acceptance as a function of mean life.*

Ans: Assuming different failure rates, the mean life and probability of acceptance can be computed from Table *G*. Following tabulation shows such calculations and Fig 14.5 shows the OC curve of the plan.

Failure rate per hour λ	*Mean life hr, θ = 1/λ*	*Expected average number of failures in 5000 test hours (5000 λ)*	*Probability of acceptance*
0.00002	50000	0.1	0.995
0.00005	20000	0.25	0.974
0.00006	16667	0.30	0.963
0.00008	12500	0.40	0.938
0.0001	10000	0.50	0.910
0.000125	8000	0.625	0.870
0.00015	6667	0.75	0.827
0.00020	5000	1.0	0.736
0.00025	4000	1.25	0.645
0.00040	2500	2.00	0.406
0.00050	2000	2.50	0.331
0.00060	1667	3.00	0.199
0.00080	1250	4.00	0.092
0.0010	1000	5.00	0.040

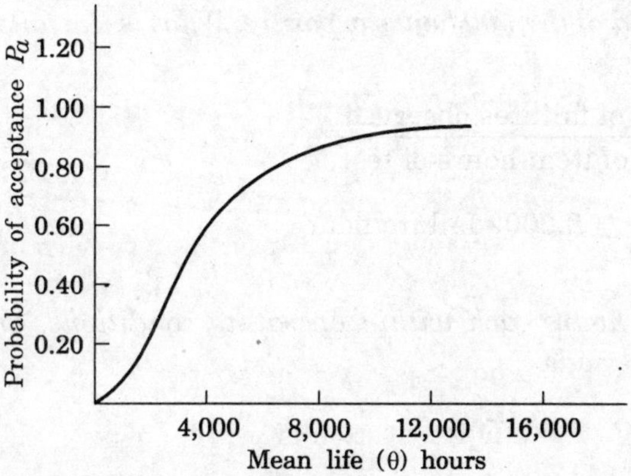

FIGURE 14.5: OC curve for a test of 5,000 items hours with an acceptance number of 1.

Q. 14.23: *The acceptance sampling plan of Q. 14.22 was stipulated for an approximate value of 0.10 for the Producer's Risk of rejection of a lot having a mean life of 10,000 h and for an approximate value of 0.10 for the Consumer's Risk of acceptance of a lot having a mean life of 1,000 h. Use Table G to compute the respective values of these two risks.*

Ans: From Q. 14.22, for a mean life of 10,000 h, the probability of acceptance is 0.910. Hence Producer's Risk = 1.0 – 0.910 = 0.09.

Also for a mean life of 1,000 h, the probability of acceptance is 0.040. Hence consumer's Risk is 0.04.

Q. 14.24: *The MTBF of an equipment is 500 h. What is the faiture rate expressed in*

(*a*) *% failures/ 1,000 h ?* (*b*) *failures/ 106 h ?* (*c*) *failures/hour ?*

Is MTBF a guaranteed failure free period ?

Ans: (*a*) $$MTBF = \frac{10^5}{\text{\% Failures/1,000 h}}$$

$$\text{\%Failures/1,000 h} = \frac{10^5}{500} = 200$$

(*b*) $$MTBF = \frac{10^6}{\text{Failures}/10^6 \text{ h}}$$

$$\text{Failures}/10^6 \text{ h} = \frac{10^6}{500} = 2,000$$

(*c*) $$MTBF = \frac{1}{\text{Failure/hour}}$$

$$\text{Failures/hour} = \frac{1}{500} = 0.002$$

The MTBF figure is **not** a guaranteed failure-free period. It is a mean values of operating times between failures.

Q. 14.25: *Ten transformers were tested for 500 hours each within prescribed operating conditions, and one transformer failed exactly at the end of the 500 hours exposure. What is the failure rate for this type of transformer ?*

Ans: $$\lambda = \frac{\text{number of failures observed}}{\text{number of item hours of test}}$$

$$= \frac{1}{10 \times 500} = 0.0002 \text{ failure/hour}$$

Q. 14.26: *Ten motors were tested for 500 hours each within operating conditions, and four motors failed after the following test time periods.*

motor 1	fails after	50 h
motor 2	fails after	150 h
motor 3	fails after	250 h
motor 4	fails after	450 h

What is the failure rate for this type of motor.

Ans: $$\lambda = \frac{4}{(1 \times 50) + (1 \times 150) + (1 \times 250) + (1 \times 450) + 6(500)}$$

$$= \frac{4}{3900} = 0.00102 \text{ failure/hour}$$

Q. 14.27: *To understand the MTBF concept, assume that the telephone company performs a life test on a large number of special voice amplifier for a 1,000 h period. The elapsed time from the start of the test to the occurrence of each failure is recorded. A total of 12 failures were* *experienced. The occurrence of last failures were coincident with the termination of the test. The record of the failures times and calculated failure-free periods is shown in the following table.*

Elapsed time	*Failure-free period (h)*
50	50
200	150
210	10
280	70
300	20
490	190
530	40
540	10
630	90
710	80
880	170
1000	120
Total	1,000

(*a*) *Calculate MTBF.*

(*b*) *What inference do you draw from the calculated value of MTBF and the data given in the problem ?*

Ans: (*a*) $$MTBF = \frac{1,000}{12} = 83.3 \text{ h}$$

(*b*) The *MTBF* is 83.3 h, even though the failure-free periods range from 10 to 190 h. Translated into equipment service operations, service calls may be expected, on average, once every 83.3 h during the 1,000 h operating period.

Q. 14.28: *The following table indicates the time a lot of electronic parts operated until failure. The times are presented in the order in which the trials were measured and included 30 measurements made with a constant failure rate of 0.0005 per h.*

(*a*) *Rearrange the data values in order of increasing magnitude.*

(*b*) *Compute the respective estimates of mean life in hours that would have been approximate after 1,000, 3,000, 5,000 and 7,713 hours of testing.*

Set of observation	*Time until failure (hours)*				
	1	*2*	*3*	*4*	*5*
1	2,737	1,281	1,855	1,472	2,638
2	2,147	4,522	428	3,727	7,713
3	961	617	6,715	714	3,303
4	714	4,025	5,618	1,474	1,567
5	1,285	3,132	501	1,661	2,148
6	456	3,913	1,846	2,114	2,713

Ans: (*a*) The values arranged in the increasing magnitude are shown in the following table.

428	961	1,661	2,638	3,913
456	1,281	1,846	2,713	4,015
501	1,285	1,855	2,737	4,522
617	1,472	2,114	3,132	5,018
714	1,474	2,147	3,303	6,715
714	1,567	2,148	3,727	7,713
Total				73,997

(*b*)

$$\theta \text{ after 1,000 hour} = \frac{428 + 456 + 501 + 617 + 714 + 714 + 961 + 1{,}000(30 - 7)}{6}$$

$$= \frac{27{,}391}{6} = 4{,}565.17 \text{ h.}$$

$$\theta \text{ after 3,000 hours} = \frac{428 + ... + 2{,}737 + 3{,}000(30 - 21)}{21}$$

$$= \frac{59{,}329}{21} = 2{,}777.57 \text{ h}$$

$$\text{after 5,000 hours} = \frac{428 + ... + 4{,}522 + 5{,}000(30 - 27)}{27}$$

$$= \frac{68{,}951}{21} = 2{,}553.74 \text{ h}$$

$$\theta \text{ after 7,713 hours} = \frac{73{,}997}{30} = 2{,}466.57 \text{ h}$$

Q. 14.29: *For the rearranged data of Q. 14.28 compute to the nearest two decimal places the fractions surviving after 500, 1,000, 1,500, 2,000, 3,000, 4,000, 5,000 and 7,000 hours respectively. Compare these observed values with the appropriate values for probability of survival that you obtain from the column in Table G headed c = 0.*

Ans: Failure upto 500 hours = 2

$$\text{Fraction surviving} = \frac{28}{30} = 0.93$$

$$H\lambda = 500 \times 0.0005 = 0.25$$

$$\text{Probability of survival} = e^{-H\lambda}$$

$$= e^{-0.25}$$

From Table G under the column headed $c = 0$,

$$e^{-0.25} = 0.779$$

Using similar computations, following table lists out the actual fraction surviving and probability of survival from Table *G*.

Age H (h hours)	*Probability of survival as computed from Table G*	*Actual fraction surviving among the 30 parts*
500	0.779	0.93
1,000	0.607	0.77
1,500	0.472	0.63
2,000	0.368	0.50
3,000	0.223	0.30
4,000	0.135	0.17
5,000	0.082	0.10
7,000	0.030	0.03

Q. 14.30: *An electronic device has a failure rate of 500 failures/10^6 h. One identical standby unit is used to increase the reliability of the basic device. The operating time is 1,000 h. The reliability of the failure sensing and switching element is P (FSS) = 0.97. Figure 14.6 shows the schematic of the system. What is the system reliability ?*

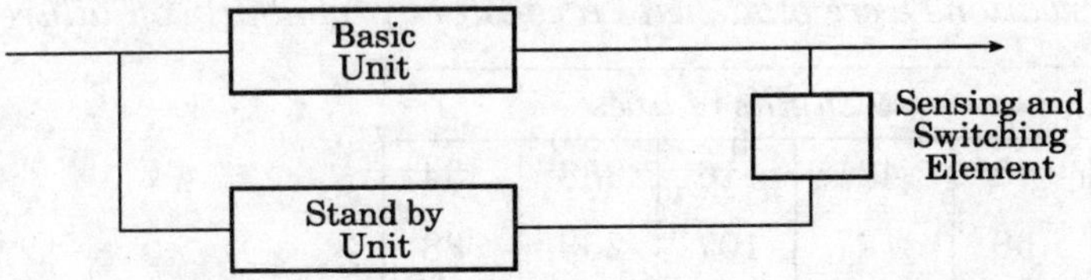

FIGURE 14.6 Standly redundancy with sensing and switching element.

Ans: The expected number of failures

$$H\lambda = 1{,}000 \times 500 \times 10^{-6} = 0.5$$

$$P = e^{-0.5}\,[1 + 0.5\,(0.97)]$$

From Table *G*, $e^{-0.5} = 0.607$

$$P = 0.607\,(1 + 0.485)$$

$$= 0.607 \times 1.485 = 0.901395$$

Q. 14.31: *The failure rate of an electronic subsystem is 0.0005 failures/hour. If an operational period of 500 h with a probability of success of p = 0.95 is desired, what level of parallel redundancy is needed ?*

Ans: $P_{(\text{system})} = 1 - Q^n$

$P_{(\text{system})} = 0.95,$

$Q^n = 1 - 0.95 = 0.05$

Since $P_{(\text{subsystem})} = e^{-H\lambda} = e^{500\,(.0005)}$ *i.e.* $= e^{-0.25}$

From Table *G*, $e^{-0.25} = 0.779$

Also since $P + Q = 1$, therefore $Q = 1 - P$

$= 1 - 0.779$ *i.e.* $= 0.221$

Also since $Q^n = 0.05$, therefore $(0.221)^n = 0.05$. The exponent n is the unknown and represents the number of parallel subsystems required to obtain a system reliability of 0.95. We therefore have to ascertain how many times 0.221 has to be multiplied by itself of obtain a value as close to 0.05 as possible, but no more than 0.05.

Let us try with $n = 2$, which means one subsystem in parallel redundancy with the original system,

$$(0.221)^2 = 0.048841$$

The answer $Q^n = 0.048841$ is satisfactory, since it is slightly less than the limit of 0.05.

Trying two subsystems in parallel redundancy with the original subsystem would have rendered.

$$(0.221)^3 = 0.0107938$$

This result is considerably lower than the required 0.05, hence we surmise that one unit in parallel redundancy with the original unit is all that is needed to assure not less than $P =$ 0.95 reliability.

Since $Q^n = (0.221)^n$ turned out to be 0.048841 instead of 0.05, the reliability of the system will be slightly above the desired P of 0.95.

Q. 14.32: *The following lengths of lives, measured in numbers of successive trials to failure, were obtained when **60** sets of observations were made with a constant probability of failure of **0.01**.*

Set of observations	*Lengths of lives*				
1 – 5	45	431	16	388	34
6 – 10	59	27	107	233	88
11 – 15	276	84	7	40	13
16 – 20	1	106	121	24	233
21 – 25	277	156	261	35	81
26 – 30	2	24	42	56	131
31 – 35	31	47	6	179	2
31 – 40	36	128	20	78	112
41 – 45	301	22	4	121	20
46 – 50	44	7	163	245	74
51 – 55	51	23	107	3	10
56 – 60	31	62	142	296	101

*Rearrange the foregoing **60** numbers in order of increasing magnitude.*

*The above arrangement may be viewed as representing a distribution of lives in hours that might have been found of simultaneous tests to failure had been made of random sample of **60** items from a universe that had a constant failure rate of **0.01** per hour. Compute the respective estimates of mean life in hours that would have been appropriate after the following numbers of hours of test ;*

(*a*) *30* (*b*) *60*

(*c*) *80* (*d*) *100 and 431.*

Ans: The 60 lives in the sequence of increasing magnitude are tabulated below :

1	16	34	59	107	223
2	20	35	62	112	233
2	20	36	74	121	245
3	22	40	78	121	261
4	23	42	81	128	276
6	24	44	84	131	277
7	24	45	88	142	296
7	27	47	101	156	301
10	31	51	106	163	388
13	31	56	107	179	431

(*a*) Mean life after 30 hours of test : $= \dfrac{1 + 2 + ... 30(60 - 18)}{18}$

$= 82.8$ hours

(*b*) Mean life after 60 hours : $= \dfrac{1 + 2 + ... + 59 + 60(60 - 31)}{31}$

$= 81.4$

(*c*) Mean life after 80 hours : $= \dfrac{1 + 2 + ... + 78 + 80(60 - 34)}{34}$

$= 90.5$

(*d*) Similar calculations will show that mean life after 100 and 431 hours are 95.9 and 97.6 hours respectively.

Q. 14.33: *What is the minimum MTBF for a piece of equipment if the probability of survival is to be at least 85% for 4,000 h of operation ?*

Ans: $P = 0.85 = e^{-H\lambda}$

For a P of 0.85, Table G by computation shows under column $c = 0$ that

$$H\lambda = 0.162$$

Since $$H = 4,000$$

$$\lambda = \frac{0.162}{4,000}$$

$$\text{MTBF} = \frac{1}{\lambda} = \frac{4,000}{0.162} = 24,691 \text{ h (min).}$$

Q. 14.34: *What is the highest failure rate, expressed in failures / 106 h, that a piece of equipment can have if it is to operate with a probability of survival of 90% for 5,000 h ?*

Ans: $$P = 0.90$$

For a P of 0.90, Table G shows (by interpolation) that $H\lambda = 0.105$.

Since $H = 5,000$ h, $\lambda = 0.105/5,000 = 0.000021$ failure/hour = 21 failures /106 h.

Q. 14.35: *The failure of an electronic device is λ = 21 failures / **106** h. Two standby units are added to the system. What is MTBF of the system ?*

Ans:
$$\text{MTBF} = \frac{3}{\lambda}$$

The failure rate = 21 failures $/10^6$ h = 21×10^{-6} failure/hour

$$\text{MTBF} = \frac{3}{21 \times 10^{-6}}$$
$$= 143{,}000 \text{ h}$$

Q. 14.36: *Calculate the probability of survival of a piece of equipment that is to operate for **500** h and which consists of four subsystems having the following MTBF's :*

Subsystem A : *MTBF = 5,000 h*
Subsystem B : *MTBF = 3,000 h*
Subsystem C : *MTBF = 15,000 h*
Subsystem D : *MTBF = 15,000 h*

Ans:
$$\lambda_A = \frac{1}{5{,}000} \text{ failures/hour}$$
$$\lambda_B = \frac{1}{3{,}000} \text{ failures/hour}$$
$$\lambda_C = \frac{1}{15{,}000} \text{ failures/hour}$$
$$\lambda_B = \frac{1}{15{,}000} \text{ failures/hour}$$
$$\lambda'_{total} = \lambda_A + \lambda_B + \lambda_C + \lambda_D$$
$$= \frac{1}{5{,}000} + \frac{1}{3{,}000} + \frac{1}{15{,}000} + \frac{1}{15{,}000}$$
$$= \frac{1}{1{,}500} = 0.00066 \text{ failures/hour}$$
$$P = e^{-500(0.00066)} = e^{-0.33}$$
$$= 0.71892.$$

Q. 14.37: *An electronic system consists of a power supply, a receiver, and an amplifier. The equipment is to operate for **1000** h. The failure rates are*

λ for supply = 25 failures $/10^6$ h
λ for receiver = 30 failures $/10^6$ h
λ for power amplifier = 15 failures $/10^6$ h

What is the probability of survival of this equipment ?

Ans:
$$P_{Powersupply} = e^{-1000\,(25 \times 10^{-6})}$$
$$= e^{-0.025} = 0.97531$$

$$P_{receiver} = e^{-1000\,(30 \times 10^{-6})}$$
$$= e^{-0.03} = 0.97045$$
$$P_{amplifier} = e^{-1000\,(15 \times 10^{-6})}$$
$$= e^{-0.015} = 0.98511$$
$$P_{Equipment} = 0.97531 \times 0.97045 \times 0.98511 = 0.93239$$

The same answer could have been obtained by adding the expected number of failure Hλ of three components of the system.

$$H\lambda \text{ of power supply} = 1{,}000\,(25 \times 10^{-6})$$
$$H\lambda \text{ of receiver} = 1{,}000\,(30 \times 10^{-6})$$
$$H\lambda \text{ of amplifier} = 1{,}000\,(15 \times 10^{-6})$$
$$\text{Total } H\lambda = 1{,}000\,(70 \times 10^{-6}) = 0.07$$
$$P_{equipment} = e^{-\text{total } H\lambda} = e^{-0.07} = 0.93239$$

In general terms, survival probability of a system containing a number of subsystems in a series configuration is

$$P = e^{-H(\lambda_1 + \lambda_2 + \lambda_3 + ...)}$$

Q. 14.38: *An acceptance sampling plan for life testing requires that a sample of 40 items be tested with replacement of 500 hours. If no more than five of items fail, the lot is accepted. Otherwise it is rejected.*

(a) Assuming that the failure rate is constant, compute the mean life for which the Producer's Risk of lot rejection is 0.05.

(b) Compute the mean life for which the Consumer's Risk of lot acceptance is 0.10.

Ans: If λ is the constant failure rate,

$$\frac{1}{\lambda} = \theta \text{ is the mean life.}$$

(*a*) Producer's Risk = 0.05

Probability of acceptance = 1 – 0.05 = 0.95

From Table *G*, under the column headed $c = 5$, for a value of 0.95, μ_{np} is computed to be 2.6. This μ_{np} corresponds to our $(40 \times 500)\lambda$. Hence

$$\lambda = \frac{2.6}{40 \times 500} = 0.00013$$

$$\theta = \frac{1}{\lambda} = \frac{1}{0.0013} = 7692 \text{ h.}$$

(*b*) Consumer's Risk = 0.10

Probability of acceptance = 0.10

From Table *G*, under the column headed $c = 5$, for a value of 0.10, $(40 \times 500)\lambda$ is computed to be 9.32

Hence $$\lambda = \frac{9.32}{(40 \times 500)} = 0.000466$$

$$\theta = \frac{1}{\lambda} = \frac{1}{0.000446} = 2146 \text{ h.}$$

Q. 14.39: *Assume that a failure is designated as the occurrence of 00 or 99 in one of the pairs of random numbers shown in Table X. App. 1. Start counting in the upper left hand corner of the table, and count downwards in the left-hand column from the left and so on. Record the number of successive trials to failure in tabular form. Continue until 20 values have been detained. Rearrange these values in order of increasing magnitude.*

Ans: From Table *X*, App. 1 counting in the manner as mentioned in the problem, the length of first 20 lives is as follows.

4, 11, 17, 100, 23, 59, 133, 27, 11, 42, 164, 96, 47, 3, 184, 12, 6, 63, 42, 105.

Following table gives the arrangement of these lives in increasing magnitude.

3	12	42	100
4	17	47	105
6	23	59	133
11	27	63	164
11	42	96	184

Q. 14.40: *Assume that the values in your table of Problem 12.26 represents the hours to failure obtained when a sample of 20 electronic components is being tested until each component fails. Compute the respective estimates of mean life in hours that would have been appropriate after the following numbers of hours of test*

(*a*) *10,* (*b*) *20,* (*c*) *30,* (*d*) *184*

Ans: (*a*) Estimated mean life after 10 hours :

$$\frac{3+4+6+10(20-3)}{3} = \frac{183}{3} = 61$$

Similar computations show that

(*b*) Estimated mean life after 20 hours is computed to be 46.3

(*c*) Estimated mean life after 30 hours is computed to be 49.3

(*d*) Estimated mane life after 184 hours is computed to be 57.4.

Q. 14.41: *In the qualification test which requires 418,000 item hours of test has an acceptance number of 3.*

(*a*) *Approximately what mean life in hours corresponds to a Producer's Risk of 0.05 ?*

(*b*) *To a Consumer's Risk of 0.10 ?*

Ans: (*a*) If Producer's Risk is 0.05, the probability of acceptance is 0.95.

From Table *G*, under the column headed $c = 3$, for the probability of acceptance of 0.95, the $\mu_{np} = (4{,}18{,}000)\ \lambda$ is computed to be 1.36. Hence $\lambda = 1.36/4{,}18{,}000$

Or, $$\text{mean life} = \frac{1}{\lambda} = \frac{418{,}000}{1.36} = 3{,}07{,}000 \text{ h}$$

(*b*) If Consumer's Risk is 0.10, the probability of acceptance is 0.10.

From Table *G*, under the column headed $c = 3$, for the probability of acceptance of 0.10, the $\mu_{np} = (4{,}18{,}000\ \lambda)$ is computed to be 6.677. Hence $\lambda = 6.667/418000$

Or, $$\text{mean life} = \frac{1}{\lambda} = \frac{418{,}000}{6.677} = 62{,}600 \text{ h.}$$

Q. 14.42: *In the acceptance test for individual lots, **11,000** item hours of test are required with an acceptance numbers of **1**.*

(*a*) *Approximately what mean life in hours corresponds to a Producer's Risk of **0.05** ?*

(*b*) *To a Consumer's Risk of **0.10**.*

Ans: (*a*) If Producer's Risk is 0.05, the probability of acceptance is 0.95.

From Table *G*, under the column headed $c = 1$, for probability of acceptance of 0.95, the $\mu_{np} = (11{,}000\ \lambda)$ is computed to be 0.352.

Hence $\lambda = 0.352/11{,}000$, or mean life $= 1 = 11{,}000/0.352 = 31{,}250$

(*b*) Similarly for Consumer's Risk of 0.10, mean life is found to be 2,820 hours.

Q. 14.43: *In the test for continued qualification applied to a series of **10** lots, **110,000** item hours of test are required with an acceptance number of **2**.*

(*a*) *Approximately what mean life in hours corresponds to a Producer's Risk of **0.15** ?*

(*b*) *To a Consumer's Risk of **0.10** ?*

Ans: (*a*) If Producer's Risk is 0.05, the probability of acceptance is 0.95.

From Table G, under the column headed $c = 2$, for probability of acceptance 0.95, the $\mu_{np} = 110{,}000\ \lambda$ is computed to be 0.8209. Hence $\lambda = 0.8209/110{,}000$.

Hence the mean life $= \dfrac{1}{\lambda} = 110{,}000/0.8209$

$= 134{,}000$ hours.

(*b*) For a Consumer's Risk of 0.10, the mean life is found to be 20,600 hours.

Q. 14.44: (*a*) *A certain type of electronic component has a uniform failure rate of **0.00001** per hour. What is its reliability for a specified period of service of **10,000** h? of **2,000** h?*

(*b*) *Although an acceptance procedure is being used to ensure the failure rate of not more than **0.00001** mentioned in (a), it happens that a producer qualifies who has a λ of **0.0000125**. What now will be the respective values of reliability for service of **10,000** h? and **2,000** h?*

Ans: (*a*) Reliability $= e^{-H/\theta} = e^{-H\lambda}$

For $H = 10{,}000$ h, reliability $= e^{-(10{,}000)\,(0.00001)}$

$= e^{-0.1} = 0.905$

For $H = 2{,}000$ h, reliability $= e^{-(2{,}000)\,(0.00001)}$

$= e^{-0.02} = 0.980$

(*b*) For $H = 10{,}000$ h, reliability $= e^{-(10{,}000)\,(0.0000125)}$

$= e^{-0.125}$

$= 0.883$

For $H = 2{,}000$ h, reliability $= e^{-(2{,}000)\,(0.0000125)}$

$= e^{-0.0125}$

$= 0.975.$

Q. 14.45: *Given a θ of **5,000** h and a uniform failure rate, what is the reliability associated with a specified service period of **200** h.*

Ans: Reliability $= e^{-H/\theta}$

For $h = 200$, reliability $= e^{-200/5000}$

$= e^{-0.01}$

$= 0.961.$

Q. 14.46: *It is desired to have a reliability of at least **0.990** for a specified service period of **8,000** h on the assumption of a uniform failure rate. What is the least value of θ that will yield this desired reliability ?*

Ans: Reliability $= e^{-H/\theta}$

$0.990 = e^{-8000/\theta}$

Also $e^{-0.010} = 0.990$

Hence $0.010 = 8{,}000/\theta$

$\theta = 8{,}000/0.01$

$= 800{,}000$ h.

Q. 14.47: *An electronic component has a uniform failure rate of **0.00002** per hour. Using Table G, compute the reliability of the component's service for a specified period of **20,000** hours of operation. If two of these components are used in series such that the failure of either one causes the system to fail, compute the reliability of service of **20,000** h.*

Ans: Reliability $= e^{-H\lambda}$.

Table G gives the values of $e^{-H\lambda}$ under the column headed $c = 0$ against the corresponding value of c or $H\lambda$.

Reliability $= e^{-(20{,}000)(0.00002)}$

$= e^{-0.4}$

From table G, under the column headed $c = 0$, probability of survival is 0.670.

Since the two such components are being used in series and failure of either one causes the failure of the system, the reliability of the system $= (0.670)^2 = 0.4489$.

Q. 14.48: *An item is required to have a failure rate no greater than **0.10%** per **1000** h of operation.*

*(a) Assuming a constant failure rate, what is the probability that one of these units will survive for a required **2,000** h service. (b) Determine the minimum acceptable failure rate where the probability of survival for a required **2,000** h of operation is **0.999**.*

(c) Find the MIL-STD-690 B FRSP-90 qualification sampling plan that meets with requirement.

Ans: (*a*) Failure rate $\lambda = 0.10\%/1{,}000 \text{ h} = 0.000001/\text{h}$

Probability of survival $= e^{-H\lambda} = e^{-2000)\,(0.00001)} = e^{-6.992}$

$= 0.998$

(*b*) $e^{-2000\lambda} = 0.999 = e^{-0.001}$

$\lambda = .001/2000 = 0.0000005$

(*c*) For failure rate of 0.10%/1000 h the FR level symbol is *P*. For FRSP-90, a total of 23,90,000 unit hours test would be required with no failure.

PART-2

QUALITY MANAGEMENT

CHAPTER

15

Modern Quality Management and Improvement

15.1 THE MEANING OF QUALITY

We may define quality in many ways. People use different definitions of quality in different contexts. Consider the following examples.

- A European company ordered some semiconductor components from a Japanese supplier. The order stated something like, '10,000 items required, with a defect rate of 0.03%'. The consignment duly arrived in two containers. The larger carried 9,997 good components and the smaller held the three defective items, clearly labelled. The supplier could not understand why the customer wanted the defectives but they were sent all the same.
- A traditional, local family-run clothes shop near our home closed down. Its place was taken by a 'factory seconds' chain store selling rejected textiles, mainly clothing. Prices are much lower and the new shop has a brasher and cheaper image compared with its predecessor. There were complaints. The RWA newsletter carried letters grumbling about the way such shops have lowered the tone of the town and the quality of the shops in the centre.

In everyday use, we speak of high quality as being superior to low quality. In so doing, we imply that some characteristic, such as designed life, has a higher value to us. A pair of shoes is, in these terms, of high quality if it gives five years' wear instead of two. Yet, what of the people who do not want shoes to last five years? To these customers, fitting the fashion may rank more highly than fitting the foot! In short, they prefer a different combination of attributes. Clearly, in any product, there are many. Customers search for those that most closely fit what they want.

We can summarize the overlapping ideas about quality as follows:

Quality defined by the customer. This perspective, preferred by marketing managers, looks for quality definition through what has become known as the *voice of the customer*. It is particularly critical in the delivery of personal services, where each customer comes along with individual needs and evaluation criteria. Yet, the variety of interpretations that the definition implies poses a problem for mass producers. They must interpret varied needs into more formal standards when they design their products and delivery systems. This perspective has been incorporated into ISO 9000 and its replica—Indian Standard IS/ISO 9000.

Quality in use. Many individually specified attributes relate to product application. These include *performance* (will it do the job?), *reliability* (under individually defined conditions), *serviceability* (again, after particular use) and *fit* (especially the aesthetic relation to other products to which it will be related). *Safety* is another feature that many would include, although it is not easy for individuals to make detailed appraisals.

Government, industry and independent organizations provide some data for some products. For instance, looking at a car gives little guide to its safety. From 1997, the European New Car Assessment Programme has helped consumers to compare safety. It tests for front and side impact to assess 'crashworthiness'.

Quality as grade or features. In referring to quality, many customers are using the term to mean grade. For instance, Rhodes's *Carron Lodge* Cheshire Cheese (First Prize, Nantwich Show, 2001) is a higher grade (said to be better quality) and more expensive than a basic product. The range of *features*, such as the number of cycle options on a washing machine, is another aspect of this confusion.

Quality to guide processes. Operations managers need standards, preferably defined by or agreed with the customer, to provide clear yardsticks. They can then decide whether they have achieved their target of *right first time*. In this view, if different bottling plants all produce their cola drinks to the specifications laid down by each syrup maker, then their quality is satisfactory. Customer brand preferences do not feature in this assessment.

Quality as product attribute. For some, the notion of quality is an attribute of the product itself, independent of intended use. Legal standards for many products, such a marmalade chocolate, sausages, petrol and electric cable are defined within such frameworks.

Quality as Service Characteristics. Despite many similarities between goods and services, many have noted special definitions in the latter. Five factors important in service quality assessment forming the basis of the SERVQUAL model, are:

- *Reliability*, giving the promised service precisely and dependably
- *Responsiveness*, helping customers promptly with their varying needs
- *Tangible factors*, the condition of facilities and the appearance of staff
- *Assurance*, the demeanour and knowledge of staff and the way they convey trust and confidence
- *Empathy*, caring and offering individual attention.

From foregoing discussion, it is obvious that most people have a conceptual understanding of quality as relating to one or desirable characteristics that a product or service should possess. Although this conceptual understanding is certainly a useful starting point, we will give a more precise and useful definition.

Quality has become one of the most important consumer decision factors in the selection among competing products and services. The phenomenon is widespread, regardless of whether the consumer is an individual, an industrial organization, a retail store, a bank or financial institution, or a military defence programme. Consequently, understanding and improving quality are key factors leading to business success, growth, and enhanced competitiveness. There is a substantial return on investment from improved quality and from successfully employing quality as an integral part of overall business strategy. In this chapter, we provide operational definitions of quality and quality management. We begin with a brief discussion of the different dimensions of quality and some basic terminology.

15.2 DIMENSIONS OF QUALITY

The quality of a product can be described and evaluated in several ways. It is often very important to differentiate these different dimensions of quality. Garvin (1987) provides an excellent discussion of eight components or dimensions of quality. We summarize his key points concerning these dimensions of quality as follows:

1. ***Performance*** (*Will the product do the intended job?*) Potential customers usually evaluate a product to determine if it will perform certain specific functions and determine how well it performs them. For example, we could evaluate spreadsheet software packages for a PC to determine which data manipulation operations they perform. We may discover that one outperforms another with respect to the execution speed.

2. Reliability (*How often does the product fail?*) Complex products, such as many appliances, automobiles, or airplanes, will usually require some repair over their service life. For example, we should expect that an automobile will require occasional repair, but if the car requires frequent repair, we say that it is unreliable. There are many industries in which the customer's view of quality is greatly impacted by the reliability dimension of quality.

3. Durability (*How long does the product last?*) This is the effective service life of the product. Customers obviously want products that perform satisfactorily over a long period of time. The automobile and major appliance industries are examples of businesses where this dimension of quality is very important to most customers.

4. Serviceability (*How easy is it to repair the product?*) There are many industries in which the customer's view of quality is directly influenced by how quickly and economically a repair or routine maintenance activity can be accomplished. Examples include the appliance and automobile industries and many types of service industries (how long did it take a credit card company to correct an error in the bill?).

5. Aesthetics (*What does the product look like?*) This is the visual appeal of the product, often taking into account factors such as style, colour, shape, packaging alternatives, tactile characteristics, and other sensory features. For example, soft-drink beverage manufacturers have relied on the visual appeal of their packaging to differentiate their product from other competitors.

6. Features (*What does the product do?*) Usually, customers associate high quality with products that have added features; that is, those that have features beyond the basic performance of the competition. For example, we might consider a spreadsheet software package to be of superior quality if it had built-in statistical analysis features while its competitors did not.

7. Perceived Quality (*What is the reputation of the company or its product?*) In many cases, customers rely on the past reputation of the company concerning quality of its products. This reputation is directly influenced by failures of the product that are highly visible to the public or that require product recalls, and by how the customer is treated when a quality-related problem with the product is reported. Perceived quality, customer loyalty, and repeated business are closely interconnected. For example, if we make regular business trips using a particular airline, and the flight almost always arrives on time and the airline company does not lose or damage your luggage, we will probably prefer to fly on that carrier instead of its competitors.

8. Conformance to Standards (*Is the product made exactly as the designer intended?*) We usually think of a high-quality product as one that exactly meets the requirements placed on it. For example, how well does the hood fit on a new car? Is it perfectly flush with the fender height, and is the gap exactly the same on all sides? Manufactured parts that do not exactly meet the designer's requirements can cause significant quality problems when they are used as the components of a more complex assembly. An automobile consists of several thousand parts. If each one is just slightly too big or too small, many of the components will not fit together properly, and the vehicle (or its major subsystems) may not perform as the designer intended.

15.3 DIMENSIONS OF SERVICE QUALITY

Service quality is critical in a service company as there is no tangible product, the company will judged on that service.

Consider a large hotel chain. Customer satisfaction is critical if the hotel is going to survive in the long-run. The hotel chain could use the following measures to asses customer satisfaction.

Examples of suitable quality measures could be:

- the length of time at reception.
- the facilities in the hotel.
- the cleanliness of the rooms
- the quality of food
- the helpfulness of its staff.
- the parting gift etc.

[**Note:** This list is not exhaustive, any suitable measure which can help determine customer satisfaction and can be measured could be used.]

Many of these could be measured using customers comment codes or using mystery shoppers. *Mystery shopping* involves use the facilities as if they were a customer and report back on their findings.

Cleanliness and condition of service facilities can be measured by the regular completion of detailed checklist showing when each area has been cleaned.

Service Quality Example

BAA (British Airports Authority) is a large company which operates many of the UK's airport. The company uses regular customer surveys for measuring customer perceptions of a wide variety of service quality attributes, including for example, the cleanness of its facilities the helpfulness of its staff and the ease of finding one's way around the airport, as per Table 15.1.

The quality measure and the mechanisms used to gather information will depend on the 'quality issue.'

TABLE 15.1 SERVICE QUALITY DIMENSION

Service Quality Dimension	*Measure*	*Mechanisms*
Access	Waking distance/ease of finding way around	surveys operational data
Aesthetics	Staff appearance/airport appearance, quality of catering	Surveys inspection
Availability	Equipment availability	Internal fault monitors
Cleanliness	Environment and Equipment	Surveys/inspection
Comfort	How crowded it is	Surveys/inspection
Communication	Information clarity/clarity of labelling and pricing	Surveys/inspection
Competence	Staff efficiency	Management Inspection
Courtesy	Courtesy of staff	Surveys/inspection
Friendliness	Staff efficiency	Surveys/inspection
Reliability	Equipment faults	Surveys/inspection
Responsiveness	Staff responsiveness	Surveys/inspection
Security	Efficiency of security check/number of urgent safety reports	Surveys/inspection

We see from the foregoing discussion that quality is indeed a multifaceted entity. Consequently, a simple answer to questions such as "What is quality?" or "What is quality improvement?"

is not easy. The **traditional** definition of quality is based on the viewpoint that products and services must meet the requirements of those who use them.

15.4 DEFINITIONS OF QUALITY

The most prevalent and in common parlance we may define quality as follows:

***Quality** means fitness for use.*

There are two general aspects of fitness for use:

1. quality of design and

2. quality of conformance.

All goods and services are produced in various grades or levels of quality. These variations in grades or levels of quality are intentional, and, consequently, the appropriate technical term is *quality of design*. For example, all automobiles have as their basic objective providing safe transportation for the consumer. However, automobiles differ with respect to size, fixtures, appearance, and performance. These differences are the result of intentional design differences among the types of automobiles. These design differences include the types of materials used in construction, specifications on the components, reliability obtained through engineering development of engines and gear trains, and other accessories or equipment.

Quality of conformance is how well the product conforms to the specifications required by the design. Quality of conformance is influenced by a number of factors, including the choice of manufacturing processes, the training and supervision of the workforce, the types of process controls, tests, and inspection activities that are employed, the extent to which these procedures are followed, and the motivation of the workforce to achieve quality.

Unfortunately, this definition has become associated more with the conformance aspect of quality than with design. This is in part due to the lack of formal education most designers and engineers receive in quality engineering methodology. This also leads to much less focus on the customer and more of a "conformance-to-specifications" approach to quality, regardless of whether the product, even when produced to standards, was actually "fit-for-use" by the customer. Also, there is still a widespread belief that quality is a problem that can be dealt with solely in manufacturing, or that the only way quality can be improved is by "goldplating" the product.

We prefer a **modern** definition of quality:

***Quality** is inversely proportional to variability.*

Note that this definition implies that if variability in the important characteristics of product decreases, the quality of the product increases.

As an example of the operational effectiveness of this definition, a few years ago, one of the automobile companies in the United States performed a comparative study of a transmission that was manufactured in a domestic plant and by a Japanese supplier. An analysis of warranty claims and repair costs indicated that there was a striking difference between the two sources of production, with the Japanese-produced transmission having much lower costs, as shown in Fig. 15.1. As part of the study to discover the cause of this difference in cost and performance, the company selected random samples of transmissions from each plant, disassembled them, and measured several critical quality characteristics.

Figure 15.2 is generally representative of the results of this study. Note that both distributions of critical dimensions are centered at the desired or target value. However, the distributions of the critical characteristics for the transmissions manufactured in the United States takes up about 75% of the width of the specifications, implying that very few nonconforming units would be produced. In fact, the plant was producing at a quality level that was quite good, based on the generally accepted view of quality within the company. In contrast, the Japanese plant produced transmissions for which the same critical characteristics take up only about 25% of the specification band. As a result, there is considerably less variability in the critical quality characteristics of the Japanese-built transmissions in comparison to those built in the United States.

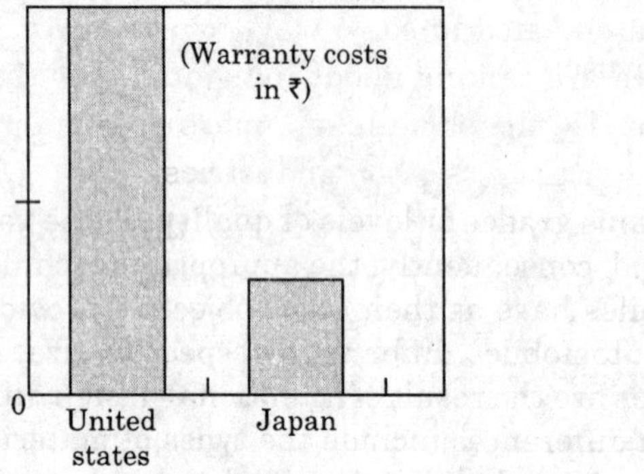

FIGURE 15.1 Warranty costs for transmissions.

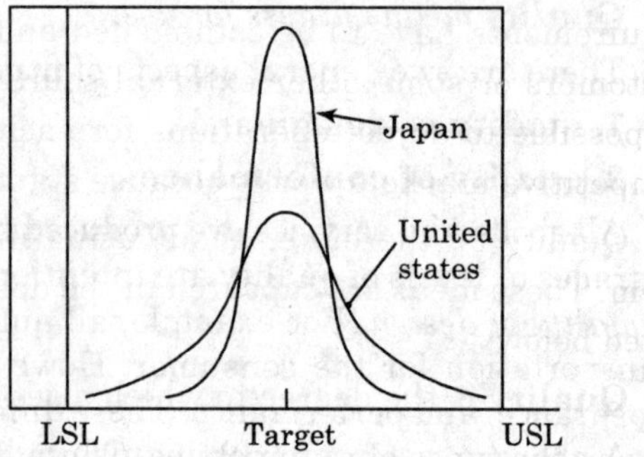

FIGURE 15.2 Distributions of critical dimensions for transmissions.

This is a very important finding. Jack Welch, the retired chief executive officer of General Electric, has observed that customer doesn't see the mean of your process (the target in Fig. 15.2), he only sees the variability around that target that you have not removed. In almost all cases, this variability has significant customer impact.

There are two obvious questions here: Why did the Japanese do this? How did they do this? The answer to the "why" question is obvious from examination of Fig. 15.1. Reduced variability has directly translated into lower costs (the Japanese fully understood the point made by Welch). Furthermore, the Japanese-built transmission shifted gears more smoothly, ran more quietly, and were generally perceived by the customer as superior to those built domestically. Fewer repairs and warranty claims means less rework and the reduction of wasted time, effort, and money. Thus, quality truly is inversely proportional to variability. Furthermore, it can be communicated very precisely in a language that everyone (particularly managers and executives) understands—namely, money.

How did the Japanese do this? The answer lies in the systematic and effective use of the methods described in this book. It also leads to the following definition of quality improvement.

***Quality improvement** is the reduction of variability in processes and products.*

Excessive variability in process performance often results in waste. For example, consider the wasted money, time, and effort that is associated with the repairs represented in Fig. 15.1. Therefore, an alternate and frequently very useful definition is that quality improvement is the reduction of waste. This definition is particularly effective in service industries, where there may not be as many things that can be directly measured (like the transmission critical dimensions in Fig. 15.2). In service industries, a quality problem may be an error or a mistake, the correction of which requires effort and expense. By improving the service process, this wasted effort and expense can be avoided.

While the above definitions of quality are well understood and need to be stressed by a customer when ordering or looking for services, we do need a more usable definition of quality combining attributes and standards with the purpose to which the product is to be put. Crosby has been influential in this argument. "Quality has to be defined as conformance to requirements, not as goodness... The setting of requirements may simply involve only answers to questions. Requirements, like measurements, are communications."

In stressing conformance to requirements, Crosby is emphasising two features. First, quality is about matching, that is conforming to, some standard. Second, these standards, or requirements have to be established and communicated in some way from their origin, be it customers or some other external source. If we are talking about individual service, it may be possible to adjust operations for each client. By the same token, mass production within competitive markets works because standards exist across whole industries.

Quality is, therefore, about using information to set standards and then conforming to them. These ideas are captured in the definitions within the international standard, ISO 9000, listed below:

> **Quality** is the degree to which a set of inherent characteristics fulfils requirements.
>
> A characteristic is a distinguishing feature. It can be: physical (such as the strength of a material); sensory (smell, taste etc.); behavioural (honesty, courtesy, truthfulness); temporal (reliability, punctuality, availability); ergonomic (physiological or safety related); or functional (such as maximum speed).
>
> **Requirements** are needs or expectations that are stated, implicit or mandatory. They can have many sources, including those indirectly affected by a transaction. Therefore, an aircraft design should consider the interests of passengers and crew, users of other aircraft and all who may be affected by its flight. Implicit, or *generally implied*, requirements are based on common practice among the organization, its customers and others.

15.5 IMPORTANCE OF QUALITY

The story of a supplier sorting defectives from good items emphasises how Japanese companies gained competitive advantage from supplying quality goods. The remarkable progress of the Japanese consumer goods manufacturers is further, more solid evidence. Quality is a strategic factor that works through virtuous cycles to build market share and reduce costs. Figure 15.3 illustrates some key relationships. The quality improvement area of the diagram has **two** zones related to product improvement, making it more suited to customers' needs, and process improvements, ensuring better conformance to standards. Improved quality increases demand and enables the firm to charge higher prices for the value differentiation that it offers. An important second-order effect is the way customers learn about quality and continue to feedback their demands into product design. Achieving customer satisfaction is not, therefore, a one-off process; rising standards create demand for even higher standards in the competitive market place. Within the organization, process improvements have direct impact on costs and also show feedback as the habit of continual development is self-reinforcing. Lastly, the increased profits both provide the funds for, and justify policies devoted to, quality improvement.

Managers in Japanese firms have recognized these interactions since the 1950s. It may be difficult, initially, to accept that improving quality will lead to improved productivity but the fewer delays, mistakes and rework more than pay for themselves in terms of rises in net output.

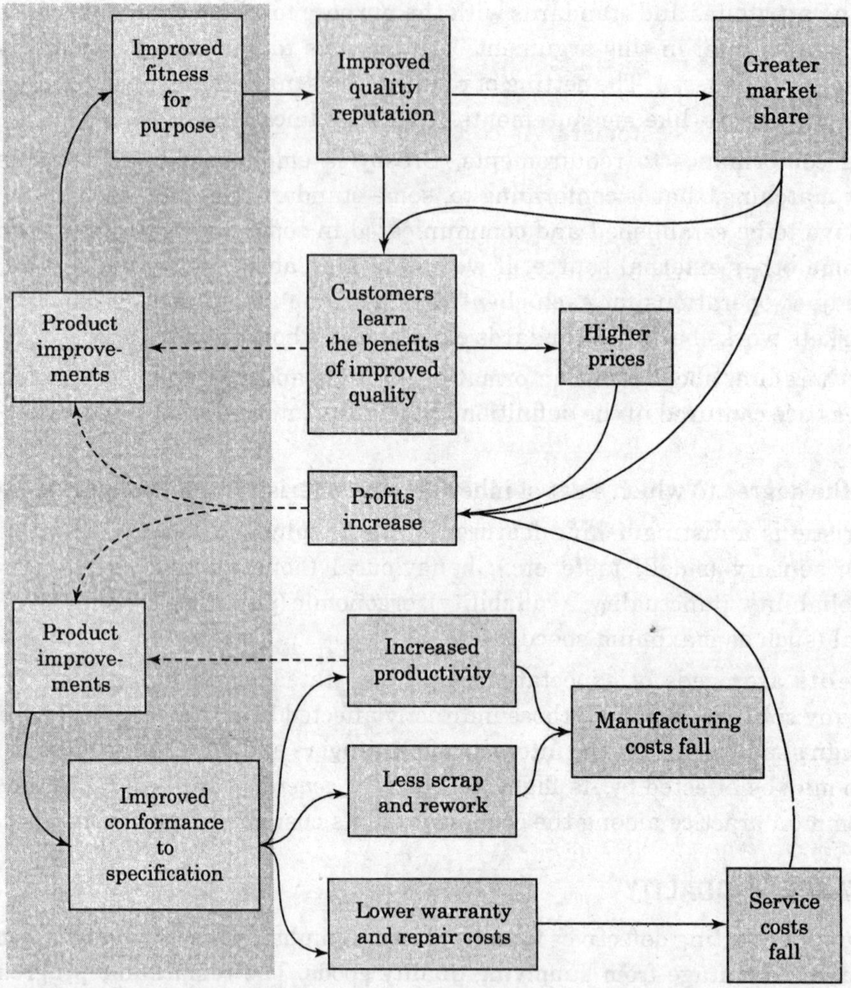

FIGURE 15.3 Various cycles in quality improvement.

Deming used a simple example to make the point. He referred to a production line running with 11% defective output, a level that the management was unaware of. The line was well controlled, showing consistent performance over time. The main cause of the defects was that both operators and inspectors did not understand sufficiently the kind of work that was acceptable or unacceptable. To them, 11% was normal. The manager and two supervisors made a special study and, in seven weeks, came up with a practical definition of work standards. They displayed this for everyone to see. Defects fell to 5%. The corresponding benefits, were achieved at very little cost. Productivity rose 6% and, as Deming noted, 'Customer happier. Everybody happier.'

Defects are not free. Someone is paid to make them, resources are used and, as Deming's example shows, opportunities of making saleable products are lost. There is a danger if this argument is overstressed. Problems are not always so serious that, in Crosby's words, quality is free. We should recognize that there are many operational situations where some improvement in quality will bring reduced operating costs, so much so that there will be net gains to the organization.

15.6 SERVICE QUALITY

Service operations often echo the manufacturing line of Deming's case. Quality standards are ill defined and consequently difficult to implement. At the same time, their effect can be critical in winning and holding on to customers. As cost pressure reduces the firm's service offering capacity, so competitive forces and the experience of good quality intensify demands, as in Fig. 15.3. The solution is not to spend more and do more but to be more effective. Quality must be seen through the eyes of the customer who only recognizes what he or she gets out of the service process, not what the firm puts in. Why provide quality service? There are good reasons. The satisfied customer will not only do more business in the future but will recommend the firm to others. The dissatisfied customer will not only reduce profitability directly but also will deter new customers. In addition to the effects in customers, poor service is demoralising for staff. They spend time coping with complaints and are frustrated when nothing seems to be done to relieve them and eventually customers stop doing business with the non-quality firm.

The importance of quality is to recognize that, although '... everyone is doing his best,' the 'best efforts are not sufficient.' Without leadership focused on consistently improving quality, these best efforts cause a random walk; such a walk takes you from your starting point an unknown direction and distance.

15.7 QUALITY AS STRATEGY

The two illustrations given below speak of the importance and strategic aspect of quality:

- In 2006 British Airways announced the rollout of an upgraded in-flight entertainment system for Club World and first-class passengers setting a new industry benchmark in the air.
- Caterpillar has a 48-hour parts delivery service, and if this is not achieved anywhere in the world then the customer receives an apology and the part free. The product is also maintained as one that is reliable and does not fail. Thus Caterpillar maintains its market despite being more expensive than its competitors.

15.8 LEGAL ASPECTS OF QUALITY

Consumerism and product liability are important reasons why quality assurance is an important business strategy. Consumerism is in part due to the seemingly large number of failures in the field of consumer products and the perception that service quality is declining. Highly visible field failures often prompt the questions of whether today's products are as good as their predecessors and whether manufacturers are really interested in quality. The answer to both of these questions is yes. Manufacturers are always vitally concerned about field failures because of heavy external failure costs and the related threat to their competitive position. Consequently, most producers have made product improvements directed toward reducing field failures. For example, solid-state and integrated-circuit technology has greatly reduced the failure of electronic equipment that once depended on the electron tube. Virtually every product line of today is superior to that of yesterday.

Consumer dissatisfaction and the general feeling that today's products are inferior to their predecessors arise from other phenomena. One of these is the explosion in the number of products. For example, a 1% field-failure rate for a consumer appliance with a production volume of 50,000 units per year means 500 field failures. However, if the production rate is 500,000 units per year and the field-failure rate remains the same, then 5,000 units will fail in the field. This is equivalent, in the total number of dissatisfied customers, to a 10% failure rate at the lower production level. Increasing production volume increases the liability exposure of the manufacturer. Even in situations in which the failure rate declines, if the production volume increases more rapidly than the decrease in failure rate, the total number of customers who experience failures will still increase.

A second aspect of the problem is that consumer tolerance for minor defects and aesthetic problems has decreased considerably, so that blemishes, surface-finish defects, noises, and appearance problems that were once tolerated now attract attention and result in adverse consumer reaction. Finally, the competitiveness of the marketplace forces many manufacturers to introduce new designs before they are fully evaluated and tested in order to remain competitive. These "early releases" of unproved designs are a major reason for new product quality failures. A few years back a renowned company in India had to call back its entire sold product because of early release of unapproved and tested new gear box design. Eventually, these design problems are corrected, but the high failure rate connected with new products often supports the belief that today's quality is inferior to that of yesterday.

Product liability is a major social, market, and economic force. The legal obligation of manufacturers and sellers to compensate for injury or damage caused by defective products is not a recent phenomenon. The concept of product liability has been in existence for many years, but its emphasis has changed recently. The first major product liability case occurred in 1916 and was tried before the New York Court of Appeals. The court held that an automobile manufacturer had a product liability obligation to a car buyer, even though the sales contract was between the buyer and a third party—namely, a car dealer. The direction of the law has always been that manufacturers or sellers are likely to incur a liability when they have been unreasonably careless or negligent in what they have designed, or produced, or how they have produced it. In recent years, the courts have placed a more stringent rule in effect called strict liability. Two principles are characteristic of strict liability. The *first* is a strong responsibility for both manufacturer and merchandiser, requiring immediate responsiveness to unsatisfactory quality through product service, repair, or replacement of defective product. This extends into the period of actual use by the consumer. By producing a product, the manufacturer and seller must accept responsibility for the ultimate use of that product—not only for its performance, but also for its environmental effects, the safety aspects of its use, and so forth.

The *second* principle involves advertising and promotion of the product. Under strict product liability all advertising statements must be supportable by valid company quality or certification data, comparable to that now maintained for product identification under regulations for such products as automobiles.

These two strict product liability principles result in strong pressure on manufacturers, distributors, and merchants to develop and maintain a high degree of factually based evidence concerning the performance and safety of their products. This evidence must cover not only the quality of the product as it is delivered to the consumer, but also its durability or reliability, its protection from possible side effects or environmental hazards, and its safety aspects in actual use. A strong quality-assurance program can help management in ensuring that this information will be available, if needed.

We now present some quality engineering terminology generally used in quality control, its improvement and management.

15.9 QUALITY ENGINEERING TERMINOLOGY

Every product possesses a number of elements that jointly describe what the user or customer thinks of as quality. These parameters are often called quality characteristics. Sometimes these are called critical-to-quality (CTQ) characteristics. Quality characteristics may be of several types:

- **Physical:** length, weight, voltage, viscosity
- **Sensory**: taste, appearance, color
- **Time Orientation:** reliability, durability, serviceability

Note that the different types of quality characteristics can relate directly or indirectly to the dimensions of quality discussed in Sections 15.2 and 15.3.

Quality engineering is the set of operational, managerial, and engineering activities that a company uses to ensure that the quality characteristics of a product are at the nominal or required levels and that the variability around these desired levels is minimum. The techniques discussed in this book form much of the basic methodology used by engineers, managers and other technical professionals to achieve these goals.

Most organizations find it difficult (and expensive) to provide the customer with products that have quality characteristics that are always identical from unit to unit, or are at levels that match customer expectations. A major reason for this is variability. There is a certain amount of variability in every product; consequently, no two products are ever identical. For example, the thickness of the blades on a jet turbine engine impeller is not identical even on the same impeller. Blade thickness will also differ between impellers. If this variation in blade thickness is small, then it may have no impact on the customer. However, if the variation is large, then the customer may perceive the unit to be undesirable and unacceptable. Source of this variability include differences in materials, differences in the performance and operation of the manufacturing equipment, and differences in the way the operators perform their tasks. This line of thinking led to the previous definition of quality improvement.

Since variability can only be described in statistical terms, **statistical methods** play a **central role** in quality improvement efforts. In the application of statistical methods to quality engineering, it is fairly typical to classify data on quality characteristics as either **attributes** or **variables** data. Variables data are usually continuous measurements, such as length, voltage, or viscosity. Attributes data, on the other hand, are usually discrete data, often taking the form of counts. Such as the number of loan applications that could not be properly processed because of missing required information, or the number of emergency room arrivals that have to wait more than 30 minutes to receive medical attention. We have already described statistical-based quality engineering tools for dealing with both types of data in Part 1 of this book.

Quality characteristics are often evaluated relative to **specifications**. For a manufactured product, the specifications are the desired measurements for the quality characteristics of the components and sub-assemblies that make up the product, as well as the desired values for the quality characteristics in the final product. For example, the diameter of a shaft used in an automobile transmission cannot be too large or it will not fit into the mating bearing, nor can it be too small, resulting in a loose fit, causing vibration, wear, and early failure of the assembly. In the service industries, specifications are typically in terms of the maximum amount of the time to process an order or to provide a particular service.

A value of a measurement that corresponds to the desired value for that quality characteristic is called the **nominal** or **target value** for that characteristic. These target values are usually bounded by a range of values that, most typically, we believe will be sufficiently close to the target so as to not impact the function or performance of the product if the quality characteristic is in that range. The largest or highest allowable value for a quality characteristic is called the **upper specification limit** (USL_x or simply U), and the smallest allowable value for a quality characteristic is called the **lower specification limit** (LSL_x or simply L). Some quality characteristics have specification limits on only one side of the target. For example, the compressive strength of a component used in an automobile bumper likely has a target value and a lower specification limit, but not an upper specification limit.

Specifications are usually the result of the engineering design process for the product. Traditionally, design engineers have arrived at a product design configuration through the use of engineering science principles, which often results in the designer specifying the target values for the critical design parameters. Then prototype construction and testing follow. This testing is often done in a very unstructured manner, without the use of statistically based experimental design procedures, and without much interaction with or knowledge of the manufacturing processes that must produce the component parts and final product. However, through this general procedure, the specification limits are usually determined by the design engineer. Then the final product is released to manufacturing. We refer to this as the **over-the-wall** approach to design.

Problems in product quality usually are greater when the over-the-wall approach to design is used. In this approach, specifications are often set without regard to the inherent variability that exists in materials, processes, and other parts of the system, which results in components or products that are nonconforming; that is, **nonconforming products** are those that fail to meet one or more of its specifications. A specific type of failure is called a **nonconformity**. A nonconforming product is not necessarily unfit for use; for example, a detergent may have a concentration of active ingredients that is below the lower specification limit, but it may still perform acceptably if the customer uses a greater amount of the product. A nonconforming product is considered defective if it has one or more defects, which are nonconformities that are serious enough to significantly affect the safe or effective use of the product. Obviously, failure on the part of a company to improve its manufacturing processes can also cause nonconformities and defects.

The over-the-wall design process has been the subject of much attention in the past 30 years. CAD/CAM systems have done much to automate the design process and to more effectively translate specifications into manufacturing activities and processes. Design for manufacturability and assembly has emerged as an important part of overcoming the inherent problems with the over-the-wall approach to design, and most engineers receive some background on those areas today as part of their formal education. The recent emphasis on concurrent engineering has stressed a team approach to design, with specialists in manufacturing, quality engineering, and other disciplines working together with the product designer at the earliest stages of the product design process. Furthermore, the effective use of the quality improvement methodology in this book, at all levels of the process used in technology commercialization and product realization, including product design, development, manufacturing, distribution, and customer support, plays a crucial role in quality improvement.

15.10 A BRIEF HISTORY OF QUALITY CONTROL AND IMPROVEMENT

Quality always has been an integral part of virtually all products and services. However, our awareness of its importance and the introduction of formal methods for quality control and improvement have been an evolutionary development. Table 15.2 presents a timeline of some

TABLE 15.2 A TIMELINE OF QUALITY METHODS

1700–1900	Quality is largely determined by the efforts of an individual craftsman. Eli Whitney introduces standarized, interchangeable parts to simplify assembly.
1875	Frederick W. Taylor introduces "Scientific Management" principles to divide work into smaller, more easily accomplished units—the first approach to dealing with more complex products and processes. The focus was on productivity. Later contributors were Frank Gilbreth and Henry Gantt.
1900–1930	Henry Ford—the assembly line—further refinement of work methods to improve productivity and quality; Ford developed mistake-proof assembly concepts, selfchecking, and in-process inspection.
1908	W. S. Gosset (writing as "Student") introduces the t-distribution—results from his work on quality control at Guinness Brewery
1920s	AT&T Bell Laboratories forms a quality department—emphasizing quality, inspection and test, and product reliability. B. P. Dudding at General Electric in England uses statistical methods to control the quality of electric lamps.
1924	W.A. Shewhart introduces the control chart concept in a Bell Laboratories technical memorandum.
1928	Acceptance sampling methodology is developed and refined by H.F. Dodge and H.G. Romig at Bell Labs.
1931	W.A. Shewhart publishes Economic Control of Quality of Manufactured Product— outlining statistical methods for use in production and control chart methods.
1932	W.A. Shewhart gives lectures on statistical methods in production and control charts at the University of London.
1940	The U.S. War Department publishes a guide for using controls charts to analyze process data.
1940–1943	Bell Labs develop the forerunners of the military standard sampling plans for the U.S. Army.
1944	Industrial Quality Control begins publication.
1946	The American Society for Quality Control (ASQC) is formed as the merger of various quality societies. The International Standards Organization (ISO) is founded. Deming is invited to Japan by the Economic and Scientific Services Section of the U.S. War Department to help occupation forces in rebuilding Japanese industry. The Japanese Union of Scientists and Engineers (JUSE) is formed.

...(Contd.)

1946–1949	**Deming** is invited to give statistical quality control seminars to Japanese industry.
1948	**G. Taguchi** beings study and application of experimental design.
1950	**Deming** begins education of Japanese industrial managers; statistical quality control methods begin to be widely taught in Japan.
	K. Ishikawa introduces the cause-and-effect diagram.
1951	**A.V. Feigenbaum** publishes the first edition of his book, *Total Quality Control.*
	JUSE establishes the Deming Prize for significant achievement in quality control and quality methodology.
1954	**Jospeh M. Juran** is invited by the Japanese to lecture on quality management and improvement. British statistician E.S. Page introduces the cumulative sum (CUSUM) control chart.
1957	**J.M. Juran** and F.M. Gryna's *Quality Control Handbook* is first published.
1975–1978	Books on designed experiments oriented toward engineers and scientists begin to appear.
	Interest in quality circles begins in North America—this grows into the total quality management (TQM) movement.
1980s	The works of Taguchi on designed experiments first appear in the United States.
1987	ISO publishes the first quality systems standard.
	Motorola's six-sigma initiative begins.
1988	The Malcolm Baldrige National Quality Award is established by the U.S. Congress.
	The European Foundation for Quality Management is founded; this organization administers the European Quality Award.
1990s	ISO 9000 certification activities increase in U.S. industry; applicants for the Baldrige award grow steadily; many states sponsor quality awards based on the Baldrige criteria.
1997	Motorola's six-sigma approach spreads to other industries.
1998	The American Society for Quality Control becomes the American Society for Quality (see www.asq.org), attempting to indicate the broader aspects of the quality improvement field.
2000s	ISO 9000:2015 standard is issued. Supply-chain management and supplier quality become even more critical factors in business success. Quality improvement activities expand beyond the traditional industrial setting into many other areas including financial services, health care, insurance, and utilities.

of the important milestones in this evolutionary process. We will briefly discuss some of the events on this timeline.

Frederick W. Taylor introduced some principles of scientific management as mass production industries began to develop prior to 1900. Taylor pioneered dividing work into tasks so that the product could be manufactured and assembled more easily. His work led to substantial improvements in productivity. Also, because of standardized production and assembly methods, the quality of manufactured goods was positively impacted as well. However, along with the standardization of work methods came the concept of work standards—a standard time to accomplish the work, or a specified number of units that must be produced per period. Frank Gilbreth and other extended this concept to the study of motion and work design. Much of this had a positive impact on productivity, but it often did not sufficiently emphasize the quality aspect of work.

Furthermore, if carried to extremes, work standards have the risk of halting innovation and continuous improvement, which we recognize today as being a vital aspect of all work activities.

Statistical methods and their application in quality improvement have had a long history. In 1924, Walter A. Shewhart of the Bell Telephone Laboratories developed the statistical control chart concept, which is often considered the formal beginning of statistical quality control. Toward the end of the 1920s, Harold F. Dodge and Harry G. Romig, both of Bell Telephone Laboratories, developed statistically based acceptance sampling as an alternative to 100% inspection. By the middle of the 1930s, statistical quality-control methods were in wide use at Western Electric, the manufacturing arm of the Bell System. However, the value of statistical quality control was not widely recognized by industry.

World War II saw a greatly expanded use and acceptance of statistical quality-control concepts in manufacturing industries. Wartime experience made it apparent that statistical techniques were necessary to control and improve product quality. The 1950s and 1960s saw the emergence of reliability engineering, the introduction of several important textbooks on statistical quality control, and the viewpoint that quality is a way of managing the organization.

In the 1950s, designed experiments for product and process improvement were first introduced in the United States..The initial applications were in the chemical industry. These methods were widely exploited in the chemical industry, and they are often cited as one of the primary reasons that the U.S. chemical industry is one of the most competitive in the world and has lost little business to foreign companies. The spread of these methods outside the chemical industry was relatively slow until the late 1970s or early 1980s, when many Western companies discovered that their Japanese competitors had been systematically using designed experiments since the 1960s for process improvement, new process development, evaluation of new product designs, improvement of reliability and field performance of products, and many other aspects of product design, including selection of component and system tolerances. This discovery sparked further interest in statistically designed experiments and resulted in extensive efforts to introduce the methodology in engineering and development organizations in industry, as well as in academic engineering curricula.

Since 1980, there has been a profound growth in the use of statistical methods for quality and overall business improvements in the United States. This has been motivated, in part, by the widespread loss of the business and markets suffered by many U.S. companies that began during the 1970s. For example, the U.S. automobile industry was nearly destroyed by foreign competition during this period. One U.S. automobile company estimated its operating losses at nearly $1 million per hour in 1980. The adoption and use of statistical methods have played a central role in the re-emergence of U.S. industry. Various management systems have also emerged as frameworks in which to implement quality improvement. The statistical methods—central to quality management have already been discussed in detail in PART-1 of this book. However a brief mention of these at appropriate places in appears again at appropricate places in this PART also.

15.11 QUALITY MANAGEMENT

To meet the increasing importance of consistent quality conformance in today's markets, companies have highlighted the dimension of quality management within their own organizations. As quality conformance levels in one organization are affected by the ability of its suppliers and after down the line agencies/vendors to meet the specification of the services and products they deliver, knowing how well suppliers are able to conform consistently to these standards is a key element of managing quality.

What drives these developments is more than the efficient management of company's business processes. It is also the requirements of today's markets and the expectation of today's customers. Companies who early on proactively improved quality also succeeded in gaining market advantage by changing the role of quality conformance from a qualifier to an order-winner. This was notably so with emerging Japanese companies in several manufacturing sectors from automobiles through to televisions and office equipment. Disadvantaged by these significantly higher quality conformance levels, European and US companies were forced to address the quality gap to prevent further loss of market share and as a matter of commercial necessity. The result is that by the turn of the last century, quality's competitive role had reverted to that of a qualifier but involving much more exacting standards of conformance. The role of quality conformance within the set of competitive dimensions that relate to the markets of most organizations is now clearly recognized. And the response of operations to the provision of this key requirements has appropriately raised the profile of and changed attitudes to the key task of managing quality throughout organizations.

But the need for quality improvement to be applied at all levels and address all aspects of organizations has become an increasingly high-profile requirement. After the scandals at World Com, Enron, Tyco, Parmalat and the rest, the need to apply the same level of rigour to corporate governance as is now the expectation in operations has become sharply apparent.

To reflect such changing needs, the *Malcolm Baldrige Award criteria for 2004 now specifically include 'Governance and social responsibility results'* (see Chap. 18). In India we have Rajiv Gandhi National Quality Award (RGNQA) on the same principles. In theory there is no reason (while there is much sense) why quality approaches should not be applied to corporate boards in terms of independent directors, governance, accounting compliance or executive compensation. Those companies that take this next step may well be the ones that prosper and succeed in today's competitive environment or at least the ones that do not fall into disrepute and destruction.

The *key to good quality lies in good management*, a point central to the views of all the main contributors to improving quality. Management has the responsibility and has to give the lead in changing the systems and processes that create quality problems. A key part of this provision is to train everyone how to use the tools and techniques to enable the quality offering to be consistently met. Sound quality management relies heavily on contributions from empowered staff and, in turn, this requires access to appropriate tools.

15.11.1 Evolution of Quality Management

The evolution of the quality management has, to some extent, come full circle. In pre-Industrial Revolution times, skilled craftsmen were responsible for both undertaking tasks and ensuring that they were completed to specification. The Industrial Revolution saw the advent of high volume requirements and with it the separation of the making or providing task from the responsibility for quality–ensuring that specification were met. One outcome was that inspection was performed by non-producers and completed after the work was finished. However, since the 1970s systems for monitoring and managing quality have evolved rapidly, as illustrated in Fig. 15.4. Since this time inspection activities were first replaced or supplemented by quality control, then enhanced by quality assurance developments, with many organizations now

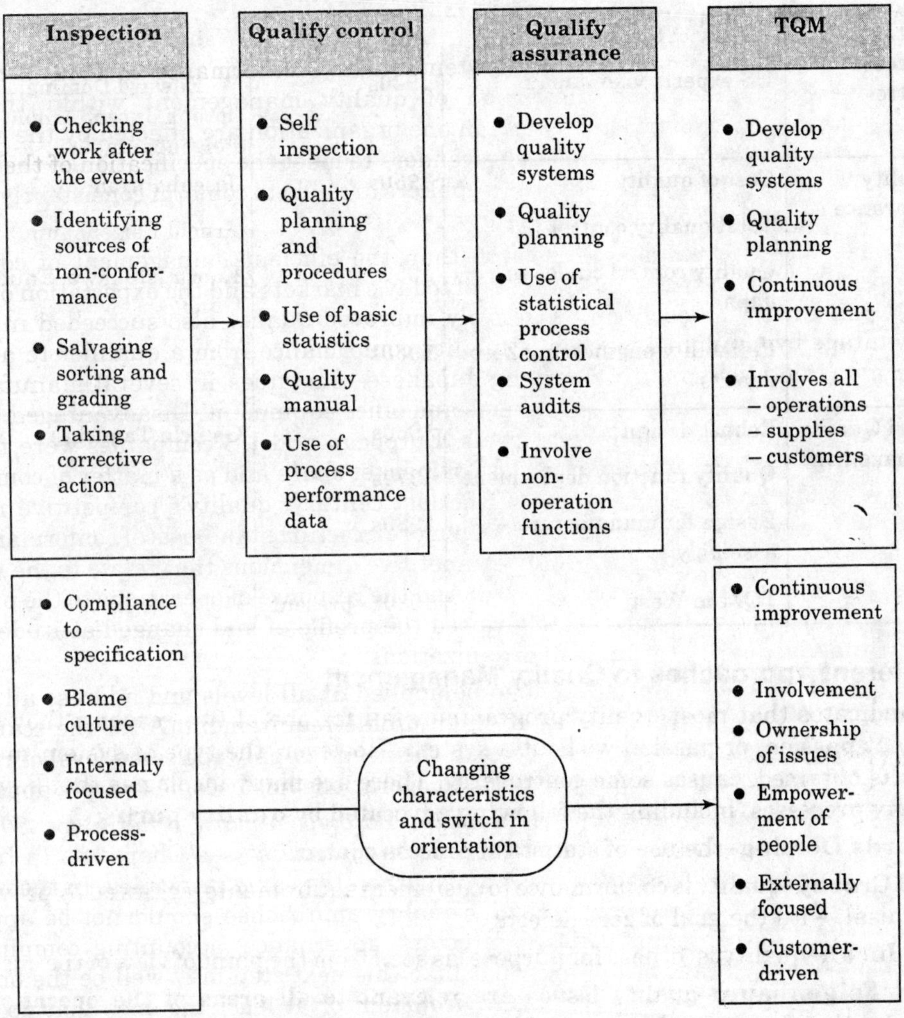

FIGURE 15.4 Evolution of quality management.

working towards total quality management (TQM) that returns the responsibility for quality conformance to those who have the task of providing the service or product.

It is interesting to note some major events in the quality evolution in Table 1.2. The "key figures" in the Table 15.3 are thinkers of quality now acknowledged as Quality Gurus. A reference to a few well known of them forms the subject matter of Chap. 17.

TABLE 15.3 MAJOR EVENTS IN QUALITY EVOLUTION

Emphasis	*Major themes*	*Dates*	*Key figures*
Inspection	Craft production	Prior to 1900s	
	Inspection	1900s	
	Standardized parts and gauging	1900s	
	Control charts and acceptance sampling	1920s	Walter Shewhart, Harold Dodge, Harry Romig

...(Contd.)

Statistical process control	Theory of SPC US experts visit Japan	1931 1940s	Walter Shewart W. Edward Deming, Joseph Juran, Arnold Feigenbaum
Quality assurance	Cost of quality Total quality control Quality control circles in Japan Reliability engineering Zero defects	1950s 1950s 1960s	Joseph Juran Arnold Feigenbaum Kaoru Ishikawa, Taiichi Ohno
Total Quality management	Robust design Quality function deployment Design for manufacture/ assembly TQM in West	1960s 1970s 1980s 1980s –present	Genichi Taguchi

15.11.2 Different Approaches to Quality Management

Experience indicates that most quality programmes fail for one of two reasons: they have a system without passion, or passion without a system. However, the type of system to follow, and the results obtained, causes some controversy. There are many ideologies that have been used in quality processes, including the following advocated by **quality gurus**:

W Edwards Deming–the use of statistical process control.

Philip B Crosby–quality is conformance to customer requirements, achieved by prevention not appraisal, with the goal of zero defects.

Joseph Juran–quality is 'fitness for purpose' as seen from the point of view of the customer.

Armand Feigenbaum–quality issues are relevant to all areas of the operation of a business, with systems and processes being designed to reduce the likelihood of sub-optimal production.

Kauro Ishikawa–the use of quality circles and techniques such as the fishbone diagram.

Genichi Taguchi–developed a mathematical model of loss, measuring costs incurred or profits forgone.

We will revisit the world recognized Quality Gurus in Chap. 17.

SOLVED QUESTIONS

Q. 15.1: *This MCQ contains five parts. Maximum 5 minutes are allocated for answering the MCQ.*

(*i*) From an operations perspective, quality concerns:

(*a*) Determining customers' needs and embodying these in the design specifications of services and products

(*b*) Consistently meeting service and product design specifications

(*c*) Both (*a*) and (*b*)

(*ii*) The first step in the quality conformance procedure is to:

(*a*) Identify causes of below-standard quality

(*b*) Define the quality characteristics

(*c*) Measure and control the quality characteristics

(*iii*) Which of the following is **not** a consideration when setting quality levels:

(*a*) Where in the operations process to check conformance to the quality standards .

(*b*) Which variables to check

(*c*) How to undertake the check(s)

(*iv*) Quality can be defined as:

(*a*) Fitness of use

(*b*) Highest possible standard

(*c*) Highest standard at acceptable

(*d*) Something that exceeds customer specification

(*v*) In today's world, quality information documentation is called

(a) end-item narrative (b) hardware

(c) data pack (d) software

(e) warrantee.

Ans. : (*i*) (*b*); (*ii*) (*b*); (*iii*) (*b*); (*iv*) (*a*); (*v*) (*d*).

Q. 15.2: *State whether the following statements are technically True (T) of False (F) ?*

(*a*) Quality is always measured through inspection.

(*b*) Quality is always measured using samples.

(*c*) Control charts can only be used with samples.

(*d*) Control charts can only be used by specialists.

Ans. : (*a*) F; (*b*) F; (*c*) F; (*d*) F

Q. 15.3: *(a) What is the simplest definition of 'quality' in your opinion?*

(b) Elaborate the definition of 'quality'.

(c) Give ISO 9000 definition of 'quality',

(d) Simply define 'quality system'.

Ans. : (*a*) The quality of a product or service is to do reliably what it is supposed to and to satisfy customer expectations.

(*b*) A simple definition of quality is 'conformance to requirements". However a better definition is "the totality of features and characteristics of a product or service that bear upon its ability to satisfy stated or implied need.

(*c*) The totality of features and characteristics of a product, process or service that bear on its ability to satisfy *stated* and implied needs.

Stated needs imply contractual obligations and would be specified in a written document

Impleed needs are the expectations of the customers and the these needs are probably not in writing.

(*d*) The organizational structure, responsibilities, procedures, processes and resources for implementing quality management.

Q. 15.4: *Quality can be divided into* ***process quality*** *and* ***product quality****. What is included in these two components of quality?*

Ans. : Product quality includes those features which appear in the final product. They can include specifications, together with added features which provide value for the customer; **process quality** includes the ability to produce at relatively low cost, with assured delivery and flexibility. Product and process quality must combine in order for a competitive quality offering to take place.

Q. 15.5: *Mention only* ***(do not describe)*** *the following:*

(a) Product quality dimensions

(b) Service quality dimensions

Ans. : (*a*) **Product quality dimensions:**

1. Performance	2. Features	3. Flexibility
4. Durability	5. Conformance	6. Serviceability
7. Aesthetics	8. Perceived quality	

(*b*) **Service quality dimensions**

1. Timeliness	2. Courtesy	3. Consistency
4. Convenience	5. Completeness	6. Accuracy

Q. 15.6: *Mention in simple term how will you judge the quality of a product or service? What are the implications of your criteria set for judging the quality of a product or service?*

Ans. : (*a*) In simple terms, the quality of a product or service can be judge on the following criteria.

(*i*) How well made a product is, or how well performed if it is a service.

(*ii*) How well it serves its purpose.

(*iii*) How it measures up against its rivals.

The implications of above criteria can be

- That quality is something that requires care on the part of the provider.
- That quality is largely subjective - it is in the eye of the beholder, the customer.

Q. 15.7: *(a) Give a reference of several definitions of the term "quality". What is your definition of quality?*

(b) How can quality problems be diagnosed?

(c) What steps lead towards conformance to specifications?

Ans.: (*a*) The term "quality" has several definitions. Among the approaches are the *transcendent approach* which views quality meaning innate excellence the manufacturing as based approach which views quality as being "free of errors" the *user-based approach* which views quality as 'fit for purpose', the *product based approach* which views quality as "measurable set of characteristics" and the *value-based approach* which views quality as a balance between "cost and price".

However, a practical definition of quality considering all these approaches is as consistent conformance to customer's expectations.

(*b*) At a broad level, quality is best modelled as the gap between customers' expectations concerning the product or service and their perceptions concerning the product or service. Modelling quality this way will allow the development of a diagnostic tool which is based around the perception-expectation gap. If such a gap exists it is likely to be caused by one or more of the gaps between factors which influence expectations and perceptions. These are four main gaps:

1. The gap between a customer's specification and the operation's specification.
2. The gap between the product or service concept and the way the organization has specified it.
3. The gap between the way quality has been specified and the actual delivered quality.
4. The gap between the actual delivered quality and the way the product or service has been described to the customer. It is the gap no. 3 (between the specification of quality and the actual quality delivered) which is of particular concern to operations managers.

(*c*) The following six steps will lead to conformance to specifications:

1. Define quality characteristic.
2. Define how to measure each of the quality characteristic.
3. Set quality standards for each characteristic.
4. Control quality against these standards.
5. Find and correct the cause of poor quality.
6. Continue to make improvement.

Q. 15.8: *(a) Mention briefly the history of quality.*

(b) Once there was a craze for English (Western) goods but now this craze has shifted for Japanese goods. What is the role of quality in such a shift over? Explain your answer with reference to Western and Japanese methods of implementing quality aspects in their products.

Ans. : (*a*) Many Japanese companies were successful in achieving revolutionary rates of quality improvement after the second world war. Since that time, quality has become a global standard.

(*b*) During the time of western organization dominance, the Japanese were rebuilding their economic infrastructure and began to work at selling their products to the rest of the world. At first the buying public viewed the Japanese products suspiciously. This was hardly surprising as the Japanese organizations often built little more than poor quality copies of western goods.

It wasn't until the 1950s that the importance of quality began to become more meaningful in the eyes of the purchaser. This was largely due to the promotion of the quality concept for goods and services by the quality gurus Deming and Juran. Their messages were largely ignored in the West – after all, why change a winning formula? The Japanese however realized that this was their opportunity and seized it in their bid for competitive advantage. They listened carefully to Deming and Juran's messages and implemented them.

When western organizations finally began to consider quality issues, they made use of them as inspection tools at the end of production runs. The Japanese on the other hand were working with quality as a method of *prevention – making the product right first time and every time.* Whilst both sides were now implementing quality, the Japanese benefitted most. This was down to cost. By producing goods and services *right first time,* there was no need for inspection, rejection and rework. Many people correctly assume the Western processes were extensive but few guess that their elimination could realistically have saved an organization 25% of its sales revenue.

The availability of quality goods at lower cost and without loss of time from Japanese organizations naturally shifted the balance in their favour.

Q. 15.9: *(a) Mention one or two benefits of quality improvement.*

(b) Briefly advise the difference between: technical quality and functional quality.

Ans. : (*a*) Quality improvement programmes can result in substantial savings and higher revenues. Quality improvement also has a non-financial and qualitative effects that improve a company's long term performance.

(b) Technical quality refers to the relatively quantifiable aspects of a product that can easily of technical quality include the waiting time at a super market checkout and the reliability of a new car. However, the consumers are also influenced by how the technical quality is delivered to them. This is known as functional quality, and it cannot be measured as objectively as the elements to technical quality. In the case of the queue at a supermarket checkout, functional quality is influenced by such factors as the environment in which queuing takes place and consumers perception of the manner in which queues are handled by the supermarket's staff.

Q. 15.10: *(a) Simply define quality management?*

(b) How will you explain to an industrial worker the meaning and objective of quality management?

(c) List out important tasks in quality management.

Ans. : (*a*) The aspect of the overall management function that determines and implements the quality policy.

(*b*) It makes quality the central concern of the business. Too often, quality is either confused with addressing customer complaints which inevitably leads to it being viewed negatively, or is viewed as a direct measure of the product or service itself. Instead, all activities that are involved should be considered. Quality should be inherent in every facet of the business and not just a "bolt-on extra".

(*c*) Quality management encompasses any activities undertaken by the organization to ensure that an organization's products or services are of the required quality. It includes quality control and assurance activities. Quality management involves:

- Establishing standard of quality for a product or service.
- Establishing procedures or production method which ought to ensure that these required standard of quality are met in a suitability high proportion of cases.
- Monitoring actual quality.
- Taking control action when actual quality falls below standard.

Q. 1.11: *(a) Why the word "quality" is often found in the mission statement of companies?*

(b) Simply define "quality policy."

(c) What is meant by quality policies of a company?

(d) Can you high light the various quality statements found in companies? Add a brief description to each.

Ans. : (*a*) Quality has been a dominant theme in management thinking for quite sometime. Consideration of quality is a fundamental part of business strategy and now in the age of increasing competition, quality is must for survival. Quality is also an important feature of process and e-business design. Hence we find a "quality" in the mission statements of companies.

(*b*) The overall quality intentions and direction of an operation as regards quality, as formally expressed by top management.

(*c*) Quality policies define the overall intentions and directions of an organization related to quality as formally expressed by top management.

(*d*) Statement of quality policy may be divided into three types:

(*i*) The mission statement is a brief statement of overall quality policy and commitment set down at the most senior level of management. It will probably refer to customer satisfaction, ISO 9000 and the importance of good quality practice.

(*ii*) The corporate policy statement expands upon the mission statement. The eight quality principles in ISO 9000 provide a good basis for drafting this policy. Additionally it should also conform to five requirements.

1. It should be appropriate to the needs of the organization and its customers.
2. It should involve all members of the organization.
3. It should provide an outline of the organization's goals and objectives.
4. It should be communicated and implemented throughout the organization.
5. It should be understood by everyone involved.

(*iii*) Process-specific policies will relate directly to the organization's processes and quality requirements. These should be adequate to manage quality in all key processes.

Q. 15.12: *State at least five core issues in quality management.*

Ans.: important core issues in quality management non recognized and practised in industries are stated below:

1. *Intense focus on the customer.* The customer includes not only outsiders who but the organization 's products or service but also internal customers ho interact with and serve other in the organization.
2. Concern for *continual improvement.* Quality management is a commitment to never being satisfied. "Very good" is not good enough. Quality can always be improved.
3. *Process-focused.* Quality management focuses on work processes as the quality of goods and services is continually improved.
4. *Improvement in the quality of everything the organization does.* Quality management uses a very broad definition of quality. It relates not only to the final product but also to how the organization handles delivers, how rapidly it responds to complaints, how politely the phones are answered, and the like.
5. *Accurate measure.* Quality management uses statistical techniques to measure every critical variable in the organization's operations. These are compared against standard or benchmarks to identify problems, trace them to their roots, and eliminate their causes.
6. *Empowerment of employees.* Quality management involves the people on the line in the improvement process. Teams are widely used in quality management programs as empowerment vehicles for finding and solving problems.

Q. 15.13: *In your opinion, what organizations are likely to become the success stories of the new millennium. Why?*

Ans.: In modern business environment, one change has been the switch in emphasis away from quantity to *quality*. Consumers and customers have become more sophisticated and discerning in their requirements. They want new products, superior on-time delivery performance and an immediate response to their requirements. Many organizations are therefore turning to quality to help them to survive the competitive modern business environment. *By developing new products quickly and supplying them on time at a consistently high level of quality such organizations are likely to become the success stories of the new millennium.*

Q. 15.14: *How does conformance quality differ from quality of design?*

Ans. : Quality of design measures how closely the characteristics of products or services match the needs and functional requirements of customers.

Conformance of quality is the performance of a product or service according to design and production specification. Figure 15.5 Illustrates the difference.

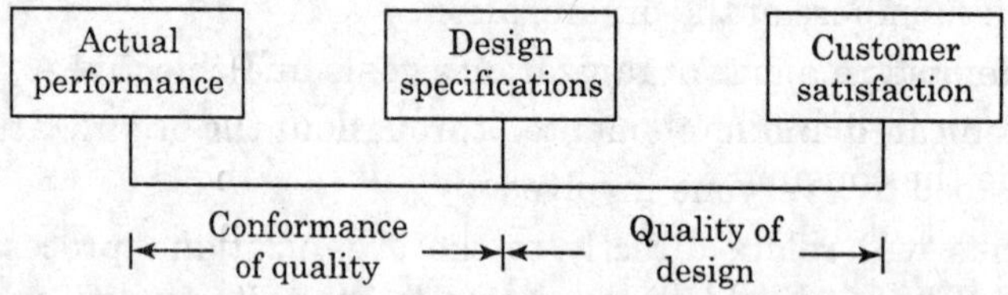

FIGURE 15.5 Difference between quality conformance and quality of design.

To travel the road from actual performance to customer satisfaction, companies must meet design specifications through conformance quality, but they must also design products to satisfy customers through quality of design.

Q. 15.15: *Give a brief description of different aspects of design for quality.*

Ans. : Quality needs to be 'built in' at various stages in the process of designing a product or service. Three distinct stages are:

- Product design stage
- Production engineering stage
- Administration

(a) Product design stage: The product or service specifications should provide a balance between price and quality (of sales and delivery, as well as manufacture). Whether the product or service will be competitive is dependent on this balance.

Modern manufacturing business use Computer Aided Design (CAD) in product design. CAD helps identify the following:

(*i*) Opportunities of *reduce the number of parts* in a product overall. The fewer the number of parts, the less parts there are to go wrong.

(*ii*) Opportunities to *use parts or materials that are already used* by other products. The more common parts overall, the less chance there is of a product failing to meet quality standards due to a rogue supplier.

(*iii*) Opportunities to *improve physical characteristics* such as shape, size or weight or positioning of controls and so on to make the product more user-friendly.

(b) Production engineering stage: Production engineering is the *process of designing the methods for making a product* (or service) *to the design specification*. It sets out to make production methods as efficient as possible.

(c) Administration: *Information systems* should be get the required information to the right person at the right time; *distribution systems* should be designed to get the right person at the right time; and so on.

Q. 15.16: *(a) What is the ordinary meaning of quality? How this meaning is different in industrial context?*

(b) Quality is to be considered from the important of both customers and producers. How ?

(c) State the core issues in

- *Product design,*
- *Process design and*
- *Process control.*

Ans. : (*a*) Quality is defined *as the totality of features and characteristics of a product which bears on its ability to meet stated or implied needs.* Ordinarily quality implies same degree of excellence or superiority.

In an industrial context, it is defined in a much more functional way. Here quality is more concerned with 'fitness for purpose' or 'fitness for use'. Fitness for use includes two elements : *Quality of design* which can include the consumer satisfactions built into the product. *Quality of conformance* in other words is a lack of defects/non-conformities in the finished goods.

(*b*) Quality must be considered from the viewpoint of both the consumer and the producer (service provider)

The customer – according to *Deming* the customer is the most important part of the production line. Quality should be aimed at the needs of the customer, present and future. This is driven by what the consumer wants and will pay for.

The producer – the product should be designed to meet or exceed the customer's expectations. Once a product has been properly designed, the role of operations, manager is to ensure that the product actually produced meet the design specification. This is done through product design, process design, process control and conformance to specification.

(*c*) **Core issues in product design**

(*i*) Assess consumer needs

(*ii*) Design a product to meet those needs at the least cost

(*iii*) Involve customers, suppliers and manufacturing personnel.

(*iv*) SET-product specifications.

Core issues in process design

(*i*) Process must be designed to meet final product design specification

(*ii*) Design process while product is being designed to avoid inefficiencies in production or the need to redesign the product.

(*iii*) SET-process limits.

Core issues in process control

(*i*) Ensure that the process actually produces a product that meets specification.

(*ii*) This will happen if the process was designed correctly and if it is kept in control

(*iii*) Keep the process within limits.

Q. 15.17: *(a) What is the traditional approach to quality? What problems do you see with this approach? Highlight the important issues in your opinion.*

(b) What does the abandonment of mass inspection to assess quality imply?

Ans. : (*a*) There has been a rise in awareness of quality and the systems that support it, to the extent that it has become of *strategic significance*. Quality is now considered to be of fundamental importance to many organizations. Indeed, many firms pursue *a strategy of differentiation based on high quality.*

There was a time when quality was not measured as an output target, and when managers considered it something to be added on to a product rather than something that was integral to it. Quality control applied largely to manufacturing and meant *inspection*, or identifying when defective items are being produced at an unacceptable level.

There are many problems with this approach.

(*i*) The inspection process itself *does not add value*; if it could be guaranteed that no defective items were produced, there would be no need for a separate inspection function.

(*ii*) The *production of substandard products is a waste* of raw materials, machine time, human effort and overhead cost.

(*iii*) The inspection department takes up possibly expensive *land and warehousing space.*

(*iv*) The production of defects is not compatible with *newer production techniques* such as just-in-time: there is no time for inspection.

(*v*) *Working capital* is tied up in inventories that cannot be sold.

In other words the mass inspection approach builds waste into the process, which is not acceptable: the resources it consumes can be put to better use.

(*b*) The abandonment of mass inspection to assess quality implies that quality must be built in from the beginning, not added on at the end.

Q. 15.18: *(a) Mention the history of quality in brief.*

(b) How employees can be supported in persuing quality?

(c) Name **(only)** *the three quality management processes.*

(d) State the difference between quality and grade.

Ans. : (*a*) Many Japanese companies were successful in achieving revolutionary rates of quality improvement after the second world war. Since that time, quality has become a global standard.

(*b*) Empowerment of employees—giving employees the authority, knowledge and resources to do what is necessary to fulfill their jobs—is part of creating quality within an organization.

(*c*) The major quality process are:

(*i*) quality planning

(*ii*) quality assurance

(*iii*) quality control

(*d*) Quality and grade are not the same. *Quality* is the sum of the characteristic of a product that allow it to meet the demands or expectations of the customer. Quality is all about fulfilling requirements.

Grade, is a category or rank given to entities having the same functional use but different technical characteristics. For example, there are different grade of paint, different grades of metal, and even different grades of travel.

Low quality is always a problem, but low grade may not be. Depending on the requirements of the customer, low grade may be completely acceptable, but low quality never is.

Q. 15.19: *Mention briefly the similarities between modern quality management principles and project management principles.*

Ans. : Modern quality management complements good project management practices. Both disciplines recognize the importance of:

- *customer satisfaction* — understanding, managing and influencing needs so that customer expectations are met or exceeded.
- *prevention over inspection* — the cost of avoiding mistakes is always much less than the cost of correcting them.
- *management responsibility* — success requires the participation of all members of the team, but it remains the responsibility of management to provide the resources needed to succeed.
- *processes within phases* — the repeated PDCA cycle described by Deming is strikingly similar to the feedback loops between project phases.

Q. 15.20: *What is gold plating with respect to quality and what are its impact?*

Ans. : The customer while drawing the specifications for the product he/she wishes to buy also fixes the price to be paid for the product. Gold plating is the process of adding extra features that may drive up costs and alter schedules. The vendor should strive to deliver what was expected. Figure 1 shows a curve relating cost and level of quality and gold plating.

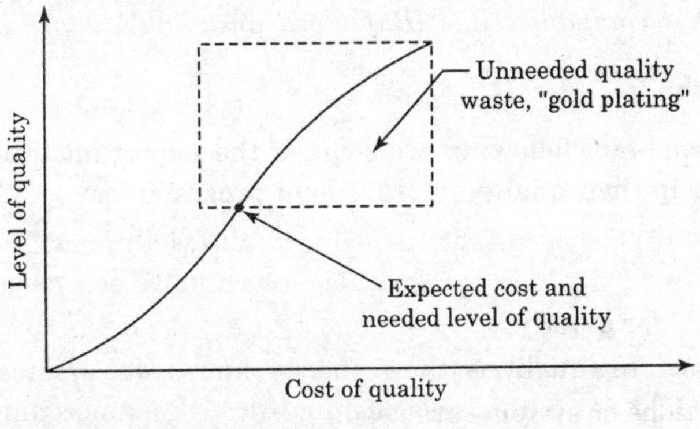

FIGURE 15.6 Gold Plating

Q. 15.21: *(a) What are the two elements in Juran's definition of quality?*

(b) Draw a suitable diagram to indicate the quality management hierarchy and add a little explanation.

Ans. : (*a*) Two elements in Juran's definition of quality are:

1. Quality of design
2. Quality of conformance.

(*b*) Quality management is the set of managerial actions taken to ensure that operation systems perform adequately on the quality performance dimensions. To implement quality policy is the main task of quality management.

Figure 15.7 shows an hierarchy of quality management. It is possible to identify five development systems as shown.

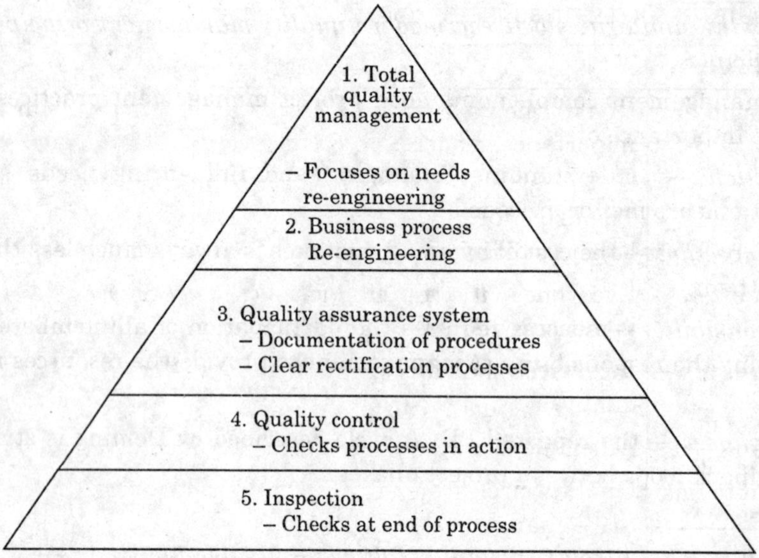

FIGURE 15.7 Quality Management

Q. 15.22: *Which of the following is responsible for the success of Japanese industries*

(i) Design Quality *(ii) Conformance quality.*

(b) Mention at least ten traits that companies like IBM, Ford and TATA share in their quality improvement programmes.

Ans. : (*a*) (*ii*) Conformance Quality

(*b*) As per the latest studies carried out, following are some of the important traits that companies like IBM, TATA etc. share in their quality improvement programmes:

1. Management obsessed with quality.
2. A guiding system or ideology.
3. Quality is measured and reward for quality.
4. Training in technologies for assessing qualities.
5. Teams involving multiple functions or systems are used.
6. Concentration on small improvements.
7. Constant stimulation.
8. Creation of a shadow or parallel organization structure devoted to quality improvement.
9. Everyone concerned is involved.
10. Quality improvement is a never-ending journey and it is the primary source of cost reduction.

Q. 15.23: *A business is to be successful if it is to survive. In this era of fierce competition, quality and economy are the two dominant attributes of successful business. Can you briefly give a few aspects of quality and their brief description in this regard.*

Ans. : Quality related aspects and their brief description for a successful business are given below in Table 15.4.

TABLE 15.4 ATTRIBUTES OF SUCCESSFUL BUSINESS

Trait or quality	*Description*
Quality obsession	Given the assumption that quality is of paramount importance, leaders should tackle quality issues the moment they arise.
Passionate systems	The drive for quality should not just be a system; it should be an ideology with a system.
Measurement of quality	Everyone in the organization should understand how quality is measured.
Quality rewards	Incentives should be given to those who consistently provide quality.
Quality training	All employees should receive training on quality.
Multi-function teams	Quality circles should be established, with the power to drive change.
Small improvements	Any quality improvement, however small, should be celebrated and rewarded.
Quality teams and structures	A structure of quality teams should be established to closely examine all aspects and processes of the business.
Total involvement	Suppliers and distributors should be included in any quality drive or vision.
Quality and cost	There is a direct relationship between quality (which reduces wastage, etc.) and profitability. All employees should be aware of this.
Quality utopia	Having achieved specific quality goals, new ones should be set to strive towards.

Q. 15.24: *You have joined the quality department of a new manufacturing organization. You have just been informed by the MD that 'something drastic has to be done about the quality'. In his view quality is the responsibility of your department and he has suggested that you take a tougher line with those responsible for quality problems, raise quality standards, increase inspection frequency, and give more authority to quality control inspectors.*

Evaluate the suggestions made by MD.

Ans. : In general terms, the suggestions made by the MD reflect a mistaken view of quality and how it is assured. His emphasis is 'reactive' rather than 'pro active', is 'feedback' based rather than 'feedforward', and is concerned with quality control rather than quality assurance. Specifically.

- His initial statement that 'something drastic has to be done about quality' does not seem to be based on any kind of systematic analysis or measurement. Nor does it suggest that the MD understands the meaning of quality, which according to Crosby is 'conformity to requirements'.
- His statement that 'quality is the responsibility of your department' ignores the fact that quality is the responsibility of all staff at all stages, in all departments and at all levels.

- The 'taugher line' suggests a punishment-oriented approach which contradicts the advice of Deming 'to drive out fear' and to seek co-operation.
- 'Raising quality standards' without targeting particular areas, and without understanding why such quality improvement is necessary, is likely to be a costly and unproductive exercise.
- 'Increasing inspection rates' and 'giving greater authority to quality control inspectors' reinforces the 'control' approach, and the 'specialist' emphasis discussed earlier.

Q. 15.25: *In Q. 15.24 You have evaluated the suggestions given by the MD. What will be your approach to solve the quality issue raised by MD?*

Ans. : (*a*) There can be an alternative approach which involves viewing quality control as part of he more strategic approach to quality—quality assurance. This requires the following steps.

- An analysis of existing quality performance and problems. Such an analysis should involve all levels and all departments, and should concert itself with the customers, with the competitions, and with suppliers as well as the activities of the firm itself. *Crosby* advocates the creation of 'quality committees' composed of members drawn from different departments.
- Calculating the 'cost of quality', which involves measuring the costs of not 'getting it right first time', and includes 'prevention costs', 'appraisal costs', and 'failure costs'. Such an analysis should identify a size able potential cost saving (or, to quote *Crosby*, 'quality is free')
- The careful selection and monitoring of suppliers, perhaps involving an 'active rather than a passive relationship.
- The design of the product, to ensure an appropriate level of quality.
- The installation of quality information systems which measure and feedback quality performance to those involved, and which can serve as the basis for targets.
- Quality improvement, perhaps involving in the creation of quality circles.
- Quality staff, which involves investment in recruitment, selection, training, development, appraisal and reward.

In conclusion, such an approach is essential long-term, and requires a shift in thinking about quality at all levels. The essential ingredient in this cultural shift is a 'right first time' mentality which encompasses all activities that impinge on quality. In short, the MD and other staff need to be educated in 'total quality management'.

CHAPTER

16

Quality Costs

16.1 QUALITY COSTS-TWO DIFFERENT APPROACHES

Financial control are an important part of business management. These financial controls involve a comparison of actual and budgeted costs, along with analysis and action on the differences between actual and budget. It is customary to apply these financial controls on a department or functional level. For many years, there was no direct effort to measure or account for the costs of the quality function. However, many organizations now formally evaluate the cost associated with quality. There are several reasons why the cost of quality should be explicitly considered in an organization. These include the following:

1. The increase in the cost of quality because of the increase in the complexity of manufactured products associated with advances in technology.
2. Increasing awareness of life-cycle costs, including maintenance, spare parts, and the cost of field failures.
3. Quality engineers and managers can most effectively communicate quality issues in a way that management understands.

As a result, quality costs have emerged as a financial control tool for management and as an aid in identifying opportunities for reducing quality costs.

Generally speaking, quality costs are those categories of costs that are associated with producing, identifying, avoiding or repairing that do not meet the 'requirements'. Generally manufacturers and service organizations use **three** categories of quality costs: ***(i)* Prevention costs**, (P-costs) ***(ii)* Appraisal costs** (A-costs), ***(iii)* Failure costs**–internal and external failure costs (F-costs). This is known as PAF cost model of quality. It is sometimes useful to subdivide the three categories of quality costs into **two** broad groups as follows:

1. **Group 1** – Cost of Making sure that quality mistakes do not happen. These include the prevention costs and appraisal costs of quality. (i.e., P and A-costs)
2. **Group 2** – Cost of fixing quality mistakes. These include the internal failure and external failure quality costs. (i.e., F-costs)

Table 16.1 shows Group 1 and Group 2 costs and Table 16.2 highlights the characteristics being measured while spending the money in PAF costs.

It may be noted that group 1 i.e., P-costs and A-costs contribute to conformance, together are also called Cost of Conformance (COC) and cost of internal failure and cost of external failure, i.e., F-costs contribute to non-conformance together are also called cost of non-conformance (CONC). This method of classify the quality costs is knowns as Process cost approaches.

Many manufacturing and service organizations currently use two basic approaches for collection and presentation of the cost of quality (COQ) data as illustrated in Fig. 2.1

- PAF—COQ approach
- Process cost approach

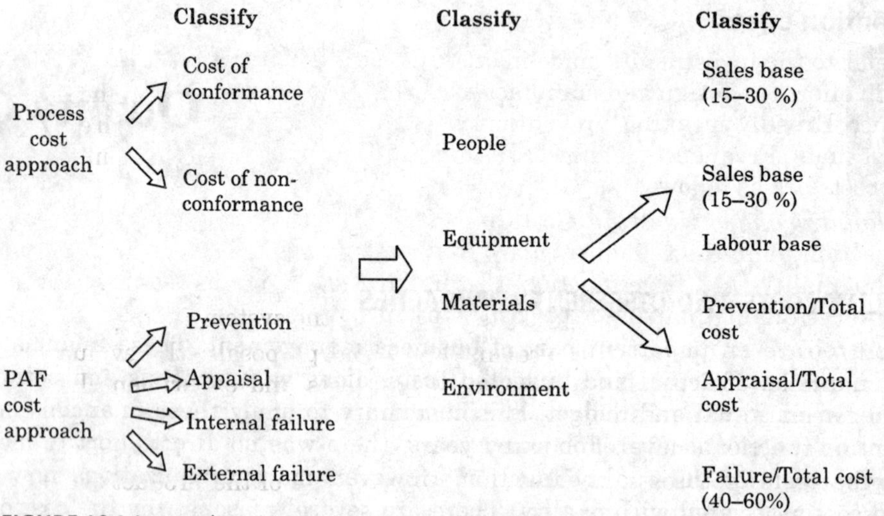

FIGURE 16.1 Approaches to reporting the cost of quality

TABLE 16.1 : TWO QUALITY COSTS

Group 1 (cost of conformance)	*Group 2 (costs of non-conformance)*
Prevention Costs	**Internal Failure Costs**
Quality planning and engineering	Scrap
New products review	Rework
Product/process design	Retest
Process control	Failure analysis
Burn-in	Downtime
Training	Yield losses
Quality data acquisition and analysis	Downgrading (off-specing)
Appraisal Costs	**External Failure Costs**
Inspection and test of incoming material	Complaint adjustment
Product inspection and test	Returned product/material
Materials and services consumed	Warranty charges
Maintaining accuracy of test equipment	Liability costs
	Indirect costs

TABLE 16.2 : CHARACTERISTIC TO BE MEASURED IN PAF MODEL

Category	*Characteristic being measured*
Prevention	The costs of ensuring that the required level of quality of service is met
Appraisal	Measuring what level of quality of service is provided
Failure	The costs of getting it wrong and putting its right – can be categorised as either internal or external failure

16.2 DESCRIPTION OF QUALITY COSTS

Following is short run of different types of quality costs in PAF model.

16.2.1 Prevention costs

These costs refer to the investments made in quality before production begins. These costs are associated with efforts in design and manufacturing that are directed toward the prevention of nonconformance. Broadly speaking, prevention costs are all costs incurred in an effort to "make it right the first time". Frequently referred to as quality assurance, the important subcategories of prevention costs are as follows:

Quality planning and engineering. Costs associated with the creation of the overall quality plan, the inspection plan, the reliability plan, the data system, and all specialised plans and activities of the quality-assurance function; the preparation of manuals and procedures used to communicate the quality plan; and the costs of auditing the system.

New products review. Costs of the preparation of bid proposals, the evaluation of new designs from a quality viewpoint, the preparation of tests and experimental programs to evaluate the performance of new products, and other quality activities during the development and preproduction stages of new products or designs.

Product/process design. Costs incurred during the design of the product or the selection of the production processes that are intended to improve the overall quality of the product. For example, an organization may decide to make a particular circuit component redundant because this will increase the reliability of the product by increasing the mean time between failures. Alternatively, it may decide to manufacture a component using process A rather than process B, because process A is capable of producing the product at tighter tolerances, which will result in fewer assembly and manufacturing problems. This may include a vendor's process, so the cost of dealing with other than the lowest bidder may also be a prevention cost.

Process control. The cost of process-control techniques, such as control charts, that monitor the manufacturing process in an effort to reduce variation and build quality into the product.

Burn-in. The cost of preshipment operation of the product to prevent early-life failures in the field.

Training. The cost of developing, preparing, implementing, operating, and maintaining formal training programs for quality.

Quality data acquisition and analysis. The cost of running the quality data system to acquire data on product and process performance; also the cost of analyzing these data to identify problems. It includes the work of summarizing and publishing quality information for management.

It is worthwhile to note that a study conducted sometimes back indicated that the added cost of prevention (which resulted in better Japanese goods) was half the cost of rectifying goods made by American manufacturers.

16.2.2 Appraisal costs

Appraisal costs are those costs associated with measuring, evaluating, or auditing products, components, and purchased materials to ensure conformance to the standards that have been imposed. These costs are incurred to determine the condition of the product from a quality viewpoint and ensure that it conforms to specifications. The major subcategories of appraisal costs are as follows:

Inspection and test of incoming material. Costs associated with the inspection and testing of all material. This subcategory includes receiving inspection and test; inspection, test, and evaluation at the vendor's facility; and a periodic audit of the quality-assurance system. This could also include intraplant vendors.

Product inspection and test. The cost of checking the conformance of the product throughout its various stages of manufacturing, including final acceptance testing, packing and shipping checks, and any test done at the customer's facilities prior to turning the product over to the customer. This also includes life testing, environmental testing, and reliability testing.

Materials and services consumed. The cost of material and products consumed in a destructive test or devalued by reliability tests.

Maintaining accuracy of test equipment. The cost of operating a system that keeps the measuring instruments and equipment in calibration.

16.2.3 Internal failure costs.

Internal failure costs are incurred when products, components, materials, and services fail to meet quality requirements, and this failure is discovered prior to delivery of the product to the customer. These costs would disappear if there were no defects in the product. The major subcategories of internal failure costs follow.

Scrap. The net loss of labour, material, and overhead resulting from defective product that cannot economically be repaired or used and to be sold as second quality.

Rework. The cost of correcting nonconforming units so that they meet specifications. In some manufacturing operations rework costs include additional operations or steps in the manufacturing process that are created to solve either chronic defects or sporadic defects.

Retest. The cost of reinspection and retesting of products that have undergone rework or other modifications.

Failure analysis. The cost incurred to determine the causes of product failures.

Downtime. The cost of idle production facilities that results from non-conformance to requirements. The production line may be down because of nonconforming raw materials supplied by a supplier, which went undiscovered in receiving inspection.

Yield losses. The cost of process yields that are lower than might be attainable by improved controls (for example, soft-drink containers that are overfilled because of excessive variability in the filling equipment).

Downgrading/off-specing. The price differential between the normal selling price and any selling price that might be obtained for a product that does not meet the customer's requirements. Downgrading is a common practice in the textile, apparel goods, and electronics industries. The problem with downgrading is that products sold do not recover the full contribution margin to profit and overhead as do products that conform to the usual specifications.

16.2.4. External failure costs

External failure costs occur when the product does not perform satisfactorily after it is delivered to the customer. These costs would also disappear if every unit of product conformed to requirements. Subcategories of external failure costs follow.

Complaint adjustment. All costs of investigation and adjustment of justified complaints attributable to the nonconforming product.

Returned product/material. All costs associated with receipt, handling, and replacement of the nonconforming product or material that is returned from the field.

Warranty charges. All costs involved in service to customers under warranty contracts.

Liability costs. Costs or awards incurred from product liability litigation.

Indirect costs. In addition to direct operating costs of external failures, there are a significant number of indirect costs. These are incurred because of customer dissatisfaction with the level of quality of the delivered product. Indirect costs may reflect the customer's attitude toward the company. They include the costs of loss of business reputation, loss of future business, and loss of market share that inevitably results from delivering products and services that do not conform to the customer's expectations regarding fitness for use.

An *important* and *notable* aspect of cost of external failure is that it is most unusual to find any computations which take into account the consequential losses. For example, there is the time spent in placating an irate customer; the loss of machine time; the effect on scheduling; the costs associated with the purchase of replacement materials etc. The cost of stockholding associated products which must be held in temporary storage awaiting the arrival of satisfactory replacement parts is never included in the figures. Neither are any estimates relating to the loss of sales revenue.

16.3 ANALYSIS AND USE OF QUALITY COSTS

How large are quality costs ? The answer, of course, depends on the type of organization and the success of their quality improvement effort. In some organizations quality costs are 4% or 5% of sales, whereas in others they can be as high as 35% or 40% of sales. Obviously, the cost of quality will be very different for a high-technology computer manufacturer than for a typical service industry, such as a department store or hotel chain. In most organizations, however, quality costs are higher than necessary, and management should make continuing efforts to appraise, analyze, and reduce these costs.

The usefulness of quality costs stems from the leverage effect; that is, rupees invested in prevention and appraisal have a payoff in reducing rupees incurred in internal and external failures that exceeds the original investment. For example, a rupee invested in prevention may return ‘ 10 or ‘ 100 (or more) in savings from reduced internal and external failures.

Quality-cost analyses have as their principal objective cost reduction through identification of improvement opportunities. This is often done with a Pareto analysis. The Pareto analysis consists of identifying quality costs by category, or by product, or by type of defect or nonconformity. For example, inspection of the quality-cost information in Table 16.3 concerning defects or nonconformities in the assembly of electronic components onto printed circuit boards reveals that insufficient solder is the highest quality cost incurred in this operation. Insufficient solder accounts for 42% of the total defects in this particular type of board and for almost 52% of the total scrap and rework costs. If the wave solder process can be improved, then there will be dramatic reductions in the cost of quality.

How much reduction in quality costs is possible? Although the cost of quality in many organizations can be significantly reduced, it is unrealistic to expect it can be reduced to zero. Before that level of performance is reached, the incremental costs of prevention and appraisal will rise more rapidly than the resulting cost reductions. However, paying attention to quality costs in conjunction with a focused effort on variability reduction has the capability of reducing quality costs by 50% or 60% provided that no organized effort has previously existed. This cost

TABLE 16.3 MONTHLY QUALITY-COSTS INFORMATION FOR ASSEMBLY OF PRINTED CIRCUIT BOARDS

Type of Defect	*Percent of Total Defects*	*Scrap and Rework Costs*
Insufficient solder	42%	₹3,75,000 (52%)
Misaligned components	21	1,20,000
Defective components	15	80,000
Missing components	10	51,000
Cold solder joints	7	50,000
All other causes	5	46,000
Totals	**100**	**₹ 7,22,000**

reduction also follows the Pareto principle; that is, most of the cost reductions will come from attacking the few problems that are responsible for the majority of quality costs.

In analyzing quality costs and in formulating plans for reducing the cost of quality, it is important to note the role of prevention and appraisal. Many organizations devote far too much effort to appraisal and not enough to prevention. This is an easy mistake for an organization to make, because appraisal costs are often budget line items in manufacturing. On the other hand, prevention costs may not be routinely budgeted items. It is not unusual to find in the early stages of a quality-cost program that appraisal costs are eight or ten times the magnitude of prevention costs. This is probably an unreasonable ratio, as rupees spent in prevention have a much greater payback than do rupees spent in appraisal.

Generating the quality-cost figures is not always easy, because most quality-cost categories are not a direct component in the accounting records of the organization. Consequently, it may be difficult to obtain extremely accurate information on the costs incured with respect to the various categories. The organization's accounting system can provide information on those quality-cost categories that coincide with the usual business accounts, such as, for example, product testing and evaluation. In addition, many companies will have detailed information on various categories of failure cost. The information for cost categories for which exact accounting information is not available should be generated by using estimates, or, in some cases, by creating special monitoring and surveillance procedures to accumulate those costs over the study period.

The reporting of quality costs is usually done on a basis that permits straightforward evaluation by management. Managers want quality costs expressed in an index that compares quality cost with the opportunity for quality cost. Consequently, the usual method of reporting quality costs is in the form of a ratio, where the numerator is quality-cost rupees and the denominator is some measure of activity, such as (1) hours of direct production labour, (2) rupees of direct production labour (3) rupees of processing costs, (4) rupees of manufacturing cost, (5) rupees of sales, or (6) units of product.

16.4 SOME GENERAL COMMENTS ON QUALITY COSTS

As explained earlier, the failure to control quality results in extra costs. Put another way, the failure to plan and manage quality means too much expenditure on the quality costs listed above. Almost certainly, the excess will lie in the failure category. Figure 16.2 shows the relationship between the organization's ability to match the quality to customers' expectation and direct quality costs. Where the quality capability is low, failure costs are high and dominate the total. With improving capability, both failure and appraisal costs can be cut, resulting in better performance overall. The change takes time and the response is itself dynamic. Consequently, the organization should not seek a stable optimum position. The costs of quality should continue to fall as it learns new approaches within an ever more exacting environment.

The **two main thrusts** of a quality plan are, therefore, prevention (quality assurance) and appraisal (inspection and control). Clearly, we should avoid the costs of failure. Such a policy is called the ZD or zero defects policy. However, the cost of avoiding all failures may be prohibitive and the technology to do so may not be available. Despite all efforts, if failures occur, the organization should make an effective response. This is especially true if the problem becomes known after supply to the customer.

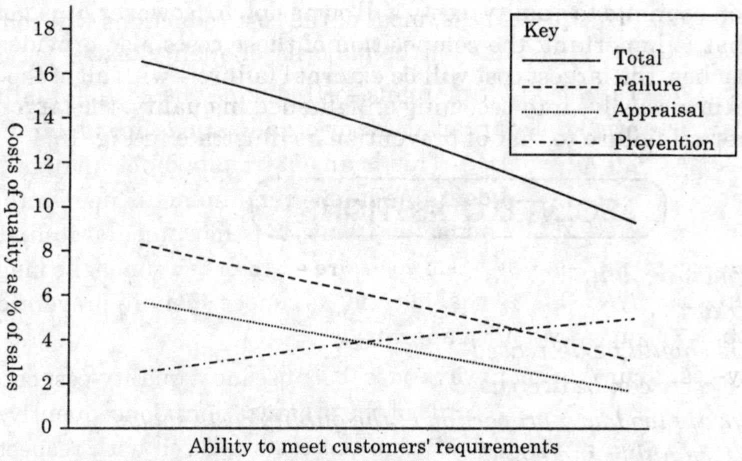

FIGURE 16.2 Quality costs fall as the organization becomes more capable.

In view of prohibitive cost and nonavailability of the required technology and competitive market, Fig. 16.3 suggests that some optimum level of quality will always be set so that some level of defects is acceptable, since the costs of prevention approach almost infinity as 100 percent conformance is approached. However, under the quality management philosophy of ZD (i.e. zero defect) the ultimate goal of operations is 100 percent conformity. In part, this is based on Philip Crosby's idea that 'quality is free', in which he argues that the benefits from improving quality more than pay for their costs.

Quality is free. It is not a gift, but it is free. What costs money are the unquality things—all the actions that involve not doing jobs right the first time.

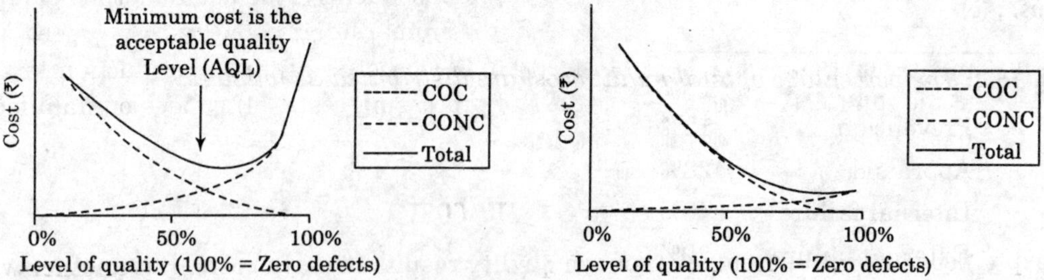

FIGURE 16.3 A cost of quality model of optimum level of quality.

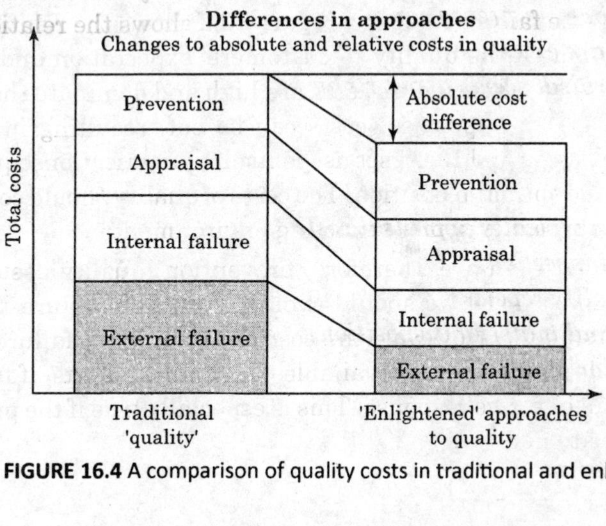

FIGURE 16.4 A comparison of quality costs in traditional and enlightened approaches to quality.

When an organization commits to quality, costs will come down. However, it is not just the total sum of the costs that is important; the composition of these costs also provides insight. Under traditional approaches, the largest cost will be external failure – with all of the strategic losses this may bring. As firms evolve into becoming enlightened in quality, the largest portion of cost changes from external failure to that of prevention as illustrate in Fig. 16.4.

SOLVED QUESTIONS

Q. 16.1: *We can draw conclude that:*

From the following cost data,

(a) prevention costs should be decreased

(b) internal failure costs can be decreased

(c) prevention costs are too low a proportion of the quality costs shown

(d) appraisal costs should be increased

(e) nothing can be concluded.

₹ 10,000	equipment design
150,000	scrap
180,000	re-inspection and retest
45,000	loss or disposition of surplus stock
4,000	vendor quality surveys
40,000	repair

Ans. : (*c*)

Q. 16.2: *The percentage of total quality cost are distributed as followes:*

Prevention	12%
Appraisal	28%
Internal failure	40%
External failure	20%

We conclude

(a) we should invest more money in prevention

(b) expenditures for failures are excessive

(c) the amount spent for appraisal seems about right

(d) nothing.

Ans. : (*d*)

Q. 16.3: *Of the following, which are typically appraisal costs ?*

(a) quality audits and final inspection

(b) quality planning and quality reports

(c) drawing control centers and material dispositions

(d) vendor surveys and vendor faults

(e) none of the above.

Ans. : (*d*)

Q. 16.4: *When analyzing quality cost data gathered during the initial stages of a new management emphasis on quality control and corrective action as part of a product improvement programme, one normally expects to see*

(*a*) *increased prevention costs and decreased appraisal costs*

(*b*) *increased appraisal costs with little change in prevention costs*

(*c*) *decreased internal failure costs*

(*d*) *decreased total quality costs*

(*e*) *all of these.*

Ans. : (*b*)

Q. 16.5: *Quality costs are best classified as*

(*a*) *cost of inspection and test, cost of quality engineering, cost of quality administration, and cost of quality equipment*

(*b*) *direct, indirect, and overhead*

(*c*) *cost of prevention, cost of appraisal, and cost of failure*

(*d*) *unnecessary*

(*e*) *none of the above.*

Ans. : 1. (*c*); 2 (*d*); 3. (*a*); 4. (*b*); 5. (*c*).

Q. 16.6: *(a) Is there any relationship between quality costs and quality levels ?*

(*b*) *List four costs of performance.*

(*c*) *List four costs of failure.*

(*d*) *Which area of cost is usually increased in a quality programme ?*

Ans. : (*a*) There is no simple relationship.

(*b*) *Prevention costs–these include training, component, plant and design.*
Appraisal costs–these include–inspection, testing and stock.

(*c*) Internal–This includes scrap, rework, stock, idle capacity, damage to plant, motivation.
External–This includes goodwill, compensation, rectification, administrative costs.

(*d*) Prevention, e.g. training.

Q. 16.7: *(a) Name only **(do not define/explain)** the three main costs of quality.*

(b) Which of the costs of quality in (a) are controlled by a good management?

(c) How the costs of quality is reported in TQM programme?

Ans. : (*a*) Three main costs of quality are (PAF costs):

1. Prevention costs
2. Appraisal costs
3. Failure costs – internal and external

(*b*) Out of above the two costs controlled by management are

- Prevention costs
- Appraisal costs.

(*c*) To implement a TQM programme, costs of quality must be highlighted separately within accounting reports so that all employees are aware of the cost of quality.

Q. 16.8: *(a) State the equation of total cost of quality (COQ).*

(b) State how will you proceed to complete the cost of poor quality (QOPQ)?

Ans. : (*a*) Cost of quality (COQ) = P-costs + A-costs + F-costs (i.e., PAF cost) (*b*) Poor quality results in (*i*) losing the business, (*ii*) loss in the opportunities to enhance the prices of the product or services. Hence COPQ = PAF costs + Lost opportunities (in terms of money).

Q. 16.9: *A newly formed bike manufacturing company in order to boost up its sale during lockdown period in India is keeping quality management processes in place.*

(a) What are the consequences?

(b) What is the remedy?

Ans. : (*a*) Any company that does not have quality management processes in place will usually find that failure cost F-costs, far exceed the P-and A-costs.

(*b*) **Remedy:** By implementing planned appraisal and prevention audits, the total cost of quality will reduce . This is a proactive process requiring commitment from all members of the company/organization.

Q. 16.10: *Present day trend is to categories the quality costs into following four types: Appraisal, prevention, internal failure and external failure costs. With reference to above four types of quality costs, advise under which category (ies) the cost of following items is to be identified:*

1. *Vendor rating*
2. *Final inspection of products and services*
3. *Administration of quality programmes*
4. *Re-inspection and investigation of failure causes.*
5. *Loss of goodwill*
6. *Loss of further business*
7. *Financial compensation paid to customers outside litigation.*
8. *Sale as second quality.*
9. *Management/overhead costs.*

Ans. : According to present practice, the categoris are as follows:

Appraisal costs	- Item No. 1, 2 and 9.
Prevention costs	- Item No. 3
Internal failure costs	- Item No. 4 and 8
External failure costs	- Item No. 5, 6 and 7.

Q. 16.11: *Categorise the following activities into cost of quality.*

(i) SQC tools (ii) vendor assessment (iii) calibration of measuring and test equipment (iv) customer returns (v) lower production yields (vi) loss of market share (vii) black-listing for future business (viii) getting on holiday list for sometime (ix) Overtime.

Ans. : Categories are as follows:

Prevention	-	(*i*)
Appraisal	-	(*iii*), (*ii*)
Internal Failure	-	(*v*), (*ix*)
External Failure	-	(*iv*), (*vi*), (*vii*), (*viii*)

Q. 16.12: *For supply of higher pressure gas pipeline, pipes were purchased from a reputed and approved manufacturer. During the construction of pipeline, one of the pipes failed under specified* *hydrotest. As a consequence, the supply company had to replace the pipe at a short notice and had to pay a heavy penality as per conditions. Is it a case of external failure quality cost? Why?*

Ans. : The pipes were supposed to be supplied as per specifications. As the pipe failed during hydrotest at site, it is a case of external failure quality cost as financial compensation had to be paid along with replacement of damaged pipe. Loss of goodwill and probable 'blacklisting' of manufacturer is another dominant factor of external failure quality cost.

Q. 16.13: *Following are* ***not*** *considered the COQ. Why?*

(a) Paying extra to programmers to help deadlines.

(b) The cost of contracting another company to make parts of the product.

Ans. : (*a*) COQ is the time and money spent to prevent, find, or repair defects.

(*b*) Any activity that helps us to find, prevent or fix defects in the product is included in COQ. Activities done to make a product are not counted in COQ.

Q. 16.14: *State the Explicite and Implicit costs of quality.*

Ans. : ***Explicit costs*** of quality are those that are recorded in accounting records, to be separately highlighted with the implementation of a TQM programme.

Implicit costs of quality are not recorded in accounting records. They tend to be of two forms:

- Opportunity costs such as the loss of future sales to a customer dissatisfied with faulty goods.
- Costs which tend to be subsumed within other account headings such as costs which result from the disruptions caused by stockouts due to faulty purchases.

Q. 16.15: *Mention some non-financial quality measures*

Ans. : Although cost of quality reports provide a useful summary of the costs, effort and progress of quality, non-financial quality measures may be more appropriate for lower levels of management. Some examples of such measures.

- Number of customer complaints
- Number of warranty claims
- Number of defective units delivered to customers as a percentage of total units delivered

---

Q. 16.16: *(a) Fill in the blank:*

The cost of training for quality is categorized as ________ *cost* (P, A, F).

(b) What do you see as the cost of training?

Ans. : (*a*) P

(*b*) The costs of training for quality include :

- the cost of the non-productive time taken to learn new attitudes and skills;
- the cost of qualified instructors or training courses and materials as necessary;
- the cost of mistakes when learning on the job, including wasted materials and lost time.

Q. 16.17: *For the following quality cost, given a table categorized there in (i)* P, A, F *costs (ii)* COC *and* CONC *category*

(a) Reworking rejected output *(b) customer return*

(c) Quality circles *(d) Inspection of finished goods.*

Ans. :

Costs	*P, A, F categories*	*COC and CONC categories*
a	F-internal	CONC
n	F-external	CONC
c	P	COC
d	A	COC

Q. 16.18: *(a) Which two of the following are examples* P. *cost of quality?*

(i) Inspection of raw material.

(ii) Training cost of operational staff.

(iii) Return of non conformity products

(iv) Machine break down repairs

(v) Routine repairs and maintenance

(b) Classify the rest ***three*** *in the COC and CONC category.*

Ans. : (*a*) P- cost : (*ii*) and (*v*);

(*b*) COC : (*i*); CONC : (*iii*), (*iv*)

Q. 16.19: *(a) Show a typical cost of quality report of a manufacturing company.*

(b) What are the uses of this kind of report?

Ans. : (*a*) A typical cost of quality report for the financial year ending 31st March, 2020 is shown below.

Cost of Quality-Report year ending March 31, 2020			
			Cost as % of annual revenue
	₹ '000	₹ '000	(₹ 1 crore)
Prevention costs			
Design of quality control equipment	100		
Quality control training	90		
		190	1.9
Appraisal costs			
Inspection of goods inwards	80		
Inspection of WIP	80		
		160	1.6
Internal failure costs			
Scrap	150		
Rework	200		
		350	3.5
External failure costs			
Returns	500		
Contribution forgone on lost sales	350		
Handling customer complaints	150		
		1,000	10.0
		1,700	17.0

Some figures in the above report, such as the contribution forgone due to sales lost because of poor quality, may have to be estimated, but it is always better to include an estimate rather than omit the category from the report.

(*b*) The report has the following uses:

(*i*) By expressing each cost category as a percentage of sales revenue, comparisons can be made with previous periods, divisions within the group or other organizations, thereby highlighting problem areas. A comparison of the proportion of external failure costs to sales revenue with the figures for other organizations, for example, can provide some idea of the level of customer satisfaction.

(*ii*) It can be used to make senior management aware of *how much is being spent* on quality-related costs.

(*iii*) It can provide an indication of *how total quality costs could be reduced by a more sensible division of costs between the four categories.* For example, an increase in spending on prevention costs should reduce the costs of internal and external failure and hence reduce total spending.

Q. 16.20: *Z Ltd is a MSME manufacturing unit. Its monthly costs are made up as follows:*

1.	Cost of re-inspecting previously finished goods after reworking them	6,000
2.	Cost of scrap	12,000
3.	Cost of calibrating and testing equipment	8,500
4.	Cost of inspecting of incoming material	1,000
5.	Cost of conductive supplier (external provider) capability survey	2,000

Which one of the following options identifies *Z*'s monthly *P*-costs, *A*-costs and *CONC* non-conformance cost (CONC)? Give reasons.

Option	*P-cost* (₹)	*A-cost* (₹)	*CONC* (₹)
A	10,500	1,000	6,000
B	2,000	1,000	12,000
C	2,000	9,500	18,000
D	N/L	21,500	1,000

Ans. : Option C.

Reason: (1) is internal failure costs. These are CONC. Likewise, (2) scrap cost are internal failure costs of non-conformance i.e., CONC, (3) Cost of calibrating test equipment are identified as A-costs. Similarly (4) cost of inspection of increasing material are classified as also classified as A-cost.

(5) Costs of conducting supplier (external provider) are P-cost incurred to prevent poor quality in products and services.

In view of above, the follows cost-category analysis gives as the correct option as C only

P-cost : ₹ 2000

A-cost: ₹ 8,500 + ₹ 1,000 i.e., ₹ 9,500

CONC : ₹ 6,000 + ₹ 12,000 i.e., ₹ 18,000

Q. 16.21: *Following information has been supplied for company XYZ*

Revenue cost	*(₹ ,000)* *320,000*
1. Design engineering	5,000
2. Warranty	8,930
3. Estimated lost contribution from public knowledge for poor quality	9,561
4. Training	560
5. Process engineering	3,450
6. Customer support for repaired unit	645
7. Product testing	65
8. Transportation cost per repaired unit	546
9. Inspection	13,800
10. Rework	7,545

Prepare a cost analysis that shows the P-costs, A-cost and F-cost (i) internal failure (ii) external failure for company XYZ. Your statement should show cost heading as % of turnover and clearly show the total cost of quality (including any opportunity cost)

Ans. :

	₹ ,000	**% of revenue**
Prevention cost : 1 + 5 + 4 i.e.,	9,010	$\left(\frac{9010}{32,000} \times 100\right) = 2.82$
Appraisal costs : 9 + 7 i.e.	13,865	4.33
Internal failure costs : 10 i.e.,	7,545	2.36
External failure costs : 2 + 6 + 18 i.e.,	10,141	3.17
Sub total	40,561	12.68%
Opportunity costs	9,561	2.99%
Total Quality costs	50,112	15.66

Q. 16.22: *(a) Mention briefly the main stages in the implementation of PAF quality costing system.*

(b) State the Explicit and Implicit cost of quality.

(c) Can you present the Explicit quality costs in a tabular form?

Ans. : Following six steps are usually required for the implementation of PAF quality costing system:

1. Establish senior management support for the philosophy of measuring quality improvement through the report of quality costs.
2. Establish a cost of quality action team comprising staff from a range of functions including furiance and quality assurance.
3. Identify the quality costs using the four categories—i.e., prevention, appraisal, internal failure and external failure.

4. Collate and validate the quality cost information to ensure both the accuracy of the data and consistency in the interpretation and establish procedures for the ongoing preparation and presentation of quality cost reports.
5. Introduce awareness training for employees to emphasize the reasons for identifying quality costs and the relationship with programmers for quality improvement in reducing the failure costs.
6. Prepare and distribute the quality cost reports as a mechanism for focusing and measuring quality improvement and ensuring reaction by the recipients

(*b*) ***Explicit costs*** of quality are those that are recorded in accounting records, to be separately highlighted with the implementation of a TQM programme.

Implicit costs of quality are not recorded in accounting records. They tend to be of two forms:

- *Opportunity costs* such as the loss of future sales to a customer dissatisfied with faulty goods.
- *Costs which tend to be subsumed* within other account headings such as costs which result from the disruptions caused by stockouts due to faulty purchases.

(*b*) Table 16.5. Gives the explicit quality costs.

TABLE 16.5: EXPLICIT QUALITY COSTS

Quality related cost	*Example*
Prevention costs	Quality engineering Design/development of quality control/inspection equipment Maintenance of quality control/inspection equipment Administration of quality control/ Training in quality control
Appraisal costs	Acceptance testing Inspection of goods inwards Inspection costs of in-house processing Performance testing
Internal failure costs	Failure analysis Re-inspection costs Losses from failure of purchased items Losses due to lower selling prices for sub-quality goods Costs of reviewing product specifications after failures
External failure costs	Administration of customer complaints section Costs of customer service section Product liability costs Cost of repairing products returned from customers Cost of replacing items due to sub-standard product/ marketing errors

Q. 16.23: *The Managing Director of a manufacturing company based in India has recently returned from a conference on modern manufacturing. One of the speakless at the conference presented a paper entitled 'Compliance versus conformance–The quality control issue'. The M.D. would like you to explain to him some of the concepts that he heard about at the conference.*

You are required to prepare a report that discussed quality costs and their significance of the company. Your report should include examples of the different quality costs and their classification within a manufacturing environment.

Ans. : Report

To: Managing Director
From: Management Accountant
Subject: Quality
Date: ....

Introduction

This report provides the basis for discussion at the company's next board meeting. It outlines the approaches to quality that may be adopted by the company, in particular the conflict between 'Conformance' and 'Non-Conformance' in terms of costs and the perceptions of our customers.

Quality costs

There are two board approaches to the quality issue which can have their own costs, some of which are easier to identify and measure than others.

1. Costs of conformance; and 2. Costs of non-conformance.

Costs of conformance (COC) are the costs that are incurred in order to try to ensure that the quality of the final products or services meets the customers' expectations. This category can be sub-analysed into two further groups:

1. Appraisal costs: which are the costs incurred in testing/measuring and checking the product or service to ensure that it meets the quality targets that have been set, examples include the operating costs of test equipment; and

2. Prevention costs: which are costs that are incurred n order to prevent poor quality products or services from being produced; examples include training costs and routine maintenance of production equipment.

Cost of non-conformance (CONC) are the costs that arise as a consequence of failing to meet the quality target. This category can also be sub-analysed into to further groups

1. Internal failure costs – which are costs of reworking and correcting items of poor quality that have been discovered prior to despatch to customers; and

2. External failure costs – which are cost associated with poor quality products or services being delivered to the customer such as the cost of the customer complaints.

Significance of quality costs

In the moder environment, with increased levels of competition and increasingly demanding customers who except the products and services being provided to them to be of the highest quality, an organization is required to carefully consider its target marked and the price/quality relationship that its customers will demand.

The decision to incur inspection and appraisal costs is often seen as an attempt to minimise the costs of failure as there is clearly a relationship between incurring conformance costs and avoiding non-conformance costs. It is necessary to determine the level of failure that would be acceptable to customer given the specific price/quality relationship referred to above.

It is possible to achieve 100% quality in respect of a ll item delivered to customer but his would require that every item would have to be checked individually prior to its despatch. Clearly this would be time consuming and costly.

An alternative approach would be to rest a sample of the items to be delivered to customers and rely on that sample being representative of the entire consignment. Clearly this would be less time consuming and there fore less costly but there is an increased risk one or more the items delivered would not be of the appropriate quality, thus increasing non-conformance costs.

Conclusion

This report has provided a basis of discussion at our next board meeting.

Q. 16.24: *LL designs and makes a single product, the X4, used in the telecommunications industry. The organization has a goods received store which employs who carry out random checks to ensure materials are of the correct specification. In addition to the random checks, a standard allowance is made for failure due to faulty materials at the completion stage and the normal practice is to charge the cost of any remedial work required to the cost of production for the month. Once delivered to the customer, any faults discovered in the X4 during its warranty period become and expensive of the customer support department. At the end of each month, management reports are prepared for the board of directors. These identify the cost of running the stores and the number of issues, the cost of production and the number of units manufactured, and the cost of customer support. You are required to answer the following :*

(a) Briefly discuss why the current accounting system fails to highlight the cost of quality.

(b) Identify four general categories (or classifications) of LL's activities where expenditure making up the explicit cost of quality will be found.

(c) Give one examples of a cost of quality not normally identified by accounts system.

Ans. : (*a*) Failure of the current accounting system to highlight the cost of quality is as follows:

Traditionally, the cost of scrapped units, wasted materials and reworking have been subsumed within the costs of production by assigning the costs of an expected level of loss (a normal loss) to the costs of good production, while accounting for other cost of poor quality within production or marketing overheads. Such costs are therefore not only considered as inevitable but are not highlighted for management attention. Moreover, tradition accounting reports tend to ignore the hidden but real costs of excessive inventory levels (held to enable faulty material to be replaced without hidering production) and the facilities necessary for storing that inventory.

(*b*) There are four recognized categories of cost identifiable within an accounting system which make up the cost of quality.

1. Prevention costs
2. Appraisal costs
3. Interval costs
4. External costs

(*c*) Quality costs which are not identified by the accounting system tend to be of two forms.

(*i*) Opportunity costs such as the loss of future sales to a customer dissatisfied with faulty goods.

(*ii*) Costs which tend to be subsumed within other account headings such as those acts which costs which result form the disruption caused by stockouts due to faulty purchases.

CHAPTER

17 Quality Gurus & Their Philosophy and Attitudinal Changes

17.1 QUALITY IMPROVEMENT

Statistical techniques including statistical process control (SPC) and design of experiments (DOX) along with other problem solving tools are the technical basis for quality control and improvement. However, to be used most effectively and beneficially, these techniques must be implemented within and be part of management system that is focused on quality improvement. The management system of an organization must be organized to properly direct the overall quality improvement philosophy and ensure its deployment in all aspects of the business. The effective management of quality involves successful execution of three activities: quality planning, quality assurance, and quality control and improvement.

Quality planning is a strategic activity, and it is just as vital to an organization's long-term business success as the product development plan, the financial plan, the marketing plan, and plans for the utilization of human resources. Without a strategic quality plan, an enormous amount of time, money, and effort will be wasted by the organization dealing with faulty designs, manufacturing defects, field failures, and customer complaints. Quality planning involves identifying customers, both external and those that operate internal to the business, and identifying their needs [this is sometimes called listening to the **voice of the customer (VOC)**]. Then products or services that meet or exceed customer expectations must be developed. The eight dimensions of quality discussed earlier in Chap. 15, are an important part of this effort. The organization must then determine how these products and services will be realized. Planning for quality improvement on a specific, systematic basis is also a vital part of this process.

Quality assurance is the set of activities that ensures the quality levels of products and services are properly maintained and that supplier and customer quality issues are properly resolved. Documentation of the quality system is an important component. Quality system documentation involves four components: policy, procedures, work instructions and specifications, and records. Policy generally deals with what is to be done and why, while procedures focus on the methods and personnel that will implement policy. Work instructions and specifications are usually product-, department-, tool-, or machine-oriented. Records are a way of documenting the policies, procedures, and work instructions that have been followed. Records are also used to track specific units or batches of product, so that it can be determined exactly how they were produced. Records are often vital in providing data for dealing with customer complaints, corrective actions, and, if necessary, product recalls. Development, maintenance, and control of documentation are important quality assurance functions. One example of document control is ensuring that specifications and work instructions developed for operating personnel reflect the latest design and engineering changes.

Quality control and improvement involve the set of activities used to ensure that the products and services meet requirements and are improved on a continuous basis. Since variability is often a major source of poor quality, statistical techniques, including SPC and designed experiments (DOX), are the major tools of quality control and improvement. Quality improvement is often done on a project-by-project basis and involves teams led by personnel with specialized knowledge of statistical methods and experience in applying them. Projects should be selected so that they have significant business impact and are linked with the overall business goals for quality identified during the planning process. The techniques in this book are integral to successful quality control and improvement.

The next section provides a brief overview of some of the key elements of quality management. We discuss some of the important quality philosophies; and the three aspects of *quality planning, quality assurance, and quality control and improvement* will be woven into the discussion.

17.2 QUALITY LEADERS / GURUS AND THEIR IDEAS OF QUALITY

Many people have contributed to the statistical methodology and other methodologies of quality improvement and management. Interest in quality as weapon took root in the West with the tide of imports of Japanese consumer products. The ideas and philosophies then spread from the factory into all organizations from service business and non-profitable organizations to government operations and administration. However, in terms of implementation and management philosophy, these six individuals emerge as the leaders (also known as **Quality 'Gurus'**): W.E. Deming, J.M. Juran, A.V. Feigenbaum; Kaoru Ishikawa, Genichi Taguchi and Philips B. Crosby. These quality leaders have moulded the attitude of a generation of managers.

17.2.1 W. Edwards Deming

W. Edwards Deming was educated in engineering and physics at the University of Wyoming and Yale University. He worked for Western Electric and was influenced greatly by Walter A. Shewhart, the developer of the control chart. After leaving Western Electric in 1930s, Deming held government jobs with the U.S. Department of Agriculture and the Bureau of the Census. His methods of statistical control achieved great improvements in the productivity and quality of the 1940 census. This work led to invitations to train industrialists and military personnel and he worked with many thousands of US military engineers and technicians to improve quality. Following the World War II Deming visited Japan in 1946 as a representative of the economic and scientific section of the US Department of War. With its manufacturing base destroyed by the US Air Force, Japanese managers listened intently on how to rebuild their manufacturing processes based on quality systems. Beginning in 1950s, thousands of Japanese managers attended Deming's course in Statistical Process Control. He became a leading consultant to Japanese industries and convinced their top management of the power of statistical methods and the importance of quality as a competitive weapon. *This commitment to and use of statistical methods has been a key element in the Japan's industrial recovery and expansion together with economy.*

While Deming based his work on advanced statistical methods, his contribution lay in presenting ideas in a simple way. The results were both impressive and influential, so much so that eventually the Japanese Union of Scientists and Engineers (JUSE) created the Deming Prize for quality improvement in his honour and it remains Japan's leading quality prize as on today.

Deming's main argument against *traditional quality control* was that it *focussed on the product rather than the process.* His basic philosophy is that **quality** and **productivity** *increase* as **process variability** (the unpredictability of the process) **decreases**. Deming advocated the use of *statistics to measure process variability*, which was chief culprit of poor quality. He then argued for continual investigation and fine tuning to improve the production system incrementally. He proposed a framework for this continuous improvement by recommending the PDCA cycle (which we shall return to a little later), as a model to guide improvement.

It was only early 1980s that Deming's work was recognized in his own country. Until his death in 1994, Deming was an active consultant and speaker spreading his message to large audiences throughout the US and around the world. Some companies (and governments) blame unions for having a negative impact on worker productivity but Deming insists that management is 90% of the problem. Organization need to address the problems of the quality of direction being given to the workforce, the resources available to get the job done efficiently and the opportunities for workers to contribute ideas about how to do the job better.

Deming, in his book **Quality, Productivity and competitive Position**, suggest that improving quality leads to improved productivity, reduce costs, more satisfied customers and increased profitability. His system for management to improve quality and competitiveness covers the following main areas.

- The organisation should have a constant purpose of improving their product or service.
- Quality objectives should be agreed and action taken to accomplish them.
- Systems for production and service delivery should be improved, eliminating all waste.
- Consideration of quality and reliability should be just as important as price when choosing a supplier.
- Attention must be paid to training people so they are better at their jobs and understand how to optimise production.
- Mass inspection of goods ties up resources and does not improve quality.
- Education and self improvement should be encouraged in all members of the organisation. Management should enable staff to take a pride in their work.
- Barriers between staff areas should be broken down.

The Deming's above philosophy is an important framework for implementing quality and productivity improvement. This philosophy is summarized in his 14 points for management in which he emphasizes the need for statistical control methods, participation, education, openness, and purposeful improvement. **Deming's 14 points** are as follows:

1. Create a constancy of purpose focused on the improvement of products and services.
2. Adopt a new philosophy that recognizes we are in a different economic era.
3. Do not rely on mass inspection to "control" quality.
4. Do not award business to suppliers on the basis of price alone, but also consider quality.
5. Focus on continuous improvement.
6. Practice modern training methods and invest in on-the-job training for all employees.
7. Improve leadership, and practice modern supervision methods.
8. Drive out fear.
9. Break down the barriers between functional areas of the business.
10. Eliminate targets, slogans, and numerical goals for the workforce.
11. Eliminate numerical quotas and work standards.
12. Remove the barriers that discourage employees from doing their jobs.

13. Institute an ongoing program of education for all employees.
14. Create a structure in top management that will vigorously advocate the first 13 points.

Deming also encouraged the Japanese to adopt a systematic approach to problem solving, which later became known as the Deming or **Plan-Do-Check-Act** (PDCA) cycle, shown in Fig. 17.1(*a*) and illustrated in Fig. 17.1(*b*). The cycle is not original. As with many of his ideas, Deming's contribution was to draw them together and apply them rigorously and vigorously to the quality question. Deming, however, referred to it as the **Shewhart cycle**, named after his teacher W.A. Shewhart. He subsequently replaced "Check" by '**study**' as that word reflects the actual meaning more nearly accurately and pragmatically; and the cycle become **PDSA Cycle**. However, the Japanese continue to call this as Deming cycle and current literature including ISO 9001 continues to call this as Deming's PDCA cycle. We shall also refer to this as Deming's PDCA cycle or Deming wheel appropriately.

In **Plan,** we propose a change in the system that is aimed at improvement. In **Do**, we carry out the change, usually on a small or pilot scale to ensure that to learn the results that will be obtained. **Check** consists of analyzing the results of the change to determine what has been learned about the changes that were carried out. In **Act**, we either adopt the change or, if it was unsuccessful, abandon it. The process is almost always iterative, and may require several cycles for solving complex problems.

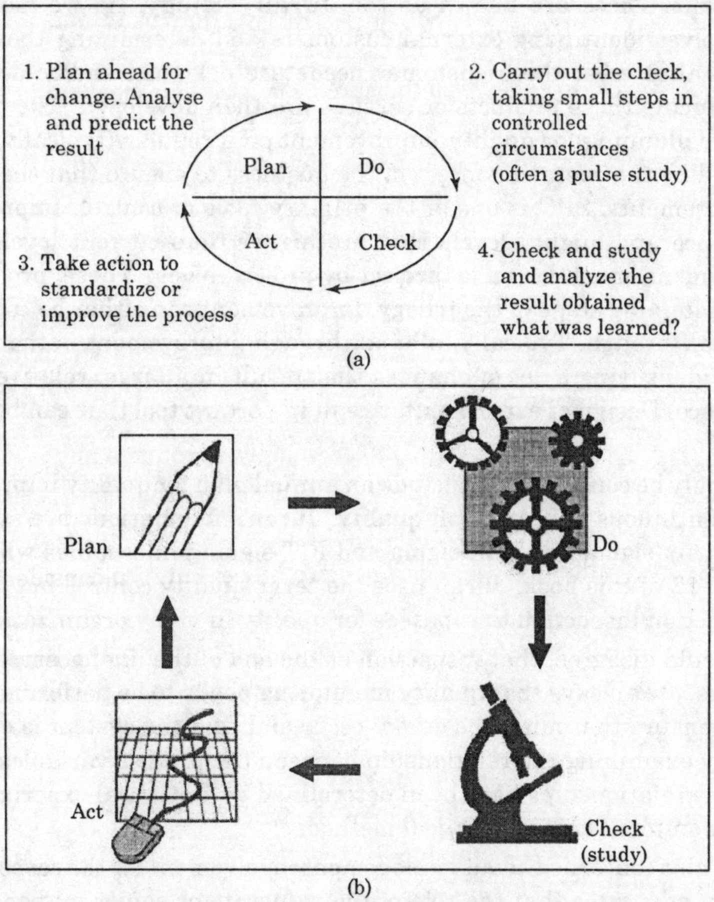

FIGURE 17.1 (*a*) Presentation; (*b*) Illustration of Deming's PDCA cycle

17.2.2 Joseph M. Juran

Juran was born in 1904. He is one of the founding fathers of the quality-control and improvement field. Like Deming, Juran's background was in statistics.

Juran was also associated with Japan's emergence as the bench mark for quality products. He was a key educator of the Japanese in quality management.

Juran defines quality as 'fitness for purpose'. This can be described loosely as 'that which relates to the evaluation of a product or service for its ability to satisfy a given need'. The elements of the theory are:

- quality of design, which can include customer satisfaction that is built into the product.
- quality of conformance, or a lack of defects
- abilities
- field services

Because customer incorporate such things as 'value for money' in their fitness for purpose' equation, Juran's theory is looking at quality from the point of view of the customer and is a more practical concept. Juran was the first guru to emphasize that quality is achieved by communication. His quality management philosophy focuses on three components: **planning, control,** and **improvement**. These are known as the **Juran Trilogy**. As we have noted previously, **planning** involves identifying external customers and determining their needs. Then products or services that meet these customer needs are designed and/or developed, and the processes for producing these products or services are then developed. The planning process should also involve planning for quality improvement on a regular (typically annual) basis. **Control** is employed by the operating forces of the business to ensure that the product or service meets the requirements. SPC is one of the primary tools of control. Improvement aims to achieve performance and quality levels that are higher than current levels. Juran emphasizes that improvement must be on a project-by-project basis. These projects are typically identified at the planning stage of the trilogy. Improvement can either be continuous (or incremental) or by breakthrough. Typically, a breakthrough improvement is the result of studying the process and identifying a set of changes that result in a large, relatively rapid improvement in performance. Design of experiments are in important tool that can be used to achieve breakthrough.

Juran's trilogy can simply be considered to include an annual plan for quality improvement and cost reduction, and continuous education on quality. Juran's foundations are still valid, and are embedded with in six-sigma and lean-sigma and FIT sigma philosophies which form the select matter of Chap. 22 of this book. Juran uses the term 'quality control' but this does not refer to the post-production inspection that passes for quality in many organizations.

He argues, and few would disagree, that inspection at the end of the line, postproduction, is too late to prevent errors. Juran says that quality monitoring needs to be performed during the production process to ensure that mistakes do not occur and that the system is operating effectively. He does this by examining the relationship between the process variables and the resultant product. Once the relationships have been determined by statistical experiment, the process variables can be monitored using statistical methods.

Like Deming, Juran is also concerned about management involvement for the responsibility of the quality. He strongly advocates that the role of the corporate or senior management is more than making policies; they have to show relationship through action – they have to walk the talk, not just give orders and set targets. He says that *quality is not free* and that investment (often substantial) in training, including statistical analysis, is needed at all levels of the organization. Juran also believed in the use of quality circles. As he describes them, quality circles are small teams of staff with a common interest who are brought together to solve quality problems.

In 1979, Juran founded a training consultancy, the Juran Institute, and through this, spread his ideas about partnerships and teamwork, internal customers, problem-solving techniques and application of Pareto analysis to quality issues. Like Deming, however, Juran continued to speak on the quality into his nineties.

17.2.3 Armand Feigenbaum

Armand Feigenbaum was a doctoral student at the Massachusetts Institute of Technology in 1950s. Feigenbaum is recognized for his work in raising quality awareness in the USA. Feigenbaum emphasises the relevance of quality issues in all areas of the operation of a business. He believes that 'prevention is better than cure' stressing the importance of identifying the costs of quality in economic and accounting terms.

Organisations adopting his ideas are encouraged to change the role of the quality control function from inspecting and rejecting output to one in which quality is given a planning role, involving the design of systems and procedures to reduce the likelihood of sub-optimal production.

The term **Total Quality Management (TQM)** originated from his book **Total Quality Control,** first published in 1951. He defines TQM as '*an effective system for integrating the quality development, quality maintenance and quality improvement efforts of the various groups in an organization so as to enable production and service at the most economical levels which allow for full customer satisfaction*'.

This book influenced much of the early philosophy of quality management in Japan in the early 1950s. In fact, many Japanese companies used the term "total quality control" to describe their efforts. He proposed a three-step approach to improving quality: **quality leadership, quality technology,** and **organizational commitment.** By **quality technology**, Feigenbaum means statistical methods and other technical and engineering techniques which form the subject matter of PART 1 and chaps 18 to 22 of PART 2 of this book.

Feigenbaum was one of the first writers to recognize that quality must be determined from the customer's perspective, and not the designer's (or the engineer's or the marketing department's) concept of what quality is. Feigenbaum also said that the best does not mean outright excellence, but means the best for satisfying certain customer conditions. In other words, as 'best' means sufficiently good to meet the circumstances. Feigenbaum emphasises the relevance of quality issues in all areas of the operation of a business. He believes that '*prevention is better than cure*', stressing the importance of identifying the costs of quality in economic and accounting terms.

Feigenbaum is concerned with organizational structure and a systems approach to improving quality. He proposed a 19-step improvement process, of which use of statistical methods was step 17. He initially suggested that much of the technical capability be concentrated in a specialized department. This is in contrast to the more modern view that knowledge and use of statistical tools need to be widespread. However, the organizational aspects of Feigenbaum's work are important, as quality improvement does not usually spring forth as a "grass roots" activity; it requires a lot of management commitment to make it work.

Feigenbaum, like Deming and Juran, found that *measurement is necessary*, but whereas Deming and Juran tended to measure production and outputs, Feigenbaum concentrated on measurement to evaluate whether good service and product met the desired level of customer satisfaction.

17.2.4 Kauro Ishikawa

A professor at the university of Tokyo, Ishikawa advocated quality ideas before the Second World War. Although modern quality management practices have their roots in the USA, some of the best Japanese principle offer significant lessons to western organisation. Studies have shown that the success of some Japanese companies has been due to progress in design quality, especially in miniaturisation, rather than conformance quality.

The late Ishikawa has been credited with originating the concept of *quality circles* (QC) and quality control. The Ishikawa *cause and effect diagram,* (C & E) known as the 'fishbone diagram' because of its shapes illustrates the relationship between possible causes and effect and helps to discover the source of the problem.

Ishikawa claimed that there had been a period of over-emphasis on statistical quality control (in Japan), and as a result people disliked quality control. They saw it as something unpleasant because they were given complex and difficult tools rather than simple ones. Furthermore, the resulting standardization of products and processes and the creation of rigid specification of standards became a burden that not only made change difficult but made people feel bound by regulations. Ishikawa saw the worker participation as the key to the successful implementation of TQM. Quality circles, he believed, were an important vehicle to achieve this.

17.2.5 Genichi Taguchi

He encouraged interactive team meetings between workers and managers to criticize and develop product design.

Taguchi developed a mathematical model of loss, measuring costs incurred or profits forgone relative to some baseline of performance. In his terms loss is more than cost. Quality is the loss imparted to society form the time the product is shipped'. Because goods use up time and resource in production a measure of quality is the fact that this 'loss' is minimised.

Taguchi identifies two aspects of quality control; off-lien and on-line.

- *Off-line quality* control incorporates systems design, parameter design and tolerance design. Systems design should reflect appropriate technology.
- *On-line quality* control aims to minimise the loss due to variations between goods produced, weighing the cost of the variation against the cost of correcting the variation. Examples of these variations could include slight difference in weight between identical parts or slight differences in time to produce something.

Quality Loss Function (QLF). Taguchi argued that what has become the conventional way of looking at specifications is too naive. The conformance perspective, with its specification width, $(U - L)$ [i.e. upper specification limit (U) – lower specification limit (L)] creates too sharp a distinction between acceptable items just inside the boundary and unacceptable ones just outside. The existence of the tolerance band, moreover, creates an attitude of mind that believes that all items falling inside the band are of equal value. Therefore, compared with real concentration on the target, this conformance-orientated quality leads to a greater proportion of products being further from it.

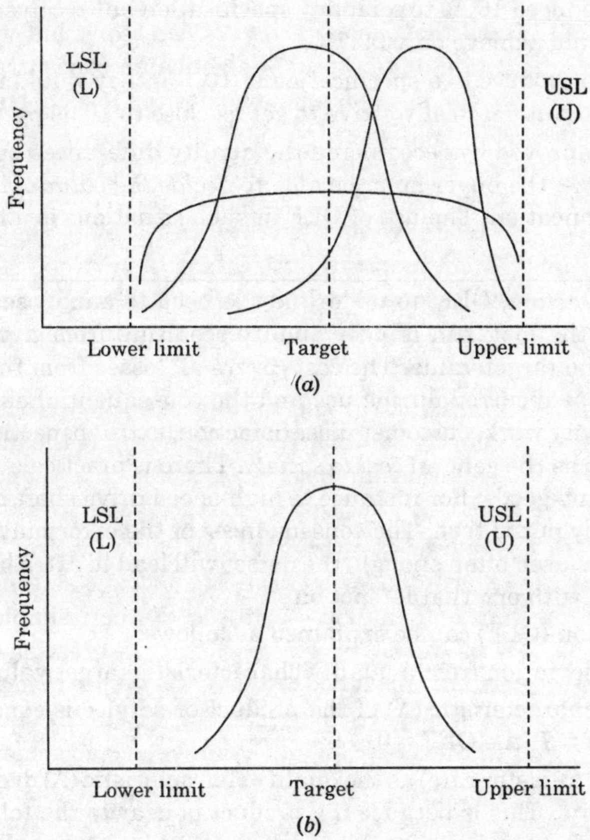

FIGURE 17.2 Conformance versus target-orientated quality.

The difference is illustrated in Fig. 17.2. Figure 17.2(*a*) shows the outputs of three conformance-orientated manufacturing processes. It does not matter whether the frequency distribution is centred on the target, or indeed whether there is any evidence of the process producing a peaked value, all of the output is acceptable. In Fig. 17.2(*b*), by the same token, it is clear that the process has been set to achieve the target. Taguchi saw the latter as better practice.

Example 17.1 ***Identical specification, identical televisions?***

In the late 1970s, Sony had found that customers preferred a particular colour density in their television pictures. We can call this value 10. Dissatisfaction rose with deviation from 10, so Sony set limits at 7 and 13.

Sets were manufactured in San Diego and Tokyo. The ones produced in the American plant had colour values uniformly spread throughout the range 7 to 13. All output was inspected and no sets outside the limits were despatched. A customer was just as likely to be given a set with a 7.8 screen as one with 10.2. Meanwhile, the Tokyo products clustered near the target of 10, although about 3 per 1,000 fell outside the range. The output was not inspected.

Colour differences were not easy to perceive but they could be noticed. If a customer compared a new television, made to 13.1, with a neighbour's achieving 12.9, there would be not detectable difference and no dissatisfaction. Yet if it were compared with a demonstration model built to 10, the customer would see the difference and demand repair visits until the set had been put right. Sony San Diego produced 100% to company specification but received more complaints than Sony Tokyo, which could achieve only 99.7%.

If American workers were asked to produce to a specification of 10 ± 3, they would readily do so. The Japanese, in addition, would automatically strive to get as close to 10 as possible.

Purchasing can, in principle, be improved by recognising the quality differences between acceptable suppliers. If this is to be done, the buyer must be able to *decide the value of quality differentials* that exist within the specification. The use of QLF in such situations is a helpful parameter.

Taguchi proposed a *quality loss function*, QLF, to underline the need to aim close to the target. It estimates the total cost in the long run of poor quality resulting from a product moving away from exactly matching the target value. The cost covers all losses from the time the product is delivered, including those incurred during use and the consequential effects of failure. It comprises service and warranty work, customer dissatisfaction, extra inspection and scrap as well as what Taguchi refers to as the general *cost to society*. There is practical support for this view in the manufacture of many goods. For instance, a high-speed drive shaft may be made within tolerance but very slightly out of true. The consequences of the error may never reveal themselves but if the assembly is used often enough, the defect will lead to extra bearing wear and premature failure compared with one that is 'spot on'.

The Taguchi's Quality Loss Function (QLF) can be explained as follows:

1. Costs are associated with *any* deviation from a quality characteristic target value (T).
2. QLF is zero when the quality characteristic (X) of the product or service is exactly on the target (T) value i.e. when $X = T$, the QLF = 0.
3. The loss rises exponentially (*i.e.* at faster rate) as the quality characteristic (X) drifts and gets closer to the tolerance limits. This is because if a product is near to the tolerance limits it is more likely to be a defective or service than a perfect one. *i.e.* loss in not equal to zero when the quality characteristic is within the specification limits *i.e.* when X is within tolerance band (*i.e.* with upper specification limit and (U) and lower specification limit (L).
4. QLF can be represented by an equation

$$L(X) = k(X - T)^2 \qquad ...(17.1)$$

where k is constant of proportionality.

$L(X)$ = The monetary loss per unit of product when the quality characteristic is equal to the value.

X = The quality characteristic (For example lengths, voltage concentration water) etc.

T = The target value of characteristic X.

k = The proportionality constant which depends upon the financial significance of the product to the society.

The expression for loss implies a continuous function whereby the loss increases as soon as the value of characteristic varies from the target. This approach is contrasted with the traditional viw of quality in which the cost of non-conformance is only incured once the product characteristic falls outside the specification limits *i.e.* when X is outside the U or L.

The features resulting from the QLF being considered as a quadratic expression are:

1. The loss is minimized the when $X = T$;
2. The loss initially increases slowly but increases more rapidly as the value of X away from the target T.

3. The loss is expressed in financial terms.

By adopting this approach to quality engineering, whereby the objective is to produce characteristics which meet the target rather than simply fall within specifications, a more robust design is produced. This is particularly true for the design of complex products (such as assembly of components of an aeroplane) in which the cumulative effect of components being away from target value can have a significant impact upon the overall reliability of the product. The QLF also enables tolerance design to be undertaken from the viewpoint of the overall loss to society rather tolerances being selected simply on the basis of material or process capability.

Example 17.2 ***The use of QLF determining manufacturing tolerances.***

Suppose, the setting of the tracking angle for the front wheels of a motor car which has a target value of –1.5 degrees. If the cost of resetting the tracking angle at the end of the production line is ₹ 400, what should the manufacturing tolerance be? From a QLF perspective, the design of the tolerances requires an evaluation of the tracking angle at which the manufacturer justifiably spends ₹ 400, correting the vehicle. Assuming the cost of rectifying a tracking problem (which occurs at angle of + 1°), for a customer who returns the new vehicle to the dealer under warranty is ₹ 15,000, then the manufacturing tolerance can be calculated a shown in Fig. 17.3. From Fig.17.3.

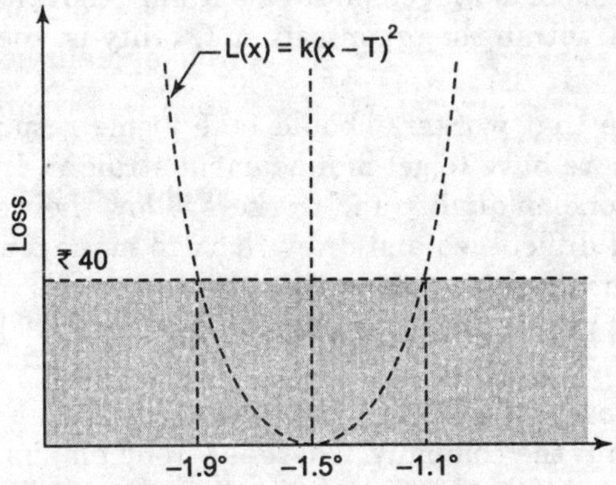

FIGURE 17.3 Taguchi's Quality loss function

$$L(X) = k(X-T)^2$$

for

$$X = +1^\circ \text{ (or } 1^\circ\text{)},\ L = ₹\ 15{,}000$$

$$T = -1.5^\circ$$

$$k = \frac{15{,}000}{[1-(-1.5)]^2} = \frac{15{,}000}{(2.5)^2}\ \textit{i.e.}\ ₹\ 2{,}400$$

The manufacturing tolerance can therefore be found by calculating the value of tracking angle (X) which corresponds to a loss of ₹ 400. Hence, again using

$$L(X) = k(X-T)^2$$

where

$$k = 2{,}400 \text{ and } L(X) = 400$$

$$(X-T)^2 = \frac{400}{2{,}400}$$

or

$$X - T = \pm\sqrt{\frac{400}{2{,}400}} = \pm 0.4$$

The manufacturing tolerance is therefore plus or minus 0.4 degree (*i.e.* $\pm$ 0.4°). If the vehicle is manufactured with the tacking angle tolerances outside these limits, then the manufacturer should reet the tracking angle otherwise the loss to society is not optimized.

17.2.6 Philip B. Crosby

Crosby is another theorist on quality. He is so prominent in America that General Motors bought a 10% stake in his firm. His thinking is base on his background working on the Pershing missile Programme, where the main objectives were zero defects (ZD). The zero defects concept and his assertion that a product should not have to corrected once it is built (right first time) are embodies in his four standards.

- Quality is conformance to standards.
- Prevention is the system for advancing quality, not appraisal.
- The important of quality is measure by the cost of not having quality.
- The importance of quality is measured by the cost of not having quality.

The problem for Crosby's standards is that quality must be judged as the customer perceives it, as Milliken and IBM in the USA, after pounding away at quality for many years, have found that a second revolution is required – become more responsive to customers. Crosby firmly believes that quality is not comparative, it either conforms to customer requirements or its is unacceptable. It is the role of management to make sure that the customer's need are reflected in the specifications set within the organisation. Quality is, therefore, an attribute and not a variable.

He does not believe that workers should take prime responsibility for poor quality; the reality, he says, is that we have to get management straight. In the Crosby scheme of things, management sets the tone on quality and workers follow their example; whilst employees are involved in operational difficulties and draw them to management's attention, the initiative comes from the top. Zero defects means that the company's objective is 'doing things right first time'. This will not prevent people from making mistakes, but will encourage everyone to improve continuously.

In the Crosby approach, the quality improvement message is spread by creating a core of quality specialists within the company. There is strong emphasis on the top-down approach, since he believes that senior management is entirely responsible for quality.

The ultimate goal is to train all the staff and give them the tools for quality improvement, to apply the basic precept of prevention management in every area. This is aided by viewing all work as a process or series of actions conducted to produce a desired result. A process model can be used to ensure that clear requirements have been defined and understood by both the supplier and the customer. He also views quality improvement as an ongoing process. Crosby's quality improvement process is based upon the *five* absolutes of quality management:

1. Quality is defined as conformance to requirements, not as 'goodness' or 'elegance'.
2. The system for causing quality is prevention, not appraisal.
3. The performance standard must be zero defects, not 'that's close enough'.
4. The measurement of quality is the price of nonconformance (PONC), not indices.
5. There is no such thing as a quality problem. His 14 quality steps are:

Cross by 14 quality steps are:

1. Establish management commitment.
2. Form interdepartmental quality teams.
3. Establish quality measurement.

4. Evaluate the cost of quality.
5. Establish quality awareness.
6. Instigate corrective action.
7. Ad hoc committee for the zero defects programme.
8. Supervise employee training.
9. Hold a zero defects day.
10. Employee goal setting.
11. Error cause removal.
12. Recognition for meeting and exceeding goals.
13. Establish quality councils.
14. Do it over again.

Quality vaccine. To help quality management an integral part of an organization's activities, Crosby introduced the concept of the quality vaccine, Fig. 17.4. This idea describes a corporate quality state that improves the overall health of a firm by addressing and correcting many of its problems. Corporate integrity represents the honest commitment to improve performance and satisfy customers in the most effective way. The concept embodies the firm's policy commitment to offer services and products that are right first time, every time. Communications represent the flow of information through the whole supply chain, emphasizing the need for regular exchanges of information on quality problems, performance, progress and related issues. The final elements is the systems and procedures designed to maintain the new quality management environment.

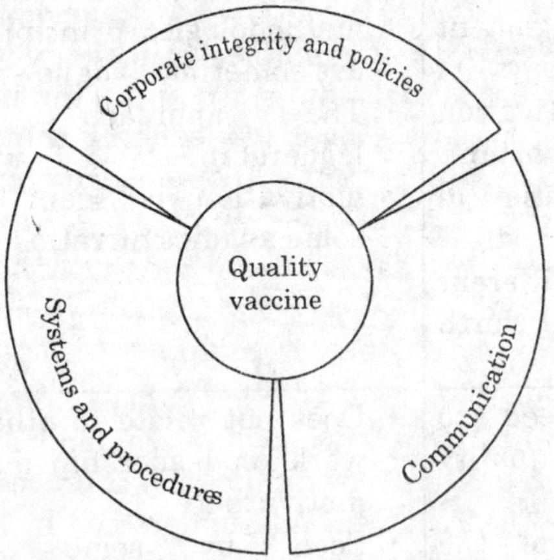

FIGURE 17.4 Crosby's quality vaccine.

Compared with the work of the other Gurus just described, Crosby's change programme is more behavioural. It stresses management and organizational processes rather than the application of statistical methods. While this enables a fit with current cultures and hierarchies it gives little detail of the practical tools of analysis that are essential in quality improvement.

17.3 RELATIVE STRENGTHS AND WEAKNESSES OF QUALITY GURUS

While above is a brief description of the philosophies of Deming, Juran, Feigenbaum, 'Crosby' Ishikawa and Taguchi, it is not an exhaustive catalogue of the other efforts and those who have contributed to the understanding and improving the quality and quality movement. All of these Gurus highlighted both common aspects and differences of their viewpoints. Author is of the opinion that there are more similarities than differences among them and the similarities are what is more important. All of these gurus have stressed upon the importance of quality as an essential competitive weapon, the important role that management must play in implementing quality improvement, the customer voice and quality cost being the central in all such improvement and the importance of statistical methods and allied techniques in the "quality transformation" of an organization.

Table 3.3 summarizes the strengths and weaknesses of each guru's approach.

TABLE 3.3 RELATIVE STRENGTHS AND WEAKNESSES OF THE QUALITY GURUS

Quality 'guru'	*Strengths of approach*	*Weaknesses of approach*
Feigenbaum	• Provides the total approach to quality control management (TQM) • Places the emphasis on the importance of management • Includes socio-technical systems thinking • Participation by all staff is promoted	• Does not discriminate between different kinds of quality context • Does not bring together the different management theories into one coherent whole
Deming	• Provides a systematic and functional logic which identifies stages in quality improvement • Stresses that management comes before technology • Leadership and motivation are recognized as important • Emphasizes role of statistical and quantitative methods • Recognizes the different contexts of Japan and North America	• Does not treat situations which are political or coercive • Action plan and methodological principles are sometimes vague • The approach to leadership and motivation is seen by some as idiosyncratic
Juran	• Emphasizes the need to move away from quality hype and slogans • Stresses the role of the customer both internal and external • Management involvement and commitment are stressed	• Does not relate to other work on leadership and motivation • Seen by some as undervaluing the contribution of the worker by rejecting bottom-up initiatives • Seen as being stronger on control systems than the human dimension in organizations

...(Contd.)

Ishikawa	• Strong emphasis on the importance of people and participation in the problem-solving process • A blend of statistical and people-orientated techniques • Introduces the idea of quality control circles and cause-and-effect diagrams	• Some of his problem solving method seen as simplistic • Does not deal adequately with moving quality circles from ideas to action
Taguchi	• Approach pulls quality back to the design stage • Recognizes quality as a societal issues as well as an organizational one • Methods are developed for practising engineers rather than theoretical statisticians	• Strong on process control • Difficult to apply where performance is difficult to measure (e.g. in the service sector) • Quality is seen as primarily controlled by specialists rather than managers and workers • Regarded as generally weak on motivation and people management issues
Crosby	• Provides clear methods which are easy to follow • Worker participation is recognized as important • Strong on explaining the realities of quality and motivating people to start the quality process.	• Seen by some as implying that workers are to blame for quality problems • Seen by some as emphasizing slogans and platitudes rather than recognizing genuine difficulties • Zero defects sometimes seen as risk avoidance • Insufficient stress given to statistical methods.

SOLVED QUESTIONS

Q. 17.1: *Select the right answer for the following:*

(i) A point *central to the views of all the main contributors (Quality gurus) or improving quality is:*

(a) The key to good quality lies in good management

(b) The concept of quality vaccine

(c) Slogans, posters and exhortations.

(ii) *Deming's quality philosophy focuses on:*

(a) The cost of quality and used data to shock management into action (*b*) Making and impact in a few months and in that way, stir the management into action.

(*c*) Quality as a management responsibility that required fundamental change and a long-term time frame.

(*iii*) Which of the following is not recognized as quality guru?

(*a*) Juran (*b*) Pareto

(*c*) Crosby (*d*) Deming

(*iv*) *Fishbone diagram is the same as a(n) – chart.*

(*a*) Ishikawa (*b*) Pareto

(*c*) flow (*d*) control

(*v*) *In consumer products, the complaint rate is most directly measure of*

(*a*) product quality (*b*) customer satisfaction

(*c*) market value (*d*) rejection rate

(*e*) specification conformance

Ans. : (*i*) (*a*); (*ii*) (*c*); (*iii*) (*b*); (*iv*) (*a*); (*v*) (*b*).

Q. 17.2: *(a) Mention the two elements in Juran's definition of quality as 'Fitness for purpose.'.*

(b) How does Taguchi define quality.

Ans. : Two elements are

(*i*) Quality of design.

(*ii*) Quality of conformance.

(*b*) Losses caused after shipment by product's functional variability.

Q. 17.3: *Advise the relevance of Deming's 14 points and other frame works for guiding management's pursuit of quality.*

Ans. : Deming's 14 points provide an all-encompassing framework for guiding management's pursuit of quality. The Malcolm Baldrige National Quality Award criteria and Juran's trilogy also provide valuable frame work.

Q. 17.4: *Which is **NOT** emphasized in quality management*

(a) Customer satisfaction *(b) Team responsibility*

(c) Phases within process *(d) Prevention over inspecting.*

Give reasons for your selected and rejected option(s).

Ans. : Correct option is (*c*).

Reason: Phases with in processes is a made-up term and is not stressed in quality management. (*a*) is incorrect because quality of management does stress that the customer's specifications should be taken into account (the implication being that if the customer's specifications are satisfied, the customer should be satisfied with the product). (*b*) is incorrect because Deming's philosophy stresses that the entire team has responsibility toward quality. (*d*) is incorrect because prevention over inspection is a big thrust of quality management, stressing that is costs less to prevent a problem than it does to fix one.

Q. 17.5: *(a) Name the famous quality gurus and in a single sentence mention their ideology for quality processes.*
(b) Mention the main elements of Juran's theory.
(c) Mention Deming's system of management for quality improvement and competitiveness.
[No explanation is called for parts (a) and (b)]

Ans. : (*a*) The ideologies used by famous quality gurus are as follows:

- **W Edwards Deming**—the use of statistical process control.
- **Philip B Crosby**—quality of conformance to customer requirements, achieved by prevention not appraisal, with the goal of zero defects.
- **Joseph Juran**—quality is 'fitness for purpose' as seen from the point of view of the customer.
- **Armand Feigenbaum**—quality issues are relevant to all areas of the operation of a business, with systems and processes being designed to reduce the likelihood of sub-optimal production and hence TQM.
- **Kauro Ishikawa**—the use of quality circles and techniques such as the fishbone diagram.
- **Genichi Taguchi**—developed a mathematical model of loss, (QLF) measuring costs incurred or profits forgone.

(*b*) Main elements of Juran theory for quality improvement are

- quality of design, which can include customer satisfaction that is built into the product
- quality of conformance, or a lack of defects
- abilities
- field service.

(*c*) Deming's system for management to improve quality and competitiveness covers the following main areas:

- The organization should have a constant purpose of improving their product or service.
- Quality objectives should be agreed and action taken to accomplish them.
- Systems for production and service delivery should be improved, eliminating all waste.
- Consideration of quality and reliability should be just as important as price when choosing a supplier.
- Attention must be paid to training people so they are better at their jobs and understand how to optimise production.
- Mass inspection of goods ties up resources and does not improve quality.
- Education and self improvement should be encouraged in all members of the organisation. Management should enable staff to take a pride in their work.
- Barriers between staff areas should be broken down.

Q. 17.6: *(a) What is Dr. Juran's simple definition of quality?*
(b) Mention briefly the main points of 'quality planning road map' of Dr. Juran.

Ans. : (*a*) Dr. Juran's definition of quality: Fitness for use (purpose)

(*b*) Dr. Juran developed the idea of quality trilogy: *quality planning, quality control and control improvement*. These three aspects of company-wide strategic quality planning are further broken down in Juran's 'quality planning road map' into following key elements shown in table below:

Juran's Quality Planning Road Map		
1.	Quality planning	• Identify who are the customers • Determine the needs of those customers • Translate those needs into our language • Develop a product that can respond to those needs • Optimise the product features so as to meet our needs and customer needs
2.	Quality control	• Prove that the process can produce the product under operating conditions • Transfer the process to operations
3.	Quality improvement	• Develop a process which is able to produce the product • Optimise the process

Q. 17.7: *Feigenbaum's quality concept is TQM. Present in a tabular form the name of some quality gurus including Feigenbaum and their quality concepts and quality tools for quality management.*

Ans. : The table gives below the famous quality gurus, their quality philosophy and their suggested tools for quality improvement.

Quality Gurus: 1. Deming, 2. Juran, 3. Feigenbaum, 4. Ishikawa, 5. Taguchi, 6. Crosby

Guru	*Their Quality Concepts*	*Their Suggested Tools*
1.	Management philosophy and reduction of variability	SQC Techniques, PDCA cycle
2.	Planning, Quality costs, Fitness for use, quality is not free	Juran's Triology-Planning, control and improvement, use of statistical tools etc.
3.	Total Quality Management, Prevention is better than cure	Statistical methods; cost of quality etc.
4.	No emphasis on quality control; customers being both internal and external to the organization	Quality circles and Fish bone diagrams
5.	Minimum Prototyping; Conformance- oriented quality leads to a greater proportion of products being further away from it	Statistical tools and quality lost function (QLF)
6.	Awareness, Zero Defects, Right First Time	Management responsibility creation a core of quality specaialists within a company

Q. 17.8: *Mention briefly the difference of approach recommended by Juran and Deming for quality management.*

Ans. : Juran acknowledges that managing for quality is not easy and requires important changes, but he does not believe it requires as great a managerial effort as Deming considered necessary.

Deming believes that the manager's job is to seek out and correct the causes of failure, rather than merely identify failures after they occur. The goal of Dèming's fourteen points therefore lies in altering the behaviour of managers and employees so that companies can become low-cost, high-quality and high productive.

Q. 17.9: *(a) What could be the background of Crosby's concept of ZD?*

(b) State four main standards of quality achievement as per Crosby.

(c) Do you see any problem with Crosby's standards in (b)?

(d) How Crosby's thinking on quality makes one to think that quality is an attribute and not a variable?

Ans. : (*a*) Crosby's concept of ZD (Zero Defect) is perhaps based on his background working on the Pershing missile programme, where the main objectives were zero defects.

(*b*) Crosby's ZD concept and his assertion that a product should not have to be corrected once it is built (right first time) are embodied in his four standards:

1. Quality is conformance to standards.
2. Prevention is the system for advancing quality, not appraisal.]
3. The goal should be zero defects.
4. The importance of quality is measured by the cost of not having quality.

(*c*) The problem for Crosby's standards is that quality must be judged as the customer perceives it. He asserts that his process is customer-oriented but companies, such as Milliken and IBM in the USA, after pounding away at quality for many years, have found that a second revolution is required—to become more responsive to customers.

(*d*) Crosby firmly believes that quality is not comparative, it either conforms to customer requirements or it is unacceptable. It is the role of the management to make sure that the customer's need are reflected in the specifications set within the organization. Quality is, therefore, an attribute and not a variable.

Q. 17.10: *There have been marked different, traditional approaches to quality aspects/ management in the West and Japan. Make a concise table so that these differences are quite evident to corporate management.*

Ans. : The traditional Western and Japanese approaches to quality are summarised in the following tabulation.

Quality issues	*The West*	*Japan*
Concept of quality	Static	Continuous improvement
Focus of activity	Volume/profit	Quality/customer satisfaction
Quality responsibility	Quality Control department	Mainly Workers
Quality training	For QC staff	For all workers
Solving quality problems	QC staff & engineering	Employees, supervisors and managers
Quality targets	Set by QC staff	Set by top managers
Role of QC experts	Inspection	Helping workers

Q. 17.11: *Juran says "quality is not free" while Crosby says "quality is free". Are these two statements not conflicting? Express your opinion on the issue.*

Ans. : Both the statements "quality is not free" and "quality is free" are true and there is no conflict between these statements. It is the question of timing. When you plan the quality improvement, investment has to be made in buying new machines, training of the persons and change in the attitude of the management personnel. It is in this sense that quality is not free. Once it is achieved and the system is set for improved quality and continuous improvement is a norm, then there is hardly noticeable investment and it is in this sense that quality is free.

Q. 17.12: *Distinguish quality assurance (QA) systems from quality control (QC) systems.*

Ans. : Both have different philosophy on quality

- QC systems attempts to control quality whereas
- QA systems attempt to create quality

QA involves managing each stage of production to minimize errors (a third party, negative intervention process). QC inspects afterwards.

QA checks quality in a positive way encouraging worker ownership for quality and "zero defects". QA prevents before hand.

Q. 17.13: *(a) The three C's of quality are: (i) Commitment, (ii) Competence (iii) Communication. What is the fourth C of of quality?*

(b) Distinguish between quality control and inspection.

Ans. : (*a*) Continuous improvement.

(*b*) Quality control involves setting controls for the process of manufacture or service delivery. It is a aimed at preventing the manufacture of defective items or the provision of defective services.

Quality control happens at various stages in the process of designing a product or service.

(*i*) Product design stage
(*ii*) Production engineering stage
(*iii*) Administration

Inspection is concerned with looking at products made, supplies delivered and services provided, to establish whether they are up to specification. It is a technique of identifying when defective items are being produced at an unacceptable level. Inspection is usually carried out at three main points:

(*i*) Receiving inspection – for raw materials and purchased components;
(*ii*) Floor or process inspection for W-I-P; and
(*iii*) Final inspection or testing for finished goods.

Q. 17.14: *(a) State two main improvement method in Deming's philosophy.*

(b) State two important elements in Juran's definition of quality.

(c) How Juran's idea about quality improvement are different from those of Deming's?

Ans. : (*a*) Use of SQC and PDCA cycle of quality improvement.

(*b*) Juran's defines quality as "fitness for use" and it includes :

(*i*) Quality of design (*ii*) quality of conformance

(*c*) While Deming's ideas are wide ranging and expand into considerations of leadership and management style, Juran was concerned with identifying specific improvements for enhancing quality. Juran's ideas are different in the following ways.

(*i*) The best approach to enhancing quality is to 'identify specific opportunities, evaluate their viability by using conventional methods such as return on investment, plan the selected project carefully, monitor their results'.

(*ii*) Juran believes in the law of diminishing returns there is an economic level of quality beyond which it is pointless to strive, because the costs outweigh the benefits.

(*iii*) Juran believes that most quality problems derive from management systems and processes rather than poor workmanship.

Q. 17.15: *(a) Who proposed the idea of Quality Circle (QC) for quality improvement? What is the real reason for instituting Quality Circle? What is the other contribution of the proposer of QC in the field of quality improvement.*

(b) Which of the following is responsible for the success of Japanese industries:

(i) design quality (ii) conformance quality

(c) Write a short note on Feignbaum's idea of quality, highlighting the important issues.

(d) What are Crosby's concept of quality? What is his methodology to implement his concepts?

Ans. : (*a*) Ishikawa in Japan proposed the idea of QC. Quality Circle are mainly management stimulated. Whatever the stated reasons are for instituting QC, the *real* reason for having QC is to motivate employees to improve quality.

The other contribution of Ishikawa is Fish-bone diagrams or cause-and-effect diagrams to solve quality problems.

(*b*) Design quality

(*c*) Armand Feigenbaum appended the word 'total' to quality, thus emphasising the relevance of quality issues to *all areas of the operations of a business.* He is also noted for assessing the economic value of quality, as the value of many quality improvement measures are not exactly self-evident. In other words he stressed the importance of identifying the costs of quality, and the lack of quality, to prove that, in economic and accounting terms, 'prevention is better than cure'.

This involves changing the role of the quality control function (which inspected and rejected output) to one in which quality provided an effective system for quality maintenance.

(*i*) An *inspection* role is carried out after the event, after the wasteful and substandard production.

(*ii*) A *planning* role would involve the design of systems and procedures to reduce the likelihood of sub-optimal production.

(*d*) Philip B Crosby is chiefly known for two concepts:

Zero defects : there should never be any defects in a product. Some consider this to be an impossible ideal, and invoke the concept of diminishing returns. Alternatively it can be seen as a slogan to employees.

Right first time is another idea which holds that a product should not have to be corrected once it is built. It is thus a corollary of the zero defects concept. Crosby proposes four standards that flesh out these concepts.

(*i*) Quality is *conformance to requirements*, (*ii*) The system for advancing quality is *prevention*, not appraisal, (*iii*) The goal should be *zero defects.* (*iv*) The importance of quality is measured by the cost of not having quality.

Crosby's ideas demonstrate a fundamental shift from a 'supervisory' culture of quality assurance to one where each individual takes full responsibility for his work quality is everyone's responsibility.

CHAPTER

18 Quality Improvement Tools & Techniques

18.1 TOOLS FOR IMPROVING QUALITY

The first step in improving the quality of an operation is data collection. Data can help uncover operations requiring improvement and the extent of remedial action needed. Eight tools for organizing and presenting data to identify areas for quality improvement are shown in Fig. 18.1. The functions of each of these tools are also stated for immediate use.

Checklists. Data collection through the use of a checklist (also called as tally sheet or tick chart) is often the first step in the analysis of quality problems. A checklist is a form used to record the frequency of occurrence of certain product or service characteristics related to quality. The characteristics may be measurable on a continuous scale (such as weight, diameter, time, or length) or on a yes-or-no basis (such as paint discoloration, odors, rude servers, or too much grease).

Histograms and Bar Charts. The data from a checklist often can be presented succinctly and clearly with histograms or bar charts (Fig. 18.1). A **histogram** summarizes data measured on a continuous scale, showing the frequency distribution of some quality characteristic (in statistical terms, the *central tendency* and *dispersion* of the data). Often the **mean (average)** of the data is indicated on the histogram. A **bar chart** is a series of bars representing the frequency of occurrence of data characteristics measured on a yes-or-no basis. The bar height indicates the number of times a particular quality characteristic was observed.

Pareto Chart. When managers discover several quality problems that should be addressed, which should be attacked first? Vilfredo Pareto, a nineteenth-century Italian scientist whose statistical work focused on inequalities in data, proposed that most of the "activity" is caused by relatively few of the factors. In a restaurant quality problem, the activity could be customer complaints and the factor could be "discourteous waiter." For a manufacturer, the activity could be product defects and a factor could be "missing part." Pareto's concept, called the 80-20 (or 80/20) rule, is that 80 percent of the activity is caused by 20 percent of the factors. By concentrating on the 20 percent of the factors (the "vital few"), managers can attack 80 percent of the quality problems.

The few vital factors can be identified with a *Pareto chart*, a bar chart organized so that the factors are plotted in decreasing order of frequency. The factors are listed along the horizontal axis. The chart has two vertical axes, the one on the left showing frequency as in a histogram and the one on the right showing the cumulative percentage of frequency. The cumulative frequency curve identifies the few vital factors that warrant managerial attention.

Chart-list

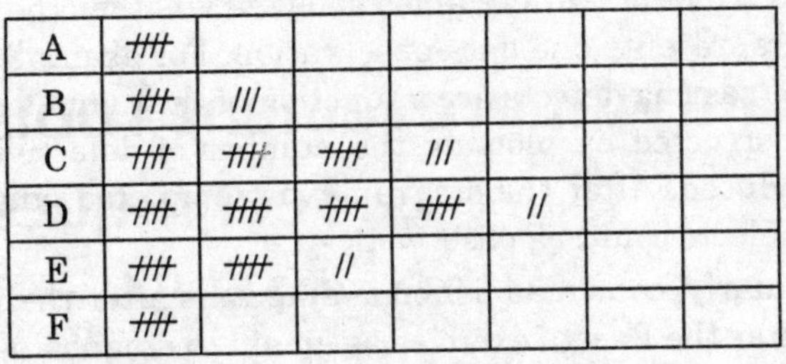

- Simplifies data collection and analysis
- Spots problem areas by frequency of location, type, or cause

Histogram

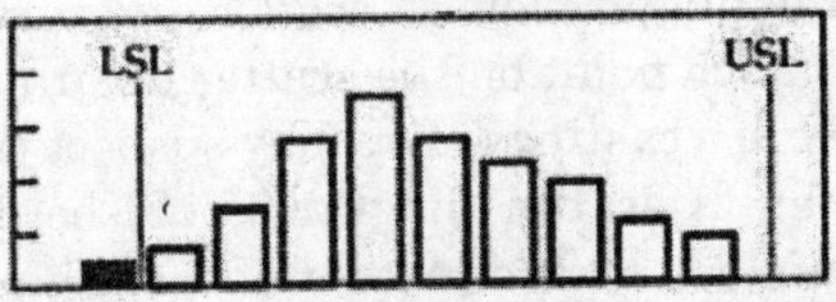

- The shape shows the nature of the distribution of the data
- The central tendency (average) and variability are easily seen
- Specification limits can be used to display the capability of the process.

Pareto Chart

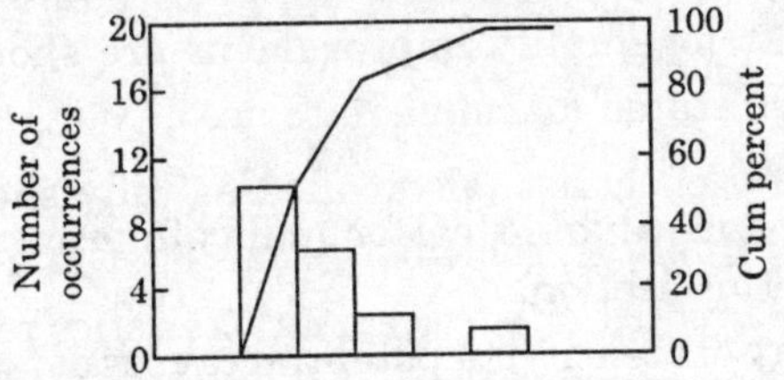

- Identifies most significant problems to be worked first
- Historically 80% of the problems are due to 20% of the factors
- Shows the vital few

Scatter Diagram

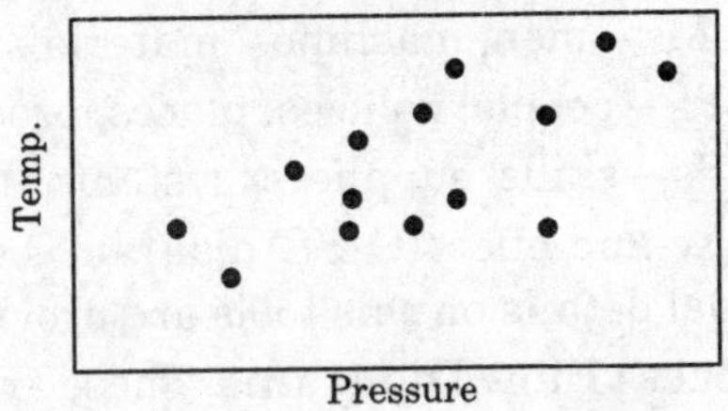

- Identifies the relationship between two variables
- A positive, negative, or no relationship can be easily detected

Cause-and-Effect (Fishbone) Diagram

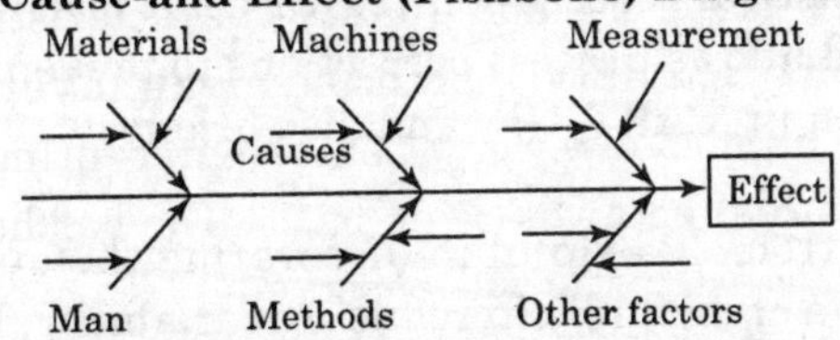

- All contributing factors and their relationships are displayed
- Identifies problem areas where data can be collected and analyzed

Process Flow Diagram

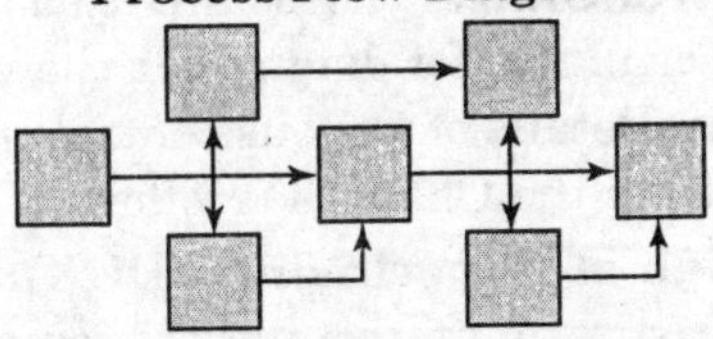

- Expresses detailed knowledge of the process
- Identifies process flow and interaction among the process steps
- Identifies potential control points

Control Chart

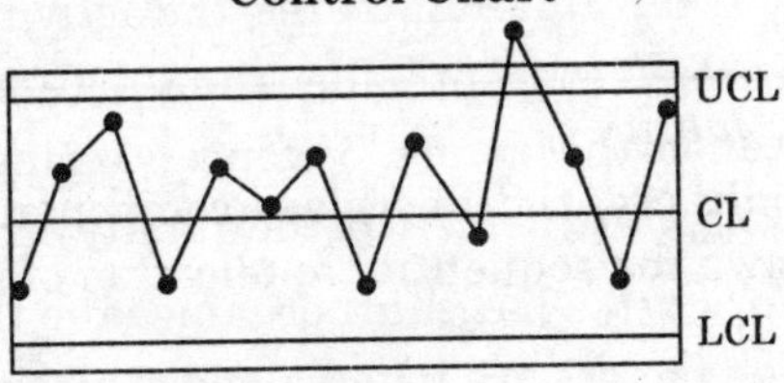

- Helps reduce variability
- Monitors performance over time
- Allows process corrections to prevent rejections
- Trends and out-of-control conditions are immediately detected.

Design of Experiments (DOX)

- Useful in process development and troubleshooting
- Identifies magnitude and direction of important process variable effects
- Greatly reduces the number of runs required with a process experiment
- Identifies interaction among process variables
- Useful in engineering design and development
- Focuses on optimizing system performance

FIGURE 18.1 Quality improvement tools.

Scatter Diagrams. Sometimes managers suspect that a certain factor is causing a particular quality problem. A *scatter diagram* is a plot of two variables showing whether they are related. Each point on the scatter diagram represents one data observation. For example, the manager of a castings shop may suspect that casting defects are a function of the diameter of the casting. A scatter diagram could be constructed by plotting the number of defective castings found for each diameter of casting produced. After the diagram was completed, any relationship between diameter and number of defects could be observed.

Cause-and-Effect (CPE) Diagrams. Popularly known as fishbone diagrams after their characteristic shape, these are normally used after the Pareto exercise as an aid to diagnosing the causes of main problem. Initially, possible causes would be brainstormed to produce a diagram. This would then be used to investigate the true cause (s). The four main 'bones' of the diagram are sometimes set in advance. These can help get the process started, but can also inhibit the development of ideas. Possible starting points include:

- 4 Ms – men, machines, materials, methods
- 4Ps – people, policies, places, procedures
- 4Ss – skills, suppliers, systems, surroundings.

Cause-and-effect (C & E) diagram is an important and valuable tool for quality improvement, additional details on this tools are provided later in this section.

Process Flow Diagrams. These are a useful way of identifying potential causes of failure. In manufacturing they can highlight vulnerable stages in the operation, as well as causes of inefficiency and delay. In services the use of flow charts which discriminate between the operation of the server and of the customer, can indicate areas where the service would appear to be functioning correctly but is not actually working well from the customer's viewpoint. flow-charting the customer can also indicate procedures that are unnecessarily complex.

Control Charts. These are used as part of statistical process control (SPC). It is a very powerful tool for diagnosing the variability and allows process corrections to prevent rejections. Details of various control charts are given in PART-1(B) and also briefly mentioned in the Chap. that follows.

Design of Experiments (DOX). These are extremely helpful in discovering the quality characteristics of interest in the process. These play a crucial role in reducing variability. Each of the tools for improving quality may be used independently, but the power of these tools is greatest when they are used in conjunction with each other. In solving a quality problem, managers often must act as detectives, sifting data to clarify the issues involved and deducing the causes. We call this process *data snooping*. Example 18.1 demonstrates how the tools can be used for data snooping.

Example 18.1: *Identifying Causes of Poor Headliner Quality.*

The Wellington Fiber Board Company produces headliners, the fiberglass components that form the inner roof of passenger cars. Figure 18.2 shows the sequential application of several tools for improving quality.

Step 1. A checklist of different types of defects was constructed from last month's production records.

Step 2. A Pareto chart prepared from the checklist data indicated that broken fiber board accounted for 72 percent of the quality defects. The manager decided to dig further into the problem of broken fiber board.

Step 3. A cause-and-effect diagram (C & E) for broken fiber board identified several potential causes for the problem. The one strongly suspected by the manager was employee training.

Step 4. The manager reorganized the production reports according to shift because the personnel on the three shifts had varied amounts of experience. A bar chart indicated that the second shift, with the least experienced work force, had most of the defects. Further investigation revealed that workers were not using proper procedures for stacking the fiber boards after the press operation, causing cracking and chipping.

Though the second shift was not responsible for all the defects, finding the source of many defects enabled the manager to improve the quality of her operations.

Step 1. Checklist

Defect type	*Tally*	*Total*
A. Tears in fabric	////	4
B. Discoloured fabric	///	3
C. Broken fiber board	~~////~~ ~~////~~ ~~////~~ ~~////~~ ~~////~~ ~~////~~ ~~////~~ /	36
D. Ragged edges	~~////~~ //	7
	Total	50

Step 2. Pareto Chart

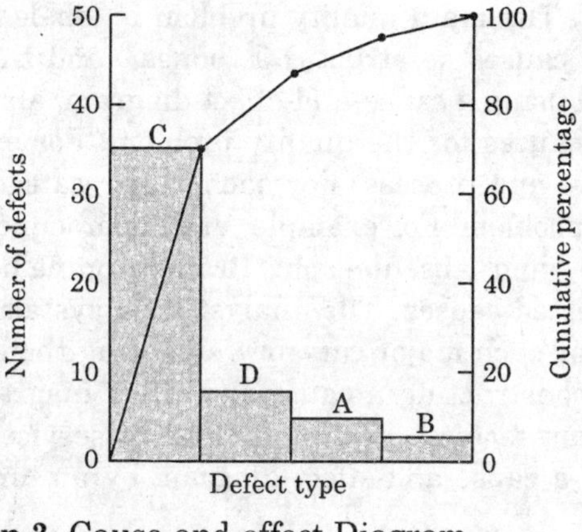

Step 3. Cause-and-effect Diagram

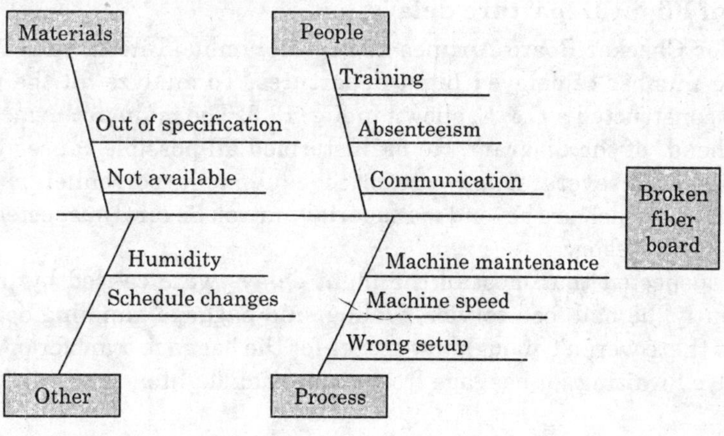

Step 4 Bar Chart

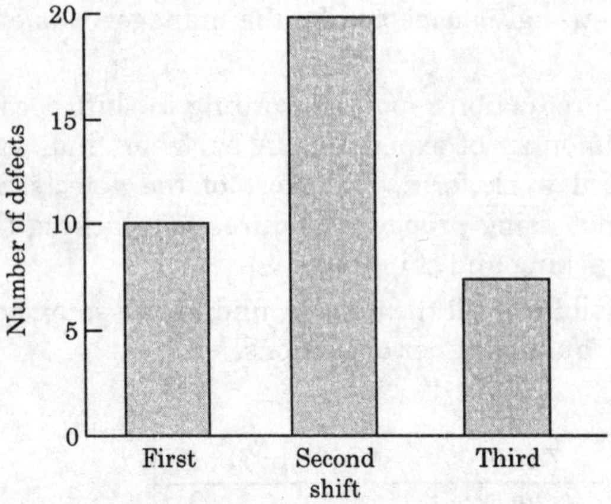

FIGURE 18.2 Application of the tools for improving quality.

18.1.1 Cause-and-Effect (C & E) Diagrams

The Cause-and-Effect (C & E) diagrams are valuable way of starting an investigation into and opening up discussion about quality questions. These are also known as *Ishikawa diagrams* after the Japanese quality guru who popularized them, or *fishbone diagrams* after their characteristic shape. They would normally be used after the Pareto exercise as an aid to diagnosing the causes of the main problems. The main quality problem is labeled as the fish's "head", the major categories of potential causes as structural "bones," and the likely specific causes as "ribs". When constructing and using a cause-and-effect diagram, an analyst identifies all the major categories of potential causes for the quality problem. For example, these might be personnel, machines, materials, and process. For each major category, the analyst lists all the likely causes of the quality problem. For example, under personnel might be listed "lack of training," "poor communication," and "absenteeism." Brainstorming helps the analyst identify and properly classify all suspected causes. The analyst then systematically investigates the causes listed on the diagram for each major category, updating the chart as new causes become apparent. The process of constructing a cause-and-effect diagram calls management and worker attention to the primary factors affecting product or service quality Example 18.2 demonstrates the application of a cause-and-effect diagram by an airline for analysis of flight departure delays.

Example 18.2 Analysis of Flight Departure delays.

The operations manager for Checker Board Airlines at Port Columbus International Airport noticed an increase in the number of delayed flight departures. To analyze all the possible causes of that problem, he constructed a C & E, shown in Fig. 18.3. The main problem, delayed flight departures, is the "head" of the diagram. He brainstormed all possible causes with his staff and together they identified several major categories: equipment, personnel, materials, procedures, and "other factors," which are beyond managerial control. Several suspected causes were identified for each major category.

The operations manager suspected that most of the flight delays were caused by problems with materials. Consequently, he had food service, fueling, and baggage handling operations examined. He learned that there weren't enough tow trucks for the baggage transfer operations and that planes were delayed waiting for baggage from connecting flights.

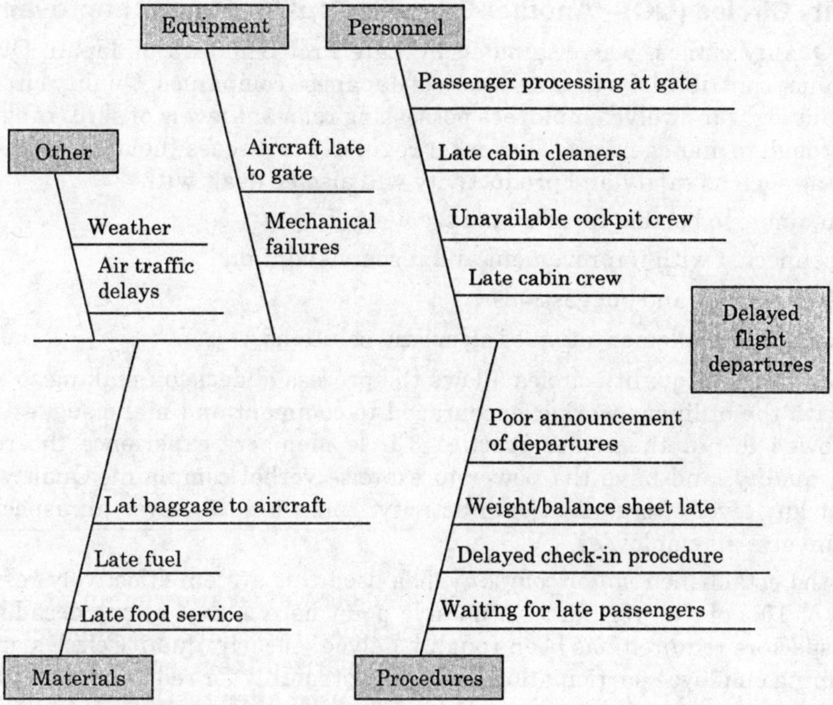

FIGURE 18.3 C & E diagram for Example 18.2

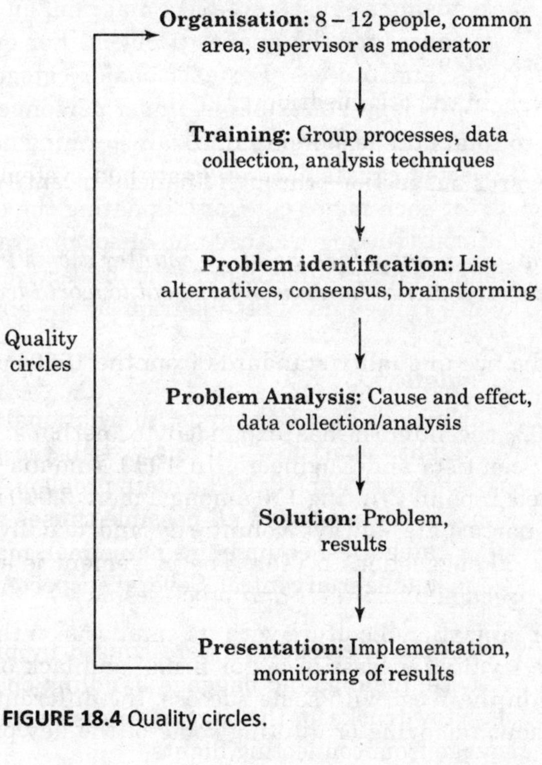

FIGURE 18.4 Quality circles.

18.1.2 Quality Circles (QC)—Another Effective Tool for Quality Improvement

The idea of Quality circles, was originated by Late Prof Ishikawa of Japan. Quality circles have made major contributions to the success of Japanese companies. Quality circle (Fig. 18.4) consist of about eight to twelve employees possessing relevant levels of skill, ranging from the shop-floor through to management. They meet regularly to discuss the major aspect of quality, but other areas such as safety and productivity will also be dealt with.

The main aim is to be able to offer management:

- ideas connected with improvement and recommendation
- possible solutions and suggestions
- organising the implementation of ideas and solutions.

The development of quality circles allows the process of decision making to start at shop floor level, with the ordinary worker encouraged to comment and make suggestions, as well as being allowed to put them into practice. Circle members experience the responsibility for ensuring quality, and have the power to exercise verbal complaint. Quality circles may be applied at any level of organizational activity, being used to cover all aspects and could conceivably involve all employees.

Jaguar, the established *motor company,* has used this system effectively resulting in the involvement of 10% of the workforce. A notable point here is that in one decade the number of quality inspectors required has been roughly halved. Clearly, quality circles are a practical means of gaining employee participation; they are not mainly for reducing costs, although this aspect will be a major topic for discussion. Other benefits are: increased awareness of shop-floor problems, members gain confidence over problem solving etc., greater output, improved quality and shop-floor participation.

Among many variants, QCs may:

- have people from one or several work groups
- have people from one or several levels in the organisation
- have a nominated leader or decide to rotate the leadership role
- be stimulated by a scheme that rewards suggestions through financial incentives.

In the 1960s Juran said:

The quality-circle movement is a tremendous one which no other country seems to be able to imitate. Through the development of this movement, Japan will be swept to world leadership in quality.

Certainly Japan did make a rapid advance in quality standards from the 1960s onwards, and quality circles were part of this advance.

From the first QC in Japan in 1962, the number has expanded to, perhaps, 100,000 registered with the Union of Japanese Scientists and Engineers. In 1990 Yamaha had 700 circles, Toyota 6,700 and the medium-sized Toppan Printing 150 among a mere 2,000 workers. More than 13 million Japanese people participate, always voluntarily and usually outside working time. Each QC generates about 50 suggestions a year. The movement is seen as a driving force behind the *continuous improvement of products and processes.*

The QC fits well into the Japanese organizational culture with its emphasis on the group, as opposed to the individual, its lifetime loyalty (at least in major firms) and lack of serious demarcation of job roles. Although tried in the West with some success, the different context makes the idea difficult to transfer without removing or diluting some of the key principles that make QCs work.

In Asia, this system has not met with desired success so far due to fierce competition among workers, fear of losing job (on sharing trade secret) etc.

Equally, putting this system into practice can prove difficult. The well-established system of hierarchical management is difficult to penetrate, and to some organizations it would present extreme changes. Some systems may not be able to accommodate such change, for example the armed forces or police force where a powerful hierarchy has developed.

18.2 BREAKTHROUGH IMPROVEMENT

Breakthrough improvement (or 'innovation'-based improvement as it is sometimes called) assumes that the main vehicle of improvement is major and dramatic change in the way the operation works. The introduction of a new, more efficient machine in a factory, or the total redesign of a computer-based hotel reservation system, are all examples of breakthrough improvement. The impact of these improvements is relatively sudden, abrupt and represents a step change in practice (and hopefully performance). Such improvements are rarely inexpensive, usually calling for high investment of capital, often disrupting the ongoing workings of the operation, and frequently involving changes in the product/service or process technology. The solid line in Fig. 18.5 illustrates the pattern of performance with several breakthrough improvements.

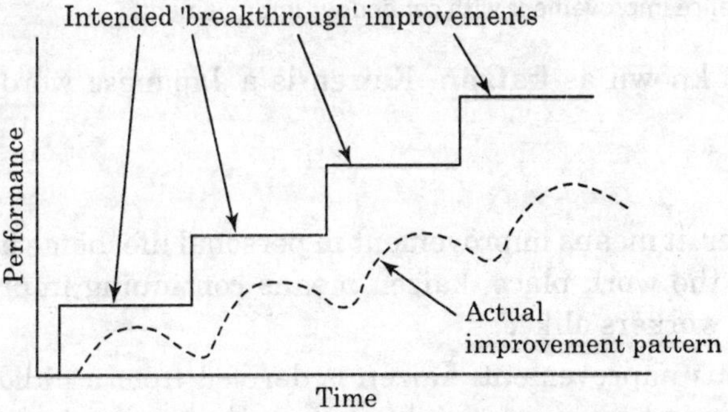

FIGURE 18.5 The intended and actual pattern of performance improvement with breakthrough improvement.

One criticism of the breakthrough approach to improvement is that such major improvements are, in practice, difficult to realize quickly and impossible to realize instantly as is implied by Fig. 18.5. The following experience reported recently is typical.

'I was once involved in the start-up of a major green-field site petrochemical plant. That is obviously a major step. The first time that the plant was 'switched on' it ran for a fraction of a second. With much hard work, energy and dedication, the engineers and the workforce succeeded, after about six months, in reaching 99 per cent capacity utilization. Once the start-up period was over, however, dedication and energy went back to normal levels and capacity utilization slipped slightly.'

The improvement pattern illustrated by the broken line in (Fig. 18.5) is regarded by some as being more representative of what really occurs when operations rely on pure breakthrough improvement.

18.3 CONTINUOUS IMPROVEMENT

Continuous improvement, as the name implies, adopts an approach to improving performance which assumes more and smaller incremental improvement steps. For example, modifying the way a product is fixed to a machine to reduce change-over time, or simplifying the operation sequence when taking a hotel reservation is an example of incremental improvements. While there is no guarantee that such small steps towards better performance will be followed by other steps, the whole philosophy of continuous improvement attempts to ensure that they will be. Continuous improvement is not concerned with promoting small improvements per se. It does see small improvements, however, as having one significant advantage over large ones - they can be followed relatively painlessly by other small improvements (Fig. 18.6).

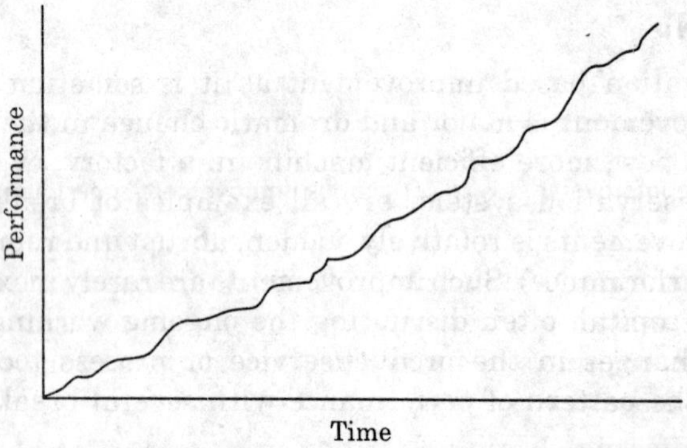

FIGURE 18.6 The pattern of performance improvement with continuous improvement.

Continuous improvement is also known as **kaizen**. Kaizen is a Japanese word, and its definition is as follows:

18.3.1 Kaizen

Kaizen means improvement. Moreover, it means improvement in personal life, home life, social life and work life. When applied to the work place, kaizen means continuing improvement involving everyone — managers and workers alike.'

The Japanese word for continuous improvement: kaizen is derived from a philosophy of gradual day-by-day betterment of life and spiritual enlightenment. Kaizen has been adopted by Japanese business to denote gradual unending improvement for the organization. The philosophy is the doing of little things better to achieve a long-term objective. Kaizen is 'the single most important concept in Japanese management - the key to Japanese competitive success'.

Kaizen moves the organization's focus away from the bottom line, and the fitful starts and stops that come from major changes, towards continuous improvement of service. Japanese firms have for many years taken quality for granted. Kaizen is now so deeply ingrained that people do not even realize that they are thinking it. The philosophy is that not one day should go by without some kind of improvement being made somewhere in the company. The far-reaching nature of Kaizen can now be seen in Japanese government and social programmes.

All this means trust. The managers have to stop being bosses and trust the staff; the staff must believe in the managers. This may require a major paradigm change for some people. The end goal is to gain a competitive edge by reducing costs and improving the quality of the service. In order to determine the level of quality to aim for, it is first necessary to find out what the customer wants and to be very mindful of what the competition is doing.

The daily aim should be accepted as being kaizen - that is, some improvement somewhere in the business.

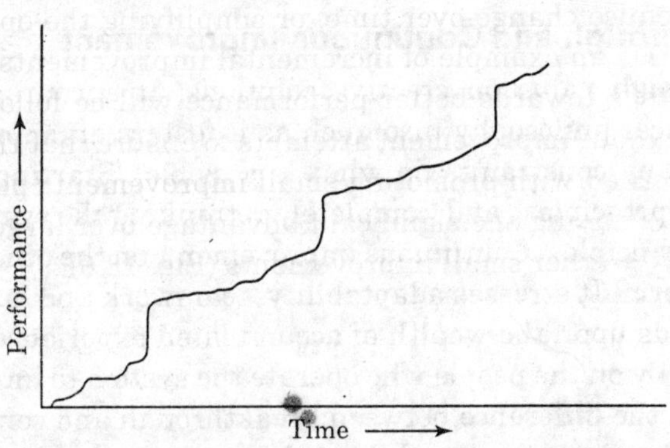

FIGURE 18.7 The pattern of performance improvement with continuous improvement superimposed on to breakthrough improvement.

In continuous improvement it is not the rate of improvement which is important, it is the *momentum* of improvement. It does not matter if successive improvements are small; what does matter is that every month (or week, or quarter, or whatever period is appropriate) some kind of improvement has actually taken place.

Notwithstanding the fundamental differences between the two approaches, it is possible to combine the two, albeit at different times. Large and dramatic improvements can be implemented as and when they seem to promise significant improvement steps, but between such occasions the operation can continue making its quiet and less spectacular kaizen improvements (Fig. 18.7).

TABLE 18.1 SOME FEATURES OF BREAKTHROUGH AND CONTINUOUS IMPROVEMENT

Attribute	*Breakthrough improvement*	*Continuous improvement*
Effect	Short-term but dramatic	Long-term and long-lasting but undramatic
Pace	Big steps	Small steps
Time frame	Intermittent and non-incremental	Continuous and incremental
Change	Abrupt and volatile	Gradual and constant
Involvement	Select a few 'champions'	Everybody
Approach	Individualism, individual ideas and efforts	Collectivism, group efforts, systems approach
Stimulus	Technological breakthroughs, new inventions, new theories	Conventional knowhow and state of the art
Risks	Concentrated - 'all eggs in one basket.	Spread-many projects simultaneously
Practical requirements	Requires large investment but little effort to maintain it	Requires little investment but great effort to maintain it
Effort orientation	Technology	People
Evaluation criteria	Results for profit	Process and efforts for better results

18.3.1. Differences between breakthrough and Continuous Improvement

Breakthrough improvement places a high value on creative solutions. It encourages free thinking and individualism. It is a radical philosophy insomuch as it fosters an approach to improvement which does not accept many constraints on what is possible. 'Starting with a clean sheet of paper', 'going back to first principles', and 'completely rethinking the system' are all typical breakthrough improvement principles. Continuous improvement, on the other hand, is less ambitious, at least in the short term. It stresses adaptability, teamwork and attention to detail. It is not radical; rather it builds upon the wealth of accumulated experience within the operation itself, often relying primarily on the people who operate the system to improve it. One analogy which helps to understand the difference between breakthrough and continuous improvement is that of the sprint and the marathon. Breakthrough improvement is a series of explosive and impressive sprints. Continuous improvement, like marathon running, does not require the expertise and prowess required for sprinting; but it does require that the runner (or operations manager) keeps on going.

Table 18.1 clearly distinguishes between the breakthrough and continuous improvement.

18.3.2 The PDCA Cycle

As mentioned in Chap. 17, Deming may have made more progress with a more subtle attack on the backward ways of western management, yet, in spite of a rather curmudgeonly approach, Deming was eventually listened to because of his experience of Japan and the simple rigour of his problem-solving approach. He pressed for the adoption of informed decision making based on good-quality data. He advocated the Plan-Do-Check Act (PDCA) cycle (Fig. 18.8). He called this the *Shewhart cycle* in honour of his teacher and the founder of statistical quality control but the Japanese, and others, call it the *Deming cycle*, while many other call it *Deming Cycle* or *Wheel*.

The PDCA cycle is the sequence of activities which are undertaken on a cyclic basis to improve activities.

In using the PDCA cycle, managers are encouraged to start with small changes about things that are really important. The approach is set in the tradition of research and trial and-error experimentation. Actions and reflections are grounded in observed data. In this belief in experimentation, Deming is close to Taguchi. The cycle starts with the P (for plan) stage and its total four steps are stated below:

- **Plan.** This involves an examination of the current method or the problem area being studied. Immediate step is to collect and analyse data so as to formulate a plan of action which is intended to improve performance. Once a plan of improvement has been agreed the next step is D (for do stage).
- **Do.** This is the implementation stage during which the plan is tried out in the operation. This stage may itself involve a mini-PDCA cycle as the problems of implementation are resolved. Next comes the C (for check) stage.
- **Check.** In this step the new implemented solution is evaluated to see whether it has resulted in the expected performance improvement. Finally, at least for this cycle comes the A (for act stage).
- **Act.** During this stage the change is consolidated or standardized if it has been successful. Alternatively, if the change has not been successful, the lessons learned from the "trial" are formalized before the cycle starts again.

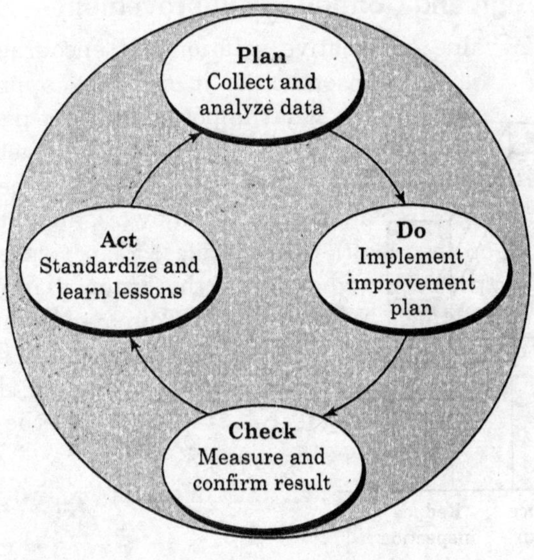

FIGURE 18.8 Deming's PDCA cycle/wheel

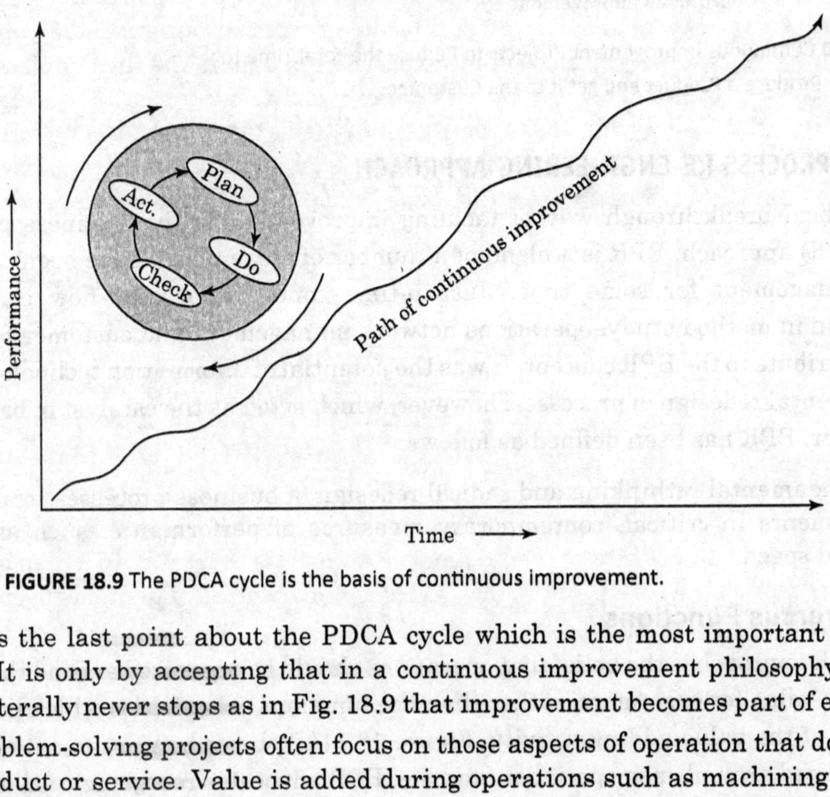

FIGURE 18.9 The PDCA cycle is the basis of continuous improvement.

It is the last point about the PDCA cycle which is the most important - the cycle starts again. It is only by accepting that in a continuous improvement philosophy the PDCA cycle quite literally never stops as in Fig. 18.9 that improvement becomes part of every person's job.

Problem-solving projects often focus on those aspects of operation that do not add value to the product or service. Value is added during operations such as machining a part or serving a customer. The idea of continuous improvement is that activities that do not add value are wasteful and should be reduced or eliminated. Figure 18.10 illustrates schematically how reducing time on non-value added activities such as materials handling, repairs, and inspection reduces the time needed to deliver a product to a customer after an order received by Timken Company.

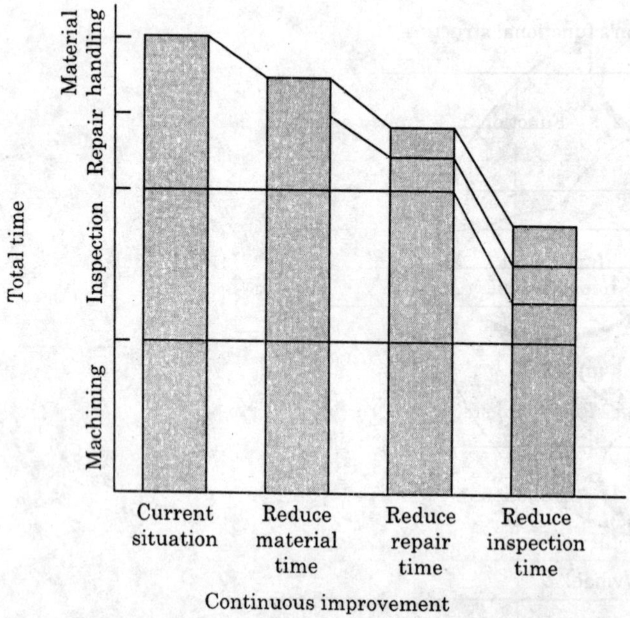

FIGURE 18.10 Continuous Improvement Projects to Reduce the Total Time to Produce a Product and get it to the Customer

18.4 BUSINESS PROCESS RE-ENGINEERING APPROACH

Typical of the radical breakthrough way of tackling improvement is the 'business process reengineering' (BPR) approach. BPR is a blend of a number of ideas which have been current in operations management for some time. Just-in-time concepts, process flow charting, critical examination in method study, operations network management and customer-focused operations, all contribute to the BPR concept. It was the potential of information technologies to enable the fundamental redesign of processes, however, which acted as the catalyst in bringing these ideas together. BPR has been defined as follows:

BPR is the fundamental rethinking and radical redesign of business processes to achieve dramatic improvements in critical, contemporary measures of performance, such as cost, quality, service and speed.

18.4.1 Process versus Functions

Underlying the BPR approach is the belief that operations should be organized around the total process which adds value for customers, rather than the functions or activities which perform the various stages of the value-adding activity. Figure 18.11(*a*) shows how organizations are traditionally organized around each specialist function. BPR advocates reorganization around the processes themselves, as in Fig. 18.11(*b*).

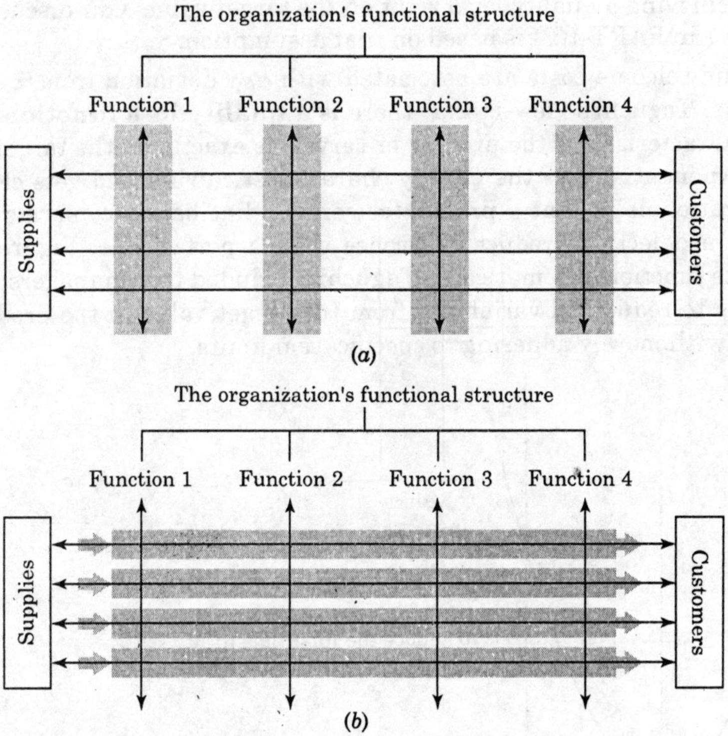

FIGURE 18.11 (*a*) An organization organized by function, (*b*) an organization organized by process.

18.4.2 Principles of BPR

Even if BPR is not an entirely original idea, it can be seen as a useful collection of principles which embody the breakthrough approach. The main principles of BPR have been summarized as follows.

- Rethink business processes in a cross-functional manner which organizes work around the natural flow of information (or materials or customers). This means organizing around outcomes of a process rather than the tasks which go into it.
- Strive for dramatic improvements in the performance by radically rethinking and redesigning the process.
- Have those who use the output from a process perform the process. Check to see if all internal customers can be their own supplier rather than depending on another function in the business to supply them (which takes longer and separates out the stages in the process).
- Put decision points where the work is performed. Do not separate those who do the work from those who control and manage the work. Control and action are just one more type of supplier-customer relationship which can be merged.

18.5 TAGUCHI'S QUALITY ENGINEERING

As stated in Chap. 17, Taguchi's quality engineering is an approach that involves combined engineering and statistical methods to reduce costs and improve quality by optimizing product design and manufacturing processes. Before Taguchi, managers often assumed that the goal in achieving quality was to produce products or services that fell anywhere within the design tolerances. Managers thought that the cost of achieving a quality level close to the tolerance limits equaled the cost of achieving a quality level right on the target value. Our discussion of process capability in Chap. 7 in PART-1(B) is based on that assumption.

Taguchi believes that unwelcome costs are associated with *any* deviation from a quality characteristic's target value. Taguchi's view is that there is a **quality loss function** (QLF) is zero when the quality characteristic of the product or service is exactly on the target value and that the value rises exponentially as the quality characteristic drifts and gets closer to the tolerance limits. The rationale is that a product or service that barely conforms to the specifications is more like a defective product or service than a perfect one. Figure 18.12 shows Taguchi's quality loss function schematically. Taguchi concluded that managers should continually search for ways to reduce all variability from the target value in the production process and not be content with merely adhering to specification limits.

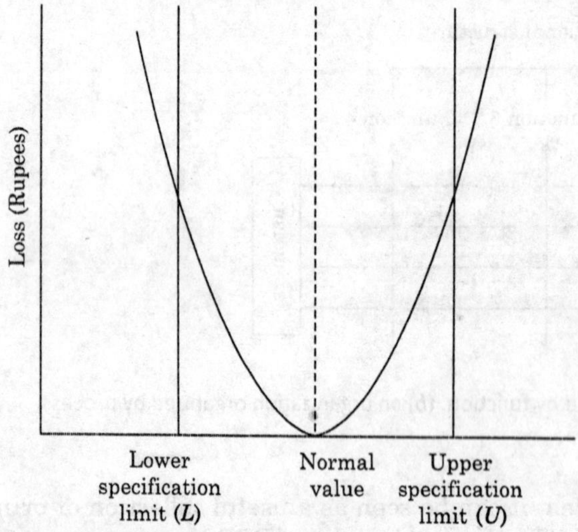

FIGURE 18.12 Taguchi's Quality Loss Function.

Using quality engineering techniques, engineers, managers, and production workers hypothesize critical factors affecting the quality of a selected product or service in team interaction sessions. They design and conduct an experiment to gather data and use statistical techniques to determine which factor(s) contribute most to quality problems. They then determine what would optimize performance and proceed to make the needed changes.

A follow-up experiment is conducted to verify the results. Users believe that quality engineering aids communication among functional groups because it requires them to solve a problem cooperatively. It also permits efficient fine tuning of processes, requiring fewer adjustments with more predictable effects from each adjustment. That can be helpful in achieving and maintaining process capability.

18.5.1 Quality Loss Function (QLF)

As stated earlier in Chap. 17, Taguchi's QLF defines the monetary loss to the society as a quadratic expression based upon the variation from the target value. Taguchi's QLF is illustrated below for designing and manufacturing tolerances.

Manufacturing tolerances can be designed based upon the quality loss function to optimise the loss to the society. The relationship between the characteristic y to the loss $L(y)$ can be used to establish the point at which the loss to society (the combined producer's loss and consumer's loss) is minimized.

Taguchi's QLF can be used for determining the manufacturing tolerances as illustrated below:

Consider, for example, the setting of the tracking angle for the front wheels of a car which has a target value of – 1.5 degrees. If the cost of resetting the tracking angle at the end of the production line is ₹ 400, what should the manufacturing tolerance be? From a quality loss function perspective the design of the tolerances requires an evaluation of the tracking angle at which the manufacturer justifiably spends ₹ 400, correcting the vehicle. Assuming the cost of rectifying a tracking problem (which occurs at an angle of + 1°) for a customer who returns the new vehicle to the dealer under warranty is ₹ 15,000 (including the cost of worn tyres!) then the manufacturing tolerance can be calculated as shown in Fig. 18.13. From Fig. 18.13.

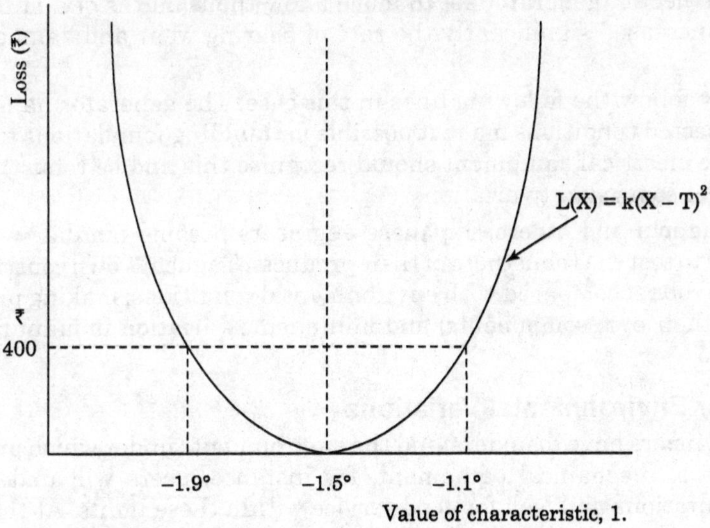

FIGURE 18.13 Tolerance design using the quality of loss function.

$$L(X) = k\,(X - T)^2$$

for $\quad X = 1°,\ L = ₹\,15000,\ T = -\,1.5°$

hence $$k = \frac{15{,}000}{[1-(-1.5)^2]} = \frac{15{,}000}{(2.5)^2} = ₹\ 2400$$

The manufacturing tolerance can therefore be found by calculating, the value of tracking angle (X) which correspondence to a loss of ₹ 400. Hence:

$$L\,(X) = 400 = k(X - T)^2$$

$$\therefore \quad (X - T)^2 = \frac{400}{2400}$$

$$\therefore \quad (X - T) = \pm\sqrt{\frac{400}{2400}} = \pm\,(0.4)$$

$$\therefore \quad X = -\,1.5 \pm (0.4)$$

The manufacturing tolerance is therefore plus or minus 0.4 degrees. If the vehicle is manufactured with the tracking outside these limits then the manufacturer should reset the tracking angle otherwise the loss to society is not optimized.

This approach to tolerance design attempts to integrate both the manufacturer's and the customer's quality cost requirements.

18.6 ROBUST QUALITY

Taguchi used the QLF in developing the idea of *robust quality*. Robustness refers to *quality in use*, that is the performance of a product when it has been used, misused, overloaded (a little), knocked about in service, not overhauled on schedule and so on. Customers assess products as much by how they perform outside the specification as how they conform to it in the first place. Naturally, designers attempt to overcome the effects of degradation by building in extra strength at key points. However, as Taguchi emphasises, many problems come not from weaknesses in individual items but from the interactions between slight variations in one item with others with which it forms systems.

In one case, a very slight design deficiencies in the foundations of a power station hall allowed the alignment of an electric generator set to move a few thousandths of a millimeter out of true. The vibrations increased significantly the rate of bearing wear and damaged the generator windings.

Taguchi's argument may follow the following lines in this case. The generator hall should be built properly. Yet, unexpected conditions make it possible for building foundations to move. Therefore, good design of the electrical equipment should recognise this and be robust, that is operate successfully inspite of some slight variations.

Through the work of Taguchi and others, Japanese engineers became familiar with the design of experiments (DOX) to test the robustness of their products. Taguchi's own contribution focused on: making products robust compared with environmental conditions; making products insensitive to variations in their own components; and minimising variation in manufacture. We shall look at each in turn.

18.6.1 Robustness Under Environmental Variations

To design for robustness, engineers have to understand the environments under which products are to be used. In the case of mechanical equipment, for instance, users will understand something of a product's limitations and look for good service within these limits. At the same time, they want to cope beyond this and will often look for the extra reliability, or at least ease of repair. The Land Rover car for example, built its reputation on both counts. Taguchi's contribution to the study of robustness was to propose a formal method for its investigation. An interesting Example 18.3 set in the field of home economics is given below.

Example 4.3 Robust muffins

Let us say we are considering the launch of a new muffin mix. We can, in the laboratory, develop mixes and test them under ideal conditions. Yet, the success of such a product depends largely on its quality in use, that is whether it will produce good outcomes in domestic environments. In the home, for example, oven temperatures are unreliable and, as anyone who cooks will know, baking time is approximate.

It may be that the mix that gives the best muffin under experimental conditions is not the best for sale. Alterations in the formulation may result in a product that is slightly less good. Yet; the design may be more robust in that it produces an acceptable output over a wider range of baking temperatures and times.

A Taguchi experiment would then vary the design factors - the amounts of plain flour, baking powder, salt, egg and milk powders and sugar – and assess the sensitivity of the outcome to the environmental factors already mentioned. The difficulty is that it is possible to conduct an endless number of trials. Taguchi proposed a means of designing the experiment in terms of which variables to change and by how much. These are set out in special arrays intended to allow the trials to home in on good results quickly. The search is not for the best muffin mix but for one that gives good results across a wide range of conditions.

18.7 MAKING PRODUCTS INSENSITIVE TO VARIATIONS IN THEIR OWN COMPONENTS

Since many products have an assembly of components, it is clear that the performance of the product will vary if the component performances vary. Given the inevitability of some component variation, engineers seek ways of minimising these effects on the assembly. To illustrate the point, let us look at the choice of length of a clock pendulum.

The relationship between the period T and the length l of a pendulum is nonlinear as in Fig. 18.14. When a clock manufacturer makes pendulums with small length variations, these will become variations in period. As Fig. 18.14 shows, however, the period variations depend on the length of the pendulum and are smaller when the pendulum is longer.

The effect can be seen from the formula for period and its differential:

$$T = 2\pi\sqrt{\frac{l}{g}}; \quad \text{and} \quad \sqrt{\frac{dT}{dl}} = \frac{\pi}{\sqrt{l \times g}}$$

Therefore, if the length variation depends only on the cutting machine and not on the total length of the pendulum, the designer should make the pendulum as long as possible.

This simple example demonstration is invalid if the manufacturing variation increases with the pendulum length. The basic notion is important, however. We can design products, such as electronic circuits, whose performance is insensitive to their components. This is especially important when those components can be neither made nor adjusted precisely.

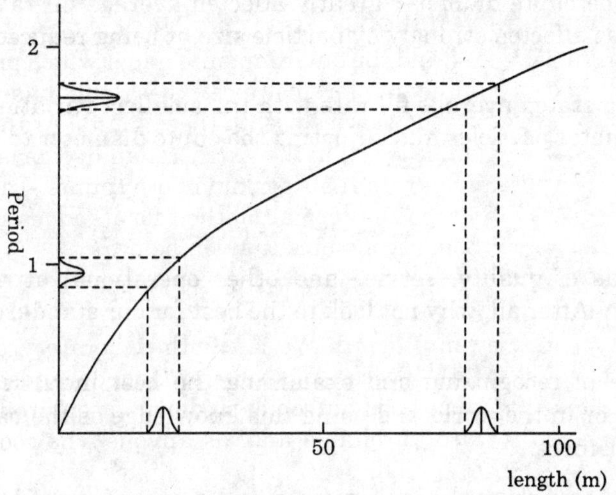

FIGURE 18.14 Pendulum Errors.

18.7.2 Minimising Variations in Manufacture

Variability is the enemy of mass production. Reducing it will reduce waste and scrap. As with the preceding examples, Taguchi argued that well-designed experiments would find ways of reducing variability caused by combinations of process factors. The approach can be illustrated by reference to a machine for filling detergent cartons (Table 18.2)

TABLE 18.2 FLOW OF DETERGENT IN EXPERIMENT

Chute A		*Particle size*	
		Low	High
Diameter	Small	1.2 (0.011)	1.4 (0.031)
	Large	3.5 (0.008)	3.3 (0.045)
Chute B		*Particle size*	
		Low	High
Diameter	Small	1.0 (0.015)	1.3 (0.027)
	Large	2.8 (0.009)	3.2 (0.030)

It is commercially important for the weight of detergent entering each carton and hence the fill rate, to be carefully controlled. Three factors affect the fill rate (kilograms per second) of the cartons: the chute diameter, the particle size of the detergent and the shape of the chute. Table 4.2 shows the experimental results using two values for particle size and chute diameter and with two chute shapes. The figures give average flow rates and standard deviations, both in kg/sec. It can be seen that only the chute diameter greatly affected average fill rate. The variation in the fill rate, however, was affected strongly by particle size, it being reduced if the particles were smaller.

If, then, the aim was to achieve a stated average fill rate with the smallest variation, this could be done by choosing small diameter particles and adjusting the chute diameter to hit the target rate.

18.8 BENCHMARKING

As a source of ideas and standards of quality, service and other operational attributes, benchmarking has obvious attraction. After all, why not look to the best for our standards? We can define the term as follows:

Benchmarking is the practice of recognizing and examining the best industrial and commercial practices in an industry or in the world and using this knowledge as the basis for improvement in all aspects of the business.

More than imitation, this is a thorough analysis of success and a spreading of learning throughout the organization. Most of the world's largest companies practise benchmarking, albeit using a diffuse range of approaches and seeking benefit in disparate aspects of business.

The method follows the ideas of Feigenbaum who explained it as a continuous process of comparing business practices. The aim is to identify improvements and put them into effect. This implies uncovering critical performance measures to be used in the comparison with examples of what is now called 'best practice'. A systematic approach, based on exchange, benefits all participants. Therefore, studies are best based on direct comparisons rather than stopping at analysis of anonymous in-firm or industry averages. Care is needed to avoid overreliance on the comparison and an uncritical aping of good (and bad) practices.

There are seven overlapping types of benchmarking. Set out in Table 18.3, the list includes three categories based on *level* in the organization; the last four represent what we may call benchmarking *direction*. The table shows how each may be used in the improvement of quality. Some authors suggest that firms should start with relatively easy internal comparisons (for example of parallel production units on different sites) through to more complex strategic appraisals. Yet others show there is little evidence for this in practice.

18.8.1 The Benchmarking Process

The many variants of the proposed process have themes related to the Deming- PDCA cycle. Figure 4.15 shows one such variant shows. The team starts by building a good working knowledge of the processes carried out in the process chosen for the study (1). They then develop an understanding of the key success factors within the industry, and, from these, select a number of factors for benchmarking (2). This can be a difficult process as data, and the means of measuring them, may not be available. The third stage is data collection (3). How to do this depends on the benchmarking direction. Internal data should be readily available while those on competitors may come from industry reports and similar analyses. Data analysis, at the next step, begins to reveal the differences sought (4). Yet, these need checking to avoid reliance on errors. At the next stage (5), the action plan begins to emerge together with its implementation. Finally, the team reviews progress and appraises the success of their improvements (6). This last stage suggests modifications to the benchmarking criteria as well as to other elements of the loop. In this way, it echoes the PDCA cycle.

TABLE 18.3 BENCHMARKING TYPES

	Type of benchmarking	*Basis of comparison for quality*
Benchmarking level	Process	Tools and processes to improve quality; comparison of product design and supply; good for detailed learning
	Performance	Performance measures to compare the organization with others and with customers' expectations; counters backward creep
	Strategic	Quality strategy; infrastructure; management processes
Benchmarking direction	Generic	Organizations using similar processes or technologies, not necessarily in the same industry; sharing not difficult
	Functional	Organizations in same sector or industry at the detailed process or technology level; may be available through professional net-work
	Internal	Activities, functions or divisions of the same organization; results may be unconvincing
	Competitor	Recognized 'best in class' competitors to establish standards; very convincing but may be inaccessible

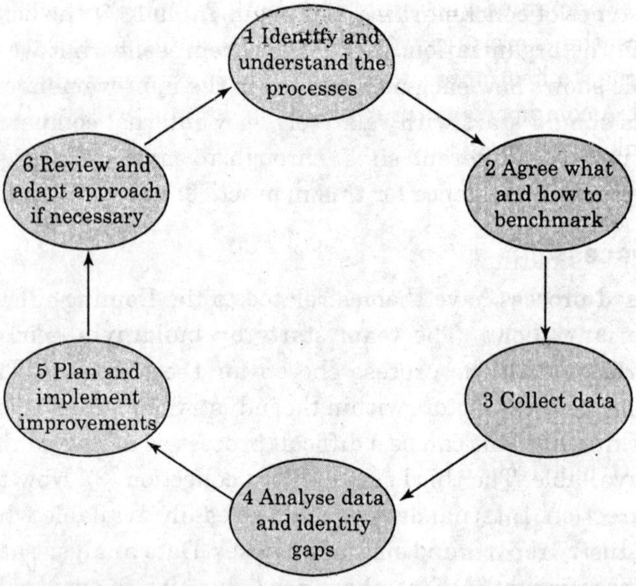

FIGURE 18.15 Benchmarking cycle

Outlined in this way, the process sounds straightforward. It can, however, run into problems with other companies, particularly fierce rivals. Yet much information is published already, products contain a wealth of data and can be readily bought or observed, and responses to different companies can be discussed with customers. Some advice for use when approaching other companies is:

- *Don't go fishing.* This means that study should have a clear purpose and its scope should be limited to support areas that need improvement.
- *Send out the people who will have to make the changes.* This means letting people see for themselves. Raising awareness in this way is a great step along the path of change.
- *Exchange information.* The target company may well be involved in its own benchmarking exercise. Information exchange is a possibility and a firm should not be asking any question that it is not prepared to answer itself. Commonly, a study is welcomed by the target organization.
- *Steer away from legal problems.* Sharing information on price, market share and related issues may suggest price and market fixing, which are illegal. Some companies forbid their managers even talking to people from rivals for this reason. The need to protect sensitive information about new products is also a factor.
- *Keep obtained information secure.* An organization that shares information with a benchmarking partner may be alarmed if this is passed on to a competitor.

18.8.2 Benchmarking in Action

Outside the industry, imaginative comparisons can be made between common or related functions. For instance: TCL has measured its training methods against those of the Royal Mail; a US regional airline compared its aircraft turnarounds with motor racing pit stops; other companies have looked worldwide to set best practice standards for research and development.

Benchmarking can be both eye opening and a stimulus to action. When studying engine repair processes, British Airways found that technicians on Japanese Airlines took 40 minutes to turn round a 747 while BA's people took three hours. The process also has its limits, however.

It works well for high-performance companies whose internal appraisal compares well with the best. Yet, for moderate performers, the exercise may only generate confusion and low morale. It is rather like someone swimming, to keep himself fit and also sometimes to his lengths to see whether he is improving at all. A comparison with the Olympic champion is pointless. Low-performing companies should think in the same way. There are plenty of basic actions they can take, from team building to improving links with customers, before they start to worry about becoming world class.

Benchmarking is used best for evaluating existing products, processes and infrastructure among firms that are aiming for excellence. As mentioned, it does not help in the innovation area where firms jealously guard their proposals from competitors' eyes. Anyhow, innovation is neither about imitation nor about catching up. To develop standards for the future, one must go to the customers.

18.9 QUALITY FUNCTION DEPLOYMENT (QFD)

Good companies incorporate customers' needs and expectations into their product planning processes. Market research takes the lead in finding out about these expectations. The design process converts them into specific products with specified performance. These should both satisfy the expectations and be capable of being supplied at reasonable cost. A major difficulty with this rational procedure is that customers' needs are expressed in different terms to those used by the suppliers.

Take, for example, the design of a popular camera. Customers may not know very much about camera design, especially as the average replacement rate spans several generations of technology. For the most part, they are likely to express their needs in terms such as convenient, flexible and simple to use. Of course, there are those with more knowledge who will talk in terms of centre field auto-focus, zoom ratio and red-eye reduction. We are talking, however, about a popular camera here and the firm is trying to reach the mass market. How does the company convert the customers' wishes into a viable product?

Quality function deployment is a methodology enabling firms to evaluate their current products and assess new proposals and the processes needed to supply them. It is both a philosophy, in that it implies a set of beliefs about the way products should be designed and supplied, and a communication tool, for it is used to underpin the links among marketers, designers and operations people. The goals are improved interpretation of what elements create customer satisfaction and dissatisfaction, quicker and more successful design, and more effective teamwork among all parties. QFD is defined as:

QFD is a system for translating consumer requirements into appropriate company requirements at every stage, from research, through product design and development, to manufacture, distribution, installation and marketing, sales and service.

18.9.1 Origin of QFD

The procedure was introduced at Mitsubishi Heavy Industries in 1972. By 1976, Toyota had taken it up, further developing the method and using it with its suppliers. This company had had, in the 1970s, a bad reputation for 'body durability' (that is to say, rust). It made rapid strides, both on that characteristic and in shortening and improving the design process. Through QFD, the start-up costs (those attributed to implementing the design in the production process by adjusting virtually every element) were reduced drastically. By the mid-1980s, the effect was such that 90% of design changes at Toyota were complete *before the manufacturing start-up*. The typical western company was still revamping its designs months after launch. Many U.S. companies including Digital Equipment, Texas Instruments, Hewlett-Packard, AT&T, ITT, Ford, General Motors, Polaroid, and Deere & Company have employed QFD approach to their benefit.

18.9.2 The Matrices

QFD has been applied using seven steps whose results are laid out in a set of special matrices and tables linked as in Figure 18.16. The form of the figure gives the technique its name - **House of Quality**. The steps are as follows:

1. *Identify customer attributes,* CAs. At this stage, it is important to record these attributes in the customers' words. Using the *voice of the customer* avoids having their needs interpreted (that is, misinterpreted) by designers and engineers. Note that the customers need not be for consumer goods. The approach works equally well for services or for intermediate products sold to other organizations. Customers' requirements will, in some industries, be backed up by those of regulators. For instance, many standards covering motor car design are set by the government.
2. *Identify engineering characteristics, ECs.* Now the process uses the language of the engineer. Product features specify components, layouts, sequences, performance and so on. The features should be measurable so that they can be evaluated in comparison. The units of measurement are recorded in the diagram.

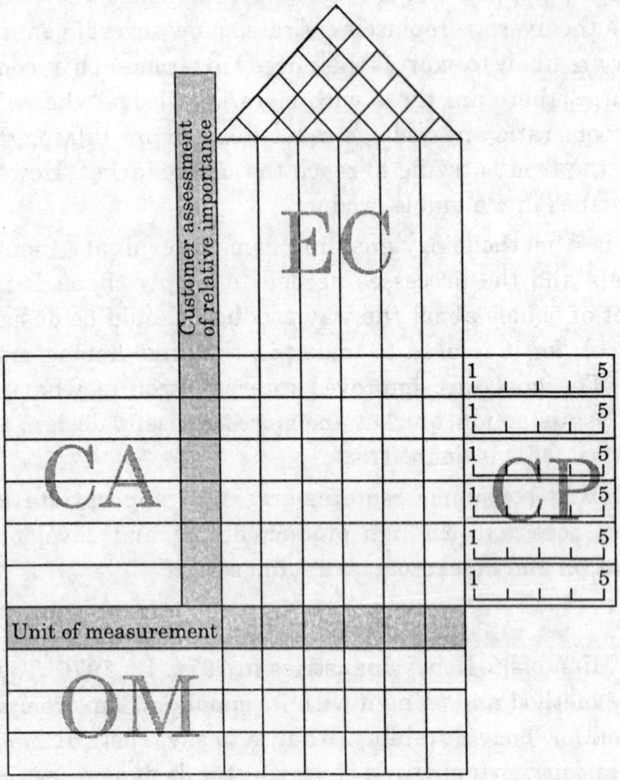

FIGURE 18.16 The House of Quality

3. *Compare CAs and ECs.* This step uses the central matrix with the CAs listed to the left and the ECs across the top. Any cell with a relationship has an entry with a symbol indicating its strength. An EC can affect several CAs. For example, incorporating a high-quality, wide-range exposure meter in a camera addresses the CAs of ease of use and flexibility. It may be, however, that an engineering characteristic does not bear on any CA. In that case, the question is whether the EC contributes to product value or is unnecessary.
4. *Establish links between pairs of ECs.* Another matrix, forming the 'roof' of the house, summarises interrelationships between the EC pairs. Again, symbols represent strong or weak links. Recording them in a matrix enables the team to understand how changes in one element affect others. For instance, thickening the material in a vehicle frame will increase strength and safety but will add weight and therefore reduce acceleration.
5. *Evaluate competitors' products, CPs.* The method here is to rank or score rival products against the CAs. An extension is to establish weightings for the CAs to facilitate trade-offs among them. This evaluation process is done readily for existing products through standard market research procedures. The weightings or rankings appear as the 'chimney' of the house.
6. *Assess the ECs of the rival products as the basis for development targets.* Testing, inspecting and dismantling the rival products, if they are goods, form this step. Field observations assess competitors' services. Results appear as a set of objective measures (OMs) to form the house foundations. From a comparison of rival OMs of ECs, development priorities will be set out.
7. *Select ECs for development into detailed design, process design and operations.* This step not only confirms the main design specification but underscores the detailed attributes that need to be incorporated into the product to satisfy the CAs. The House of Quality, therefore, feeds the voice of the customer right through into the manufacturing or supply processes.

Example 18.4 A Practical Illustration of QFD

To show how this works out in practice, let us return to the example of camera design. We will consider the sector for compact automatic cameras without zoom lens. This is a crowded sector with about a dozen leading suppliers and much 'feature' competition. Figure 18.17 shows how information would be set out. The CAs include notions such as 'easy to use', which ranks first, to 'easy to carry', which ranks fifth in the abbreviated list shown here. ECs list the main devices to be included in the EC specification. The roof matrix shows that the firm knows how to, say, design an automatic focus and exposure system with integrated flash and low power consumption. Yet, the flash itself consumes more battery power, particularly if it incorporates the red-eye reduction system. Further, electric film winding consumes power and adds weight. Hence, we have some negative symbols in the roof. The central matrix relates the ECs to the CAs. ECs of auto-focus and exposure strongly support 'easy to use', as does, to a lesser extent, electric film winding.

Units for the ECs are shown below the central matrix. They are metres, grams, milliwatts and f-numbers. OMs for the firm's current product and two leading rivals appear in the foundations. The three are compared with CAs in the CP area on the right. The array presents designers with a view of the problem they face and suggests where they may concentrate their efforts. At present, the firm's camera compares poorly with rivals on CAs, especially the most important, ease of use. Improvements to the controls for the focusing, exposure and, possibly, flash units seem to be a development priority.

Naturally, studies would have to be conducted in much more detail and a practical House of Quality would contain many more rows and columns than the cutdown version shown here.

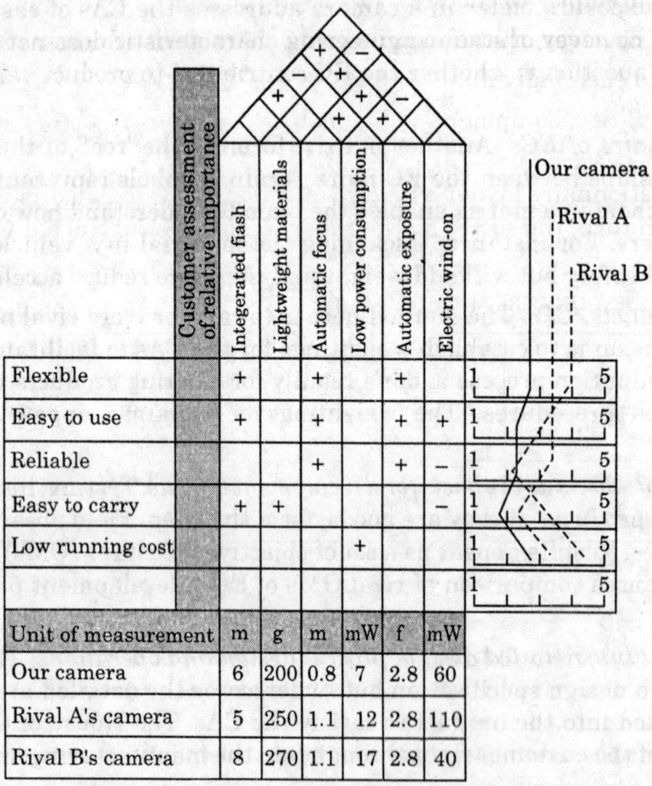

	Customer assessment of relative importance	Integerated flash	Lightweight materials	Automatic focus	Low power consumption	Automatic exposure	Electric wind-on
Flexible		+		+		+	
Easy to use		+		+		+	+
Reliable				+		+	−
Easy to carry		+	+				−
Low running cost					+		
Unit of measurement		m	g	m	mW	f	mW
Our camera		6	200	0.8	7	2.8	60
Rival A's camera		5	250	1.1	12	2.8	110
Rival B's camera		8	270	1.1	17	2.8	40

FIGURE 18.17 House of Quality: Camera Development.

18.9.3. A Flexible Procedure

It may be pointed out that the house is not a rigid procedure. It helps teams to set targets and summarise data in usable form. Like any good methodology, it acts as a guide, framework and agenda setter. The decisions still have to be made by the participants. The procedure is not rigid in another sense. Although one form of the process has been set out here, development teams would customise the House of Quality to suit their own needs. Details of how to select and evaluate rivals' products, for example, depend on the industrial setting. It is also clear that the process will differ if the firm intends to develop a new product, in which case the comparison procedure would be more open ended. Yet again, in the supply of services the terminology would change. The essence of the House of Quality, however, remains the same. It sustains the effort to convert the voice of the customer into real product characteristics.

18.10 THE SERVQUAL MODEL

Sometimes to accelerate the implementation of quality improvement it is proposed to measure the gap between what customers expected and their perceptions of the service experience. The size of this gap would indicate areas of improvement. The SERVQUAL questionnaire containing 22 pairs of questions derived from a larger survey. They are grouped in to five categories, called the dimensions of service quality, as follow:

- *reliability:* dependable and accurate performance as promised
- *responsiveness:* responding promptly to customer's needs
- *assurance:* competence and courtesy of staff, coupled with their ability to show trust
- *empathy:* caring attention to each individual
- *tangibles:* appearance of facilities, equipment, personnel; environmental factors such as noise and temperature.

Table 18.4 illustrates the questionnaire layout with two questions on tangible dimensions of a library service. Taking each in turn, the scores on the Likert scales are subtracted to yield the satisfaction measure.

TABLE 18.4 PART OF SERVQUAL QUESTIONNAIRE APPLIED TO A LIBRARY

		My expectation of the library service is		*My perception of the library services is*	
	When it comes to :	*Low*	*High*	*Low*	*High*
1.	Having physical facilities that are visually appealing	1 2 3 4 5 6 7		1 2 3 4 5 6 7	
2.	Having staff who give users individual attention	1 2 3 4 5 6 7		1 2 3 4 5 6 7	

To allow for the varying importance of the dimensions in different settings, the questionnaire often asks subjects to weight the categories by sharing 100 points across them. The results of the weighted survey are then assembled in a report such as Table 18.5. We can see that, although the respondents reported the greatest gap in empathy, they found that dimension less important than assurance. The weighted score ranked the latter more highly.

TABLE 18.5 SERVQUAL SCORES WITH WEIGHTING

	SERVQUAL score (P – E)	*Weights %*	*Weighted SERVQUAL*	*Rank*
Tangibles	– 0.37	18.7	– 0.31	5
Reliability	– 0.41	23.8	– 0.44	4
Responsiveness	– 0.48	23.3	– 0.51	3
Assurance	– 0.67	19.8	– 0.60	1
Empathy	– 0.82	14.5	– 0.54	2
Overall	– 0.53	100	– 0.48	

Criticism of SERVQUAL has been based on the importance of expectations and questions on the general application of the five-factor structure. In detail, interpreting the meaning of the $(P - E)$ gap is difficult. In the wider, marketing context, others comment that the service dimension is only one element of the marketing mix. Notwithstanding these reactions, service organisations in many fields have taken up the model. For instance, the Accounts Commission for Scotland recommends it for the assessment of local government services.

18.11 STATISTICAL METHODS FOR QUALITY CONTROL

Almost all quality gurus have emphasized the importance of statistical methods for quality control and reduce variability. Use of statistical methods also is one of the tenets of ISO 9001. Though we shall look into the details of these methods in Chap. 5 (PART-2), a brief of these methods is just presented here. In statistical quality control (SQC) focus is on three major areas: **Statistical Process Control (SPC), Scientific Acceptance Sampling (SAS)** and a lesser extent **Design of Experiments (DOX) and Reliability**. The key concepts associated with SPC were developed by Walter Shewart at Bell Laboratories in 1920 while SAS is credited to Dodge-Romig team in 1930.

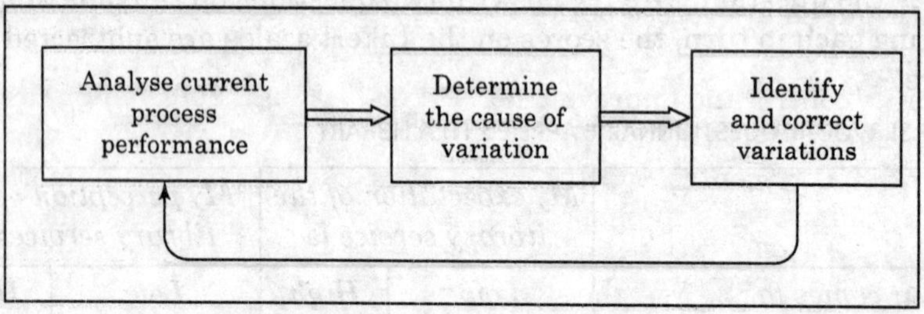

FIGURE 18.18 Process control activities.

Statistical process control (SPC) measures the performance of a process. Statistical process control (SPC) can be used to monitor and correct quality as the product or service is being produced, rather than at the conclusion of the process. SPC uses control charts to track the performance of one or more quality variables or attributes. Samples are taken of the process outputs, and if they fall outside the acceptable range then corrections to the process are made. This allows operations to improve quality through a sequence of activities, Fig. 18.18.

A **control chart** is one of the primary techniques of SPC. A typical control chart is shown in Fig. 18.19. This chart plots the averages of measurements of a quality characteristic (variable or attribute) taken from the process versus time (or the sample number). The chart has a center line (CL), and upper and lower control limits (UCL and LCL in Fig. 18.19). The center line represents where the process characteristic should fall if there are no unusual sources of variability are present. The control limits are determined from some simple statistical consideration as discussed in PART-1(B). Usually control charts are applied to the output variable(s) in a system such as in Fig. 18.19. However, in some cases they can be usefully applied to the inputs as well.

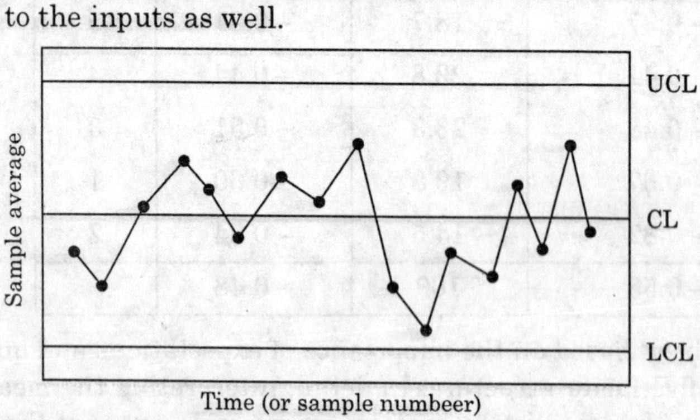

FIGURE 18.19 A typical control chart.

The control chart is a very useful process monitoring technique; when unusual sources of variability are present, sample averages will plot outside the control limits. This is a signal that some investigation of the process should be made and corrective action to remove these unusual sources of variability taken. Systematic use of a control chart is an excellent way to reduce variability.

A **design of (DOX) experiment** (DOX) is extremely helpful in discovering the key variables influencing the quality characteristics of interest in the process. A designed experiment is an approach to systematically varying the controllable input factors in the process and determining the effect these factors have on the output product parameters. Statistically designed experiments are invaluable in reducing the variability in the quality characteristics and in determining the levels of the controllable variables that optimize process performance. Often significant breakthroughs in process performance and product quality also result from using designed experiments.

The third area of quality control and improvement that we discuss is **scientific acceptance sampling (SAS)**. This is closely connected with inspection and testing of product, which is one of the earliest aspects of quality control, dating back to long before statistical methodology was developed for quality improvement. Inspection can occur at many points in a process. Acceptance sampling, defined as the inspection and classification of a sample of units selected at random from a larger batch or lot and the ultimate decision about disposition of the lot, usually occurs at two points: incoming raw materials or components, or final production.

Several different variations of acceptance sampling are shown in Fig. 18.20. In Fig. 18.20(*a*) the inspection operation is performed immediately following production, before the product is shipped to the customer. This is usually called **outgoing inspection**. Figure 18.20(b) illustrates incoming inspection; that is, a situation in which lots of batches of product are sampled as they are received from the supplier. Various *lot-dispositioning* decisions are illustrated in Fig. 18.20(c).

Sampled lots may either be accepted or rejected. Items in a rejected lot are typically either scrapped or recycled, or they may be reworked or replaced with good units. This latter case is often called **rectifying inspection**.

Customers would ideally like 100 percent of the products which they obtain to be inspected and acceptable, but this is practically impossible particularly where quantity offered for inspection and decision (acceptance/rejection/rectification) is enormous, SAS is the only method where destructive testing is involved. Therefore some lower quality level

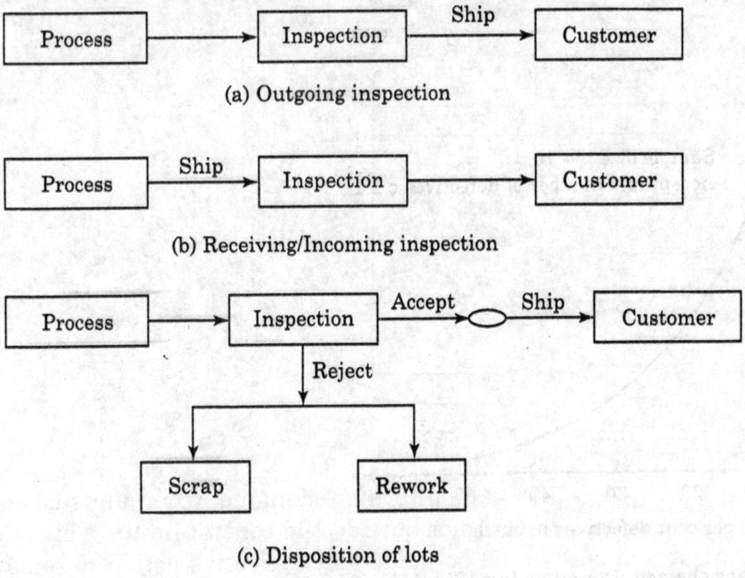

FIGURE 18.20 Variations of acceptance sampling.

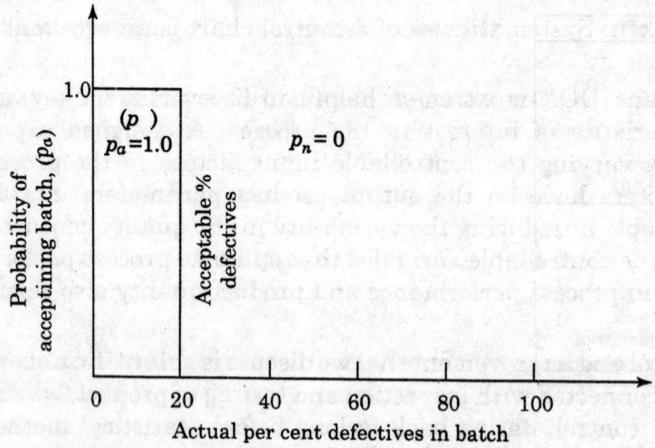

FIGURE 18.21 The probability of accepting batches, with 100% inspection (acceptable percentage defective 20%)

must, of necessity, be agreed. Even so only by 100 percent inspection (and even then, only if there are no errors during inspection) can be absolutely certain that a batch or sample conforms to this agreed standard. In Fig. 18.21, 100 percent inspection has been used, so we can be 100 percent certain that batches do, or do not, conform to the agreed quality level, which is maximum of 20 per cent defectives per batch (again assuming no mistakes during inspection).

A curve such as this is known as an *operating characteristic* curve and shows the probability of accepting batches with various percentage defectives. Operating characteristic (OC) curves can be calculated and drawn for any sampling plan if we specify:

(*a*) the sample size n;

(*b*) the acceptance number c, *i.e.* the maximum allowance number of defects in the sample

An example for a sampling plan with $c \leq 1$ and $n = 10$ is shown in Fig. 18.22. Sampled lots may either he accepted or rejected. Items in a rejected lot are typically either scrapped or recycled, or they may be reworked or replaced with good units. This latter case is often called **rectifying inspection**.

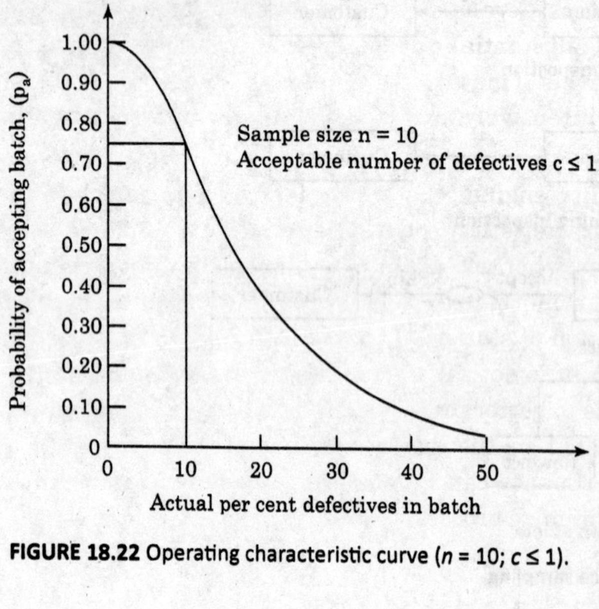

FIGURE 18.22 Operating characteristic curve (n = 10; $c \leq 1$).

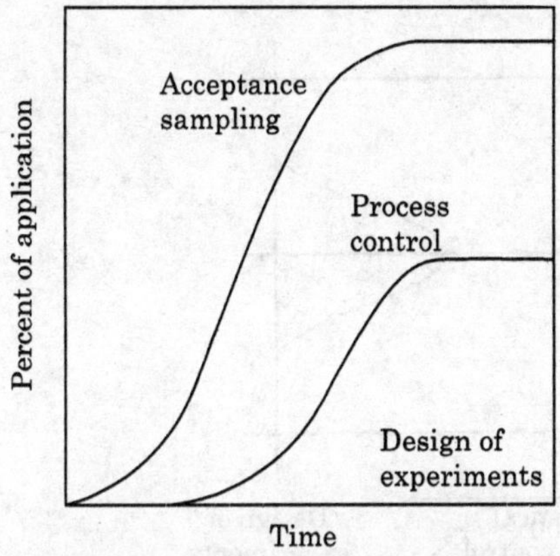

FIGURE 18.23 Phase diagram of the use of quality-engineering methods.

Modern quality assurance systems usually place less emphasis on acceptance sampling and attempt to make statistical process control and designed experiments the focus of their efforts. Acceptance sampling tends to reinforce the conformance-to-specification view of quality and does not have any feedback into either the production process or engineering design or development that would necessarily lead to quality improvement.

Figure 18.23 shows the typical evolution in the use of these techniques in most organizations. At the lowest level of maturity, management may be completely unaware of quality issues, and there is likely to be no effective organized quality improvement effort. Frequently there will be some modest applications of acceptance-sampling and inspection methods, usually for incoming parts and materials. The first activity as maturity increases is to intensify the use of sampling inspection. The use of sampling will increase until it is realized that quality cannot be inspected or tested into the product.

At that point, the organization usually begins to focus on process improvement. Statistical process control and experimental design potentially have major impacts on manufacturing, product design activities, and process development. The systematic introduction of these methods usually marks the start of substantial quality, cost, and productivity improvements in the organization. At the highest levels of maturity, companies use designed experiments and statistical process control methods intensively and make relatively modest use of acceptance sampling.

The primary **objective** of quality engineering efforts is the **systematic reduction of variability** in the key quality characteristics of the product. Figure 18.24 shows how this happens over time. In the early stages, when acceptance sampling is the major technique in use, process "fallout," or units that do not conform to the specifications, constitute a high percentage of the process output. The introduction of statistical process control will stabilize the process and reduce the variability. However, it is not satisfactory just to meet requirements—further reduction of variability usually leads to better product performance and enhanced competitive position, as was vividly demonstrated in the automobile transmission example discussed earlier. Statistically designed experiments can be employed in conjunction with statistical process monitoring and control to minimize process variability in nearly all industrial settings.

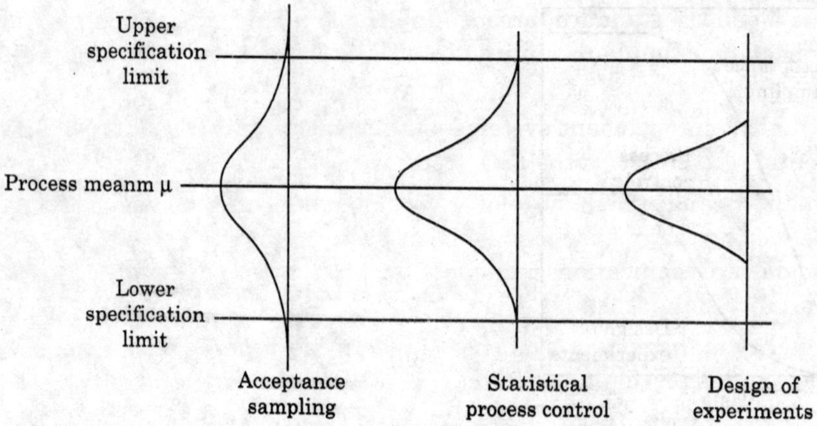

FIGURE 18.24 Application of quality-engineering techniques and the systematic reduction of process variability.

18.12 ISO 9000—INTERNATIONAL QUALITY STANDARD

Quality management systems involve the use of quality standards against which actual performance is monitored. These may be:

- set internally by operations management, for their own particular operation
- external standards set for a particular industry, or for all industries and organizations in general, depending on the nature of the quality item.

In a bid to secure international quality recognition between organizations, a set of internationally recognized standards has been devised.

ISO 9000 is a family of standards and guidelines for quality management systems developed by the International Organizations for Standardization (ISO) - Switzerland. They provide organizations with a model based on best practice in quality management systems and have been implemented by organization throughout the world, many of whom have been certified as conforming to the standards. The ISO 9000 standards set out eight principles of quality management for organizations to apply:

- customer focus
- leadership
- involvement of people
- process approach
- a system approach to management
- continuous improvement
- a factual approach to decision making
- mutually beneficial supplier relationships.

ISO 9000 provides a framework for quality assurance throughout the world. Oddly, this does not mean it is recognized in every country. Some nations insist upon dealing only with organizations that hold their own nation ISO equivalent standard. Examples of ISO equivalents are: the IS: 14000, UK BS5750, the Australian AS3900.

The purpose of ISO 9000 and its *nationalised cousins* is to guarantee to anyone buying products or services that their build quality meets requirements. This is achieved by outlining standards, procedures and features of the management system controlling the business.

The ISO 9000 is a generic standard, broadly applicable to any type of organization and is often used to demonstrate a supplier's ability to control its processes. The three standards of ISO 9000 are:

- ISO 9000: 'Quality management systems–fundamentals and vocabulary'. This defines the fundamental terms used in the ISO 9000 series of standards.
- ISO 9001 'Quality management systems–requirements'. This specifies the requirements that must be met by the quality management system within an organization if it is to meet the standard. Organizations can apply to obtain a certificate for meeting the ISO 9001 : 2015 quality standards.
- ISO 9004 'Quality management systems – guidelines for performance improvements'. This provides guidelines for the continual improvement of the quality management system in an organization.

To qualify for ISO status an organization must have its quality standards and procedures assessed by a third party. Once ISO standing is achieved, the standards and procedures are audited on a regular basis to guarantee their use and maintenance.

ISO 9000 accreditation holds a number of benefits:

- The framework supplies a disciplined approach to work
- When writing and developing ISO procedures, organizations identify unnecessary areas of work and eliminate them – thus saving money.
- It can help to reduce waste, mistakes, customer complaints and costs.
- Holding ISO status is a strong marketing tool for an organization.

A detailed description of ISO 9000 standard forms the subject matter of Chap. 20 of this book.

18.13 TOTAL QUALITY MANAGEMENT (TQM)

In earlier chapters before this, we saw many and varied definitions of quality that are use. Some people argue that to them, a quality car is one with the right badge on the front. Others argue a quality car is one that does not break down between services.

Total Quality Management offers a standard interpretation for its role in the world of quality.

Total means that every member of an organization is concerned with the product or service being sold to the customer.

Quality is more difficult to define. Laws throughout the world refer to quality products as those that are *fit for purpose*. Alternatively, we see a quality good or service as one that *conforms to or exceeds customer requirements.*

This is in line with Juran and Crosby's thinking quality as continuously meeting customer's requirements.

Management is the activity led from top that makes the entire process work. It makes use of personnel, capital and any other resources available.

Total quality management (TQM) is a philosophy of quality management that originated in Japan in the 1950s. As seen from above, TQM is a system that integrates the quality management efforts of all groups in an organization and, it is argued, has been a significant factor in Japanese global business success. It has a number of important features.

- The basic principle that the cost of preventing mistakes is less than the cost of correcting them once they occur and the cost of lost, potential future sales. The aim should therefore be to get things right first time consistently—Crosby's philosophy.
- This contrasts with the 'traditional' approach that less than 100% quality is acceptable as the costs of improvement from say 90% to 100% outweigh the benefits.

To ensure an organization sustains competitive advantage and meets its financial targets, TQM focuses primarily on:

- **Customers** – what do they specifically want?
- **Processes** – are they efficient and effective?
- **Workforce empowerment** – can individuals make decisions for themselves?
- **Continuous improvement** – is the workforce aware they can make improvements to the ways in which they perform their jobs?
- **Leadership** – often requiring training.
- **Measurement** – of outputs, profits and effectiveness.

Whilst TQM is obviously concerned with quality, we can see from the focus list above that it strives for quality by tackling all the issues that could potentially create poor quality goods or services. If there are no excuses for poor output then it simply cannot exist!

There are many other aspects of TQM. Chapter 21 discusses all such aspects in detail.

18.14 QUALITY AWARDS

In order to promote quality movement and quality improvement are many industry and company honours; the **Sweeney award**, offered among the suppliers of McDonald's for example.

However, total quality management is a mature integration of systems techniques and behaviour and consequently no single assessment criterion is available or appropriate.

There is a need however, to be able to validate an organization's claim to total quality and a need for companies to measure their own comparative level of quality development. In response to these needs a number of international quality assessment mechanisms have been developed. The four best known awards important as on date are:

1. the Deming Prize (primarily used in Japan)
2. the Malcom Baldrige Award (primary used in United States)
3. the European Quality Award (primary used in Europe)
4. the Rajiv Gandhi National Quality Award (used in India).

18.14.1 The Deming Prize

Recognizing Deming's important effect on the performance of manufacturing firms, the *Deming Prize* was instituted by the Union of Japanese Scientists and Engineers (UJSE) in 1951 and is awarded to those companies, initially in Japan, but more recently opened to overseas companies, which have successfully applied 'company-wide quality control' based upon statistical quality control. There are several categories of winners including individuals, factories and divisions. There are also ten major assessment categories: policy and objectives, organization and its operation, education and its extension, assembling and disseminating of information, analysis, standardization, control, quality assurance, effects and future plans.

Hundreds of applications are made for the prize each year. The applications are required to submit a detailed description of quality practices. This is a significant activity in itself and many companies claim a great deal of benefit from having done so. A shortlist is then created and site visits are made by inspectors to the organizations on the shortlist. The site visits include company presentations, in-depth questioning by examiners, top management meetings and the opportunity for examiners to see any parts of the plant and question any worker.

18.14.2 Malcolm Baldrige National Quality Award

All organizations will have to produce high-quality products and services if they are to be competitive in the years ahead. The emphasize that point, in August 1987, Congress signed into law the Malcolm Baldrige National Quality Improvement Act, creating the Malcolm Baldrige National Quality Award (*MBNQA*). Named for the late secretary of commerce, who was a strong proponent of enhancing quality as a means of reducing the trade deficit, the award promotes, recognizes, and publicizes quality strategies and achievements.

It is given annually to recognize U.S. organizations for performance excellence. Awards are given to organizations in five categories: manufacturing, service, small business, health care, and education. Three awards may be given each year in each category. Many companies have received this award. The more familiar firms include Motorola, IBM, Xerox, Federal Express, Ritz-Carlton Hotels, AT & T, Cadillac and Texas instruments. Many organizations compete for the awards, and many companies use the performance excellence criteria for self-assessment. The award is administered by NIST (the National Institute of Standards and Technology).

The application and three-stage review process for the Baldrige award is rigorous, but often the process helps companies define what quality means for them. The seven major criteria for the award are:

1. leadership in creating and sustaining a visible quality culture,
2. effectiveness in collecting and analyzing information for quality improvement and planning,
3. effectiveness in integrating quality requirements into the strategic planning process,
4. success in utilizing the full potential for the work force for quality improvement,
5. effectiveness of the company's systems for assuring quality control,
6. results of quality achievement and improvement, as demonstrated by quantitative measures, and
7. business prospects.

The performance excellence criteria and their interrelationships are shown in Fig. 18.25. The point values for these criteria in the MBNQA are shown in Table 18.6. The criteria are directed towards results, where results are a composite of customer satisfaction and retention, market share and new market development, product/service quality, productivity and operational effectiveness, human resources development, supplier performance, and public/corporate citizenship. The criteria are nonprescriptive. That is, the focus is on results, not the use of specific procedures or tools.

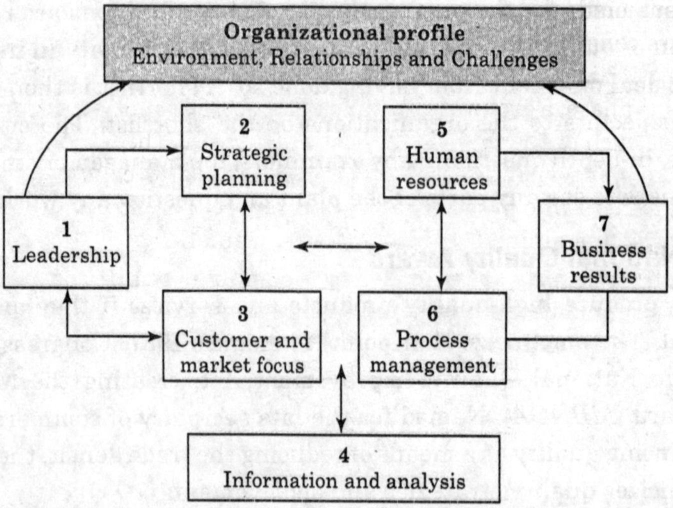

FIGURE 18.25 The structure of the MBNQA performance excellence criteria.

TABLE 18.6 PERFORMANCE EXCELLENCE CATEGORIES AND POINT VALUES

	Categories and items	*Points*	*Value*
1	LEADERSHIP		
	• organizational leadership	80	
	• social responsibility	40	120
2	STRATEGIC PLANNING	40	85
	• strategy development	45	
	• company strategy		
3	CUSTOMER AND MARKET FOCUS		
	• customer and market knowledge	40	
	• customer satisfaction and enhancement	45	85
4	MEASUREMENT, ANALYSIS AND KNOWLEDGE MANAGEMENT	50	
	• measurement and analysis of organizational performance	40	90
	• information and knowledge management		
5	HUMAN RESOURCE FOCUS		
	• work systems	35	
	• employee education, training and development	25	
	• employee well-being and satisfaction	25	85
6	PROCESS MANAGEMENT		
	• management of product and service processes	45	
	• management of business processes	25	
	• management of support processes	15	85
7	BUSINESS RESULTS		
	• customer-focused results	125	
	• financial and market results	125	
	• human resource results	80	
	• organizational effectiveness results	120	450
Total Points			1000

The MBNQA process is shown in Fig. 18.26. An applicant sends the completed application to NIST. This application is then subjected to a first-round review by a team of Baldrige examiners. The board of Baldrige examiners consists of highly qualified volunteers from a variety of fields. Judges evaluate the scoring on the application to determine if the applicant will continue to **consensus**. During the consensus phase, a group of examiners who scored the original application determines a consensus score for each of the items. Once consensus is reached and a consensus report written, judges then make a site-visit determination. A site visit typically is a one-week visit by a team of four to six examiners who produce a site-visit report. The site-visit reports are used by the judges as the basis of determining the final MBNQA winners.

As shown in Fig. 18.26 feedback reports are provided to the applicant at up to three stages of the MBNQA process. Many organizations have found these reports very helpful and use them as the basis of planning for overall improvement of the organization and for driving improvement in business results.

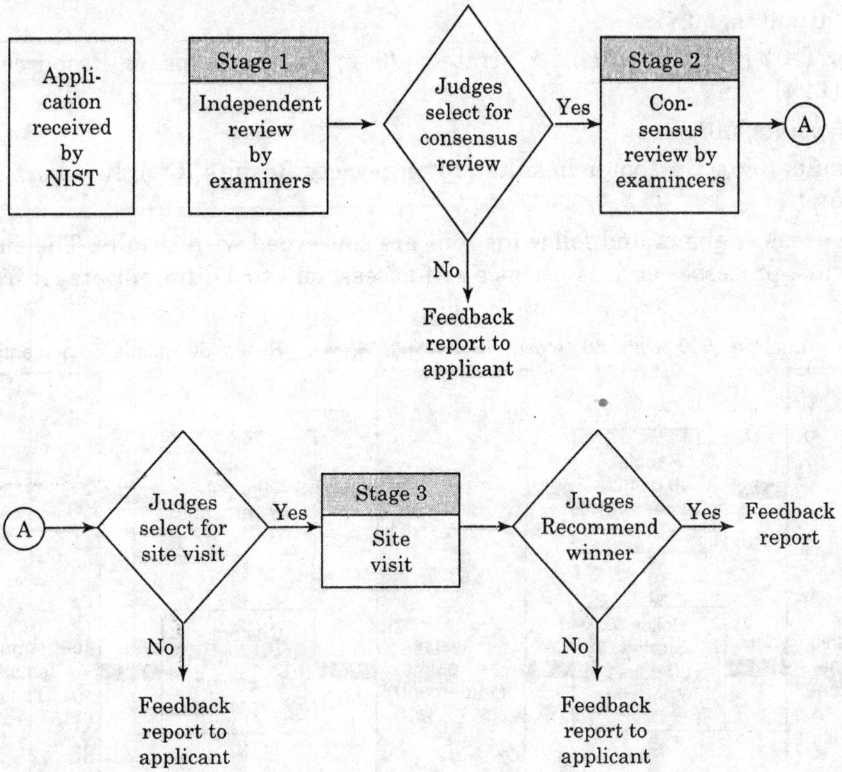

FIGURE 18.26 MBNQA process.

18.14.3 European Quality Award (EQA)

In 1988, 14 leading West European companies formed the European Foundation for Quality Management (EFQM) and by the year 2000 it had over 850 members. One of EFQM's core objectives is to recognize quality achievement and to this end it launched the European Quality Award (EQA) in 1992. The EQA is awarded to the most successful exponent of total quality management in Western Europe each year. European quality prizes are awarded to a number of companies that demonstrate excellence in the management of quality as their fundamental process for continuous improvement. To receive a prize, companies must demonstrate that their approach to total quality management has contributed significantly to satisfying the expectations of customers, employees and others with an interest in the nine areas divided into **enablers** and **results**. Each year participating companies initially apply for their own national award and the top firms from each country go into the EQA competition. The scoring system reflects the 'approach', 'development' and 'results' aspects as outlined under the section on the Baldrige Award.

The EQA classifies the areas of assessment into either **enables** or **results**. The enablers are the business activities which are employed to produce the results. This represents an important approach to self assessment by encouraging organizations to understand, appreciate and balance the efforts which are put in and the performances which result. Each of the nine elements in the EQA model is assessed through a comprehensive self-appraisal questionnaire to measure an organization's quality development. The EQA (Fig. 18.27) also has categories and a total of 1000 points are awarded, with weight reflecting the levels of importance and emphasis

Enablers (500 points, 50%)

Leadership (10%); People (9%); & strategy (8%); Partnerships & Resources (9%); Processes (14%)

Results (500 points, 50%)

People Results (9%); Customer Results (20%); Society Results (6%); Key Performance Results (15%)

The first five areas enablers and following four are concerned with results. The emphasis is on results, not just processes and its use as a self-assessment tool differentiates it from ISO 9000 series.

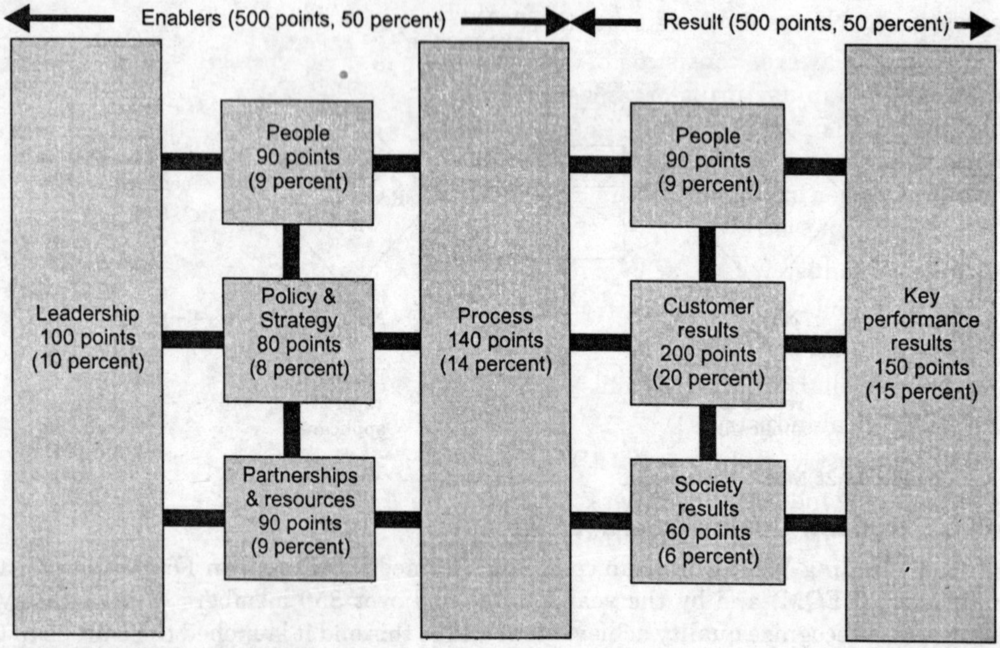

FIGURE 18.27 Structure of EQA.

18.14.4 Rajiv Gandhi National Quality Award (RGNQA)

The award has been designed in line with similar awards, like Malcolm Baldrige National Quality Award in USA, Deming Prize in Japan and European Quality Award and are given annually (once in one financial year).

It is on the similar lines as EQA. As with MBNQA and EQA it is also a 1000 point rating award with 500 marks reserved for enablers and 500 marks for results as per Table 18.7.

TABLE 18.7 PERFORMANCE PARAMETERS AND POINT VALUES

Parameter	*Marks*	
	Large Scale	*Small Scale*
Enablers		
Leadership	100	200
Policies; objectives and strategies	100	–
Human resource management	50	100
Resource	100	–
Processes	150	100
Results		
Customer focused results	200	200
Employees' satisfaction	50	–
Impact on environment and society	100	200
Business results	150	200
Total	1000	1000

RGNQA was instituted by Bureau of Indian standards (BIS) in 1991 and given on the basis of assessment by National Award Committee (NAC).

There are five awards consisting of one for **large scale** manufacturing organizations, one for **small scale** manufacturing organization, one for large scale service sector organizations, one for small scale service sector organizations and one for **BEST OF ALL**. In addition, there are eight commendation certificates each for large scale and small scale manufacturing organizations as per industrial sectors given below:

1. Biotechnology;
2. Chemical industry;
3. Electrical and electronic industry;
4. Food and drug industry;
5. Gems, Jewellary and allied industry;
6. Metallurgical industry;
7. Textile industry; and
8. Engineering industry and others.

Further, there are six commendation certificates each for large scale and small scale service organizations in the following sectors:

1. Education,
2. Finance,
3. Health Care,
4. Information Technology;
5. Utilities, and
6. Others.

While the award *does not* amount to a product or service endorsement for the recipients, it is primarily given because the receipient organization has shown it has an outstanding system for managing its products, services, human resources, customer relationships etc.

An organization is eligible to compete for the award, if it satisfies all the following conditions:

(*a*) Applicant organization is located in India.

(*b*) Applicant organization has been in existence for at least three years as on last date of the application.

(*c*) Applicant organization is situated at one place or a unit of an organization housed at one location.

(*d*) Applicant organization has not been convicted by any court for deficiency in product or service and/or found guilty of financial irregularities by any regulatory authority or court for the period for which applying and three years prior to the period for which applying. An undertaking to this effect will have to be submitted.

(*e*) Applicant organization is not manufacturing products, like ***tobacco*** and ***liquor*** etc. which are injurious to health.

A Sub-unit which performs only support functions for the parent organization such as, sales, marketing, distribution, finance, human resources and health are not eligible. [A Subunit is a Unit or Division of a larger organization (Parent organization) which owns or has organizational and/or financial control of sub-unit]

Further, if an applicant organization has earlier received an award, it is not eligible to apply for an award for next three awards. However, this condition will not apply to those applicant organizations which have received commendation certificate.

18.15 AUTHOR'S OBSERVATION ON QUALITY AWARDS

From the composition of the awards it can be seen that all the three awards—EQA, Baldrige and RGNQA Awards focus on customer satisfaction and quality improvement and results are disseminated widely. The Deming Prize is narrower, stressing problem prevention using statistical methods.

All three - Baldrige, EQA and RGNQA awards are on 1000-point scale and include society results among their criteria and acknowledge how improved quality benefits more people than the parties to the immediate transaction. This perspective is also present in ISO 9004, where the broader 'interested parties' replace the 'customer'.

It may be noted that the purpose of standards certification and registration (for example registration to ISO 9001) and of quality awards are quite different. Certification does not guarantee the quality of any particular product or service. What it does is to ensure clients/ customers that a firm's systems and procedures conform to certain minimum requirements.

The objective of RGNQA, Baldrige Award or EQA Award is to enhance competitiveness. The main purpose of quality awards is to recognize innovative activities by management and excellence in service to customers and lay heavy emphasis on customer satisfaction, competitive quality results comparison, executive leadership, employee involvement and public responsibility etc.

18.16 5S

It is group of five Japanese words starting from letter 'S'–Seri, Seition, Seiso, Seikatsu and Shitsuke.

1. **Seri** (or sorting) means sorting and organizing the items as critical, important, frequently used, useless (not needed as of now). Critical items should be kept for use nearby and items that are not to used in near future, or obsolete items should be discarded. It thus involves differentiating between the necessary unneccessary items for the job in hand. It is infact technical house keeping in industry it saves floor space and avoids wastages.
2. **Seition.** (Or systematic arrangements or putting things in order). It is rational orderly and methodical arrangement of all items. This helps in *sarving valuable productive time* in industries.
3. **Seiso.** (Cleaning up). This involves cleaning up the workplace, making free from burrs, grease, oil, waste, hanging wires and leakage of oil. Such an activity *helps in avoiding accidents.*
4. **Seikatsu.** (personal cleanliness). This is concerned with personal hygiene. It makes the worker *presentable and smart and more confident* and better quality of work.
5. **Shitsuke.** (discipline) boosts the morale of the works force and helps in *avoiding wastage* of all kind.

Following 5S, it is believed enhances the quality and production.

SOLVED QUESTIONS

Q. 18.1: *Select the correct option in for the following*

(i) In general, quality tools and techniques can be categorized as:

(a) Design Tools (b) Process tools

(c) Either (a) or (b)

(ii) Which of the following is not an example of a quality tool or techniques?

(a) Network analysis (b) C & E diagrams

(c) OLF

(iii) Which of the following is ***not*** example of a quality award?

(a) six-sigma (b) ISO-9000

(c) RGNQA (d) EQA

(iv) Which of the following tools and techniques is used to show which categores of defects are most common?

(a) control charts (b) Pareto charts

(c) Run charts (d) Flow chart

(v) Which tool or techniques is used to analyze treads?

(a) Scatter chart (b) Run charts

(c) Pareto charts (d) Histograms

(vi) Which quality control tools is used to analyze processes by visualizing them graphically:

(a) Check list (b) Flow charts

(c) Pareto charts (d) Histograms

Ans. (c) The Cause and Effect (C&E) diagrams are also known as Ishikawa diagrams or fishbone diagrams. In QC, these are used to show how different factors relate together and might be tied to potential problems. C&E diagrams are used as part of an approach to improve quality problems and trying to uncover the underlying causes.

(a) Pareto law is also known as 80/20 rule. This rule states that 80% of the problems come from 20% of the causes but there are variations on this theme.

(b) A scatter diagram is a powerful tool for spotting trends in data. Scatter diagrams are made using two variables (a dependent variable and an independent variable).

(d) JIT is a manufacturing method that brings inventory down to zero (or near-zero levels). It forces a focus on quality, since there is no excess inventory on hand to use.

Q. 11. (a) What is the most usual way to modelling continuous improvement process?

(b) List out some benefits of continuous improvement.

Ans. (a) The most usual way of modelling continuous improvement is Plan-Do-Check-Act (PDCA) cycle, by which the stages of problem solving are seen as forming a never-ending cycle.

(b) Benefits of continuous improvement:

- Better performance which produces increased profits
- Improvements in customer satisfaction
- Increases in staff morale
- Improvement on a continual, step-by-step basis is more prudent than changing things all at once
- Better communication within the organisation
- Improvements in relations with suppliers
- Better use of resources
- More efficient planning.

Q. 12. (a) What is necessarily required for quality improvement?

(b) What is the process of continuous improvement?

(You answer for (a) and (b) should state the core issues only)

Ans. (a) Quality improvement requires close cooperation among functions (design, operation, marketing, purchasing and others). Quality function deployment (QFD) uses a chart called the house of quality, to encourage interfunctional planning and communication.

(b) Continuous improvement involves identifying benchmarks of excellent practice and instilling a sense of ownership so that employees will continually identify changes and improvements that should be made.

Q. 13. (a) Khan is the project manager of a multi-location project. His core-team wants to use design of experiments to look for ways to improve quality. Which of the following are advantages design of experiments ?

(a) It allows the project manager to move the relationship of changes to control the project costs with the best resources available.

(b) It allows the project manager to experiment with the project design to determine which variables are causing the failure.

Ans. : (*a*) The Cause-and-Effect (C&E) diagrams are also known as Ishikawa diagrams or fishbone diagrams. In QC these are used to show how different factors relate together and might be tied to potential problems. C&E diagrams are used as part of an approach to improve quality problems and trying to uncover the underlying cause.

(*b*) Pareto law is also known as 80/20 rule. This rule states that 80% of the problems come from 20% of the causes but there are variations on this theme.

(*c*) A scatter diagram is a powerful tool for spotting trends in data. Scatter diagrams are made using two variables (a dependent variable and an independent variable).

(*d*) **JIT:** A manufacturing method that brings inventory down to zero (or near zero) levels. It forces a focus on quality, since there is no excess inventory on hand to waste.

Q. 18.7: *(a) What is the most usual way to madelling continuous improvement:*

(b) Lost out some benefits of continuous improvement.

Ans. : (*a*) The most usual way of modelling continuous improvement is Plan-Do-Check-Act cycle (PDCA cycle), by which the stages of problem solving are seen as forming a never ending cycle.

(*b*) Benefits of continuous improvement

- Better performance, which produces increased profits
- Improvements in customer satisfaction
- Increases in staff morale
- Improvement on a continual, step-by-step basis is more prudent than changing things all at once
- Better communication within the organisation
- Improvements in relations with suppliers
- Better use of resources
- More efficient planning

Q. 18.8: *(a) What is essentially required for quality improvement?*

(b) What is the process of continuous improvement?

Your answer for (a) and (b) should state the core issues only.

Ans. : (*a*) Quality improvement requires close cooperation among functions (design, operations, marketing, purchasing, and others). Quality function deployment (QFD) uses a chart called the "house of quality" to encourage interfunctional planning and communication.

(*b*) Continuous improvement involves identifying benchmarks of excellent practice and instilling a sense of ownership so that employees will continually identify changes and process improvements that should be made.

Ans. : *(a) Tina is the project manager of a manufacturing project. She and her project team are using design of experiments to look for ways to improve quality. Which of the following best describes design of experiments ?*

(i) It allows the project manager to move the relationship of activities to complete the project work with the best resources available.

(ii) It allows the project manager to experiment with the project design to determine what variables are causing the flaws.

(iii) It allows the project manager to experiment with variables to attempt to improve quality.

(iv) It allows the project manager to experiment with the project design document to become more productive and to provide higher quality.

(b) Mention briefly about DOX and its role in quality improvement.

Ans. : (*a*) (*iii*)

Reason : of all the option presented (*iii*) is the best. DOX uses experiments and "what-if' Scenarios to determine what variables are affecting quality option (*i*) is incorrect because DOX in regard to quality is not interested in changing relationship of activities to complete project work. Option (*ii*) and (*iv*) are also incorrect because DOX will not be changing project design to determine where flows exist or to become more productive.

(*b*) Design of Experiments (DOX) is a technique of examining controlled changes of input factors and the observation of resulting changes in outputs – *i.e.* the response to input changes. The technique is applied in quality management, most notably by Ishikawa and Taguchi in Japan.

Q. 18.10: *(a) Explain objectively what quality improvements is.*

(b) What do you understand by continuous improvement in quality.

(c) What is a run chart?

Ans. : (*a*) Any quality improvement can be objectively regarded as an improvement only if it reduces the net loss to society.

(*b*) Continuous improvement involves searching for need ways to improve work quality and performance.

(*c*) A run chart is one of the basic tools of quality improvement. It is a long line graph that severs the trend and variances over a time.

Q. 18.11: *(a) What is a flow chart?*

(b) What is a Pareto chart or diagram? Can you draw a suitable diagram to make your answer understandable?

Ans. : (*a*) A flow chart is one of the seven basic tools of quality. We use it to analyze processes that are part of the project in order to look for quality problems etc.

(*b*) A Pareto chart is an ordered histogram used to distinguish critical problems and serves the magnitude of the different causes. The most frequent cause is usually (but not always) the most improvement cause. Figure show an example of Pareto chart

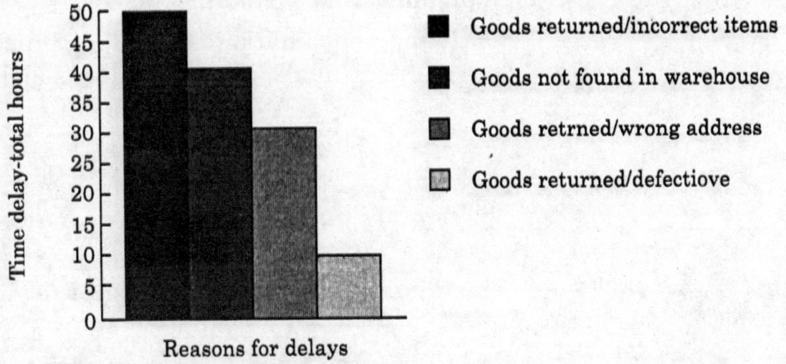

Fig. 18.28 An example of a Pareto chart

[illegible]

[illegible]

(b) [illegible] quality improvement [illegible]

5. (a) What is a flow chart?

the customer's intended use, product or service support, and aesthetic may take on greater importance. One TQM responsibility of marketing is to listen to customers and report changing perceptions of quality.

(*c*) Responsibility for quality is shared by all employees in the organization. Employee involvement programmes include leadership in changing organizational culture, individual development, awards and incentives, and teamwork.

(*d*) Top management commitment and leadership are necessary to attain and sustain revolutionary rates of quality improvement.

(*e*) Benchmarking and focusing on customers are two important things managers can do to increase quality.

Q. 18.16: *Name **(only)** the main dimensions of quality management? Give examples of improvement methods which can be used for each of those dimensions.*

Ans. : The main dimensions of quality management are

1. people 2. system 3. tool and techniques

Examples of improvement methods are:

People—team working, empowerment etc.

System—ISO 9000

Tools—SPC, problems solving tools, QFD etc.

Q. 18.17: *(a) What is the difference between ISO 9000 and a quality award?*

*(b) Mention only **(do not describe)** some practices to improve quality in an organization.*

(c) Name a few leading quality gurus.

Ans. : (*a*) The difference between ISO 9000 and a quality award is that ISO is a way to improve quality, whereas an award is a once-only quality recognition.

(*b*) Practices to improve quality in an organization include poka yoke, continuous improvement, Taguchi methods, Activity based costing, sample design, Just-intime, Benchmarking and perhaps Re-engineering.

(*c*) Leading quality management authorities include Edward Deming, Joseph Juran, Crosby, Armand Feigenbaum, Kazai Ishikawa and Taguchi.

Q. 18.18: *(a) Name the Enablers and Results in EQA? How much points the Enablers and Results have been allocated in EQA?*

(b) What is the major difference between EQA and quality enabling standards?

(c) Name one Indian Award for Quality and its model.

Ans. : (*a*) The five enablers are:

(*i*) Leadership (*ii*) People
(*iii*) Policy (*iv*) Partnership and resources
(*v*) Process

The four results are:

(*i*) People results (*ii*) Customer results
(*iii*) Society results (*iv*) Key performance results

Enablers account for 500 points and results also account for 500 points.

(*b*) The major difference between the EQA and quality enabling standards is that the EQA is concerned with what a company has achieved and is achieving—enablers are interested in how results are being achieved.

(*c*) One famous Indian Award for Quality is Rajiv Gandhi National Quality Award (RGNQA). This is modelled on the EQA.

Q. 18.19: *(a) What is the total point value in Baldrige Award?*

(b) What is the total point value in EQA and RGNQA?

(c) What aspects are reflected under the scoring system of each of above awards?

(d) Does the RGNQA amount to a product or service endorsement for the recipients? If your answer is No, then explain.

(e) A liquor manufacturing company has come into existence in India. Is it eligible for RGNQA after 2 years of existence? after 5 years of existence with excellent quality management?

Ans. : (*a*) 1000 points.

(*b*) 1000 points.

(*c*) All the three awards scoring system reflect:

(*i*) approach

(*ii*) deployment

(*iii*) results.

(*d*) No. The award is given because an organization has shown that it has an outstanding system for managing its products, services, human resources, customer relationships etc. As part of the evaluation, an organization is asked to describe its system for assuring the quality of its goods and services. It also must supply information on quality improvement and customer satisfaction efforts and results. That does not mean that a recipient's products or services are endorsed.

(*e*) No. Minimum period for the eligibility of award is 3 years. But the liquor being injurious to health, it is not eligible for applying for RGNQA even.

Q. 18.20: *(a) State the purpose of MBNQA. Is it an International Award?*

(b) Do you see Baldrige Award as a broad measure of quality development?

(c) In MBNQA which is the most heavily weighted criterion for award?

(d) What aspects are reflected in MBNQA scoring system?

Q. 18.21: *Draw a simple diagram of EQA showing nine elements. How many enablers are there in this EQA? What is the total quantum of marks of enablers?*

Ans. : (*a*) The purpose of MBNQA is to stimulate American companies to improve quality and productivity, to recognize achievements, to establish criteria for a wider quality effort and to provide guidance on quality improvement.

It is given in US only and to US companies. So it is **not** an international award.

(*b*) Yes.

(*c*) It is customer focus and satisfaction.

(*d*) The MBNQA scoring system reflects following three different aspects :

Approach	-	appropriateness of methods
	-	effectiveness of methods
	-	evidence of innovation

Ans. : (*a*) Ishikawa in Japan proposed the idea of QC. Quality Circle are mainly management stimulated. Whatever the stated reasons are for instituting QC, the real reason for having QC is to motivate employees to improve quality.

The other contribution of Ishikawa is Fish-bone diagrams or cause-and-effect diagrams to solve quality problems.

(*b*) A quality circle consists of a group of employees, often from different areas of the organisation, who meet regularly to discuss problems of quality control in their area of work, and perhaps of suggest way of improving quality. It is also a way to encourage innovation. The aim of quality circles is to improve employee development and morale so as to create a sense of ownership of the quality of products and services.

Teamwork, in the form of quality circles and group problem-solving activities, is the cornerstone of continuous improvement.

(*c*) A quality circle is a multidisciplinary group of staff whose brief is to identify, investigate and solve work-related problems. The concept of quality circle is important for two reasons.

(*i*) The concept of a circle never ends, hence the constant search for improvement.

(*ii*) Within a quality circle there is no hierarchy. Rather like the Arthurian round table, all players are equal.

(*d*) Following is the distinction between QC and QC.

Quality control (QC)	*Quality Circles (QC)*
Traditionally Western approach to production	Associated with Japanese production
Involves inspection of work by 3rd party	Involves collaborative effort
Rejects defective work that is sampled	Allows idea shearing, problem solving and ongoing quality improvement

Q. 18.25: *Are the QC (quality circles) successful in India. State the reasons for your answer.*

Ans. : No.

QC are not successful in India.

In India quality circles are not successful because of losing technical secreats and fear of criticism from management through not openly.

Q. 18.26: *XYZ limited owns 154 stores selling food and drink. Each store is located in a major town, with the stores being spread across a large geographical area in four different countries. A range of 3,500 different products are sold, its prices and layout of each store being dertermind by the local store manager.*

The MD of XYZ limited has recently receives a report from the management accountant indicating that the profitability between the stores varies significantly. In an initial attempt to determine why this is happening the MD has asked you, a newly approved assistant management accountant to explain the methods of bench marking that can be used within XYZ limited.

You are required to address the issue be explaining the method of benchmarking available to XYZ limited, providing any two specific examples of benchmarking activities that can take place for each of the methods identified.

Ans. : There are three main types of benchmarking.

1. Internal benchmarking assumes there are differences in the work processes of an organisation as a result of geographical differences, local organisational history, customs, differences among business units, and relationships amoung managers and employees. The different locations can then be compared and the best practices or activities identified. They can then be transferred to other locations and performance improvements obtained.

   As XYZ Limited has stores in many different location, the processes in each stored can be compared to determine whether or not there are any location that are more efficient or have lower costs than another.

2. Competitive benchmarking, where a company such as XYZ limited identifies specifci information about a competitor's products, processes, and business results, and then makes comparisons with those of its won organization.

   XYZ Limited needs a similar company to compare itself with. This may be difficult to achieve as most companies tend to keep details of profits and processes relatively secrete. Staff visiting similar stores and noting prices or accessing competitors {S websites an obtaining the information on-line could obtain Price comparisons.

   XYZ Limited could investigate whether any other stores would be willing to participate in a joint benchmarking scheme.

3. Activity benchmarking involves the identification of state-of-the-art products, services, or processes of an organization that may or may not be a direct competitor. The objective is to identify best practices in any type of organization that has established a reputation for excellence in specific business activities.

   Regarding the actual processes, comparisons with a different type of organization may yield some useful information.

   If we know that details is needed on a specific area, such as providing quality training, then an organization known for providing good training for its staff can be approached to obtain ideas and comparison some form of joint agreement may be have to be signed.

   As an alternative, consultants could be employed to provide a report on best practice and this could be used as a benchmark within XYZ Limited.

Q. 18.27: *What is QFD? Explain in details.*

Ans.: QFD is a bench marking approach developed in Japan. It takes the customer's requirements as the starting point to improve performance by converting customer's perceptions of supplier's performance into an improvement agenda. QFD reduces the design time and design cost substantially while maintaining and even enhancing product design quality.

In QFD cross-functional teams use a series of interaction matrices in order to transform the customer needs into product specifications (Fig. 18.30). The first matrix is called 'house of quality'. It relates data generated from market research on customer needs and wants to propose performance characteristics of the product (engineering design inputs). The second QFD matrix relates potential product features to the delivery of performance characteristics. The third and fourth matrices bring process characteristics and production requirements into the engineering and marketing relationships.

SOLVED QUESTIONS

Q. 19.1: *(a) State the goal of SQC.*

(b) What is random sampling.

(c) State one situation where sampling is essential.

*(**Note :** Answers must be brief and touch only the core issues)*

Ans. : (*a*) The ultimate objective of statistical quality control is not to find out if units are good or bad, but to avoid the production of poor quality items in the first place. It is always more economic to produce products that conform, rather than having to repair products later that do not conform. In addition to measurable costs, there is the intangible customer damage.

(*b*) A random sample is one where each unit in the lot has an equal chance of being selected. It is because of this randomness that the sample is considered representative of the lot. In random sampling, either attributes or variables can be measured and compared to standards.

(*c*) Situations where the *destructive testing* is involved call essentially for sampling.

Q. 19.2: *Give a summary of some common types of control charts used in SPC works.*

Ans. : Some common types of control charts used in *SQC* works are summarized below:

Variable charts ($\bar{X}$, R, X)

Attribute charts (p, c)

Charts	*Measure recorded*	*Explanation*
$\bar{X}$	Averages of small samples of measurements	To pick out changes in process settings; very common
R	Standard deviation (or range) of small samples of measurements	In combination with $\bar{X}$ to detect sudden changes in process variation
X	Measurements of single items	Only one observation is practicable; more difficult to interpret than $\bar{X}$
p	Proportion of defective items	Decisions are whether to accept or reject
c	Number of defects	Samples are of same size; identifies different types of defect when decision is whether to accept or reject

---

Q. 19.3: *Draw the control chart decision tree.*

Ans. : Knowing the purpose of control charts, the decision tree is depicted in Fig. 19.1. It makes the selection of control charts easier. First, the type of data to be collected is decided. Data are either variable (measurable quality characteristics) or attribute (non-measurable but countable quality characteristics). Examples of variable data are values read from a micrometer. A Go-gauge and Not-go gauge, however, gives attributes data, since it determines if a diameter is satisfactory or non-satisfactory, without actually measuring it. If the decision is to collect variable data, two control charts are always required, one to monitor "the process average" and another one to monitor "changes in the dispersion of the process." The control chart used to monitor the process average is normally the $\bar{X}$ chart. The chart to monitor changes in dispersion, however, depends on the sample size.

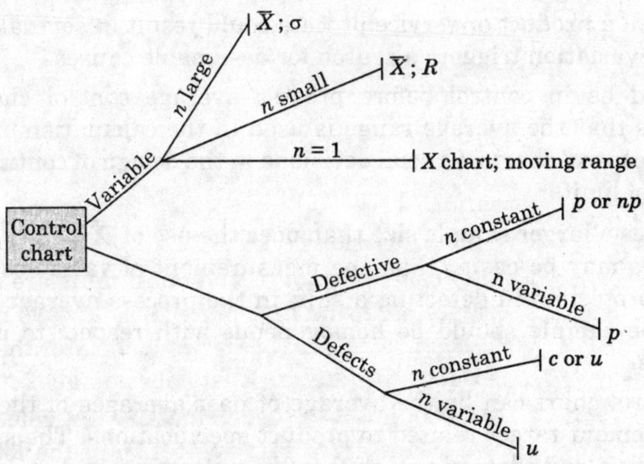

FIGURE 19.1 Control chart decision tree.

Q. 19.4: *You have conducted a two-day short cause and SQC methods–SPC and SAS. You wish to give hand-out at the end of the course. Prepare a such a brief hand out mentioning only the core points*

Ans. : The SQC techniques are mainly used in manufacturing and services.

- In manufacturing, statistical quality control is the sampling and analysis of units of determine if these are in accordance with specifications. In services, statistical quality control is often carried out to determine customer satisfaction.
- The ultimate objective of statistical quality control is not to find out if situations or units are bad, but to avoid poor quality in the first place. It is more economic to operate in a quality mode than to have to repair damage later.
- There are statistical quality control measures for attributes, whether a product works or not, or for variables, to see whether a product is within a specified range.

Two basic SQC techniques are:

- SPC (Statistical Process Control)
- SAS (Scientific Acceptance Sampling)

Other techniques such as reliability, and C & E diagram, etc. are called allied techniques or quality management techniques.

SPC–core points

- A key to meeting design specifications in a product or service is to reduce output variability. When a process is in a state of statistical control, outputs subject to common causes of variation follow a staqble probability distribution. When assignable causes of variation are present, the process is out of statistical control. Statistical process control (SPC) methods are used to detect the presence of assignable causes of variation.
- Inspection stations may be located at three points in the process: where incoming materials are received, at selected points in the process, and at the end of the process. Inspection identifies whether processes need corrective action.
- Statisical process control charts are useful for measuring the current quality generated by the process and for detecting whether the process has changed to the detriment of quality. Thus *R*-charts are used to monitor process variability, $\bar{X}$ charts and *p* charts identify abnormal variations in the process average, and c-charts are used for controlling

the number of defects when a product or service process could result in several defects. The presence of abnormal variation triggers a search for assignable causes.

- Process variability should be in control before process average control charts are constructed. The reason is that the average range is used in the calculation of control limits for process average control charts. Crucial decisions in the design of control charts are sample size and control limits.
- The use of p-charts requires a larger sample size than does the use of $\bar{X}$-charts, but the measurement of attributes may be easier than the measurement of variables. Larger samples provide greater protection in detecting a shift in the process average than do smaller samples. Also, the sample should be homogeneous with respect to potential causes of quality problems.
- The central line of a control chart can be the average of past averages of the quality measurement or a management target related to product specifications. The spread in control limits affects the chances of detecting a shift in the process average or range, as well as the chances of searching for assignable causes when none exist.
- A process can be in statistical control but still not be capable of producing all of its output within design specifications. The process capability ratio and the process capability index are quantitative measures used to assess the capability of a process.

SAS-core points

- Acceptance sampling is concerned with the decision to accept or reject a batch (or lot) of goods. The design of the acceptance sampling process includes decisions about sampling versus complete inspection, attribute versus variable measures, AQL, α, LTPD, β, sample size, and the acceptable number of defective items in the sample.
- Management can select the best plan (choosing sample size n and acceptance number c) by using an operating characteristic (OC) curve.
- Attribute sampling can be done with single-sampling double-sampling, or sequential-sampling plans. When the lot proportion defective is either very low or very high, the last two have an advantage over single-sampling plans because the average number of items (ANI) needed to make a decision is smaller.
- When less than 100 percent of the lot is inspected, the sample may not be an accurate representation of the lot. There are risks of accepting poor quality materials or rejecting good quality materials. The OC curves provide a graphic display of the performance of a sampling plan. They show how the probability of accepting a lot decreases with an increasing proportion defective in the lot.
- When rectified inspection is used to replace defective items with good items, the material leaving the inspection area (outgoing) will have a very high quality level. The average outgoing quality will depend on the original quality of the lot and the sampling plan used to identify and correct defects. Sampling plan parameters may be adjusted to provide an acceptable average outgoing quality limit.
- Computers are used to monitor vast amounts of quality performance data and to develop sampling plans that may cover thousands of parts, products, and services.

CHAPTER

20

ISO 9000 Standards

20.1 EMERGENCE OF QUALITY STANDARDS

International trade has implications for quality standards. Standards, as Crosby argued, are communications. They pass between customers and suppliers to convey information about the clients' needs summarised in conventional form. The European Union made harmonisation of standards as one of the main planks of its construction of the single market.

20.1.1 Product Standards

Product standards have existed ever since the creation of assay offices to ensure that gold was not being alloyed with other metals by unscrupulous traders. Gradually, the British Standards Institute (BSI) along with parallel organizations, such as Deutsche Industrienormen (DIN) and the American National Standards Institute (ANSI), have developed product standards covering items from reinforced concrete and rolled steel sections to cables and thread. Table 20.1 gives a small extract from one of the early British Standard specifications, for steel beams in its many tables and multiple editions, BS 4 gets out the dimensions of standard steel sections that could be used by engineers to select and specify beams to use in their designs. Standardization in specification and manufacture reduced design time for engineers, stimulated a competitive market and enabled the more efficient producers to gain economies of scale.

Industry standards and norms have developed along other paths. These include: industry agreements, such as the emerging specifications for digital television; the success of a leading design or brand, such as the personal computer: or almost by chance, as evidenced by the dimensions of wallpaper, cloth, railway track and vinyl records. Nowadays, many product standards are backed by statute, often at the international level. There are many international regulations covering product specifications from the strength of vehicle seat belts to the noise emitted by domestic lawn mowers.

The BSI kitemark, Indian **ISI** mark and other quality labels are recognized as marks of product quality and safety. Not only must the product regularly pass tests within the standards, but also the supplier must undergo assessment of the process underpinning consistent quality. Despite these advantages, product standards have several drawbacks:

TABLE 20.1 EXTRACT FROM I-BEAMS, BS 4 (1932)

Depth × breadth (in)	*Weight per foot (lb)*	*Area (in²)*	*Modulus (in⁴)*
3 × 3	8.5	2.52	3.81
$4 \times 1\frac{3}{4}$	5	1.47	3.66
4 × 3	10	2.94	7.79
5 × 3	11	3.26	13.68

- *Limited scope.* The time taken to agree standards, and the difficulty of reaching agreement, means that they relate to only to a limited range of the products in general circulation.
- *Limited applicability to assemblies.* Product standards often apply only to components, or a few features, of assemblies. For instance, standards in domestic equipment usually refer to their electrical safety and not to their performance.
- *Applied only to some properties of a product.* BS 476, for example, specifies testing methods for fire resistance of building materials. The attachment of this label to a batch of, say, decorative panels will say nothing about their acoustic or other properties.
- *Complexity.* The multiplicity of standards almost takes away the point of having them. Lacking common standards, many companies and purchasing authorities have felt obliged to issue their own specifications. Government purchasing, especially of military equipment, became subject to standards and conventions such as the 05 standards of the Ministry of Defence and NATO's Allied Quality Assurance Publication.

Since many items of military hardware were very complex and had to have quality built into every component, defence procurement authorities required suppliers to have their manufacturing processes open to inspection. Indeed, when small companies manufactured supplies for the MoD, an external inspector had to observe every stage. From the frustration, confusion and costs of this system, and the burgeoning number of standards in the civil sector, grew a new approach, concentrating on the processes themselves.

20.1.2 Process Standards

The first major process standard, BS 5750 was published in the United Kingdom in 1979. It responded to the need to externally validate those many situations where product certification was not practicable. A national standard usable by organizations of all sizes, it was built around basic quality disciplines. It ensured that procedures could consistently meet the specifications set out by the company. Quality in every process had to be evidenced with relevant documentation. Compliance with the provisions of the standard, validated by an inspection organised by the British Standards Institute (BSI), led to certification and an inclusion in the *QA Register*. Unannounced checks were made up to four times a year.

Recognising the benefits of BS 5750, the **International Organization for Standardization (ISO)** *not* IOS (as its pro-nounciation sounds much like chaos), Geneva, Switzerland (logo juxtaposed), a worldwide federation of national standards bodies having 140 members at present, one in each country, adopted it as the core of the first version of ISO 9000 in 1987. Its formal title BS EN ISO 9000 identifies it as the national, European and international quality process standard.

20.2 ISO 9000

ISO 9000 series of standard represents an international consensus on good management practices with the aim of ensuring that the organization can time and time again deliver the product or services that meet the client's quality requirements. The good practices have distilled into a set of standardized requirements for a quality management system, regardless of what an organization does, its size, or whether it is the private, or public sector.

The series first adopted in 1987, defines internationally accepted standards for business quality. They provide a framework that governs the activities and procedures for managing quality that customers expect of a supplier to demonstrate the effective control of its processes. Most countries have their own equivalent, mostly identical, standards, but accept ISO 9000 as the internationally recognized and accepted certification.

The ISO 9000 quality standards have now been adopted by many organizations worldwide. A company registering for ISO 9000 certification is required to submit its quality standards and procedures to external inspection. If it receives a certificate, it will be subjected to continuing audit. The aim of an ISO 9000 certificate is to provide an **assurance** to customers (and suppliers) of the organization that its products are made, or its services are delivered, in a way that meets ISO's **standards** for quality. But, as the cartoon in Fig. 20.1 is intended to highlight, certification is not a cosmetic exercise.

FIGURE 20.1 ISO 9000 Certification—What it is not!

It should be noted that

(*i*) these standards are not about the quality of the product in any absolute sense, but about the capability of use organizations to meet its ours claim.

(*ii*) ISO 9000 does not guarantee quality. Nor ISO certificated company can be taken for granted to meet product specification.

20.3 QUALITY SYSTEM

Quality systems include all activities that contribute to quality directly or indirectly. Product quality depends upon many variables , such as the quality of the components or materials used: type of equipment for fabrication and design standard, testing, maintenance procedures, training and experience of the supervisory staff, the level of workman ship, quality awareness of the workers; and sometimes humidity, level of dust particles in the area whose the product is produced. In case of manufacture of optical fibre, the environmental conditions are dominant of quality of the product.

20.4 QUALITY MANAGEMENT SYSTEM (QMS)

A Quality Management system (QMS) refers to the organized structure of responsibilities, activities, resources and events that together provide procedures and methodology of implementation of ensure the capability of an organization to meet its quality requirements and continually improve its performance.

To achieve this, a QMS needs to be capable of

1. Demonstrating continuous improvement
2. Preventing non-conformance.
3. Assisting self-evaluation

This QMS will consist of rules, procedures and instructions prepared in accordance with agreed standards in quality standards in micro, small or medium (MSME) organisation this may not be written down, but in most organizations, it involves written down procedures, instructions and other documents. This are stated in the **Quality Manual** as well as the associated are processes, procedures and work instructions. This documents hierarchy is shown in Fig. 20.2.

Benefits resulting from well-documented system, applicable to any type of organizations, are that:

- everyone involved understands his/her roles
- responsibilities of all activities are clear and identified
- there is a focus on critical activities, which are no forgotten or ignored
- when quality problems do occur there is a feedback system that enables identification of the cause.
- corrective and preventative processes are already established to ensure that necessary and permanent improvements can be made.

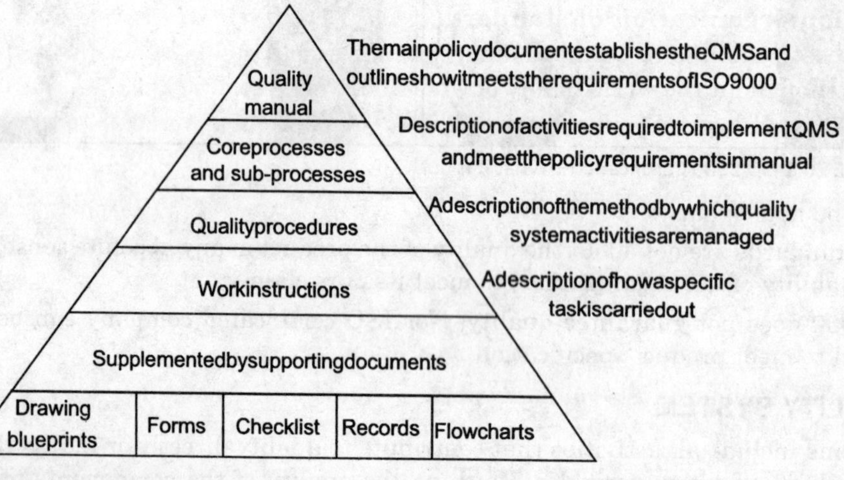

FIGURE 20.2 structure of QMS

20.4.1 Implementing QMS

Delivering products which meet the desired level to quality will only occur if all the factors that have an impact on quality are managed effectively.

A QMS should pervade the whole organizations recognising the quality impact of all area of organisation. These are a number of ways of implementing QMS. For example ISO 9001-2015 recommends the design should be based on **eight** principles mentioned in Sec. 20.6.

20.5 QUALITY STANDARDS

Quality Management systems involve the use of quality standards against which actual performance is monitored. These may be

1. **Internal standards** set by operations management, for their our particular operation.

These are many smaller self-assessment models for business/organization improvement in Europe, one of the most popular is European quality Foundation (EQF) model. This provides a structured methodology for organizations of measure their own performance in the areas that are critical to their business.

The model provides a basis for measurement of **enables** (leadership, policies, strategies, processes and resources) and **"results"** in relation to customers, employees and society and performance indicators.

Criticism of this and other similar schemes include the expenses (in terms of time) and the fact that scoring out of 1000 lakhs of rupees for, is largely subjective.

However this may be noted that the cost of conformance is the cost of operating a QMS. The more rigorous the QMS, the lower the cost of non-conformance will be.

2. **External standards** set for a particular industry or all industries and organizations in general, depending on the nature of quality of item. External standard for quality management system is ISO 9000 (Latest edition.)

20.6 ISO 9000 FAMILY OF STANDARDS

ISO 9000 is a family of standards and guidelines for quality management systems developed by the **internation organization of standardization**. They provide organizations with a model based on best practices in quality management systems and have been implemented by organizations thoughout the world, many of whom have been certified as conforming to the standard. ISO 9000 standards set out eight principles of quality management for organizations to apply for ISO certification.

1. Customer focus
2. Leader
3. Involvement of people
4. Process approach
5. A system approach to management
6. Continuous improvement
7. A factual approach to decision making
8. Mutually beneficial supplier (or external provider) relationship.

External Quality standards are voluntary, but if adopted, the level of the quality with in the industry will rise.

Many countries particularly in Europe had multiple external quality standards. The British quality standard BS 5750 particularly influenced the development of quality standards by the International Organization for Standardization (ISO) Fig. 20.3, in Switzerland, which issued ISO 9000 series of standards. These were revised time to time and currently, as per latest revision in 2015, four quality standards in the ISO family are:

1. **ISO 9000:** 2015
2. **ISO 9001:** This specifies the requirements management system within an organizations if it is to meet the can apply to obtain a certificate for meeting the ISO 9001 : 2015 quality standards.
3. **ISO 9002 :** 2018
4. **ISO 9004 :** 2018(E)

Other standards in the ISO 9000 range cover specific topics. For example, ISO 9006 deals with quality management in project management; ISO 9011 sets out guidelines on the internal and external audits of quality management.

FIGURE 20.3

In member countries of ISO, the ISO 9000 standards are being reproduced as **replica** of these standards and given a standar number as per their system. For example in India earlier, IS 14000 was an eaxct replica of ISO 9000 and so on.

But as per current practice, India has adopted ISO 9000 standars in their original from but renamed them as IS/ISO 9000 and so on. The earlier IS 14000 a replica of ISO 9000 is abolished.

20.6.1 Main Features of the ISO 9000 Family Standards

1. The ISO 9000 family standards constitute a quality management system and form an effective quality management tool.
2. It is a top-down management system that defines responsibility and activities the organization.
3. WHAT is required, but how a decision taken by organizations. It respects autonomy of the organizations and is tool that allow the organizations to individual expression.

20.7 QMS AS PER ISO 9000 STANDARDS

Figure 20.4 represents the QMS approach as per ISO 9000 standards. It is a sets out eight principles of quality management that organisation should apply. These principles are seen to be fully compatible with the objectives and approach deployed in six-sigma process.

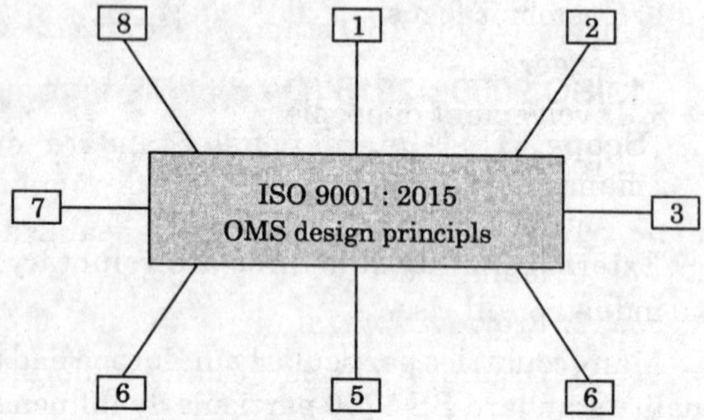

FIGURE 20.4

1. **Customer focus.** There must be a customer focus. This means obtaining measurements of customer requirements, not just measurements of customer satisfaction. Measurements of customer requirements can be obtained by proactive methods (such as market research) or reactive methods (such as finding data from customer returns or complaints)
2. **Leadership.** Management must take an active role in implementing and sustaining quality improvement.
3. **Involvement approach.** Management must ensure that all employees are aware of how their activities contribute towards the achievement of quality objectives.
4. **Process approach.** There should be a process-based approach to quality management. In a process-based approach, the business is seen as a series of individual processes, with outputs from one process sometimes beings the input to and linkages between the different processes.
5. **System approach.** To management groups of related process, system should be managed in an integrated quality.
6. **Continuous improvement** is should be a permanent objective of the organization.
7. **Factual approach to decision making.** Decisions affecting qualify should be based on data about work processes that has been gathered and analysed.
8. **Mutually beneficial supplier relationships.** Relationships with suppliers should be based on open-ness and mutual trust, with a sharing of information about quality.

Most recently concern has moved form goods to procedures. The capability of organizations to produce consistent quality is recognized, rather then the quality of the output itself. Again this is not new, supply partnerships frequently depend upon the customer validating the suppliers capability (Vendors registration by some big companies, for example), but the practice has developed to the point that these standards are now required.

It should be noted that these standards are not about the quality of product in any absolute sense, but about the capability of the organization to meet its our claims.

The international organization for standardization's quality standards require conformity of documented practices. Certification requires that the company produces a comprehensive documentation relating to areas of activity that have a bearing on quality. The company must then demonstrate conformity to this documentation. In other words, it must have appropriate quality procedures which it follows. Continued certification requires periodic third party inspection to ensure that the procedures are still current and still being applied. The ISO 9000 portfolio of standards include guidance on what standards are appropriate for activity in question and what documentation should be produced.

ISO 9000 does not guarantee quality

However it may be noted that ISO certified company cannot be taken for granted to meet product specifications.

20.8 CURRENT ISO STANDARDS FOR QUALITY MANAGEMENT

Currently, four ISO standards for quality management are being followed in worldwide:

1. ISO 9000 : 2015 (Quality Management Systems-Fundamentals and Vocabulary)

Scope. This International Standard describes the fundamental concepts and principle management which are universally applicable to the following:

1. Organizations seeking sustained success through the implementation of quality management system,
2. Providers of training, assessment or advice in quality management.
3. Organizations performing conformity assessments against ISO 9001.

2. ISO 9001 : 2015 (Quality Management Systems Requirements)

Scope. This international standard specifies requirements for a quality management system when an organization.

1. needs to demonstrate its ability to consistently provide products and services that meet customer and applicable statutory and regulating requirements, and
2. aims to enhance customer satisfaction through the effective application of the system, including processes for improvement of the systems and the assurance of conformity to customer and applicable statutory and regulatory requirements.
3. It recommends PDCA (or PDSA) cycle can be applied to all processess and to the quality management system as a whole.
4. Some main changes from its earlier edition of 2008 are follows:

ISO 9001 : 2008	ISO 9001 : 2015
(*a*) Document, quality manual document procedure	Document information
(*b*) Work environment	Environment for the operations of process
(*c*) Supplier	External provider

5. ISO certificate, the one shown in Fig. 20.5 for quality management to organizations is provided against this standard only (Fig. 20.5) and this certificate is valid for a period of 3 years only and after that it is to be renewed for an additional fee.

Though the company is certified as ISO 9001 yet it is generally known as **ISO 9000 certified** company.

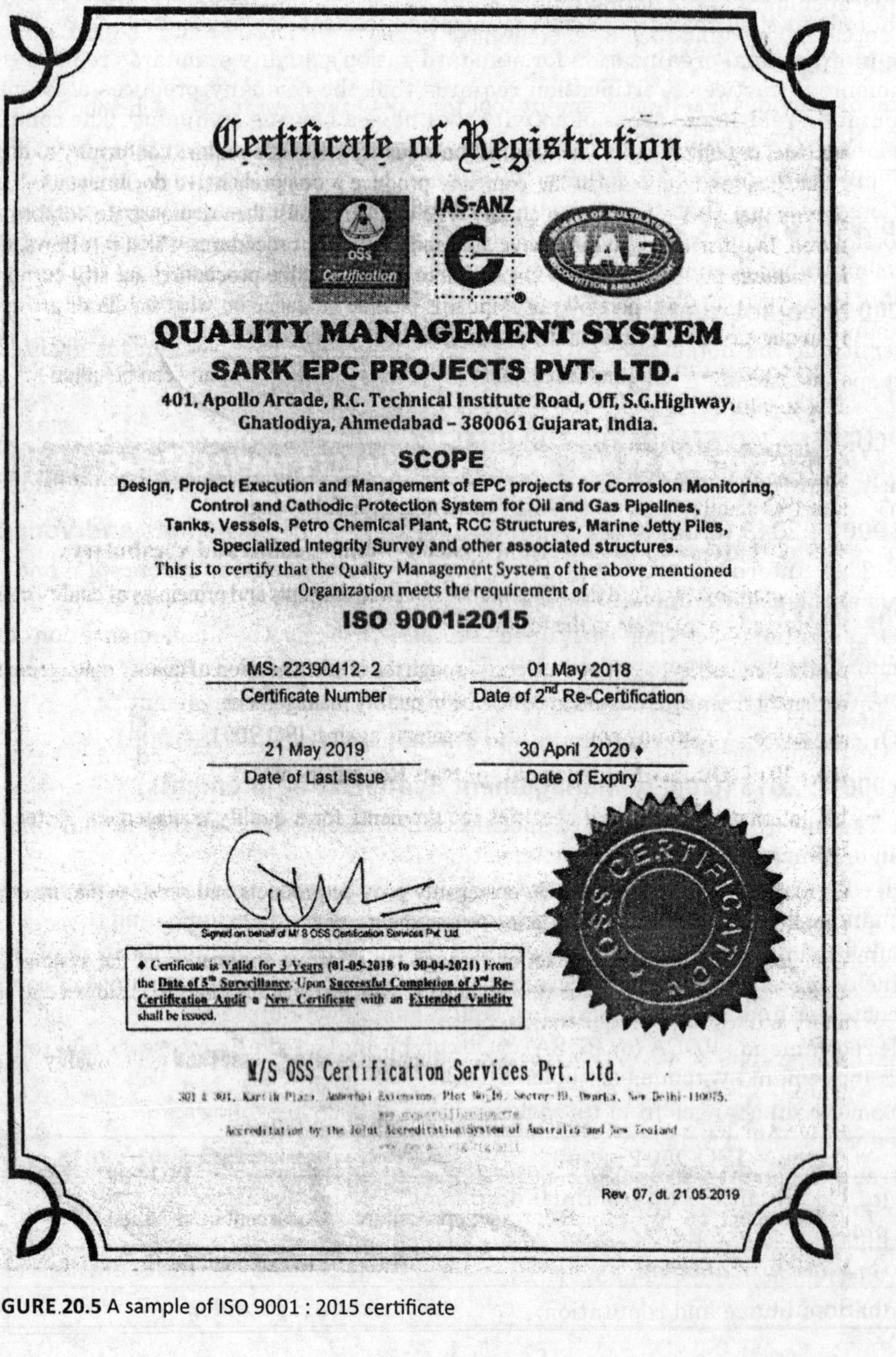
Certificate of Registration

QUALITY MANAGEMENT SYSTEM

SARK EPC PROJECTS PVT. LTD.

401, Apollo Arcade, R.C. Technical Institute Road, Off, S.G.Highway, Ghatlodiya, Ahmedabad – 380061 Gujarat, India.

SCOPE

Design, Project Execution and Management of EPC projects for Corrosion Monitoring, Control and Cathodic Protection System for Oil and Gas Pipelines, Tanks, Vessels, Petro Chemical Plant, RCC Structures, Marine Jetty Piles, Specialized Integrity Survey and other associated structures.

This is to certify that the Quality Management System of the above mentioned Organization meets the requirement of

ISO 9001:2015

MS: 22390412- 2	01 May 2018
Certificate Number	Date of 2nd Re-Certification
21 May 2019	30 April 2020 ♦
Date of Last Issue	Date of Expiry

Signed on behalf of M/S OSS Certification Services Pvt. Ltd.

♦ Certificate is Valid for 3 Years (01-05-2018 to 30-04-2021) From the Date of 5th Surveillance. Upon Successful Completion of 3rd Re-Certification Audit a New Certificate with an Extended Validity shall be issued.

M/S OSS Certification Services Pvt. Ltd.

Accreditation by the Joint Accreditation System of Australia and New Zealand

Rev. 07, dt. 21.05.2019

FIGURE 20.5 A sample of ISO 9001 : 2015 certificate

3. ISO 9002 : 2018

It is an implementational standard of ISO 9001 : 2015.

4. ISO 9004 : 2018 [E]

Quality management—Quality of an organization—Guidance to achieve sustained success.

Scope. This document gives guidelines for enhancing an organizations ability to achieve sustained success. This guidance is consistent with the quality management principles given in ISO 9000 : 2015.

This document provides a self-assessment tool to review the extent to which the organization has adopted the concepts in this document.

This document is applicable to any organization, regardless of its size and activity.

20.8.1 Indian Standards For Quality Management

In India earlier we had IS 14000 corresponding to ISO 9000. This IS 14000 was an exact replica of ISO 9000. This practice of adopting exact ISO standard and giving a different IS number has been abandoned now and at present we in India have four quality management standards as follows:

IS/ISO 9000 : 2015
IS/ISO 9001 : 2015
IS/ISO 9002 : 2018
IS/ISO 9004 : 2018 (E)

The above removes the confusion in numbers which existed earlier.

20.9 QUALITY CERTIFICATION

If an organization's QMS is to provide a proper level of assurance to existing and potential customers, it is necessary for the organization to achieve **quality certification**. This is an externally provided acknowledgement that the QMS is adequate in its provisions and its operation. Certification can only be provided by **accredited certifying bodies**.

At first, some companies found the registration effort very onerous. Yet, certification spread and many companies across the globe are now ISO certified as the registration as a condition of joining lists of approved suppliers. International sourcing was facilitated by this common approach. By 1998, 127,000 organizations had joined, with 54,000 in the United Kingdom and many companies across the globe are now have the ISO certification and , many recognize the range of benefits listed Table 20.2.

TABLE 20.2 BENEFITS OF QUALITY MANAGEMENT REGISTRATION

Internal:
Clearly defined responsibilities.
Procedures form a point of reference for all staff.
Reduced costs of failure.
Strengthened morale and motivation.
External:
Enhanced marketability to customers buying only from registered suppliers.
Greater customer confidence.
Enhanced image and reputation.

20.9.1 ISO Certified/Registered or ISO Compliant?

When a company claims that they are **ISO 9000 certified** or **registered**, they mean that **an independent registrar** has audited their processes and certified that they meet the ISO requirements. It means that a **registrar has given a written assurance** that ISO's quality management system standard has been met.

When an organization says that they are **ISO 9000 compliant**, they mean that they have **met ISO's quality system requirements**, but have **not been formally certified** by an independent registrar. In effect, they are **self-certified**. Of course, an official certificate does tend to carry more weight in the market place.

Organizations are granted certified or **compliant** status on the basis that their processes rather than their products and services meet ISO 9000 requirements. The ISO 9000 standards are process standards, not **product standards.** The logic is that high quality processes ensure high quality output.

20.10 CERTIFYING BODY (CB) AND ITS ROLE

Once the decision is made to go in for ISO 9000 certification, (with prerequisite conditions fully met with–updation of organization's quality manual and procedures and ensuring the compliance of the same); the next step is to choose a Certifying Body (CB). The role of the CB is to conduct an in-depth assessment of the quality system of the organization in order to determine whether it meets the standards set out in ISO 9000. The CB requires a fee, which is negotiated according to the size of the organization and the complexity of the quality system. The quality manual and procedures must be submitted, but otherwise documentation is kept very simple. The CB then:

- Reviews documentation.
- Vists the premises to interview quality staff and other employees and to generally see the total quality system in practice.
- Produces a report which either conforms that the standard has been met or indicates the changes needed in the system to meet the standard.

A very important and careful step is to choose an appropriate CB. Since most of the companies are certified to ISO 9001, for quality management system-defined as an assembly of components, such as the management responsibility, process and resources and being in line with the EFQM Excellent Model in terms of the *direction-process-people-performance* a number of documents are available from ISO, IAF, IQNet, BIS, and BSI Web sites covering issues related to certification to ISO 9001: 2015.

- ISO (International Organization of Standardization) is the body issuing the standard. They do not perform audits or accredit certification bodies.
- IAF (International Accreditation Forum) is an association of national accreditation bodies and sets policies for mutual recognition of certificates by member bodies. If your certification body is accredited by a member of IAF, the CBs certificates will be recognized everywhere else in the world.
- IQNet is an association of Certification Bodies but does not include all CBs.

Most industralized nations will maintain at least one accredited CB entitled to award certification to applicant company. Less developed countries may elect not to maintain their own national inspectorate but permit other countries' approved inspectorate, *e.g.* those of countries they export to assess their local manufacturers. Any country wishing to gain recognition of its own national inspectorate has to seek the approval of an accredition board of representatives from countries having approved inspection organizations or has to be a member of IAF. For example:

NABCB (National Accredition Board for certification Bodies) in India is a constituent of Quality Council of India (QCI). It is an autonomous body promoted jointly by Indian Industry and Govt. of India. NABCB offers accredition of *CB*s as per International Standards and Guidelines for Quality Management System (QMS) and Environment Management System (EMS).

NACCB (National Accredition Council for certification Bodies) formed in 1984, is the British Authority for accredition of third-party registrars of quality systems.

RAB (Registrar Accredition Board) is a subsidiary of ASQC. RAB is a US organizations whose dual mission is to recognize the competence and reliability of registrars of quality system and to achieve international recognition of registrations issued by RAB-accredited registrars. The RAB also certifies quality system auditors.

RvA. Dutch council for Accredition-A body equivalent to NACCB, NABCB etc.

In Britain, it is reported there are now well over 15 organizations including LRQA, NQA, BSI, DNV, BM, TRADA etc. recognized by their NACCB. LRQA (Lloyd's Register for Quality Assurance) was accredited by NACCB in 1986. In the same year it was also accredited for quality management system certification by the Dutch by the Council for Accredition RvA.

In India, many Indian and foreign CB are accredited. Indian Register of Quality System (IRQS) is accredited by RvA. Bureau of Indian Standards (BIS) quality management system certification activity has been accredited by Raad Voor Accredited (RvA) of Netherlands to carry out ISO 9001:2015 certification on 23 business sectors.

It is not necessary that one CB is accredited for certification with only one member of IAF. For example IRQS is accredited to NABCB and also RvA. Similarly DNV is accredited to NABCB and also RvA etc. It is usual for CB to indicate the agency to which they are accredited to while issuing the certificate. Generally the CB prefers the accredition organization of the country (if it happens to be accredited for certification in that country). For example, if DNV mentions NABCB while working for any company in India.

Figure 20.6 shows the insignia of CB and their accrediting agencies mentioned in the letter heads of some companies.

The certificate once issued is valid for 3 years only. With the provision of annual surveillance. However it can be withdrawn after one year if on surveillance, the things are not OK. After 3 years reassessment is done for revalidation of certificate. Fig. 20.5 shows a typical ISO certificate for the information only. It is mandatory for CB to state itself on the certificate the name of the company, the services it is providing, date of registration and validity date of the issued certificate.

FIGURE 20.6 Insignia of CBS and their Accreditation Organization.

20.11 THE THREE PILLARS OF ISO 9000

ISO 9000 Certification is only of any value in markets where it provides the confidence needed for free trade. ISO 9000 as a symbol has become synonymous with certification, quality management systems, documentation and internal audits to such an extent that if one were to dispense with ISO 9000 certification, one also ceases to maintain a quality management system, ceases to conduct audits and ceases to use documentation. We have to divorce certification from systems and systems from standards and correct a few misconceptions.

ISO 9000 Certification is ***optional*** and whether or not any organization is ISO 9000 certificated, it does not by itself affect the performance of an organization. It is a flag of confidence that is visible to others with whom you trade. Certification is inextricably linked to the standard.

ISO 9000 is a series of standards and their use is ***optional.*** They do not affect the performance of an organization although their use can assist organizations improve performance. The standards can be used without being linked with certification.

All organizations have a quality management system but its formalization is optional. The system enables the organizations to achieve its objectives and therefore exists independently of whether or not ISO 9000 is used and whether not ISO 9000 Certification is obtained.

These three pillars are illustrated in Fig. 20.7 showing that an organization can sustain and improve its performance without using ISO 9000 as a standard and without using ISO 9000 Certification. Remove the two outer pillars and the organization remains stable! The foundation upon which the three pillars stand is the body of knowledge that represents the field of quality management. Most of this knowledge is channelled through the management system, somewhat less is channelled through the standard (ISO 9000) and a particular branch of the body of knowledge is channelled through certification. An organization could absorb and apply all relevant knowledge and therefore obtain no additional support from ISO 9000 standards or ISO 9000 certification. Another organization may absorb and apply some knowledge directly from the foundation but require the support of the ISO 9000 standards to help understanding and application. A third organization may absorb and apply little knowledge directly from the foundation and require both the support of the ISO 9000 standards and ISO 9000 certification to maintain a stable and robust management system.

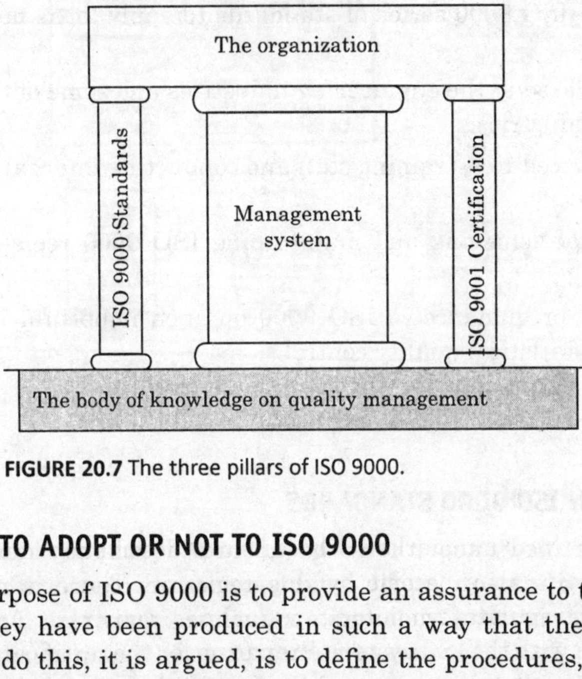

FIGURE 20.7 The three pillars of ISO 9000.

20.12 TO ADOPT OR NOT TO ISO 9000

The purpose of ISO 9000 is to provide an assurance to the purchasers of products or services that they have been produced in such a way that they meet their requirements. The best way to do this, it is argued, is to define the procedures, standards, and characteristics of the management control system which governs the operation. Such a system will then help to ensure that quality is 'built into' the operation's transformation processes. This is why ISO 9000 is seen as providing benefits both to the organizations adopting it (because it gives them detailed guidance on how to design their control procedures) but most especially to customers (who have the assurance of knowing that the products and services they purchase are produced by an operation working to a defined standard). However, the adoption of ISO 9000 is not seen as beneficial by all authorities, and has been subject to some criticism. The following are just some of the advantages and disadvantages associated with ISO 9000.

Advantages

- Many operations do find that it provides a useful discipline to stick to "sensible' procedures.
- Many operations have benefited in terms of error reduction, reduced customer complaints and reduced costs of quality.
- The ISO 9000 audit (when an organization is inspected to see if it warrants the award of the ISO, or local country, accreditation) is generally accepted and takes the place of other audits such as customer audits.
- Adopting ISO 9000 procedures can identify existing procedures which are not necessary and can be eliminated.
- Gaining the certificate demonstrates to actual and potential customers that the company takes quality seriously; it therefore has a marketing benefit.

Disadvantages

- The emphasis on standards and procedures encourages 'management by manual' and over-systematized decision making.
- Choosing which of the various ISO 9000 series of standards to apply for is not always easy.
- The standards are too much geared to the engineering industries and some of the terms used are unfamiliar in other industries.
- The whole process of writing procedures, training staff and conducting internal audits is expensive and time consuming.
- Similarly, the time and cost of achieving and maintaining ISO 9000 registration is excessive.
- There is little encouragement or guidance in ISO 9000 on such important issues as continuous improvement and statistical quality control.
- The ISO procedures are document conscious. Importance of time element in results is not emphasized.

20.11 AUTHOR'S OBSERVATIONS ON ISO 9000 STANDARDS

As mentioned earlier, to become certified under the ISO standard, a company must select a **registrar** and prepare for a **certification audit** by this registrar. There is no single independent authority that licenses, regulates, monitors, or qualifies registrars. As we will discuss later, this is a serious problem with the ISO system. Preparing for the certification audit involves many activities, including (usually) an initial or phase I audit that checks the present quality management system against the standard. This is usually followed by establishing teams to ensure that all components of the key clause are developed and implemented, training of personnel, developing applicable documentation, and developing and installing all new components of the quality system that may be required. Then the certification audit takes place. If the company is certified, then periodic **surveillance audits** by the registrar continue, usually on an annual (or perhaps six-month) schedule.

Many organizations have required their suppliers to become certified under ISO 9000, or one of the standards that are more industry-specific. Examples of these industry-specific quality system standards are AS 9100 for the aerospace industry; ISO/TS 16949 and QS 9000 for the automotive industry; and TL 9000 for the telecommunications industry. Many components of these standards are very similar to those of ISO 9000.

Much of the focus of ISO 9000 (and of the industry-specific standards) is on formal documentation of the quality system; that is, on **quality assurance** activities. Organizations usually must make extensive efforts to bring their documentation into line with the requirements of the standards; this is the Achilles' heel of ISO 9000 and other related or derivative standards. There is far too much effort devoted to documentation, paperwork, and bookkeeping and not nearly enough to actually reducing variability and improving processes and products. Furthermore, many of the third-party registrars, auditors, and consultants that work in this area are not sufficiently educated or experienced enough in the **technical** tools required for **quality improvement** or how these tools should be deployed. They are all too often unaware of what constitutes modern engineering and statistical practice, and usually are familiar with only the most elementary techniques. Therefore, they concentrate largely on the documentation, record keeping, and paperwork aspects of certification.

There is also evidence that ISO certification or certification under one of the other industry-specific standards does little to prevent poor quality products from being designed, manufactured, and delivered to the customer. ***For example, in 1999-2000, there were numerous incidents of rollover accidents involving Ford Explorer vehicles equipped with Bridgestone/Firestone tyres. There were nearly 300 deaths in the United States alone attributed to these accidents, which led to a recall by Bridgestone/Firestone of approximately 20.5 million tyres. Apparently, many of the tyres involved in these incidents were manufactured at the Bridgestone/Firestone plant in Decatur, Illinois. In an article on this story in Time magazine (September 18, 2000), there was a photograph (p. 38) of the sign at the entrance of the Decatur plant which stated that the plant was "QS 9000 Certified" and "ISO 14001 Certified" (ISO 14001 is an environmental standard).***

Although the assignable causes underlying these incidents have not been fully discovered, there are clear indications that despite quality systems certification, Bridgestone/Firestone experienced significant quality problems. ***ISO certification alone is no guarantee that good quality products are being designed, manufactured, and delivered to the customer. Relying on ISO certification is a strategic management mistake.***

It has been estimated that ISO certification activities are approximately a $50 billion annual business, worldwide. Much of this money flows to the registrars, auditors, and consultants. This amount does not include all of the internal costs incurred by organizations to achieve registration, such as the thousands of hours of engineering and management effort, travel, internal training, and internal auditing. It is not clear whether any significant fraction of this expenditure has made its way to the bottom line of the registered organizations. Furthermore, there is no assurance that certification has any real impact on quality (as in the Bridgestone/Firestone tyre incidents). Many quality engineering authorities believe that ISO certification is largely a waste of effort. Often, organizations would be far better off to "just say no to ISO" and spend a small fraction of that $50 billion on their quality systems and another larger fraction on meaningful variability reduction efforts, develop their own internal (or perhaps industry-based) quality standards, rigorously enforce them, and pocket the difference.

SOLVED QUESTIONS

Q. 20.1: *Select the technically correct option in the following:*

(*i*) QMS is best described as

(*a*) The strategy for delivering what the customers requires

(*b*) The planned quality checks in the next stage.

(*c*) ISO : 9001

(*ii*) Quality Assurance is

(*a*) External auditors visiting the organization.

(*b*) The activity of providing evidence that quality related activities are being performed effectively.

(*c*) Producing quality plan

(*iii*) What is the purpose of a Quality Plan?

(a) To show how quality is to be achieved on a project/product

(*b*) To show how quality is to be achieved in an organization

(*c*) To audit the quality control work

Ans. : (*i*) (*a*); (*ii*) (*b*); (*iii*) (*a*)

Q. 20.2: *Select the correct option and advise why other options the incorrects*

The ISO 9000 is :

(*a*) Product standard (*b*) Quality management standard

(*c*) Environmental standard (*d*) Seal of meeting specifications

Ans. : Correction option is (*b*).

Reason(s) for rejecting options (*a*), (*c*) and (*d*) are as follows :

Option (*a*) is incorrect as ISO 9000 is not a product standard. Option (*c*) is also incorrect as the environment standard is ISO 14000. As ISO does not guarantee adherence to specifications, hence option (*d*) is also incorrect.

Q. 20.3: *Answer the following questions briefly*

(a) What is the meaning of quality?

(b) What is ISO 9000?

(c) What is ISO certification? What is the time validity of this certificate?

(d) What is Indian standard equivalent to ISO 9001?

Ans. : (*a*) Quality. The quality of a product or service to reliably do what it's supposed to and to satisfy customer expectations.

(*b*) ISO 9000. A series of international quality management standards that set uniform guidelines for process to ensure that products conform to customer requirements.

(*c*) ISO certification indicates conformance with a rigorous set of international quality standards. Its validity is for 3 years.

(*d*) India has adopted the ISO 9001 with a name IS/ISO 9001.

Q. 20.4: *Answer the following questions briefly.*

(a) What does an ISO certificate mean?

(b) What four aspects of quality are particularly important in software?

(c) What are alpha testing and beta testing of a product?

(d) What is meant by control of documents information?

(e) What should be the qualities of quality criteria?

Ans. : (*a*) The aim of an ISO 9000 certificate is to provide on assurance to customers (and suppliers) of the organization that its products are made, or its services are delivered, in way that meets ISO's standard for quality.

(*b*) Functionality, reliability, usability; build quality.

(*c*) There are two types of product testing, namely alpha testing and beta testing

- *Alpha testing* is conducted in-house, in a laboratory setting or some part of the developing firm's regular operations.
- *Beta testing* takes place on the premises of the intended market users. It is quite common in the software market where beta versions of new software are provided to computer experts for testing.

(*d*) It is important to ensure that only the latest issue of quality related documents information as drawings and instructions is used. Such documents must be approved before use and marked as controlled copy etc.

(*e*) The quality criteria themselves have to have three qualities

- They must be specific
- They must be measurable
- They must be achievable.

Q. 20.5: *Give short answer for the following questions*

(a) What is the meaning of quality process?

(b) IS ISO 9000 certification a point scoring system? (Yes/No)

(c) What is the difference between ISO certificated and ISO compliant companies?

(d) State the difference between a quality process and a quality procedure.

Ans. : (*a*) A quality process is a statement of the specific way to carry out an activity or a process.

There are two types of quality process : *core business processes* and *supporting processes.*

Core business processes combine in a logical sequence that proceeds from a market opportunity through to the delivery of a satisfactory product or service. The process owner for the overall sequence of core business processes would normally be the CEO or equivalent.

Supporting processes supplement the core business processes by providing the necessary infrastructure. These processes will be owned by functional directors or managers.

Both core business processes and supporting processes must be fully documented possibly using diagrams in a hierarchy of detail.

(*b*) No.

(c) An ISO certified company has its procedures checked and verified by an independent auditor while the claim of an ISO compliant company that it meets the ISO requirements has not verified.

(*d*) A quality process is a set of inter-related interfacing activities which transform inputs into outputs while a quality procedure is a specified way to carry out an activity or a process.

Q. 20.6: *(a) Why does organisation should have ISO 9000 certificate? Would it be worth while to gain certification? Why should you implement quality standard?*

(b) (i) What are the potential benefits of training for quality?

(ii) What are the potential benefits of quality control?

Ans. : *(a)* This quality standard is largely aimed at manufacturing companies. It is useful to some companies because it demonstrates they are in control of their business, and have proved it to a certification body. ISO 9000 registration is a good way of measuring progress and monitoring maintenance of the standard. It reduces the need for customer supplier demonstration of quality assurance procedures by its introduction and ensures that the organization product is compatible with world quality procedures.

There are many different reasons for implementing the standard.

(i) Pressure from large customers

(ii) To maintain contracts with existing customers.

(iii) To use the constraints of the standard to prevent scrap

(iv) To reduce auditing of the quality system by customers.

(v) To make reference to the standard on company letterhead paper

(vi) To get the ISI symbol on the company's product.

(viii) To enforce discipline on employees

(b) (i) The potential benefits of training for quality include improved quality of output, improved productivity and greater job satisfaction and commitment on the part of the employees.

*(ii)*The benefits of quality control come from the savings in quality-related costs from improvements in customer relations and hopefully (because of the quality of the final product) increased sales revenue due to increased sales demand.

Q. 20.7: *(a) What do you understand by Quality Management System (QMS)?*

(b) State ***(do not describe)*** *the eight Quality Management Principles as per ISO 9001 : 2015?*

(c) State at least three benefits of having a QMS.

Ans. : *(a)* If an organization is to deliver products and services of the necessary level of quality, it must actively manage all the factors that have an impact on quality. In fact, there are very few aspects of any organization that can be regarded as having no influence on quality, so an effective quality management system (QMS) is likely to have complex remifications. The ISO definition of QMS is perhaps, over-simplistic: 'a management system to direct and control an organisation with regard to quality'. A fuller definition is as follows:

A quality management system is the organization structure of responsibilities, activities, resources and events that together provide procedures and methods of implementation to ensure the capability of an organization to meet quality requirements.

This definition gives a good indication of what is involved in a QMS. Much of it is present in organisations that do not claim to have a QMS as such: the difference is that the organization that uses a QMS manages these common elements in a way that contribute to quality management. For example, any manufacturing organization, no matter how rudimentary, will perform the activity of procurement. Procurement as part of a QMS will, for example, take positive steps to ensure that purchased material conform consistently to the appropriate quality standards; non-QMS procurement may or may not do the same, but even if it does it is unlikely that the procedures concerned will be documented and applied consistently.

The quality management system pervades the whole organizations sine it is unlikely that there will be any of its aspects that do not have the potential to affect the quality of its outputs. Two very obvious features are the quality manual and the job of quality manager, but many other elements have their part to play. These include staff and management generally, customer requirements, suppliers inputs, product design and development and customer service activities.

(*b*) All QMS are designed around the eight quality management principles given in ISO 9001 : 2015

- Customer focus
- Leader
- Involvement of people
- Process approach
- A system approach to management
- Continuous improvement
- A factual approach to decision making
- Mutually beneficial supplier relationship.

(*c*) Having an effective QMS will have the following advantages:

1. An improvement in the organization's ability to delivers outputs of consistently satisfactory quality.
2. An improved level of staff commitment based on the pride in the work.
3. Improved customer relationships, with fewer complaints and increased turnover.

Q. 20.8: *(a) Distinguish between ISO 9000, IS/IOS 9000 and ISO 14000?*

(b) Mention a few reasons as why sometimes companies do not like ISO 9000?

Ans. : (*a*) ISO 9000 is international standard of quality management systems.

IS/ISO 9000 is Indian equivalent of ISO 9000 standard for quality management system.

ISO 140001 is an internation standard the environment management systems. It has two important additional features.

(*i*) organisations must identify the environmental aspects inherent in their activities.

(*ii*) define the impacts they have on the environment, and they must identify and obey any environment legislation which applies to them.

(*b*) Many companies dislike ISO 9000. There are five main criticisms are as follows :

1. It is bureaucratic
2. It is internally focused
3. It is imposed by a customer
4. The company dislikes being assessed by an outsider
5. The company does not want to pay for it

Q. 20.9: *(a) What is QCI? Where it is located? Draw its logo.*

(b) What is IAF? What is its logo? What is the importance of June 12, 2012?

(c) Draw the logo of Indian Standard Institition?.

Ans. : (*a*) QCI is the quality council of India. Its offices are located in New Delhi. Its emblem is shown in Fig. 20.8:

QCI

FIGURE 20.8 Logo of QFC

(*b*) International Accreditation Forum (IAF) is an association of Conformity Assessment Accreditation bodies and other bodies interested in conformity assessment which exists primarily to facilitate world trade by working to remove technical barriers that may flow from demands for certification and/or registration of management systems. Its emblem is shown in Fig. 20.9.

FIGURE 20.9 Logo of IAF

(*c*) The logo of ISI is shown below in Fig. 20.10.

FIGURE 20.10 Logo of ISI

Q. 20.10: *(a) How the definition of 'quality' has changed after induction of ISO 9000?*

(b) Do you agree with the statement that ISO 9000 is not a quality system?

(c) Choose the correct statement: ISO 9000 ensures:

(i) high quality (ii) Constant quantity

(d) Fill in the blank: ISO 9000 is associated with .... (QA/QC)

Ans. : (*a*) Before the induction of ISO 9000, the usual definition of quality used by Britishers and Americans was:

"The totality of features and characteristics of a product or service that bear on its ability to satisfy stated or implied needs."

After the induction of ISO 9000 in 1987, the definition of quality has undergone changes and it is defined now as: "Quality is the degree to which a set of inherent characteristics fulfills requirements."

(*b*) ISO 9000 is an international standard that helps organizations follow their own quality procedures. ISO 9000 is *not* a quality system, but a method of following procedures created internally to an organization.

(*c*) (*ii*) Constant quality

(*d*) quality assurance (QA).

Q. 20.11: *(a) "ISO 9000 is a set of quality standards for companies doing business in the European Community". Do you agree with this statement? (Yes or No).*

(b) Is it legal for supplier/service organizations in India or anywhere in the world to have an ISO certification in order to do the business?

(c) What is meant by a company stating they are ISO 9000 certified?

(d) For a company designing and manufacturing items, what type of information are likely to be included in its quality plan if it is operating to ISO 9000?

(e) Can it be believed that ISO 9000 certified companies have good quality? Why or Why not?

Ans. : (*a*) Yes.

(*b*) No. ISO certification is only optional. However, ISO certified companies are preferred to others in the same business.

(*c*) It means that the company has been issued with a certificate by a government accredited certification body as conforming to the standards laid down in ISO 9000 and are being periodically reassessed to ensure conformance.

(*d*) As per ISO 9000, the quality plan should include the sequence of operations required for production and quality controls over the process, how the quality system is to work; how the requirements of the standard are to be met; quality procedures; quality responsibilities; quality checks—how, by who, when.

(*e*) The ISO 9000 standard does not itself relate to quality; it simply outlines a systematic approach to documentation. It is for this reason that the ISO 9000 standards are relatively short. Thus, there is a danger that companies who have been certified to ISO 9000 believe they have good quality. This is not true; ISO 9000 accreditation simply means that the company concerned has comprehensive and consistent set of documents outlining business practices. It does not mean these practices are optimal or even effective.

Q. 20.12: *(a) Mention briefly the eight quality-management principles enshrined in ISO 9000: 2015 series of standards.*

(b) Do these principles bear any relationship with the objectives and approach deployed in the Six-Sigma process?

(c) Is it always essential to have ISO 9000 certification for quality system?

(d) What is the time validity of ISO 9000 certificate?

Ans. : (*a*) The ISO 9000-2015 series of standards is based on the eight quality management principles:

1. **Customer focus:** organizations depend on their customers and, therefore, should understand current and future customer needs, meet customer require-ments and strive to exceed customer expectations.
2. **Leadership:** leaders establish unity of purpose and the direction of the organization. They should create and maintain an internal environment in which people can become fully involved in achieving the organization's objectives.
3. **Involvement of people:** people at all levels are the essence of an organization, and their full involvement enables their abilities to be used for the organization's benefit.
4. **Process approach:** a desired result is achieved more efficiently when related resources and activities are managed as a process.
5. **System approach to management:** identifying, understanding and managing a system of inter-related processes for a given objective improves the organization's effectiveness and efficiency.
6. **Continual improvement:** continual improvement should be a permanent objective of the organization.

7. **Factual approach to decision-making:** effective decisions are based on the analysis of data and information.
8. **Mutually beneficial supplier relationships:** an organization and its suppliers are interdependent, and a mutually beneficial relationship enhances the ability of both to create value.

(*b*) The above eight quality-management principles are seen to be fully compatible with the objectives and approach deployed in the Six-Sigma process.

(*c*) No. It is not always necessary to have ISO 9000 certification for practising quality system.

(*d*) The validity of ISO 9000 certificate is for 3 years only. Revalidation is required after every 3 years.

Q. 20.13: *(a) Is EN 29000 identical to ISO 9000 or IS/ISO 9000?*

(b) State briefly the advantages and disadvantages of ISO 9000 or equivalent standards for business firms.

Ans. : (*a*) EN 29000, ISO 9000 and IS/ISO 9000 are totally identical standards.

(*b*) The main **advantages** for business in the publication of quality system standards are as follows:

1. They provide a common framework for assessing the management of quality and this removes the variability of traditional customer assessments.
2. They provide for an international 'currency' in terms of the evaluation of a company's quality management which is important in export markets.
3. They provide an internal focus for quality development which, because it is externally assessed, assists in the management of change process.

The main **disadvantages** of these universally applied quality system evaluation standards are, however, as follows:

1. They represent a 'minimum' standard and therefore do not provide for longterm competitive advantage.
2. They are mainly directed towards manufacturing or manufacturing engineering industries and therefore require interpretation for other business sectors.
3. They are written in general terms and therefore open to interpretation.

Q. 20.14: *(a) How can you say that ISO 9000: 2015 covers manufacturing and nonmanufacturing industries?*

(b) What is the significance of ISO 9000 certification on the letterhead of an organization?

Ans. : (*a*) The ISO 9000 standards are comprehensive in their coverage, ranging from product or service development to after-sales service. However, they have tended to have a clear bias towards the manufacturing sector. That is, after all, where the process started and where greatest use continues to be made of the standards. The ISO 9000: 2015 family of standards, launched at the end of 2015, attempts to harmonize all the standards and remove the manufacturing bias. ISO 9001: 2008 and ISO 9004: 2009 is a further step in this direction.

(*b*) ISO 9000 certification means that an organization constantly meets rigorous standards (which are well documented) of management of quality of product and services. To retain certification the organization is audited annually by an outside accredited body. ISO 9000 on the letterhead of an organization demonstrates to its employees, to its customers and to other interested bodies that it has an effective quality assurance system in place.

Q. 20.15: *What is QMS ? Explain.*

Ans. : A Quality Management System (QMS) is the organized structure of responsibilities, activities, resources and events that together provide procedures and methods of implementations to ensure the capability of an organization to meet quality requirements. To achieve this a QMS needs to be capable of:

- demonstrating continuous improvement
- preventing non-conformity
- assisting self-evaluation

This QMS will consist of the documented rules, procedures and instructions prepared in accordance with agreed standards. These are stated in the quality manual as well as the associated core processes, procedures and work instructions. The document hierarchy is shown below in Fig. 20.11.

FIGURE 20.11 Document pyramid.

Q. 20.16: *Choose mark (√/×) on the correct statement(s) from the following on QMS:*

(i) It does not dictate the quality of individual goods and services

(ii) It aims to ensure that quality management systems of a suitable standard are in place.

(iii) It does not cover every quality issue; it deals with quality system not of achievement.

(iv) It guarantees the control action

(v) It is an indicator of performance.

Ans. : (*b*) (*i*) (√) ; (*ii*) (√) ; (*iii*) (√) ; (*iv*) (×) ; (*v*) (√)

Q. 20.17: (*a*) *What is a 'quality manual' of any organization? What are its main parts?*

(*b*) *Write briefly the various aspects of quality policies.*

Ans. : (*a*) A **quality manual** is a document specifying the quality management system of an organization. There are two important aspects to the nature of the quality manual.

- Practical details and instructions for the operation of quality procedures and systems.
- Quality assurance sought by external agencies such as customers and certification bodies.

The quality manual is fundamental to quality management.

The quality manual is likely to contain a wide range of material: this can be grouped into a number of categories.

1. Policies relating to quality.
2. The organizational structure that relates to quality management: this is likely to be identical with the overall structure of the organization, or nearly so.
3. Details of quality procedures: thus category includes a wide range of documentation.

(*b*) Quality policies include a mission statement, a corporate policy statement and process specific policies.

Quality policies define the overall intentions and direction of an organization related to quality for formally expressed by top management.

Statement of quality policy may be divided into three types:

1. *Mission statement* referring to customer satisfaction, ISO 9000 and importance of good quality practice.
2. *Corporate policy statement* based upon eight quality management principles mentioned in ISO 9000.
3. *Process-specific policies* will relate directly to the organization's processes and quality requirements. They should be adequate to manage quality in all key processes.

Q. 20.18: *(a) What is ISO definition of QMS? Do you agree with it fully? If not, give your definition of QMS.*

(b) Quality assurance (QA) and Quality control (QC) are important aspects of QMS. Define these terms and explain the same to a group of students.

Ans. : (*a*) The ISO definition of QMS is "a management system to direct and control an organization with regard to quality".

This definition is perhaps over simplistic. A fuller definition will be "a quality management system is the organizational structure of responsibilities, activities, resources and events that together provide procedures and methods of implementation to ensure the capability of an organization to meet quality requirements.

(*b*) ISO 9000: 2015 definition of QC and QA are as follows:

- QC is the part of quality management focussed on fulfilling quality requirements.
- QA is the part of quality management focussed on providing confidence that quality requirements will be fulfilled.

It is a *common misconception* that QA is just a more upto date version of QC. In order to be clear in the matter the following explanation is worthwhile.

Quality control is about the things the organization has to do to be sure that the quality of its output is as it should be. It is about activities such as supervision, inspection, checks and measurements and applies to all parts of the organization's value chain.

If QC is about fulfilling quality requirements, it is clear from the definition of QA that it is about providing confidence that all the necessary QC activities are operating as they should and that a proper level of quality is therefore being achieved. QA is therefore concerned with the things that make QA systems and activities effective. These things include quality policies, relevant management and training and documentation such as quality seconds. The purpose of QA is two fold.

1. To provide assurance to a customer that the standard of workmanship within a contractor's premises is of the desired level and that all products leaving that particular firm are at, or above a certain fixed minimum level of specification.
2. To ensure that manufacturing and service standards are uniform between an organization's department or offices and that they remain constant despite changes in personnel.

Q. 20.19: *(a) Briefly mention the procedure for ISO certification.*

(b) Why ISO certificate is necessary?

Ans. : (*a*) The following gives briefly the stepwise procedure for ISO certification.

Stepwise Procedure for ISO Certification

- Letter of intention sent to the ISO certifying Body (CB)
- Questionnaire received by the firm
- Optional visit by ISO CB and evaluation report
- ISO Committee requirements:

Contract information	Reference guide and preliminary
Preliminary questionnaire	Examination and evaluation of submitted documents

- ISO Audit

Audit report submitted to firm	Response by firm

In some case, additional audit

Valuation and Certification by ISO Committee Certification, for 3 years

- Periodic visits
- Contract renewal

(*b*) Certification is important because it conveys a signal that the certified firm is operating structured manner for quality improvement and TQM. Certification can be obtained from national and international organizations such as BIS, IR, DNV etc.

Q. 20.20: *Discuss the scope of the ISO Standard **9000** used for the third-party evaluation company's quality assurance system. Describe the stages involved in the implementation within a small manufacturing company of a quality assurance programme to comply with the Standard.*

Ans. : ISO 9000 covers a company's quality systems from material reception through to final test and despatch. The areas covered include:

- material reception and specification procedures;
- design and documentation control;
- manufacturing procedures and control;
- final inspection and test procedures;
- specification of sampling plans;
- calibration systems;
- controls for nonconforming materials;

- identification of inspection standard;
- audit and review.

The implementation discussion should include:

- identification of appropriate part;
- identifying the quality objectives;
- identify responsible senior manager;
- planning to take into account all the company's activities;
- development of a quality policy and programme;
- document procedures and quality manual;
- review systems.

Q. 20.21: *(a) What are the main contributions made by implementation of ISO 9000 towards the quality development of a manufacturing?*

(b) In which areas of quality system development is the use of statistical techniques appropriate? Describe how you would introduce acceptance samplings as part of an ISO 9000 implementation programme.

Ans. : (a) Main contributions are:

1. To provide basic systems foundation and definition of requirement.
2. To give company wide view of quality.
3. To enforce externally 'policed' quality commitment.

(b) Quality systems may include statistical techniques in the following areas:

Acceptance sampling to control incoming materials (4.10.2); in-process inspection (4.10.3); final inspection (4.10.4) and SPC in process control (4.9).

Introduction of acceptance sampling includes:

1. Definition of procedures and criteria;
2. Adoption of Dodge Romig Samples Scheme, MIL-STD 105 E or BS 6000.

Q. 20.22: *(a) Simply advise how the cost of quality is affected by implimentation of ISO 9000?*

(b) What are the main areas associated with quality accreditions?

(c) What are the criticisms of quality accredition?

Ans. : (*a*) ISO 9000 incurrs appraisal costs and prevention costs (specification and vendor control)

(*b*) For organizations pursing a philosophy of quality management accreditation is an official external recognition. Organizations seek to get approval of a controlling body in order to achieve accreditation of a nationally or internationally recognized quality standard (such as ISO 9000). Main areas include:

- responsibilities,
- procedures,
- processes required to implement quality manage-ment in the organization.

(*c*) Main criticisms of quality accredition are:

- Documentation is expensive (in terms of time) to produce.

- Rigid policies and procedures discourage innovation and initiative.
- The schemes encourage bureaucracy.
- The formal methods may not be consistent with ways of working in small and medium-sized organizations.

Q. 20.23: *(a) Distinguish between a quality process and a quality procedure.*

(b) What are the main provisions of ISO 9001: 2008?

(c) Why external audits for ISO certification are not so effective? What is the remedy?

(d) Is it necessary to keep hard copies of quality manuals etc.?

Ans. : (*a*) The difference is summarized in the definitions given below:

A quality process is a set of inter-related or interfacing activities which transform inputs into outputs.

A quality procedure is use specified way to carry out an activity or a process.

(*b*) Main provisions of ISO 9001: 2008 are:

1. Quality management system,
2. Management responsibility
3. Resource management
4. Product/service relatization
5. Measurement.

(*c*) External audits are held after some specified periods. The external audit requirements of the ISO 9000 series are more towards compliance checks after an activity has started or been completed. This type of check confirms that procedures are being kept to, or that an outcome complies with standard. Where mistakes are found, they are retrospective. Audit highlights where errors have occurred and this indicates the need for corrective action for the future, but they do not stop the error happening in the first place. To be effective internal audits are to be in place. Internal auditors should be there to help and guide, not to trap and catch. If the audit is preventative – that is, before the events rather than after – so much the better.

(*d*) It is **not** essential to keep hard copy of quality manuals etc. Indeed, when the people have customer terminal at hand they are more likely to search the computer than to leaf through large manuals. Also, with a computer system it is easier to update the records with the latest procedures and to ensure that the user acknowledges receipt of change when using the system. In this way the system can be kept almost instantly updated, and staff can be encouraged to make improvement suggestions.

Q. 20.24: *(a) What is the significance of the Fig. 20.12 with reference to ISO 9001?*

(b) What are the benefits of continuous imporvement?

(c) How many minimum written quality procedures are required by ISO 9001: 2015?

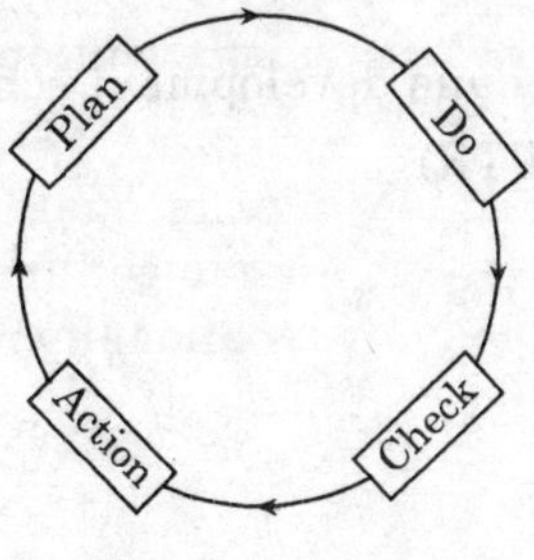

FIGURE

Ans. : (*a*) Figure 20.12 represents a Deming's PDCA cycle for continuous improvement. Need for continuous improvement has been emphasized in ISO 9001: 2015.

(*b*) Benefit of continuous improvement:

1. Better performance which increases profits.
2. Improvement in customer satisfaction.
3. Increase in staff morale.
4. Improvement on a continual, step-by-step is more prudent them changing things abruptly.
5. Better communication within the organization.
6. Improvements in relations with suppliers.
7. Move efficient planning.

(*c*) ISO 9001: 2015 mandates a minimum of six specific written quality procedures. These cover two QMS processes an four MAI (Measurement, Analysis and Improvement) processes:

- control documents
- control records
- internal audit
- product failures
- corrective action
- prevention action

Q. 20.25: (*a*) *What are the main areas associated with quality accredition?*

(*b*) *What benefits may organization achieve from participating in a quality certification scheme?*

Ans. : (*a*) For organizations with a quality philosophy, accredition means official external recognition Organizations get approval of controlling body to achieve accredition of a nationally or internationally recognized quality standard.

Main areas include:

- responsibility
- procedures
- process required

(*b*) Benefits from adopting a quality scheme include:

1. improved marketing by linking to a 'brand' or 'logo'.
2. helps improve quality within the organization
3. helps to maximise performance
4. helps organizations and staff show competency
5. may attract better staff
6. can help develop staff training and development schemes.
7. no need of past track record (PTR).

CHAPTER

21 Total Quality Management (TQM)

21.1 TOTAL QUALITY MANAGEMENT

The evolution of quality management stimulated, at least in part, by the impact of the demand by customers for higher quality conformance levels and the increasing competitiveness in world markets has resulted in the need to address quality management in all aspects of a business, including customers and suppliers. Quality management becomes total when it is applied to everything a business does. Thus TQM can be defined as follows :

TQM is the process of applying a zero defect philosophy to the management of all resources and relationships within the organization as a means of developing and sustaining a culture of continuous improvement which focuses on meeting customers' expectations.

TQM requires that the principles of quality management are applied in all aspects of and at every level in an organization. It is a company-wide approach to quality management with improvements being undertaken on a continuous basis by everyone.

TQM as a philosophy of quality management originated in Japan in the 1950s. TQM is a system that integrates the quality management efforts of all groups in an organization and, it is argued, that it has been a significant factor in Japanese global business success. It has a number of important features.

The alphabet T, Q and M signify the following:

- **Total** – means that everyone in the value chain is involved in the process, including employees, customers and suppliers.
- **Quality** – products and services must meet the customers' requirements.
- **Management** – management must be fully committed and encourage everyone else to become quality conscious.
- The basic principle of TOM that the cost of *preventing* mistakes is **less than** the *cost of correcting them* once they occur *and the cost of lost potential future sales*. The aim should therefore be to get things right first time consistently.
- This contrasts with the 'traditional' approach that less than 100% quality is acceptable as the costs of improvement from say 90% to 100% outweigh the benefits.

21.2 UNDERSTANDING THE TQM

The philosophy of TQM is based on the idea of a series of quality chains, which may be broken at any point by one person or service not meeting the requirements of the customer. The key to TQM is for everyone in the organization to have well-defined customers – an extension of the word, beyond the customers of the company, to anyone to whom an individual provides a service. Thus the 'Paint shop' staff would be customers of the 'Assembly shop' staff who would themselves be the customers of the 'Machine shop' staff. The idea is that the supplier-customer relationships would form a chain extending from the company's original suppliers through to its ultimate consumers. Areas of responsibility would need to be identified and a manager allocated to each, and then the customer/supplier chain established. True to the principle outlined above, the quality requirements of each customer within the chain would be assessed, and meeting these would then become the responsibility of the 'suppliers' who form the preceding link in the chain.

Quality has to be managed –it will not just happen. To meet the requirements of TQM, a company will probably need to recruit more staff and may also need to change the level of services or offer to its customers, which includes 'internal' customers. This would probably entail costs in terms of the redesign of systems, recruitment and training of staff, and the purchase of appropriate equipment.

Some essential characteristics of organizations that follow TQM programmes are as follows:

1. Organization-wide there must be acceptance that the only thing that matters is the customer.
2. There should be recognition of the all-pervasive nature of the customer-supplier relationship, including internal customers; passing sub-standard material to another division is not satisfactory.
3. Instead of relying on inspection to a predefined level of quality, the cause of the defect in the first place should be prevented.
4. Each employee or group of employees must be personally responsible for defect-free production or service in their domain.
5. There should be a move away from 'acceptable' quality levels. Any level of defects must be unacceptable.
6. All departments should try obsessively to get thing right first time; this applies to misdirected phone calls and typing errors as much as to production.
7. Quality certification programmes should be introduced.
8. The cost of poor quality should be emphsised; good quality generates savings.

21.2.1 Emergence of TQM

TQM as a theory was developed after the Second World War by US academics such as Armand Feigenbaum and W. Edwards Deming. As a practical notion, it had its first major impact in Japan where American ideas caught on as part of the rebuilding of the country following the war. It then caught on in the West where it continues to be a source of fascination and debate. There is an important difference in timescale between East and West as regards quality and TQM. For example, the Deming Quality Award started in Japan in 1951, whereas the quality standard BS 5750 was not introduced in the West until

TABLE 21.1 THE GURUS OF TQM

Gurus	*Their contributions to TQM*
A Feigenbaum	Responsible for the idea of total quality control management which is popular in Japan.
W E Deming	Father of quality control. Emphasised quality as a top management and strategic activity. Famous for his '14 points for quality improvement'.
J M Juran	Emphasised a more user-based approach to quality management based on 'fitness for purpose'. Concerned with management responsibility for quality and the involvement of individual workers in quality improvements.
K Ishikawa	Originated quality circles and cause effect (C & E) diagrams. Saw quality circles as a way of involving employees to make TQM work
G Taguchi	Emphasised the importance of engineering in quality through design combined with statistical methods of process control. Originated the idea of quality loss on a product/service from the time it was created (quality loss function or QLF)
P B Crosby	The idea of cost of quality and zero defects was his main concern – he developed a zero defects programme in his book *Quality is Free* (1979)

1979, and it wasn't until 1987 that the US introduced the Baldridge Award. Company-wide quality control was common in Japanese companies by the late 1970s, but did not begin in the west until the early 1980s. Table 21.1 outlines briefly the major contribution of some key thinkers (gurus) on quality leading to TQM. A detailed description on quality gurus and their philosophy has already appeared in Chap. 3, however, a passing reference of them in Table 21.1 again is a tribute to these quality gurus.

While not an exhaustive catalogue of those who have contributed to TQM thinking, the above list in Table 21.1 does give the flavour of how TQM developed. Even from these brief summaries of their work, it is evident that each 'guru' stressed a different set of issues from which emerged the TQM approach to operations improvement. Each contributor, with hindsight, is seen as having made some particularly significant points, and as having perhaps neglected other issues, now seen as important.

21.2.2 TQM Stages

As we have seen that quality has many different meanings. However, the customer orientation is central to the quality definition. An organizational definition of quality will help to prevent misunderstanding and avoid different interpretations being made by people and the various functions within the business.

Quality systems have been evolving rapidly in recent years. During the last forty years simple inspection (I) activities have been replaced or supplemented by quality control (QC), quality assurance (QA) has been developed and refined and the most progressive companies are now working towards total quality management (TQM). In this progress four fairly discrete stages can be identified as:

- inspection (I)
- quality control (QC)
- quality assurance (QA)
- total quality management (TQM)

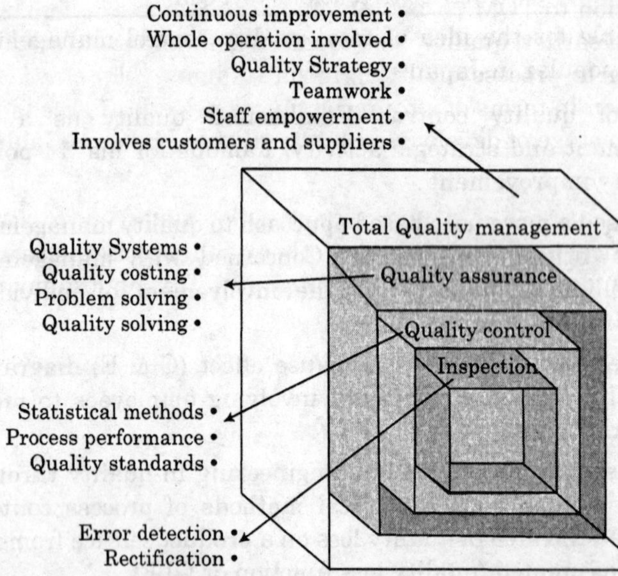

FIGURE 21.1 The stages of TQM.

The terms used here indicate levels in a hierarchal circumfacent system of quality management (Fig. 21.1) and do not necessarily correspond to the usual definitions.

1. **Inspection** – a basic, fire-fighting system of quality control involving error detection and correction.
2. **Quality control** – a more rigorous quality management system involving self inspection, statistical process control (SPC) and quality standards.
3. **Quality assurance** – a preventative-based system emphasising product and process design, planning, and process control.
4. **Total quality management** – all the previous three and more as depicted in Fig. 21.1.

Each stage as illustrated in Table 21.2 is a progression which absorbs the previous stage until we get to the final stage, which is TQM. The key development between total quality management and other forms of quality management is its strategic focus on empowerment and improvement. It involves maximising the potential of people right across the organization in a continuing drive for improvement of all activities.

TABLE 21.2 STAGES OF DEVELOPMENT IN QUALITY AND RELATED ACTIVITIES

Stage of development	*Activities*
Inspection	Salvaging, sorting, grading and corrective actions
Quality control	Quality manuals, product testing, basic quality planning, including statistics
Quality assurance	Third party approvals, advanced planning, systems audits, SPC
Company-wide QC	Quality measured in all areas of the firm
TQM	Continuous improvement; involvement of suppliers and customers; employee involvement and teamwork

It is interesting to revisit and scan Table 15.2 of Chap. 15 for major events in quality evolution starting from Inspection to TQM.

The development from inspection to TQM reveals the increasing strategic importance of quality over time. As we mentioned earlier, quality used to mean conformance to specification: the nature of this was conforming to process quality criteria (in-house). By the 1980s and 1990s, however, quality became seen in terms of a total commitment from all areas including the supply chain. The scope of each stage of developments in quality is shown in Table 21.2.

21.3 TQM PHILOSOPHY

Although TQM does include statistical process control and other quality tools and techniques, the outermost layer of TQM is often described as being a philosophy. This philosophy has four basic elements:

1. involving everyone in the company through teamwork, trust and empowerment
2. continuous improvement
3. identification of customers and their needs, and then focusing on them
4. using tools and techniques jointly to resolve quality problems.

21.3.1 Teamwork, Trust and Empowerment

The holistic approach of TQM distinguishes it from conventional approaches where the responsibility is assigned to a 'quality department'. For some, it even goes beyond the quality circle which can be seen as a means of management delegating some quality responsibilities while retaining most of the control. Indeed, Japanese workers sometimes see QCs as coercive. The holistic goal is commitment and sharing of the quality issue among all employees so that the contribution of each is both recognized and influential.

Empowerment can only occur when people are well trained, given access to relevant information, know and use the best techniques, are involved in the decisions and receive appropriate rewards. Most quality problems relate to materials, designs, specifications and processes and have little to do with poor employee performance. Yet, these same employees are usually well aware of the shortcomings of the production system and can be invaluable in finding solutions.

21.3.2 Continuous Improvement

Continuous improvement is based on three basic concepts or cornerstones : (1) *Quality*, (2) *Process Improvement* and (3) *Team work*.

Quality is defined by the needs of our customers (both internal and external). *Quality alone does not make us a "World Class Company".*

Process improvements: Lack results from the lack of complacency in our process. It helps us succeed in becoming a "World Class Company". We strive for Process Improvements through **technology** and the innovative ideas of our Partners.

Teamwork among departments and locations is essential in providing the best possible solutions to our challengers. T**hrough Teamwork we differentiate ourselves from our competition,** we become more than our machines.

All three Cornerstones must be present for continuous improvement to work. If one is left out we lose the battle to become Better than the Best. "Quality without Teamwork leaves us competing against ourselves. Teamwork without Process Improvements leaves us vulnerable to our competition. Process Improvements without Quality leaves us without customers."

Some pragmatic factors for quality improvement are as follows:

1. Total commitment from senior management
2. The opportunity for all employees to contribute to the continuous improvement process. Tactical and operational level staff, rather than senior management, usually have the information required. The most successful continuous improvement programs are the ones that have the highest staff involvement.
3. Good, objective information about the organization's environment so that its outcomes (what it does) and its processes (how it does it) can be evaluated
4. Employee's awareness of thier role in the achievement of the organization's strategy
5. Management of the performance and contribution of employees
6. Good communications throughout the organization
7. Implementation of recognized quality management systems and standards
8. Measurement and evaluation of progress against key performance indicators (KPI) and benchmarks (BM). Some organizations have found that simply displaying productivity and quality data every day or week raises production and quality because staff can tell when they are doing things right, and so find themselves in a personal continuous improvement cycle.

It is claimed that if these areas are regularly reviewed, change can be managed effectively and continuous improvement becomes a natural part of the organizational processes. It should create steady growth and development by keeping the organization focused on its aims, priorities and performance.

21.3.3 Being Customer Centred

We have seen that both Ishikawa and Juran advocated the notion that, in the TQM organization, everyone has customers. They may be internal or external. Internal customers are other members of the organization who rely on the next person along the quality chain for inputs to get their work done. Sometimes, people's work can be so interconnected that they are *mutually dependent*, that is each is the other's customer. Whatever the relationship, they are all part of quality chains. When it comes to quality, the internal customer is very much like an external one. The difficulty of the customer's work, and the quality of the output, are strongly affected by the quality of the input.

As for external customers, it is obvious that the TQM company will require *all employees* who deal with them to be committed to satisfying their needs.

21.3.4 Tools and Techniques

Some important tools for solving quality problems have already been mentioned in Chap. 18 and these can be used need-based. Most quality problems can be resolved by simple steps using common sense. Procedures for putting common sense into practice are:

- *Go to gemba (workplace).* This is the most important rule.
- *Standardization.* Standards are the basis of both continuing activity and improvement. If there are no standards, they should be introduced. If the standards are failing, they should be modified.
- *Don't get it, don't make it, and don't send it.* Based on the premise that quality is everyone's job, one should be determined not to receive rejects, create them or pass them on.

- *Speak with data.* Collecting data is the starting point of analysis. People should be prepared to measure before changing anything.
- *Ask why.* Problem solving means asking why as often as necessary to find the root cause. Only then can the problems be eradicated.

Some people argue that quality cannot be sustained without quality measurement techniques. This is undoubtedly true, but the emphasis in the TQM organization is less on the measurement and more on the use of appropriate measures to support continuous improvement. Matching the complexity of quality tools with the training and experience of the users is a vital part of involving people at all levels. The tools are clearly a necessary but not sufficient basis for a TQM programme.

The four basic elements of TQM philosophy discussed above, lead us to the practical definition of TQM.

Based an above understanding TQM, Table 21.3 gives seven TQM principles.

TABLE 21.3 Principles of Total Quality Management

TQM principle	*Description*
Committed and effective leaders	A commitment to, and a belief in, the principles of TQM by those key decision-makers at the top of the organizational structure is essential. They have to portray this commitment to the lower levels of management in an effective style of leadership by providing resources to make changes happen.
Planning	It is imperative that all changes are planned effectively, particularly as the TQM approach may be fundamentally different from the approach currently adopted by an organization. All planned changes must be integrated through the whole organization with cooperation throughout all levels and functions. With quality, or improved quality, as the key dimension, a longer-term strategy will be adopted throughout the organization's functions, from new product design through to getting the product to the end-user.
Monitoring	A continuous monitoring system will be put into place so that the process of continuous improvement can be supported and developed. Problem identification and the implementation of solutions will be sought.
Education and training	Without education and training, employees and management will lack expertise and awareness of quality issues. It will be difficult to implement changes in organizational behaviour unless there is a comprehensive and effective educational scheme which not only seeks to provide the initial information and understanding of techniques, but constantly updates those techniques in order to reinforce under-standing. Without this investment, short-term TQM benefits will be difficult to achieve, as will the long-term impact of TQM through conventional measurements such as increased efficiency and general growth.

...(Contd.)

Teamwork	The development of empowered cooperative teams is an essential prerequisite of TQM. Under this system teams are encouraged to take the initiative and often given responsibilities which would have formerly been management roles. Without this involvement and empowerment TQM is almost impossible to implement as it requires both the participation and the commitment of individuals throughout the organization.
Evaluation and feedback	It is imperative that individuals within the organization see the fruits of their labour. TQM means that there should be an integral system which not only provides positive feedback but also rewards for achievement. The evaluation and feedback of TQM will invariably involve the measurement of achievement in both internal and external targets, notably through **benchmarking.**
Long-term change	As TQM becomes embedded and very much a fact of life in the ways in which employees think and processes are carried out, there is a permanent change to the way in which attitudes, working practices and overall behaviour are approached.

21.4 TQM AND PEREFORMANCE MEASURES

Performance measures of TQM must embrace every activity of the organization.

Because TQM embraces every activity of a business, **performance measures should not be confined to the production process.** Measures should also cover the work of sales, distribution and administration departments, the efforts of external suppliers and the reaction of external customers.

In many cases the measure used will be non-financial ones. They may be divided into three types as per Table 21.4.

TABLE 21.4 PERFORMANCE MEASURE FOR TQM

Type of measure	*Example*
Measuring incoming supplies	Percentage of defective items per delivery Number of returns per supplier
Monitoring work done as it proceeds	Number of rejects per production run Ratio of waste material to used material
Measuring customer satisfaction	Complaints per 10,000 units sold satisfaction Number of claims under warranty

21.5 PROS AND CONS OF TQM

There is an on going debate about the effectiveness of TQM. Table 21.5 summarises some of the salient points.

TABLE 21.5 PROS AND CONS OF TQM

Arguments for TQM	*Arguments against TQM*
It can reduce product defect ratzes or customer complaints	Management is unable to make the necessary commitment
Getting employees on board improves productivity	Over-complex tools, systems and standards
People take pride in, and responsibility for, their products	It is stressful for employees who can be over-empowered
Quality cascades through the whole organization at every level	The time and resources needed to implement it are too great
Quality throughout the supply chain improves product supply and distribution	It is impossible to improve continually
Continuous improvement keeps people challenged	People are expected to do more but are not paid any more
Everybody has a customer focus	TQM is not suitable for all organizations (and the culture change required is too great)
People use their brains to solve problems	It takes too long to implement
Reduces costs and improves bottom line	It increases costs and harms bottom line

Supports of TQM will come back at the opposition and suggest that there are ways around their objections, such as ensuring reward systems that harmonise with any new tasks (taking a whole system view) or setting aside training days for management and staff. Whatever the opinions, TQM has thrown up a lot of ideas, and organizations do not have to implement it to benefit from some of these ideas, for example, some organizations implement teamworking practices even though they do not choose to adopt TQM.

However, TQM has certainly has brought changes in traditional attitude as can be seen from Table 21.6 which compares traditional attitude and attitude with TQM on several important criteria.

TABLE 21.6 CHANGING VIEWS OF QUALITY MANAGEMENT

Criteria	*Traditions Attitude*	*Attitude with TQM*
Importance	quality is a technical issue	quality is a strategic issue
Cost	high quality costs money	high quality saves money
Responsibility	quality control department	everyone in the organization
Target	meet specifications	continuous improvement
Measured by	average quality level	zero defects
Emphasis	detecting defects	preventing defects
Attitude	inspect quality in	build quality in
Defined by	organization	customers

21.6 TQM—BENEFITS AND LIMITATIONS

Manufacturing and service organizations are under increasing pressure for more effective use of the few resources that are available. Technology and quality management have emerged to play a major role in the success or failure of enterprises. To successfully manage operations, managers will need to view the quality management function on the basis of systems requirements. Specific operations within in organization should be viewed as components of a large system that must be integrated to achieve the overall quality objective of the organization. TQM facilitates an appreciation of reintegration of advanced technology, a revision of the corporate culture, upgrade of production infrastructure, and better utilization of human resources. It is the people aspects of managing quality that make TQM very essential. TQM is not in effect in an organization if it does not affect all the people and all the products all the time. TQM fosters a new attitude toward quality. TQM offers the following advantages:

- Higher productivity.
- Better employee relations.
- Cooperative coordination of efforts.
- Interaction with subsystem environments.
- Uniformity and consistency of quality objectives.
- Specification of the interrelationships of subsystems.
- Systematic solution of quality problems in an organization.
- Coordinated adjustment of functions to solve quality problems.
- Dynamic integration of activities into an effective total system.
- Increased probability, frequency, and consistency of making good products.

Limitations of TQM. At its core, total quality management is a simple idea. The large firms may go for TQM easily; the smaller firms may feel forced to do so and grumble about the costs of consultants and the appraisal process itself. European firms may not have committed themselves to TQM as much as Japanese, and it appears, North American ones. We can examine this further by looking at costs and people.

Costs. Quality programmes eventually pay for themselves. 'Quality is free' because the total costs of prevention are less than the costs of failure. Initial costs of prevention are prohibitive as these are mainly related to reorganization and training.

People. There may be problems within the work groups during transition. To participate in TQM, through quality circles is voluntary, to work under the restructured operating system is mandatory cultural, language and structural constants create further barriers.

21.7 BUSINESS PROCESS REENGINEERING (BPR)

The notion of Business Process Reegineering (BPR) being incorporated into the subject of quality may seem unusual, but the quality world has much to gain from it.

BPR is concerned with radically re-thinking and re-designing processes to bring about improvements in performance. This means we may have to scrap old processes – probably the familiar and easy ones we have been working with for many years – and start again with a clean sheet of paper.

An obvious question here is why ? In order to arrive at a logical decision whether to go in for BPR is to answer the following questions:

- Is the organization working perfectly?
- Is there room for improvement?

- Each time an improvement is made, is it merely tacked on to the end of the present process?
- Does this make it more difficult to work?

If the answer is yes then why not scrap the old method with its complicated ways and begin again – a fresh?

The underlying thought behind BPR is that operations should be organized around the processes that add value to goods and services for the customer. Operations should not be organized around *what we can do*.

21.7.1 Principles of BPR

Basic principles of BPR are:

- Redesigning processes around what the product or service requires rather than having the product or service evolving around the processes
- By redesigning processes there will be a dramatic increase in performance
- Making employees see the results of their outputs – possibly through job rotation
- Make people responsible for making decisions for the work they do

With these points in mind, it is *not unfair* to argue that BPR very similar to TQM. The *difference* is that TQM is concerned with an entire organization, while BPR is concerned with possibly just one individual process within an organization.

21.8 AUTHOR'S OBSERVATIONS ON TQM

TQM is philosophy of strategic implementation and managing quality improvement activities on an organization-wide basis. TQM began in the early 1980s, with the philosophies of Deming and Juran as the focal point. It evolved into a broader spectrum of concepts and ideas, involving participative organizations and work culture, customer focus, supplier quality improvement, integration of the quality system with business goals, and many other activities to focus all elements of the organization around the quality improvement goal. Typically, organizations that have implemented a TQM approach to quality improvement have quality councils or high-level teams that deal with strategic quality initiatives, workforce-level teams that focus on routine production or business activities, and cross functional teams that address specific quality improvement issues.

TQM has only had moderate success for a variety of reasons, but frequently because there is insufficient effort devoted to widespread utilization of the technical tools of variability reduction. Many organizations saw the mission of TQM as one of training. Consequently, many TQM efforts engaged in widespread training of the workforce in the philosophy of quality improvement and a few basic methods. This training was usually placed in the hands of human resources departments, and much of it was ineffective. The trainers often had no real idea about *what* methods should be taught, and success was usually measured by the percentage of the workforce that had been "trained," not by whether any measurable impact on business results had been achieved. Some general reasons for the lack of conspicuous success of TQM include:

(1) lack of topdown, high-level **management commitment** and **involvement**;
(2) inadequate use of statistical methods and insufficient recognition of variability reduction as a prime objective;
(3) general as opposed to specific business-results-oriented objectives; and
(4) too much emphasis on widespread **training** as opposed to focused technical **education**.

Another reason for the erratic success of TQM is that many managers and executives have regarded it as just another "program" to improve quality. During the 1950s and 1960s, programs such as **Zero Defects** and **Value Engineering** abounded, but they had little real impact on quality and productivity improvement. During the heyday of TQM in the 1980s, another popular program was the Quality is Free initiative, in which management worked on identifying the cost of quality (or the cost of nonquality, as the Quality is Free devotees so cleverly put it). Indeed, identification of quality costs can be very useful (we discuss quality costs in Chapter 2), but the Quality is Free practitioners often had no idea about what to do to actually improve many types of complex industrial processes and technology. The aim to get things right first time consistently was not stressed upon in the right proportion. Inspite of claiming TQM, in their plants, the Japanese auto major Honda had to recall its 58,000 units of city Sedan car in India in February, 2011 for replacing defective springs. In fact, the leaders of this initiative had no knowledge about performance of their products and customers' feed back and statistical methodology and completely failed to understand its role in quality improvement. When TQM is wrapped around an ineffective program such as this, disaster is often the result.

SOLVED QUESTIONS

Q. 21.1: *TQM is about :*

(*a*) moving towards cost reduction.

(*b*) involving everyone in quality.

(*c*) moving towards perfect quality.

(*d*) getting the right quality level.

(*e*) management being concerned about quality.

Ans. : (*c*) but (*b*) is a stage 2.

Q. 21.2: *Which of the following options is true for implementory TQM in a business?*

(*a*) Improvement is the responsibility of the quality department.

(*b*) Mistakes should be criticised and corrected.

(*c*) supplier and customers need to be part of the improvement process.

Ans. : (*c*)

Q. 21.3: *In a TQM environment, which of the following be classification.*

(*i*) Cost of repairing products returned from customer

(*ii*) Product liabilities costs.

(*iii*) Cost of customer service section.

(*iv*) Cost of providing replacement items due to marketing errors.

(*a*) *None of above* (*b*) *All of above*

(*c*) (*i*) *only* (*d*) (*ii*) *only*

Ans. : (*b*)

Q. 21.4: (*a*) *State whether the following statements are TRUE (T) or FALSE (F).*

(*i*) TQM is a fixed duration programme.

(*ii*) TQM is not a programme, it is a process which is continuous and involves everyone.

(iii) ISO 9000 series is associated with QA.

(iv) Training is an essential element of TQM.

(v) Benefits of TQM can be measured in monetary terms.

(vi) TQM is now being applied in service industries as well as manufacturing industries.

(vii) TQM and scientific management have same approach.

(b) Explain briefly the meaning associated with each letter of TQM.

(c) State its four main principles.

Ans. : *(a)* *(i)* F *(ii)* T *(iii)* T *(iv)* T *(v)* F *(vi)* T *(vii)* F

(b) The meaning associated with each letter of TQM is:

Total – involving every person in the organization and every aspect of its operation (the definition of organization may be extended to include suppliers and customers)

Quality– a customer-control definition is usually employed, with ultimate aim of maximizing customer benefit.

Management – although everyone is involved, the role of management is paramount. The senior executive must be fully committed and this commitment must flow down the hierarchy.

(c) Four main principles of TQM are:

1. Recognition of the customers importance
2. The involvement of everyone in quality improvement
3. Viewing every business activity as a process with potential for improvement
4. The goal of continuous improvement.

Q. 21.5: *Answer the following question in a word or two:*

(a) Who should you consult when seeking quality improvement?

(b) What does W. Edward Deming say is the alternative to Total Quality?

(c) Who is responsible for the idea that TQM companies should distinguish between vital few and the trivial many?

(i) ***Juran*** *(ii)* ***Deming*** *(iii)* ***Pareto*** *(iv)* ***Shewhart***

(d) CQI stands for:

(i) Constant quality increments

(ii) Continuous quality improvement

(iii) Continuous quality increases

(iv) Complete quality implementation.

Ans. : *(a)* Your staff

(b) Failure

(c) *(i)*

(d) *(ii)*

Q. 21.6: *A company on its letter head has stated "ISO & TQM certified company".*

Can any company print the above statement on its letterhead? Why or why not?

Ans. : A company can be ISO certified but there is no certification for TQM as of now. Hence the company cannot print such a statement.

Q. 21.7: *How TQM has lead to remove confusion on the meaning of quality?*

Ans. : It makes quality the central concern of the business. Too often, quality is either confused with addressing customer complaints which inevitably leads to it being viewed negatively, or is viewed as a direct measure of the product or service itself. Instead, all activities that are involved should be considered. Quality should be inherent in every facet of the business and not just a "bolt-on extra".

Q. 21.8: *What is the simplest objective of TQM?*

Ans. : The simplest objective of TQM is:

'Do the right things, right the first time, every time.

Q. 21.9: *"The aim of TQM is for a process to go out of control less than 10% of the time". Advise whether it is True or False statement.*

Ans. : It is a False statement.

Q. 21.10: *What do you understand by bench marking and concurrent engineering?*

Ans. : **Benchmarking** is a comparative measure. It is used to establish goals for continuous improvement. Forms of benchmarking include competitive, functional and internal **concurrent engineering** results in a better match between product design and production process capabilities. The higher quality and shorter product development times associated with concurrent engineering are competitive advantages.

Q. 21.11: *Compare and contrast Benchmarking and BPR.*

Ans. : Both benchmarking and BPR

- can bring about radical changes
- can utilize IT to bring about improvement
- strive for superior performance
- are involved in learning and improved efficiency

Whereas benchmarking focuses on other providers, BPR focuses on customers.

Whereas benchmarking concentrates on key measures, BPR looks at entire processes.

Whereas benchmarking is continuing process, BPR might be one-off exercise.

Q. 21.12: *What is the difference between quality costs of ISO and TQM?*

Ans. : ISO 9000 incurs appraisal costs and prevention costs (specifications and under control) white TQM involves investment in prevention though improvement activities.

Q. 21.13: *Mention briefly three important principles of TQM, adding a very brief explanation for each.*

Ans. : The important principles of TQM are as follows:

1. The *first* and *major* TQM principle is to *satisfy the customer* the person who pays for the product or service.
2. The *second* TQM principle is to satisfy the suppler, which is person or organization from whom we satisfying the internal supplier is by empowering the workers. Empowerment has two key aspects:
   (*i*) Allowing workers to have the freedom to decide how to do the necessary work, using the skills they possess and acquiring new skills as necessary to be an effective team member.
   (*ii*) Making workers responsible for achieving production targets and for quality control.
3. The *third* principle of TQM is continuous improvement. The aim should be get it right first time (*ii*) get at right next time.
   Workers are often a source of continuous improvements. They can provide suggestions or how to improve a process and eliminate waste or necessary work.

Q. 21.14: *(a) What was TQM originated?*

(b) State the fundamental of TQM?

(c) Can we have a TQM certified company?

(d) How does TQM work?

(e) What are its development stages?

(f) What is quality assurance?

Ans. : (*a*) TQM is a philosophy of quality management that originated in Japan in the 1950s.

(*b*) Fundamentals of TQM:

- Prevention of errors before their occur.
- Continual improvement
- Real participation by all
- Management commitment

(*c*) We do not have any certification from Govt. or and outside party for a company to be TQM. Hence we cannot have a TQM certified company.

(*d*) TQM increases customers satisfaction by boosting quality. It does this by motivating the work force and improving the way the company operates.

(*e*) Inspection ⇒ Quality control ⇒ Quality assurance ⇒ TQM.

(*f*) QA is the system of policies, procedures and guidelines that establishes and maintains the specified standards of product qualities as to generate adequate confidence that the product or service will satisfy the given requirements for quality.

Q. 21.15: *(a) Give a simple definition of TQM.*

(b) What is the aim of TQM?

(c) State ***(do not describe)*** *two commercial advantages of TQM?*

(d) What are the basic requirements for introduction of TQM?

(e) What is ISO 9000 ?

Ans. : (*a*) TQM is the process of applying a zero defect philosophy to the management of all resources and relationships within an organization as a means of developing and sustaining a culture of continuous improvement which focusses on meeting customer expectations.

(*b*) TQM is a management philosophy aimed at continuous improvement in all areas of operation. TQM initiative aims to achieve continuous improvement in quality productivity and effectiveness. It does this by establishing management responsibility for processes as well as output.

(*c*) It reduces wastages and mistakes and therefore leads to contracts being completed on time schedule without unnecessary remedial work. In addition, due to built in fault logging procedures it is unlikely that problems will be duplicated in future.

(*d*) Some basic requirements are for introduction of TQM are listed below:

1. Leadership
2. Organization wide introduction
3. Changing corporate orientation
4. Motivation
5. Robustness
6. Cost Orientation
7. Customer orientation

(*e*) ISO 9000 is internationally recognized 'total' quality standard. It specifically relates to quality system.

Q. 21.16: *(a) What is the important aim of TQM:*

(b) Why in JIT production, TQM is necessary?

Ans. : (*a*) TQM considers that the costs of prevention are less than the costs of correction. One of the main aims of TQM is to achieve zero rejects and 100% quality.

In JIT (Just-in-time) there are negligible inventories. There is no buffer stock. If there is a problem in production there is nothing to fall back on. JIT philosophy is based on perfect quality with zero defects. A TQM system is therefore necessary. In a JIT system quality is the responsibility of each employee.

Q. 21.17: *(a) How JIT is related to quality?*

(b) Use the words and phrases 1 to 8 in the table provided below to complete the following paragraphs by filling:

1	Quality	2	Output	3	Productions problems	4	TQM
5	Customer goodwill	6	Quality	7	Delays	8	Buffer inventory

(i) In a company operations on JIT principles the absence of inventories deprives production of a saftely net or '______'. This exposes the business to production problems or '______' and, ultimately, to lost sales and damages ______.

(ii) In this context, adoption of a ______ philosophy is key. In this ______ is a feature rooted in the production process and every individual is responsible for the quality of his/her ______.

(iii) This will encourage good quality at all times and therefore minimise ______ that would otherwise occur due to poor ______.

SOLUTION: (*a*) JIT is a manufacturing method that brings inventory down to zero (or near zero) levels. It forces a focus on quality, since there is no excess inventory on hand to waste.

(*b*) (*i*) 8 , 7, 5

(*ii*) 4, 1 or 6, 2

(*iii*) 3, 1 or 6.

Q. 21.18: *(a) Why Indian companies more and more are adopting TQM?*

(b) What is TQM? Explain.

(c) What are the Characteristics of an organization that has successfully implemented TQM?

(d) How TQM and Malcolm B. Baldrige Award are related?

Ans. : (*a*) Recent years have witnessed a renewed emphasis on delivering superior-quality products and services to customers. With foreign competition steadily eating away the profitability and the market shares of Indian companies, more and more of them are adopting total quality management (TMQ) to become more competitive.

(*b*) TQM is a process of managing complex changes in the organization with the aim of improving quality.

The TQM concept essentially is a business philosophy that was used by the Japanese to gain competitvie advantage. It is now being discovered and used by Indian organizations. TQM can be defined as a systematic effect at continuous quality improvement of all process, products, services, and human resources throughtout the organization, undertaken with an objective of improving customer satisfaction.

(*c*) The characteristics of an organization that has successfully implemented TQM are as follows:

- A TQM company strives for a continuous improvement in quality. To achieve this continuous improvement process (CIP), everyone in the organization must be trained and educated continuously.
- Teams and network are another cornerstone of the TQM organization. Cross-functional teams must be formed, and they must work together. The teams must be inherently motivated and should be empowered to set their own objective.
- Quantifiable measures of progress must be established, and rewards should be based on these measures. One of the most commonly used tools to set quantifiable measures is benchmarking. Competitive benchmarking means comparing the company's processes, practices and products to the world's best, including those in other industries.

(*d*) Adoption of TQM is one of the prerequisite for competing Malcolm Baldrige Award for quality.

Q. 21.19: *(a) What are the main differences between traditional quality management and TQM?*

(b) How can a company embracing TQM move forward and what is the role of an accountant in this?

Ans. : (*a*) TQM puts customers at the forefront of quality decision making. Customers' needs and expectations are always considered first in measuring achieved quality.

TQM takes an organization-wide perspective. It holds that all part of the organization have the potential to make a positive contribution to quality. *Central to this idea is the concept of the internal customer-supplier chain.*

TQM places considerable emphasis on the role and responsibilities of every member of staff within an organization to influence quality. It often encourages the idea of empowering individuals to improve their own part of the operation.

The implied cost models of TQM are very different from those used in the traditional approach to quality. Traditionally, the emphasis was placed on finding an optimum amount of quality effort which minimized the costs associated with quality. By contrast, TQM emphasizes the balance between different types of quality cost. It argues that increasing the amount of cost and effort placed on prevention will give a more-than-equivalent reduction in other costs. This idea is often summarized in the phrase 'right first time'.

TQM also places a heavy emphasis on the ideas of problem solving and continuous improvement.

(*b*) To move forward a company that is embracing TQM needs:

1. A leadership that inspires.
2. An employee - led customer service
3. Employees motivation to achieve TQM
4. Simplification of work
5. Elimination of waste.

The accountant's role is to provide performance measures that motivate staff to simplify their work and to eliminate waste in all forms including waste time.

Q. 21.20: *(a) Where did the idea of TQM come from?*

(b) What are the main implementation issues in TQM?

(c) How do quality awards and models contribute towards TQM?

Ans. : (*a*) Although the origins of TQM go back to the 1940s and '50s, the term was first formally used in 1957 by Feigenbaum. Many authorities have contributed to the development of the idea, however. These authorities include Feigenbaum, Deming, Juran, Ishikawa, Taguchi, and Crosby.

The emphasis placed on various aspects of TQM varies among these authorities but the general thrust of their arguments is similar.

TQM can be seen as being an extension of the traditional approach to quality –inspection-based quality control being replaced by the concept of quality assurance which in turn has been superseded by TQM.

(*b*) A number of factors appear to be influential in ensuring the success of TQM. These are:

- the existence of a fully worked-out quality strategy;
- top-management's support;
- steering group to guide the initiative;
- group-based improvements;
- an adequate recognition and rewards scheme;
- an emphasis on appropriate training.

TQM is a mature integration of system techniques and behaviour and consequently no single assessment criterion is available or appropriate.

There is a need however, to be able to validate an organization's claim to total quality and a need for companies to measure their own comparative level of quality development. In response to these needs a number of international quality assessment mechanisms have been developed. The three most important of these are:

1. the European Quality Award (EQA)
2. the Malcom Baldrige National Quality Award (MBNQA)
3. the Deming Awards
4. Rajiv Gandhi National Quality Award (RGNQA)

The EQA and RGNQA are based on nine point models which distinguish between 'enablers' of quality and the 'results' of quality. These are often now used as self certification models.

Q. 21.21: *(a) Simply define TQM. What is the focus of TQM?*

(b) What is Poka Yoke?

(c) State the outputs associated with three quality management processes:

(i) Plan quality; (ii) Perform QA, (iii) Perform QC

(d) Define Kaizen.

Ans. : (*a*) TQM: A quality theory popularized after World War II that states that everyone in the company is responsible for quality and is able to make a difference in the ultimate quality of the product. TQM applies to improvements in processes and in results. TQM also includes statistical process control.

TQM shifts the primary quality focus away from the product that is produced and looks instead at the underlying process of how it was produced.

(*b*) Poka yoke: Mistake proofing a process by focussing on potential problems before they occur. This is a Japanese term and method designed to design out potential problems. This is particularly important when it is critical that processes do not fail e.g. a nuclear power plant.

(*c*) The primary outputs associated with three quality management processes are shown in the table below:

Process	*Primary Outputs*
(*i*) Plan Quality	• Quality management plan • Quality metrics • Quality checklists
(*ii*) Perform QA	• Changes requests • Quality control measurements
(*iii*) Perform QC	• Validated changes • Validated deliverables

(*d*) Kaizen: It is a Japanese management term. It is a philosophy that stresses constant process improvement in the form of small changes in products or services.

Q. 21.22: *(a) Mention a few tools and techniqes of TQM.*

(b) Why TQM initiatives are prone to failure?

Ans. : (*a*) TQM there is no simple methodology to achieve TQM. However based upon the teachings of quality Curus– Deming, Juran, Taguchi and Ishikaur, following are some toosl and techniques to emtrace TQM. Examples of TQM tools include the following:

- flowcharting
- statistical process control (SPC)
- Pareto analysis
- cause and effect diagrams
- employee and customer surveys

Examples of techniques include:

- benchmarking
- cost of quality
- quality function deployment

- failure mode effects analysis
- design of experiments

(*b*) TQM initiatives have been prone to failure because of common mistakes. These include:

- allowing external forces and events to drive a TQM initiative
- an overwhelming desire for quality awards and certificates
- organising and perceiving TQM activities as separate from day-to-day work responsibilities
- teating TQM as an add-on with little attention given to the required changes in organisation and culture
- senior management underestimating the necessary commitment to TQM

Q. 21.23: *(a) State **one** of the most **important** principles of TQM.*

*(b) What is **benchmarking**?*

*(c) Explain the meaning of **TQM philosophy** and its relevance to the modern economic environment.*

*(d) What is the difference between **TQM** and **scientific management?***

Ans. : (*a*) The most **important principle** of TQM is customer driven focus.

(*b*) **Benchmarking** is a continuous, systematic process that measures products, services, and practices against those of industry leaders. Companies use benchmarking to understand better how outstanding companies do things so that they can improve their own operations.

(*c*) **TQM's** central concept is that 'quality' is the key strategic variable in a business and that it is a variable that is amenable to organizational culture. The key concepts associated with the provision of quality in an organization are 'empowerment' and 'teams'. TQM is very much the antithesis of the traditional 'command and control' concept associated with the budgeting that we often encounter. TQM involves the devolution of authority to multi-skilled, empowered teams in the organization. It is claimed that TQM provides the organizational flexibility needed to cope with the environment where product life cycle are short, products are highly customised and products have a high service element. The empowerment and motivation of individual staff to deal directly with customers is therefore critical to success.

(*d*) **TQM** rejects the notion that quality is the responsibility of specialists, human factors are extremely important. Hence in TQM employee involvement (EI) is crucial to process while **scientific management**, individual workers are expected to follow instructions.

Q. 21.24: *(a) In TQM what is the significance of Words-Total, Quality and Management?*

(b) What are the issues on which are under focus of TQM?

(c) Why do we implement TQM?

(d) State benefits of TQM.

Ans. : (*a*) Total Quality Management (TQM) offers a standard interpretation for its role in the world of quality.

Total means that every member of an organization is concerned with the product or service being sold to the consumer.

Quality is more difficult to define. Laws throughout the world refer to quality products as those that are fit for purpose. Alternatively, we see a quality good or service as one that conforms to or exceeds our requirements.

Management is the activity that makes the entire process work. It make use of personnel, capital and any other resources available.

(*b*) To ensure that an organization sustains competitive advantage and meets its financial targets, TQM focuses primarily on:

- Customer – what do they specifically want?
- Processes – are they efficient and effective?
- Workforce empowerment – can individual make decisions for themselves?
- Continuous improvement – is the workforce aware they can make improvements to the ways in which they perform their jobs?
- Leadership – often requiring training
- Measurement – of outputs, profits and effectiveness.

(*c*) From the focus list in (b) above, it is obvious that TQM strives for quality by tackling all the issues that could potentially create poor quality goods or services. The reason for implementing TQM are:

- Survival
- Elimination of waste
- To compete with the world-wide increase in competition
- To empower employees
- A marketing tool – customers now take more interest in how goods and services are produced

(*d*) Benefits of TQM are:

- Elimination of waste
- Employee empowerment leading to self managed teams
- Enhanced products and services
- Increase in competitive advantage
- Increase in market share
- Increase in productivity
- Increase in profits
- Motivated workforce

Q. 21.25: *(a) What is the role of ISO 9000 in TQM?*

(b) Is ISO 9000 quality system series registration a prerequisite for TQM?

Ans. : (*a*) ISO 9000 and associated standards are concerned with the systems and procedures which support quality. These are intended to assure purchasers of products and services that they have been produced in a way which meets customer requirements. ISO 9000 has received some criticism as being over-bureaucratic and inflexible.

(*b*) A quality system is a fundamental pillar to an organization's approach to TQM and it helps to ensure that any improvements made are held in place; (Fig. 21.2). However ISO 9000 quality system series registration is not a prerequisite for TQM. Some organizations, in particular those from the non manufacturing sector, have analyzed and improved their systems and working practices and then have gone straight to TQM.

The guidance provided in ISO 9001, and the independent assessment surveillance, is an indisputable aid in developing and maintaining the procedures, controls and discipline required in a quality management system. The system should help to ensure that more people within the organization are touched by quality and, in this way, quality awareness is raised.

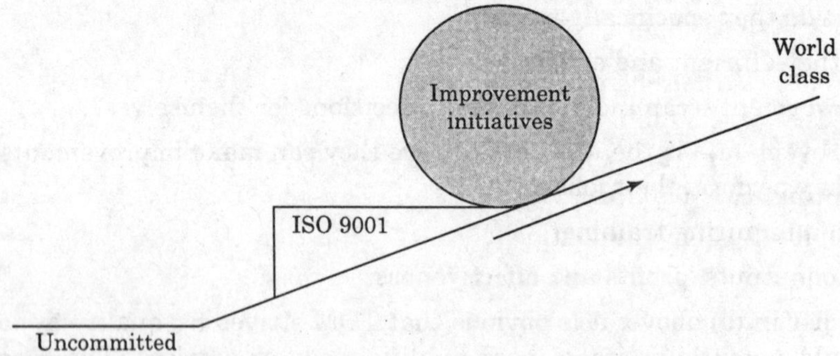

FIGURE 21.2 : Quality improvement and the ISO 9000 series.

Q. 21.26: *(a) Simply and briefly advise what is meant by TQM?*

(b) Does TQM include implementation of ISO 9000 series standards?

(c) Can it be said that TQM has its roots in statistics?

(d) How does TQM fit into operations strategy?

Ans. : (*a*) Total quality management (TQM) is a concept that has emereged recently as a way to achieve a systems approach to quality management. Total quality management refers to a total commitment to quality. This implies an overall integrated approach to all aspects of quality considering all the people, all the hardware, all the software, and the organizational resources. This required the total participation of everyone. High-quality performance should be required from all the people at all times.

(*b*) It is one of the ways of TQM. Practically it includes implementation of ISO 9000.

(*c*) Yes

(*d*) TQM is a philosophy of how to approach the organization of quality improvement that stresses the 'total' of TQM. It puts quality and improvement generally at the heart of everything that is done by an operation. It provides a checklist of how to organize operations improvement. It has also been developed into a more prescriptive form as in the EFQM Excellence Model, developed by the European Foundation for Quality Management (EFQM).

Q. 21.27: *(a) What is the role of quality management function?*

(b) For a company which has implemented ISO 9000 what are the main activities involved in moving towards a total quality management (TQM) company?

(c) Discuss the benefits of implementation of ISO 9000 before embarking upon TQM.

Ans. : (*a*) The role of quality management function encompasses the following:

- Management led company-wide interpretation of quality.
- Customer focus and conformance to specification.
- Quality improvement teams and change in management style.

(*b*) Stages in development covered in Fig. 21.3 are as:

System orientation	⇒	**Improvement orientation**	⇒	**Prevention orientation**
ISO 9000		Team based problem solving		Advance quality planning

FIGURE 21.3 Stages for an ISO company towards TQM

(*c*) Benefits of adopting ISO 9000 initial are:

- In provides a reliable system 'foundation'.
- Procedures provide a mechanism for capturing improvement.
- First stage in workforce orientation and training.

Q. 21.28: *Describe in brief the use of following techniques in the implementation of TQM:*

(a) quality costs; *(b) supplier assessment;*

(c) process control charts; *(d) quality improvement teams.*

Ans. : Implementation of techniques includes the following:

(*a*) Quality costs collected in terms of prevention, appraisal and internal/external failure used as basis for improvement measurement—focus on prevention. Categories of cost should be identified.

(*b*) Supplier assessment including third party accreditation using ISO 9000 and the scope of such assessment, i.e. contract revision → design control → purchasing → process control → inspection → corrective action → storage/handing, etc. Cost of ownership and focus on specification.

(*c*) Process control implementation via identification through pilot study of C*p* and C*pk*. Identify process is under control then employ control charts UCL/LCL ± 3 sigma. Operation of preventative approach to the control of process variability. Widespread application in TQM.

(*d*) QITs operating company-wide (deployed teams and quality circles) to focus on improvement projects. Description of types of teams, organizational structure through quality improvement councils and facilitations.

Q. 21.29: *(a) What are the main business benefits of TQM?*

(b) How does the cost of quality for a manufacturing company change during each of the stages implementing TQM.

(c) Why do so many companies experience difficulties in implementing TQM and how difficulties overcome?

Ans. : (*a*) The main business benefits of TQM are:

1. Reduced cost of quality.
2. Improved customer service and retention.
3. Reduced process and development lead times.

(*b*) The changes in the cost of quality are indicated in Fig. 21.4.

Stage 1	Stage 2	Stage 3
System Orientation	Improvement	Prevention
20% →	15% →	8% → 5%

FIGURE 21.4 Changes in cost of quality

Typical distribution of costs, investment in prevention less than failure.

(*c*) Problems in implementing TQM:

1. Improving all three dimensions - people, systems and tools and techniques simultaneously.
2. Regenerating ongoing continuous improvements
3. Sustaining management commitment

These difficulties are overcome by using:

- Combination of systems, techniques and people development;
- Changing focus of TQ implementation
- long, term senior management commitment

Q. 21.30: *(a) Do we essentially need ISO 9000 for TQM?*

(b) What are the basic four Ps and three Cs of a new simple TQM?

Ans. : (*a*) With TQM aim is continuous improvement and, with the continuing impetus for quality, improvement being driven from best ISO can be seen as a step on the way to TQM, at worst it might actually inhibit TQM, as it relies on the setting of top-down standards and controls and might deter staff from suggesting changes. A true TQM organization does not need ISO, but if ISO is insisted on by a customer it can be made to fit into overall TQM plan.

(*b*) **Planning, People** and **Processes** are the keys to delivering quality products and services to customers and generally improving overall **Performance**. These **four** Ps form a structure of 'hard management necessities' for a new simple TQM model.

The three Cs of **Culture**, **Communication**, and **Commitment** provide the glue of 'soft outcomes' of the model which will take organizations successfully into the twenty-first century.

Q. 21.31: *(a) Do you agree with the statement "ISO 9000 are to some extent contrary to the philosophy of TQM". Explain your answer.*

(b) If (a) is justified then how ISO 9000 is useful in relation to TQM for an organization?

Ans. : (*a*) TQM means more than just the basics as outlined in ISO 9000; indeed, ISO 9000 could be seen running contrary to the philosophy of TQM. In fact it is important to recognize the limitations of the ISO 9000 series. They are not and do not profess to be a panacea for the business's ills. Many companies have misguidedly expected that by adopting an ISO 9000 standard they will achieve success comparable to that of the over-publicised Japanese. One must not forget that the ISO 9000 standards did not exist when the Japanese quality performance improved so spectacularly: many Japanese firms did not need such written standards, and probably still don't.

ISO 9000 exists primarily to give customers confidence that the product or service being provided will meet certain specified standards of performance, and that the product or service will always be consistent with those standards. Indeed, some customers will insist that suppliers are ISO accredited.

There are also internal benefits for organizations that seek ISO 9000 accreditation. First, by adopting how to go about establishing and documenting a quality improvement system. To achieve accreditation, an organization has to prove that every step of the process is documented and that the specifications and check procedures shown in the documentation are always complied with. The recording and documenting of each step is a long and tedious job; perhaps the most difficult stage is agreeing on what exactly the standard procedure is.

If an organization does not have a standard way of doing things, trying to document methods will prove difficult and many interesting facts will emerge. The act of recording exactly what is happening and then determining what the one set method should be is in itself a useful exercise. Non-value-adding activities will be unearthed and hopefully, overall a more efficient method will emerge and be adopted as standard procedure. Determining a standard does not imply that the most efficient method is being used; the standard adopted only means that there is now a standard method (not necessarily the most efficient), that the method is recorded.

Q. 21.32: *What are Business Process Re-engineering (BPR) and TQM? State the difference between the two.*

Ans. : TQM is a continuous process improvement and was adopted by companies during the 1980s. However, in the 1990s, many of these companies began experimenting with more radical change approaches by introducing business process reengineering (BPR). TQM and BPR share many characteristics, such as customer focus, process orientation and committment to improved performance. However, there are also a number of differences between the two processes; below:

- Goal improvement

  BPR: radial, sometimes ten-fold levels of improvement in time, cost and quality of process

  TQM: around 10% improvement in any given year
- Starting point

  BPR: new start with a clean sheet of paper.

  TQM: starting from the current state of the process.
- Control measurement

  BPR: attempts to identify the technological or organizational process factors that will maximize variation and create fruitful change.

  TQM: stresses the rigour of statistical process control to minimize unexplained variation in each process.
- Both BPR and TQM are process-orientated
- *BPR:* the focus is on cross-functional processes.

  TQM: the focus is on functional processes.
- Rigorous measurement of process performance

  BPR: cost of process.

  TQM: cost of quality.
- Investment of time before significant results

  BPR: time for training and culture change.

  TQM: time to establish information systems and an organizational structure.

As on-going polemic regarding the implementation of TQM and BPR is: which comes first? Many project organizations re-engineer processes prior to the introduction of a quality system to ensure that the latest IT enablers are incorporated in the system. If a quality system is developed without sufficient investigation of the processes involved, then it is likely that the system will need major development as the project proceeds.

Fundamental differences between TQM and BPR

Factors	*TQM*	*BPR*
Nature of implementation	Bottom-up	Top-down
Main control measure	Cost of quality	Cost of process
Type of change way of doing a job	Evolutionary: a better a new way of doing business	Revolutionary:
Culture change	Culture/structural change	
Process focus	Functional	Cross-functional
Method	Adds value to the existing process	Redesigns the business process
Improvement	Incremental (continuous)	Dramatical
Risk	Moderate	High
Scope of change	Organization processes	Core business
Role of technology	Statistical control	IT enabler

Q. 21.33: *(a) Mention in simple terms how will you judge the quality of a product or service? What are the implications of you criteria set for judging the quality of a product or service.*

(b) How your answer in (a) above changes in the context of TQM?

(c) State some characteristics of total quality management programmes.

Ans. : (*a*) In simple terms, the quality of a product or service can be judged on the following criteria.

(*i*) How well made a product is, or how well performed if it is a service.

(*ii*) How well it serves its purpose.

(*iii*) How it measures up against its rivals.

The implications of above criteria can be

- That quality is something that requires care on the part of the provider.
- That quality is largely subjective - it is in the eye of the beholder, the customer.

(*b*) In the context of TQM, quality means getting it right first time and improving continuously.

(*c*) Some of the characteristics of total quality management programmes are :

1. Organization wide there must be acceptance that the only thing that matters is the customer.
2. There should be recognition of the all-pervasive nature of the customer-supplier relationship, including internal customers; passing sub-standard material to another division is not satisfactory.

3. Instead of relying on inspection to a predefined level of quality, the cause of the defect in the first place should be prevented.
4. Each employee or group of employees must be personally responsible for defect-free production or service in their domain.
5. There should be a move away from 'acceptable' quality levels. Any level of defects must be unacceptable.
6. All departments should try obsessively to get thing right first time; this applies to misdirected phone calls and typing errors as much as to production.
7. Quality certification programmes should be introduced.
8. The cost of poor quality should be emphasised; good quality generates savings.

Q. 21.34: *XYZ Bank has over 2 million customers and nearly 6,00,000 credit card holders. The bank employs 4,000 staff in 10 locations through out the country and each week handles over 5 million transactions. A new chief executive set an agenda some years ago to focus on the features, benefits and drawbacks of contemporary approaches to the management of quality. Since this time XYZ has been involved in implementing a TQM programme. As part of an induction briefing for new staff of XYZ you are required to make a presentation.*

Requirements:

(a) Explain the critical elements of XYZ's TQM approach to Quality improvement Customer care and Quality Assurance.

(b) If a subsidiary company wished to introduce TQM how could it plan to communicate the quality approach to its managers.

Ans. : (*a*) The critical elements of XYZ's TQM approach in the presentation can be summarised as: Quality improvement programme

- Identification, elimination and prevention of processing errors, rework and wastage via systematic audit processes.
- Design control of all processes, products and services.
- The development of beneficial partnerships with all external suppliers.
- A shift in culture so that the whole workforce becomes active in the quality process. Customer care programme (focusing on the needs of the external customer and internal customer relationships)
- Market research to understand customer needs and current customer perceptions of products and service quality.
- Staff perception: research to ascertain staff attitude to quality and their interactions with external customers. (Staff interaction with customers will determine the customer perception of the service).
- A complaints-handling service designed to be highly and speedily responsive to customer issues.
- Effective and regular customer care training for all staff.
- Effective customer communication and reporting procedures to keep customers informed on organi-zational issues.

Quality assurance programme

This should lay down the standards for performance and implement and manage a quality management system, ensuring compliance to standards (ISO 9000).

- Ensure XYZ is a ISO-registered firm with latest relevant ISO standard.
- Benchmark against other banks and service providers to monitor performance and to ensure constant awareness of external quality assurance programmes.

Often quality programmes are undertaken for the wrong reasons.

It is important that organizations ensure that both internal and external quality needs are assessed and addressed.

(*b*) Plan to communicate quality to internal managers

Stage 1. Present TQM philosophy to the senior management team to instill TQM at the top level.

Stage 2. Set up quality groups/circles within departments to tackle specific quality issues.

Stage 3. Run TQM workshops and training sessions for group co-ordinators to ensure the quality message is received.

Stage 4. Establish departmental/group quality standards. Possibly implement reward systems for quality improvements.

Stage 5. Agree quality performance data/standards for each department to monitor quality achievements.

Q. 21.35: *The divisional managing director of the organization that you work for has proposed a total quality management (TQM) programme to help change prevailing attitudes and improve results. You have been asked to prepare a report for the next management board meeting basis for constructive discussion as to how the TQM programme should be implemented.*

Requirements:

(a) Explain the critical success factors for the implementation of a programme of Total Quality Management (TQM).

(b) Explain the categorization of quality costs and how such categorization could be of assistance in the establishment of a TQM programme.

Ans. : (*a*) Total Quality Management (TQM) can be defined as follows: Integrated and comprehensive system of planning and controlling all business functions so products or services are produced which meet or exceed customer expectations. TQM is a philosophy of business behaviour, embracing principles such as employee involvement, continuous improvement at all levels and customer focus, as well as being a collection of related techniques aimed at improving quality such as full documentation of activities, clear goal setting and performance measurement from the customer perspective.

The key factors in the success of TQM:

- There is a concentration on continuous improvement. This means that small improvements are as important as large leaps in technology. Such improvements may be changes in production flow, product specification or manufacturing methods.
- There needs to be widespread commitment to improvement in quality. All those involved in the company are part of the TQM environment: from board to shop floor.
- TQM should focus on the customer, not on just a single area of a business. This customer focus means the perspective of the company changes from its present obvious production/ sales/research one. Within the company, all sections may see themselves as potential customers of other sections and potential suppliers to other sections. This refocussing is vital in this company.
- TQM is about designing quality into the product and the production process. This means there must be a close working relationship between sales, production, distribution and research.
- Concentration on short-term profit needs to be abandoned in favour of longterm quality improvement, which will itself lead to long-term profit improvement. This implies being prepared to invest in changes for the future.

- There is a need for a fundamental culture change. Management, in particular, needs to use feedback and appraisal to find better ways of doing things. Failure to meet targets is probably inevitable, but needs to be met with positive, rather than negative, comment.
- There needs to be a clear willingness to discuss and measure quality. This may involve setting standards and gathering information that perhaps has previously been ignored. Feedback information, which need not be quantitative or financial, must be fed back quickly and in an intelligible way.
- Reward systems need to be reorganized to enable and encourage quality, rather than to prevent it happening. Thus, incentive schemes based on improvement suggestions would be a very rapid way of improving quality.

Other factors that might have been identified, though these are by no means always vital:

- Training in areas where the company is felt to be weak. The TQM programme should identify these. Training possibly needs to be external.
- The establishment of project teams to change procedures.
- The establishment of quality circles.
- The establishment of regular reporting of key indicators of quality.

It is difficult to select factors that are more crucial than others: the particular ones of importance will depend on the company and the areas of shortfall. The most crucial over-all area, especially in the company quoted, appears to be the building up of teamwork.

(*b*) Quality cost is normally defined as the 'cost of ensuring and assuring quality, as well as the loss incurred when quality is not achieved' and may be measured in four ways. These four methods have often been called the 'cost of not achieving quality':

- **Prevention cost:** The cost of ensuring that poor quality does not happen, e.g. training, planning and administration, checking design is adequate, etc.
- **Appraisal cost:** The cost of discovering poor-quality items. This would include quality control, inspections, etc.
- **Internal failure cost:** The cost, internal to the company, caused by poor quality. Costs include rework costs, scrap, re-engineering, retooling, etc.
- **External failure cost:** The cost of poor quality incurred outside the company: this includes direct costs, such as warranties, repair and after sales service, and indirect costs such as lost customer goodwill.

These costs are very difficult to isolate and judge. In each area, there is often a need to opportion costs (e.g. training, planning and administration) and there are many areas, especially the external failure cost, where costs cannot be calculated, for example, the opportunity cost of lost sales as a result of poor quality service.

Nevertheless, striving towards measuring quality costs keeps this issue on the management's agenda. The presence of multiple measures of quality can be helpful in presenting a balanced approach to control and the identification of the key areas for an individual organization.

Some companies regard the cost of quality as zero, because if TQM is achieved, then none of the costs above will be incurred and so cost is actually reduced. Others see the above costs of quality as being avoidable non-value-adding and therefore costs that might be reduced. This latter view is central to the understanding of how the cost of quality can assist TQM: discovering the cost of wasted resources we have been using to meet current customer standards. It is these costs that need to be reduced and doing so is central to a programme of cost reduction.

CHAPTER

22

Six-Sigma

22.1 UNDERSTANDING THE SIX-SIGMA (6σ)

After TQM we are now in a position to discuss the enigma of **six-sigma.** Sigma (σ) is a classical Greek letter that is used in mathematical and statistical models to signify the standard deviation firm the mean i.e., variation from the average value of the quality characteristic. The more the value of σ, the more is the variation. In an ideal situation, the variation from the mean is ±3σ. Figure 22.1 shows a normal distribution as a model for quality characteristic with specification limits at three standard deviations (i.e., ±3σ) on either side of the mean (with the amid at value of quality characteristic $X\mu_o = T$). It is obvious from Fig. 22.1 (*a*) that 99.73% of the product will have the given quality characteristic within ±3σ meaning thereby that 0.27% or 2700 parts per million will be defective or non conforming with respect to the given quality characteristic *X* where amid at value is μ_o.

Products (or assemblies) with numerous components such as a motor car or an aeroplane and specialized fighter plane (like Rafale) have many components in their assembles or subassemblies and hence have many chances of failure or rather fatal failure if the components with then characteristics outside their boundary limits of ±3σ are assembled at random in mass production. Hence lesser the variation in the given quality characteristics i.e., lesser the value of σ for the given of quality characteristic, the lesser the chances of failure. Realising this fact, **Motorola** developed a six-sigma (i.e. 6-σ) programme in the late 1980s, that as a response to the demand for their products.

However, as we know that variation in mass manufacture is inevitable i.e., variation is bound to occur and hence we specify the value of quality characteristic. It is therefore the aim in six-sigma that variation in quality characteristic, i.e., ±6σ should be within Upper specification limit (i.e., USL_X or *U*) and lower specification limit (i.e. LSL_X or *L*) so that we get only 2 parts per billion (or almost nil) products outside the $(U - L)$ tolerance band

Figure 22.1 (*a*) shows a normal probability distribution as a model for a quality characteristic with specification limits at ±3σ on either side of the mean.

Now it turns out that in this situation the probability of producing a product within these specifications is 0.9973, which corresponds to 2700 parts per million (ppm) defective. This is referred to as **three-sigma quality performance**, and it actually sounds pretty good. However, suppose we have a product that consists of an assembly of 100 independent components or parts and all 100 of these parts must be nondefective for the product to function satisfactorily. The probability that any specific unit of product is nondefective is

$$0.9973 \times 0.9973 \times \ldots \times 0.9973 = (0.9973)^{100} = 0.7631$$

That is, about 23.7% of the products produced under three-sigma quality will be defective. This is not an acceptable situation, because many products used by today's society are made up of many components. Even a relatively simple service activity, such as a visit by a family of four to a fast-food restaurant, can involve the assembly of several dozen components. A typical automobile has about 100,000 components and an airplane has between one and two million!

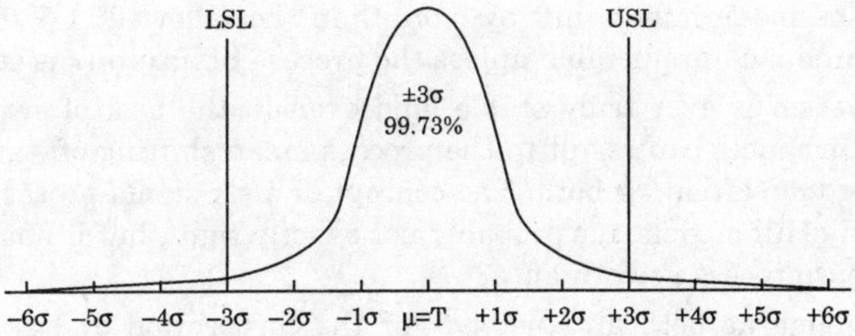

Spec. Limits	Percent inside specs	ppm Defective
±1 Sigma	68.27	317300
±2 Sigma	95.45	45500
±3 Sigma	99.73	2700
±4 Sigma	99.9937	63
±5 Sigma	99.999943	0.57
±6 Sigma	99.9999998	0.002

(*a*) Normal distribution centered at the target (T)

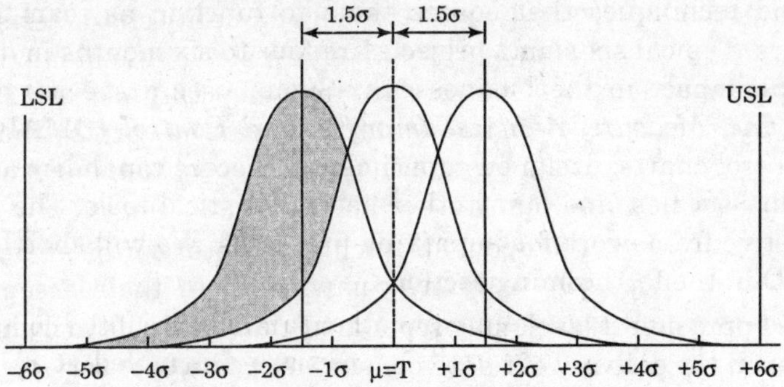

Spec. Limits	Percent inside specs	ppm Defective
±1 Sigma	30.23	697700
±2 Sigma	69.13	608700
±3 Sigma	93.32	66810
±4 Sigma	99.3790	6210
±5 Sigma	99.97670	233
±6 Sigma	99.999660	3.4

(*b*) Normal distribution with the mean shifted by ±1.5s from the target.

FIGURE 22.1 The Motorola Six-Sigma concept.

The Motorola six-sigma concept is to reduce the variability in the process so that the specification limits are at least *six standard deviations* from the mean. Then, as shown in Fig. 22.1a, there will only be about 2 parts per *billion* defective. Under **six-sigma quality**, the probability that any specific unit of the hypothetical product above is nondefective is 0.9999998, or 0.2 ppm, (practically zero defective) a much better situation.

When the six-sigma concept was initially developed, an assumption was made that when the process reached the six-sigma quality level, the process mean was still subject to disturbances that could cause it to shift by as much as 1.5 standard deviations off target. This situation is shown in Fig. 22.1(*b*). Under this scenario, a six-sigma process would produce about 3.4 ppm defective.

There is an apparent inconsistency in this. As we stated in Chap. 3, PART-1(A) on SQC, we can only make predictions about process performance when the process is **stable**; that is, when the mean (and standard deviation, too) is **constant**. If the mean is drifting around, and ends up as much as 1.5 standard deviations off target, a prediction of 3.4 ppm defective may not be very reliable, because the mean might shift by *more* than the "allowed" 1.5 standard deviations. Process **performance** isn't predictable unless the process **behaviour** is stable.

However, no process or system is ever truly stable, and even in the best of situations, disturbances occur. These disturbances can result in the process mean shifting off-target, an increase in the process standard deviation, or both. The concept of a six-sigma process is one way to **model** this behavior. Like all models, it's probably not exactly right, but it has proven to be a useful way to think about process performance.

Motorola established six-sigma as both an objective for the corporation and as a focal point for process and product quality improvement efforts. In recent years, six-sigma has spread beyond Motorola and has come to encompass much more. It has become a program for improving corporate **business performance** by both *improving quality* and paying attention to reducing costs. Companies involved in a six-sigma effort utilize specially trained individuals, called *Green Belts* (GBs), *Black Belts* (BBs), and *Master Black Belts* (MBBs) lead teams focused on projects that have both quality and business (economic) impacts for the organization. The "belts" have specialized training and education on statistical methods and the quality and process improvement tools and techniques that equips them to function as team leaders, facilitators, and problem solvers. Typical six-sigma projects are four to six months in duration are selected for their potential impact in the business. Six-Sigma uses a specific five-step problem-solving approach: *Define, Measure, Analyze, Improve, and Control* **(DMAIC)**. The DMAIC framework utilizes control charts, designed experiments, process capability analysis, measurement systems capability studies, and many other basic statistical tools. The DMAIC approach is an extremely effective framework for improving processes. We will shortly give a fuller representation of DMAIC in the forthcoming sections.

The goals of six-sigma, a 3.4 ppm defect level, may seem artificially or arbitrarily high, but it is easy to demonstrate that even the delivery of relatively simple products or services at high levels of quality can lead to the need for six-sigma thinking. For example, consider the visit to a fast-food restaurant mentioned above. The customer orders a typical meal: a hamburger (bun, meat, special sauce, cheese, pickle, onion, lettuce, and tomato), fries, and a soft drink. This product has ten components. Is 99% good quality satisfactory? If we assume that all ten components are independent, the probability of a good meal is

$$P\{\text{Single meal good}\} = (0.99)^{10} = 0.9044$$

which looks pretty good. There is better than a 90% chance that the customer experience will be satisfactory. Now suppose that the customer is a family of four. Again, assuming independence, the probability that all four meals are good is

$$P\{\text{All meal good}\} = (0.9044)^4 = 0.6690.$$

This isn't so nice. The chances are only about two out of three that all of the family meals are good. Now suppose that this hypothetical family of four visits this restaurant once a month. The probability that all visits result in good meals for everybody is

$$P\{\text{All visits during the year good}\} = (0.6690)^{12} = 0.0080.$$

This is obviously unacceptable. So, even in a very simple service system involving a relatively simple product, very high levels of quality and service are required to produce the desired high-quality experience for the customer.

Business organizations have been very quick to understand the potential benefits of six-sigma and to adopt the principles and methods. Between 1987 and 1993, Motorola reduced defectivity on its products by approximately 1300%. This success led to many organizations adopting the approach.

22.1.1 Why Six-Sigma?

Six-Sigma is not just a statistical approach to measure variance; it is a process and culture to achieve operational excellence. Following its success, particularly in Japan, Total Quality Management (TQM) seemed to be everywhere. Sayings synonymous with TQM, such as work smarter not harder, right first time and every time, zero defects, quality is free, fitness for purpose, and the customer is king, became so over-used as to become hackneyed cliches. Although TQM was the 'in' management tool in the 1980s, by the 1990s it was regarded by many (especially in the USA) as an embarrassing failure and was written off as a concept that promised much but failed to deliver to its expectation. Some believe that TQM swung too far towards the 'soft' issues of culture, consensus and staff involvement - the 'country club' approach. In any event, research by Turner (1993) has shown that any quality initiative needs to be reinvented at regular intervals to keep the enthusiasm level high. Against this background, six-sigma emerged to replace the 'tired' TQM philosophy.

Six-Sigma began in 1985 when Bill Smith, an engineer with Motorola, recommended the reinserting of hard-nosed statistics into the blurred philosophy of TQM. It should be remembered that Deming, Juran and Feigenbaum, the pioneers of TQM, were statisticians and had all preached the need for measurement and control charts. Indeed, in Japan there was never a dilution of the statistical roots of TQM. Only in the USA and Europe, with the 'soft' politically correct approach to staff and the idea that if customer service is high ('have a nice day') the numbers (bottom line) will look after themselves, was the statistical approach to TQM lost. Although six-sigma began in Motorola, in 1980s its greatest successes have been in Allied Steel and General Electric. Following the merger of these two organizations, General Electric has become the worldwide leader for six-sigma.

22.2 OBJECTIVE OF SIX-SIGMA

Six Sigma is a quality management programme to achieve 'six sigma' levels of quality, derived from TQM.

- It is a performance measurement framework first pioneered by Motorola in the 1980s, which has developed into a system for process improvement.
- Six Sigma has been used for both manufacturing and service businesses.
- Six Sigma can be implemented across the whole business, but in practice it is generally used for individual processes.
- Six Sigma is designed to decrease wastage and improve products and services, leading to greater customer satisfaction and lower costs. Companies implementing Six Sigma report high levels of savings from projects.
- Six Sigma is a data-driven approach, based on statistical measurements of variation from a standard or a norm and the use of quantitative data for processes.
- The aim of the approach is to achieve a reduction in variations and the number of 'faults' that go beyond an accepted tolerance limit. The ultimate aim of a Six Sigma project is to reduce the variation in process output so that there are no more than 3.4 defects per million opportunities – the Six Sigma level of programme.
- Performance measures are based on customer requirements. While targets may appear very high at first, it should be remembered that just one defect can result in a lost customer.

- The Six-Sigma is a frame work that makes use of the range of tools such as
  - Statistical measures
  - Fish bone diagrams
  - Pareto analysis
  - DOX.

22.3 THE DMAIC CYCLE

The common tool used in Six Sigma is **DMAIC**. On identification of area to be improved by six-sigma, DMAIC–the six-sigma problem solving process is employed. The DMAIC methodology covers the following steps.

- *D* – Define – defining the problem, clarifying the purpose of the project and developing the project plan.
- *M* – Measure – data collection to quantify the problem, measuring the key processes that are critical to quality.
- *A* – Analyze – analysis of data to find the root cause of the problem, considering the process itself, materials, environmental factors and the activities of staff involved in the process. The results from the analysis may lead to modifications in the definition of the problem.
- *I* – Improve – developing solutions and implementing them.
- *C* – Control – monitoring changes, and dealing with problems arising. The control process will focus on key performance measures.

Figure 22.2 shows the different stages of the DMAIC process and the important possible output from each step and Table 22.1 summarizes the tools commonly used in six-sigma projects.

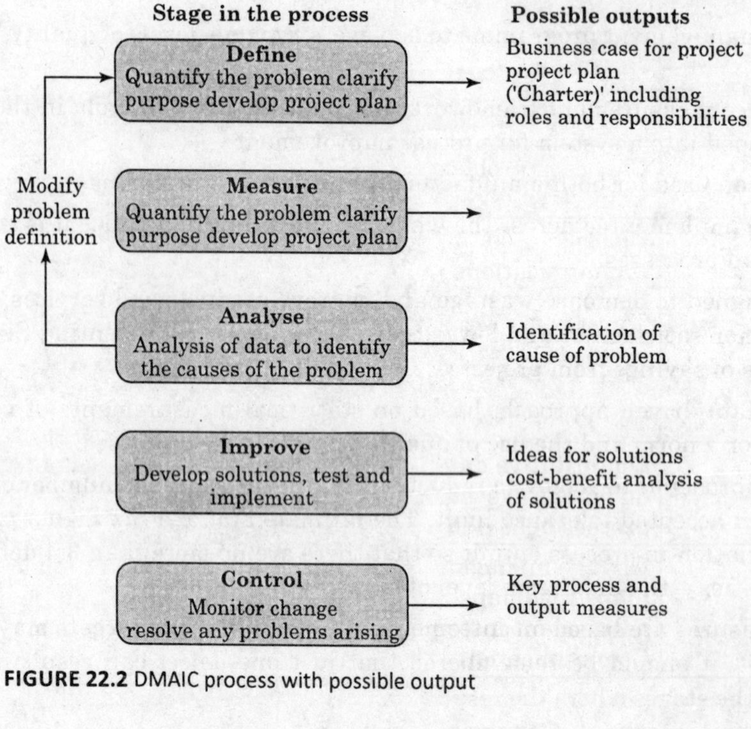

FIGURE 22.2 DMAIC process with possible output

TABLE 22.1 THE TOOLS COMMONLY USED IN SIX-SIGMA PROJECTS.

Type of tool/technique			Example deliverables	6α Stage*	Example tools
Data Collection	Quantitative		Quantitative data Number of defects	*D, M, C*	Surveys Automated data collection tools check sheets(e.g. defect check sheets) Group voting
	Qualitative		Customer opinions (qualitative)	*D*	Focus groups Interviews Workshops
Data analysis	Quantitative	Graphical	Distribution charts Patterns/trends identified	*A, C*	Control Charts Run Charts Capability analysis Pareto charts Scatter plots
	Quantitative	Numerical (statistics)	Statistical indicators	*A*	ANOVA Capability indices Sigma level
	Qualitative		Well Organized qualitative information clarity	*D, A*	7M tools (affinity diagrams, interrelationship diagrams, etc.)
Creativity/Idea generation			New ideas Solutions to problems	*D, M, A, I*	Brain Storming Nominal group technique THE (Technology/ Human/Environment) Six Thinking Hats
Knowledge discovery			Causes of problems	*A*	Ishikawa tool 5 Whys
Formalising/ Communication			Clear communications plans	*D, M, C*	Project charter Process documentation Operational definitions Gantt Charts Flow Charts SIPOC Dashboards
Simulation/Testing			Quantitative data on potential system/ process behaviour	*I*	Monte Carlo simulations Pilot tests
Change management			Change management plans/roadmaps Risk assessment internal Communication	*I, C*	Force field analysis SSC (Stop, Start, Continue)

* Stage refers to some of the stages where the respective types of tools are used most often. The stages are: D = Define, M = Measure, A = Analyse, I = Improve, C = Control.

22.3.1 Additional Tools in Six-Sigma

In recent years, two other tool sets have become identified with six-sigma. These are

1. DFSS
2. LEAN SYSTEMS

Many organizations regularly use one or both of these approaches as an integral part of these six-sigma implementation.

Design for six-sigma is an approach for taking the variability reduction and process improvement philosophy of six-sigma upstream from manufacturing or production into the design process, where new products (or services or service processes) are designed and developed. Broadly speaking, **DFSS** is a structured and disciplined methodology for the efficient commercialization of technology that results in new products, services, or processes. By a product, we mean anything that is sold to a consumer for use; by a service, we mean an activity that provides value or benefit to the consumer. DFSS spans the entire development process from the identification of customer needs to the final launch of the new product or service. Customer input is obtained through **voice of the customer (VOC)** activities designed to determine what the customer really wants, to set priorities based on actual customer wants, and to determine if the business can meet those needs at a competitive price that will enable it to make a profit. VOC data is usually obtained by customer interviews, by a direct interaction with and observation of the customer, through focus groups, by surveys, and by analysis of customer satisfaction data. The purpose is to develop a set of critical to quality (CTQ) requirements for the product or service. Traditionally, six-sigma is used to achieve operational excellence, while DFSS is focused on improving business results by increasing the sales revenue generated from new products and services and finding new applications or opportunities for existing ones. In many cases, an important gain from DFSS is the reduction of development lead time; that is, the cycle time to commercialize new technology and get the resulting new products to market. DFSS is directly focused on increasing value in the organization. Many of the tools that are used in operational six-sigma are also used in DFSS. The DMAIC process is also applicable, although some organizations and practitioners have slightly different approaches (**DMADV**, or *Define, Measure, Analyze, Design,* and *Verify,* is a popular variation).

Lean systems are designed to eliminate waste. By waste, we mean unnecessarily long cycle times, or waiting times between value-added work activities. Waste can also include rework (doing something over again to eliminate defects introduced the first time) or scrap. Rework and scrap are often the result of excess variability, so there is an obvious connection between six-sigma and lean. An important metric in lean is the process cycle efficiency (PCE) defined as

$$\text{Process cycle efficiency} = \frac{\text{Value-add time}}{\text{Process cycle time}}$$

where the value-add time is the amount of time actually spent in the process that transforms the form, fit, or function of the product or service that results in something for which the customer is willing to pay. PCE is a direct measure of how efficiently the process is converting the work that is in-process into completed products or services. Process cycle time is also related to the amount of work that is in-process through Little's Law:

$$\text{Process cycle time} = \frac{\text{Work-in-process}}{\text{Average completion rate}}$$

The average completion rate is a measure of capacity; that is, it is the output of a process over a defined time period. For example, consider a mortgage refinance operation at a bank. If the average completion rate for submitted applications is 100 completions per day, and there are 1,500 applications waiting for processing, the process cycle time is

$$\text{Process cycle time} = \frac{1500}{100} = 15 \text{ days}$$

Often the cycle time can be reduced by eliminating waste and inefficiency in the process, resulting in an increase in the completion rate.

Lean also makes use of many tools of industrial engineering and operations research. One of the most important of these is **discrete-event simulation**; in which a computer model of the system is built and used to quantify the impact of changes to the system that improve its performance. Simulation models are often very good predictors of the performance of a new or redesigned system. Both manufacturing and service organizations can greatly benefit by using simulation models to study the performance of their processes.

Ideally, six-sigma/DMAIC, DFSS, and lean tools are used simultaneously and harmoniously in an organization to achieve high levels of process performance and significant business improvement. Figure 22.3 highlights many of the important complimentary aspects of these three sets of tools.

Six-Sigma (often combined with DFSS and Lean) has been much more successful than its predecessors, notably TQM. The project-by-project approach and the focus on obtaining improvement in bottom-line business results has been instrumental in obtaining management commitment to six-sigma. Another major component in obtaining success is driving the proper deployment of statistical methods into the right places in the organization. The DMAIC problem-solving framework is an important part of this.

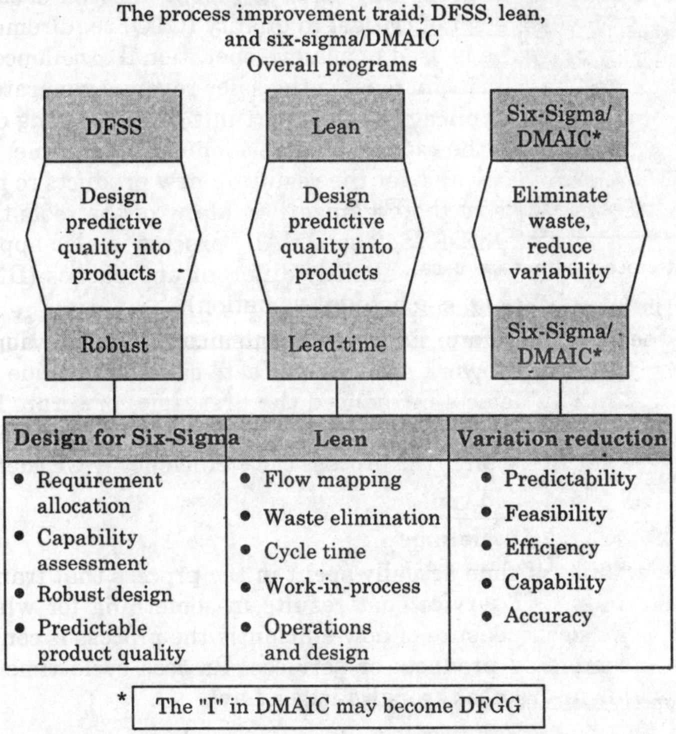

FIGURE 22.3 Six-Sigma/DMAIC, lean, and DFSS: How they fit together.

22.4. USE OF SIX-SIGMA IN SERVICE INDUSTRIES

It might be considered that six-sigma relates better to manufacturing, and, as stated above, the publicised successes have been in manufacturing and engineering operations. However, American Express, very much a service operation, began a successful six-sigma pilot in 1998, and is now rolling out the six-sigma programme worldwide. Additionally, much of the success of General Electric (GE) was in the GE Capital division (the financial services operation that accounts for over 40 per cent of GE's business). Bob Galvin, the former Chief Executive Officer of Motorola, has stated that the lack of initial six-sigma emphasis in the non-manufacturing areas was a mistake that cost Motorola at least $5 billion over a fouryear period.

One reason for this misconception is that service organizations are usually unaccustomed to looking at their processes in the traditional systematic 'input-process-output' manner of manufacturing, Fig. 22.4. A simplified input-process-output (IPO) diagram for a sales process, as shown in Fig. 22.5 illustrates the point that a process is a process regardless of the type of operation or organization. All processes have inputs and outputs; likewise, all processes have customers, suppliers and quality criteria.

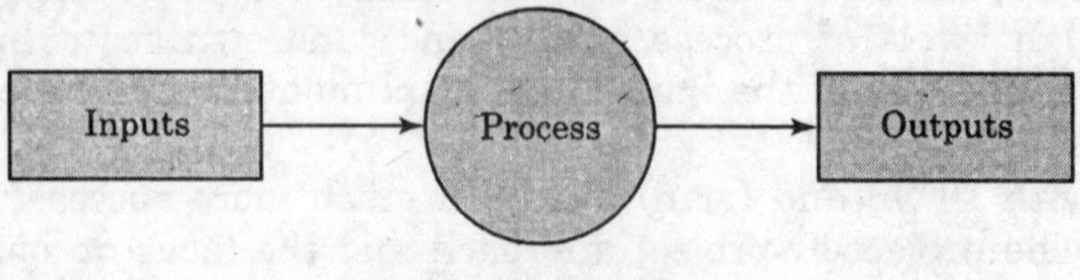

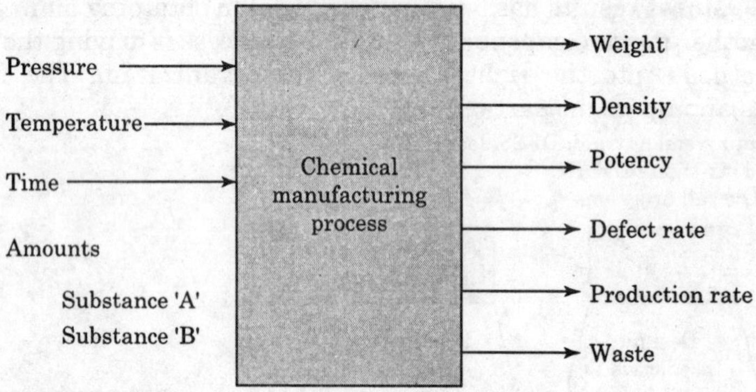

FIGURE 22.4 The Sigma input-process-output approach.

The objective of six-sigma is to gain significant breakthroughs and improved results by doing things better, faster and cheaper. Therefore, six-sigma has to incontrovertibly applicable to service industries.

Example sales office

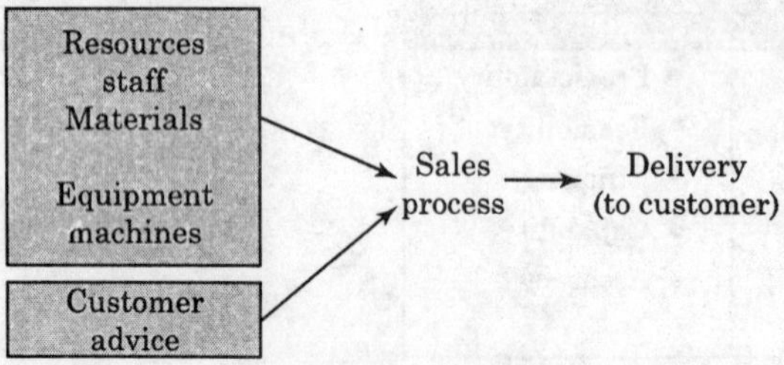

FIGURE 22.5 Simplified input-process-output diagram for a sales process.

22.5. THREE GENERATION OF SIX-SIGMA

Since its origin in late 1980s, there have been three generations of six-sigma implementation.

Generation I of six-sigma focused on defect elimination and basic variability.

In **Generation II**, Six-sigma the emphasis on variability and defect reduction remained, but now there was a strong effort to these efforts to projects and activities that improved business performance through cost reduction.

In **Generation III**, Six-Sigma has the additional focus of creating value throughout the organization and for its stake holders.

Many different kinds of businesses have embraced Six-Sigma and made its part of the culture of doing business.

22.6. SIX-SIGMA ORGANIZATION STRUCTURE (TEAM ROLES)

Following the rigorous application of six-sigma in many organizations (industrial and others), a proven structured approach has emerged for product and process improvement. Fig. 22.6 shows the structure of a six-sigma team. Through six-sigma for any project is specific but the top management must have a total commitment to the implementation of six-sigma and accomplish the following tasks:

1. Establish a Six Sigma leadership team
2. Develop and roll out a development plan for the training of Master Black-Belts, Black Belts, Green Belts and Yellow belts.
3. Assign Master Black Belts to identify and own critical projects related to key business issues.
4. Provide support to Black Belts to make breakthrough improvements in critical projects.
5. Encourage Green Belts to identify and implement 'just do it' projects.
6. Set aggressive Six Sigma targets.
7. Continuously evaluate the Six Sigma implementation and deployment programmes and make changes if necessary.

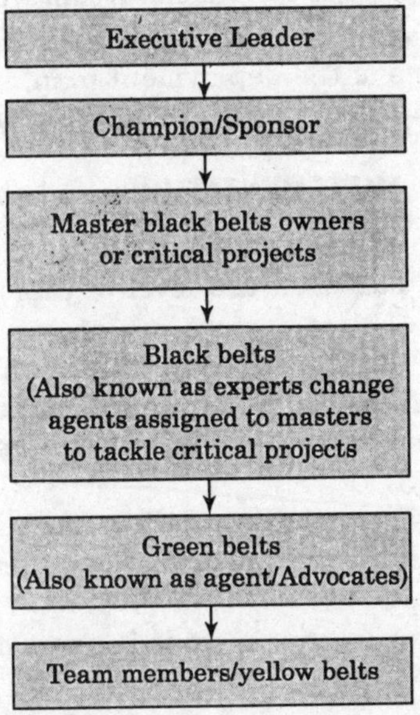

FIGURE 22.6 Structured organizations of Six-Sigma

22.6.1 Definition of Belts in Six-Sigma

(*a*) The **Executive Leader** is often a senior manager often a board member, who is responsible for six-sigma across the whole organizations.

(*b*) A Six Sigma **Champion** is the manager who initiates or sponsors a six-sigma project.

(*c*) **Master Black Belts (MBBs)** are experts in the use of six-sigma analytical tools. They work as consultants to six-sigma teams and may have a training or coaching role.

(*d*) **Black Belts (BBs)** are experts in the methodology they work alongside teams undertaking six-sigma projects. Black Belts works full-time on six-sigma.

(*e*) **Green Belts (GBs)** are also trained in six-sigma but work full-time elsewhere. They may be team members or part-time team leaders.

(*f*) **Yellow Belts (YBs)** are team members and act as support staff.

22.6.2 Education and Training of Six-Sigma Team Members

Business aligment planning, assures that Six-Sigma Projects align with business strategy and drive results. Preliminary project selection criteria start with projects having potential substantial savings (US $ 1 million or more). During the leadership education programme, which usually lasts for five days. Master Black Belts are selected and Masters are assigned to key business issues and projects. Intensive Master Black Belt training tasks three to four weeks. While the Masters are being trained, the selection process for those to be trained as Black Belts is carried out.

Master Black Belts (MBBs) have a through understanding of the improvement process, DMAIC, Six-Sigma associated statistics and change management. Master Black Belts are capable of leading and managing significant end-to-end projects, and also coaching Green Belts.

Black Belt training is a combination of formal classroom training and onsite project work. Training is spread over four to five months, and indicates four or five weeks of classroom work, with the balance onsite project work.

Green Belts (GBs) have an awareness of Six-Sigma principles and in particular apply the DMAIC cycle to work with and support Black Belts in end-to-end projects. Green Belt training is usually spread over six to seven weeks, including given days to formal classroom work.

External consultants and experienced trainers are usually needed to manage and train he first development wave. For the second and third waves of the deployment plan, in-house Master Black Belts take charge of both the training and the management of specific projects.

22.7 KEY REQUIREMENTS FOR SUCCESSFUL SIX-SIGMA IMPLEMENTATION

These are a number of key requirements for the implementation of six-sigma.

1. Six-Sigma should be focused on the customer and based on the level of performance acceptable to the customer.
2. Six-Sigma targets for a process should be related to the main drivers of performance.
3. To maximise wavings, Six-Sigma needs to be part of a wider performance management programme that is linked to the strategy of the organization. It should not be just about doing things better but about doing things differently.
4. Senior managers within the organization have a key role in driving the process.
5. Training and education about he process throughout the organization are essential for success.
6. Six-Sigma sets a tight targets, but accepts some failure – the target is not zero defects.

22.8 APPLICATION OF SIX-SIGMA

1. Six-Sigma is used by a number of large companies to improve processes in e-business environments.
2. It is used to enhance an organization's ability to meet targets and to provide value for money product or service.
3. It is used for process redesign.

22.9. SOME CRITICISMS AND LIMITATIONS OF SIX-SIGMA

Literature on Six Sigma contains some criticisms of the process and identifies a number of limitations as follows.

- Six Sigma has been criticised for its focus on current processes and reliance on data. It is suggested that this could become too rigid and limit process innovation.

- Six-Sigma is based on the use of models that are by their nature simplifications of real life. Judgement needs to be used in applying the models in the context of business objectives.
- The approach can be very time consuming and expensive. Organisations need to be prepared to put time and effort into its implementation.
- The culture of the organization must be supportive – not all organizations are ready for such a scientific process.
- The process is heavily data-driven. This can be a strength, but can become over-bureaucratic.
- Six Sigma can give all parts of the organization a common language for process improvement, but it is important to ensure that this does not become jargon but is expressed in terms specific to the organization and its business.

22.10 SOME SOFTWARE PACKAGES USED FOR SIX-SIGMA PROJECTS

A number of software packages are available in the market. However, some frequently used softwares are

1. Quality Companion
2. Sigma Flow
3. Sigma Sense
4. Minitab
5. Statistics.

SOLVED QUESTIONS

Q. 22.1: *Select the right answer (s) from the following*

(*i*) Six-Sigma gives a precision of
  (*a*) 100% (*b*) 99.73%
  (*c*) 99.99% (*d*) 97.93%

(*ii*) First company to celopt six-sigma approach is
  (*a*) Motoyama (*b*) Motorola
  (*c*) Samsung (*d*) Toyoto

(*iii*) Six-Sigma has replaced TQM soft approach policy to same extent
  (*a*) correct (*b*) incorrect
  (*c*) same times (*d*) matter of opinion

(*iv*) Belts in Six-Sigma refer is
  (*a*) level of responsibility (*b*) a belt during working time
  (*c*) decoration (*d*) grade of the employee in the company

(*v*) The focus of six sigma is mainly on reduction of
  (*a*) manpower (*b*) cost
  (*c*) variability (*d*) delays

(*vi*) Which of the following is not an example of a quality award?
  (*a*) Six-Sigma (*b*) ISO 9000
  (*c*) RGNQA

(*vii*) Which of the following is the main objective of Six-Sigma
  (*a*) Developing of Pareto diagrams
  (*b*) Reducing monetary investment while improving output quality
  (*c*) Developing detanted control charts for critical processes
  (*d*) Reducing variation from the target value in critical processes

(*viii*) We **do not** have ________ certified company

(*a*) ISO (*b*) Six-Sigma

(*c*) TQM (*d*) PDSA

(*ix*) Six-Sigma is a business driven, multi-dimensional structured approach to

(*a*) increasing customer satisfaction (*b*) Reduce process

(*c*) lowering non conformance (*d*) all of (a), (b) & (c)

(*x*) ________ is an example of SQC technique

(*a*) design of disassembly (*b*) SCM

(*c*) Six-Sigma (*d*) Quality circles

Ans. : (*i*) (*c*); (*ii*) (*b*); (*iii*) (*a*); (*iv*) (*a*); (*v*) (*c*); (*vi*) (*a*); (*vii*) (*d*); (*viii*) (*b*), (*c*) & (*d*); (*ix*) (*d*); (*x*) (*c*).

Q. 22.2: *State whether the following statements are technically True or False*

(*i*) Six-Sigma is a time bound programme.

(*ii*) In Six-sigma team Master Black Belts are experts in the use of Six-Sigma analytical tools.

(*iii*) Six-Sigma is same as ±3σ from the mean.

(*iv*) A company can its letter head can write Six-Sigma certified company.

(*v*) Six-Sigma is used in process redesign.

(*vi*) The definition of world class "implies quality, timeliness, flexibility and competitiveness.

(*vii*) In quality circles there is no formal training but in Six-Sigma team these is proper training.

(*viii*) In Six-Sigma the 'Belt' refers to the training and experience.

Ans. : (*i*) True; (*ii*) True; (*iii*) False; (*iv*) False; (*v*) True; (*vi*) True; (*vii*) True; (*viii*) True.

Q. 22.3: *Read the following statement:*

With one-sigma, 68.27 percent of product or services will meet customer requirements and there will be 317300 defects per million opportunities.

Make ***similar*** *statements for three sigma and six-sigma.*

Ans. : The statements for three-sigma and six-sigma can be made easily with the use of normal distribution curve.

- With three-sigma, 99.73 per cent of products or services will meet customer requirements and there will be 2700 defects per million opportunities.
- With six-sigma, 99.99966 per cent of products or services will meet customer requirements and there will be 3.4 defects per million opportunities.

Q. 22.4: *In one sentences only, describe Six-Sigma.*

Ans. : Six-Sigma is a quality standard that established a goal of no more than 3.4 defects per million units or procedures.

Q. 22.5: *Name the two principal focets of Six-Sigma initiative.*

Ans. : 1. Statistical mode

2. Continual improvement processes

Q. 22.6: *Name the three components of continual improvement process under Six-Sigma.*

Ans. : The Six-Sigma continual improvement process is made up of *three* primary components:

1. The Judo-like organizational structure of Belts.

2. The development of cane competencies in participants.
3. The project-by-project approach.

Q. 22.7: *Mention at least three situations in which six-sigma is used.*

Ans. : Six-Sigma is used in the following situations

1. When problems are common place and not well defined.
2. When there are unknown causes of error.
3. In complex situation with many variables.

Q. 22.8: *What potential problems can you see with the use of six-sigma in an organization with which you are familiar?*

Ans. : Depending upon the organization with which any one is familiar, answers will vary, but may include the following as a minimum:

1. Its reliance on the data.
2. Focuses on what is happening not what could have happened.
3. Based on models and assumptions that will need to be modified when applied in the real world.
4. Expensis.
5. Can become meaningless jargon.
6. Can be bureaucratic.
7. Could be viewed as another management fad.

Q. 22.9: *(a) Name the basic tool of six-sigma process.*

(b) Mention briefly the aim of six-sigma in any serving organization with its resources.

Ans. : (*a*) The basic tool of six-sigma process is DMAIC.

(*b*) The two key objectives of any serving organization with its resources are customer service and efficient use of its resources and these objectives are often in conflict. The aim of six-sigma is to reduce the conflict by fully understanding what the customer really wants and then designing the product and process to minimize the costs of production.

Q. 22.10: *What is six-sigma quality management philosophy?*

Ans. : Six-Sigma is a popular philosophy of quality management that focuses on achieving very high levels of quality by controlling the process and reducing defects (a defect is defined as anything that does not meet the customer's quality standards).

At the three-sigma quality level, 99.73% of all output meet quality standards. At the six-sigma level, it is 99.99966% of all outputs that meet quality standards. This means that when quality reaches six-sigma standards, the results will be such that only 3.4 out of every 1,000,000 outputs do not meet quality standards.

Six-Sigma quality strives to make the overwhelming majority of the bell curve fall within customer quality limits.

Q. 22.11: *What is primary focus of six-sigma?*

Ans. : Six-Sigma puts a primary focus on quantifying, measuring, and controlling the quality of products, services, and results. It is based on the underlying theory that anything will vary if measured to a fine enough level. The goal is to refine the process so that human error and outside influence no longer exist, and these variations are completely random.

If done properly, the statistical outcome should follow the bell curve. The goal is to make six standard deviations (sigmas) of the outputs fall within the customer's quality limits.

Q. 22.12: *What is the main focus of Six-Sigma approach?*

Ans. : The Six-Sigma approach focuses on continually improving the efficiency and effectiveness of all processes, tasks and transactions within any organization. This is achieved mainly on a project-by-project basis by a critical mass of members, trained in performance-enhancement methods, within a receptive and company culture and perpetuating infrastructure.

Q. 22.13: *How Six-Sigma approach leads to continual improvement in process?*

Ans. : The Six-Sigma continual-improvements process is based on the premise that each and every activity in any organizations is looked upon as a process. Every individual process has a supplier, a customer, resources and controls. Every organization consists of a myriad of interrelated processes. The improvement process focuses on business critical issues and opportunities with the intention of enhancing profit margins, competitiveness, customer satisfaction and generally adding value. It is made up three primary components.

Q. 22.14: *Mention briefly the measure of process performance under Six-Sigma.*

Ans. : The Six-Sigma statistical model provides a universal measure of process performance called a Sigma measure. The higher the value of Sigma the better the performance. A value of Six-Sigma corresponds with 3.4 adverse events (*e.g.* faults) per million opportunities. Six-Sigma is generally considered to be **world class**. This world-class standard of Six-Sigma provides the marketing name for the Six-Sigma initiative. It is suggested that many, if not most, organizations operate at round 2-4 Sigma. This has the effect of generating considerable waste and customer dissatisfaction.

Q. 22.15: *In which type of industries, we strive* **higher** *than six-sigma quality?*
[Your answers should touch the main issue(s) and in brief].

Ans. : Six-Sigma quality levels may not be high enough for all projects or all industries. For instance, the pharmaceutical industry, the airline industry, and power utilities typically strive for higher levels of quality than six sigma would specify in some areas of their operations.

Q. 22.16: *What are the key requirements for successful six-sigma implementation?*

Ans. : There are a number of key requirements for the implementation of six-sigma:

- Six-Sigma should be focused on the customer and based on the level of performance acceptable to the customer.
- Six-Sigma targets for a process should be related to the main drivers of performance.
- To maximize savings, six-sigma needs to be part of a wider performance management programme that is linked to the strategy of the organization. It should not be just about doing things better but about doing things differently.
- Senior managers within the organization have a key role in driving the process.
- Training and education about the process throughout the organisation are essential for success.
- Six-Sigma sets a tight target, but accepts some failure— the target is not zero defects.

Q. 22.17: *List the steps to be taken in applying six-sigma to redesigning processes and list the personnel to be involved.*

Ans. : The stages involved in the redesigning of a process using six-sigma are:

1. Identification of problem, 2. Plan project, 3. Analyse the existing process, 4. Design new process, 5. Acquire and/or develop resources for implementation of the redesigned process, 6. Manage the change, 7. Review.

Those likely to be involved are process team members **green belts**, **black belts** and **master black belts** working alongside a **champion** sponsoring the project.

Q. 22.18: *A company wishes to adept and implement six-sigma philosophy. Make a list of items it needs.*

Ans. : Following items are required for implementation of six-sigma philosophy.

1. The tools, 2. Methodology, 3. Training, 4. Matrices, 5. Total commitment from Top Management, 6. Significant culture change.

Q. 22.19: *List out* **(do not explain)** *some key success factors differentiating six-sigma from TQM.*

Ans. : The key success factors differentiating six-sigma from TQM are:

1. The emphasis on statistical science and measurement.
2. Structured training plans at different levels (Champion, Master Black Belt, Black Belt and Green Belt). Even the worldwide organizations of American Society for Quality will be establishing a new certificate exam for six-sigma Black Belts, which truly demonstrates how institutionalized the six-sigma process has become.
3. The project-focused approach with a single set of problem-solving techniques such as DMAIC (Define, Measure, Analyse, Improve and Control).
4. The reinforcement of Juran's tenets, such as top management leadership, continuous education and annual savings plan.
5. That the effects are quantified in tangible savings (as opposed to TQM, where it was often said we can't measure the benefits, but if we didn't have TQM who knows what losses might have occurred?)

This last point, the quantification of tangible savings, is a major selling point for six-sigma.

It is usually possible to measure the Cost of Poor Quality (COPQ) with the sigma level at which the process consistently performs. The COPQ if the performance level is at six-sigma will be less than 1 percent of cost of sales, whereas at three sigma (three sigma is regarded by many organizations as a very acceptable level of process quality) the corresponding COPQ will range from 25-30 percent of cost of sales.

Q. 7.20: *When the existing companies embark on six-sigma, what are the most likely challenges for change over?*

Ans. : For the existing companies embarking on six-sigma, there are many challenges, of which the two most significant are:

Initiative fatigue - the confusion and tiredness of staff when there is a succession of new initiatives to generate productivity and quality (e.g. a succession of maddening management fads that keep front-line staff from doing their jobs!).

The fear of statistical complexity - staff either see six-sigma as 'too hard' or as statistical mumbo jumbo. Or because they can't understand, or are afraid that they will be shown up, they find it more comfortable to denigrate rather than to learn.

Q. 7.21: *(a) What is Motorola Corporation's six sigma quality programme ?*

(b) Consider a normally distributed process with a target value of the mean $\mu = 20$ and $\hat{\sigma}$ of 2. The $U = 32$, and $L = 8$, so that if the process is centered at the target value, $Cp = C_{pk} = 2.0$. This is a process it is assumed that the mean may dreft as much as $1.5\hat{\sigma}$ off target without causing serious problems. Set up a control chart for monitoring the mean of this Six-Sigma process with a sample size $n = 4$.

Ans. : (*a*) This programme popularized by Motorola Corporation has a goal of reducing the process variation such that the spread between specification limits is 12 σ and the process mean is centered on exactly mid-way the specifications. This means that the specification limits are six sigma from the mean. Six sigma translates into a $C_{pk} = 2$.

(*b*) $\sigma_{\bar{X}} = \dfrac{\hat{\sigma}}{\sqrt{n}} = \dfrac{2}{\sqrt{4}}$ *i.e.* 1

If the mean drifts towards higher side then new mean $(\mu) = 20 + 1.5\,(\hat{\sigma}) = 20 + 1.5(2)$ i.e. 23

If the mean drift toward lower side, then new mean $(\mu) = 20 - 1.5\,(\hat{\sigma}) = 20 - 1.5(2) =$ i.e. $= 17$

Hence $UCL_{\bar{X}} = 23 + 3\,(\sigma_{\bar{x}})$ i.e. $23 + 3(1)$ i.e. 26

$LCL_{\bar{X}} = 17 - 3\,(\sigma_{\bar{x}})$ i.e. $17 - 3(1)$ i.e. 14

Q. 22.22: *Six-Sigma and Quality Circles both are comprise specific teams. What is the difference between the two?*

Ans. : Though there are many common things in Six-Sigma and QC but some significant differences are:

1. **Choice of project.** In QC members often identify and choose projects in their own area of work while Six-Sigma the projects are chosen by managers and may cross functional boundaries.
2. **Extent of training.** In QC pre-project training for QC members is kept to a bare minimum. Members are further trained appropriately, on the job, as a project proceeds. These is actually to formal training. With Six-Sigma there is quite lengthy pre-project training.
3. **Outcome expectations.** Unlike QC, with Six-Sigma significant 'bottom line' savings are the principal, if not the sole focus.

Q. 22.23: *What is meant by the term* **"World Class"**.

Ans. : The term "World Class" implies capability to deliver innovative and quality products at a lower cost, when the customer wants them at a level better than the competitor.

Any definition of "World Class" will now include the **five** aspects of **quality, timeliness, flexibility, innovative** and **competitiveness**. The point is that what was best practice ten years ago is not what best practice is today because of the rapid changes in technology.

Q. 22.24: *What is the basic criterion of awarding certificates to Black Belts and Master Black Belts?*

Ans. : Black Belts are awarded a certificate after:

- Completing three weeks of formal classroom Black Belt training
- Completing one week of change management and project management training
- Completing, as a team leader, an end-to-end $1 million Black Belt project
- Demonstrating Six Sigma commitment, evidence by mentoring Green Belts and preparation of Green Belt training material.

Master Black Belts are awarded Master' certificates after:

- Black Belt certification
- Completion of five end-to-end Black Belt projects as team leader.
- Delivery of three Green Bell training sessions
- Demonstrating commitment to the Six Sigma philosophy through mentoring Black Belts and/or Green Belt Projects.
- Designing Black Belt training materials.

Q. 22.25: *How Pareto charts are useful in Six-Sigma projects?*

Ans. : In Six-Sigma projects Pareto charts can be used when there is a need to determine the relative importance of elements such as

1. Different projects that are proposed to sponsors for them to confirm priorities (project selection).
2. Different characteristics for customers (Define);
3. Relative importance of different matrics that are being considered for use (Measure):
4. The key factors affecting the quality of a product or service (Analyse);
5. Selecting the best alternatives for process improvement (improve).

The Pareto analysis can also identify whether the Pareto 80/20 rule applies in a situation. Whilst there are a number of instances when the belief that 80 percent of defects come from 20 percent of causes will hold true, it **cannot be assumed to be a cast-iron rule.** In reality the Pareto may not apply and the *Six Sigma* team will need to show whether it is relevant or not by hard analysis.

In a process improvement project, when the Pareto principle applies to the causes of defects, it gives an indication of what the main area that need attention are. When Pareto does not apply it is an indication that another dimension may need to be explored to identify issues.

For example, if there are ten main causes for defects and no Pareto effect, then the team could use the cost needed to eliminate each cause as a third dimension, and add it as a weight to the chart to produce a new, weighted Pareto chart that can aid the decision process much better by showing the cheapest solution that will have the biggest impact.

Q. 22.26: *What is and What is not Six-Sigma?*

Ans. : Six-Sigma is a disciplined methodology for defining, measuring, analyzing, improving and controlling the quality in every one of the company's product, processes with ultimate goal of improving quality by removing defects and their causes in business process. Six-Sigma is normally executed by people known as Green Belts (part time). Black Belts (full time) and Master Black Belts (full time trainers and coaches).

Six-Sigma is all about reducing the variation of a process. It requires an understanding of the relationship between input variables (*Xs*) and the dependent output variable (*Y*). Six-Sigma equates in percentage terms to 99.9997% accuracy or to 3.4 defects per million.

Which Sigma Level to strive for is dependent upon market conditions, competitor's performance and customer expectations. A good example is the airline industry, where it would be inconceivable that only 99% of flights landed safely. In contrast, most airline baggage handing processes are generally performing at 3-Sigma (93% accuracy).

Six-Sigma has evolved into a powerful business philosophy and an instrument for driving **cultural change**. As is the case with Lean, Six-Sigma also relies on the application and deployment of best management practice in a structured manner.

Six-Sigma is **neither** a too much **statistical methodology** and **nor** it is any **quick fix** that will overcome corporate inefficiency and save crores of rupees.

Q. 22.27: *How does Six-Sigma compare with other improvement initiatives?*

Ans. : A number of improvement initiatives are, or have been at some time, in common currency. These are described at the appreciation level and compared with the Six-Sigma process. It will be noted that Six-Sigma adopts, and builds upon, many of the best-practice methods and practices applied in other initiatives. It is unique, however, in respect of its enabling and perpetuating infrastructure of 'Judo' belts. It also aims to combine and refocus a whole range of improvement tools that, hitherto, have been largely deployed in a fragmented manner. This fragmentation of deployment of various tools and techniques in a number of organization is illustrated in Fig. 22.7. Such organization don't deploy these very useful methods in a cohesive manner.

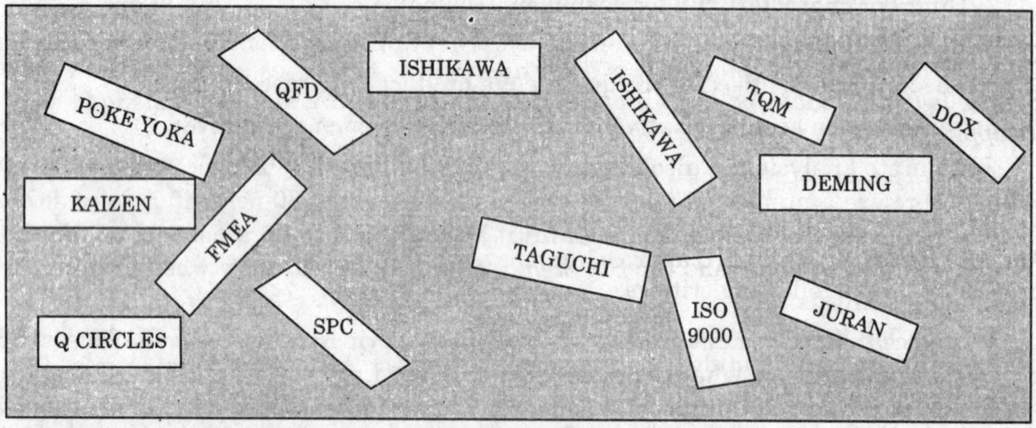

FIGURE 22.7 Fragmented deployment of improvement tools prior to Six-Sigma

Figure 22.8 portrays the Six-Sigma process as one that orientates a number of existing, seemingly disparate, practices towards a common goal. The result is seen as a cohesive set of existing practices, focused, marshalled, driven and managed by a unique Six-Sigma infrastructure.

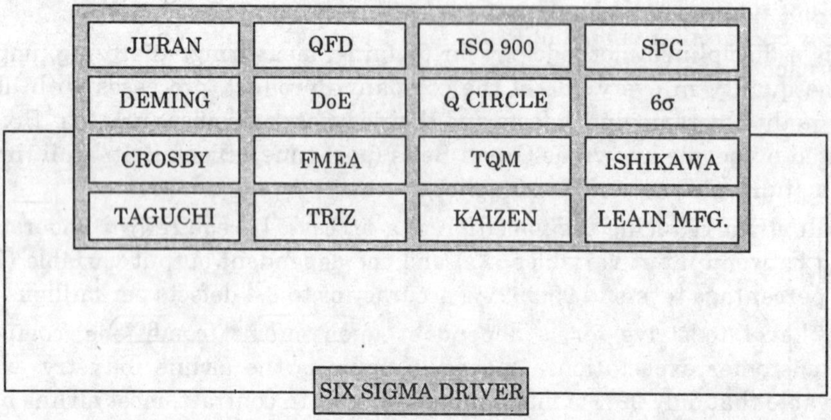

FIGURE 22.8 Six-Sigma as an orientating mechanism for selected elements of various approaches.

Q. 22.28: *Write a general note an Six-Sigma for management.*

Ans. : Six-Sigma is the most recent manifestation of many quality improvement initiatives such as TQM, the EFQM, Quality Circles and Zero Defects.

Initially focussed on statistical control of processes such as manufacture of engineered terms to a particular tolerance, but now has a much wider management application. Its purpose as on today can be described as follows:

- to provide a universal performance metric, or measure that can be applied to any product, process, service regardless of its relative complexity, a world class performance bench mark and the marketing name for the Six-Sigma improvement initiative.

The overall approach of improvement using Six-Sigma is usually summarized as DMAIC (5 stages) but it is useful to add 3 more stages to Six-Sigma projects to have (IDMADICC). Additional stages are:

- Identify the project
- Develop the improvements, pilot and verify
- Communicate new knowledge gained; transfer solution to similar areas.

Q. 22.29: *(a) DMAIC methodology is a key approach to process as system improvement in Six-Sigma. Is it applicable for every project? If not, then what are the conditions to be satisfied for its applicability for process improvement?*

(b) Is there any variation to DMAIC approach?

(c) Write briefly on the tools used in Six-Sigma.

Ans. : *(a)* No, Usually DMAIC approach can be applied in cases where the process improvement project meets the following criteria.

1. It is compled and the causes of the problem are not completely known *e.g.,* high payroll error rates where multiple systems are used to generate payroll data.
2. There is judged to be enough room for improvement to make the project worthwhile investing time and effort e.g., reducing recruitment time to hire.
3. There is no obvious or predetermined solution available – if one knows how to solve the problem then just do it. However, sometimes the obvious solution is nearly a quick-fix that masks the true underlying problem *e.g.* low customer satisfaction scores relating to the HR Shared Service Centre.

(b) One variation **is IDMADICC**. The other is **DMADV** this is often less used and is relevant when a new operation is being implemented Figure 22.9. shows the two main (DMAIC and DMADV) approaches to Six-Sigma improvements.

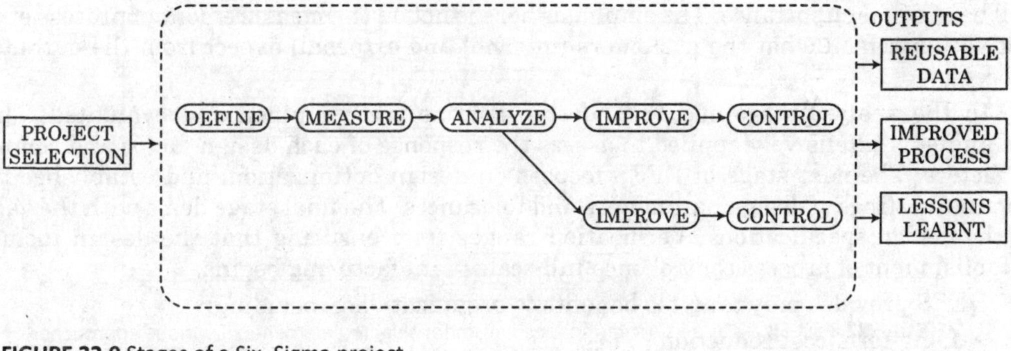

FIGURE 22.9 Stages of a Six- Sigma project.

Processes are so badly fragmented that a complete new design is needed.

(c) The best known element of Six-Sigma is its focus on empirical methods based on statistics and quantitative data. For these, a wide range of statistical tools are used such as distributions, descriptive statistics or more advanced ones such as various methods for analyzing fluctuations or uncertainty within a process.

However, process improvement projects are complex and cannot be limited simply to the quantitative dimensions, So Six-Sigma also uses qualitative tools to capture data and insights which are not numerically based.

Q. 7.30: *(a) What is the difference between (DFSS) and (DFFS)?*

(b) Write an explanatory note on Design for FIT SIGMA.

Ans. : (*a*) While DFSS refers to Design For Six-Sigma, DFFS refers to Design For FIT SIGMA.

(*b*) Design for FIT SIGMA (DFFS) utilizes the most powerful tools and methods known for developing optimal designs. These tools and methods include both DMAIC and DOX, and are capable of interfacing with any existing product development process of any organization. There are differences between DMAIC and DFFS, but the similarities are such that both approaches are compatible; one relates to process improvement and the other to product development and process. Both require a rigorous, disciplined approach.

The comparison is:

DMAIC	*DFFS*
Define	Define
Measure	Measure
Analyse	Analyse
Improve	Design
Control	Validate

In the context of DFFS, the first step. Define, has two objectives:

1. To get the project running, including the full involvement of the marketing function.
2. To agree and define critical quality factors as seen by the customer. In six-sigma language this is referred to as Critical to Quality Factors (CTQ). It is important that the customers' requirements are understood when defining the CTQs, six-sigma refers to this as Quality Function Deployment (QFD).

The second step of the DFFS project includes not only understanding customer needs but also measuring and prioriting them. In many cases customer needs will be several, but not all will be of equal importance. The emphasis here is not on the measurement of process efficiency, but very much on what the customers (internal and external) expect from the outputs of the process.

In the analyse stage of DFFS, design options are examined and evaluated. The DOX technique is extensively applied to assess the response of each design factor and combination of factors. The next stage of DFFS focuses on design optimization, and establishes the best nominal settings of design parameters and tolerances. The final stage deals with the validation of the design specifications. Verification ranges from ensuring that the design includes the establishment of process control once full-scale manufacturing begins.

DEFS provides may tangible benefits to organizations, including:

- Long-term cost reduction
- Reduction of time to market
- Definition of customers' needs, which improves quality in meeting these needs.

All of the above might sound straightforward, but experience has shown that there is a steep learning curve with the first project. There is also a need for a through understanding and application of the appropriate statistical tools. An extended version of DFFS, which has an even more in-depth customer focus, is known as Design for Customer Impact (DFC).